Introduction to AutoCAD® 2013

A Modern Perspective

Introduction to AutoCAD® 2013

A Modern Perspective

Paul Richard

Jim Fitzgerald

PEARSON

Boston Columbus Indianapolis New York San Francisco Upper Saddle River
Amsterdam Cape Town Dubai London Madrid Milan Munich Paris Montreal Toronto
Delhi Mexico City São Paulo Sydney Hong Kong Seoul Singapore Taipei Tokyo

Editorial Director: Vernon R. Anthony
Acquisitions Editor: Sara Eilert
Editorial Assistant: Nancy Kesterson
Director of Marketing: David Gesell
Executive Marketing Manager: Derril Trakalo
Senior Marketing Coordinator: Alicia Wozniak
Marketing Assistant: Crystal Gonzalez
Project Manager: Alicia Ritchey
Associate Managing Editor: Alexandrina Benedicto Wolf
Operations Specialist: Deidra Skahill
Art Director: Jayne Conte
Cover Designer: Bruce Kenselaar
Cover Image: Cozyta/Fotolia.com
AV Project Manager: Janet Portisch
Full-Service Project Management: Mohinder Singh, Aptara®, Inc.
Composition: Aptara®, Inc.
Printer/Binder: Edwards Brothers Malloy
Cover Printer: Lehigh-Phoenix Color/Hagerstown
Text Font: ITC Bookman Std

Library of Congress Cataloging-in-Publication Data

Richard, Paul (Paul Fritz)
Introduction to AutoCAD 2013: a modern perspective/Paul Richard, Jim Fitzgerald.
p. cm.
ISBN-13: 978-0-13-295475-4
ISBN-10: 0-13-295475-3
1. Computer graphics. 2. AutoCAD. I. Fitzgerald, Jim, 1964- II. Title.
T385.R4945742 2013
620'.0042028553—dc23

2012022938

10 9 8 7 6 5 4 3 2 1

PEARSON

ISBN-10: 0-13-295475-3
ISBN-13: 978-0-13-295475-4

Features of *Introduction to AutoCAD® 2013*

Introduction to AutoCAD® 2013 presents a modern approach to using AutoCAD. That is, it addresses advances in technology and software evolution and introduces commands and procedures that reflect a modern, efficient use of AutoCAD 2013. Features include:

A **"Quick Start"** chapter at the beginning of the book allows users to get up to speed in no time to create and even plot AutoCAD drawings. Quick Start topics and concepts are linked to corresponding chapters later in the book, providing a motivational preview and allowing users to delve into detailed topics of instruction as they choose, at their own pace.

2 chapter**two**

Quick Start Tutorial

CHAPTER OBJECTIVES

- Explore CAD's uses and benefits
- Understand fundamental CAD concepts
- Tour the AutoCAD user interface
- Explore the different AutoCAD data input methods
- Display and manipulate m drawings simultaneously
- Maximize AutoCAD's **Info** system features

Chapter Objectives, with a bulleted list of learning objectives for each chapter, provide users with a road map of important concepts and practices that will be introduced in the chapter.

Key Terms are bold and italic within the running text, briefly defined in the margin, and defined in more detail in the Glossary at the end of the book to help students understand and use the language of the computer-aided drafting world.

Dimension Styles

dimension style: A collection of dimension settings that control how dimension objects act and are displayed.

Now that you have created a basic
we start dimensioning, we need to
sions to reflect industry standards.
are controlled through ***dimension***
collection of dimension settings sav
object takes on the look and behavi
a dimension style called *Standard* a
Standard dimension style or create
exercise, you'll take a quick tour th
style settings.

DRAFTING SETTINGS

Menu:	Tools | Drafting Settings...
Command Line:	DSETTINGS
Command Alias:	DS or SE

Drawing tools can
the top of your keyboa
line. Each method is li
this chapter.

Most of the drawi
settings. For instance
and off, whereas the g
is controlled via the d
settings are managed
Figure 5-3.

Command Grids appear in the margin alongside the discussion of the command. These grids provide a visual of the action options using the Ribbon, Standard Toolbar, Pull-Down Menu, Command Line, or Command Alias, ensuring that the student is in the right place at the right time and correctly following the authors' direction.

Discipline Icons are placed in the margin alongside each project and identify the discipline to which each project applies: **M** Mechanical, **G** General, **A** Architectural, or **E** Electrical. These icons allow instructors to quickly identify homework assignments that will appeal to the varying interests of their students and allow students to work on projects that have the most interest and relevance depending on their course of study.

5 chapterfive

Chapter Projects

G **Project 5-1:** *Calculator* [

1. Start a new drawing using the **aca**
2. Draw the figure shown in Figure 5- snap settings. Toggle the **Object S** The borders around the perimeter a 1/16″. The spacing between the bu

NEW to AutoCAD 2013

- **Command Line Interface** Provides access to line where it is possible to enter commands ar display the history of previously entered comm interface is also where AutoCAD displays man tings and other important messages
- **Model/Layout Tabs** The **Model** and **Layout** switch between model space and different pap
- **Status Bar** Minidashboard for AutoCAD that ing interactively displaying the current mouse location, toggling different drawing tools on an model space and paper space layouts, setting workspaces, and more
- **InfoCenter** Allows you to search for useful ir topic by entering key words or phrases, provid

New to AutoCAD 2013 icons flag features that are new to the 2013 version of the AutoCAD software, creating a quick "study guide" for instructors who need to familiarize themselves with the newest features of the software to prepare for teaching the course. Additional details about these new features can be found in the Online Instructor's Manual.

Exercises throughout the chapters provide step-by-step walk-through activities for the student, allowing immediate practice and reinforcement of newly learned skills.

EXERCISE 1-1 **Using Cartesian Coordinates**

1 Using pencil and paper, lay out a Cartesian coordinate similar to the one shown in Figure 1-3.

2 Draw a line from the coordinate point (2,1) to the coord (4,5).

3 Draw a line from the origin (0,0) at an approximate ang the edge of the grid.

4 Draw a line from the coordinate point (−2,−1) to the or

TIP

You can increase or decrease the layout preview image size by holding down the <Ctrl> key while rolling the mouse wheel in and out.

NOTE

Move the mouse past the edge of the row of images to display layouts that extend beyond the edge of the screen.

FOR MORE DETAILS

See page 655 in Chapter 15 for more detailed information about using the **PUBLISH** command for quickly plotting multiple drawings and layouts.

Tip, Note, and **For More Details** boxes highlight additional helpful information for the student.

URLs in the margin direct students to the online student data files.

To access student data files, go to www.pearsondesigncentral.com.

EXERCISE 16-4 **Inserting a Drawing File as a Block**

1 Continue from Exercise 16-3.

2 Start the **INSERT** command to display the **Insert** dialog

3 Select the **Browse...** button to display the **Select Drawin** box and locate the ***EX16-4.DWG*** drawing file in the stud

4 Select the ***EX16-4.DWG*** file, and select the **Open** button the **Insert** dialog box.

5 Select **OK** to insert the block anywhere in the drawing as Figure 16-14.

6 Save the drawing.

1 chapterone

Chapter Summary

The information and concepts explained in this chapter form
the rest of this textbook. In this chapter we explored the use
the benefits that it provides. We also looked at some fundam
concepts such as drawing things real-world size, using Cartesi
to precisely locate drawing information, measuring angles co
and managing object properties.
In addition, an in-depth tour of the AutoCAD ribbon-bas
and the different ways that you can input data were provide
can optimize command and data entry. The techniques for n
tiple open drawings and displaying different window configu
explained so that you can easily share information between
increase productivity exponentially.

End-of-Chapter material, easily located by shaded bars on page edges, includes:

- Chapter Summary
- Chapter Test Questions
- Chapter Projects

to help students check their own understanding of important chapter concepts.

Chapter Projects are organized by discipline to allow for application of skills to various fields, and numbered consistently among the chapters for easy back-and-forth reference. The end-of-chapter projects offer three different levels of difficulty consisting of basic, intermediate, and advanced that require students to use all the commands and skills they have learned cumulatively.

5 chapterfive

Chapter Projects

G Project 5-1: *Calculator* [BASIC]

1. Start a new drawing using the **acad.dwt** template.
2. Draw the figure shown in Figure 5-68 using the appropr
snap settings. Toggle the **Object Snap** button on and of
The borders around the perimeter and around the scree
1/16″. The spacing between the buttons is 1/8″. **Do not**
dimensions.
3. Save the drawing as ***P5-1***.

SUPPLEMENTS

Instructor Resources

Instructor's Manual that includes an updated outline of the material for each chapter.

PowerPoint Presentation for use in lectures or as a supplement to class activities.

Download Instructor Resources from the Instructor Resource Center

To access supplementary materials online, instructors need to request an instructor access code. Go to www.pearsonhighered.com/irc to register for an instructor access code. Within 48 hours of registering, you will receive a confirming email including an instructor access code. Once you have received your code, locate your text in the online catalog and click on the Instructor Resources button on the left side of the catalog product page. Select a supplement, and a login page will appear. Once you have logged in, you can access instructor material for all Prentice Hall textbooks. If you have any difficulties accessing the site or downloading a supplement, please contact Customer Service at http://247pearsoned.custhelp.com/.

Preface

We live in a digital world where the trend in technology is to duplicate reality as much as possible. As time goes on, more and more industries and fields require the use of AutoCAD drafting and design software. AutoCAD has long been, and will remain, the industry standard for generating top-of-the-line CAD drawings in the least amount of time possible.

Introduction to AutoCAD® 2013: A Modern Perspective offers a complete guide for students and professionals who want to enter the interesting world of computer-aided drafting using AutoCAD. This book covers all aspects of the AutoCAD program's 2D tools, from the basic concepts to the most powerful tools used in design and engineering.

In this book, readers will find an interesting combination of theory and many complex projects and exercises, as well as clear and descriptive illustrations. Real design problems starting from scratch will be solved throughout the projects. In addition, many other short exercise sections are included to ensure full comprehension of the commands.

Concepts are explained clearly in easy-to-understand language and are accompanied by descriptive illustrations, which will help the reader to understand each topic and to speed up the learning process. By following the steps in each project, readers will see results immediately and will understand the development process as they go along, rather than just entering instructions.

After using this book, readers will realize that AutoCAD is the premier software for generating 2D drawings. Its ease of use, combined with its ability to create complex drawings, makes it the first choice among many design and drafting professionals.

About This Book

This book can serve as a reference for designers, draftspersons, or anyone with a basic knowledge of technical drawing who wants to learn how to use the AutoCAD program to create his or her work. The projects and the exercise sections are designed to enhance and help the reader retain the content learned in each chapter.

You do not need to be an expert draftsperson to use this book, but you should have some drafting background. This book focuses more on using AutoCAD as a tool for creating 2D CAD drawings. Occasionally, industry standards are referenced as they relate to a topic. Unfortunately, it is impossible to address standards thoroughly because each industry and discipline is different.

It is also assumed that you have some knowledge of computers and basic file management. Because some of the topics in the later chapters are rather technically advanced, having some computer background is helpful. A basic technical background is required because AutoCAD has many Internet and network-enabled features that facilitate the sharing of electronic information.

In addition to learning the basic AutoCAD tools, you will also learn to recognize and use these tools to achieve specific goals. A number of challenging end-of-chapter projects from varying disciplines progress through multiple chapters so you can see how a drawing is put together from beginning until end. Brief definitions of the commands involved, as well as notes containing tips and warnings, will give you extra help in understanding the commands.

Chapter Organization

The book is organized into seven parts that advance in complexity as you go through each chapter. Each subsequent chapter is meant to build on the preceding chapters so you can see the steps typically taken to create a set of drawings from start to finish.

PART ONE—An Introduction to AutoCAD

Chapter 1: Introduction to AutoCAD introduces you to fundamental CAD concepts and the AutoCAD interface.

Chapter 2: Quick Start Tutorial allows you to hit the ground running so that you learn the basics necessary to start a new drawing, create and modify some objects, add annotation features, and print out your work. All topics are then explained in detail in the subsequent chapters.

PART TWO—Drafting Skills: Drawing with AutoCAD

Chapter 3: Controlling the Drawing Display shows you how to move around in a drawing by panning and zooming. It also introduces some different display performance settings.

Chapter 4: Basic Drawing Commands provides an overview of the basic drawing commands such as **LINE** and **CIRCLE** so you can create a simple drawing.

Chapter 5: Drawing Tools and Drafting Settings explains the different drawing tools and settings available to help you create and modify your work.

Chapter 6: Managing Object Properties shows how to set up and apply different layer systems and manage other object properties.

PART THREE—Understanding Editing Techniques: Basics Through Advanced

Chapter 7: Basic Editing Techniques explains how to select groups of AutoCAD objects that can be modified as a single unit. Grips are introduced to teach you how to modify objects directly by simply selecting them in your drawing.

Chapter 8: Advanced Editing Techniques introduces some of the more advanced modify commands that allow you to perform complex operations.

PART FOUR—Working with Complex Objects

Chapter 9: Drawing and Editing Complex Objects looks at creating and editing complex polyline-based objects with multiple line segments.

Chapter 10: Pattern Fills and Hatching provides information about incorporating different predefined pattern fills and hatch patterns into your drawings to create filled areas.

PART FIVE—Annotating Drawings

Chapter 11: Adding Text shows the different ways to manage and create text in a drawing.

Chapter 12: Working with Tables explains how to insert and modify different types of tables in a drawing, including those linked to Microsoft Excel spreadsheets and those extracted from object information in a drawing.

Chapter 13: Dimensioning Drawings outlines the different dimensioning tools and shows how to manage their appearance using dimension styles.

PART SIX—Outputting Your Work

Chapter 14: Managing Paper Space Layouts shows you step by step how to set up paper space layouts for plotting using industry standard techniques, including multiple layouts and multiple scaled viewports.

Chapter 15: Plotting and Publishing provides an overview of the different plotting tools and settings, including how to batch plot a group of drawings using the **PUBLISH** command.

PART SEVEN—Advanced Drawing and Construction Methods

Chapter 16: Blocks and Block Attributes explains how to create complex named symbols that can be inserted anywhere in a drawing or drawings. Dynamic block attribute text examples are explained to show how to update individual blocks quickly, as well as extract alphanumeric information to a table or external file.

Chapter 17: Working with External References shows you how to reference external files (drawings, images, DWF, DGN, and PDF files) into your current drawing so that you can coordinate and communicate work without having to open the referenced file.

Chapter 18: Drawing Management Tools and Utilities provides an overview of AutoCAD's drawing utilities for fixing and/or restoring drawings. Purging a drawing to reduce file size and complexity is demonstrated. Object linking and embedding are explained so that you can share information with other programs. AutoCAD's **Action Recorder** tool is introduced so you can automate repetitive commands. The **Measure** tools and the **QuickCalc** calculator are explained so you can both measure and calculate numeric values using drawing object data. Preserving data integrity by deleting duplicate objects using the **OVERKILL** command and web-based collaboration tools are introduced.

Features New to This Edition

Chapter 1

- The command line interface has been enhanced to include color, transparency, and increased flexibility for displaying history and accessing recent commands. You can dock the command line at the top or bottom of the AutoCAD window or let it float to maximize the drawing area.
- New **Layout** tab added to ribbon with 2D tools for creating and managing layouts, page setups, and viewports. Additionally, includes advanced model documentation tools for automatically creating 2D projected views, sections, and details from 3D models.
- New **Annotation Monitor** button added to status bar that toggles on and off annotation monitoring, which provides feedback regarding the status of annotation objects that are associated with views, sections, and details that have been automatically created using AutoCAD's advanced 3D model documentation tools.
- A new **Welcome Screen** is automatically displayed when you launch AutoCAD 2013 that provides easy access to drawings, learning tools, and online content.
- The online **Help** system has been significantly restructured to provide faster search-based results.

Chapter 2

- It is now possible to dynamically preview changes to an object before applying a change.

Chapter 8

- Enhanced array functionality helps you create objects in a pattern faster and easier than ever before.

Chapter 9

- The **PLINEREVERSEWIDTHS** system variable provides increased flexibility when reversing the direction of polylines that have varying widths.

Chapter 10

- It is possible to select more than one hatch boundary area at a time in your drawing and update them all simultaneously using the **Hatch Editor** context tab of the ribbon.

Chapter 11

- You can use the **Strikethrough** button to put a line through selected text.

Chapter 17

- Point cloud files can be referenced in a drawing using the **POINTCLOUDATTACH** command.
- Xref path tools that allow you to change, remove or set a path to be relative.

Chapter 18

- **Autodesk® 360** provides web-enabled, typically referred to as cloud-based, features, services, and other products that allow you to design, visualize, simulate, and share your work with others anytime, anywhere via the Internet.

Acknowledgments

Content Contributors

Appendix A

Dr. Gerald L. Bacza
Coordinator and Professor: Drafting/Design/CAD Engineering Technology
Fairmont State Community and Technical College

Chapter 18: Drawing Management Tools and Utilities

Kelly Keala
Clackamas Community College, OR

Drawings and Drawing Expertise

Kimi Barham
Student, Clackamas Community College, OR

The authors also like to thank the following individuals for their helpful reviews: Dede Griffith, Lee College; Lloyd W. Lunde, Southeast Technical Institute; Ronald M. Mauno, Michigan Tech and Susan Campbell, Glendale Community College.

Style Conventions in *Introduction to AutoCAD® 2013*

Text Element	Example
Key Terms—Boldface and italic on first mention (first letter lowercase, as it appears in the body of the text). Brief definition in margin alongside first mention. Full definition in Glossary at back of book.	Views are created by placing ***viewport*** objects in the paper space layout.
AutoCAD commands—Bold and uppercase.	Start the **LINE** command.
Ribbon and panel names, palette names, toolbar names, menu items, and dialog box names—Bold and follow capitalization convention in AutoCAD toolbar or pull-down menu (generally first letter cap).	The **Layer Properties Manager** palette The **File** menu
Panel tools, toolbar buttons, and dialog box controls/buttons/input items—Bold and follow the name of the item or the name shown in the AutoCAD tooltip.	Choose the **Line** tool from the **Draw** panel. Choose the **Symbols and Arrows** tab in the **Modify Dimension Style** dialog box. Choose the **New Layer** button in the **Layer Properties Manager** palette. In the **Lines and Arrows** tab, set the **Arrow size:** to**.125**.
AutoCAD prompts—Dynamic input prompts are set in a different font to distinguish them from the text. Command line prompts are set to look like the text in the command line, including capitalization, brackets, and punctuation. Text following the colon of the prompts specifies user input in bold.	AutoCAD prompts you to *Specify first point:* Specify center point for circle or [**3P 2P T**tr (tan tan radius)]: **3.5**
Keyboard Input—Bold with special keys in brackets.	Type **3.5 <Enter>**

Brief Contents

Contents

NEW to AutoCAD 2013

New to AutoCAD 2013

Introduction to AutoCAD® 2013

A Modern Perspective

chapterone
Introduction to AutoCAD

CHAPTER OBJECTIVES

- Explore CAD's uses and benefits
- Understand fundamental CAD concepts
- Tour the AutoCAD user interface
- Explore the different AutoCAD data input methods
- Display and manipulate multiple AutoCAD drawings simultaneously
- Maximize AutoCAD's **InfoCenter** and help system features

Introduction

This textbook is designed to allow you to "hit the ground running" using AutoCAD so that you can quickly start creating accurate technical drawings using accepted industry drafting standards. The next chapter (Chapter 2, Quick Start Tutorial) shows you the minimum you need to know in order to create and plot an AutoCAD drawing starting from scratch. These introductory concepts and techniques are then linked to detailed information about each topic so you can explore them at your own pace.

Before you can do any of that though, we need to cover some basics. This chapter introduces you to some fundamental CAD concepts and the AutoCAD ***user interface*** so you are prepared to hit the ground running in Chapter 2.

user interface: The commands and mechanisms the user interacts with to control a program's operation and input data.

What Is CAD?

In a little over a generation's time the methods used to create technical drawings have fundamentally changed from using pencil and paper to the use of computer-aided drafting, better known as CAD. The analog world of drafting boards, T squares, triangles, and even the romantic french curve (see Figure 1-1) has given way to the digital world of computers. No longer must you refill your mechanical pencil when you run out of lead, find your eraser when you make a mistake, or walk across the room to share a design with another person.

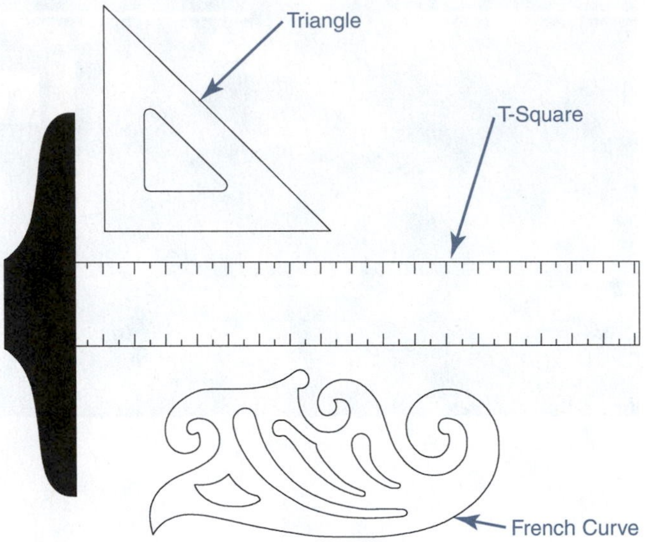

Figure 1-1
A T square, a triangle, and a french curve

Using CAD, you can draw something once and copy it hundreds, or even thousands, of times. Changing a design can be as simple as pushing a button. Drawings can be shared instantaneously across the room or even around the world. These and the other benefits of CAD include the following:

- Increased productivity
  - Drawing content can be continuously reused.
  - Text and dimensions can be created and updated automatically.
  - Hatch and pattern fills can be placed with a single pick of the mouse.
  - Revising and editing drawings can be done quickly with minimum effort.
  - ***Parametric design*** tools allow you to constrain drawing objects based on your design intent.

parametric design: Design process that utilizes both variable and constrained dimensions that automatically update the drawing objects they are assigned to so that many different variations of a base design can be accurately represented.

- Improved precision
  - Digital information is accurate to 14 decimal places.
  - Geometry is precisely located using the Cartesian coordinate system.
  - It is possible to snap to control points and features on existing drawing geometry to accurately locate drawing information.
  - Polar and object tracking features can be utilized for precise angular measurements.
- Better collaboration
  - Drawings can be shared across a network (locally and globally).
  - Drawings can be referenced and updated in real time with notification.
  - Revisions and markups can be managed electronically via email and Internet-based collaboration sites such as **AutoCAD WS.**

Figure 1-2
Sample 3D presentation drawing in AutoCAD

- 3D visualization and analysis (see Figure 1-2)
  - 3D animations and walk-throughs can be easily generated to allow you and potential clients to visualize a design before it is constructed.
  - Interference checking can be done to ensure that parts do not run into each other before they are created.
  - Engineering calculations such as finite element analysis (FEA) and other structural calculations can be performed automatically.
  - Computer prototypes can be created and tested, eliminating the time and materials needed to manufacture a real-world prototype.

All these benefits are explored in this textbook, except for 3D visualization and analysis, which is beyond the scope of this text. The following chapters explain how to utilize the tools provided in AutoCAD to create and share the most accurate technical drawings in the quickest and most efficient manner. Using AutoCAD you will learn how to do the following:

- Set up and lay out different types of AutoCAD 2D drawings using AutoCAD model space and paper space techniques.
- Quickly create accurate 2D drawing information using AutoCAD's precision drafting aids.
- Edit and modify 2D drawing information in a productive fashion.
- Annotate and dimension drawings using AutoCAD's automated annotation and dimensioning features.
- Create section views utilizing AutoCAD's predefined and custom hatch and pattern fills.
- Utilize and manage CAD standards including:
  - Layers
  - Linetypes

    - Text styles
    - Dimension styles
- Coordinate drawing information with other team members using external reference files.
- Create and manage symbol libraries using AutoCAD's **Content Explorer, DesignCenter,** and tool palettes.
- Output your drawings to different plotting devices with specific colors and lineweights.
- Share your drawings online using **AutoCAD WS** so it is possible to view and edit your drawings using a mobile device or web browser.

Fundamental CAD Concepts

Because CAD-based drafting is a digital pursuit, some of the concepts that apply to its analog "on the board" cousin are a bit different. It is important that you are aware of and understand these concepts before we begin any drawing.

Drawing Actual Size

sheet size: The size of the paper on which a drawing is printed or plotted.

Board drafting requires that you select a scale before you begin a drawing. This is to ensure that whatever it is that you are drawing fits properly on the selected paper, or ***sheet size.***

Large objects are scaled down so that you can see the complete design on the sheet while smaller objects are scaled up so that you can clearly discern finer details.

Unlike drawing on the board, CAD-based drafting does not require design information to be scaled as it is drawn. Everything is drawn actual size as it exists in the real world. This means that the layout of a floor plan that is 100′-0″ × 50′-0″ is actually drawn 100′-0″ long × 50′-0″ wide in AutoCAD. The scaling process occurs when the drawing is being set up to be printed or plotted to ensure that your drawing fits properly on the desired sheet size.

FOR MORE DETAILS

See page 819 in Appendix A for detailed information about standard sheet sizes.

Using CAD, you have a theoretically infinite amount of space within your CAD drawing file to create your design. A drawing can be as large as our entire solar system or small enough to fit on the head of a pin. To help navigate within this infinite drawing space, AutoCAD provides a number of display tools that allow you to zoom and pan around a drawing similar to the zoom and pan functions found on a camera. This allows you to zoom up close to your drawing for detailed work or zoom out so that you can view the complete drawing.

NOTE

Annotation features like text and dimensions have their own unique scaling issues. You must typically scale annotation features so that they appear at the correct size in relation to the actual size drawing you are creating. For instance, 1/8″-high text appears as a tiny speck next to a 100′-0″-long wall. AutoCAD provides an **Annotation Scale** feature that helps automate the process. This feature is explained later in the "Annotation Scale" section on page 8.

> **FOR MORE DETAILS**
>
> AutoCAD's display tools are described in detail in Chapter 3.

The Cartesian Coordinate System

The primary means of locating information in an AutoCAD drawing is the Cartesian coordinate system. The Cartesian coordinate system is a grid-based system where points are represented by their *x* and *y* coordinate values separated by a comma as follows:

x,y

For example, a point located at $x = 4$ and $y = 2$ is represented as follows:

4,2

There is also a *z* coordinate, but we'll talk about that later. For now, think of your computer screen as a 2D sheet of paper where the origin of the coordinate system (0,0) is in the lower left-hand corner of your screen as shown in Figure 1-3.

Positive *x* and *y* coordinate values are represented in the upper right quadrant of the grid. Because it is easiest to work with positive coordinates exclusively, this is where most of your drawings will be created.

Right-Hand Rule

As alluded to earlier, the Cartesian coordinate system also has a *z* coordinate that is used to locate points in 3D space. The *Z*-axis runs perpendicular to the XY plane shown in Figure 1-3.

Figure 1-3
The Cartesian coordinate system

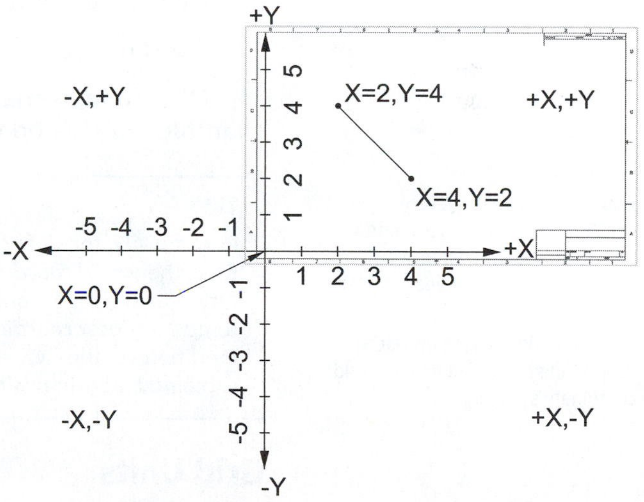

right-hand rule: Easy-to-understand reference that can be used to determine the positive and negative direction of the *X*-, *Y*-, and *Z*-axes.

The easiest way to represent this concept is to rely on what is known as the ***right-hand rule***—it's as easy as 1-2-3.

To start, clench your right hand into a fist with your palm facing toward you.

1. Extend your thumb to the right.
2. Uncurl your pointer finger so that it points straight up.
3. Uncurl your middle finger so that it points toward you.

Your hand should now look similar to the one shown in Figure 1-4. Using the right-hand rule, your thumb represents the positive *X*-axis, your pointer finger represents the positive *Y*-axis, and your middle finger represents the positive *Z*-axis.

Figure 1-4
The right-hand rule

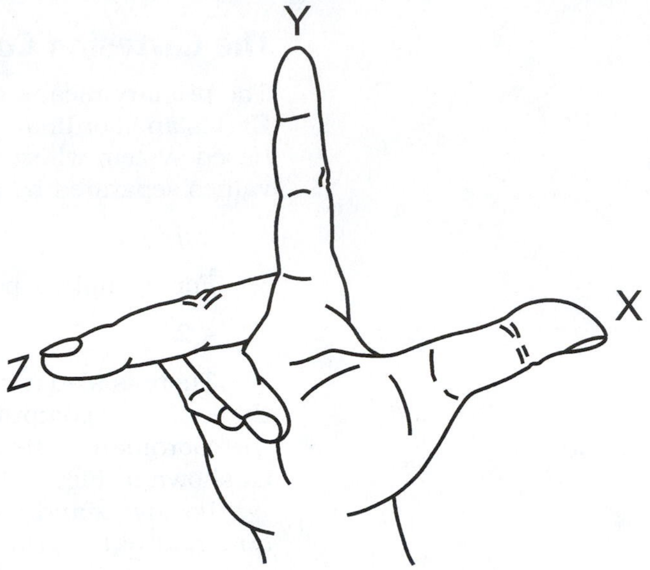

Your palm, and by extension, your computer screen, represents the 2D XY plane where $z = 0$. Using this analogy, positive z values are toward you, or above the screen, while negative z values are away from you, or into the screen.

By default, the z coordinate value is set to 0. Because of this, there is no need to specify a z coordinate value when you locate 2D points. If the z coordinate is omitted, it is interpreted as 0. For instance, to locate a 2D point where $x = 4$ and $y = 2$, you can enter either of the following:

4,2,0 or 4,2

Of course, it makes sense to type the least amount possible, so all examples in this book rely on the shorthand version.

world coordinate system (WCS): The default coordinate system in AutoCAD upon which all objects and user coordinate systems are based.

user coordinate system (UCS): A user-defined variation of the world coordinate system.

> **TIP**
>
> In AutoCAD, the default Cartesian coordinate system explained in this section is referred to as the ***world coordinate system***, or ***WCS***. It is possible to change the origin and orientation of the *X*-, *Y*-, and *Z*-axes for high-level drawing operations by creating your own temporary ***user coordinate system***, or ***UCS***. A temporary UCS can be quickly created and modified via the UCS icon in the lower left corner of the AutoCAD drawing window, as explained later in this chapter. For more information, please consult the AutoCAD Help.

Grid Units

In AutoCAD, one unit on the Cartesian coordinate grid system can represent whatever you want it to represent. A unit can be 1 inch, 1 foot, 1 millimeter, 1 meter, 1 nautical league, or even 1 ***parsec.***

parsec: A unit of astronomical length.

Fortunately for us, the majority of the drafting and design world works in either inches (imperial) or millimeters (metric) where the following applies:

Imperial:

1 grid unit = 1 inch

Metric:

1 grid unit = 1 millimeter

There are of course exceptions to this unwritten rule, most notably in the civil design field. Because civil engineers work with drawings that cover large areas (parcel plans, highway plans, etc.), it is common for them to work in decimal feet or decimal meters where the following applies:

Imperial:

1 grid unit = 1 foot

Metric:

1 grid unit = 1 meter

Unless otherwise noted, most of the examples and drawing problems in this book will rely on 1 unit = 1 inch for imperial-type drawings and 1 unit = 1 millimeter for metric-type drawings.

> **TIP**
>
> The default drawing setup in AutoCAD is an imperial-type drawing where 1 grid unit = 1 inch. Setting a drawing up for the metric system where 1 grid unit = 1 millimeter is described on page 136 in Chapter 4.

Angle Measurement

By default, angles in AutoCAD are measured counterclockwise from 0°, which is due east, or right, on the positive *X*-axis as shown in Figure 1-5. Using this system of angle measurement, 90° is north, 180° is west, and 270° is south. It is possible to change the default 0° base angle to any of the other three compass directions, or a custom angle, as well as change the default angle measurement direction from counterclockwise to clockwise.

Figure 1-5
AutoCAD base angle and direction

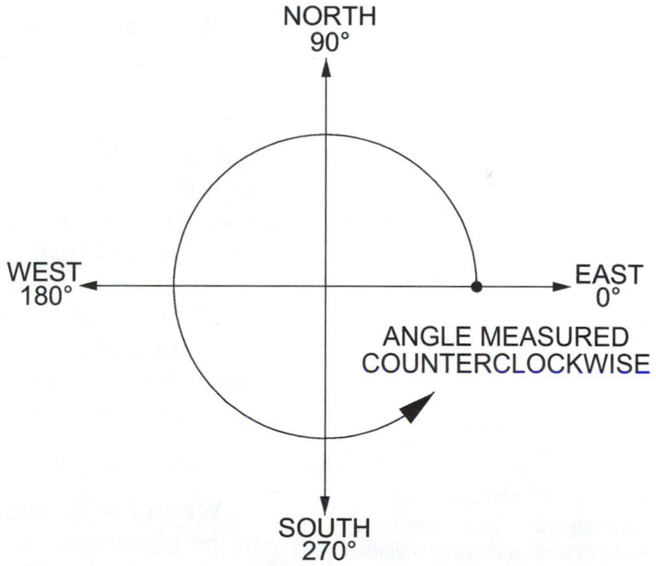

AutoCAD provides five different types of angle unit settings so you can enter angles in a format that applies to the type of work you are doing. Most architects and engineers prefer angles in decimal units (e.g., 45.00°), or degrees, minutes, and seconds (e.g., 45°00′00″), while those in the civil engineering world rely on surveyor units (e.g., N45°0′0″E).

> **FOR MORE DETAILS**
>
> Setting different angle unit settings as well as setting a different base angle and angle direction is described on page 138 in Chapter 4.

> **TIP**
> You can also enter negative angle measurements when working in AutoCAD to input an angle that is measured in the clockwise direction. For example, an angle of 315° can also be entered as −45°.

EXERCISE 1-1 **Using Cartesian Coordinates**

1. Using pencil and paper, lay out a Cartesian coordinate grid system similar to the one shown in Figure 1-3.
2. Draw a line from the coordinate point (2,1) to the coordinate point (4,5).
3. Draw a line from the origin (0,0) at an approximate angle of 135° to the edge of the grid.
4. Draw a line from the coordinate point (−2,−1) to the origin (0,0).
5. Draw a line from the origin at an approximate angle of −30° to the edge of the grid.

Annotation Scale

As mentioned earlier in the section "Drawing Actual Size," the lines, circles, and other geometry that represent your design are drawn to their exact "real-world" specifications; the scaling occurs when you set your drawing up to plot on the desired sheet size.

To accommodate this scaling process, the size of annotation features such as text and dimensions must be adjusted accordingly when they are added to your drawing. This ensures that they print out at the correct size after they are scaled up or scaled down. Most organizations rely on drafting standards that define specific text heights, arrowhead sizes, and other annotation specifications so that drawings maintain a consistent appearance. The proper scaling of annotation features is very important so that drafting standards are always maintained.

As an example, annotation features on a drawing that is going to be scaled to 1/2 of its original size when it is printed must be scaled up by the reciprocal of 1/2, or 2 times, when they are created. With this in mind, if your drafting standards require that text print out 1/8″ high, you must apply the following formula:

1/8″ × 2 = 1/4″-high text

scale factor: Multiplier that determines the size of annotation features when a drawing is plotted or printed.

When the drawing is then plotted, the 1/4″-high text is scaled by 1/2 and prints out at the correct standard text height of 1/8″. See Figure 1-6. In this example, 2 is considered the scale factor. The ***scale factor*** is the

Figure 1-6
1/4″ text scaled to 1/8″ at plot time

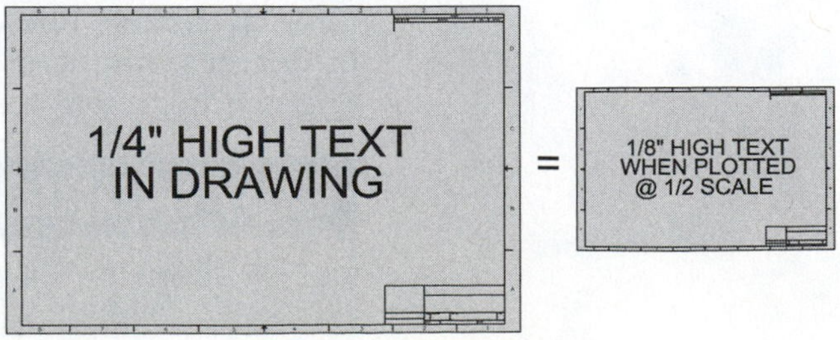

reciprocal of the plotted scale. Calculating the scale factor in the preceding example is easy because the plotted scale is a simple ratio of 1:2. It's obvious that the reciprocal of 1:2 is 2.

FOR MORE DETAILS

See page 813 in Appendix A for more information about standard annotation specifications and the steps necessary to calculate other scale factors, based on standard drawing scales. Page 813 in Appendix A also contains a list of the most common standard drawing scales, their corresponding scale factors, and even suggested text sizes and dimension scales.

Calculating, *and applying*, scale factors for all the different annotation-type objects can be a tedious, time-consuming process. Fortunately, it is possible to automate the process using the AutoCAD **Annotation Scale** feature. Annotation objects such as text and dimensions have an annotative property that, when enabled, automatically scales the objects according to the scale selected. The annotation scale is controlled via an easily accessible list of the same standard drawing scales found in Appendix A. Annotation objects can even have more than one annotation scale so that they are displayed at the correct size on multiple different scale drawings!

NOTE

There are other things in a drawing that are affected by the annotation scale besides just text and dimensions. Special linetype definitions and hatch patterns can also be affected.

FOR MORE DETAILS

See pages 238–239 in Chapter 6 for details regarding scaling linetype definitions. See page 395 in Chapter 10 for more information about scaling hatch patterns. See page 418 in Chapter 11 for more information about the **Annotation Scale** feature.

Object Properties

In AutoCAD, the lines, circles, text, dimensions, and just about everything else that make up a drawing are commonly referred to as *objects*. All these drawing objects have properties associated with them that control their appearance and behavior. Some properties are unique to a particular type of object, especially properties that relate to an object's geometry. For example, a circle object has a radius, whereas text has a height. Other object properties are shared by all the objects in a drawing. These general object properties are introduced in the following sections.

Layers. Before the advent of CAD, drafters and designers coordinated their drawings by physically overlaying them on top of each other. The paper, known as *vellum*, was translucent so that as you layered each drawing on top of the previous one, the drawing(s) underneath were still visible. This allowed the drafters and designers to compare the work on each individual drawing and coordinate them as a complete system. See Figure 1-7.

Figure 1-7
Overlay drafting

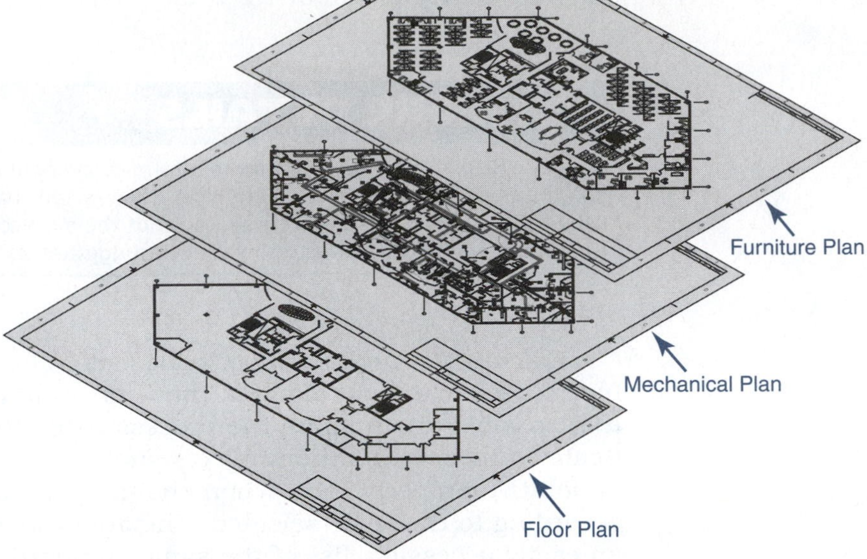

Flash forward to the digital world of the twenty-first century. Using CAD, this concept of physically "layering" multiple drawings one on top of another has morphed into the ability to separate distinct drawing information using named layers. Typically, the name of the layer reflects the type of information that resides on it. For instance, a layer named **WALL** might contain drawing information that relates to the walls of a floor plan, while a layer named **DOOR** might contain the lines and arcs that represent the doors. In fact, numerous standard layer-naming conventions and guidelines have been created that allow people to share CAD drawings and understand what type of drawing information resides on each layer.

CAD-based layers provide much more functionality and control than their analog vellum-based cousins. Layers in CAD can be turned off and on so that you can create multiple views of your drawing information. For instance, text and dimensions can be put on their own unique layers so that they can be turned off when you want to concentrate on your design. Similar drawing information can be grouped on specific layers so that you can coordinate between different disciplines. The electrical wiring might be located on a layer named **ELEC** while the mechanical heating ductwork might be located on a layer named **HVAC**. Basically, layers give your drawings a level of intelligence that allows you to indicate what objects in a CAD drawing represent in the real world.

Besides controlling the visibility of drawing information, layers also can be used to control the color, linetype, lineweight, and transparency of an object. You can even use layers to determine whether an object is plotted or not.

FOR MORE DETAILS

Layer property management is discussed in greater detail in Chapter 6.

Colors

Colors can serve multiple purposes in an AutoCAD drawing:

1 They separate drawing information so that it is easily identifiable on the computer screen.

2 They allow printing and plotting with specific line thicknesses.

3 They allow color output on color printing and plotting devices.

The first use of colors is fairly obvious. One of the easiest ways to differentiate between different drawing information on the computer screen is by using color. You might set up your drawing so that all the walls are green, the doors are blue, and the text is yellow. This color coding makes your drawing easier to comprehend and work with.

The second use of colors might seem a bit obscure to many new AutoCAD users—to control line thicknesses when plotting. This use of colors was introduced very early on in AutoCAD's life as one of the only means of plotting a drawing with varying line thicknesses, a necessity for most organizations. This color-based approach to controlling lineweights is still in use today because of the time and effort necessary to update legacy systems. For this reason, it is a good idea to at least have a basic understanding of how the color-based approach works.

Without getting into too much detail, color-based plotting is based on the fact that each color in AutoCAD is associated with an integer value. This relationship is referred to as the *AutoCAD Color Index,* or *ACI.* The ACI consists of 255 colors numbered from 1 to 255, with the first seven colors represented as follows:

1 = Red

2 = Yellow

3 = Green

4 = Cyan

5 = Blue

6 = Magenta

7 = White

In the early days, plotting was done on pen plotters using numbered ink pens with varying pen tip sizes that created different line thicknesses. The numbered plotter pens were associated with the information in the drawing via the object's color. For example, red drawing objects plot with pen #1 because the color red = 1 in AutoCAD's Color Index. This color–to–plot pen relationship is referred to as a plotter's "pen mapping." Thankfully, this antiquated approach to controlling plotter pens is quickly being heaped on the trash bin of history as the much simpler approach of using AutoCAD's lineweight property becomes more popular.

plot style: A collection of property settings that is applied when the drawing is plotted to control the appearance of the drawing objects on the printed drawing.

NOTE

There is another approach to controlling line thicknesses on a plot using ***plot styles.*** It is possible to assign a unique plot style directly to an object that will control the object's appearance on the printed page.

FOR MORE DETAILS

See page 817 in Appendix A for detailed information about standard line thicknesses. Plotting with lineweights and plot styles is discussed in detail in Chapter 15.

Linetypes

Manually drawing objects with different linetypes on the board is a very tedious process, if not an art form. A mechanical pencil and a scale must be utilized so that you can accurately measure out the dashes, dots, and/ or gaps over the distance of a line.

Fortunately, AutoCAD provides more than 40 different predefined linetypes that can be applied directly to your line work with a click of a button. Figure 1-8 shows examples of linetypes that come with AutoCAD.

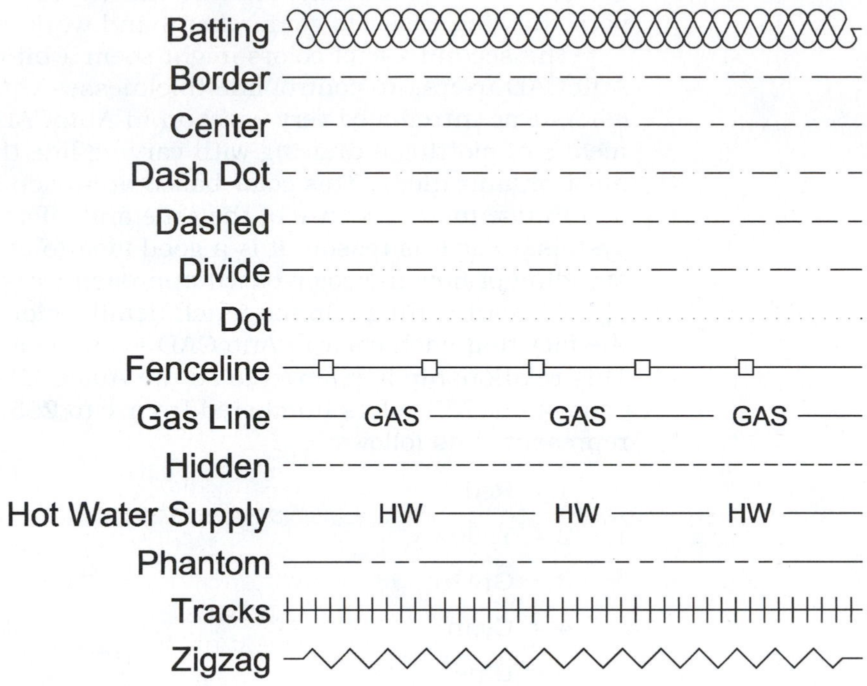

Figure 1-8
Examples of default AutoCAD linetypes

> **TIP**
> The dashes, dots, and gaps that make up a linetype definition are also affected by the scale factor described earlier. Their size must be adjusted to accommodate the plot scale in the same fashion as the other annotation features in order for them to print out at the right size.

> **FOR MORE DETAILS**
> See page 817 in Appendix A for a detailed description of different linetype standards. Linetypes and linetype scaling are explained in detail in Chapter 6.

Lineweights

In AutoCAD, the term *lineweight* is used to refer to a line's thickness. Different drafting standards dictate how line thicknesses should be applied in technical drawings.

Drawing different line thicknesses on the board requires that you use different pencils with different lead thicknesses. AutoCAD provides graphical lineweights that you can assign to your line work, which allows you to see different line thicknesses on the screen *before* you plot your drawing. There are more than 20 different lineweights available in both imperial (inches) and metric (millimeters) format.

FOR MORE DETAILS

See page 817 in Appendix A for detailed information regarding line thickness drafting standards. AutoCAD lineweights are discussed in detail beginning on page 232 in Chapter 6.

Transparency

It is possible to make objects transparent in AutoCAD so that you can see through them and view objects that are below. The level of transparency can be adjusted up or down so that you can control the visibility of the objects. By default the transparency level is set to 0, which means all objects are opaque and you cannot see through them.

FOR MORE DETAILS

See page 233 in Chapter 6 for more information about controlling object transparency.

Controlling Object Properties

The common approach to controlling the general object properties discussed in the previous sections is to set the desired object property active, or current, before drawing an object. An object assumes the current object properties when it is drawn. This does not mean you cannot change an object's properties after it is drawn. In fact, there are a multitude of tools in AutoCAD to help you accomplish this.

FOR MORE DETAILS

Controlling AutoCAD object properties is discussed in detail beginning on page 221 in Chapter 6.

EXERCISE 1-2 **Researching CAD Layer Guidelines**

1. Using the Internet, search for websites with information about the "AIA layer guidelines." (*Note: AIA is the abbreviation for the American Institute of Architects.*)
2. Describe the AIA layer-naming scheme and how it is organized.
3. Find an example of at least one other layer standard or guideline.

Model Space and Paper Space

AutoCAD has two distinct drawing environments: model space and paper space. Model space is the 3D drawing environment described in "The Cartesian Coordinate System" section earlier that is used for the drawing ***model,*** or 3D representation of your design. Model space contains most of the line work, text, and dimensions that make up a drawing.

model: The geometry (lines, circles, etc.) created in a drawing that defines the object or objects drawn.

Paper space is the 2D environment used for laying out different views of the model space information on a standard sheet size and scale for plotting purposes. This 2D page setup is known as a ***layout*** in AutoCAD and typically consists of one or more views of your drawing along with a border and title block.

layout: 2D page setup created in paper space that represents the paper size and what the drawing will look like when it is printed.

Metaphorically speaking, an AutoCAD paper space layout can be thought of as a 2D sheet of paper that hovers over your 3D model space drawing. Scaled views are created by cutting holes in the paper so you can see the 3D drawing model below. See Figure 1-9.

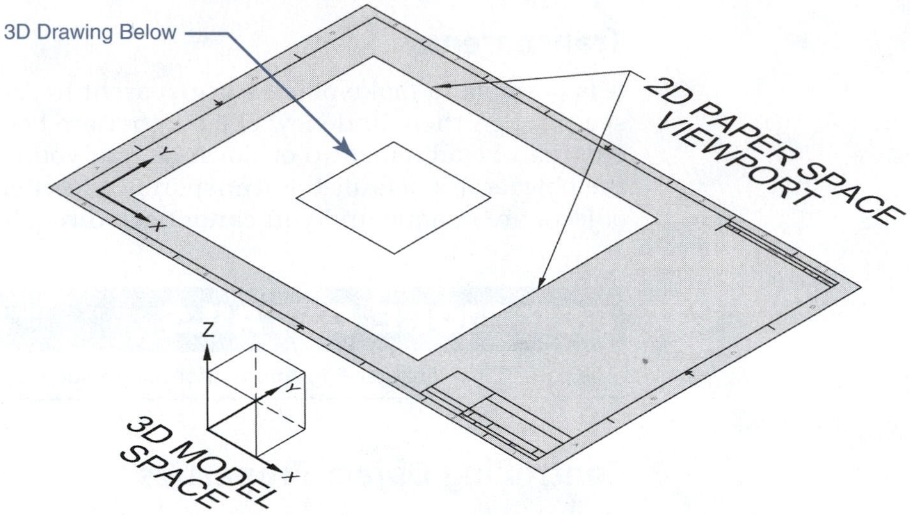

Figure 1-9
Model space and paper space

> **TIP**
>
> It is possible to have multiple layouts in an AutoCAD drawing. Each layout can be a different sheet size and can also contain multiple scaled views.

> **FOR MORE DETAILS**
>
> Layouts and views are discussed in detail in Chapter 14.

AutoCAD File Types. By default, a drawing in AutoCAD is saved as a file with a .DWG file extension. For example, a floor plan drawing might be saved with the file name

Floor Plan.dwg

A file name can be up to 256 characters long and can include most of the alphanumeric characters, including spaces ( ), dashes (-), and underscores (_). A file name *may not* include any of the following special characters:

\ / | : " * ? > <<

Windows is not case sensitive, so you can mix uppercase and lowercase letters when naming a file and Windows will not distinguish between them. For instance, the file name in the example above:

Floor Plan.dwg

is the same as

FLOOR PLAN.DWG

Proper file naming, and by extension, proper file management, is one of the most important aspects of using CAD effectively.

> **TIP**
>
> By default, every time you save a drawing in AutoCAD, a backup file with the .BAK file extension is created. The backup file is the last saved version of the .DWG drawing file. This allows you to always have the last saved version of your drawing to "roll back" to if something happens to the current .DWG file.

Some of the other common file types and extensions used by AutoCAD are listed in the following table.

AutoCAD File Types

File Extension	Description
AC$	Temporary AutoCAD file. Created automatically by AutoCAD
BAK	AutoCAD drawing backup file. Created automatically when a drawing is saved
DWG	AutoCAD drawing file
DWF/DWFx	AutoCAD Design Web Format file
DWL	AutoCAD drawing lock file. Created automatically by AutoCAD
DWS	AutoCAD Drawing Standards file
DWT	AutoCAD drawing template
DXB	Binary AutoCAD design exchange format file
DXF	ASCII AutoCAD design exchange format file
PLT	AutoCAD plot file
SV$	AutoCAD automatic save file

If you are unsure of a file type, consult the Windows Help and Support Center.

A First Look at AutoCAD

AutoCAD is one of the more complex software applications. There are a myriad of commands, menus, toolbars, palettes, and dialog boxes. The following sections explain all these features and how they work so you can get the most out of the AutoCAD user interface.

The AutoCAD User Interface

Because AutoCAD is a program for drawing, the focal point is the drawing window. This is where you create your drawing. Everything else surrounding the drawing window helps you accomplish this task. The ribbons, panels, menus, toolbars, and other tools that you interact with to create your drawings are collectively referred to as the *user interface*. These user interface items are controlled, in turn, using what are referred to as AutoCAD ***workspaces.***

workspace: A named configuration of menus, toolbars, and palettes that are grouped and organized so that you can work in a custom, task-oriented drawing environment.

The user interface for the default AutoCAD **Drafting & Annotation** workspace is shown in Figure 1-10.

The major interface features provided in the **Drafting & Annotation** workspace are as follows:

- **Application Menu** Clicking on the **Application Menu** button displays a menu of commonly used AutoCAD file tools and drawing utilities, as well as providing quick access to open or recently opened drawings. It's also possible to access the **Options** dialog box and exit AutoCAD via buttons at the bottom of the menu

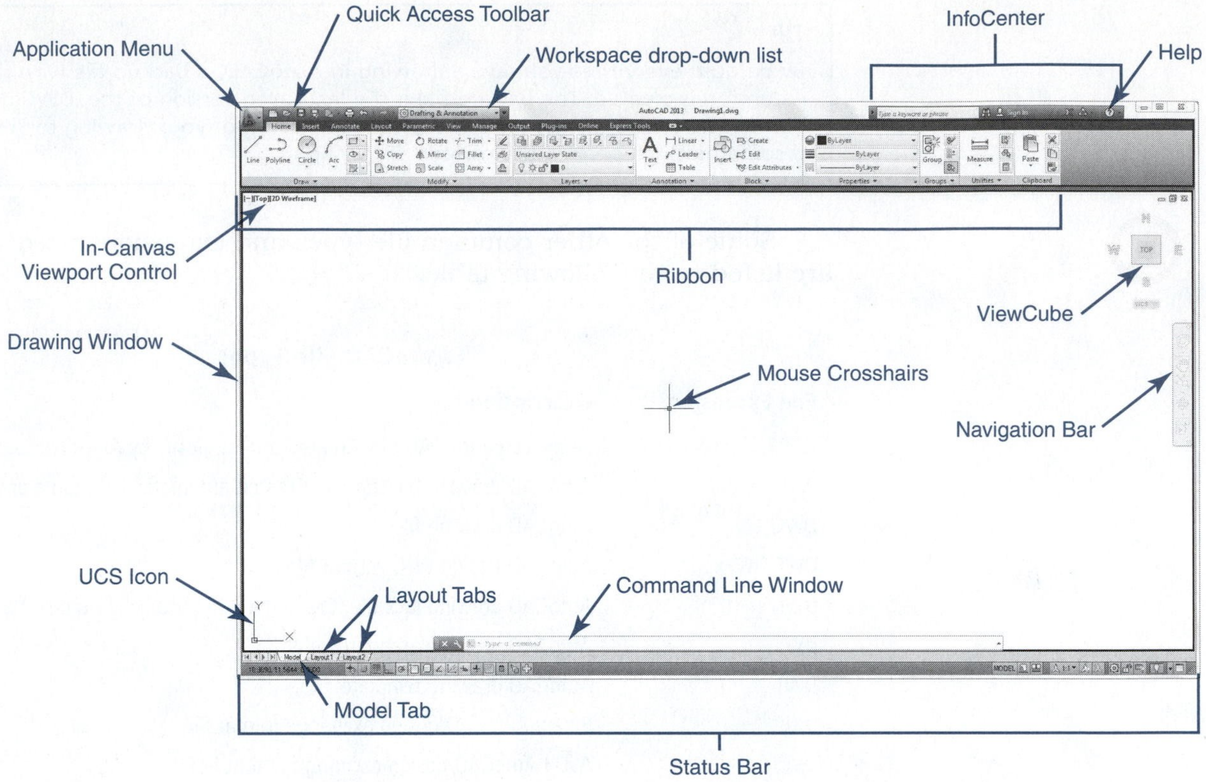

Figure 1-10
The default AutoCAD user interface

- **Quick Access Toolbar** Provides easy access to all the most commonly used tools such as **New, Open, Save, Save As…, Plot, Undo,** and **Redo**
- **Workspace List** Provides easy access to all of the default and custom workspaces so you can easily switch your drawing environment
- **Ribbon** Provides easy access to most of the AutoCAD tools via task-specific tabs and panels. Each tab has multiple panels containing related tools. Panels with a black arrow on the bottom center can be expanded to access additional tools
- **In-Canvas Viewport Control** Allows you to change viewport settings, views, and visual styles directly in the AutoCAD drawing window below
- **Drawing Window** The theoretically infinite space where you create the lines, circles, text, and so on that make up your drawing using the Cartesian coordinate system explained earlier
- **Mouse Crosshairs** Used for locating points and selecting objects when working in a drawing. The crosshairs switch back to a pointer when the mouse is outside of the drawing window
- **ViewCube** Allows you to easily switch between different views in your drawing using your mouse
- **Navigation Bar** Provides easy access to most commonly used navigation tools so you can control what is displayed on your screen
- **UCS Icon** Represents the current user coordinate system (UCS); by default, this is set to the world coordinate system (WCS) explained earlier in this chapter where the *X*-axis is aligned horizontally and the *Y*-axis is aligned vertically

NEW to AutoCAD 2013

- **Command Line Interface** Provides access to the AutoCAD command line where it is possible to enter commands and their options, as well as display the history of previously entered commands. The command line interface is also where AutoCAD displays many default command settings and other important messages
- **Model/Layout Tabs** The **Model** and **Layout** tabs allow you to quickly switch between model space and different paper space layouts
- **Status Bar** Minidashboard for AutoCAD that does many things, including interactively displaying the current mouse crosshairs coordinate location, toggling different drawing tools on and off, switching between model space and paper space layouts, setting the scale factor, managing workspaces, and more
- **InfoCenter** Allows you to search for useful information about a topic by entering key words or phrases, provides access to **Autodesk Exchange**, the online destination for application downloads, **Autodesk 360**, AutoCAD product updates, and AutoCAD Help

NEW to AutoCAD 2013

The Welcome Screen

The **Welcome Screen** shown in Figure 1-11 provides quick and easy access to drawings, learning tools, and online content.

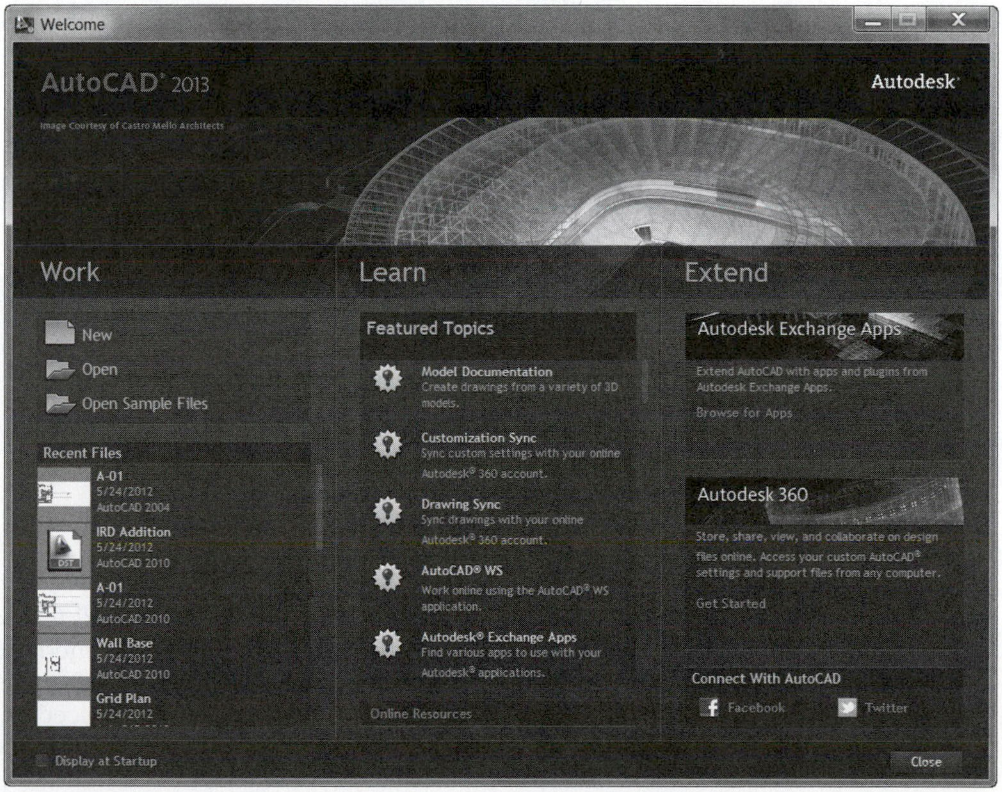

Figure 1-11
The **Welcome Screen** window

The **Work** panel on the left of the **Welcome Screen** allows you to create new drawings or open your existing drawings and sample files. The **Recent Files** list provides quick access to your most recently used drawings.

The **Learn** panel in the middle of the **Welcome Screen** provides featured topics about what's new in AutoCAD 2013, including links to additional online learning resources.

The **Extend** panel on the right of the **Welcome Screen** provides access to Autodesk® Exchange Apps and allows you to connect to **Autodesk 360** and other AutoCAD social media resources, including Facebook and Twitter.

You can prevent the **Welcome Screen** from displaying automatically each time you start AutoCAD by deselecting the **Display at Startup** check box at the lower left corner of the **Welcome Screen** window.

> **TIP**
>
> It is always possible to display the **Welcome Screen** window after it has been closed by selecting it from the **Help** drop-down menu on the **InfoCenter** toolbar or by entering **WELCOMESCREEN** at the command line.

Workspaces

Most of the features that define the user interface for a particular setup (e.g., ribbons, panels, menus, toolbars, etc.) are managed using what are referred to as AutoCAD *workspaces*.

The **Drafting & Annotation** workspace is the default current workspace when you start AutoCAD. The **Drafting & Annotation** workspace, shown in Figure 1-10, turns off all of AutoCAD's 3D tools and features so that you have quick and easy access to all of the 2D tools required for this textbook.

AutoCAD comes with other standard workspaces that you can switch to at any time by selecting the **Workspace** drop-down list on the right side of the **Quick Access** toolbar at the top left of the AutoCAD window, as shown in Figure 1-12.

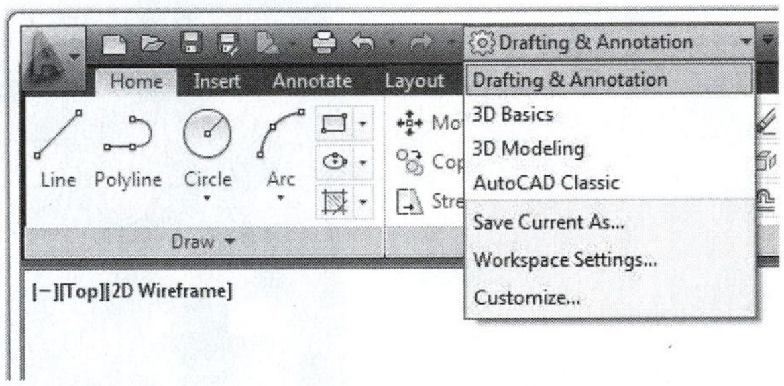

Figure 1-12
Workspace drop-down list on **Quick Access** toolbar

The **3D Basics** workspace is intended for users who are new to 3D by combining the most commonly used 3D modeling commands.

The **3D Modeling** workspace turns off most of the 2D AutoCAD tools and replaces them with AutoCAD's advanced 3D tools and features.

Switching to the **AutoCAD Classic** workspace turns off the ribbon at the top of the AutoCAD drawing window and turns on the traditional pull-down menus and toolbars found in earlier releases of AutoCAD.

> **NOTE**
>
> - You can also switch workspaces using the **Workspace Switching** button on the right side of the AutoCAD status bar at the bottom of the AutoCAD drawing window.
> - The **Drafting & Annotation** workspace is the default workspace used for all of the exercises in this textbook. If it is not your current workspace, you should set it current now.

Figure 1-13
Quick Access toolbar

Quick Access Toolbar

The **Quick Access** toolbar shown in Figure 1-13 provides quick and easy access to the following commonly used AutoCAD tools so that they are always available:

- **New** Creates a new drawing file based on the selected AutoCAD template file
- **Open** Opens an existing AutoCAD drawing or template file
- **Save** Saves the drawing in its current location if it has been saved previously. Otherwise, performs a "Save As" the first time so that the drawing file name and location can be specified
- **Save As...** Displays the **Save As** dialog box so you can rename the drawing and/or change the file type to an earlier version of AutoCAD
- **Plot** Prints a drawing to the specified printing device or file type with the settings specified
- **Undo** Allows you to undo one or more recent commands
- **Redo** Allows you to reverse the effect of the last undo command

Clicking on the down arrow on the right side of the **Quick Access** toolbar displays the flyout menu shown in Figure 1-14 so you can add or remove common tools.

Selecting **More Commands...** from the menu allows you to add additional commands via the **Customize User Interface** (CUI) dialog box.

In addition, the **Show Menu Bar** option allows you to turn on the pull-down menus traditionally located across the top in previous releases of AutoCAD. The **Show Below the Ribbon** option moves the **Quick Access** toolbar below the ribbon.

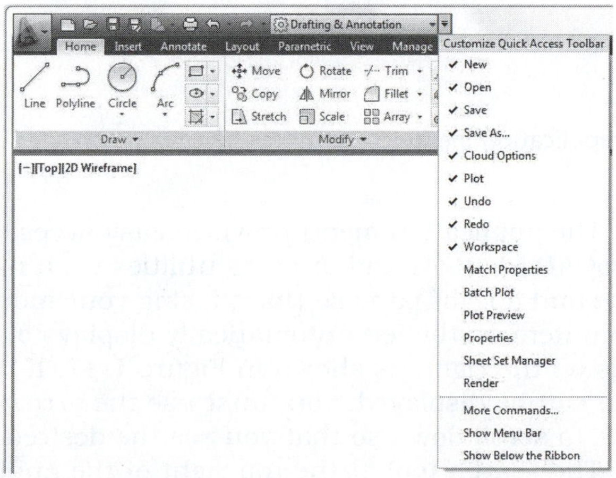

Figure 1-14
Quick Access toolbar flyout menu

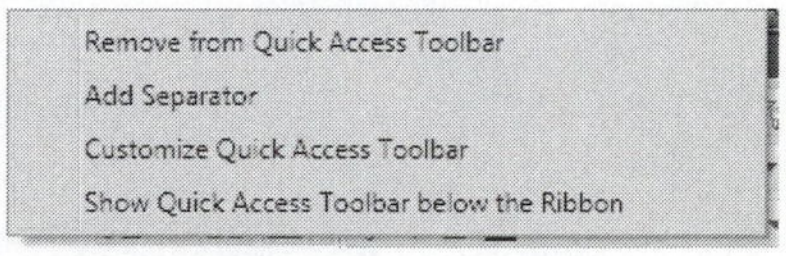

Figure 1-15
Quick Access toolbar shortcut menu

Right-clicking on the **Quick Access** toolbar displays the shortcut menu shown in Figure 1-15 that provides some of the same options as the flyout menu discussed above plus a few more. Using the right-click menu you can remove tools, add separators between tools, add additional commands via the **Customize User Interface** (CUI) dialog box, or move the toolbar below the ribbon.

Application Menu

Clicking on the big **A** button at the top left of the AutoCAD window displays the application menu shown in Figure 1-16.

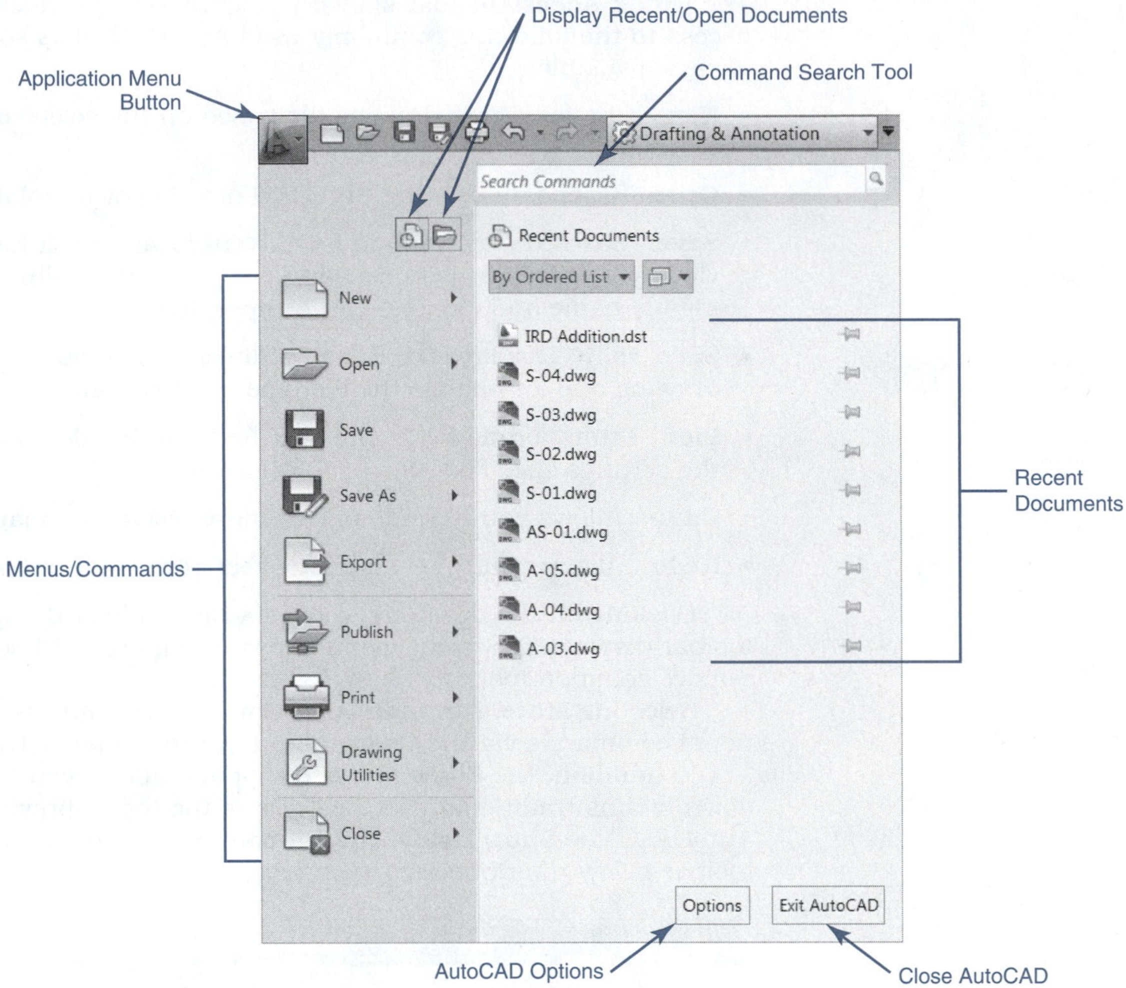

Figure 1-16
Displaying the application menu

The application menu provides easy access to commonly used AutoCAD file tools and drawing utilities via a menu that is split into a left pane and a right pane so that placing your mouse pointer over the main menu item on the left automatically displays a submenu list of related tools on the right, as shown in Figure 1-17. If the submenu list is longer than can be displayed, you must use the arrow at the bottom of the right pane to scroll down so that you see the desired menu item.

The search tool at the top right of the application menu allows you to search through all of the AutoCAD tools by specifying key terms. For example, if you start typing **L-I-N-E** in the search field, AutoCAD dynamically displays all the tools that include the word LINE, as shown in Figure 1-18. Click on an item in the list to initiate the associated AutoCAD tool.

Additional Time-Saving Application Menu Features. In addition to easy access to AutoCAD file tools and drawing utilities, it is also possible to view and access recently opened drawings or drawings that are currently

Figure 1-17
The **Print** submenu

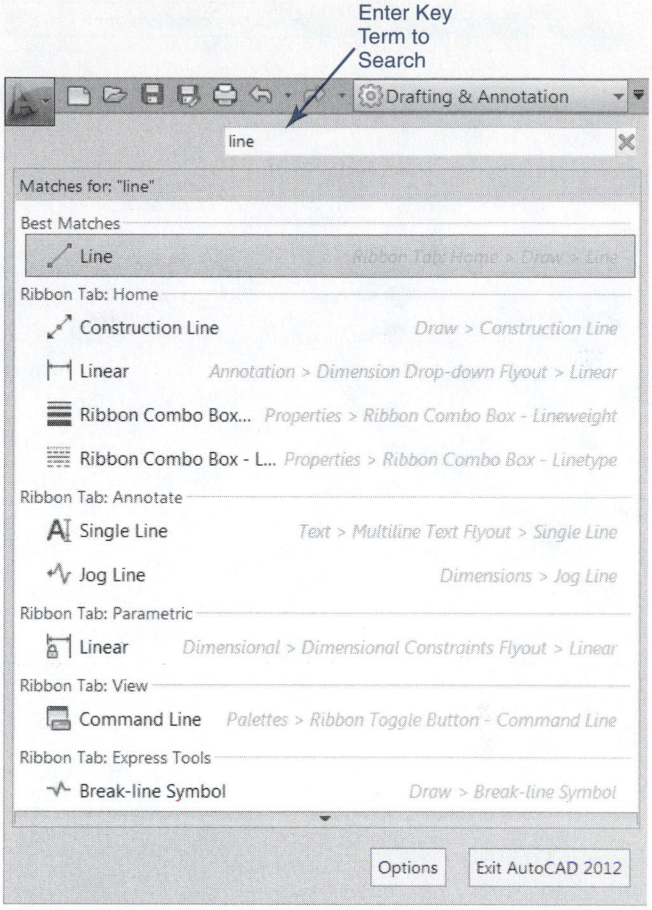

Figure 1-18
Using the **Application Menu** search tool

open in other windows via the two buttons at the top of the application menu shown in Figure 1-16. For example, selecting the **Recent Documents** button displays a list of recently opened drawings, as shown in Figure 1-19.

By default, recent drawings are displayed in an ordered list of when they were last accessed. It is possible to group drawings by access date, size, or file type via the **By Ordered List** drop-down menu at the top left.

The **View icon** button directly to the right of the **By Ordered List** drop-down menu allows you to change the file display from icons to small, medium, or large preview images. Additionally, briefly hovering the cursor over the drawing name displays a preview image. If you do not move your cursor for a few split seconds, the preview is expanded to include other important file information as shown in Figure 1-20.

AutoCAD Options. The **Options** button at the bottom right of the application menu displays the AutoCAD **Options** dialog box shown in Figure 1-21. The **Options** dialog box is your one-stop shop for controlling and maintaining most AutoCAD features and settings such as the color of different window elements, size of the cursor crosshairs, default print settings, and so on. Because it is accessed so often, it is located on the application menu for easy access. It can also be found at the bottom of most AutoCAD right-click shortcut menus discussed later in the chapter. You'll want to remember this because accessing and using the **Options** dialog box is discussed often throughout the rest of the textbook.

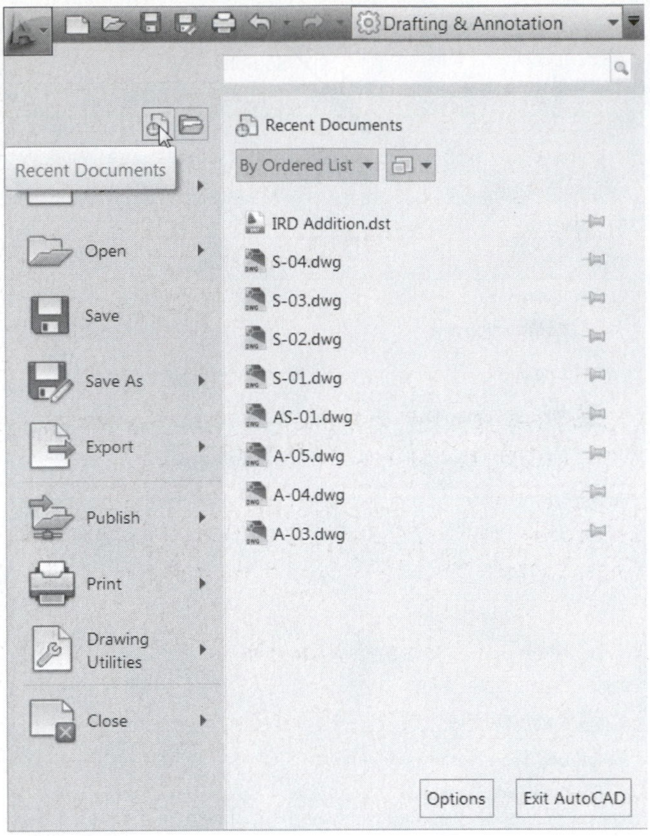

Figure 1-19
Viewing recently opened drawings

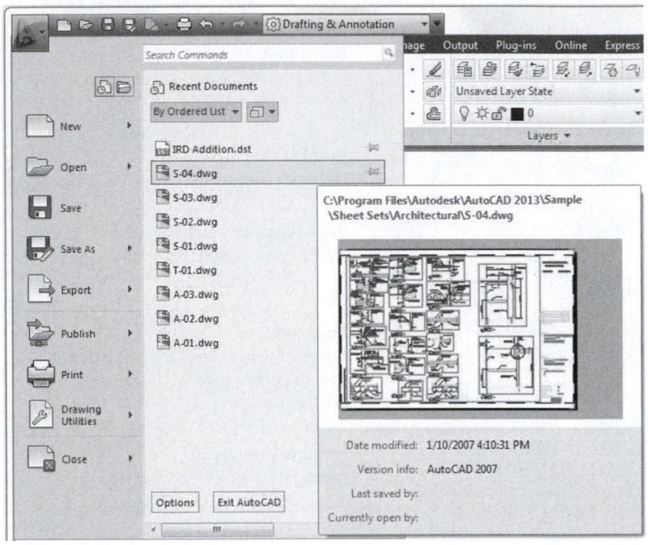

Figure 1-20
Displaying a preview image

Figure 1-21
The AutoCAD **Options** dialog box

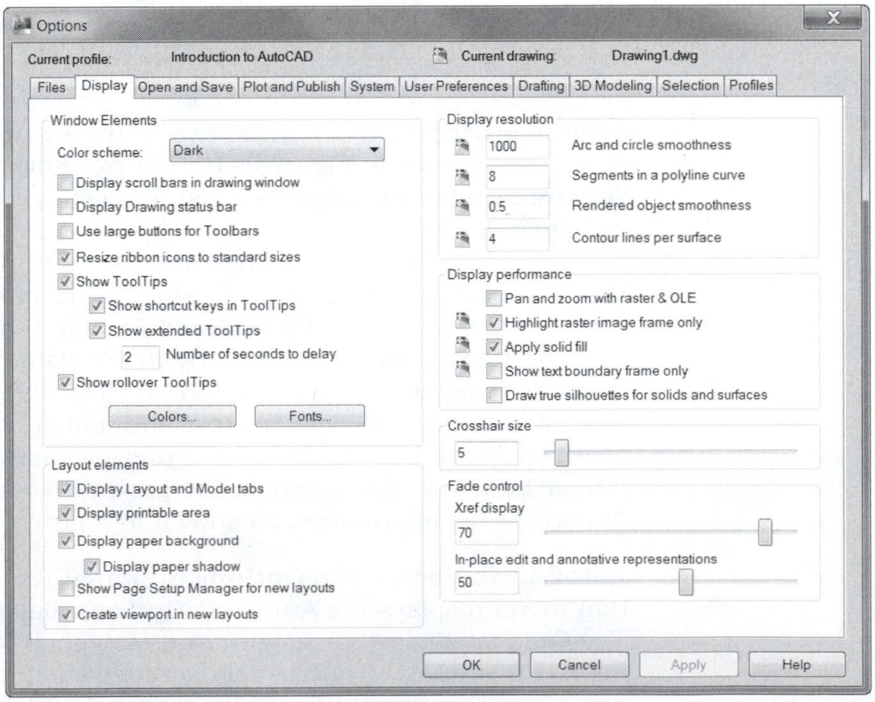

Ribbon

The ribbon at the top of the AutoCAD window shown in Figure 1-22 provides quick and easy access to the most used AutoCAD tools and features via a variety of task-specific tabs and panels.

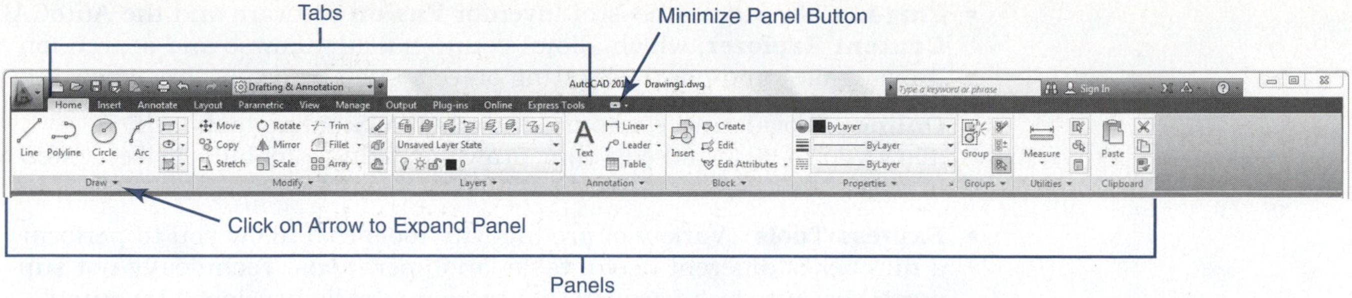

Figure 1-22
Ribbon

Each task-specific tab contains multiple panels that, in turn, contain related tools. In addition, panels with a black arrow next to the panel name can be expanded to access additional tools as shown in Figure 1-23.

Figure 1-23
The **Draw** ribbon panel with additional tools displayed

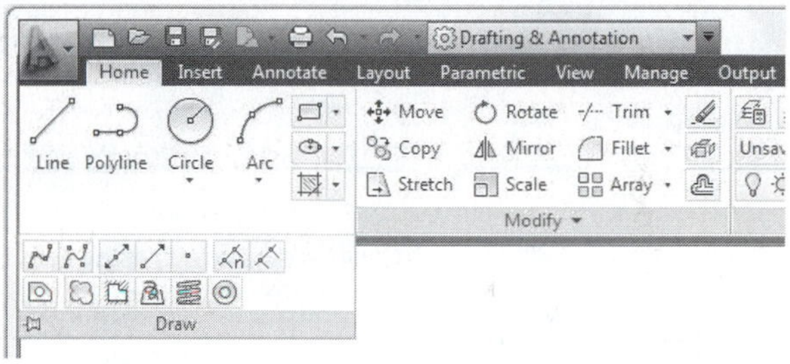

The default tab is the **Home** tab shown in Figure 1-22, which provides access to the most commonly used AutoCAD tools and features. The other tabs and their associated tools are as follows:

- **Insert** Tools for working with blocks and block attributes, external references, point clouds, importing different file formats, managing drawing data, and inserting content via **DesignCenter** and Autodesk **Seek**
- **Annotate** Tools for creating and modifying text and dimensions, creating leader notes and tables, marking up and revising drawings, and managing annotation scaling features

NEW to AutoCAD 2013

- **Layout** 2D tools for creating and managing layouts, page setups, and viewports. Additionally, includes advanced model documentation tools for automatically creating 2D projected views, sections, and details from 3D models
- **Parametric** Tools for establishing and maintaining geometric constraints and dimensional relationships
- **View** Tools for navigating in a drawing, managing named views, managing the user coordinate system (UCS), managing visual styles, managing viewports, turning different palettes on and off, viewing and switching multiple open drawings, and controlling the display of different AutoCAD interface features
- **Manage** Tools for recording and playing command macros, customizing the AutoCAD interface, loading and running custom programs, and managing CAD standards
- **Output** Tools for plotting and publishing drawings, creating DWF and PDF files, and sharing drawings using Autodesk **Seek**

- **Plug-ins** Provides access to Inventor **Fusion** software and the AutoCAD **Content Explorer,** which allows you to quickly browse and search for drawing files and named drawing objects such as layers, linetypes, etc.
- **Online** Provides access to the **AutoCAD WS** online tools, which allow you to view and edit your drawings using a mobile device or web browser
- **Express Tools** Variety of productivity tools that allow you to perform a number of different useful tasks and operations. Technically not supported by Autodesk because they were originally developed by outside users

Clicking on another tab swaps the current tools displayed with the set of tools selected so that a minimum amount of space is required for the tools you need and the drawing space is always maximized. In Figure 1-24 the **Annotate** tab has been selected so that the tools for adding text, dimensions, and other annotation features are now displayed.

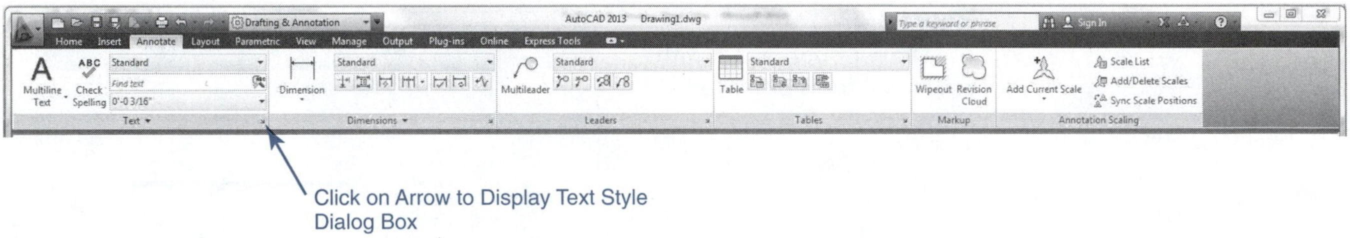

Figure 1-24
Annotate tab of the ribbon

> **TIP**
>
> The small arrows pointing down on the right side of some panel title bars shown in Figure 1-24 are buttons that when clicked display the style dialog box for the corresponding panel. For instance, clicking on the down arrow button on the right side of the **Text** panel displays the **Text Style** dialog box.

> **FOR MORE DETAILS**
>
> See page 419 in Chapter 11 for more information about creating and managing text styles.

Controlling the Ribbon Display. The ribbon has a number of different display features and options. Right-clicking on a panel tab displays the shortcut menu shown in Figure 1-25.

Figure 1-25
The ribbon right-click menu

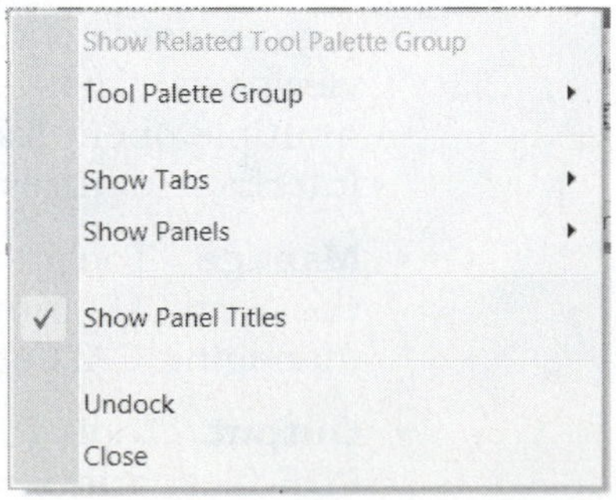

Using the right-click menu, you can turn different ribbon tabs and panels on and off by selecting them from their corresponding submenus. You can turn off all the panel titles at the bottom of the ribbon by deselecting the **Show Panel Titles** option.

The arrow buttons on the right side of the **Express Tools** tab shown in Figure 1-26 allow you to maximize the size of the drawing display window even further.

Clicking on the down arrow on the far right displays the menu shown in Figure 1-26 that allows you to minimize the ribbon using three different options.

Selecting the **Minimize to Panel Buttons** option collapses all the panels so that only the ribbon tabs and button representations are displayed. Placing your mouse pointer over a button temporarily displays the panel so you can select the desired tool similar to Figure 1-27. The panel then collapses back to the button-only display when you move your mouse pointer back over the drawing window.

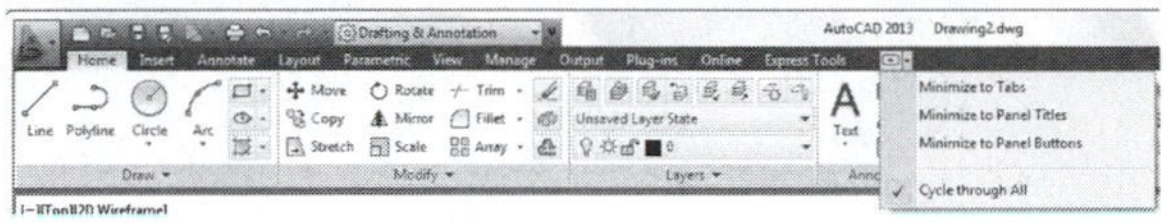

Figure 1-26
The ribbon **Minimize** menu

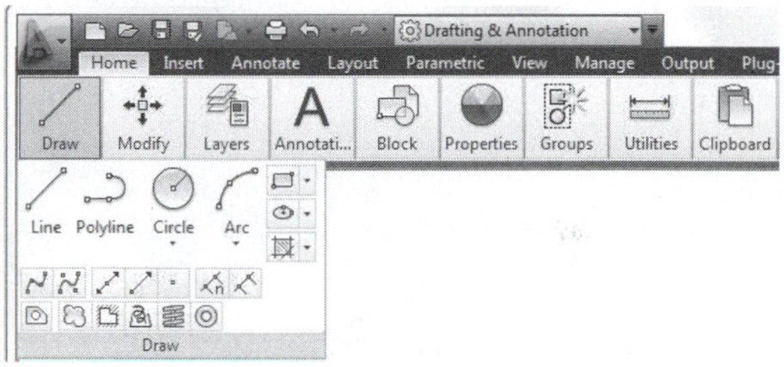

Figure 1-27
Single ribbon panel temporarily displayed

Selecting the **Minimize to Panel Titles** option collapses all the panels so that only the ribbon tabs and panel titles are displayed. Placing your mouse pointer over a panel title temporarily displays the panel so that you can select the desired tool similar to Figure 1-27. The panel then collapses back to the title-only display when you move your mouse pointer back over the drawing window.

Selecting the **Minimize to Tabs** option collapses all the panels and their titles so that all that is visible are the ribbon tabs across the top. You must click on the tab to display its respective ribbon temporarily while you choose the desired tool. The ribbon then disappears when you move your cursor back over the drawing window.

TIP

Clicking on the arrow button to the immediate left of the down arrow that displays the **Minimize** options menu discussed previously (see Figure 1-26) allows you to cycle between the full ribbon and the current **Minimize** option.

You can reorganize ribbon tabs, or panels within individual tabs, by simply dragging and dropping them to a different location on the ribbon using your mouse. It is even possible to drag panels completely off the ribbon and create separate, what are called "sticky," panels, which float above your drawing window.

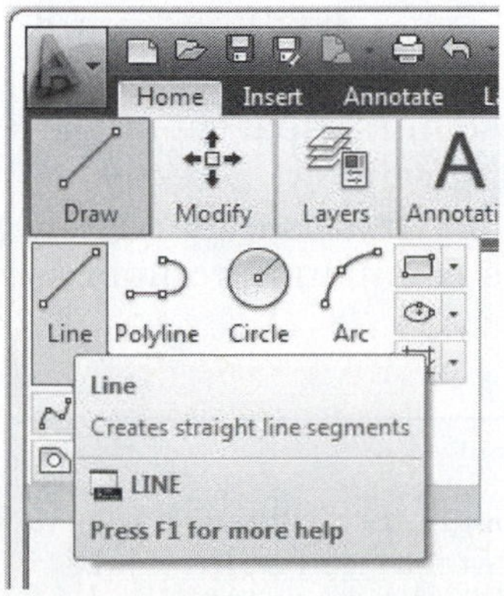

Figure 1-28
Line tooltip

Tooltips

You may have already noticed that information about a tool automatically appears directly at your mouse pointer if you hover the pointer over a tool for a short period of time. This useful feature is commonly referred to as a *tooltip*. The tooltip for the **Line** tool is shown in Figure 1-28.

The best part is that if you hover the mouse pointer for a split second more without moving, the tooltip expands to display additional information if it is available, sometimes even including helpful graphics, as shown in Figure 1-29.

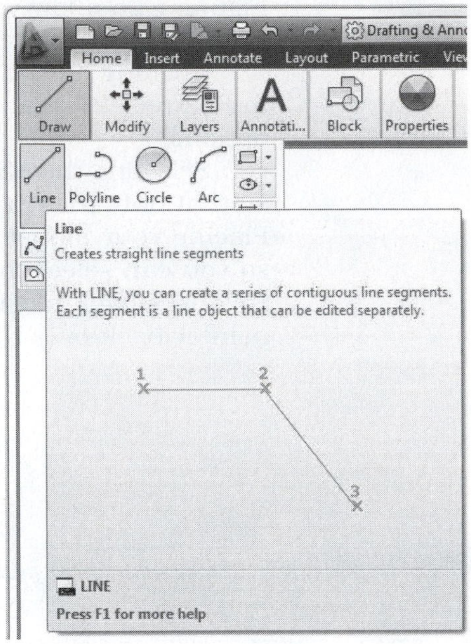

Figure 1-29
Line tooltip with additional information displayed

In addition, pressing the **<F1>** function key on your keyboard will display the complete AutoCAD online help topic for the current tool for even more detailed information. The AutoCAD online help system is discussed in detail at the end of this chapter.

NEW to AutoCAD 2013

The Command Line Interface

The *command line interface* provides access to the AutoCAD command line (see Figure 1-30). The AutoCAD command line allows you to enter AutoCAD commands by typing them on the keyboard. It is also one of the ways AutoCAD communicates with you via command prompts and messages.

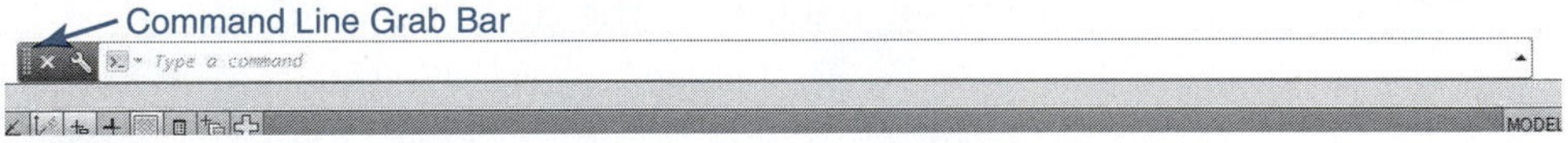

Figure 1-30
The command line interface

By default, the command line is displayed in a semitransparent single row that floats above the bottom of AutoCAD drawing window. Directly above the command line is a command prompt history that is dynamically updated so you can keep track of all of the previous command prompts as you work through a command.

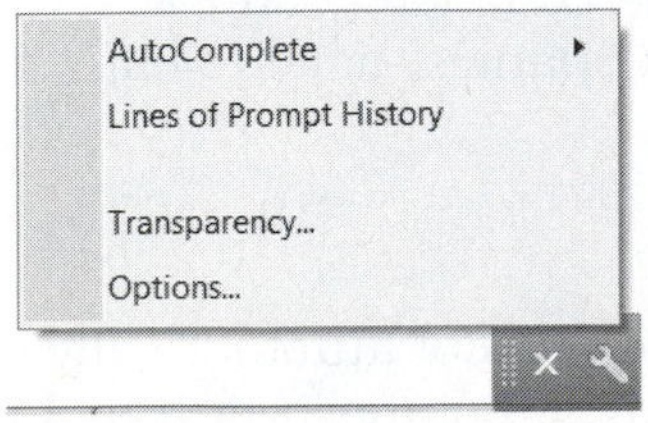

Figure 1-31A
Command line options menu

> **TIP**
>
> The default number of lines displayed in the command prompt history is three. You can change the number of lines displayed by clicking on the wrench icon on the left of the command line interface shown in Figure 1-31A and selecting the **Lines of Prompt History** option.

NOTE

Command line transparency can be controlled by clicking on the wrench icon on the left of the command line shown in Figure 1-31A and selecting **Transparency**... from the flyout menu to display the **Transparency** dialog box.

The command line interface provides a number of other customizable features and options including a clickable list of the most recently entered commands and an **AutoComplete** feature, which automatically suggests and completes commands as you type. All of these features and options are described in detail in the following sections.

Entering Commands via the Keyboard. AutoCAD commands can be entered by typing them at the keyboard. For instance, the command to draw a line can be entered by typing **Line<Enter>** at the command line as follows:

Line<Enter>

AutoCAD commands are not case sensitive so you can enter any combination of uppercase and lowercase characters with the same result.

TIP

When AutoCAD is awaiting a command, an icon that looks like ">_" is displayed on the left of the command line along with the prompt to "*Type a command*". When a command is active, the ">_" icon is replaced with command's icon along with the command name to let you know you are currently in a command.

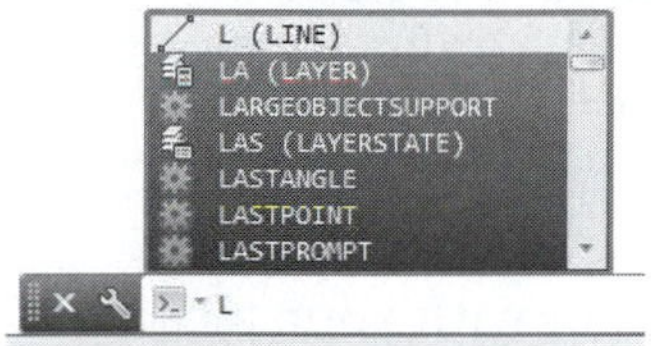

Figure 1-31B
The **AutoComplete** list

system variable: A named setting maintained by AutoCAD that controls an aspect of a drawing or the drawing environment.

By default, AutoCAD provides an **AutoComplete** feature that allows you to begin typing a command, and AutoCAD automatically completes the entry with an AutoCAD command or system variable. If you pause for a split second, a list is displayed as shown in Figure 1-31B that allows you to cycle through all the commands and ***system variables*** that start with the letters you typed and select from the list. As you type, the list is refined to match the characters you are typing.

NOTE

The different **AutoComplete** features and options can be controlled by clicking on the wrench icon on the left of the command line shown in Figure 1-31A to display a flyout menu with all the command line options. Displaying the **AutoComplete** submenu allows you to turn on/off the auto-append feature, the suggestion list, the command icon display, whether system variables are displayed, and to adjust the delay time before the **AutoComplete** features are displayed.

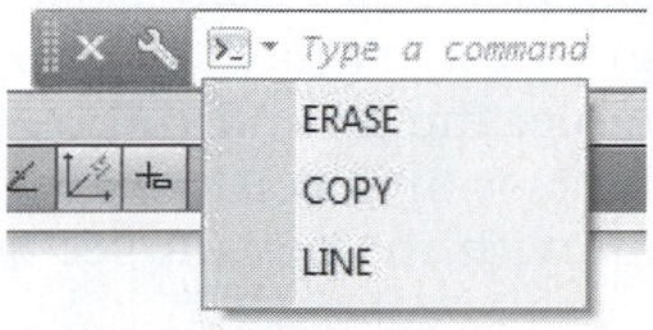

Figure 1-31C
Command history

TIP

Clicking on the down arrow icon on the left side of the command line shown in Figure 1-31C displays a flyout menu of the most recently used commands so you can quickly reenter a recent command by simply clicking on it.

command alias: An abbreviated definition of a command name that enables you to enter commands faster at the keyboard by typing the first one or two letters of the command.

Most commands can also be abbreviated to speed up their entry. The abbreviated version of a command is known as a ***command alias.***

Typically, the command alias is the first one or two letters of the full command. The abbreviation for the **LINE** command is **L:**

L<Enter>

FOR MORE DETAILS

A complete list of command aliases is provided in Appendix C.

TIP

Hitting the **<Enter>** key or the spacebar when no command has been typed will reenter the last command. This is a time-saving device that allows you to enter the same command repeatedly. For this reason, the most productive way to work in AutoCAD is to group like operations together. This allows you to "stay in the command" without losing focus jumping around to other ribbons, panels, and commands. Always try to focus on one operation.

Entering Command Options at the Command Line. Many commands have options that the user can select by entering a designated response using the keyboard. Options are always displayed as a list in square brackets with clickable options displayed in blue and separated by spaces. The **ZOOM** command prompts you with the following options at the command line:

Specify corner of window, enter a scale factor (nX or nXP), or

[**A**ll **C**enter **D**ynamic **E**xtents **P**revious **S**cale **W**indow **O**bject] <real time>:

NOTE

The spacebar at the bottom of the keyboard works exactly the same as the **<Enter>** key in AutoCAD. Because it is larger, some people prefer using it over the **<Enter>** key because it is easier and faster to get to. The spacebar is especially helpful when used as described in the preceding TIP to repeat commands!

Options can be selected either by clicking on them with your mouse or by entering them at the keyboard. If you enter the option via the keyboard, you can either type in the complete option keyword or, more simply, type in whatever letter is displayed in blue and capitalized in the option keyword. For example, to use the **ZOOM** command with the **Window** option, you can enter either **Window** or **W** in response to the **ZOOM** command prompt. The **Previous** option can be entered as **P,** the **Extents** option as **E,** and so on. Obviously, typing a shortened abbreviation is faster than typing the complete word so their liberal use is suggested.

Default Command Options. Sometimes a command will display a default option indicated with the option displayed between angle brackets. The default can be selected by simply hitting the **<Enter>** key. For instance, the default option for the **ZOOM** command is always **<real time>**. This means if you simply hit the **<Enter>** key in response to the **ZOOM** options prompt, you will be automatically placed in the **Zoom Realtime** mode.

AutoCAD remembers some command options so you don't have to type them the next time you use the command. For example, the default radius for a circle always reflects the radius you entered the last time you created a circle. The following is a **CIRCLE** command prompt with the default set to 2.0000 units.

Specify radius of circle or [**D**iameter] <2.0000>: **<Enter>**

If you are creating another circle with a radius of 2.0000 units, hit the **<Enter>** key, and voilà!

Canceling a Command with the <Esc> Key. The **<Esc>** key at the top left of the keyboard cancels, or aborts, an active command. It is probably the most used keyboard key in AutoCAD! When you hit the **<Esc>** key, the current command is immediately aborted.

Hitting the **<Esc>** key will also "unselect" any objects that are currently selected in the drawing window.

> **FOR MORE DETAILS**
>
> How to select objects in the drawing window is explained in detail in Chapter 7.

The Command History. AutoCAD remembers every command entered in an AutoCAD session from the time you start AutoCAD up until the very last command you enter. This is known as the command history. You can display the command history by selecting the up arrow on the right side of the command line as shown in Figure 1-32 or by hitting the **<F2>** key. The command history is distinguished from the active command line using a gray background color. You can scroll backward and forward through the command history using the arrow keys on your keyboard. The up arrow scrolls backward through the command history, whereas the down arrow scrolls forward. You can scroll backward or forward to any command in the history and run it again by hitting the **<Enter>** key.

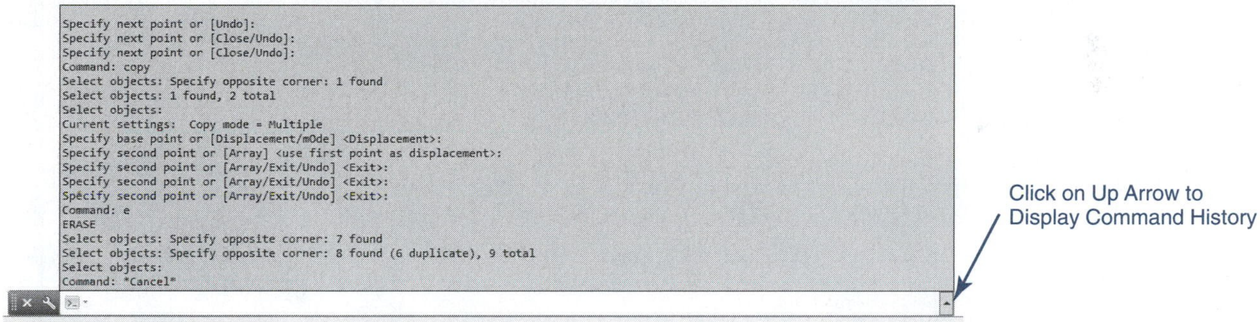

Figure 1-32
Resizing command line interface

You can change the color used for the command history background color and other command line interface features via the **Drawing Window Colors** dialog box, which can be displayed by selecting the **Colors...** button on the **Display** tab of the **Options** dialog box.

Resizing, Moving, and Docking the Command Line Interface. The command line can be resized, moved, and even docked at the top or bottom of the AutoCAD window. To resize the command line interface so you can see more lines of text, place your mouse pointer over the top or bottom edge of the command line interface so that the pointer switches into a double arrow. Hold down your left mouse button and drag up or down, and the window size changes accordingly.

The command line can also be moved by clicking on the grab bar on the left side and dragging it with your mouse. If you move the command line near an edge of the drawing window, it will snap to the edge. If you want to place the window near the edge without snapping, simply hold down the **<Ctrl>** key while moving it.

You can dock the command line at either the top or the bottom of the AutoCAD drawing window by dragging it using the grab bar to the top or the bottom.

Turning the Command Line Interface Off. The command line interface can be turned off by simply selecting the **X** on the command line grab bar on the left. It can be turned back on using the **<Ctrl>+9** keyboard combination. When the command line is turned off, commands can still be entered with the keyboard using *dynamic input*, which is explained in the next section.

The Full Text Window. It is possible to switch to a larger separate command line window known as the **Text** window by pressing **<Ctrl>+<F2>** function key at the top of your keyboard. Pressing **<Ctrl>+<F2>** once will display the **Text** window, as shown in Figure 1-33. The **Text** window can be minimized, maximized, and resized using standard Windows techniques. Pressing **<Ctrl>+<F2>** again toggles the window off.

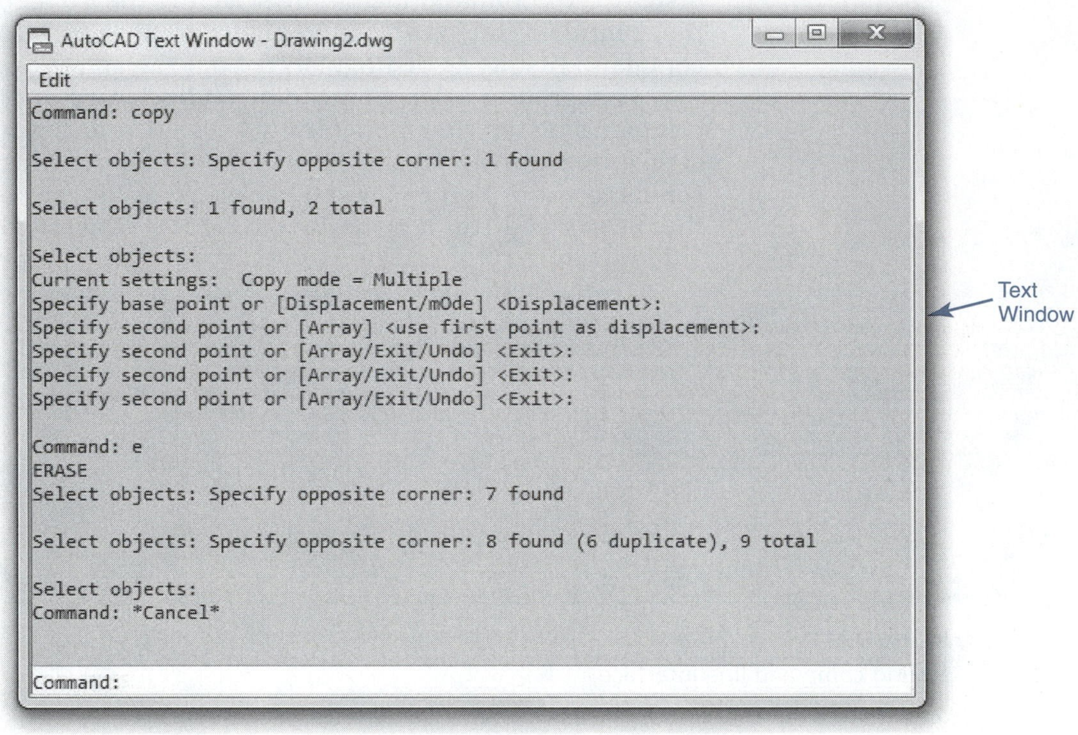

Figure 1-33
The **Text** window

You'll notice that there is an **Edit** pull-down menu in the **Text** window. Selecting it displays the menu shown in Figure 1-34.

This menu gives you even more command line options. You can run recent commands, select old commands and paste them to the command line to repeat them, and even copy the complete command history.

Figure 1-34
Text window menu

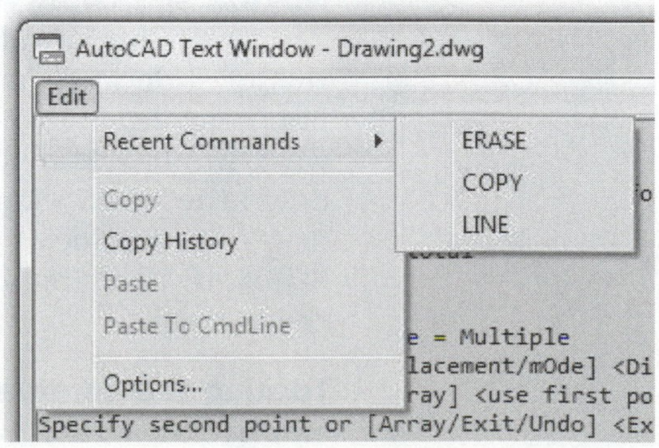

Dynamic Input

Dynamic input is a set of related input display features that allows you to enter information near the mouse cursor so you can focus on your drawing instead of constantly switching focus to the command line.

Viewing and Entering Data Near the Mouse Cursor. When the **Dynamic Input** feature is turned on, you input data at the cursor by toggling between different input fields. Figure 1-35 shows the **Pointer Input** feature, which allows you to enter *x* and *y* coordinate values right at the cursor. Coordinates are entered by typing the *x* coordinate value and the *y* coordinate value separated by a comma. When you enter the comma, the *x* value is locked, and input changes to the *y* value. You can also use the **<Tab>** key to switch between the *x* and *y* values. Hitting **<Enter>** accepts both values.

Dynamic input also provides a **Dimension Input** feature that displays temporary dimensions as you draw that you can dynamically update to create objects ***parametrically.*** The values that you enter in the dimension input fields are the values used to create the object. See Figure 1-36.

parametric: Automated creation of a drawing based on a given set of dimensions referred to as parameters.

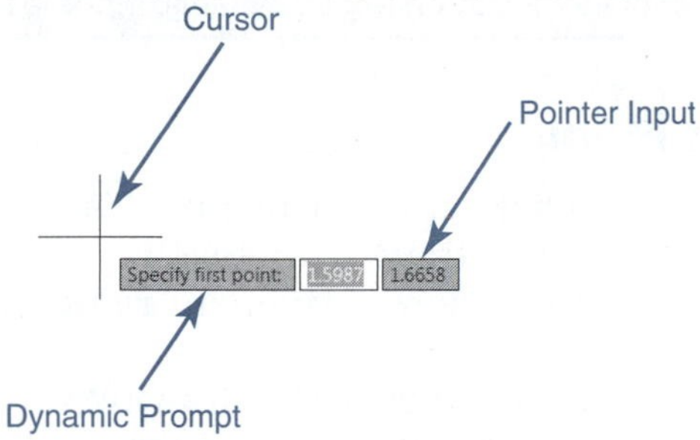

Figure 1-35
Viewing and entering data near the mouse cursor

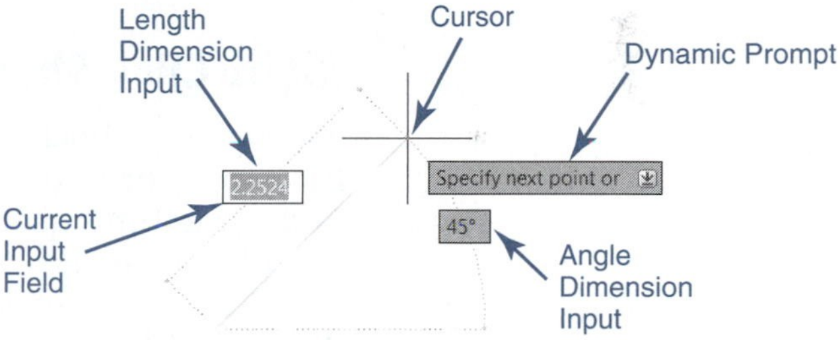

Figure 1-36
Using dynamic dimensions to create a line

The **<Tab>** key allows you to toggle between the different input fields. For instance, pressing the **<Tab>** key in the example shown in Figure 1-36 switches the input field from the dynamic length dimension to the dynamic angle dimension as shown in Figure 1-37.

Figure 1-37
Using the <Tab> key to toggle through input fields

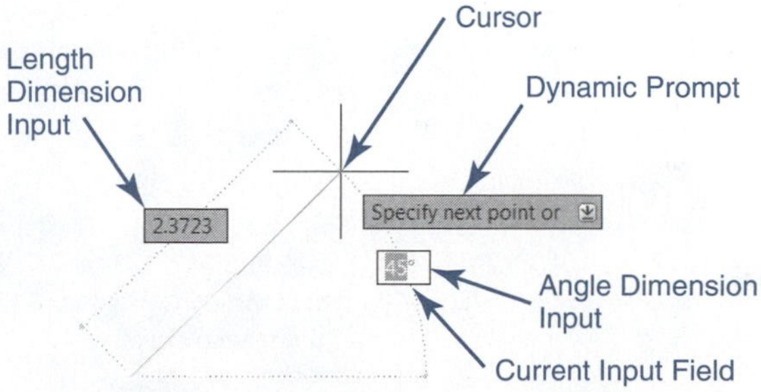

Selecting Command Options Near the Mouse Cursor. Earlier we saw that command options can be specified by selecting them with your mouse or by typing all or part of them at the AutoCAD command line. By using the **Dynamic Prompt** feature you can also select command options using either your mouse or the keyboard. If you press the down arrow key on your keyboard, a list of the valid command options is displayed near the

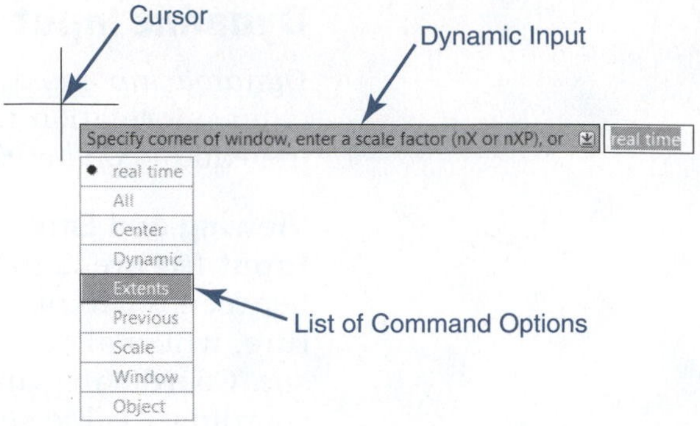

Figure 1-38
Selecting **ZOOM** command options using dynamic input

cursor as shown in Figure 1-38. You can either use your mouse to select the desired option or navigate up and down the list using the arrow keys on your keyboard. Using this method, you must press **<Enter>** when the desired option is indicated.

FOR MORE DETAILS

See page 197 in Chapter 5 for more information about dynamic input features and settings.

Right-Click Shortcut Menus

AutoCAD is chock-full of right-click shortcut menus. They're everywhere. If you're ever in doubt, right-click with your mouse, and you are bound to find something useful. Some of the more prominent right-click menus are introduced next.

If you right-click with your mouse over the drawing window when no drawing objects are selected, the **Default** shortcut menu shown in Figure 1-39 is displayed.

If you right-click when objects are selected in the drawing window, the **Edit** shortcut menu shown in Figure 1-40 is displayed so that you can modify the selected object(s).

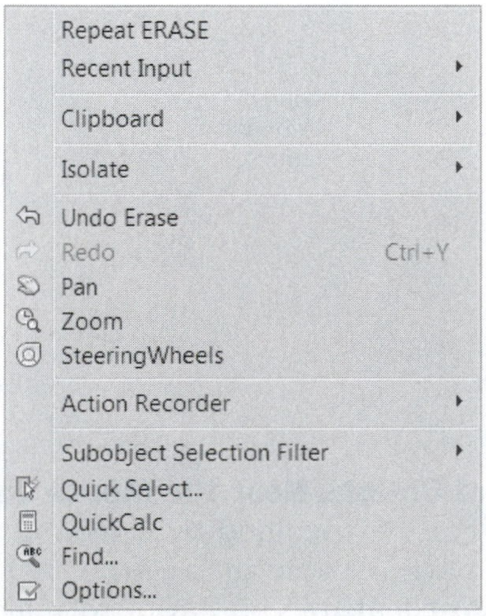

Figure 1-39
Default shortcut menu

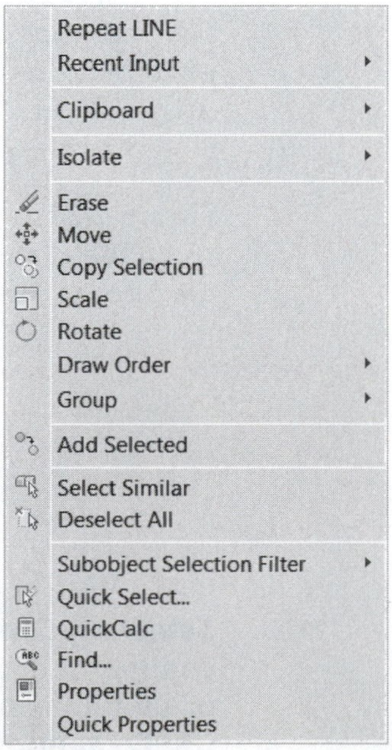

Figure 1-40
Edit shortcut menu

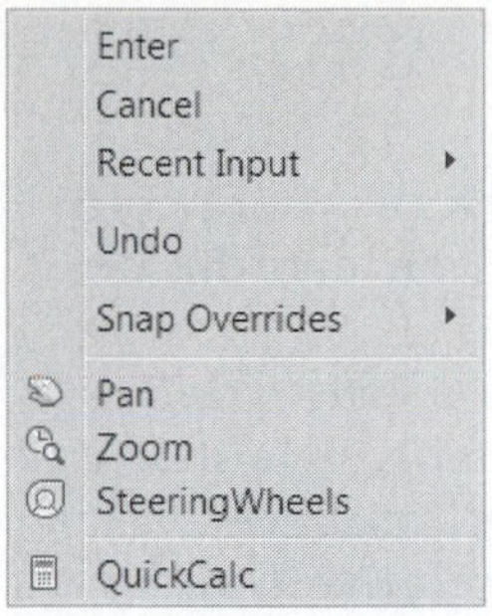

Figure 1-41
Command shortcut menu

If you right-click when a command is active, the **Command** shortcut menu shown in Figure 1-41 is displayed, providing access to different command options, etc.

Accessing Recent Input. It is possible to access recent command input using the keyboard up and down arrow keys or the right-click shortcut menu shown in Figure 1-42.

The **Recent Input** feature is a time-saving feature that allows you to recall recently entered data values so you don't have to type them again regardless of whether the values were entered via the keyboard in the first place. AutoCAD remembers all the input values from all the input methods.

Figure 1-42
Accessing recent input

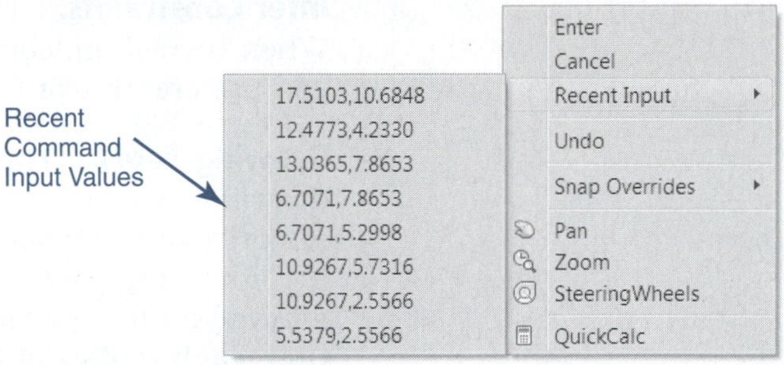

> **TIP**
> If you use the right-click menu to list the recent input when no command is active, AutoCAD will display a list of recently used commands.

Status Bars

There are two different status bars in AutoCAD: the *drawing status bar*, which is at the bottom of every individual drawing window, and the *application status bar*, which is located at the very bottom of the AutoCAD window shown earlier in Figure 1-10.

The drawing status bar is used primarily for controlling the annotation and viewport scale in each drawing and is explained in detail in Chapter 14. It is turned off by default.

The application status bar, on the other hand, is always on because it controls so many different things. It is like a minidashboard for AutoCAD (see Figure 1-43).

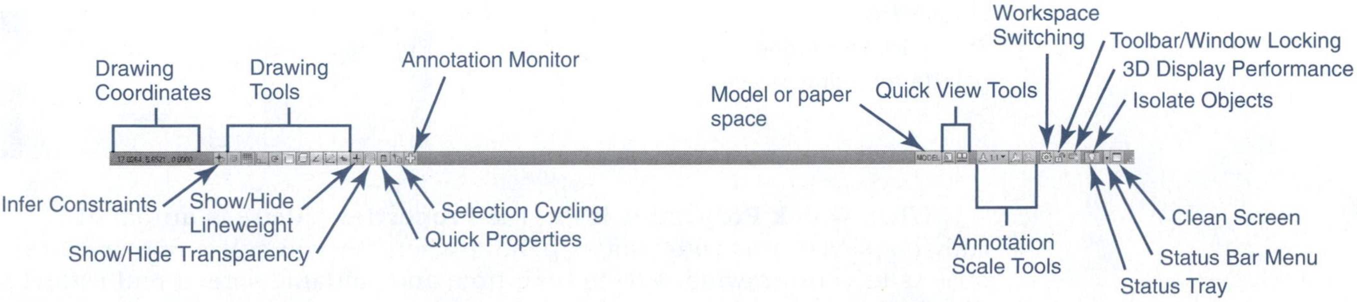

Figure 1-43
The application status bar

> **NOTE**
> You can turn on the drawing status bar on the **Display** tab of the **Options** dialog box introduced earlier on page 21.

Like your car's dashboard, the application status bar provides a myriad of different features and functionality:

Drawing Coordinates. The coordinate display keeps track of where your mouse crosshairs are located by interactively displaying their coordinates as you move your mouse.

You can disable the coordinate display by clicking on it with your mouse. Right-clicking on the coordinate display button displays a shortcut menu that allows you to switch between relative, absolute, and geographic coordinate display. The difference between absolute and relative coordinates is explained in Chapter 4.

Infer Constraints. This toggles automated geometric constraints on and off. When turned on, constraints are automatically applied between the object you are creating or editing and the points associated with the object snaps.

Drawing Tools. The drawing tool buttons allow you to toggle different drawing tools on and off interactively as you work in your drawing. The majority of the tools are explained in detail in Chapter 5.

Each drawing tool button has its own unique right-click menu that allows you to control that tool's specific settings and features. In addition, each tool's right-click menu has a **Display** submenu that allows you to remove any of the drawing tool buttons from the status bar, as well as switch from the icon-type buttons that have pictures back to the traditional text-only style shown in Figure 1-44 that was used in earlier releases of AutoCAD.

Figure 1-44
Drawing tool buttons in text-only mode

Show/Hide Lineweight. This button toggles lineweight display on and off.

Show/Hide Transparency. This button toggles object transparency on and off.

Quick Properties. The **Quick Properties** button toggles on and off the **Quick Properties** feature that allows you to quickly view and modify object properties directly where the objects are located on your screen via a trimmed down **Properties** palette like the one shown in Figure 1-45.

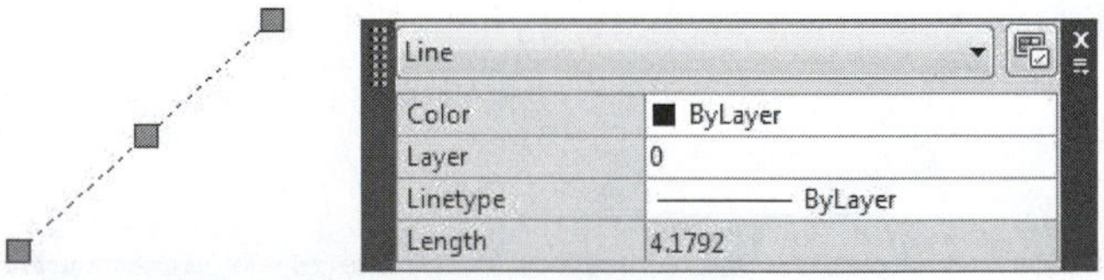

Figure 1-45
The **Quick Properties** palette for a line object

When **Quick Properties** is on, the **Properties** palette is automatically displayed near your mouse pointer whenever you select one or more objects in your drawing, saving both time and valuable screen real estate! The **Quick Properties** feature and the **Properties** palette are explained in detail in Chapter 6.

Selection Cycling. The **Selection Cycling** button toggles on and off selection cycling, which provides more control over selecting overlapping objects. When **Selection Cycling** is on and you try to select an object that overlaps with other objects, AutoCAD displays a list of all the overlapping objects, allowing you to choose exactly which object you want.

NEW to AutoCAD 2013

Annotation Monitor. The **Annotation Monitor** button toggles on and off annotation monitoring, which provides feedback regarding the status of annotation objects that are associated with views, sections, and details that have been automatically created using AutoCAD's advanced 3D model documentation tools.

MODEL/PAPER. The **MODEL/PAPER** button switches the drawing environment to the last active paper space layout if you are currently in model space. Select it so it switches to **PAPER.** If you are in paper space and select the button and change it to **MODEL,** the last viewport will become active so you can work "through" the viewport (same as double-clicking on a viewport).

Quick View Drawings and Layouts Tools. The **Quick View Drawings** and **Quick View Layouts** tools allow you to visually switch between open drawings or layouts via a horizontal row of preview images. The **Quick View Drawings** tool is explained later in this chapter. See Chapter 14 for more information about the **Quick View Layouts** tool.

Annotation Scale Tools. As mentioned earlier in the "Fundamental CAD Concepts" section, it is possible to automate the process of creating annotation objects such as text and dimensions at the correct size for the final plotted drawing scale using the **Annotation Scale** feature located on the right side of the status bar (see Figure 1-43). Clicking on the **Annotation Scale** button displays a menu with a list of predefined scales, as shown in Figure 1-46.

When annotation objects that have their *annotative* property enabled are added to the drawing, they will automatically scale up or down by the current annotation scale so that you do not have to scale them manually.

The two buttons to the right of the **Annotation Scale** allow you to add and view annotation objects at multiple scales so that it is possible to reduce redundant annotation information in your drawings.

In the past, drawings that had multiple scales had to have separate copies of all the annotation objects such as text and dimensions at different scales to account for each drawing scale factor. Typically, different scale representations of the annotation objects were located on separate layers so that they could be turned on and off for each scale as needed. It was a very complex process, and because it required redundant information, it was prone to errors and omissions.

Chapters 11 through 14 discuss in detail how to utilize the AutoCAD **Annotation Scale** features to add and manage different annotation objects.

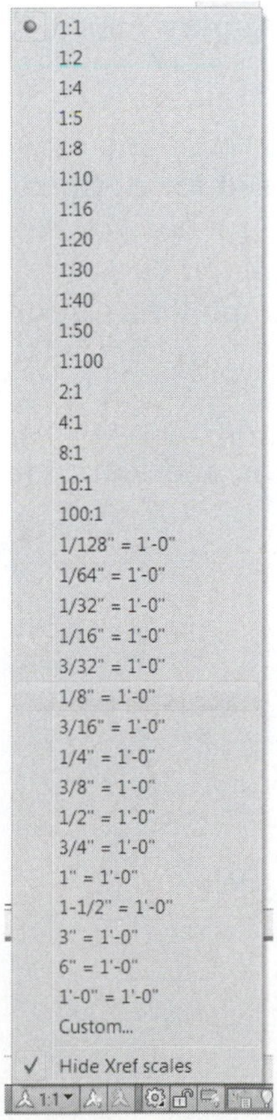

Figure 1-46
The **Annotation Scale** menu

Workspace Switching. The **Workspace Switching** button allows you to switch between AutoCAD's default workspaces, save a custom workspace, control workspace settings, and customize workspaces.

Workspaces allow you to save and restore the on/off status and positions of the ribbon, palettes, pull-down menus, and toolbars so that you can set up different work environments for different tasks. For instance, you might set up a dimensioning environment that has all the AutoCAD dimension tools turned on while most of the other AutoCAD tools are turned off so that you can focus strictly on the task of dimensioning.

To save your own custom workspace, you first set up the AutoCAD environment in the way you wish to save it by turning on and off the features you want and positioning them accordingly. Click on the **Workspace Switching** button and select **Save Current As...** from the menu and then enter a workspace name.

To restore a saved workspace, click on the **Workspace Switching** button and select it from the list.

The **Workplace Settings...** menu item allows you to control which workspaces are displayed, the menu order, and whether workspace changes are automatically saved when switching workspaces.

The **Customize...** menu item displays the AutoCAD **Customize User Interface** (CUI) dialog box for more high-level-type customization tasks.

The **Display Workspace Label** menu item toggles on and off the text label display that indicates the current active workspace directly on the status bar.

Toolbar/Window Locking. The **Toolbar/Window Locking** tool allows you to lock toolbars, palettes, and other AutoCAD features so you do not accidently move them. Locking the various AutoCAD user interface features is discussed later in this chapter after most of the different interface features have been covered.

3D Display Performance. This controls features that affect display performance when working in 3D. Options include turning on and off adaptive degradation and hardware acceleration, as well as accessing the **Performance Tuner** dialog box so you can fine-tune your 3D display settings.

Isolate Objects. The **Isolate Objects** button displays a small menu that allows you to control object visibility independent from layer visibility using the following two options:

- **Isolate Objects** Only selected objects remain visible in the drawing. All other objects are hidden
- **Hide Objects** Selected objects are hidden. All other objects are visible

Objects that are isolated or hidden can be restored at any time using the **End Object Isolation** tool that is added to the **Object Display** menu after objects have been selected.

Status Tray. On the far right of the status bar is the status tray. The status tray dynamically updates with different icons that are used for notification features and different task-specific settings depending on what you're doing. For instance, after a plot is complete a notification balloon is displayed in the status tray with information about whether the plot was successful, as shown in Figure 1-47.

Status Bar Menu. The **Status Bar** menu shown in Figure 1-48 allows you to control different status bar features. You can remove buttons and features

Figure 1-47
Plot status notification balloon

Figure 1-48
The **Status Bar** menu

by deselecting them, turn on/off the separate **Drawing Status Bar,** and control when/how often notification balloons are displayed in the status tray.

Clean Screen Toggle. The **Clean Screen** toggle temporarily turns off most of AutoCAD's graphical interface features such as the ribbon, palettes, and toolbars and maximizes your drawing area so that you have more room to draw. Clicking on the **Clean Screen** toggle again turns everything back on again. The **Clean Screen** toggle is explained in detail in Chapter 3.

In-Canvas Viewport Control

The in-canvas viewport control located in the upper left corner of the AutoCAD drawing window is comprised of the three separate shortcut menus shown in Figures 1-49A through 1-49C. These menus allow you to quickly change viewport settings, views, and visual styles directly in the drawing window.

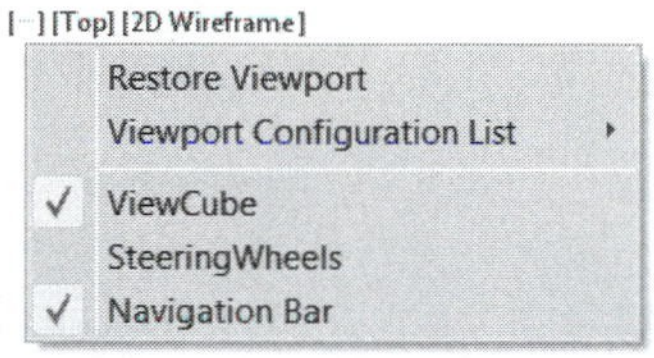

Figure 1-49A
The in-canvas viewport control

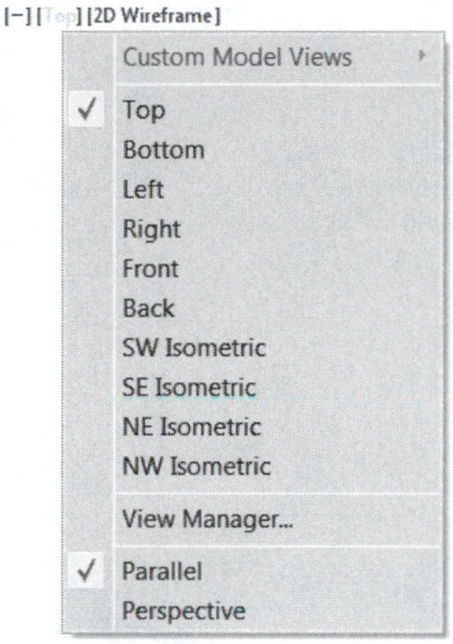

Figure 1-49B

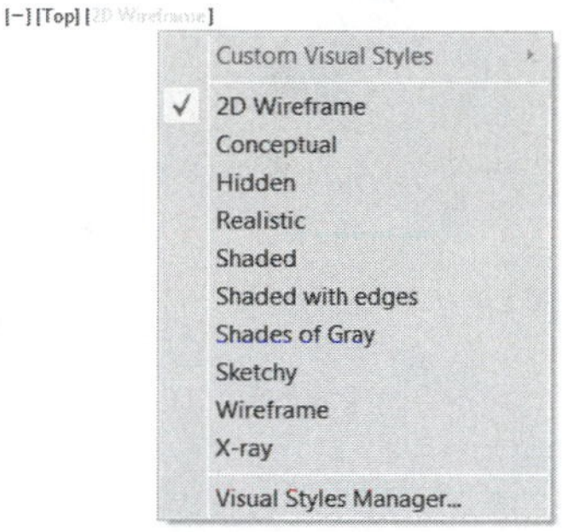

Figure 1-49C

The first menu on the left, which is displayed when you click on the "-" symbol, is the most useful in the 2D world for it controls the ViewCube and navigation bar displays explained in the following sections. You can ignore the other menus when working strictly in 2D drawings.

> **TIP**
>
> You can turn the in-canvas viewport control on and off via the **Display the Viewport Controls** check box on the bottom left of the **3D Modeling** tab of the **Options** dialog box.

ViewCube

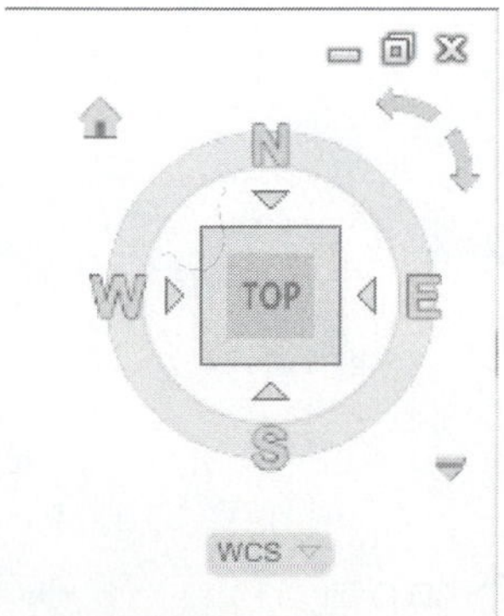

Figure 1-50
The **ViewCube** tool

The **ViewCube** tool, shown in Figure 1-50 at its default position in the upper right corner of the AutoCAD drawing window, is a clickable and draggable interface that you can use to switch between standard and isometric views of your model.

The **ViewCube** tool provides visual feedback about the current viewpoint of the drawing model as view changes occur. When your mouse pointer is positioned over the **ViewCube** tool, it becomes active so that it is possible to drag or click and switch to one of the available preset views, roll the current view 90° clockwise or counterclockwise, or switch to an isometric view of the model.

Considering that the **ViewCube** tool is more of an advanced 3D tool, it might be best to turn it off for now. The easiest way to do that is via the shortcut menu shown earlier in Figure 1-49A, which is displayed when you select the "-" symbol on the in-canvas viewport control. It is also possible to turn the **ViewCube** tool on and off from the **3D Modeling** tab of the **Options** dialog box. To turn off the **ViewCube** tool in the 2D drawing environment, uncheck the **2D Wireframe visual style** check box under the **Display the ViewCube** section at the bottom left of the dialog box shown in Figure 1-51.

Figure 1-51
Turning off the **ViewCube** tool in the **Options** dialog box

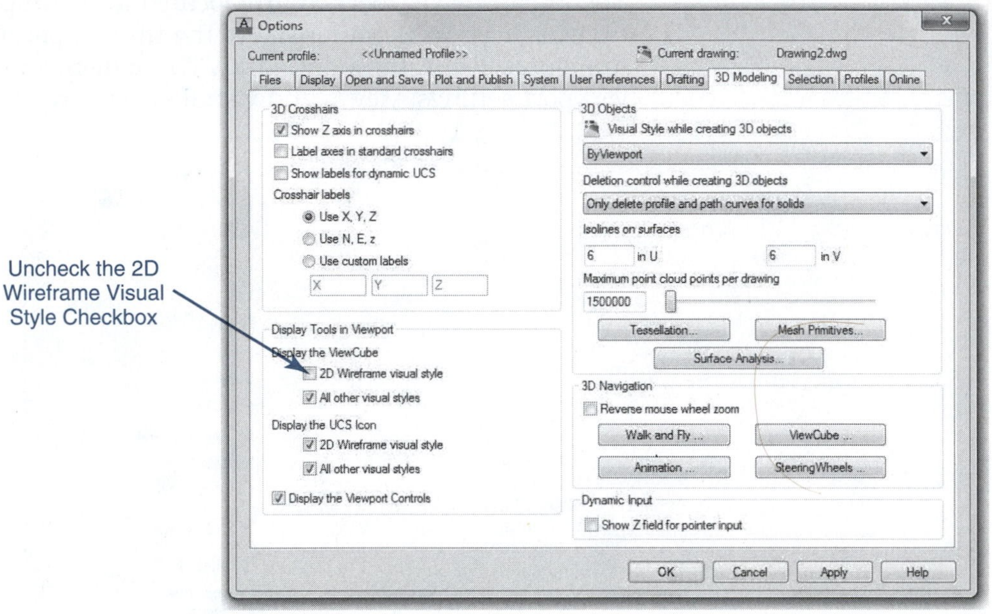

TIP

Remember that it is possible to quickly display the **Options** dialog box by right-clicking and selecting **Options...** from the bottom of most shortcut menus.

Navigation Bar

The navigation bar shown in Figure 1-52 provides quick and easy access to frequently used navigation tools including **SteeringWheels, Pan, Zoom, 3D Orbit,** and **ShowMotion.**

Figure 1-52
The navigation bar

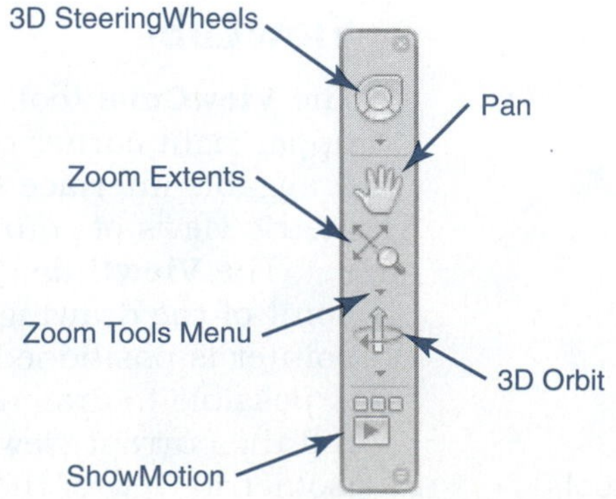

The **Pan** and **Zoom** tools are of most interest because they allow you to navigate the 2D drawing display so that you can view all of the information in the drawing at the scale necessary to do your work. The other tools are primarily for 3D use and are beyond the scope of this textbook. Consult the AutoCAD Help if you want more information about the 3D tools.

Clicking on the **Pan** tool changes your mouse pointer to a hand icon that indicates that you can click and hold your left mouse button down to drag the drawing around the drawing display. You can press **<Enter>** or **<Esc>** to close the **Pan** tool. Right-clicking will display a handy shortcut menu that also allows you to exit or to switch to a few different **Zoom** tools that are useful.

The **Zoom** tool defaults to **Zoom Extents**, which will zoom in or out in order to fill the drawing display with the extents, or outermost reaches, of the drawing. Selecting the down arrow at the bottom of the **Zoom Extents** tool displays a complete menu of different **Zoom** tools, as shown in Figure 1-53.

Figure 1-53
The different **Zoom** tools

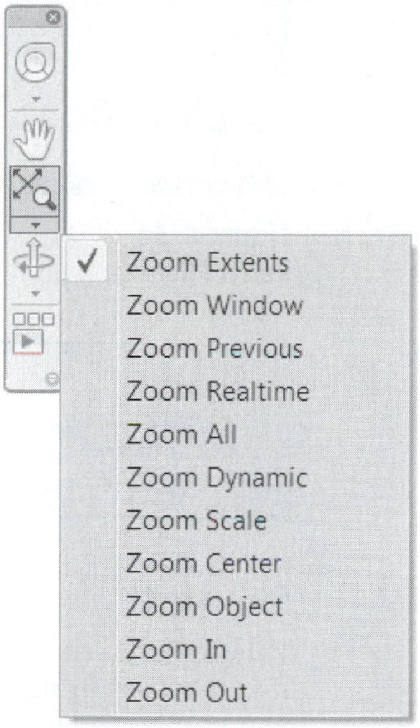

The main **Zoom** tools are introduced in Chapter 2, and all of the **Zoom** tools are explained in detail in Chapter 3 so that you can get around and navigate your drawings.

> **TIP**
>
> The easiest way to turn the navigation bar on and off is by selecting the "-" symbol on the in-canvas viewport control in the upper left of the drawing window to display the shortcut menu and deselect the **Navigation Bar** option. Alternatively, you can also use the **NAVBAR** command. To turn the navigation bar on or off, type **NAVBAR<Enter>** and then specify **On** or **Off**.

Dialog Boxes

Dialog box is the term used to describe any of the graphical windows displayed in response to a command that allows you to select and specify various command options. AutoCAD has many different dialog boxes. Selecting the **Open** tool from the **Quick Access** toolbar displays the **Select File** dialog box shown in Figure 1-54. This dialog box is common to many file-related commands. The common file dialog boxes work very similarly to Windows Explorer as explained earlier.

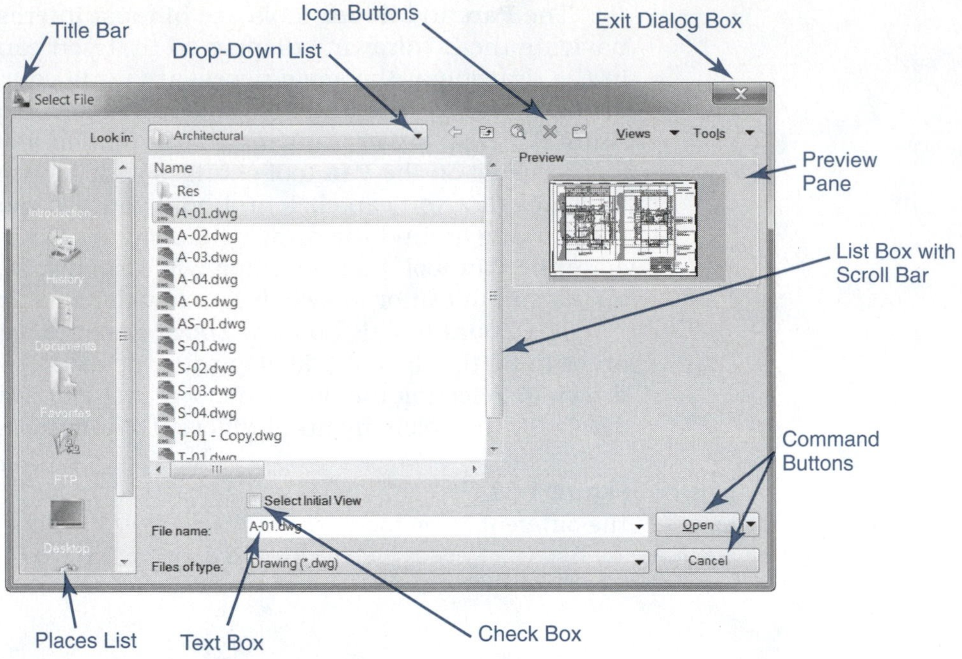

Figure 1-54
Select File dialog box

> **TIP**
>
> The common file dialog boxes contain a right-click shortcut menu that provides the same commands and options found in Windows Explorer so that you can perform different file operations without leaving AutoCAD.

Palettes

Palettes are separate windows that provide additional AutoCAD functionality. The cool thing is that palettes can be continuously displayed so that you can work between the palette and your drawing, like an artist creating a painting. Because of this capability, palettes have a special feature called **Auto-hide** that can be set to automatically hide a palette when you are not using it, freeing up your drawing window for actual drawing.

The easiest way to turn palettes on and off is via the **Palettes** panel on the **View** tab of the ribbon shown in Figure 1-55.

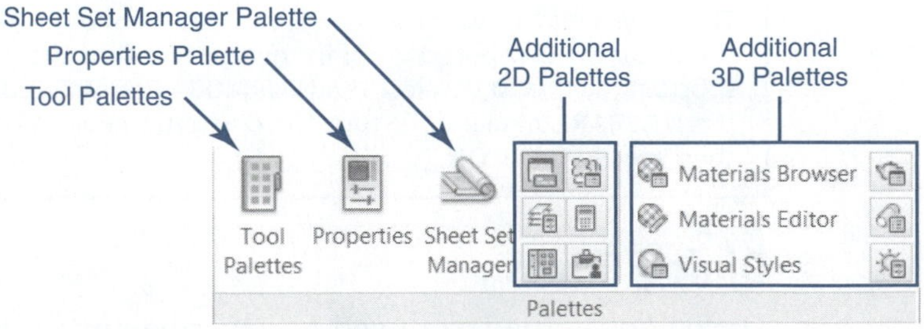

Figure 1-55
Palettes panel buttons

Tool Palettes. *Tool palettes* provide easy access to commands, hatch patterns, and blocks via a series of tabbed palettes as shown in Figure 1-56. To switch to a palette, select the corresponding tab. You can select a tool palette item either by clicking on its icon or by dragging an icon into your drawing window.

Figure 1-56
Tool palettes

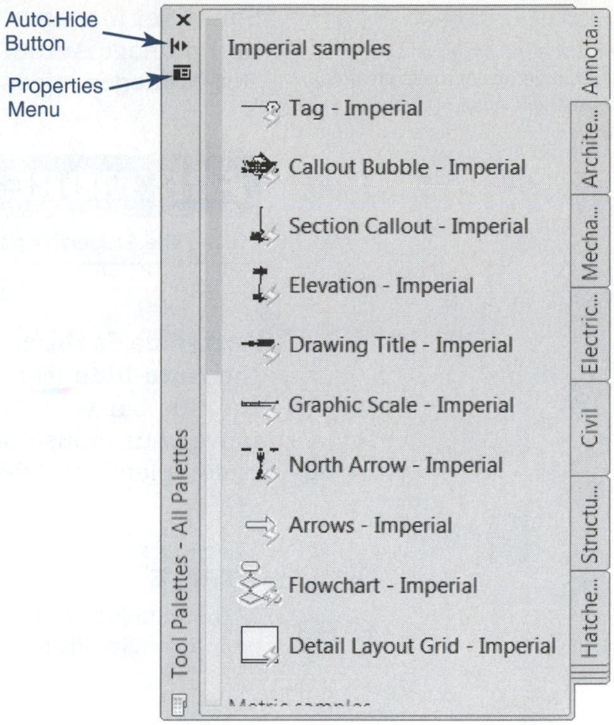

Tool palettes are meant to be customized, allowing you to add and organize your own commands, blocks, and hatch patterns. The default content is provided as a sample of what you can do. Creating custom tool palettes with your own blocks, hatch patterns, and commands is discussed later in the book.

Properties Palette. The **Properties** palette is your one-stop shop for managing the drawing object properties explained earlier. In Figure 1-57, the properties of a line are displayed in the **Properties** palette.

Figure 1-57
The **Properties** palette

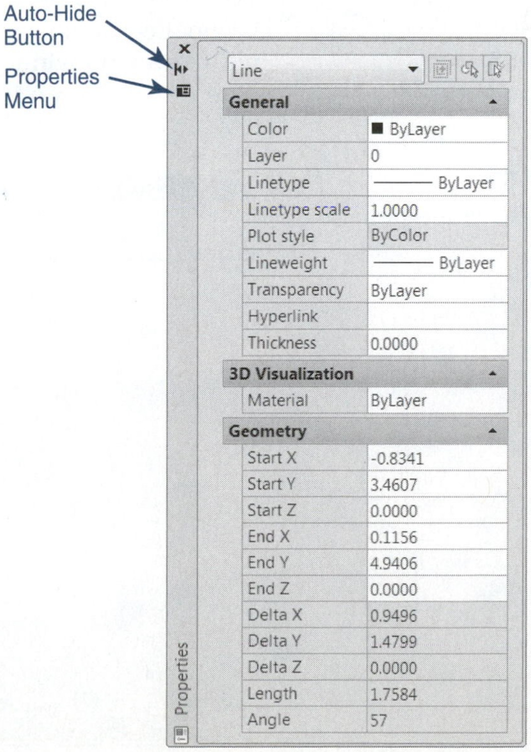

sheet set: An organized and named collection of sheets created from multiple AutoCAD drawing files.

Sheet Set Manager Palette. The **Sheet Set Manager** is used to create and manage AutoCAD ***sheet sets.*** For further information about the **Sheet Set Manager,** please consult AutoCAD Help.

FOR MORE DETAILS

Using the **Properties** palette is thoroughly detailed on page 244 in Chapter 6.

Auto-hide Feature. As mentioned, it is possible to "hide" a palette using the **Auto-hide** feature. When **Auto-hide** is on, the palette collapses so only the title bar is visible when your mouse is not over the palette. When you move your mouse back over the palette's title bar, the palette expands so it is completely visible again.

NOTE

The **Auto-hide** feature can be used when a palette is docked by selecting the "-" button on the right side of the title bar.

The easiest way to turn the **Auto-hide** feature on and off is by clicking on the **Auto-hide** arrow icon on the palette's title bar, as shown in Figure 1-57. **Auto-hide** can also be turned on and off using the **Palette Properties** shortcut menu explained in the next section.

Figure 1-58
Palette Properties menu

Palette Properties. Each of the palettes introduced previously has similar properties that are controlled by clicking on the **Properties** icon on the palette's title bar, as shown in Figure 1-57. Selecting the **Properties** icon on any palette displays a **Properties** shortcut menu similar to the one shown in Figure 1-58. Using the **Palette Properties** menu, you can turn the **Auto-hide** feature on and off and indicate whether a palette can be docked or not. A palette can be docked on either the left or right side of your drawing window. The **Properties** palette is shown docked on the right side of the screen in Figure 1-59.

Figure 1-59
Docking the **Properties** palette

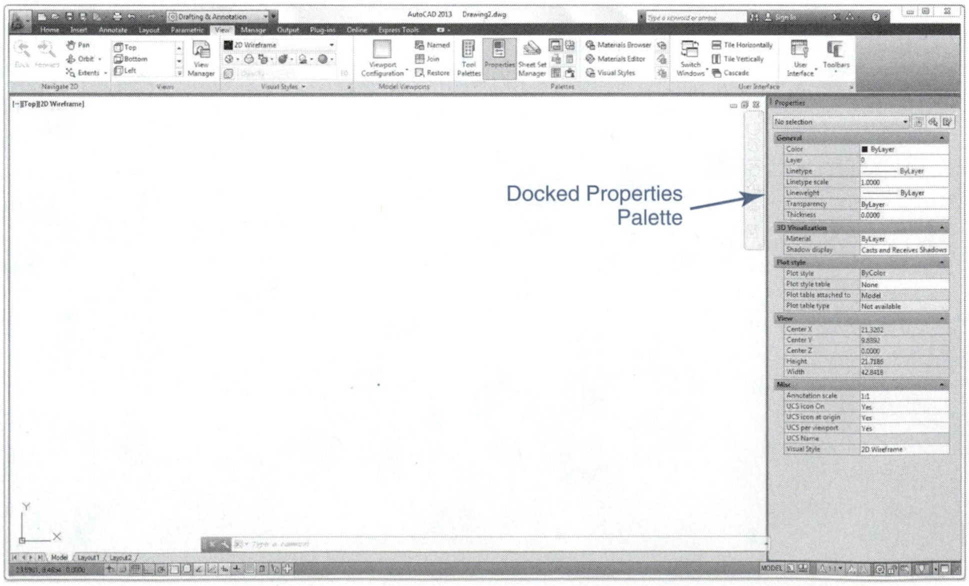

The **Anchor Left** and **Anchor Right** options on the **Palette Properties** menu allow you to dock a palette on the left or right of the AutoCAD window with the **Auto-hide** feature on so that the palette is reduced to a thin strip represented by the palette title bar, as shown in Figure 1-60.

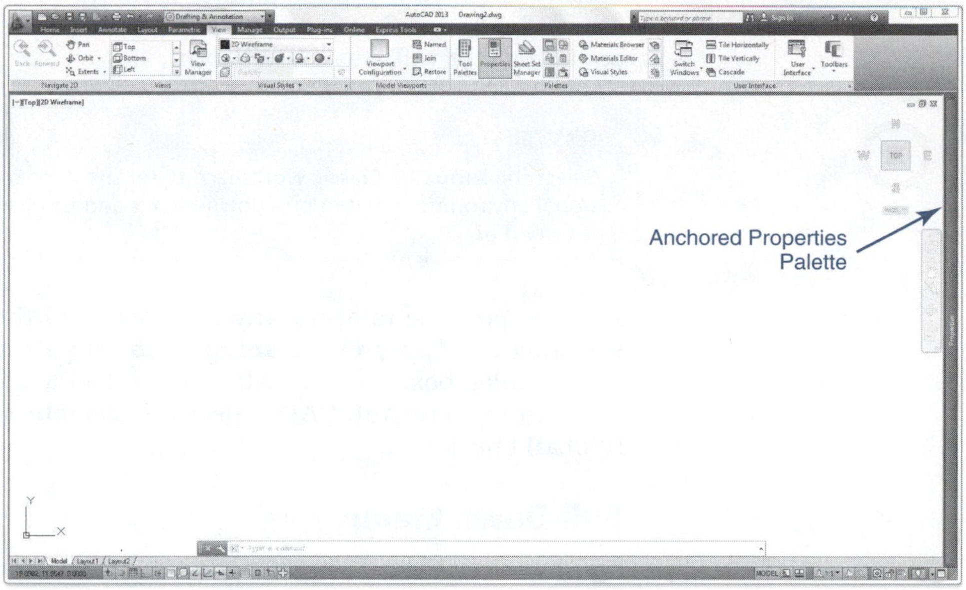

Figure 1-60
Properties palette anchored on the right with **Auto-hide** turned on

Placing your mouse pointer over the title bar displays the palette temporarily so that you can make any changes or updates. Turning the **Auto-hide** feature off when a palette is anchored will change it back to the docked mode shown earlier.

Transparency. It is possible to make palettes transparent so that you can see the drawing under, or through, the palette. The **Transparency...** menu item on the **Palette Properties** menu displays the **Transparency** dialog box shown in Figure 1-61.

Figure 1-61
The **Transparency** dialog box

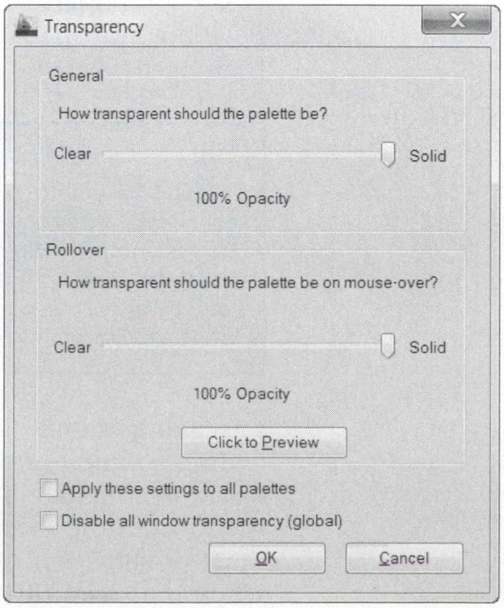

The slider bar at the top in the **General** area controls the overall transparency of palettes. By default, palettes are set to 100% opacity so that you cannot see through them. Sliding the bar to the left makes the palettes more transparent.

By default, palettes that are transparent will change back to 100% opacity when your mouse pointer is above them so that you can see them. The slider bar in the middle in the **Rollover** area allows you to change it so the palette will stay transparent.

NOTE

Select the **AutoCAD Classic** workspace to set the AutoCAD interface back to the traditional environment where pull-down menus and toolbars are turned on and the ribbon is turned off.

It is possible to apply any changes to all the palettes in AutoCAD by selecting the **Apply these settings to all palettes** check box at the bottom of the dialog box. To make all palettes 100% opaque and turn off transparency throughout AutoCAD, select the **Disable all window transparency (global)** check box.

Pull-Down Menus

The pull-down menus across the top of the AutoCAD window provide access to most of the AutoCAD commands. You'll notice that the menus are organized in the same order from left to right as in other Windows programs. The **File** menu is on the far left and the **Help** menu is on the far right, with many of the same menus in between **(Edit, View, Insert, Format, Tools,** and **Window).** Most of these menus contain similar commands and behavior.

TIP

You can also turn on the pull-down menus by selecting **Show Menu Bar** from the **Quick Access** toolbar flyout menu shown in Figure 1-14.

Putting your mouse pointer over a pull-down menu heading and clicking the mouse will display the pull-down menu. The **File** pull-down menu is shown in Figure 1-62. To select a menu item on a pull-down menu, position your mouse over the desired menu item so it is highlighted and then click with your mouse.

TIP

It is also possible to select a menu item via the keyboard by selecting the **<Alt>** key on your keyboard in combination with the underlined character on the pull-down menu. For instance, the **File** pull-down menu can be displayed by holding down the **<Alt>** key in combination with the **F** key on your keyboard. You can then select the desired menu item by hitting the key for the underlined letter in the menu label. Hitting the **N** key while the **File** pull-down menu is displayed selects the **New...** menu item.

Cascading Menus. Menu items with an arrow on the right indicate a cascading submenu. Simply placing your cursor over a menu item with an arrow will display the cascading menu. The **Drawing Utilities** cascading menu from the **File** pull-down menu is shown in Figure 1-63. The three dots, or ellipses, next to a menu item indicate that a dialog box is displayed when that menu item is selected.

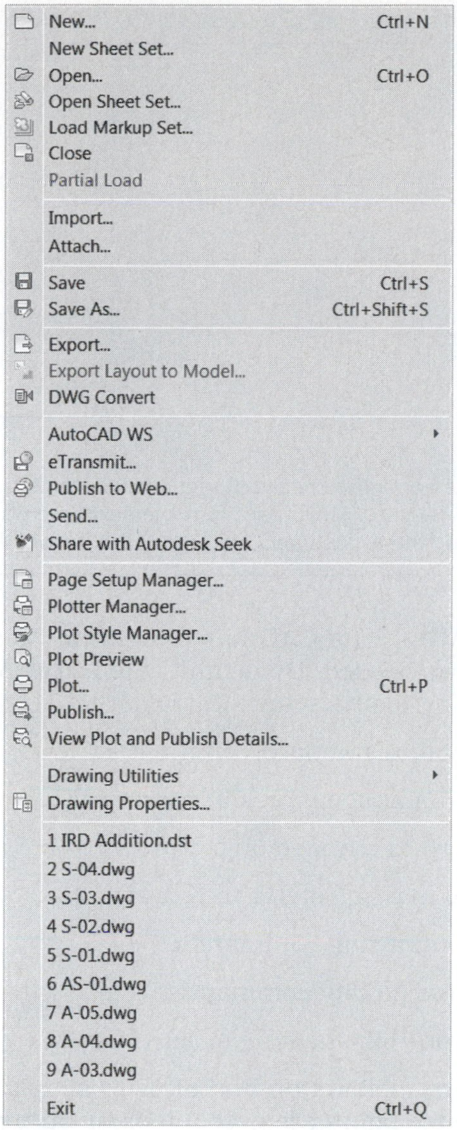

Figure 1-62
The **File** pull-down menu

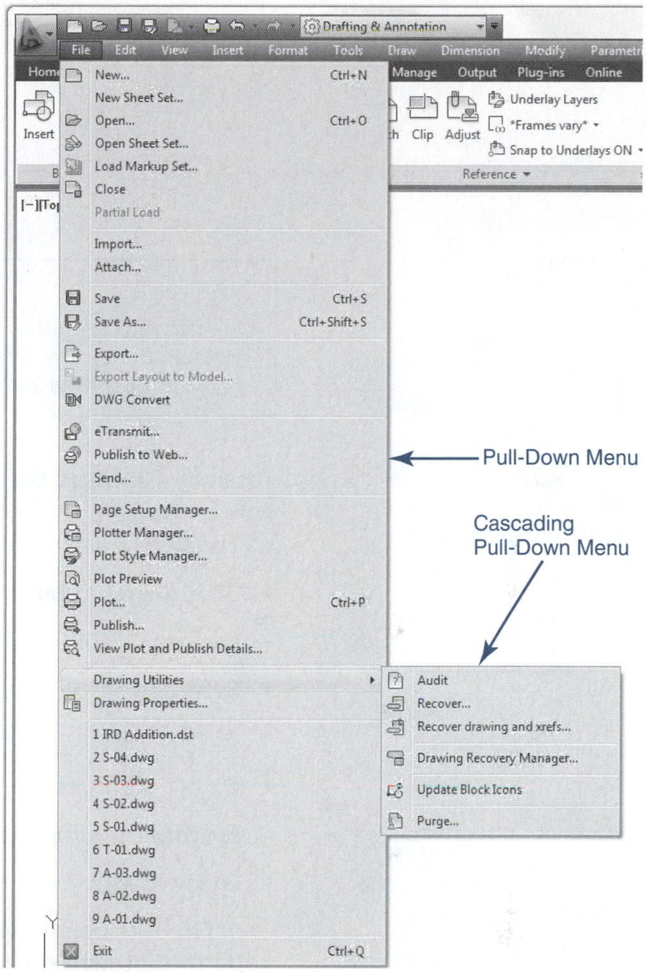

Figure 1-63
Cascading pull-down menu

Toolbars

They say a picture is worth a thousand words. Toolbars provide an easy-to-use graphical interface to most of the AutoCAD commands by using pictures called *toolbar icons* to represent different commands. The **Standard** toolbar is shown in Figure 1-64. You will probably recognize some of the icons from other Windows programs. Toolbar buttons provide quick access to a command because they require only one click of the mouse.

Figure 1-64
The **Standard** toolbar

Toolbar Flyouts. A toolbar button with a small arrow indicates that it is a toolbar flyout. A toolbar flyout button displays a subtoolbar with additional buttons when it is selected. It is the toolbar equivalent of a cascading menu. Figure 1-65 shows the **Zoom** toolbar flyout.

Figure 1-65
Zoom toolbar flyout menu

> **TIP**
>
> The last toolbar button selected on a toolbar flyout menu will become the button shown on the main toolbar after it is selected. This means that the next time you need the command you don't have to display the flyout menu; you can select it from the main toolbar.

Turning Toolbars On and Off. AutoCAD has more than 30 toolbars that can be turned on and off as needed. By default, the **AutoCAD Classic** workspace has the following toolbars turned on:

- **Standard** toolbar Contains standard commands
- **Layers** toolbar Used to manage layers in a drawing
- **Properties** toolbar Used to manage object properties
- **Styles** toolbar Used to manage styles in a drawing
- **Draw** toolbar Contains drawing commands
- **Modify** toolbar Contains modify commands
- **Draw Order** toolbar Controls stacking order of objects

The easiest way to turn toolbars on and off is to simply right-click with your mouse when the mouse pointer is over a toolbar button. This displays the **Toolbar** shortcut menu shown in Figure 1-66, which lists all the toolbars with a check mark next to those that are currently on.

Selecting a toolbar that is not currently checked will turn it on and place it on the screen wherever it was located when it was last displayed. You can then move it and place it where you want using the techniques explained in the next section.

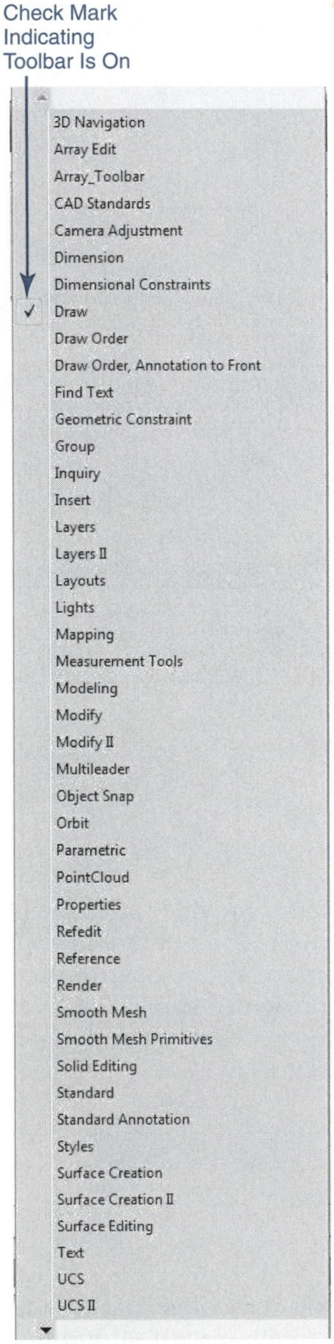

Figure 1-66
Turning toolbars on and off

> **TIP**
>
> You can also turn toolbars on and off when you are working in the **Drafting & Annotation** workspace via the **Windows** panel on the far right side of the **View** tab of the ribbon. Select the **Toolbars** button to display a list of all menus that are currently loaded and their corresponding toolbars.

Moving and Placing Toolbars. Toolbars can exist in two states—floating and docked. Floating means that the toolbar is located somewhere (floating) over your drawing window with the title shown at the top and the window-close **X** visible in the upper right corner. The **Dimension** toolbar is shown floating in Figure 1-67. When a toolbar is floating, you can move it by placing your mouse pointer over the title bar on top, clicking with your left mouse button, and dragging the toolbar where you want it.

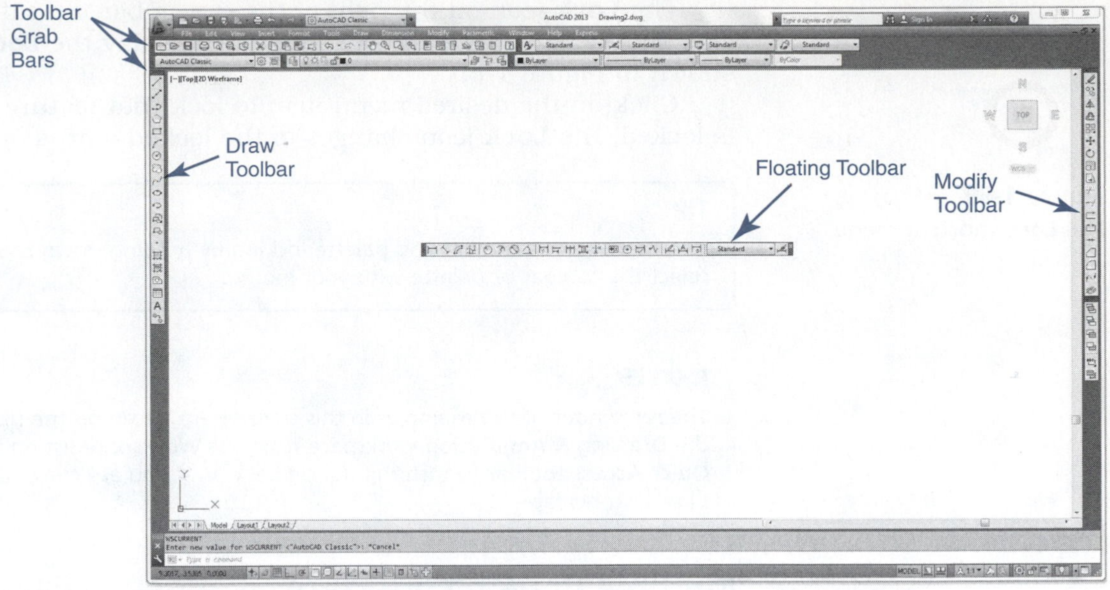

Figure 1-67
Floating toolbar

You can dock a toolbar by dragging it to any side of the drawing window. In Figure 1-67 the **Draw** and **Modify** toolbars are docked. To dock a toolbar, simply drag it to any of the four sides of the drawing window until the shadow line changes shape, indicating it is ready to be docked, and then release the mouse button. In Figure 1-68 the **Dimension** toolbar has been docked on the left side of the screen. To float a toolbar that has been docked, select the grab bars (Figure 1-68) at the top or left side of the toolbar with your mouse pointer, and drag the toolbar into the drawing window to the desired location.

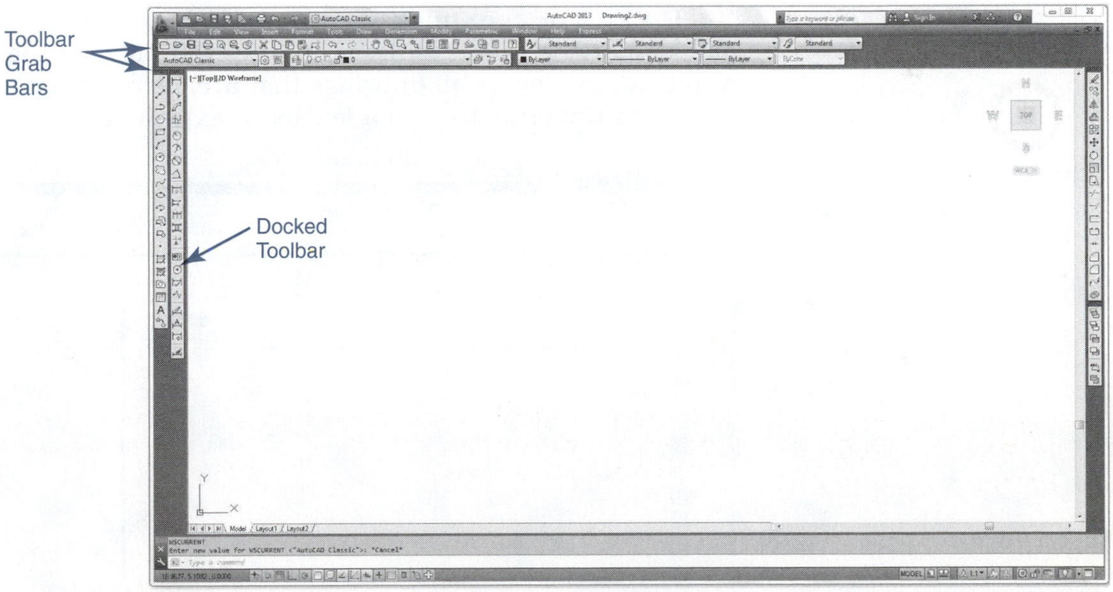

Figure 1-68
Docking a toolbar

Locking Toolbars and Windows. As you can see, manipulating toolbars and windows is easy—almost too easy. To eliminate any accidental changes, AutoCAD provides the ability to lock them.

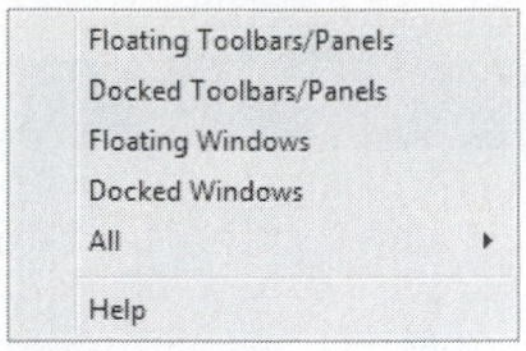

Figure 1-69
The **Lock** shortcut menu

The **Lock** icon on the right of the status bar indicates the current lock status. Select it with your mouse to display the **Lock** shortcut menu shown in Figure 1-69.

Click on the desired menu item to lock that feature. Once any feature is locked, the **Lock** icon changes to the locked status on the status bar.

> **TIP**
>
> You can override toolbar and palette locking by holding down the <**Ctrl**> key while you select the toolbar or palette with your mouse.

> **NOTE**
>
> The remainder of the examples in this chapter are based on the ribbon interface. Select the **Drafting & Annotation** workspace from the **Workspace** list on the right side of the **Quick Access** toolbar to turn the ribbon back on if you are currently using the **AutoCAD Classic** workspace.

Multiple Drawing Interface

AutoCAD has what is known as a *multiple drawing interface,* or *MDI.* This just means you can open more than one drawing at a time. This allows you to do things such as compare multiple related drawings simultaneously so you can coordinate your work and, even better, copy drawing information between drawings using *drag-and-drop* techniques. In order to facilitate these features, you must be able to quickly switch between open drawings as well as organize your open drawing windows on your screen.

Switching Between Open Drawings. The **Quick View Drawings** button located on the right side of the status bar shown earlier in Figure 1-43 is the best way to switch among open drawings because it provides preview images of the drawings; plus, you can also preview and switch to any layout within a drawing.

Clicking on the **Quick View Drawings** button on the status bar displays a horizontal row of drawing preview images at the bottom of the AutoCAD window of all drawings that are currently open and a toolbar displayed underneath with a few tools, explained later. See Figure 1-70.

Figure 1-70
The **Quick View Drawings** tool

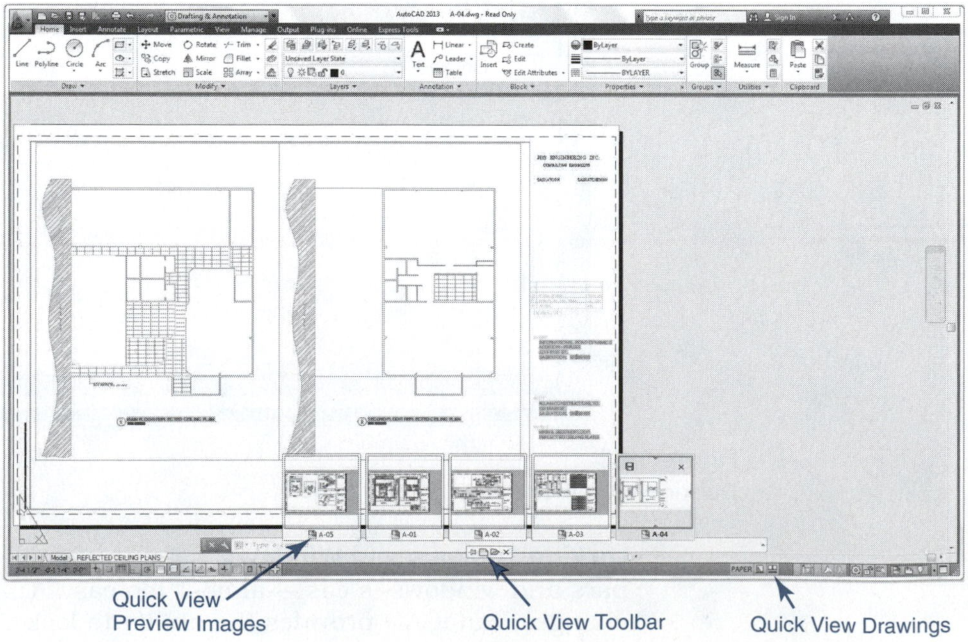

> **TIP**
> You can move the mouse past the edge of the image strip to view drawing images that extend beyond the screen. You can increase or decrease the size of the drawing preview images by pressing the <Ctrl> key while rolling the mouse wheel up or down.

When you move your mouse pointer over a **Quick View** drawing preview, preview images of all the layouts in that drawing, including model space, display above the drawing preview images as a separate image bar as shown in Figure 1-71.

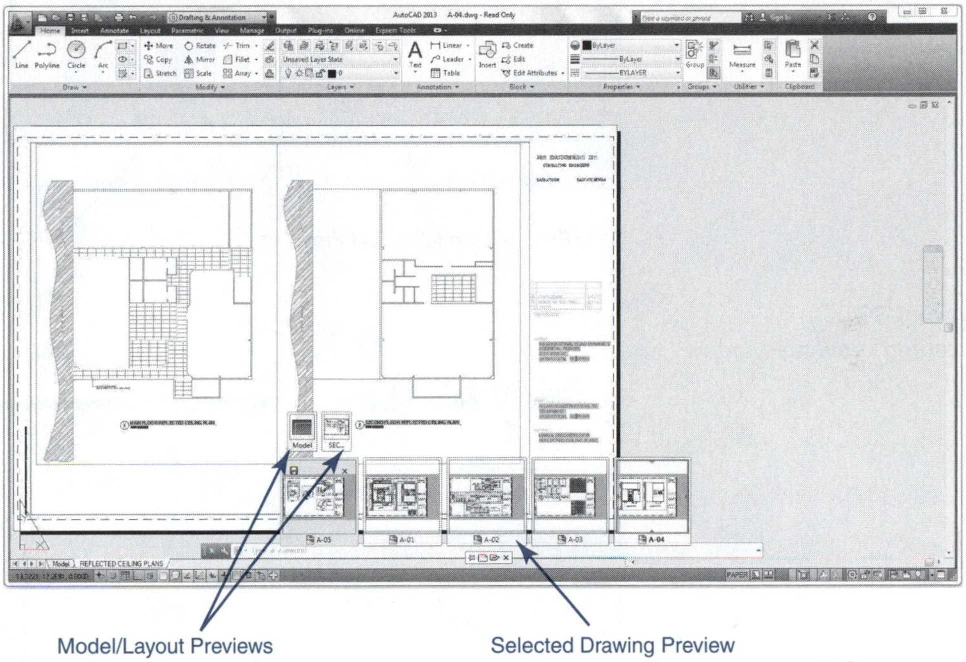

Figure 1-71 The **Quick View Drawings** tool with a drawing selected

Clicking a preview image will switch AutoCAD's focus to that drawing. It is also possible to save or close a drawing via its preview image by clicking on the corresponding **Save** and **Close** icons in the upper corners of the preview window.

To see a larger view of the layouts, simply move your mouse pointer over a layout preview image. AutoCAD enlarges the size of all the layout images and reduces the size of the drawing images. **Plot** and **Publish** icons are also displayed in the upper corners of the current layout preview, making it possible to print directly from the preview (see Figure 1-72).

Moving the cursor back over a drawing preview reverses the process and returns the drawing preview images back to their larger size and the layout preview images back to their smaller size.

Additional tools are provided via the **Quick View** toolbar, which is automatically displayed below the **Quick View** drawing preview images as shown in Figure 1-70. Using these tools you can pin the row of **Quick View** drawings open so that it remains visible while you work in the drawing editor. You can use the **Close** tool to turn off the **Quick View** drawings when you no longer want them displayed. The **New** button creates a new drawing and displays the preview at the end of the **Quick View** toolbar. You can easily open existing drawings using the **Open** tool.

The Windows Panel on the View Tab of the Ribbon. The **Windows** panel on the **View** tab of the ribbon shown in Figure 1-73 also allows you to

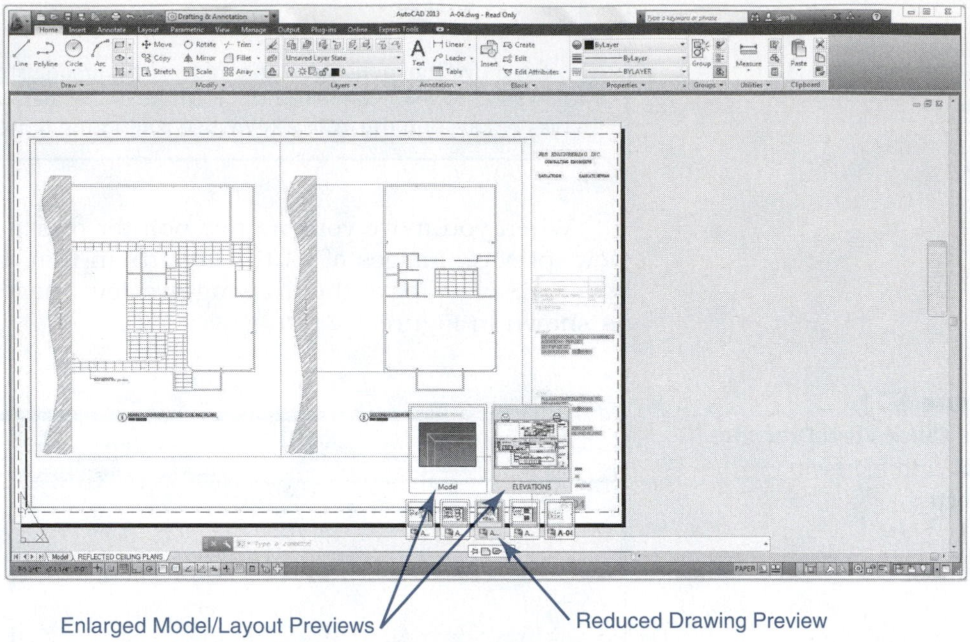

Figure 1-72
The **Quick View Drawings** tool with a layout selected

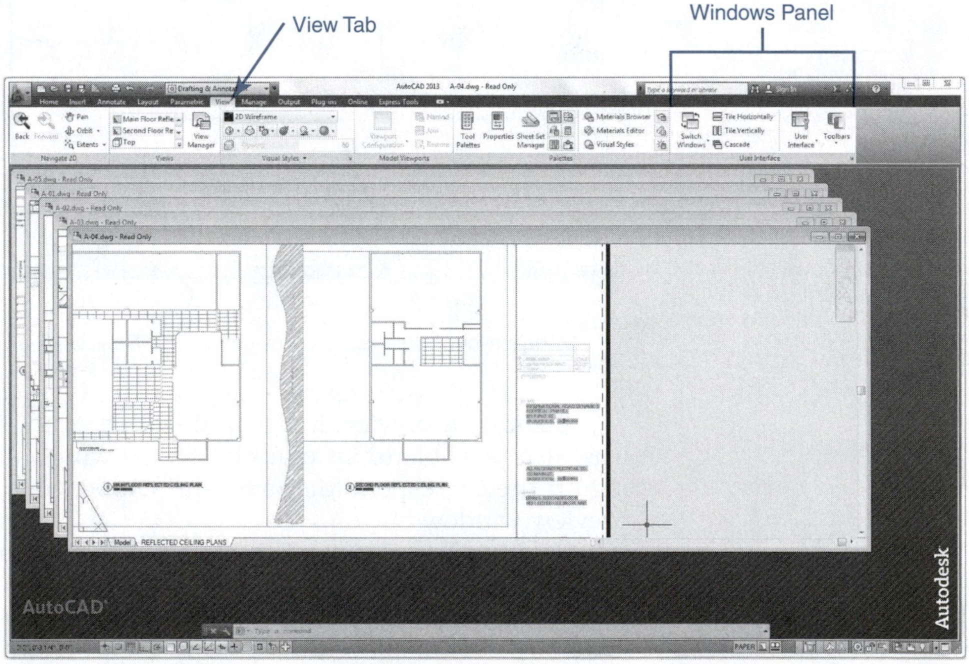

Figure 1-73
Cascading drawing windows

quickly switch among open drawings and provides a number of window display options for viewing multiple drawings.

Cascading Windows. The **Cascade** option displays all open drawings stacked in a tiered fashion so that you can see all open drawings one on top of another as shown in Figure 1-73. You can then switch to another drawing by simply clicking on the desired drawing's title bar.

Tiling Windows Horizontally. The **Tile Horizontally** option fills the drawing window with all the open drawings tiled in a horizontal fashion as shown in Figure 1-74.

Tiling Windows Vertically. The **Tile Vertically** option fills the drawing window with all the open drawings tiled in a vertical fashion as shown in Figure 1-75.

Figure 1-74
Tiling windows horizontally

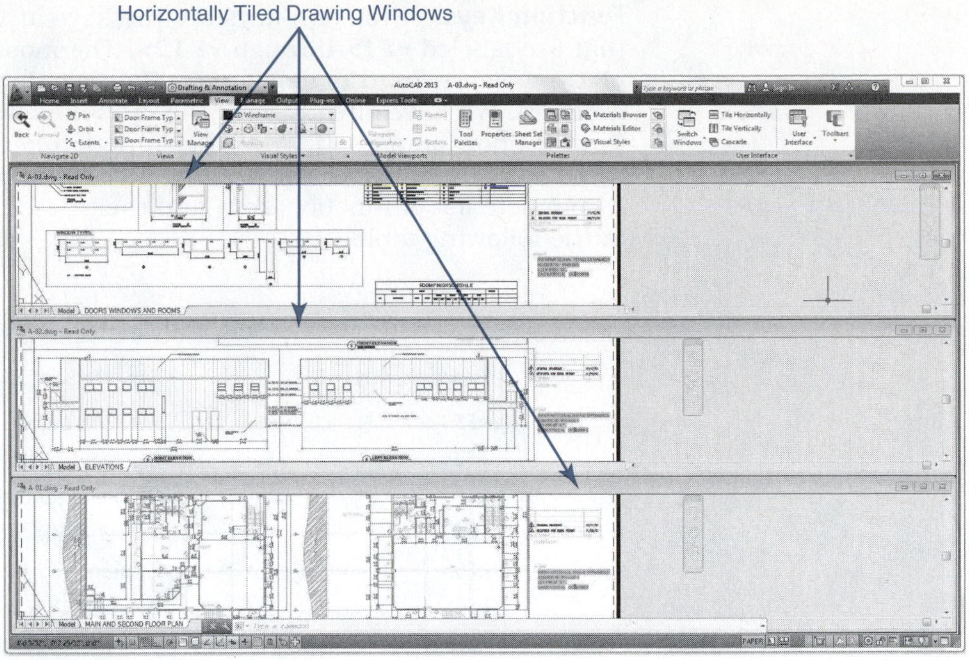

Figure 1-75
Tiling windows vertically

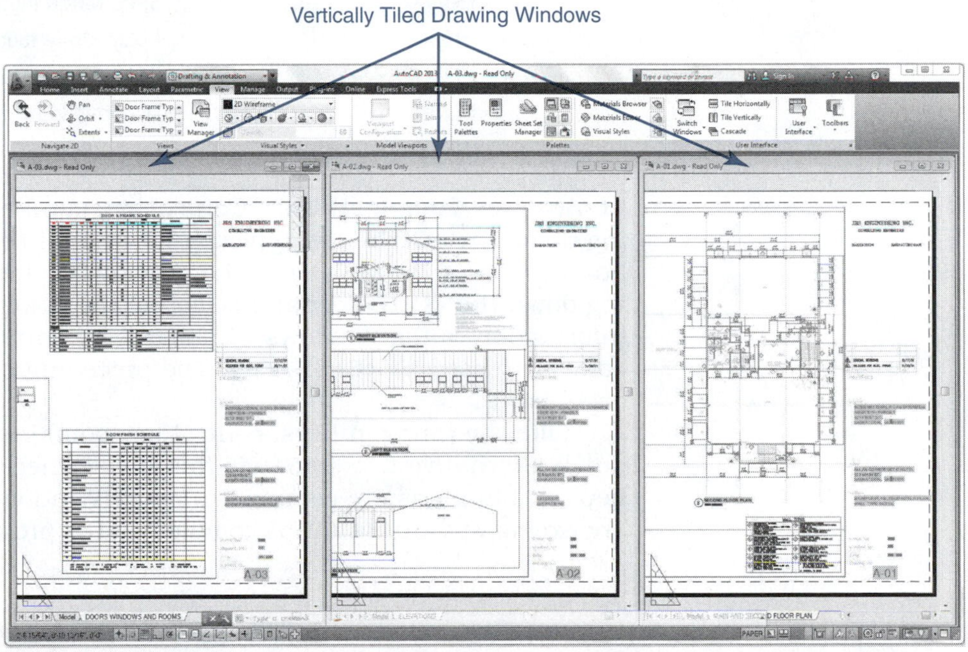

> **TIP**
>
> Tiling the open drawings either horizontally or vertically is best when you need to share information between drawings. With the drawings tiled, you can use drag-and-drop techniques to copy information from one drawing to another!

Keyboard Commands

AutoCAD has a number of other keyboard commands besides the **<Esc>** key that cancels a command in progress and the **<F2>** function key that displays the **Text** window. Keyboard commands provide quick access to a number of commands and options.

Function Keys. Function keys are the keys at the top of most keyboards that are labeled **<F1>** through **<F12>.** The most famous function key is **<F1>,** which is used to display the **Help** window in almost every Windows program. We have already seen the **<F2>** key, which toggles the AutoCAD **Text** window on and off. The other function keys also work as toggles, mostly as alternates for the drafting aids found on the AutoCAD status bar. A complete list of function keys and their associated functions is provided in the following table.

AutoCAD Function Keys

Function Key	Description
<F1>	AutoCAD online help system
<F2>	Command history toggle
<F3>	**Object Snap** toggle
<F4>	**Tablet Mode** toggle
<F5>	**Isoplane** toggle
<F6>	**Dynamic UCS** toggle
<F7>	**Grid Display** toggle
<F8>	**Ortho Mode** toggle
<F9>	**Snap Mode** toggle
<F10>	**Polar Mode** toggle
<F11>	**Object Snap Tracking** toggle
<F12>	**Dynamic Input** toggle

Control Key Combinations. Control key combinations are created by holding down the **<Ctrl>** key, typically located on the bottom row of your keyboard, while selecting some other key on the keyboard. For example, holding down the **<Ctrl>** key and selecting the **C** key at the same time copies information to the Windows Clipboard. A control key combination is typically expressed as **<Ctrl>+Key**. The preceding copy example is expressed as **<Ctrl>+C**.

Like the function keys, control key combinations are provided as a quick alternative to commands found elsewhere in AutoCAD. Some control key combinations are common to many Windows programs, whereas some are exclusive to AutoCAD. A complete list is provided in the following table.

AutoCAD Control Key Combinations

Combination	Description
<Ctrl>+A	Select all
<Ctrl>+B	**Snap Mode** toggle
<Ctrl>+C	**COPYCLIP** command
<Ctrl>+D	**Dynamic UCS** command
<Ctrl>+E	**Isoplane** toggle
<Ctrl>+F	**Osnap** toggle
<Ctrl>+G	**Grid Display** toggle
<Ctrl>+H	**Pickstyle** toggle
<Ctrl>+I	**Coordinate Display** toggle
<Ctrl>+J	Repeats last command

(*Continued*)

Combination	Description
<Ctrl>+K	**HYPERLINK** command
<Ctrl>+L	**Ortho Mode** toggle
<Ctrl>+M	Repeats last command
<Ctrl>+N	**NEW** command
<Ctrl>+O	**OPEN** command
<Ctrl>+P	**PLOT** command
<Ctrl>+Q	**QUIT** command
<Ctrl>+R	**Viewport** toggle
<Ctrl>+S	**SAVE** command
<Ctrl>+T	**Tablet Mode** toggle
<Ctrl>+U	**Polar Mode** toggle
<Ctrl>+V	**PASTECLIP** command
<Ctrl>+W	**Object Snap Tracking** toggle
<Ctrl>+X	**CUTCLIP** command
<Ctrl>+Y	**REDO** command
<Ctrl>+Z	**UNDO** command
<Ctrl>+0	**Clean Screen** toggle
<Ctrl>+1	**Properties Manager** toggle
<Ctrl>+2	**DesignCenter** toggle
<Ctrl>+3	**Tool Palettes** toggle
<Ctrl>+4	**Sheet Set Manager** toggle
<Ctrl>+5	Not Used
<Ctrl>+6	**dbConnect Manager** toggle
<Ctrl>+7	**Markup Set Manager**
<Ctrl>+8	Quick Calculator
<Ctrl>+9	**Command line** toggle

TIP

The <Ctrl>+<Alt> keyboard combination allows you to cycle through all your open drawings so that you can quickly switch the active drawing window.

InfoCenter

InfoCenter is your one-stop shop for AutoCAD information and help. Conspicuously located at the top far right of the AutoCAD window (see Figure 1-76), InfoCenter allows you to:

- Search multiple sources simultaneously for AutoCAD information using keywords and phrases
- Display the **Autodesk Exchange** window
- Connect to **Autodesk 360**

Figure 1-76
InfoCenter

- Access product updates
- Access AutoCAD help

To search for information, enter a keyword or phrase in the **InfoCenter** search box on the left of the **InfoCenter** bar and either press **<Enter>** or click on the **Search** icon directly on the right.

Selecting the **Sign In** link from the drop-down list to the right of the **InfoCenter** search box displays the **Autodesk Accounts** dialog box so you can sign in to **AutoCAD Online Services**. If you do not have an Autodesk ID, you can create one. It is free and takes only a minute. Once you have an ID, you can use it to access all of your Autodesk products and services, beta programs, trial software, community resources, and more.

Selecting the icon with the big **X** to the right of the **Sign In** box displays the **Autodesk Exchange** window where you can download different AutoCAD apps.

The question mark icon and down arrow on the far right of the **InfoCenter** bar provide access to all of the AutoCAD help facilities.

NEW to AutoCAD 2013

The Help System

AutoCAD provides substantial search-based online help. As mentioned in the "Keyboard Commands" section, the quickest way to activate the help system is by hitting the **<F1>** function key. You can also access help by clicking on the **Question Mark** on the far right of the **InfoCenter** toolbar shown in Figure 1-76, or by entering a question mark **<?>** at the keyboard. In addition, clicking on the down arrow to the right of the **Question Mark** on the right side of the **InfoCenter** toolbar displays the **Help** drop-down menu where you can select the **Help** menu item. Using any of these methods displays the AutoCAD 2013 help, as shown in Figure 1-77.

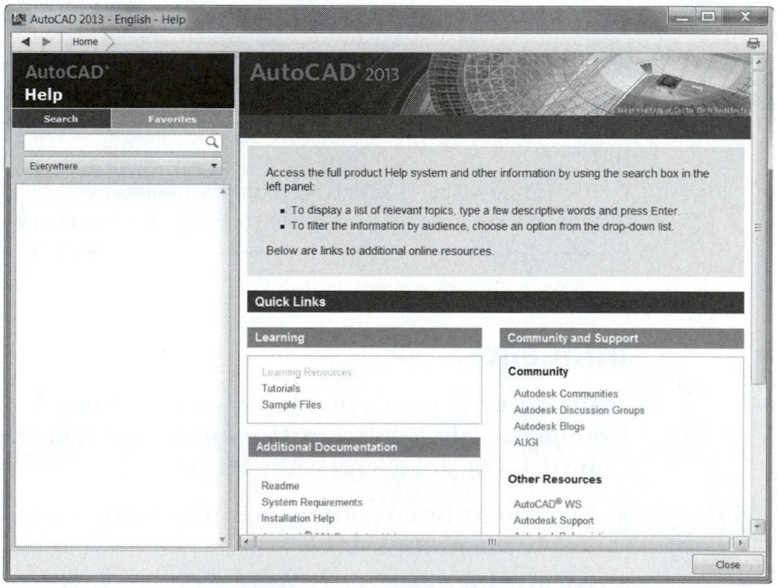

Figure 1-77
AutoCAD **Help**

> **TIP**
>
> It is possible to download online help and set AutoCAD to access help from your local drive instead by selecting **Download Offline Help** from the **Help** drop-down menu and deselecting the **Access online help when available** setting from the **Help and Welcome Screen** area on the right side of the **System** tab in the **Options** dialog box.

EXERCISE 1-3 Exploring the AutoCAD User Interface

1. Start AutoCAD.
2. Click on the big **A** button of the application menu on the upper left of the AutoCAD window to display the list of AutoCAD menus.
3. Select each menu to display its contents.
4. Select the **Home** tab of the ribbon at the top of the AutoCAD window.
5. Click on the black arrow in the middle of the **Draw** panel title to display the expanded panel and all the **Draw** tools.
6. Click on the black arrow on the middle bottom of the **Circle** tool to display the **Circle** subpanel with all the **Circle** options.
7. Click on the **3-Point Circle** tool to start the **CIRCLE** command.
8. Hit the **<Esc>** key to cancel.
9. Notice that the **3-Point Circle** tool is now the default **Circle** tool option displayed on the **Draw** panel.
10. Right-click with your mouse on any ribbon tab to display the shortcut menu and click on the **Show Panel Titles** option to unselect it (unchecked) so all panel titles are turned off.
11. Right-click with your mouse on any ribbon tab to display the shortcut menu and click on the **Show Panel Titles** option again to select it (checked) so all panel titles are turned back on.
12. Click on the **Minimize to Panel Titles** option on the right of the **Express Tools** tab at the top right to turn off the panels and display only the panel titles.
13. Put your mouse pointer over the **Modify** panel title to display the full **Modify** panel.
14. Click on what is now the **Minimize to Tabs** option on the right of the **Express Tools** tab at the top right to turn off the panel titles and display only the tabs.
15. Click on the **Annotate** tab of the ribbon to display those tools.
16. Click on the down arrow button to the right of the **Express Tools** tab at the top right to turn the ribbon back on again.
17. Resize the command line interface so it displays six lines.
18. Hit the **<F1>** function key to display AutoCAD Help.
19. Locate any topic using any of the methods explained in this chapter.

1 chapterone

Chapter Summary

The information and concepts explained in this chapter form the basis for the rest of this textbook. In this chapter we explored the uses of CAD and the benefits that it provides. We also looked at some fundamental CAD concepts such as drawing things real-world size, using Cartesian coordinates to precisely locate drawing information, measuring angles counterclockwise, and managing object properties.

In addition, an in-depth tour of the AutoCAD ribbon-based interface and the different ways that you can input data were provided so that you can optimize command and data entry. The techniques for navigating multiple open drawings and displaying different window configurations were explained so that you can easily share information between drawings and increase productivity exponentially.

Finally, the powerful **InfoCenter** feature and the help system were introduced so that you know where to go when you have a question and need an answer fast. The best part of this is that many of these tools are integrated with the Internet, so that you always have the most up-to-date information.

Chapter Test Questions

Multiple Choice

Circle the correct answer.

1. The main benefit of using CAD is:

a. Increased productivity

b. Improved precision

c. Better collaboration

d. All of the above

2. What is the Cartesian coordinate system?

a. A grid-based system with an *X*- and *Y*-axis

b. A grid-based system with an *X*-, *Y*-, and *Z*-axis

c. A system for coordinating your work

d. None of the above

3. The default units in AutoCAD are:

a. Millimeters c. Feet

b. Inches d. Meters

4. By default, angles in AutoCAD are measured:

a. Clockwise c. Using radians

b. Counterclockwise d. Using a protractor

5. Layers in AutoCAD are used for the following:

a. Controlling object colors

b. Organizing drawing information

c. Controlling an object's visibility

d. All of the above

6. Paper space is primarily used for:
   a. Creating 3D models for visualization
   b. Laying out multiple 2D sheets for plotting purposes
   c. Storing extra copy paper
   d. All of the above
7. The default three-letter file extension for AutoCAD is:
   a. DWL — c. DWG
   b. DWT — a. BAK
8. What keyboard key cancels any active command?
   a. **<Tab>** key — c. **<F2>** key
   b. **<F1>** key — d. **<Esc>** key
9. What keyboard key toggles the full text command window on and off?
   a. **<F1>** key — c. **<F2>** key
   b. **<Esc>** key — d. **<Tab>** key
10. What keyboard key toggles between input fields when using the **Dynamic Input** feature?
   a. **<F2>** key — c. **<Tab>** key
   b. **<F1>** key — d. **<Esc>** key

Matching

Write the number of the correct answer on the line.

a. Cartesian coordinate system ______	1. 3D drawing environment where most of a drawing's line work and text reside
b. Right-hand rule ______	2. Main window in AutoCAD where you create and modify drawing objects
c. Scale factor ______	3. Grid-based system where points are represented by their x and y coordinate values
d. Layer ______	4. 2D environment used to lay out a drawing for plotting
e. Model space ______	5. Technique for visualizing the X-, Y-, and Z-axes
f. Paper space ______	6. Multiplier applied to annotation features such as text and dimensions
g. Drawing window ______	7. Interface used to enter commands using the keyboard and display command prompts
h. Command line ______	8. Feature that allows you to enter input information near the mouse cursor
i. Dynamic input ______	9. AutoCAD minidashboard at the bottom of the AutoCAD window
j. Status bar ______	10. Object property used to organize drawing information

True or False

Circle the correct answer.

1. **True or False:** Using CAD requires that you scale your drawing as you create it so everything will fit on the printed paper size.

2. **True or False:** You must always specify a z coordinate when locating 2D points in CAD, even if z = 0.
3. **True or False:** A grid unit always equals 1 inch.
4. **True or False:** Angles in AutoCAD are always measured counterclockwise.
5. **True or False:** Annotation features such as text and dimensions must usually be scaled by the reciprocal of the drawing's plotted scale to appear the correct size.
6. **True or False:** All objects in an AutoCAD drawing have a layer property.
7. **True or False:** The color property of objects can be used to determine the object's line thickness when it is plotted.
8. **True or False:** Model space is where you create most of the line work and text that represents your design.
9. **True or False:** AutoCAD creates a backup file with a BAK extension each time you save a drawing.
10. **True or False:** The main focus of the AutoCAD user interface is the drawing window.

2 chapter two

Quick Start Tutorial

CHAPTER OBJECTIVES

- Create a new drawing
- Save your work
- Switch between model space and layout space
- Draw some basic AutoCAD objects
- Toggle the **Snap Mode, Ortho Mode, Polar Tracking,** and **Grid Display** buttons on and off
- Navigate around the drawing
- Examine and change object properties
- Create drawing layers and move objects from one layer to another
- Add basic dimensions
- Make some basic modifications to your drawing
- Add text to your drawing
- Set up and plot your drawing

Introduction

This chapter will give you an overview of a typical AutoCAD drawing session. You examine some of the basic operations you will do on a day-to-day basis when using AutoCAD, including starting an AutoCAD session, drawing and modifying some objects, and saving and plotting your drawing. All the topics touched on in this chapter will be explained in greater detail in the following chapters. Let's start by creating a new drawing.

Creating a New Drawing

drawing template: A drawing used as a starting point when creating a new drawing. Drawing templates can contain page layouts, borders, title blocks, layer settings, and many other settings or drawing objects you use on a regular basis.

When AutoCAD starts, it places you in a blank drawing by default. This blank drawing is based on a number of default AutoCAD settings, which are stored in a ***drawing template.*** In addition to this default template, AutoCAD gives you other templates to choose from, which can save you time in setting up your drawing.

Using a Template

AutoCAD provides a number of predefined templates with default settings for various drawing disciplines. These drawing templates typically have title blocks in them and predefined settings for text, dimensioning, and plotting. You can also create your own templates or save any drawing as a template.

You can create a new drawing by selecting **New** from the **Quick Access** toolbar. This displays the **Select template** dialog box (see Figure 2-1), which allows you to select one of these predefined templates as a starting point.

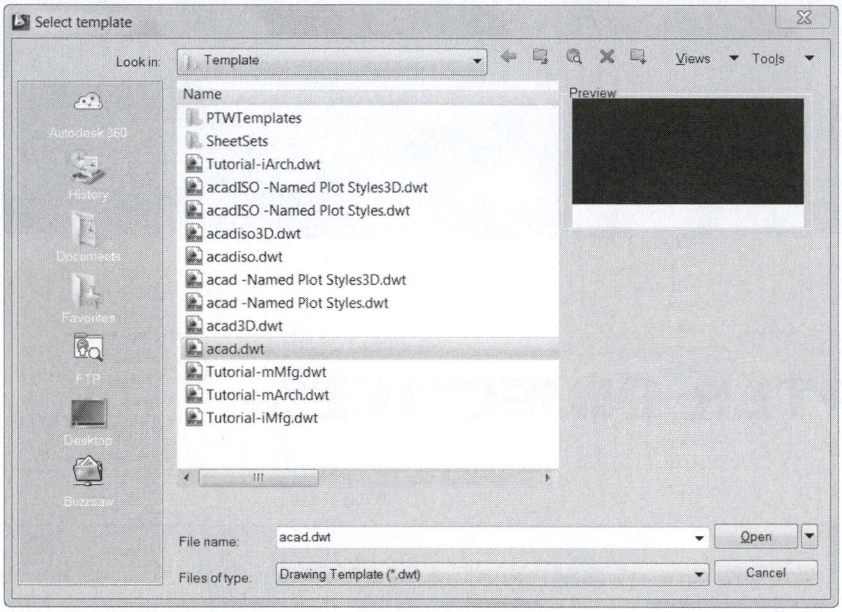

Figure 2-1
The **Select template** dialog box

Saving Your Work

When you create a new drawing using a template, it is initially named *Drawing* followed by an incremental number (Drawing1.dwg, Drawing2.dwg, Drawing3.dwg, etc.), indicating its place in the series when it was created. The drawing does not exist as a file on your computer or network until you save it at least once by selecting **Save** from the **Quick Access** toolbar, which runs the **QSAVE** command.

> **NOTE**
>
> The template files that contain "ISO" in the file name are set up for metric units. In fact, the acadiso.dwt template is the default metric template.

The **QSAVE** command is short for "Quick Save," although it is not so quick the first time you use it. The first time you use **QSAVE,** the standard Windows **Save Drawing As** file dialog box shown in Figure 2-2 is displayed so that you can give the drawing a file name and folder location to store the file on your computer or network. Subsequent use of the **QSAVE** command simply updates the file in its specified location, hence the "Quick" part.

Select the drive or device where you want to save the file by selecting it from the **Save in:** drop-down list at the top, and navigate to the desired folder using the Explorer-type interface in the middle. Enter the drawing name in the **File name:** list box or select a previous name from the

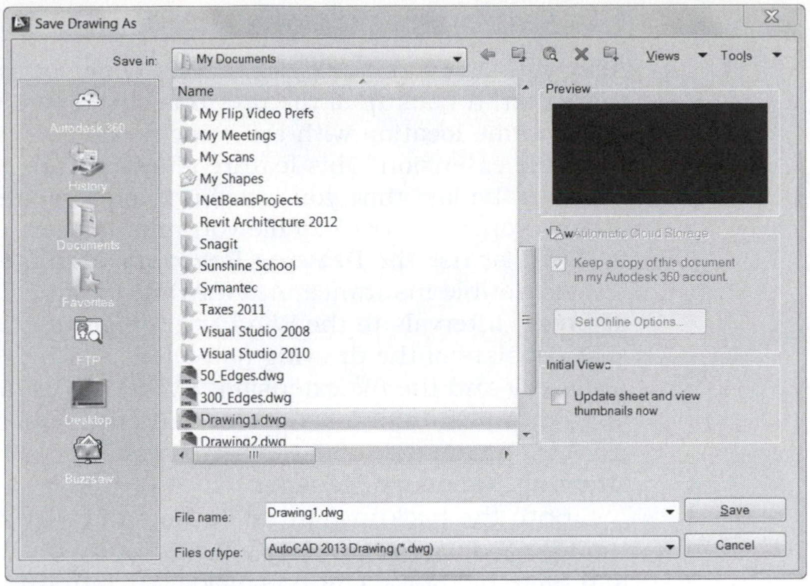

Figure 2-2
The **Save Drawing As** file dialog box

drop-down list. Select the **Save** button to save the drawing in the specified folder and close the dialog box.

> **TIP**
>
> You can use the **SAVEAS** command to save your drawing to a new location or to change the file name. You can access the **SAVEAS** command by choosing **Save As...** from the **Quick Access** toolbar. In addition to changing the location and name of your file, the **SAVEAS** command allows you to save your drawing to an earlier version of AutoCAD or to convert it to a DXF (Design eXchange Format) file. This allows you to share your drawing data with earlier versions of AutoCAD or with other CAD packages. You can also use the **SAVEAS** command to save your drawing as a drawing template. See Chapter 18 for more on file formats and exchanging drawing data.

> **FOR MORE DETAILS**
>
> See page 14 in Chapter 1 for more information about naming drawing files and the other AutoCAD file types.

Now that the drawing is named, each time you use the **QSAVE** command from now on, by clicking on the **Save** icon on the **Quick Access** toolbar, AutoCAD will update the file in the specified location and overwrite the last saved version. You should save your drawing often using the **QSAVE** command to ensure that you don't lose too much work if an unexpected and/or catastrophic failure occurs. A good rule of thumb is to save your drawing every 10 to 15 minutes. Get in the habit of choosing **Save** from the **Quick Access** toolbar or by using the **<Ctrl>+S** keyboard combination.

> **TIP**
>
> By default, the current file name and path is always displayed in the title bar at the top of the AutoCAD window. Keeping your eye on the title bar after a drawing is saved is a good way to keep track of the file you're currently working on.

File Safety Precautions

After you save a drawing once, every time you use the **QSAVE** command thereafter, a backup of the previous saved version of the drawing is saved in the same location with the same name as the drawing, except with a .BAK file extension. This feature allows you to recover drawing information up until the last time you saved it if for some reason this is necessary. In order to open the backup file you must either rename the .BAK extension to .DWG or use the **Drawing Recovery Manager**.

As double insurance, AutoCAD automatically saves your drawing at preset intervals to the Windows Temporary folder using a file name that consists of the drawing name followed by six numbers generated by AutoCAD and the file extension .SV$. The default interval between saves is 10 minutes. In order to restore an automatically saved file with the .SV$ extension, you must either rename the extension to .DWG or use the **Drawing Recovery Manager**.

Both the backup copy and automatic save options can be changed via the **File Safety Precaution** settings found on the bottom left of the **Open and Save** tab of the **Options** dialog box introduced on page 21 in Chapter 1. It is recommended that you leave both features on. Someday you will be glad you did!

NOTE

The automatic save feature is meant to be used as a failsafe so that you can recover drawing information when things go wrong. It should not be relied on as a primary means of saving your work. In fact because the automatic save files (.SV$) are saved to the Windows Temporary folder, their life span is unpredictable, and they may be deleted at any time.

TIP

The **Drawing Recovery Manager** typically displays automatically the next time you start AutoCAD after a system crash so you can restore either the backup (BAK) file or the autosave file if they are available. To display the **Drawing Recovery Manager** manually, you must go to the **Drawing Utilities** menu on the application menu (big red **A**).

EXERCISE 2-1 Setting Up a Drawing

1. Choose **New** from the **Quick Access** toolbar to display the **Select template** dialog box shown in Figure 2-1. The **Select template** dialog box opens in the default AutoCAD **Template** folder.

To access student data files, go to **www.pearsondesigncentral.com.**

2. Select the **Look in:** list at the top of the dialog box, and open the **Chapter 2** folder in the student data files.
3. Select the **ansi-a.dwt** template file, and select the **Open** button to start a new drawing with the predefined **ansi-a** title block shown in Figure 2-3.
4. Choose the **Save** button from the **Quick Access** toolbar, and save your drawing as ***CH2_EXERCISE*** using the **Save Drawing As** file dialog box shown in Figure 2-2.

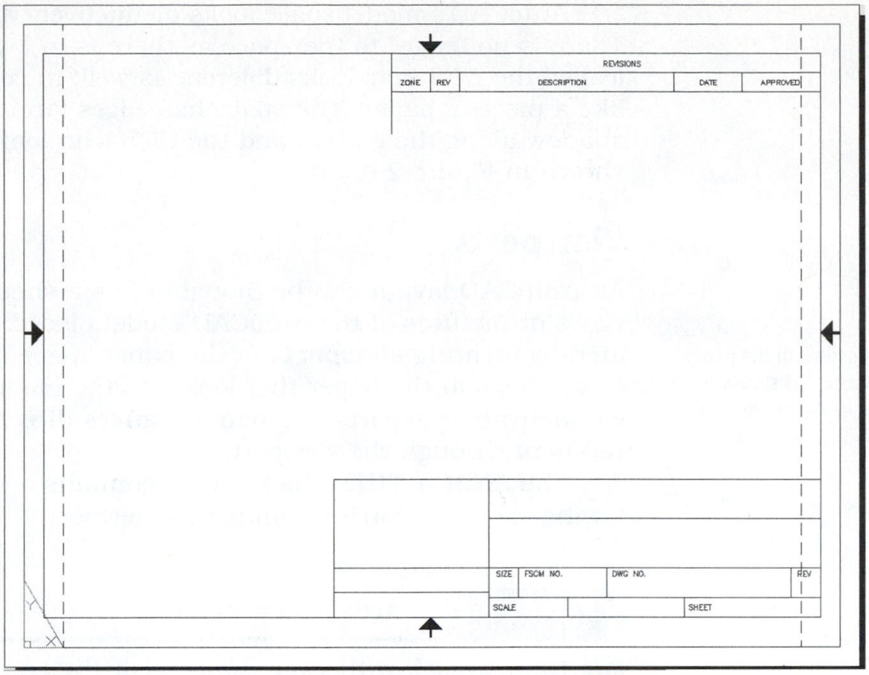

Figure 2-3
A new drawing created from a template

Model Space and Layout Space

Chapter 1 discussed AutoCAD's two distinct drawing environments, model space and layout space. Generally speaking, model space is used for creating the geometry of your drawing. Objects that exist in the physical world (walls, doors, mechanical parts, etc.) are generally drawn in model space. Objects that exist only on a piece of paper (annotation, dimensions, notes, title blocks, etc.) are generally placed in layout space. Each drawing has only one model space but can have multiple layout spaces, each with its own name.

The drawing template used in this chapter has one layout named **ANSI A Title Block**. You can switch between model space and the layout using the tabs at the bottom of the drawing window shown in Figure 2-4.

Figure 2-4
The **Model** and **Layout** tabs

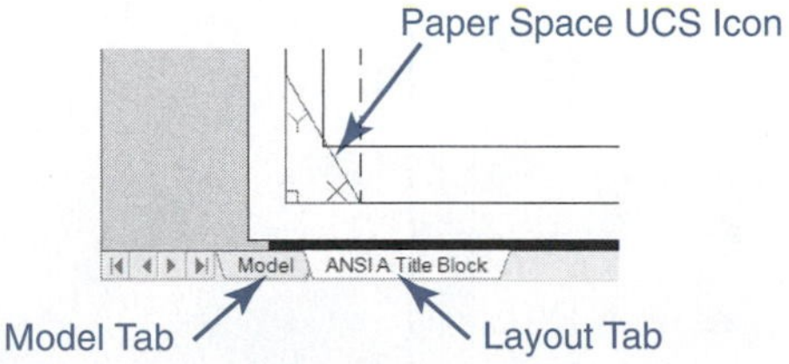

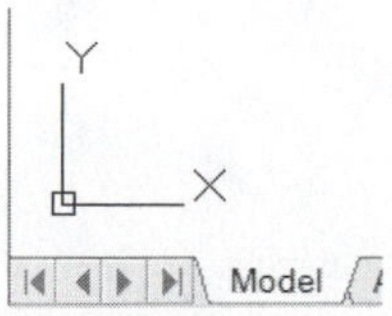

Figure 2-5
The AutoCAD model space UCS icon

EXERCISE 2-2 **Switching Between Model and Layout Space**

1. Click on the **Model** tab. AutoCAD switches to model space, and the model space UCS icon is displayed (see Figure 2-5).
2. Click on the **ANSI A Title Block** tab. AutoCAD switches back to layout space.
3. Save your drawing.

AutoCAD's model space looks distinctively different from layout space. There is no "edge" to the space as there is in layout space. The XY icon (called the *UCS icon*) looks different as well. In contrast, layout space looks like a piece of paper. The space has edges (and the appearance of a shadow along the edges), and the UCS icon looks like a page corner, as shown in Figure 2-4.

Viewports

viewport: A window in the paper space environment that shows the view of the model space environment.

An AutoCAD layout can be thought of as a sheet of paper with scaled views or pictures of the AutoCAD model placed on it. These views are created by creating ***viewports*** in the paper space layout. Viewports are holes or windows in the paper that look into the model space environment. You can activate viewports and make changes directly to the model space environment through the viewport.

The **ANSI A Title Block** layout contains a single viewport. In the following exercise, you'll examine this viewport.

EXERCISE 2-3 Activating a Viewport

1. Double-click with your mouse near the center of the drawing within the border outline. AutoCAD outlines the viewport so it becomes bold (see Figure 2-6).
2. Drag your mouse around the screen. Notice that the crosshairs appear only inside the viewport. When you drag the cursor outside the viewport, the crosshairs turn into a pointer.
3. Double-click outside the viewport to close the viewport and return to layout space.
4. Save your drawing.

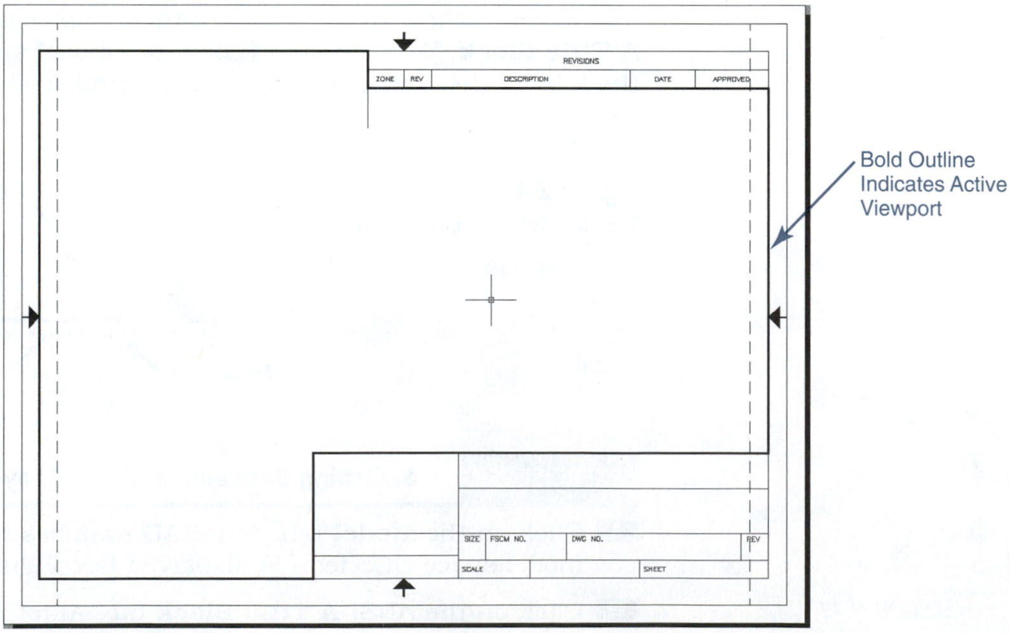

Figure 2-6
The active model space viewport

NOTE

You can also use the **MODEL/PAPER** button on the status bar to activate a single viewport. Switching from **PAPER** to **MODEL** makes a viewport active. Switching back to **PAPER** returns you to layout space.

The drawing template used in this chapter contains a single viewport; however, you can create multiple viewports in each layout.

FOR MORE DETAILS

Chapter 14 provides detailed information about model space, paper space, layouts, and how to create and control viewports.

Communicating with AutoCAD

objects: Graphical drawing elements, such as lines, arcs, circles, polylines, and text.

When you create a drawing, you are placing AutoCAD ***objects*** in the drawing. There are different types of objects (lines, arcs, circles, text, etc.). Each type of object has a unique set of properties. When you create an object, AutoCAD will ask you to specify the various aspects of that object. This is done primarily through prompts for information at both the command line interface and the cursor.

The Command Line

The command line interface is at the bottom of the drawing area by default (see Figure 2-7). This is one place where AutoCAD communicates with you. When you select a tool, AutoCAD will display the command name in the command line and then prompt you for more information. The command line can be docked at the top or bottom of the drawing window and moved. It can also be turned off completely, but this is not recommended.

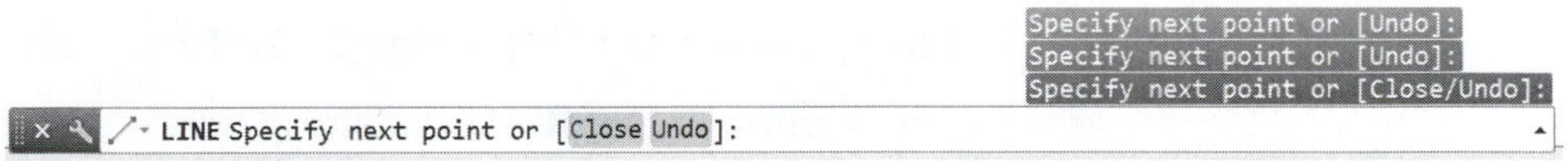

Figure 2-7
The command line interface

FOR MORE DETAILS

See page 29 in Chapter 1 for detailed information about controlling the display of the command line interface.

Dynamic Input

Dynamic input (see Figure 2-8) uses a command prompt that moves with your cursor and provides instant, dynamic feedback as you move around the drawing. Dynamic input provides you with active, heads-up feedback that allows you to read and respond to AutoCAD's prompts without changing focus away from your drawing. Dynamic input can be turned on and off by toggling the **Dynamic Input** button on the status bar.

Figure 2-8
Dynamic input

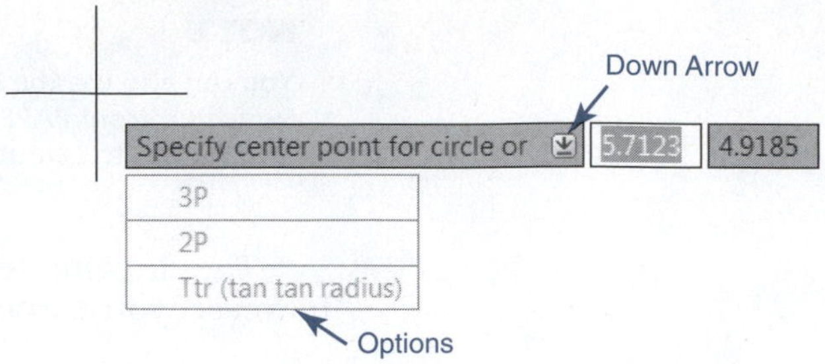

Whether you use dynamic input, the command line interface, or both, the general process you'll follow when creating drawing objects is:

1. Start a command.
2. Read AutoCAD's prompt.
3. Pick points and/or respond to prompts.
4. Press **<Enter>** or **<Esc>** to end the command.

Sometimes the AutoCAD prompts can be difficult to decipher. There are some general conventions that AutoCAD uses.

- AutoCAD will ask you to *specify* a placement point (for example, the start point of a line or arc or the center point of a circle). You can specify a placement point by picking a point on the screen, typing in a coordinate, or using an object snap.
- When there are multiple ways to create an object, AutoCAD will display a down arrow next to the dynamic input prompt (see Figure 2-8). Press the down arrow key to see the list of command options.
- At the command line, options are enclosed in square brackets [] and are separated by a space. You specify an option by selecting it with your mouse or by typing in the blue highlighted capital letter(s) shown for that option. For example, when drawing a circle, AutoCAD gives you the following prompt and options:

  Specify center point for circle or [**3P** **2P** **T**tr (tan tan radius)]:

In this example, AutoCAD is asking you either to specify the center point of the circle or to select one of three options (3P, 2P, or Ttr). To specify the **Ttr** option, you would either pick it with your mouse or type **T** and press **<Enter>**.

TIP

AutoCAD remembers the numerical values you enter. That means the next time you use the same command, the value you entered previously is displayed in chevrons < > so that you can simply press the **<Enter>** key to use the value again.

FOR MORE DETAILS

See Chapter 4 for more on coordinate entry methods and all the specifics on the **CIRCLE** command and its options.

Keep in mind that when you specify a point or select an option, AutoCAD will continue to ask you for more information until it has everything it needs to create that object.

EXERCISE 2-4 Drawing a Line

1. Select the **Model** tab to switch to model space.
2. Choose the **Line** tool from the **Draw** panel (see Figure 2-9). AutoCAD prompts you to *Specify first point:*.

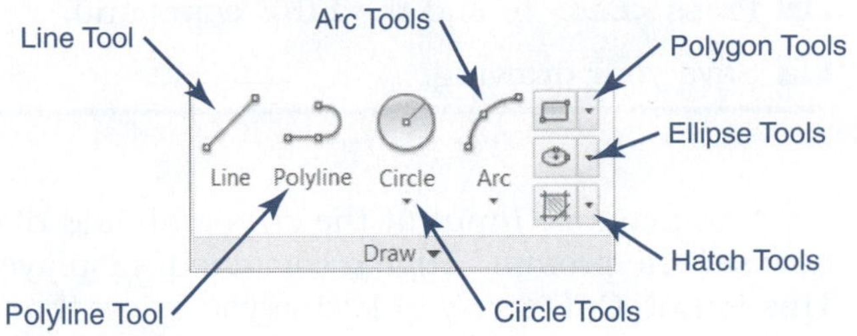

Figure 2-9
The **Line** tool on the **Draw** panel

3. Look at the command line. AutoCAD shows the following:

   LINE Specify first point:

   LINE is the command you started when you chose the **Line** tool. AutoCAD is asking where you want to start the line.

4. Pick anywhere on the screen to start the line. You should now have a ***rubber-band*** line extending from the first point you specified along with dynamic information about the length and direction of the rubber-band line (see Figure 2-10).

rubber band: A live preview of a drawing object as it is being drawn. The rubber-band preview allows you to see objects as they are being created.

5. AutoCAD prompts you to *Specify next point or* ↓. The down arrow indicates that a command option is available. Press the down arrow key, and you'll see the **Undo** option appear (see Figure 2-11).

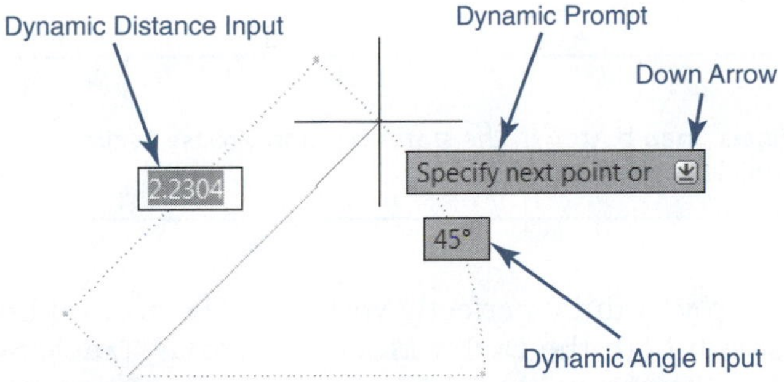

Figure 2-10
Dynamic display information

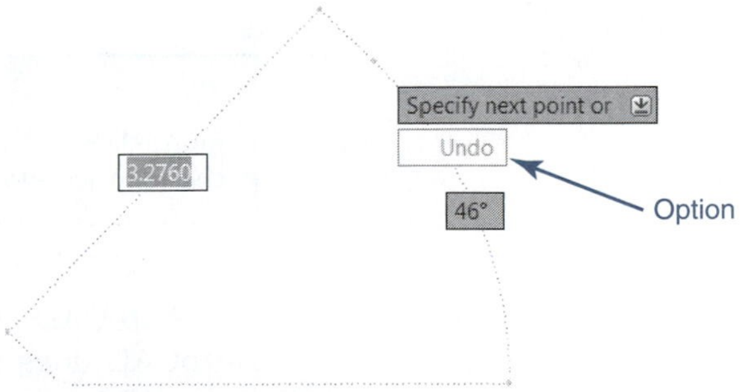

Figure 2-11
Dynamic display options

6. Look again at the command line. It shows:

   LINE Specify next point or [**U**ndo]:

   You can now either specify the next point on the line, choose the **Undo** option from the dynamic display, pick the **Undo** option from the command line with your mouse, or type **U<Enter>** to undo that point.

7. Pick another point anywhere on the screen. AutoCAD will draw a single line segment and automatically start drawing another line segment. AutoCAD again prompts you to *Specify next point or* ↓.

8. Press the down arrow and select **Undo** from the option list. The second point you specified is "undone," and the rubber-band line is now extending from the first point you selected.

9. AutoCAD again prompts you to *Specify next point or* ↓. Pick another point on the screen. AutoCAD draws that line segment and repeats the prompt.

10. Press **<Esc>** to end the **LINE** command.

11. Save your drawing.

The dynamic input at the cursor should disappear and you should now see the prompt "*Type a command*" displayed at the command line. This is AutoCAD's way of letting you know that it is idle and ready for the next command.

> **TIP**
>
> You can repeat the last command you used by pressing either **<Enter>** or the spacebar at the command prompt. In most cases, AutoCAD interprets pressing the spacebar the same as pressing **<Enter>**. The exception to this is when you are typing in a line of text where spaces are expected.

Object Snaps, Ortho Mode, and Polar Tracking

object snaps/osnaps: Geometric points on objects such as the endpoints or midpoint of a line or the center of an arc or circle.

Because precision is important, AutoCAD can look for key points on objects and select those points automatically. These key points are known as ***object snaps*** or ***osnaps***.

By default, AutoCAD will look for the endpoints of lines and arcs and the center points of circles. You can turn object snapping on and off by selecting the **Object Snap** button on the status bar.

> **TIP**
>
> Right-click on the **Object Snap** button in the status bar and choose **Settings...** to change the default object snap setting.

orthographic: 90° increments.

AutoCAD can help you draw perfectly vertical or horizontal lines. AutoCAD does this with both the **Ortho Mode** and **Polar Tracking** buttons. When turned on, **Ortho** mode (which stands for ***orthographic***) will restrict the crosshairs movement to either horizontal or vertical movement. **Ortho** mode takes effect only when you are specifying a point relative to another point (when specifying the second point of a line, for example).

> **TIP**
>
> The **<F8>** key will toggle **Ortho** mode on and off.

polar tracking: A process in which AutoCAD will lock the cursor movement to predefined angles.

Polar tracking is similar to **Ortho** mode, except it simply indicates when the crosshairs are close to a vertical or horizontal angle. When you get close to these directions, AutoCAD will display an alignment path and a tooltip showing you how far and in what direction you have dragged your crosshairs (see Figure 2-12). When the alignment path is visible, the point you pick will be placed along that alignment path at the distance indicated.

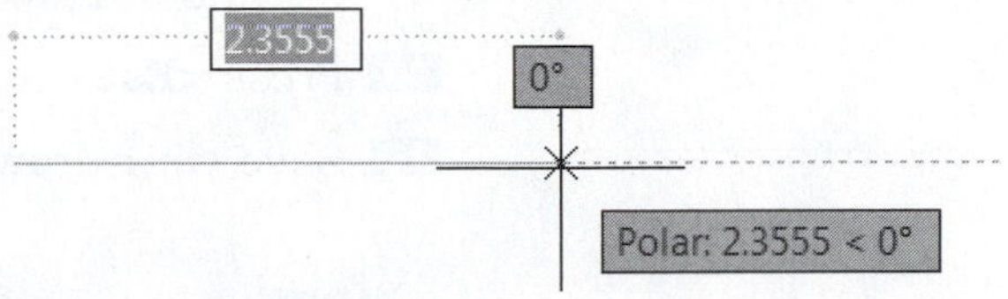

Figure 2-12
Polar tracking

> **TIP**
>
> The **<F10>** key will toggle polar tracking on and off. By default, polar tracking is set to select angles in increments of 90°. Right-click on the **Polar Tracking** button in the status bar and choose **Settings...** to change the default increment angle and to detect specific angles to track.

> **FOR MORE DETAILS**
>
> See Chapter 5 for a complete list of object snaps and how to use them and for more on using the **Ortho Mode** and **Polar Tracking** buttons.

EXERCISE 2-5 Using Object Snaps, Ortho Mode, and Polar Tracking

1. Toggle the **Object Snap** button on.
2. Select the **Line** tool from the **Draw** panel.
3. Move the crosshairs close to the start of the first line and let it sit there for a moment. A square will appear at the end of the line along with a tooltip that says *Endpoint* (see Figure 2-13).

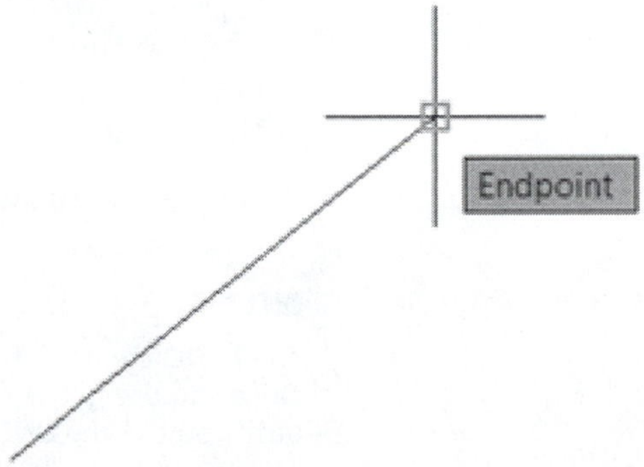

Figure 2-13
The **Endpoint** osnap

4. Pick near the end of the line. AutoCAD will automatically select the endpoint of that line.
5. Toggle the **Polar Tracking** button on.
6. Drag the crosshairs straight up until the polar tracking appears. Notice the polar tracking shows a distance and direction (90°).
7. Pick a point approximately 1 inch 90° above the end of the line.

Chapter 2

8. Toggle the **Polar Tracking** button off and the **Ortho Mode** button on.
9. Drag the crosshairs around the screen. The crosshairs are now restricted to horizontal and vertical movement only.
10. Drag the cursor to the right and type **3<Enter>.** AutoCAD draws a line 3 units long to the right.
11. Press **<Esc>** to end the **LINE** command.
12. Save your drawing.

direct distance entry: The process of specifying a point by dragging the AutoCAD cursor to specify direction and typing in a distance.

> **NOTE**
>
> The last line you drew was done using a method called ***direct distance entry***. This is a combination of cursor movement and keyboard input in which you drag your cursor to indicate direction and use the keyboard to type in the distance. Direct distance input can be used any time you need to specify a coordinate location. Used with the **Ortho Mode** and **Polar Tracking** controls, it can greatly simplify coordinate entry.

Undo/Redo

AutoCAD keeps a running history of all the commands you've issued within a single drawing session. This allows you to back up to any point in the drawing session. The **UNDO** command will take you back through your drawing session, one command at a time, all the way back to the start of your drawing. If you go back too far, the **REDO** command will move you forward, one command at a time, until you've restored everything.

EXERCISE 2-6 Using Undo/Redo

1. From the **Quick Access** toolbar, choose **Undo** (or press **<Ctrl>+Z**). The lines created with the previous **LINE** command will disappear. Look at the command prompt and see that the lines were undone. The **Redo** button is now active in the **Quick Access** toolbar.
2. Choose the **Redo** tool. The lines will reappear.
3. Choose the **Undo** tool until all the lines are gone (model space is empty). If you go back too far (for example, back into paper space), use the **Redo** tool to get back to an empty model space.
4. Save your drawing.

> **NOTE**
>
> The **REDO** command can be used only immediately after using the **UNDO** command. Once you use **REDO** and resume drawing, you cannot use the **REDO** command again until you use the **UNDO** tool.

Grid and Snap

In addition to using polar tracking and object snaps, you can also control the crosshairs movement by turning on **Snap** mode. **Snap** mode simply locks the crosshairs movement to a predefined increment.

Along with **Snap** mode, you can also display a visual grid on the screen. The **Grid Display** button toggles the display grid on and off. The grid is simply a visual display; it does not print and does not control the cursor movement. The grid and snap settings are not the same thing and are set separately.

> **TIP**
> The <F7> key toggles **Grid Display** on and off. <F9> toggles **Snap Mode** on and off.

EXERCISE 2-7 Using Grid Display and Snap Mode

1 Toggle the **Grid Display** button off and toggle the **Snap Mode** button on.

2 Move the cursor around and notice how it jumps from one point to another. The coordinate readout is locked into .5 unit increments (see Figure 2-14).

Figure 2-14
Coordinate readout

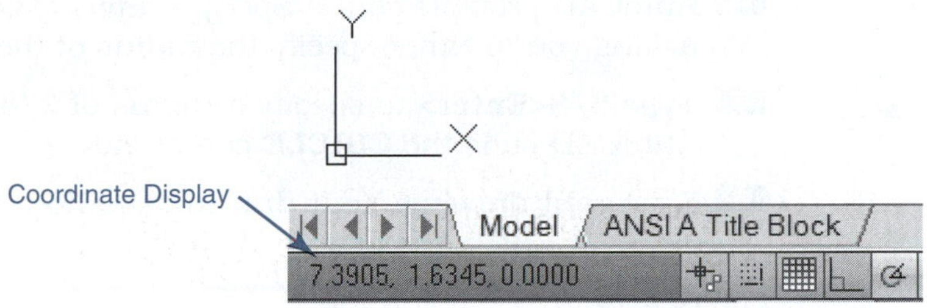

3 Toggle the **Grid Display** button on and toggle the **Snap Mode** button off. Now move your cursor around the screen and look at the coordinate readout on the cursor. Notice that the cursor is no longer jumping from point to point, and the coordinate readout is no longer locked to .5 unit increments.

4 Toggle the **Snap Mode** button on and pick the **Line** tool from the **Draw** panel.

5 Move your cursor to the coordinate 4,2 and pick that point. Continue picking points in a counterclockwise direction to draw the outline shown in Figure 2-15.

Figure 2-15
Drawing with **Snap** mode

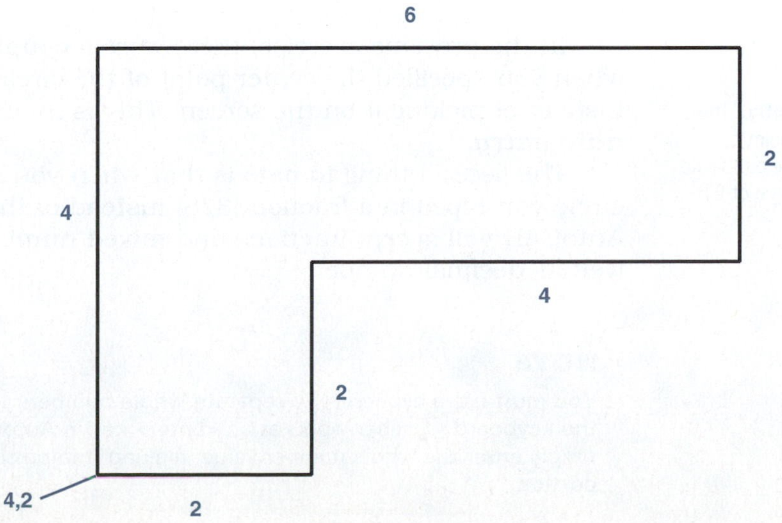

6 Press <Enter> or <Esc> to end the **LINE** command.

7 Save your drawing.

Draw a Circle

Let's add a hole to our drawing. To do that, we'll place a circle on the drawing using the **CIRCLE** command.

EXERCISE 2-8 Drawing a Circle

1 Toggle the **Grid Display** and **Snap Mode** buttons off.

2 Choose the **Center, Radius** tool from the **Draw** panel. AutoCAD prompts you: *Specify center point for circle or* ↓. AutoCAD is asking you to either specify a center point location or choose an option.

3 Type **9,5<Enter>**. AutoCAD places the center of the circle at the coordinate 9,5 and starts dragging a preview of the circle.

4 AutoCAD prompts you to *Specify radius of circle or [Diameter]:*. It is asking you to either specify the radius of the circle or choose an option.

5 Type **3/8<Enter>** to specify a radius of 3/8″. The circle is drawn, and AutoCAD ends the **CIRCLE** command.

6 Save your drawing. Your drawing should now resemble Figure 2-16.

Figure 2-16
Drawing a circle

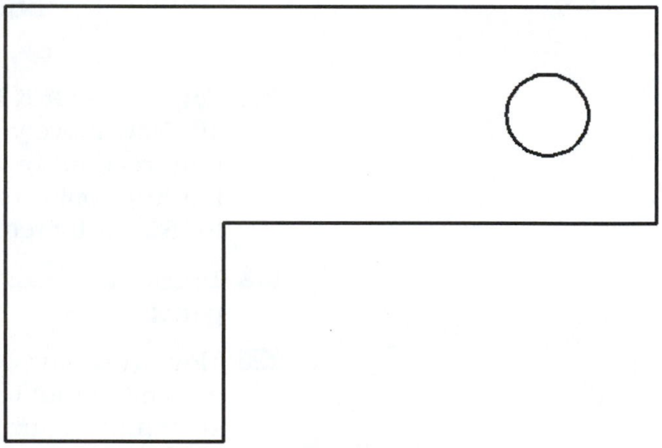

In the previous exercise, there were a couple of things to notice. First, when you specified the center point of the circle, you typed the coordinate instead of picking it on the screen. This is an example of ***absolute coordinate entry.***

absolute coordinate entry: The process of specifying a point by typing in a coordinate. The coordinate is measured from the origin or 0,0 point in the drawing.

The second thing to note is that when you specified the radius of the circle you typed in a fraction (3/8) instead of the decimal number (.375). AutoCAD will accept fractions and mixed numbers (for example, 1-3/8) as well as decimal numbers.

NOTE

You must use a hyphen (-) to separate whole numbers and fractions as shown because the keyboard spacebar works as an <Enter> key in AutoCAD. Pressing the spacebar will simply enter the whole number value, making it impossible to enter the fractional portion.

FOR MORE DETAILS

See page 140 in Chapter 4 to learn more about coordinate entry methods.

Navigating Around the Drawing

In order to work effectively, you must be able to navigate around the drawing by controlling what is displayed on your screen. Sometimes it is necessary to zoom in close to your drawing to do detailed work, while at other times, you might need to zoom out to see the big picture. If you are zoomed in close, but the portion of the drawing you need to work on next is off the edge of the screen so it is not visible, you need to be able to shift the display to view that area of the drawing. In AutoCAD this is referred to as panning.

The easiest way to navigate around the drawing is using the **Pan** and **Zoom** tools located on the navigation bar shown in Figure 2-17.

Selecting the **Pan** tool changes the cursor to a little hand icon that you click and drag in the drawing window to shift your display. If necessary, you can click and drag repeatedly until you reach the desired location in the drawing. When you reach the area of the drawing you want to display, press the **<Enter>** or **<Esc>** key to exit.

There are a number of **Zoom** tools to select from. The default **Zoom** tool is **Zoom Extents,** which is explained next. Clicking on the down arrow at the bottom of the **Zoom Extents** button displays the shortcut menu shown in Figure 2-18 with all of the different **Zoom** tools.

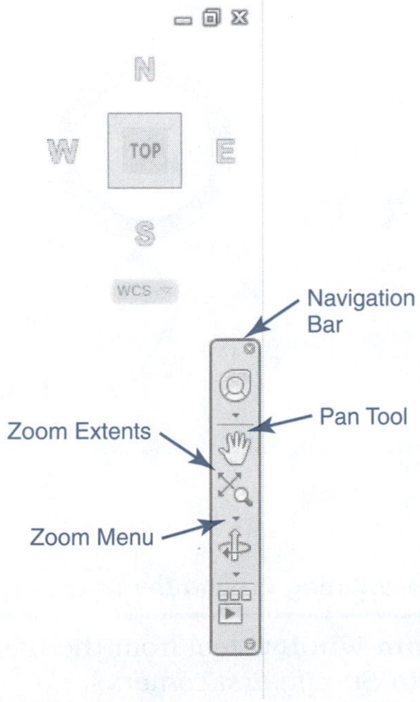

Figure 2-17
The **Pan** and **Zoom** tools on the navigation bar

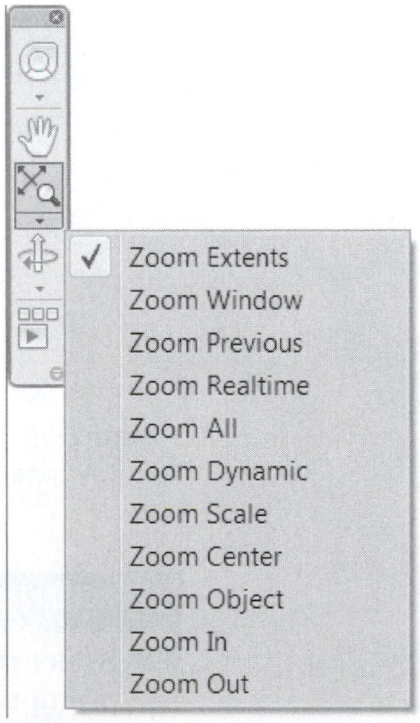

Figure 2-18
The **Zoom** tools

Some of the more useful **Zoom** tools include:

- **Zoom Extents** Displays everything visible in your drawing by fitting the outermost extents of your drawing information within the AutoCAD drawing window. Good command to use if you "lose" your work off the screen and you want to get it back

- **Zoom Window** Allows you to define a rectangular window area to zoom up on by specifying two corner points of a boundary area
- **Zoom Previous** Restores the previous pan/zoom display so you can back up through your pan/zoom history. It DOES NOT undo any other commands; it affects only the display. AutoCAD keeps track of up to 10 previous views
- **Zoom Realtime** Changes the cursor to a magnifying glass icon with a plus/minus sign indicating that you can click and drag the mouse up the screen to zoom in closer to the drawing, and click and drag the mouse down the screen to zoom out farther from the drawing

FOR MORE DETAILS

See Chapter 3 for a complete explanation of all the **Zoom** tools.

The **Pan** and **Zoom** tools, as well as other useful navigation tools, are also available on the **Navigate 2D** panel located on the **View** tab of the ribbon shown in Figure 2-19. The **View Back** tool allows you to step back through views similar to the **Zoom Previous** tool, whereas the **View Forward** tool allows you to step forward through views after the **View Back** tool has been used one or more times.

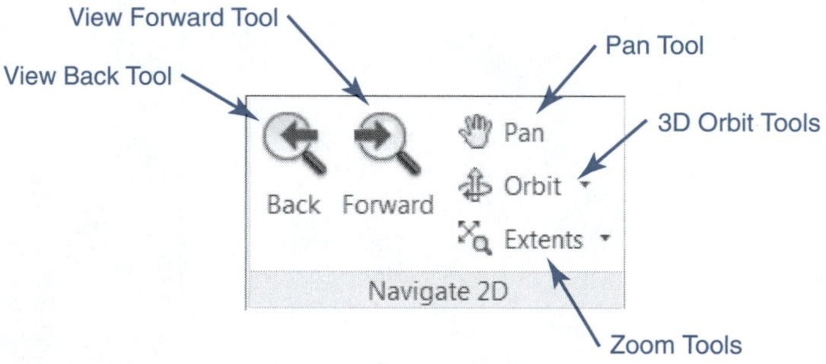

Figure 2-19
The **Navigate 2D** panel

EXERCISE 2-9 **Navigating Around the Drawing**

1. Select the **Zoom Window** tool from the navigation bar. AutoCAD prompts you to *Specify first corner:*.
2. Pick a point slightly below and to the left of the circle. AutoCAD prompts you to *Specify opposite corner:*.
3. Pick a point slightly above and to the right of the circle. AutoCAD will zoom into the area you selected.
4. Select the **Zoom Previous** tool from the navigation bar. AutoCAD switches back to the previous view.
5. Select the **Zoom Extents** tool from the navigation bar. AutoCAD fills the display with the drawing.

6. Select the **Zoom Previous** tool again to return to the original display.
7. Select the **Zoom Realtime** tool from the navigation bar.
8. Hold down the mouse button and drag your mouse up and down the screen. AutoCAD zooms in and out accordingly. Press **<Esc>** to exit the command.
9. Select the **Pan** tool from the navigation bar.
10. Hold down the mouse button and drag your mouse back and forth across the screen. AutoCAD pans the display accordingly. Press **<Esc>** to exit the command.
11. Using the **Pan** and **Zoom** tools, pan and zoom your drawing as needed.
12. Save your drawing.

Zooming with a Wheel Mouse

If you use a wheel mouse with your computer, AutoCAD will make use of the scroll wheel. When you scroll the wheel up and down, AutoCAD will zoom in and out, respectively. The zoom will be centered about the location of the cursor.

Pressing and holding down the scroll wheel allows you to dynamically pan around the drawing.

> **TIP**
>
> Using the scroll wheel is a system behavior and not technically a command. Because of this, you can use the dynamic zoom and pan of the scroll wheel at any time during the drawing process, even while in the middle of a command.

Object Properties

properties: The settings that control how and where a drawing object is shown in the drawing.

As mentioned earlier in this chapter, when you create a drawing, you are placing AutoCAD objects in the drawing. When you create an object, AutoCAD will ask you to specify the various aspects or ***properties*** of that object. Chapter 1 described how some properties are common to all objects (for example, layer and color) and other properties are unique to a given type of object (for example, the radius of a circle or the height of text).

> **NOTE**
>
> If you hover the cursor over an object so that the object is highlighted and pause for a second, the object type, color, layer, and linetype are displayed.

When you double-click on most objects, AutoCAD displays the **Quick Properties** palette. This palette displays the properties of the selected object. Figure 2-20 shows the **Quick Properties** palette for a line segment. If more than one object is selected, AutoCAD will show only common properties of all the selected objects. You can change the properties of any selected object by changing their values in the **Quick Properties** palette.

Figure 2-20
The **Quick Properties** palette

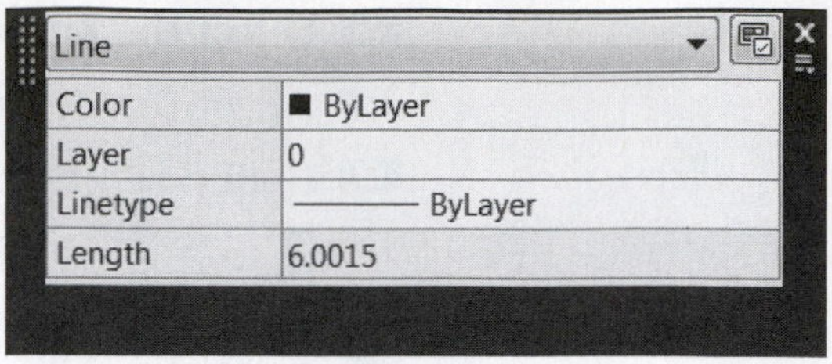

EXERCISE 2-10 **Using the Quick Properties Palette**

1. Drag your cursor over the circle in the drawing. The circle will highlight when the cursor hovers over it and its general properties are displayed.
2. Double-click on the circle in your drawing. The circle will change to a dashed line to indicate that it has been selected. Blue boxes will also appear on the circle. The **Quick Properties** palette will display the object properties for that circle.
3. Select the **Diameter** box and type **1<Enter>**. The circle will immediately change its size. Notice that the values for radius, circumference, and area update as well.
4. Change the **Center X** value to **5**.
5. Change the **Center Y** value to **3**.
6. Press **<Esc>** to deselect the circle.
7. Double-click on the line on the far right of the drawing. The **Quick Properties** palette now shows the properties for that object.
8. While the line is still selected, select the circle. AutoCAD now shows only the properties that are common to those two objects.
9. Press **<Esc>** to clear the selection. Your drawing should resemble Figure 2-21.
10. Save your drawing.

Figure 2-21
The modified circle

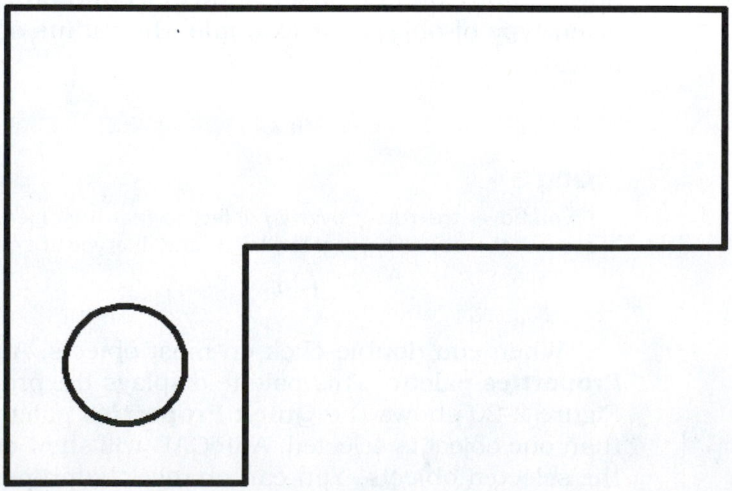

NEW to AutoCAD 2013

TIP

You can dynamically preview changes to an object before applying the changes. For example, if you select the circle in Figure 2-21 and then use the **Quick Properties** palette to change the color property, the circle dynamically changes color as you pass the cursor over each color in the list.

Layers

As you saw in the previous exercise, some properties are common to all objects. These include color, linetype, lineweight, layer, and transparency. Color is fairly obvious; it is the display color of the object on the screen. Linetype refers to how the line is displayed—for example, a dashed line, dotted line, continuous line, etc. Lineweight is the plotted width of the object (think of it as pen width). Transparency controls the visibility of objects so you can see through them.

You can assign a color, linetype, lineweight, and transparency level to each object individually; however, when your drawing grows in complexity, you can quickly find it difficult to manage each object individually. This is where layers come to the rescue.

FOR MORE DETAILS

Page 9 in Chapter 1 provides a brief description of how layering is used in CAD. Chapter 6 provides a complete description of layers and other object properties.

Layers give you a way to group objects together logically. The objects are still separate but share common properties and can be manipulated as a group.

Each layer consists of a name, color, linetype, lineweight, transparency level, and a number of on/off settings. When you draw an object, the properties of the current layer are applied to that object. The quickest and easiest way to manage layers is via the **Layers** panel on the **Home** tab of the ribbon shown in Figure 2-22. The **Layer** drop-down list allows you to set the current drawing layer (see Figure 2-22). The **Layer Properties Manager** palette allows you to create and manage drawing layers.

Figure 2-22
The **Layers** panel on the **Annotate** tab of the ribbon

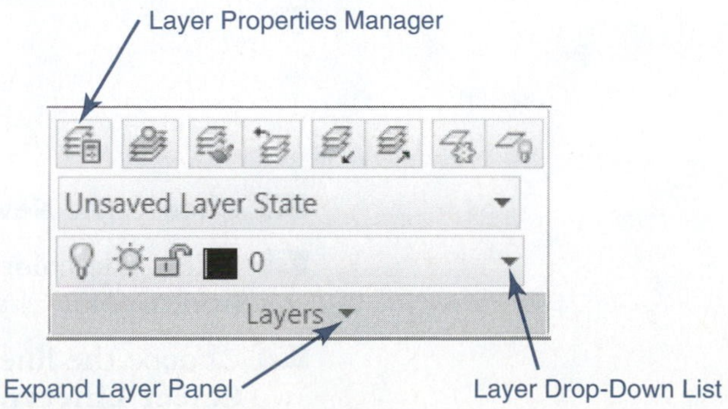

Chapter 2

EXERCISE 2-11 Creating New Layers

1 Choose the **Layer Properties** tool from the **Layers** panel. The **Layer Properties Manager** palette appears (see Figure 2-23). There are three layers currently defined. Layer **0** is the default layer included in every drawing. The **Title Block** and **Viewport** layers came from the drawing template.

Figure 2-23
The **Layer Properties Manager** palette

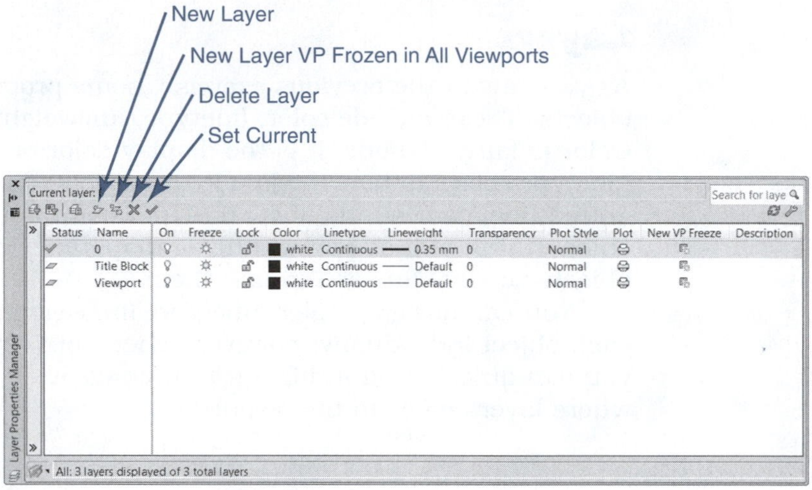

2 Choose the **New Layer** button at the top of the palette (see Figure 2-23). Type **Dim<Enter>** for the name.

3 Press **<Enter>** again. AutoCAD will create another new layer. Type **Object <Enter>** for the name.

4 Choose the color setting for the **Object** layer you just created. This will display the **Select Color** dialog box (see Figure 2-24). Choose the color red (index color 1) and choose **OK** to close the dialog box.

Figure 2-24
The **Select Color** dialog box

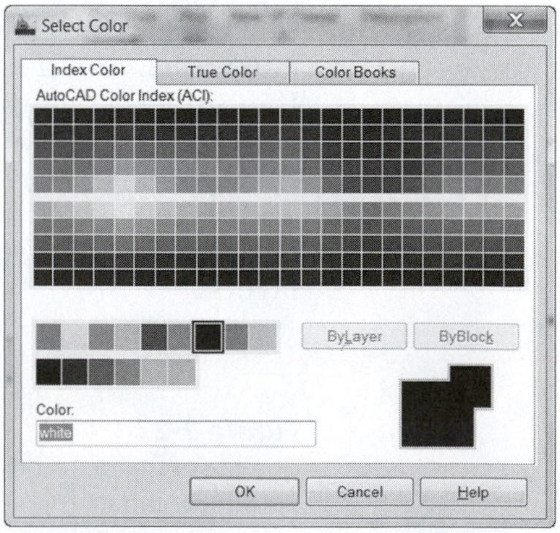

5 Choose the **New Layer** button and create a layer named **Center**.

6 Select the color setting for the **Center** layer. Set the color to blue (index color 5) and choose **OK** to close the **Select Color** dialog box.

7 Choose the linetype setting for the **Center** layer. This displays the **Select Linetype** dialog box (see Figure 2-25).

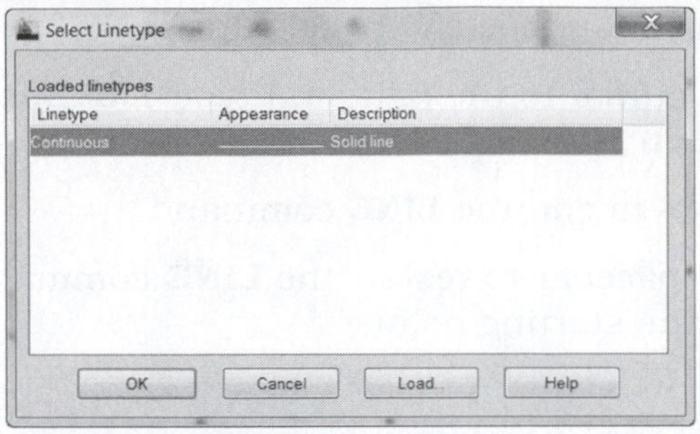

Figure 2-25
The **Select Linetype** dialog box

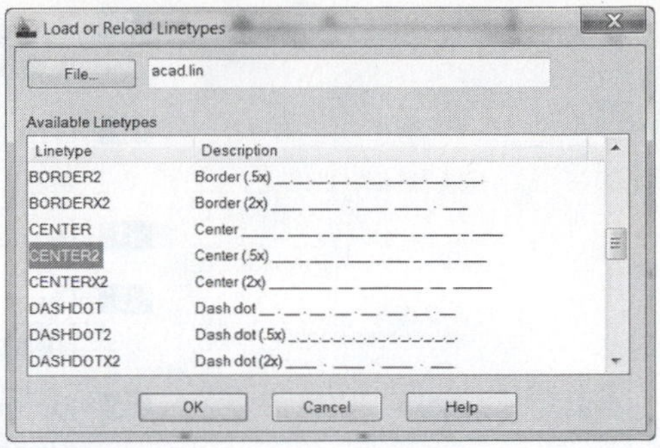

Figure 2-26
The **Load or Reload Linetypes** dialog box

8. Choose the **Load...** button. This displays the **Load or Reload Linetypes** dialog box (see Figure 2-26).
9. Scroll down through the list to see the available linetypes. Next to each line is a text representation of what the linetype looks like. Select the **CENTER2** linetype and choose **OK**. This loads this linetype definition into the drawing and returns you to the **Select Linetype** dialog box.
10. In the **Select Linetype** dialog box, select the **CENTER2** linetype you just loaded and choose **OK**. This assigns the linetype you just loaded to the layer and returns you to the **Layer Properties Manager** palette.
11. Choose the **Layer Properties** button to close the **Layer Properties Manager** palette.
12. Save your drawing.

So far, the appearance of your drawing hasn't changed. All you have done at this point is to define some new layers.

EXERCISE 2-12 Drawing on a Layer

1. From the **Layers** panel, choose **Center** from the **Layer** drop-down list (see Figure 2-27). This sets the layer **Center** as the current drawing layer.

Figure 2-27
The **Layer** drop-down list

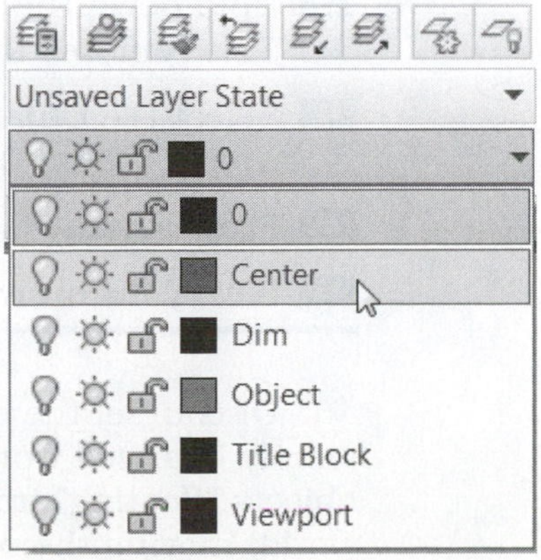

2. Toggle the **Ortho Mode** button to on and choose the **Line** tool. Type **4.25,3<Enter>** to specify the starting point.
3. Drag your cursor to the right and type **1.5<Enter>** to specify the length and direction of the line segment.
4. Press **<Esc>** to end the **LINE** command.
5. Press the spacebar to restart the **LINE** command. Type **5,2.25<Enter>** to specify the starting point.
6. Drag the cursor up and type **1.5<Enter>** to specify the length and direction of the line segment.
7. Press **<Esc>** to end the **LINE** command. Your drawing should now resemble Figure 2-28.
8. Save your drawing.

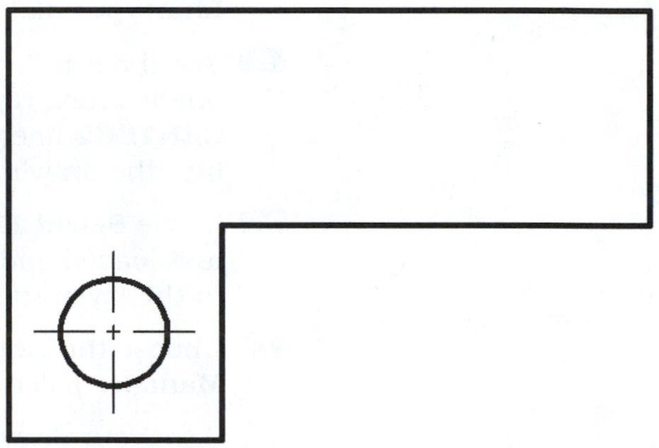

Figure 2-28
Adding centerlines to the drawing

The new lines have the color and linetype of the **Center** layer. The rest of the drawing was created on Layer **0.** In the next exercise, you'll move those objects from Layer **0** to the **Object** layer.

EXERCISE 2-13 Moving Objects to Another Layer

1. In the drawing area, pick a point below and to the left of your figure. AutoCAD prompts you to *Specify opposite corner or* ↓. A blue selection window will drag from the point you picked.
2. Pick a point above and to the right of your figure. This will select all the objects inside the box you just specified.
3. Hold down the **<Shift>** key and pick the two centerlines you just drew. This removes those lines from the selection.
4. Select the **Object** layer from the **Layer** drop-down list. The objects "move" to the **Object** layer and take on the properties of that layer.
5. Press **<Esc>** to clear the selection.
6. Save your drawing.

Of course, the objects didn't actually move. Their layer property was simply changed from **0** to **Object.** However, you can think of this as the objects "floating" from one layer to another or (in the pin-board drafting world) moving the objects from one overlay sheet to another.

Freeze and Thaw a Layer

Your drawing objects are now organized into a few logical layers. Next we'll look at some methods of manipulating layers in your drawing.

EXERCISE 2-14 **Freezing and Thawing Layers**

1. Select Layer **0** from the **Layer** drop-down list. This sets Layer **0** as the current layer.
2. From the **Layer** drop-down list, click on the sun icon next to layer **Center** (see Figure 2-29). The sun icon will change to a snowflake. Now pick anywhere in your drawing to close the **Layer** drop-down list. This ***freezes*** the **Center** layer and hides it from view.
3. From the **Layer** drop-down list, click on the snowflake icon next to layer **Center**. The snowflake now turns back to a sun. Pick anywhere in the drawing area to close the **Layer** drop-down list. This ***thaws*** the **Center** layer, making it visible again.
4. Save your drawing.

freeze/thaw: Hiding or displaying the contents of a drawing layer. Objects on a frozen layer are ignored by AutoCAD, are not shown in the drawing, and cannot be edited.

Figure 2-29
The **Layer** drop-down list

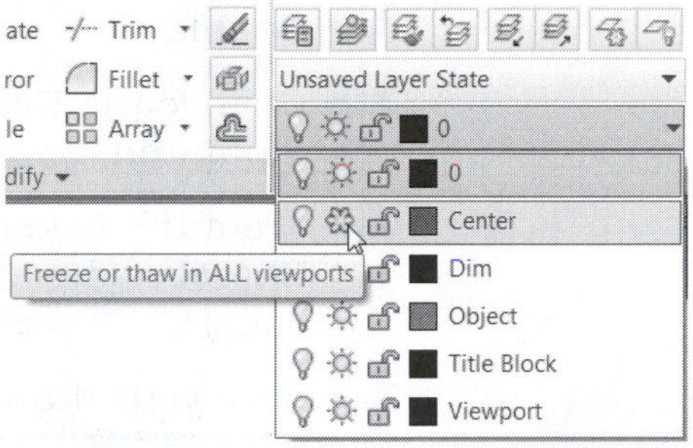

When layers are frozen, AutoCAD acts as though the objects on those layers don't exist. Objects on frozen layers are hidden from view and cannot be changed while the layer is frozen. The current drawing layer cannot be frozen.

AutoCAD also has an **On/Off** setting for layers (represented by the lightbulb in the **Layer** drop-down list). While turning layers off will hide them from view, objects on those layers can still be modified (i.e., erased). For this reason, freezing and thawing layers is generally preferred to turning layers on and off.

NOTE

Unlike the **Freeze** option, it is possible to make a layer current that has been turned off, but it is not recommended for the simple fact that you cannot see what you are drawing.

Lock and Unlock a Layer

Although the **Freeze** option will prevent objects from being modified, it also hides them from view. The **Lock/Unlock** setting allows you to prevent objects from being modified while still keeping them displayed on screen.

EXERCISE 2-15 Locking and Unlocking Layers

1 From the **Layer** drop-down list, click on the open-lock icon next to layer **Object** (see Figure 2-30). The open-lock icon will change to a closed lock. Pick anywhere in your drawing to close the **Layer** drop-down list.

Figure 2-30
Locking the **Object** layer

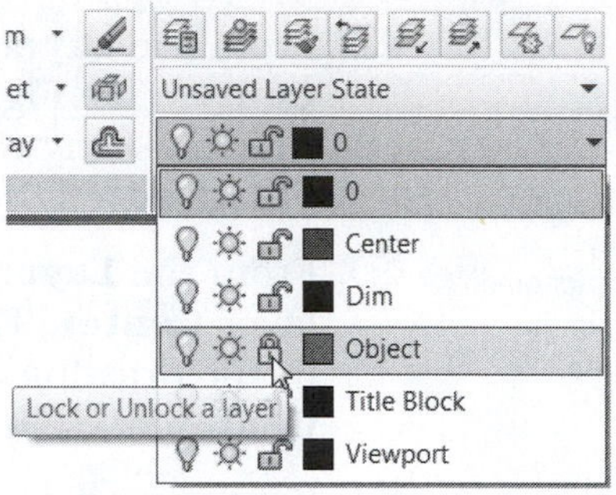

2 Double-click on the circle so the **Quick Properties** palette opens.

3 Change the **Radius** property of the circle to **1**. AutoCAD rejects the input and maintains the 0.5 **Radius** value.

4 From the **Layer** drop-down list, click on the lock icon next to layer **Object** and pick anywhere in the drawing to close the **Layer** drop-down list. The **Object** layer is now unlocked.

5 Save your drawing.

This section has touched on only a few key elements of layering and AutoCAD's layer management tools. Layer management is a crucial element of using AutoCAD effectively.

FOR MORE DETAILS

Chapter 6 explains how to use AutoCAD's layer management tools and describes some of the issues involved in layer management.

Dimension Styles

dimension style: A collection of dimension settings that control how dimension objects act and are displayed.

Now that you have created a basic drawing, it's time to dimension it. Before we start dimensioning, we need to set up the appearance of the dimensions to reflect industry standards. The look and behavior of dimensions are controlled through ***dimension styles***. A dimension style is simply a collection of dimension settings saved with a certain name. A dimension object takes on the look and behavior of its dimension style. AutoCAD uses a dimension style called *Standard* as a default, but you can modify the Standard dimension style or create new ones as needed. In the following exercise, you'll take a quick tour through some of the various dimension style settings.

FOR MORE DETAILS

There are a lot of settings, and the following exercise goes through them quickly: don't get overwhelmed. Chapter 13 gives a detailed description of dimensioning and dimension style settings.

EXERCISE 2-16 Changing Dimension Styles

1. Select the **Annotate** tab of the ribbon to display the different annotation tools.
2. Choose the **Dimension Style** tool from the **Dimensions** panel by selecting the down arrow on the right side of the panel title bar, as shown in Figure 2-31. The **Dimension Style Manager** dialog box appears (see Figure 2-32).

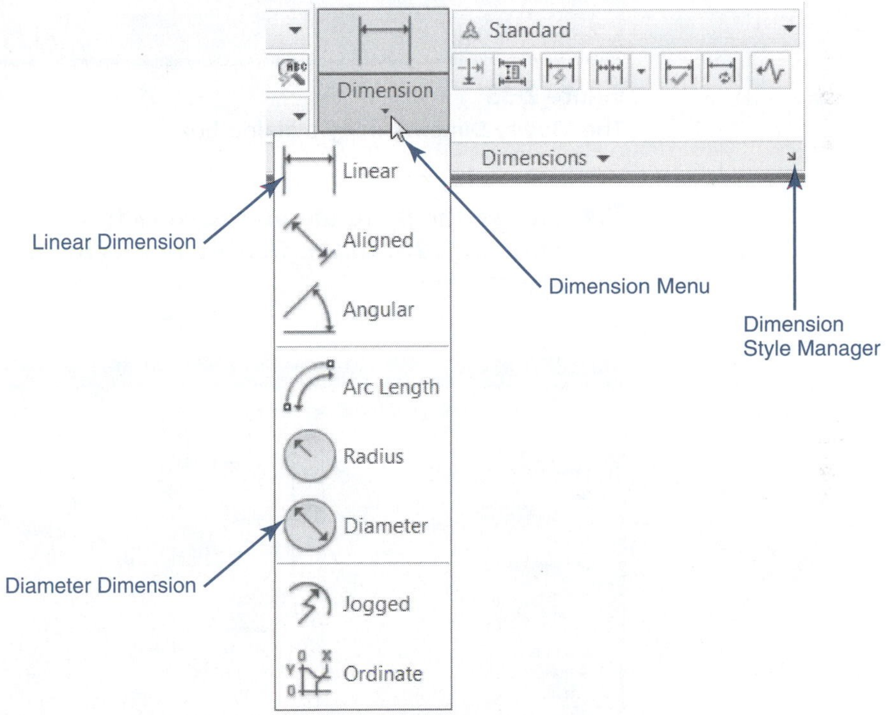

Figure 2-31
The **Dimensions** panel on the **Annotate** tab of the ribbon

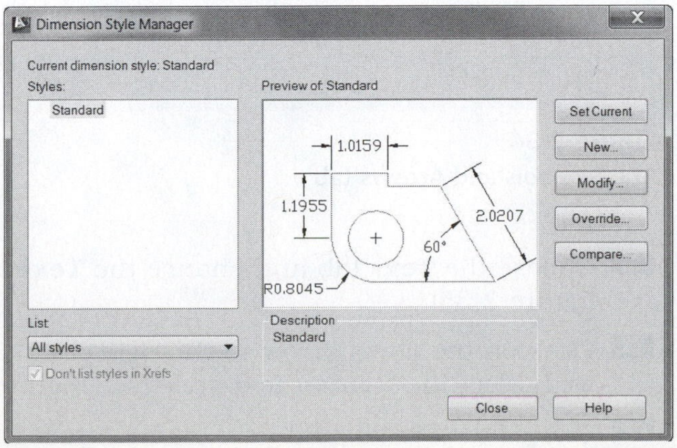

Figure 2-32
The **Dimension Style Manager** dialog box

3. Choose the **Modify...** button to modify the **Standard** dimension style. The **Modify Dimension Style** dialog box appears (see Figure 2-33).

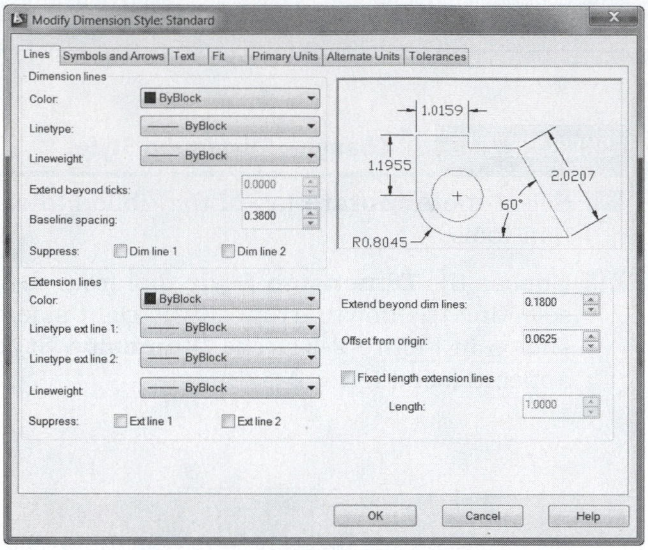

Figure 2-33

The **Modify Dimension Style** dialog box

4. Choose the **Symbols and Arrows** tab and change the **Arrow size** value to **.125.** In the **Center marks** area, change the type to **None** (see Figure 2-34).

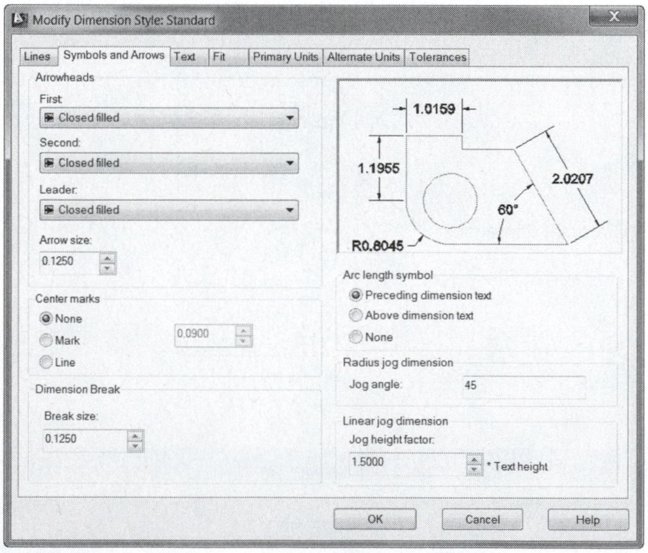

Figure 2-34

The **Symbols and Arrows** tab

5. Choose the **Text** tab and change the **Text height** value to **.125** (see Figure 2-35).

6. Click on the down arrow to the right of the **Text style:** drop-down list and select the **Roman** text style (see Figure 2-36).

7. Choose the **Fit** tab and turn on the **Annotative** option (see Figure 2-37).

Figure 2-35
The **Text** tab

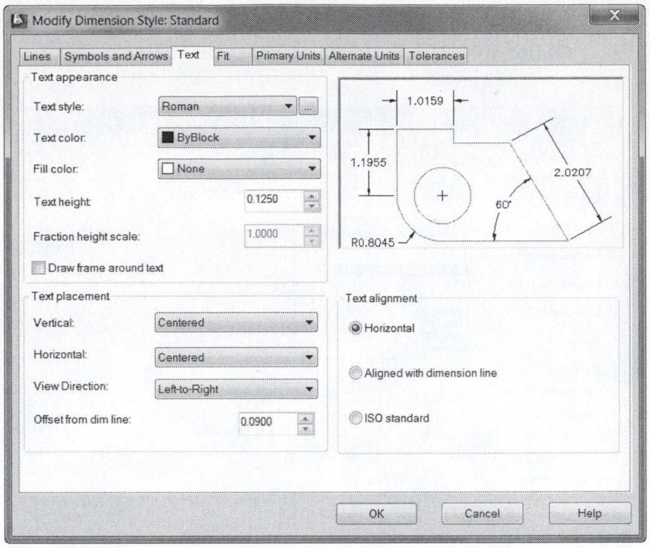

Figure 2-36
The **Text style:** drop-down list

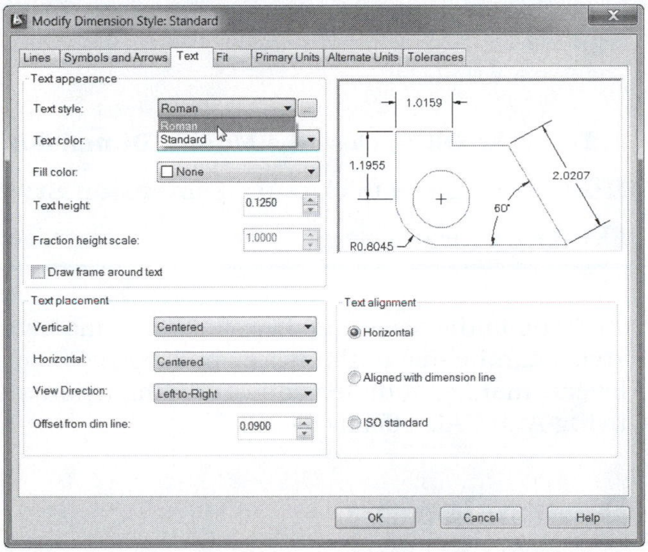

Figure 2-37
The **Fit** tab

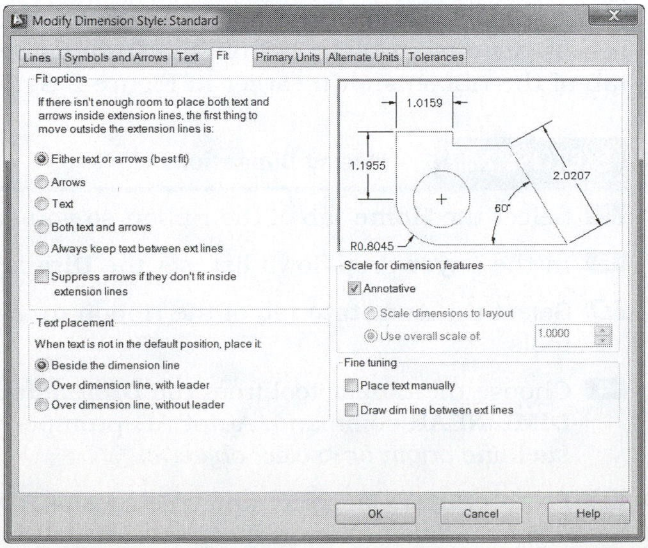

8 Choose the **Primary Units** tab and select **0.00** from the **Precision** drop-down list (see Figure 2-38).

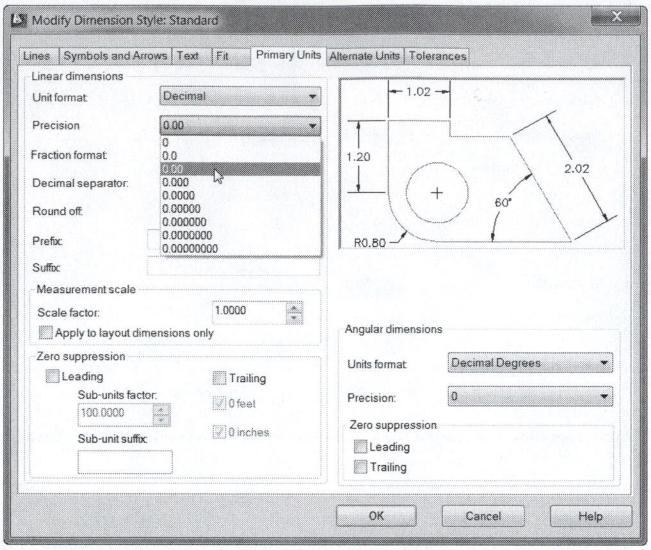

Figure 2-38
The **Primary Units** tab

9 Choose **OK** to close the **Modify Dimension Style** dialog box.

10 Choose **Close** to close the **Dimension Style Manager** dialog box.

11 Save your drawing.

Due to the sheer number of options, modifying and managing dimension styles can be one of the more challenging aspects of AutoCAD. As with layers, managing dimensions and dimension styles is a crucial element of using AutoCAD effectively.

Dimensioning

AutoCAD's dimensioning tools can easily measure distances and place dimensions on your drawing. You tell AutoCAD what type of dimension you want to place and what object or points you wish to dimension, and AutoCAD will measure and place the dimension on the drawing. You can access the dimension tools from the **Dimensions** panel on the **Annotate** tab of the ribbon shown earlier in Figure 2-31.

EXERCISE 2-17 Placing Dimensions

1 Select the **Home** tab of the ribbon so you can access the **Layers** panel.

2 In the **Layer** drop-down list, set the **Dim** layer current.

3 Select the **Annotate** tab of the ribbon to switch back to the annotation tools.

4 Choose the **Linear** tool from the **Dimensions** panel to start the **DIMLINEAR** command. AutoCAD prompts you to *Specify first extension line origin or <select object>:*.

5 Press **<Enter>** to select an object. AutoCAD prompts you to *Select object to dimension:*.

6 Pick the line at the bottom of the drawing (point 1 in Figure 2-39). AutoCAD starts dragging a dimension from that line and prompts you to *Specify dimension line location or* ↓.

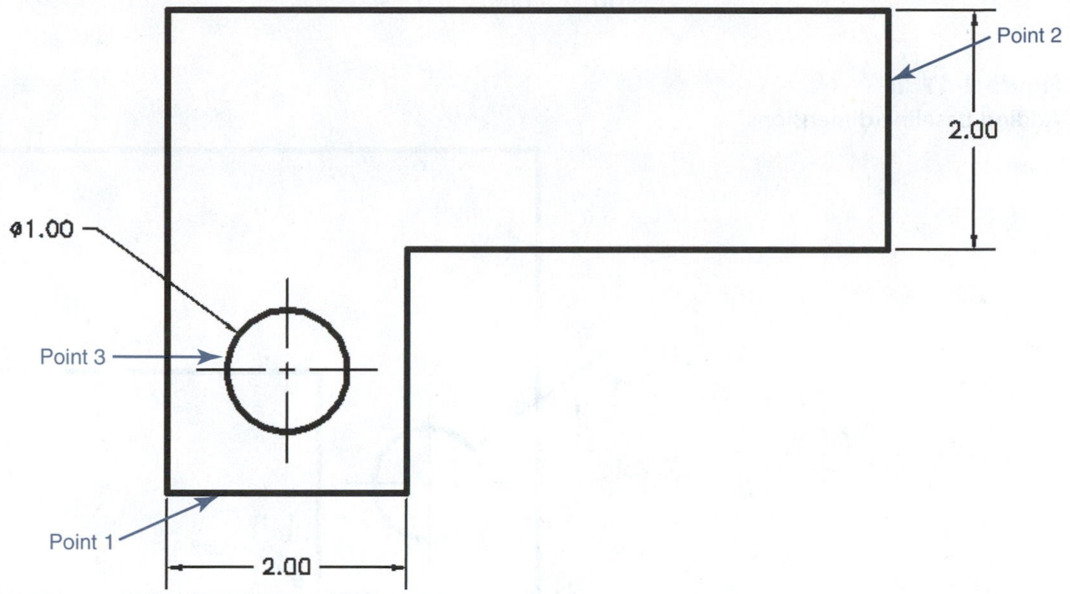

Figure 2-39
Adding dimensions

7 Pick a point below the line. The dimension is placed, and the **DIMLINEAR** command ends.

8 Press **<Enter>** to restart the **DIMLINEAR** command.

9 Press **<Enter>** to select an object and pick the line at the right side of the drawing (point 2 in Figure 2-39).

10 Drag the dimension to the right and pick a point to place it. The **DIMLINEAR** command ends.

11 From the **Dimensions** panel, choose **Diameter** to start the **DIMDIAMETER** command. AutoCAD prompts you to *Select arc or circle:*.

12 Select the circle and pick a point above and to the left of the circle (point 3 in Figure 2-39). The **DIMDIAMETER** command ends.

13 Choose the **Baseline** tool from the **Dimensions** panel, as shown in Figure 2-40 to start the **DIMBASELINE** command. AutoCAD starts dragging a dimension from the end of the last linear dimension. AutoCAD prompts you to *Specify a second extension line origin or* ↓.

Figure 2-40
The **Baseline** tool on the **Dimensions** panel

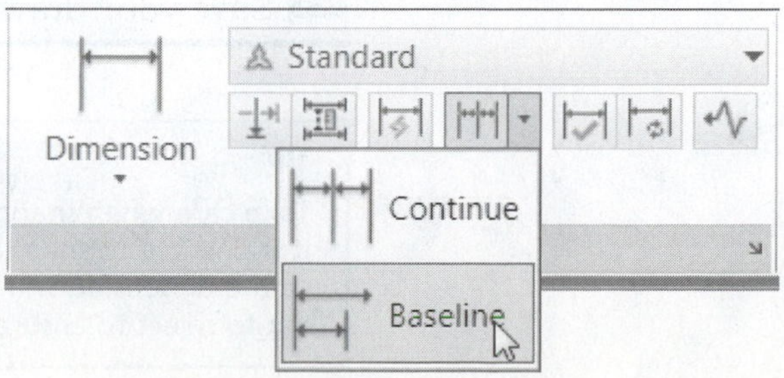

14 Press the down arrow and choose the **Select** option from the menu. AutoCAD prompts you to *Select base dimension:.*

15 Pick the left dimension line of the first dimension you created (point 1 in Figure 2-41). A dimension line rubber-bands from the dimension you selected.

Figure 2-41
Adding baseline dimensions

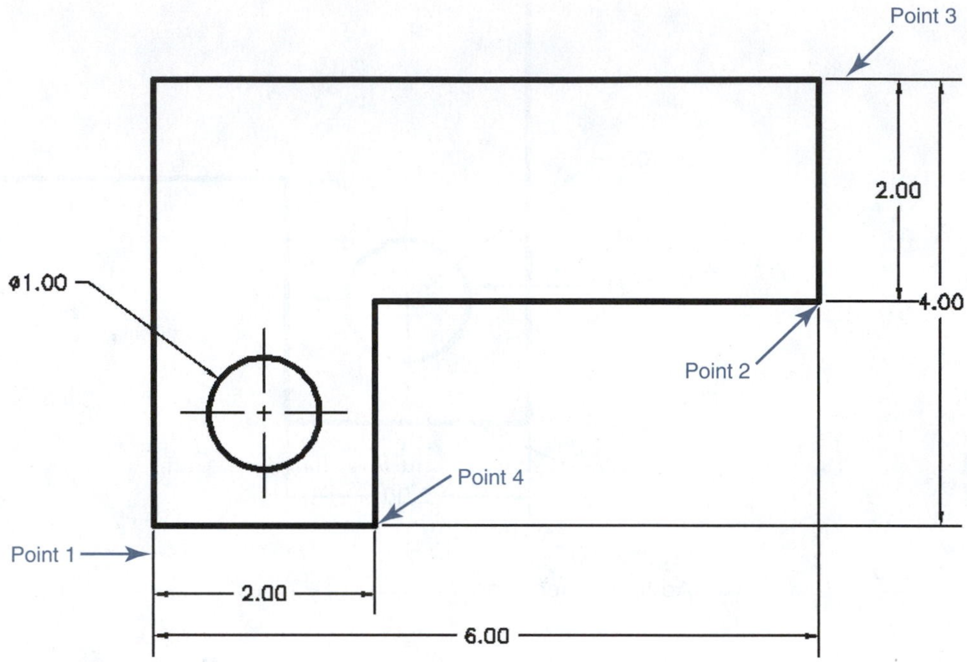

16 Make sure your **Object Snap** toggle is turned on on the status bar, and move your cursor near point 2 shown in Figure 2-41. When the **Endpoint** object snap appears, pick that point to select the endpoint of that line. AutoCAD will place the dimension and start dragging a new dimension.

17 AutoCAD again prompts you to *Specify a second extension line origin or* ↓. Press the down arrow and choose the **Select** option from the menu. AutoCAD prompts you to *Select base dimension:.*

18 Pick the upper dimension line of the vertical dimension (point 3 in Figure 2-41).

19 Move your cursor near point 4 shown in Figure 2-41. When the **Endpoint** object snap appears, pick that point to select the endpoint of that line. AutoCAD will place the dimension and start dragging a new dimension.

20 Press **<Esc>** to end the **DIMBASELINE** command.

21 Save your drawing.

TIP

Take care when snapping to endpoints that are connected to dimension extension lines. It is possible to snap to the extension line endpoint instead of the object line endpoint, so the dimension will be incorrect. You can always zoom closer to the point you are trying to select to ensure proper dimension placement.

Chapter 2

You now have some basic dimensions on your drawing. The look and orientation of the dimensions are controlled by the dimension style.

associativity: A link between drawing objects and dimension objects. Associative dimensions will update and follow the drawing objects to which they are linked.

One of the unique aspects of dimensions is their ability to update automatically as the drawing changes. This feature is called ***associativity***, which means that dimensions are associated with the geometry and will automatically update when the geometry changes. In the next section, we'll look at some ways to modify your drawing and see how the associative dimensions follow along.

Modifying Drawing Objects

So far, we've looked at modifying object properties through the **Quick Properties** palette. One of the most powerful benefits of CAD systems is their unique ability to make changes to your drawing. This section introduces you to some of the basic tools used to modify your drawing.

Selection Sets

As with the drawing tools, AutoCAD has a general process for modifying objects, which is to:

1. Select an editing tool.
2. Specify which object(s) you want to modify.
3. Read the prompt.
4. Specify points and answer prompts.
5. Press **<Enter>** or **<Esc>** to end the command.

building a selection set: The process of specifying the objects you wish to edit.

The process of specifying which objects you want to edit is called ***building a selection set***.

It is possible to preselect the objects you want to modify. If any objects are selected prior to starting a command, AutoCAD will use these objects as the selection set and will skip the *Select objects:* prompt.

FOR MORE DETAILS

See Chapter 7 for more on building selection sets.

EXERCISE 2-18 **Moving Objects**

1. Make sure the **Object Snap** and **Polar Tracking** toggles on the status bar are turned on.
2. Select the **Home** tab of the ribbon so you can access the **Modify** panel.
3. Choose the **Move** tool from the **Modify** panel on the **Home** tab of the ribbon. AutoCAD prompts you to *Select objects:*.
4. Select the circle. AutoCAD again prompts you to *Select objects:*.
5. Select the two centerlines and press **<Enter>** to stop the selection process. AutoCAD prompts you to *Specify base point or* ↓.

6 Move the cursor near the edge of the circle. When the **Center** object snap appears, pick that point to specify the center of the circle. AutoCAD starts dragging the objects from the center of the circle and prompts you to *Specify second point of displacement or <use first point as displacement>:*.

7 Drag the object straight up until the 90° polar tracking alignment path appears (see Figure 2-42). Once it appears, type **2<Enter>**. The circle, lines, and dimensions move up 2″.

8 Save your drawing.

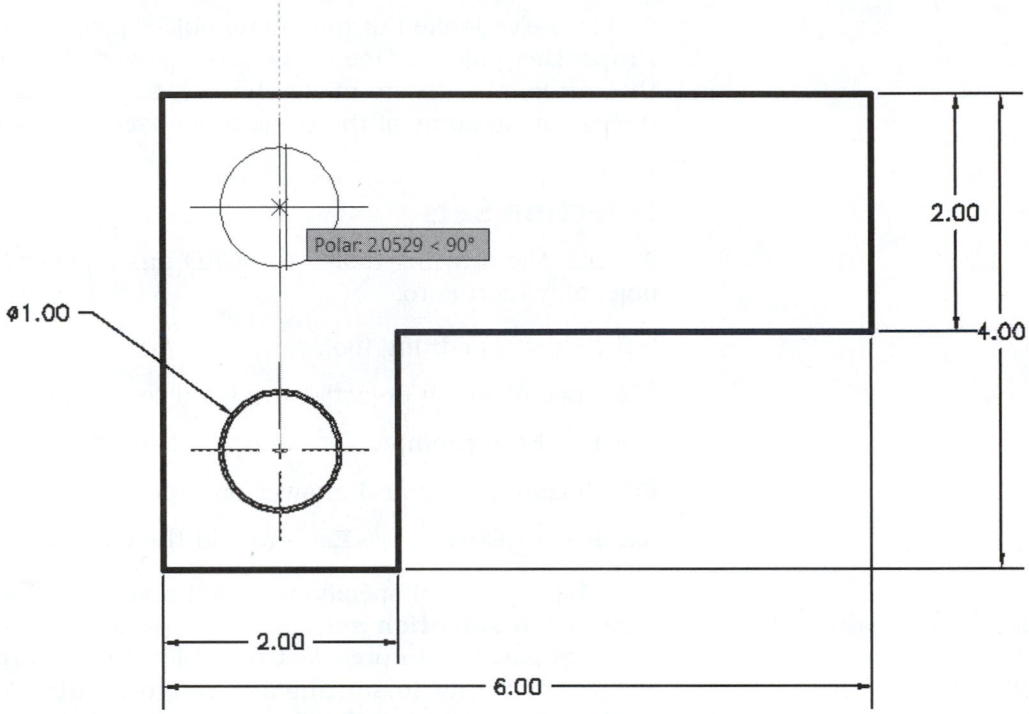

Figure 2-42
Moving objects

When you started the **MOVE** command, AutoCAD needed to know which objects you wanted to move. The *Select objects:* prompt repeated until you pressed **<Enter>**, telling AutoCAD you had finished selecting objects. Once you finished selecting objects, AutoCAD then went on to complete the command. It asked you to specify where you wanted to move the objects from (the base point) and where you wanted to drag the objects to (the second point).

Notice that even though you didn't select the dimension, it moved as well. This is because of the associativity of the dimension with the circle.

Now, let's look at selecting the objects you want to modify first and then selecting the modify command.

EXERCISE 2-19 Selecting First

1 Pick a point on the screen above and to the right of the circle (point 1 in Figure 2-43). AutoCAD will prompt you: *Specify opposite corner or* ↓.

Figure 2-43
Dragging a crossing window

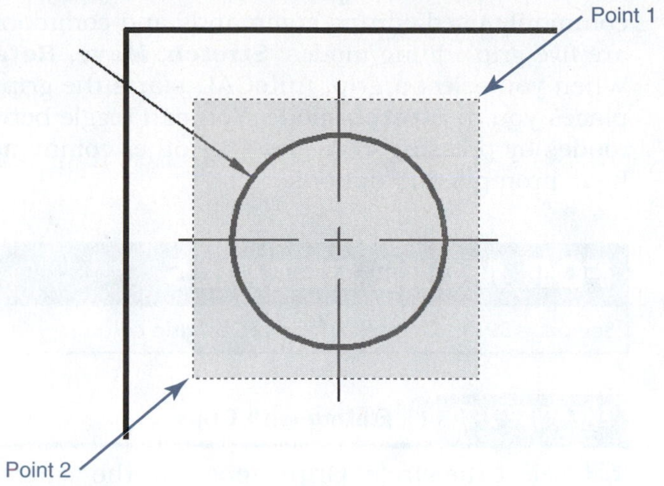

crossing window: A method of selecting objects in a selection set by specifying a rectangular area. Anything that touches the crossing window area is selected.

2. Drag the cursor down and to the left of the circle. AutoCAD will drag a dashed rectangle with a green background from the first point you picked (see Figure 2-43). This is called a ***crossing window***.
3. Pick a point below and to the left of the circle (point 2 in Figure 2-43). AutoCAD will select all the objects that are inside or touch the edge of the crossing window you picked.
4. Choose the **Erase** tool from the **Modify** panel. AutoCAD immediately erases the selected objects.
5. Choose the **Undo** tool from the **Quick Access** toolbar to bring the objects back.
6. Save your drawing.

FOR MORE DETAILS

The crossing window is one of a number of ways to select objects. Page 276 in Chapter 7 discusses crossing windows and other ways to select objects.

Notice that AutoCAD did not prompt you to select objects. Because you selected the objects before you started the command, AutoCAD assumed that those were the objects you wanted to erase. AutoCAD doesn't care whether you select the objects before or after you start the command. If no objects are selected, AutoCAD will simply ask you to select them before it continues with the command.

Grip Editing

grips: Editing points that appear at key locations on drawing objects.

You may have noticed in previous exercises that when you preselect objects, the objects highlight and little squares show up on them. These squares are known as ***grips***. Grips appear when you select objects when there is no active command. Grips are located at strategic points on an object. For example, on a circle, grips appear at the center and the four quadrants of the circle. On lines, grips appear at the ends and midpoints of the line. On dimensions, they appear on the dimension text and the ends of the dimension lines and arrows.

Grips give you a quick way to modify objects by giving you access to commonly used editing commands and commonly used object points. There are five grip editing modes: **Stretch, Move, Rotate, Scale**, and **Mirror**. When you select a grip, AutoCAD starts the grip editing command and places you in **Stretch** mode. You can toggle between the different editing modes by pressing **<Enter>**. Like other commands, the grip editing modes have prompts and options.

FOR MORE DETAILS

See page 301 in Chapter 7 for more on grip editing.

EXERCISE 2-20 Editing with Grips

1. Select the circle. Grips appear at the center point and the four quadrants of the circle.
2. Select the two centerlines. Grips appear at the endpoints and midpoint of the lines. The grip at the center of the circle coincides with the midpoints of the two lines (see Figure 2-44).

Figure 2-44
Grips

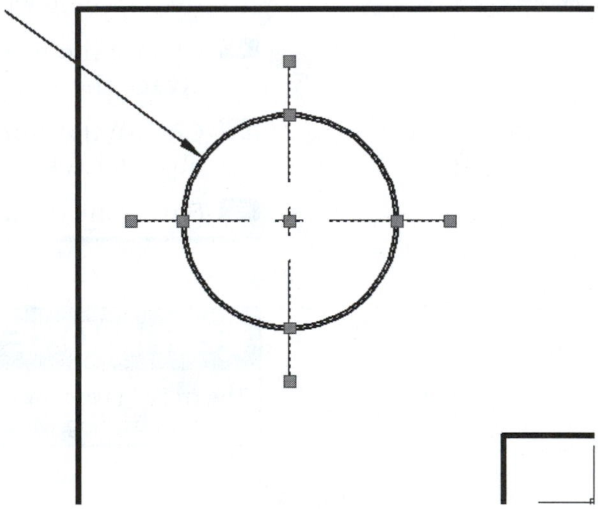

3. Click on the center grip. The grip turns red, and AutoCAD prompts you to *Specify stretch point or* ↓. AutoCAD is now in **Stretch** mode. AutoCAD is prompting you to specify a stretch point.
4. Move your cursor to the right until the polar tracking appears. Once it appears, type **3.5<Enter>**. AutoCAD moves the center of the circle 3.5″ to the right (see Figure 2-45).
5. Press **<Esc>** to exit **Grip Edit** mode and clear the selection set.
6. Select the diameter dimension on the circle. Grips appear at the middle of the text and at two points on the circle.
7. Pick the text grip and drag the text above and to the right of the circle. Pick a point outside of the drawing to place the text (see Figure 2-46).
8. Press **<Esc>** to exit **Grip Edit** mode and clear the selection set.
9. Save your drawing.

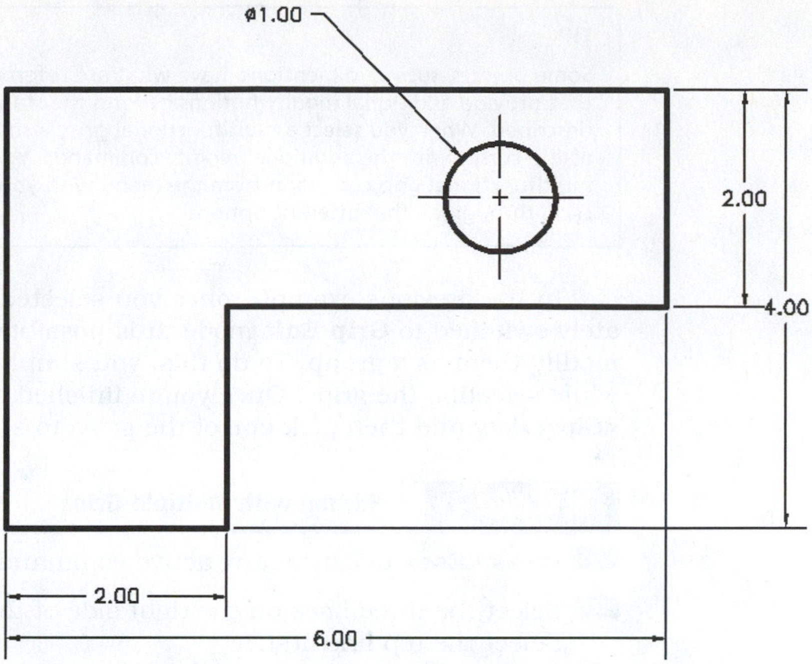

Figure 2-45
The modified circle

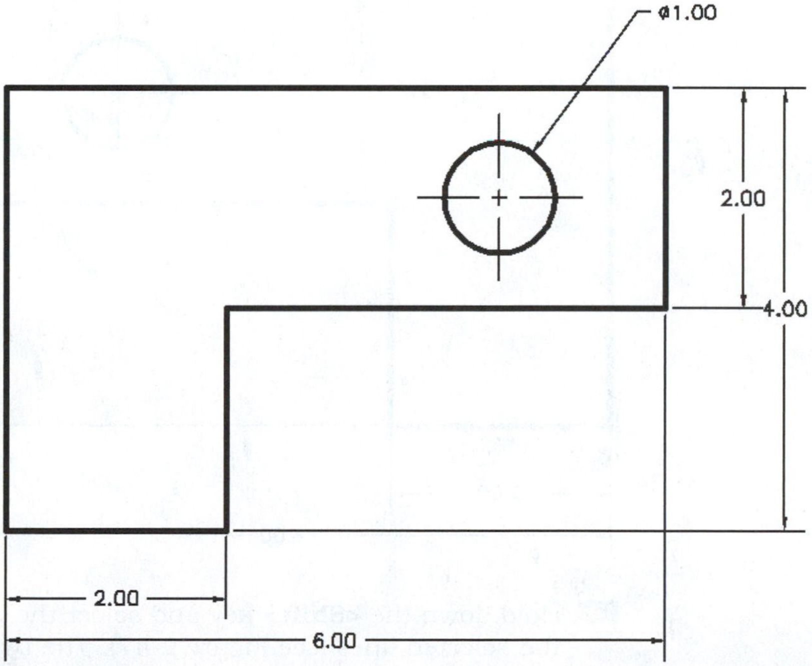

Figure 2-46
The modified dimension

Notice that when you *stretched* the center and midpoints of the objects, the end result was that the objects moved. It's a subtle distinction but worth noting. AutoCAD defines circles by a center point (the center grip) and a radius (the quadrant grips). Since you stretched only the center point, only the location of the circle changed, not its size. The same thing applies to the line; because you stretched just the midpoint of the line, the size and direction of the line didn't change, only its location.

> **TIP**
>
> Some objects, such as dimensions, have what are referred to as multifunctional grips that provide additional modify options beyond the standard grip editing modes just described. When you select a multifunctional grip, a small pop-up menu is displayed at the cursor with the additional modify commands. You can either pick the desired multifunctional grip command from the menu with your mouse or use the **<Ctrl>** key to cycle through all the different options.

In the previous example, once you selected a grip, AutoCAD immediately switched to **Grip Edit** mode. It is possible to select multiple grips and modify them as a group. To do this, you simply hold down the **<Shift>** key while selecting the grips. Once you're finished selecting grips, release the **<Shift>**key and then pick one of the grips to start the editing process.

EXERCISE 2-21 Editing with Multiple Grips

1. Press **<Esc>** to cancel any active commands and clear any selections.
2. Select the three lines on the right side of the drawing (see Figure 2-47). Select the top line first.

Figure 2-47
Selecting multiple grips

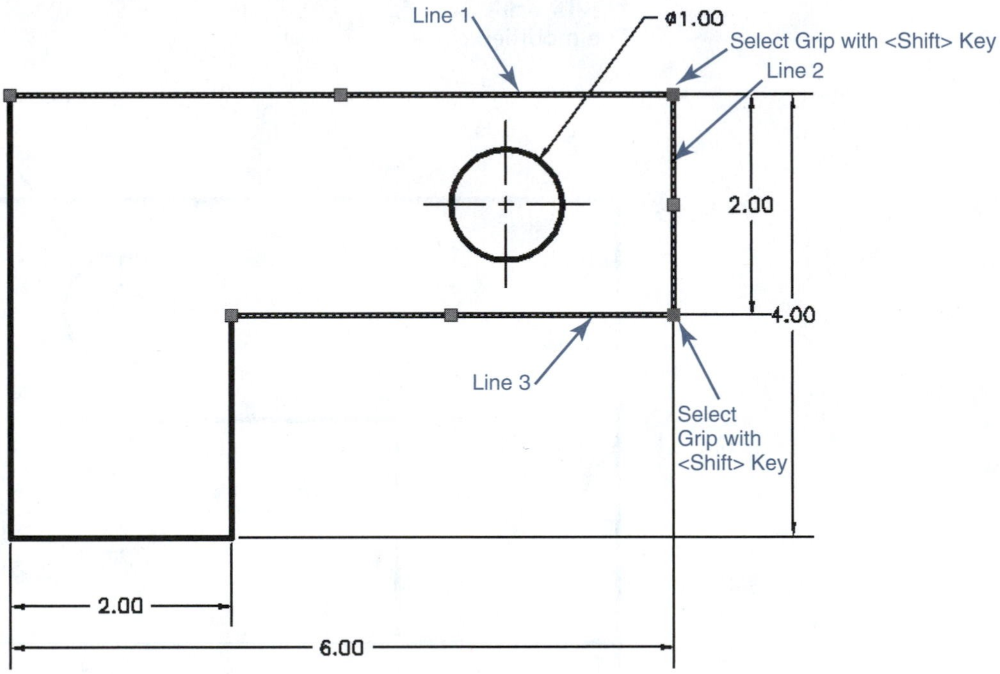

3. Hold down the **<Shift>** key and select the two grips at the corners of the selected lines (see Figure 2-47). The two grips are highlighted, but grip editing has not started.
4. Release the **<Shift>** key and select either one of the highlighted grips. AutoCAD now enters **Grip Edit** mode.
5. Drag the grip to the left until the polar tracking alignment path appears at 180°. Once the polar tracking appears, type **.5<Enter>** into the dynamic input box (see Figure 2-48).
6. AutoCAD stretches the longest line to a length of 5.5 (see Figure 2-49).
7. Press **<Esc>** to exit **Grip Edit** mode and clear the selection set.
8. Save your drawing.

Figure 2-48
Grips and dynamic input

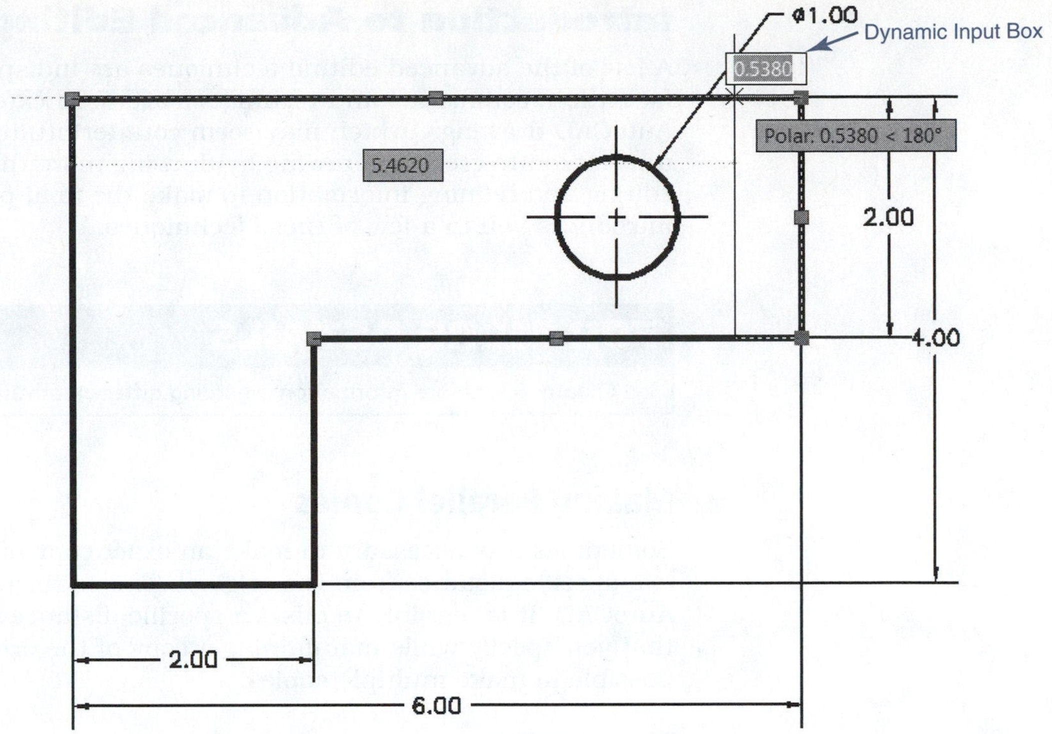

Figure 2-49
The stretched objects

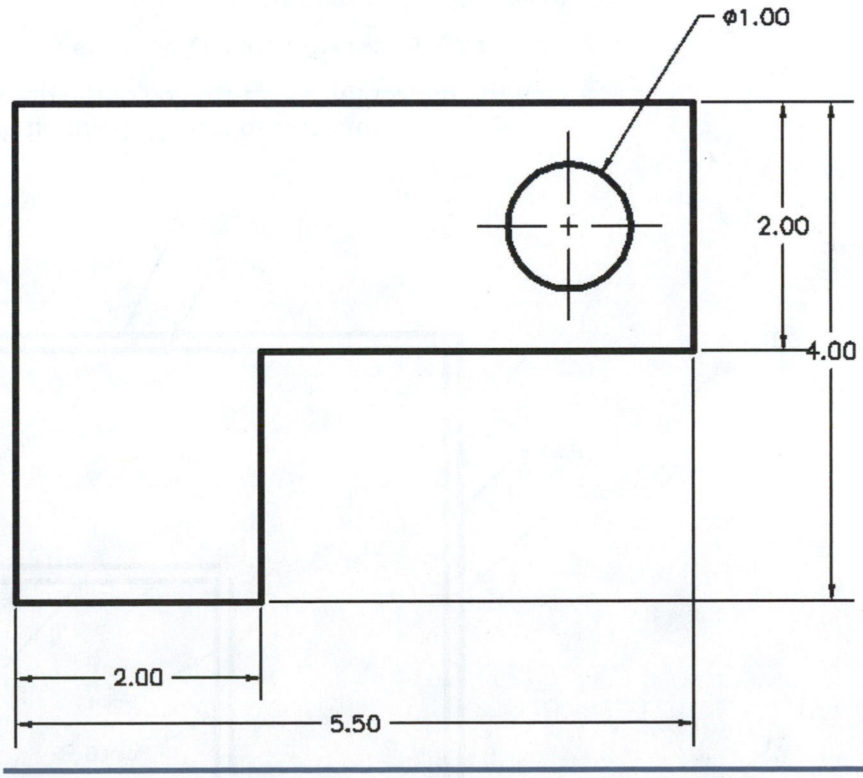

The order in which you select the lines is important. The first line you selected determined which dimension would appear in the dynamic input box. You should have also seen the associative dimensions in action again. The dimensions updated to follow the changes in the geometry.

Introduction to Advanced Editing Techniques

A few of the advanced editing techniques are indispensable in AutoCAD. In fact, these commands and techniques are used extensively when creating AutoCAD drawings, which may seem counterintuitive. Using CAD, it is not uncommon to create a drawing by drawing more than you need and then editing and refining information to make the final product. This section introduces you to a few of these techniques.

FOR MORE DETAILS

See Chapter 8 for more information regarding different advanced editing techniques.

Making Parallel Copies

Sometimes it is necessary to make an exact copy of a line or circle that is a specific distance from the original. This is referred to as an *offset* in AutoCAD. It is possible to offset a specific distance or even through a point that you specify while maintaining a copy of the original object. It is even possible to make multiple copies.

EXERCISE 2-22 **Offsetting Objects**

1. Choose the **Offset** tool from the **Modify** panel. AutoCAD prompts you to *Specify offset distance or* ↓.
2. Type **.125<Enter>**. AutoCAD prompts you to *Select object to offset or* ↓.
3. Pick the horizontal line at the top of the drawing (point 1 in Figure 2-50). AutoCAD prompts you to *Specify point on side to offset or* ↓.

Figure 2-50
Offsetting lines

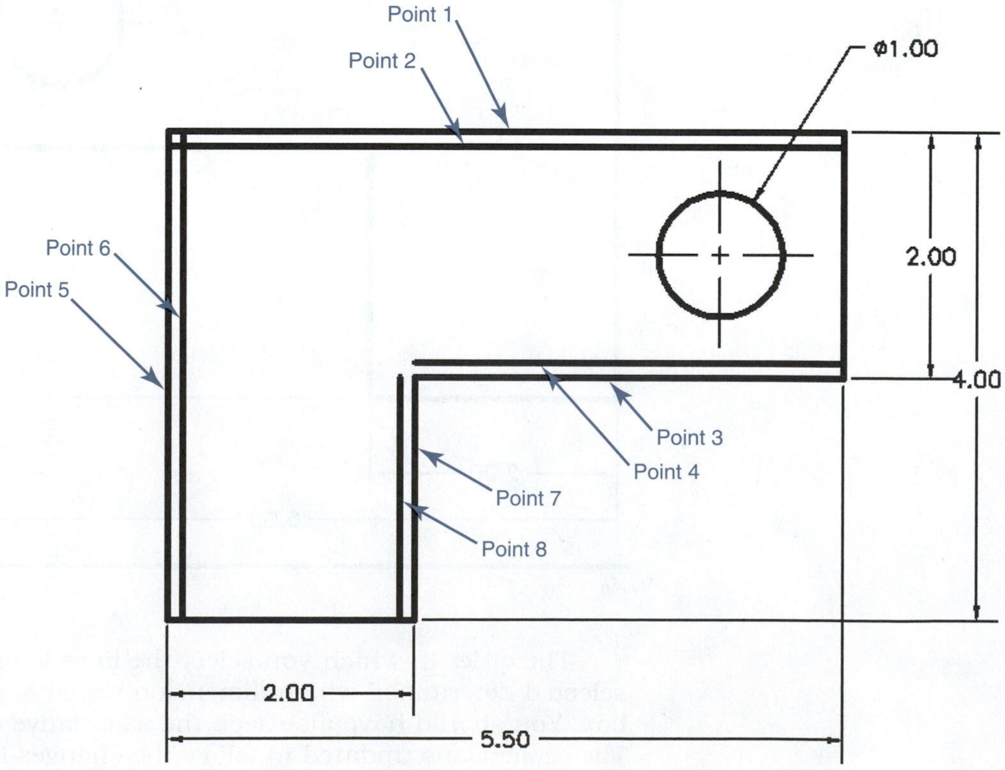

4. Pick a point below that line (point 2 in Figure 2-50). AutoCAD places a copy of the line .125″ below the original. AutoCAD prompts you again to *Select object to offset or* ↓.
5. Pick the next horizontal line down from the top of the drawing (point 3 in Figure 2-50). AutoCAD prompts you to *Specify point on side to offset or* ↓.
6. Pick a point above that line (point 4 in Figure 2-50). AutoCAD places a copy of the line .125″ above the original. AutoCAD prompts you again to *Select object to offset or* ↓.
7. Pick the vertical line on the left side of the drawing (point 5 in Figure 2-50). AutoCAD prompts you to *Specify point on side to offset or* ↓.
8. Pick a point to the right of that line (point 6 in Figure 2-50). AutoCAD places a copy of the line .125″ to the right of the original and prompts you again to *Select object to offset or* ↓.
9. Pick the next vertical line to the right of the drawing (point 7 in Figure 2-50). AutoCAD prompts you to *Specify point on side to offset or* ↓.
10. Pick a point to the left of that line (point 8 in Figure 2-50). AutoCAD places a copy of the line .125″ to the left of the original and prompts you again to *Select object to offset or* ↓.
11. Save your drawing.

Fixing Overlapping Lines and Closing Gaps

Often it is necessary to "clean up" lines that overlap and/or do not meet exactly so that there is a gap. Remember that the key to using AutoCAD effectively is to draw everything as precisely as possible. There is no room for even the tiniest overlap or gap. These small errors can propagate larger errors when dimensions are added or parts are mated together. AutoCAD provides a number of methods for cleaning up your drawings quickly.

> **TIP**
>
> When cleaning up line work it is often necessary to zoom in closer so that you can pick points precisely. The easiest way to zoom in and out is to use the mouse wheel if you have one. Otherwise, you can always use the navigation bar.

EXERCISE 2-23 Trimming and Extending Objects

1. Choose the **Trim** tool from the **Modify** panel. The current command settings are displayed at the command line, and AutoCAD prompts you:

   Current settings: Projection=UCS, Edge=None

   Select cutting edges...

   Select objects or <select all>:
2. Select lines 1–4 shown in Figure 2-51 and press **<Enter>**. AutoCAD prompts you to *Select object to trim or shift-select to extend or* ↓.

Figure 2-51
Trimming and extending lines

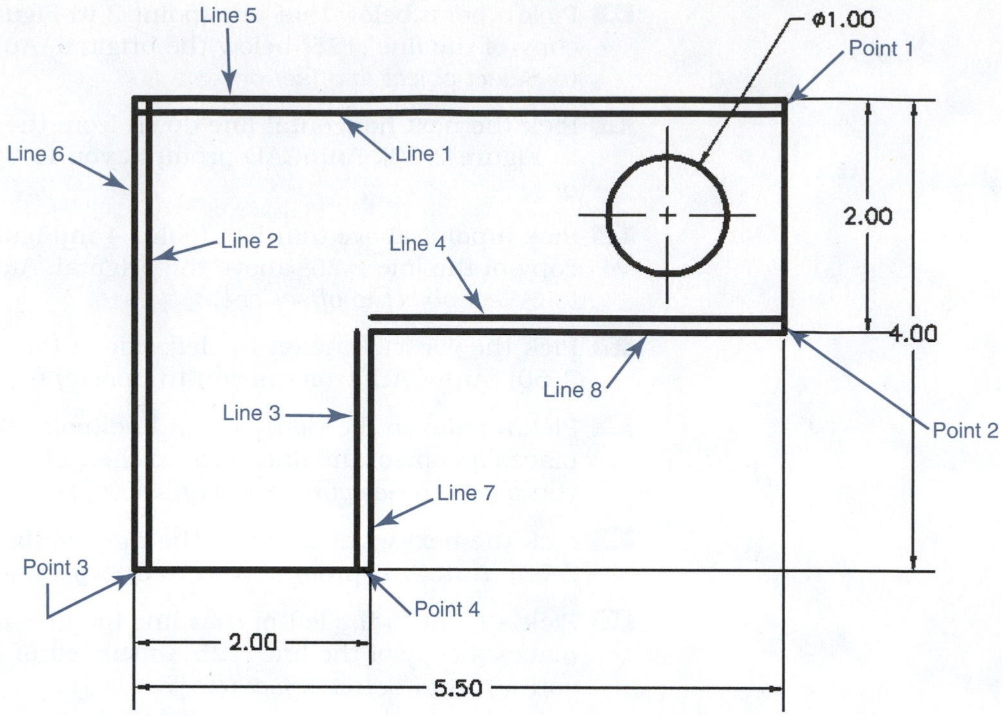

3 Pick a point on the short line segment shown at point 1 in Figure 2-51. The vertical line is trimmed, and AutoCAD prompts you again to *Select object to trim or shift-select to extend or* ↓.

4 Pick the line segments shown at points 2, 3, and 4 in Figure 2-51. The lines are trimmed.

5 Press **<Enter>** to exit the **Trim** tool. Notice that the dimensions automatically update to reflect the new sizes.

6 Choose the **Extend** tool from the **Modify** panel. The current command settings are displayed at the command line, and AutoCAD prompts you:

Current settings: Projection=UCS, Edge=None

Select boundary edges...

Select objects or <select all>:

7 Select lines 3 and 4 in Figure 2-51 and press **<Enter>**. AutoCAD prompts you to *Select object to extend or shift-select to trim or* ↓.

8 Press the down arrow on your keyboard or type **E<Enter>** and select the **Extend** option.

9 Pick a point toward the top of line 3 in Figure 2-51. The vertical line is extended, and AutoCAD prompts you again to *Select object to extend or shift-select to trim or* ↓.

10 Pick a point on the left of line 4 in Figure 2-51. The line is extended.

11 Press **<Enter>** to exit the **Extend** tool.

12 Choose the **Fillet** tool from the **Modify** panel. The current command settings are displayed at the command line, and AutoCAD prompts you:

Current settings: Mode = TRIM, Radius = 0.0000

Select first object or ↓.

13 Select lines 1 and 2 near the upper left corner in Figure 2-51. Both lines are trimmed to form a closed corner by creating a fillet with a radius of 0.0″.

14 Choose the **Erase** tool from the **Modify** panel and erase lines 5, 6, 7, and 8 (see Figure 2-51).

15 Your drawing should now look like Figure 2-52. Use grips to select the dimension extension line origin as shown and attach it back to the corner of the drawing using an **Endpoint** object snap. Make sure the **Object Snap** button is on.

16 Save your drawing.

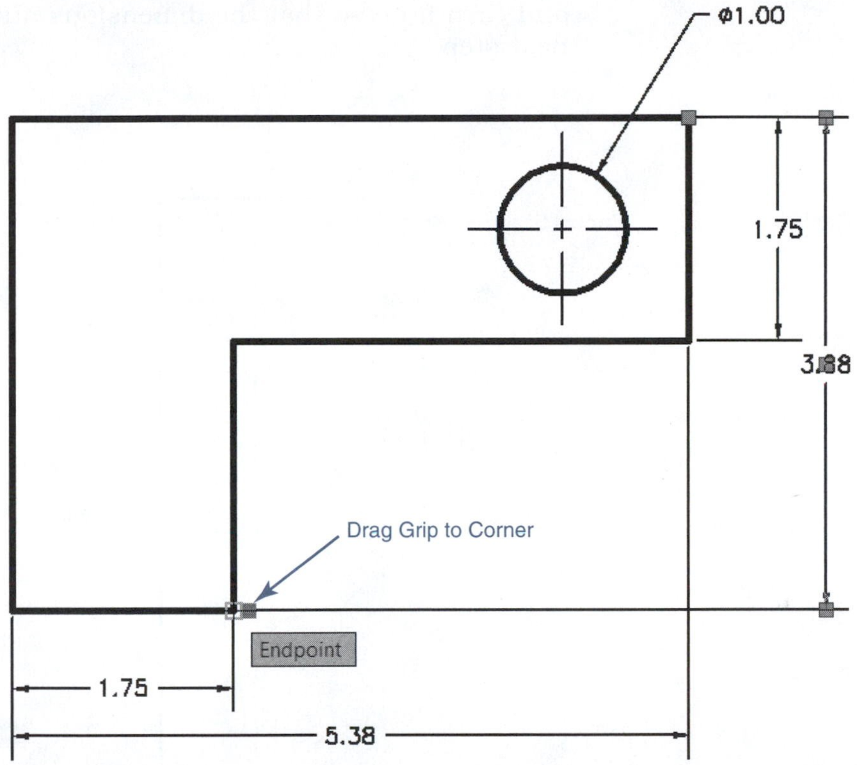

Figure 2-52
The updated drawing

Cleaning Up Layout Space

Now that we have some basic dimensions on the drawing, let's go back to the layout space and make some adjustments to the viewport and the title block so we can get the drawing ready for plotting.

Setting the Viewport Scale

Remember that in layout space (paper space), viewports are simply holes or windows into the model space environment. You can activate a viewport to zoom and pan around model space and even make changes to your model. You can also assign a viewport scale to each viewport. By setting the viewport scale, you are telling AutoCAD to display the model at a certain scale factor (full-scale, half-scale, 1/8″ = 1′-0″, etc.) within that viewport. The viewport in the **ANSI A Title Block** layout was part of the template file used to create the drawing. In the next exercise, you'll set the scale of the viewport and adjust the position of the model within the title border.

EXERCISE 2-24 Setting the Viewport Scale

1 Choose the **ANSI A Title Block** tab at the bottom of the drawing to switch to layout space. The geometry from model space will show up in the viewport.

2 Choose the **Zoom All** tool from the **Zoom** tools on the navigation bar. This will fill the drawing area with your layout sheet.

3 Double-click inside the viewport to activate it. The viewport will highlight, and the crosshairs will appear only inside the viewport.

4 Click on the **Automatically Add Scales** icon at the far right of the **Viewport Scale** button on the status bar shown in Figure 2-53, and turn it on so that the dimensions automatically scale in the next step.

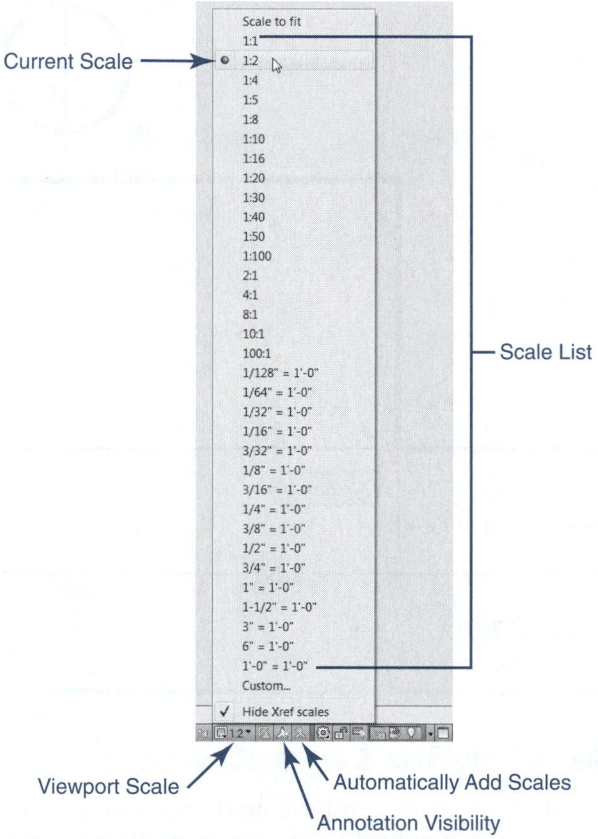

Figure 2-53
Setting the viewport scale

5 Click on the down arrow to the right of the **Viewport Scale** button on the status bar shown in Figure 2-53 to display the scale list and choose **1:2**. Your drawing will zoom so that your model is half-scale (1:2) on your layout (paper).

6 Choose **Pan** from the navigation bar, and pan your drawing so that it looks like Figure 2-54.

7 Save your drawing.

Figure 2-54
The scaled viewport

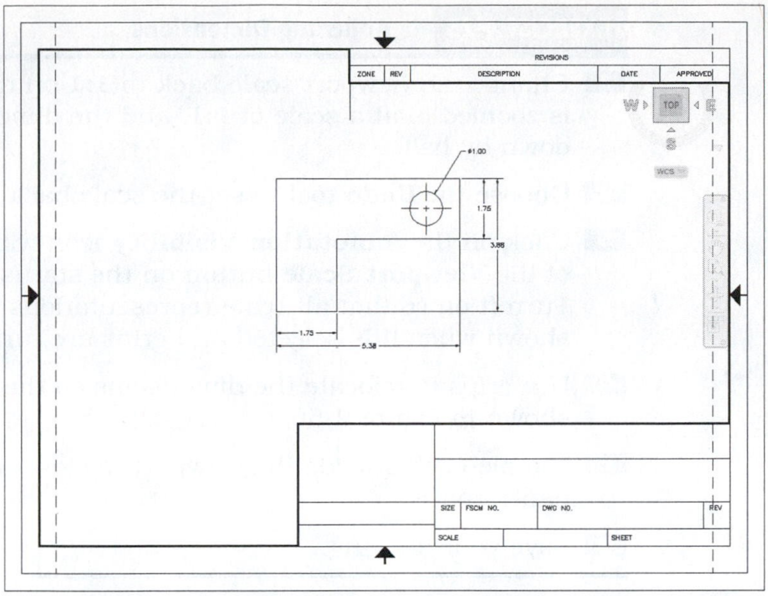

Notice that the dimension features are now twice as large as they were before you set the viewport scale. This is because the dimension style was set up earlier with the **Annotative** feature turned on (see Figure 2-37). When combined with turning on the feature that automatically scales annotative objects, as done in step 4 of Exercise 2-24, this setting actually creates another set of dimensions for the new viewport/annotation scale so that you can view your drawing at different scales and have all the annotation objects display at the correct size.

> **TIP**
>
> It is possible to display all of an annotation object's scale representations when you select it so that each size is visible. You can grip edit the current scale's representation without affecting any of the other scale representations. For instance, by using grips, you can relocate one scale representation while leaving the others in their current locations, as shown in Figure 2-55.

Figure 2-55
The adjusted dimensions

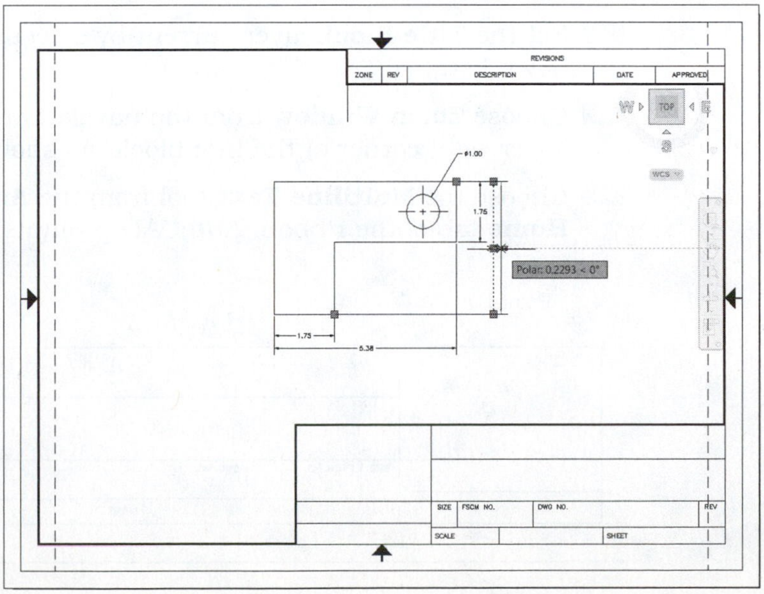

EXERCISE 2-25 **Adjusting Dimensions**

1. Change the viewport scale back to **1:1** on the status bar. The view is zoomed in at a scale of 1:1, and the dimension features are scaled down by half.
2. Choose the **Undo** tool to set the scale back to **1:2**.
3. Click on the **Annotation Visibility** icon with the lightbulb to the right of the **Viewport Scale** button on the status bar shown in Figure 2-53. Turn it on so that all scale representations of an annotation object are shown when it is selected and grips are turned on.
4. Use grips to relocate the dimensions so that they no longer overlap, as shown in Figure 2-55.
5. Double-click outside the viewport to close the viewport and switch to paper space.
6. Save your drawing.

Text

Now, let's update the title block and place some text. When placing text in a drawing, AutoCAD will ask you to define a box in which to place the text. Once that text box is defined, a miniature text editor appears where you specified, and you can start typing your text. The text editor has a number of formatting features found in many text editors (fonts, bold, justification, etc.). You can insert predefined text fields (such as the file name, date, plot scale, etc.) and can also import text from an external text file.

FOR MORE DETAILS

Chapter 11 describes the various options for placing and formatting text.

EXERCISE 2-26 **Placing Text**

1. Make sure that you are still in paper space and that the viewport is not active.
2. Set the **Title Block** layer current by selecting it from the **Layer** drop-down list.
3. Choose **Zoom Window** from the navigation bar, and zoom up on the lower right corner of the title block, as shown in Figure 2-56.
4. Choose the **Multiline Text** tool from the **Annotation** panel on the **Home** tab of the ribbon. AutoCAD prompts you to *Specify first corner:*.

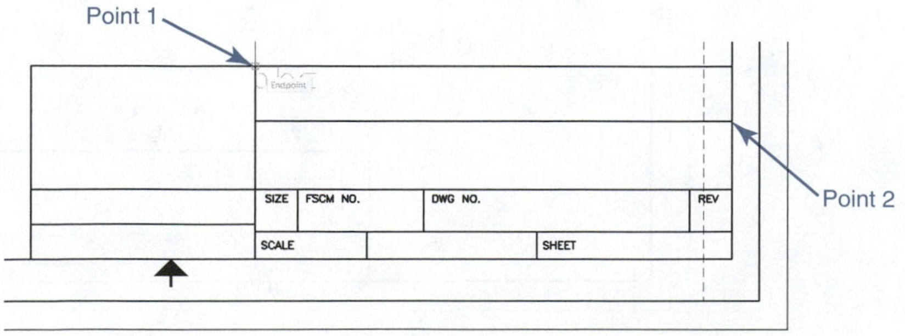

Figure 2-56
Defining a text box

5 Pick the endpoints at point 1 and point 2 shown in Figure 2-56. The **Text Editor** context tab of the ribbon replaces the **Home** tab of the ribbon at the top of the screen, and a flashing text cursor is displayed at the upper left corner of the text box. This indicates where the text will appear when you type.

6 In the **Style** panel, first set the current text style to **Roman,** then set the text height to **.125**.

7 Choose the **Justification** button in the **Paragraph** panel and choose **Middle Center MC** from the menu. The flashing cursor will move to the middle of the text box.

8 In the text box, type **Introduction to AutoCAD** and choose **Close Text Editor** from the **Close** panel. AutoCAD places the text centered in the text box you specified.

9 Press **<Enter>** to repeat the **MTEXT** command.

10 Pick the endpoints at point 1 and point 2 shown in Figure 2-57. The **Text Editor** context tab of the ribbon replaces the **Home** tab of the ribbon at the top of the screen, and a flashing text cursor is displayed at the upper left corner of the text box.

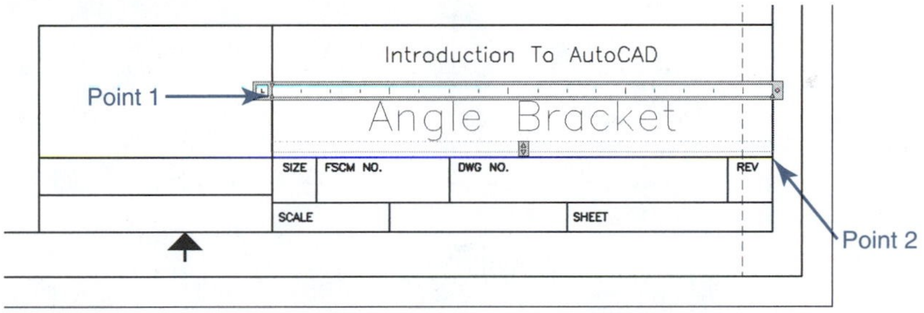

Figure 2-57
Placing more text

11 Set the style to **Roman** again, then set the text height to **.250** and choose **Middle Center MC** from the **Justification** menu.

12 Type **Angle Bracket** in the text box and then choose **Close Text Editor** to end the command.

13 Save your drawing.

So far, you've simply typed in the text you want to display. You may want to place text that is specific to the drawing (such as the drawing file name) or that is dynamic (for example, the plot time or date the drawing was last revised). AutoCAD provides you with a number of predefined text fields that will display various drawing or system information. In the following exercise, you'll use a text field to create the text.

EXERCISE 2-27 Using a Text Field

1 Choose the **Multiline Text** tool from the **Annotation** panel on the **Home** tab of the ribbon, and select the endpoints at point 1 and point 2 shown in Figure 2-58. The **Text Editor** context tab of the ribbon replaces the **Home** tab of the ribbon at the top of the screen, and a flashing text cursor is displayed at the upper left corner of the text box.

2 Set the style to **Roman**, then set the text height to **.125** and the justification to **Middle Center MC**.

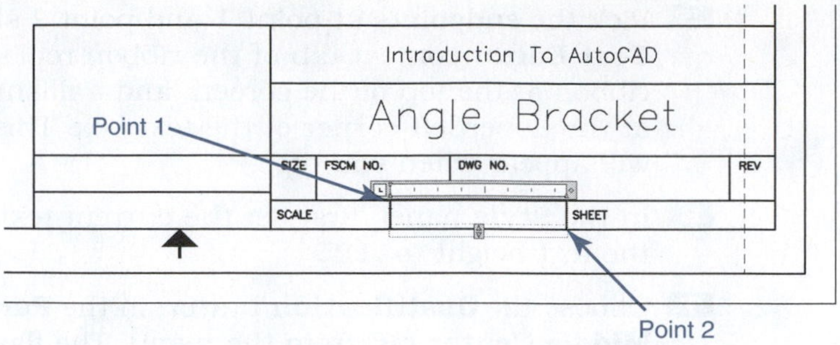

Figure 2-58
Placing a text field

3 Choose **Field** from the **Insert** panel. This displays the **Field** dialog box (see Figure 2-59).

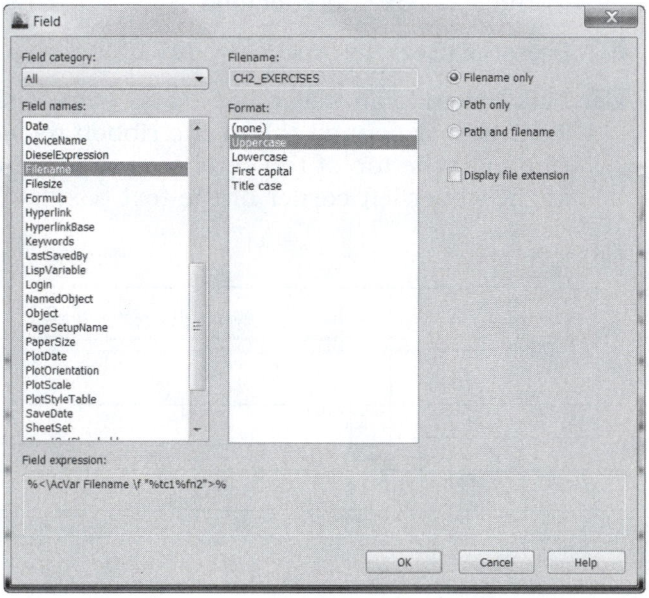

Figure 2-59
The **Field** dialog box

4 From the **Field names:** list, choose **Filename**.

5 In the **Format:** area, choose **Uppercase**.

6 Select the **Filename only** option and uncheck the box on the **Display file extension** setting (see Figure 2-59).

7 Choose **OK** to insert the field into the drawing. The **Field** dialog box will close.

8 Choose **Close Text Editor** to end the command. The drawing file name ***CH2_EXERCISE*** appears in the title block (see Figure 2-60). The field text is highlighted to indicate that it is a field value.

9 Choose **Zoom Extents** from the navigation bar.

10 Save your drawing.

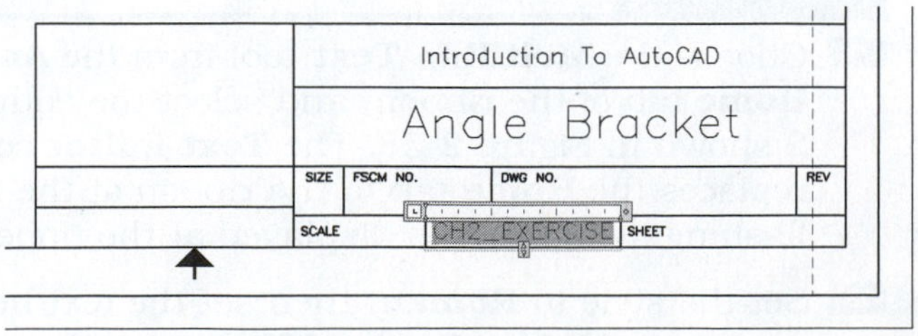

Figure 2-60
The **Filename** text field

As you can see from the **Field** dialog box (see Figure 2-59), there are a number of predefined fields. Using field names is a great time-saver. By default, the field is updated every time you regenerate, save, or plot your drawing. So, any changes to the drawing file name will automatically update the text.

FOR MORE DETAILS

Page 452 in Chapter 11 covers text fields and how to use them.

Plotting and Page Setups

page setup: A collection of plot settings that are applied to a drawing layout.

When you plot a drawing, AutoCAD needs to know a number of different settings (printer, paper size, orientation, margins, color settings, plot scale, etc.). You can specify these settings each time you plot, but for consistency, AutoCAD allows you to save all these settings to a ***page setup***. A page setup is simply a group of plot settings saved to a user-specified name. In the following exercise, you will make changes to the page setup associated with the **ANSI A Title Block** layout.

EXERCISE 2-28 Page Setup

1. Select the **Output** tab of the ribbon to display the plotting tools and options.
2. Choose **Page Setup Manager** from the **Plot** panel. This displays the **Page Setup Manager** dialog box shown in Figure 2-61.
3. Choose **New...** to display the **New Page Setup** dialog box (see Figure 2-62).

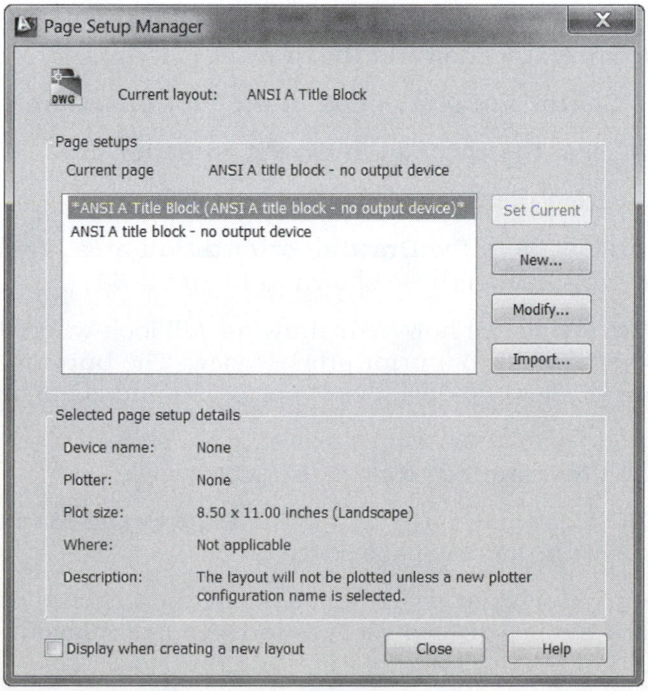

Figure 2-61
The **Page Setup Manager** dialog box

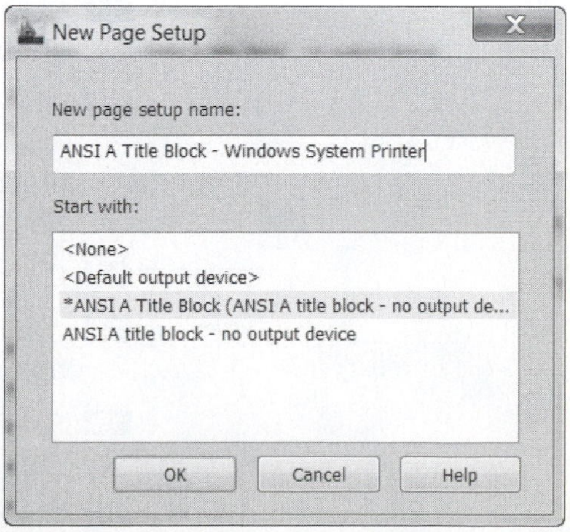

Figure 2-62
The **New Page Setup** dialog box

4. Enter **ANSI A Title Block—Windows System Printer** as the new page setup name and choose **OK**. This displays the **Page Setup** dialog box (see Figure 2-63).

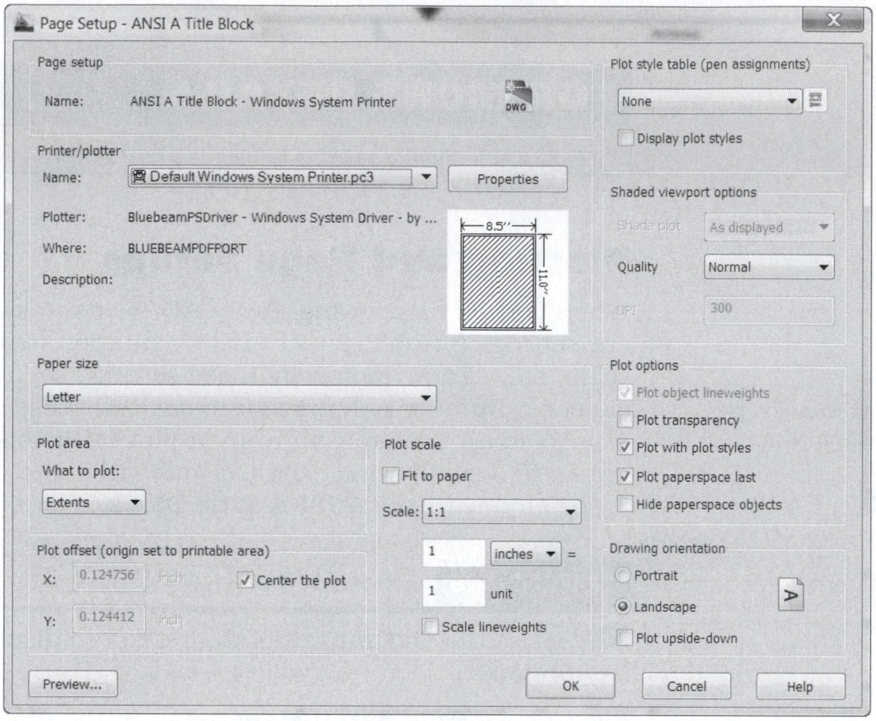

Figure 2-63
The **Page Setup** dialog box

5. From the **Printer/plotter** list, select **Default Windows System Printer.pc3**. This is your default Windows printer.
6. From the **Paper size** list, choose **Letter**.
7. Choose **Extents** from the **What to plot:** list. This tells AutoCAD to plot everything currently shown in the drawing.
8. Check the **Center the plot** option in the **Plot offset** area.
9. If checked, clear the check from the **Fit to paper** box.
10. Choose **1:1** from the **Scale** drop-down list.
11. Choose **Landscape** in the **Drawing orientation** area. Your selections should be the same as those shown in Figure 2-63.
12. Choose **Preview** to see how your drawing will look when it is printed. AutoCAD will switch to a print preview view. The buttons at the top of the print preview window allow you to pan and zoom around the preview.
13. Choose the **Close** button to close the preview window.
14. Choose **OK** to save the page setup. The **Page Setup Manager** dialog box returns with the new page setup listed.
15. Select the page setup you just created and then choose **Set Current**. This applies the page setup settings to the current layout.
16. Choose **Close** to close the **Page Setup Manager** dialog box.
17. Save your drawing.

TIP

In order for the centerline dashes and gaps to show up correctly, you must set the value of the **PSLTSCALE** system variable to **0**. The **PSLTSCALE** variable controls whether or not linetypes are scaled automatically by the viewport scale when working in paper space. See page 605 in Chapter 14 for details.

NOTE

Many times a page setup has the same name as the layout space; however, they are not the same thing. Be careful not to confuse the page setup with the drawing layout. The layout is a drawing space where your drawing objects (title blocks, viewports, etc.) reside. The page setup is a collection of plot settings that are applied to the layout when you plot the drawing.

Notice the dashed line that appears around the edge of the layout (see Figure 2-64). This dashed line represents the printable area on your drawing. It's not an actual drawing object (you can't select it), but only a visual indication of what part of your drawing will be printed. If any part of your drawing extends outside this dashed line, those parts will be clipped from the final print. To fix this, you can adjust the plot scale of your drawing, move or adjust the geometry within your drawing, or adjust the margins of your printer.

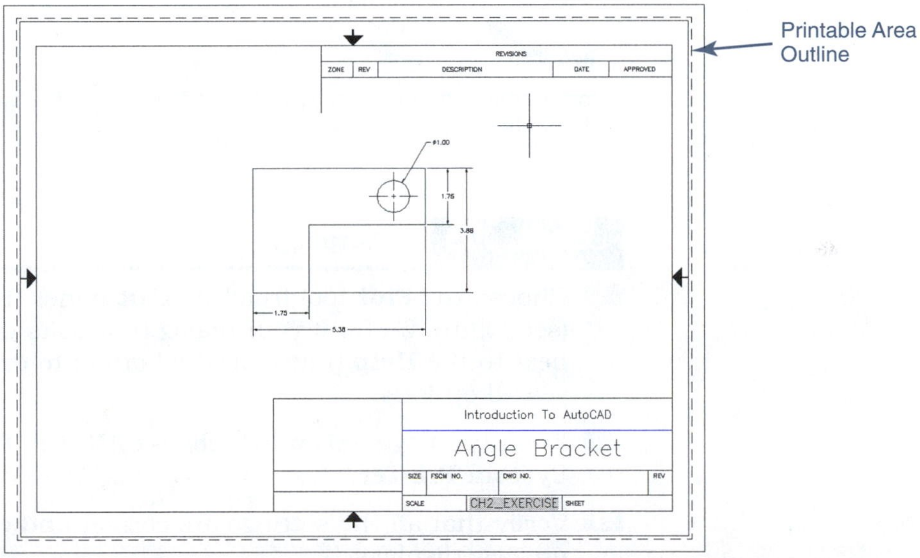

Figure 2-64
The printable drawing area

FOR MORE DETAILS

See Chapter 14 for more on page setups.

Plotting

When you plot a drawing in AutoCAD, you are presented with the **Plot** dialog box (see Figure 2-65). The **Plot** dialog box has all the same settings as the **Page Setup** dialog box (in fact, you can use the **PLOT** command to create page setups). These options allow you to make last-minute changes

Figure 2-65
The **Plot** dialog box

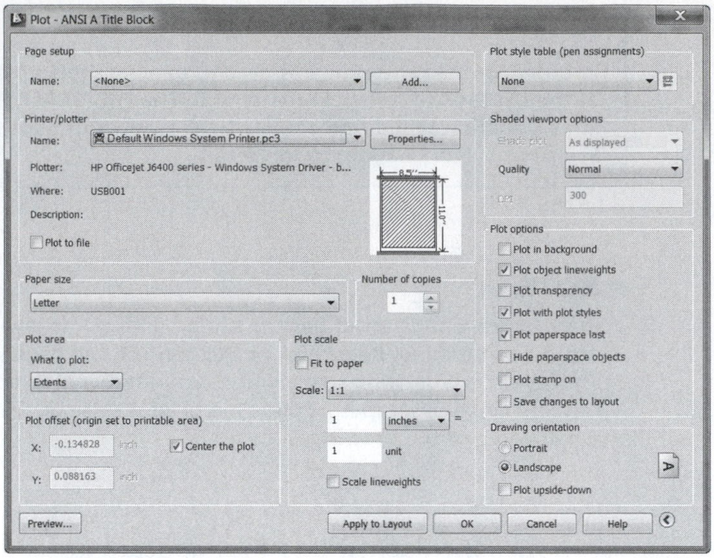

to your page setup or temporarily override settings contained in the page setup. For example, your page setup may be defined for a C- or D-size plot, but you may want to create a quick check plot on an A-size sheet. The **PLOT** command allows you to change your plot setting without going through the process of creating a new page setup.

In the following exercise, you'll create a plot using the page setup you just created.

NOTE

In the following exercise, your printer features and settings may differ from those shown here.

EXERCISE 2-29 Plotting

1. Choose the **Plot** tool from the **Plot** panel. The **Plot** dialog box appears (see Figure 2-65). If your dialog box looks different, choose the arrow next to the **Help** button at the bottom to expand the dialog box and see all options.
2. From the **Page setup** list, choose **ANSI A Title Block—Windows System Printer**.
3. Verify that all the settings are correct and choose **Preview....** The plot preview displays.
4. Choose the **Plot** button to plot your drawing to your default Windows system printer. A plot progress bar will appear briefly, and AutoCAD will return to the command prompt when the plot is complete.
5. Save your drawing.

Figure 2-66
The **Plot and Publish** balloon

Once the plot is complete, AutoCAD will display a balloon in the notification tray in the lower right corner of the status bar (see Figure 2-66). This indicates the results of the **PLOT** command and reports any errors that may have occurred. To view the plot results, click on the indicated link to display the **Plot and Publish Details** box. Here you can view the results of all plots submitted during the current AutoCAD session.

Chapter Summary

You have now walked through a typical AutoCAD drawing session. In this chapter we have gone through the steps to quickly create a new drawing based on an existing AutoCAD template drawing that already has a title block and border established. We saw that templates help us to be more productive by saving the time it would normally take to create a border each time we start a new drawing, as well as help promote CAD standards by having everything pre-established.

We then created a simple drawing using AutoCAD's precision drawing aids and then modified it using different AutoCAD modify commands and techniques, including grips. Then, after most of the line work was complete, we annotated the drawing by adding associated dimensions that automatically update when the drawing is modified and created title block text that included a field to automatically insert the drawing name.

In the final steps, we set the drawing up to plot on an 8-1/2 × 11 (ANSI A) size paper by setting the drawing scale to 1:2 using the predefined **Viewport Scale** list on the right side of the status bar. Because we took advantage of AutoCAD's automated **Annotation Scale** feature, we then had to adjust the location of the dimensions that were automatically scaled up. After everything was nice and tidy, we plotted the drawing using the default Windows system printer.

Chapter Test Questions

Multiple Choice

Circle the correct answer.

1. Model space is:
   a. Only for three-dimensional objects
   b. Limited in size so you must scale your model appropriately
   c. Generally used to draw objects that exist in the real world
   d. Generally used to draw objects that exist only on paper
2. In the following command line prompt, what would you type to use the **Ttr** option?
   Specify center point for circle or [**3P 2P T**tr (tan tan radius)]:
   a. **3P<Enter>**
   b. **(tan tan radius)<Enter>**
   c. **2P<Enter>**
   d. **T<Enter>**
3. Which of the following settings does **not** allow you to control point specifications?
   a. Grid
   b. Snap
   c. Ortho
   d. Polar
4. The command line:
   a. Cannot be moved
   b. Can be turned off
   c. Is the only way to communicate with AutoCAD
   d. Cannot be docked

5. Scrolling the wheel of a wheel mouse will:
   a. Scroll the text in the command line
   b. Do nothing
   c. Pan the drawing up and down
   d. Zoom the drawing in and out
6. Which of the following is **not** a property common to all objects?
   a. Length
   b. Layer
   c. Color
   d. Lineweight
7. Dimensions:
   a. Can be placed only in model space
   b. Can be placed only in paper space
   c. Must be erased and redrawn if the model changes
   d. Are controlled by their associated dimension style
8. Grips appear:
   a. At key points on drawing objects
   b. On a separate layer
   c. Every time you click on the screen
   d. Only in model space
9. A page setup:
   a. Is the same thing as a paper space layout
   b. Can be defined only in a drawing template
   c. Is a collection of plot settings
   d. Must have the same name as a paper space layout
10. The dashed line that appears around the edge of a layout:
    a. Can be erased if needed
    b. Is on its own layer and can be turned off if desired
    c. Shows a visual indication of the area that will be printed
    d. Shows up on the printed drawing

Matching

Write the number of the correct answer on the line.

a. Drawing template ______

b. Objects ______

c. Dimension style ______

d. Page setup ______

e. Grips ______

f. Object snaps ______

1. The process of moving around the drawing by shifting the display
2. The settings that control how and where a drawing object is shown in the drawing
3. A link between drawing objects and dimension objects
4. The process of specifying the objects you wish to edit
5. A collection of plot settings that are applied to a drawing layout
6. A drawing file used as a starting point when creating new drawings

g. Object properties ______

h. Panning ______

i. Associativity ______

j. Building a selection set ______

7. Editing points that appear at key locations on drawing objects when they are selected
8. Graphical drawing elements, such as lines, arcs, circles, polylines, and text
9. Geometric points on objects such as the end-points or midpoint of a line or the center of an arc or circle
10. A collection of dimension settings that control how dimension objects act and are displayed

True or False

Circle the correct answer.

1. **True or False:** There is only one layout allowed in a drawing file.
2. **True or False:** A layout can have only one viewport.
3. **True or False:** There is only one model space allowed in a drawing file.
4. **True or False:** Polar tracking can be set to detect any angle.
5. **True or False:** You can only use the **REDO** command immediately after using the **UNDO** command.
6. **True or False:** Objects on a layer that is frozen can be seen but not modified.
7. **True or False:** Objects on a layer that is turned off can still be modified.
8. **True or False:** To move an object, you must always select the object first and then start the **MOVE** command.
9. **True or False:** You can override page setup settings when you plot.
10. **True or False:** Dimensions can update to follow changes to your geometry.

3 chapterthree
Controlling the Drawing Display

CHAPTER OBJECTIVES

- Zoom in and out of a drawing
- Pan around a drawing
- Refresh the drawing display
- Toggle the ribbon and all toolbars and palettes off and on
- Make arcs and circles appear smoother
- Increase drawing display regeneration speed by turning off text and solid fill areas

Introduction

The AutoCAD drawing display window is one of the most important features of the AutoCAD user interface. It is here where you do most of your work creating and modifying the objects that make up your drawing. AutoCAD provides a number of tools and settings that allow you to control how and what drawing information is displayed in the drawing display window. The drawing display tools and their settings are explained in detail in this chapter.

Zooming In and Out of a Drawing

The AutoCAD drawing display window is like a camera lens. You control what's displayed in your drawing by zooming in to get a closer look and by zooming out to see the big picture, similar to a camera.

Unlike most cameras, AutoCAD provides a number of different ways to control the zooming process. The **Zoom** tools are located on the navigation bar located on the right side of the drawing window, as shown in Figure 3-1.

All of the **Zoom** tools can be displayed by selecting the **Zoom Extents** tool to display the **Zoom** flyout menu shown in Figure 3-2. As you can see, there are many different **Zoom** tools available. Some of the tools are holdovers from early releases of AutoCAD and are beginning to show their age. They still exist in AutoCAD for legacy reasons, for the most part. You will need to refer to the AutoCAD Help for information regarding the legacy **Zoom** tools. The next section covers most of the **Zoom** tools that are still relevant today.

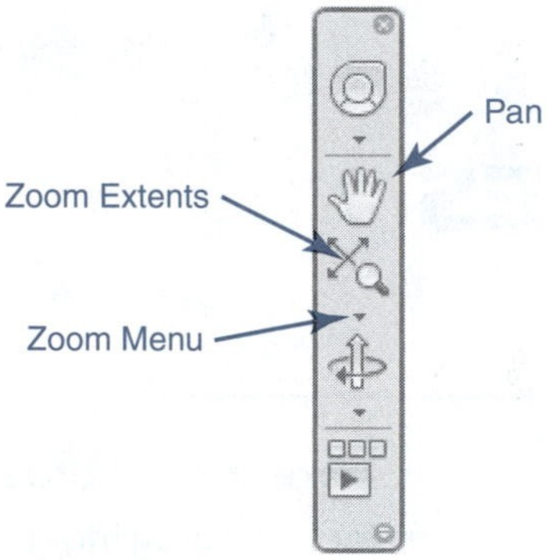

Figure 3-1
The navigation bar

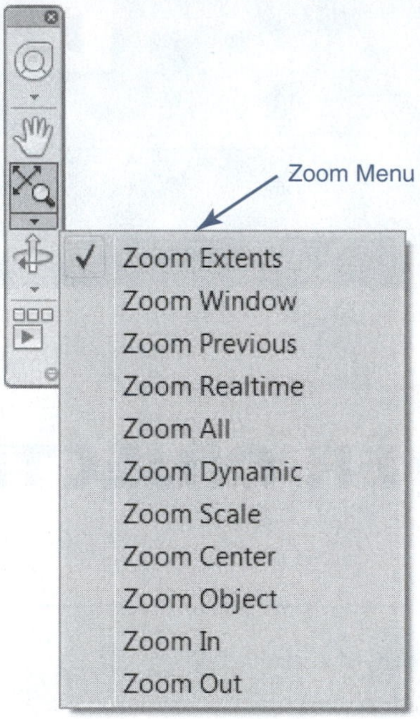

Figure 3-2
The **Zoom** flyout menu

> **TIP**
> You can turn the navigation bar on and off by selecting the "–" symbol on the in-canvas viewport control on the upper left of the drawing window to display the shortcut menu and selecting/deselecting the **Navigation Bar** option. Alternatively, you can turn the navigation bar on and off via the **NAVBARDISPLAY** system variable. Setting **NAVBARDISPLAY** to **1** turns on the navigation bar and setting **NAVBARDISPLAY** to **0** turns it off.

ZOOM EXTENTS	
Ribbon & Panel:	View | Navigate 2D Extents
Navigation Bar:	
Zoom Toolbar:	
Menu:	View | Zoom | Extents
Command Line:	ZOOM
Command Alias:	Z

Zoom Tools

The following **Zoom** tools are the easiest to use and provide the most "bang for the buck" when you need to zoom in and out of your drawing quickly. You will likely find yourself using the **Zoom** tools explained in this section most often out of the many different **Zoom** tools provided by AutoCAD.

Zoom Extents. The **Zoom Extents** tool is very useful because it allows you to view everything in your drawing on your screen quickly. AutoCAD calculates the extents of the outermost objects in your drawing that are not on a frozen layer and then zooms out so that everything is visible. This is especially helpful when you are zoomed in on a small area of your drawing and you draw an object that goes off the screen. Using **Zoom Extents** allows you to see the complete object.

> **TIP**
>
> Sometimes when you use the **Zoom Extents** tool, it may appear that there is nothing in your drawing—don't panic. Usually this means that there is some rogue object out in the nether regions of your drawing. If you zoom out just a little, you can usually find the object and determine its identity so that you may move or delete it.

EXERCISE 3-1 Using the Zoom Extents Tool

To access student data files, go to **www.pearsondesigncentral.com.**

1. Open drawing ***Willhome*** located in the student data files.
2. Select the **Model** tab so that model space is active.
3. Select the **Zoom Extents** tool on the navigation bar and zoom to the extents of the drawing.
4. Zoom in on an area of the drawing using your mouse wheel or any of the techniques introduced in Chapter 2.
5. Select the **Zoom Extents** tool again.
6. All the drawing information is now displayed in the drawing display window.

> **NOTE**
>
> If there are no objects in your drawing or everything is on layers that are currently frozen, the **Zoom Extents** tool will zoom to the limits of your drawing. See page 139 in Chapter 4 for more information about controlling drawing limits.

ZOOM WINDOW	
Ribbon & Panel:	View | Navigate 2D Window
Navigation Bar:	
Zoom Toolbar:	
Menu:	View | Zoom | Window
Command Line:	ZOOM
Command Alias:	Z

Zoom Window. The **Zoom Window** tool allows you to define a rectangular area, or window, using two mouse pick points so that you can quickly zoom in on a specific area of your drawing. The windowed area is zoomed *and* centered at a scale that fills your drawing display area.

After selecting the **Zoom Window** tool, you are prompted to select the two corner points of the window. Select two points in your drawing to define the rectangular area you wish to zoom on as shown in Figure 3-3.

The display is zoomed immediately after selecting the second corner point, as shown in Figure 3-4.

EXERCISE 3-2 Using the Zoom Window Tool

1. Continue from Exercise 3-1.
2. Select the **Zoom Window** tool on the **Zoom** flyout menu on the navigation bar. AutoCAD prompts you to *Specify first corner:*.
3. Pick a point in your drawing. AutoCAD places the first point and drags a rectangular rubber-band line from that point and prompts you to *Specify opposite corner:*.
4. Size the rectangle so that the information you want to zoom in on is within the windowed area, and pick another point in your drawing (see Figure 3-3).
5. After you pick the second point, the windowed area is zoomed to fill the drawing display window (see Figure 3-4).

Figure 3-3
Defining the **Zoom Window** area

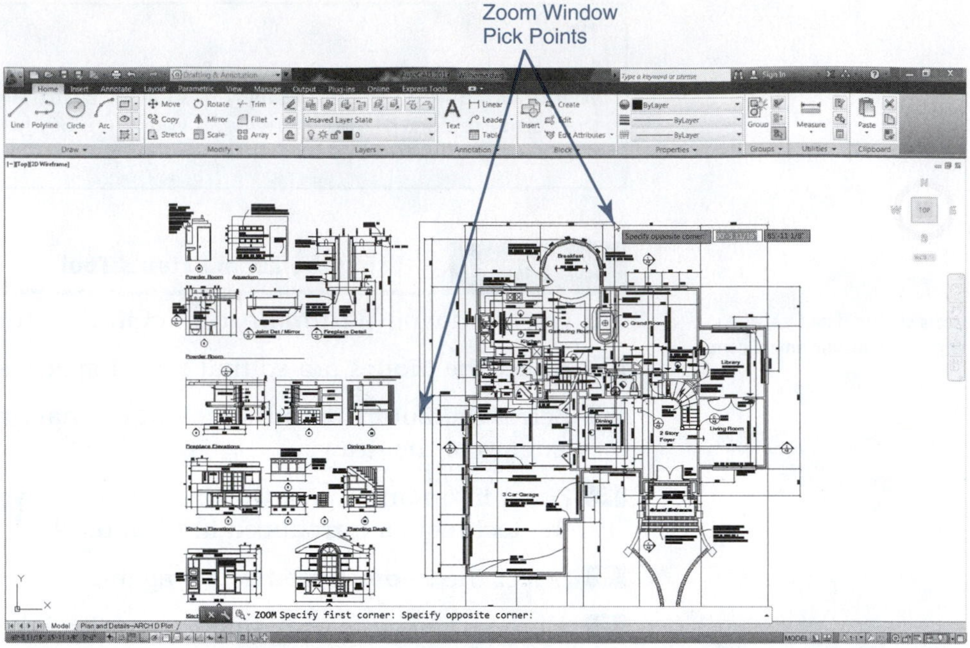

Figure 3-4
Display after second window corner point is selected

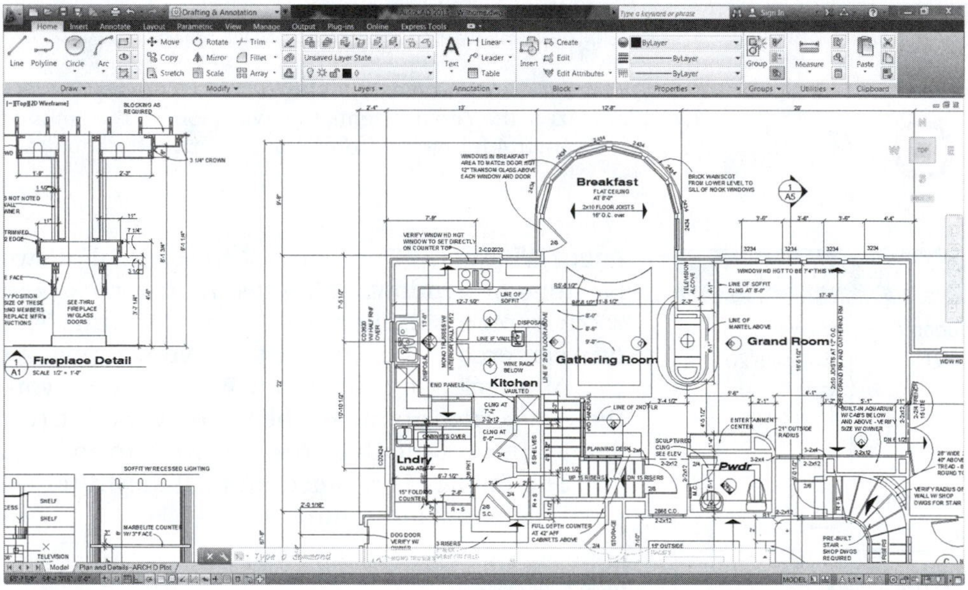

ZOOM PREVIOUS	
Ribbon & Panel:	View | Navigate 2D Previous
Navigation Bar:	
Standard Toolbar:	
Menu:	View | Zoom | Previous
Command Line:	ZOOM
Command Alias:	Z

Zoom Previous. The **Zoom Previous** tool is probably the most popular of the **Zoom** tools because it allows you to restore the previous drawing display. In fact, you can restore up to 10 previous views, so that you can step back in time. This capability allows you to zoom in on an area of your drawing to get close to your work (see Figure 3-4) and then quickly return to the previous overall view (see Figure 3-3). From there you can zoom in on other areas and then zoom back out again. The combination of the **Zoom Window** tool and the **Zoom Previous** tool provides one of the easiest, most efficient ways to navigate around your drawing.

AutoCAD stores up to 10 previous views. The following message is displayed at the command line if there is no previous view to display:

Command: No previous view saved.

EXERCISE 3-3 Using the Zoom Previous Tool

1. Continue from Exercise 3-2.
2. Select the **Zoom Extents** tool and zoom to the extents of the drawing.
3. Follow the steps shown in Exercise 3-2, and zoom in on an area of the drawing so that the drawing display looks similar to Figure 3-4.
4. Select the **Zoom Previous** tool on the navigation bar.
5. The drawing information displayed in the drawing display window returns to the previous view.
6. Continue selecting the **Zoom Previous** tool until AutoCAD displays the following prompt at the command line:

   No previous view saved.

NOTE

The **Zoom Previous** tool *does not* undo any drawing or editing commands and affects the display *only*.

ZOOM REALTIME	
Ribbon & Panel:	View | Navigate 2D  Realtime
Navigation Bar:	
Standard Toolbar:	
Menu:	View | Zoom | Realtime
Command Line:	ZOOM
Command Alias:	Z

Zoom Realtime.

Zoom Realtime. Zooming in "realtime" simply means that the zooming process is interactive. As you zoom in, objects grow larger on the screen; as you zoom out, objects grow smaller.

Selecting the **Zoom Realtime** tool causes the mouse pointer to change to the magnifying glass icon shown in Figure 3-5.

Notice that there is a plus sign at the top right of the magnifying glass and a minus sign at the bottom left. Holding your mouse button down and moving the magnifying glass toward the top of the screen zooms in and increases the display magnification (+). See Figures 3-6A and 3-6B. Holding the button down and moving the magnifying glass toward the bottom of the screen zooms out and decreases the display magnification (–).

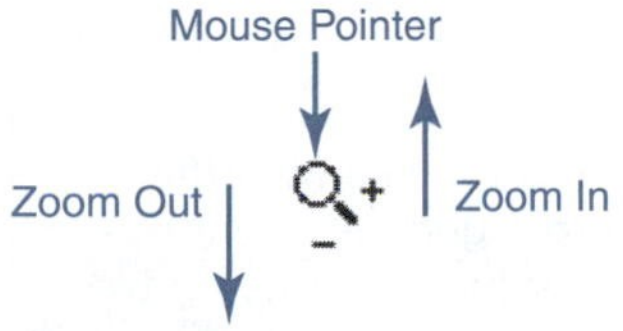

Figure 3-5
The **Zoom Realtime** mouse pointer icon

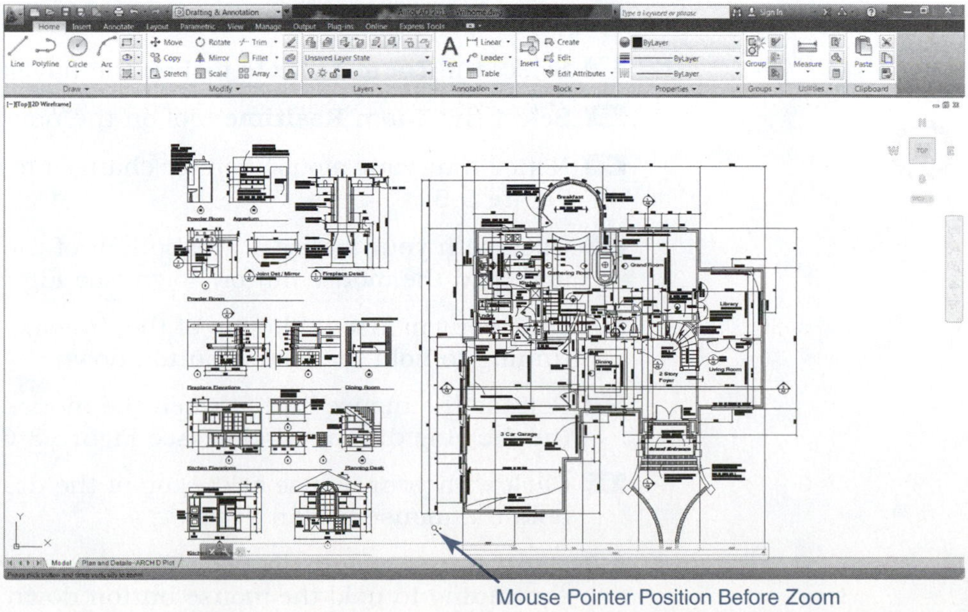

Figure 3-6A
Original **Zoom Realtime** mouse pointer position (bottom of screen)

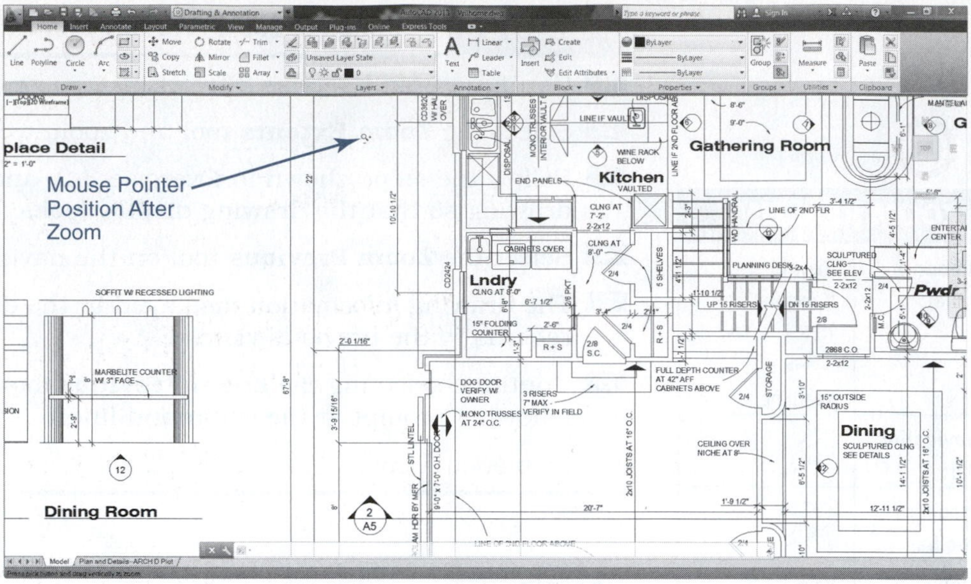

Figure 3-6B
New **Zoom Realtime** mouse pointer position (top of screen)

If you run out of mouse pad during the process of moving your mouse up or down the screen, just pick up your mouse, reposition it, and repeat the process. When you are finished zooming and the drawing display appears at the desired magnification factor, press **<Enter>** or **<Esc>** to complete the zoom process.

> **TIP**
>
> If you reach a point in zooming in or out when the display will not zoom any farther and appears stuck, don't worry. This just means that you need to regenerate your display using the **REGEN** command. The **REGEN** command is discussed in detail later in the section "Cleaning Up the Drawing Display."

EXERCISE 3-4 Using the Zoom Realtime Tool

1. Continue from Exercise 3-3.
2. Select the **Zoom Extents** tool on the navigation bar.
3. Select the **Zoom Realtime** tool on the navigation bar.
4. Notice that your mouse pointer changes to a magnifying glass (see Figure 3-5).
5. Click with your mouse at the bottom of the drawing display window and hold the mouse button down (see Figure 3-6A).
6. Drag your mouse to the top of the drawing display window while continuing to hold the mouse button down.
7. Release the mouse button when the mouse pointer reaches the top of the drawing display window (see Figure 3-6B).
8. Click with your mouse at the top of the drawing display window and hold the mouse button down.
9. Drag your mouse to the bottom of the drawing display window while continuing to hold the mouse button down.

10 Release the mouse button when the mouse pointer reaches the bottom of the drawing display window.

11 Press **<Enter>** or **<Esc>** to complete the zoom process.

ZOOM ALL

Ribbon & Panel:	View | Navigate 2D All
Navigation Bar:	
Zoom Toolbar:	
Menu:	View | Zoom | All
Command Line:	ZOOM
Command Alias:	Z

Zoom All. The **Zoom All** tool zooms either to the extents of the drawing in a fashion similar to the **Zoom Extents** tool discussed earlier or to the outer reaches of the drawing area that have been established using the **Drawing Limits** settings (**LIMITS** command).

FOR MORE DETAILS

See page 139 in Chapter 4 for more information about adjusting the drawing area using the **LIMITS** command.

If the defined drawing area is smaller than the outermost drawing extents, the **Zoom All** tool zooms to the drawing extents, just like the **Zoom Extents** tool does. If the drawing area is larger, or past the drawing limits, the **Zoom All** tool will zoom to the larger area.

TIP

The **Zoom All** tool can be used in a paper space layout to center the layout, or paper, in the center of your drawing window while leaving a small margin around the edges of the sheet. The **Zoom Extents** tool can be used too, but the edge of the drawing window abuts the edge of the paper with no margin.

EXERCISE 3-5 Using the Zoom All Tool

1 Continue from Exercise 3-4.

2 Select the **Zoom Extents** tool and zoom to the extents of the drawing.

3 Select the **Zoom All** tool. Notice that the drawing zooms out even farther. This is because the drawing area or limits are set to an area much larger than the extents of the drawing.

4 Select the **Zoom Extents** tool again to zoom back to the drawing extents.

Using the Mouse Wheel

If you have a wheel mouse, you can use the wheel to zoom in and out. Rolling the wheel toward the computer (away from you) zooms into your drawing. Rolling the wheel away from the computer (toward you) will zoom out of your drawing.

NOTE

The **ZOOMWHEEL** system variable controls the default zoom direction when rolling the mouse wheel. Setting **ZOOMWHEEL** to **0** (default) zooms in when rolling the wheel forward, and setting **ZOOMWHEEL** to **1** zooms out when rolling the wheel forward.

Each click of the mouse wheel zooms in or out by 10%. You can change this zoom scale factor via the **ZOOMFACTOR** system variable. The **ZOOMFACTOR** default value is 60 and can be set to a value of between 3 and 100.

> **TIP**
>
> The mouse wheel also acts as a mouse button. In fact, it can be used to either pan your drawing display or display the **Object Snap** shortcut menu (see the next section, "Panning Around a Drawing"). It's also a little-known fact that double-clicking the wheel button will zoom to the extents of your drawing just like the **Zoom Extents** tool!

EXERCISE 3-6 Using the Mouse Wheel to Zoom In and Out

1. Continue from Exercise 3-5.
2. Roll the mouse wheel forward toward your computer screen.
3. The drawing display zooms in as you roll the mouse wheel forward.
4. Roll the mouse wheel away from the computer screen or toward yourself.
5. The drawing display zooms out as you roll the mouse wheel backward.
6. Double-click the mouse wheel button.
7. The drawing display is zoomed to the extents of the drawing.

> **NOTE**
>
> In order to do this exercise, you must have a mouse with a thumb wheel.

pan: The process of moving your drawing from side to side in the display window so the location of the view changes without affecting the zoom scale.

PAN	
Ribbon & Panel:	View | Navigate 2D
Navigation Bar:	
Standard Toolbar:	
Menu:	View | Pan | Realtime
Command Line:	PAN
Command Alias:	P

Panning Around a Drawing

When you move a camera from side to side to change the subject matter displayed in the camera lens, it is referred to as *panning*. Borrowing yet another term from the world of photography, AutoCAD uses the term ***pan*** to describe the process of moving your drawing from side to side in the drawing display window.

Just as the subject matter doesn't move when you pan a camera, your drawing doesn't actually move, just what's shown in the display window so that you can view another area.

The different methods used to pan around your drawing are explained in the following sections.

The Pan Tool

The **Pan** tool allows you to pan your drawing so that you can recenter it in the drawing display without affecting the current zoom display scale factor. This allows you to view drawing information quickly that might not be visible because it is off the side of the drawing display. The **Pan** tool is located on the navigation bar shown in Figure 3-1.

After you select the **Pan** tool, your mouse pointer changes to the hand icon shown in Figure 3-7.

Using the **Pan** tool, you simply grab on to the drawing with your "hand" by clicking with your mouse and then drag the drawing across the drawing display window by holding the mouse button down. See Figures 3-8A and 3-8B.

Figure 3-7
The **Pan** mouse pointer icon

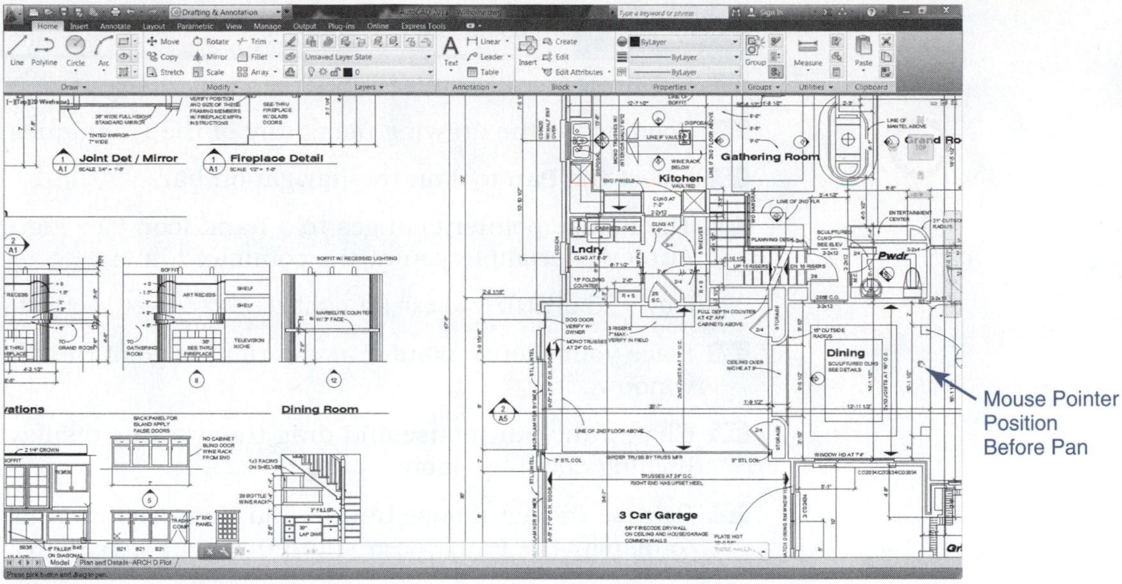

Figure 3-8A
Original **Pan** mouse pointer position (right side of screen)

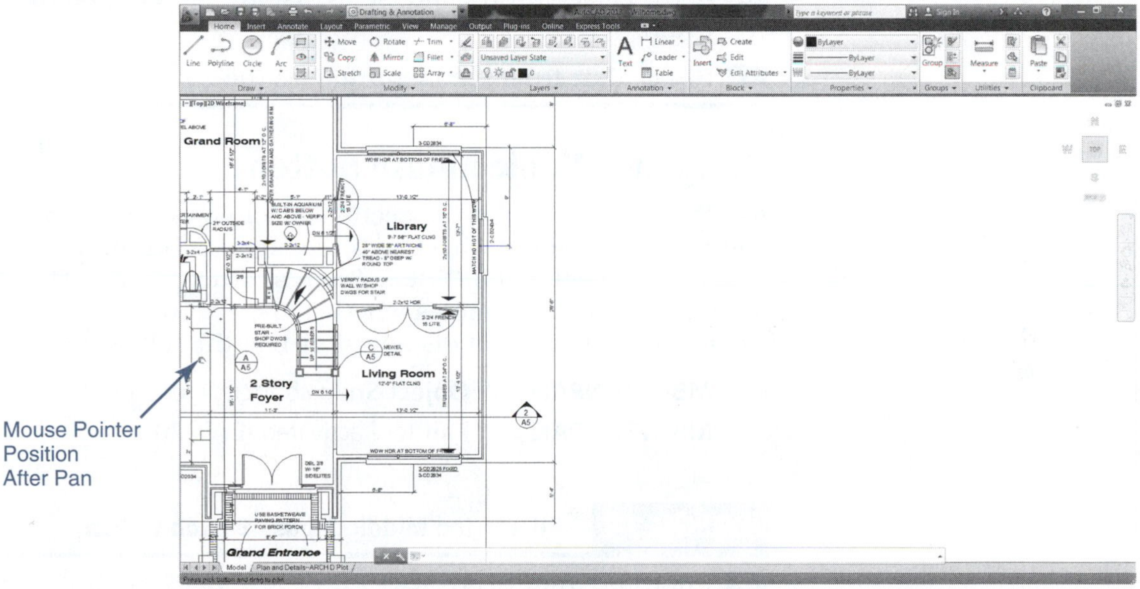

Figure 3-8B
New **Pan** mouse pointer position (left side of screen)

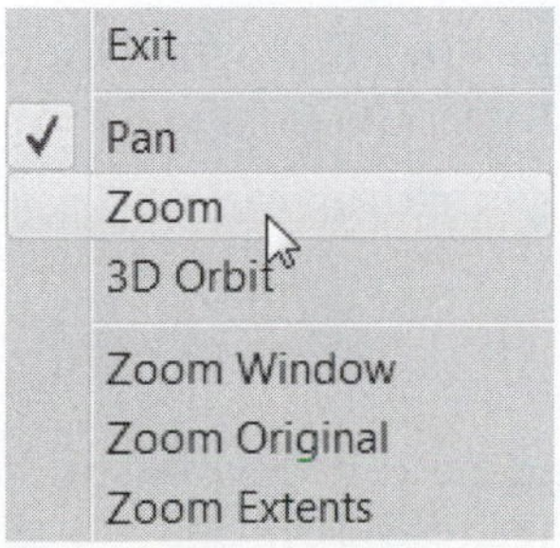

Figure 3-9
Pan/Zoom shortcut menu

As with the **Zoom Realtime** tool, if you run out of mouse pad during the process of moving your mouse across the screen, just pick up your mouse, reposition it, and repeat the process. When you are finished panning and the drawing display contains the desired drawing information, press **<Enter>** or **<Esc>** to complete the panning process.

> **TIP**
>
> You can quickly switch between the **Pan** tool and the **Zoom Realtime** tool by right-clicking to display the shortcut menu shown in Figure 3-9.

EXERCISE 3-7 Using the Pan Tool

1. Continue from Exercise 3-6.
2. Zoom in on the drawing using any of the techniques explained earlier.
3. Select the **Pan** tool on the navigation bar.
4. The mouse pointer changes to a hand icon (see Figure 3-7), and AutoCAD prompts you at the command line:

   Press ESC or ENTER to exit, or right-click to display shortcut menu.
5. Place your mouse pointer at the right edge of the drawing display window.
6. Click with your mouse and drag the drawing display to the left by holding down the mouse button.
7. Release the left mouse button and then click the right mouse button to display the **Pan/Zoom** shortcut menu (see Figure 3-9).
8. Select **Zoom** from the menu to switch to the **Zoom Realtime** tool.
9. Zoom in and out of the drawing a few times using the **Zoom Realtime** tool.
10. Right-click with the mouse to display the **Pan/Zoom** shortcut menu again.
11. Select **Exit** from the menu to end the command.

Using the Middle Mouse Button

As alluded to earlier in the section "Zooming In and Out of a Drawing," you can also use the wheel on a mouse as a button to either activate the **Pan** tool or display the **Object Snap** shortcut menu. The **MBUTTONPAN** system variable determines whether the **Pan** tool is activated or the **Object Snap** shortcut menu is displayed. It has the following settings:

MBUTTONPAN = 0: Object Snap shortcut menu displayed

MBUTTONPAN = 1: Pan tool activated (Default)

EXERCISE 3-8 Using the Middle Mouse Button to Pan

1. Continue from Exercise 3-7.
2. Select the **Zoom Extents** tool and zoom to the extents of the drawing.
3. Zoom in on the drawing using any of the techniques explained earlier.
4. Click the center mouse button or mouse wheel and hold it down. The mouse pointer changes to the hand icon (see Figure 3-7).
5. Hold the button down and pan back and forth in your drawing.
6. Release the button.
7. Hold down the **<Ctrl>** key on your keyboard.
8. Click the center mouse button or mouse wheel and hold it down. The mouse pointer changes to the joystick icon (see Figure 3-10).
9. Hold the button down and pan around in your drawing.

Figure 3-10
Pan tool in "joystick" mode

NOTE

In order to do this exercise you must have a mouse with a center button or a thumb wheel, and the **MBUTTONPAN** system variable must be set to **1.**

TIP

Holding down the **<Ctrl>** key when you use the middle button of your mouse to activate the **Pan** tool will put you in "joystick" mode (see Figure 3-10) so that the mouse pointer acts like a game joystick.

Panning and Zooming Transparently

transparent command: A command that can be used without interrupting the currently active command.

One of best things about the **Pan** and **Zoom** display tools is that you can use them ***transparently***.

This ability allows you to pan and zoom in the middle of drawing or editing. For instance, you can begin drawing a line by selecting the first point in an overall view (see Figure 3-11A), use the **Zoom Window** tool to zoom closer to your work, and select the endpoint (see Figure 3-11B).

Check out the command line interface in Figure 3-11B. When you are prompted for the corner points to define the window area, both prompts are preceded with double arrows (>>) to indicate the command is transparent. After the zoom process is complete and control passes back to the **LINE** command, AutoCAD displays the following prompt at the command line:

Resuming the LINE command.

The transparent display commands can be used in conjunction with almost every draw or modify command and can substantially increase both your precision and your productivity.

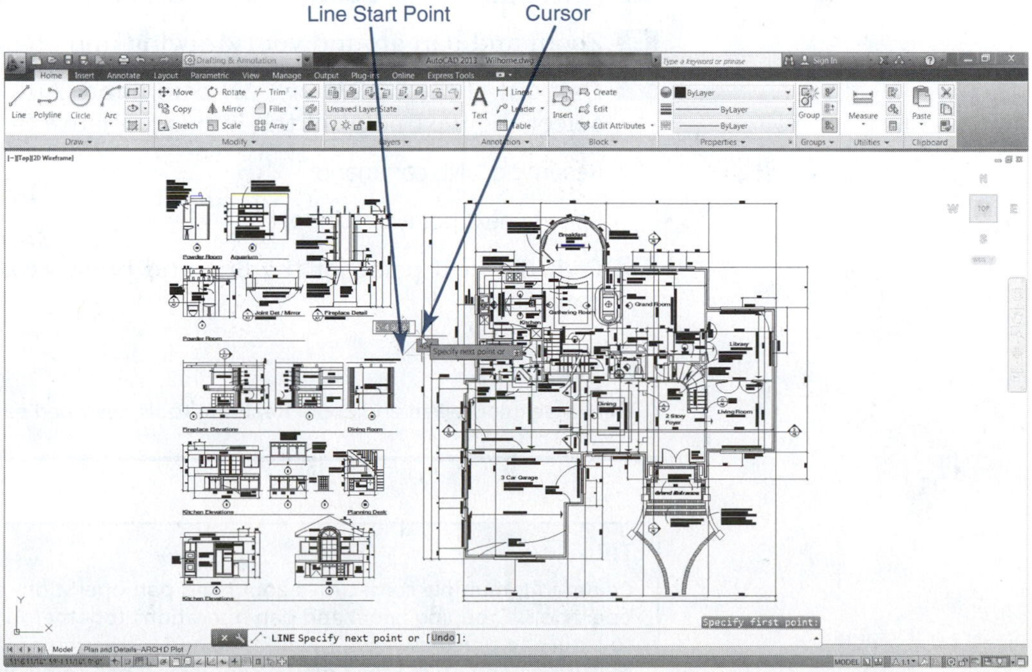

Figure 3-11A
A transparent **Zoom** command

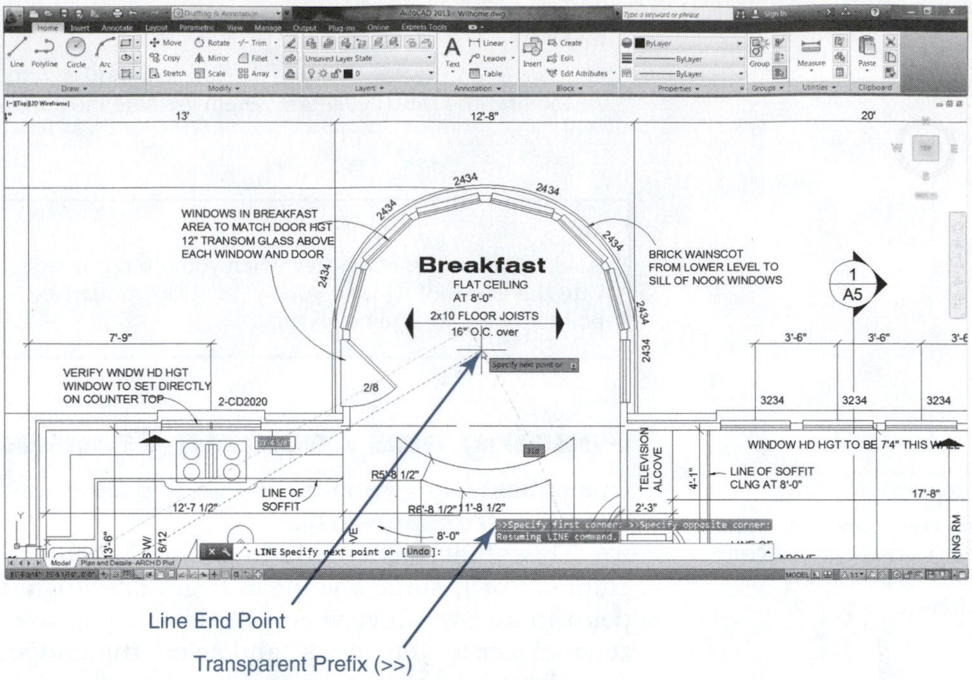

Figure 3-11B
A transparent **Zoom** command

EXERCISE 3-9 Panning and Zooming Transparently

1. Continue from Exercise 3-8.
2. Select the **Zoom Extents** tool and zoom to the extents of the drawing.
3. Select the **Line** tool from the **Draw** panel. AutoCAD prompts you:

   Specify first point:

4. Pick a point in your drawing to begin the line (see Figure 3-11A).
5. Select any of the **Zoom** or **Pan** tools explained so far in this chapter.
6. Zoom and pan around your drawing and change the drawing display.
7. Exit out of the **ZOOM** or **PAN** command. AutoCAD prompts you to select the next point of the line (see Figure 3-11B):

   Resuming LINE command.

   Specify next point or [**U**ndo]:

8. Pick the next point for the line and press **<Enter>** to end the **LINE** command.

NOTE

The wheel mouse **Pan** and **Zoom Realtime** tools described earlier also work transparently.

TIP

By default, multiple consecutive zoom and pan operations are grouped into a single operation. Grouping zoom and pan operations together minimizes the steps required to return to previous views, saving time and increasing productivity. You can turn this feature on and off via the **Combine zoom and pan commands** check box in the **Undo/Redo** area at the bottom right of the **User Preferences** tab of the **Options** dialog box.

Cleaning Up the Drawing Display

Occasionally it is necessary to "clean up" or refresh the drawing display area so that objects appear correctly. Information on layers that were frozen and then thawed may not appear in some cases, and the display smoothness of arc and circle objects can look jagged. AutoCAD provides a way to "regenerate" the display, but only via command line entry using the commands described in the following section.

The REGEN Command

The **REGEN** command recalculates, or regenerates, your drawing display, updating all drawing objects. Information that is on layers that did not reappear after a layer was thawed is redisplayed; and all curved objects such as circles, arcs, and splines are recalculated so that they appear much smoother.

Figure 3-12 shows what occasionally happens when you zoom in on a circle after being zoomed out in a drawing.

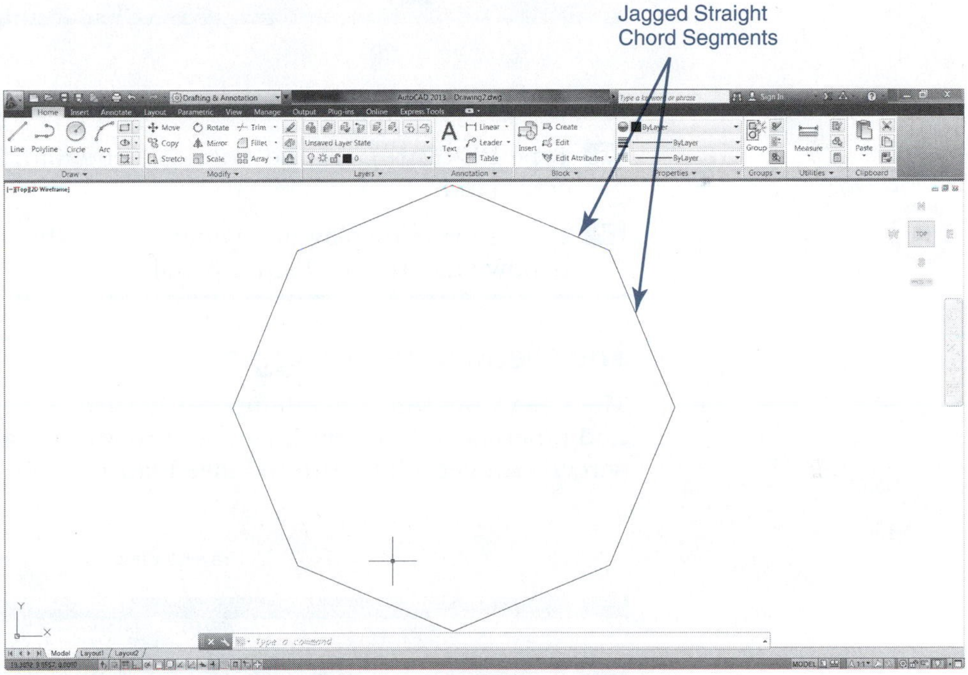

Figure 3-12
Zoomed circle before the **REGEN** command is used

AutoCAD approximates the curve using straight chord segments. This approximation is done primarily to accelerate display performance. To smooth out the curve, you can enter **REGEN<Enter>,** or **RE<Enter>,** at the AutoCAD command line. Entering either will totally recalculate the display so that the curve is smoothed out as shown in Figure 3-13.

EXERCISE 3-10 Regenerating the Drawing Display

1. Start a new drawing using the **acad.dwt** drawing template.
2. Select the **Zoom All** tool to zoom to the limits of the drawing.
3. Draw a tiny circle at the center of the drawing display using the **CIRCLE** command introduced in Chapter 2.
4. Select the **Zoom Window** tool and zoom in so the circle fills the drawing display.

Figure 3-13
Zoomed circle after the **REGEN** command is used

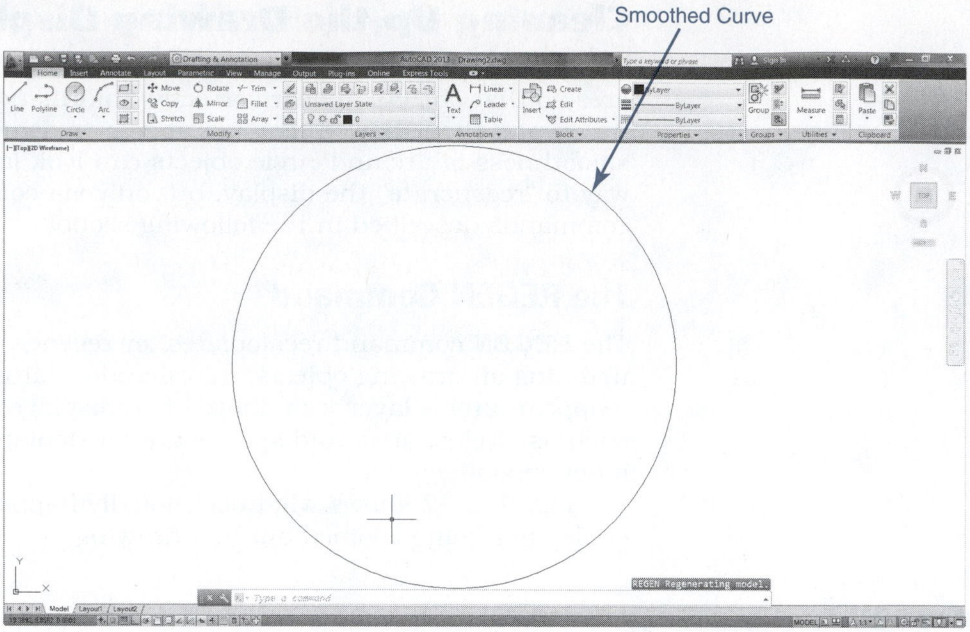

5 The perimeter of the circle should appear jagged (see Figure 3-12).

6 Type **RE<Enter>** at the AutoCAD command line to run the **REGEN** command.

7 The drawing display is regenerated so that the perimeter of the circle is now smooth (see Figure 3-13).

The Clean Screen Toggle

The **Clean Screen** toggle temporarily turns off the ribbon and any toolbars and palettes so that you have more room to draw because sometimes the screen can get a bit cluttered (see Figure 3-14).

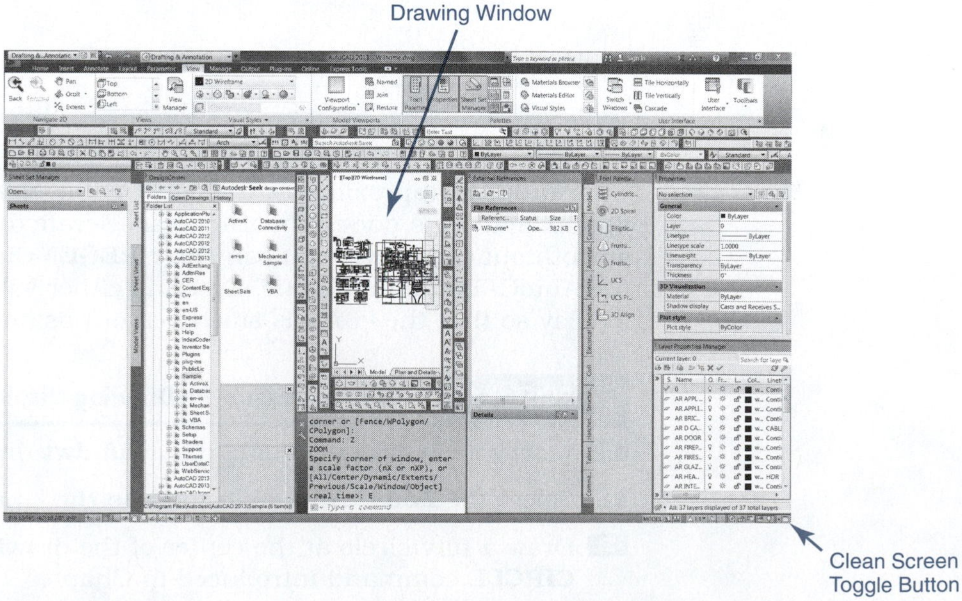

Figure 3-14
Where's my drawing?

Figure 3-14 is an extreme example of what your screen might look like if you turned on every AutoCAD toolbar and palette. Fortunately, AutoCAD provides a way out of this mess.

The **CLEANSCREENON** command turns the ribbon, toolbars, and palettes off, and the **CLEANSCREENOFF** command turns them back on. You can toggle **Clean Screen** on and off by clicking on the button on the right side of the status bar, as shown in Figure 3-14.

Selecting **Clean Screen** will turn off the ribbon, toolbars, and palettes and maximize your drawing area as shown in Figure 3-15.

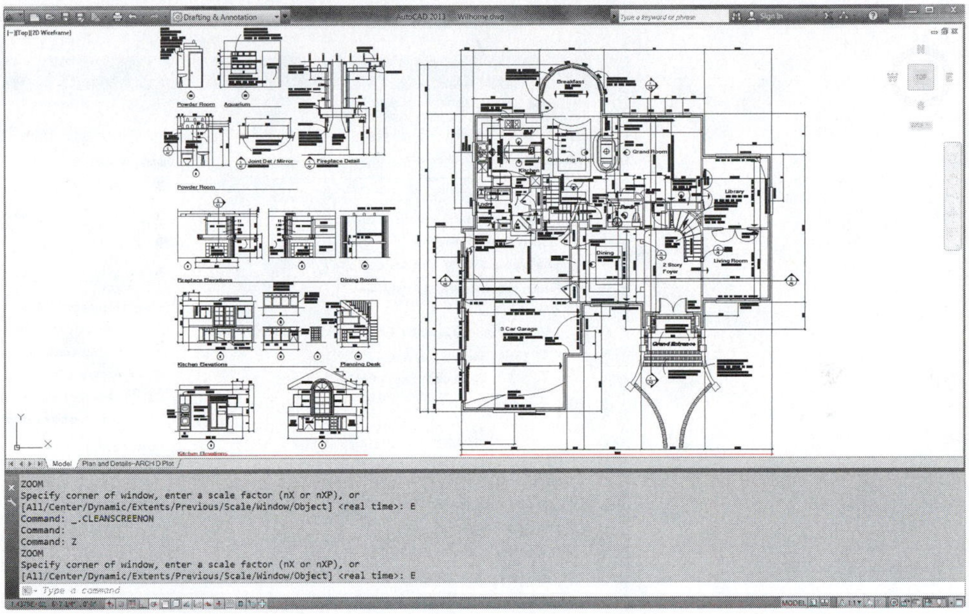

Figure 3-15
Drawing display with **Clean Screen** turned on

When **Clean Screen** is turned on, your drawing display is maximized to completely fill your Windows desktop so that the Windows taskbar is no longer available. You must turn **Clean Screen** off to access the Windows taskbar again.

> **TIP**
> You can also use the **<Ctrl>+0** keyboard combination to toggle **Clean Screen** on and off.

EXERCISE 3-11 Toggling Clean Screen On and Off

1. Continue from Exercise 3-10.
2. Select the **Clean Screen** button on the right side of the status bar.
3. The ribbon and any toolbars are temporarily turned off, and the drawing display area is increased.
4. Select the **Clean Screen** button on the status bar again.
5. The ribbon and any toolbars that were turned off are turned back on again, and the drawing display returns to its previous size.
6. Use the **<Ctrl>+0** keyboard combination to turn **Clean Screen** on and off again.

Drawing Display Resolution and Performance

There are a number of AutoCAD settings that can be used to control the resolution of drawing objects on your screen and, in turn, enhance your computer's performance when regenerating the drawing display. With the advent of high-performance computers and workstations, some of the settings described in this section have lost a little significance.

All the display settings can be managed on the **Display** tab of the **Options** dialog box (see Figure 3-16).

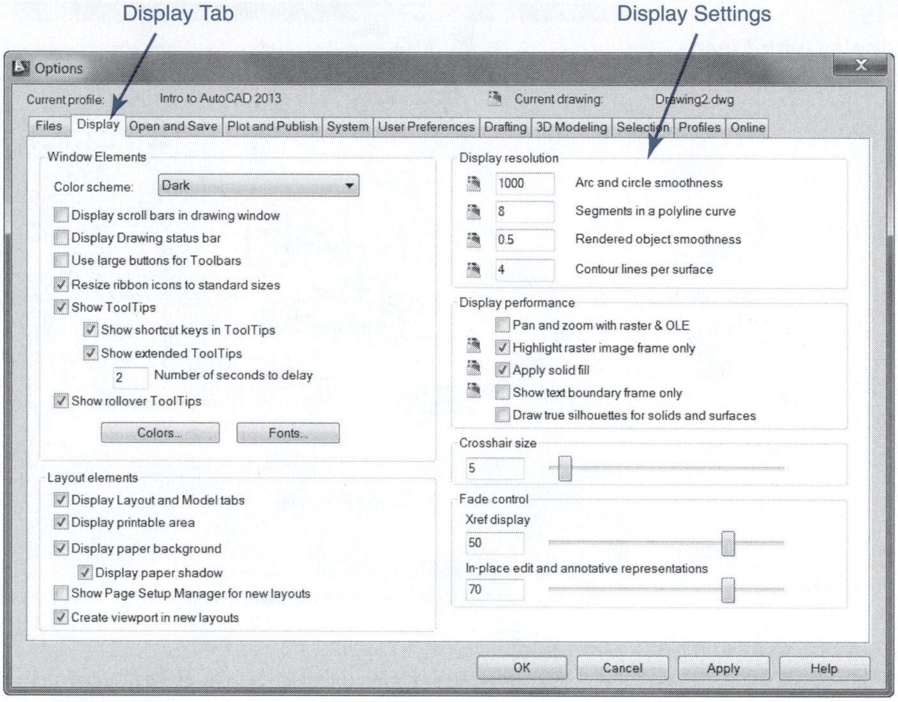

Figure 3-16
Display tab of **Options** dialog box

Controlling Arc and Circle Smoothness

AutoCAD uses short vectors, or chords, to represent radial geometry such as arcs, circles, ellipses, and splines on the drawing display. These chords are not typically noticeable until you zoom in on a curved surface like a circle without regenerating your drawing (see Figure 3-12).

The number of chords used to represent a curve and determine its smoothness is controlled via the **Arc and circle smoothness** setting on the **Display** tab of the **Options** dialog box shown in Figure 3-16. Settings can range from 1 to 20,000. The default setting is 1000. Setting this number higher makes curved surfaces appear smoother by increasing the number of vectors used to represent each curve. This increased resolution does come at a cost in performance, however. The higher the number, the longer it takes to regenerate your drawing.

EXERCISE 3-12 **Controlling Arc and Circle Smoothness**

1. Continue from Exercise 3-11.
2. Select the **Options** button from the bottom of the application menu list to display the **Options** dialog box.

3. Select the **Display** tab.
4. Increase the **Arc and circle smoothness** setting in the **Display resolution** area at the top right of the dialog box from the default value of **1000** to **10,000**.
5. Select **OK** to close the **Options** dialog box and return to the drawing.
6. Select the **Zoom Extents** tool to zoom to the limits of the drawing.
7. Draw a tiny circle at the center of the drawing display using the **CIRCLE** command introduced in Chapter 2.
8. Select the **Zoom Window** tool and zoom in so the circle fills the drawing display (see Figure 3-12).
9. The perimeter of the circle should appear smooth (see Figure 3-13).

NOTE

The **Arc and circle smoothness** setting can also be controlled via the **VIEWRES** command. Type **VIEWRES** at the AutoCAD command line and enter a value between 1 and 20,000. This **VIEWRES** setting is saved with the drawing.

Turning Text Display On and Off

Text is one of the most resource-intensive object types in an AutoCAD drawing because of its detail. If you have a large drawing with lots of text (see Figure 3-17A), regenerating a drawing can become a time-consuming task. To help, AutoCAD provides a way to turn text off in a drawing so that only a boundary frame outline of the text is visible (see Figure 3-17B).

This allows you to still locate each text object in a drawing but not have to regenerate it in finite detail. To turn off text display in a drawing, select the **Show text boundary frame only** check box on the **Display** tab of the **Options** dialog box shown in Figure 3-16. After turning the text display off, you must regenerate the drawing in order to see the results.

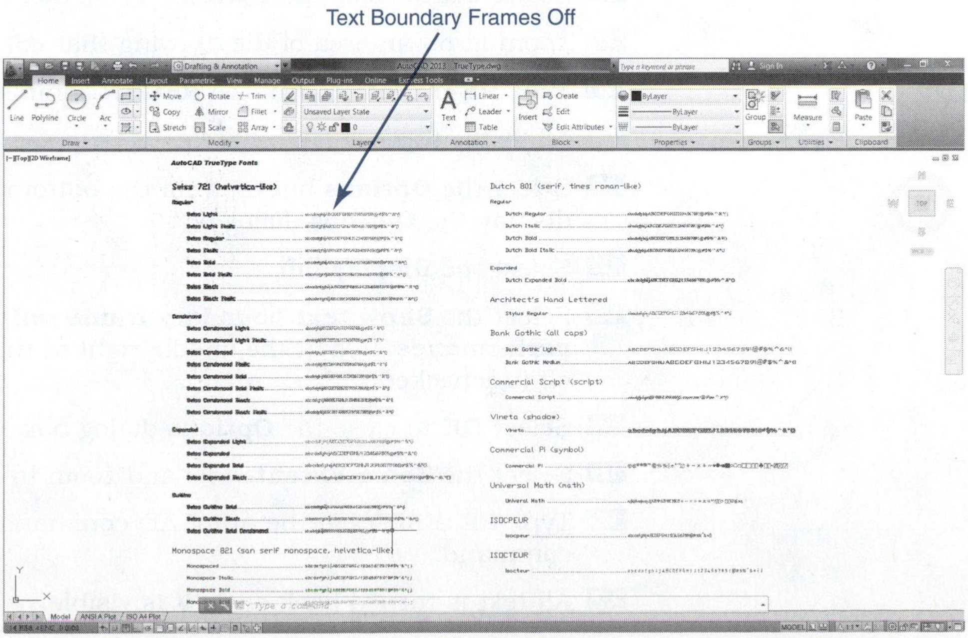

Figure 3-17A
Text display on

Figure 3-17B
Text display off

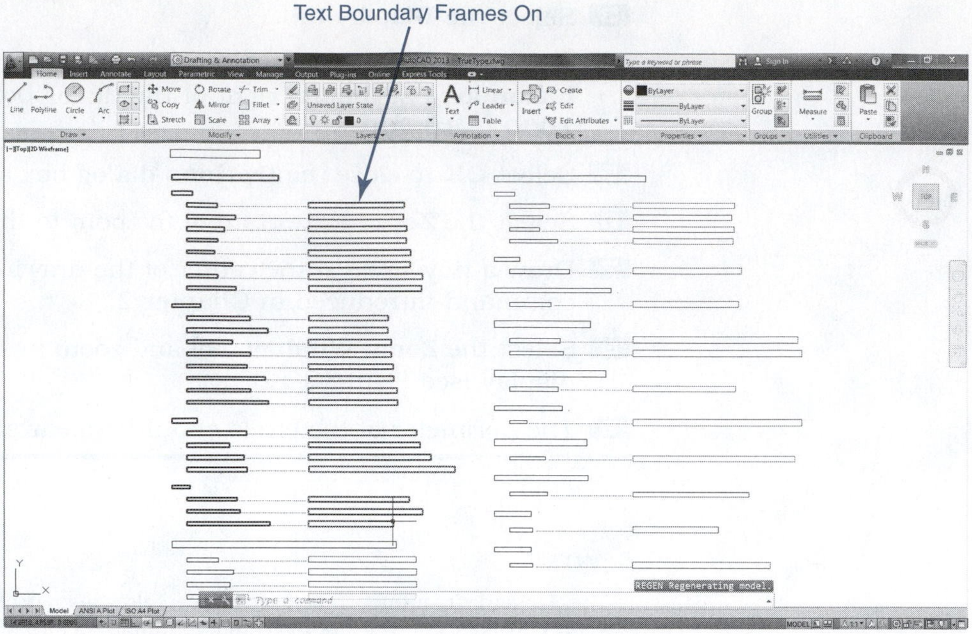

EXERCISE 3-13 Turning Text Display On and Off

To access student data files, go to **www.pearsondesigncentral.com.**

1. Open drawing ***Willhome*** located in the student data files.
2. Select the **Model** tab so that model space is active.
3. Select the **Zoom Extents** tool and zoom to the extents of the drawing.
4. Select the **Options** button from the bottom of the application menu to display the **Options** dialog box.
5. Select the **Display** tab.
6. Select the **Show text boundary frame only** option in the **Display performance** area at the middle right of the dialog box so it is turned on (checked).
7. Select **OK** to close the **Options** dialog box and return to the drawing.
8. Zoom in on an area of the drawing that contains text.
9. Type **RE<Enter>** to run the **REGEN** command.
10. All text is turned off so only the rectangular boundary frames are visible.
11. Select the **Options** button from the bottom of the application menu to display the **Options** dialog box.
12. Select the **Display** tab.
13. Select the **Show text boundary frame only** option in the **Display performance** area at the middle right of the dialog box so it is turned off (unchecked).
14. Select **OK** to close the **Options** dialog box and return to the drawing.
15. Select the **Zoom Extents** tool and zoom to the extents of the drawing.
16. Type **RE<Enter>** at the AutoCAD command line to run the **REGEN** command.
17. All text is turned back on so it is visible.

NOTE

The **Show text boundary frame only** setting can also be controlled via the **QTEXTMODE** system variable. Setting **QTEXTMODE = 1** turns off text display and turns on text boundary frames. Setting **QTEXTMODE = 0** will turn text back on in a drawing. This **QTEXTMODE** setting is saved with the drawing.

Turning Fills On and Off

Like text, hatch patterns and solid filled areas are also very resource-intensive. Many hatched and/or solid filled areas in a drawing can significantly increase the time it takes to regenerate the drawing display. Fortunately, you can turn off hatch patterns and solid fills by deselecting (unchecking) the **Apply solid fill** check box on the **Display** tab of the **Options** dialog box shown in Figure 3-16. After turning solid fill areas off, you must regenerate the drawing in order to see the results.

EXERCISE 3-14 Turning Fill Areas On and Off

To access student data files, go to **www.pearsondesigncentral.com.**

1. Open drawing ***Plot Screening and Fill Areas*** located in the student data files.
2. Select the **Model** tab so that model space is active.
3. Select the **Zoom Extents** tool and zoom to the extents of the drawing.
4. Select the **Options** button from the bottom of the application menu to display the **Options** dialog box.
5. Select the **Display** tab.
6. Select the **Apply solid fill** option in the **Display performance** area at the middle right of the dialog box so that it is turned off (unchecked).
7. Select **OK** to close the **Options** dialog box and return to the drawing.
8. Type **RE<Enter>** at the AutoCAD command line to run the **REGEN** command.
9. All filled areas are now turned off.
10. Select the **Options** button from the bottom of the application menu again to display the **Options** dialog box.
11. Select the **Display** tab.
12. Select the **Apply solid fill** option in the **Display performance** area at the middle right of the dialog box so that it is turned on (checked).
13. Select **OK** to close the **Options** dialog box and return to the drawing.
14. Type **RE<Enter>** at the AutoCAD command line to run the **REGEN** command.
15. All filled areas are now turned back on.

NOTE

The **Apply solid fill** setting can also be controlled via the **FILLMODE** system variable. Setting **FILLMODE = 0** turns off hatching, solid fills, gradient fills, and wide polylines. Setting **FILLMODE = 1** turns hatching, solid fills, gradient fills, and wide polylines back on in a drawing. This **FILLMODE** setting is saved with the drawing.

Chapter Summary

Mastering the drawing display tools and settings explained in this chapter will help to make you a more productive and precise drafter. The navigation bar on the right side of the drawing window provides you quick and easy access to all the **Zoom** and **Pan** tools you will ever need to get around in your drawings. Because there is not one display tool that provides all of the ideal functionality, practice using a combination of different tools to navigate around your drawing as you are working. You might find that you are more comfortable with some tools than others.

Sometimes it is necessary to clean up the drawing display so that arcs and circles appear smooth and you are sure all of the drawing information is displayed correctly. Typically, this requires that you enter the **REGEN** command via the keyboard. To help reduce the need to regenerate the display as often, you can adjust the display settings via the **Display** tab of the **Options** dialog box and optimize drawing performance.

Chapter Test Questions

Multiple Choice

Circle the correct answer.

1. To make drawing objects appear larger on the screen, you should:

a. Zoom out
b. Zoom in
c. Get a bigger computer monitor
d. Pan

2. The **Zoom** tools are located on the:

a. Navigation bar
b. Status bar
c. Application menu
d. None of the above

3. The **Zoom Realtime** tool allows you to:

a. Zoom in and zoom out
b. Zoom interactively
c. Draw faster
d. All of the above

4. The **Zoom Window** tool zooms in your drawing when you:

a. Choose a view
b. Pick two points
c. Pick one point
d. Specify a scale factor

5. To move the drawing display area back and forth without changing the drawing's zoom scale factor, you should use:

a. **Pan** tool
b. Middle mouse button
c. Scroll bars
d. All of the above

6. The system variable that controls whether the middle mouse button activates the **Pan** tool is:

a. **MOUSEPANBUTTON**
b. **MIDDLEBUTTONPAN**
c. **MBUTTONPAN**
d. **MPAN**

7. Entering a command transparently allows you to:

a. Not see the command at the command line interface
b. Use the command while another command is already active

c. Temporarily turn off the drawing display
d. All of the above

8. Double-clicking the mouse wheel will:
   a. Display the **Object Snap** shortcut menu
   b. Put the mouse in joystick mode
   c. Pan the display
   d. Zoom extents
9. The **Clean Screen** toggle allows you to:
   a. Minimize the drawing window
   b. Turn off the ribbon, toolbars, and palettes
   c. Erase all objects displayed on the screen
   d. Clear smudge marks off your screen

Matching

Write the number of the correct answer on the line.

a. **Zoom Realtime** tool ______
b. **Zoom Window** tool ______
c. **Zoom Previous** tool ______
d. **Zoom Extents** tool ______
e. **ZOOMFACTOR** system variable ______
f. **Zoom All** tool ______
g. **Pan** tool ______
h. **VIEWRES** system variable ______

1. Zooms to the outermost visible drawing objects
2. Returns to the previously zoomed view
3. Zooms to the drawing limits
4. Zooms interactively
5. Controls mouse thumb wheel zoom increment
6. Controls arc and circle smoothness
7. Pans interactively
8. Zooms to a user-defined rectangular area

True or False

Circle the correct answer.

1. **True or False:** The mouse pointer changes from an arrow to a microscope when the **Zoom Realtime** tool is selected.
2. **True or False:** If you zoom in as far as you can using the **Zoom Realtime** tool and you cannot zoom any farther, you should use the **REGEN** command to recalculate your display.
3. **True or False:** The **Zoom Previous** tool will also undo the last command.
4. **True or False:** The mouse wheel button always activates the **Pan** tool.
5. **True or False:** It is possible to zoom past the extents of a drawing using the **Zoom All** tool.
6. **True or False:** When zooming using the mouse wheel, each click of the wheel zooms in or out by 10%.
7. **True or False:** The mouse pointer changes from an arrow to a hand when the **Pan** tool is selected.
8. **True or False:** Any command can be used transparently when another command is active.

Chapter Project

G Project 3-1: *Controlling the Drawing Display* [BASIC]

To access student data files, go to **www.pearsondesigncentral.com.**

1. Open drawing ***Willhome*** located in the student data files.
2. Select the **Model** tab so that model space is active.
3. Select the **Zoom Extents** tool and zoom to the extents of the drawing.
4. Use the **Zoom Object** tool to zoom in on the "Breakfast" room label text at the top of the floor plan.
5. Double-click on the text and change it to "Breakfast Nook" using the **Edit Text** dialog box.
6. Zoom to the extents of the drawing.
7. Turn off the text display so only the text boundary boxes are visible.
8. Regenerate the drawing.
9. Turn off all solid fill areas.
10. Regenerate the drawing.
11. Increase the arc and circle smoothness factor to 10,000.
12. Regenerate the drawing.
13. Save the drawing as ***P3-1***.

4 chapterfour

Basic Drawing Commands

CHAPTER OBJECTIVES

- Create a new drawing
- Establish the drawing units
- Set the drawing limits
- Create lines, circles, and arcs
- Create ellipses and elliptical arcs
- Create point objects and control their size and appearance
- Measure and divide using point objects

Introduction

The vast majority of 2D drawings are comprised of three basic drawing elements: lines, circles, and arcs. The size, location, color, line width, and linetype may vary. They may even be combined or joined together to create more complex objects. But most drawings can be broken down to these three basic elements. Chapter 2 gave you a quick introduction to these basic drawing objects. In this chapter, we'll take a closer look at these basic drawing commands as well as ellipses and points. We'll also examine some ways to control precisely the placement of AutoCAD objects and take a closer look at the various ways to create new drawings.

Drawing Setup

AutoCAD provides a number of ways to get started in a drawing. In Chapter 2, you used a drawing template to quickly start a new drawing with a number of preconfigured settings. Templates make starting a drawing quick and easy.

Templates

Drawing templates are simply drawings that have been set up and saved as templates with the file extension *dwt*. AutoCAD comes with a number of predefined templates for various page sizes and industry standards. They typically have specific unit settings, title blocks, layer definitions, page layouts, dimension styles, and so on. The template **acad.dwt** is the default template. When you start a new session of AutoCAD, the blank drawing you see is created from the **acad.dwt** drawing template.

Any drawing can be saved as a template. To save a drawing as a template, choose **Save as** from the **Quick Access** toolbar, and choose **AutoCAD Drawing Template** to display the **Save Drawing As** dialog box (see Figure 4-1).

Figure 4-1
Creating a drawing template

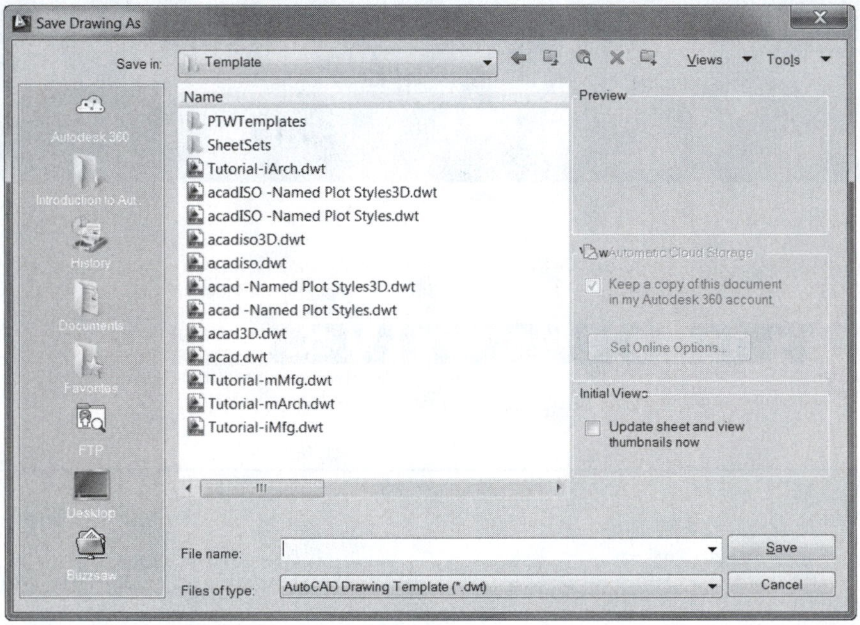

By default, drawing templates are stored in a folder named **Template** that is created by AutoCAD.

> **TIP**
>
> You can specify a different default template folder by changing the **Default Template File Location** setting under **Template settings** on the **Files** tab of the AutoCAD **Options** dialog box.

UNITS	
Application Menu:	Drawing Utilities 0.0
Toolbar:	None
Menu:	Format | Units...
Command Line:	UNITS
Command Alias:	UN

Units

Typically, the first step in setting up your drawing is to set the drawing units. Chapter 1 discussed the fact that AutoCAD is, for the most part, a unitless environment. One unit in AutoCAD can represent any measurement you want (1 inch, 1 foot, 1 millimeter, 1 meter, 1 nautical league, or even 1 parsec). The **UNITS** command allows you to control how AutoCAD displays units. It is located on the **Drawing Utilities** menu on the application menu (big **A**).

> **NOTE**
>
> The **UNITS** command controls only how units are displayed in the drawing. It does not control how geometry is stored nor does it control the precision of the geometry.

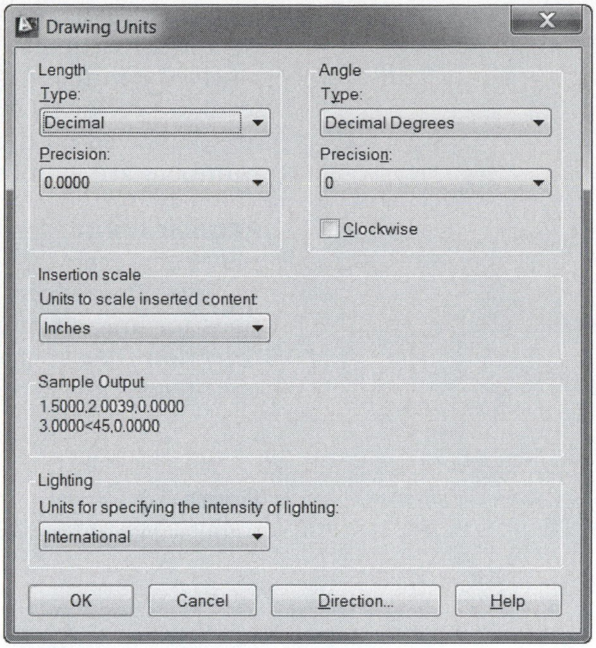

Figure 4-2
The **Drawing Units** dialog box

The **UNITS** command displays the **Drawing Units** dialog box (see Figure 4-2).

The **Drawing Units** dialog box allows you to set how both linear and angular measurements are displayed.

Linear Units. The **Length** settings control how linear units are displayed. You can choose from among five different linear unit display options: **Decimal, Engineering, Architectural, Fractional**, and **Scientific**. They are described in the following table.

Decimal	This is the default format for displaying units. The **Decimal** setting is unitless in that decimal units can represent any unit of measurement. In general, you should note on your drawing which drawing units you are using.
Engineering	Engineering units are based on imperial feet-inch units. 1 unit is 1″ and 12 units are 1′. Inches are displayed in decimal units. For example, 15½″ would be displayed as 1′-3.5″.
Architectural	Architectural units are similar to engineering units except inches are displayed as fractions. For example, 15½″ would be displayed as 1′-3.5½″.
Fractional	Fractional units are similar to decimal units except that numbers are represented as fractions. For example, 15.5 units would display as 15½″. Like the **Decimal** setting, the **Fractional** setting is unitless.
Scientific	Scientific unit display uses exponential notation. For example, 15.5 would display as 1.5500E + 01 (1.55×10^1). Like the decimal and fractional unit displays, scientific unit display is unitless.

NOTE

You can enter feet (′) and inches (″) only when drawing units are set to either **Architectural** or **Engineering.** If you try to enter either unit designation when drawing units are set to anything else, AutoCAD will reject the entry and display the following ambiguous message at the command line:

Point or option keyword required.

If you are using dynamic input, a bright red border is displayed around the distance input box, and you are forced to reenter a valid input value.

There is also a **Precision:** drop-down list that allows you to set the round-off setting for each unit type. The precision setting controls how precisely the number is displayed. The units are rounded off to the specified level of precision. It is important to note that this affects only how units are displayed on the screen. AutoCAD still stores numbers accurately; the numbers are simply rounded off when displayed on screen.

Angular Units. The **Angle** area controls how angles are input and displayed.

The **Precision:** drop-down list works the same for angular units as it does for linear units. The **Clockwise** check box allows you to change the direction that angles are measured. By default, angles are measured in a counterclockwise direction (see Figure 4-3).

Figure 4-3
Angular measurements

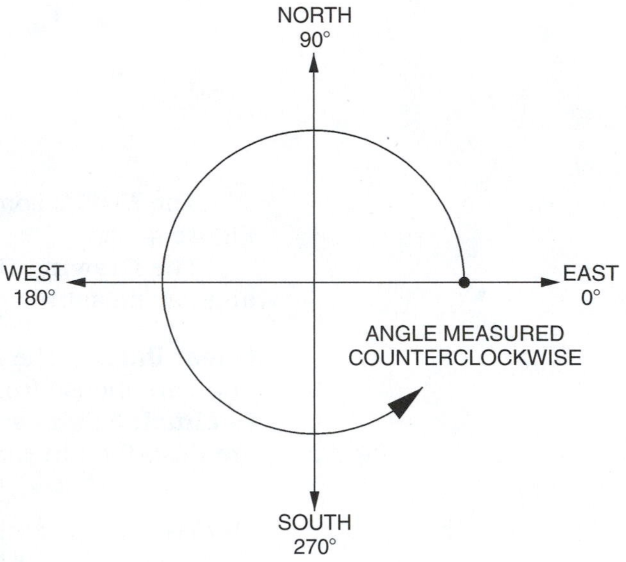

Decimal Degrees	This is the default format for displaying angular measurements. 1 unit equals 1 degree.
Deg/Min/Sec	Degrees/Minutes/Seconds. With this format, there are 360 degrees in a full circle, 60 minutes in 1 degree, and 60 seconds in 1 minute. A 30-degree angle would display as 30d0′0″ where d denotes degrees, ′ denotes minutes, and ″ denotes seconds. Latitude and longitude are typically displayed using Deg/Min/Sec.
Grads	400 grads = 360 degrees. 1 grad is roughly 0.9 degree.
Radians	Radians are measured as multiples of pi (Π). 2 pi radians (~6.28r) equals 360 degrees. Pi radian (3.14r) is 180 degrees.
Surveyor's Units	Surveyor's units show angles as bearings, using N or S for north or south, degrees/minutes/seconds to denote how far east or west the angle is from direct north or south, and E or W for east or west. For example, N 45d0′0″ E represents 45 degrees from north in the east direction (45 degrees in decimal units). Angles are always less than 90 degrees and are displayed in the Deg/Min/Sec format. You can simply use E, N, W, and S to represent 0, 90, 180, and 270 degrees, respectively.

Putting a check in the **Clockwise** box changes the direction of angular measurement so that 90 degrees is south, and 270 degrees is north.

EXERCISE 4-1 **Setting the Drawing Units**

1. Start a new drawing using the **acad.dwt** drawing template.
2. On the application menu, choose **Units** from the **Drawing Utilities** menu. The **Drawing Units** dialog box is displayed.
3. In the **Length** area, choose **Decimal** from the **Type:** drop-down list and set the **Precision** to **0.00** (2 decimal places).
4. In the **Angle** area, choose **Decimal Degrees** from the **Type:** drop-down list and set the **Precision** to **0.0** (1 decimal place).
5. Make sure there is no check in the **Clockwise** box and the **Insertion scale** is set to **Inches**. Choose **OK** to close the dialog box.
6. Save your drawing as ***CH4_EXERCISE***.

Setting the Drawing Area

AutoCAD provides an unlimited space for you to create your drawing. Chapter 1 discussed the concept of drawing objects their actual size. You'll want to set up a large drawing area to draw large objects and a small drawing area to draw small ones. In model space, the drawing area is not critical and can be changed at any time. In layout (paper) space, the drawing area determines the paper size. The drawing area is set up using the **LIMITS** command in model space.

LIMITS	
Ribbon & Panel:	None
Toolbar:	None
Menu:	Format | Drawing Limits...
Command Line:	LIMITS
Command Alias:	None

NOTE

The **Zoom All** command will zoom your drawing to fit the drawing area to your screen.

When you start the **LIMITS** command, AutoCAD will ask you to specify two points: the lower left corner and the upper right corner. These two corners determine the drawing area.

EXERCISE 4-2 **Setting the Drawing Limits**

1. Continue from Exercise 4-1.
2. Type **limits <Enter>**. AutoCAD prompts you to *Specify lower left corner or* ↓.
3. Press **<Enter>** to accept the default setting of 0,0. AutoCAD then prompts you to *Specify upper right corner <12.00,9.00>:*.
4. Type **11,8.5<Enter>** to set the upper right corner. You now have an 11 × 8.5 drawing area.
5. Save your drawing.

LINE	
Ribbon & Panel:	Home | Draw 
Draw Toolbar:	
Menu:	Draw | Line
Command Line:	LINE
Command Alias:	L

Drawing Lines

In Chapter 2, we used the **LINE** command to create some simple geometric shapes. Lines are one of the fundamental drawing objects in AutoCAD. As you've seen, when you start the **LINE** command, AutoCAD prompts you for the first (or start) point and then prompts you for the next point. AutoCAD then simply draws a straight line segment between those two points. AutoCAD will continue to prompt you for the next point and continue to draw line segments until you either press **<Enter>** or cancel the command by pressing **<Esc>**.

While drawing line segments, you have two options available: **Undo** and **Close**. The **Undo** option will delete the last line segment and resume drawing from the end of the previous line segment.

The **Close** option will draw a line segment from the last specified point to the point specified at the start of the **LINE** command. For example, in Figure 4-4, if you draw line segments from point A to B to C and to D, selecting the **Close** option would draw a line segment from point D to A. The **Close** option is available only after three points are specified.

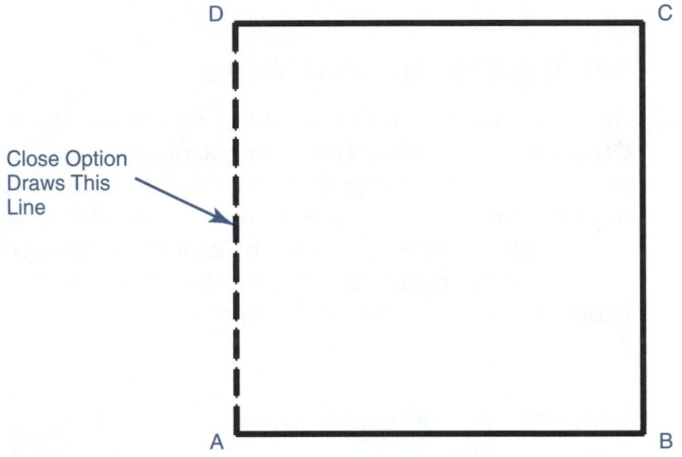

Figure 4-4
Using the **Close** option

Coordinate Entry Methods

As you've seen, to place objects in AutoCAD, you need to specify where in the drawing you want to place them. For example, when drawing a line, AutoCAD prompts you to *Specify first point:* and to *Specify next point:*. This process of specifying point locations is called ***coordinate entry***. AutoCAD uses two basic types of coordinate systems: Cartesian coordinates and polar coordinates.

coordinate entry: The process of specifying point locations.

Cartesian Coordinates

In Chapter 1, we discussed the Cartesian coordinate system, where 0,0 is the origin and a point location is described as an *x* and *y* coordinate (see Figure 4-5).

Using this system, it's possible to describe accurately any position on a two-dimensional plane. However, while it is possible to use basic Cartesian coordinates all the time, it is not always practical or efficient to do so. For example, let's look at a 2 × 2 square with its lower left corner located at the coordinate 3,2. To describe this square using Cartesian coordinates, you would need to calculate the location of each corner by taking the starting coordinate (3,2) and adding the dimensions to the respective *x* and *y* coordinates (see Figure 4-6).

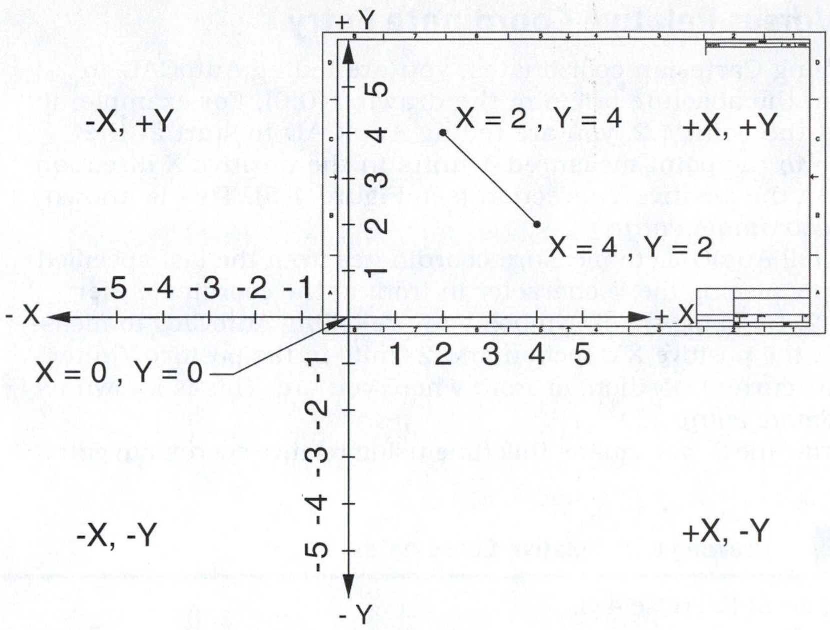

Figure 4-5
The Cartesian coordinate system

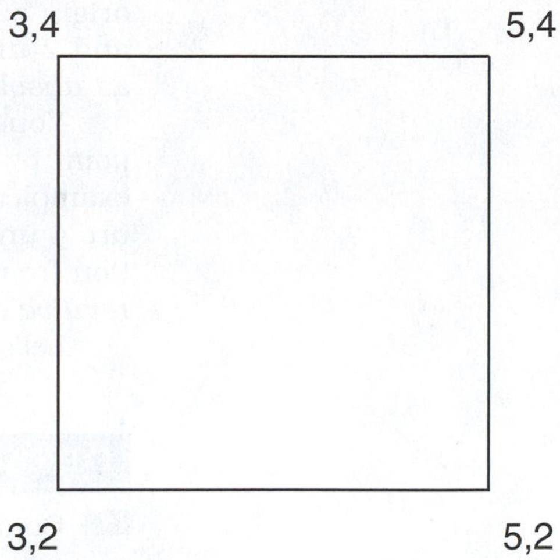

Figure 4-6
2 × 2 square coordinates

EXERCISE 4-3 **Drawing with Cartesian Coordinates**

1. Continue from Exercise 4-2.
2. Toggle the **Dynamic Input** setting off.
3. Start the **LINE** command. AutoCAD prompts you to:

   Specify first point:
4. Type **3,2<Enter>**. AutoCAD places the first point and prompts you to:

   Specify next point or [**U**ndo]:
5. Type **5,2<Enter>**. AutoCAD places the second point and prompts you to:

   Specify next point or [**U**ndo]:
6. Type **5,4<Enter>**. AutoCAD places the third point and prompts you to:

   Specify next point or [**C**lose **U**ndo]:
7. Type **3,4<Enter>**. AutoCAD places the fourth point and prompts you to:

   Specify next point or [**C**lose **U**ndo]:
8. Select the **Close** option to close the square and end the **LINE** command.
9. Save your drawing.

Although drawing using only Cartesian coordinates is possible, it's not an efficient way to draw. The coordinates in the previous exercise are fairly simple, but the problem is made more difficult if the square is rotated or the points do not lie on easily determined coordinates.

To address these issues, AutoCAD gives you some additional ways of specifying coordinates.

Absolute Versus Relative Coordinate Entry

When specifying Cartesian coordinates, you are telling AutoCAD to measure from the absolute origin of the drawing (0,0). For example, if you specified the point 4,2, you are telling AutoCAD to start at the origin and go to the point measured 4 units in the positive X direction and 2 units in the positive Y direction (see Figure 4-5). This is known as *absolute coordinate entry*.

You can tell AutoCAD to measure coordinates from the last specified point by simply placing the @ character in front of the coordinate—for example, @4,2. By using the @ symbol, you are telling AutoCAD to measure 4 units in the positive X direction and 2 units in the positive Y direction from your current position, or from where you are. This is known as *relative coordinate entry*.

Let's redraw the 2 × 2 square, this time using relative coordinate entry.

EXERCISE 4-4 Drawing with Relative Coordinates

1. Continue from Exercise 4-3.
2. Toggle the **Dynamic Input** setting back on.
3. Start the **LINE** command. AutoCAD prompts you to:

   Specify first point:

4. Type **6,2<Enter>**. AutoCAD places the first point and prompts you to:

   Specify next point or [**U**ndo]:

5. Type **@2,0<Enter>**. AutoCAD places a point 2 units to the right of the first point and prompts you to:

   Specify next point or [**U**ndo]:

6. Type **@0,2<Enter>**. AutoCAD places a point 2 units above the second point and prompts you to:

   Specify next point or [**C**lose **U**ndo]:

7. Type **@-2,0<Enter>**. AutoCAD places a point 2 units to the left of the third point and prompts you to:

   Specify next point or [**C**lose **U**ndo]:

8. Select the **Close** option to close the square and end the **LINE** command. Your drawing should now resemble Figure 4-7.
9. Save your drawing.

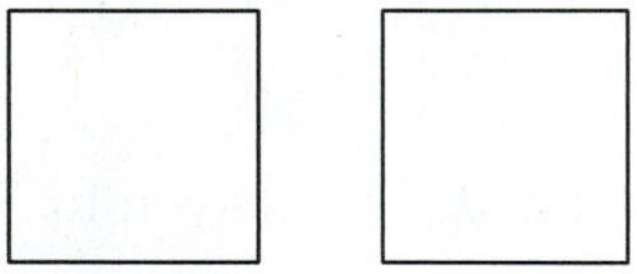

Figure 4-7
Drawing with relative coordinates

You used absolute coordinate entry to place the first point (6,2), but each subsequent point was measured from the last placed point—i.e., from where you were.

> **TIP**
>
> When **Dynamic Input** is turned on, all coordinates you enter after the first point are automatically relative. AutoCAD enters the @ prefix automatically so you don't have to. If you want to enter an absolute coordinate, you just prefix the coordinate with the # symbol (e.g., #2,4**<Enter>**).

Chapter 4

Polar Coordinates

Cartesian coordinates work well when drawing objects have mostly right angles or when coordinates lie on a well-defined grid. However, when drawing objects that have angles other than 90°, calculating coordinate locations is quite a bit more difficult. Let's take our 2 × 2 square and rotate it 45° (see Figure 4-8).

To calculate the location of these coordinates, you'll need to either use the Pythagorean theorem ($x^2 + y^2 = z^2$) or use AutoCAD's polar coordinates.

Polar coordinates use distance and direction to specify locations. For example, if you specify a location of 2<0, 2 is the distance, < is the angle indicator, and 0 is the direction in degrees. The coordinate 2<0 tells AutoCAD to measure 2 units in the 0° direction from the origin (0,0). Remember from Chapter 1 that in AutoCAD, angles are measured counterclockwise from 0°, which is east, or to the right, of the origin along the positive *X*-axis.

Like Cartesian coordinates, polar coordinates can be either absolute (measured from 0,0) or relative (measured from the last specified point). Also, angles can be positive (counterclockwise) or negative (clockwise). Figure 4-9 shows some examples of polar coordinate entry and the resulting point locations.

Now, let's draw the rotated 2 × 2 square using polar coordinate entry.

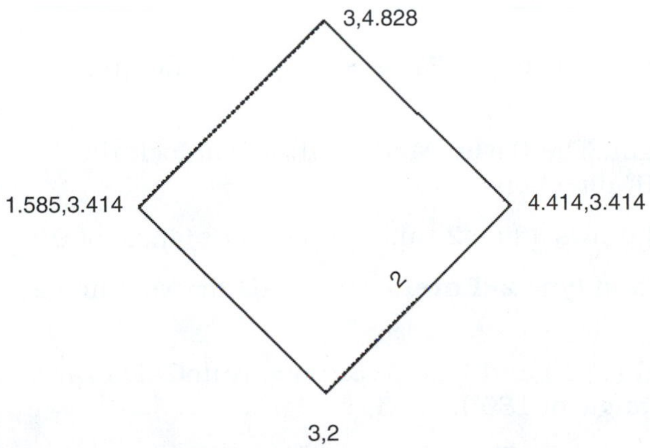

Figure 4-8
The rotated 2 × 2 square

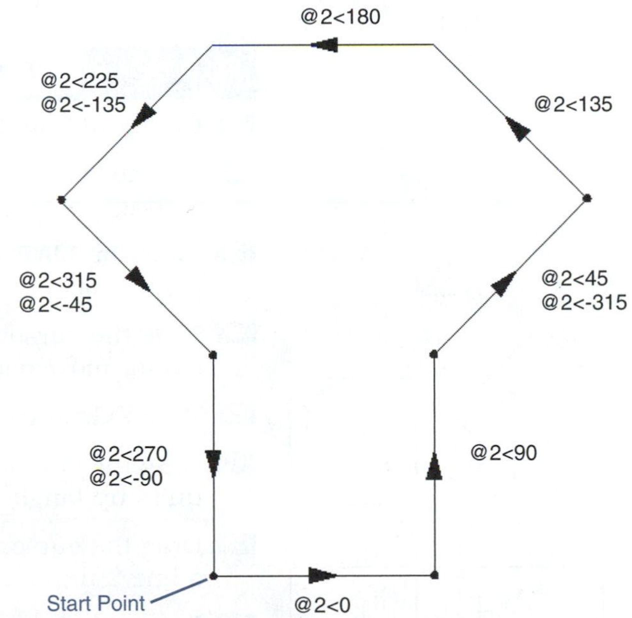

Figure 4-9
The polar coordinate examples

EXERCISE 4-5 **Drawing with Polar Coordinates**

1. Continue from Exercise 4-4.
2. Start the **LINE** command. Type **4,5<Enter>** to specify the first point. AutoCAD starts drawing the line and prompts you for the second point.
3. Type **@2<45<Enter>**. AutoCAD draws a line segment 2 units long at an angle of 45° from the first point.

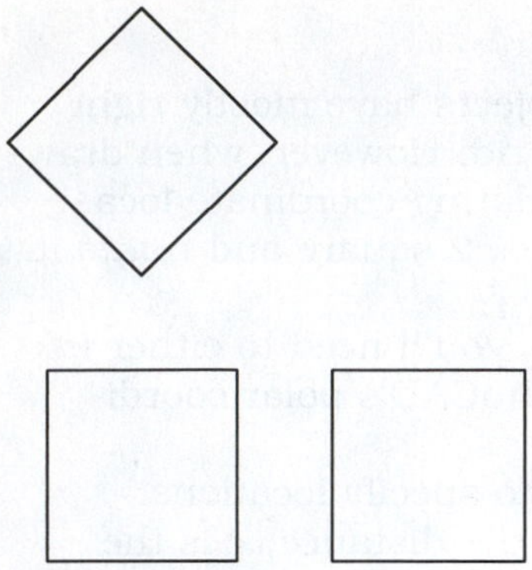

Figure 4-10
Drawing with polar coordinates

4. Type **@2<135<Enter>**. AutoCAD draws a line segment 2 units long at an angle of 135° from the second point.
5. Type **@2<–135<Enter>**. AutoCAD draws a line segment 2 units long at an angle of –135° from the third point.
6. Select the **Close** option to close the square and end the **LINE** command. Your drawing should now resemble Figure 4-10.
7. Save your drawing.

NOTE

Absolute coordinate entry, whether Cartesian or polar coordinates, is rarely used. The majority of points are specified using either object snaps (see Chapter 5) or some form of relative coordinate entry.

Dynamic Input

As you saw in Chapter 2, AutoCAD's dynamic prompt moves with your cursor and provides instant feedback as you move around the drawing. One of the advantages of dynamic input is the immediate coordinate and dimensional information it provides while drawing. Using dynamic input, you can use the cursor location to determine the angle and dimensions of the objects as they are being drawn. This is best explained with an example.

EXERCISE 4-6 Drawing with Dynamic Input

1. Continue from Exercise 4-5.
2. On the status bar, turn on both the **Ortho Mode** and **Dynamic Input** settings.
3. Start the **LINE** command and type **6,5<Enter>** to specify the first point.
4. Drag the cursor to the right. The **Ortho Mode** setting will lock the cursor movement to the 0° direction.
5. Type **2<Enter>**. AutoCAD draws a line 2 units to the right (angle of 0°).
6. Drag the cursor up (90°) and type **2<Enter>**. AutoCAD draws a line 2 units up (angle of 90°).
7. Drag the cursor to the left (180°) and type **2<Enter>**. AutoCAD draws a line 2 units to the left (angle of 180°).
8. Press the down arrow and choose **Close** from the list of options. AutoCAD closes the square and ends the **LINE** command. Your drawing should now resemble Figure 4-11.
9. Save your drawing.

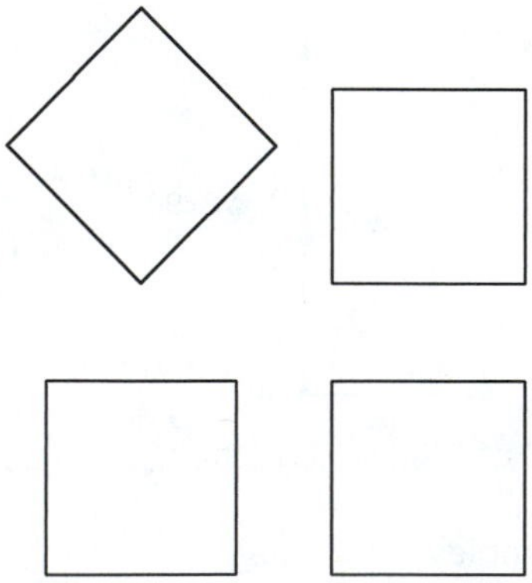

Figure 4-11
Drawing with dynamic input

Dynamic input automates the process of specifying relative coordinates. When **Dynamic Input** is turned on, all dimensions and coordinates you type are measured from the last specified point. Dynamic input also allows you to see the length and direction visually without having to calculate the direction angles. You simply point the way and tell AutoCAD how far to go.

FOR MORE DETAILS

Chapter 5 covers more ways of specifying coordinate locations and demonstrates how to combine Cartesian, polar, and direct distance coordinate entry methods with object snaps and polar tracking.

We've seen that AutoCAD remembers the last specified coordinate. When inputting relative coordinates, AutoCAD will measure coordinates from the last specified point. The **LINE** command can also make use of the last point. When you start the **LINE** command, AutoCAD prompts you to specify the first point. If you simply press **<Enter>**, AutoCAD will start the line from the last specified point.

Drawing Circles

A circle is another basic AutoCAD drawing object. By default, AutoCAD asks for a center coordinate and a radius distance. However, there are a number of other ways to draw a circle. When you start the **CIRCLE** command, AutoCAD prompts you to *Specify center point for circle or*↓. If you choose the down arrow, you'll see that you have other options for drawing a circle.

Altogether, there are six different options for creating a circle: **Center Radius, Center Diameter, 2 Point, 3 Point, Tangent Tangent Radius,** or **Tangent Tangent Tangent**.

Center Radius

CIRCLE	
Ribbon & Panel:	Home | Draw 
Draw Toolbar:	
Menu:	Draw | Circle
Command Line:	CIRCLE
Command Alias:	C

This is AutoCAD's default method for creating a circle. You can specify the center point using any of the coordinate entry methods. Once you have the center point placed, AutoCAD will then display a rubber-band line and drag a circle from the center point. You can specify the radius either by picking a point on the screen or by typing in a radius value.

EXERCISE 4-7 **Drawing a Circle**

1. Continue from Exercise 4-6.
2. Toggle the **Ortho Mode** setting off.
3. Start the **CIRCLE** command. AutoCAD prompts you to *Specify center point for circle or*↓.
4. Type **1,3<Enter>.** AutoCAD places the center of the circle and starts dragging the radius. A preview image of the circle appears (see Figure 4-12). AutoCAD prompts you to *Specify radius of circle or*↓.

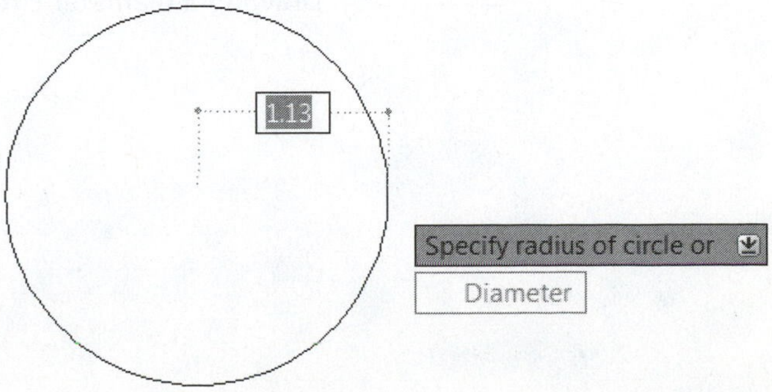

Figure 4-12
The preview image of the circle

Figure 4-13
Drawing a circle

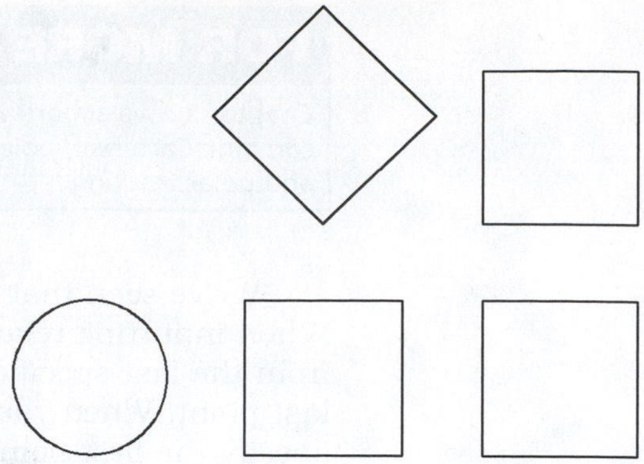

5. Type **1<Enter>** to specify a radius of 1. AutoCAD creates the circle and ends the **CIRCLE** command. Your drawing should now look like Figure 4-13.
6. Save your drawing.

Center Diameter

This is similar to the **Center Radius** option. Once you specify a center point, AutoCAD prompts you to *Specify radius of circle or* ↓.

You can then select the **Diameter** option using your mouse or by typing **D<Enter>**. AutoCAD will then prompt you for the diameter of the circle. The rubber-band line will now stretch out twice the radius of the circle, and the dynamic input will be located at the center of the circle. You can specify the diameter either by picking a point on the screen or by typing in a diameter.

EXERCISE 4-8 Drawing a Circle Using Center Diameter

1. Continue from Exercise 4-7.
2. Start the **CIRCLE** command. AutoCAD prompts you to *Specify center point for circle or* ↓.
3. Type **4,3<Enter>**. AutoCAD places the center of the circle and starts dragging the radius. AutoCAD prompts you to *Specify radius of circle or* ↓.
4. Choose **Diameter** from the options list. AutoCAD prompts you to *Specify diameter of circle:*. Notice that the default value is the diameter of the last circle drawn (2.00).

Figure 4-14
Drawing a diameter circle

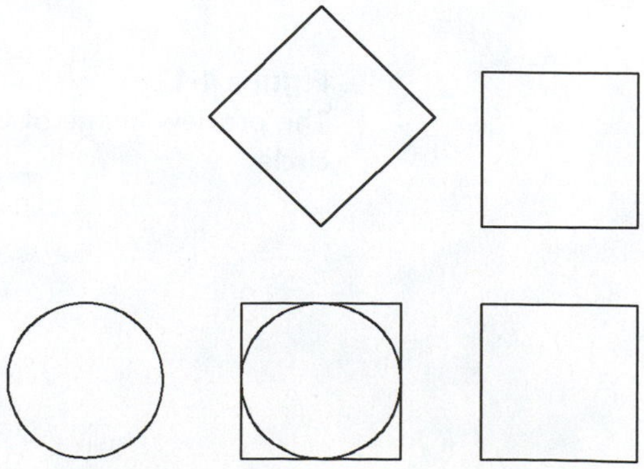

5 Press **<Enter>** to accept the default diameter value. AutoCAD places the circle and ends the **CIRCLE** command. Your drawing should resemble Figure 4-14.

6 Save your drawing.

2 Point Circle

A 2 point circle is defined by specifying two points on the diameter of the circle. To use this option, start the **CIRCLE** command and either type **2P<Enter>** at the prompt or choose **2P** from the options list. AutoCAD then asks you to specify the first point of the circle's diameter and the second point and will draw a circle whose diameter passes through the two points.

EXERCISE 4-9 Drawing a 2 Point Circle

1 Continue from Exercise 4-8.

2 Toggle the **Ortho Mode** setting on.

3 Start the **CIRCLE** command. AutoCAD prompts you to *Specify center point for circle or* ↓.

4 Select **2P** from the options list. AutoCAD prompts you to *Specify first endpoint of circle's diameter:*.

5 Type **7,2<Enter>** to specify the first point on the circle's diameter. AutoCAD prompts you to *Specify second endpoint of circle's diameter:*.

6 Drag the cursor up and type **2<Enter>** to place the second point on the circle's diameter. AutoCAD draws the circle and ends the **CIRCLE** command.

7 Save your drawing. Your drawing should resemble Figure 4-15.

Figure 4-15
Drawing a 2 point circle

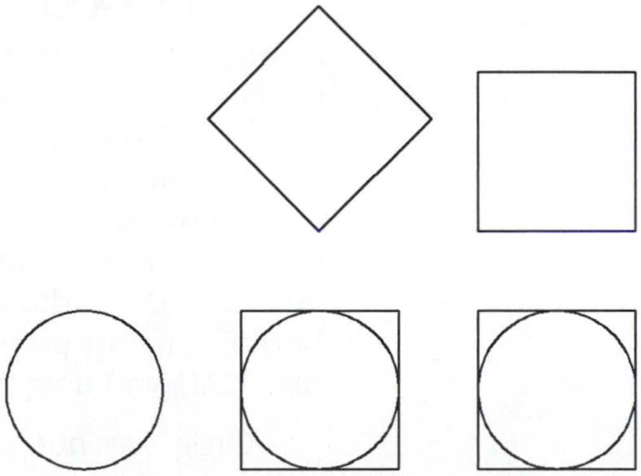

3 Point Circle

A 3 point circle is defined by specifying three points on the circle's circumference. To use this option, start the **CIRCLE** command and type **3P<Enter>** or choose **3P** from the options list. AutoCAD asks you to specify the first point on the circle, then the second point. Once you specify the second point, AutoCAD will prompt you for the third and will drag a circle that passes through the first two points. AutoCAD will not display the preview circle until the first two points are specified.

EXERCISE 4-10 **Drawing a 3 Point Circle**

1. Continue from Exercise 4-9.
2. Start the **CIRCLE** command. AutoCAD prompts you to *Specify center point for circle or ↓.*
3. Select **3P** from the options list. AutoCAD prompts you to *Specify first point on circle:.*
4. Type **7,5<Enter>** to specify the first point on the circle.
5. Type **1,1<Enter>** to specify the second point on the circle. The dynamic input places the point at the middle of the right side of the square. AutoCAD now displays the preview circle. AutoCAD prompts you to *Specify third point on circle:.*
6. Drag your cursor to the left and type **2<Enter>** to place the last point on the circle. AutoCAD creates the circle and ends the **CIRCLE** command.
7. Save your drawing. Your drawing should resemble Figure 4-16.

Figure 4-16
Drawing a 3 point circle

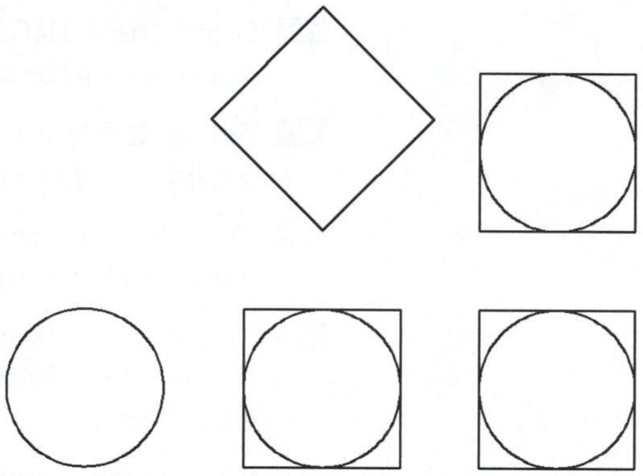

Tangent Tangent Radius

A tangent tangent radius, or TTR, circle is defined by two points of tangency on existing objects and a radius value. This method of creating a circle is a bit different from the other methods. First, the points of tangency must be on existing objects. AutoCAD uses the **Tangent** object snap to get the points of tangency. Second, the exact points of tangency are determined only after you specify the radius. Because of this, you can't drag and pick the radius of the circle. Last, it is possible to specify a combination of tangent points and a radius that cannot be created. In this case, AutoCAD will simply tell you:

Circle does not exist.

EXERCISE 4-11 **Drawing a TTR Circle**

1. Continue from Exercise 4-10.
2. Start the **CIRCLE** command. AutoCAD prompts you to *Specify center point for circle or ↓.*
3. Select **Ttr** from the options list. AutoCAD prompts you to *Specify point on object for first tangent of circle:.*
4. Drag your cursor over the lower left side of the rotated box (see Figure 4-17). AutoCAD will display the **Deferred Tangent** object snap.

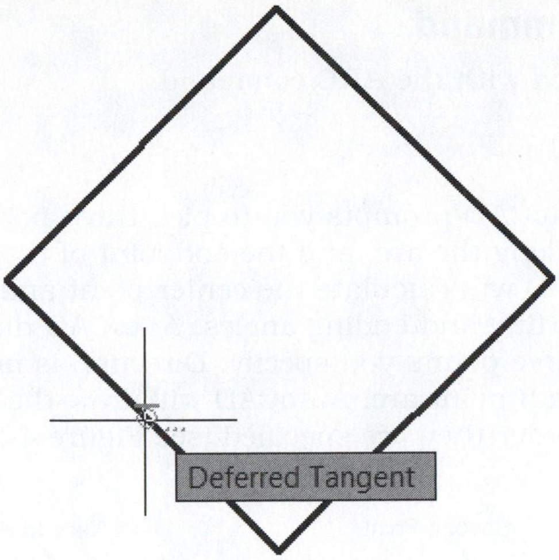

Figure 4-17
The **Deferred Tangent** object snap

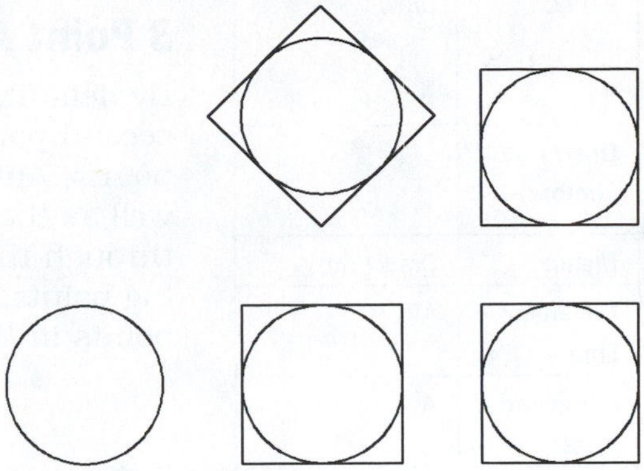

Figure 4-18
Drawing a **TTR** circle

5. Pick anywhere along the line to select the first tangent point. AutoCAD prompts you to *Specify point on object for second tangent of circle:*.
6. Pick anywhere along the lower right line to select the second tangent point. AutoCAD prompts you to *Specify radius of circle <1.00>:*.
7. Press **<Enter>** to accept the default circle radius (1.00). AutoCAD creates the circle and ends the **CIRCLE** command.
8. Save your drawing. Your drawing should resemble Figure 4-18.

Tan, Tan, Tan. When choosing the **CIRCLE** command from the **Draw** panel, you'll notice that there is yet another option listed: **Tan, Tan, Tan.** This is technically *not* an option of the **CIRCLE** command. It is simply a method of constructing a circle using the **3P** option of the **CIRCLE** command along with AutoCAD's **Tangent** object snap.

Drawing Arcs

Arcs are another type of basic drawing object. An arc is simply a segment of a circle. Like circles, arcs are defined by a center point and radius, but they also include a starting angle and an ending angle (see Figure 4-19). The part of the circle between the start and end angles defines the arc segment. Keep in mind that, by default, AutoCAD measures angles in a counterclockwise direction, with 0 along the positive portion of the *X*-axis. Likewise, arcs are also drawn in a counterclockwise direction. This means that by default, AutoCAD will draw the arc segment from the starting angle in a counterclockwise direction toward the ending angle.

Figure 4-19
How arcs are defined

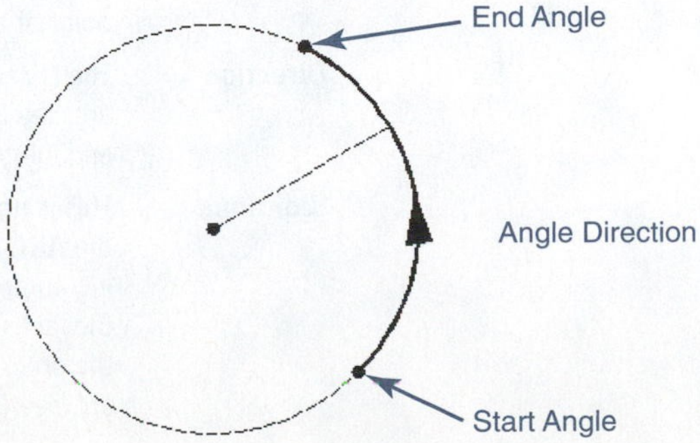

ARC	
Ribbon & Panel:	Home | Draw 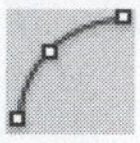
Draw Toolbar:	
Menu:	Draw | Arc
Command Line:	ARC
Command Alias:	A

The ARC Command

Arcs are created with the **ARC** command.

3 Point Arc

By default, AutoCAD prompts you to pick three points: a start point, a second point along the arc, and the endpoint of the arc. From these three points, AutoCAD will calculate the center point and radius of the arc as well as the starting and ending angles. AutoCAD draws an arc segment through the three points you specify. Direction is not important when picking points for a 3 point arc. AutoCAD will draw the arc through the three points in the order they are specified (see Figure 4-20).

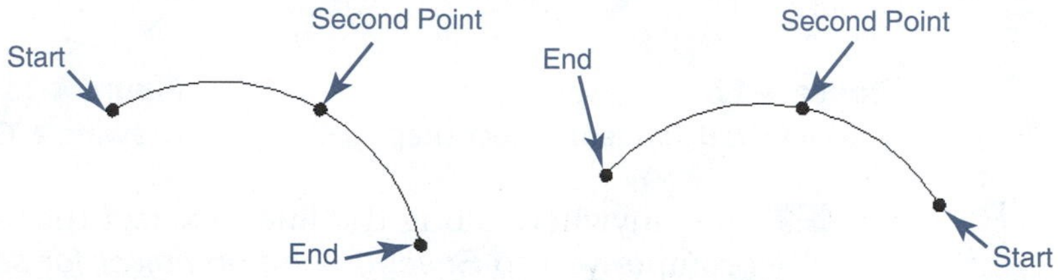

Figure 4-20
3 point arcs

You may find that, while easy to use, the 3 point method of drawing an arc is not always practical. You may not know the exact location of a second point on the arc, or even the start point or endpoint of the arc. You might know the radius of the arc, the center point, the included angle, or some combination of these properties.

Arc Options

AutoCAD provides a number of options for constructing arcs. These options can be used in various combinations, depending on what information you know. The options are described next.

Start	The **Start** option defines the start point of the arc.
End	The **End** option defines the endpoint of the arc.
Center	The **Center** option defines the center point of the arc.
Radius	The **Radius** option defines the radius of the arc. This option can be used only after the start point and endpoint of the arc are defined.
Angle	The **Angle** option defines the included angle of the arc. This is the difference between the starting angle and the ending angle. The **Angle** option is available only after the start point and either the endpoint or the center point have been picked.
Length	The **Length** option defines the length of the chord between the start point and endpoint of the arc (see Figure 4-21).
Direction	The **Direction** option defines the direction of a line tangent to the start point of the arc (see Figure 4-21). The **Direction** option can be used only after the start point and endpoint of the arc have been defined.
Continue	This is not technically an option, but a behavior of the **ARC** command. When you start the **ARC** command, if you press **<Enter>** at the first prompt, AutoCAD will start drawing an arc segment tangent to the previous line or arc segment drawn. AutoCAD uses the last specified point as the start point and determines the tangent direction from the previous line or arc segment. AutoCAD then prompts you for the endpoint of the arc (see Figure 4-21).

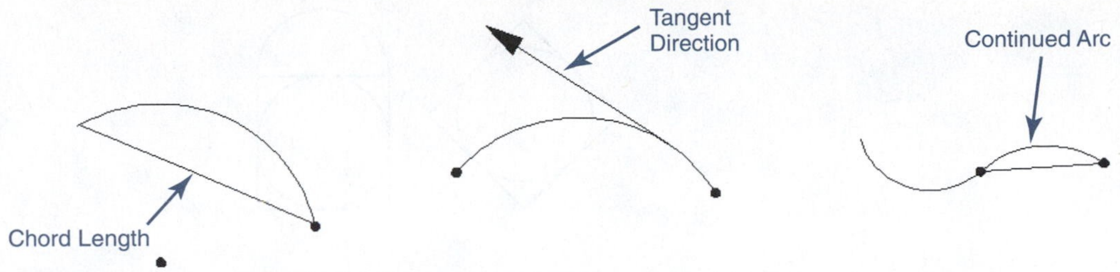

Figure 4-21
Arc options

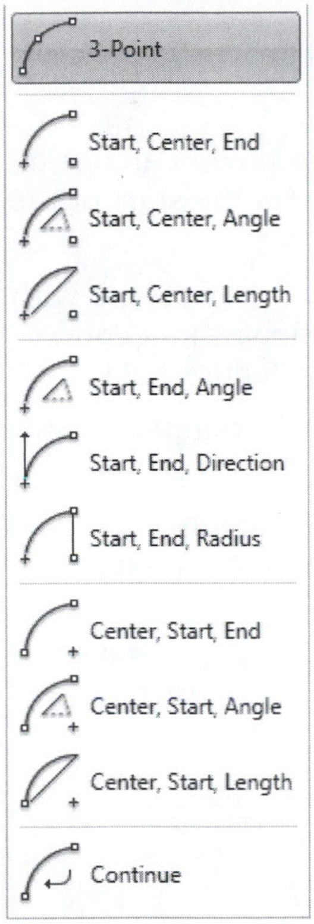

Figure 4-22
The **Home|Draw|Arc** menu

Using the ARC Command

When you start the **ARC** command, AutoCAD will prompt you to *Specify start point of arc or* ↓. You can specify the start point, choose the **Center** option, or press **<Enter>** to create an arc tangent to the previous line or arc segment. Depending on the options you choose, AutoCAD will present you with other options. There are 10 different combinations of options for drawing an arc.

When accessing the **ARC** command from the **Draw** panel, you'll see the 10 different combinations of options used to draw arcs (see Figure 4-22). When using these menu options, AutoCAD will automatically type the options for you after each point selection.

> **TIP**
> Before drawing an arc, take a moment to consider what information you know about the arc. This will help you decide which **ARC** command options to use.

Let's look at some examples of drawing arcs.

EXERCISE 4-12 Drawing Arcs

1. Continue from Exercise 4-11.
2. Choose **Start, End, Radius** from the **Draw** panel. AutoCAD prompts you to *Specify start point of arc or* ↓.
3. Type **8,7<Enter>** to start the arc at the top right corner of the upper right box. A rubber-band line stretches from the point. AutoCAD prompts you to *Specify end point of arc:*. Notice that AutoCAD has specified the **End** option for you.
4. Type **6,7<Enter>** to specify the upper left corner of the square. A preview image of the arc appears, and a rubber-band line stretches from the end of the arc. AutoCAD has also specified the **Radius** option for you. AutoCAD prompts you to *Specify radius of arc:*.
5. Type **1<Enter>** to specify a radius of 1. AutoCAD draws the arc. Your drawing should look like Figure 4-23.
6. Choose **Start, End, Angle** from the **Draw** panel. AutoCAD prompts you to *Specify start point of arc or* ↓.
7. Type **0,3<Enter>** to start the arc at the left quadrant of the circle on the left of your drawing. A rubber-band line stretches from the point. AutoCAD prompts you to *Specify end point of arc:*.

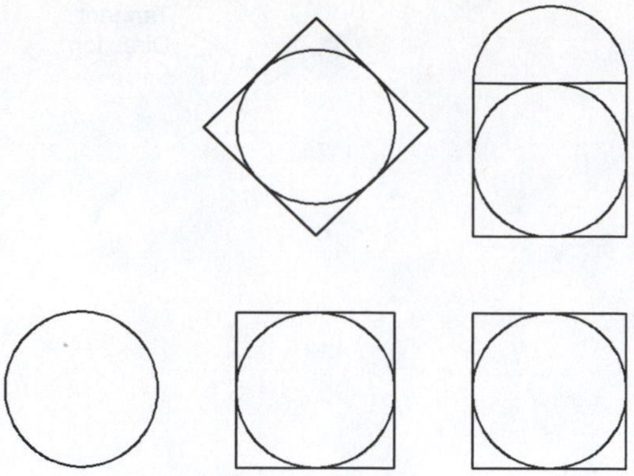

Figure 4-23
Start, End, Radius arc

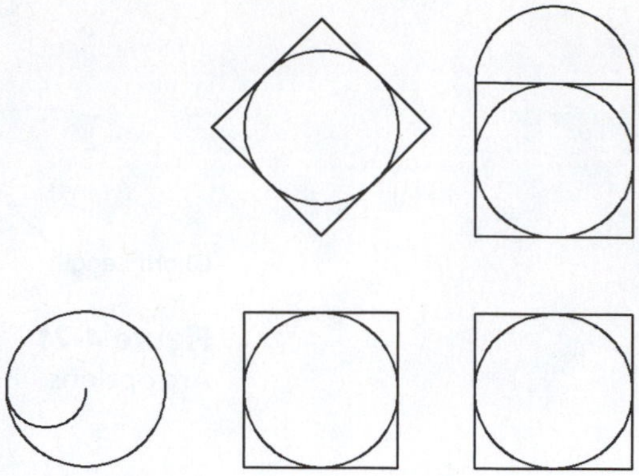

Figure 4-24
Start, End, Angle arc

8 Type **1,3<Enter>** to specify the center of the circle. A preview image of the arc appears, and a rubber-band line stretches from the start of the arc. AutoCAD prompts you to *Specify included angle:*.

9 Drag the cursor up and type **180<Enter>.** AutoCAD draws an arc with a 180° included angle from the start point to the endpoint in a counterclockwise direction. Your drawing should look like Figure 4-24.

10 Press **<Enter>** to repeat the **ARC** command. AutoCAD prompts you to *Specify start point of arc or* ↓.

11 Press **<Enter>** to continue an arc from the end of the last arc. AutoCAD stretches a tangent arc from the end of the last arc and prompts you to *Specify endpoint of arc:*.

12 Drag the cursor to the right and type **1<Enter>** to specify the right quadrant of the circle. AutoCAD places the arc tangent to the first arc. Your drawing should look like Figure 4-25.

13 Save your drawing.

Figure 4-25
A continued arc

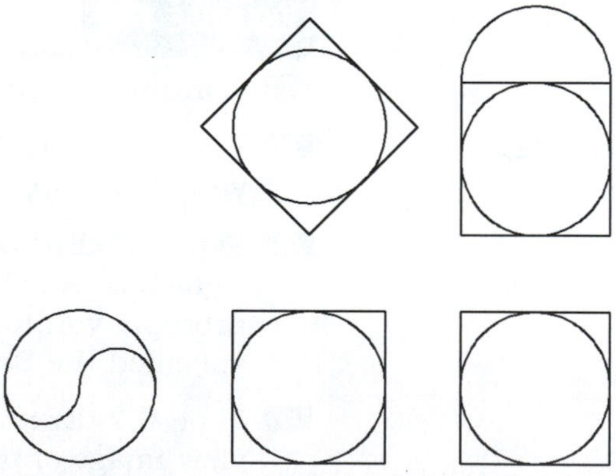

ELLIPSE	
Ribbon & Panel:	Home | Draw 
Draw Toolbar:	
Menu:	Draw | Ellipse
Command Line:	ELLIPSE
Command Alias:	EL

Drawing Ellipses

An ellipse (or oval) is similar in definition to a circle except that it has both a major and a minor radius (see Figure 4-26).

An ellipse is created with the **ELLIPSE** command.

You can construct an ellipse either by specifying the center point and points on the major and minor radii or by picking points on the major and minor axes.

Let's draw an ellipse.

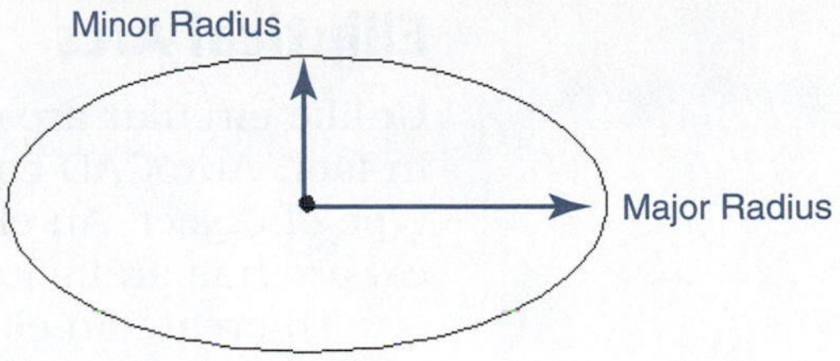

Figure 4-26
An ellipse

EXERCISE 4-13 **Drawing an Ellipse**

1. Continue from Exercise 4-12.
2. Toggle the **Ortho Mode** setting on.
3. Start the **ELLIPSE** command. AutoCAD prompts you to *Specify center of ellipse:*.
4. Type **1,6<Enter>**. AutoCAD drags a rubber-band line from the point. AutoCAD prompts you to *Specify endpoint of axis:*.
5. Pick a point 1 inch to the right of the first point. A rubber-band line stretches from the center point. AutoCAD prompts you to *Specify distance to other axis or* ↓.
6. Drag the mouse around to see how the shape of the ellipse changes as you move it. Pick a point 0.5 inch above the center point to create the ellipse. Your drawing should look like Figure 4-27.
7. Save your drawing.

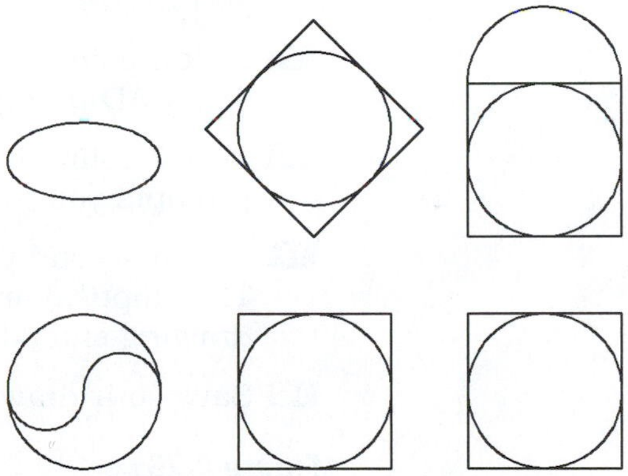

Figure 4-27
An ellipse

When drawing an ellipse, once you specify the major axis (by picking either a center and major radius or two points on the major axis), you'll have a **Rotation** option available. The **Rotation** option allows you to draw the ellipse as though it is a circle being viewed from an angle. Imagine holding a hula hoop directly in front of you so it looks like a circle. Now imagine tilting the hula hoop away from you. The outline of the tilted circle is now an ellipse. When using the **Rotation** option, you are specifying that tilt angle. A tilt angle of 0 will draw a circular ellipse (the major and minor axes are equal). You can specify a maximum tilt angle of 89.4°. Figure 4-28 shows the results of different rotation angles.

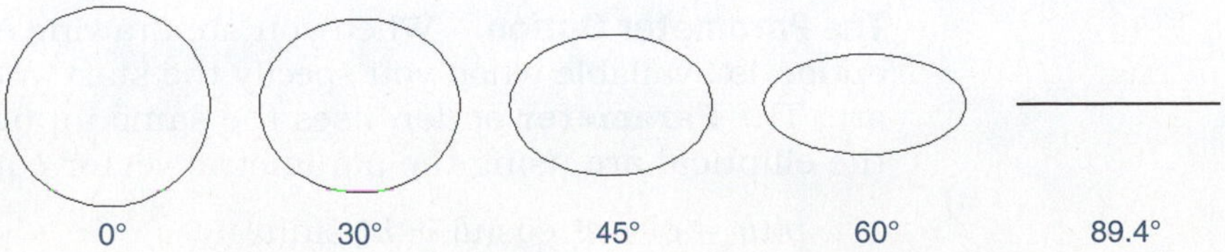

Figure 4-28
The **Rotation** option values of the **ELLIPSE** command

Elliptical Arcs

Unlike circular arcs, elliptical arcs are drawn with the **ELLIPSE** command. In fact, AutoCAD considers an ellipse and an elliptical arc as the same type of object. An ellipse has an included angle of 360, whereas an elliptical arc has an included angle less than 360.

To create an elliptical arc, start the **ELLIPSE** command and select the **Arc** option or choose the **Ellipse Arc** tool from the **Draw** panel. Once you have defined the ellipse, you are prompted for the start angle and end angle. Like circular arcs, AutoCAD draws the elliptical arcs from the start angle to the end angle in a counterclockwise direction.

EXERCISE 4-14 Drawing an Elliptical Arc

1. Continue from Exercise 4-13.
2. Select the **Undo** tool and undo the ellipse drawn in Exercise 4-13.
3. Toggle the **Ortho Mode** setting on.
4. Choose the **Ellipse Arc** tool from the **Draw** panel. AutoCAD prompts you to *Specify axis endpoint of ellipse or* ↓.
5. Type **0,6<Enter>**. AutoCAD drags a rubber-band line from the point. AutoCAD prompts you to *Specify other endpoint of axis:*.
6. Pick a point 2 inches to the right of the first point. AutoCAD will calculate the midpoint of that line and use it for the center of the ellipse. A rubber-band line stretches from this center point. AutoCAD prompts you to *Specify distance to other axis or* ↓.
7. Pick a point 0.5 inch above the center point to create the ellipse. AutoCAD prompts you to *Specify start angle or* ↓.
8. Pick a point at 0° along the ellipse to specify the start angle. AutoCAD prompts you to *Specify end angle or* ↓.
9. Pick a second point at 90° along the ellipse to specify the end angle. The elliptical arc is created between the start and end angles. Your drawing should look like Figure 4-29.
10. Save your drawing.

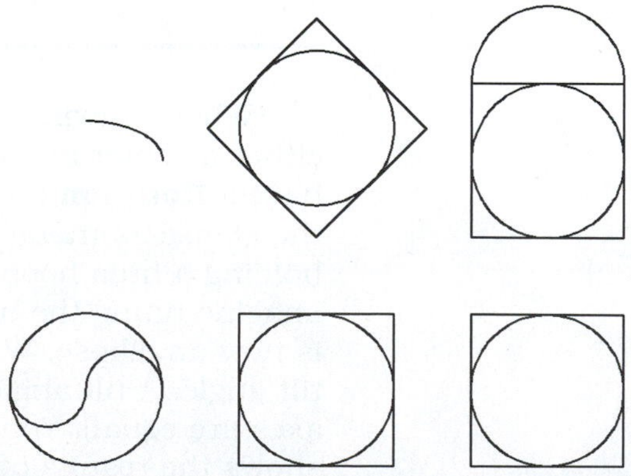

Figure 4-29
The **Angle** option of the **ELLIPSE** command

The Parameter Option. When you are drawing elliptical arcs, the **Parameter** option is available when you specify the start and end angles of the elliptical arc. The **Parameter** option uses the same input as start angle but creates the elliptical arc using the parametric vector equation

$$p(u) = c + a^* \cos(u) + b^* \sin(u)$$

where c is the center of the ellipse, and a and b are its major and minor axes, respectively.

FOR MORE DETAILS

See the AutoCAD **Help** file for more detailed information on using the **Parameter** option.

Points

point: A one-dimensional object that is defined as a single coordinate in space. Points have no length or width, only a coordinate location.

Another basic drawing object is the ***point***. To draw a point, AutoCAD simply prompts you to specify a point.

POINT	
Ribbon & Panel:	Home | Draw 
Draw Toolbar:	
Menu:	Draw | Point
Command Line:	POINT
Command Alias:	PO

POINT STYLE	
Ribbon & Panel:	None
Toolbar:	None
Menu:	Format | Point Style...
Command Line:	DDPTYPE
Command Alias:	None

EXERCISE 4-15 Drawing a Point

1. Continue from Exercise 4-14.
2. Start the **POINT** command. AutoCAD prompts you to *Specify a point:*.
3. Pick a point on the screen. AutoCAD will place a point object.
4. Press **<Enter>** or **<Esc>** to end the command.

Points can be difficult to see. By default, points appear as dots with no real size or shape. When you zoom in on a point, it does not get larger. If you place a point directly on top of another object, you might not see it at all. However, you can change the appearance of points to make them easier to spot.

Point Styles

When you start the **POINT** command, AutoCAD shows you the current value of the **PDMODE** and **PDSIZE** system variables in the command line.

```
Current point modes: PDMODE=0.0000
PDSIZE=0.0000
```

NOTE

Keep in mind that the point style and the point size are global settings, meaning that all the points in the drawing are affected by these settings. You cannot have one point displayed using one point style and another point with a different style.

These variables control the look (style) and size of points in your drawing. The **DDPTYPE** command allows you to set the **PDMODE** and **PDSIZE** system variables.

NOTE

You can choose a point style that will make all points invisible (**PDMODE = 1**). When this point style is selected, points in your drawing will not be displayed on your screen but can still be moved, copied, erased, etc.

When you start the **DDPTYPE** command, the **Point Style** dialog box appears (see Figure 4-30).

You can choose the desired point style as well as specify a display size for the points. Point size can be entered as an absolute size (for example, 0.1″) or

Figure 4-30
The **Point Style** dialog box

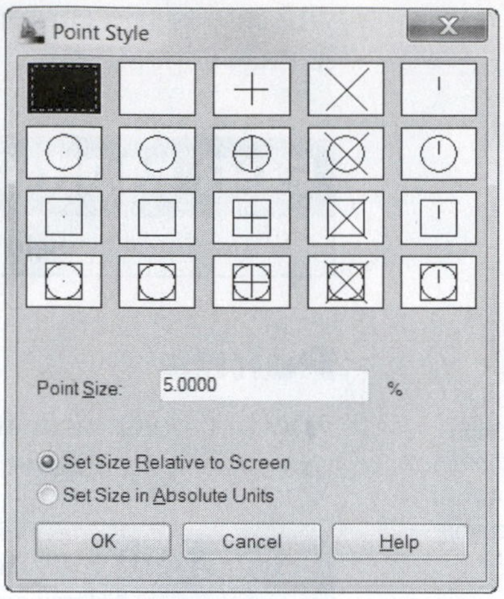

as a relative size (a percentage of the display height). When using a relative point size, AutoCAD will recalculate the point size every time the drawing regenerates.

EXERCISE 4-16 Changing the Point Style

1. Continue from Exercise 4-15.
2. Type **DDPTYPE <Enter>**. The **Point Style** dialog box is displayed.
3. Choose the point style shown in Figure 4-31 and choose **OK** to close the dialog box.
4. Type **REGEN<Enter>** to regenerate your drawing. AutoCAD updates the point display.
5. Save your drawing.

Figure 4-31
Choosing a point style

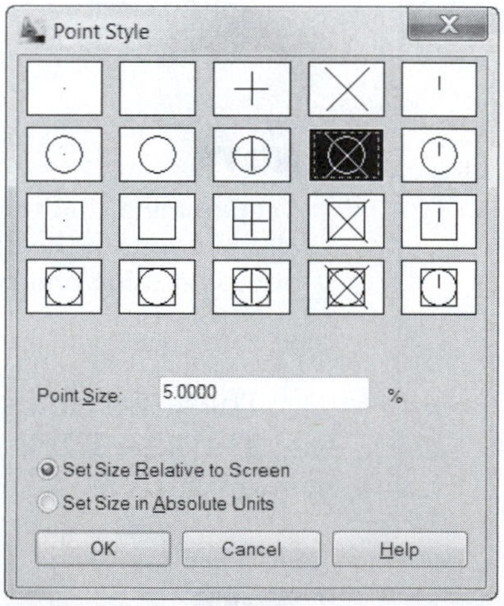

The values for **PDMODE** and their associated shapes are shown in Figure 4-32.

When you use the **POINT** command, the values shown for **PDSIZE** will be either positive numbers or negative numbers. Positive numbers indicate an absolute size, and negative numbers indicate a percentage of the view-port height. For example, a **PDSIZE** value of −**10.0** would make points 10% of the current display area. A value of **(+)10** would create points that were

Figure 4-32
PDMODE values and their associated point styles

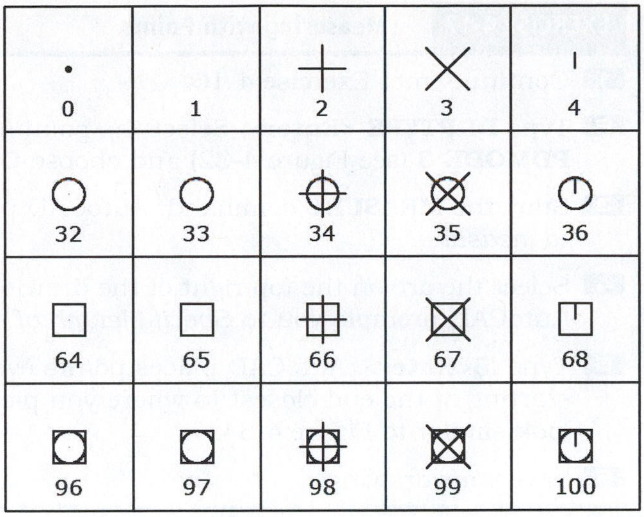

10 units tall. A **PDSIZE** value of **0.0** will default the point size to 5% of the current display height. The **PDSIZE** variable has no effect when **PDMODE** is set to **0** (a dot) or **1** (blank).

Points can be used for a number of things, including simple markers, and AutoCAD uses them when dimensioning. Points are also used as measurement indicators in the **MEASURE** and **DIVIDE** commands.

MEASURE	
Ribbon & Panel:	Home | Draw 
Toolbar:	None
Menu:	Draw | Point | Measure
Command Line:	MEASURE
Command Alias:	ME

DIVIDE	
Ribbon & Panel:	Home | Draw 
Toolbar:	None
Menu:	Draw | Point | Divide
Command Line:	DIVIDE
Command Alias:	DIV

Measure and Divide

The **MEASURE** and **DIVIDE** commands are used to automatically place point objects at regular intervals along an existing object. The **MEASURE** command places points at a specified distance along an object, whereas the **DIVIDE** command places points so that the object is divided into a specified number of segments.

> **NOTE**
> Although the command names imply otherwise, the **MEASURE** and **DIVIDE** commands are simply methods of placing point objects. The **DISTANCE** command allows you to measure distances, and the **BREAK** command (Chapter 8) allows you to break an object into multiple pieces.

Measure. The **MEASURE** command will prompt you to select an object and then ask you to specify a length. AutoCAD will then place points along the object at the specified interval, starting at the end closest to where you selected the object. For example, in Figure 4-33, if you selected the arc near point 1, AutoCAD would measure the distances from endpoint 1. If you selected the arc near point 2, AutoCAD would measure the distances starting at endpoint 2.

Points are not placed on the endpoints of objects, and points are placed until the remaining distance is less than the specified distance.

Figure 4-33
Selecting the object to be measured

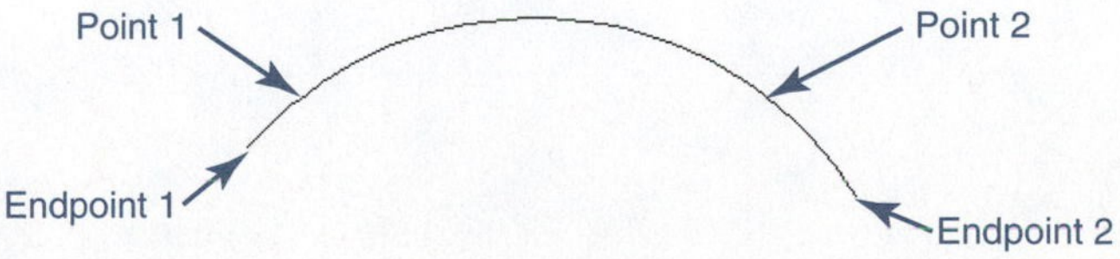

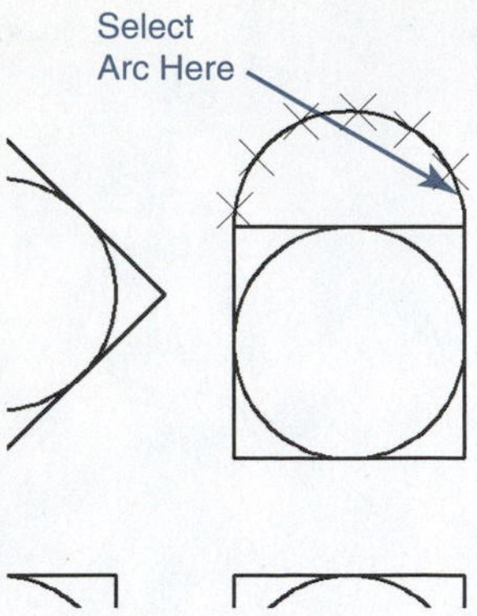

Figure 4-34
Placing points with **MEASURE**

EXERCISE 4-17 Measuring with Points

1. Continue from Exercise 4-16.
2. Type **DDPTYPE <Enter>.** Select the point style that corresponds to **PDMODE 3** (see Figure 4-32) and choose **OK**.
3. Start the **MEASURE** command. AutoCAD prompts you to *Select object to measure:*.
4. Select the arc on the top right of the drawing, as shown in Figure 4-34. AutoCAD prompts you to *Specify length of segment or* ↓.
5. Type **.5<Enter>**. AutoCAD places points every .5 unit along the arc starting at the end closest to where you picked. Your drawing should look similar to Figure 4-34.
6. Save your drawing.

Divide. The **DIVIDE** command prompts you to select an object and then asks for the number of segments. The number must be an integer between 2 and 32767; decimals or fractions are not allowed. AutoCAD will then place points along the object at equal intervals that divide the object into the specified number of segments.

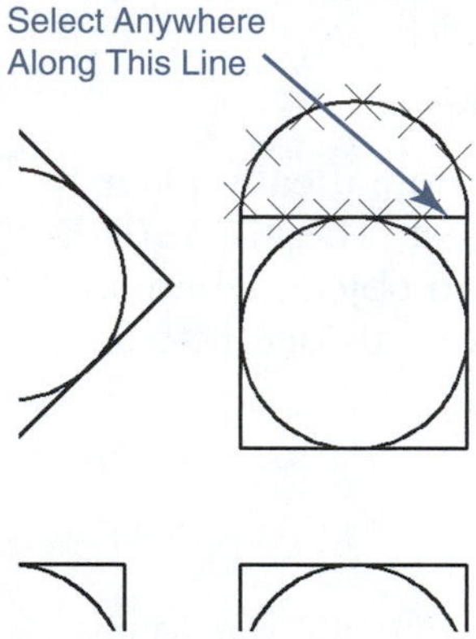

Figure 4-35
Placing points with **DIVIDE**

EXERCISE 4-18 Dividing Objects with Points

1. Continue from Exercise 4-17.
2. Start the **DIVIDE** command. AutoCAD prompts you to *Select object to divide:*.
3. Pick anywhere along the line object on the top right of the drawing, as shown in Figure 4-35. AutoCAD prompts you to *Enter the number of segments or* ↓.
4. Type **5<Enter>**. AutoCAD places 4 points along the line that divide the line into 5 equal pieces. The line object has not been changed or broken. Points have just been placed on top of the line. Your drawing should now look like Figure 4-35.
5. Save your drawing.

Like the **MEASURE** command, the **DIVIDE** command does not place points at the endpoints of objects. It will always place one point less than the number of segments you specify (for example, specifying 5 segments creates 4 points, 10 segments creates 9 points, etc.).

Both the **MEASURE** and **DIVIDE** commands have a **Block** option. This option allows you to substitute a block reference for the point objects.

FOR MORE DETAILS

See page 651 in Chapter 16 for more detailed information about blocks.

Chapter Summary

The quickest and easiest way to start a new drawing is to base it on a predefined AutoCAD drawing template, or DWT, file. When you start the **NEW** command, AutoCAD automatically opens the default **Template** folder and displays a list of predefined DWT template drawings that come with AutoCAD. Some even have predefined borders and title blocks. You can use these drawings as a starting point for your new drawings, or you can create your own using the **SAVEAS** command. Either way, it is a great time-saving feature.

AutoCAD comes with five different linear and angular unit settings that can be changed using the **UNITS** command. If you are using the default **acad.dwt** template, drawing units are set to decimal inches. Setting linear units to either **Architectural** or **Engineering** allows you to input feet by using the apostrophe (') after a number and inches by using the quote symbol ("). Using the **LIMITS** command, you can define a drawing area in model space that can be used to define the grid area and area displayed when the **ZOOM** command is used with the **All** option.

Point coordinates can be entered using a variety of different methods in AutoCAD. The most basic is absolute coordinate entry where you specify an *x* and a *y* position. Relative coordinates allow you to place points "relative" to the last point using the @ prefix, whereas polar coordinates allow you to specify a distance and angle using the < symbol to separate the two. Dynamic input allows you to automatically combine all of the methods visually at the current cursor location.

Finally, learning how to master drawing basic objects such as lines, circles, and arcs lays the groundwork for creating the more complex objects and techniques discussed later in the textbook. Elliptical objects can be used to represent circles shown at a specific angle of rotation or by indicating a major and a minor axis. Point styles allow you to represent points so that they are useful for dividing objects into a specific number of equal segments or measuring the specified distance along an object.

Chapter Test Questions

Multiple Choice

Circle the correct answer.

1. The @ symbol is used to denote:

a. Relative coordinate entry
b. Polar coordinate systems
c. Cartesian coordinate systems
d. Absolute coordinate entry

2. Drawing templates have the file extension:

a. DWF
b. DWT
c. DXF
d. DWG

3. Which drawing units are specifically based on imperial (feet-inches) units?

a. Decimal and engineering
b. Engineering and architectural
c. Architectural and fractional
d. Fractional and scientific

4. Which of the following is an example of polar coordinate entry?
   a. 3,0 c. 3<90
   b. 3>90 d. 90<3
5. Which of the following is an example of relative coordinate entry?
   a. 3<4 c. 3d90
   b. 3<90 d. @3,4
6. By default, in which direction are positive angles measured in AutoCAD?
   a. 90° c. Counterclockwise
   b. Clockwise d. Depends on where you pick
7. Which of the following is **not** a valid method of drawing a circle?
   a. **Center Radius** c. Tangent tangent radius
   b. 2 points on the diameter d. Center circumference
8. Which of the following is **not** a valid method for constructing an arc?
   a. **Start, End, Length** c. **Start, Center, Length**
   b. **Start, End, Radius** d. **3-Point**
9. Drawing templates:
   a. Cannot be created in AutoCAD
   b. Cannot contain geometry; only drawing settings are stored
   c. Can contain both geometry and drawing settings
   d. Can be stored only in a specific folder on your computer
10. Points:
    a. Do not plot
    b. Cannot be erased or modified
    c. Cannot change their appearance
    d. Are stored as a single coordinate in space

Matching

Write the number of the correct answer on the line.

a. Drawing template ______	1. A system of locating points using the *X*- and *Y*-axes
b. Cartesian coordinate system ______	2. N32d8′26″E
c. Scientific unit display ______	3. Command used to place points at a specified interval along an object
d. **DIVIDE** ______	4. The active drawing area. In layout space, it determines the size of your paper
e. Circle ______	5. A drawing object defined by a center point and a radius length
f. **MEASURE** ______	6. A drawing file used as a starting point when creating new drawings
g. Point objects ______	7. 1.4200E+01
h. Architectural units ______	8. Command used to place points at equal distances along an object

i. Drawing limits _____

j. Surveyor's units _____

9. 4'-8 3/16"

10. A system of locating points using distance and direction

True or False

Circle the correct answer.

1. **True or False:** The **UNITS** command controls how precisely coordinates are stored in the drawing.
2. **True or False:** The **Length** option in the **ARC** command determines the actual arc length.
3. **True or False:** An ellipse must have different major and minor axis lengths.
4. **True or False:** Architectural units are based on imperial (feet-inch) units.
5. **True or False:** A circle can be drawn tangent to three objects.
6. **True or False:** Point objects do not plot.
7. **True or False:** The **MEASURE** command is used to measure the distance between two points.
8. **True or False:** The **DIVIDE** command will break an object into equal length pieces.
9. **True or False:** Drawings can use only imperial or metric units.
10. **True or False:** Point styles can be set separately for each point.

Chapter Projects

G Project 4-1: *Lines, Circle, and Arcs* [BASIC]

1. Start a new drawing using the **acad.dwt** template.
2. Draw the lines, circles, and arcs shown in Figure 4-36. **Do not** draw dimensions. *Hint:* Use the **Tan, Tan, Tan** circle option to place the corner circles.
3. Save the drawing as ***P4-1***.

Figure 4-36

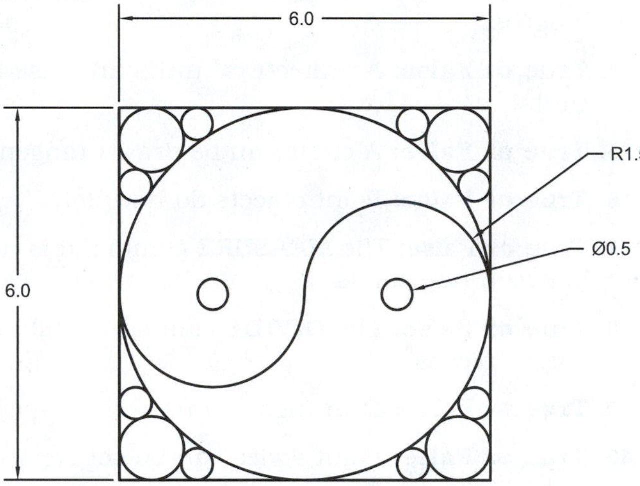

M Project 4-2: *B-Size Mechanical Border* [INTERMEDIATE]

1. Start a new drawing using the **acad.dwt** template.
2. Set the limits for a 17″ × 11″ drawing area.
3. Draw the border as shown in Figure 4-37. **Do not** draw dimensions.
4. Zoom to the drawing extents.
5. Save the drawing to a template file as ***Mechanical B-Size.DWT***.

A Project 4-3: *Architectural D-Size Border (36 × 24)* [ADVANCED]

1. Start a new drawing using the **acad.dwt** template.
2. Set linear units to **Architectural** with precision set to **1/16″**.
3. Set angular units to **Deg/Min/Sec** with precision set to **0d00′00″**.
4. Set limits to **36″ × 24″** for a D-size drawing.
5. Draw the border as shown in Figure 4-38. **Do not** draw dimensions.

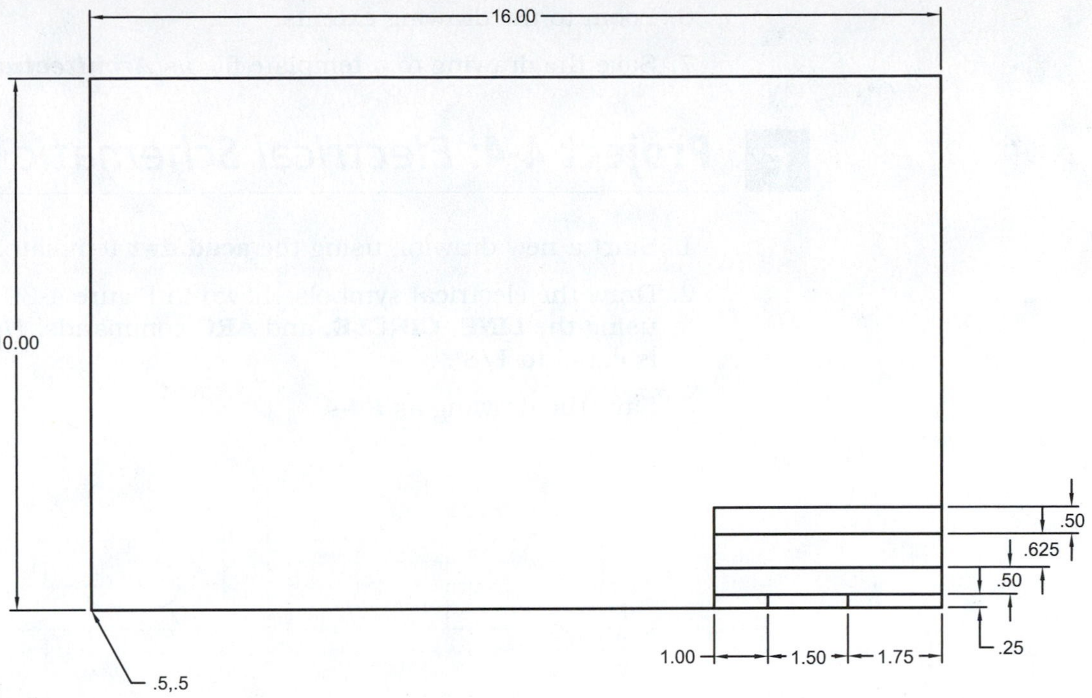

Figure 4-37

Figure 4-38

6. Zoom to the drawing extents.
7. Save the drawing to a template file as ***Architectural D-Size.DWT***.

E Project 4-4: *Electrical Schematic* [BASIC]

1. Start a new drawing using the **acad.dwt** template.
2. Draw the electrical symbols shown in Figure 4-39 at the sizes shown using the **LINE, CIRCLE,** and **ARC** commands. *Hint:* Each grid square is equal to 1/8″.
3. Save the drawing as ***P4-4***.

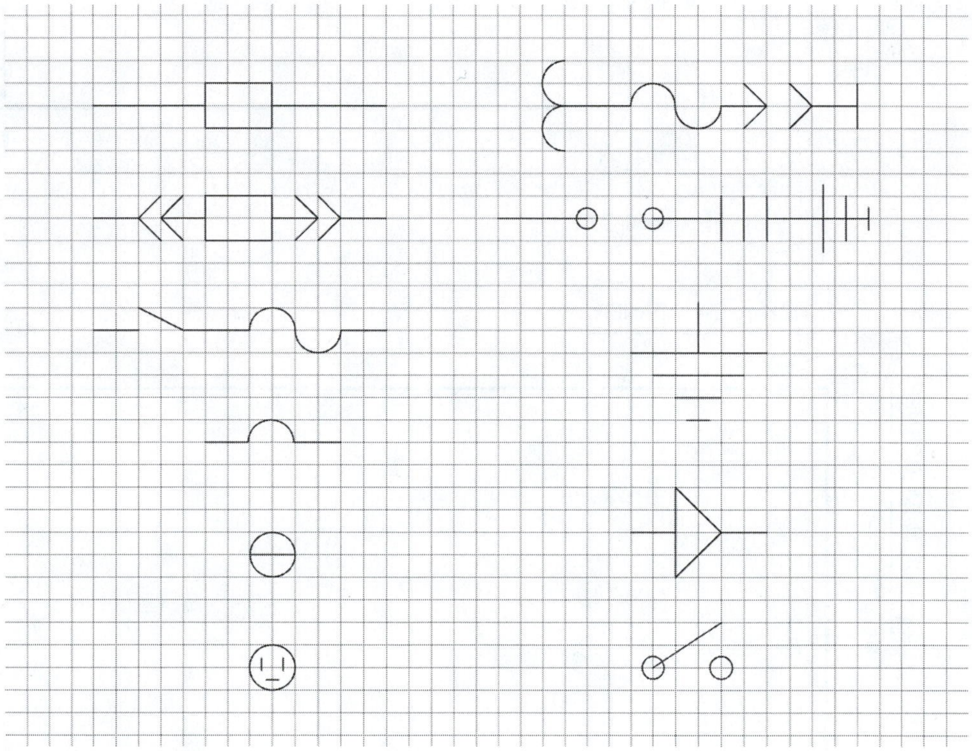

Figure 4-39

A Project 4-5: *Residential Architectural Plan* [ADVANCED]

1. Start a new drawing using the **acad.dwt** template.
2. Set linear units to **Architectural** with **Precision** set to **1/16″**.
3. Set the drawing limits so that the lower left limit is at **0,0** and the upper right limit is at **80′-0″, 60′-0″**.
4. Select the **Zoom All** tool to zoom out to the new larger drawing area.

5. Draw the building outline as shown in Figure 4-40. Place the corner of the building at 0,0 as shown. **Do not** include dimensions. *Hint:* Draw the outline in a counterclockwise direction.

6. Save the drawing as ***P4-5***.

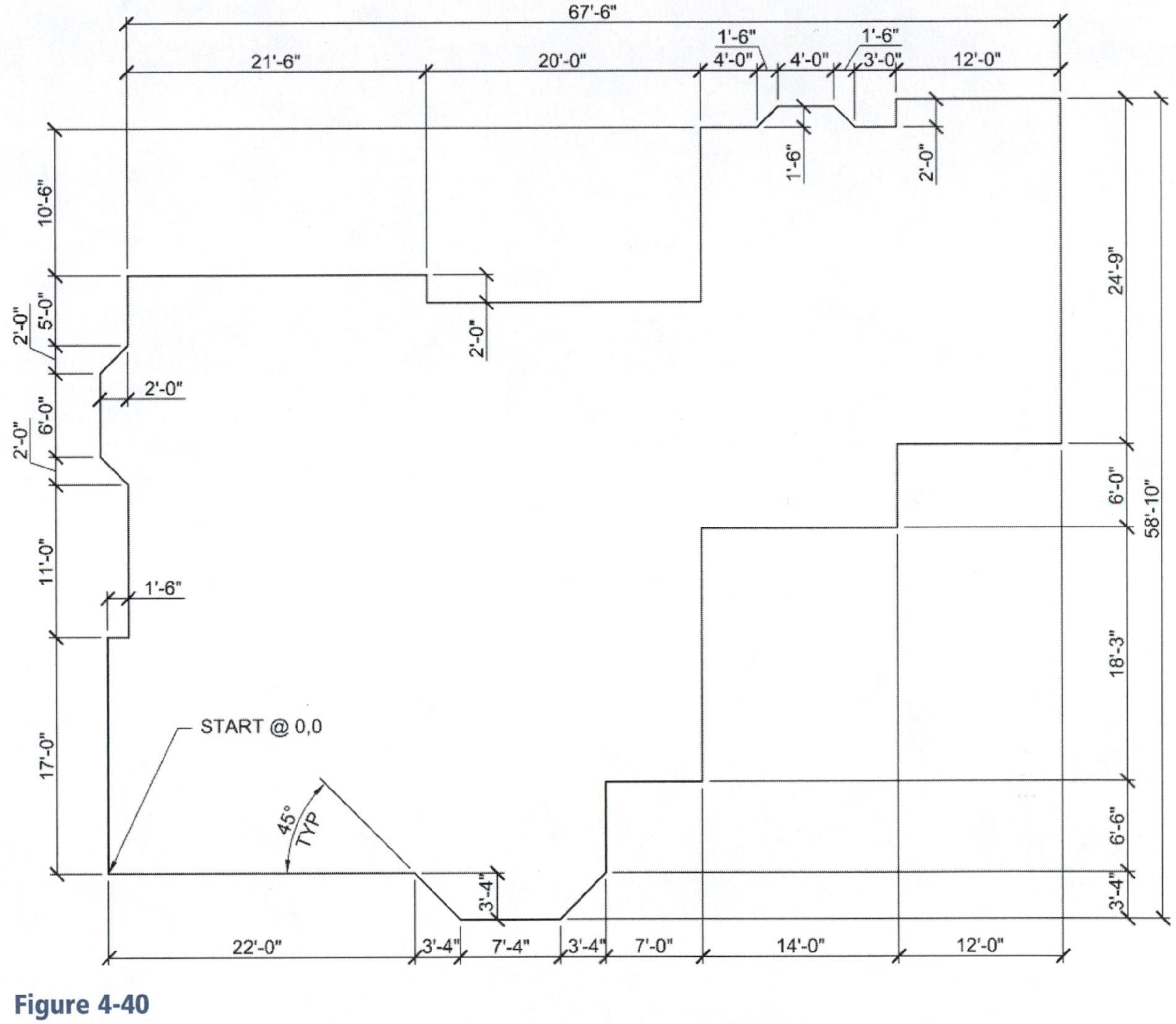

Figure 4-40

5 chapter five

Drawing Tools and Drafting Settings

CHAPTER OBJECTIVES

- Use the **Grid Display** and **Snap Mode** drawing tools to locate points quickly and precisely
- Draw orthogonally using the **Ortho Mode** drawing tool
- Draw at angles using the **Polar Tracking** drawing tool
- Use basic object snaps to locate points precisely relative to existing objects
- Defer object snaps to locate complex points
- Use advanced object snaps to locate points using acquired points and alignment paths
- Locate points relative to multiple objects by using the **Object Snap Tracking** feature to display multiple intersecting alignment path tracking vectors
- Control dynamic input settings
- Use construction lines to increase productivity and precision when creating multiple-view drawings

Introduction

Recall from Chapter 1 that two of the most important benefits of using CAD to create technical drawings are increased productivity and improved precision.

These benefits are achieved in AutoCAD primarily through the use of the drawing tools and drafting settings explained in this chapter.

Drawing tools are toggles that can be turned on and off as needed by clicking on the appropriate status bar buttons located at the bottom of the AutoCAD display window shown in Figure 5-1.

Figure 5-1
The AutoCAD status bar

Right-clicking with your mouse over a drawing tool button allows you to switch the status bar button display from icons to the traditional text-only label display by unchecking the **Use Icons** menu item, as shown in Figure 5-2.

Additional button-specific menu items are also included on each button's right-click shortcut menu so that you can quickly access the selected drawing tool's settings and features. The shortcut menu for the **Snap Mode** tool is shown in Figure 5-2.

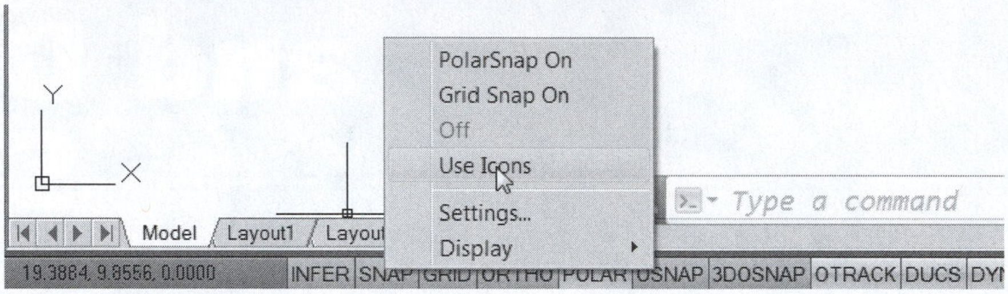

Figure 5-2
The status bar with traditional text-only buttons displayed

DRAFTING SETTINGS	
Menu:	Tools | Drafting Settings...
Command Line:	DSETTINGS
Command Alias:	DS or SE

Drawing tools can also be turned on and off using the function keys at the top of your keyboard, or they can be typed in at the AutoCAD command line. Each method is listed with the corresponding drawing tool throughout this chapter.

Most of the drawing tools work in conjunction with different drafting settings. For instance, the **Grid Display** button turns a grid display on and off, whereas the grid spacing (X and Y distance between grid lines) is controlled via the drafting settings. The grid spacing and other drafting settings are managed using the **Drafting Settings** dialog box shown in Figure 5-3.

NOTE

Any of the drawing tool buttons discussed in this chapter can be removed from the status bar via the **Status Bar** menu. To display the **Status Bar** menu, click on the down arrow at the far right of the status bar.

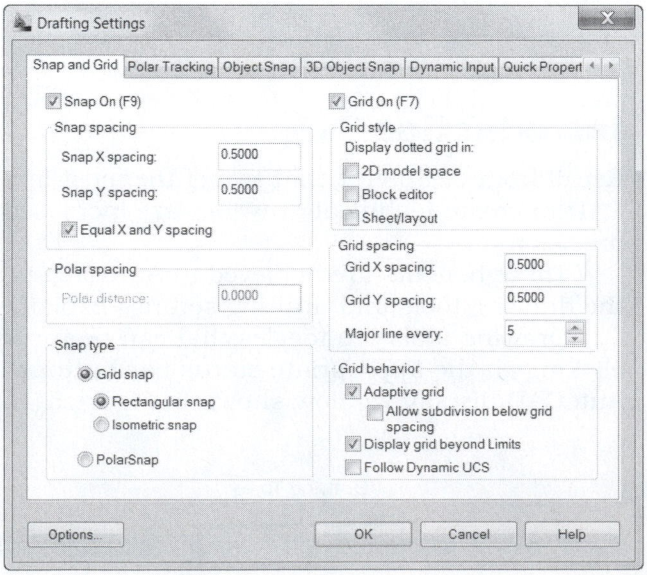

Figure 5-3
The **Drafting Settings** dialog box

FOR MORE DETAILS

See the section "Keyboard Commands" on page 51 in Chapter 1 for a complete list of function keys. See the "Status Bars" section on page 33 in Chapter 1 for more information about turning status bar features on and off.

The **Drafting Settings** dialog box can be displayed by selecting **Drafting Settings...** from the **Tools** menu or typing **DSETTINGS**. Even easier, you can right-click on any of the drawing tool buttons on the status bar to display a shortcut menu like the one shown in Figure 5-4 and select the **Settings...** menu item.

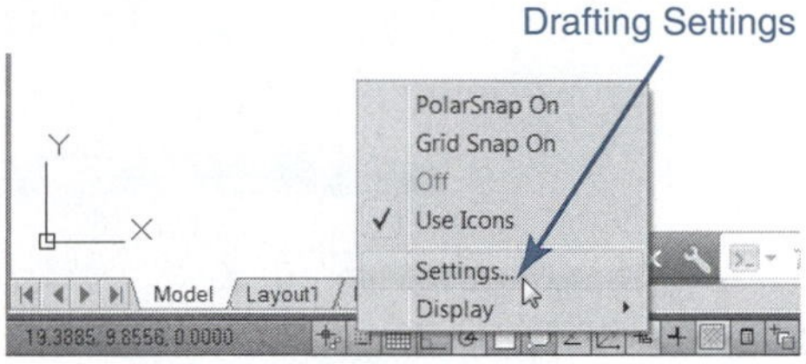

Figure 5-4
Drawing Tools right-click shortcut menu

TIP

All the drawing tools and drafting settings can be accessed when a command is active. This means that you can turn drawing tools on or off or change your drafting settings in the middle of most commands on an as-needed basis.

Grid Display

GRID DISPLAY	
Status Bar:	[grid icon] or GRID
Function Key:	F7
Command Line:	GRID
Keyboard Combo:	Ctrl+G

The *grid display* is a rectangular pattern of evenly spaced lines you can turn on in your drawing to help you visually locate points. It is similar to using a sheet of graph paper when drawing with pencil and paper, except that you can control the distance between the lines and can change them at any time using the **Drafting Settings** dialog box. The grid display does not plot and is provided strictly as a visual aid. *The grid display does not affect the cursor movement*—this feature is controlled by the **Snap** mode explained in the next section.

Figure 5-5 shows a drawing with the grid display turned on with the default spacing of 0.50″ between the lines in both the horizontal and vertical axes.

Setting the Grid Style

It is possible to set the grid display back to the old dot-style display on the **Snap and Grid** tab of the **Drafting Settings** dialog box shown in Figure 5-6. In fact, you can control it at different levels: 2D model space, the **Block Editor**, and in paper space layouts.

Setting the Grid Spacing

The horizontal and vertical spacing between the grid lines is controlled on the **Snap and Grid** tab of the **Drafting Settings** dialog box shown in

Figure 5-5
Grid display turned on

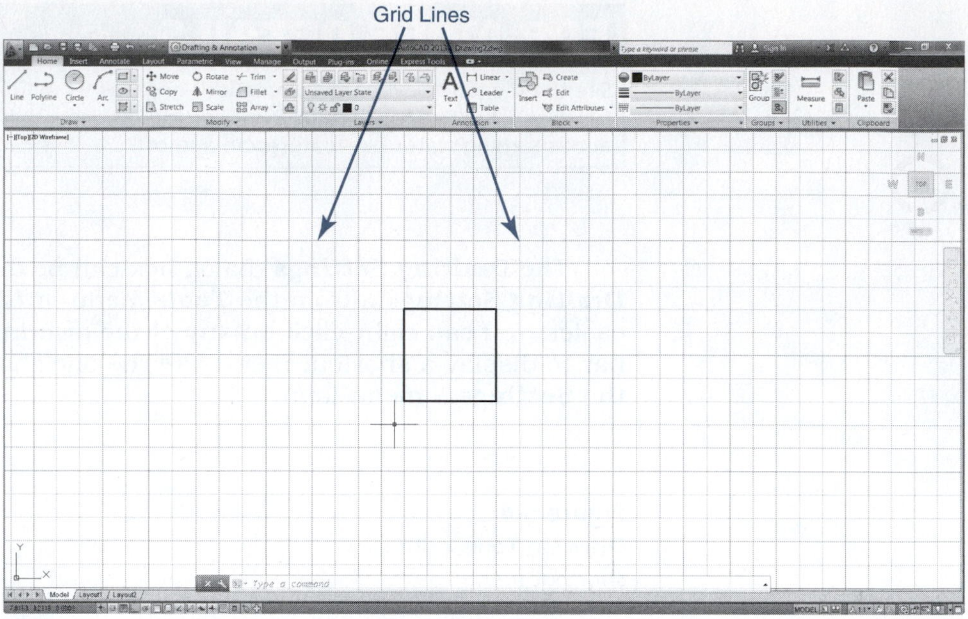

Figure 5-6
Grid display settings

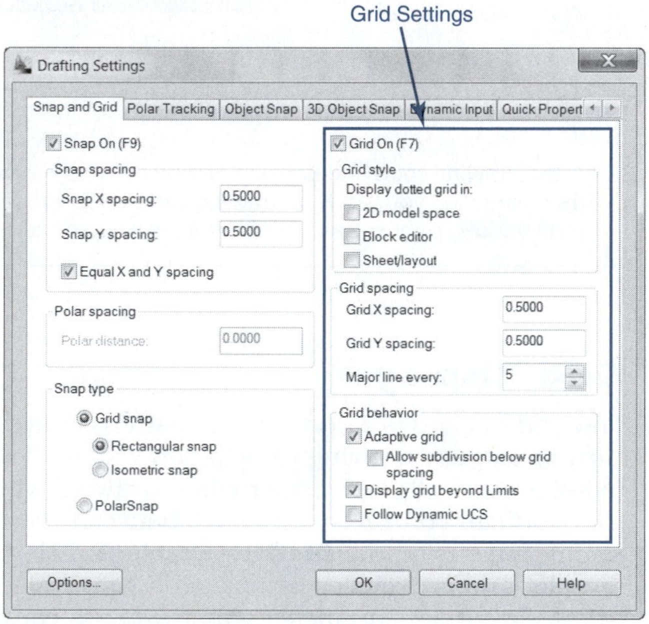

Figure 5-6. You can change the distance between the lines by specifying the **Grid X spacing** for the horizontal distance and the **Grid Y spacing** for the vertical distance. The X and Y distances are typically set to an equal value. In fact, when you try to change one distance, the other distance is updated automatically.

The **Major line every**: setting specifies the frequency of major grid lines compared to minor grid lines.

Controlling Grid Display Behavior

The settings in the **Grid behavior** section of the **Drafting Settings** dialog box are primarily used to control the appearance of the grid lines that are displayed when the current visual style is set to any visual style except **2D Wireframe**.

The **Adaptive grid** setting limits the density of the grid when the drawing is zoomed out using the **Major line every**: setting introduced earlier to turn minor grid lines off.

The **Allow subdivision below grid spacing** setting generates additional, more closely spaced grid lines when zoomed in. The spacing and frequency of these minor grid lines is determined by the frequency of the major grid lines.

The **Display grid beyond Limits** setting allows you to display the grid beyond the area specified by the **LIMITS** command.

The **Follow Dynamic UCS** setting is a 3D tool that allows you to automatically update the grid plane to follow the XY plane of the dynamic UCS.

SNAP MODE	
Status Bar:	[icon] or SNAP
Function Key:	F9
Command Line:	SNAP
Keyboard Combo:	Ctrl+B

Snap Mode

The **Snap Mode** drawing tool controls the movement of your cursor so that you can select points in your drawing only at specific X and Y increments. It is typically used in conjunction with the grid display explained in the previous section. The grid display provides the visual reference, whereas the **Snap** mode forces your pick points to be located precisely at specific coordinate locations.

By default, the X and Y spacing for both tools are set the same so that your cursor "snaps" directly to the grid display lines when both drawing tools are turned on at the same time. It is possible to set the X and Y spacing for grid and snap to different values, although it is recommended that they relate to each other to avoid confusion.

> **TIP**
>
> When **Snap Mode** is on, your cursor will not snap to grid points when selecting objects—only when specifying points. **Snap Mode** is temporarily turned off during the selection process so that it is easier to select objects.

Setting the Snap Spacing

The horizontal and vertical spacing between the snap points is controlled on the **Snap and Grid** tab of the **Drafting Settings** dialog box shown in Figure 5-7. You can change the distance between the snap points by

Figure 5-7
Snap mode settings

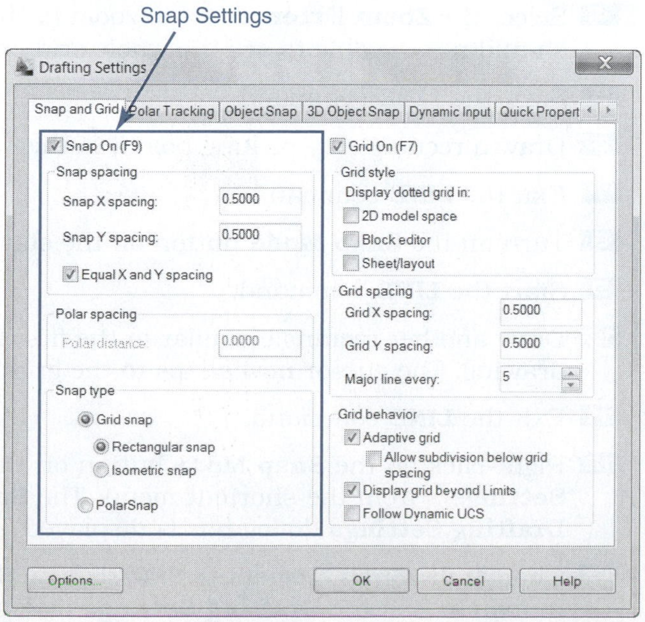

specifying the **Snap X spacing** for the horizontal distance and the **Snap Y spacing** for the vertical distance. The X and Y distances are typically set to an equal value. By default, when you try to change one distance the other distance is updated automatically. You must uncheck the **Equal X and Y spacing** check box shown in Figure 5-7 before setting values that are not the same.

As mentioned, it is possible to set the snap X and Y spacing to different values than the grid X and Y spacing, but it is suggested that one is an increment of the other. For instance, you might set the snap X and Y spacing to 0.25″, while the grid X and Y spacing remains at 0.50″. With these settings, your cursor will still snap to each grid and halfway between each grid line.

Setting the Snap Type and Style

There are two major types of **Snap** modes: **Grid snap** and **Polar snap.** You can switch between the different types using the option buttons in the **Snap type** section of the **Drafting Settings** dialog box shown in Figure 5-7. The default mode is **Grid snap,** which has two different styles:

- **Rectangular snap (default)** Traditional orthogonal snap pattern with rows and columns of snap points at the specified X and Y spacing
- **Isometric snap** Angled snap pattern where snap points are aligned at 30°, 90°, and 150° angles at the specified spacing so you can create isometric drawings

Polar snap mode is used with the **Polar Tracking** drawing tool so that you can snap to points along polar tracking vectors at the specified spacing. Polar tracking and the **Polar snap** mode are explained later in this chapter.

EXERCISE 5-1 Creating a Drawing Using Snap Mode and Grid Display

1. Start a new drawing using the **acad.dwt** drawing template.
2. Turn off all the drawing tool buttons on the status bar.
3. Turn on the **Grid Display** button on the status bar.
4. Select the **Zoom Extents** tool to zoom to the limits of the drawing. You should now be able to see the whole grid on the drawing display.
5. Start the **LINE** command.
6. Draw a rectangle by picking points in the drawing.
7. Exit the **LINE** command.
8. Turn on the **Snap Mode** button on the status bar.
9. Start the **LINE** command.
10. Draw another rectangle similar to the first by picking points in the drawing. The cursor now snaps to the grid lines on the screen.
11. Exit the **LINE** command.
12. Right-click on the **Snap Mode** button on the status bar and select **Settings...** from the shortcut menu. The **Snap and Grid** tab of the **Drafting Settings** dialog box is displayed (see Figure 5-7).
13. Change the **Snap X spacing** to **0.25**. The **Snap Y spacing** will change to match. Exit the **Drafting Settings** dialog box by selecting **OK**.

14 Start the **LINE** command.

15 Draw another rectangle by picking points in the drawing. The cursor now snaps both to the grid lines and to points halfway between the grid lines.

16 Exit the **LINE** command.

17 Save your drawing as ***CH5_EXERCISE1***.

ORTHO MODE	
Status Bar:	or ORTHO
Function Key:	F8
Command Line:	ORTHO
Keyboard Combo:	Ctrl+L

Ortho Mode

The **Ortho Mode** drawing tool restricts your cursor movement to the horizontal (*X*-) and vertical (*Y*-) axes so you can quickly draw horizontal and vertical lines at right angles (90°) to each other. This right-angle approach to drafting is often referred to as drawing "orthogonally"; hence the term *ortho*. Drawing with **Ortho** mode turned on allows you to draw rectangular objects quickly and be assured that all the angles are square.

> **NOTE**
>
> The **Ortho Mode** and **Polar Tracking** drawing tools described later in this chapter cannot be on at the same time. Turning the **Ortho Mode** button on immediately turns the **Polar Tracking** button off, and vice versa.

When **Ortho Mode** is turned off, the rubber-band line that indicates the cursor movement points at any angle you move your cursor, as shown in Figure 5-8A. When **Ortho Mode** is turned on, the rubber-band line that indicates the cursor direction follows the horizontal or vertical axis, depending on which axis is nearer to the cursor at the time, as shown in Figure 5-8B.

AutoCAD overrides **Ortho** mode when you enter coordinates at the command line or use any of the object snaps explained later in this chapter.

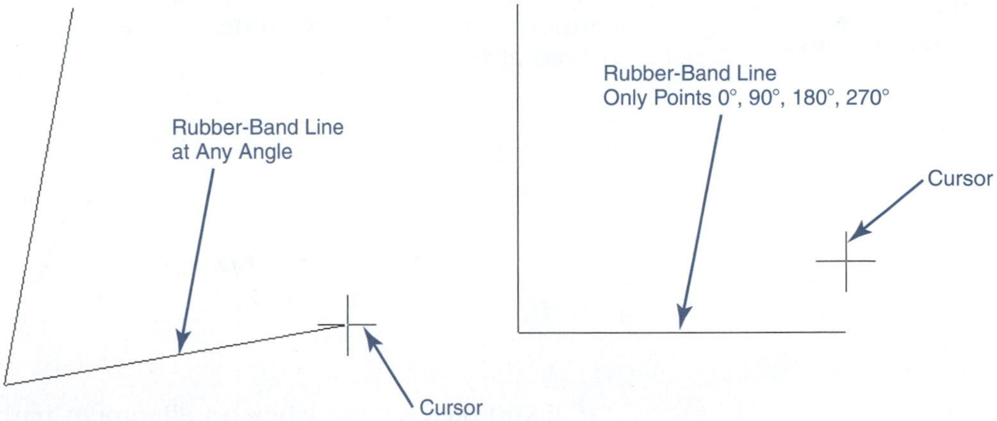

Figure 5-8
A Ortho Mode turned off
B Ortho Mode turned on

EXERCISE 5-2 Creating a Drawing Using Ortho Mode

1 Continue from Exercise 5-1.

2 **UNDO** or **ERASE** all of the line work from Exercise 5-1.

3 Turn off all the drawing tool buttons on the status bar.

4 Select the **Zoom Extents** tool to zoom to the limits of the drawing.

5 Turn the **Ortho Mode** button on.

6. Start the **LINE** command.
7. Type **2,2<Enter>** to specify the first point.
8. Drag the cursor to the right. The **Ortho** mode setting will lock the cursor movement to the 0° direction.
9. Type **2<Enter>**. AutoCAD draws a line 2 units to the right (angle of 0°).
10. Drag the cursor up (90°) and type **2<Enter>**. AutoCAD draws a line 2 units up (angle of 90°).
11. Drag the cursor to the left (180°) and type **2<Enter>**. AutoCAD draws a line 2 units to the left (angle of 180°).
12. Select the **Close** option. AutoCAD closes the square and exits the **LINE** command.
13. Save your drawing. Your drawing should look like Figure 5-9.

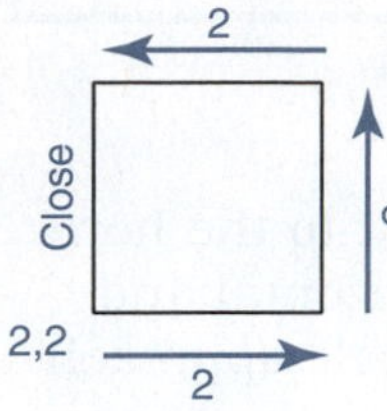

Figure 5-9
Drawing using **Ortho** mode

Polar Tracking

AutoTracking: AutoCAD feature that helps you draw objects at specific angles or in specific relationships to other objects.

POLAR TRACKING	
Status Bar:	[icon] or POLAR
Function Key:	F10
Command Line:	None
Keyboard Combo:	None

AutoCAD provides a feature called ***AutoTracking™*** that helps you to draw objects at specific angles using dashed lines known as *alignment paths.*

The **Polar Tracking** drawing tool utilizes AutoTrack so you can quickly draw and modify objects using preset polar angles. Polar tracking works by displaying a dashed alignment path and a polar tracking tooltip as you move your cursor around in a drawing that temporarily restricts your cursor movement to preset angle increments.

By default, the increment angle is set at 90° so that an alignment path is displayed at every 90° (0°, 90°, 180°, 270°, and 360°) when the **Polar Tracking** button is turned on. This provides the same basic functionality of the **Ortho Mode** drawing tool explained earlier in the chapter. As noted earlier, when you turn the **Polar Tracking** button on, the **Ortho Mode** button gets turned off automatically, and vice versa. Both drawing tools cannot be on at the same time. Figure 5-10 shows an alignment path displayed at 0°.

Figure 5-10
Polar tracking alignment path

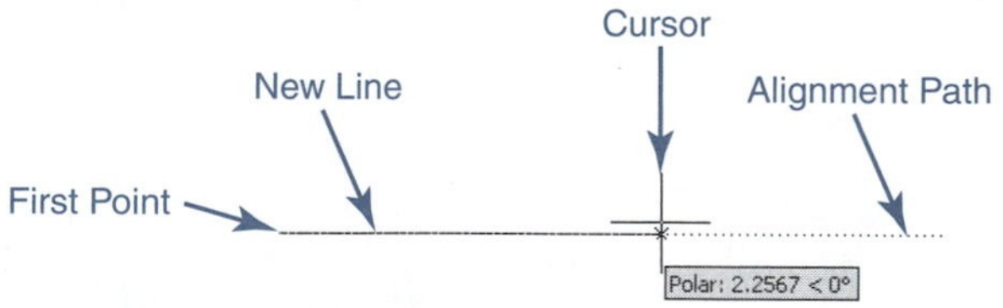

If you pick a point when an alignment path is displayed, the point is located at the distance and angle displayed in the polar tracking tooltip. Even better, it is possible to use the direct distance coordinate entry method explained in Chapter 4 to locate a point at a specified distance along an alignment path. Any time an alignment path is displayed, you can enter a distance, and AutoCAD will follow the alignment path the distance specified. For example, if you enter **2** in response to the *Specify next point or [**U**ndo]:* prompt while the 0° alignment path is displayed, as shown in Figure 5-10, a horizontal line segment 2 units long is created. Combining polar tracking with direct distance coordinate entry is one of the fastest and easiest ways to locate points in your drawings.

TIP

Polar tracking is not just for drawing objects. It also works with AutoCAD's modify tools. For example, using polar tracking, you can move objects at a specific angle and distance.

FOR MORE DETAILS

Using the AutoCAD **MOVE** command is explained on page 284 in Chapter 7.

Setting the Polar Tracking Angle and Measurement Method

The polar tracking settings are controlled on the **Polar Tracking** tab of the **Drafting Settings** dialog box shown in Figure 5-11.

Figure 5-11
Polar tracking settings

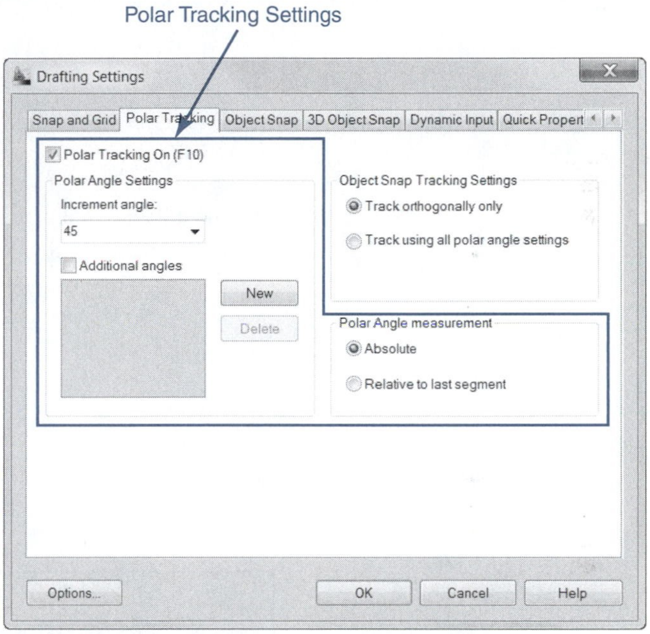

The polar tracking angle is set in the **Polar Angle Settings** area on the **Polar Tracking** tab. There are two polar angle settings:

- **Increment angle** A list of default preset angles ranging from 5° through 90° that controls the increment angle that polar tracking alignment paths are displayed. In Figure 5-11, a default increment angle of 45° has been selected so that a polar tracking alignment path will be displayed at every increment of 45° (0°, 45°, 90°, 135°, 180°, 225°, 270°, and 315°).
- **Additional angles** Additional angles that can be added using the **New** button. *These angles are not incremental.* Polar tracking alignment paths will be displayed only at each additional angle specified.

The polar tracking measurement method is set in the **Polar Angle measurement** area on the right side of the **Polar Tracking** tab. There are two **Polar Angle measurement** options:

- **Absolute** All polar tracking angles are measured from the current AutoCAD base angle setting. The default base angle setting is 0° due east or to the right.

- **Relative to last segment** Polar tracking angles are measured relative to the last segment, and the absolute angle is ignored.

Figures 5-12A through D show a square that is rotated at 45° being drawn with the **Polar Tracking** button turned on with an increment angle setting of 45° using the absolute method of angle measurement.

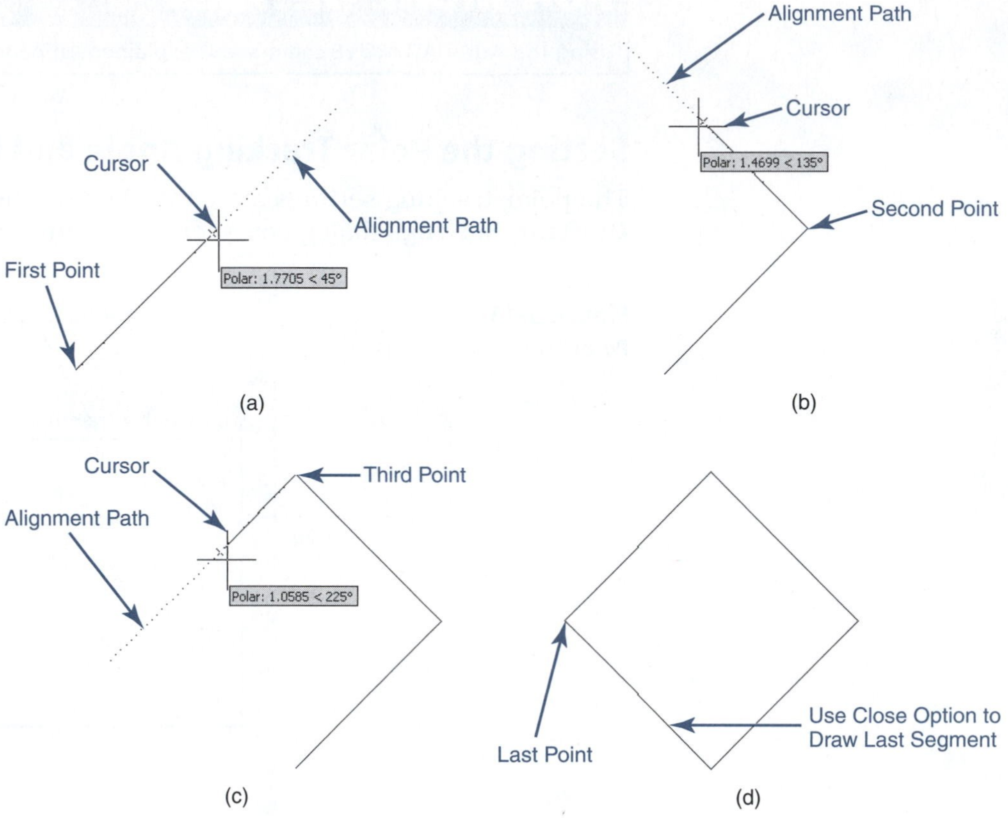

Figure 5-12
A Polar tracking alignment path at 45° **B** Polar tracking alignment path at 135° **C** Polar tracking alignment path at 225° **D** Completed 45° square

> **TIP**
>
> The AutoTrack settings are controlled via the **Drafting** tab of the **Options** dialog box. You can toggle on and off the following features: polar tracking alignment vectors, AutoTrack tooltips, and full-screen tracking vectors.

EXERCISE 5-3 Creating a Drawing Using Polar Tracking

1. Continue from Exercise 5-2.
2. Turn off all the drawing tool buttons on the status bar.
3. Right-click on the **Polar Tracking** button on the status bar and select **Settings...** from the shortcut menu. The **Polar Tracking** tab of the **Drafting Settings** dialog box is displayed (see Figure 5-11).
4. Change the **Increment angle** list box setting to **45°**. Make sure that the **Polar Angle measurement** setting is set to **Absolute**. Exit the **Drafting Settings** dialog box by selecting **OK**.
5. Turn the **Polar Tracking** button on.
6. Start the **LINE** command.
7. Type **3,5.5<Enter>** to specify the first point.

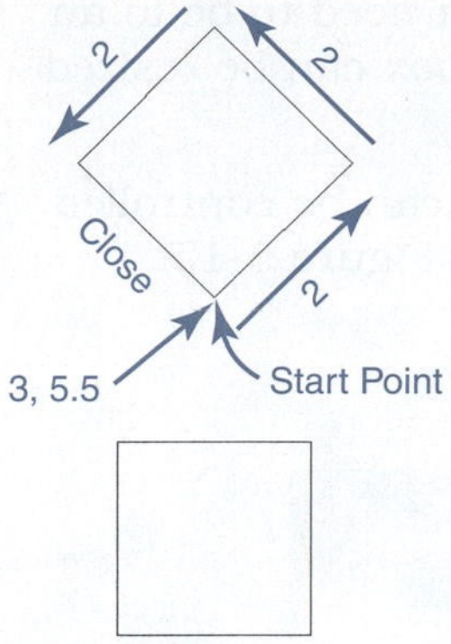

Figure 5-13
Drawing using polar tracking

8. Drag the cursor up to the right until a polar tracking alignment path is displayed at 45°.
9. Type **2<Enter>** while the alignment path is displayed. AutoCAD draws a line 2 units at the angle of 45°.
10. Drag the cursor up to the left until a polar tracking alignment path is displayed at 135°.
11. Type **2<Enter>** while the alignment path is displayed. AutoCAD draws a line 2 units at the angle of 135°.
12. Drag the cursor down to the left until a polar tracking alignment path is displayed at 225°.
13. Type **2<Enter>** while the alignment path is displayed. AutoCAD draws a line 2 units at the angle of 225°.
14. Select the **Close** option. AutoCAD closes the square and exits the command.
15. Save your drawing. Your drawing should look like Figure 5-13.

Object Snaps

Object snaps, or *osnaps* as they are sometimes called, are among the most essential features available in AutoCAD. Object snaps allow your cursor to snap to exact locations relative to existing objects in your drawing so that you can locate points precisely when you are drawing or editing. Using object snaps, you can snap to the endpoint of a line (Figure 5-14A); the center point of a circle (Figure 5-14B), or if a line and circle overlap, their point of intersection (Figure 5-14C), just to name a few. There are more than 15 different types of object snaps ranging from the basic to the advanced.

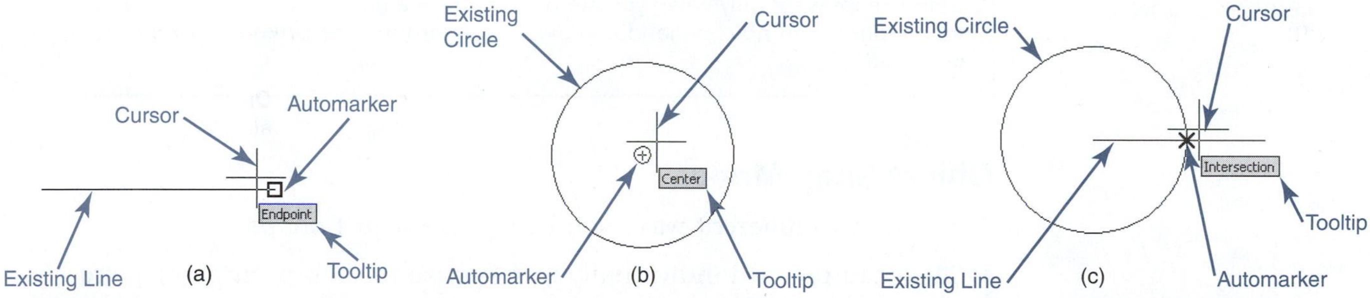

Figure 5-14
A Endpoint object snap **B Center** object snap **C Intersection** object snap

To help you use object snaps most effectively, a visual aid called *AutoSnap* is provided. AutoSnap provides the following features, most of which are on by default:

- **Marker** Displays the object snap type and location when the cursor moves over or near an object
- **Magnet** Feature that attracts and locks the cursor onto the object snap point when your cursor gets near an AutoSnap marker
- **Tooltip** Text description of the type of object snap you are snapping to in a small box at the cursor location

- **Aperture box** Boxed area that defines how close you need to be to an object to snap to an object snap point. The aperture box can be resized and turned on or off

All these settings, and a few others explained later, can be controlled on the **Drafting** tab of the **Options** dialog box shown in Figure 5-15.

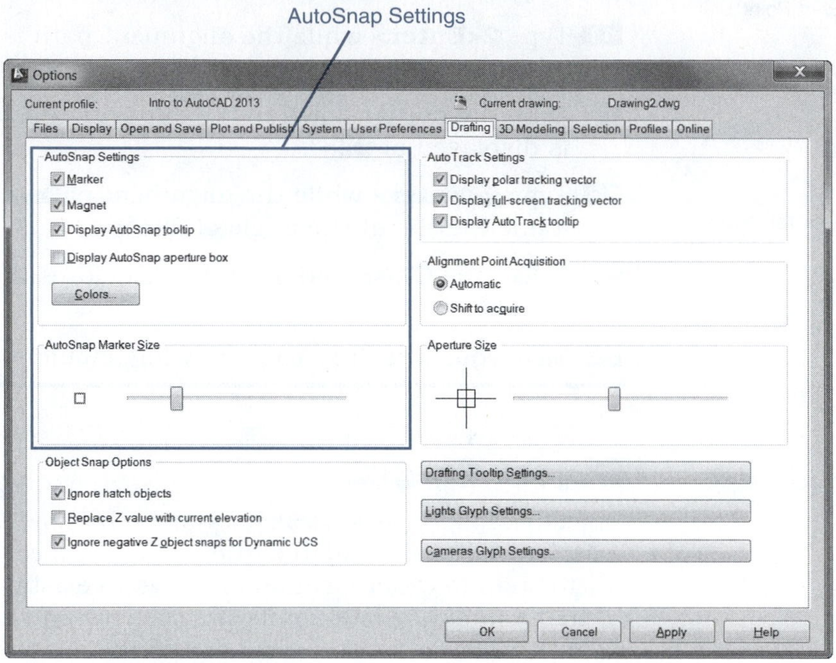

Figure 5-15
AutoSnap Settings on **Drafting** tab of the **Options** dialog box

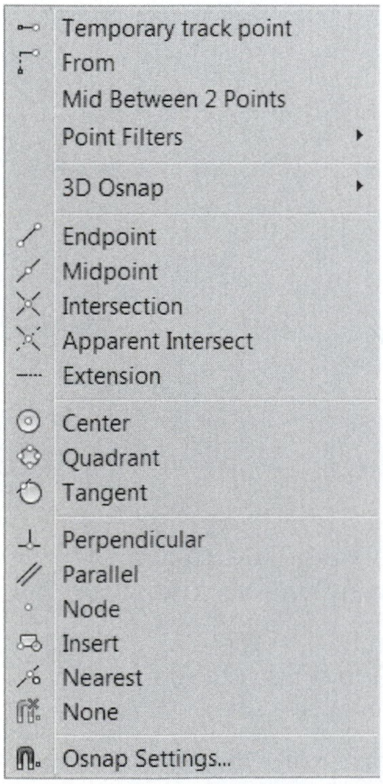

Figure 5-16
Right-click **Object Snap** shortcut menu

> **TIP**
>
> Object snaps work only when you are prompted for a point. If you try to use an object snap alone when no command is active, the error message *Unknown command* is displayed.

Object Snap Modes

There are two different ways you can utilize object snaps:

- They can be used individually in response to each prompt for point coordinate information.
- You can turn on one or more object snaps on the **Object Snap** tab of the **Drafting Settings** dialog box so that they are automatically active each time you are prompted to select a point.

Entering an object snap individually in response to a request for point information makes the object snap active for only one cursor pick point. *Each time AutoCAD prompts for a point you must respond with another object snap.* There are a couple of ways to enter an object snap using this approach:

- Select the object snap from the **Object Snap** right-click shortcut menu (see Figure 5-16). The **Object Snap** shortcut menu is displayed by holding down the **<Shift>** key on your keyboard while right-clicking with your mouse.

- Type the desired object snap at the command line in response to a point request. The following is an example of activating the **Endpoint** object snap by typing **end** at the command line in response to a prompt for a point:

  Specify first point: **end**

  Most object snaps can be specified by entering the first three or four characters of the object snap name. In fact, if you observe the command line while selecting an object snap using the right-click shortcut menu, you can glean what is being entered at the command line so you can type it in the next time.

The second approach to using object snaps is to turn on a select number of object snaps via the **Object Snap** tab of the **Drafting Settings** dialog box (see Figure 5-17) so that they are automatically activated each time you are prompted for a point location.

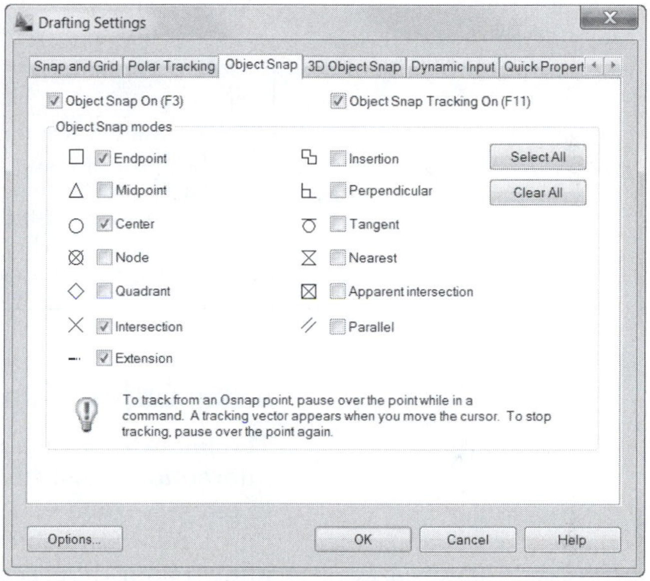

Figure 5-17
Setting running object snaps

This technique is typically referred to as *setting running object snaps* because the selected object snaps are always running in the background as you draw.

When your cursor gets close to any running object snap feature when you are selecting points in your drawing, an AutoSnap marker is automatically displayed so you can quickly snap to the corresponding feature.

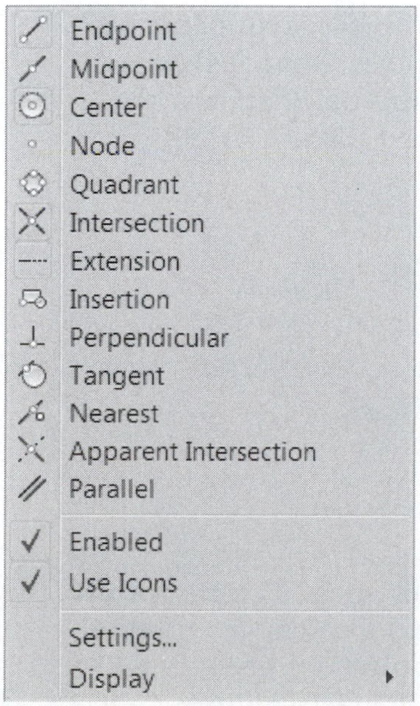

Figure 5-18
Object Snap shortcut menu

> **TIP**
> You can also set running object snaps by right-clicking on the **Object Snap** button and selecting the desired object snap from the shortcut menu shown in Figure 5-18.

Using running object snaps is typically considered the most efficient approach because it allows you to quickly locate objects precisely in your drawing without having to activate an object snap each time you need it. If you do need a particular object snap that is not currently active, you can always fall back on one of the individual object snap selection approaches explained earlier:

- Use the **<Shift>** key and the right-click shortcut menu.
- Type the object snap name at the command line.

When you activate an individual object snap this way, it is considered an override because you are temporarily suppressing any active running object snaps for a single point selection using the currently selected object snap. After a point is selected, all the running object snaps are active again until another object snap override is selected or object snaps are turned off using the **Object Snap** button on the status bar.

Sometimes when using running object snaps, you might need to select a point in your drawing without using any of the active running object snaps. The easiest thing to do is to disable running object snaps by turning off the **Object Snap** button on the status bar. It is also possible to activate the **None** object snap using one of the individual override methods. The **None** object snap turns object snaps off temporarily.

> **TIP**
>
> As you will discover in this chapter, there are many different object snaps that provide a wide array of features and functionality. You will want to be judicious as you start exploring and turning on different running object snaps. You definitely don't want to turn them all on at the same time. This will create confusion as you try to select points in your drawing. Select a few you use most often as running object snaps and then select others on an as-needed basis using the override approach.

Basic Object Snaps

The following object snaps are basic in nature and require minimal user interaction. Most involve a single point selection near the feature you want to snap to—end of a line, center of a circle, intersecting objects, and so on. Some of the object snaps in this section provide an additional feature, known as a ***deferred point***.

deferred point: Object snap feature that allows you to "build" the object snap point using multiple point selection input by deferring the first point selected.

Deferred object snaps allow you to "build" the object snap point by selecting additional points and/or objects. When an object snap is deferred, there is an ellipsis (...) displayed after the object snap AutoSnap marker, indicating that there are more selections required (see Figure 5-19).

Figure 5-19
Deferred object snap

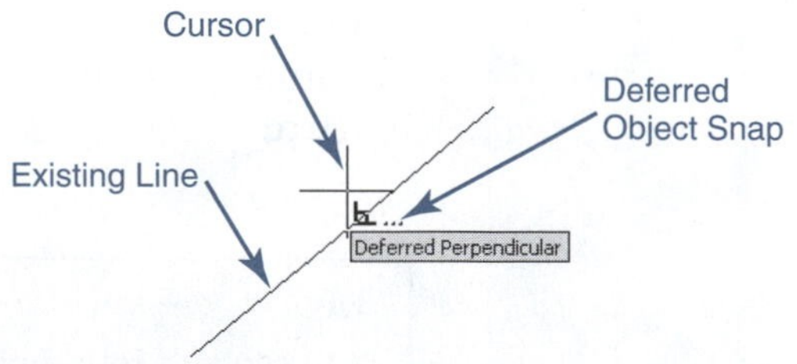

Endpoint. **Endpoint** is easily the most used object snap. The **Endpoint** object snap snaps to the closest endpoint of an arc, elliptical arc, line, multiline, polyline, spline, region, or ray. The **Endpoint** object snap will also snap to the closest corner of a trace, solid, or 3D face. Figures 5-20A and B show how to snap to the endpoint of a line using the **Endpoint** object snap when drawing a line.

Figure 5-20
A Using the **Endpoint** object snap—Step 1 **B** Using the **Endpoint** object snap—Step 2

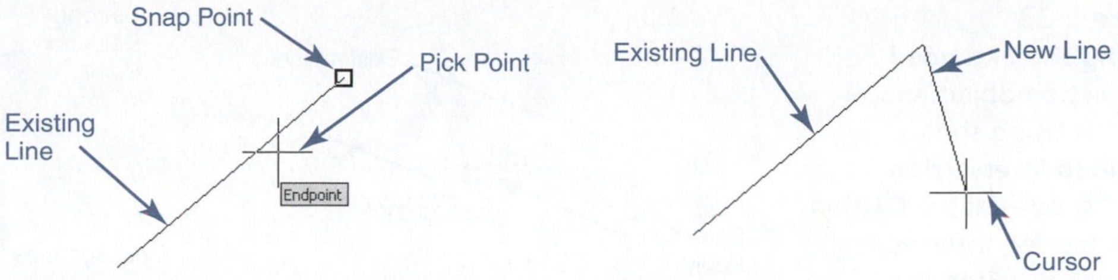

Midpoint. The **Midpoint** object snap snaps to the midway point of an arc, ellipse, elliptical arc, line, multiline, polyline, region, solid, spline, or Xline. The selected object is bisected exactly at the halfway point. Figures 5-21A and B show how to snap to the midpoint of a line using the **Midpoint** object snap when drawing a line.

Figure 5-21
A Using the **Midpoint** object snap—Step 1 **B** Using the **Midpoint** object snap—Step 2

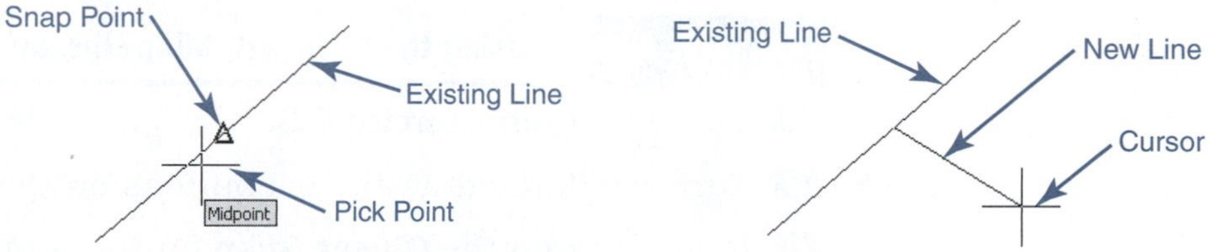

Intersection. The **Intersection** object snap snaps to the intersection of two objects. The two objects can be any combination of the following: arc, circle, ellipse, elliptical arc, line, multiline, polyline, ray, region, spline, or Xline. Figures 5-22A and B show how to snap to the intersection of two lines using the **Intersection** object snap when drawing a line.

Figure 5-22
A Using the **Intersection** object snap—Step 1 **B** Using the **Intersection** object snap—Step 2

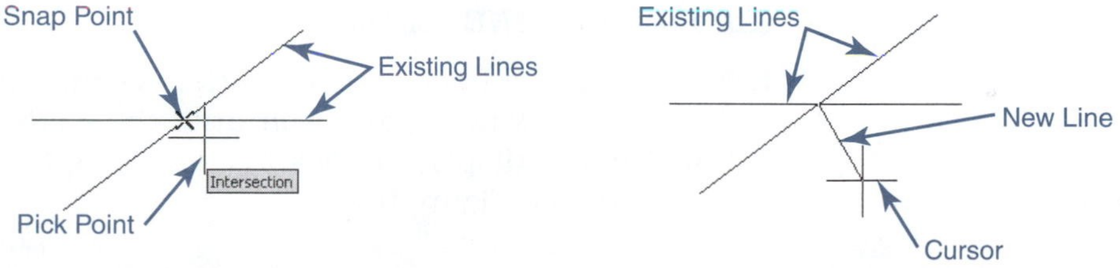

It is also possible to snap to the intersection of two objects that do not physically cross in your drawing but would intersect if either of them, or both, were extended. The **Extended Intersection** object snap snaps to the implied intersection of two objects. This extension mode occurs automatically through the deferred pick point process explained earlier. If you do not pick close to the physical intersection of two objects when using the **Intersection** object snap, AutoCAD automatically puts you in **Extended Intersection** mode and displays the **Extended Intersection** AutoSnap marker (Figure 5-23A).

Remember that any time you see the ellipsis (...) next to an AutoSnap marker it means AutoCAD is waiting for more input. If you move your cursor over the other object that would intersect if it were extended, the typical **Intersection** AutoSnap marker is displayed (Figure 5-23B).

As soon as the **Intersection** AutoSnap marker is displayed, you can pick a point, and it will snap to the implied intersection (Figure 5-23C).

> **TIP**
> **Extended Intersection** is not available as a running object snap.

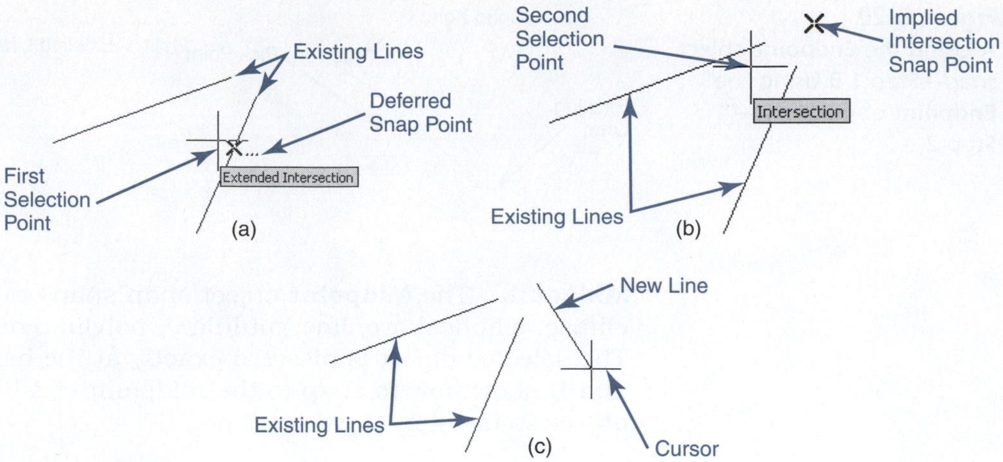

Figure 5-23
A Using the **Extended Intersection** object snap—Step 1 **B** Using the **Extended Intersection** object snap—Step 2 **C** Using the **Extended Intersection** object snap—Step 3

EXERCISE 5-4 Using the Endpoint, Midpoint, and Intersection Object Snaps

1. Continue from Exercise 5-3.
2. Turn off all the drawing tool buttons on the status bar.
3. Right-click on the **Object Snap** button on the status bar and select **Settings...** from the shortcut menu. The **Object Snap** tab of the **Drafting Settings** dialog box is displayed (see Figure 5-17).
4. Select the **Clear All** button to clear any running object snaps. Turn on the **Endpoint, Midpoint,** and **Intersection** object snaps. Exit the **Drafting Settings** dialog box by selecting **OK.**
5. Turn on the **Object Snap** button on the status bar.
6. Start the **LINE** command.
7. Place your cursor over the bottom corner of the rotated square on the top of the drawing and wait until the **Endpoint** AutoSnap marker and tooltip are displayed. Pick a point while the AutoSnap marker is displayed (see Figure 5-24).

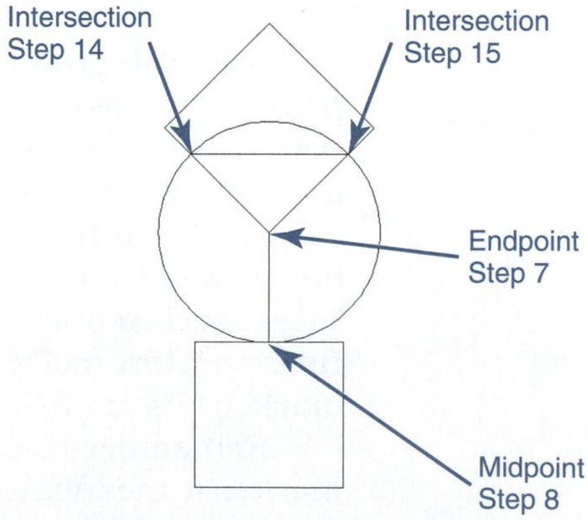

Figure 5-24
Using **Endpoint, Midpoint,** and **Intersection** object snaps

8. Place your cursor over the middle of the top line of the square on the bottom of the drawing and wait until the **Midpoint** AutoSnap marker and tooltip are displayed. Pick a point while the AutoSnap marker is displayed (see Figure 5-24).
9. Press **<Enter>** to end the **LINE** command.
10. Start the **CIRCLE** command.

11 Choose the same point selected in step 7 to locate the circle center point.

12 Choose the same point selected in step 8 to indicate the circle radius.

13 Start the **LINE** command.

14 Place your cursor over the intersection on the left side of the circle and bottom left angled line of the rotated square and wait until the **Intersection** AutoSnap marker and tooltip are displayed. Pick a point while the AutoSnap marker is displayed (see Figure 5-24).

15 Place your cursor over the intersection on the right side of the circle and bottom right angled line of the rotated square and wait until the **Intersection** AutoSnap marker and tooltip are displayed. Pick a point while the AutoSnap marker is displayed (see Figure 5-24).

16 Hit **<Enter>** to end the **LINE** command.

17 Save your drawing. Your drawing should look like Figure 5-24.

Apparent Intersection. The **Apparent Intersection** object snap snaps to the visual intersection of two objects that are not in the same plane in 3D space so they don't physically intersect but appear to intersect when viewed from certain angles. Its use is reserved for working in 3D drawings.

Center. The **Center** object snap snaps to the center of an arc, circle, ellipse, or elliptical arc. Figures 5-25A and B show how to snap to the center of a circle using the **Center** object snap when drawing a line.

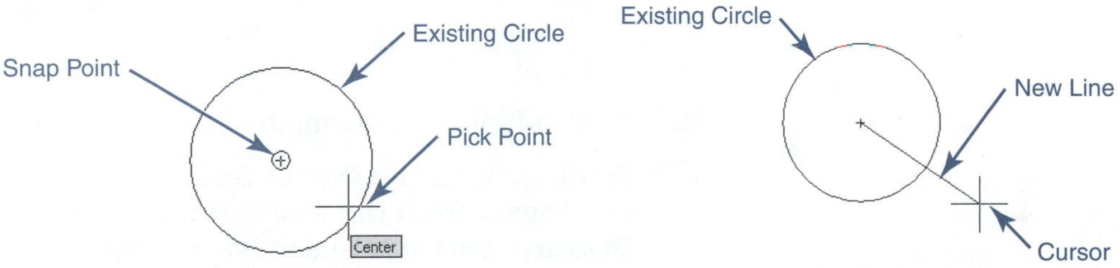

Figure 5-25
A Using the **Center** object snap—Step 1 **B** Using the **Center** object snap—Step 2

TIP
You can pick a center point by selecting either near the center or near the edge of a circle.

Quadrant. The **Quadrant** object snap snaps to one of the four quadrant points (0°, 90°, 180°, or 270°) of an arc, circle, ellipse, or elliptical arc. The quadrant point selected is the one closest to where you select the object. Figures 5-26A and B show how to snap to the 0° quadrant point of a circle using the **Quadrant** object snap when drawing a line.

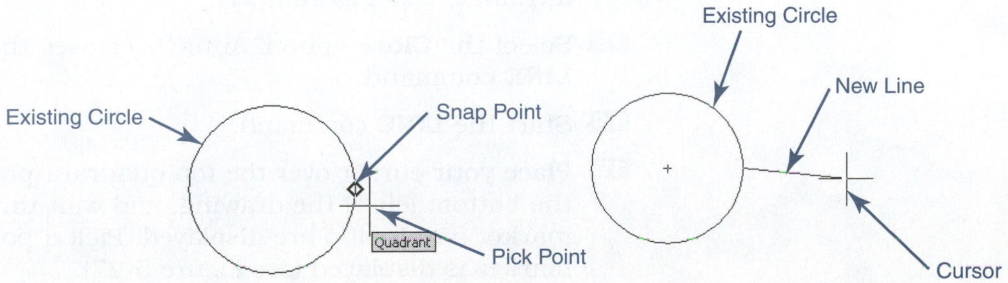

Figure 5-26
A Using the **Quadrant** object snap—Step 1 **B** Using the **Quadrant** object snap—Step 2

EXERCISE 5-5 Using the Center and Quadrant Object Snaps

1. Start a new drawing using the **acad.dwt** drawing template.
2. Select **Zoom Extents** to zoom to the limits of the drawing.
3. Start the **CIRCLE** command. AutoCAD prompts you to *Specify center point for circle or*↓.
4. Type **2,2<Enter>**. AutoCAD prompts you to *Specify radius of circle or*↓.
5. Type **1<Enter>** to specify a radius of 1″.
6. Repeat steps 4 and 5 to create two more 1″-radius circles at the coordinate locations of **(4,5)** and **(6,2)** (see Figure 5-27).

Figure 5-27
Using the **Center** and **Quadrant** object snaps

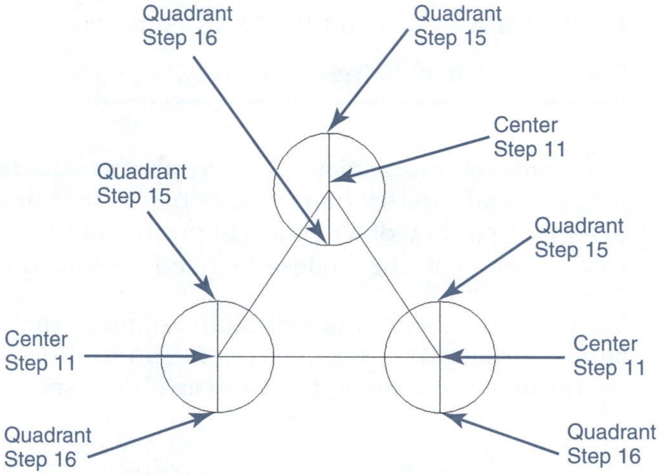

7. Turn off all the drawing tool buttons on the status bar.
8. Right-click on the **Object Snap** button on the status bar and select **Settings...** from the shortcut menu. The **Object Snap** tab of the **Drafting Settings** dialog box is displayed (see Figure 5-17).
9. Select the **Clear All** button to clear any running object snaps. Turn on the **Center** and **Quadrant** object snaps. Turn the **Object Snap On** check box on in the upper left corner. Exit the **Drafting Settings** dialog box by selecting **OK**.
10. Start the **LINE** command.
11. Place your cursor over the center of the circle on the bottom left of the drawing, and wait until the **Center** AutoSnap marker and tooltip are displayed. Pick a point while the AutoSnap marker is displayed (see Figure 5-27).
12. Repeat step 11 for the other two circles and draw three lines to create a triangle (see Figure 5-27).
13. Select the **Close** option. AutoCAD closes the triangle and exits the **LINE** command.
14. Start the **LINE** command.
15. Place your cursor over the top quadrant point (90°) of the circle on the bottom left of the drawing, and wait until the **Quadrant** AutoSnap marker and tooltip are displayed. Pick a point while the AutoSnap marker is displayed (see Figure 5-27).

16 Place your cursor over the bottom quadrant point (270°) of the circle on the bottom left of the drawing, and wait until the **Quadrant** AutoSnap marker and tooltip are displayed. Pick a point while the AutoSnap marker is displayed (see Figure 5-27).

17 Repeat steps 14 through 16 to create vertical lines from quadrant to quadrant on the other two circles.

18 Save your drawing as ***CH5_EXERCISE5***. Your drawing should look like Figure 5-27.

Tangent. The **Tangent** object snap snaps to the tangent of an arc, circle, ellipse, elliptical arc, or spline. Figures 5-28A and B show how to snap to the tangent of a circle using the **Tangent** object snap when drawing a line.

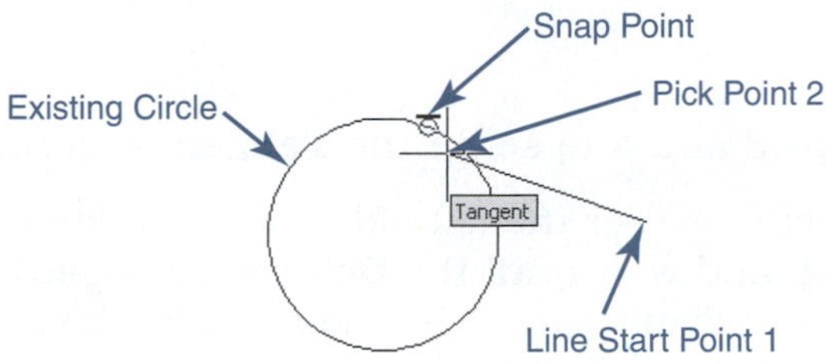

Figure 5-28A
Using the **Tangent** object snap—Step 1

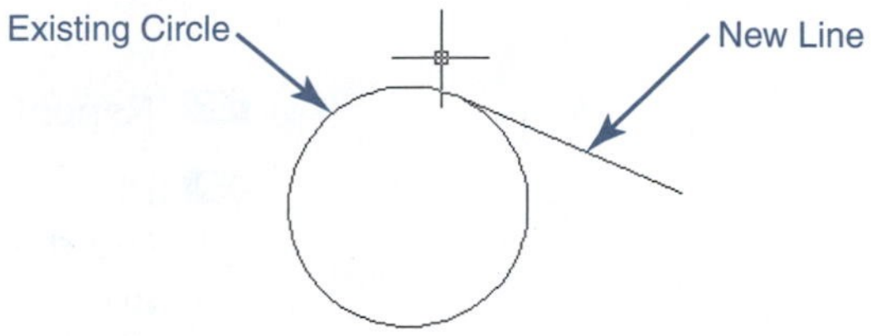

Figure 5-28B
Using the **Tangent** object snap—Step 2

It is possible to defer a tangent point by first selecting the object you want to be tangent to before picking any other points. Picking a circle first displays the **Deferred Tangent** AutoSnap marker (Figure 5-29A).

Again, the ellipsis (...) next to an AutoSnap marker means AutoCAD is waiting for more input. Pick another point to locate the end of the line (Figure 5-29B).

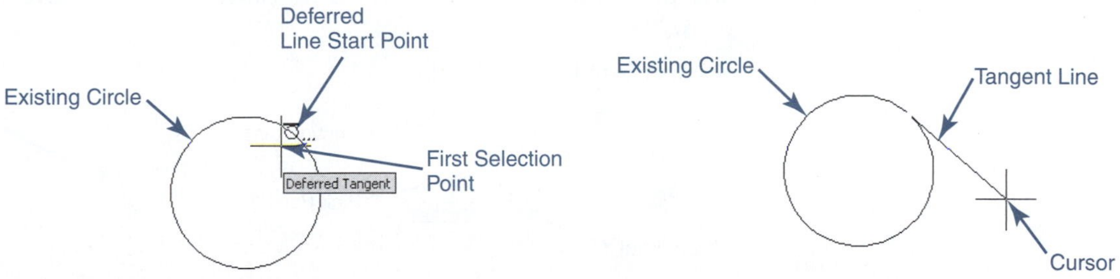

Figure 5-29
A Using the **Deferred Tangent** object snap—Step 1 **B** Using the **Deferred Tangent** object snap—Step 2

EXERCISE 5-6 Using the Tangent Object Snap

1 Continue from Exercise 5-5.

2 Start the **LINE** command.

3 Hold down the **<Shift>** key on your keyboard while right-clicking with your mouse to display the **Object Snap** shortcut menu (see Figure 5-16).

4 Select the **Tangent** object snap from the menu.

5 Place your cursor over the left side of the circle on the bottom left of the drawing, and wait until the **Deferred Tangent** AutoSnap marker and tooltip are displayed. Pick a point while the AutoSnap marker is displayed (see Figure 5-30).

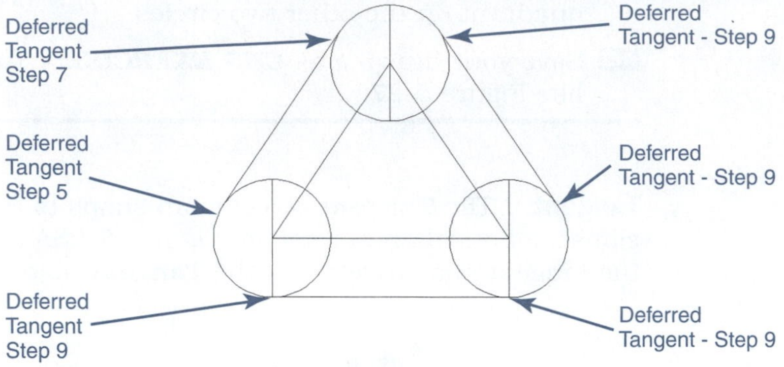

Figure 5-30
Using the **Tangent** object snap

6 Repeat steps 3 and 4 to select the **Tangent** object snap again.

7 Place your cursor over the left side of the circle on the top middle of the drawing, and wait until the **Deferred Tangent** AutoSnap marker and tooltip are displayed. Pick a point while the AutoSnap marker is displayed (see Figure 5-30).

8 There should now be a line segment tangent to both circles.

9 Repeat steps 2 through 7 and create two more line segments tangent to the other two circles (see Figure 5-30).

10 Save your drawing. Your drawing should look like Figure 5-30.

Perpendicular. The **Perpendicular** object snap snaps to a point perpendicular to an arc, circle, ellipse, elliptical arc, line, multiline, polyline, ray, region, solid, spline, or Xline. Figures 5-31A and B show how to draw a line perpendicular to another line using the **Perpendicular** object snap.

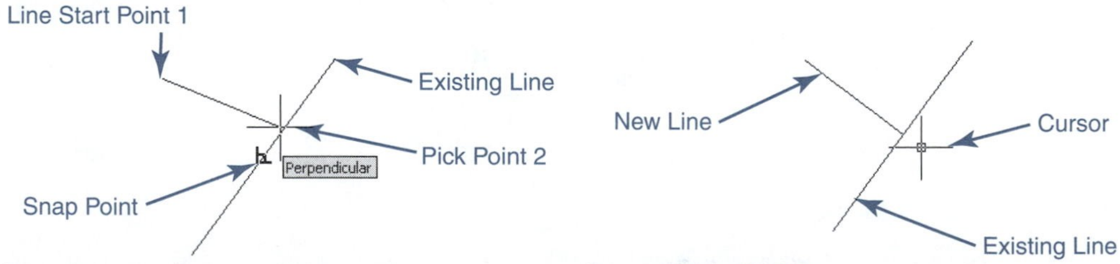

Figure 5-31
A Using the **Perpendicular** object snap—Step 1 **B** Using the **Perpendicular** object snap—Step 2

It is possible to defer a perpendicular point by first selecting the object you want to be perpendicular to before picking any other points. Picking a line first displays the **Deferred Perpendicular** AutoSnap marker (see Figure 5-32A).

Again, the ellipsis (...) next to an AutoSnap marker means AutoCAD is waiting for more input. Pick another point to locate the end of the line, which in turn determines where the new line attaches to the existing line (see Figure 5-32B).

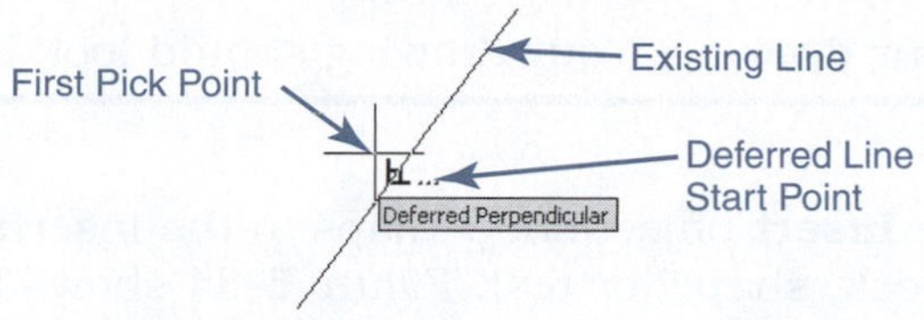

Figure 5-32A
Using the **Deferred Perpendicular** object snap—Step 1

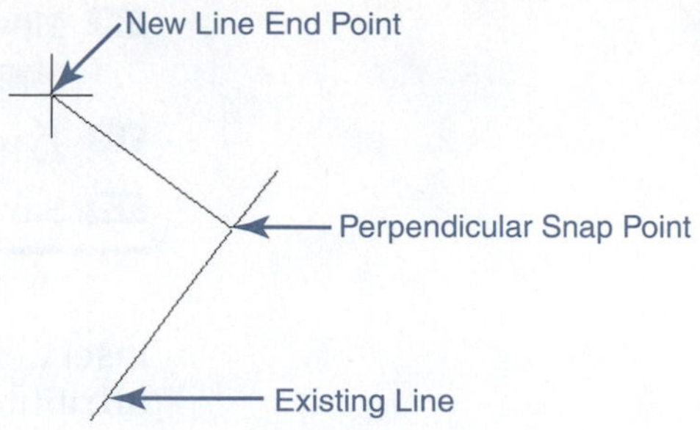

Figure 5-32B
Using the **Deferred Perpendicular** object snap—Step 2

EXERCISE 5-7 Using the Perpendicular Object Snap

1. Continue from Exercise 5-6.
2. Turn off all the drawing tool buttons on the status bar.
3. Right-click on the **Object Snap** button on the status bar and select **Settings...** from the shortcut menu. The **Object Snap** tab of the **Drafting Settings** dialog box is displayed (see Figure 5-17).
4. Select the **Clear All** button to clear any running object snaps. Turn on the **Perpendicular** object snap. Turn the **Object Snap On** check box on in the upper left corner. Exit the **Drafting Settings** dialog box by selecting **OK**.
5. Start the **LINE** command. AutoCAD prompts you to *Specify first point:*.
6. Type **8,6<Enter>**. AutoCAD prompts you to *Specify next point or* ↓.
7. Place your cursor over the angled line on the right side of the triangle, and wait until the **Perpendicular** AutoSnap marker and tooltip are displayed. Pick a point while the AutoSnap marker is displayed (see Figure 5-33).

Figure 5-33
Using the **Perpendicular** object snap

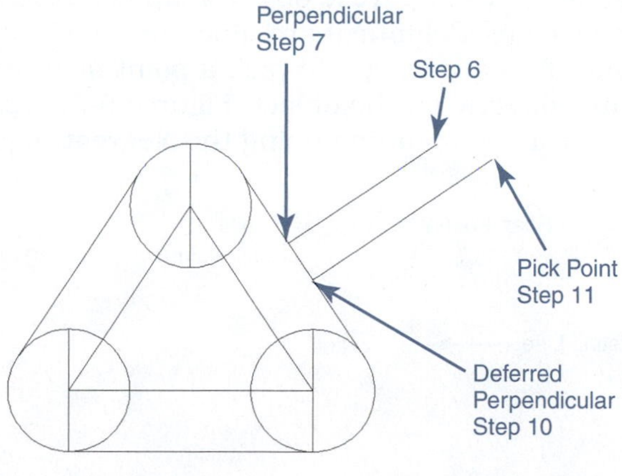

8. Type **<Enter>** to end the **LINE** command.
9. Start the **LINE** command again.
10. Place your cursor over the angled line on the right side of the triangle, and wait until the **Deferred Perpendicular** AutoSnap marker and tooltip are displayed. Pick a point while the AutoSnap marker is displayed (see Figure 5-33).

11 Move your cursor up to the right and pick another point to create a perpendicular line segment (see Figure 5-33).

12 Type **<Enter>** to end the **LINE** command.

13 Save your drawing. Your drawing should look like Figure 5-33.

Insert. The **Insert** object snap snaps to the insertion point of an attribute, block, shape, or text. Figure 5-34 shows how to snap to the insertion point of a text object using the **Insert** object snap.

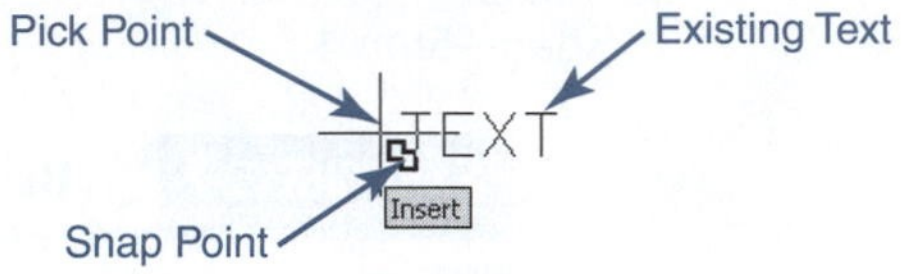

Figure 5-34
Using the **Insert** object snap

Node. The **Node** object snap snaps to a point object, dimension definition point, or dimension text origin. Figures 5-35A and B show how to snap to a point created using the **DIVIDE** or **MEASURE** command and the **Node** object snap when drawing a line.

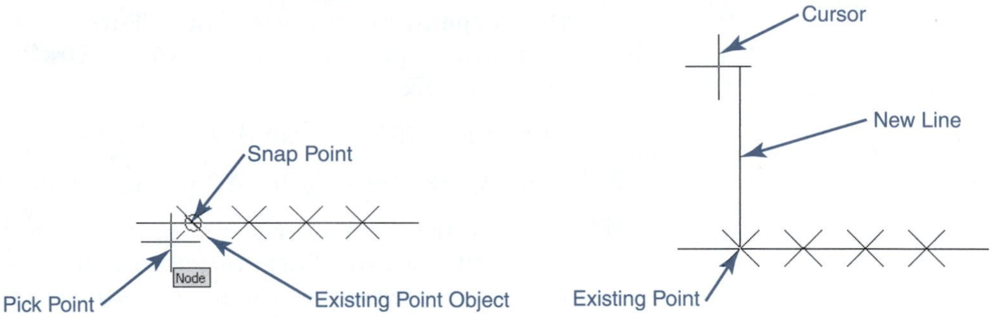

Figure 5-35
A Using the **Node** object snap—Step 1 **B** Using the **Node** object snap—Step 2

Nearest. The **Nearest** object snap snaps to the nearest point on an arc, circle, ellipse, elliptical arc, line, multiline, point, polyline, ray, spline, or Xline. This allows you to pick a point near an object and be assured that it snaps directly on the object. Figures 5-36A and B show how to snap to a point exactly on a line using the **Nearest** object snap when drawing a line.

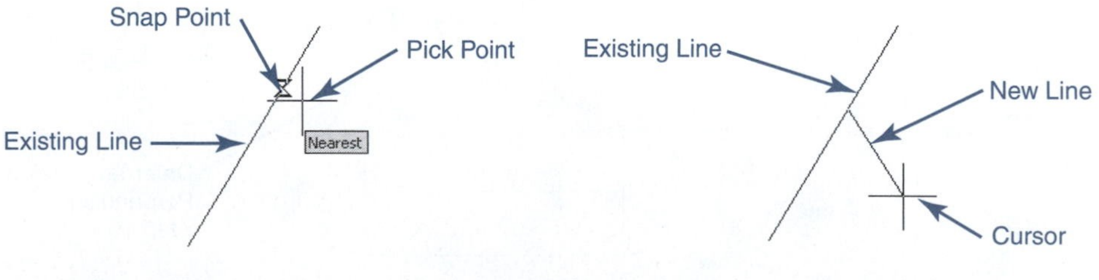

Figure 5-36
A Using the **Nearest** object snap—Step 1 **B** Using the **Nearest** object snap—Step 2

None. The **None** object snap allows you to snap to nothing ... literally. The **None** object snap temporarily disables any running object snaps set on the **Object Snap** tab of the **Drafting Settings** dialog box for the next picked point. This makes it possible to pick a point in your drawing that doesn't snap to any objects that might be nearby, particularly when you are working in close quarters. You can always turn the **Object Snap** button off on the status bar at any time as well, but then you have to turn it back on when you need object snaps enabled again.

Advanced Object Snap Modes

The following object snaps are more advanced than those introduced in the previous section. The object snaps in this section require additional information to build the snap point based on the geometry of an existing object, or even objects. This can range from entering an offset distance to acquiring points that are used to display alignment paths (see Figure 5-37).

Figure 5-37
Acquired point and alignment path

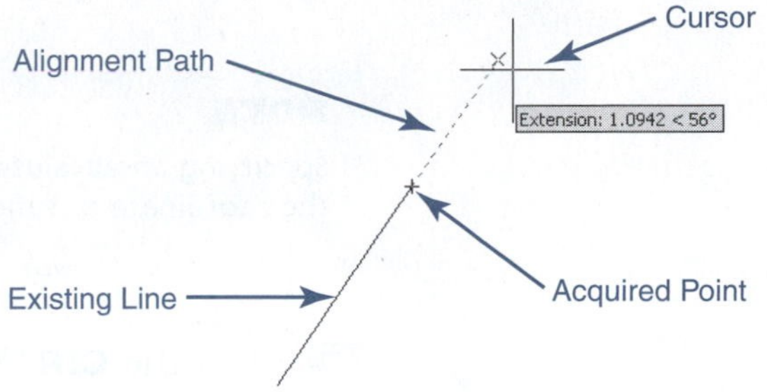

acquired point: Object tracking feature used to locate a point as an intermediate location in order to locate temporary alignment paths.

Some ***acquired points*** are selected automatically by simply moving your cursor over an object, whereas others require that you explicitly pick a point in the drawing.

The difference between the two methods of acquiring points is highlighted in the following sections to help reduce any confusion.

From. The **From** object snap allows you to specify a relative distance from a selected point and is typically used in conjunction with other object snaps. The distance can be entered either as a relative Cartesian coordinate using the format @X,Y (for example, @2,2) or as a polar coordinate using the distance and angle format (for example, @2<45). Figures 5-38A and B show how to snap to a point that is 0.5″ to the right and 0.5″ above the endpoint of a line using the **From** object snap.

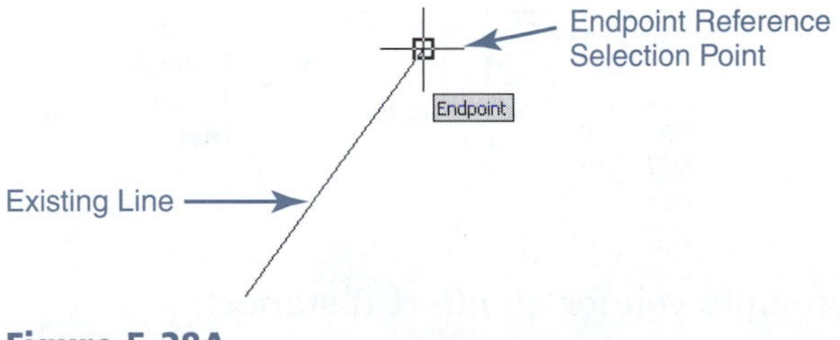

Figure 5-38A
Using the **From** object snap—Step 1

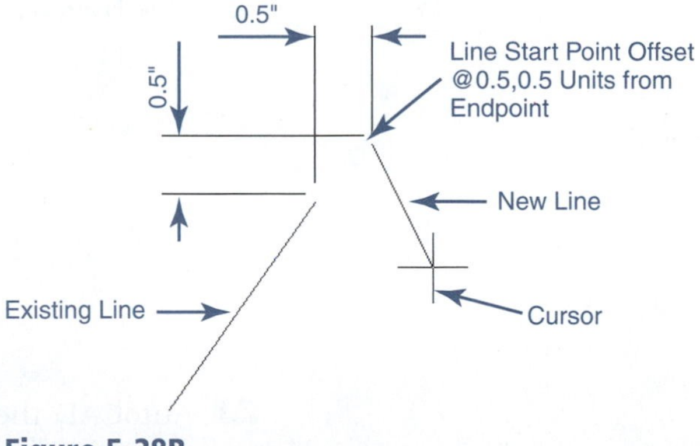

Figure 5-38B
Using the **From** object snap—Step 2

FOR MORE DETAILS

See page 142 in Chapter 4 for more information about relative coordinate entry.

EXERCISE 5-8 **Using the From Object Snap**

1. Create a 2 × 2 square using the steps in Exercise 5-2 on pages 185–186.
2. Turn off all the drawing tool buttons on the status bar.

3 Right-click on the **Object Snap** button on the status bar and select **Settings...** from the shortcut menu. The **Object Snap** tab of the **Drafting Settings** dialog box is displayed (see Figure 5-17).

4 Select the **Clear All** button to clear any running object snaps. Turn on the **Endpoint** object snap. Turn the **Object Snap On** check box on in the upper left corner. Exit the **Drafting Settings** dialog box by selecting **OK**.

> **NOTE**
>
> Specifying an absolute coordinate without the @ symbol will simply locate the point at the coordinate specified.

5 Start the **CIRCLE** command. AutoCAD prompts you to *Specify center point for circle or* ↓.

6 Hold down the **<Shift>** key on your keyboard while right-clicking with your mouse to display the **Object Snap** shortcut menu (see Figure 5-16).

7 Select the **From** object snap from the menu. AutoCAD prompts you for a base point:

Base point:

8 Place your cursor over the endpoints on the bottom left corner of the square, and wait until the **Endpoint** AutoSnap marker and tooltip are displayed. Pick a point while the AutoSnap marker is displayed (see Figure 5-39).

Figure 5-39
Using the **From** object snap

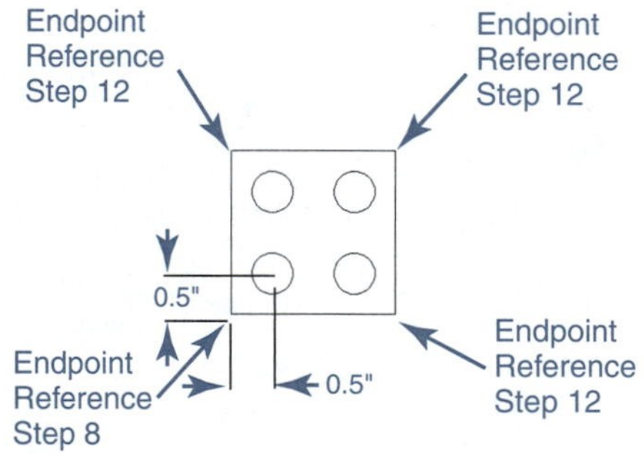

9 AutoCAD then prompts you for an offset distance:

<Offset>:

10 Type @**.5,.5<Enter>**. AutoCAD locates the center point of the circle and prompts you for a radius:

Specify radius of circle or ↓.

11 Type **.25<Enter>**.

12 Repeat steps 5 through 11 to locate three more circles with a 0.25 radius a half inch in from each corner (see Figure 5-39).

13 Save your drawing as ***CH5_EXERCISE8***. Your drawing should look like Figure 5-39.

Mid Between 2 Points. The **Mid Between 2 Points** object snap allows you to locate a snap point midway between two points and is typically used in conjunction with other object snaps so that you can locate the point precisely. Figures 5-40A through C show how to snap midway between the endpoints of two lines using the **Mid Between 2 Points** object snap when drawing a circle.

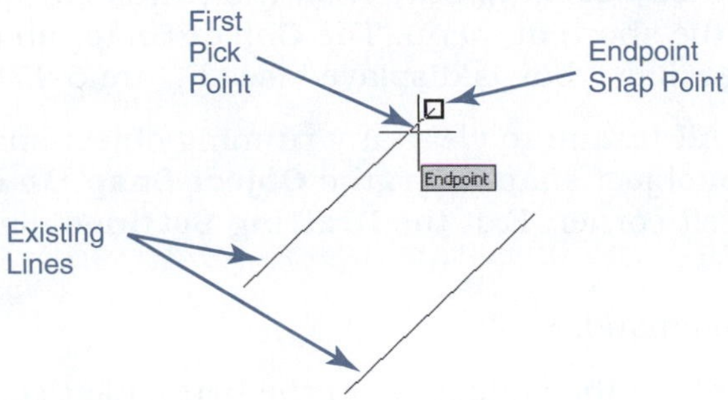

Figure 5-40A
Using the **Mid Between 2 Points** object snap—Step 1

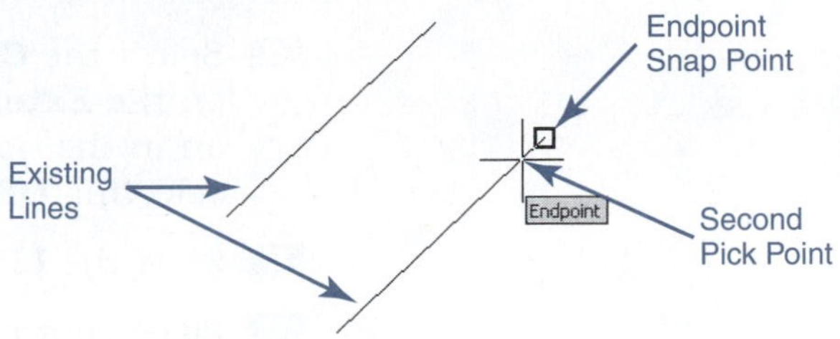

Figure 5-40B
Using the **Mid Between 2 Points** object snap—Step 2

Figure 5-40C
Using the **Mid Between 2 Points** object snap—Step 3

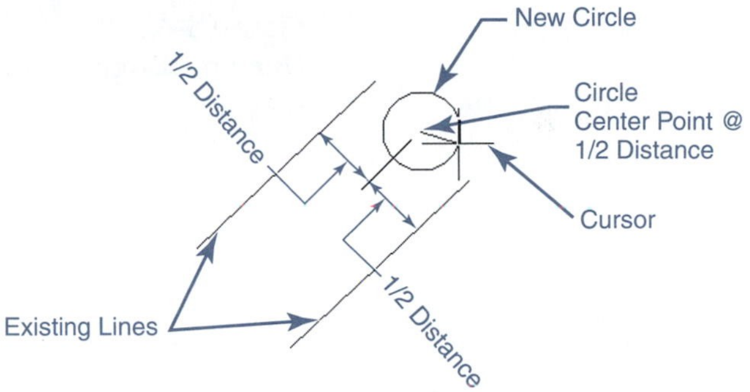

Extension. The **Extension** object snap allows you to display an alignment path along the extension of an arc, elliptical arc, line, multiline, polyline, region, or ray by acquiring an endpoint on one or more objects.

A point is acquired by simply moving your cursor over an endpoint of a valid object type. You *do not* need to pick a point to acquire it when using the **Extension** object snap. A small cross is displayed after a point is acquired. You can deselect an acquired point by moving your cursor back over the acquired point so the cross disappears.

After a point is acquired, you display an alignment path by moving your cursor in the object's extension direction. Once the alignment path is displayed, you can locate a point by picking a point on the path or by using direct distance entry to specify a distance to travel along the vector. Figures 5-41A and B show how to locate a line start point on the extension alignment path of a line using the **Extension** object snap.

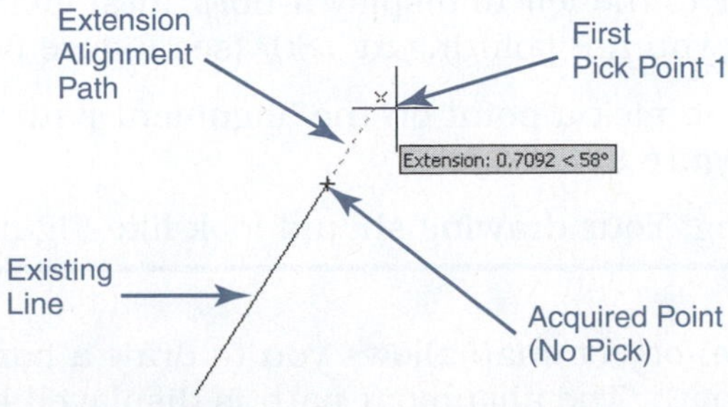

Figure 5-41A
Using the **Extension** object snap—Step 1

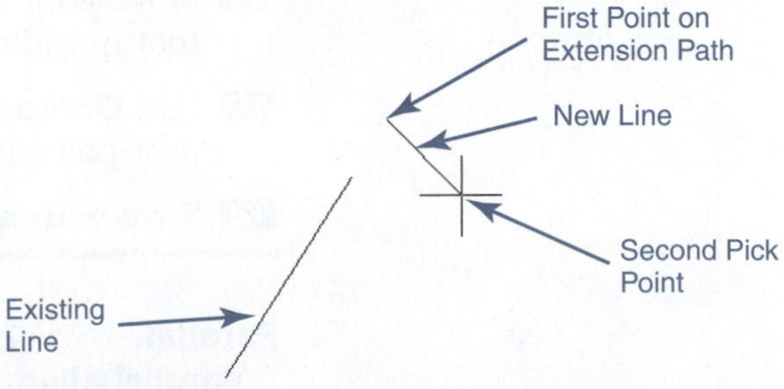

Figure 5-41B
Using the **Extension** object snap—Step 2

EXERCISE 5-9 Using the Extension Object Snap

1. Continue from Exercise 5-8.
2. Turn on the **Ortho Mode** button on the status bar.
3. Right-click on the **Object Snap** button on the status bar and select **Settings...** from the shortcut menu. The **Object Snap** tab of the **Drafting Settings** dialog box is displayed (see Figure 5-17).
4. Select the **Clear All** button to clear any running object snaps. Turn on the **Extension** object snap. Turn the **Object Snap On** check box on in the upper left corner. Exit the **Drafting Settings** dialog box by selecting **OK**.
5. Start the **LINE** command.
6. Place your cursor over the endpoints on the bottom left corner of the square to acquire a point (see Figure 5-42).

Figure 5-42
Using the **Extension** object snap

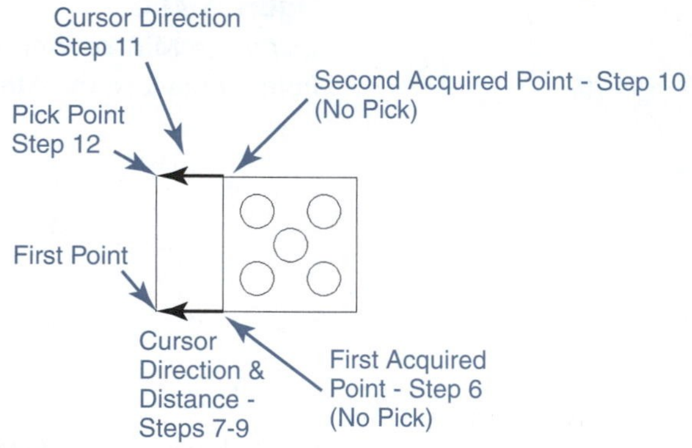

7. Move your cursor to the left of the corner to display a horizontal alignment path and tooltip indicating you are pointing at 180° (see Figure 5-42).
8. Type **1<Enter>**.
9. AutoCAD uses direct distance entry to place a point 1 unit from the lower left corner along the 180° horizontal extension alignment path (see Figure 5-42).
10. Place your cursor over the endpoints on the top left corner of the square to acquire another point (see Figure 5-42).
11. Move your cursor to the left to display a horizontal alignment path and tooltip indicating you are pointing at 180° (see Figure 5-42).
12. Use **Ortho** mode to pick a point on the alignment path 90° from the first point (see Figure 5-42).
13. Save your drawing. Your drawing should look like Figure 5-42.

Parallel. The **Parallel** object snap allows you to draw a parallel line using a parallel alignment path. The alignment path is displayed by acquiring a point on the line segment to which you want to draw a parallel line when AutoCAD prompts you for the second point of a line.

Chapter 5

A **Parallel** object snap point is acquired by moving your cursor over the desired line segment. You *do not* need to pick a point to acquire it when using the **Parallel** object snap. When you move your cursor over a line segment after selecting the **Parallel** object snap, the **Parallel** AutoSnap marker is displayed, and a point is acquired showing a small cross. You can deselect an acquired point by moving your cursor back over the acquired point so the cross disappears.

After a point is acquired, you display a parallel alignment path by moving your cursor in the parallel direction. Once the alignment path is displayed, you can locate a point by picking a point on the path or by using direct distance entry to specify a distance to travel along the vector. Figures 5-43A and B show how to draw a line parallel to another line using the **Parallel** object snap when drawing a line.

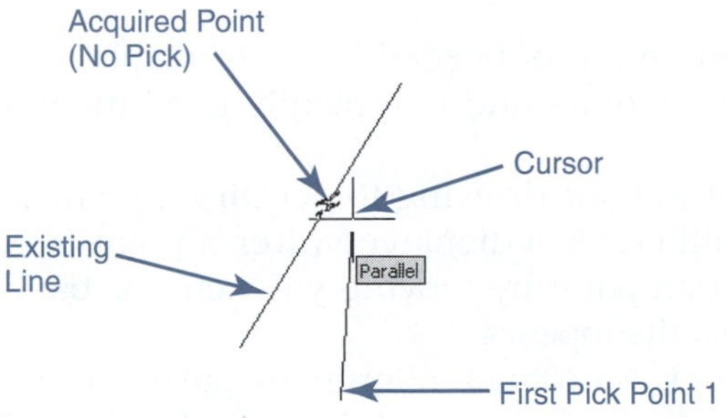

Figure 5-43A
Using the **Parallel** object snap—Step 1

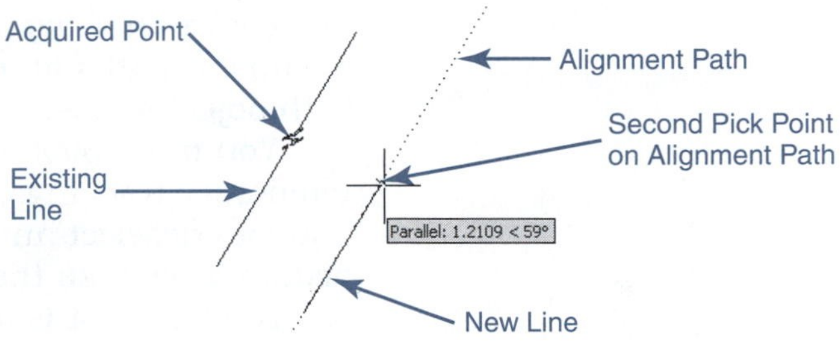

Figure 5-43B
Using the **Parallel** object snap—Step 2

Object Snap Tracking

Object snap tracking relies on the AutoTracking feature (explained earlier in the "Polar Tracking" section) to display alignment paths at orthogonal or polar angle settings using points you select in your drawing using object snaps. The angle settings used, polar or orthogonal, are controlled in the **Object Snap Tracking Settings** section on the **Polar Tracking** tab of the **Drafting Settings** dialog box shown in Figure 5-44.

Figure 5-44
Object Snap Tracking Settings

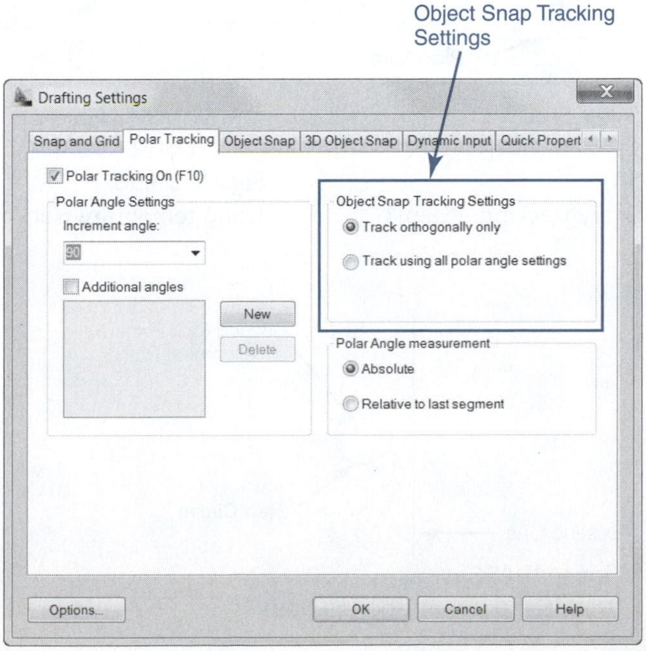

By default, object snap tracking is set to track orthogonally at horizontal and vertical angles. There are two types of object snap tracking:

- Temporary tracking
- Object snap tracking mode

Temporary tracking works like an object snap override to display tracking alignment paths on an as-needed basis at picked points. The object snap tracking mode works with running object snaps so that when it is turned on, tracking alignment paths are automatically displayed at all the currently running object snap points. Both types of tracking are explained in detail in the following sections.

Temporary Tracking

Temporary tracking is used on an as-needed basis to display AutoTrack alignment paths at acquired points and is typically used in conjunction with object snaps.

You must pick a point in your drawing to acquire a point when using temporary tracking. A small cross is displayed after a point is acquired. You can deselect an acquired point by moving your cursor back over the acquired point so the cross disappears.

After a point is acquired, AutoTrack alignment paths are displayed at the angles specified on the **Polar Tracking** tab of the **Drafting Settings** dialog box. Once the alignment path is displayed, you can locate a point by picking a point on the path or by using direct distance entry to specify a distance to travel along the alignment vector. Figures 5-45A through C show how to locate the center point of a circle by tracking horizontally from the midpoint of a vertical line.

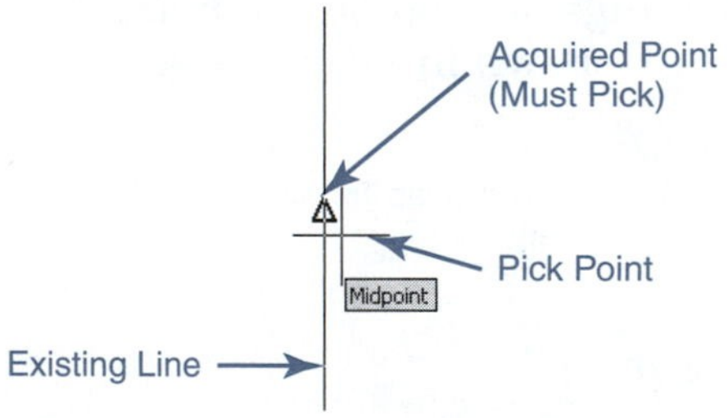

Figure 5-45A
Using temporary tracking—Step 1

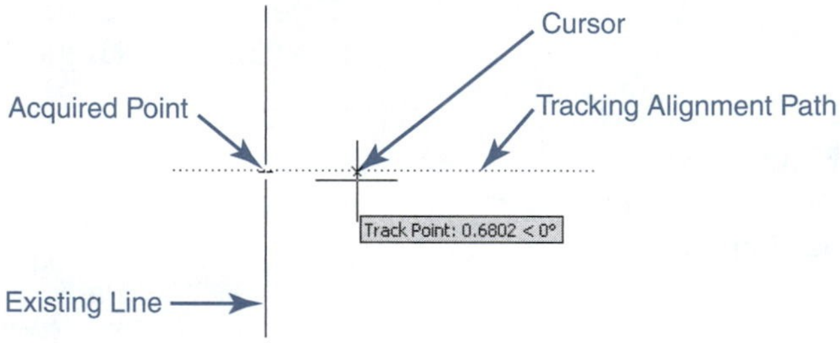

Figure 5-45B
Using temporary tracking—Step 2

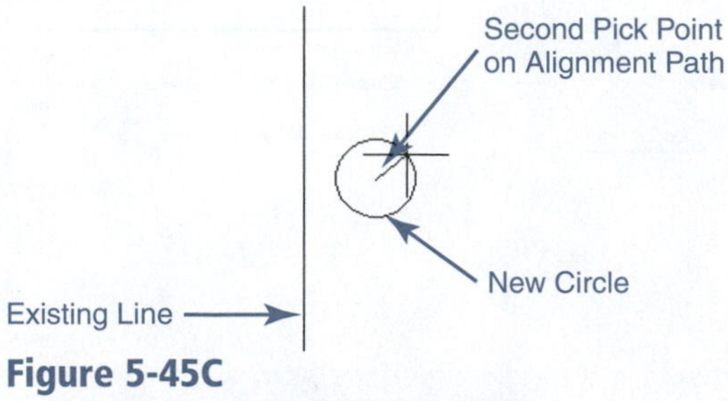

Figure 5-45C
Using temporary tracking—Step 3

OBJECT SNAP TRACKING	
Status Bar:	 or OTRACK
Function Key:	F11
Command Line:	None
Keyboard Combo:	None

Object Snap Tracking

The **Object Snap Tracking** drawing tool works with running object snaps so that when object snap tracking mode is turned on, AutoTrack alignment paths can be displayed by acquiring a point at any currently running object snap point.

Unlike with temporary tracking, when object snap tracking mode is on, you *do not* have to pick a point to acquire it. You just move your cursor over an object snap point, and a small cross (+) is displayed, indicating the point is acquired. You can deselect an acquired point by moving your cursor back over the acquired point so the cross disappears.

After a point is acquired, AutoTrack alignment paths are displayed at the angle specified on the **Polar Tracking** tab of the **Drafting Settings** dialog box. Once the alignment path is displayed, you can locate a point by picking a point on the path or by using direct distance entry to specify a distance to travel along the alignment vector.

Intersecting Alignment Paths

Both temporary tracking and object snap tracking allow you to display multiple AutoTrack alignment paths so that you can locate points relative to multiple objects in your drawing. When you use AutoTracking, each point you snap to displays its own alignment path. If multiple alignment paths cross, it is possible to snap to their point of intersection by putting your cursor over the intersection until a small cross appears that looks similar to an acquired point and then picking a point. Figures 5-46A

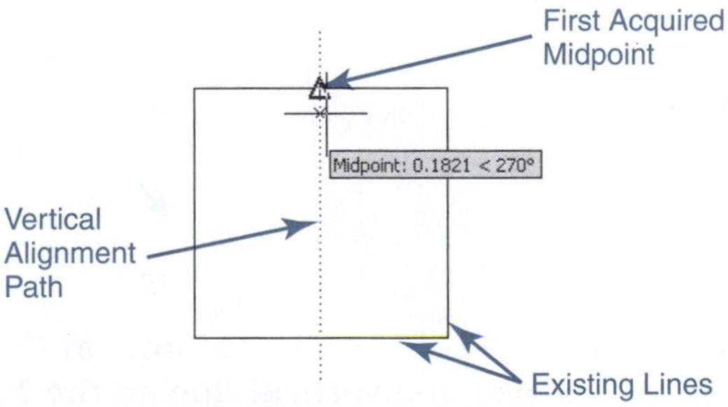

Figure 5-46A
Intersecting alignment paths—Step 1

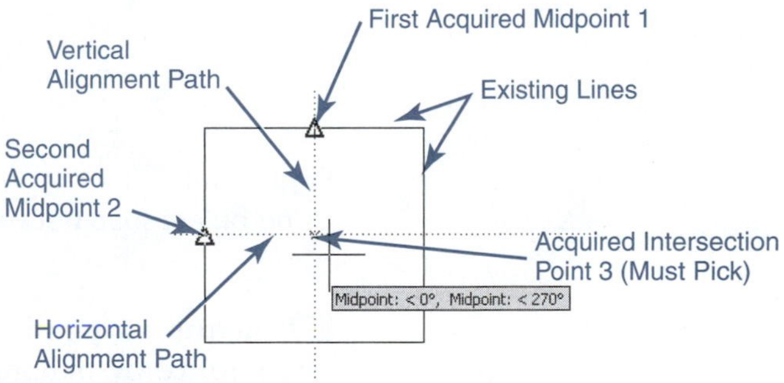

Figure 5-46B
Intersecting alignment paths—Step 2

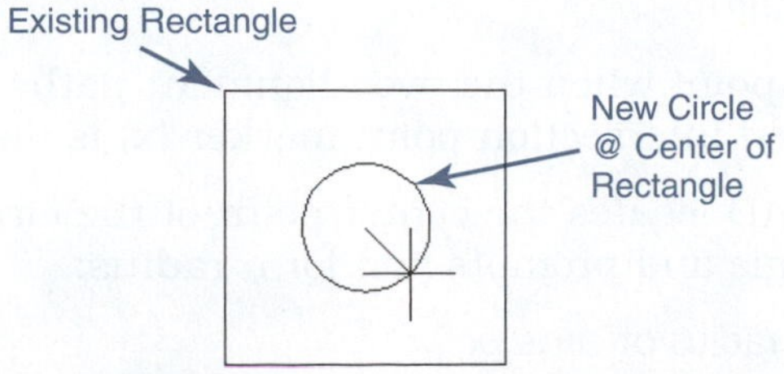

Figure 5-46C
Intersecting alignment paths—Step 3

through C show how to locate the center of a circle using the intersection point of vertical and horizontal AutoTrack alignment paths.

EXERCISE 5-10 Using Object Snap Tracking

1. Continue from Exercise 5-9.
2. Turn off all the drawing tool buttons on the status bar.
3. Right-click on the **Object Snap** button on the status bar and select **Settings...** from the shortcut menu. The **Object Snap** tab of the **Drafting Settings** dialog box is displayed (see Figure 5-17).
4. Select the **Clear All** button to clear any running object snaps. Turn on the **Midpoint** object snap. Turn the **Object Snap On** check box on in the upper left corner. Exit the **Drafting Settings** dialog box by selecting the **OK** button.
5. Turn on the **Object Snap Tracking** button on the status bar.
6. Start the **CIRCLE** command. AutoCAD prompts you to *Specify center point for circle or* ↓.
7. Acquire a point at the middle point of the horizontal line on the top of the square by placing your cursor over the horizontal line so the **Midpoint** AutoSnap marker and tooltip are displayed. *Do not* pick a point (see Figure 5-47).

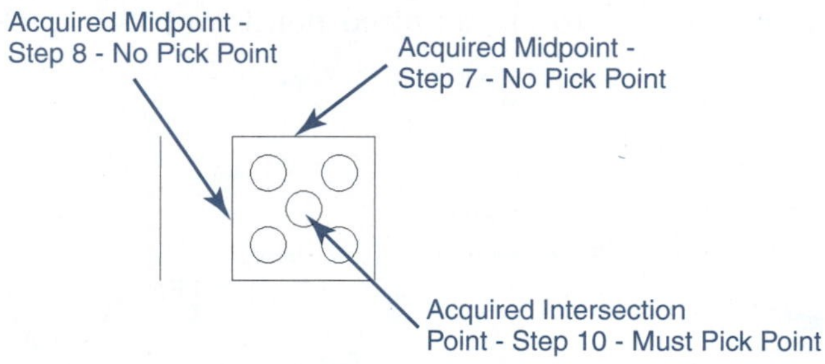

Figure 5-47
Using object snap tracking

8. Acquire a point at the middle point of the vertical line on the left of the square by placing your cursor over the vertical line so the **Midpoint** AutoSnap marker and tooltip are displayed. *Do not* pick a point (see Figure 5-47).
9. Move your cursor to the middle of the rectangle to display both a horizontal alignment path with tooltip and a vertical alignment path with tooltip.
10. Pick a point when the two alignment paths cross and the small acquired intersection point marker (x) is displayed (see Figure 5-47).
11. AutoCAD locates the center point of the circle at the center of the rectangle and prompts you for a radius:

    Specify radius of circle or ↓.
12. Type **.25<Enter>**.
13. Save your drawing. Your drawing should look like Figure 5-47.

TIP

AutoCAD provides a keyboard feature for overriding the current object snap settings temporarily when AutoCAD is prompting for a point. It is referred to as a *temporary override*. Typically, an override consists of a keyboard combination that includes the <Shift> key. In fact, holding down the <Shift> key by itself when selecting a point temporarily puts AutoCAD in **Ortho** mode. The following table provides a complete list of temporary overrides:

Temporary Override	Description
<F3>	Toggles **OSNAP**
<F6>	Toggles **UCSDETECT**
<F8>	Toggles **ORTHOMODE**
<F9>	Toggles **SNAPMODE**
<F10>	Toggles Polar Tracking
<F11>	Toggles Object Snap Tracking
<F12>	Toggles Dynamic Input
<Shift>	Toggles **ORTHOMODE**
<Shift>+’	Toggles **OSNAP**
<Shift>+,	Object Snap Override: Center
<Shift>+.	Toggles Polar Tracking
<Shift>+/	Toggles **UCSDETECT**
<Shift>+;	Enables Object Snap Enforcement
<Shift>+]	Toggles Object Snap Tracking
<Shift>+A	Toggles **OSNAP**
<Shift>+C	Object Snap Override: Center
<Shift>+D	Disable All Snapping and Tracking
<Shift>+E	Object Snap Override: Endpoint
<Shift>+L	Disable All Snapping and Tracking
<Shift>+M	Object Snap Override: Midpoint
<Shift>+P	Object Snap Override: Endpoint
<Shift>+Q	Toggles Object Snap Tracking
<Shift>+S	Enables Object Snap Enforcement
<Shift>+V	Object Snap Override: Midpoint
<Shift>+X	Toggles Polar Tracking
<Shift>+Z	Toggles **UCSDETECT**

DYNAMIC INPUT	
Status Bar:	or DYN
Function Key:	F12
Command Line:	None
Keyboard Combo:	None

Dynamic Input

As mentioned in Chapter 1, dynamic input is a set of related input and display features that allows you to enter information near the mouse cursor so you can focus on your drawing instead of constantly switching focus to the command line for command prompts and data entry.

The **Dynamic Input** interface consists of three different components:

- **Pointer Input**
- **Dimension Input**
- **Dynamic Prompts**

Each of these different components is explained in the following sections.

Pointer Input

When **Pointer Input** is on, the coordinate location of the mouse crosshairs is displayed as *x* and *y* values in a tooltip near the cursor. As you move your mouse the coordinate values are dynamically updated to reflect the cursor's new location. The pointer input for the first point of a line is shown in Figure 5-48.

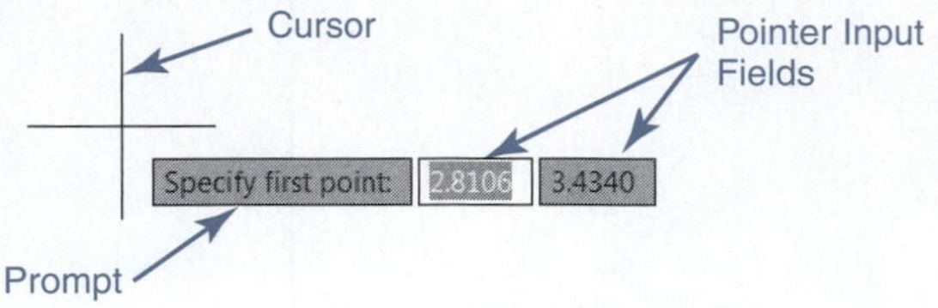

Figure 5-48
Using pointer input

The pointer input tooltip consists of *x* and *y* input fields that you can update with a coordinate value of your choice via the keyboard using the same comma-delimited format used for entering coordinates at the command line by typing **X,Y<Enter>**. Entering the comma after the *x* value locks the input field for *x* and shifts focus to the *y* input field. Entering the desired *y* value and hitting **<Enter>** accepts the coordinate value.

> **TIP**
>
> It is also possible to use the <Tab> key to switch between the *x* and *y* coordinate input fields.

Dimension Input

When **Dimension Input** is on, distance and angle values are displayed in multiple tooltips near the cursor when a command prompts for a second point. The values in the dimension tooltips change as you move the cursor. The dimension input for the second point of a line is shown in Figure 5-49.

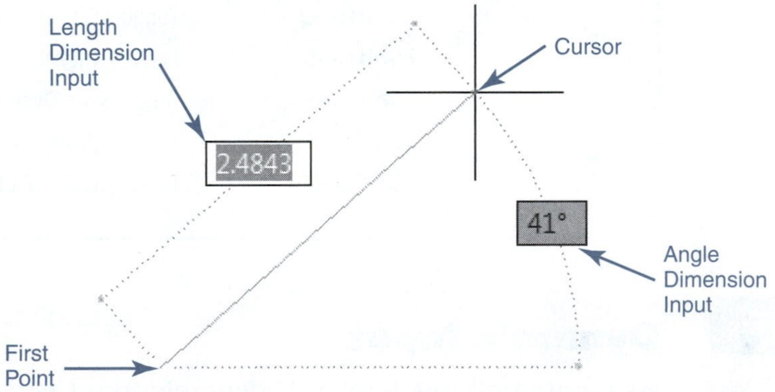

Figure 5-49
Using dimension input

You can use the **<Tab>** key to switch between the different length and angle dimension input fields. When you use the **<Tab>** key, focus switches to another dimension input field while locking the previous field. Using this feature, you can input a length for a line and then press the **<Tab>** key to switch to the angle field to specify the angle. Any angle you input will create a line at that angle with the length previously entered in the length field. This process also works in reverse so that you can press the **<Tab>** key to enter the angle first and then press the **<Tab>** key again to enter the length. Now a line will be created at the preset input angle at any length specified.

NOTE

If you enter an invalid value in any dimension input field, the value highlights automatically so you can enter a new value.

Dynamic Prompts

When **Dynamic Prompts** is on, command prompts and options are displayed in a tooltip near the cursor. You can type a response in the dynamic prompt input field instead of at the command line. The dynamic prompt for the **POLYGON** command is shown in Figure 5-50.

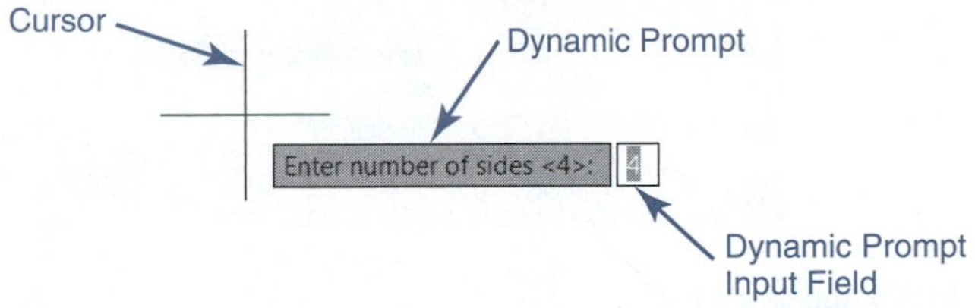

Figure 5-50
Using dynamic prompts

Dynamic Prompts also allows you to select command options near the cursor using the arrow keys on your keyboard. If a command has options, a down arrow is displayed in the dynamic prompt tooltip. Pressing the down arrow key displays the command options in a shortcut menu near the cursor. The **ZOOM** command options are shown in Figure 5-51.

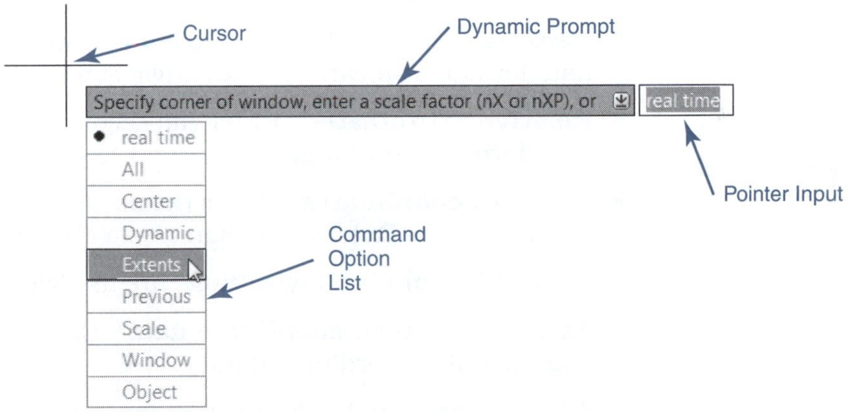

Figure 5-51
Selecting dynamic prompt options

You can use your up and down arrow keys to navigate to the desired option and hit **<Enter>**, or you can select an option with your mouse pointer.

Dynamic Input Settings

The dynamic input settings are managed on the **Dynamic Input** tab of the **Drafting Settings** dialog box shown in Figure 5-52.

The following sections explain the different dynamic input settings.

Pointer Input Settings. You can turn **Pointer Input** on and off via the **Enable Pointer Input** check box. The **Settings...** button displays the **Pointer Input Settings** dialog box shown in Figure 5-53. This dialog box allows you to control the format and visibility of the pointer input coordinate tooltips.

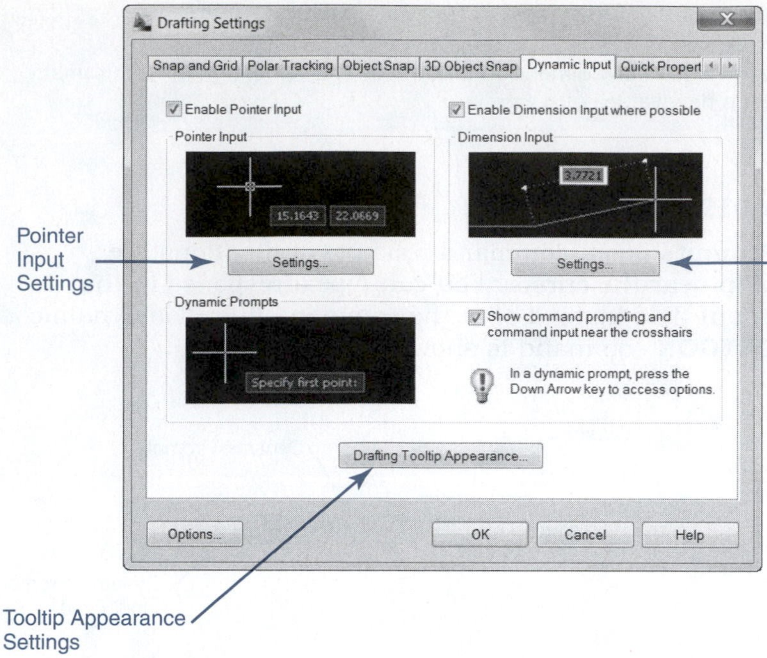

Figure 5-52
Dynamic input settings

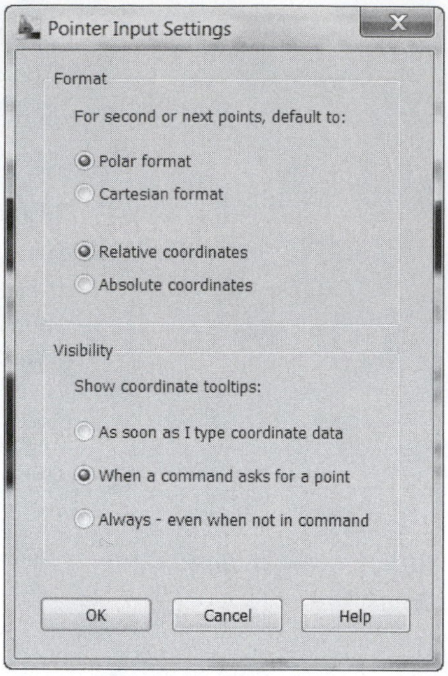

Figure 5-53
The **Pointer Input Settings** dialog box

The different format settings are as follows:

- **Polar format** Enter the second or next point in polar coordinate format. Enter a comma (,) to change to Cartesian format.
- **Cartesian format** Enter the second or next point in Cartesian coordinate format. You can enter an angle symbol (<) to change to polar format.
- **Relative coordinates** Enter the second or next point in relative coordinate format. Enter a pound sign (#) to change to absolute format.
- **Absolute coordinates** Enter the second or next point in absolute coordinate format. Enter an at sign (@) to change to polar format.

The different visibility settings are as follows:

- **As soon as I type coordinate data** Displays tooltips only when you start to enter coordinate data
- **When a command asks for a point** Displays tooltips whenever a command prompts for a point
- **Always - even when not in command** Always displays tooltips when **Pointer Input** is turned on

Dimension Input Settings. You can turn **Dimension Input** on and off via the **Enable Dimension Input where possible** check box (see Figure 5-52). The **Settings...** button displays the **Dimension Input Settings** dialog box shown in Figure 5-54. This dialog box allows you to control the visibility of the dimension input coordinate tooltips when you are editing using grips.

The different visibility settings are as follows:

- **Show only 1 dimension input field at a time** Displays only the distance dimension input tooltip when you are using grips
- **Show 2 dimension input fields at a time** Displays the distance and angle dimension input tooltips when you are using grips

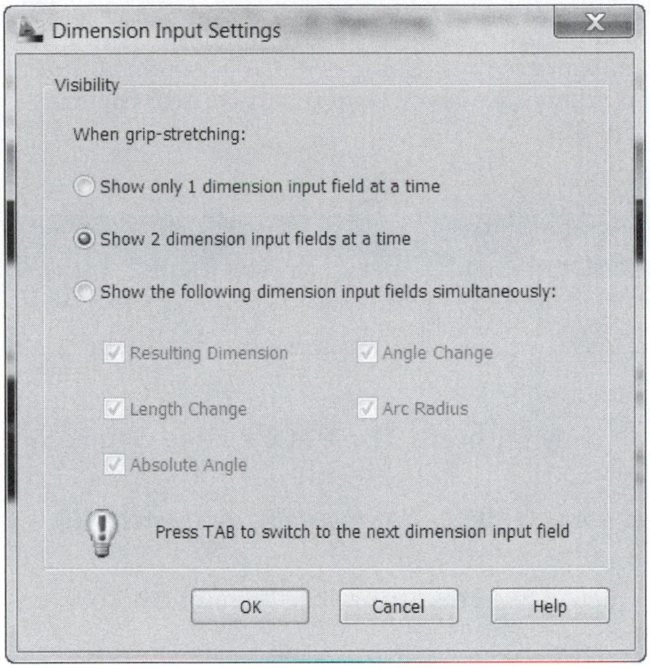

Figure 5-54
The **Dimension Input Settings** dialog box

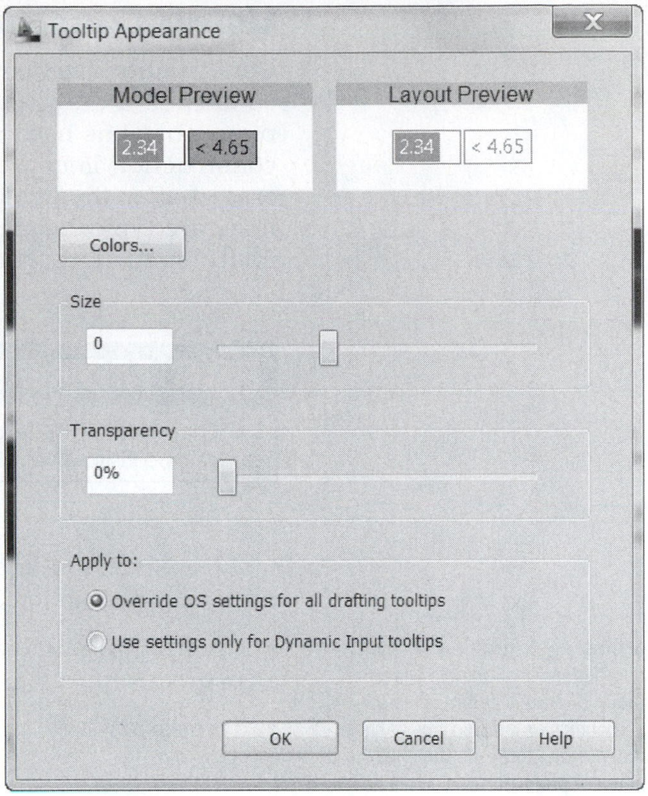

Figure 5-55
The **Tooltip Appearance** dialog box

- **Show the following dimension input fields simultaneously** Displays the selected dimension input tooltips when you are using grips. You can select one or more of the check boxes

Dynamic Prompts. You can turn **Dynamic Prompts** on and off via the **Show command prompting and command input near the crosshairs** check box (see Figure 5-52).

Controlling the Drafting Tooltip Appearance. The **Drafting Tooltip Appearance...** button displays the **Tooltip Appearance** dialog box shown in Figure 5-55. This dialog box allows you to control the color, size, and transparency of the dynamic input tooltips.

To change the color of the tooltip in both model space and layout space, select the **Colors...** button to display the **Drawing Window Colors** dialog box. The **Drawing Window Colors** dialog box allows you to change the tooltips in both environments by selecting the proper **Context** setting.

To change the size of tooltips, you can either move the slider to the right to make tooltips bigger or move it to the left to make tooltips smaller. The default size is 0.

To change the transparency of tooltips, you can either move the slider to the right to make tooltips more transparent or move it to the left to make them less transparent. A value of 0 makes the tooltips opaque.

You can choose to apply your changes using the following:

- **Override OS settings for all drafting tooltips** Applies the settings to all tooltips, overriding the settings in the operating system
- **Use settings only for Dynamic Input tooltips** Applies the settings only to the drafting tooltips used in dynamic input

Using Construction Lines

Construction lines are temporary lines that are used to help you lay out, or construct, a drawing. Using construction lines to create drawings is a technique that has been around since the early days of drafting. On the board, construction lines were typically drawn with very light lines that could be erased after the final drawing was created. Using AutoCAD, construction lines are typically created on a separate layer so you can control their visibility by turning them on and off.

FOR MORE DETAILS

See Chapter 6 for detailed information on using layers to separate drawing information to control the visibility of objects.

Construction lines serve many purposes. Some of the more common uses of construction lines are:

orthographic projection: The two-dimensional graphic representation of an object formed by the perpendicular intersections of lines drawn from points on the object to a plane of projection.

- Creating multiple views of a mechanical drawing using ***orthographic projection***
- Temporary locating of geometric features using object snaps and offset distances
- Creating architectural elevations based on features located on an existing floor plan, and vice versa
- Bisecting an angle

One of the classic uses of construction lines is in the creation of multiple views of a mechanical drawing using orthographic projection. See Figure 5-56.

Using construction lines, you can create one view of a part (e.g., front, top, side) and then locate horizontal and vertical (orthographic) construction lines on key points of the part using the object snaps explained earlier in the chapter to project the points as construction lines in other views. You can then create the other views by drawing directly over the top of the construction lines using the **Intersection** object snap introduced earlier. Once you complete all the necessary views to describe the part, you can erase or turn off the construction line layer, and you have a finished drawing.

Using the construction line approach, you have to measure distances only once when you create the first view of the part. Most, if not all, of the other views can then be created by projecting construction lines from the original view, which you know is accurate. Theoretically, if you draw the part correctly in the first view, all the other views that are based on it should also be correct. Using construction lines is a great time-saving technique that increases production and promotes precision.

CONSTRUCTION LINE	
Ribbon & Panel:	Home | Draw 
Draw Toolbar:	
Menu:	Draw | Construction Line
Command Line:	XLINE
Command Alias:	XL

The XLINE Command

In AutoCAD, construction lines are referred to as *Xlines* and extend infinitely in both directions. This infinite property allows you to zoom or pan as far as necessary and always have the construction lines visible so you can reference them. Construction lines are created using the **XLINE** command.

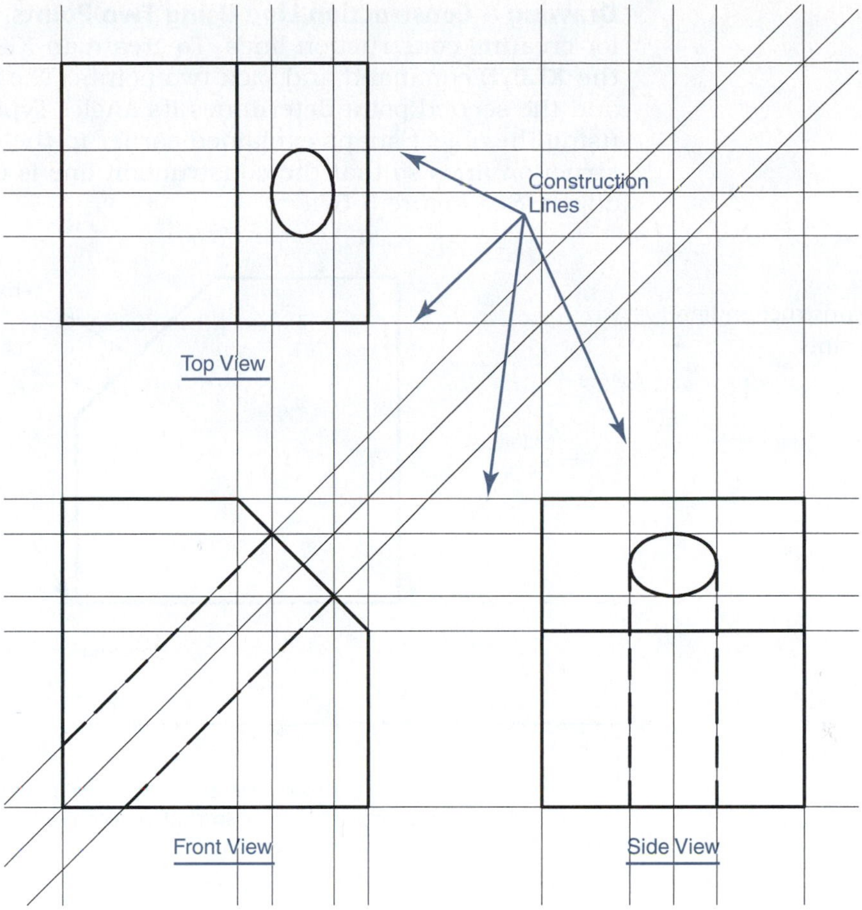

Figure 5-56
Multiview drawing using orthographic projection

NOTE

The **Zoom Extents** tool is unaffected by Xline objects. Any Xlines that exist in a drawing are ignored when zooming to the drawing extents.

There are a number of different ways to create construction lines using the **XLINE** command:

- Using two pick points
- Horizontally
- Vertically
- Offset from an existing line
- Specified angle
- Bisected angle

The **XLINE** command options are explained in the following sections.

FOR MORE DETAILS

See page 114 in Chapter 3 for more information about using the **Zoom Extents** tool.

Drawing a Construction Line Using Two Points. This is the default option for creating construction lines. To create an Xline using two points, select the **XLINE** command and pick two points. The first point locates the Xline, and the second point determines its angle. Typically you select points using the object snaps explained earlier in the chapter when creating construction lines so that the construction line is drawn relative to an existing object. See Figure 5-57.

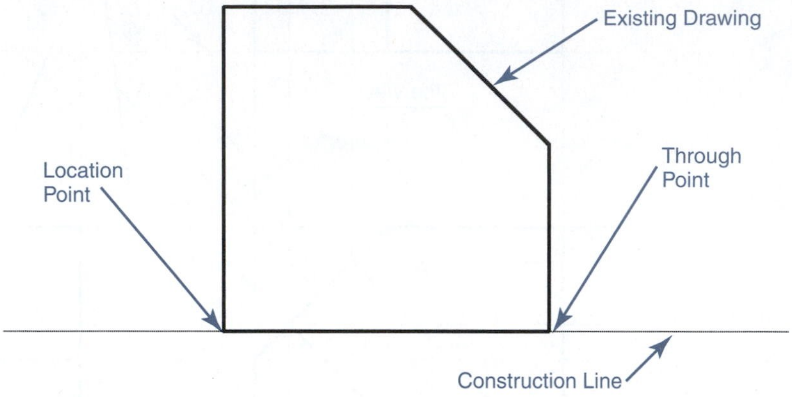

Figure 5-57
Drawing a construction line using two points

> **TIP**
>
> The first point you select to create a construction line using two points becomes the midpoint of the construction line so that you can snap to it using the **Midpoint** object snap later.

Drawing Horizontal and Vertical Construction Lines. Horizontal and vertical construction lines are the two most popular **XLINE** command options because they help facilitate the creation of multiview drawings using orthographic projection.

To create a horizontal construction line, select the **XLINE** command and type **H<Enter>** at the command line or select **Hor** from the list of **Dynamic Input** command options. To create a vertical construction line, select the **XLINE** command and type **V<Enter>** at the command line or select **Ver** from the list of **Dynamic Input** command options. You then select a single point to locate the horizontal or vertical construction line in your drawing. AutoCAD continues to prompt for points until you type **<Enter>** so you can create as many construction lines as needed. See Figures 5-58A and B.

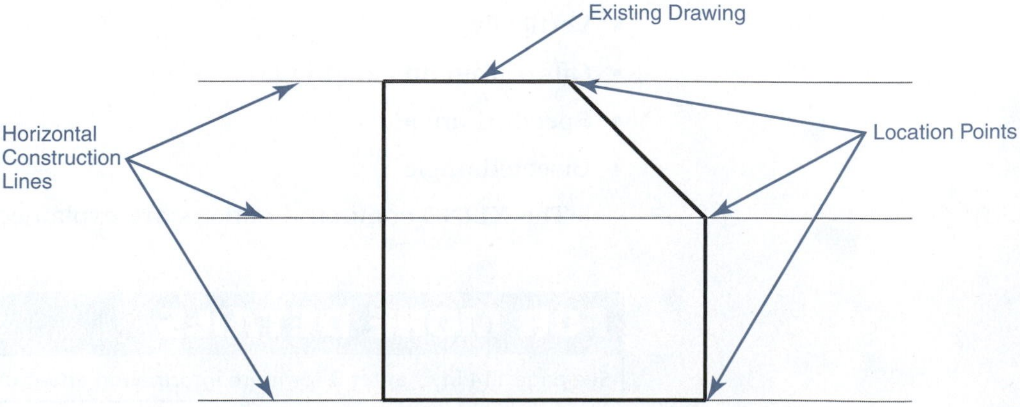

Figure 5-58A
Drawing horizontal construction lines

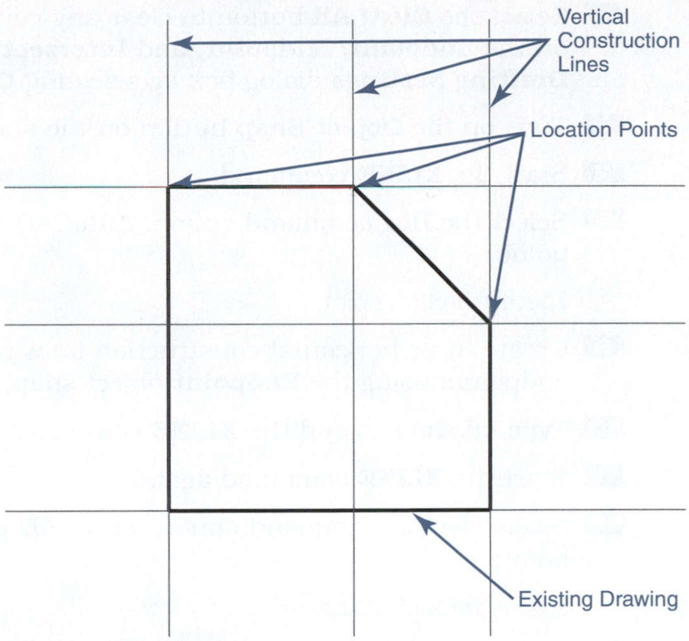

Figure 5-58B
Drawing vertical construction lines

EXERCISE 5-11 Drawing Horizontal and Vertical Construction Lines

1. Start a new drawing using the **acad.dwt** drawing template.
2. Create the drawing shown in Figure 5-59.

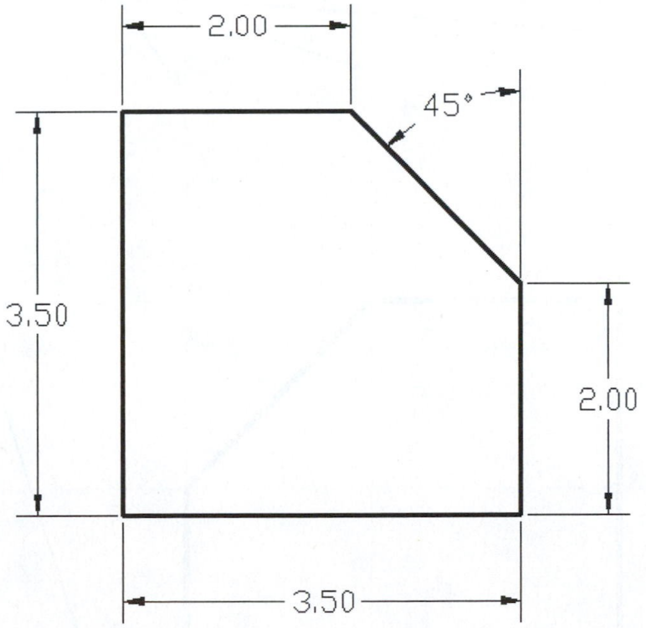

Figure 5-59
Front view of part

3. Turn off all the drawing tool buttons on the status bar.
4. Right-click on the **Object Snap** button on the status bar and select **Settings...** from the shortcut menu. The **Object Snap** tab of the **Drafting Settings** dialog box is displayed (see Figure 5-17).

5 Select the **Clear All** button to clear any running object snaps. Turn on the **Endpoint, Midpoint,** and **Intersection** object snaps. Exit the **Drafting Settings** dialog box by selecting **OK**.

6 Turn on the **Object Snap** button on the status bar.

7 Start the **XLINE** command.

8 Select the **Hor** command option. AutoCAD prompts you for a through point:

Specify through point:

9 Create three horizontal construction lines by snapping to the three endpoints using the **Endpoint** object snap, as shown in Figure 5-58A.

10 Type **<Enter>** to end the **XLINE** command.

11 Start the **XLINE** command again.

12 Select the **Ver** command option. AutoCAD prompts you for a through point:

Specify through point:

13 Create three vertical construction lines by snapping to the three endpoints using the **Endpoint** object snap, as shown in Figure 5-58B.

14 Type **<Enter>** to end the **XLINE** command.

15 Save your drawing as ***CH5_EXERCISE11***. Your drawing should look like Figure 5-60.

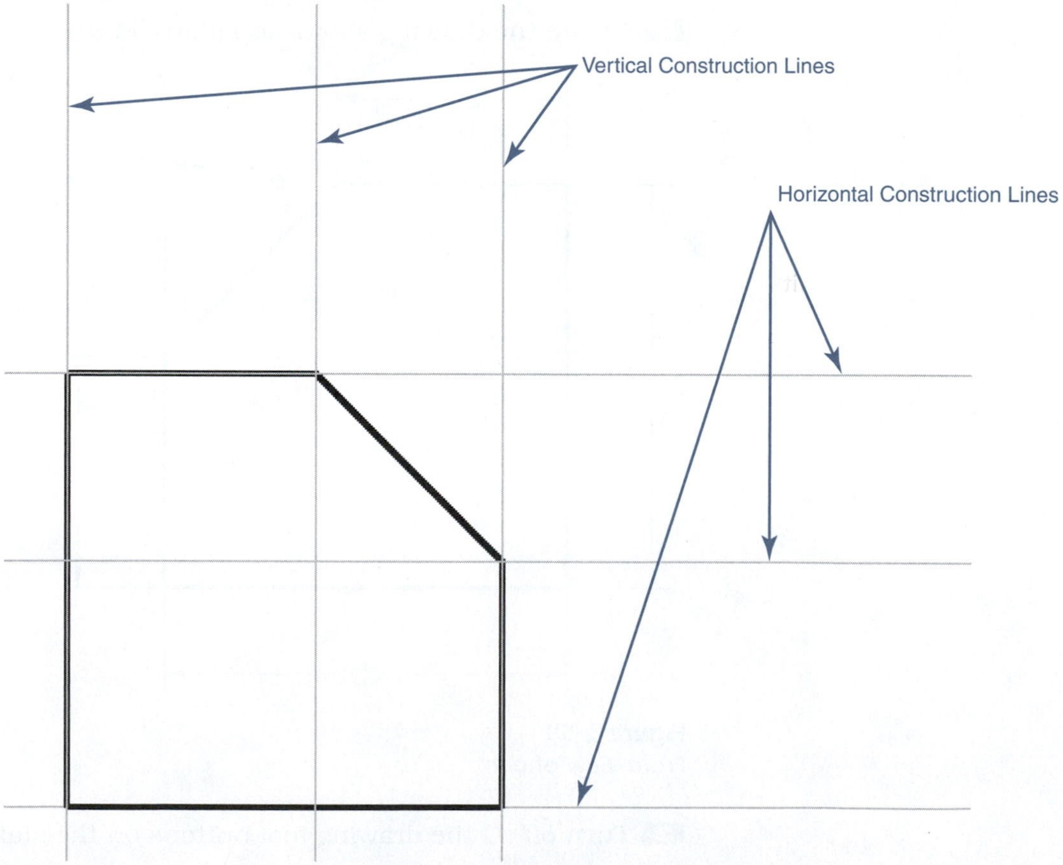

Figure 5-60
Drawing horizontal and vertical construction lines

Offsetting Objects with Construction Lines. To further facilitate the layout and construction of a drawing, you can offset an existing line object (line, polyline, etc.) with a parallel construction line by either specifying a distance or picking a through point.

To offset an object, start the **XLINE** command and select the **Offset** option. The offset distance either can be entered via the keyboard, or it can be indicated by selecting the point in the drawing you want to offset through. The default is to enter the distance at the keyboard.

Both options require that you select the line object you want to offset (see Figure 5-61A) and then pick a point on either side of the selected line object to indicate the direction you want to offset (see Figure 5-61B). If you are using the **Through** option, the pick point is also used to locate the line.

AutoCAD will continue to prompt you to select objects to offset until you press **<Enter>** so that it is possible to offset multiple objects at a time.

Figure 5-61A
Offsetting an object with a construction line

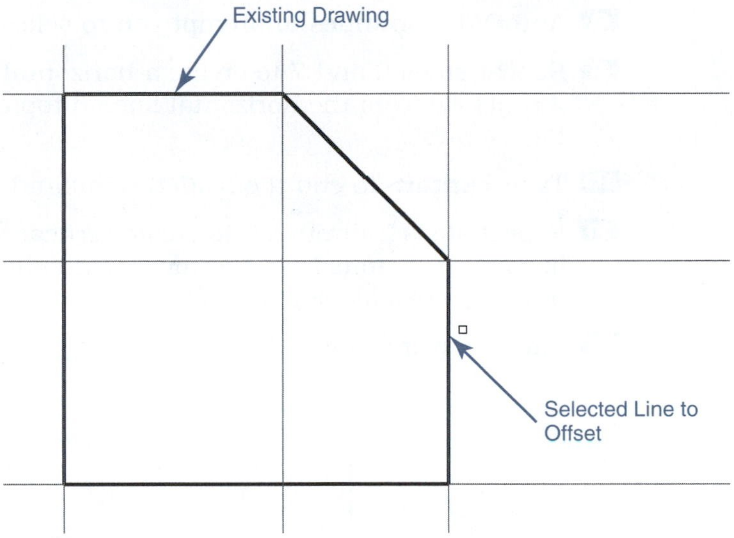

Figure 5-61B
Offsetting an object with a construction line

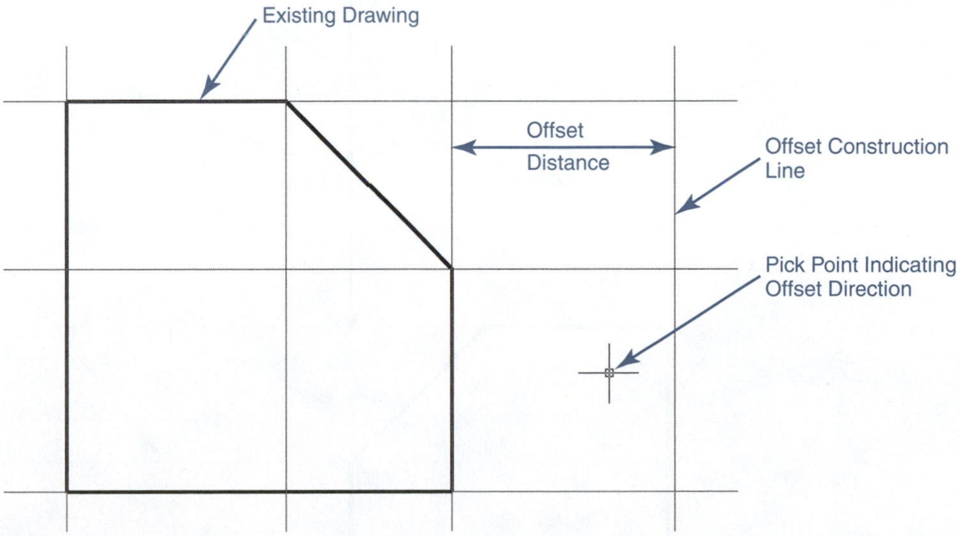

EXERCISE 5-12 **Offsetting Objects with Construction Lines**

1 Continue from Exercise 5-11.

2 Select the **XLINE** command from the **Draw** panel.

3. Select the **Offset** option.
4. AutoCAD prompts you for an offset distance or through point:

   Specify offset distance or ↓.
5. Type **2<Enter>**. AutoCAD prompts you to select the object you want to offset:

   Select a line object:
6. Select the vertical line, as shown in Figure 5-61A. AutoCAD then prompts you for the side you wish to offset:

   Specify side to offset:
7. Pick a point on the right side of the object, as shown in Figure 5-61B, to indicate that you want to create a vertical construction line offset on the right-hand side of the line.
8. AutoCAD continues to prompt you to select line objects.
9. Repeat steps 6 and 7 to create a horizontal construction line offset 2 units up from the horizontal line on top of the part, as shown in Figure 5-62.
10. Type **<Enter>** to end the **XLINE** command.
11. Repeat steps 2 through 9 to create vertical and horizontal construction lines offset 3 units from the construction lines you just created so your drawing looks like Figure 5-62.
12. Save your drawing.

Figure 5-62
Offsetting objects with construction lines

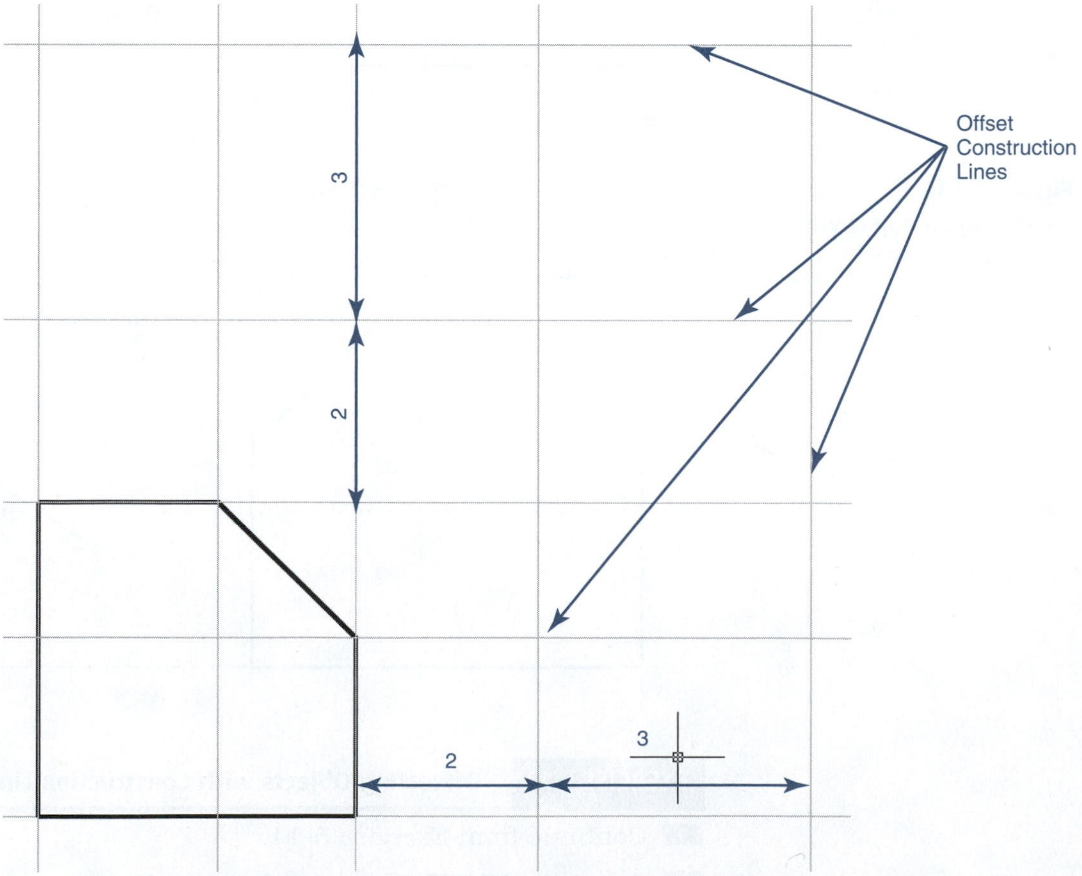

Drawing Angular Construction Lines. Construction lines can be created at an angle either by specifying an angle from the horizontal axis 0° or by referencing an angle from an existing line.

To create a construction line at an angle, start the **XLINE** command and select the **Angle** option. By default, AutoCAD prompts you for an angle. Enter the desired angle and locate the construction line by selecting a point. Figure 5-63 shows a 45° construction line located at the **Midpoint** object snap of an angled line.

Using the **Reference** option allows you to select a line object and use its existing angle as a base angle. You can then enter the angle relative to the selected line object. For instance, to create the 45° construction line shown in Figure 5-63 using the **Reference** option, you would first select the existing angled line and then input the desired angle relative to the selected line. Inputting 90° creates a construction line perpendicular to the angled line, which just so happens to also be 45° from the *X*-axis.

Figure 5-63
Drawing a construction line at an angle

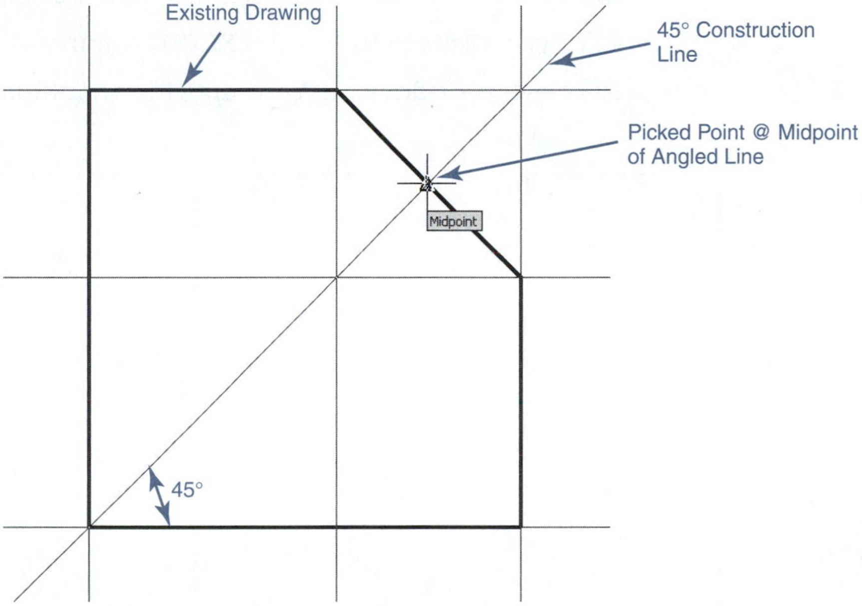

EXERCISE 5-13 **Drawing Angular Construction Lines**

1. Continue from Exercise 5-12.
2. Start the **XLINE** command.
3. Select the **Angle** option.
4. AutoCAD prompts you to enter an angle:

   Enter angle of xline (0) or ↓.

5. Type **45<Enter>**. AutoCAD prompts you for a through point:

   Specify through point:

6. Select the **Midpoint** object snap of the angled line as shown in Figure 5-63.
7. Type **<Enter>** to end the **XLINE** command.
8. Start the **XLINE** command again.
9. Select the **Offset** option.

10. AutoCAD prompts you to specify an offset distance:

    Specify offset distance or ↓.

11. Type **.5<Enter>**. AutoCAD prompts you to select the object you want to offset:

    Select a line object:

12. Select the angled construction line you just created. AutoCAD then prompts you for the side you wish to offset:

    Specify side to offset:

13. Pick a point on the bottom right side of the angled construction line.
14. Select the angled construction line again. AutoCAD then prompts you for the side you wish to offset:

    Specify side to offset:

15. Pick a point on the top left side of the angled construction line.
16. Type **<Enter>** to end the **XLINE** command.
17. Save your drawing. Your drawing should look like Figure 5-64.

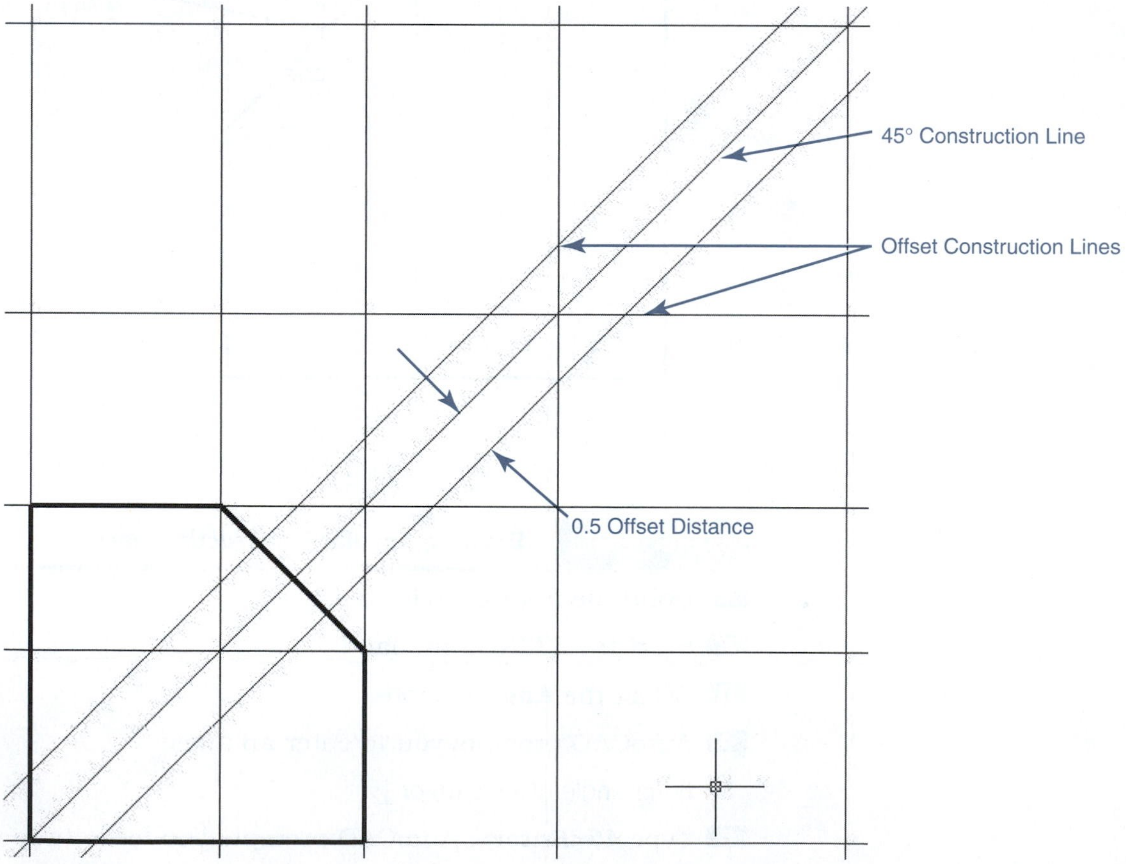

Figure 5-64
Drawing angular construction lines

Bisecting an Angle with a Construction Line. You can split an angle into two equal parts by creating a construction line at the bisector of an existing angle using the **XLINE** command's **Bisect** option.

To create a construction line at the bisector of an angle, start the **XLINE** command and select the **Bisect** option. AutoCAD prompts you to select a vertex point, an angle start point, and an angle endpoint, as shown in Figure 5-65.

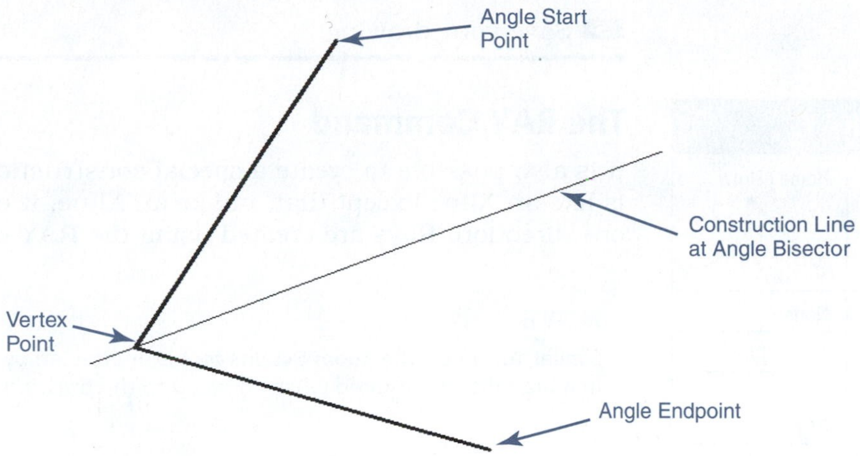

Figure 5-65
Drawing a construction line at an angle

AutoCAD will continue to prompt you to select angle endpoints until you press **<Enter>** so that it is possible to bisect multiple related angles at the same time.

EXERCISE 5-14 Creating the Final Drawing Using Construction Lines

1. Continue from Exercise 5-13.
2. Create the remaining horizontal and vertical construction lines shown in Figure 5-66.

Figure 5-66
Creating the final drawing using construction lines

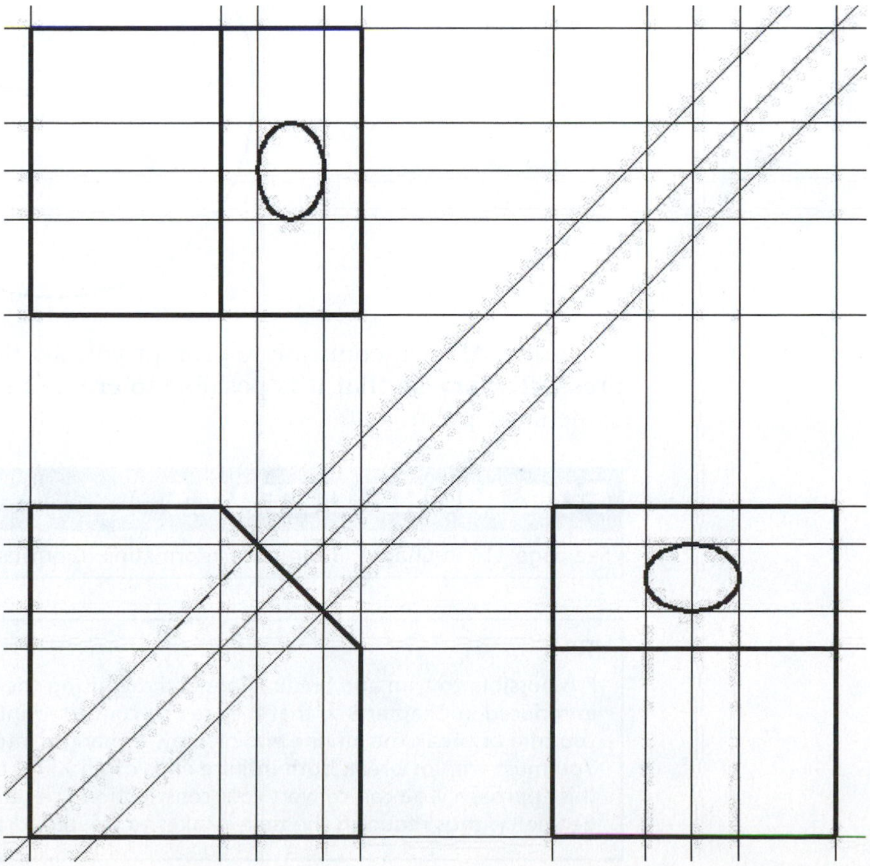

3. Use the **Intersection** object snap with the **LINE** and **ELLIPSE** commands to create the final drawing shown in Figure 5-66. Hidden lines are not required.

4. Erase all the construction lines using the **ERASE** command.

5. Save your drawing.

RAY	
Ribbon & Panel:	Home | Draw 
Toolbar:	None
Menu:	Draw | Ray
Command Line:	RAY
Command Alias:	None

The RAY Command

It is also possible to create a special construction line known as a *ray* that is like an Xline except that, unlike an Xline, it extends to infinity in only one direction. Rays are created using the **RAY** command.

> **NOTE**
>
> Similar to Xlines, the **Zoom Extents** tool is unaffected by ray objects. Any rays that exist in a drawing are ignored when zooming to the drawing extents.

After selecting the **RAY** command, AutoCAD prompts you to pick a start point and a through point to indicate the direction and angle of the ray, as shown in Figure 5-67.

Figure 5-67
Drawing a ray

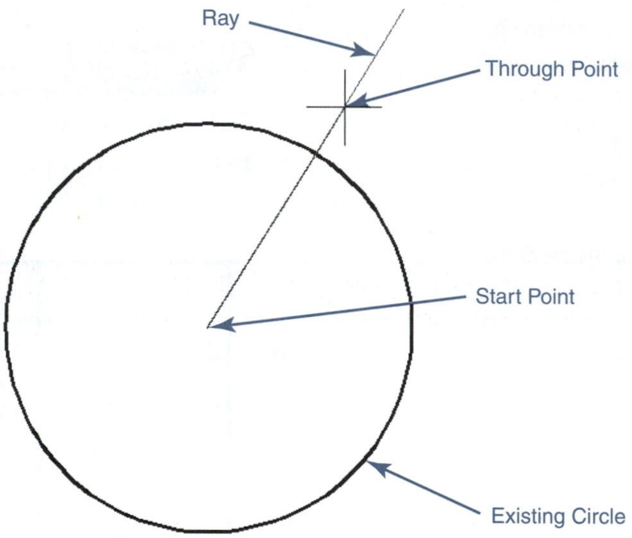

AutoCAD will continue to prompt you for through points until you press **<Enter>** so that it is possible to create multiple rays that share the same start point.

> **FOR MORE DETAILS**
>
> See page 114 in Chapter 3 for more information about using the **Zoom Extents** tool.

> **TIP**
>
> It is possible to trim and break Xlines and rays using the advanced editing commands introduced in Chapter 8 so that they can be converted into regular AutoCAD lines. When you trim or break the infinite end of a ray, it changes into a line with two endpoints. You must trim or break both infinite ends of an Xline to change it into a line. Using this approach, you can convert your construction lines directly into the final drawing geometry, thus reducing the time it takes to create a drawing.

Chapter Summary

Mastering the different drawing tools and drafting settings explained in this chapter will increase your drafting exponentially. Being able to locate points quickly and accurately using object snaps is one of the main keys to being more productive. Knowing that a point is located exactly where you intend it makes you a more confident, assured drafter. It's these qualities that help you to succeed in creating quality CAD drawings in a timely fashion.

Dynamic input allows you to enter information directly at your cursor so that you can focus on your drawing and not have to look back and forth to the command line all of the time. Plus, when **Dynamic Input** is on, you can use your **Tab** key to switch between input fields so you can lock in distances and angles. As an added bonus, you can also select command options on the screen by pressing the down arrow key on your keyboard whenever command options are available.

Using construction lines to lay out drawings is an age-old art that not many people know about these days. This is a shame because they can help you become a faster, more accurate drafter. Not only do construction lines allow you to measure once, and then draw twice, or more, they also can speed up the creation of floor plan drawings and even schematics. Using the **XLINE** command with the **Offset** option and some basic object snaps, you can lay out a drawing lickety-split. Put the construction lines on a layer that has its **No Plot** property on, and voilà, you can leave your construction lines on in your drawing but they will not show up on your plots!

FOR MORE DETAILS

See page 234 in Chapter 6 for information on setting up a layer so that it does not plot but you can still see information in your drawing.

Chapter Test Questions

Multiple Choice

Circle the correct answer.

1. Most of AutoCAD's drawing tools can be toggled on and off by:
   a. Selecting the buttons on the status bar
   b. Using keyboard function keys
   c. Typing them at the command line
   d. All of the above
2. The rectangular grid display area is determined by the:
   a. Units setting
   b. Drawing limits
   c. Zoom scale factor
   d. Size of your computer monitor

3. The two major different snap styles are:
   a. Rectangular and polar
   b. Rotated and isometric
   c. Horizontal and vertical
   d. Rows and columns
4. The **Ortho Mode** drawing tool restricts your cursor movement to:
   a. 45° angles
   b. 90° angles
   c. Horizontal axis
   d. Vertical axis
5. Polar tracking works by displaying a dashed line referred to as:
   a. Construction line
   b. Vector path
   c. Alignment path
   d. Tracking path
6. Object snaps can be selected by:
   a. Right-clicking on the **Object Snap** button on the status bar
   b. Using the right-click shortcut menu
   c. Typing them at the command line
   d. All of the above
7. Turning an object snap on via the **Object Snap** tab of the **Drafting Settings** dialog box is referred to as:
   a. Making an object snap permanent
   b. Setting a running object snap
   c. Creating an object snap override
   d. Setting the default object snap
8. An ellipsis (...) next to an object snap AutoSnap marker indicates the object snap is:
   a. Implied
   b. Delayed
   c. Waiting for AutoCAD to regen
   d. Deferred
9. Object snap tracking can display alignment paths:
   a. At all polar increment angles
   b. Horizontally
   c. Vertically
   d. Horizontally and vertically
10. Construction lines are used for:
    a. Laying out your drawing
    b. Creating different views using orthographic projection
    c. Bisecting angles
    d. All of the above

Matching

Write the number of the correct answer on the line.

a. Grid display ______
b. **Snap** mode ______
c. **Ortho** mode ______
d. Polar tracking ______
e. Running object snap ______
f. Object snap override ______
g. Acquired point ______
h. Alignment path ______
i. Object snap tracking ______
j. Construction line ______

1. Displays dashed alignment paths that temporarily restrict cursor to preset angle increments
2. Object snap tracking vector used to locate a point
3. Temporary object snap that can be used for one pick point
4. Rectangular pattern of evenly spaced lines displayed on the screen
5. Controls movement of cursor to specific x and y increments
6. Restricts cursor movement to the horizontal (X-) and vertical (Y-) axes
7. Displays dashed alignment paths at object snap points
8. Temporary lines used to lay out a drawing
9. Object snaps that are on continuously
10. Selected point used to create complex object snaps

True or False

Circle the correct answer.

1. **True or False:** It is possible to remove drawing tool buttons temporarily from the status bar.
2. **True or False:** Drawing tools can be toggled on and off when a command is active.
3. **True or False:** The grid display controls the cursor movement.
4. **True or False:** The snap and grid spacing must always be the same.
5. **True or False:** It is possible to use the **Ortho Mode** and **Polar Tracking** drawing tools at the same time.
6. **True or False:** Polar tracking angles are always measured from the AutoCAD base angle (0°).
7. **True or False:** Object snaps work only when you are prompted for a point at the command line.
8. **True or False:** It is possible to snap to the intersection of two lines even if they don't visually cross but would if they were extended.
9. **True or False:** You must always pick an acquired point when using object snaps.
10. **True or False:** Construction lines extend to your drawing limits.

chapterfive

Chapter Projects

G Project 5-1: *Calculator* [BASIC]

1. Start a new drawing using the **acad.dwt** template.
2. Draw the figure shown in Figure 5-68 using the appropriate grid and snap settings. Toggle the **Object Snap** button on and off as needed. The borders around the perimeter and around the screen area are 1/16″. The spacing between the buttons is 1/8″. **Do not** draw the dimensions.
3. Save the drawing as ***P5-1***.

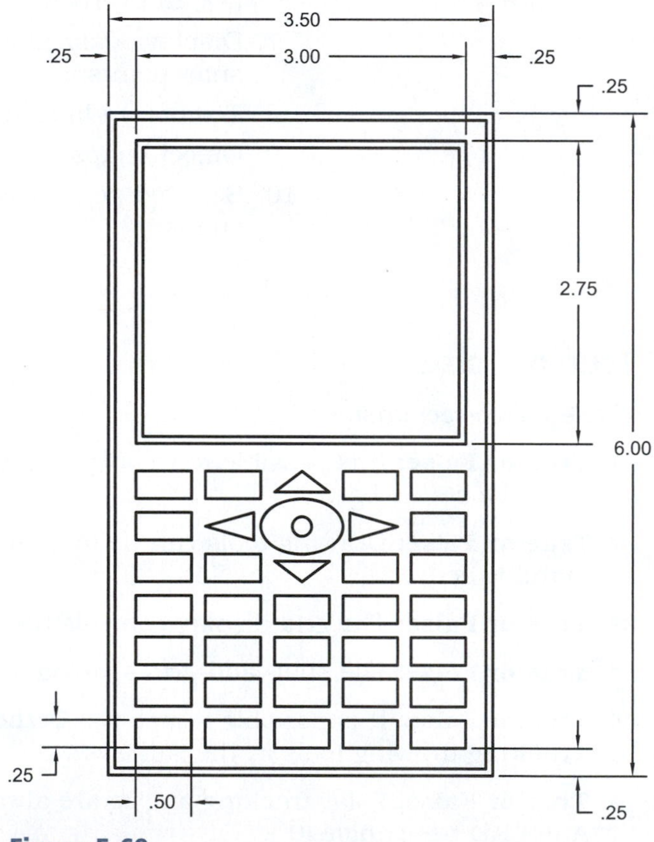

Figure 5-68

M Project 5-2: *B-Size Mechanical Border, continued from Chapter 4* [INTERMEDIATE]

1. Open the template file ***Mechanical B-Size.DWT*** from Chapter 4.
2. Add the line work shown in Figure 5-69. **Do not** draw dimensions.
3. Save the drawing template file.

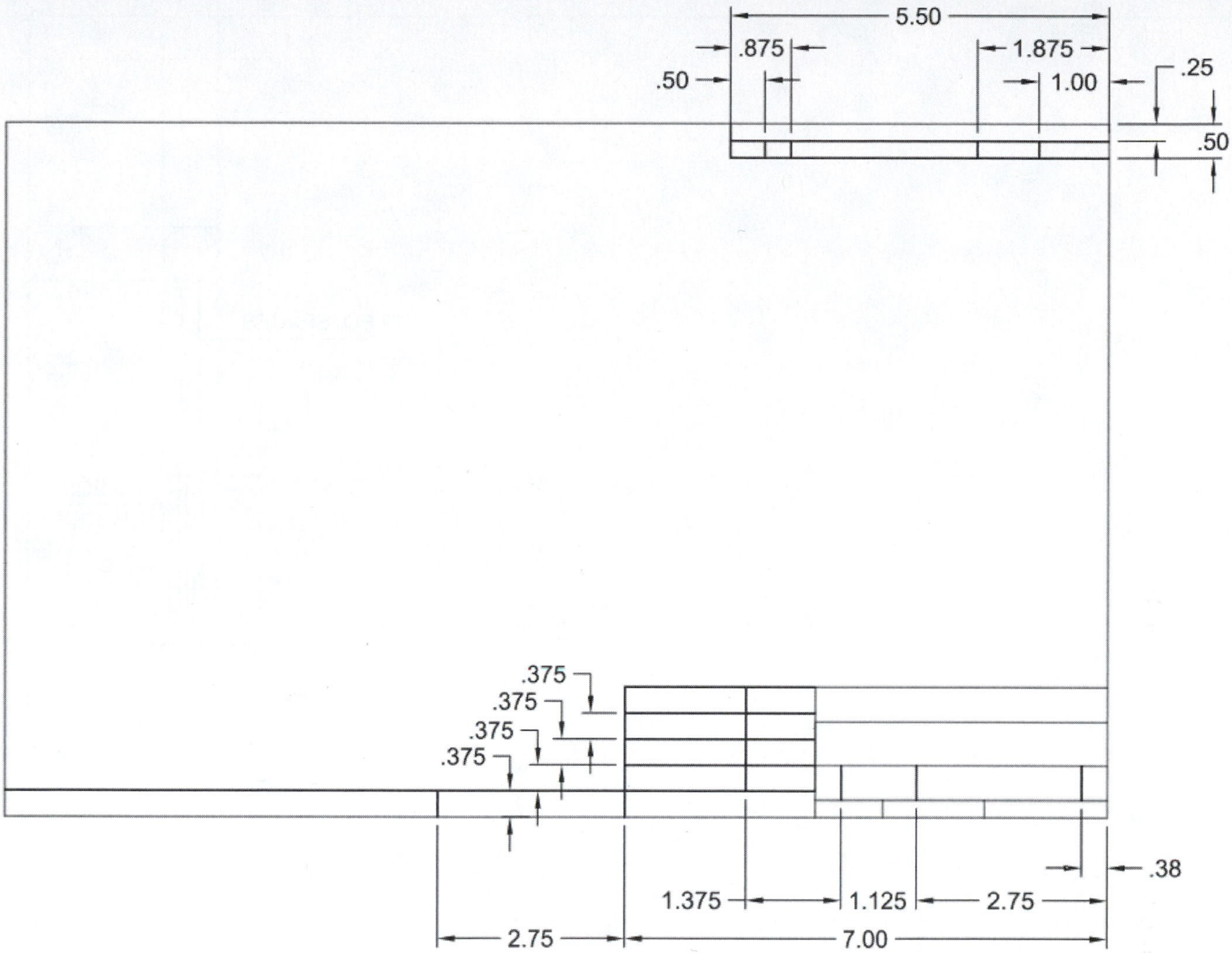

Figure 5-69

A Project 5-3: *Architectural D-Size Border, continued from Chapter 4* [ADVANCED]

1. Open the template file ***Architectural D-Size.DWT*** from Chapter 4.
2. Add the line work as shown to the border as shown in Figure 5-70 using construction lines and object snaps to your advantage. *Hint:* You can use the **DIVIDE** command to lay out the equally spaced title block lines.
3. Save the drawing template file.

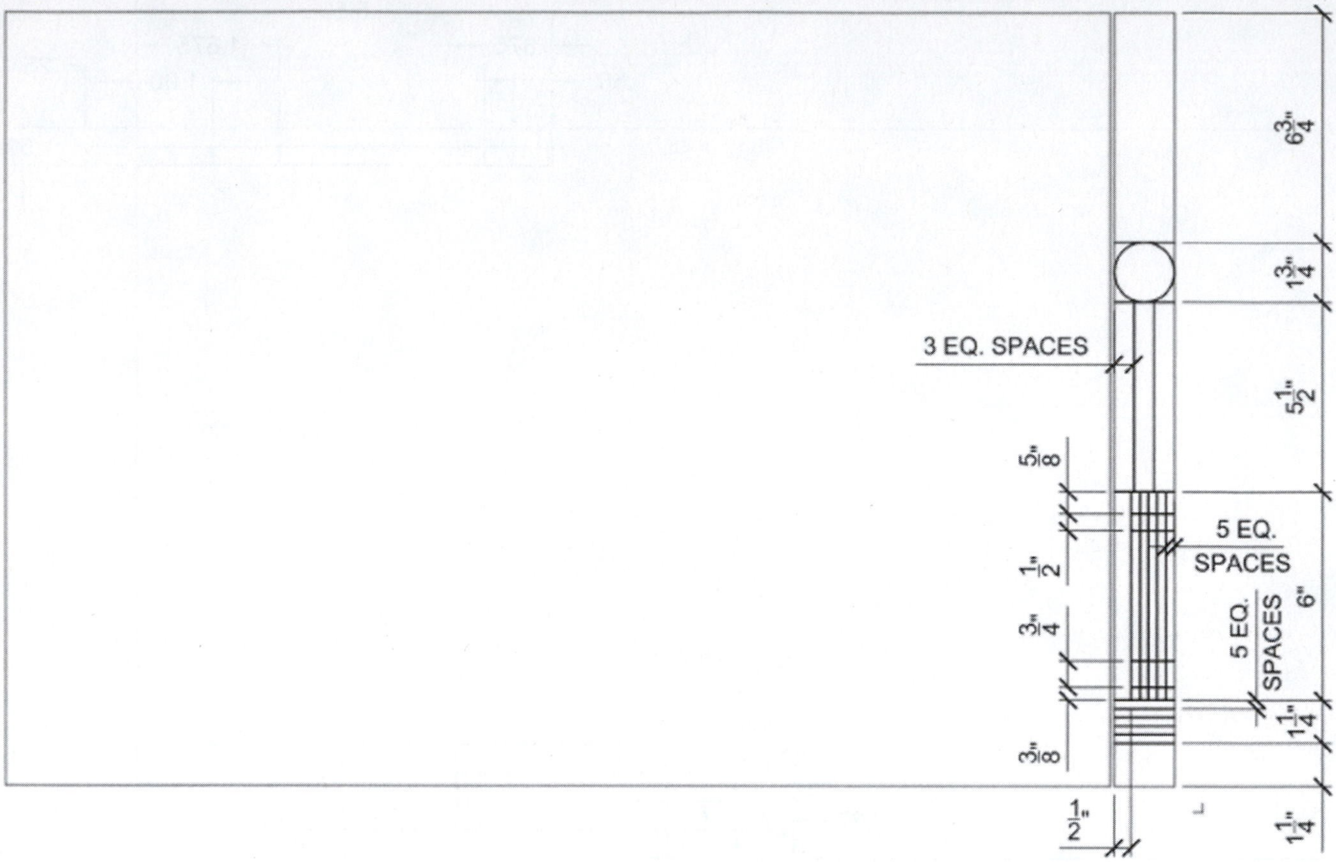

Figure 5-70

E Project 5-4: *Electrical Schematic, continued from Chapter 4* [BASIC]

1. Open drawing ***P4-4*** from Chapter 4.
2. Set the **Grid Display** and **Snap Mode** spacing to **0.125**.
3. Draw the electrical schematic shown in Figure 5-71. *Hint:* Use the grid display and **Snap** mode to draw the lines and object snaps to locate the electrical symbols.
4. Save the drawing as ***P5-4***.

chapter six
Managing Object Properties

CHAPTER OBJECTIVES

- Create layers
- Set layer properties
- Load linetypes
- Modify the properties of drawing objects
- Use **DesignCenter** and **Content Explorer** to import layers from other drawings
- Create layer filters and groups
- Manage layer states
- Control object visibility

Introduction

Precise, accurate, and clear drawings are a primary goal of any drafter. However, equally important in CAD is creating a well-organized drawing. Chapter 2 gave you a brief overview of object properties and layering. In this chapter, we'll take a closer look at object properties, how to effectively use layers to organize your drawing, and how to control the look and final output of your drawing.

Common Object Properties

Every object in AutoCAD has five primary properties associated with it: color, linetype, lineweight, transparency, and layer. These properties control how objects are displayed in your drawing and also control how objects are plotted. Color controls the color of an object and can also be used to control the plotted lineweight of an object, linetype controls the line pattern (dashed, dotted, etc.) used to display objects, lineweight (or pen width) controls the width of objects when plotted, and transparency allows you to control the ability to see through objects.

layer: A collection of object properties and display settings that are applied to objects.

A ***layer*** is a collection of color, linetype, and lineweight properties that can be used to organize the objects in your drawing. Layers are the primary way in which drawing information is organized.

The concept of layering goes back to the days of manual drafting in which transparent overlays were used to control the content of a blueprint. For example, an architect might create an architectural base print showing the location of walls, doors, windows, and so on. An electrical engineer might then create a transparent overlay showing the location of the electrical equipment, outlets, and such. To create the electrical plan blueprint, you would take the architectural base print, place the electrical overlay on top of it, and run the stack of drawings through the blueprint machine. The resulting print would show the electrical drawing layer over the top of the architectural base drawing.

Layering in AutoCAD works in a similar way. By assigning a layer to an AutoCAD object, you are, in effect, putting those objects on a transparent overlay. You can then turn these layers on and off and control which objects are shown in the drawing.

LAYER	
Ribbon & Panel:	Home | Layers 
Layers Toolbars:	
Menu:	Format | Layer...
Command Line:	LAYER
Command Alias:	LA

Layers

When you create a layer, you provide a name for that layer and then assign it a color, linetype, lineweight, and transparency level. Any objects placed on that layer will then, by default, take on the color, linetype, lineweight, and transparency level associated with that layer.

AutoCAD comes with a predefined layer, called Layer **0**. By default, everything on Layer **0** is drawn with color 7 (white/black), has a continuous linetype, uses the default lineweight (.25 mm or .01 inch) for plotting, and has a transparency level of 0, which is opaque. You can change the color, linetype, lineweight, and transparency settings for Layer **0**, but you cannot delete or rename Layer **0**.

Layers are created with the **LAYER** command.

The LAYER Command

When you start the **LAYER** command, AutoCAD displays the **Layer Properties Manager** palette (see Figure 6-1). The **Layer Properties Manager** palette works like all other palettes. It can be docked, hidden, or closed as needed.

Figure 6-1
The **Layer Properties Manager** palette

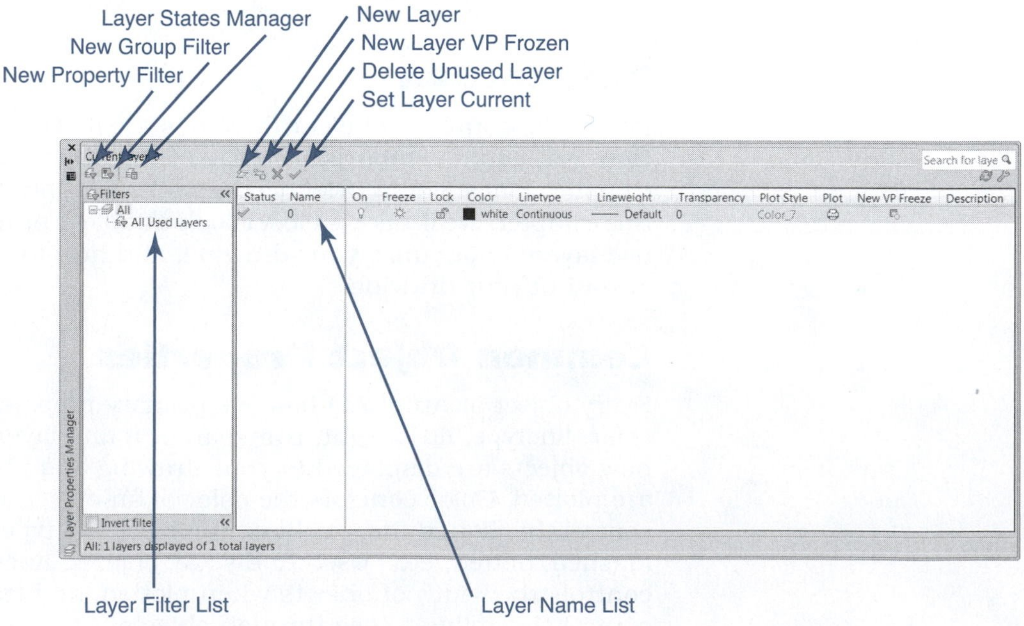

The **Layer Properties Manager** palette allows you to create and control all aspects of your layers. The palette is divided into two main areas; the layer filters are listed on the left, and the list of layers is shown on the right.

Layer filters allow you to show only layers that match a certain criterion—for example, all the layers that start with the letter "E" or all the layers that are red. The list of layers shows the layers currently defined in your drawing along with their current settings.

> **TIP**
>
> You can collapse the **Layer Filter** list by clicking on the double arrows on the top and bottom on the right side of the **Filters** pane.

Layer Name List

The list of layers is divided into columns with each column representing a layer setting. The column headings can be resized by dragging the divider bar between each column. You can also sort the layers by any of the columns by clicking on the column heading. To change a setting for a layer, simply click on the setting. To change the settings for multiple layers, first select the layers by holding down either the **<Shift>** or **<Ctrl>** key and selecting the layers, then click on the setting you want to change. The change will be applied to all the selected layers.

Controlling the Column Display. Clicking on a column heading at the top of the layer list in the **Layer Properties Manager** will toggle the display order of the layers in ascending or descending order using the information in the column header you click on.

You can resize a column by dragging the vertical bar between columns with your mouse, as well as rearrange the display order of the columns by dragging and dropping the column headings to different locations.

Right-clicking on a column heading displays a shortcut menu that allows you to turn different property columns on and off, maximize column widths, or reset everything back to the default. You can also display the **Customize Layer Columns** dialog box to turn multiple columns off simultaneously and rearrange the column order via the **Customize...** menu item.

Layer List Right-Click Shortcut Menu. Right-clicking anywhere in the layer list in the **Layer Properties Manager** displays the shortcut menu shown in Figure 6-2.

This shortcut menu provides a number of handy, time-saving features and capabilities. Many of the features and capabilities can be found elsewhere in the **Layer Properties Manager**, but a few are unique to the right-click menu. Some of the things you can do include:

- Turn the **Layer Filter** list on the left off and on
- Show any layer filters in the **Layer Name** list on the right so you can manage them as a unit
- Remove viewport property overrides
- Select all/deselect all layers for mass property updates

You can also create and restore layer states, which allow you to manage different saved layer settings. Layer states are discussed in detail later in this chapter.

Figure 6-2
Layer list right-click shortcut menu

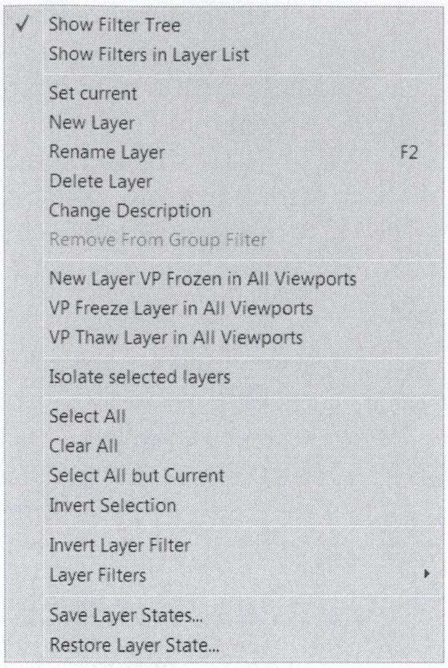

Layer Names. The layer name is the primary means of identifying a layer. Layer names can have up to 255 characters and can include letters and numbers as well as other special characters, including spaces. Layer names should convey the contents of that layer. Layer names can be based on part numbers, project names, design discipline (civil, architectural, etc.), or any other agreed-upon standard.

Layer Naming Standards. Many companies create layering standards based on their own experience and practices, or they may adopt or adapt a national or industry CAD standard. A good standard will be well documented, showing the appropriate settings and the type of drawing content that belongs on each layer.

> **NOTE**
> AutoCAD layer names can contain all but the following characters: <>/\“”:;?*|,=’

The American Institute of Architects (AIA) has published the CAD Layer Guidelines for the building industry that has been adopted by the National CAD Standards organization (http://nationalcadstandard.org). This layering standard describes a method of organizing layers based on a series of prefixes and descriptors that are easy to understand. Each discipline has a prefix; for example, all architectural layers start with A, electrical layers start with E, civil layers start with C, etc. Following the prefix is an abbreviation for the content of that layer, such as A-WALL for architectural walls or E-DEMO for electrical demolition.

To access student data files, go to **www.pearsondesigncentral.com.**

The student data files included with this book contain standard drawings for both architectural and mechanical design disciplines. The drawings contain layers set up in accordance with common industry standards.

Creating New Layers. To create a new layer, choose the **New Layer** button on the **Layer Properties Manager** palette. AutoCAD will create a new layer and automatically call it **Layer1**. The layer name is highlighted, so to rename the layer, simply type in the new name and press **<Enter>**. You can press **<Enter>** again to create another new layer.

TIP

You can also create multiple layers by typing the layer names separated by a comma. When you press the comma key, AutoCAD will end the first layer and create a new layer. This method allows you to create multiple layers easily.

EXERCISE 6-1 Creating Layers

1. Start a new drawing using the **acad.dwt** drawing template.
2. Start the **LAYER** command to display the **Layer Properties Manager** palette.
3. Choose the **New Layer** button. AutoCAD will create a layer called **Layer1**.
4. Type **Object<Enter>** to rename the new layer.
5. Press **<Enter>** to create another new layer.
6. Type **Hidden<Enter>** to rename the new layer.
7. Press **<Enter>** to create another new layer.
8. Type **Center,Dim,Title<Enter>** to create three new layers. Notice how every time you type the comma key, AutoCAD creates a new layer. You should now have a total of six layers (including Layer **0**) in your drawing.
9. Close the **Layer Properties Manager** palette.
10. Save your drawing as ***CH6_EXERCISE***.

Setting the Current Layer. To set a layer current, select the layer and choose the **Set Current** button (or press **<Alt>+C**). The current layer is the default layer for new drawing objects. Any new object will be placed on the current layer.

On/Off. The **On/Off** settings control the visibility of the layers in the drawing. Layers that are turned on are displayed, and those that are turned off do not display. However, when a layer is turned off, AutoCAD simply hides the layer from view. Objects can still be selected, modified, and even deleted when their layer is turned off.

Freeze/Thaw. The **Freeze/Thaw** settings are similar to **On/Off**. When a layer is frozen, AutoCAD ignores the objects on that layer and does not display them on screen. When a layer is frozen, AutoCAD will completely ignore the objects on that layer until that layer is thawed and the drawing regenerates. Objects on frozen layers cannot be modified until that layer is thawed. For this reason, freezing a layer is generally preferred to turning a layer off.

EXERCISE 6-2 Freeze and Thaw Versus On and Off

1. Continue from Exercise 6-1.
2. Draw a line anywhere on the screen. Since Layer **0** is current, the new line is drawn on Layer **0**.

3. Start the **LAYER** command.

4. Select the **Object** layer and choose the **Set Current** button. The **Object** layer is now the current layer.

5. Select Layer **0** and choose the sun icon in the **Freeze** column. The sun icon will change to a snowflake, indicating that the layer is frozen. Close or hide the **Layer Properties Manager** palette. The line will disappear because Layer **0** is frozen.

6. Choose the **Erase** tool from the **Modify** panel. AutoCAD prompts you to *Select objects:*.

7. Type **All<Enter>**. This tells AutoCAD to select all the objects in the drawing. In the command line, AutoCAD responds *0 found*. This tells you that AutoCAD ignored the line on the frozen Layer **0**. Press **<Esc>** to end the **ERASE** command.

8. Start the **LAYER** command again and thaw Layer **0** by selecting the snowflake in the Layer **0 Freeze** column. Select the lightbulb in the **On** column to turn off Layer **0**. Close or hide the **Layer Properties Manager** palette.

9. Choose the **Erase** tool again from the **Modify** panel and type **All<Enter>** at the *Select objects:* prompt. In the command line, AutoCAD responds *1 found*. This tells you that AutoCAD has selected the line on Layer **0**, even though the layer is turned off. Press **<Enter>** to finish the **ERASE** command. AutoCAD will erase the line.

10. Start the **LAYER** command and select the lightbulb to turn Layer **0** on. Close the palette to verify that the line was erased.

You can see that although the **On/Off** and **Freeze/Thaw** settings are similar, AutoCAD treats them very differently.

Lock/Unlock. The **Lock/Unlock** setting controls whether objects on a layer can be modified. Objects on a locked layer can be seen but not modified. To lock a layer, choose the icon in the **Lock** column for the layer you wish to lock.

Drawing objects that are on a locked layer will appear faded in the drawing to indicate their locked status. In addition, if you move your cursor over an object on a locked layer, a small lock icon appears to further warn you that it cannot be changed. You can control the level of fading used for locked layers via the expanded **Layers** panel discussed later in this chapter.

Color. The color property is the default display color for objects on a layer. To assign a color to a layer, pick the color swatch for the layer you wish to change. AutoCAD will display the **Select Color** dialog box (see Figure 6-3). The **Select Color** dialog box has three tabs: **Index Color, True Color**, and **Color Books**. The three tabs provide different ways to specify colors.

The AutoCAD Color Index (ACI). The **Index Color** tab shows the **AutoCAD Color Index** (ACI), which is the primary way colors are assigned in AutoCAD. The ACI consists of 255 colors (numbered 1–255). Colors 1–9 are called the ***standard colors*** and are shown below the main color palette. Grayscale colors are shown below the standard colors.

standard colors: Colors 1–9 of the AutoCAD Color Index.

Figure 6-3
The **Select Color** dialog box

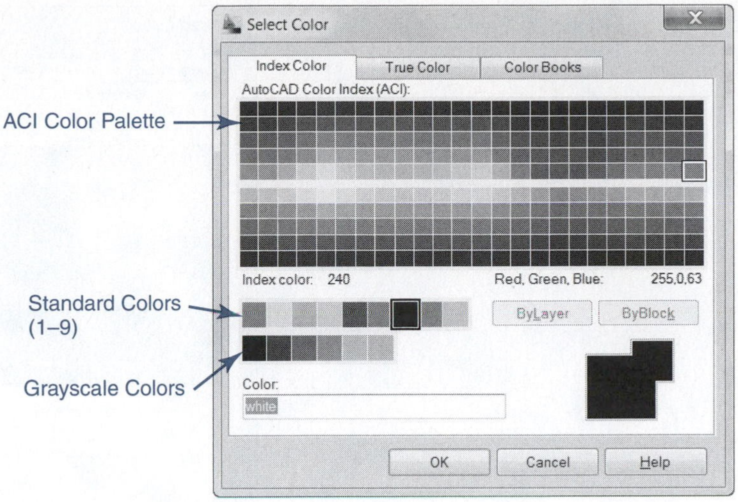

Colors 1–7 have names assigned to them. The names are shown in the following table:

ACI Number	Color
1	Red
2	Yellow
3	Green
4	Cyan
5	Blue
6	Magenta
7	White

The remaining colors are shown in the large color palette (see Figure 6-3). As you drag your cursor over the various color patches, AutoCAD will display the color number as well as the red, green, and blue components of each color. To select a color, simply click on a color patch. AutoCAD will display the color name or number in the **Color:** box. AutoCAD will also show you a preview of the selected color. If you know the color name or number you wish to use, you can simply type it into the **Color:** text area.

NOTE

Color 7 shows up as black on a white background and white on a black background.

True Color. The **True Color** tab allows you to select colors based on either the RGB (Red, Green, Blue) or HSL (Hue, Saturation, Luminance) color model (see Figure 6-4). You can select the color model you wish to use from the **Color model:** drop-down list.

The HSL color model allows you to control color properties in three ways. The **Hue:** setting refers to a color in the visible spectrum, from 0 to 360. On the color chart, a **Hue:** setting goes from 0 on the left of the chart to 360 on the right.

The **Saturation:** setting refers to the purity of that color on a scale of 0 to 100%. On the color chart, saturation values go from 0 (gray) at the bottom of the chart to 100 (the pure color) at the top of the chart.

The **Luminance:** setting represents the brightness of the color on a scale of 0 to 100%. The **Luminance:** setting is represented in the bar to

Figure 6-4
The HSL color model

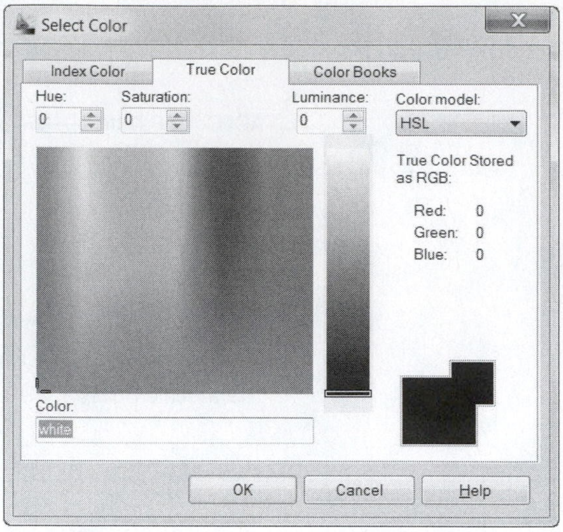

the right of the color chart. A luminance value of 0 (the bottom of the bar) gives you black, a value of 100 (the top of the bar) gives you white, and a setting of 50 represents the brightest value of the color.

When you select a color on the chart, its color is displayed in the preview area, and its RGB color values are displayed in both the color box and below the **Color model:** drop-down list.

The RGB color model (see Figure 6-5) allows you to mix colors based on the red, green, and blue components. An RGB number is a set of three numbers representing the red, green, and blue color components, respectively. Each component can have a value from 0 to 255 with 0 representing black, or no color, and 255 representing the pure color component. For example, a color setting of 255,0,0 represents red, 0,255,0 represents green, and 0,0,255 represents blue. White has an RGB value of 255,255,255, and black has an RGB value of 0,0,0.

Figure 6-5
The RGB color model

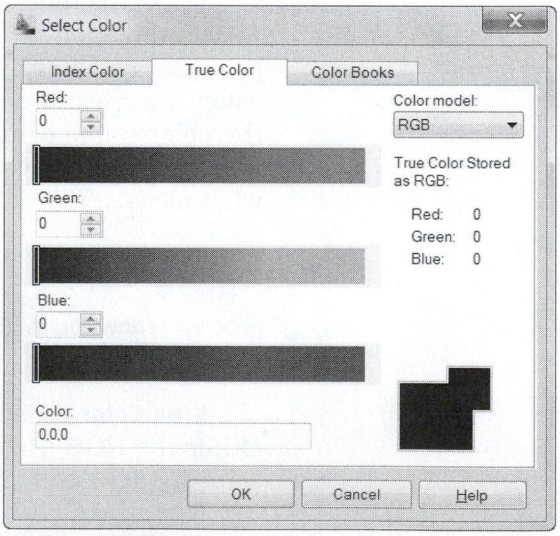

When you select the RGB color model, AutoCAD gives you three sliders to control the RGB components. You can type in a value, pick a point on each slider, or drag the indicator to a location on the slider to specify the value for each component.

Color Books. The **Color Books** tab allows you to select colors based on various color matching standards, such as Pantone, DIC, or RAL. When you select the **Color Books** tab, AutoCAD provides you with a list of available color books and a list of colors in each book (see Figure 6-6). Once

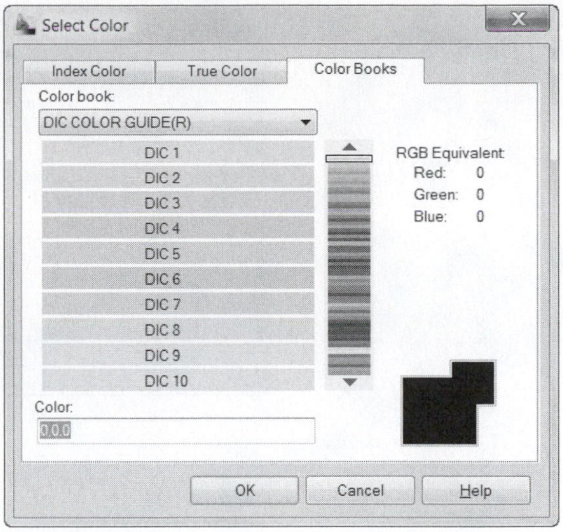

Figure 6-6
The **Color Books** tab

you select a color, AutoCAD displays its RGB color value on the right side of the dialog box and shows the color in the preview area.

EXERCISE 6-3 Setting Layer Colors

1. Continue from Exercise 6-2.
2. Start the **LAYER** command.
3. Choose the color box in the **Color** column of the **Object** layer. The **Select Color** dialog box will appear.
4. In the **Index Color** tab, select the color red (color index 1) and choose **OK** to close the dialog box.
5. Continue setting colors for the layers as follows:

   Center—**Blue (Color 5)**

   Dim—**Color 8**

   Hidden—**Green (Color 3)**

   Title—**White (Color 7)**
6. Close the **Layer Properties Manager** palette.
7. Save your drawing.

Linetypes. *Linetype* refers to the pattern (continuous, dashed, dotted, etc.) of a line. Linetypes are generally a series of lines, spaces, dots, and symbols (circles, squares, text, etc.) at preset intervals. Linetypes are used to designate a particular type of object (fence line, railroad tracks, hot water line, etc.) or a feature of an object (the hidden edge of an object, centerline of a circle or arc, etc.).

To assign a linetype to a layer, choose the **Linetype** setting for the layer you want to change. The **Select Linetype** dialog box will appear (see Figure 6-7). The **Select Linetype** dialog box shows all the currently available linetypes in your drawing. Before you can use a linetype, it must first be loaded into your drawing.

Standard Linetypes. AutoCAD comes with a large selection of standard linetypes. These linetype definitions are stored in linetype files. AutoCAD comes with two standard linetype files, ACAD.LIN and ACADISO.LIN. The standard AutoCAD linetypes are shown in the following table. You can also create and modify linetypes to meet your needs.

Figure 6-7
The **Select Linetype** dialog box

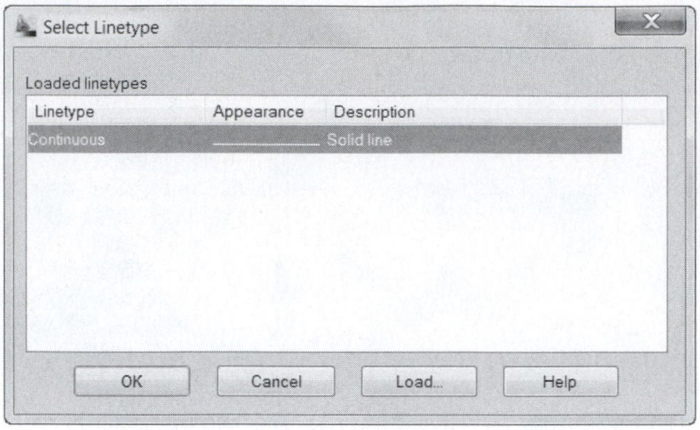

Linetype	Description
ACAD_ISO02W100	ISO dash __ __ __ __ __ __ __ __ __ __ __ __ __
ACAD_ISO03W100	ISO dash space __ __ __ __ __ __
ACAD_ISO04W100	ISO long-dash dot ____ . ____ . ____ . ____ . _
ACAD_ISO05W100	ISO long-dash double-dot ____ .. ____ .. ____ .
ACAD_ISO06W100	ISO long-dash triple-dot ____ ... ____ ... ____
ACAD_ISO07W100	ISO dot . . . .
ACAD_ISO08W100	ISO long-dash short-dash ____ __ ____ __ ____ _
ACAD_ISO09W100	ISO long-dash double-short-dash ____ __ __ ____
ACAD_ISO10W100	ISO dash dot __ . __ . __ . __ . __ . __ . __ .
ACAD_ISO11W100	ISO double-dash dot __ __ . __ __ . __ __ . __ _
ACAD_ISO12W100	ISO dash double-dot __ . . __ . . __ . . __ . .
ACAD_ISO13W100	ISO double-dash double-dot __ __ . . __ __ . . _
ACAD_ISO14W100	ISO dash triple-dot __ . . . __ . . . __ . . . _
ACAD_ISO15W100	ISO double-dash triple-dot __ __ . . . __ __ . .
BATTING	Batting SSSSSSSSSSSSSSSSSSSSSSSSSSSSSSSSSSSSSSS
BORDER	Border __ __ . __ __ . __ __ . __ __ . __ __ .
BORDER2	Border (.5x) __.__.__.__.__.__.__.__.__.__.__.
BORDERX2	Border (2x) ____ ____ . ____ ____ . ___
DASHDOT	Dash dot __ . __ . __ . __ . __ . __ . __ . __
DASHDOT2	Dash dot (.5x) _._._._._._._._._._._._._._._.
DASHDOTX2	Dash dot (2x) ____ . ____ . ____ . ___
DIVIDE	Divide ____ . . ____ . . ____ . . ____ . . ____
DIVIDE2	Divide (.5x) __..__..__..__..__..__..__..__.._
DIVIDEX2	Divide (2x) ________ . . ________ . . _
FENCELINE1	Fenceline circle ----0-----0----0-----0----0-----0--
FENCELINE2	Fenceline square ----[-----[]----[]-----[]----[]--
GAS_LINE	Gas line ----GAS----GAS----GAS----GAS----GAS----GAS--
HIDDEN	Hidden __ __ __ __ __ __ __ __ __ __ __ __ __ __
HIDDEN2	Hidden (.5x) _ _ _ _ _ _ _ _ _ _ _ _ _ _ _ _ _
HIDDENX2	Hidden (2x) ____ ____ ____ ____ ____ ____ ____
HOT_WATER_SUPPLY	Hot water supply ---- HW ---- HW ---- HW ----
TRACKS	Tracks -|-|-|-|-|-|-|-|-|-|-|-|-|-|-|-|-|-|-|-|-|-|-|-|-
ZIGZAG	Zigzag /\/_

AutoCAD's linetype files, along with the ability to create your own linetypes, mean there is a potentially unlimited number of linetypes available. In any given drawing, you will use only a limited number of these linetypes so linetypes are loaded into your drawing on an as-needed basis. To load linetypes into your drawing, choose the **Load...** button in the **Select Linetype** dialog box. This will display the **Load or Reload Linetypes** dialog box (see Figure 6-8).

> **NOTE**
> The ACADISO.LIN file contains all the linetypes included in the ACAD.LIN file but also contains linetypes that support the Japanese Industrial Standard (JIS Z 8312).

Figure 6-8
The **Load or Reload Linetypes** dialog box

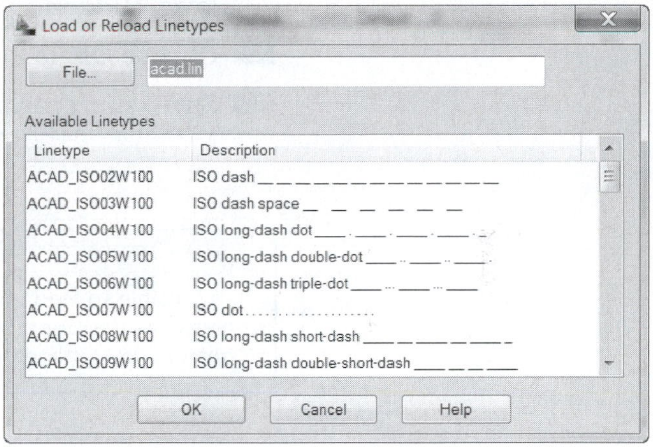

The **Load or Reload Linetypes** dialog box shows you the current linetype file and displays all the linetypes defined within that file. You can specify a different file by choosing the **File...** button and selecting the linetype file you wish to use.

To load a linetype, select a linetype from the list of available linetypes and choose **OK**. You can select multiple linetypes by holding down either the **<Shift>** or the **<Ctrl>** key while selecting linetypes. Once you choose **OK**, you are returned to the **Select Linetype** dialog box.

Once the linetypes are loaded into your drawing, you can assign a linetype to a layer by selecting a linetype in the **Select Linetype** dialog box and choosing **OK**. The selected linetype will be assigned to the layer.

> **NOTE**
> Some linetypes have multiple versions of each linetype defined in the .LIN file. Generally, these linetypes have lines and spaces that are either half or twice the size of the original. For example, in addition to the **CENTER** linetype, there are also **CENTER2** and **CENTERX2** linetypes. The **CENTER2** linetype has lines and spaces that are half (.5x) the size of the **CENTER** linetype. The **CENTERX2** linetype has lines and spaces that are twice (2x) the size of the **CENTER** linetype.

EXERCISE 6-4 **Setting the Layer Linetype**

1. Continue from Exercise 6-3.
2. Start the **LAYER** command.

3. Choose **Continuous** in the **Linetype** column of layer **Center**. This displays the **Select Linetype** dialog box.
4. Choose the **Load...** button. This displays the **Load or Reload Linetypes** dialog box.
5. Hold down the **<Ctrl>** key and select the **CENTER** and **HIDDEN** linetypes. Choose **OK** to return to the **Select Linetype** dialog box. The linetypes have now been loaded into your drawing.
6. Choose the **CENTER** linetype and choose **OK** to assign the linetype to layer **Center**.
7. Choose **Continuous** in the **Linetype** column of layer **Hidden.** This displays the **Select Linetype** dialog box.
8. Choose the **HIDDEN** linetype and choose **OK** to assign the linetype to layer **Hidden**.
9. Choose **OK** to close the **Layer Properties Manager** palette.
10. Save your drawing.

TIP

It is possible to load and manage linetypes without using the **Layer Properties Manager** palette via the **Linetype Manager** dialog box discussed later in the section "Linetype Control and Management" on page 241.

Lineweights. *Lineweight* refers to the printed width of a line. The ANSI (American National Standards Institute) standard Y14.2 recommends using two lineweights (thick and thin) to differentiate contrasting lines. The actual values you use will depend on your particular CAD standards. AutoCAD's default lineweight is .25 mm (.010″).

NOTE

Before the lineweight setting was introduced in AutoCAD, pen tables were used to map AutoCAD colors to plotted lineweights. For example, all red objects are plotted with a .35 mm pen, yellow objects with a .15 mm pen, etc. AutoCAD still supports pen tables and gives you a number of options for creating and managing them.

FOR MORE DETAILS

See page 625 in Chapter 15 for more on plotting and the use of pen tables.

To assign a lineweight to a layer, choose the value in the **Lineweight** column for that layer. This will bring up the **Lineweight** dialog box (see Figure 6-9). Select the lineweight you wish to use and choose **OK** to assign the lineweight to the layer.

Figure 6-9
The **Lineweight** dialog box

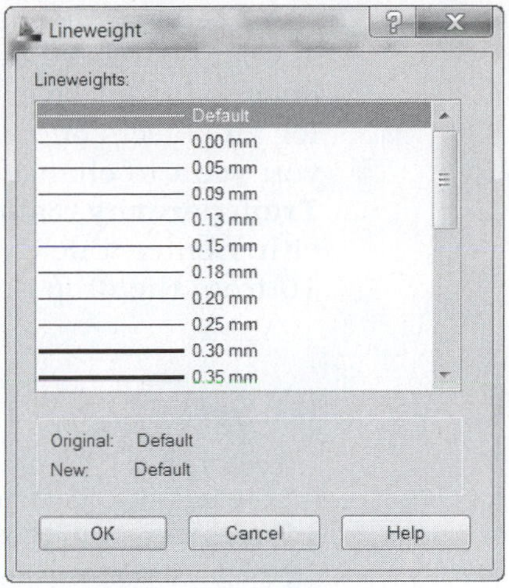

EXERCISE 6-5 Setting the Layer Lineweight

1. Continue from Exercise 6-4 and start the **LAYER** command.
2. Choose **Default** in the **Lineweight** column of layer **Object**. This displays the **Lineweight** dialog box.
3. Choose **0.60 mm** from the list and choose **OK**. This sets the lineweight for layer **Object**.
4. Hold down the **<Ctrl>** key and select the **Center, Hidden**, and **Dim** layer names. The layers will highlight.
5. Choose the **Default** icon in the **Lineweight** column of the **Center** layer, and choose **0.30 mm** from the lineweight list. Choose **OK** to set the lineweight for all the selected layers.
6. Choose **OK** to close the **Layer Properties Manager** palette.
7. Save your drawing.

NOTE

The list of available lineweights is fixed in AutoCAD. You can, however, adjust the actual value of the plotted lineweight using the **Plot Style Manager**.

Lineweight display can be turned on and off via the **Show/Hide Lineweight** button on the AutoCAD status bar. The lineweight thickness shown on your screen is only a graphical approximation and does not accurately reflect the plotted lineweight, as noted earlier. It is possible to adjust the display scale, change the default lineweight, and switch from metric units to inches using the **Lineweight Settings** dialog box shown later in the section "Lineweight Control and Management" on page 243.

Transparency. As first mentioned in Chapter 1, it is possible to make objects transparent in AutoCAD so that you can see through them and view objects below. Transparency can be assigned by layer or individually for an object, just like the color, linetype, and lineweight properties. Using the layer method to control transparency is typically preferred because it gives you the most control over your drawing information.

Transparency is controlled by specifying a value from 0 to 90, where 0 is opaque and 90 is almost completely translucent. The default transparency value for layers and objects is **0**. To change the transparency level for all objects on a layer, click in the **Transparency** column for the layer you want to change in the **Layer Properties Manager** palette. The **Layer Transparency** dialog box shown in Figure 6-10 is displayed where you can either enter a new value manually or select a new value in increments of 10 from the drop-down list.

NOTE

You can turn off transparency when plotting. The **Plot** and **Page Setup** dialogs both include a check box for transparency. Be forewarned, though, that when the **Transparency** option is enabled, AutoCAD rasterizes the entire drawing for plotting so that plot times will increase exponentially.

Figure 6-10
The **Layer Transparency** dialog box

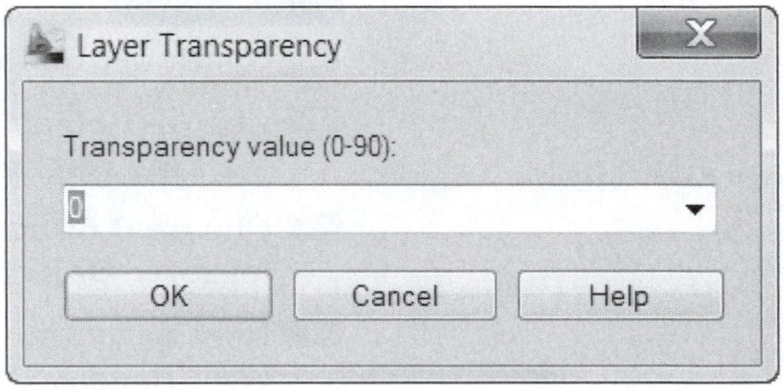

TIP

You can toggle transparency on and off via the **Show/Hide Transparency** button on the AutoCAD status bar.

Plot Style. The **Plot Style** setting is used when a drawing is set up to use named plot styles. This is a drawing setting that allows you to use unique custom styles to control the plotted pen weight and appearance of objects when they are plotted. Typically, most drawings are set up by default to use color-dependent plot styles, which cannot be changed in the **Layer Properties Manager** because they are hard-wired to the layer's color assignment.

FOR MORE DETAILS

See page 626 in Chapter 15 for more on using plot styles and the **Plot Style Manager**.

Plot/Noplot. The **Plot/Noplot** setting controls whether the contents of a layer will appear on a print of the drawing. This setting allows you to create objects in AutoCAD that will appear only in the drawing file, but not on any of the printed output of the drawing. For example, you may wish to create layers for construction lines, internal design notes, or drafting markups. To toggle the **Plot/Noplot** setting, choose the **Plot** setting for that layer. Plotting layers will show a printer icon, and nonplotting layers will have a red line through the printer icon.

New VP Freeze. The **New VP Freeze** setting freezes the selected layer in any new viewports that are subsequently created in a paper space layout. It is possible to control layer visibility per individual viewport in paper space so that you can set up multiple views in one or more layouts that each show different drawing information.

NOTE

In order to take advantage of viewport overrides, all drawing objects should be created using the ByLayer property discussed later in this chapter in the "Hard-Coded Versus Soft-Coded Properties" section.

In fact, if you are in a paper space layout and start the **LAYER** command to display the **Layers Properties Manager** palette, four columns are added to the right of the **New VP Freeze** column so that you can control all aspects of a layer's appearance per viewport using the following viewport overrides:

- **VP Color** Controls the layer color per viewport
- **VP Linetype** Controls the layer linetype per viewport
- **VP Lineweight** Controls the layer lineweight per viewport
- **VP Plot Style** Controls the layer plot style per viewport

FOR MORE DETAILS

See page 571 in Chapter 14 for more information on controlling layer properties per paper space viewport using viewport overrides.

Description. The **Description** setting allows you to add a brief description of the layer. For example, a layer named **A-Wall** might have a description of "Architectural walls." To change the description of a layer, select the layer and then single-click inside the **Description** field. A flashing text cursor will appear, allowing you to change the layer description.

Deleting a Layer

To delete a layer from your drawing, select the layer(s) from the layer list and choose the **Delete Layer** button (or choose **<Alt>+D**). A layer can be deleted only if it is not used in the drawing or if it is not the current layer. If the layer is not used and is not the current layer, AutoCAD will delete the layer. You can use **Undo** in the **Quick Access** toolbar to bring back a deleted layer.

If the layer is used in the drawing, or if it is the current layer, AutoCAD will display an error message (see Figure 6-11).

NOTE

Sometimes a layer may appear empty or unused in your drawing but you are still unable to delete it. Many times this is due to a layer being used in a block or xref. Even though the layer is currently empty, you cannot delete that layer until the block or xref that uses that layer is also deleted.

Figure 6-11
The **Delete Layer** error message

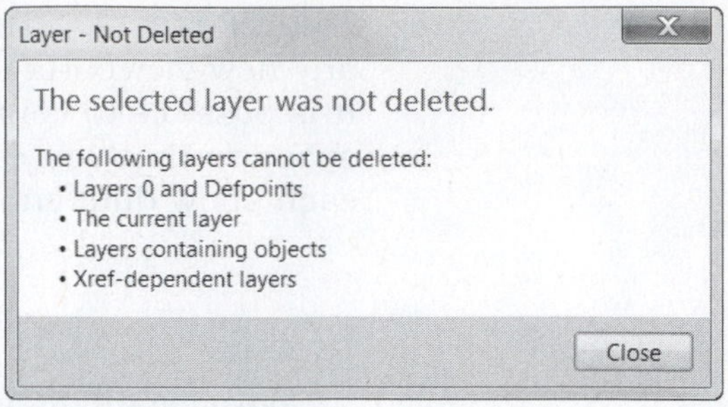

FOR MORE DETAILS

See page 778 in Chapter 18 for more on deleting blocks and xrefs from your drawing.

Layer Settings

Selecting the **Setting** button in the **Layer Properties Manager** displays the **Layer Settings** dialog box shown in Figure 6-12.

Figure 6-12
The **Layer Settings** dialog box

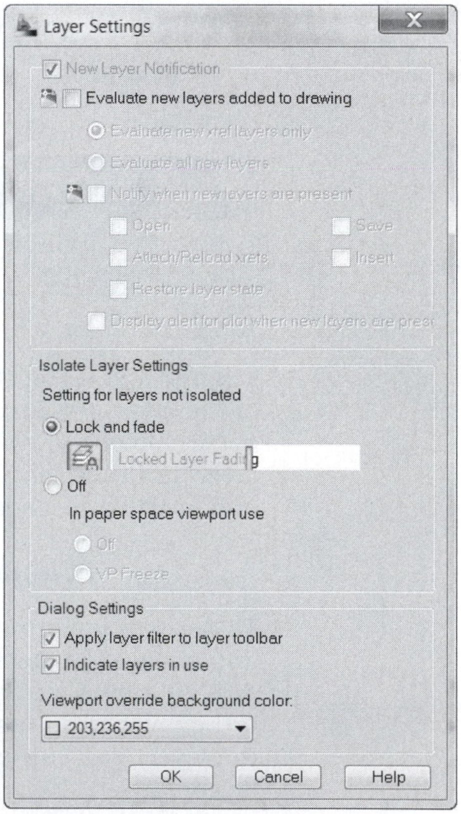

The **Layer Settings** dialog box allows you to control the **New Layer Notification** feature, apply a layer filter to the **Layer** toolbar so only filtered layers are displayed, and change the background color for viewport overrides, introduced earlier in the chapter.

The **New Layer Notification** feature prevents new layers from being added to your drawing without your knowledge by creating a list of what are referred to as *reconciled* layers, using all the existing layer names the first time you save or plot a drawing.

When the **Evaluate new layers added to drawing** check box is turned on, a **Notification** icon is displayed in the status tray at the bottom right of the AutoCAD window when a new layer is added to your drawing that does not match the reconciled layer list. Clicking on the **Notification** icon will display a list of unreconciled layers in the **Layer Properties Manager**.

You can choose to evaluate only new layers that are added when an external refereence (xref) drawing is attached or to evaluate all new layers that are added to your drawing, regardless of the source.

You can control when layer evaluation and notification is performed when the **Notify when new layers are present** check box is selected. Layer evaluation can be performed when the **Open, Save, Attach/Reload xrefs, Insert,** and **Restore layer state** options are selected.

The **Display alert for plot when new layers are present** check box allows you to control separately whether layer evaluation and notification is performed when a plot is created.

The **Isolate Layer Settings** area allows you to control how layers are isolated using the **LAYISO** command. The **LAYISO** command allows you to work on only a selected group of layers. Nonselected layers are either locked and faded or turned off. The **Isolate Layer Settings** area of the **Layer Settings** dialog box allows you to select which method to use as well as set the amount of fading that occurs.

Using Layers

In AutoCAD, the current layer is shown in the **Layer Control** drop-down list in the **Layers** panel (see Figure 6-13). This drop-down list shows you the current settings for your layers. You can change the active layer by selecting a new layer from the drop-down list. You can also toggle layer settings from this list by selecting the icon for that setting. For example, to freeze a layer, choose the drop-down list and select the **Freeze/Thaw** icon next to the layer you wish to freeze. The icon will change from a sun to a snowflake, indicating the layer has been frozen. You can use this list to toggle the **On/Off, Freeze/Thaw,** and **Lock/Unlock** settings.

Figure 6-13
The **Layers** panel

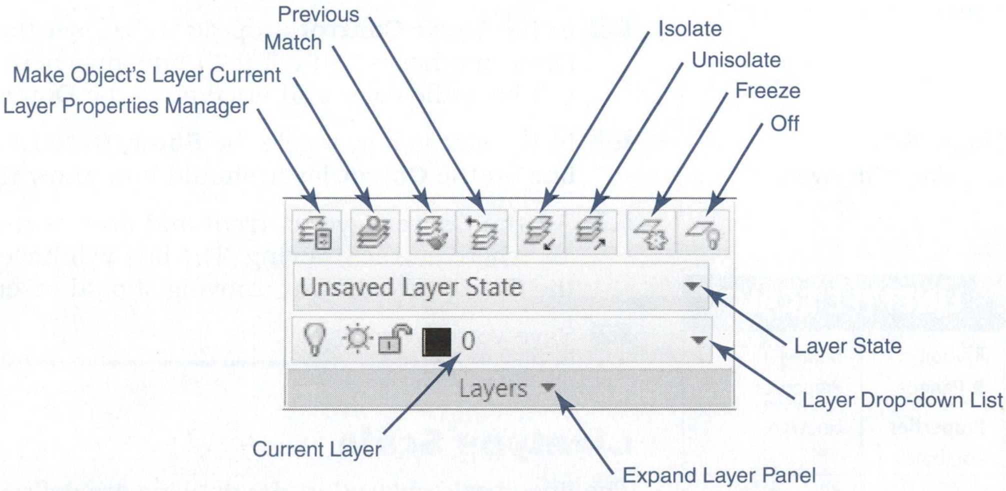

The **Layers** panel has some additional buttons. The **Make Object's Layer Current** button allows you to select an object in your drawing and have that object's layer become the current drawing layer.

The **Match** button changes the layer of one or more selected objects to match the destination layer of another object that you select in the drawing.

The **Previous** button will switch the current layer back to its previous setting. For example, if you were to change the current layer from **Object** to **Hidden,** the **Previous** button would reset the current layer to **Object**.

Selecting the **Previous** button undoes the most recent change, or set of changes, made using either the **Layer Properties Manager** or the **Layer Control** drop-down list on the **Layers** panel. Every change you make to the layer settings is tracked and can be undone with **Previous** with the following special exceptions:

- Deleted layers **Previous** does not restore deleted and/or purged layers
- New layers **Previous** does not remove any newly added layers
- Renamed layers **Previous** does not restore the original layer name

The **Isolate** button hides or locks all the objects in the drawing except for the ones you select. This allows you to work on a selected layer without worrying about accidentally modifying objects. The **Isolate Layer Settings** discussed above allows you to control how objects are isolated and displayed.

The **Unisolate** button simply undoes the **Isolate** tool. Selecting this button reverts all layers to their state prior to using the **Isolate** tool.

The **Freeze** button freezes the layer of a selected object whereas the **Off** button turns a layer off instead. Both commands have settings for how to handle viewports and block definitions that persist from session to session.

The **Layer State** drop-down list allows you to save, restore, and manage named layer states.

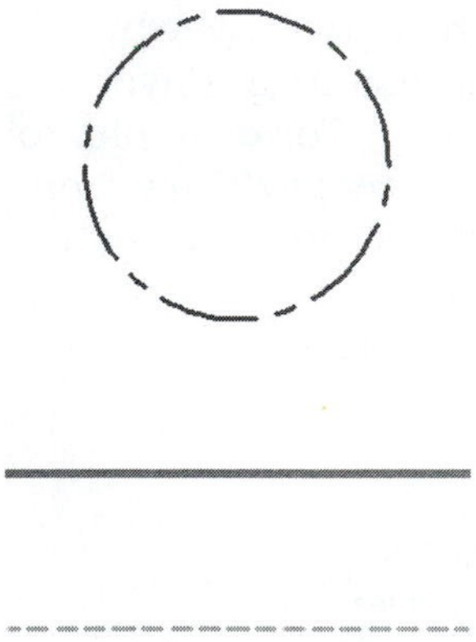

Figure 6-14
Drawing with layers

EXERCISE 6-6 Using the Layers Panel

1. Continue from Exercise 6-5.
2. In the **Layer Control** drop-down list, choose **Hidden** to set that layer current.
3. Draw a line that is approximately 3 inches long anywhere on the screen. The line will have the color and linetype of layer **Hidden**.
4. In the **Layer Control** drop-down list, set the layer **Object** current. Draw another roughly 3-inch line anywhere in the drawing. The line will have the color and linetype of the **Object** layer.
5. In the status bar, toggle the **Show/Hide Lineweight** button on. The line on the **Object** layer should now show the **.60 mm** lineweight.
6. Set the **Center** layer current and draw a circle with a 1-inch radius anywhere on the drawing. The line will have the color and linetype of the **Center** layer. Your drawing should resemble Figure 6-14.
7. Save your drawing.

LINETYPE SCALE	
Ribbon & Panel:	Home | Properties
Properties Toolbar:	Linetype
Menu:	Format | Linetype
Command Line:	LTSCALE
Command Alias:	LTS

Linetype Scale

The linetypes displayed in the drawing are defined by the linetype definitions that were loaded from the .LIN file. The linetype is defined by the length of the dashes and spaces in the line and uses the drawing units to define those lengths. For example, say a linetype is defined as a line segment .5 unit long followed by a space of .25 unit and then repeated. When drawn in a metric drawing using mm as the base unit, that linetype would be a series of .5 mm lines and .25 mm spaces.

The **LTSCALE** command allows you to set a global scaling factor for all linetypes. The **LTSCALE** command prompts you for a new linetype scale factor. The linetypes of all objects are multiplied by this scaling factor. For example, an **LTSCALE** setting of **2** would make each line segment and space twice its defined size. An **LTSCALE** setting of **.5** would make each linetype half its defined size.

It is also possible to set the LTSCALE via the **Linetype Manager** dialog box shown in Figure 6-19, although it is not obvious where it is set. In order to access any of the linetype scaling options, you must select the **Show details** button on the top right to display the details at the bottom of the dialog box (see Figure 6-20). The **Global scale factor:** setting updates the LTSCALE. See the "Linetype Control and Management" section later in this chapter for more information about the **Linetype Manager** dialog box.

EXERCISE 6-7 **Setting the LTSCALE**

1. Continue from Exercise 6-6.
2. Type **LTSCALE<Enter>**. AutoCAD prompts you to *Enter new linetype scale factor <1.0000>:*.
3. Type **.5<Enter>** to set the linetype scale. The linetype pattern of the objects on the **Hidden** and **Center** layers will scale down by 50%.
4. Save your drawing.

NOTE

The **MSLTSCALE** system variable allows you to scale linetype definitions by the current annotation scale. Setting **MSLTSCALE** to **1** turns on automatic linetype scaling. It is on by default.

Hard-Coded Versus Soft-Coded Properties

By default, when an object is created in a drawing, it takes on the color, linetype, lineweight, and transparency settings of the current layer. When this happens, its properties are defined as *Bylayer*. This means that the color, linetype, lineweight, and transparency of an object are defined by the layer on which the object resides. For example, say your drawing has a layer called **Object**, which is red, and has a continuous linetype and a lineweight of .6 mm. If you draw a line on that layer, by default it would show up as a red, continuous, .6 mm-wide line. This line is considered to have soft-coded properties in that its properties are defined indirectly by the layer on which it resides. If you were to change the layer color to blue, the object would update to reflect the changes to its layer.

It is possible to override these soft-coded properties and define the color, linetype, lineweight, and transparency directly. These are called *hard-coded* properties because the properties are assigned directly to the object, regardless of which layer it resides on.

Using the hard-coded, or override, method of assigning properties directly to objects should typically be avoided because it makes it much more difficult to manage the appearance of objects in your drawings. If a change needs to be made, you must comb through all of the objects in a drawing and update them individually. Using the Bylayer approach allows you to make changes in one place, the **Layer Properties Manager**, and update all of the objects on a layer simultaneously. For this reason, many organizations have strict rules against using hard-coded properties.

TIP

The **SETBYLAYER** command allows you to quickly update the color, linetype, lineweight, and transparency of objects to the ByLayer property.

Setting the Default Object Properties

The current settings for the color, linetype, lineweight, and transparency properties are shown in the **Properties** panel (see Figure 6-15). AutoCAD applies these current property settings to all new objects. By default, these are all set to **ByLayer**.

To change the current setting, select the setting from its respective drop-down list. Any new objects you create will take on these properties.

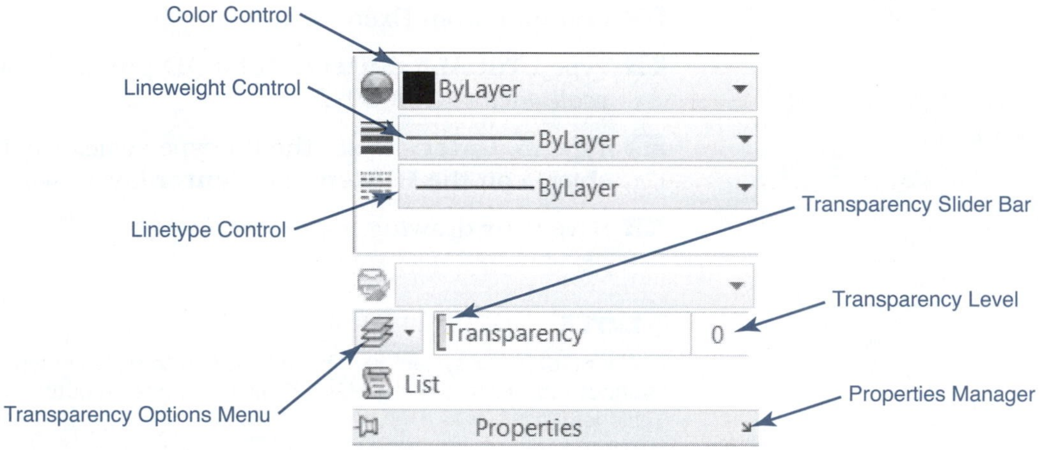

Figure 6-15
The **Properties** panel

NEW to AutoCAD 2013

TIP

Using the **Properties** panel, you can dynamically preview changes to an object before applying the change. Selected objects change dynamically as you pass the cursor over each property in the list.

COLOR	
Ribbon & Panel:	Home | Properties
Select Colors...	
Properties Toolbar:	
Red	
Menu:	Format | Color...
Command Line:	COLOR
Command Alias:	COL

Color Control and Management

In the **Color Control** drop-down list, you see a list consisting of **ByLayer, ByBlock**, color numbers 1–7, and a **Select Colors...** item (see Figure 6-16). The **Select Colors...** item starts the **COLOR** command and displays the **Select Color** dialog box (see Figure 6-17). This is the same dialog box used to select colors within the **LAYER** command. To set the current drawing color, select the color from the **Color Control** drop-down list or choose the **Select Colors...** item and select the color from the **Select Color** dialog box.

FOR MORE DETAILS

See page 657 in Chapter 16 for more on blocks and the **ByBlock** setting.

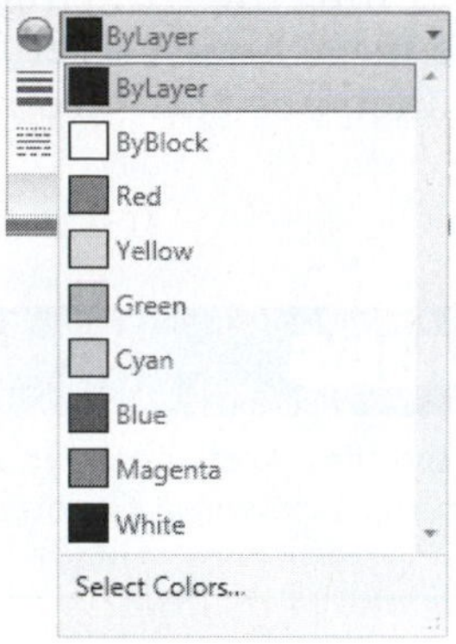

Figure 6-16
The **Color Control** drop-down list

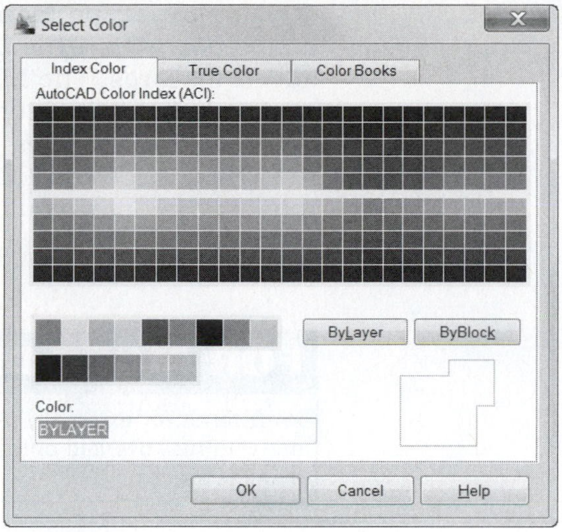

Figure 6-17
The **Select Color** dialog box

Linetype Control and Management

In the **Linetype Control** drop-down list (see Figure 6-18), you are shown a list of all the currently loaded linetypes in the drawing as well as the **ByLayer** and **ByBlock** settings and an **Other...** item. The **Other...** item starts the **LINETYPE** command, which displays the **Linetype Manager** dialog box (see Figure 6-19).

LINETYPE	
Ribbon & Panel:	Home | Properties
Other...	
Properties Toolbar:	
——— – ·CENTER	
Menu:	Format | Linetype...
Command Line:	LINETYPE
Command Alias:	LT

NOTE

In the **LAYER** command, the **Select Color** dialog box has the **ByLayer** and **ByBlock** buttons disabled. In the **COLOR** command, these buttons are enabled. These choices are also available in the **Color Control** drop-down list in the **Properties** panel. The **ByLayer** setting resets the color to its layer-defined, soft-coded color property. The **ByBlock** setting creates everything using color 7 until the objects are grouped into a block.

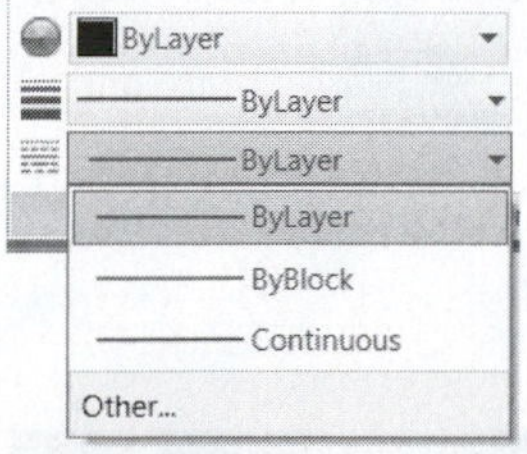

Figure 6-18
The **Linetype Control** drop-down list

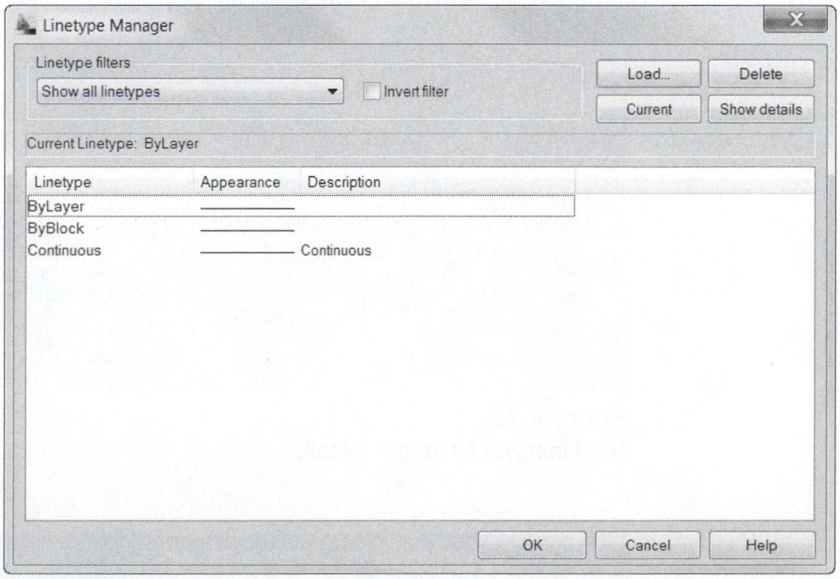

Figure 6-19
The **Linetype Manager** dialog box

The **Linetype Manager** dialog box is similar to the **Select Linetype** dialog box within the **LAYER** command (see Figure 6-7) but with a few added features. The **Linetype Manager** dialog box shows you all the currently loaded linetypes but also includes a filter that allows you to show all the linetypes loaded into the drawing, only the linetypes currently in use, or all that are used in any xref files. You can also invert the filter to show you only linetypes that are *not* in use or *not* used in xref files.

FOR MORE DETAILS

Xref stands for externally referenced files. Xrefs allow you to display the contents of other drawing files overlaid onto your current drawing. Chapter 17 describes how to use and manage xrefs.

The **Load...** button displays the **Load or Reload Linetypes** dialog box. This is the same dialog box used within the **LAYER** command and allows you to load linetypes from .LIN files.

The **Delete** button allows you to delete unused linetypes from the drawing. Only linetypes that are not currently used can be deleted.

The **Show details** button displays an additional area of the global box that shows additional information about each linetype and also allows you to set the linetype scale for all objects **(LTSCALE)**, set the current linetype scale **(CELTSCALE)**, and control whether linetypes are scaled in paper space using the current viewport scale **(PSLTSCALE)** (see Figure 6-20).

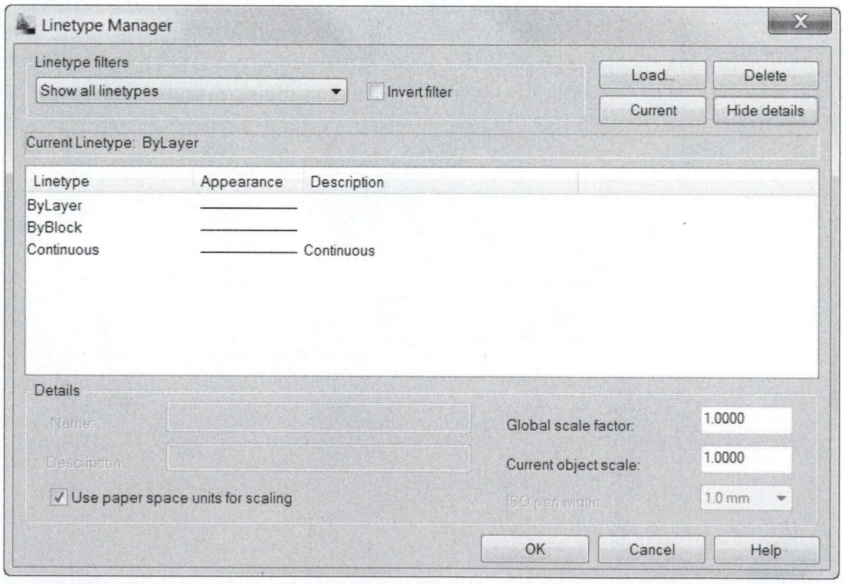

Figure 6-20
The **Linetype Manager** details

FOR MORE DETAILS

See page 605 in Chapter 14 for more information about paper space linetype scaling.

LINEWEIGHT	
Ribbon & Panel:	Home | Properties ByLayer
Properties Toolbar:	0.60 mm
Pull-down Menu:	Format | Lineweight...
Command Line:	LINEWEIGHT or LWEIGHT
Command Alias:	LW

Lineweight Control and Management

The **Lineweight Control** drop-down list shows you a list of all available lineweights. The lineweights are set to millimeter (mm) units by default. You can change the units and control other aspects of lineweight setting by selecting **Lineweight Settings...** from the bottom of the **Lineweight** drop-down list or by using the **LINEWEIGHT** command.

Either method displays the **Lineweight Settings** dialog box (see Figure 6-21), which includes controls to turn the lineweight display on and off, set the default lineweight, and switch the units from millimeters to inches. The **Adjust Display Scale** slider allows you to control the relative thickness of the lineweight display on your screen. It does not affect the plotted width of the lineweight.

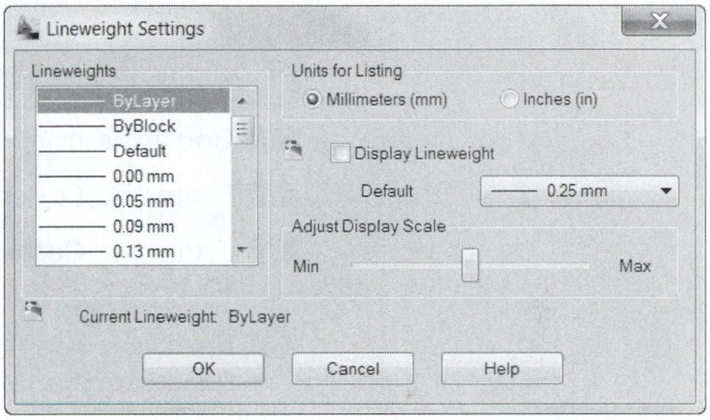

Figure 6-21
The **Lineweight Settings** dialog box

Transparency Control and Management

Just like the other object property overrides discussed thus far, it is best to use the *ByLayer* option to control transparency for maximum control of your drawing. Although you can assign transparency directly to objects, it is not advised. In fact, the default setting is **ByLayer** on the **Transparency** options menu located on the **Properties** panel of the **Home** tab of the ribbon, as shown in Figure 6-22.

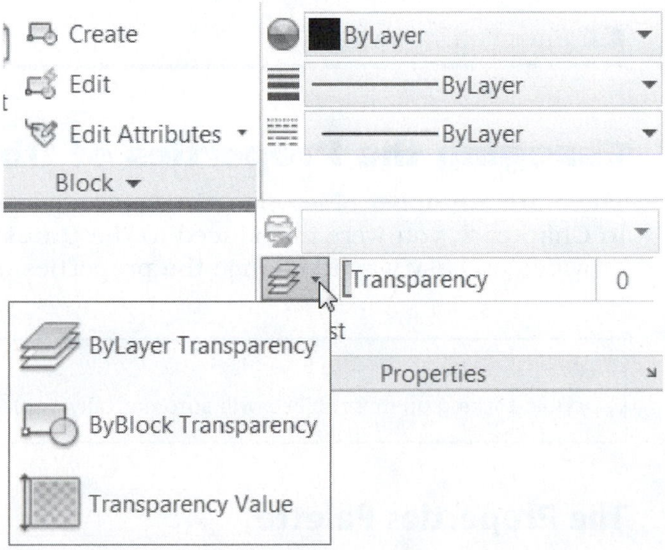

Figure 6-22
The **Transparency** options menu on the **Properties** panel

Moving the **Transparency** slider bar to the right or entering a value between 1 and 90 in the corresponding number box turns off the ByLayer method and assigns the specified transparency setting directly to any new objects created in the drawing.

The ByBlock method for assigning transparency is an advanced technique that is used with blocks and can be ignored for now. The ByBlock method of assigning object properties is discussed in Chapter 16.

> **TIP**
>
> You can also control transparency using the **CETRANSPARENCY** system variable. It has the following settings:
>
> **ByLayer:** Transparency value determined by layer
>
> **ByBlock:** Transparency value determined by block
>
> **0:** Fully opaque
>
> **1–90:** Transparency value defined as a percentage

EXERCISE 6-8 Setting Hard-Coded Properties

1. Continue from Exercise 6-7.
2. From the **Layer Control** drop-down list, set the **Object** layer current.
3. From the **Color Control** drop-down list, set the current color to **Magenta** (color 6).
4. From the **Linetype Control** drop-down list, choose **Other...** to display the **Linetype Manager** dialog box.
5. Load the **ZIGZAG** linetype from the acad.lin linetype file and set it to be the current linetype. Choose **OK** to close the **Linetype Manager** dialog box.
6. From the **Lineweight Control** drop-down list, set the current lineweight to **0.80 mm**.
7. Draw a line approximately 3 inches long above the circle. The new line will have the current color, linetype, and lineweight settings even though the **Object** layer has different properties. Your drawing should resemble Figure 6-23.
8. Save your drawing.

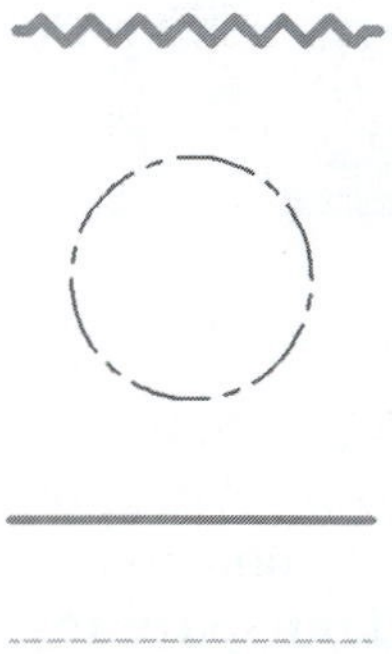

Figure 6-23
Hard-coded object properties

PROPERTIES	
Ribbon & Panel:	View | Palettes 
Standard Toolbar:	
Menu:	Modify | Properties
Command Line:	PROPERTIES
Command Alias:	PR

NEW to AutoCAD 2013

Changing the Properties of Objects

There are a number of ways to change the properties of existing objects. In Chapter 2, you were introduced to the **Quick Properties** palette, which provides an easy way to change the properties of any object.

> **TIP**
>
> Double-clicking on most objects will automatically display the **Quick Properties** palette.

The Properties Palette

As stated at the beginning of the chapter, there are five properties that are common to all objects: layer, color, linetype, lineweight, and transparency. These are shown in the **General** area of the **Properties** palette (see Figure 6-24). You can change any of the properties by selecting the value from the palette and choosing a new value. Using the **Properties** palette,

Figure 6-24
The **Properties** palette

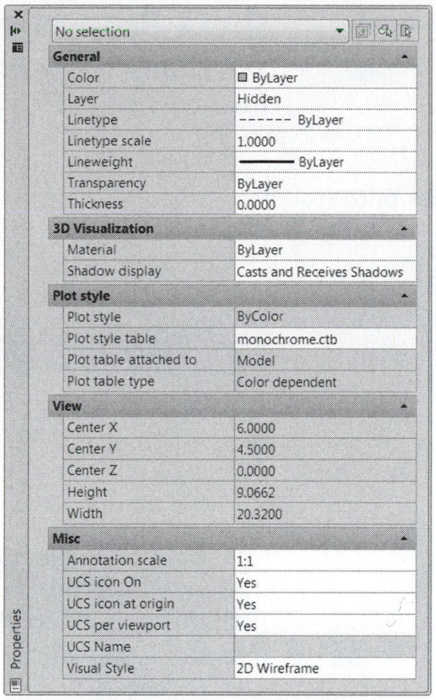

you can dynamically preview changes to an object before applying the change. Selected objects change dynamically as you pass the cursor over each property in the list.

NEW to AutoCAD 2013

TIP

You can turn the dynamic preview feature on and off via the **PROPERTYPREVIEW** system variable. Setting **PROPERTYPREVIEW** to **Off** disables the dynamic preview. Setting **PROPERTYPREVIEW** to **On** turns it back on.

NOTE

The **Thickness** property shown in the **Properties** palette is used to assign a three-dimensional "thickness" to AutoCAD objects. Although it is a common property of all objects, it is rarely used in 2D drawings and is beyond the scope of this book.

The **Linetype scale** option in the **Properties** palette allows you to change the linetype scale of individual objects. This object linetype scale factor is applied in addition to the global linetype scale set by the **LTSCALE** command. For example, a line created with an object linetype of 2 in a drawing with **LTSCALE** set to **0.5** would appear the same as a line created with an object linetype of 1 in a drawing with **LTSCALE** set to **1**.

The **Hyperlink** property allows you to assign an Internet URL or email address to an object.

FOR MORE DETAILS

See the online AutoCAD documentation for more on using the **Thickness** setting.

The Properties Panel

Another way to quickly change object properties is via the properties drop-down menus on the **Properties** panel shown earlier in Figure 6-15. To change an object's property, select the object and then choose the property you wish to change from its drop-down menu.

Quick Properties

The **Quick Properties** button on the status bar shown in Figure 6-25 turns on and off the **Quick Properties** feature.

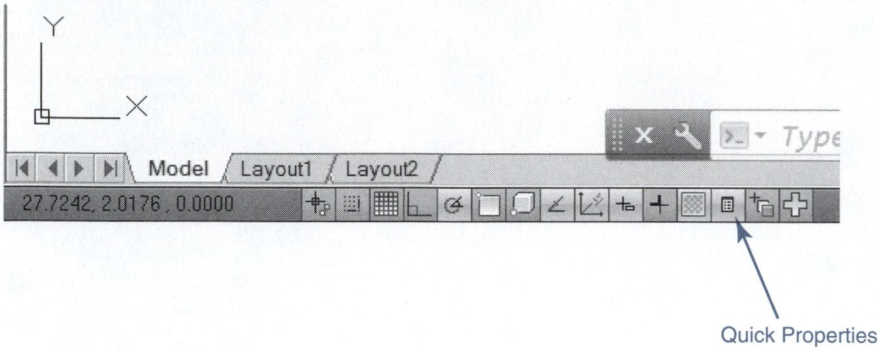

Figure 6-25
The **Quick Properties** button on the status bar

When the **Quick Properties** feature is on, a mini **Properties** palette is displayed at your current cursor location every time you select an object. It displays a short list of the major object properties, such as color, layer, and linetype, so that you can quickly make changes to the selected object (see Figure 6-26).

Figure 6-26
The **Quick Properties** palette

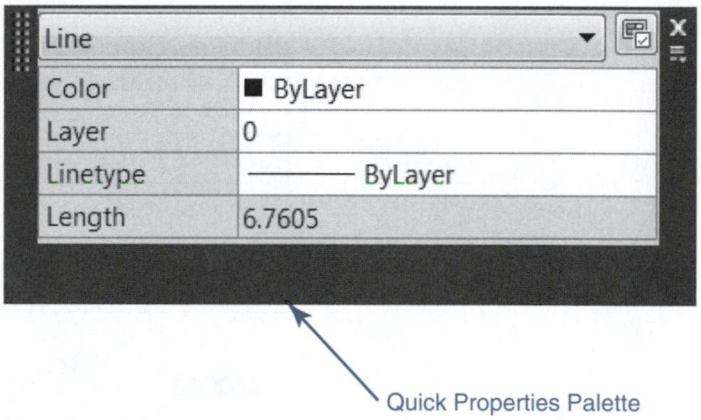

The initial properties displayed are dependent on the type of object you select. For example, text has a different list of properties than a line does. In fact, by default, only the top three properties are visible when the **Quick Properties** palette is initially displayed. Moving your mouse pointer over the palette border expands the palette to display additional properties, as shown in Figure 6-27.

You can turn off the expansion mode so all of the available properties are always displayed by deselecting the **Auto-collapse** option on the **Options** menu that is displayed when you select the **Options** button on the title bar shown in Figure 6-27. The **Location Mode** cascade menu on the **Options** menu allows you to switch the palette from always displaying at the current cursor location to being in a static mode that behaves like the other typical AutoCAD palettes so that it stays where you place it in whatever display mode you set (docked, Auto-hide, etc.). Selecting the **Settings...** menu item from the **Options** menu displays the **Quick Properties** tab of the **Drafting Settings** dialog box shown in Figure 6-28.

Using the **Quick Properties** tab you can control some of the same options mentioned previously plus certain more advanced features.

In the **Palette Display** area, you can control what type of objects will display the **Quick Properties** palette. By default, when the **Quick Properties** feature is on, the palette is displayed for every object you select. It is possible, using AutoCAD's advance **Customize User Interface** (CUI) tool, to select

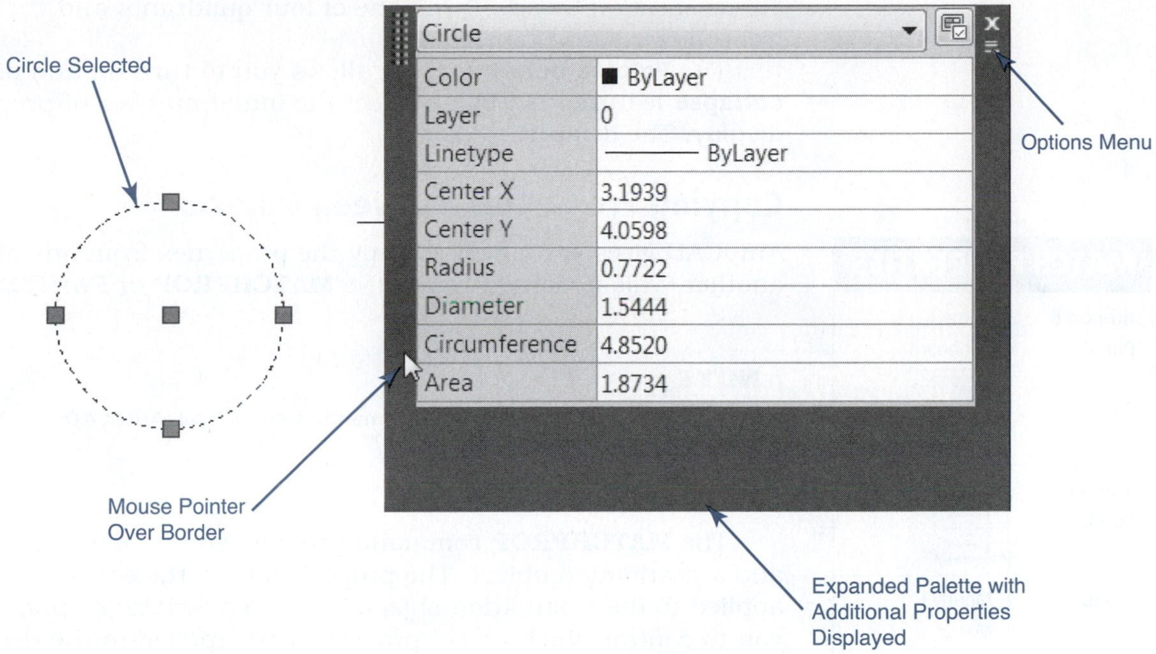

Figure 6-27
The expanded **Quick Properties** palette

Figure 6-28
The **Quick Properties** tab of the **Drafting Settings** dialog box

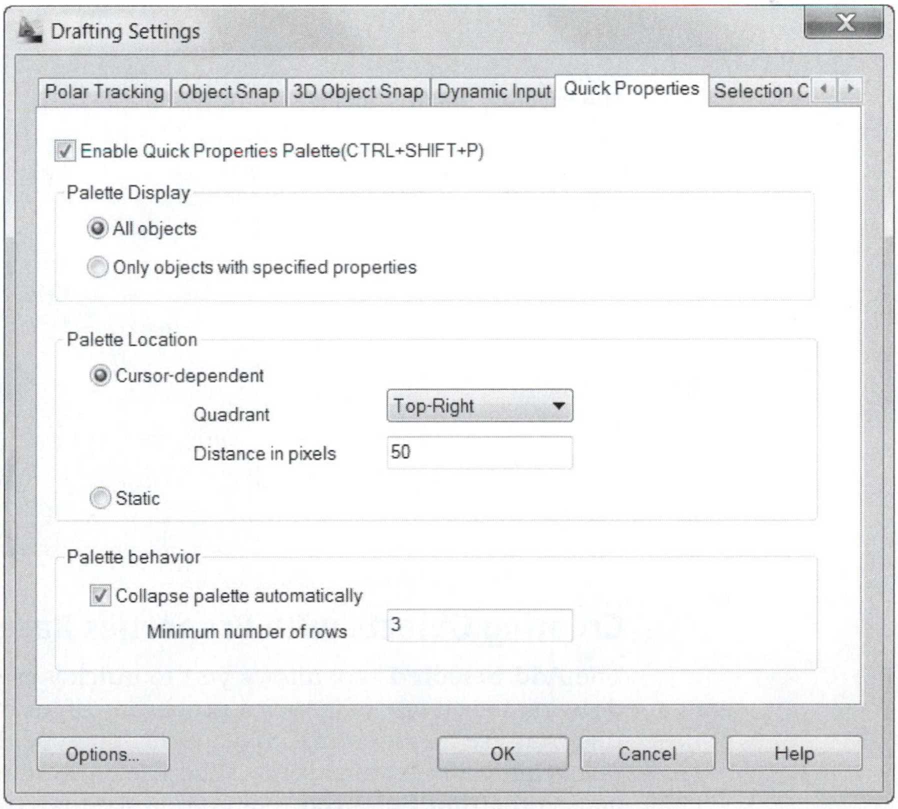

which objects will cause the **Quick Properties** palette to be displayed. Additionally, you can even tell AutoCAD which properties to display. Both of these advanced topics are beyond the scope of this textbook.

The **Palette Location** area allows you to control whether the **Quick Properties** palette is static or is displayed at the current cursor location. Additionally, you control where the palette is located relative to the current cursor location by specifying one of four quadrants and the distance away from the cursor in pixels.

The **Palette behavior** area allows you to turn on and off the **Auto-collapse** feature, as well as select the initial number of property rows to display. The default is 3 rows.

Copying Properties Between Objects

MATCH PROPERTIES	
Ribbon & Panel:	Home | Clipboard 
Standard Toolbar:	
Menu:	Modify | Match Properties
Command Line:	MATCHPROP Or PAINTER
Command Alias:	None

AutoCAD gives you a way to copy the properties from one object to another. This is done through the **MATCHPROP** or **PAINTER** command.

NOTE

The **MATCHPROP** and **PAINTER** commands are identical. AutoCAD simply has two names for the same command.

The **MATCHPROP** command prompts you to select a source object and a destination object. The properties from the source object are then applied to the destination object. There is a **Settings** option that allows you to control which object properties are applied to the destination object. When you choose the **Settings** option, AutoCAD shows you the **Property Settings** dialog box (see Figure 6-29). This shows you the properties of the source object and allows you to specify which property settings to apply to the destination object.

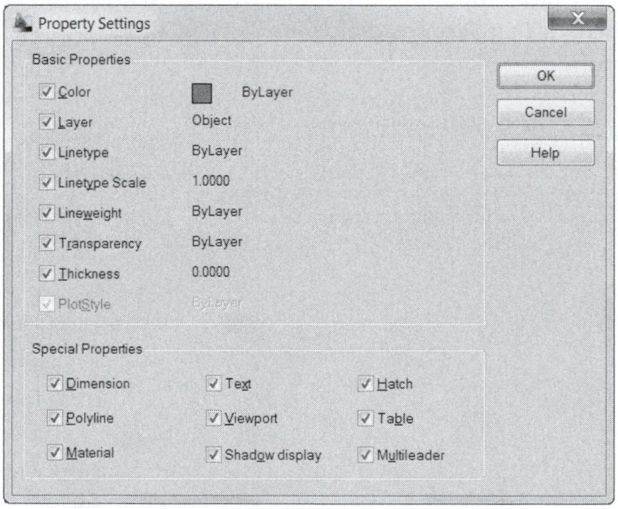

Figure 6-29
The **Property Settings** dialog box

Creating Objects with Properties Based on Existing Objects

The **Add Selected** tool allows you to quickly create a new object in your drawing based on the general properties of an existing object. The properties that are included are color, layer, linetype, linetype scale, plot style, lineweight, and transparency. The tricky thing is that the only way to access the **Add Selected** tool is to first select the existing object that you want to base on and then right-click to display a shortcut menu with the tool now included, as shown in Figure 6-30.

After selecting the **Add Selected** tool, AutoCAD starts the command that was used to create the existing object and updates the general properties to match the selected object.

In the following exercise, you'll examine some of the different ways of changing object properties.

Figure 6-30
The right-click menu with the **Add Selected** tool displayed

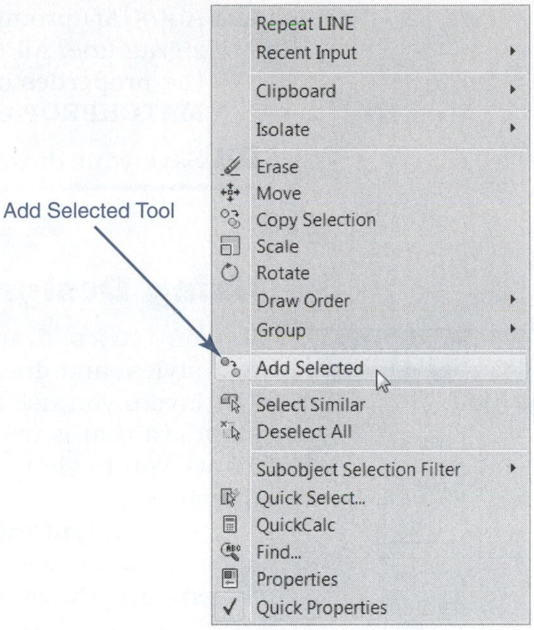

EXERCISE 6-9 Changing Object Properties

1. Continue from Exercise 6-8.
2. Set the **Object** layer current.
3. Select the circle in your drawing. Notice that values in the **Layer, Color, Linetype,** and **Lineweight** drop-down lists all change to show you the property settings for the selected circle.
4. Open the **Properties** palette.
5. Change the **Linetype scale** value to **2**. The linetype scale of the circle will double. Press **<Esc>** to clear the circle selection and close the **Properties** palette.
6. Select the line on layer **Hidden**. Again, the **Properties** drop-down lists show the values of the selected object.
7. Select the **Object** layer in the **Layer Control** drop-down list. The line is changed to the **Object** layer. Since the linetype, color, and lineweight properties of the line were all set to **ByLayer**, those properties were updated as well. Press **<Esc>** to clear line selection.
8. Turn on the **Quick Properties** button on the status bar.
9. Select the circle in the drawing. The **Quick Properties** palette is displayed.
10. Place your cursor on the bottom edge of the **Quick Properties** palette so that the expanded palette is displayed and you can access the **Diameter** property.
11. Change the diameter to **3.0**.
12. Press **<Esc>** to clear the circle selection and close the **Quick Properties** palette.
13. Start the **MATCHPROP** command. AutoCAD prompts you to *Select source object:*. Select one of the lines on the **Object** layer.

14 AutoCAD prompts you to *Select destination objects(s) or ↓*. Select the zigzag line. All the properties of the zigzag line are changed to match the properties of the **Object** line. Press **<Enter>** or **<Esc>** to end the **MATCHPROP** command.

15 Save your drawing.

Using DesignCenter to Import Layers

DESIGNCENTER	
Ribbon & Panel:	View | Palettes 
Standard Toolbar:	
Menu:	Tools | Palettes | Design Center
Command Line:	ADCENTER
Command Alias:	DC

In many cases, drawing information such as layers, linetypes, symbols, text styles, and dimension settings are common across multiple drawings. The layers you use in one drawing might be part of a company or project standard that is used over and over. AutoCAD's **DesignCenter** is a tool that allows you to share common information and settings between multiple drawings.

The **DesignCenter** palette (see Figure 6-31) is arranged in tabs that show drawings you currently have open, drawings in other local or network folders, and drawings you've recently accessed.

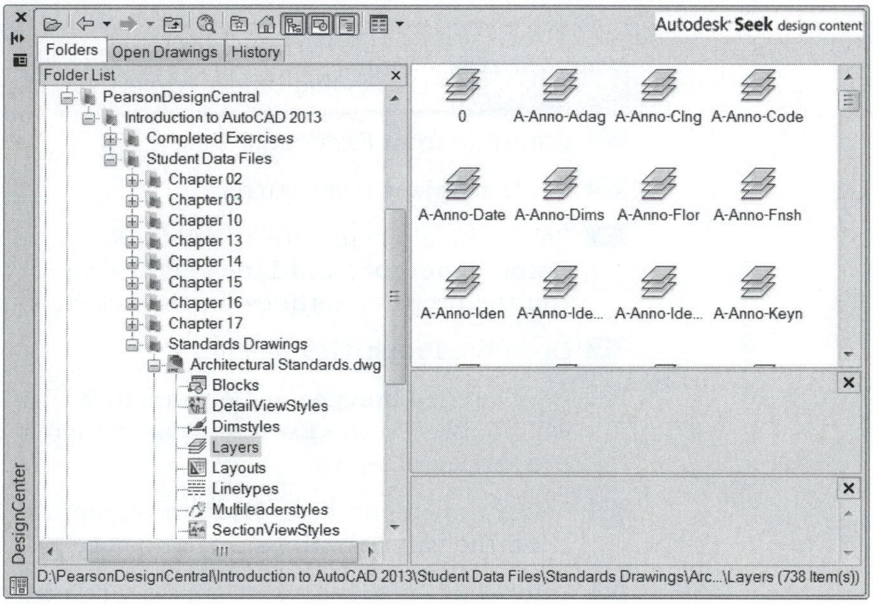

Figure 6-31
The **DesignCenter** palette

The **Folders** tab shows you a directory tree similar to what you might see in Windows Explorer. With the **Folders** tab, you can navigate to drawing files in any accessible local or network folder. The **Open Drawings** and **History** tabs show you a list of currently or recently opened drawing files.

When you select a drawing file in **DesignCenter**, AutoCAD shows you a list of drawing information contained in that drawing. The drawing information is divided into categories (Blocks, Dimstyles, Layers, Layouts, Linetypes, Multileaderstyles, Tablestyles, Textstyles, and Xrefs), and within each category are the specific objects and settings contained within that drawing. These objects and settings can be copied into your current drawing by selecting them from the list on the right and then dragging them into the drawing area of your current drawing. The settings and objects are then copied into your drawing.

NOTE

When drawing objects such as blocks and xrefs are placed in the drawing, the objects are placed on the current layer. For settings such as layer definitions, dimension styles, and other nongraphical information, only the settings are loaded into the drawing. If an object or setting with the same name already exists in your drawing, **DesignCenter** will simply ignore duplicate items and not import them.

FOR MORE DETAILS

See page 699 of Chapter 16 for more information about **DesignCenter**.

EXERCISE 6-10 **Using DesignCenter to Import Layers**

To access student data files, go to **www.pearsondesigncentral.com.**

1. Continue from Exercise 6-9.
2. Choose the **DesignCenter** button from the **Palettes** panel on the **View** tab of the ribbon. This opens the **DesignCenter** palette. Position the palette on your screen anywhere you like.
3. In the **Folders** tab, navigate to the **Standards Drawings** folder in the student data files, and select the + box next to the **Architectural Standards.dwg** file. This will show the objects and settings available in this drawing.
4. Select the **Layers** item in the list. A list of available layers will appear in the right-hand pane.
5. Select the **A-ANNO-ADAG** layer, hold down the **<Shift>** key, and select the **A-ANNO-FNSH** layer. AutoCAD will select all the layers between these two layers.
6. Press and hold your mouse button on one of the selected layers and drag the layers into your drawing area. When you release the mouse button, the layers will be copied into your new drawing. In the command line, AutoCAD will respond with

   Layer(s) added. Duplicate definitions will be ignored.
7. Start the **LAYER** command to verify that the layers have been imported into your drawing.
8. Close or hide the **DesignCenter** palette.
9. Save the drawing.

Using Content Explorer to Import Layers

The AutoCAD **Content Explorer** is considered the next generation of **DesignCenter**. The **Content Explorer** palette (see Figure 6-32) is toggled on and off via the **Explore** button on the **Plug-ins** tab of the ribbon.

Content Explorer provides access to drawing information such as layers, linetypes, text styles, dimension settings, etc. in any drawing. However, unlike **DesignCenter, Content Explorer** is built upon an index that allows you to quickly search for drawing information across multiple folders with possibly thousands of files and have the results returned instantaneously.

In addition, by using **Content Explorer** you can find specific text strings or blocks in a drawing, then automatically open the file they are contained in, and zoom up on the found objects. Try that with **DesignCenter**!

Figure 6-32
The **Content Explorer** palette

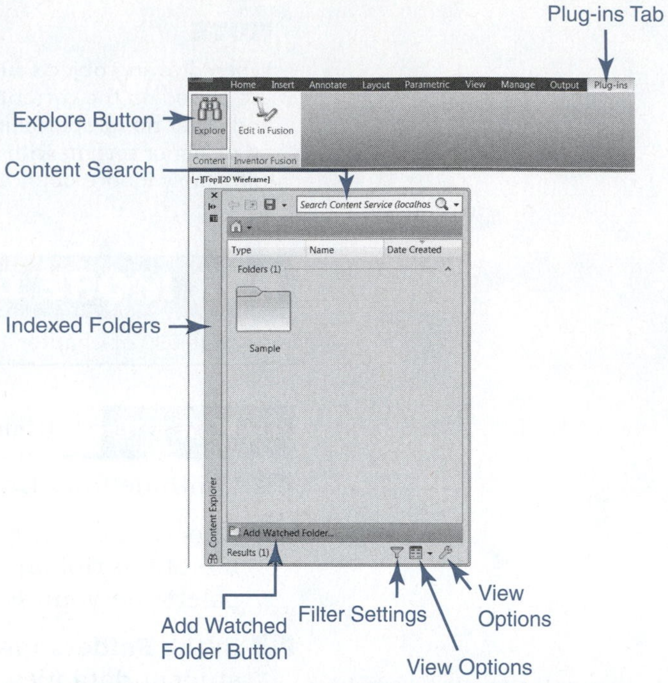

FOR MORE DETAILS

See page 714 of Chapter 16 for more information about **Content Explorer**.

EXERCISE 6-11 **Using Content Explorer to Import Layers**

1. Continue from Exercise 6-10.
2. Choose the **Explore** button from the **Content** panel on the **Plug-ins** tab of the ribbon. This opens the **Content Explorer** palette. Position the palette on your screen anywhere you like.
3. Select the **Add Watched Folder...** button near the bottom of the palette to display the **Select Watched Folder** window.
4. Navigate to the **Standards Drawings** folder in the student data files and select the **OK** button. AutoCAD will start building an index for all drawings in that folder.
5. Once the index is created, double-click on the **Standards Drawings** folder and then double-click on the **Architectural Standards.dwg** file. This will show the objects and settings available in this drawing.
6. Select the **I-LITE** layer, drag it into the drawing window, and release the mouse button to copy the layer and all of its properties to the current drawing.
7. Close or hide the **Content Explorer** palette.
8. Save the drawing.

To access student data files, go to **www.pearsondesigncentral.com.**

Layer Filters

When working in drawings that have a large number of layers, managing layer settings in a long list of layers can prove difficult. To help manage this, AutoCAD allows you to filter the list of layers. This allows you to display

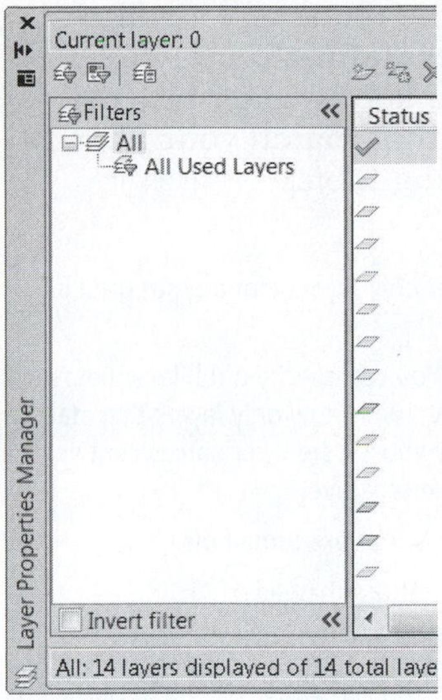

Figure 6-33
The **Layer Filters** area of the **Layer Properties Manager** palette

only the layers you are interested in or will be using. The **Layer Filter** list of the **Layer Properties Manager** palette allows you to create and manage these filters (see Figure 6-33).

The filter tree shows you a hierarchy of layers, starting with all layers. Clicking on the **All** level will list all the layers in the drawing in the layer list area. Below the **All** filter is the **All Used Layers** filter. Selecting this will filter the layer list to show only the layers that are currently in use in the drawing. The **All** and **All Used Layers** filters are predefined filters that cannot be renamed or deleted. You can create your own custom layer filters.

The Filter Tree

To activate a layer filter, simply select it from the filter tree. The filter tree is hierarchical, which means that the filter is applied to the layers on the level above it in the tree.

Below the filter tree are two boxes: **Invert filter** and **Indicate layers in use**. Putting a check in the **Invert filter** box will reverse the effects of the filter. For example, if you choose the **All Used Layers** filter, putting a check in the **Invert filter** box will show you all the unused layers.

Checking the **Indicate layers in use** option will indicate which layers have drawing information on them by making the icon in the **Status** column darker for referenced layers and lighter for layers that do not have anything on them. This is a good way to determine which layers can be deleted and which layers cannot.

Property Filters

Property filters will filter your layer list based upon certain matching criteria. For example, you might create a filter that shows you only layers that start with characters "C-," or a filter that shows only thawed layers, or only locked layers. You can also combine criteria. For example, you can create a filter that shows all layers that are both frozen and locked and contain the letter X in their name.

To create a property filter, choose the **New Property Filter** button. The **Layer Filter Properties** dialog box will appear (see Figure 6-34).

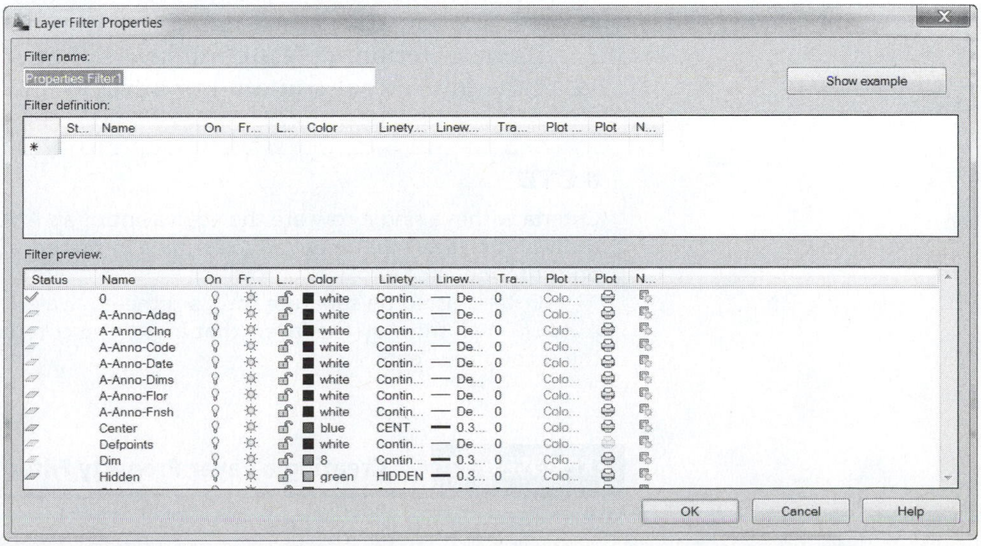

Figure 6-34
The **Layer Filter Properties** dialog box

The **Filter name:** area allows you to change the name of your filter. You create a filter by selecting criteria in the **Filter definition:** area. You can select multiple criteria on a single row. As you specify filter criteria, the **Filter preview:** area shows you all the layers that match your filter. The various filter criteria are defined in the following table:

Status	Shows only layers that are used in the drawing or only layers that are not used in the drawing.
Name	Shows only layer names that match the criteria. You can specify a full layer name or a partial name with wildcards. For example, **W*** will show only layers that start with the letter W. A name filter of ***C*** will show you all the layer names containing the letter C. The **Layer Name** filter is not case sensitive.
On	Shows only layers that are turned on or only layers that are turned off.
Freeze	Shows only layers that are frozen or only layers that are thawed.
Lock	Shows only layers that are locked or only layers that are unlocked.
Color	Shows only layers that match the color specified. You can either specify a color name or number or choose the **...** box to select from the **Select Color** dialog box. Like the layer name, you can specify a partial color number with wildcards. For example, specifying **4•** for the color will show color 4 and colors 40–49.
Linetype	Shows only layers that match the specified linetype. You can type in the linetype name or choose **...** to select the linetype from the **Select Linetype** dialog box. Partial names with wildcards are allowed.
Lineweight	Shows only layers that are a specified lineweight.
Transparency	Shows only layers with a specified transparency level.
Plot Style	Shows only layers that match a specific plot style. This option is available only in drawings where named plot styles are used. Partial names with wildcards are allowed.
Plot	Shows only layers that are set to either **Plot** or **Noplot**.
New VP Freeze	Shows only layers that are either frozen in new viewports or thawed in new viewports. This option is available only when accessed from a drawing layout (paper space).

All the criteria you specify in a row are applied to the layer list. For example, a filter row with the name criteria of "A-" and "Frozen" will show only layers that both start with "A-" *and* are frozen.

Once you specify some criteria, a new row is added to the **Filter definition:** list. Each row is applied separately to the filter. For example, if you have one row that has a name criterion of "E-" and another row that has a name criterion of "Wall," all layers that start with "E-" will be shown *and* all the layers that contain the word "WALL" will also be shown.

NOTE

Criteria within a single row are the equivalent of an AND search query. AutoCAD will show all the layers that meet *all* the criteria in that row (the first criterion *AND* the second criterion, etc.).

Criteria listed on separate rows are the equivalent of an OR search query. AutoCAD will show all the layers that match the criteria of *any* row (the first row *OR* the second row, etc.).

EXERCISE 6-12 Creating a Layer Property Filter

1. Continue from Exercise 6-11.
2. Start the **LAYER** command and choose the **New Property Filter** button. The **Layer Filter Properties** dialog box will appear (see Figure 6-35).

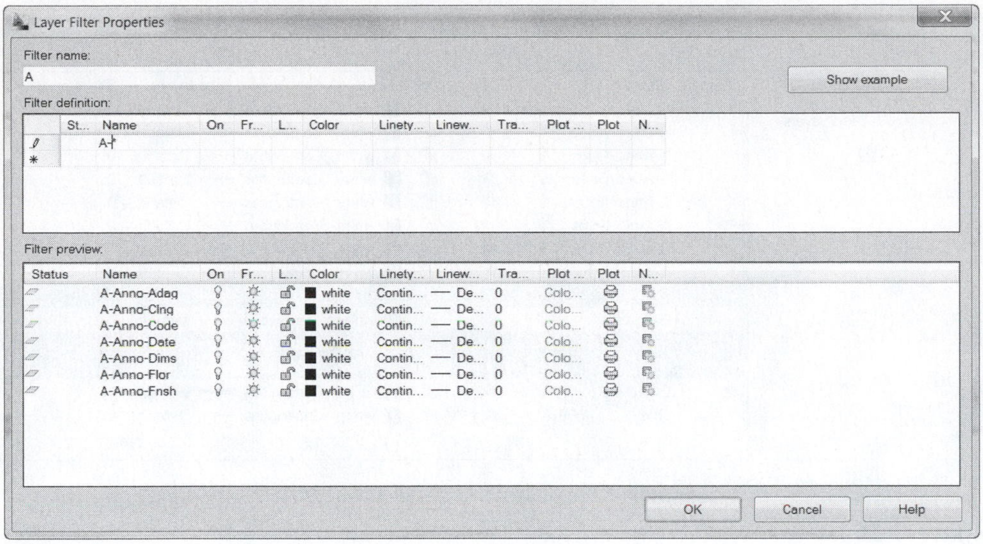

Figure 6-35
The **Layer Filter Properties** dialog box

3. Change the **Filter name** to **A** and click inside the **Name** criteria column. An asterisk (*) will appear in the **Name** column and all the layers will appear in the **Filter preview:** area.
4. Type **A-*** in the **Name** column. The **Filter preview:** area will update to show you only layer names that start with **A-**.
5. Choose **OK** to save the filter and close the dialog box. The **A** filter will now appear in the **Layer Filter** area. The filter is applied to the layer list so only the **A-** layers are shown.
6. Select the **Invert filter** box. The filter is reversed and all layers except the **A-** layers are shown.
7. Remove the check from the **Invert filter** box. Choose **OK** to end the **LAYER** command.
8. Select the **Layer Control** drop-down list. Notice that only layers that match the **A** filter are shown.
9. Save the drawing.

Group Filters

A group filter allows you to filter your layer list to show only layers you select. The layers do not need to match any particular criteria; you simply select the layers you want to include in your filter. To create a group filter, choose the **New Group Filter** button in the **Layer Properties Manager** palette. AutoCAD will create a new group filter called **Group Filter1** and highlight the name. You can then type a new name for the filter. To add layers to the filter, select the layers from the layer list on the right side and drag them onto the group filter name on the left side.

EXERCISE 6-13 Creating a Group Filter

1. Continue from Exercise 6-12.
2. Start the **LAYER** command and choose the **New Group Filter** button. AutoCAD creates a new group filter called **Group Filter1** and highlights the name. Type **Misc** for the group filter name. The layer list is now empty because the new group filter is active and has no layers in it.

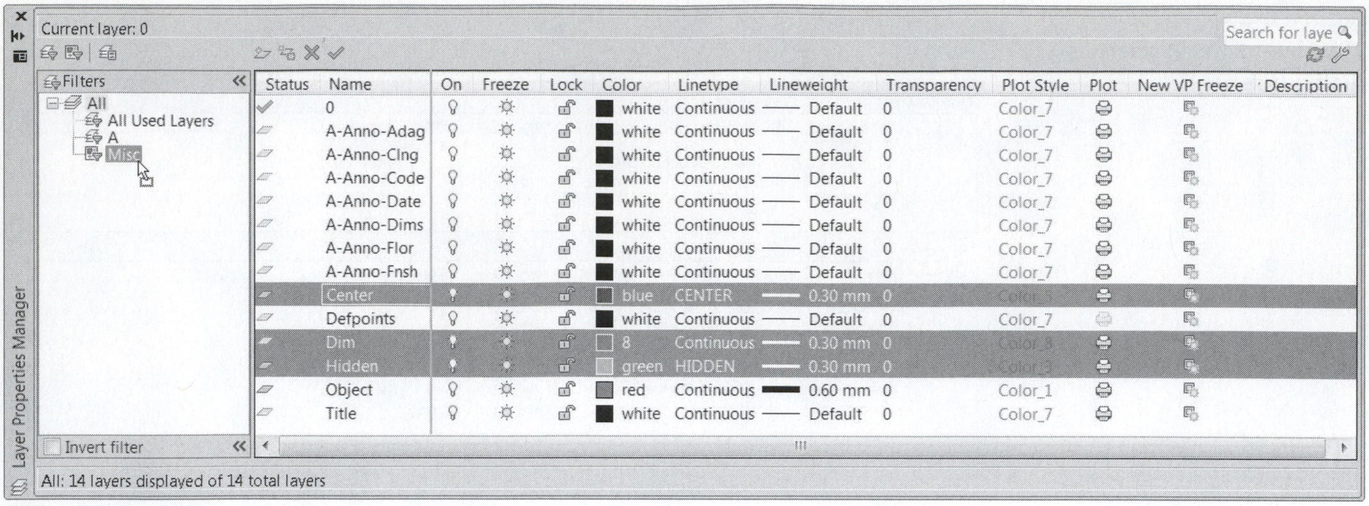

Figure 6-36
Creating a group filter

3 Select **All** in the **Layer Filter** area to show all the layers. Hold down the **<Ctrl>** key and select the **Center, Dim,** and **Hidden** layers from the layer list. Click and drag the layers onto the **Misc** filter and release the mouse button (see Figure 6-36). The selected layers are added to the group filter.

4 Select the **All** filter and choose **OK** to end the **LAYER** command.

5 Save the drawing.

Search Filter

In the top right corner of the **Layer Properties Manager** palette is a box that says **Search for layer**. This is a layer search filter that allows you to do a temporary name filter on the current list of layers. You can type in a layer name (including wildcards) to show a list of layers that match that name. The search filter cannot be saved; it works only while the dialog box is open or until you select another filter. The search filter applies only to the list of layers shown in the layer list at the time the search is done.

LAYER STATES MANAGER	
Layer Properties Manager:	
Layers Toolbar:	
Menu:	Format | Layer States Manager
Command Line:	LAYERSTATE
Command Alias:	LAS

Layer States Manager

There may be times when you have a set of layer settings that you use or need to restore at certain times. For example, you might want to freeze a set of layers before you plot, or you might want to lock certain layers before you share them with others. The **Layer States Manager** will save a snapshot of layer settings that you can then recall at any time. To create a layer state, set the layers to the setting you want to save, and then start the **LAYERSTATE** command to display the **Layer States Manager** dialog box (see Figure 6-37) by selecting the **Layer States Manager** button in the **Layer Properties Manager** palette.

Choose the **New...** button to create a new layer state. The **New Layer State to Save** dialog box appears (see Figure 6-38), and you are asked for a layer state name. You can also provide an optional description for the layer state. Once you've supplied a name, choose **OK**, and you'll be returned to the **Layer States Manager** dialog box.

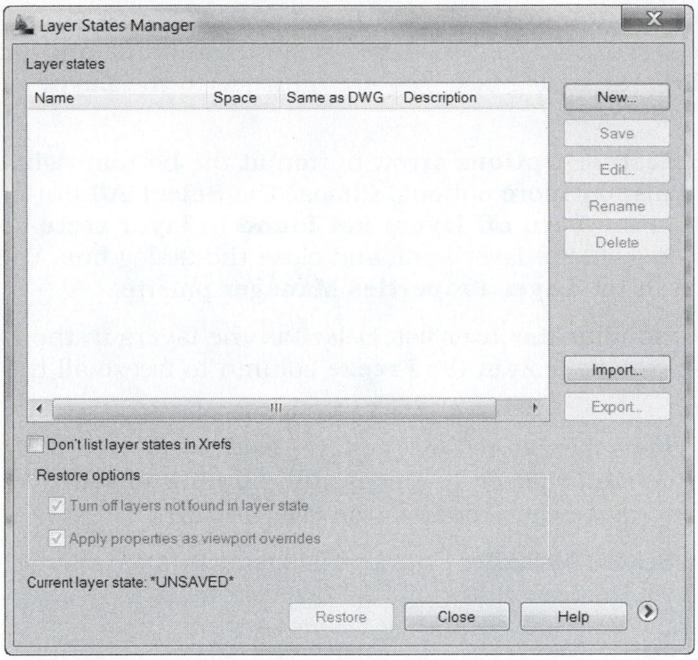

Figure 6-37
The **Layer States Manager** dialog box

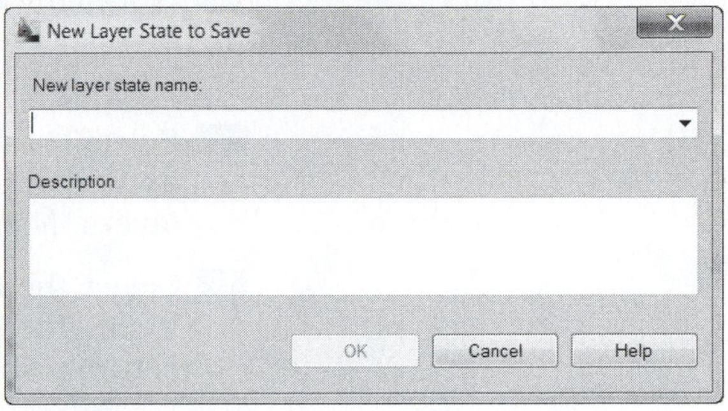

Figure 6-38
The **New Layer State to Save** dialog box

It is possible to edit a layer state directly by selecting the **Edit...** button so that the layer state does not need to be deleted and re-created. Selecting the **Edit...** button displays the **Edit Layer State** dialog box so that you can update any of the standard layer properties, add new layers, or delete existing layers from the currently selected layer state.

Selecting the **More Restore Options** arrow button at the bottom right of the dialog box displays the **Layer properties to restore** options on the right of the dialog box so you can control which layer properties you wish to save and restore. Simply select which properties you wish to maintain.

Layer states can be exported to a file. This allows you to create standard layer settings that can be shared among multiple drawings in a project or used within a company standard. Use the **Export...** and **Import...** buttons in the **Layer States Manager** dialog box to export a layer state setting or to import an existing layer state file with an LAS extension. It is also possible to import layer states directly from DWG, DWT, or DWS files.

To restore a layer state, choose the **Layer States Manager** button on the **Layer Properties Manager** palette, select the layer state you wish to restore, and then choose the **Restore** button. All the settings for that layer state will be restored.

EXERCISE 6-14 Creating and Restoring Layer States

1. Continue from Exercise 6-13.
2. Start the **LAYER** command and select the **All** filter from the filter tree.
3. Choose the **Layer States Manager** button to display the **Layer States Manager** dialog box.

4 Choose the **New...** button to display the **New Layer State to Save** dialog box. Type **Default** in the **New layer state name:** area and choose **OK** to close the dialog box. You are returned to the **Layer States Manager** dialog box.

5 Select the **More Restore Options** arrow button at the bottom right of the dialog box to display more options. Choose the **Select All** button and put a check in the **Turn off layers not found in layer state** box. Choose **Restore** to save the layer state and close the dialog box. You are now returned to the **Layer Properties Manager** palette.

6 Select the **A** filter to filter the layer list. Select all the layers in the list and select the snowflake icon in the **Freeze** column to freeze all the layers.

7 Select the **Misc** group filter to refilter the layer list. Select all the layers and set the color to **white** (color 7). Choose the **All** filter to see all layers. Notice the changes you made to the layer settings.

8 Select the **Layer States Manager** button. The **Default** layer state is highlighted. Choose **Restore** to restore the layer settings. The layer settings should now be restored to their previous state.

9 Save the drawing.

Layer Tools

There are a number of useful miscellaneous layer tools available on the expanded **Layers** panel shown in Figure 6-39, the **Layer Tools** cascade menu found on the **Format** menu shown in Figure 6-40, or via the **Layers II** toolbar shown in Figure 6-41.

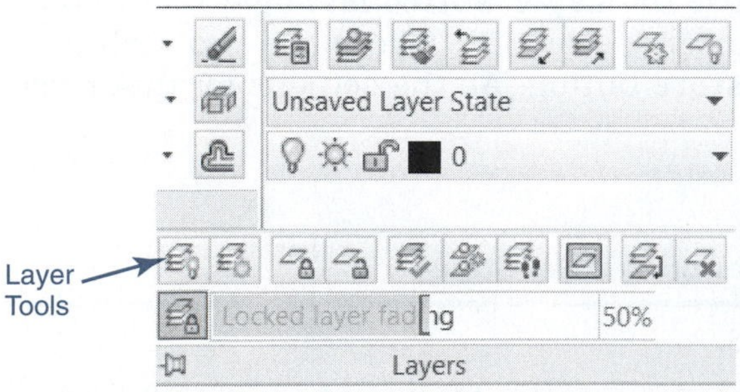

Figure 6-39
The expanded **Layers** panel

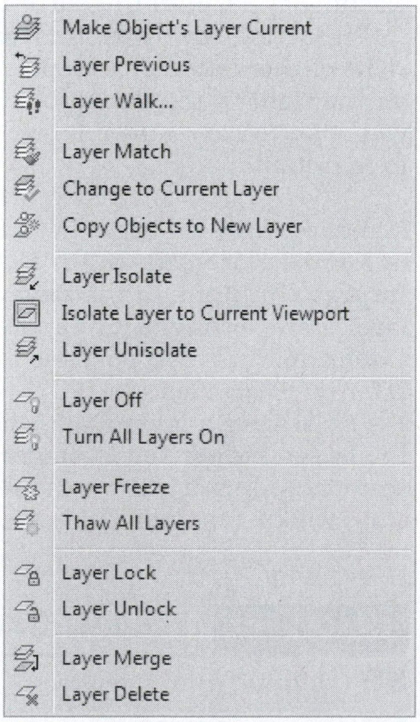

Figure 6-40
The **Layer Tools** cascade menu

Figure 6-41
The **Layers II** toolbar

The **Layer** tools and their uses are listed in the following table.

Layer Tools

Layer Tool	Command	Description
Make Object's Layer Current	LAYMCUR	Changes the current layer to match the selected object.
Layer Previous	LAYERP	Undoes the last change or set of changes made to layer settings.
Layer Walk	LAYWALK	Dynamically displays objects on selected layers.
Layer Match	LAYMCH or -LAYMCH	Changes the layer(s) of selected objects to match the layer of a selected destination object.
Change to Current Layer	LAYCUR	Moves selected objects to the current layer.
Copy Objects to New Layer	COPYTOLAYER or -COPYTOLAYER	Copies selected objects to another layer, leaving the original objects intact.
Layer Isolate	LAYISO	Isolates the layer of the selected object(s) so that all other layers are turned off.
Isolate Layer to Current Viewport	LAYVPI	Isolates an object's layer to the current viewport.
Layer Unisolate	LAYUNISO	Turns on layers that were turned off with the **LAYISO** command.
Layer Off	LAYOFF	Turns off the layer of the selected object(s).
Turn All Layers On	LAYON	Turns on all layers.
Layer Freeze	LAYFRZ	Freezes the layer of selected objects.
Thaw All Layers	LAYTHW	Thaws all layers.
Layer Lock	LAYLCK	Locks the layer of a selected object.
Layer Unlock	LAYULK	Unlocks the layer of a selected object.
Layer Merge	LAYMRG or -LAYMRG	Moves all objects from the first selected layer to the second selected layer and deletes the first layer.
Layer Delete	LAYDEL or -LAYDEL	Deletes all objects from the specified layer and purges the layer from the drawing.

Object Visibility

It is possible to control object visibility independent of layer visibility via the **Object Visibility** tools located in the status tray on the far right of the status bar shown in Figure 6-42.

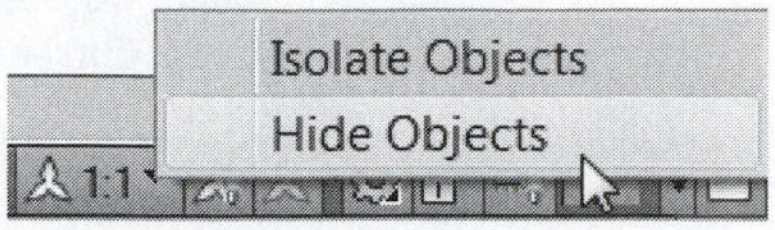

Figure 6-42
The **Object Visibility** tools

The **Isolate Objects** tool displays only the objects you select in the drawing. All other objects are hidden. The **Hide Objects** tool, on the other hand, hides all of the objects you select in the drawing. All other objects are visible.

You can use the **Isolate Objects** and **Hide Objects** tools together to display only the objects that are relevant to your current task. For example, you can first use the **Isolate Objects** tool to select an area of the drawing you want to edit using a window selection technique and then use the **Hide Objects** tool to hide individual objects within the displayed group. When you are done, you can quickly restore the original drawing display by selecting the **End Object Isolation** tool, which is displayed on the same **Object Visibility** menu when either tool is in use.

NOTE

- You can also use the **ISOLATEOBJECTS** and **HIDEOBJECTS** commands to control object visibility.
- The lightbulb icon in the status tray on the status bar appears dimmed when either the **Isolate Objects** or **Hide Objects** tool is in use.

TIP

The **OBJECTISOLATIONMODE** system variable controls whether isolated/hidden objects persist between drawing sessions. Setting **OBJECTISOLATIONMODE** to **0** will not save the isolated/hidden status of objects between drawing sessions. Setting **OBJECTISOLATIONMODE** to **1** will save any active isolated/hidden status so that it persists between drawing sessions. The default setting is **0**.

Chapter Summary

A well-organized drawing is something every CAD user should strive for. Clear and concise CAD standards and drawing objects placed on their proper layers can make the difference between a drawing that is easy to read and understand and one that is confusing. Good layer management practices are critical in group settings where multiple people will be accessing and editing your drawings. Incorporating different standard linetypes and lineweights to delineate different types of information in a drawing helps to visually communicate design intent and display drawing information in a concise fashion.

One of the beauties of CAD, as an old boss used to tell me, is the ability to update and modify a drawing quickly. To tell the truth, I think he abused that capability considering the many times he made me revise the same drawings. But, it is a fact of life in the drafting world that drawings constantly change. Using the different property management tools introduced in this chapter provides the most efficient means of implementing those changes. It's not called **Quick Properties** for nothing.

Rather than creating a bunch of layers and updating all of their corresponding properties in every drawing, it is possible to save significant amounts of time using the **DesignCenter** palette or **Content Explorer** to drag and drop multiple layer definitions from any existing drawing on your system into your current drawing. To help manage the huge amount of layers and their various properties that can end up in a drawing over its life span, AutoCAD provides a means to filter layer information so you can reduce the infoglut. On top of that, complex layer groups and their property settings can be saved to a layer state so that they may be restored later in the current drawing or even in other drawings on a whole project so that everyone is literally on the same page!

Chapter Test Questions

Multiple Choice

Circle the correct answer.

1. A layer is:

a. A separate drawing that you merge into your drawing
b. The only way to control the color of drawing objects
c. A collection of color, linetype, lineweight, and other display settings
d. A 3D setting

2. Turning a layer off:

a. Prevents objects on that layer from being seen
b. Prevents objects on that layer from being edited
c. Deletes all the objects on a layer
d. Is the same as freezing a layer

3. The color blue is AutoCAD Color Index number:
   a. 3
   b. 4
   c. 5
   d. 6
4. An RGB color number of 0,255,0 is what color?
   a. Red
   b. Green
   c. Blue
   d. Black
   e. White
5. AutoCAD linetypes:
   a. Consist of only lines and spaces
   b. Are loaded automatically when you assign them to a layer
   c. Cannot be modified
   d. Must be loaded into the drawing before they can be used
6. Deleting a layer:
   a. Deletes the layer and all the objects on the layer
   b. Deletes all the objects on a layer but keeps the layer name in the drawing
   c. Can be done only when a layer is unused
   d. Can be done at any time regardless of whether the layer is used or not
7. The **LTSCALE** setting:
   a. Is a global scale factor applied to all objects' linetypes
   b. Affects the lineweight of all objects
   c. Affects the plot scale of layout viewports
   d. Does not affect objects that have an individual object linetype scale
8. An object with a color of ByLayer:
   a. Gets its color setting from its layer
   b. Is white
   c. Is white until a hard-coded color is assigned to it
   d. Is always the same color regardless of its layer color setting
9. Property filters:
   a. Are case sensitive
   b. Can filter only layers based on a single criterion
   c. Can use wildcards
   d. Are not based on any specific criteria
10. Group filters:
   a. Are case sensitive
   b. Can filter only layers based on a single criterion
   c. Can use wildcards
   d. Are not based on any specific criteria

Matching

Write the number of the correct answer on the line.

a. Layer ______
b. Property filter ______
c. Linetype ______
d. **LTSCALE** ______
e. RGB ______
f. Lineweight ______
g. Hard-coded object properties ______
h. **DesignCenter** ______
i. Group layer filter ______
j. Layer state ______

1. A layer filter based on user-selected layer names
2. The pattern of a line
3. A color model based on red, green, and blue color components
4. Object properties set independently of an object's layer
5. A collection of color, linetype, lineweight, transparency, and display settings
6. A tool used to share design information between AutoCAD drawings
7. The printed width of a line
8. A saved collection of layer settings
9. A global scale factor applied to all linetypes
10. A layer filter based on matching criteria

True or False

Circle the correct answer.

1. **True or False:** Layer **0** cannot be deleted.
2. **True or False:** Lineweight appears only when you plot a drawing.
3. **True or False:** Linetypes can be modified and new linetypes can be created.
4. **True or False:** A layer can be deleted only if it is unused in the drawing.
5. **True or False:** The **Layer Control** drop-down list always shows all the layers in a drawing.
6. **True or False:** Layers can be imported from other drawing files.
7. **True or False:** The **MATCHPROP** and **PAINTER** commands do the same thing.
8. **True or False:** A search filter takes effect only while the **LAYER** command is active.
9. **True or False:** Layer states can be exported and shared between multiple drawings.
10. **True or False: DesignCenter** is used only to insert blocks from other drawings.

Chapter Projects

G Project 6-1: *Classroom Plan* [BASIC]

1. Start a new drawing using the **acad.dwt** template. Set the **UNITS** to **Architectural** with **1/16″** precision. Set the **LTSCALE** to **6**.
2. Create the following layers:

Name	Color	Linetype	Lineweight	Description
A-Anno-Note	7	Continuous	0.25 mm	Notes
A-Door	4	Continuous	0.30 mm	Doors
A-Eqpm	6	Continuous	0.30 mm	Equipment
A-Eqpm-Hidden	7	Hidden	0.25 mm	Hidden equipment
A-Furn	7	Continuous	0.50 mm	Furniture
A-Furn-Char	7	Continuous	0.50 mm	Chairs
A-Glaz	4	Continuous	0.30 mm	Windows
A-Wall	7	Continuous	0.50 mm	Walls

3. Draw the desk, monitor, computer tower, mouse, chair, and keyboard shown in Figure 6-43. Draw the desk on the **A-Furn** layer. Place the computer on the **A-Eqpm-Hidden** layer. Place all other objects on the **A-Eqpm** layer.
4. **Do not** draw dimensions or text.
5. Save the drawing as ***P6-1***.

Figure 6-43

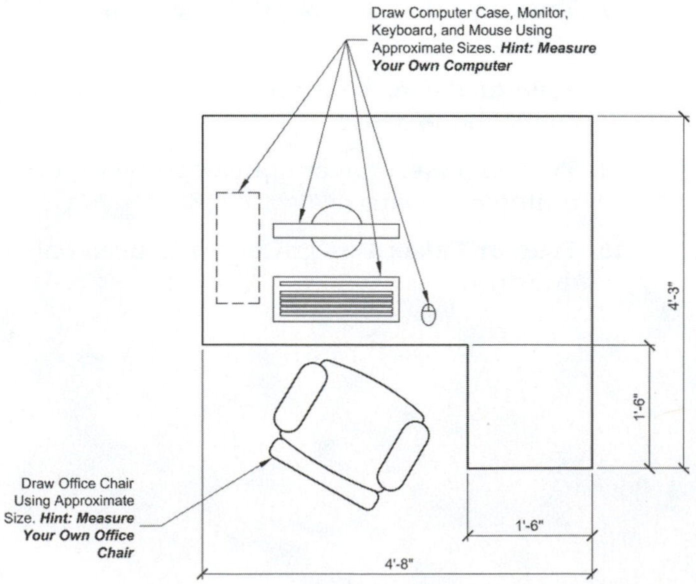

M Project 6-2: *B-Size Mechanical Border, continued from Chapter 5* [INTERMEDIATE]

1. Open the template file ***Mechanical B-Size.DWT*** from Project 5-2 in Chapter 5.
2. Create the following layers:

Name	Color	Linetype	Lineweight	Plot/Noplot	Description
Title	7	Continuous	0.50 mm	Plot	Title border and text
Logo	7	Continuous	Default	Plot	Logo
Notes	7	Continuous	0.30 mm	Plot	Notes
Viewport	9	Continuous	Default	Noplot	Viewports

3. Place the existing geometry on layer **Title**.
4. Add the line work shown in Figure 6-44 to the drawing. Use the **Title** layer for all geometry. **Do not** draw dimensions.
5. Save the drawing.

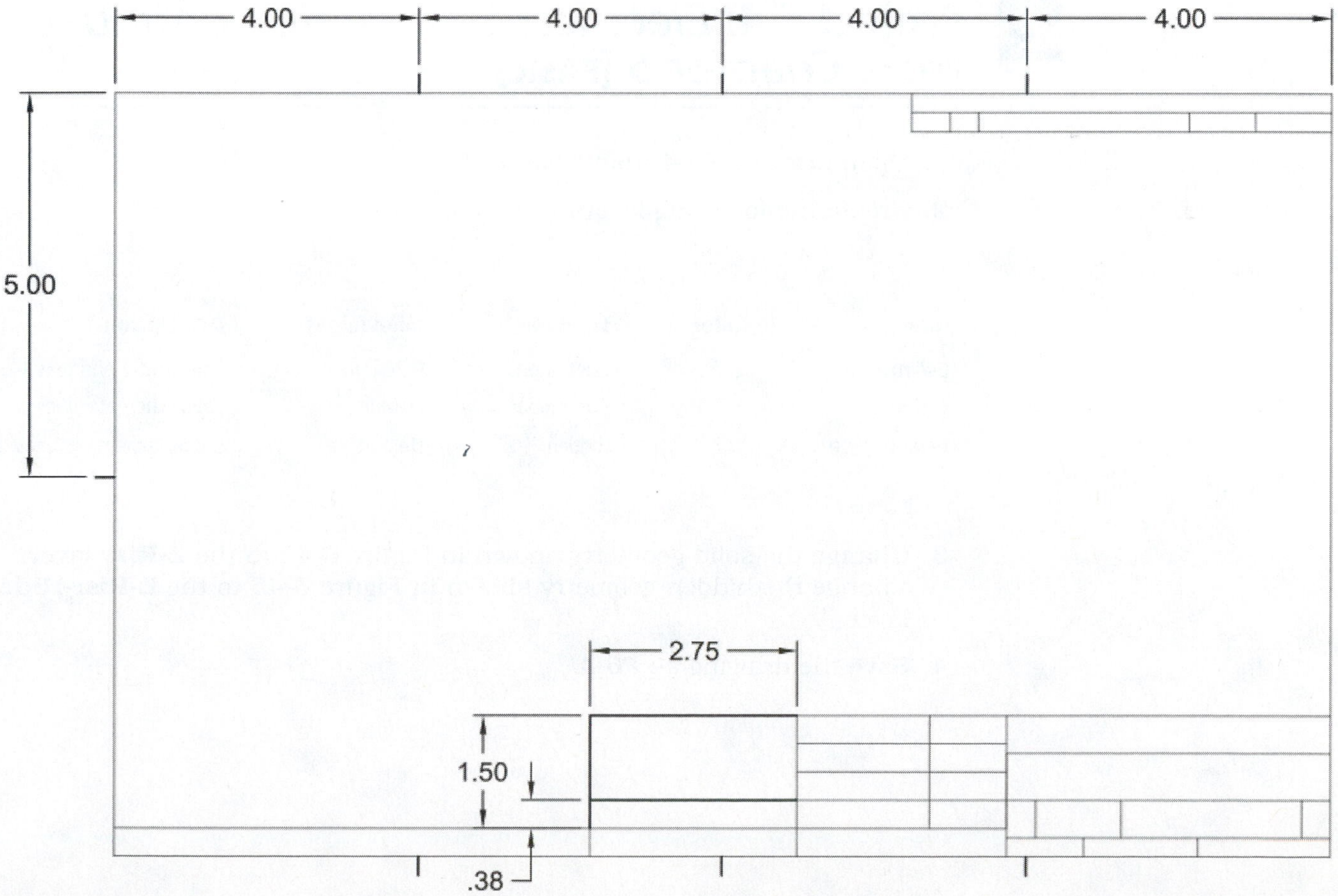

Figure 6-44

A Project 6-3: *Architectural D-Size Border, continued from Chapter 5* [ADVANCED]

1. Open the template file ***Architectural D-Size.DWT*** from Project 5-3 in Chapter 5.
2. Create the following layers:

Name	Color	Linetype	Lineweight	Plot/Noplot	Description
A-Anno-Ttlb	7	Continuous	0.50 mm	Plot	Title block/border lines
A-Anno-Ttlb-Text	1	Continuous	0.30 mm	Plot	Title block text
A-Anno-Ttlb-Logo	3	Continuous	Default	Plot	Logo
A-Anno-Vprt	7	Continuous	Default	Noplot	Viewport lines

3. Put all the existing line work on layer **A-Anno-Ttlb**.
4. Save the drawing.

E Project 6-4: *Electrical Schematic, continued from Chapter 5* [BASIC]

1. Open drawing ***P5-4*** from Chapter 5.
2. Create the following layers:

Name	Color	Linetype	Lineweight	Description
E-Anno	7	Continuous	0.30 mm	Title border and text
E-Risr	7	Continuous	Default	Solid schematic lines
E-Risr-Hide	7	Hidden	Default	Hidden schematic lines

3. Change the solid geometry shown in Figure 6-45 to the **E-Risr** layer. Change the hidden geometry shown in Figure 6-45 to the **E-Risr-Hide** layer.
4. Save the drawing as ***P6-4***.

Figure 6-45

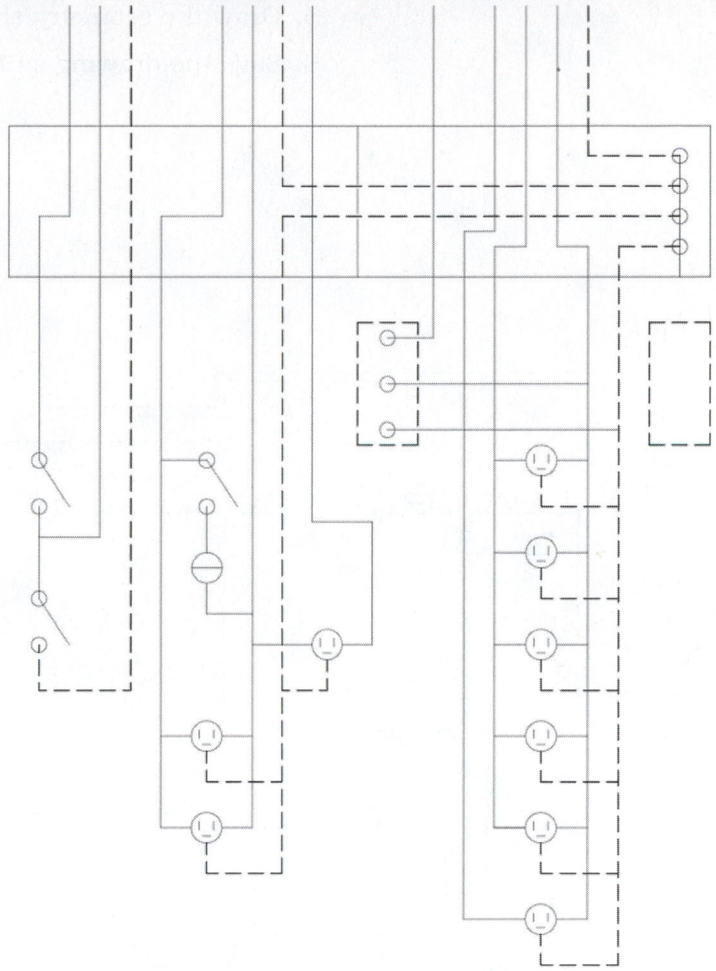

A Project 6-5: *Residential Architectural Plan, continued from Chapter 5* [ADVANCED]

1. Open drawing ***P5-5*** from Chapter 5.
2. Create the following layers:

Name	Color	Linetype	Lineweight	Description
A-Anno-Symb	7	Continuous	0.30 mm	Misc. symbols
A-Flor-Ovhd	3	Dashed	0.25 mm	Overhead skylights and overhangs
A-Door	5	Continuous	0.30 mm	Doors
A-Glaz	5	Continuous	0.30 mm	Windows
A-Wall	7	Continuous	0.50 mm	Walls
A-Wall-Pat	7	Continuous	Default	Wall hatch patterns and fills

3. Set the **LTSCALE** to **24**.
4. Place all existing walls on the **A-Wall** layer.

5. Draw the geometry shown in Figure 6-46 on the appropriate layer.
6. Save the drawing as ***P6-5***.

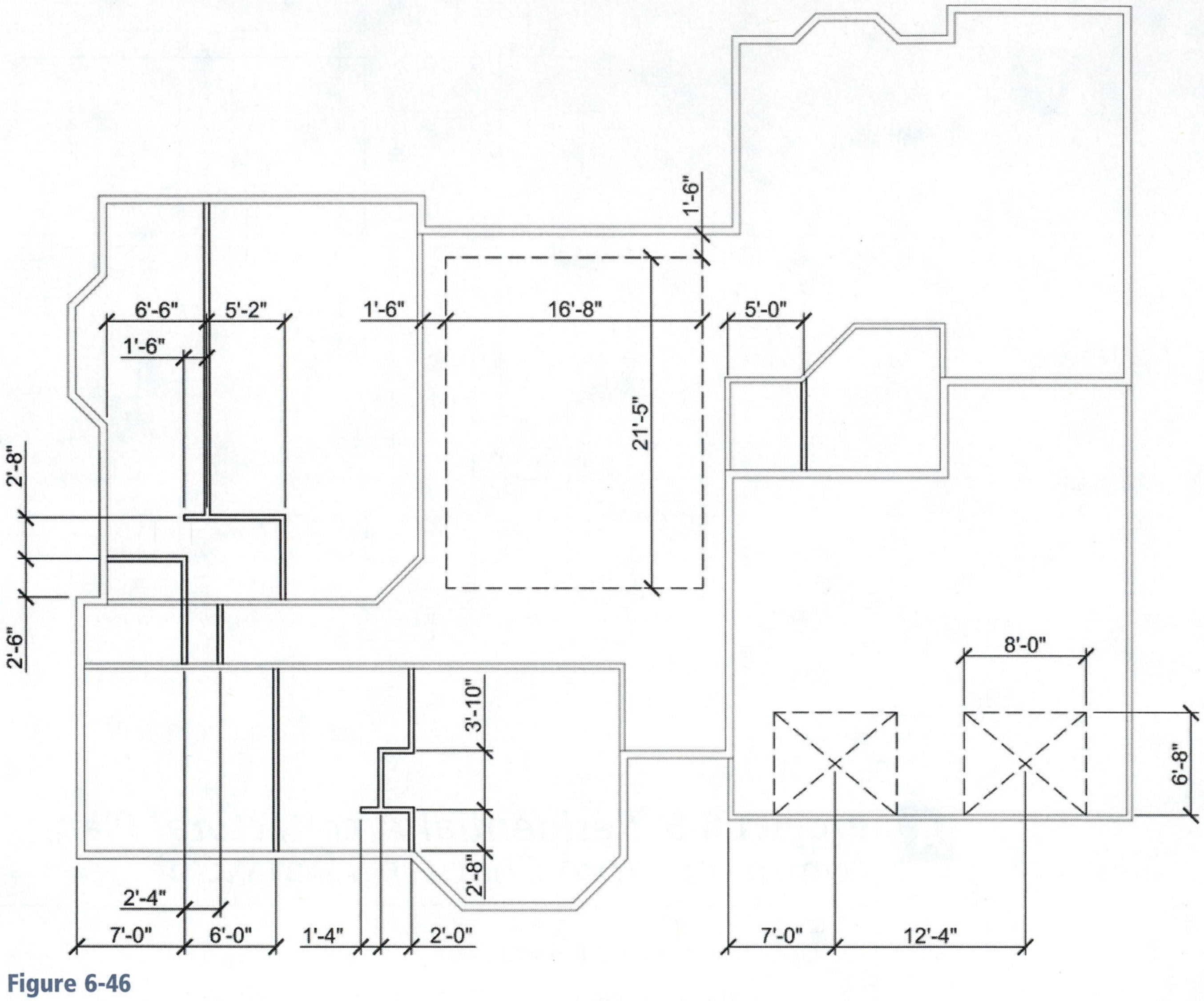

Figure 6-46

7 chapterseven

Basic Editing Techniques

CHAPTER OBJECTIVES

- Understand the difference between editing objects using the verb/noun technique and editing objects using the noun/verb technique
- Use the **ERASE** command to remove objects from a drawing
- Learn different ways to select one or more objects so that they can be modified
- Group objects
- Move objects
- Copy objects
- Mirror objects
- Rotate objects
- Scale objects
- Stretch objects
- Use grips to modify objects

Introduction

The ability to edit and modify objects quickly and with minimum effort is one of the keys to increasing your productivity when using AutoCAD. On the board, if a line is drawn in the wrong location, you must erase it and then redraw it in the correct location. In fact, most on-the-board changes require this same process—erase and redraw, erase and redraw, erase and redraw. . . . Using AutoCAD, a drawing can be edited and revised countless times without worry of burning a hole in your drawing with an electric eraser.

In AutoCAD you simply edit the existing drawing information. If a line is in the wrong location, you can just move it. You do not need to erase it and draw it again, although you can if you want. Most of the time, you will want to take advantage of the edit and modify tools provided by AutoCAD. The basic editing tools can be found on the **Modify** panel on the **Home** tab of the ribbon (see Figure 7-1).

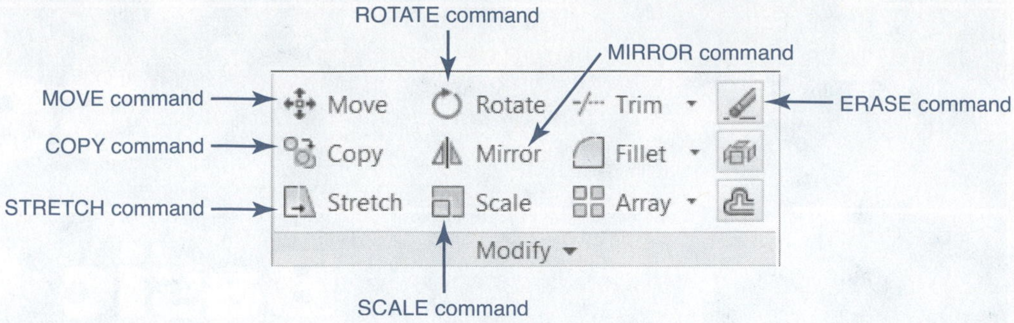

Figure 7-1
The **Modify** panel

In this chapter, you'll learn how to modify an object, or a group of objects, using two different approaches:

- Activating a modify command and then selecting the object(s) you want to modify (verb/noun)
- Selecting the object(s) to modify and then activating a modify command (noun/verb)

The noun/verb terminology might seem a little confusing at first, but if you consider that nouns represent objects (lines, circles, text, etc.) and that verbs represent actions (move, copy, rotate, etc.) it makes sense:

- Noun = Drawing object
- Verb = AutoCAD command

NOTE

You can display the **Options** dialog box using the following techniques:

- Select **Options** from the bottom of the application menu (big **A**).
- Right-click with your mouse at the command line and select **Options...** from the **Command Line** shortcut menu.
- Right-click with your mouse when nothing is selected in the drawing window, and select **Options...** from the **Default** shortcut menu.
- Type **OP** or **Options**.

The traditional approach to editing in AutoCAD is verb/noun—activate the command first and then select the object(s). The alternate noun/verb approach to editing can actually be disabled—it is on by default. The noun/verb selection mode and other object selection features are controlled on the **Selection** tab of the **Options** dialog box shown in Figure 7-2.

Many of the settings located on the **Selection** tab are explained throughout this chapter. For now, make sure that your **Selection modes** settings match those shown in Figure 7-2. Failure to do so can cause some of the examples and exercises in this chapter to behave differently than anticipated.

Figure 7-2
Selection settings on the **Selection** tab of the **Options** dialog box

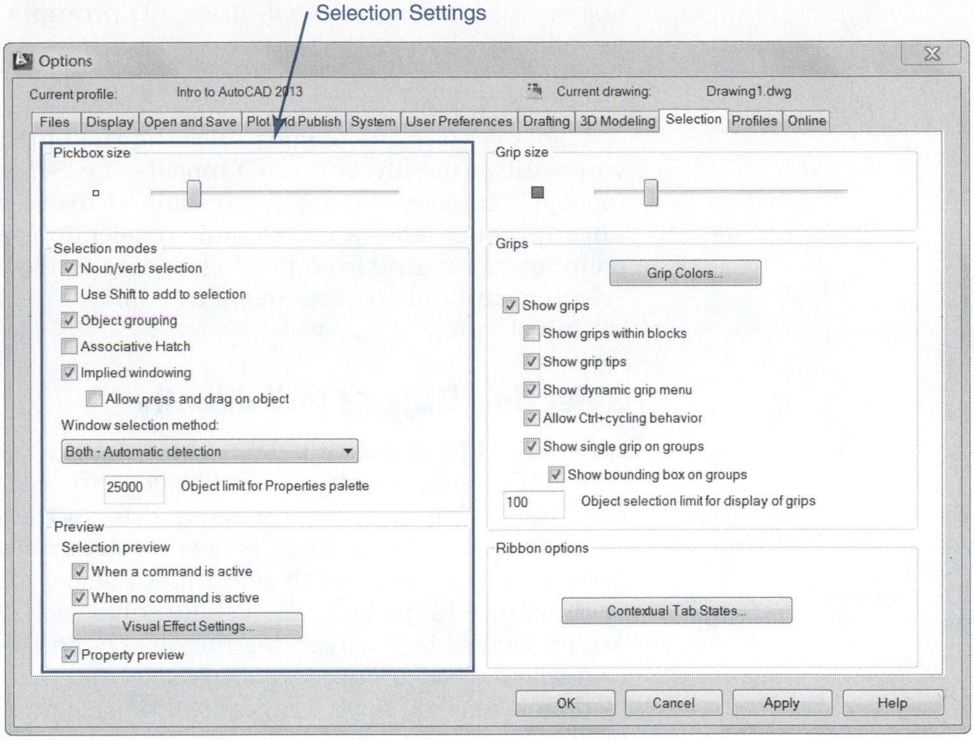

ERASE	
Ribbon & Panel:	Home | Modify 
Modify Toolbar:	
Menu:	Modify | Erase
Command Line:	ERASE
Command Alias:	E

The ERASE Command

In order to explain the different ways to select objects using either the verb/noun approach or the noun/verb approach, we first need a verb, or command. The **ERASE** command is a good candidate, considering it is probably the most used of all the modify commands. The **ERASE** command removes, or erases, the selected objects from a drawing.

> **TIP**
>
> If you erase something by accident, remember that you can always use the **UNDO** command to bring it back. You can either select the **Undo** tool from the **Quick Access** toolbar or simply type **U<Enter>** at the AutoCAD command line. Entering **U** repeatedly at the command line will undo commands one at a time until you reach the beginning of your drawing session.

Selecting Objects for Editing

As described in the introduction, there are two ways to edit information in AutoCAD—verb/noun and noun/verb. The beginning of this chapter concentrates on the traditional verb/noun approach of activating the command first and then selecting the object(s). Once we understand this approach, we can explore the noun/verb way of doing things. The basics of the modify commands remain the same.

All modify commands work by modifying objects contained in what is referred to as a ***selection set*** in AutoCAD.

selection set: One or more selected objects that are treated as one unit by an AutoCAD command.

A selection set is simply the object, or objects, that you select to be modified. Any time you activate an AutoCAD modify command, and no objects are already selected, AutoCAD prompts you to create a selection set as follows:

Select objects:

This is your cue to start selecting the object(s) in your drawing that you want to modify. AutoCAD repeats the *Select objects:* prompt until you "accept" the selection set by pressing **<Enter>** without selecting anything. This approach allows you to build a selection set using multiple selection techniques ranging from picking objects individually with your mouse to selecting multiple objects using the different selection set options explained in this chapter.

Selecting Objects Individually

Selecting objects individually is the default selection mode. Any time AutoCAD prompts you to *Select objects:* to create a selection set, the cursor crosshairs change to what is referred to as the ***pickbox***.

pickbox: Square box that replaces the cursor crosshairs whenever AutoCAD prompts you to *Select objects:*. It is used to pick objects in a drawing to create a selection set.

The size of the pickbox is used to determine how close you need to be to an object in order to select it. To select an object, it must be within or touching the pickbox. By default, objects that are within the pickbox are previewed by highlighting the objects so that they become dashed *and* thicker (see Figure 7-3). This *selection preview* feature provides you feedback regarding what object will be selected before you pick with your mouse so that you don't pick the wrong object unintentionally.

TIP

You can control the size of the pickbox and turn the selection preview feature on and off via the **Selection** tab of the **Options** dialog box shown in Figure 7-2. Other selection preview features are controlled via the **Visual Effect Settings** dialog box, which can be displayed by selecting the **Visual Effect Settings...** button in the **Selection preview** area.

Picking an object adds it to the current selection set and highlights it so it is dashed. See Figure 7-4.

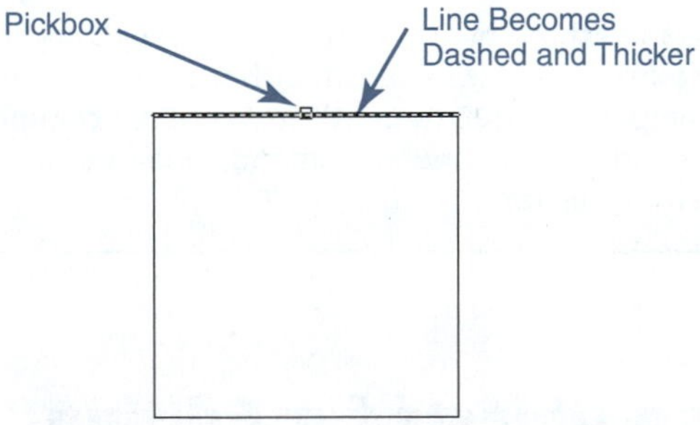

Figure 7-3
The selection preview feature

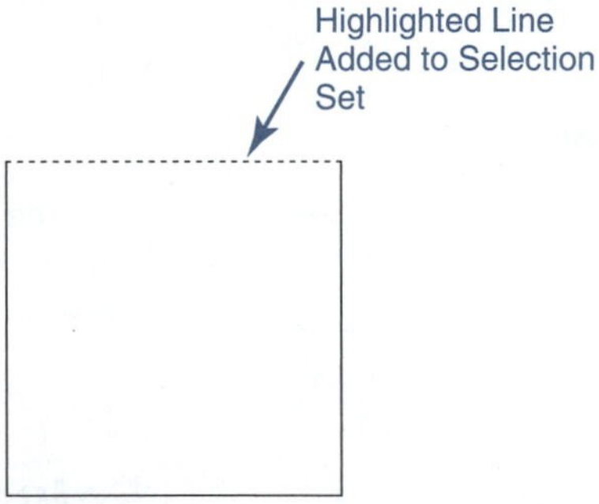

Figure 7-4
Highlighted object

You also get feedback at the command line informing you that one object was found:

Select objects: 1 found

Select objects:

AutoCAD stays in the selection mode until you press the **<Enter>** key without selecting anything to accept the selection set. This allows you to continue to add to the selection set by selecting more objects. As objects are selected, AutoCAD prompts you if the object was found and keeps a running tally of how many total objects are part of the current selection set:

Select objects: 1 found, 2 total
Select objects:

You can enter **U<Enter>** in response to the *Select objects:* prompt to undo, or deselect, the last object selected. If you have more than one object selected, you can enter **U<Enter>** repeatedly to deselect multiple objects in the order they were selected.

> **TIP**
> You can also remove selected objects from the selection set by holding down the <Shift> key and selecting the object you want to remove.

implied windowing: Feature that allows you to create a window or a crossing selection automatically by picking an empty space in a drawing to define the first corner point.

If you try to select an object and you miss because the object isn't within the pickbox, you may automatically be put in what is known as ***implied windowing*** mode, depending on whether it is turned on or not.

Implied windowing is turned on and off on the **Selection** tab of the **Options** dialog box shown in Figure 7-2. If implied windowing mode is on, AutoCAD automatically initiates the **Window** option. The **Window** option is discussed in detail a little later in this section. For the time being, you can hit the **<Esc>** key to exit the window selection mode and return to selecting objects individually.

Toggling Between Adding and Removing Objects from a Selection Set. It is possible to toggle between adding and removing objects from a selection set using the **A** (Add) and **R** (Remove) selection set options. If you type **R<Enter>** in response to the *Select objects:* prompt, AutoCAD enters the **Remove** object mode and the prompt changes to *Remove objects:*. Objects you then select are removed from the selection set so that they are no longer highlighted. AutoCAD stays in the **Remove** object mode until you enter **A<Enter>** in response to the *Remove objects:* prompt to switch back to **Add** object mode. Switching to **Add** object mode changes the prompt back to the familiar *Select objects:* prompt.

> **NOTE**
> The **Add** and **Remove** toggle also works with all the multiple object selection modes described later in this chapter.

Using the <Shift> Key to Add to a Selection Set. When selecting objects individually, it is possible to change the selection mode so that you must use the **<Shift>** key when adding objects to the current selection set. If you select the **Use Shift to add to selection** check box in the **Selection modes** area on the **Selection** tab of the **Options** dialog box (see Figure 7-2) so that it is turned on, you must hold down the **<Shift>** key when selecting more than one object. When the **Use Shift to add to selection** mode is on and you try to select more than one object *without* using the **<Shift>** key, the first object is deselected so it is no longer highlighted. By default, the **Use Shift to add to selection** mode is off.

Selecting Stacked and Overlaid Objects. It is possible to easily select overlapping objects by picking the **Selection Cycling** button on the AutoCAD status bar shown in Figure 7-5.

When selection cycling is turned on and you try to select an object that overlaps one or more other objects, AutoCAD displays a list of all the overlapping objects that you can select from, so you can select the desired object. When you pass your cursor over an object in the list, AutoCAD highlights the object in the drawing so you know which object in the list it is associated with, as shown in Figure 7-6.

Select the object from the list, and it becomes part of a new or existing selection set.

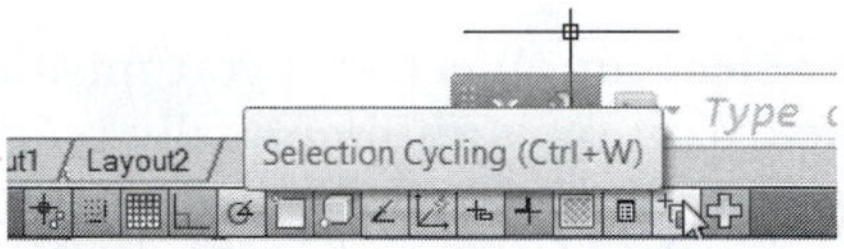

Figure 7-5
The **Selection Cycling** button on the status bar

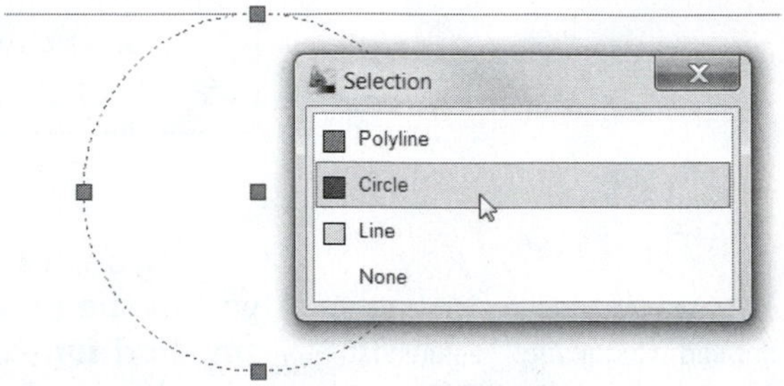

Figure 7-6
The **Selection Cycling** list of overlapping objects

> **NOTE**
>
> When you hover your cursor over any overlapping objects in a drawing, a small icon representing two overlapping squares is displayed indicating stacked objects. This is your cue that, if you pick a point, the **Selection Cycling** list in Figure 7-6 will be displayed so you can select the correct object.

EXERCISE 7-1 Selecting Objects Individually

1. Start a new drawing using the **acad.dwt** drawing template.
2. Make sure that your **Selection modes** settings on the **Selection** tab of the **Options** dialog box match those shown in Figure 7-2.
3. Draw a 2 × 2 square similar to the one shown in Figure 7-3 using the **LINE** command so that the rectangle consists of four separate line segments. *Do not use the **RECTANG** command!*
4. Start the **ERASE** command.
5. Select the top line as shown in Figure 7-4 and press **<Enter>**. The line is erased.
6. Type **U<Enter>** or select the **Undo** tool so that the line is undeleted.
7. Start the **ERASE** command again.
8. Select the top line as shown in Figure 7-4.
9. Select the other three lines in a clockwise direction using your cursor so that all the rectangle lines are highlighted.

10 Type **U<Enter>** three times so that only the top line is highlighted as shown in Figure 7-4.

11 Select the other three lines again in a clockwise direction using your cursor so that all the square lines are highlighted.

12 Hold down the **<Shift>** key, and select the vertical line on the left side of the square so it is no longer highlighted.

13 Type **R<Enter>**.

14 Select the remaining three highlighted lines so that all the square lines are no longer highlighted.

15 Type **A<Enter>**.

16 Select all four lines so that the entire square is highlighted again, and press **<Enter>** so that the square is erased.

17 Type **U<Enter>** or select the **Undo** tool so that the square is undeleted.

Selecting Multiple Objects

Oftentimes, you need to select more than one object when modifying a drawing. Suppose you need to erase a large portion of your drawing—you don't want to have to pick each object individually. Doing so would be very time-consuming. Fortunately, AutoCAD provides a number of selection set options that expedite the process of selecting multiple objects. All these options are entered via the keyboard in response to the *Select objects:* prompt. The following sections explain each of these selection set options.

W—Window Option. The **Window** option allows you to define a rectangular window selection area by prompting you to pick two corner points as shown in Figure 7-7.

By default, the windowed area is shaded a semitransparent blue color to make it obvious which objects will be selected before the second corner point is picked. This selection preview feature helps you avoid the unintentional selection of objects.

Using the **Window** option, only objects that are *completely within* the window boundary area are selected. Objects that cross the window boundary are ignored (see Figure 7-8).

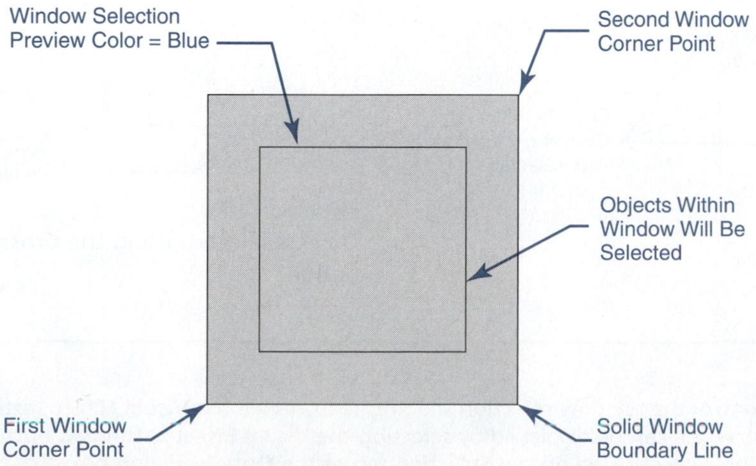

Figure 7-7
Defining the window selection area

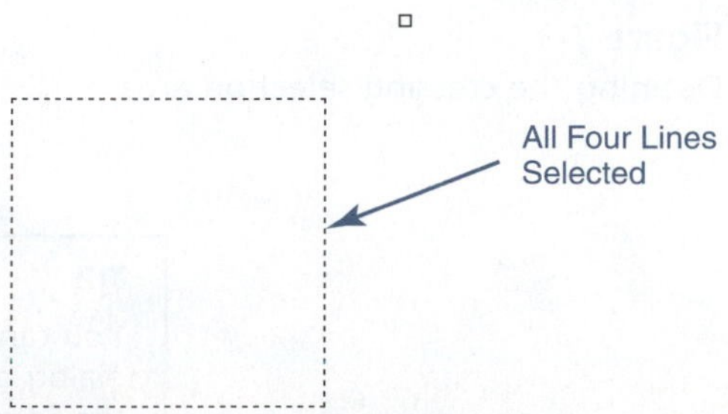

Figure 7-8
Objects selected using the **Window** option

TIP

Recall from Chapter 6 that objects on frozen or locked layers are not affected by any of the selection methods explained in the chapter. You can use this to your advantage when selecting multiple objects so that you can select a large group of objects but filter out the objects you don't want to be part of the selection set.

EXERCISE 7-2 Selecting Multiple Objects with the Window Option

1. Continue from Exercise 7-1.
2. Start the **ERASE** command.
3. Type **W<Enter>**.
4. Create a window selection similar to the one shown in Figure 7-7 and press **<Enter>** twice. The four lines of the square are erased.
5. Type **U<Enter>** or select the **Undo** tool so that the square is undeleted.

C—Crossing Option. The **Crossing** option allows you to define a rectangular window selection area by picking two corner points similar to the **Window** option, as shown in Figure 7-9.

To distinguish between the **Window** option and the **Crossing** option, the **Crossing** option window boundary is dashed (see Figure 7-9), whereas the **Window** option window boundary is solid (see Figure 7-7). In addition, the **Crossing** option windowed area is, by default, shaded a semitransparent green color (see Figure 7-9) instead of the default blue color used with the **Window** option (see Figure 7-7).

The major difference between the **Crossing** option and the **Window** option is that the **Crossing** option will select objects that *cross over* the rectangular window boundary in addition to the objects that lie completely within the window boundary area (see Figure 7-10).

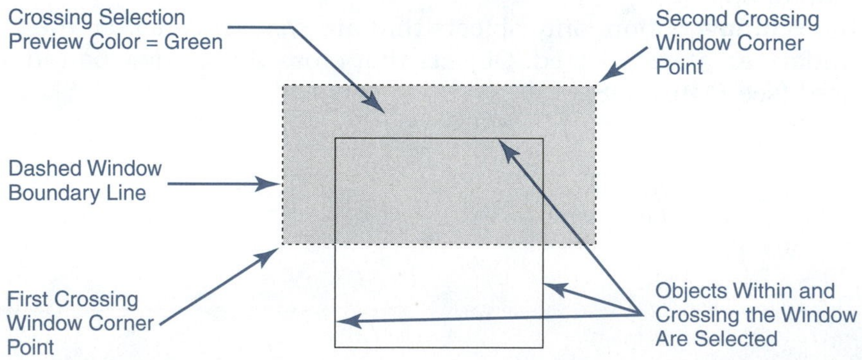

Figure 7-9
Defining the crossing selection area

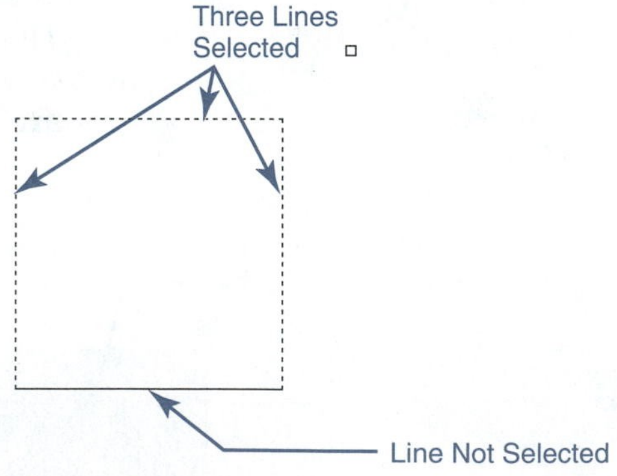

Figure 7-10
Objects selected using the **Crossing** option

TIP

You can control the window selection shading features via the **Visual Effect Settings** dialog box, which can be displayed by selecting the **Visual Effect Settings...** button in the **Selection preview** area on the **Selection** tab of the **Options** dialog box shown in Figure 7-2.

EXERCISE 7-3 **Selecting Multiple Objects with the Crossing Option**

1. Continue from Exercise 7-2.
2. Start the **ERASE** command.
3. Type **C<Enter>**.
4. Create a crossing selection similar to the one shown in Figure 7-9 and press **<Enter>** twice. The top horizontal line and the two vertical lines of the square are erased. The bottom horizontal line remains in the drawing.
5. Type **U<Enter>** or select the **Undo** tool so that the three lines are undeleted.

Press and Drag Window Mode. It is possible to define the window area for both the **Window** and **Crossing** options by picking the first window corner point and then, instead of picking the opposite corner point, simply dragging your mouse to the opposite corner location and releasing the button—eliminating the need to pick a second point. This semiautomated window creation mode is enabled by selecting the **Allow press and drag on object** check box in the **Selection modes** area on the **Selection** tab of the **Options** dialog box (see Figure 7-2). By default, the **Press and drag** window selection mode is turned on.

Implied Windowing. As mentioned earlier in the section "Selecting Objects Individually," it is possible to initiate the **Window** *or* the **Crossing** option automatically by relying on a feature called *implied windowing.* **Implied windowing** can be turned on and off on the **Selection** tab of the **Options** dialog box shown in Figure 7-2.

When **Implied windowing** is on, you can initiate either the **Window** or **Crossing** option by picking an empty space in your drawing so that no objects fall within your pickbox in response to the *Select objects or*↓ prompt. When you pick and no objects are found, AutoCAD interprets the pick point as the first corner point of a rectangular window area and prompts you to select the second corner point as follows:

Specify opposite corner:

This is where it gets interesting. If you move your cursor to the *right* of the first pick point, you initiate the **Window** option—the window boundary outline is solid, and the default shade color is blue (see Figure 7-7).

If you move your cursor to the *left* of the first pick point, you initiate the **Crossing** option—the window boundary outline is dashed, and the default shade color is green (see Figure 7-9).

The **Implied windowing** option can be a real time-saving device when selecting objects. Its use basically eliminates the need to enter either the **W** or the **C** option at the keyboard. The key is placing the first point in the correct location in response to the *Select objects:* prompt. If you know you want to use the **Crossing** option, place the first point to the right of the objects you want to select and move your cursor to the left to pick the second point. If it's the **Window** option you desire, pick to the left and move your cursor to the right.

EXERCISE 7-4 **Selecting Multiple Objects with an Implied Window**

1. Continue from Exercise 7-3.
2. Start the **ERASE** command.

3. Pick a point to the lower left of the square so that no objects are within your pickbox, and pick a point.
4. Drag your cursor up to the right of the square so that an implied window similar to the window selection shown in Figure 7-7 is created and pick a point.
5. Press **<Enter>**. The four lines of the square are erased.
6. Type **U<Enter>** or select the **Undo** tool so that the four lines are undeleted.
7. Start the **ERASE** command again.
8. Pick a point to the upper right of the square so that no objects are within your pickbox, and pick a point.
9. Drag your cursor down and to the left of the square so that an implied window similar to the crossing selection shown in Figure 7-9 is created, and pick a point.
10. Press **<Enter>**. The top horizontal line and the two vertical lines of the square are erased. The bottom horizontal line remains in the drawing.
11. Type **U<Enter>** or select the **Undo** tool so that the three lines are undeleted.

> **TIP**
>
> It is also possible to use the **Window Polygon**, **Crossing Polygon**, and **Fence** selection options discussed in the next sections when using the **Implied windowing** technique. All three of these options are available after picking the first implied window point via the command line or dynamic input.

WP—Window Polygon Option. The **Window Polygon** option allows you to define a polygonal window area using multiple pick points so that you can select multiple objects in a complex drawing that you might not be able to select using a simple rectangular window. When you enter the **WP** option, AutoCAD prompts you for the first polygon point and then prompts you for line endpoints until you press **<Enter>** as shown in Figure 7-11.

Similar to the **Window** option, the **Window Polygon** option selects only objects that are completely within the window boundary area. Objects that cross the window boundary are ignored (see Figure 7-12).

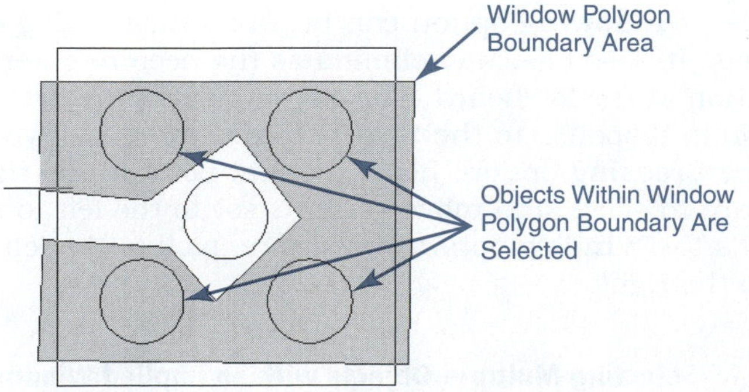

Figure 7-11
Defining the window polygon selection area

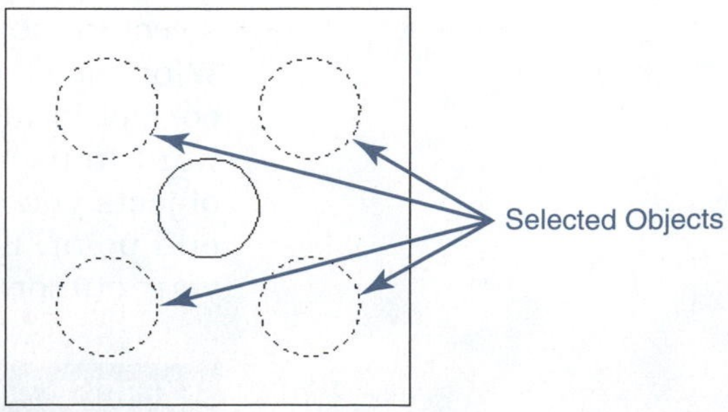

Figure 7-12
Objects selected using the **Window Polygon** option

TIP

All the multiple selection options that rely on more than two pick points have an **Undo** option that allows you to "unpick" points you have already selected so that you can relocate an errant pick point without canceling and starting over. To use the **Undo** option, type **U<Enter>** in response to a prompt for the next point, and the last point will be erased.

EXERCISE 7-5 Selecting Multiple Objects with a Window Polygon

1. Continue from Exercise 7-4.
2. Add five circles so your drawing looks as shown in Figure 7-11.
3. Start the **ERASE** command.
4. Type **WP<Enter>**.
5. Create a window polygon selection similar to the one shown in Figure 7-11, and press **<Enter>** twice. The four circles at the corners of the square are erased.
6. Type **U<Enter>** or select the **Undo** tool so that the four circles are undeleted.

CP—Crossing Polygon Option. The **Crossing Polygon** option works similarly to the **Window Polygon** option. It also allows you to define a polygonal window area using multiple pick points except that, like the **Crossing** option, objects that cross the polygon window are also selected. When you enter the **CP** option, AutoCAD prompts you for the first polygon point and then prompts you for line endpoints until you press **<Enter>** as shown in Figure 7-13.

As noted, the **Crossing Polygon** option selects objects that *cross over* the polygon window boundary in addition to the objects that lie completely within the window boundary area (see Figure 7-14).

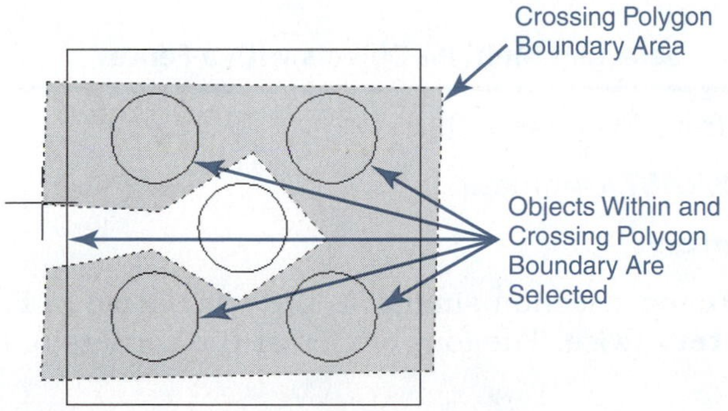

Figure 7-13
Defining the crossing polygon selection area

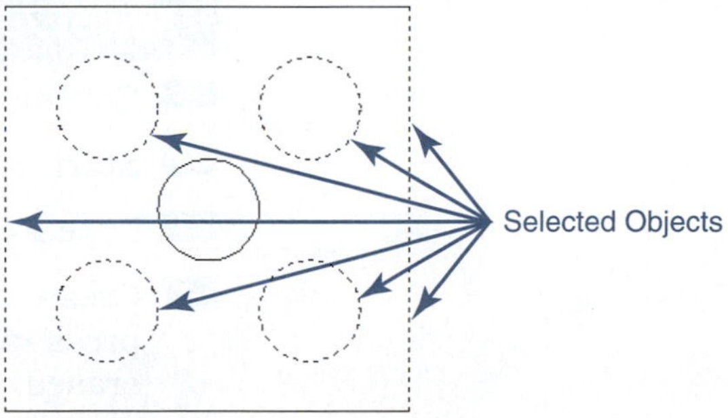

Figure 7-14
Objects selected using the **Crossing Polygon** option

EXERCISE 7-6 Selecting Multiple Objects with a Crossing Polygon

1. Continue from Exercise 7-5.
2. Start the **ERASE** command.
3. Type **CP<Enter>**.

4. Create a **Crossing Polygon** selection similar to the one shown in Figure 7-13, and press **<Enter>** twice. The four circles at the corners and the two vertical lines of the square are erased.
5. Type **U<Enter>** or select the **Undo** tool so that the four circles and two lines are undeleted.

NOTE

Both the **Window Polygon** and **Crossing Polygon** options interact the same as their **Window** and **Crossing** counterparts so that a solid window boundary is used for the **Window Polygon** option and a dashed window boundary is used for the **Window Crossing** option. The window selection shading feature settings are also shared between the corresponding options.

F—Fence Option. The **Fence** option allows you to define a multisegmented fence line that selects everything it crosses similar to the **Crossing** option. When you enter the **F** option, AutoCAD prompts you for the first fence point and then prompts you for additional fence endpoints until you press **<Enter>** as shown in Figure 7-15.

The **Fence** option selects all objects that the fence line crosses over or touches (see Figure 7-16).

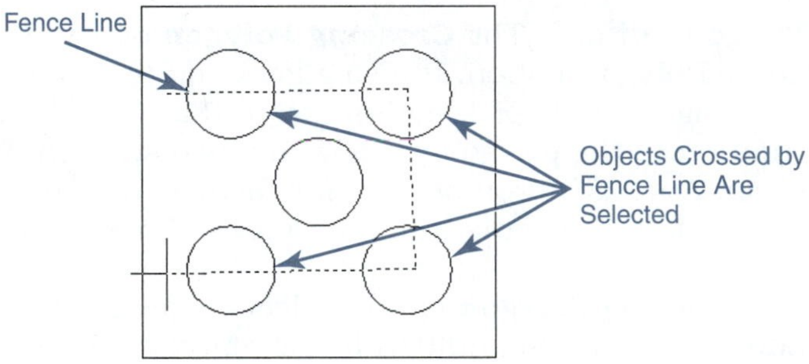

Figure 7-15
Defining the fence selection line

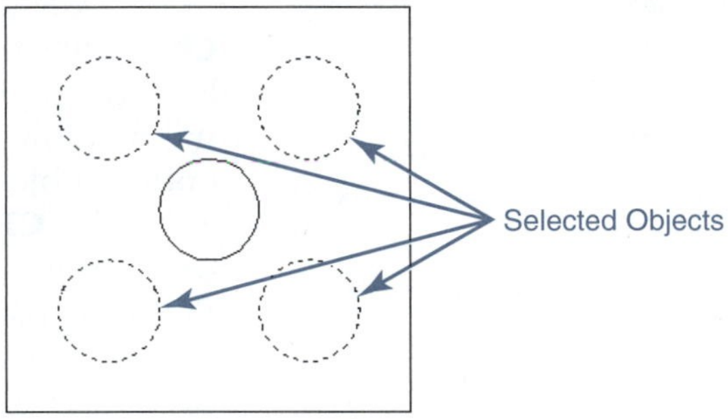

Figure 7-16
Objects selected using the **Fence** option

EXERCISE 7-7 **Selecting Multiple Objects with a Fence**

1. Continue from Exercise 7-6.
2. Start the **ERASE** command.
3. Type **F<Enter>**.
4. Create a **Fence** selection similar to the one shown in Figure 7-15, and press **<Enter>** twice. The four circles at the corners of the square are erased.
5. **Type U<Enter>** or select the **Undo** tool so that the four circles are undeleted.

Advanced Selection Techniques

The following selection set options provide additional ways to select objects without having to pick any points in your drawing.

All—All Option. The **All** option selects *all* the objects in a drawing—even those objects that lie outside the visible drawing window! Because of this, care should be taken when using it. When used properly, it can be a handy way to modify everything in a drawing.

> **TIP**
>
> Objects that are on frozen or locked layers are protected when using the **All** option so that they are not selected.

L—Last Option. The **Last** option selects the last object created in a drawing. For instance, if you draw a line in a drawing and then enter the **ERASE** command, entering **L** in response to the *Select objects:* prompt highlights and selects the line you just drew.

P—Previous Option. The **Previous** option recalls the last selection set created so that you can modify the same objects again. If no previous selection set exists, AutoCAD displays the following at the command line:

No previous selection set.

Selecting Similar Objects

The **Select Similar** tool allows you to select an object and then automatically include all of the other objects in the drawing that are of the same type and share the same properties. The easiest way to use the **Select Similar** tool is to select one or more objects and right-click to display the **Edit** shortcut menu shown in Figure 7-17, which includes the tool.

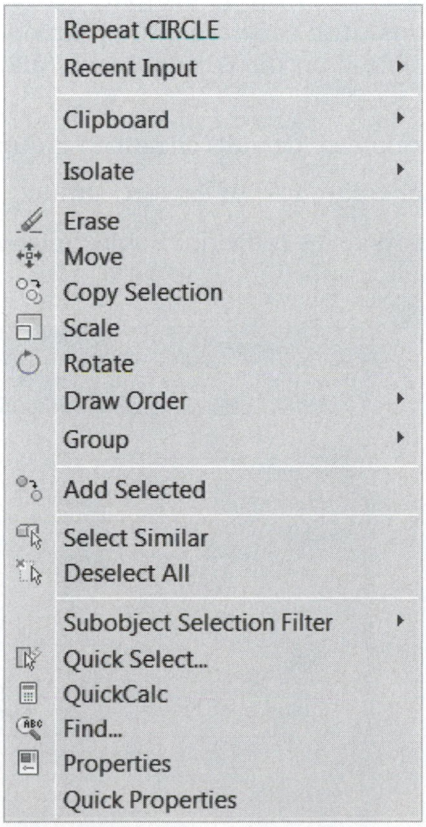

Figure 7-17
Right-click menu with **Select Similar** tool

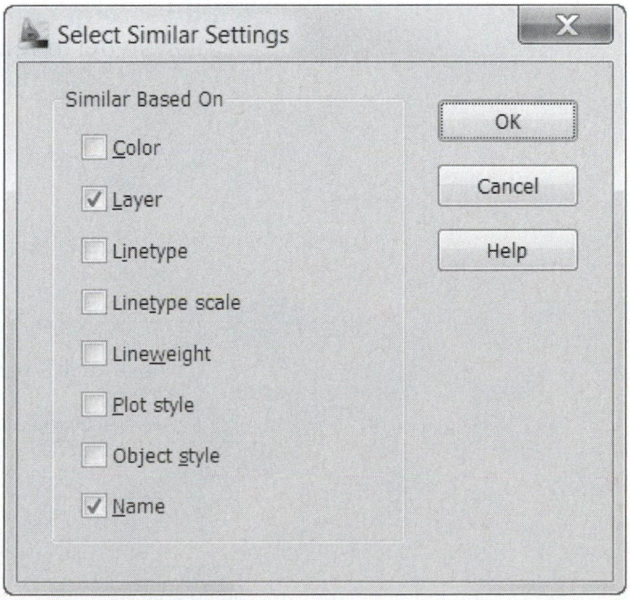

Figure 7-18
The **Select Similar Settings** dialog box

You can control which properties are matched when creating the selection set by entering **SELECTSIMILAR** at the command line. The **SELECTSIMILAR** command has a **Setting** option that displays the **Select Similar Settings** dialog box shown in Figure 7-18 so you can select the properties to filter on.

EXERCISE 7-8 Using Advanced Selection Techniques

1. Continue from Exercise 7-7.
2. Start the **ERASE** command.
3. Type **All<Enter>**.
4. Press **<Enter>** again. All the drawing objects are erased.
5. Type **U<Enter>** or select the **Undo** tool so that everything is undeleted.
6. Start the **ERASE** command again.
7. Type **L<Enter>**.
8. Press **<Enter>** again. The last object added to the drawing is erased.
9. **Type U<Enter>** or select the **Undo** tool so that the object is undeleted.

Grouping Objects

It is possible to group multiple objects together so they act as one unit using the grouping tools found on the **Groups** panel on the **Home** tab of the ribbon shown in Figure 7-19.

Groups can be either unnamed or named and are stored in the drawing between drawing sessions until they are either exploded or erased. The different grouping tools found on the **Groups** panel allow you to do the following:

- **Group** Creates an unnamed (default) or named group by selecting objects
- **Ungroup** Explodes or ungroups an existing group
- **Edit Group** Adds or removes individual objects from a group and also allows you to rename a group

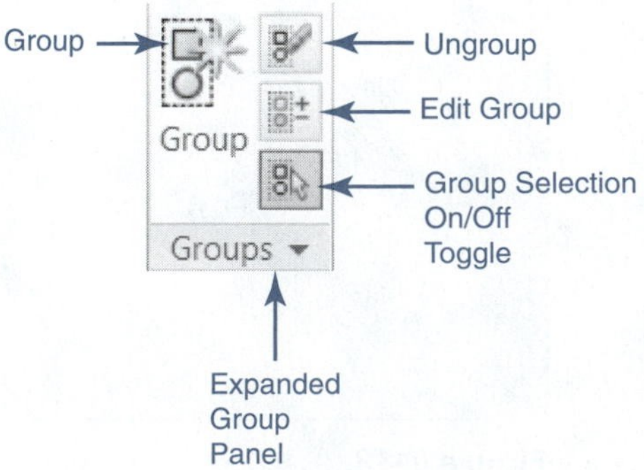

Figure 7-19
The **Groups** panel

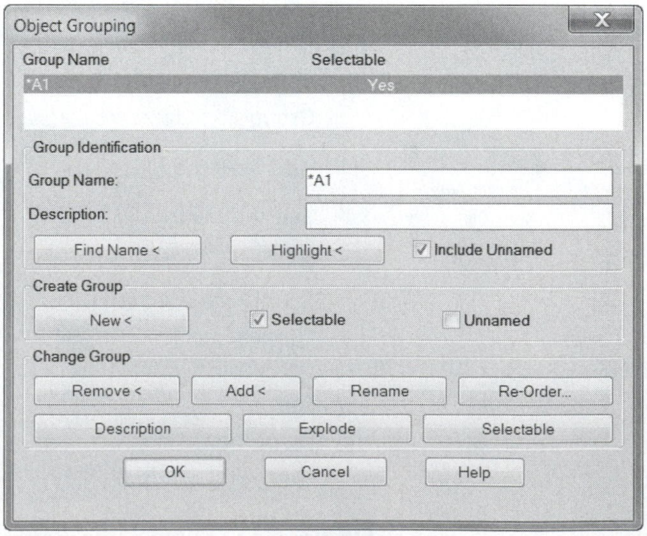

Figure 7-20
The **Object Grouping** dialog box

- **Group Selection On/Off** Turns group selection on and off so it is possible to select individual group objects if necessary

Additional group management features are provided by selecting the **Group Manager** tool on the expanded **Groups** panel accessible by clicking on the down arrow in the right of the panel title bar shown in Figure 7-19. Selecting the **Group Manager** tool displays the **Object Grouping** dialog box shown in Figure 7-20.

The different features and options in the **Object Grouping** dialog box include:

- **Group Identification**
  - **Group Name** Name of group, if there is any. Group names can be up to 31 characters long and can include letters and numbers but no spaces. It is possible to use a hyphen (-) or underscore (_). The name is always converted to uppercase
  - **Description** Description of the selected group, if there is any. Descriptions may be up to 64 characters long
  - **Find Name** Allows you to select an object and list the group(s) it belongs to in the **Group Member List** dialog box
  - **Highlight** Highlights the members of the selected group in the drawing window
  - **Include Unnamed** Determines whether unnamed groups are listed. When this check box is unselected, only named groups are displayed
- **Create Group**
  - **New** Creates a new group using the selected objects with the name and description specified
  - **Selectable** Determines whether a new group is selectable in the drawing
  - **Unnamed** Specifies that a new group has no name. A default name is assigned (*An) where "n" represents a number that increases each time a new group is created
- **Change Group**
  - **Remove** Allows you to remove objects from the selected group. You must first uncheck the **Selectable** option before you can remove any objects
  - **Add** Allows you to add objects to the selected group
  - **Rename** Renames the selected group to the name specified in the **Group Name:** text box
  - **Re-Order** Allows you to change the numerical order of objects within the selected group using the **Order Group** dialog box. By default, objects are numbered in the order in which you select them for inclusion in the group
  - **Description** Updates the selected group's description using the name entered in the **Description:** text box at the top
  - **Explode** Explodes selected group back to individual objects and removes group definition from the drawing
  - **Selectable** Toggles selected group's **Selectable** property on and off

> **TIP**
>
> The **Group Bounding Box** toggle, which is also located on the expanded **Groups** panel, allows you to control the box that is displayed around all of the objects in the group.

MOVE	
Ribbon & Panel:	Home | Modify Move
Modify Toolbar:	
Menu:	Modify | Move
Command Line:	MOVE
Command Alias:	M

Moving Objects

Now that you are familiar with all the different ways to select objects, it's time for some action. The **MOVE** command moves objects a user-supplied distance and angle.

When you start the **MOVE** command, AutoCAD prompts you to *Select objects:*. Select the object(s) you want to move and press **<Enter>** to accept the selection set. AutoCAD then prompts you to *Specify base point or* ↓. You have three options:

1. Specify a base point.
2. Select the **Displacement** option.
3. Enter a displacement distance using Cartesian coordinates.

Using the first option, you typically pick a base (*from*) point by snapping to a key object feature using an object snap. You can then pick a destination (*to*) point, and the selected objects are moved to the new location (see Figure 7-21).

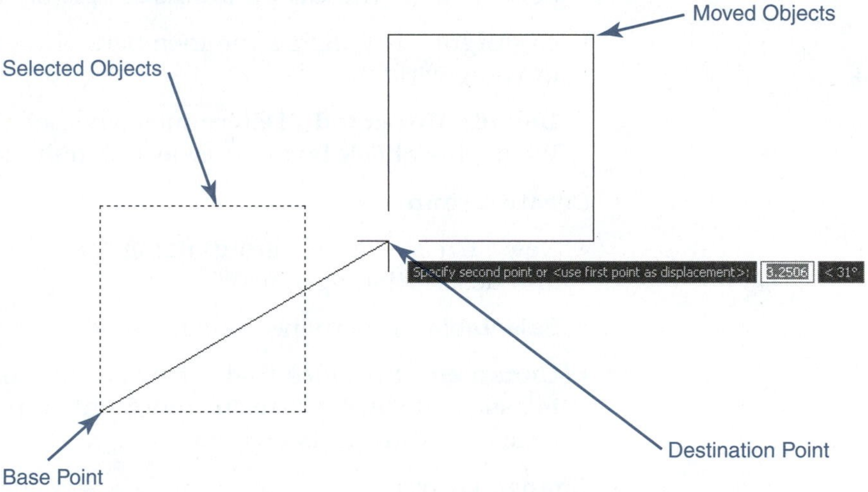

Figure 7-21
Moving objects using mouse pick points

> **NOTE**
> It is also possible to type a base point as a Cartesian coordinate value at the cursor or the command line. You can then specify a destination point either by using your mouse or by entering an absolute, relative, or polar coordinate value.

You can also use direct distance entry to locate the second point. Using direct distance, you simply point the direction you want to move the selected object(s) and type in the distance you want to travel (see Figure 7-22).

> **TIP**
> Remember that the best way to utilize direct distance entry is to use it in conjunction with either **Polar Tracking** or **Ortho Mode**. Using either of these drawing tools allows you to lock in an angle and enter a distance for precise movement.

Figure 7-22
Moving objects using direct distance

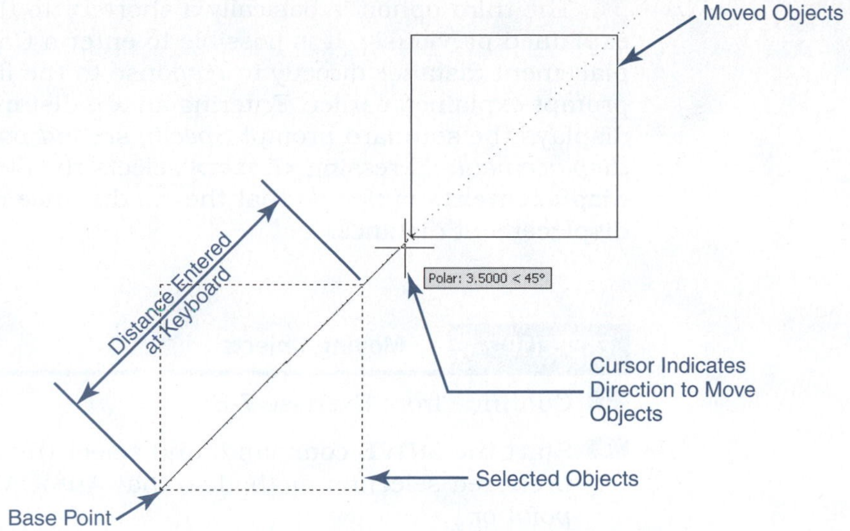

FOR MORE DETAILS

See Chapter 5 for detailed information about using the **Polar Tracking** and **Ortho Mode** drawing tools.

The **Displacement** option allows you to specify a displacement distance using rectangular or polar coordinates. The coordinate value you enter is *always* the relative distance the selected object(s) will be moved, even if you omit the @ sign.

You can enter the displacement distance using either rectangular (*x*,*y*) or polar (@distance<angle) coordinates. Entering **3,3<Enter>** results in the move operation shown in Figure 7-23.

Figure 7-23
Moving objects using the **Displacement** option

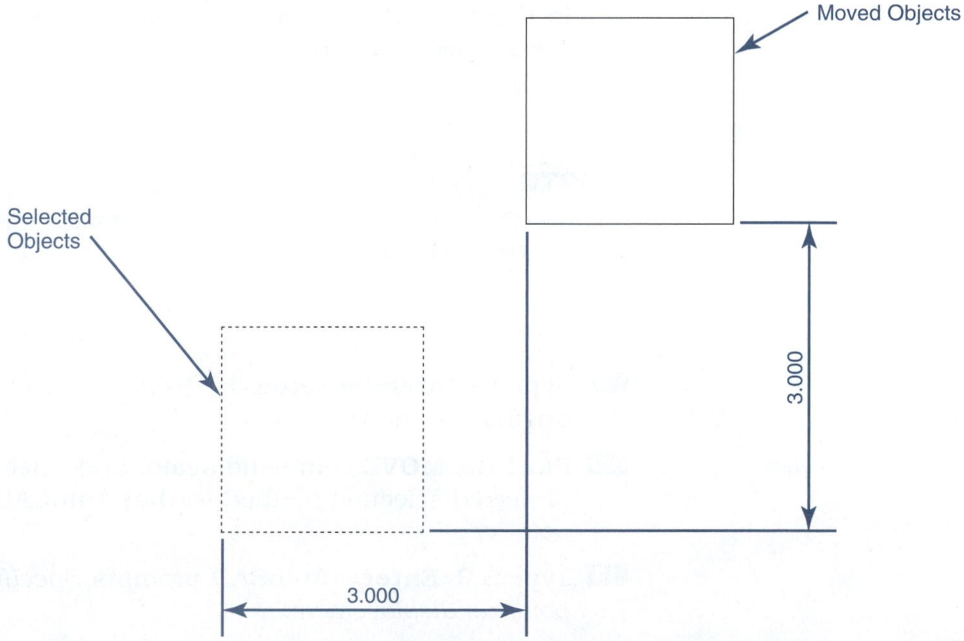

TIP

AutoCAD remembers the displacement distance entered so that it is now the default distance. The next time you use the **MOVE** command, you can just press **<Enter>** to move the same distance again.

The third option is basically a shortcut to the **Displacement** option explained previously. It is possible to enter a Cartesian coordinate displacement distance directly in response to the first *Specify base point or*↓ prompt explained earlier. Entering an *x,y* distance and pressing **<Enter>** displays the standard prompt *Specify second point or <use first point as displacement>:*. Pressing **<Enter>** selects the default **<use first point as displacement>** option so that the *x,y* distance entered is used as the displacement distance.

EXERCISE 7-9 Moving Objects

1. Continue from Exercise 7-8.
2. Start the **MOVE** command, and select the square using your preferred selection method so that AutoCAD prompts *Specify base point or*↓.
3. Snap to the lower left corner of the square using the **Endpoint** object snap as shown in Figure 7-21.
4. Move the square using a second pick point as shown in Figure 7-21.
5. Type **U<Enter>** or select the **Undo** tool so that the square is in its original location.
6. Start the **MOVE** command again, and select the square using your preferred selection method so that AutoCAD prompts *Specify base point or*↓.
7. Snap to the lower left corner of the square using the **Endpoint** object snap as shown in Figure 7-22.
8. Move your cursor so the rubber-band line points to the right as shown in Figure 7-22, and type **3<Enter>**. The square moves 3 units along the rubber-band line.

NOTE

It is possible, and quite common, to use object snaps when modifying objects, especially when selecting a base point.

9. Type **U<Enter>** or select the **Undo** tool so that the square is in its original location.
10. Start the **MOVE** command again, and select the square using your preferred selection method so that AutoCAD prompts *Specify base point or*↓.
11. Type **3,3<Enter>**. AutoCAD prompts *Specify second point or <use first point as displacement>:*.
12. Press **<Enter>** again to use the first point entered as the displacement distance. The square moves +3 units on the *X*-axis and +3 units on the *Y*-axis, as shown in Figure 7-23.
13. Type **U<Enter>** or select the **Undo** tool so that the square is in its original location.

COPY	
Ribbon & Panel:	Home | Modify 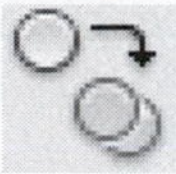
Modify Toolbar:	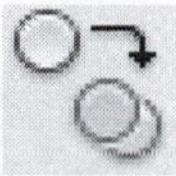
Menu:	Modify | Copy
Command Line:	COPY
Command Alias:	CO

Copying Objects

The **COPY** command copies objects a user-supplied distance and angle. Its usage is similar to the **MOVE** command except that the **COPY** command maintains the selected objects in their original location. It is possible to make multiple copies if you specify a base point.

After you start the **COPY** command and select something, AutoCAD prompts you to *Specify base point or* ↓. Similar to the **MOVE** command, you initially have these options:

1. Specify a base point.
2. Select the **Displacement** option.
3. Enter a displacement distance using Cartesian coordinates.

> **NOTE**
>
> The **mode** option allows you to switch between making multiple copies (default) and a single copy.

Using the first option, you typically pick a base (*from*) point by snapping to a key object feature using an object snap. You can then pick a destination (*to*) point, and the selected objects are copied to the new location as shown in Figure 7-24.

Figure 7-24
Copying objects using mouse pick points

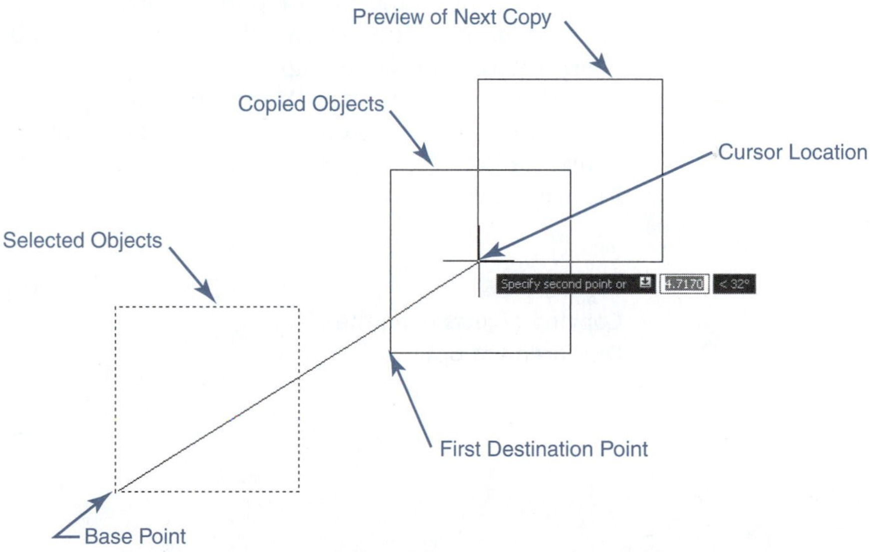

Just like the **MOVE** command, you can also rely on direct distance entry to locate the second point. Using direct distance, you simply point the direction you want to copy the selected object(s) and type in the distance you want to travel.

> **TIP**
>
> The **COPY** command has an **Undo** option when you are making multiple copies so that you can undo a copy operation if it is the wrong location. To use the **Undo** option, you can either select the option using your arrow keys or type **U<Enter>**.

If you use the first option and specify a base point, AutoCAD remains in the **COPY** command after the first copy is created so that it is possible to make multiple copies by specifying multiple destination points. After making the first copy, AutoCAD repeatedly prompts you to *Specify second point or* ↓ until you end the command, as shown in Figure 7-25.

Figure 7-25
Copying multiple objects

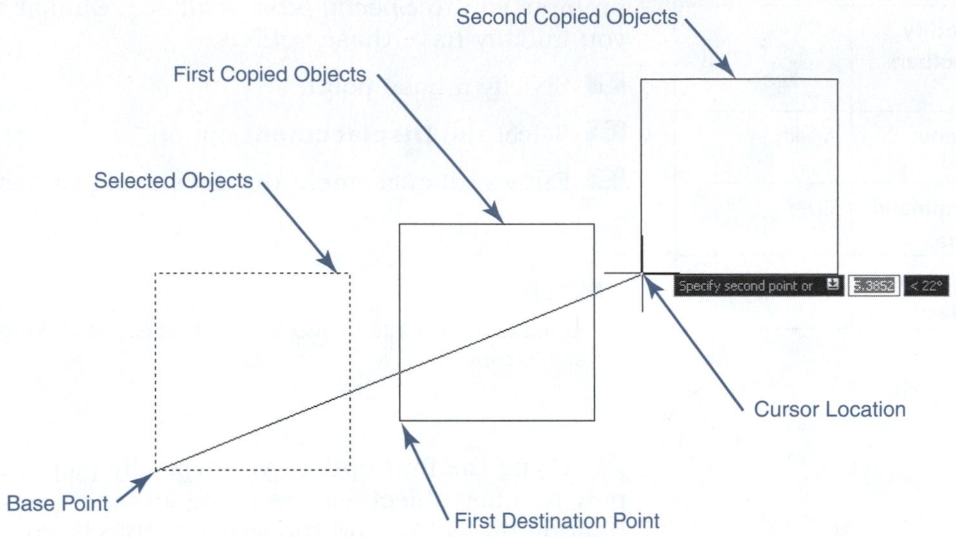

The **Displacement** option allows you to specify a displacement distance using rectangular or polar coordinates. The coordinate value you enter is *always* the relative distance the selected object(s) will be copied, even if you omit the @ sign.

After you select the **Displacement** option, you can enter the displacement distance using either rectangular (*x*,*y*) or polar (@distance<angle) coordinates. Entering **3,3<Enter>** results in the copy operation shown in Figure 7-26.

Figure 7-26
Copying objects using the **Displacement** option

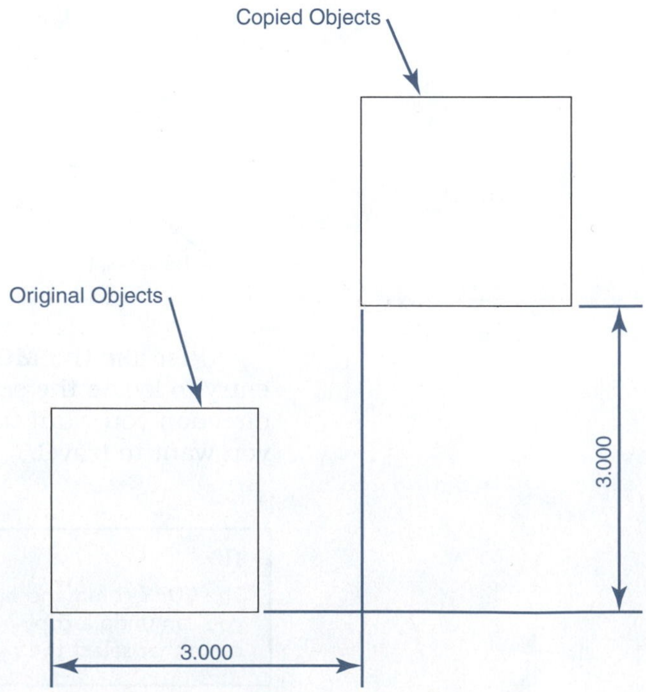

> **TIP**
>
> AutoCAD remembers the displacement distance entered so that it is now the default distance. The next time you use the **COPY** command, you can just press **<Enter>** to copy the same distance again.

Similar to the **MOVE** command, it is possible to enter a Cartesian coordinate displacement distance directly in response to the first *Specify base point or*↓ prompt explained earlier. Entering an *x,y* distance and pressing **<Enter>** twice selects the default **<use first point as displacement>** option so that the *x,y* distance entered is used as the displacement distance.

The **Array** option allows you to create a one-dimensional array of objects by specifying the total number of copies and either the distance between each copy or a total distance to automatically fit all of the copies.

EXERCISE 7-10 Copying Objects

1. Continue from Exercise 7-9.
2. Start the **COPY** command, and select the square using your preferred selection method so that AutoCAD prompts *Specify base point or*↓.
3. Snap to the lower left corner of the square using the **Endpoint** object snap, as shown in Figure 7-24. AutoCAD prompts *Specify second point or <use first point as displacement>:*.
4. Copy the square using a second pick point, as shown in Figure 7-24. AutoCAD repeatedly prompts *Specify second point or*↓.
5. Continue to pick points to make multiple copies, as shown in Figure 7-25.
6. Press **<Enter>**, select the **Exit** option, or type **E<Enter>** to end the **COPY** command.
7. Type **U<Enter>** or select the **Undo** tool so that only one square is left in its original location.
8. Start the **COPY** command, and select the square using your preferred selection method so that AutoCAD prompts *Specify second point or*↓.
9. Type **3,3<Enter>**. AutoCAD prompts *Specify second point or <use first point as displacement>:*.
10. Press **<Enter>** again to use the first point entered as the displacement distance. The square is copied +3 units on the *X*-axis and +3 units on the *Y*-axis, as shown in Figure 7-26.
11. Type **U<Enter>** or select the **Undo** tool so that only one square is left in its original location.

MIRROR	
Ribbon & Panel:	Home Modify 
Modify Toolbar:	
Menu:	Modify | Mirror
Command Line:	MIRROR
Command Alias:	MI

Mirroring Objects

The **MIRROR** command creates a mirror image of objects about a mirror axis line defined by two user-supplied line endpoints.

After you start the **MIRROR** command and select something, AutoCAD prompts you to specify the two endpoints of a line about which to mirror the selected objects as shown in Figure 7-27, while maintaining a ghost image of the original objects and displaying a preview of the mirrored objects.

Figure 7-27
Mirroring objects

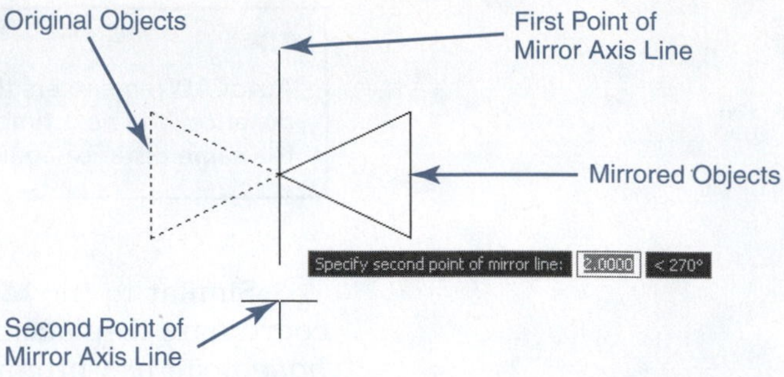

TIP

You can use either the **Ortho Mode** or the **Polar Tracking** tool to create either a horizontal or vertical mirror axis line quickly by simply picking two points.

FOR MORE DETAILS

See Chapter 5 for more information about using the **Ortho Mode** and **Polar Tracking** drawing tools.

After selecting the second point, AutoCAD prompts you to *Erase source objects?*↓. You have the option of either erasing the originally selected objects, so only the mirrored copies remain, or leaving them in the drawing. The default is *not* to erase the original objects so that you can just press **<Enter>** and end up with the mirrored object *and* the original, as shown in Figure 7-28.

Figure 7-28
Mirrored objects with original objects maintained

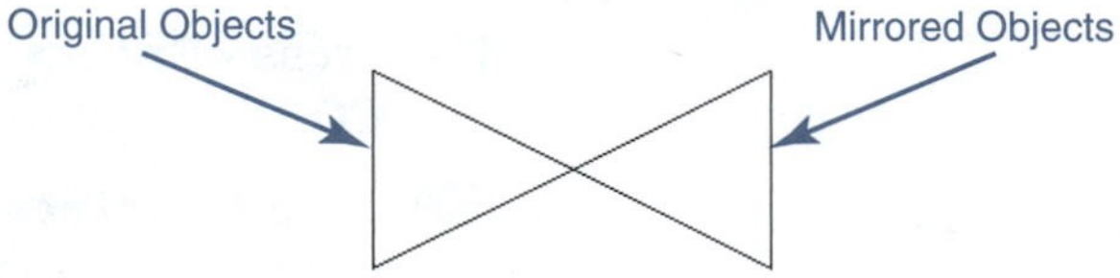

To erase the original objects, select the **Yes** option in response to the *Erase source objects?*↓ prompt. The result of erasing the original objects is shown in Figure 7-29.

Figure 7-29
Mirrored objects with original objects erased

Mirroring Text

Usually, when you mirror text you want it to retain its original left-to-right orientation so that the text isn't reversed, as shown in Figure 7-30.

The AutoCAD **MIRRTEXT** system variable controls whether or not text is reversed when it is mirrored. Setting **MIRRTEXT** to **1** (on) will cause text to be reversed when it is mirrored, as shown in Figure 7-30. Setting **MIRRTEXT** to **0** (off) retains the text's original orientation, as shown in Figure 7-31.

By default, the **MIRRTEXT** system variable is set to **0** (off).

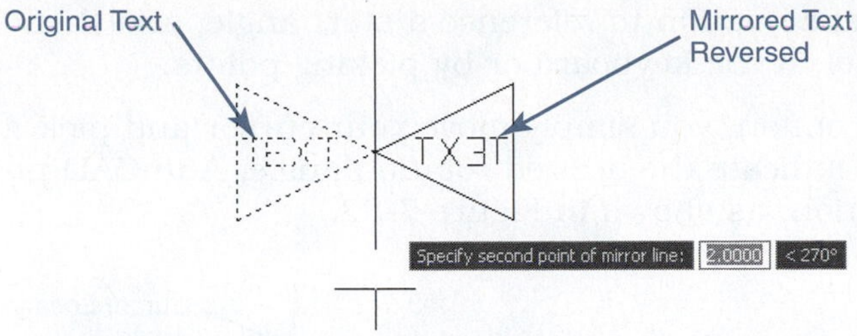

Figure 7-30
Mirrored text—Reversed

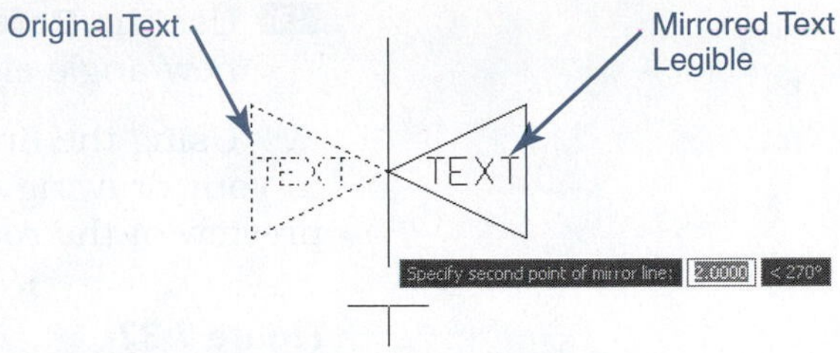

Figure 7-31
Mirrored text—Normal

EXERCISE 7-11 Mirroring Objects

1. Continue from Exercise 7-10.
2. Erase the lines that make up the square in your drawing.
3. Draw a triangle similar to the one shown in Figure 7-27.
4. Start the **MIRROR** command, and select the triangle using your preferred selection method so that AutoCAD prompts *Specify first point of mirror line:*.
5. Pick a point above the right side vertex as shown in Figure 7-27. AutoCAD prompts you to *Specify second point of mirror line:*.
6. Turn on the **Ortho Mode** drawing tool if it is not already on.
7. Pick a point directly below the first point at 270° using the **Ortho Mode** drawing tool as shown in Figure 7-27. AutoCAD mirrors the triangle and prompts *Erase source objects?* ↓.
8. Press **<Enter>** to accept the default and retain the original triangle so that the drawing looks similar to Figure 7-28.

ROTATE	
Ribbon & Panel:	Home | Modify 
Modify Toolbar:	
Menu:	Modify | Rotate
Command Line:	ROTATE
Command Alias:	RO

Rotating Objects

The **ROTATE** command rotates objects a user-specified rotation angle around a user-specified base point.

After you start the **ROTATE** command and select something, AutoCAD prompts you to *Specify base point:*. The base point is the axis of rotation about which the selected object(s) are rotated. Typically you pick a base point by snapping to a key object feature using an object snap.

NOTE

It is also possible to type in a base point as a Cartesian coordinate value at the cursor or the command line. For instance, to rotate an object using the drawing origin as the base point, you can enter **0,0<Enter>** in response to the *Specify base point:* prompt.

After specifying the base point, AutoCAD then prompts you to *Specify rotation angle or* ↓. You have three different ways you can enter the rotation angle:

1. Pick a point with your mouse that defines the rotation angle using the base point as the vertex.
2. Enter the angle at the keyboard.

3 Use the **Reference** option to reference a start angle, and then enter a new angle either at the keyboard or by picking points.

Using the first option, you simply move your cursor and pick a point in your drawing to indicate the desired rotation angle. AutoCAD provides a preview of the rotation, as shown in Figure 7-32.

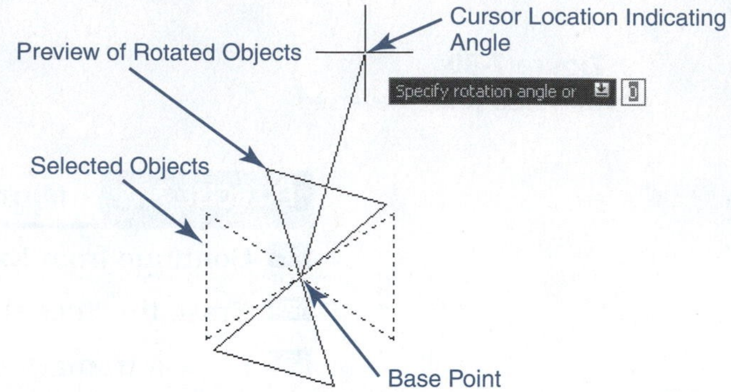

Figure 7-32
Rotating objects using your mouse

TIP

You can use either the **Ortho Mode** or **Polar Tracking** tool to quickly rotate object(s) at predefined angles.

FOR MORE DETAILS

See Chapter 5 for more information about using the **Ortho Mode** and **Polar Tracking** drawing tools.

The second option is to enter the rotation angle at the keyboard. Angles are measured using the current base angle and direction. The default base angle is 0°=East with angles measured counterclockwise. The current direction and base angle are displayed at the command line when you use the **ROTATE** command for an easy reference as follows:

Current positive angle in UCS: ANGDIR=clockwise ANGBASE=θ

Entering **45<Enter>** with the settings above rotates the selected objects, as shown in Figures 7-33A and B.

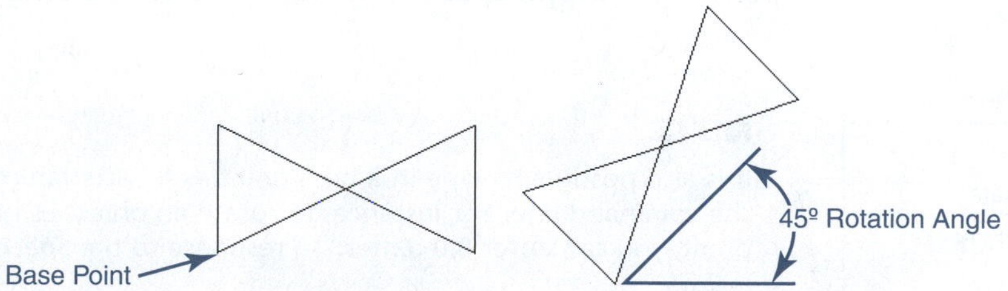

Figure 7-33
A Objects before rotating **B** Objects rotated 45°

TIP

It is also possible to enter a negative angle and rotate objects in the opposite direction of the current angle direction setting. For example, entering **–45°** is equal to entering **315°**.

FOR MORE DETAILS

See page 138 in Chapter 4 for more information about setting the base angle and direction.

The **Reference** option allows you to rotate object(s) by specifying a reference, or start angle, and then specifying a new, absolute angle to rotate to. AutoCAD determines the necessary rotation angle by calculating the difference from the reference angle to the new angle.

After you select the **Reference** option, you can either type in an angle via the keyboard, or you can select two points in your drawing that define the reference angle. The **Reference** option is invaluable if you don't know the angle of an existing object. Using object snaps, you can snap to two points on the object(s) that define its current angle, as shown in Figure 7-34.

AutoCAD then prompts you to *Specify the new angle or* ↓. You can either type in an angle via the keyboard, or you can use the **Points** option to select two points in the drawing to define the new angle, as shown in Figure 7-35.

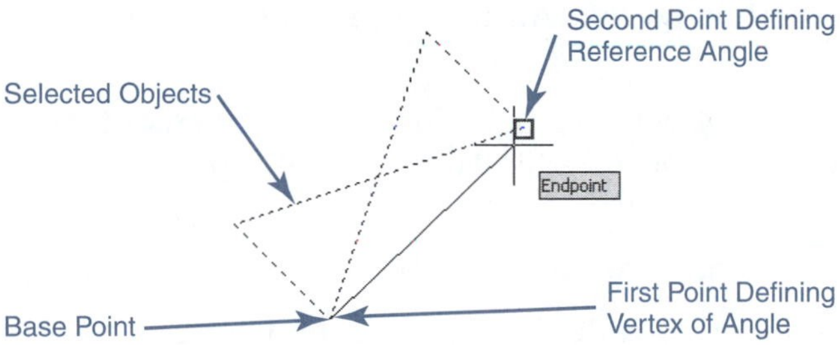

Figure 7-34
Rotating objects using the **Reference** option—Start angle

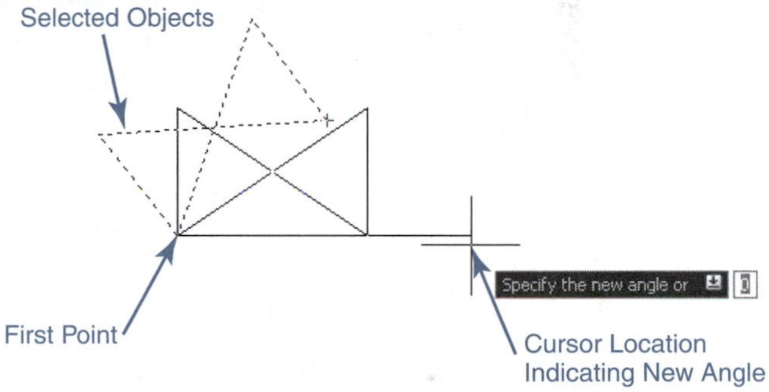

Figure 7-35
Rotating objects using the **Reference** option—New angle

Rotating and Copying Objects

It is possible to rotate and copy objects using the **Copy** option. When you select the **Copy** option, AutoCAD displays the following at the command line:

Rotating a copy of the selected objects.

You can use any of the methods explained earlier to specify a rotation angle. Figure 7-36 shows the results of using the **Copy** option and rotating the objects shown in Figure 7-33A 90° from horizontal.

Figure 7-36
Rotating and copying objects

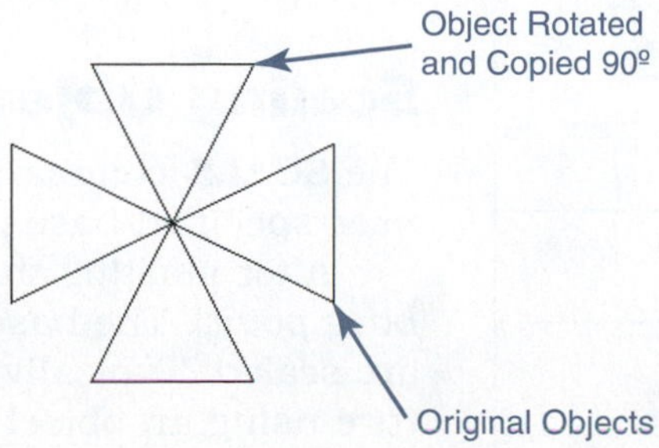

TIP

AutoCAD remembers the angle entered using any of the **ROTATE** command options so that it is now the default angle. The next time you use the **ROTATE** command, you can press **<Enter>** to rotate the same angle again.

EXERCISE 7-12 **Rotating Objects**

1. Continue from Exercise 7-11.
2. Start the **ROTATE** command, and select both triangles using your preferred selection method so that AutoCAD prompts *Specify base point or* ↓.
3. Snap to the intersection of both triangles using the **Intersection** object snap, as shown in Figure 7-32. AutoCAD prompts *Specify rotation angle or* ↓.
4. Rotate the triangles to any angle using a cursor pick point, as shown in Figure 7-32.
5. Type **U<Enter>** or select the **Undo** tool so that the triangles are oriented horizontally again, as shown in Figure 7-33A.
6. Start the **ROTATE** command again, and select the triangles using your preferred selection method so that AutoCAD prompts *Specify base point or* ↓.
7. Snap to the intersection of both triangles using the **Intersection** object snap, as shown in Figure 7-32. AutoCAD prompts *Specify rotation angle or* ↓.
8. Type **45<Enter>**. The triangles are rotated 45° as shown in Figure 7-33B.
9. Type **U<Enter>** or select the **Undo** tool so that the triangles are oriented horizontally again as shown in Figure 7-33A.
10. Start the **ROTATE** command again, and select the triangles using your preferred selection method so that AutoCAD prompts *Specify base point or* ↓.
11. Snap to the intersection of both triangles using the **Intersection** object snap, as shown in Figure 7-32. AutoCAD prompts *Specify rotation angle or* ↓.
12. Select the **Copy** option.
13. Type **90<Enter>**. The triangles are copied and rotated 90° as shown in Figure 7-36.
14. Type **U<Enter>** or select the **Undo** tool so that only two triangles are left at their original horizontal orientation.

<table>
<tr><th colspan="2">SCALE</th></tr>
<tr><td>Ribbon & Panel:</td><td>Home | Modify </td></tr>
<tr><td>Modify Toolbar:</td><td></td></tr>
<tr><td>Menu:</td><td>Modify | Scale</td></tr>
<tr><td>Command Line:</td><td>SCALE</td></tr>
<tr><td>Command Alias:</td><td>SC</td></tr>
</table>

Scaling Objects

The **SCALE** command scales objects a user-specified scale factor about a user-specified base point.

After starting the **SCALE** command, AutoCAD prompts you to *Specify base point:*. The base point is the point about which the selected object(s) are scaled. Typically you pick a base point by snapping to a key object feature using an object snap.

NOTE

It is also possible to type in a base point as a Cartesian coordinate value at the cursor or the command line. For instance, to scale an object using the drawing origin as the base point, you can enter **0,0<Enter>** in response to the *Specify base point:* prompt.

After specifying the base point, AutoCAD then prompts you to *Specify scale factor or* ↓. You have three different ways you can enter the scale factor:

1. Pick a point with your mouse that defines the scale factor.
2. Enter the scale factor at the keyboard.
3. Use the **Reference** option to reference a starting size/length and then enter a new size/length either at the keyboard or by picking points.

Using the first option you simply move your cursor and pick a point in your drawing to indicate the desired scale factor. AutoCAD provides a preview of the scaling process, as shown in Figure 7-37.

Figure 7-37
Scaling objects using your mouse

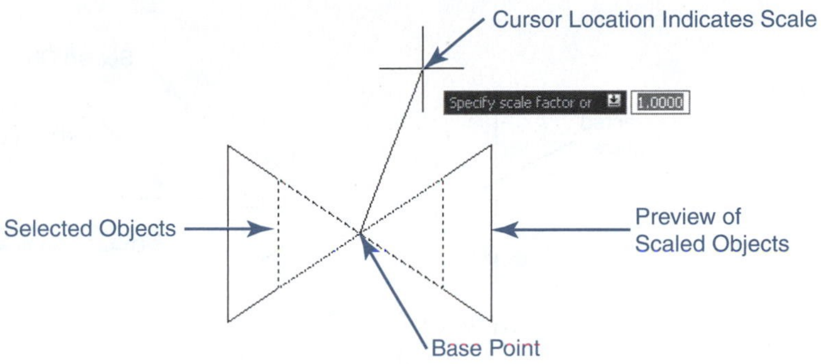

The second option is to enter the scale factor at the keyboard. A scale factor greater than 1 makes objects larger, and a scale factor less than 1 makes objects smaller. Scale factors must always be greater than zero. Entering **2<Enter>** in response to the *Specify scale factor or* ↓ prompt scales the selected objects up by a factor of 2 so that they are twice as large, as shown in Figures 7-38A and B.

Figure 7-38
A Objects before scaling
B Objects scaled by a factor of 2

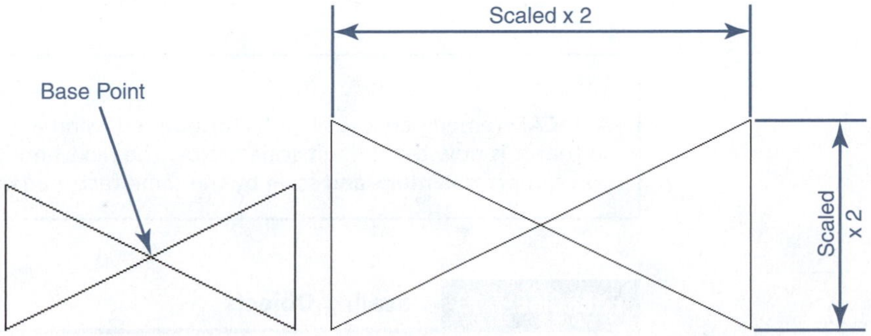

The **Reference** option allows you to scale objects by specifying a reference, or start length, and then a new, absolute length to scale to. AutoCAD determines the necessary scale factor by calculating the difference between the reference length and the new length.

After you select the **Reference** option, you can either type in a length via the keyboard, or you can select two points in your drawing that define the reference length. The **Reference** option is invaluable if you don't know the length of an existing object but you do know the length it needs to be. Using object snaps, you can snap to two points on the object(s) that define its current length, as shown in Figure 7-39.

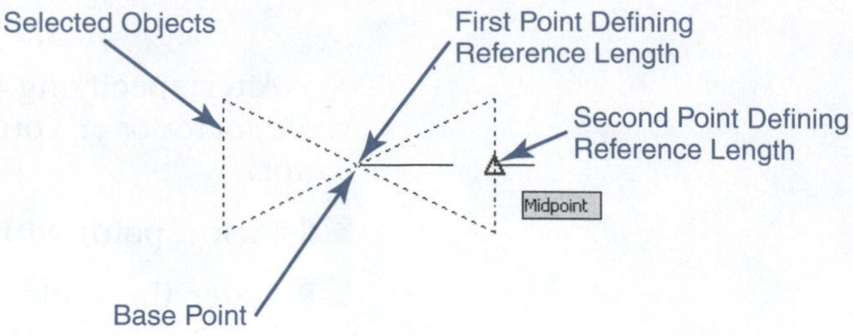

Figure 7-39
Scaling objects using the **Reference** option—Start length

AutoCAD then prompts you to *Specify new length or* ↓. You can either type in a length via the keyboard, or you can use the **Points** option to select two points in the drawing to define the new length as shown in Figure 7-40.

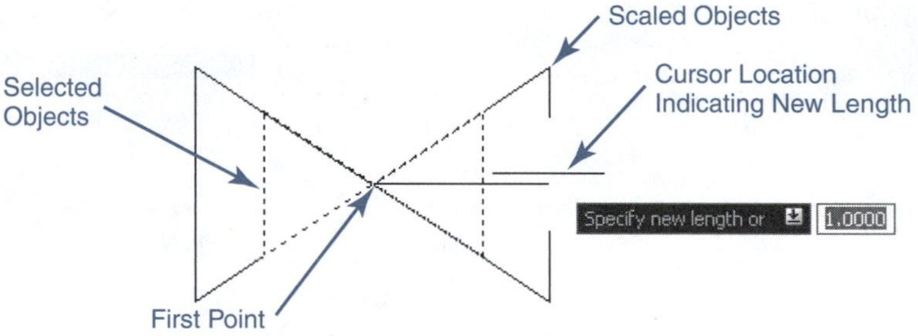

Figure 7-40
Scaling objects using the **Reference** option—New length

Scaling and Copying Objects

It is possible to scale and copy object(s) using the **Copy** option. Using the **Copy** option, AutoCAD displays the following at the command line:

Scaling a copy of the selected objects.

You can use any of the methods explained earlier to specify a scale factor.

> **TIP**
> AutoCAD remembers the scale factor entered using any of the **SCALE** command options so that it is now the default scale factor. The next time you use the **SCALE** command, you can press <**Enter**> and scale by the same factor again.

EXERCISE 7-13 Scaling Objects

1. Continue from Exercise 7-12.
2. Start the **SCALE** command, and select both triangles using your preferred selection method so that AutoCAD prompts *Specify base point or* ↓.
3. Snap to the intersection of both triangles using the **Intersection** object snap, as shown in Figure 7-37. AutoCAD prompts *Specify scale factor or* ↓.

4. Scale the triangles to any scale using a cursor pick point, as shown in Figure 7-37.
5. Type **U<Enter>** or select the **Undo** tool so that the triangles are scaled to their original size again, as shown in Figure 7-38A.
6. Start the **SCALE** command again, and select the triangles using your preferred selection method so that AutoCAD prompts *Specify base point or* ↓.
7. Snap to the intersection of both triangles using the **Intersection** object snap, as shown in Figure 7-37. AutoCAD prompts *Specify scale factor or* ↓.
8. Type **2<Enter>**. The triangles are scaled up by a factor of 2, as shown in Figure 7-38B.
9. Type **U<Enter>** or select the **Undo** tool so that the triangles are scaled to their original size again, as shown in Figure 7-38A.

STRETCH	
Ribbon & Panel:	Home | Modify 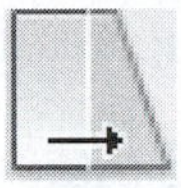
Modify Toolbar:	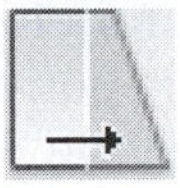
Menu:	Modify | Stretch
Command Line:	STRETCH
Command Alias:	S

Stretching Objects

The **STRETCH** command moves or stretches objects a user-supplied distance and angle using the crossing window or crossing polygon selection option. The key to the **STRETCH** command is that it moves only endpoints and vertices that lie inside the crossing selection, leaving those outside unchanged.

When you start the **STRETCH** command, AutoCAD displays the following at the command line:

Select objects to stretch by crossing-window or crossing-polygon...

AutoCAD also prompts you to *Select objects:*. You *must* select the object(s) you want to stretch using either the **Crossing** or **Crossing Polygon** selection option, as shown in Figure 7-41.

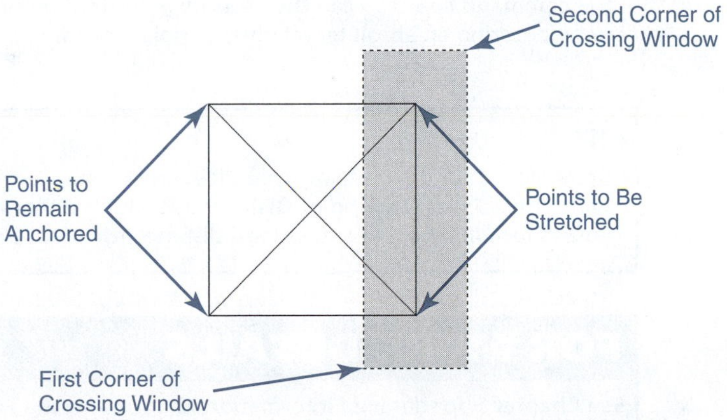

Figure 7-41
Selecting objects to stretch using a crossing selection

AutoCAD then prompts you to *Specify base point or* ↓. You have three options:

1. Specify a base point.
2. Select the **Displacement** option.
3. Enter a displacement distance using Cartesian coordinates.

TIP

You can use standard object selection methods such as picking on the object, and AutoCAD automatically treats those objects with a **MOVE** operation. You can also apply multiple crossing selections within a single **STRETCH** operation to stretch multiple object selections simultaneously.

Using the first option, you typically pick a base (*from*) point by snapping to a key object feature using an object snap. You can then pick a destination (*to*) point, and the selected objects are stretched or moved to the new location, as shown in Figure 7-42.

Figure 7-42
Stretching objects using mouse pick points

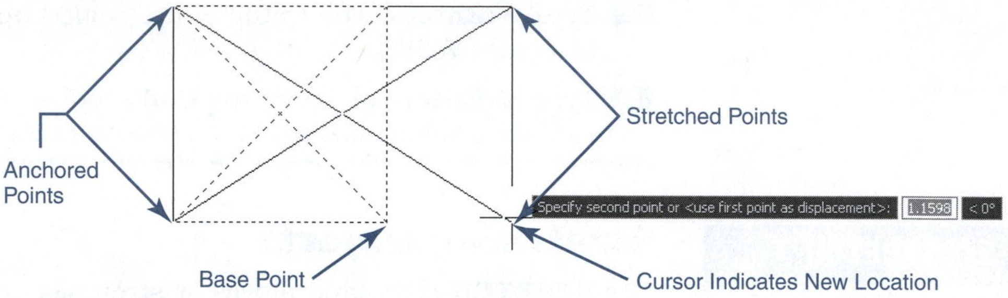

Notice in Figure 7-42 that the **STRETCH** command leaves any points or vertices outside the crossing selection anchored in place so that they are unaffected by the move. This is useful when you need to move or stretch part of a drawing but leave other portions of the drawing intact.

In the example above, you can also rely on direct distance entry to locate the second point. Using direct distance, you simply point the direction you want to stretch the selected object(s) and type in the distance you want to travel.

NOTE

It is also possible to type a base point as a Cartesian coordinate value at the cursor or the command line. You can then specify a destination point either by using your mouse or by entering an absolute, relative, or polar coordinate value.

TIP

Remember that the best way to utilize direct distance entry is to use it in conjunction with either **Polar Tracking** or **Ortho Mode**. Using either of these drawing tools allows you to lock in an angle and enter a distance for precise movement.

FOR MORE DETAILS

See Chapter 5 for detailed information about using the **Polar Tracking** and **Ortho Mode** drawing tools.

The **Displacement** option allows you to specify a displacement distance using rectangular or polar coordinates. The coordinate value you enter is *always* the relative distance the selected object(s) will be stretched, even if you omit the @ sign.

After you select the **Displacement** option, you can enter the displacement distance using either rectangular (*x*,*y*) or polar (@distance<angle) coordinates. Entering **2,0<Enter>** results in the stretch operation shown in Figure 7-43.

Figure 7-43
Stretching objects using the **Displacement** option

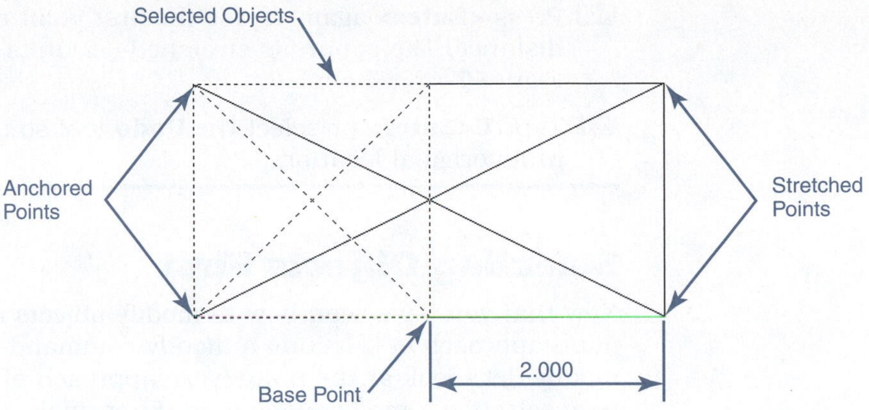

> **TIP**
>
> AutoCAD remembers the displacement distance entered so that it is now the default distance. The next time you use the **STRETCH** command, you can just press **<Enter>** to stretch the same distance again.

The third option is a shortcut to the **Displacement** option explained previously. It is possible to enter a Cartesian coordinate displacement distance directly in response to the first *Specify base point or* ↓ prompt explained earlier. Entering an *x,y* distance and pressing **<Enter>** twice selects the default **<use first point as displacement>** option so that the *x,y* distance entered is used as the displacement distance.

EXERCISE 7-14 Stretching Objects

1. Continue from Exercise 7-13.
2. Erase any existing line work in your drawing from previous exercises.
3. Draw a 2″ × 2″ square with a cross similar to the one shown in Figure 7-41.
4. Start the **STRETCH** command, and select the line endpoints on the right side of the square using the **Crossing** selection method shown in Figure 7-41 so that AutoCAD prompts *Specify base point or* ↓.
5. Snap to the lower right corner of the square using the **Endpoint** object snap, as shown in Figure 7-42. AutoCAD prompts *Specify second point or <use first point as displacement>:*.
6. Stretch the line endpoints to the right using a second pick point, as shown in Figure 7-42.
7. Type **U<Enter>** or select the **Undo** tool so that the square is its original size.
8. Start the **STRETCH** command, and select the line endpoints on the right side of the square using the **Crossing** selection method shown in Figure 7-41 so that AutoCAD prompts *Specify base point or* ↓.
9. Type **2,0<Enter>**. AutoCAD prompts *Specify second point or <use first point as displacement>:*.

10 Press **<Enter>** again to use the first point entered as the displacement distance. The square is stretched +2 units on the *X*-axis as shown in Figure 7-43.

11 Type **U<Enter>** or select the **Undo** tool so that only one square is left in its original location.

Selecting Objects First

Now that you have seen how to modify objects using the traditional verb/noun approach of selecting a modify command and then the objects to modify, let's look at the noun/verb approach of selecting objects first and *then* selecting a modify command. First, make sure that the **Noun/verb selection** check box is selected on the **Selection** tab of the **Options** dialog box, as shown in Figure 7-2. It is on by default.

> **TIP**
>
> The **PICKFIRST** system variable can also be used to control the noun/verb selection setting. Setting **PICKFIRST** to **1** (on) is the same as selecting the **Noun/verb selection** check box. Setting **PICKFIRST** to **0** (off) turns off the **Noun/verb selection** check box.

Using noun/verb selection, you can select objects either by using your cursor or by using implied windowing to create a window or crossing selection. When you select objects first using implied windowing, you have additional options. After selecting the first point in a clear area of the drawing, so you avoid selecting an object directly, it is possible to select the **Fence**, **WPolygon**, or **CPolygon** option in addition to defining a two-point rectangular window area. Selected objects are highlighted, and if grips are enabled, their grips are turned on as shown later in Figure 7-44. Grips are explained in detail in the next section. If you now select any of the modify commands introduced in this chapter, the selected objects become the default selection set for the modify command, and you are *not* prompted to select any objects. You can then use the command and any command options by applying the same techniques explained in the previous sections.

Figure 7-44
Grips displayed for a line, circle, and rectangle

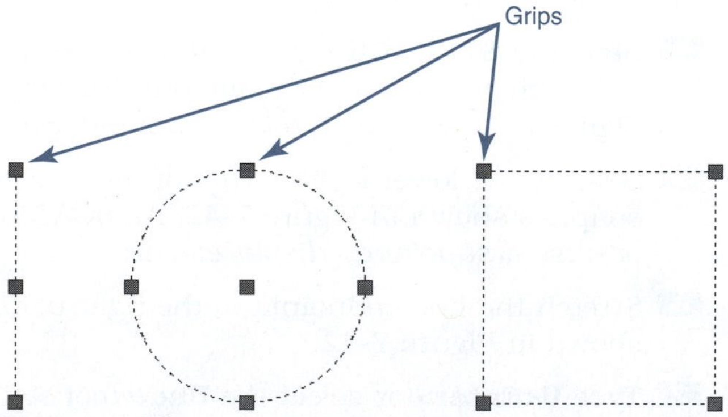

> **NOTE**
>
> Setting the **PICKAUTO** system variable to **2** allows you to start an implied window even while picking directly on an object, minimizing the need to find a clear area of your drawing.

EXERCISE 7-15 **Selecting Objects First for Editing**

1. Continue from Exercise 7-14.
2. Select all the objects in the drawing either by selecting objects individually with your mouse or by using implied windowing.
3. Select the **ERASE** command. All the objects are erased.

Using Grips to Edit

Grips are the small colored squares (default=blue) that appear at key object definition points when an object is selected, as shown in Figure 7-44.

Grips act as object handles and when selected provide quick, easy access to the five basic modify commands explained earlier in this chapter so that you can maintain your focus on your drawing. The five grip commands, or modes, are as follows:

1. **Stretch**
2. **Move**
3. **Rotate**
4. **Scale**
5. **Mirror**

Multifunctional Grips

Some AutoCAD objects such as lines, arcs, and dimensions have grips that can perform multiple functions. Hovering your cursor over a grip displays a shortcut menu similar to those shown in Figure 7-45 so you can select the desired command using your mouse or the arrow key on your keyboard.

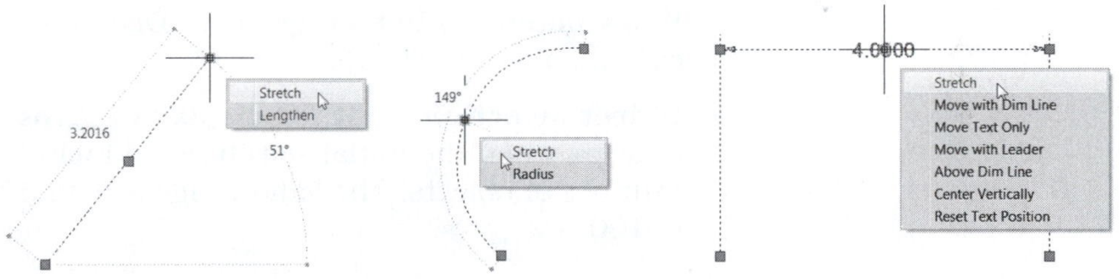

Figure 7-45
Multifunctional grips

> **TIP**
> After a grip is selected using the techniques described in the following sections, you can cycle through any available multifunctional grips by pressing the <**Ctrl**> key.

Controlling Grips

Grips are controlled on the **Selection** tab of the **Options** dialog box shown in Figure 7-46.

The different grip features and their settings are as follows:

- **Grip size** Controls the display size of grips
- **Grip Colors...** Determines the color of grips in various modes
- **Show grips** Displays grips on an object when it is selected
- **Show grips within blocks** Controls how grips are displayed on a block after you select it. If this option is selected, AutoCAD displays all grips

Figure 7-46
Grip settings on the **Selection** tab of the **Options** dialog box

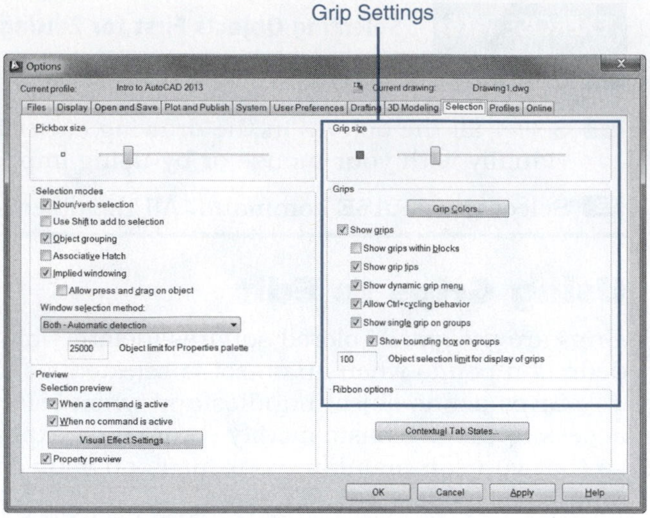

for each object in the block. If this option is cleared, AutoCAD displays one grip located at the insertion point of the block

- **Show grip tips** Displays grip-specific tips when the cursor hovers over a grip on a custom object that supports grip tips. This option has no effect on standard AutoCAD objects
- **Show dynamic grip menu** Controls the display of a dynamic menu when pausing over multifunctional grips used by polylines and splines
- **Allow Ctrl+cycling behavior** Allows the **<Ctrl>** key cycling behavior for multifunctional grips used by polylines and splines
- **Show single grip on groups** Displays a single grip for an object group
- **Show bounding box on groups** Displays a bounding box around the extents of grouped objects
- **Object selection limit for display of grips** Suppresses the display of grips when the initial selection set includes more than the specified number of objects. The valid range is 1 to 32,767. The default setting is 100.

FOR MORE DETAILS

See Chapter 16 for more information about blocks.

For the best results, make sure that your grip settings closely match those shown in Figure 7-46. Failure to do so can cause some of the examples and exercises in the following sections to behave differently than anticipated.

Selecting Grips

To select a grip, you must place your cursor within the grip box and pick with your mouse. When a grip is selected, it changes color (default=red), and you are placed in **Grip Edit** mode, as shown in Figure 7-47.

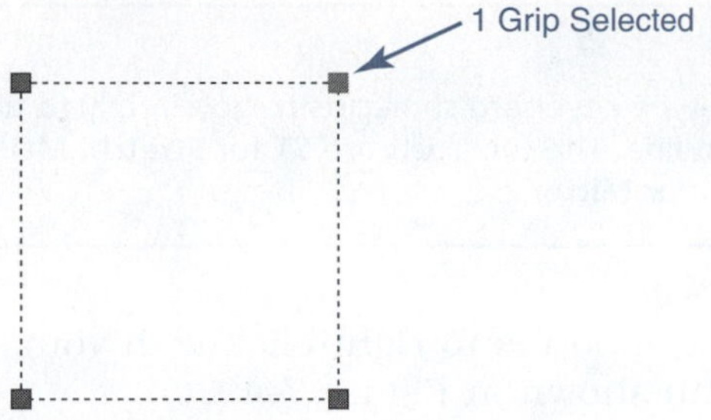

Figure 7-47
One grip selected

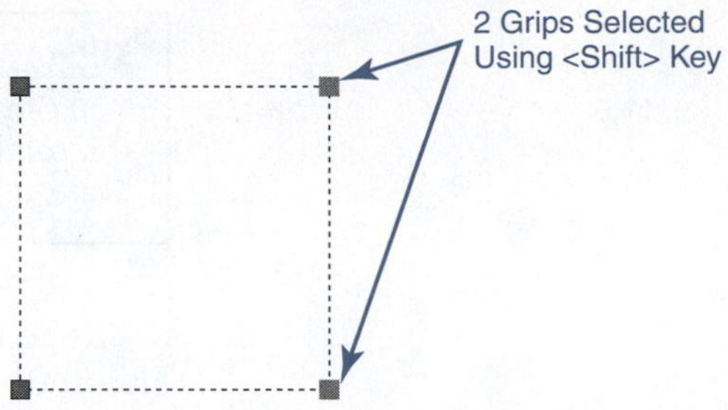

Figure 7-48
Two grips selected

It is possible to select multiple grips by holding down the **<Shift>** key before selecting the first grip. You can continue to select grips until you release the **<Shift>** key. In Figure 7-48, two grips have been selected.

To "unselect" all grips that have been selected (default=red), as shown in Figure 7-47, press the **<Esc>** key once. This changes the grips to the unselected mode (default=blue), as shown in Figure 7-47. To turn off all the grips that are unselected (default=blue), you must press the **<Esc>** key again. This will result in the object(s) being simply highlighted (dashed) with no grips displayed.

> **TIP**
> You can remove objects from the selection set by holding down the **<Shift>** key and selecting the object you want to remove.

Grip Modes

After at least one grip is selected (default=red) and you are in **Grip Edit** mode, as shown in Figure 7-48, the desired grip mode can be selected either at the command line or via the right-click **Grip** shortcut menu.

The command line approach allows you to cycle through the five different grip modes starting with **Stretch** mode by pressing the spacebar or the **<Enter>** key as follows:

** STRETCH **

Specify stretch point or [**B**ase point **C**opy **U**ndo e**X**it]:

** MOVE **

Specify move point or [**B**ase point **C**opy **U**ndo e**X**it]:

** ROTATE **

Specify rotation angle or [**B**ase point **C**opy **U**ndo **R**eference e**X**it]:

** SCALE **

Specify scale factor or [**B**ase point **C**opy **U**ndo **R**eference e**X**it]:

** MIRROR **

Specify second point or [**B**ase point **C**opy **U**ndo e**X**it]:

Each time you press the spacebar or **<Enter>**, AutoCAD cycles to the next grip mode in the order shown above, repeating the modes again when it gets back to **Stretch** mode.

> **TIP**
> You can also type keyboard shortcuts to go directly to the desired grip mode option at the command line. The shortcuts are **ST** for **Stretch, MO** for **Move, RO** for **Rotate, SC** for **Scale,** and **MI** for **Mirror**.

The other option is to right-click with your mouse to display the **Grip** shortcut menu shown in Figure 7-49.

Figure 7-49
Grip shortcut menu

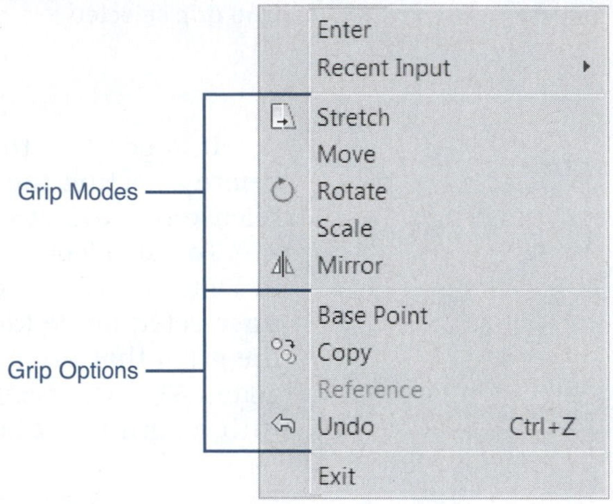

This approach allows you to go directly to the desired grip mode option without having to hit your spacebar or the **<Enter>** key multiple times.

Using either approach, the different grip modes work similarly to their traditional modify command counterparts explained earlier in the chapter and share most of the same options. Each grip mode shares the following options:

- **Base Point** Allows you to specify a new base point to use with current grip mode. By default, the base point is set to the selected grip
- **Copy** Allows you to create a copy of the selected object(s) to use with the current grip mode
- **Undo** Undoes the last grip mode operation
- **Exit** Exits the current grip mode and leaves grips on but unselected

In addition, the **Rotate** and **Scale** modes also have a **Reference** option that works exactly the same as described earlier in the **ROTATE** and **SCALE** modify command sections.

After selecting the desired grip mode either at the command line or via the **Grip** shortcut menu, the different grip mode options can be selected by selecting the first letter of the option at the command line, by selecting the option from the right-click shortcut menu, or by using your arrow keys if you are using dynamic input.

Chapter Summary

This chapter presents the basics of selecting and modifying objects in an AutoCAD drawing. The different object selection techniques explored in this chapter can be applied throughout the rest of the textbook. As you can see, there are many different ways to go about creating and modifying a selection set. Practice using, and even combining, the different selection and editing techniques and try to think "outside of the box." Sometimes you might want to pick objects first and then select a modify command; other times it makes sense to pick a command first and then the objects(s) to modify. If a collection of objects is to be used repeatedly, try grouping them together using the AutoCAD group tools so they behave as one unit.

You will use many of the basic modify commands introduced in this chapter on a daily basis. They form the basis of most of the editing that occurs in a drawing. Note that most of the modify tools work similarly and display the same prompts. This is so you can apply the knowledge learned mastering one tool across the range of modify tools and become a more productive drafter.

Grips are just another way of doing the same thing: modifying drawing information. They are quicker for simple operations, but may be more tedious for other, more complex tasks. Some of the things you can do with grips and dynamic input cannot be done as quickly any other way. Conversely, multifunctional grips can provide the quickest access to an object-specific command. It is all a matter of picking the right tool for the job. Experience is the best way to figure out which tool you should reach for in any given situation.

Chapter Test Questions

Multiple Choice

Circle the correct answer.

1. Selecting objects first and then selecting a modify command is referred to as what type of editing process?

   a. Noun/verb
   c. Grip mode
   b. Verb/noun
   d. Cut and paste

2. A selection set is:

   a. Set of commands used to select objects
   b. All currently selected objects
   c. Group of similar objects
   d. None of the above

3. The box that appears at the mouse crosshairs when you are prompted to select objects is called:

   a. Grip
   b. Aperture
   c. Pickbox
   d. Window area

4. When you are creating a selection set, you can remove objects by:

a. Typing **U<Enter>**

b. Holding down the **<Shift>** key while selecting objects

c. Entering **Remove** object mode by typing **R<Enter>**

d. All of the above features

5. The difference between the window selection method and the crossing selection method is:

a. A window boundary is a solid line, and a crossing boundary is a dashed line

b. The window method selects only objects inside the boundary, and the crossing method selects objects inside *and* objects that cross the boundary

c. By default, the window area preview is blue, and the crossing area preview is green

d. All of the above

6. Implied windowing allows you to:

a. Automatically create a window or crossing selection

b. Turn off window and crossing selection options

c. Pick one corner point to define a window and drag your mouse and release to create the other corner point

d. Select objects with your mind

7. The system variable that controls whether text is reversed when it is mirrored is:

a. **MIRRORTEXT** c. **TEXTMIRROR**

b. **MIRRTEXT** d. **MTEXT**

8. To select multiple grips, you must hold down which key when picking the first grip?

a. **<Ctrl>** c. **<Esc>**

b. **<Shift>** d. Spacebar

9. Grip modes can be selected via:

a. Command line

b. Right-click shortcut menu

c. Keyboard shortcuts

d. All of the above

10. The keyboard key that turns off (deselects) grips is:

a. **<Ctrl>** c. **<Esc>**

b. **<Enter>** d. **<Alt>**

Matching

Write the number of the correct answer on the line.

a. **ERASE** command ______

b. Selection set ______

1. Automated window and crossing selection option

2. Moves objects a user-supplied distance and angle

c. Implied window ______

d. Grips ______

e. **MOVE** command ______

f. **COPY** command ______

g. **MIRROR** command ______

h. **ROTATE** command ______

i. **SCALE** command ______

j. **STRETCH** command ______

3. Creates a mirror image of objects about a mirror axis line
4. Small squares that appear when an object is selected
5. Removes objects from a drawing
6. Rotates objects a user-specified rotation angle around a user-specified base point
7. Moves or stretches objects a user-supplied distance and angle
8. Scales objects a user-specified scale factor about a user-specified base point
9. Copies objects a user-supplied distance and angle
10. Group of one or more objects selected in a drawing

True or False

Circle the correct answer.

1. **True or False:** The traditional approach to modifying objects in AutoCAD is to select the command first and then select the objects to modify.
2. **True or False:** The traditional approach to modifying mentioned in Question 1 is referred to as the *noun/verb approach.*
3. **True or False:** It is possible to select more than one grip at a time using the **<Shift>** key.
4. **True or False:** The window and crossing selection options can be initiated automatically.
5. **True or False:** It is possible to create a window or crossing selection using only one pick point.
6. **True or False:** The **Previous** selection option will select the previous object that was added to a drawing.
7. **True or False:** The displacement distance for the **MOVE, COPY**, and **STRETCH** commands is always relative.
8. **True or False:** Text is always mirrored when you use the **MIRROR** command.
9. **True or False:** It is possible to enter a negative rotation angle when using the **ROTATE** command.

Chapter Projects

G Project 7-1: *Classroom Plan, continued from Chapter 6* [BASIC]

1. Open drawing ***P6-1*** from Chapter 6.
2. Draw the floor plan shown in Figure 7-50 using the **A-Door** and **A-Wall** layers for the doors and walls. Place the heater on the **A-Eqpm** layer. The wall next to the heater is 8″ thick; all other walls are 4″ thick. The doors are each 3′-0″ wide and the heater is 1′-0″ wide. **Do not** draw dimensions or text.
3. Use the **MOVE, COPY**, and **MIRROR** commands to place the desks in the configuration shown. Use object snaps and the **Polar Tracking** and/or **Ortho Mode** settings to ensure the desks are aligned.
4. Save the drawing as ***P7-1***.

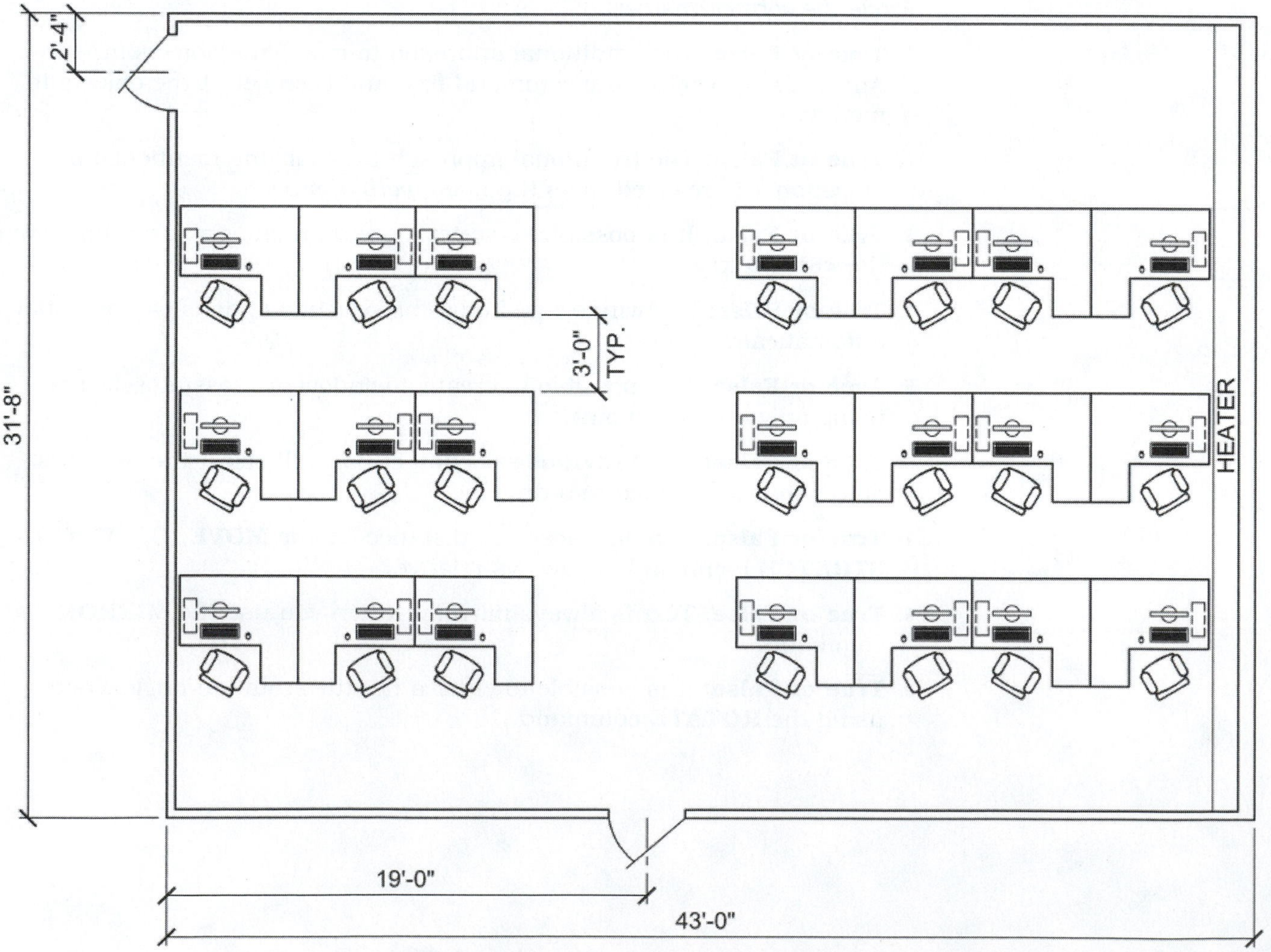

Figure 7-50

M Project 7-2: *Socket Head Cap Screws—English Units* [INTERMEDIATE]

1. Start a new drawing using the **acad.dwt** template.
2. Create two socket head cap screws based on the table shown in Figure 7-51. **Do not** draw dimensions or table.
3. Save the drawing as ***P7-2***.

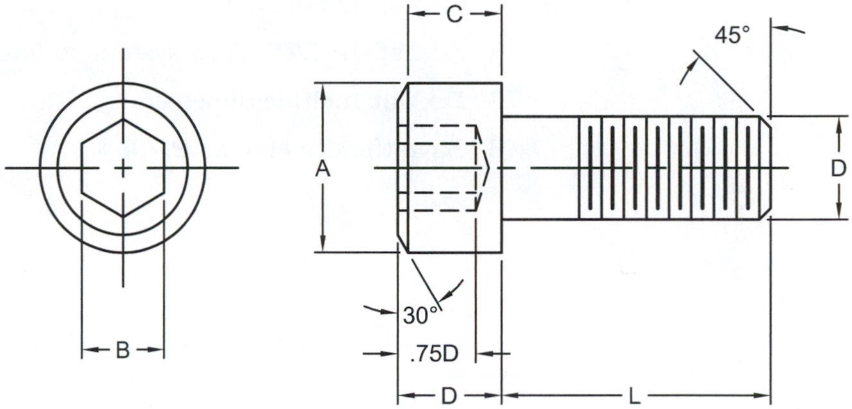

SOCKET HEAD CAP SCREW					
NOMINAL SIZE (D)	THREAD/IN	A	B	C	L
4 (.112)	40	.183	.09375	.103	1.00
5 (.125)	40	.205	.09375	.113	1.00
6 (.138)	32	.226	.109375	.125	1.25
8 (.164)	32	.270	.140625	.150	1.25
10 (.190)	24	.312	.15625	.171	1.50
¼ (.250)	20	.375	.1875	.225	1.50

Figure 7-51

M Project 7-3: *Motorcycle Head Gasket—Metric* [ADVANCED]

1. Start a new drawing using the **acadiso.dwt** template.
2. Create the following layers:

Name	Color	Linetype	Lineweight	Description
Object	7	Continuous	0.60 mm	Object lines
Hidden	1	Hidden	0.30 mm	Hidden lines
Center	2	Center	0.30 mm	Centerlines
Hatch	4	Continuous	0.30 mm	Hatch patterns and fills
Notes	3	Continuous	0.30 mm	Text and notes
Dims	2	Continuous	0.30 mm	Dimensions

3. Draw the motorcycle head gasket shown in Figure 7-52 using the appropriate layers.
4. Adjust the **LTSCALE** system so linetypes appear properly.
5. **Do not** include dimensions.
6. Save the drawing as ***P7-3***.

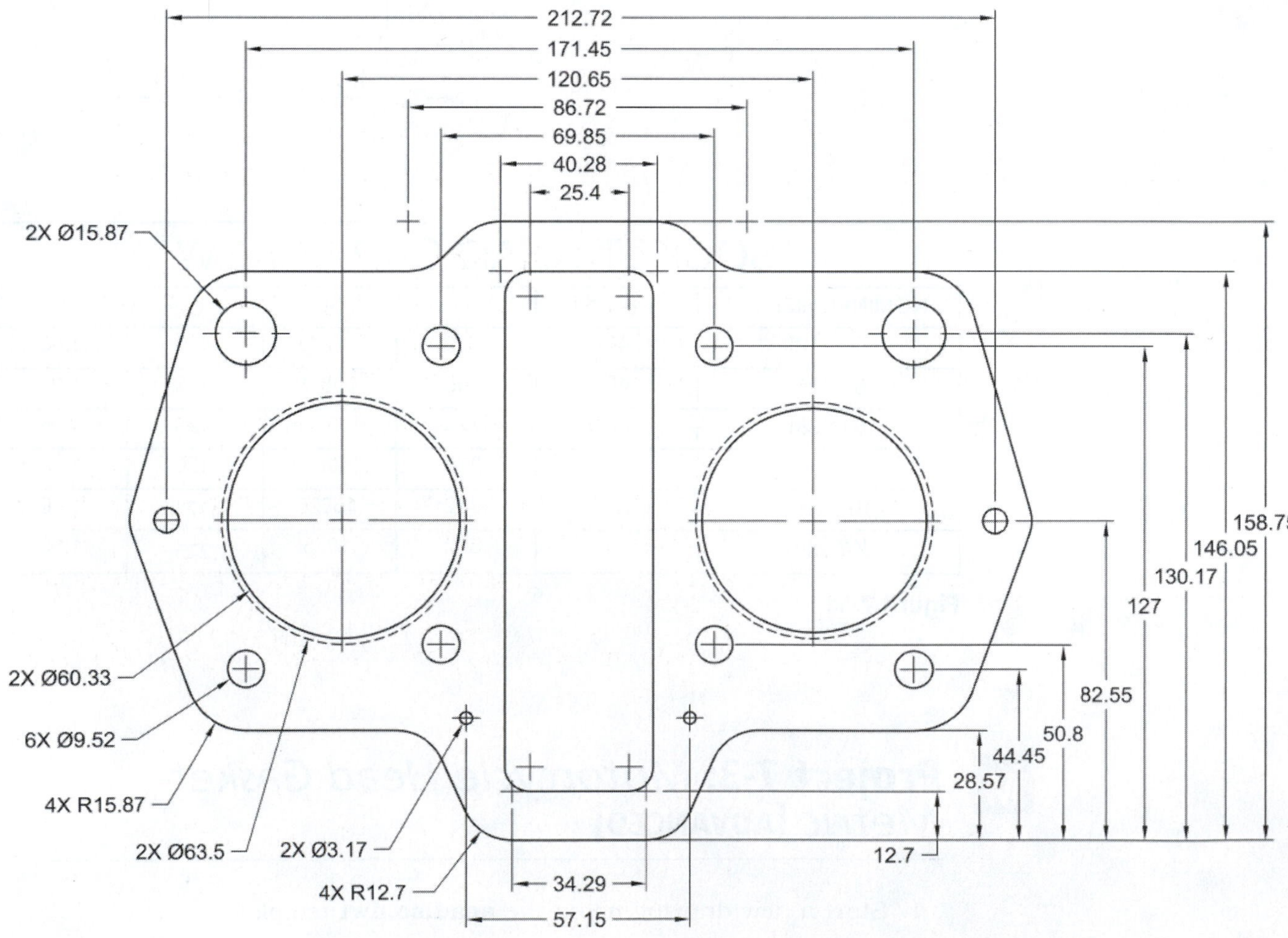

Figure 7-52

E Project 7-4: *Electrical Distribution Panel* [BASIC]

1. Start a new drawing using the **acad.dwt** template.
2. Create the following layer:

Name	Color	Linetype	Lineweight	Plot/Noplot	Description
E-Powr-Panl	7	Continuous	Default	Plot	Electrical power panels

3. Set the grid to **.5** and the snap to **.25** and draw the electrical distribution panel shown in Figure 7-53. **Do not** draw grid lines. *Hint:* The grid lines shown are spaced at .5 intervals.
4. Save the drawing as ***P7-4***.

Figure 7-53

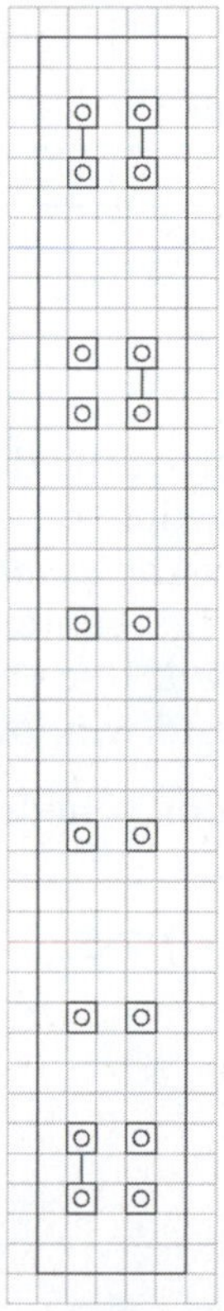

A Project 7-5: *Residential Architectural Plan, continued from Chapter 6* [ADVANCED]

1. Open drawing ***P6-5*** from Chapter 6.
2. Draw the door and window symbols shown in Figure 7-54 using the **A-Door** and **A-Glaz** layers.

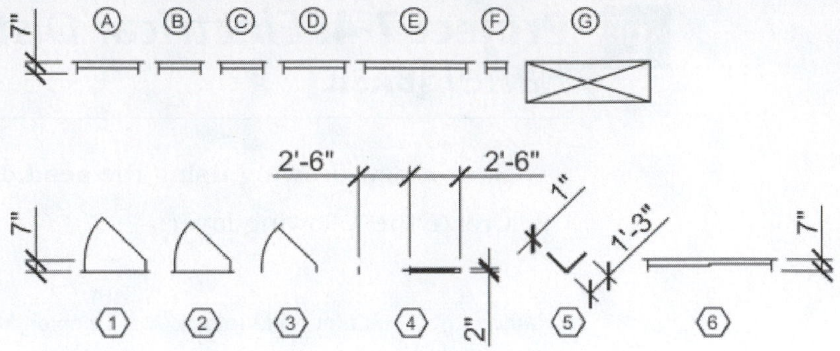

WINDOW SCHEDULE			
SYM.	SIZE	TYPE	QTY.
A	3'-0" X 3'-6"	S.H.	10
B	2'-0" X 3'-6"	S.H./FROSTED	1
C	2'-0" X 3'-0"	S.H.	4
D	3'-0" X 3'-0"	PCT.	2
E	5'-0" X 5"-0"	TEMP. PCT.	3
F	1'-0" X 3'-0"	S.H.	2
G	2'-0" X 6'-0"	GLASS SKY.	2

DOOR SCHEDULE			
SYM.	SIZE	TYPE	QTY.
1	3'-0" X 6'-8"	M.I./R.P.	1
2	2'-8" X 6'-8"	M.I./S.C.	2
3	2'-8" X 6'-8"	H.C.	8
4	2'-6" X 6'-8"	POCKET/H.C.	2
5	2'-6" X 6'-8"	H.C./BI-FOLD	2
6	6'-0" X 6'-8"	TEMP. SLIDER	2
7	8'-0" X 6'-8"	GARAGE	2

Figure 7-54

3. Add the walls and place the doors and windows as shown in Figure 7-55 according to the schedules. Use appropriate object snaps to ensure the proper placement of the symbols. Doors and windows that are not dimensioned are either centered on the interior wall or located 3″ from the nearest wall. *Hint:* Use the **Offset** option of the **XLINE** command to locate the door and window symbols.
4. **Do not** draw the door schedule or identifier symbols. **Do not** draw dimensions or text.
5. Save the drawing as ***P7-5***.

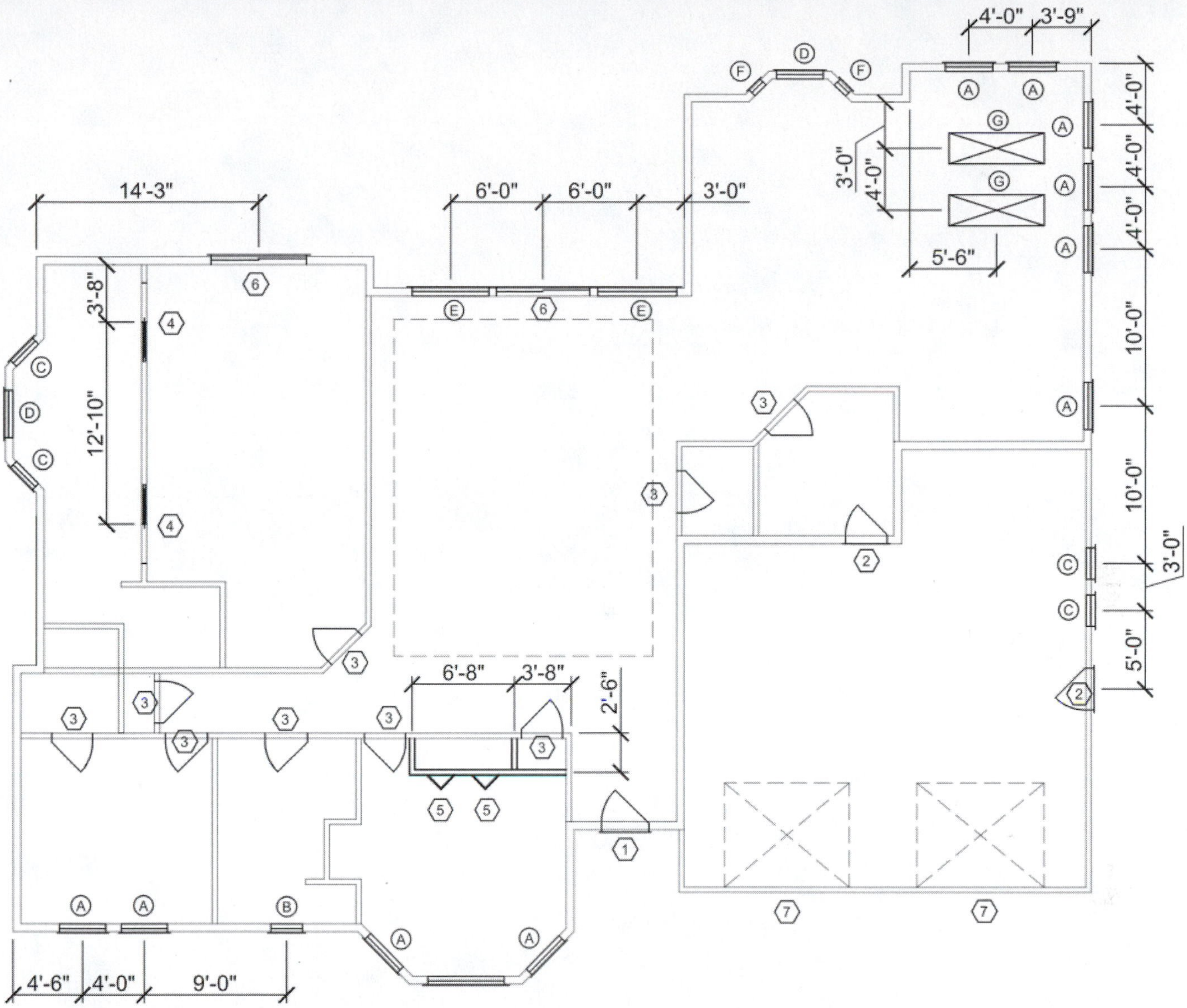

4'-0"
3'-9"
14'-3"
6'-0"
6'-0"
3'-0"
3'-0"
4'-0"
4'-0"
4'-0"
4'-0"
5'-6"
10'-0"
10'-0"
3'-0"
5'-0"
3'-8"
12'-10"
6'-8"
3'-8"
2'-6"
4'-6"
4'-0"
9'-0"

Figure 7-55

8 chapter eight
Advanced Editing Techniques

CHAPTER OBJECTIVES

- Offset objects through a specified distance
- Create rectangular, path, and polar arrays
- Trim and extend objects
- Use the **FILLET** and **CHAMFER** commands to modify intersecting objects
- Break single objects into multiple objects
- Join separate objects into a single object
- Use the **LENGTHEN** command to modify the length of an object

Introduction

As you've seen, there is usually more than one way to accomplish a given task in AutoCAD. For example, to create multiple line segments, you could simply draw multiple lines using the **LINE** command, or you could create a single line segment and copy it using grips or the **COPY** command. There are multiple ways to create arcs and circles as well as different methods for creating layers and changing object properties.

In Chapter 7, you used basic editing commands such as **MOVE, COPY**, and **ROTATE** to modify objects. In this chapter, you'll examine some editing tools that provide additional functionality. These advanced editing tools are also located on the **Modify** panel, although a few of them can be accessed only on the expanded **Modify** panel, as shown in Figure 8-1.

TIP

You can keep the expanded panel displayed while you're editing by selecting the push-pin icon on the lower left of the expanded panel. Click on the pin again to close the panel later.

Figure 8-1
The expanded **Modify** panel

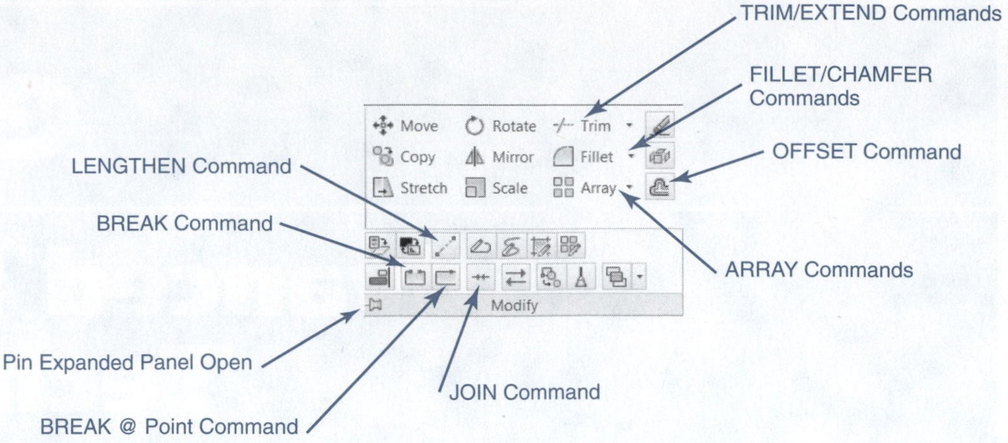

offset: To create a parallel copy of an object.

OFFSET	
Ribbon & Panel:	Home | Modify 
Modify Toolbar:	
Menu:	Modify | Offset
Command Line:	OFFSET
Command Alias:	O

Offsetting Objects

To ***offset*** an object is to make a copy of an object parallel to the original. This is similar to the **COPY** command but allows you to make parallel copies at a specified distance from the original. This can be used to make concentric arcs and circles as well as parallel lines (such as roads, walls, etc.). Offsetting is done with the **OFFSET** command.

The **OFFSET** command works by copying an object a specified distance away from the original or source object. When using the **OFFSET** command, you specify a distance, select an object to offset, and tell AutoCAD on which side of the original object you want to place the new object. To provide the offset distance, you can either specify the distance or pick a point that the new object will pass through. The **OFFSET** command has three options: **Through, Erase**, and **Layer**.

Through	Allows you to pick a point that the new object will pass through. AutoCAD measures the distance from the point to the source object.
Erase	Controls whether the source object is kept or deleted after the offset is complete. You can answer **Yes** (erase the source object) or **No** (keep the source object).
Layer	Allows you to control the layer of the new object. You can choose to have the new object take on the current layer setting or retain the layer setting of the source object.

Offsetting an Object a Specified Distance

Specifying a distance is the default method and the most commonly used. When specifying a distance, you can simply type in the distance or pick two points. If you pick two points, AutoCAD will measure the distance between the two points and use that as the offset distance.

TIP
Whenever AutoCAD asks you to provide a numeric value such as a length or distance, you can usually pick two points and have AutoCAD measure the distance.

Offsetting Through a Point

It is also possible to offset objects through a point that you pick in the drawing using the **Through** option. Typically, this is done in conjunction with object snaps so that you can snap to specific key features in your drawing. The easiest way to specify the **Through** option is to press **<Enter>** when AutoCAD prompts you to *Select object to offset or* ↓.

Offset Options

By default, the **OFFSET** command will copy the selected object on the same layer as the original, or source, object. The **Layer** option allows you to offset an object on the current layer. The **Erase** option allows you to erase the original object. The current settings are displayed at the command line each time you select the **OFFSET** command.

> **TIP**
>
> The **OFFSET** command continues to prompt you to *Select object to offset or* ↓ until you press **<Enter>** so that is possible to offset multiple objects without exiting the command. Even better, after you select an object to offset, the **Multiple** option is available so that you can make multiple copies the same distance apart by continuing to click with your mouse.

EXERCISE 8-1 **Offsetting Objects**

1. Start a new drawing using the **acad.dwt** drawing template.
2. Create two layers with the following settings:

   C-ROAD, Continuous, Color 7 (White)

   C-ROAD-CNTR, Center, Color 5 (Blue)

   Set layer **C-ROAD-CNTR** as the current layer.
3. Set the **LTSCALE** system variable to **12**.
4. Draw a line from the coordinates **100,100** to **100,250**. Zoom out using the **Zoom Extents** tool so the line is centered in the screen.
5. Set the **C-ROAD** layer current and draw a circle centered at **100,250** with a radius of **35**.
6. Start the **OFFSET** command. AutoCAD prompts you to *Specify offset distance or* ↓.
7. Press **<Enter>** to select the **Through** option. AutoCAD prompts you to *Select object to offset or* ↓.
8. Select the centerline. AutoCAD prompts you to *Specify point on side to offset or* ↓.
9. Type **QUA<Enter>** to activate the **Quadrant** object snap.
10. Move your cursor to the right side quadrant point on the circle and pick a point when the **Quadrant** object snap AutoSnap marker is displayed. The centerline is offset through the circle quadrant point on the same layer and linetype as the original centerline.
11. Type **U<Enter>** to undo the offset line and press **<Enter>** to exit the **OFFSET** command.
12. Press **<Enter>** to run the **OFFSET** command again. AutoCAD prompts you to *Select object to offset or* ↓.

13 Choose the **Layer** option and choose **Current**. The new objects will be placed on the current drawing layer. AutoCAD again prompts you to *Specify offset distance or* ↓.

14 Type **25<Enter>** to set the offset distance. AutoCAD prompts you to *Select object to offset or* ↓.

15 Select the centerline. AutoCAD prompts you to *Specify point on side to offset or* ↓. Pick anywhere off to the left of the centerline. AutoCAD will create a new line 25 units to the left of the centerline. AutoCAD again prompts you to *Select object to offset or* ↓.

16 Select the centerline again and pick anywhere off to the right of the line. AutoCAD places a new line 25 units to the right of the original. Both of the new lines are on the current layer **(C-ROAD)**.

17 Press **<Enter>** or **<Esc>** to exit the **OFFSET** command.

18 Save your drawing as ***CH8_EXERCISE1.*** Your drawing should resemble Figure 8-2.

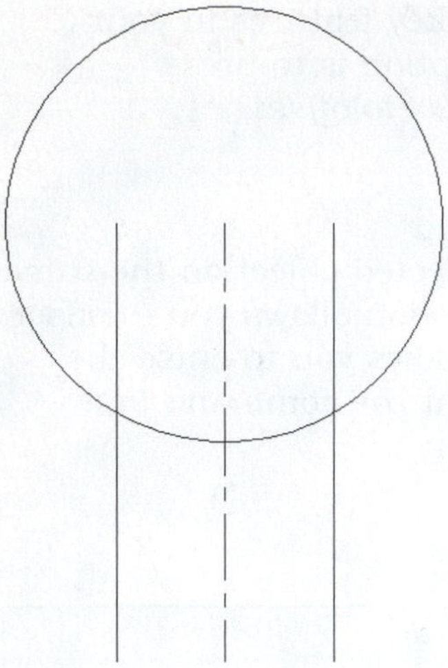

Figure 8-2
Offsetting objects

Arraying Objects

array: A rectangular, circular, or linear pattern of objects.

An ***array*** consists of multiple objects copied in a regular pattern. There are three types of arrays in AutoCAD (see Figure 8-3):

- **Rectangular** Pattern of evenly distributed objects arranged in rows and columns
- **Path** Linear pattern of evenly distributed objects that follow a predefined path
- **Polar** Circular pattern of evenly distributed objects arranged around a center point

Figure 8-3
Three different array types

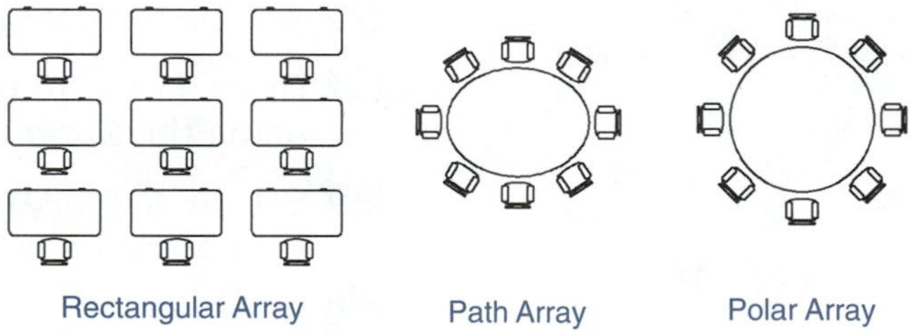

NOTE

It is possible to specify 3D levels when creating an array so that you can copy objects in the *Z*-axis. Please consult the AutoCAD Help for more information regarding any of the 3D features of the different array tools.

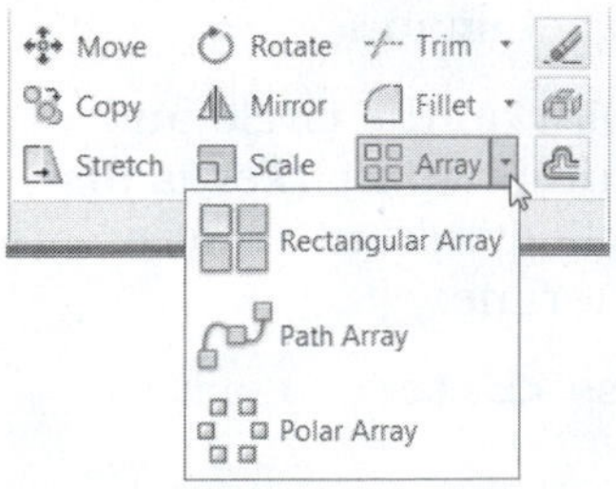

Figure 8-4
The **Array** flyout menu

The AutoCAD array tools are located on the **Array** flyout menu on the **Modify** panel on the **Home** tab of the ribbon as shown in Figure 8-4.

By default, arrayed objects are associated like AutoCAD blocks and dimensions so that they act as one complex unit and individual objects maintain a set relationship to each other. If one object in an array is selected, all of the objects in the array are highlighted. The **Array** context tab of the ribbon shown in Figure 8-5 is swapped in place of the current tab of the ribbon at the top of the AutoCAD drawing window, so it is easy to edit the array without starting over.

Figure 8-5
The **Array** context tab of the ribbon

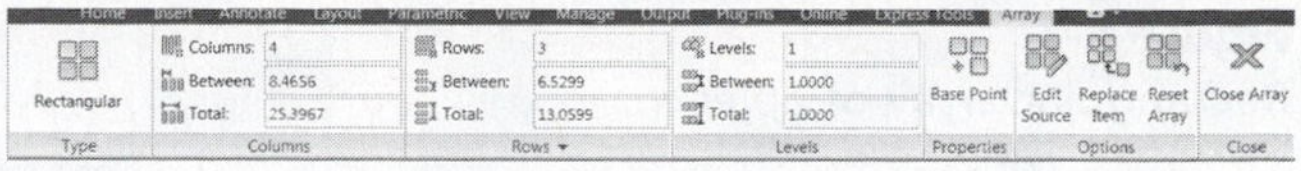

The **Array** context tab of the ribbon allows you to change any of the array properties, update or replace individual array objects, and even reset an array back to its original settings while maintaining the array's associativity. The **Edit Source** tool allows you to update a single array object individually using regular AutoCAD commands and then elect to either save or discard changes via an **Edit Array** panel that gets appended to the right end of the current tab of the ribbon.

> **TIP**
>
> It is also possible to edit array objects individually by holding the **<Ctrl>** key down while selecting the object(s) first. You can then use most of the regular modify commands as you would normally.

In addition to the **Array** context tab of the ribbon, many array options and settings are provided via right-click shortcut menus and multifunctional grips that are displayed when an array is selected in the drawing, as shown in Figure 8-6.

Figure 8-6
Multifunctional **Array** grips

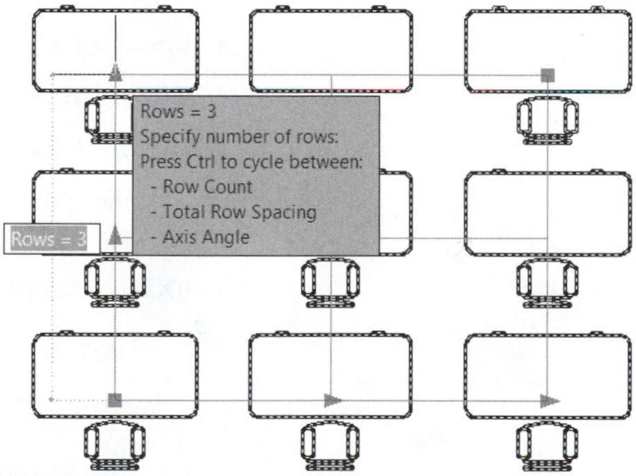

RECTANGULAR ARRAY	
Ribbon & Panel:	Home | Modify  Rectangular Array
Modify Toolbar:	
Menu:	Modify | Array | Rectangular Array
Command Line:	ARRAYRECT
Command Alias:	None

> **NOTE**
>
> It is possible to include parametric geometry and expressions when creating an array so that even more complex relationships between array objects can be established. Both of these topics are beyond the scope of this textbook, so please consult the AutoCAD Help for additional information.

Creating a Rectangular Array

The **Rectangular Array** tool allows you to copy objects equidistantly to create any combination of rows and columns (see Figure 8-7).

After you choose the **Rectangular Array** tool, select the object(s) you want to array, and press **<Enter>**, AutoCAD automatically creates a default array with 3 rows and 4 columns. AutoCAD also replaces the standard ribbon

Figure 8-7
Rectangular array of objects

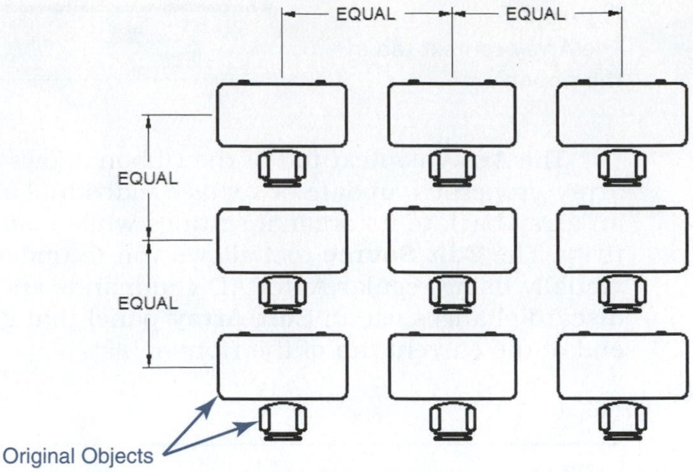

NEW to AutoCAD 2013

with the **Array Creation** context tab of the ribbon and turns on multifunctional grips. To specify different array options other than the defaults, you can either use the **Array Creation** context tab of the ribbon, pick a grip to edit in grip mode, or select one of the following command options:

- **ASsociative** Specify whether to create an array of associated objects, or individual objects
- **Base Point** Specify a new base point
- **COUnt** Specify the number of rows and columns
- **Spacing** Change spacing between rows and columns
- **COLumns** Change the number and spacing of columns
- **Rows** Change the number and spacing of rows
- **Levels** 3D setting that allows you to change the number of levels in the *Z*-axis
- **eXit** Accept all settings and end the command

> **TIP**
>
> If you want to create an old-style array that has no associativity between array objects, set the **ASsociative** option to **No** when creating the array.

EXERCISE 8-2 Creating a Rectangular Array

1. Start a new drawing using the **acad.dwt** drawing template.
2. Draw the geometry shown in Figure 8-8.
3. Select the **Rectangular Array** tool from the **Modify** panel on the **Home** tab of the ribbon.
4. Select the circle and press **<Enter>**.
5. Select the **COUnt** option.
6. Specify 3 columns and 3 rows.

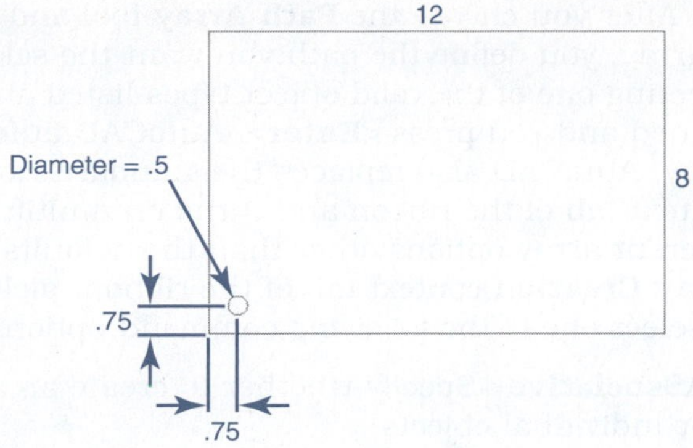

Figure 8-8
A rectangle and circle

Figure 8-9
A rectangular array

7. Select the **Spacing** option.
8. Type **5.25<Enter>** to specify the distance between columns.
9. Type **3.25<Enter>** to specify the distance between rows.
10. Press **<Enter>** again to exit the **Rectangular Array** tool.
11. Hold down the **<Ctrl>** key and select the circle at the center of the part.
12. Select the **Erase** tool, or press the **<Del>** key and erase the circle.
13. Save your drawing as ***CH8_EXERCISE2.*** Your drawing should look like Figure 8-9.

PATH ARRAY	
Ribbon & Panel:	Home | Modify Path Array
Modify Toolbar:	
Menu:	Modify | Array | Path Array
Command Line:	ARRAYPATH
Command Alias:	None

Creating a Path Array

The **Path Array** tool allows you to copy objects evenly along a path that can be defined using a line, polyline, spline, arc, circle, or ellipse. You have the option of either specifying the distance between each object or letting AutoCAD figure it out based on the total distance and number of copies, as shown in Figure 8-10.

Figure 8-10
Path array of objects

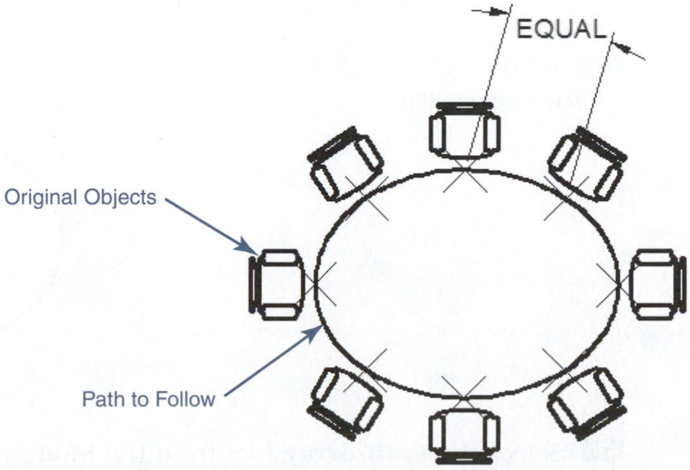

By default, path array objects are associative so that they will automatically update if the associated path curve changes. For instance, if you choose to divide the path into equal segments, the spacing between the objects automatically adjusts if the length of the path changes.

NEW to AutoCAD 2013

After you choose the **Path Array** tool and select the object(s) you want to array, you define the path you want the selected object(s) to follow by selecting one of the valid object types listed above. Once the path is defined and you press **<Enter>**, AutoCAD automatically creates a default array. AutoCAD also replaces the standard ribbon with the **Array Creation** context tab of the ribbon and turns on multifunctional grips. To specify different array options other than the defaults, you can either use the **Array Creation** context tab of the ribbon, pick a grip to edit in grip mode, or select one of the following command options:

- **ASsociative** Specify whether to create an array of associated objects, or individual objects
- **Method** Specify whether to divide the path into equal segments or measure the distance between arrayed objects
- **Base Point** Specify a new base point
- **Tangent direction** Specify how the arrayed items are aligned relative to the starting direction
- **Items** Change the total number of items
- **Rows** Change the number and spacing of rows
- **Levels** 3D setting that allows you to change the number of levels in the *Z*-axis
- **Align Items** Specify whether to align each item with the path direction or not
- **Z Direction** 3D setting that controls whether items follow their original Z direction
- **eXit** Accept all settings and end the command

EXERCISE 8-3 Creating a Path Array

1. Start a new drawing using the **acad.dwt** drawing template.
2. Draw the circle and ellipse shown in Figure 8-11.

Figure 8-11
A circle and an ellipse

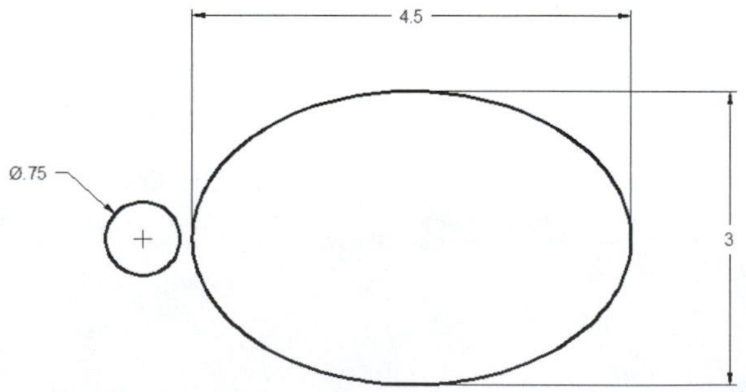

3. Select the **Path Array** tool from the **Modify** panel on the **Home** tab of the ribbon.
4. Select the circle and press **<Enter>**.
5. Select the ellipse when prompted to select a path curve.
6. Select the **Method** option.

7 Select the **Divide** option.

8 Select the **Items** option.

9 Type **8<Enter>** to specify the number of items (copies).

10 Press **<Enter>** again to exit the **Path Array** command. Your drawing should look like Figure 8-12.

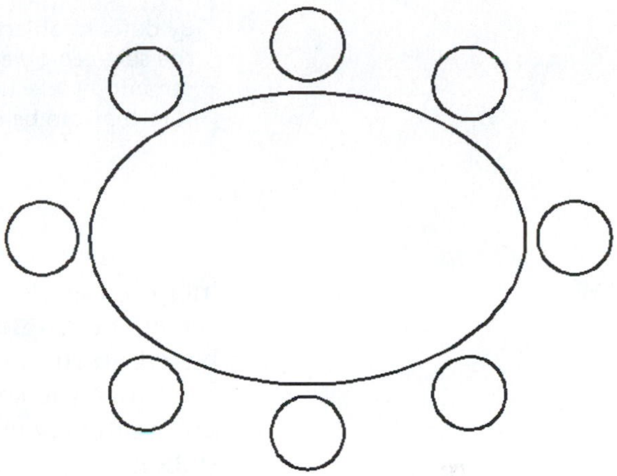

Figure 8-12
A path array

POLAR ARRAY	
Ribbon & Panel:	Home | Modify Polar Array
Modify Toolbar:	
Menu:	Modify | Array | Polar Array
Command Line:	ARRAYPOLAR
Command Alias:	None

11 Select the ellipse so grips are displayed.

12 Select one of the perimeter grips on the ellipse, and resize it by stretching the point in or out. Notice how the array objects are automatically updated based on the size of the ellipse.

13 Save your drawing as ***CH8_EXERCISE3.***

Creating a Polar Array

The **Polar Array** tool allows you to create a circular pattern of objects arranged around a center point by specifying either the number of copies to make and the angle to fill (0°–360°), or the included angle between each object as shown in Figure 8-13.

Figure 8-13
Polar array of objects

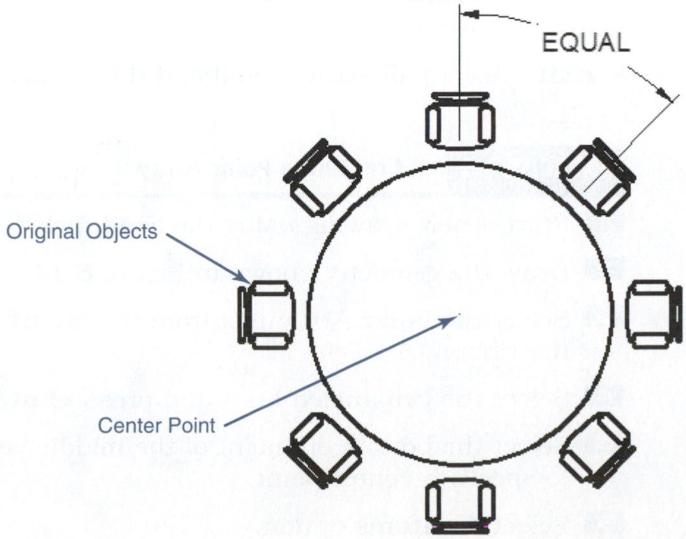

First you choose the **Polar Array** tool and select the object(s) you want to array. Then you define the center point about which to rotate the objects while they are copied by either picking a point in your drawing or inputting a coordinate value via the keyboard.

> **NOTE**
> By default, objects are aligned using a base point located at the middle, or centroid, of the selected objects as they are copied. The **Base point** option allows you to change the default by selecting a point in another location. The **Axis of rotation** option is a 3D feature that can be ignored while working in 2D.

If you enter the total number of copies, AutoCAD will calculate the included angle between objects based on the current angle to fill. If you select the **Angle between** option, AutoCAD will calculate the angle to fill based on the included angle and the total number of items specified.

Once the center point is defined and you press **<Enter>**, AutoCAD automatically creates a default array. AutoCAD also replaces the standard ribbon with the **Array Creation** context tab of the ribbon and turns on multifunctional grips. To specify different array options other than the defaults, you can either use the **Array Creation** context tab of the ribbon, pick a grip to edit in grip mode, or select one of the following command options:

NEW to AutoCAD 2013

- **ASsociative** Specify whether to create an array of associated objects, or individual objects
- **Base Point** Specify a new base point
- **Items** Change the total number of items
- **Angle Between** Change the angle between items
- **Fill Angle** Change the angle between the first and the last item in the array
- **ROWs** Change the number and spacing of rows
- **Levels** 3D setting that allows you to change the number of levels in the *Z*-axis
- **ROTate items** Specify whether items are rotated while they are arrayed or not
- **eXit** Accept all settings and end the command

EXERCISE 8-4 Creating a Polar Array

1. Start a new drawing using the **acad.dwt** drawing template.
2. Draw the geometry shown in Figure 8-14.
3. Select the **Polar Array** tool from the **Modify** panel on the **Home** tab of the ribbon.
4. Select the two angled lines and press **<Enter>**.
5. Select the bottom endpoint of the middle vertical line when prompted to specify a center point.
6. Select the **Items** option.

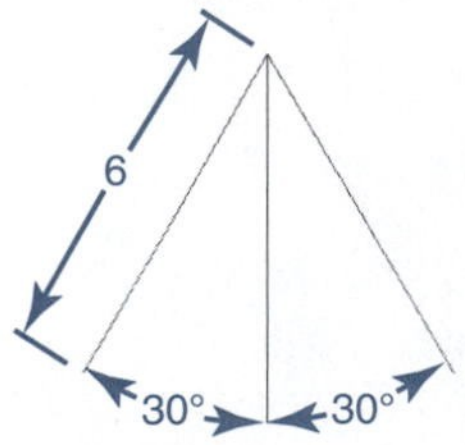

Figure 8-14
The starting geometry

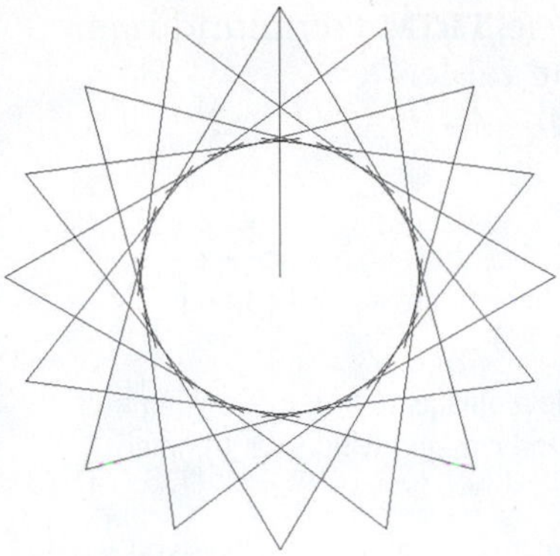

Figure 8-15
A polar array

7 Type **8<Enter>** to specify the number of items (copies).

8 Press **<Enter>** again to exit the **Polar Array** tool.

9 Select the array you just created. The **Array** context tab of the ribbon is displayed at the top of the drawing window.

10 Change the **Items** value from **8** to **16** on the top of the **Items** panel on the left side of the **Array** context tab of the ribbon. The total number of array objects will update.

11 Press the **<Esc>** key to deselect the array so it is no longer highlighted.

12 Save your drawing as ***CH8_EXERCISE4.*** Your drawing should look like Figure 8-15.

Trimming and Extending Objects

Trimming and extending is the process of lengthening or shortening objects using AutoCAD objects as the boundaries. When you trim or extend, you use existing AutoCAD objects as the boundary edges, and AutoCAD either lengthens or shortens your objects to touch those edges.

The **TRIM** and **EXTEND** commands are located on a small flyout menu on the **Modify** panel, as shown in Figure 8-16.

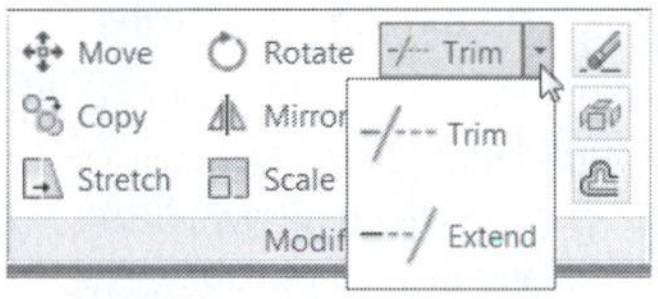

Figure 8-16
The **Trim/Extend** flyout menu

TIP

When using the flyout menu to select either the **Trim** or **Extend** tool, the last tool used becomes the default, top-level tool so that you do not need to display the flyout menu the next time you use the same command.

TRIM	
Ribbon & Panel:	Home | Modify
Modify Toolbar:	
Menu:	Modify | Trim
Command Line:	TRIM
Command Alias:	TR

Trimming Objects

Objects are trimmed using the **TRIM** command. When you start the **TRIM** command, AutoCAD prompts you to select your cutting edges. These cutting edges determine the stopping boundaries of the trimmed objects. Select the cutting edges using AutoCAD's standard selection methods. Once you've selected the cutting edges, press **<Enter>** and AutoCAD will prompt you to select the object to trim. As you pick each object, AutoCAD will trim the object back to the cutting edge. The portion of the object you select is the part that is deleted. In order for an object to be trimmed, it must cross one of the cutting edges. If AutoCAD cannot detect an intersection between the cutting edges and the object to be trimmed, it displays a message: *Object does not intersect an edge.*

Selecting Cutting Edges. In some cases, the cutting edges and the objects to be trimmed may be the same objects. AutoCAD does not distinguish between the cutting edges and the objects to be trimmed. You can select a cutting edge as an object to be trimmed.

TIP

AutoCAD will allow you to select all the drawing objects as cutting edges. To do this, simply press **<Enter>** when prompted to select the cutting edges. When you do this, AutoCAD will use all the objects in the drawing as cutting edges and simply trim an object to the closest intersecting edge.

Trim Options. After you select the cutting edges, the **TRIM** command has a number of options. They are listed in the following table.

Fence	This option allows you to select multiple objects to trim by drawing a fence line. Anything that touches the fence line will be trimmed back to the nearest cutting edge.
Crossing	Like the **Fence** option, this allows you to select multiple objects to trim by drawing a crossing window. Anything that touches the edge of the crossing window is trimmed to its nearest cutting edge.
Project	This option is for objects located in different three-dimensional planes. It allows you to trim objects that appear to intersect even though they are in different 3D planes.
Edge	The **Edge** option allows you to trim objects based on an implied intersection with a cutting edge. When this option is selected, you can set the edge mode to **Extend** or **No extend.** In **No extend** mode, an object must actually intersect with a cutting edge in order to be trimmed. With **Extend** mode, an object will be trimmed as if the cutting edge extended out to infinity (see Figure 8-17). **No extend** mode is the default setting.
Erase	The **Erase** option allows you to erase objects instead of trimming them. You may find that once you start trimming an object, you simply want to trim it all away. The **Erase** option allows you to do that within the **TRIM** command instead of exiting the command and starting the **ERASE** command.
Undo	**Undo** will undo the last trim action. If you selected a single object to trim, the **Undo** option will undo that trim. If you used either the **Fence** or **Crossing** option to select multiple objects, AutoCAD will undo all the trims done with that selection.

Figure 8-17
Extend mode settings

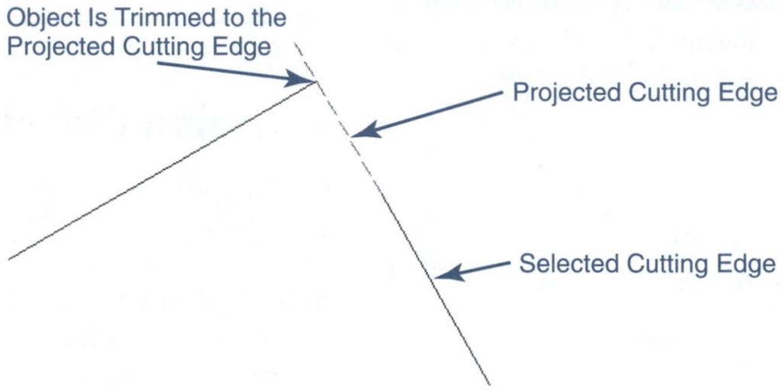

Some closed objects such as circles or ellipses require that the object intersect a cutting edge in at least two places. This is because these objects have no endpoints and must therefore be trimmed between two edges. If you attempt to trim one of these objects with only one cutting edge, AutoCAD will display the message: *Object must intersect twice.* Some objects cannot be trimmed, such as text and blocks.

EXERCISE 8-5 **Trimming Objects**

1. Start a new drawing using the **acad.dwt** drawing template.
2. Draw a circle with a radius of 5.
3. Draw three lines that are 6 units long, starting at the center of the circle at an angle of 80°, 90°, and 100°, respectively, as shown in Figure 8-18.

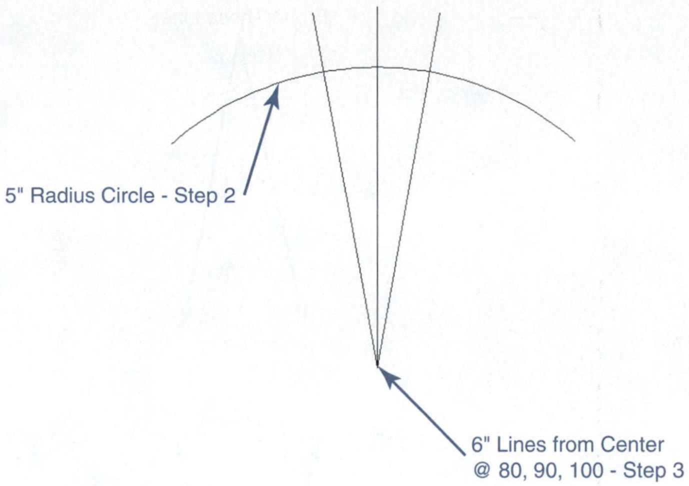

Figure 8-18
5″ Radius circle with 6″ lines from center point

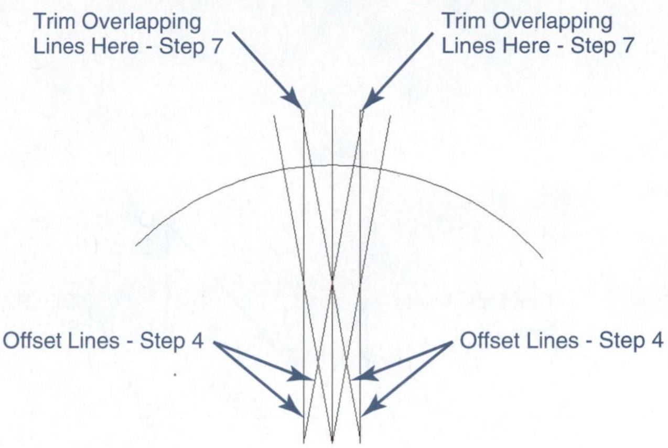

Figure 8-19
Offsetting and trimming lines

4. Use the **OFFSET** command and offset each line **.5** unit, as shown in Figure 8-19.
5. Start the **TRIM** command. AutoCAD prompts you to *Select objects or <select all>:*.
6. Press **<Enter>** to select all the objects as cutting edges. AutoCAD prompts you: *Select object to trim or shift-select to extend or* ↓.
7. Pick the points shown in Figure 8-19 to trim the objects so that all overlapping lines at the corners are cleaned up. AutoCAD continues to prompt you: *Select object to trim or shift-select to extend or* ↓.
8. Select the **eRase** option. AutoCAD prompts you to *Select objects to erase:*. Select the three vertical lines, the 80° line, and the 100° line that start at the circle center point as shown in Figure 8-19. Press **<Enter>** to erase the selected objects. Your drawing should look like Figure 8-20.
9. AutoCAD again prompts you to *Select object to trim or shift-select to extend or* ↓. Press **<Enter>** or **<Esc>** to exit the **TRIM** command.

Figure 8-20
Drawing after objects trimmed and erased

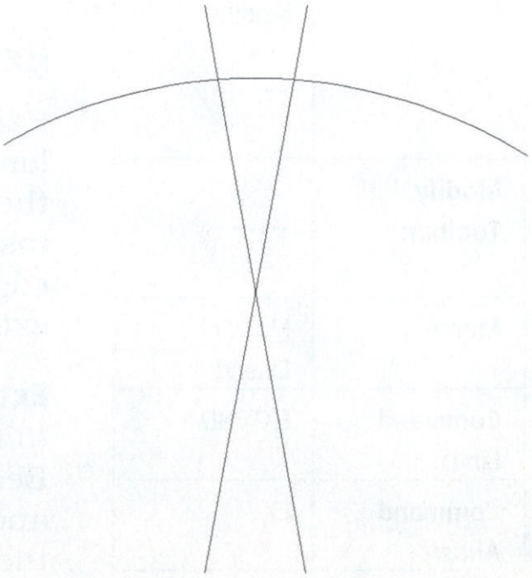

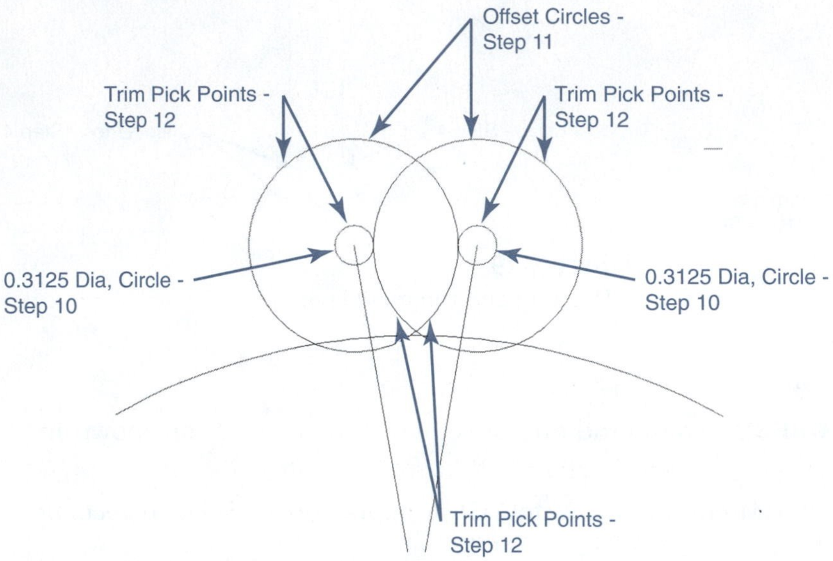

Figure 8-21
Offsetting and trimming the circles

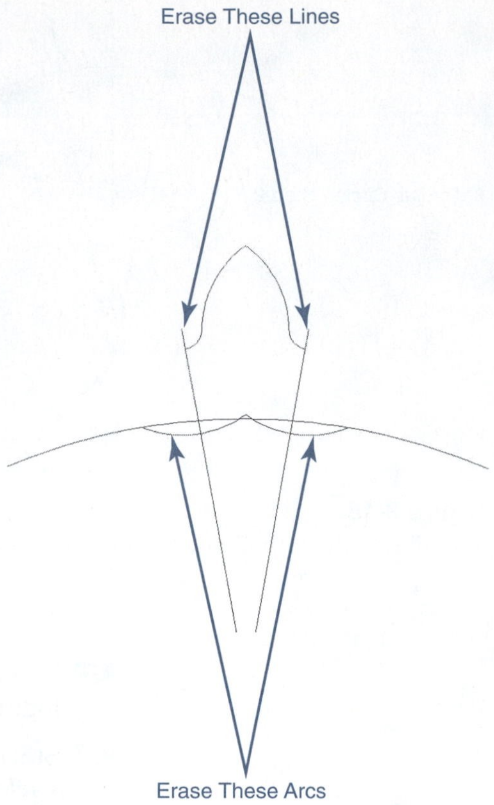

Figure 8-22
Erasing the remaining objects

10 Draw two circles with a diameter of 0.3125 by snapping to the endpoints of the angled lines as shown in Figure 8-21.

11 Start the **OFFSET** command and offset each of these circles **0.6875** toward the outside of each circle, as shown in Figure 8-21.

12 Zoom in on the two circles at the top of the drawing. Start the **TRIM** command and press **<Enter>** to select all the objects as cutting edges, and then select the six trim points shown in Figure 8-21.

13 Choose the **eRase** option and select the objects shown in Figure 8-22 to erase. Press **<Enter>** to erase the objects. Press **<Enter>** again to end the **TRIM** command.

14 Save your drawing as ***CH8_EXERCISE5.***

EXTEND	
Ribbon & Panel:	Home| Modify 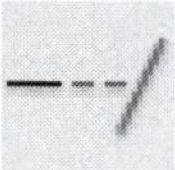
Modify Toolbar:	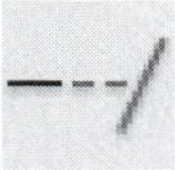
Menu:	Modify | Extend
Command Line:	EXTEND
Command Alias:	EX

Extending Objects

Extending objects is similar to trimming them; the objects simply get longer instead of shorter. The **EXTEND** command has options similar to the **TRIM** command except you are prompted to select boundary edges instead of cutting edges. Whether they are called boundary or cutting edges, the concept is the same; the edge determines where the object is extended.

Extend Options. The options for the **EXTEND** command are identical to those for the **TRIM** command with the exception of the **eRase** option. Because extending is an additive process (you are adding length to objects) and the **eRase** option is a subtractive process, this option is omitted from the **EXTEND** command.

Using the <Shift> Key to Switch Between Trim and Extend. Because the **EXTEND** and **TRIM** commands are so similar, AutoCAD provides an easy way to switch back and forth between them. You may have noticed that in the **TRIM** command, after you select the cutting edges, AutoCAD prompts you to *Select object to trim or shift-select to extend or*↓. By holding down the **<Shift>** key while selecting the objects to extend, you can use the **TRIM** command to trim objects. The same is true for the **EXTEND** command. After you select the boundary edges, AutoCAD prompts you to *Select object to extend or shift-select to trim or*↓. While the **<Shift>** key is depressed, the **EXTEND** command will trim objects, using the boundary edges as the cutting edges.

EXERCISE 8-6 **Extending Objects**

1. Continue from Exercise 8-5.
2. Start the **OFFSET** command and offset the large circle **3.5** units toward the center of the circle. Repeat the **OFFSET** command and offset the new circle **.5** unit toward the center.
3. Draw two lines, each 8 units long, from the center of the circle at an angle of 85° and 95°, respectively.
4. Draw two more short lines, each 3 units long, from the center of the circle at an angle of 60° and 120°, respectively.
5. Start the **OFFSET** command, set the **eRase** option to **Yes** so the original lines are erased, and set the offset distance to **.25**. Offset the two short lines. Offset the left-hand line to the right, and the right-hand line to the left. Your drawing should look like Figure 8-23.

Figure 8-23
Angled lines with offsets

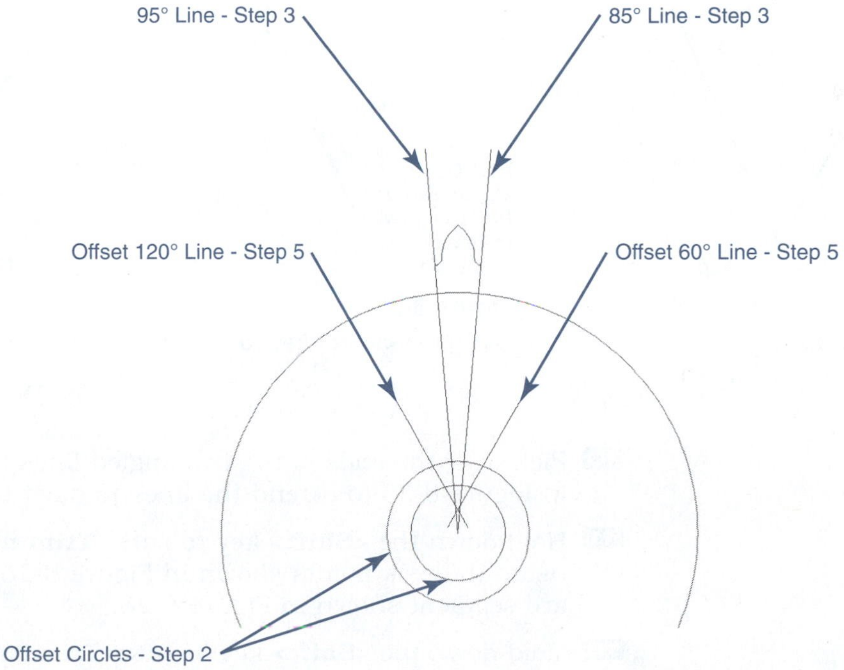

6. Zoom in on the top of the drawing and start the **EXTEND** command. AutoCAD prompts you to *Select objects or <select all>:*. Select the two 8″ long angled lines and press **<Enter>** to make them the boundary edges.

7 AutoCAD prompts you to *Select object to extend or shift-select to trim or* ↓. Pick the two small arc segments nearest to the angled lines selected in step 6 as shown in Figure 8-24 so that the arcs extend out to meet the boundary edges.

8 Select the **ERASE** command, and delete the two 8″ long angled lines used as boundary edges in step 7.

9 Zoom out to see the entire drawing and select the **EXTEND** command again. Select the two outer circles and the two angled lines as boundary edges as shown in Figure 8-25 and press **<Enter>**.

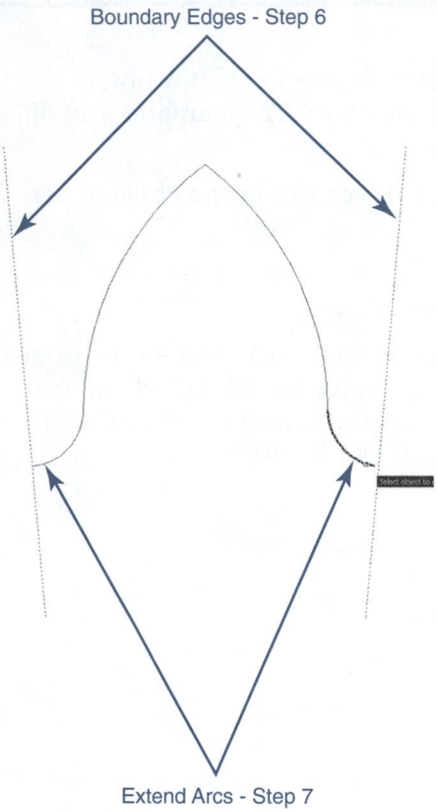

Figure 8-24
Extending the arcs

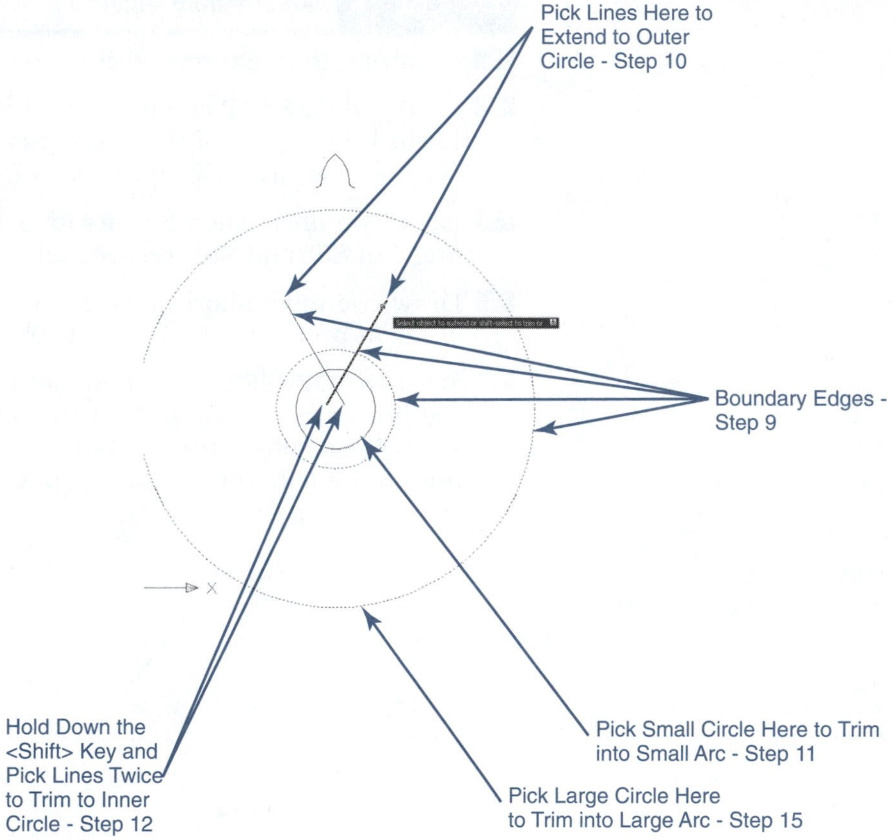

Figure 8-25
Using the **<Shift>** key to switch between **EXTEND** and **TRIM**

10 Pick near the ends of the two angled lines using the pick points shown in Figure 8-25 to extend the lines to meet the outer circle.

11 Hold down the **<Shift>** key to enter **Trim** mode. Select the inner circle using the pick points shown in Figure 8-25, and trim it into the small arc segment shown in Figure 8-26.

12 Hold down the **<Shift>** key to enter **Trim** mode. Select the two angled lines using the pick points shown in Figure 8-25, and trim them to meet the small arc segment created in step 11 as shown in Figure 8-26.

13 Press **<Enter>** to end the **EXTEND** command.

14 Start the **TRIM** command, and select the two angled lines that were extended in step 10 as cutting edges and press **<Enter>**.

15 Pick the outer circle near the bottom as shown in Figure 8-25 to trim it into the large arc segment shown at the top in Figure 8-26.

16 Press <Enter> to end the **TRIM** command.

17 Save your drawing. Your drawing should look like Figure 8-26.

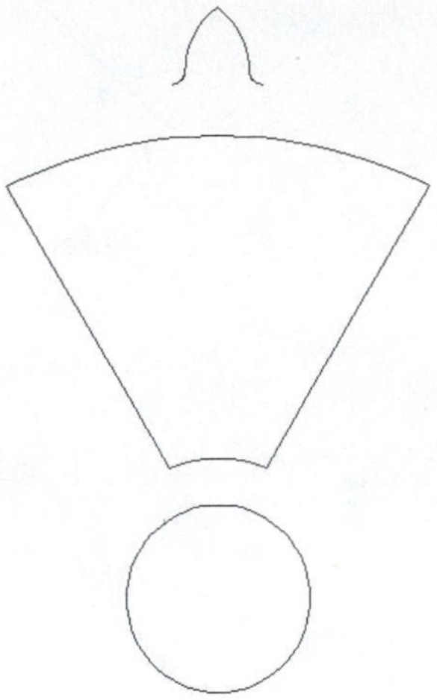

Figure 8-26
Drawing after trimming/extending lines and arcs

FILLET	
Ribbon & Panel:	Home | Modify
Modify Toolbar:	
Menu:	Modify | Fillet
Command Line:	FILLET
Command Alias:	F

Creating Fillets and Chamfers

Fillets and chamfers are rounded and angled corners, respectively. To create a fillet or a chamfer using basic drawing and editing commands would be a difficult task. The process of rounding a simple right-angle corner would involve shortening each leg by the radius of the round, and then creating an arc segment between the two shortened ends. Using **TRIM** and **EXTEND** might make the process easier, but you would still need to draw an arc or circle and use a combination of **TRIM** and **EXTEND** to clean up the intersections. Creating a chamfered or angled corner might prove easier but would still involve drawing new objects and cleaning up their intersections. The **FILLET** and **CHAMFER** commands allow you to easily add rounds and angled lines at the corner of two intersecting objects.

The **FILLET** and **CHAMFER** commands are located on a small flyout menu on the **Modify** panel, as shown in Figure 8-27.

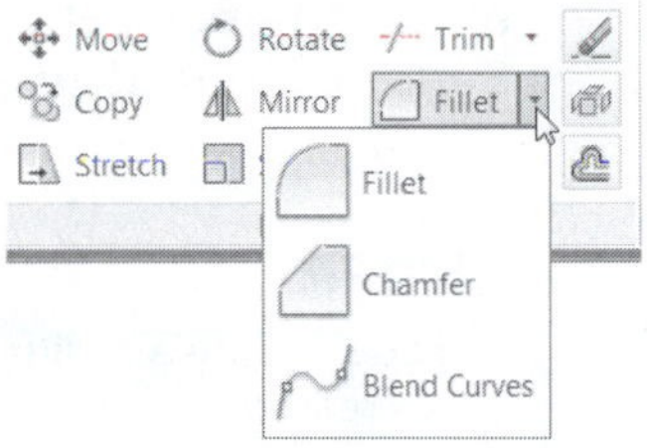

Figure 8-27
The **Fillet/Chamfer** flyout menu

NOTE

The **Blend Curves** tool located at the bottom of the flyout menu shown in Figure 8-27 allows you to create a curved spline in the gap between two selected lines or curves. Please consult the AutoCAD Help for more information about spline objects.

TIP

When using the flyout menu to select either the **Fillet** or **Chamfer** tool, the last tool used becomes the default, top-level tool so that you do not need to display the flyout menu the next time you use the same command.

Creating Fillets

To create a fillet, you specify a fillet radius and select two objects. AutoCAD will place an arc between the two objects and trim and extend the objects as needed. The points where you select the objects determines where the arc is placed. AutoCAD will place the fillet so that the selected portions will remain (see Figure 8-28).

After selecting the first object, AutoCAD provides a preview of the fillet when you pass your cursor over the second object. You can use the **Radius** option to change the radius value anytime before you select the second object.

Figure 8-28
Fillet selections

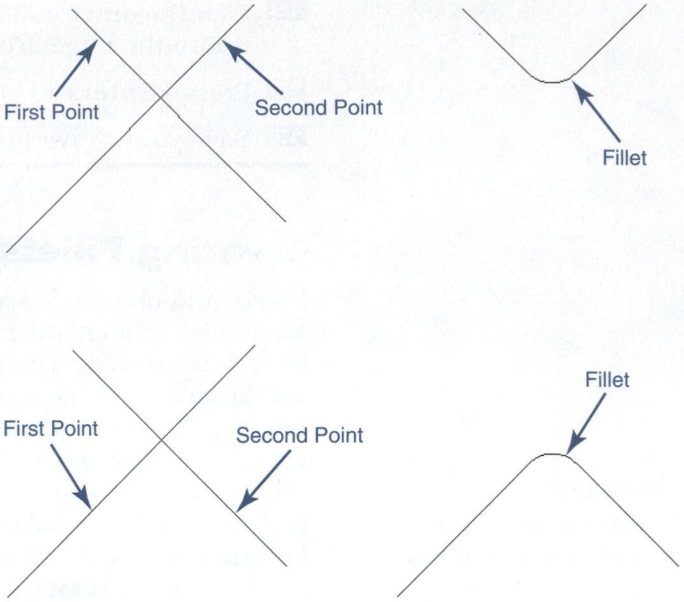

Radius Option. When you start the **FILLET** command, the current radius setting is listed at the command line. The **Radius** option allows you to set the fillet radius. The fillet radius is stored in the **FILLETRAD** system variable and once set, AutoCAD will retain the setting until you change it. Setting the **Radius** option to **0** will result in AutoCAD squaring off a corner.

NOTE

If you specify a radius that is too large or too small or try to create an arc that cannot be created, AutoCAD will return an error message. Blocks and text cannot be filleted.

TIP

It is possible to create a square corner even if the fillet radius is currently set to a value greater than 0 by holding down the <**Shift**> key when selecting the second line.

You can create a fillet between open objects (lines, arcs, and elliptical arcs) as well as closed objects (circles and ellipses). When you select a closed object, AutoCAD doesn't actually trim the closed object but simply draws a tangent fillet arc (see Figure 8-29).

Figure 8-29
Some closed objects with fillets applied

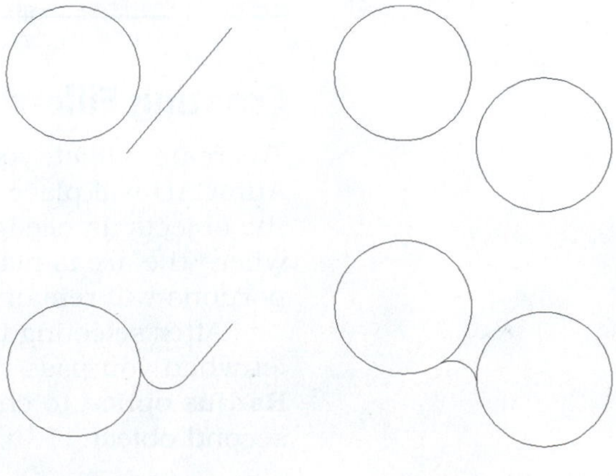

Multiple Mode. The **Multiple** option puts you into **Multiple** mode and allows you to create multiple fillets in a single command. In **Multiple** mode, the **FILLET** command simply repeats until you press **<Enter>** or **<Esc>**. The **Undo** option allows you to undo the last fillet while in **Multiple** mode.

Trim Mode. The **Trim** option allows you to turn **Trim** mode on and off. With **Trim** mode turned on, objects are trimmed or extended to the fillet arc. With **Trim** mode turned off, AutoCAD creates the fillet arc but leaves the source objects unchanged. Like the **Radius** option, the **Trim** setting is retained after the **FILLET** command is complete until you change it.

The Polyline Option. The **Polyline** option allows you to add a fillet radius to all the intersections in a polyline object.

FOR MORE DETAILS

See Chapter 9 for more on creating and editing polylines.

Capping Two Parallel Lines Using the Fillet Tool

If you fillet two parallel lines, AutoCAD will create a rounded end cap between the two lines. In this case, AutoCAD will ignore the **Radius** setting and create a 180° arc using half the distance between the lines as the radius. If the lines are different lengths, the first object you select will determine the start point of the arc. The other line will be trimmed or extended to match the first selected object (see Figure 8-30).

Figure 8-30
Capping two parallel lines

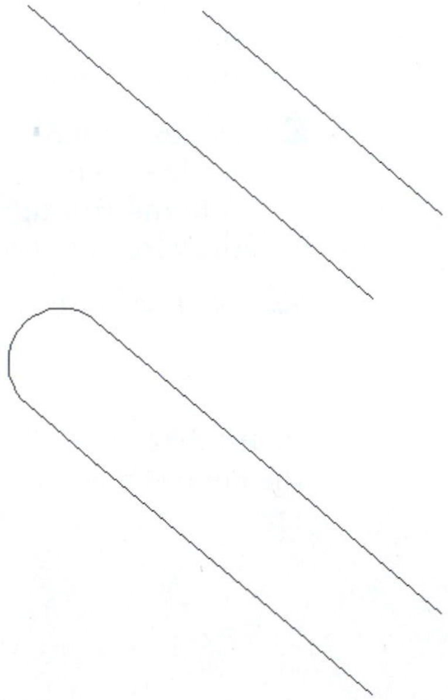

EXERCISE 8-7 **Creating a Fillet**

1. Continue from Exercise 8-6.
2. Start the **FILLET** command. AutoCAD prompts you to *Select first object or* ↓.
3. Choose the **Multiple** option to turn on **Multiple** mode.

4. Choose the **Radius** option and type **.5<Enter>** to set the fillet radius.
5. Pick the lines and arc shown in Figure 8-31 to round the outer corners. AutoCAD will round the corners and continue prompting you to select objects.

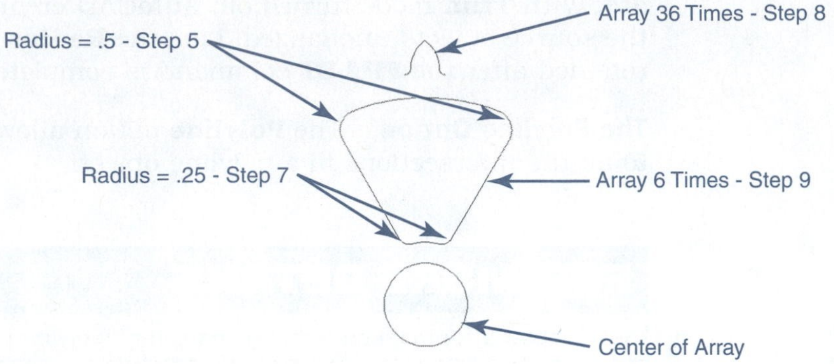

Figure 8-31
Creating fillets

6. Choose the **Radius** option and type **.25<Enter>** to set the fillet radius.
7. Pick the lines and arc shown in Figure 8-31 to round the inner corners. When you've finished rounding the four corners, press **<Esc>** to end the **FILLET** command.
8. Start the **ARRAY** command and create a polar array of the pointed geometry at the top of the drawing. Center the array about the center of the circle, and create 36 items through 360°, rotating the objects as they are copied.
9. Repeat the **ARRAY** command and create a polar array of the rounded wedge. Center the array about the center of the circle, and create 6 items through 360°, rotating the objects as they are copied. Your drawing should look like Figure 8-32.
10. Save your drawing.

Figure 8-32
The finished drawing

CHAMFER	
Ribbon & Panel:	Home | Modify
Modify Toolbar:	
Menu:	Modify | Chamfer
Command Line:	CHAMFER
Command Alias:	CHA

Creating Chamfers

The **CHAMFER** command is used to create angled corners between two intersecting objects. Drawing a chamfer between intersecting objects is similar to drawing a fillet. However, instead of a fillet radius, you need to provide two distances from the intersection along each object, or a distance and an angle for the chamfer (see Figure 8-33).

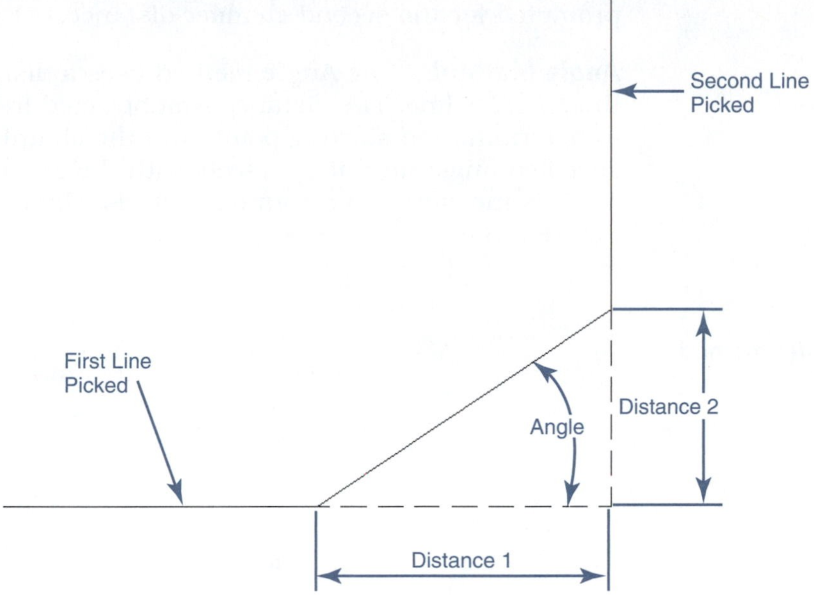

Figure 8-33
Creating a chamfer

The **CHAMFER** command has two methods for creating chamfers: distance and angle. The **mEthod** option allows you to select which chamfer method to use.

After selecting the first object, AutoCAD provides a preview of the chamfer when you pass your cursor over the second object. You can use the **Distance** or **Angle** option to change the chamfer size or angle anytime before you select the second object.

> **TIP**
>
> It is possible to create a square corner using the **CHAMFER** command similar to the **FILLET** command by setting both distances to **0**, the default setting. In fact, you can hold down the **<Shift>** key when selecting the second object and override the distance if it is greater than 0, just like with the **FILLET** command.

Distance Method. With the **Distance** method, you specify the distance from the intersection along each line. From the intersection, AutoCAD subtracts the first chamfer distance from the first object and the second chamfer distance from the second object and then draws a line between these two points. The **Distance** option allows you to set the chamfer distances. The first distance is applied to the first object you select, and the second distance is applied to the second object.

NOTE

Whereas the **FILLET** command allows you to create arcs between both straight and curved objects, the **CHAMFER** command works only on straight, linear objects (lines, straight polyline segments, Xlines, and rays).

If the chamfer distances are equal, a 45° chamfer is drawn. When you set the first distance, AutoCAD sets the default value of the second distance to the first distance. To accept this default, just press **<Enter>** when prompted for the second chamfer distance.

Angle Method. The **Angle** method uses a distance and angle to determine the chamfer line. The distance is subtracted from the first object selected to determine the starting point, and the chamfer line is drawn at the specified angle until it intersects with the second object. By default, the angle is measured in a counterclockwise direction from the first object (see Figure 8-34).

Figure 8-34
The **Angle** chamfer method

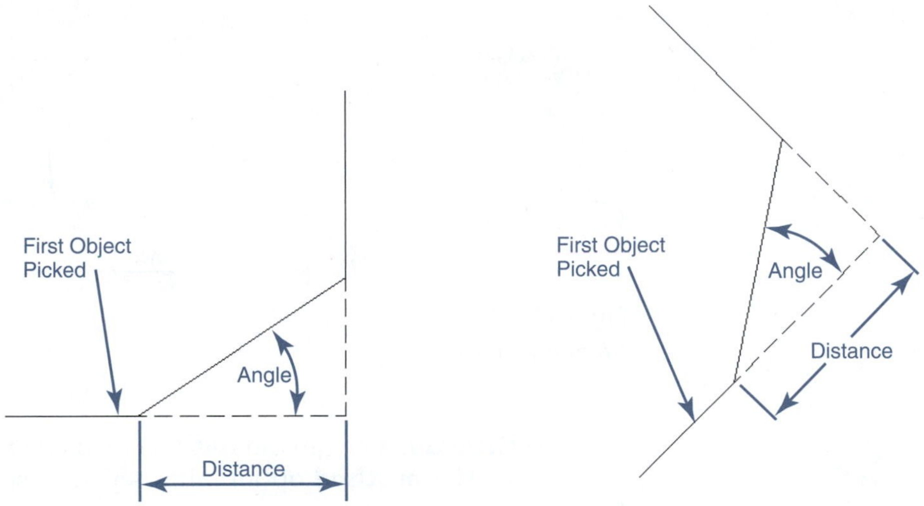

The Polyline Option. The **Undo, Polyline, Trim**, and **Multiple** options work the same way as on the **FILLET** command. When chamfering a polyline with the **Polyline** option, the first and second objects are determined by the order in which the polyline was drawn. When in doubt, or if you are not getting the results you're expecting, your best bet may be not to use the **Polyline** option and just chamfer the polyline segments individually.

FOR MORE DETAILS

See Chapter 9 for more on creating and editing polylines.

EXERCISE 8-8 **Creating a Chamfer**

1. Continue from Exercise 8-2. If you've closed the drawing, open drawing ***CH8_EXERCISE2.***
2. Start the **CHAMFER** command and select the **Angle** option. AutoCAD prompts you to *Specify chamfer length on the first line:*. Type **.75<Enter>** to set the length.

3. AutoCAD prompts you to *Specify chamfer angle from the first line:*. Type **60<Enter>** to set the chamfer angle.
4. AutoCAD prompts you to *Select first line or* ↓. Pick the objects shown in Figure 8-35. AutoCAD chamfers the corner. Note that the .75 distance is taken off of the first line you selected.
5. Because this chamfer comes very close to the hole, type **U<Enter>** to undo the last chamfer.
6. Restart the **CHAMFER** command and select the **Distance** option. Set the first distance to **.5**. AutoCAD sets the default value of the second distance to match the first. Press **<Enter>** to accept the default. AutoCAD prompts you to *Select first line or* ↓.
7. Select the **Multiple** option and chamfer the four corners of the part. Your drawing should look like Figure 8-36.
8. Save your drawing.

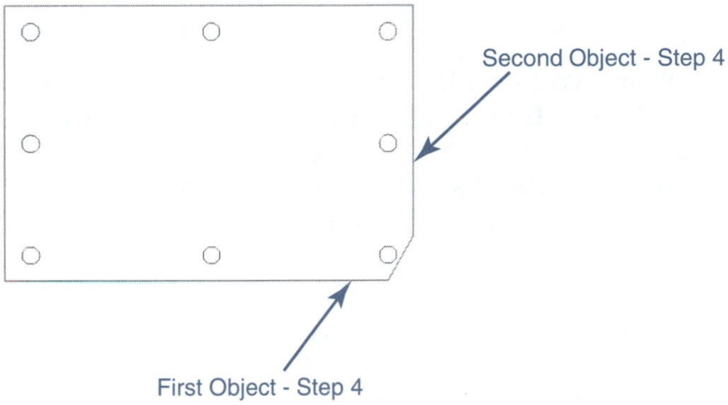

Figure 8-35
Using the **Angle** method

Figure 8-36
Creating chamfers

Breaking an Object

BREAK	
Ribbon & Panel:	Home | Modify
Modify Toolbar:	
Menu:	Modify | Break
Command Line:	BREAK
Command Alias:	BR

The **BREAK** command allows you to remove portions of an object or to break a single object into two separate objects. The **BREAK** command requires you to select an object and then select two points on the object. The portion of the object between the two points is then removed. The **BREAK** command is located on the expanded **Modify** panel shown in Figure 8-1.

Creating a Gap in an Object

When you start the **BREAK** command, AutoCAD prompts you to select an object. By default, when you select the object, the point you pick on the object becomes the first break point, and AutoCAD will prompt you to select the second break point. If the point you select is not the point you want, you can use the **First** option to repick the first break point on the selected object.

Once you specify the first break point, AutoCAD prompts you for the second break point and breaks the object between the two points.

Breaking an Object Exactly at a Point

There may be times when you want to break the object in two without creating a physical gap. To break an object without creating an opening, simply use the @ symbol to specify the second point. When you use the @ symbol, AutoCAD will place the second point at the same coordinate as the first point. The end result is the object is broken in two without creating a gap.

Breaking Circles, Xlines, and Rays

Depending on the type of object you select, the **BREAK** command will create new objects. When you break a line, AutoCAD simply creates two lines. However, when you break a circle, Xline, or ray, AutoCAD will create different types of objects.

> **NOTE**
> Circles and ellipses must be broken in two distinct locations. Using @ when specifying the second break point is not allowed.

Circle. When you break a circle, AutoCAD converts the circle to an arc. The order in which you select the points will determine which portion of the circle is kept. AutoCAD will remove the portion of the circle starting at the first in a counterclockwise direction. Figure 8-37 shows the results of selecting different points along a circle.

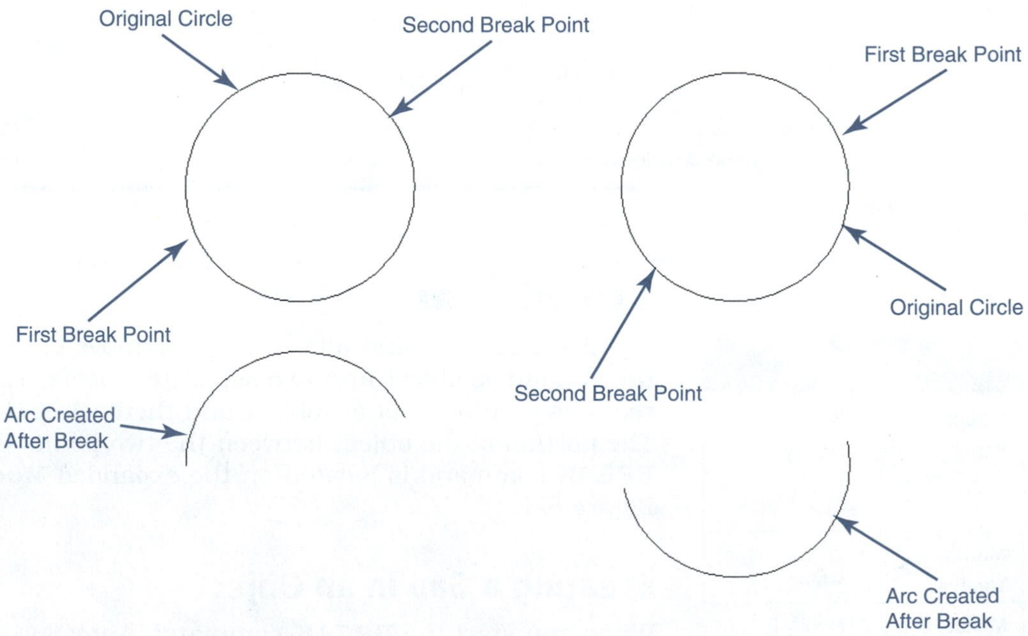

Figure 8-37
Breaking a circle

Xlines and Rays. When you break an Xline, AutoCAD will create two rays with the starting points of the rays located at the first and second break points. Breaking a ray will result in a line and a ray.

Selecting the Second Points

When you select the second break point, there are a couple of things to keep in mind. First, if you select the second point somewhere away from the object, AutoCAD will project a break point along a line perpendicular to the object passing through the selected point. Second, if the second break point lies past the end of the object, AutoCAD will simply remove everything between the first point and the end of the object. Figure 8-38 shows examples of these.

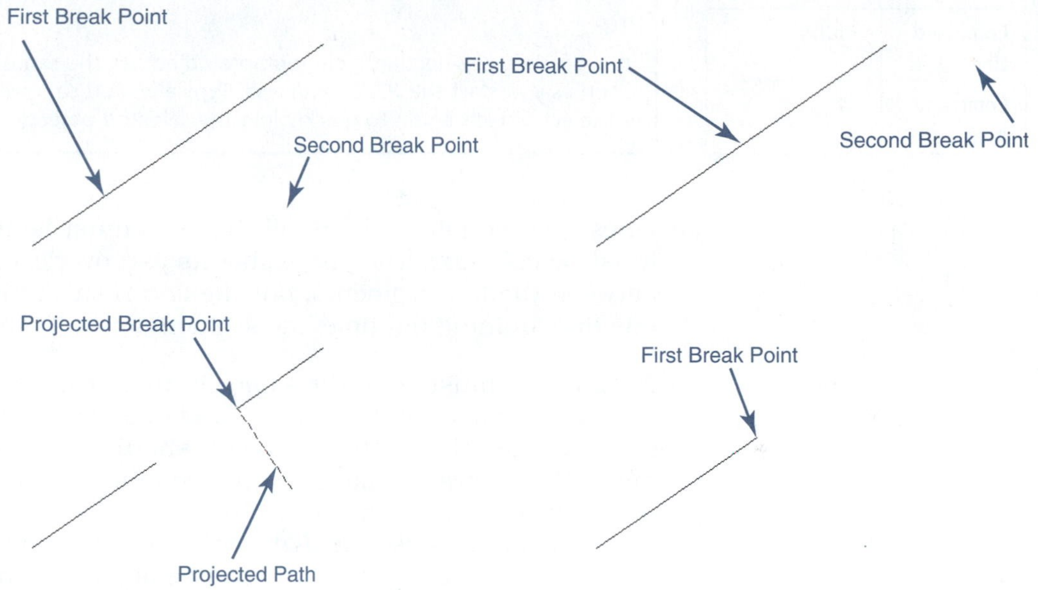

Figure 8-38
Breaking objects

EXERCISE 8-9	Breaking Objects

1. Continue from Exercise 8-1. If you've closed the drawing, open drawing ***CH8_EXERCISE1.***
2. Start the **BREAK** command and select the circle near the bottom quadrant, between the two vertical lines. AutoCAD prompts you to *Specify second break point or* ↓. Pick anywhere near the circle to break the circle into an arc segment. Don't worry about the final length of the arc segment.
3. Restart the **BREAK** command. AutoCAD prompts you to *Select object:*. Hold down the **<Shift>** key and right-click to bring up the **Object Snap** menu. Choose **Midpoint** and select the centerline. This selects the line and places the first break point at the midpoint of the line. AutoCAD prompts you to *Specify second break point or* ↓.
4. Type **@<Enter>** to break the line at the midpoint. Drag your cursor over a portion of the centerline. AutoCAD will highlight half of the centerline.
5. Start the **FILLET** command and set the radius to **25**. Turn on **Multiple** mode and add fillets between the arc and line segments. Your drawing should look like Figure 8-39.
6. Save your drawing.

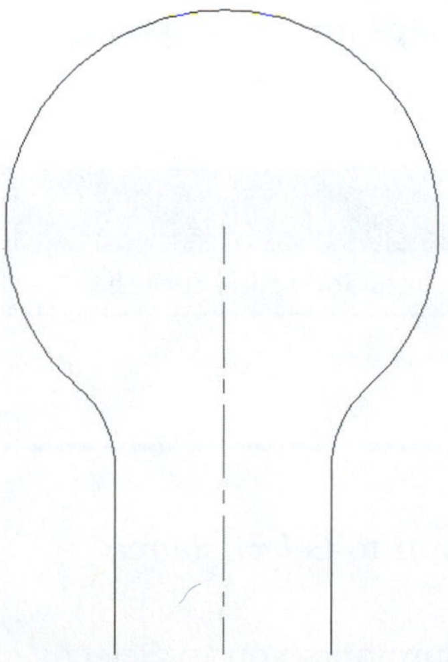

Figure 8-39
Breaking objects

JOIN	
Ribbon & Panel:	Home | Modify
Modify Toolbar:	
Menu:	Modify | Join
Command Line:	JOIN
Command Alias:	J

Joining Multiple Objects

The **JOIN** command does the opposite of the **BREAK** command by closing the gap between objects and converting multiple objects into a single object. The **JOIN** command starts by asking you to select a source object and then prompts you to select the objects to join to the source. The objects you want to join must match the source object and have different rules depending on the type of source object you choose. The **JOIN** command is located on the expanded **Modify** panel shown in Figure 8-1.

> **TIP**
>
> It is possible to select and join multiple objects at the same time by selecting them as soon as you start the **JOIN** command. Typically, you can press **<Enter>** when prompted to select objects again to quickly join the selected objects in one step.

Lines. When joining lines, all the lines must lie in the same plane and must be collinear. The line segments can overlap or there can be gaps between the line segments, but the end result must be a single, continuous line. Joining multiple line segments results in a single line object.

Arcs. Arcs must lie in the same circular path, meaning they must have the same center point and radius. Like lines, the arcs can overlap or have gaps between them. The end result should be a single continuous arc segment. If the arcs overlap to form a complete circle, AutoCAD will ask you if you want to convert the arcs into a circle.

You can also use the **JOIN** command to convert an arc into a circle. When you select an arc as the source object, AutoCAD provides a **cLose** option. Choosing this option will close the arc and convert it to a circle.

Elliptical Arcs. Elliptical arcs behave the same as circular arcs. The elliptical arcs must lie on the same elliptical path. Gaps and overlaps are allowed, and the **cLose** option is available to convert an elliptical arc into an ellipse.

Polylines. The objects must be lines, arcs, or open polylines. Gaps and overlapping are not allowed when joining polylines. All the segments must lie end-to-end in the same plane.

Spline Curves. Spline curves behave similarly to polylines. All the objects must be spline curves that lie in the same plane. Gaps and overlapping are not allowed; all the segments must lie end-to-end.

> **FOR MORE DETAILS**
>
> See Chapter 9 for more on creating polylines and editing polylines and spline curves.

EXERCISE 8-10 Joining Objects

1. Continue from Exercise 8-9.
2. Start the **JOIN** command. AutoCAD prompts you to *Select source object or multiple objects to join at once:*.
3. Select one portion of the centerline. AutoCAD prompts you to *Select lines to join to source:*. Pick the other half of the centerline and press **<Enter>**. AutoCAD joins the two lines together.

4 Drag your cursor over the centerline to verify it is a single object.

5 Save your drawing.

LENGTHEN	
Ribbon & Panel:	Home | Modify 
Toolbar:	None
Menu:	Modify | Lengthen
Command Line:	LENGTHEN
Command Alias:	LEN

Lengthening an Object

The **LENGTHEN** command allows you to lengthen or shorten drawing objects as well as get information about the length of selected objects. When you start the **LENGTHEN** command, you are asked to select an object and are given four options: **DElta**, **Percent**, **Total**, and **DYnamic**. When you select an object, the **LENGTHEN** command displays the length of the object at the command line. If the object is an arc, the included angle of the arc is also displayed. The **LENGTHEN** command is located on the expanded **Modify** panel shown in Figure 8-1.

> **TIP**
>
> The length information for most objects is displayed in the **Properties** palette. However, for some objects such as spline curves, ellipses, and elliptical arcs, the **Properties** palette doesn't display total length information. The **LENGTHEN** command is an easy way to display this information for these complex curves.

The LENGTHEN Command Options

When lengthening an object, AutoCAD must know how much length to add to or subtract from the object. Once it knows what changes to make, the **LENGTHEN** command will prompt you to select an object to lengthen. You can either select a single object or use the **Fence** selection method to drag a fence crossing line across the items you wish to lengthen. AutoCAD will keep prompting you to select objects, allowing you to lengthen multiple objects within a single command.

The **LENGTHEN** command options provide four different methods for altering the length of an object.

DElta Option. The **DElta** option allows you to specify a discrete length to add to or subtract from the object. When you choose the **DElta** option, AutoCAD asks you to enter a delta length and then prompts you to select an object. The length you specify is then added to the object at the end closest to where you select. A positive delta value will increase the length, and a negative delta will shorten the object.

The **DElta** option also includes an **Angle** option. This allows you to modify the included angle of an arc. By default, positive angles add length in the counterclockwise direction, and negative angles subtract length in the clockwise direction.

Percent Option. The **Percent** option allows you to scale the line by a percentage value. A percent value of 200 will make an object twice as long. A value of 50 will make it half as long. A value of 110 will add 10% to the length of the object. A value of 100 will leave the object unchanged.

Total Option. The **Total** option allows you to set the total length of an object. If the value is greater than the current length of the object, the object will increase in length. If the value is smaller, the object will shorten.

DYnamic Option. The **DYnamic** option allows you to specify the length of an object by dragging it around the screen. When you use this option, you are asked to select an object. AutoCAD will then ask you to specify a new endpoint for the object. You can then drag your cursor around the drawing and dynamically see the length change. To set the length, simply pick a point.

Invalid Objects

When using the **LENGTHEN** command, it's possible to ask AutoCAD to create objects that can't exist or to lengthen objects that cannot be lengthened. For example, although AutoCAD will tell you the length of a closed object like a circle or an ellipse, you can't add length to a closed object. Another example would be to try to increase the included angle of a line, or to increase the included angle of an arc beyond 360°. In cases such as these, AutoCAD will simply display a message stating that it cannot lengthen the object, and it will ignore the selected object.

EXERCISE 8-11 Lengthening an Object

1. Continue from Exercise 8-10.
2. Start the **LENGTHEN** command and select the centerline. AutoCAD replies *Current length: 100.0000* and prompts you to *Select an object or* ↓.
3. Select the **DElta** option and enter a value of **25**. AutoCAD prompts you to *Select an object to change or* ↓. Select the bottom portion of each of the vertical lines. Each line is lengthened by 25 units. AutoCAD continues to prompt you to *Select an object to change or* ↓.
4. Type **F<Enter>** to specify a **Fence** selection. Draw a fence through the three bottom lines (see Figure 8-40), and press **<Enter>** to end the selection process. AutoCAD will lengthen the three lines by another 25 units.
5. Save your drawing. Your drawing should resemble Figure 8-41.

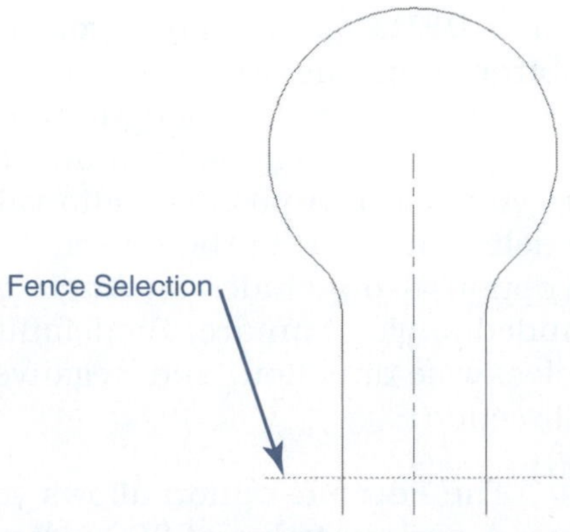

Figure 8-40
Using a **Fence** selection

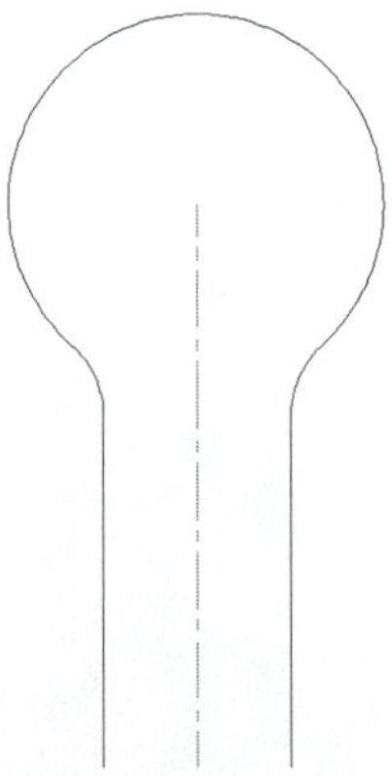

Figure 8-41
The lengthened street

Chapter Summary

The advanced editing techniques explained in this chapter, together with the basic editing techniques introduced in the last chapter, form the majority of the modification tools and methods used to update AutoCAD 2D drawings. Creating parallel copies of objects using the **OFFSET** command can be used for many different discipline-specific tasks, be it creating walls in an architectural floor plan or roadways on a civil engineering drawing. The same can be said about rectangular and polar arrays. Using a rectangular array, you can create a column grid layout on an architectural plan in practically one step. Without using a polar array, creating gears and sprockets would be very time-consuming affair. Path arrays allow you to evenly distribute copies of one or more objects along a linear or curved path a specific number of times or distance.

Trim and **Extend** tools allow you to quickly "clean up" line work that might have been created as a side effect of some of the other modify and draw tools. **Fillet** and **Chamfer** tools can be used to quickly create rounded and beveled corners, as well as to clean up corner work that overlaps or has gaps.

When there is nothing to trim or extend to, the **BREAK** command allows you to break objects at a single point or create gaps the length you specify. On the flip side, the **JOIN** command will glue objects back together when they are broken. If an object is not exactly the correct length, the **LENGTHEN** command provides a number of different ways to fix it. Contrary to its name, it can be used to shorten objects, too!

Chapter Test Questions

Multiple Choice

Circle the correct answer.

1. Copying an object parallel to an existing object is called:
   a. Filleting
   b. Chamfering
   c. Offsetting
   d. Extending

2. In a rectangular array, the row distance represents:
   a. The horizontal (X) spacing of the arrayed objects
   b. The vertical (Y) spacing of the arrayed objects
   c. The number of rows in the array
   d. None of the above

3. In the **TRIM** command, when selecting objects to trim, holding down the **<Shift>** key:
   a. Allows you to remove objects from the selection set
   b. Puts a 0 radius corner at the intersection of the two objects
   c. Allows you to select additional cutting edges
   d. Allows you to extend objects to the cutting edges

4. In the **FILLET** command, when selecting the objects to fillet, holding down the **<Shift>** key:
   a. Allows you to remove objects from the selection set
   b. Puts a 0 radius corner at the intersection of the two objects
   c. Allows you to select additional cutting edges
   d. Allows you to extend objects to the cutting edges
5. In the **TRIM** command, when asked to select cutting edges, pressing **<Enter>:**
   a. Ends the **TRIM** command
   b. Switches between **EXTEND** and **TRIM**
   c. Selects all the objects in the drawing as cutting edges
   d. None of the above
6. While creating a rectangular array, the array angle:
   a. Rotates the array
   b. Changes your rectangular array to a polar array
   c. Sets the polar array fill angle
   d. None of the above
7. When creating a polar array, entering a negative angle to fill:
   a. Will copy objects in a clockwise direction
   b. Will copy objects in a counterclockwise direction
   c. Is not allowed
   d. None of the above
8. The **BREAK** command:
   a. Will work on lines and arcs
   b. Will work on closed objects
   c. Can have the same first and second break point
   d. All of the above
9. To convert an arc to a circle:
   a. Use the **FILLET** command with a 0 radius
   b. Use the **EXTEND** command
   c. Use the **LENGTHEN** command
   d. Use the **JOIN** command
10. Breaking an Xline:
   a. Creates a line and a ray
   b. Creates two rays
   c. Converts the Xline to polyline
   d. Is not allowed

Matching

Write the number of the correct answer on the line.

a. **ARRAYPATH** command ______
b. Polar array ______
c. Fillet radius ______
d. Rectangular array ______

1. Items copied in a circular pattern
2. Moves objects a user-supplied distance and angle
3. Can convert an arc into a full circle
4. The radius of a rounded intersection

e. **JOIN** command ______

f. **BREAK** command ______

g. **LENGTHEN** command ______

h. **Extend** mode ______

i. **Erase** mode ______

j. **CHAMFER** command ______

5. Copies objects equidistantly along a path
6. Can convert a circle into an arc and turn a single object into multiple objects
7. A mode of the **OFFSET** command that deletes the source object after it is offset
8. Items copied in a rectangular pattern of rows and columns
9. A mode of the **TRIM** and **EXTEND** commands that allows you to trim or extend to implied intersections
10. Allows you to display and modify the length of objects

True or False

Circle the correct answer.

1. **True or False:** The **OFFSET** command cannot be used on closed objects.
2. **True or False:** Objects must actually touch each other for the **TRIM** command to work.
3. **True or False:** The **EXTEND** command can be used to trim objects.
4. **True or False:** A fillet radius can be drawn between two parallel objects.
5. **True or False:** The **JOIN** command requires that line segments must lie end-to-end with no gaps or overlaps.
6. **True or False:** The **LENGTHEN** command doesn't work with arcs.
7. **True or False:** Holding down the **<Shift>** key during the **CHAMFER** command allows it to draw fillet curves.
8. **True or False:** The **eRase** option of the **TRIM** and **EXTEND** commands will undo any changes made during the command.
9. **True or False:** The **BREAK** command requires two separate points when breaking a circle.
10. **True or False:** The **BREAK** command converts rays into Xlines.

Chapter Projects

G Project 8-1: *Classroom Plan, continued from Chapter 7* [BASIC]

1. Open drawing ***P7-1*** from Chapter 7.
2. Draw the remaining equipment and windows shown in Figure 8-42 using the appropriate layers. The windows are all 4′-6″ wide. **Do not** draw dimensions or text.

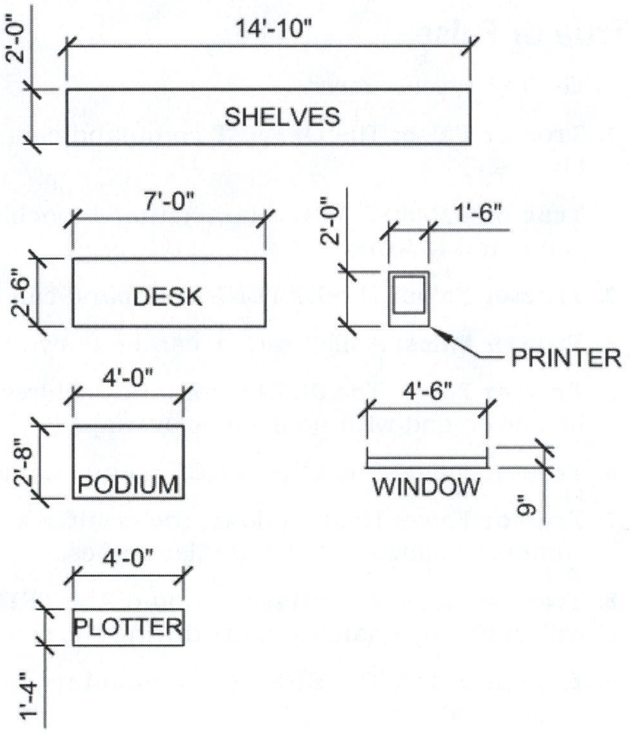

Figure 8-42

3. Locate the windows as shown in Figure 8-43. Trim the walls as necessary to allow for the window openings. Change the layout of the desks and chairs to reflect the updated plan.
4. Save your drawing as ***P8-1***.

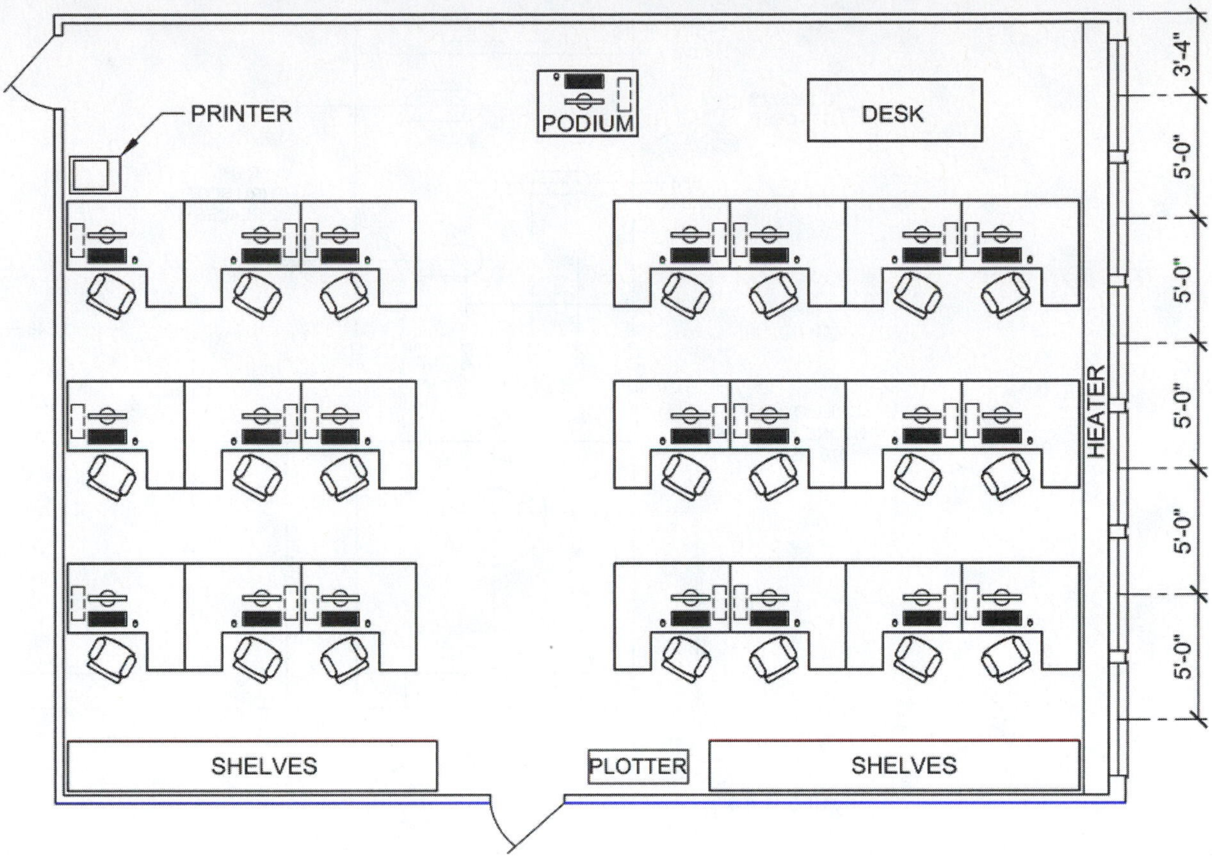

Figure 8-43

Project 8-2: *Optical Mount—English Units* [INTERMEDIATE]

1. Start a new drawing using the **acad.dwt** template.
2. Create the following layers:

Name	Color	Linetype	Lineweight	Description
Object	7	Continuous	0.60 mm	Object lines
Hidden	1	Hidden	0.30 mm	Hidden lines
Center	2	Center	0.30 mm	Centerlines
Hatch	4	Continuous	Default	Hatch patterns and fills
Notes	3	Continuous	0.30 mm	Text and notes
Dims	2	Continuous	Default	Dimensions

3. Create the three-view drawing as shown in Figure 8-44. *Hint:* Use the **FILLET** command to create the round ends of the slots.
4. Adjust the **LTSCALE** system so linetypes appear properly.
5. **Do not** include notes or dimensions.
6. Save your drawing as ***P8-2***.

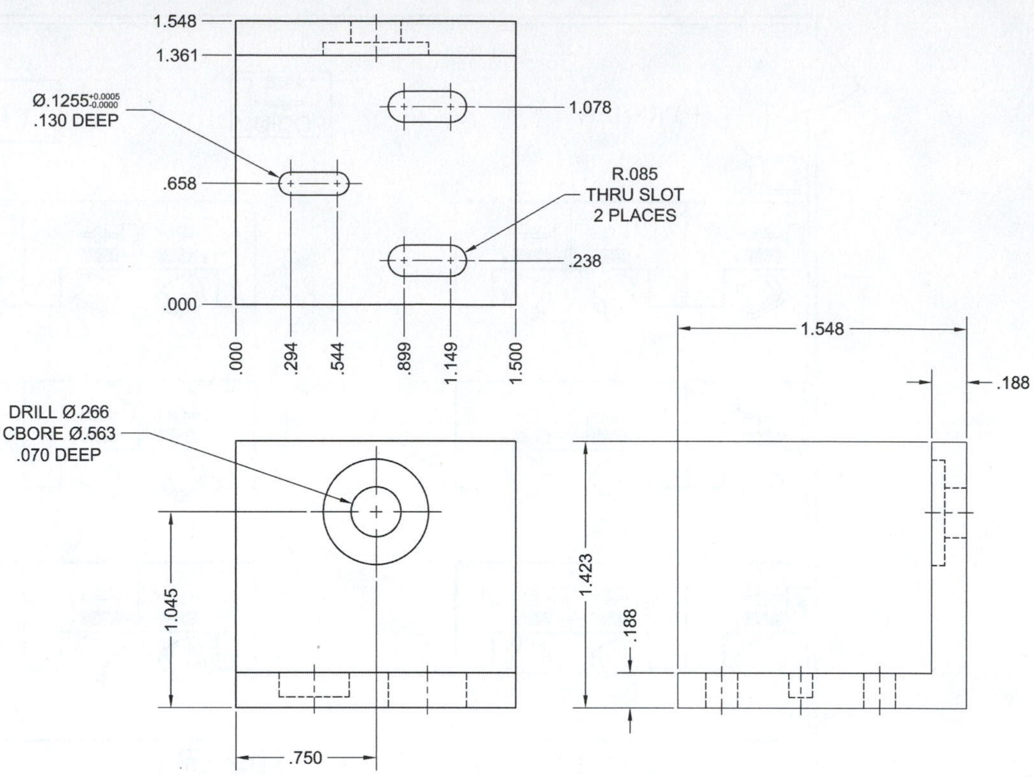

Figure 8-44

A Project 8-3: *Truss with Soffited Eave Detail* [ADVANCED]

1. Start a new drawing using the **acad.dwt** template.
2. Set linear units to **Architectural** with precision set to **1/16″**.
3. Set angular units to **Deg/Min/Sec** with precision set to **0d00′00″**.
4. Create the following layers:

Name	Color	Linetype	Lineweight	Description
A-Detl-Mbnd	1	Continuous	Default	Detail lines that represent material in the background
A-Detl-Mcut	3	Continuous	0.60 mm	Detail lines that represent material cut in section
A-Detl-P1	2	Continuous	0.30 mm	Secondary (light) lines
A-Detl-Batt	1	Batting	Default	Batt insulation
A-Detl-Pat	1	Continuous	Default	Hatch patterns and fills
A-Anno-Note	3	Continuous	0.30 mm	Note text
A-Anno-Title	3	Continuous	0.30 mm	Title text
A-Anno-Dims	1	Continuous	0.30 mm	Dimensions

5. Draw all line work that appears beyond the section cut as shown in Figure 8-45 on layer **A-Detl-Mbnd** (roof truss, break lines, vertical wall lines).

Figure 8-45

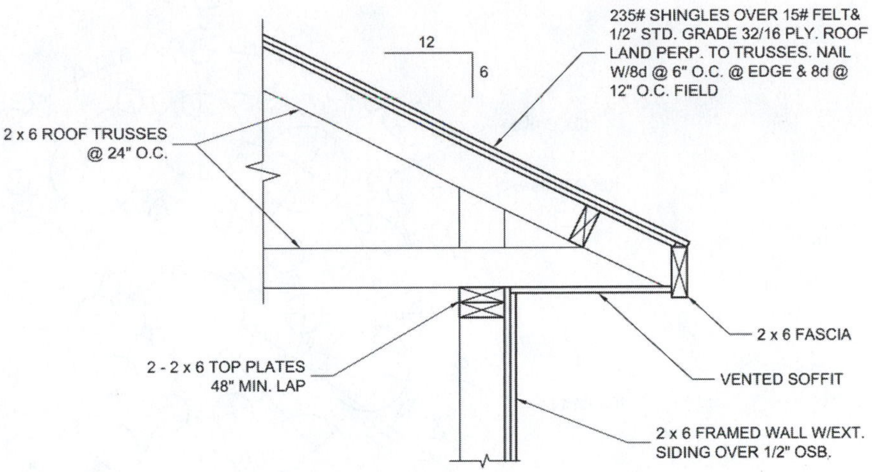

6. Draw all line work that is cut by the section as shown in Figure 8-45 on layer **A-Detl-Mcut** (lumber in section, plywood, O.S.B., siding).
7. Draw the X's that represent lumber in section as shown in Figure 8-45 on layer **A-Detl-P1**.
8. **Do not** include notes or dimensions.
9. Save the drawing as ***P8-3***.

M Project 8-4: *68-Tooth Rear Sprocket—Metric* [BASIC]

1. Start a new drawing using the **acadiso.dwt** template.
2. Create the following layers:

Name	Color	Linetype	Lineweight	Description
Object	7	Continuous	0.50 mm	Object lines
Hidden	1	Hidden	0.30 mm	Hidden lines
Center	2	Center	0.30 mm	Centerlines
Hatch	4	Continuous	Default	Hatch patterns and fills
Notes	3	Continuous	0.30 mm	Text and notes
Dims	2	Continuous	Default	Dimensions

3. Draw the sprocket as shown in Figure 8-46 using the appropriate layers. *Hint:* Draw one sprocket tooth as indicated in Detail A, and array it using the **ARRAY** command with the **Polar** option. You can use the same technique to create the holes.

Figure 8-46

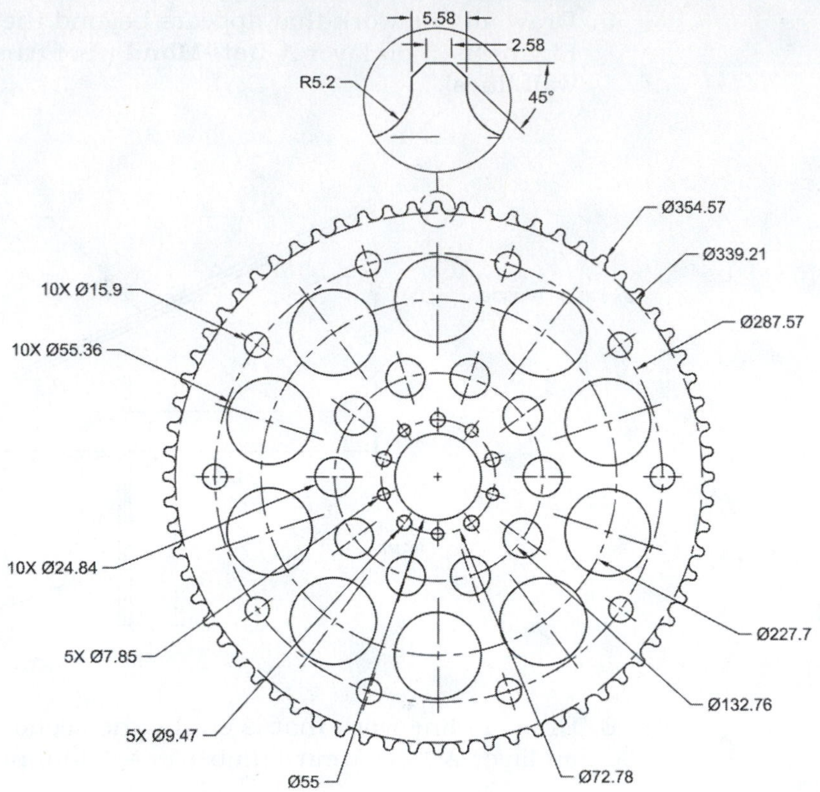

4. Adjust the **LTSCALE** system so linetypes appear properly.
5. **Do not** include notes or dimensions.
6. Save the drawing as ***P8-4***.

A Project 8-5: *Residential Architectural Plan, continued from Chapter 7* [ADVANCED]

1. Open drawing ***P7-5*** from Chapter 7.
2. Modify the floor plan as shown in Figure 8-47. Use the **TRIM, EXTEND**. and **FILLET** commands to clean up wall intersections and door/window openings. **Do not** draw dimensions or text.
3. Save your drawing as ***P8-5***.

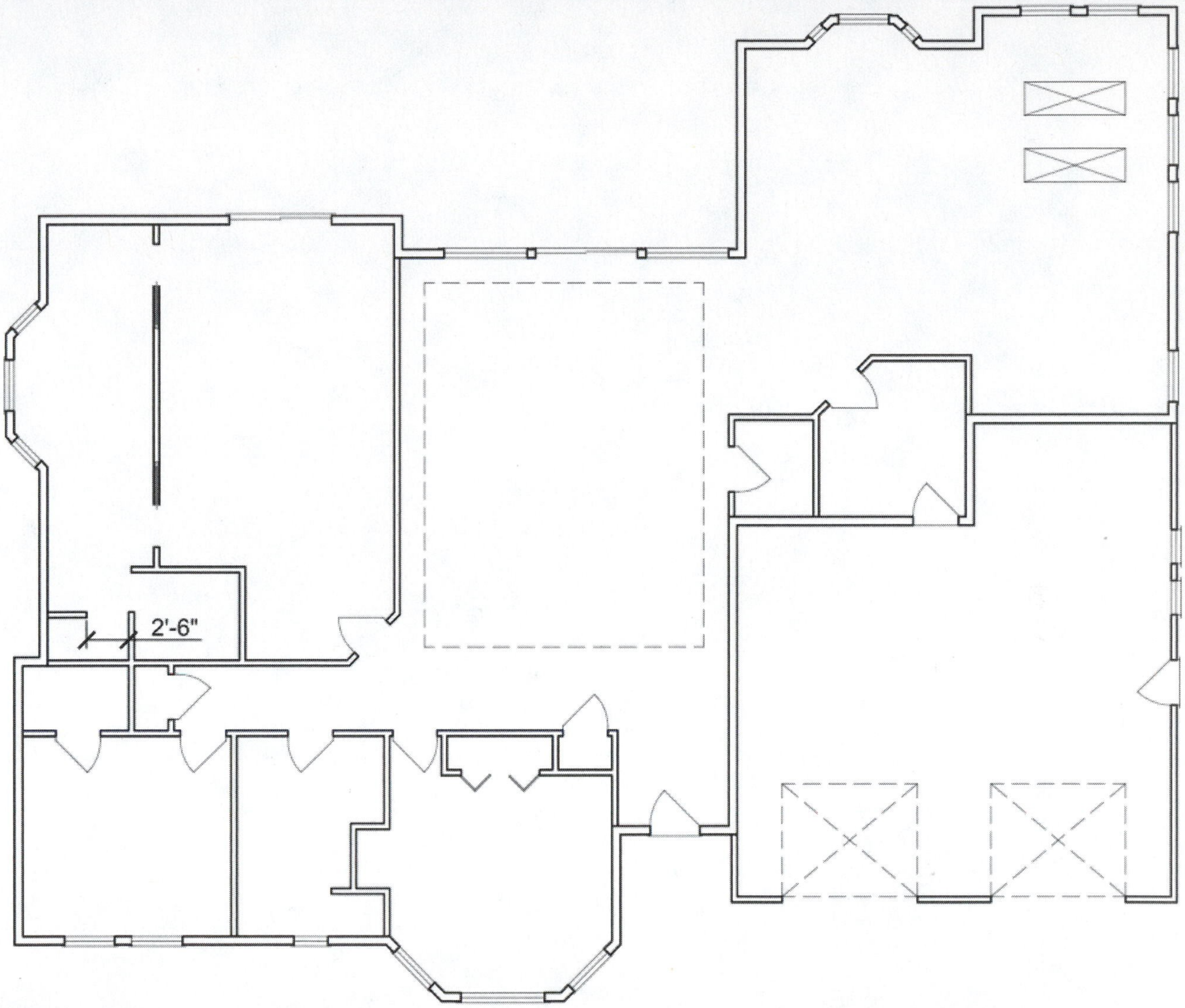

Figure 8-47

chapter nine

Drawing and Editing Complex Objects

CHAPTER OBJECTIVES

- Draw polylines with straight line segments
- Draw polyline arcs
- Create rectangles using two points
- Make multisided polygons
- Create solid and hollow donuts
- Draw revision clouds
- Edit polylines as a unit
- Explode complex objects

Introduction

AutoCAD provides a number of complex line objects that consist of multiple segments but are treated as a single line with multiple points:

- Polyline
- Rectangle
- Polygon
- Donut
- Revision cloud

Complex line objects serve many different purposes and needs. Polylines allow you to define a closed boundary that can be used to calculate an enclosed area. Polylines are also used extensively to create ***contour lines*** on civil engineering maps.

contour line: A line on a map that joins points of equal elevation.

In fact, AutoCAD uses polylines to create the rectangles, polygons, donuts, and revision clouds described in this chapter. This chapter explores the commands used to create and edit these different complex line objects. Also covered is the ability to break complex line objects down into their individual line and arc segments using the **EXPLODE** command.

Most of the commands, with the exception of the **Explode** command, are located on the **Draw** panel on the **Home** tab of the ribbon, as shown in Figure 9-1.

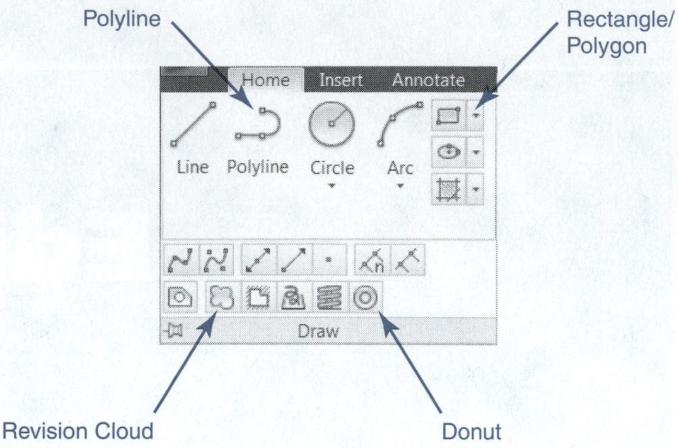

Figure 9-1
The expanded **Draw** panel with polyline commands

POLYLINE	
Ribbon & Panel:	Home | Draw
Draw Toolbar:	
Menu:	Draw | Polyline
Command Line:	PLINE
Command Alias:	PL

Drawing Polylines

A polyline is a complex line object made up of one or more connected line segments and/or arcs that are treated as a single line (see Figure 9-2).

Polylines are created using the **PLINE** command.

When you start the **PLINE** command, AutoCAD prompts you to *Specify start point:*. You can either type in a coordinate value or pick a point in your drawing similar to the **LINE** command. After you specify the first point, AutoCAD will continue to prompt you to *Specify next point or*↓ until you press **<Enter>** without specifying a point, as shown in Figure 9-3.

> **TIP**
> You can specify points when drawing a polyline using absolute, relative, or polar coordinate entry methods. It is also possible to use direct distance entry with either the **Ortho Mode** or **Polar Tracking** drawing tool.

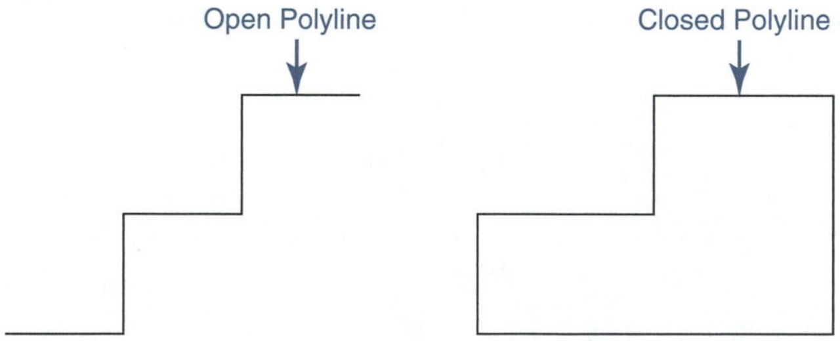

Figure 9-2
Examples of polylines

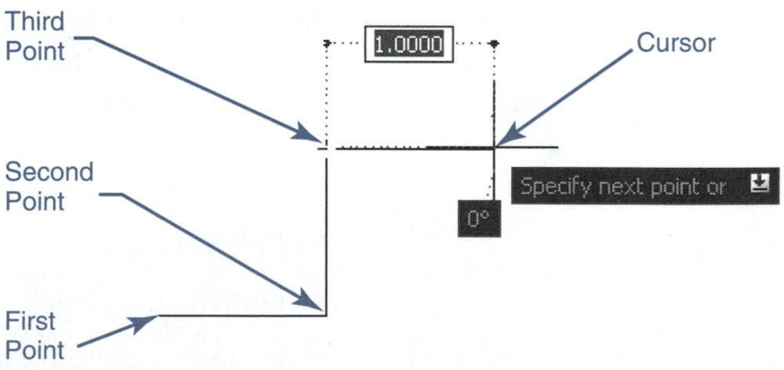

Figure 9-3
Drawing a polyline

You can create a closed polyline line using the **Close** option just as with the **LINE** command, except that the closed polyline creates a true closed polygon, unlike the **LINE** command, which creates individual line segments. The **Close** option will draw a line segment from the last point back to the start point. Figure 9-4 shows the result of selecting the **Close** option after drawing two line segments.

Figure 9-4
Drawing a closed polyline

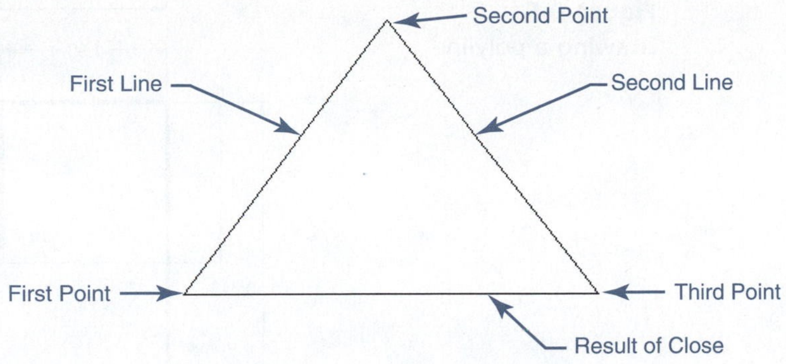

TIP

It is possible to get the area and perimeter of a closed polyline using the **LIST** command. To use the **LIST** command type **LIST** or **LI**, select the polyline, and press **<Enter>**. AutoCAD switches to the full text window and lists the area, perimeter, vertex point information, and a few other properties. You can also retrieve the same information using the **Properties** palette or the **MEASUREGEOM** command using the **Area** option.

The **PLINE** command also has a built-in **Undo** option that allows you to undo points as you draw. Using the **Undo** option repeatedly will undo all the polyline points back to the first point.

NOTE

By default, AutoCAD creates what's referred to as an optimized polyline that has the object name LWPOLYLINE. The *LW* stands for lightweight because the method in which polylines store vertex point information has been optimized. The old unoptimized polyline format still exists for legacy reasons and is referred to simply as a POLYLINE object.

TIP

You can control the type of polyline used via the **PLINETYPE** system variable. **PLINETYPE** controls both the creation of new polylines and the conversion of existing polylines in drawings from previous releases of AutoCAD. **PLINETYPE** has three settings.

0: Polylines in older drawings are not converted when opened; **PLINE** command creates old-format polylines.

1: Polylines in older drawings are not converted when opened; **PLINE** command creates optimized polylines.

2: Polylines in AutoCAD Release 14 or older drawings are converted when opened; **PLINE** creates optimized polylines.

The default setting is **2**.

EXERCISE 9-1 Drawing a Polyline

1. Start a new drawing using the **acad.dwt** drawing template.
2. Create the drawing shown in Figure 9-5 using the **PLINE** command. **Do not** draw dimensions.
3. The polyline should be closed using the **Close** option.
4. Save the drawing as ***CH9_EXERCISE1***.

Figure 9-5
Drawing a polyline

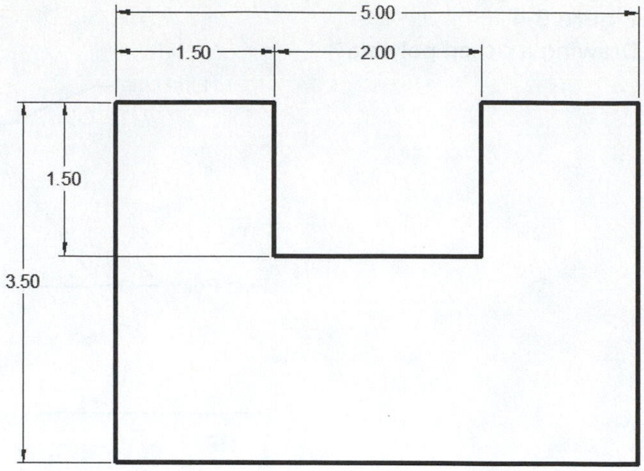

Drawing Polyline Arcs

It is possible to switch from drawing line segments to drawing arcs when creating a polyline using the **Arc** option. By default, specifying an arc endpoint creates an arc that is tangent to the last line or arc segment, as shown in Figure 9-6.

Figure 9-6
Drawing a tangent polyline arc

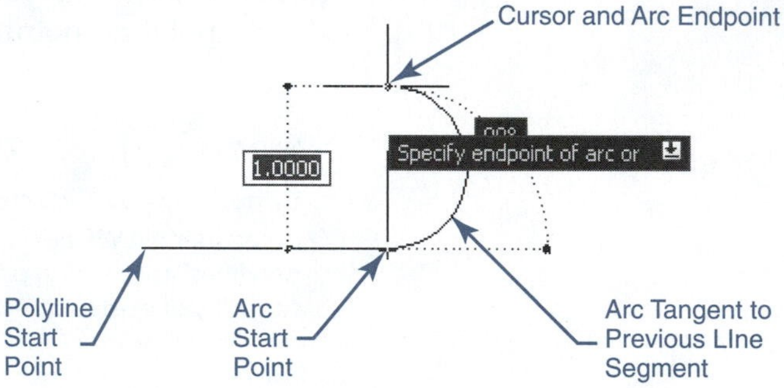

The direction of the arc is determined by where the arc endpoint is located relative to the current polyline point. If you continue to specify points in response to the *Specify endpoint of arc or*↓ prompt, AutoCAD will create multiple tangent arc segments, as shown in Figure 9-7.

Figure 9-7
Drawing multiple tangent polyline arcs

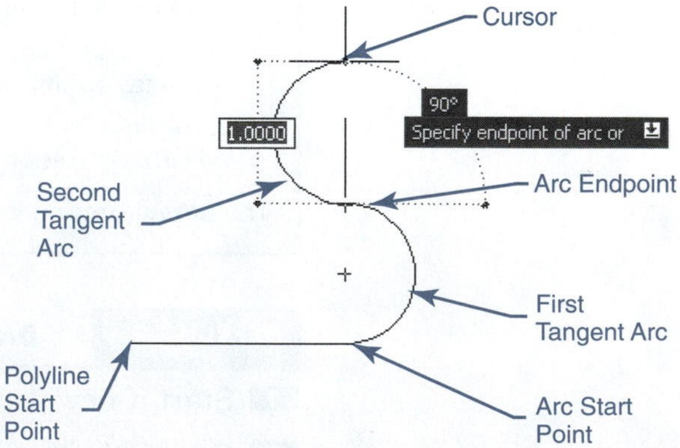

You can switch back to drawing straight line segments using the **Line** option, as shown in Figure 9-8.

There are a number of other options for creating polyline arcs, which are explained in the following sections.

Figure 9-8
Switch from a polyline arc to a straight line segment

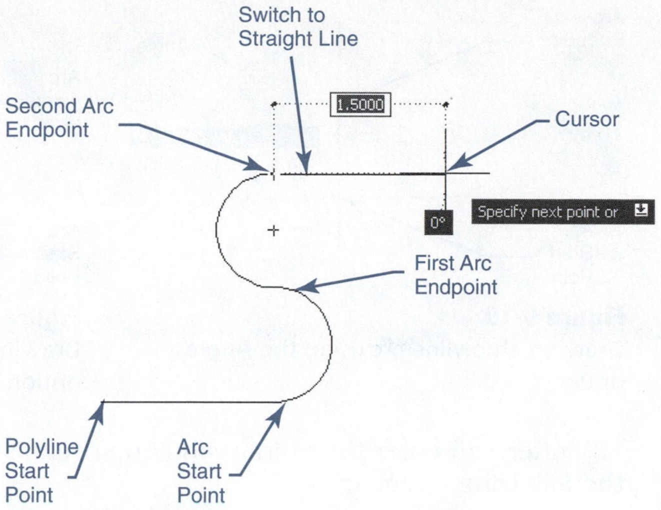

EXERCISE 9-2 Drawing Tangent Polyline Arcs

1. Continue from Exercise 9-1.
2. Create the drawing shown in Figure 9-9 using the **PLINE** command and the default tangent **Arc** option.
3. Save the drawing.

Figure 9-9
Drawing polyline arcs

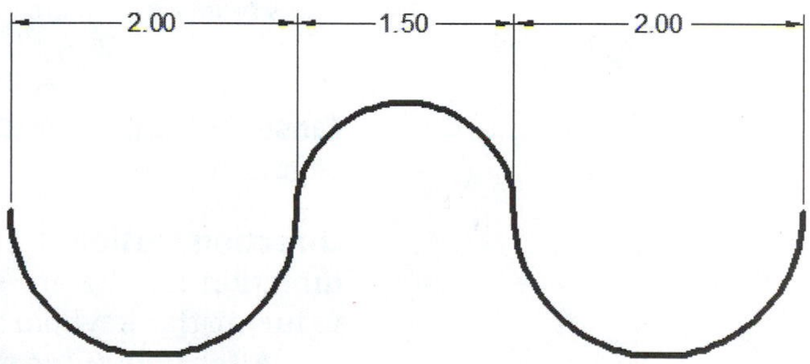

Angle Option. The **Angle** option allows you to specify the included angle of the arc segment from the start point.

After you enter the angle, you can specify an endpoint or enter one of the following options:

CEnter: Allows you to specify the center of the arc segment

Radius: Allows you to specify the radius of the arc segment. You can pick a point to indicate the direction or enter an angle at the keyboard

Figure 9-10 shows the results of drawing a polyline arc using the **Angle** option.

> **NOTE**
>
> Entering a positive number creates counterclockwise arc segments. Entering a negative number creates clockwise arc segments.

CEnter Option. The **CEnter** option allows you to specify the center of the arc segment. You can pick a point or enter a coordinate value at the keyboard.

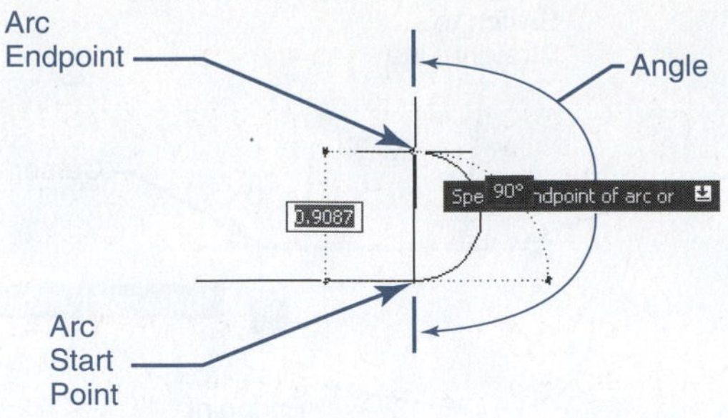

Figure 9-10
Drawing a polyline arc using the **Angle** option

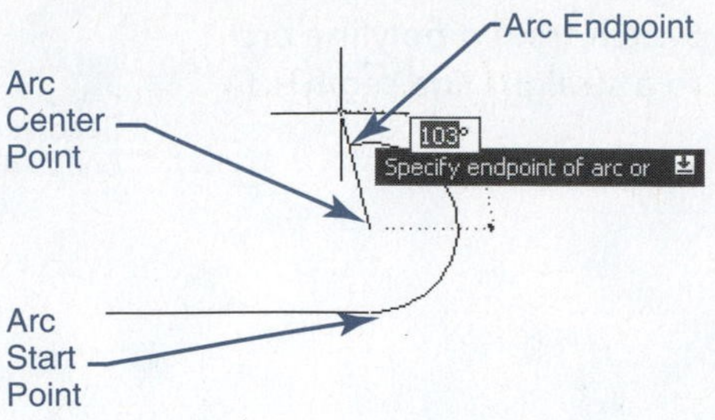

Figure 9-11
Drawing a polyline arc using the **CEnter** option

After you enter the point, you can specify an endpoint or enter one of the following options:

Angle: Allows you to enter the included angle of the arc segment from the start point

Length: Allows you to specify the chord length of the arc segment

Figure 9-11 shows the results of drawing a polyline arc using the **CEnter** option.

> **NOTE**
> AutoCAD draws the new arc segment tangent to the previous arc segment if the previous segment is an arc.

Close Option. The **Close** option allows you to close a polyline with an arc segment.

Direction Option. The **Direction** option allows you to indicate the starting direction for the arc segment. You can pick a point or enter a coordinate value at the keyboard.

After you enter the angle, you can pick a point or enter a coordinate value at the keyboard.

Figure 9-12 shows the results of drawing a polyline arc using the **Direction** option.

Figure 9-12
Drawing a polyline arc using the **Direction** option

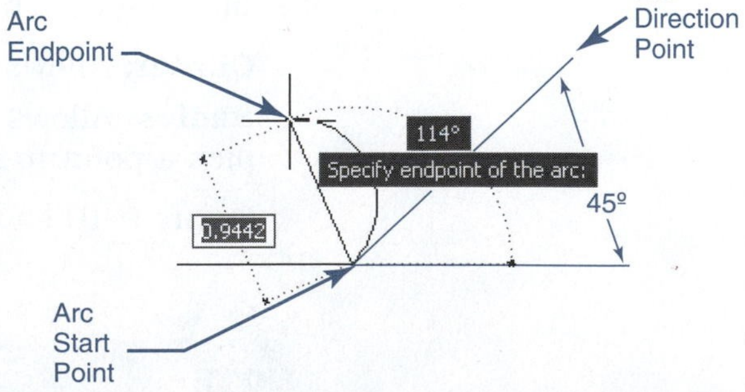

Halfwidth Option. The **Halfwidth** option allows you to specify the width from the center of a wide polyline segment to one of its edges. After you select the **Halfwidth** option, AutoCAD prompts you to *Specify starting half-width <current>:*. Enter a value or press **<Enter>** to use the current half-width. AutoCAD then prompts you to *Specify ending half-width <starting width>:*.

You can either enter a different half-width value to create a tapered arc or press **<Enter>** for a uniform width.

Figure 9-13 shows the results of drawing a polyline arc using the **Halfwidth** option.

Figure 9-13
Drawing a polyline arc using the **Halfwidth** option

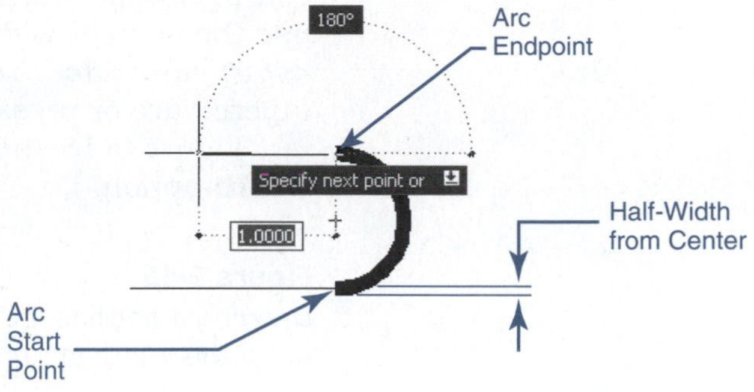

NOTE

The ending half-width becomes the uniform half-width for all new segments until you change the half-width again.

Line Option. The **Line** option exits the **Arc** option and returns to the initial **PLINE** command prompt so you can draw straight line segments.

Radius Option. The **Radius** option allows you to specify the radius of the arc segment.

After you enter the radius, you can specify an endpoint or select the **Angle** option. The **Angle** option allows you to enter the included angle of the arc segment from the start point. After you enter the angle, you can pick a point to indicate the direction or enter an angle at the keyboard.

Figure 9-14 shows the results of drawing a polyline arc using the **Radius** option.

Second Pt Option. The **Second Pt** option allows you to specify the second point and the endpoint of a three-point arc. You can pick a point or enter a coordinate value at the keyboard.

After you specify the second point, you can pick a point or enter a coordinate value at the keyboard.

Figure 9-15 shows the results of drawing a polyline arc using the **Second Pt** option.

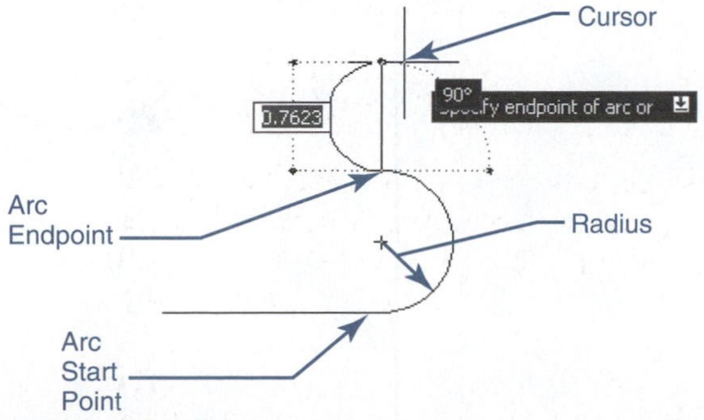

Figure 9-14
Drawing a polyline arc using the **Radius** option

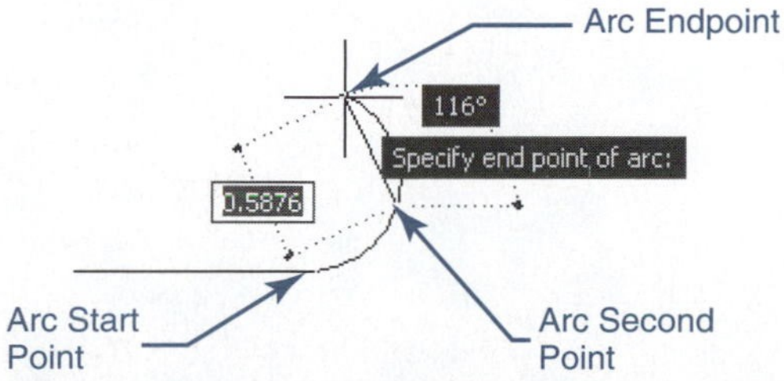

Figure 9-15
Drawing a polyline arc using the **Second Pt** option

Undo Option. The **Undo** option allows you to undo the most recent arc segment added to the polyline.

Width Option. The **Width** option allows you to change the width of the next arc segment. After you select the **Width** option, AutoCAD prompts you to *Specify starting width <current>:*. Enter a value or press **<Enter>** to use the current width. AutoCAD then prompts you to *Specify ending width <starting width>:*. You can either enter a different width value to create a tapered arc or press **<Enter>** for a uniform width.

Figure 9-16 shows the results of drawing a polyline arc using the **Width** option.

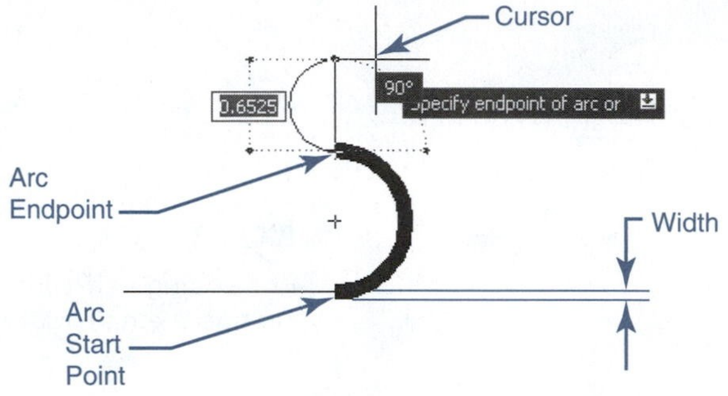

Figure 9-16
Drawing a polyline arc using the **Width** option

> **NOTE**
> The ending width becomes the uniform width for all new segments until you change the width again.

EXERCISE 9-3 Drawing Complex Polyline Arcs

1. Continue from Exercise 9-2.
2. Create the drawing shown in Figure 9-17 using the **PLINE** command and the **Arc** options covered in this section. **Do not** draw dimensions.
3. Close the polyline using the **PLINE** command's **Close** option.
4. Save the drawing.

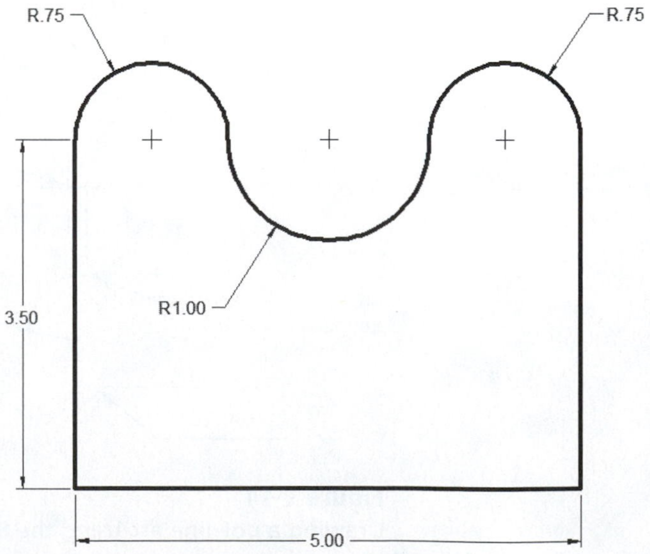

Figure 9-17
Drawing complex polyline arcs

Drawing Polylines with a Width

It is possible to assign a physical width to a polyline using the **Width** option. In fact, it is possible to vary a polyline's width between vertex points using the **Width** option so that a polyline segment can be tapered.

> **NOTE**
>
> Polyline width is not related to the lineweight property discussed in Chapter 6. Polyline width is a unique property that is assigned directly to the polyline. Because it is unrelated to the lineweight property, it is not affected by the **Show/Hide Lineweight** lineweight toggle on the status bar.

After you select the **Width** option, AutoCAD prompts you for a starting width and an ending width. This allows you to vary the width from point to point. To apply a width to all the line segments of a polyline, you simply specify an equal starting and ending width. For instance, to draw a polyline with a constant width of 0.100″, you type **.1<Enter>** when AutoCAD prompts you to *Specify starting width <0.0000>:*. AutoCAD then prompts you for the ending width of the polyline segment using the starting width as the default by prompting *Specify ending width <0.1000>:*. This allows you to simply press the **<Enter>** key to create a constant width. Figure 9-18 shows a polyline drawn with a constant width of 0.100″.

Varying a polyline width provides many unique possibilities. For instance, you can use a polyline with varying widths to create an arrow by specifying a starting width of 0.000″ to create the point, or tip, and then specifying an ending width greater than zero for the next point so the line is tapered. For instance, to create an arrow that tapers from a point to a base width of 0.25″, you would type **0<Enter>** when AutoCAD prompts *Specify starting width <0.0000>:* to create the arrow point and then type **.25<Enter>** when AutoCAD prompts *Specify ending width <0.1000>:* to indicate the base width, as shown in Figure 9-19.

You can even combine these varying width techniques with polyline arcs to create curved arrows that can be used for signage on parking lot plans and roadways, as shown in Figure 9-20.

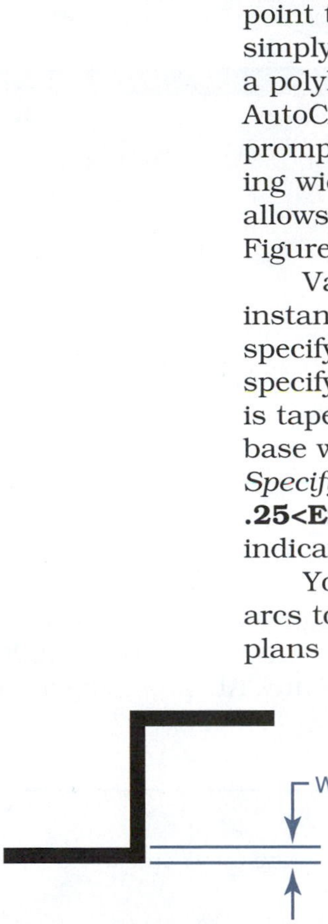

Figure 9-18
A polyline drawn with a constant width of 0.100″

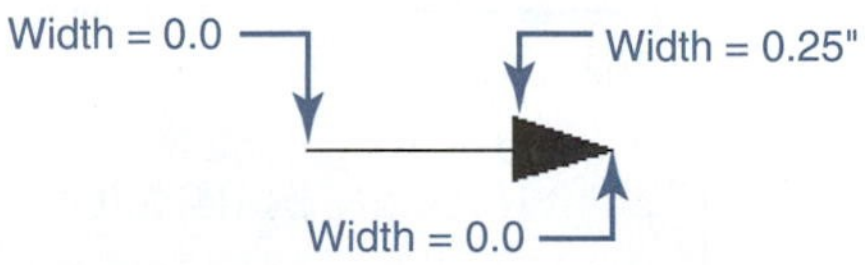

Figure 9-19
A polyline arrow created by varying the polyline width

Figure 9-20
A curved polyline arrow created using polyline arcs

EXERCISE 9-4 Drawing Polylines with a Width

1. Continue from Exercise 9-3.
2. Create a polyline with a uniform width of 0.100″ similar to the polyline shown in Figure 9-18 using the **PLINE** command and the **Width** option.
3. Create a polyline arrow that tapers from a point to a base width of 0.25″ similar to the polyline shown in Figure 9-19 using the **PLINE** command and the **Width** option.

4 Create a curved polyline arrow similar to the polyline shown in Figure 9-20 using the **PLINE** command and the **Width** and **Arc** options.

5 Save the drawing.

Drawing Rectangles

RECTANGLE	
Ribbon & Panel:	Home | Draw 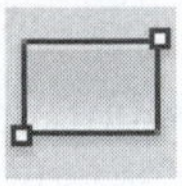
Draw Toolbar:	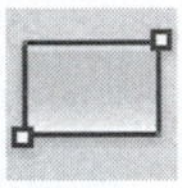
Menu:	Draw | Rectangle
Command Line:	RECTANGLE or RECTANG
Command Alias:	None

The **RECTANGLE** or **RECTANG** command draws a polyline rectangle using two user-supplied corner points.

When you start the **RECTANG** command, AutoCAD prompts you to *Specify first corner point or*↓. You can either type in a coordinate value, or you can pick a point in your drawing. After you specify the first point, you can locate the other corner point as shown in Figure 9-21.

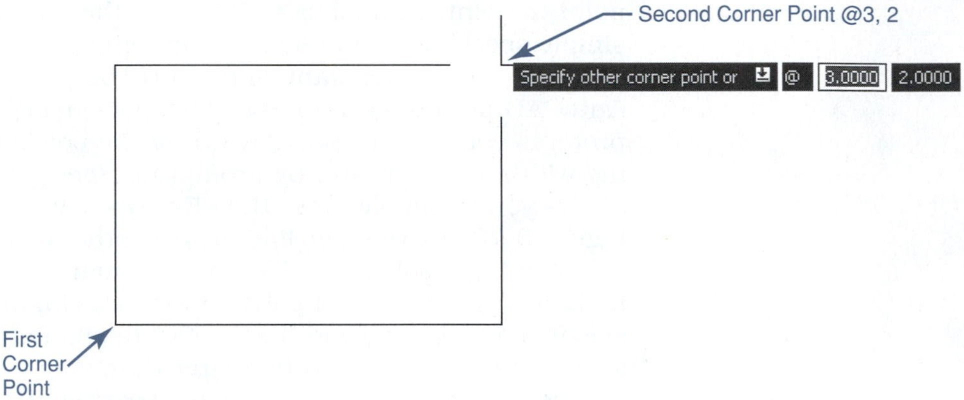

Figure 9-21
Drawing a 3 × 2 rectangle

Remember that it is always possible to enter a coordinate value any time AutoCAD prompts you for a point. In fact, if you know the length and width of the rectangle, you can enter a relative coordinate where *x* is the length and *y* is the width. For instance, to draw a 3.000″ × 2.000″ rectangle, you can type **@3,2<Enter>** when AutoCAD prompts you to *Specify other corner point or*↓.

> **TIP**
>
> If you are using dynamic input, you do not need to use the @ prefix. The second pick point is relative by default.

Entering the Length and Width. The **Dimensions** option allows you to draw a rectangle by entering the length and width in response to AutoCAD prompts. To use the **Dimensions** option, you must pick the first corner point. After you enter a length and width, AutoCAD prompts you for a direction point by prompting *Specify other corner point or*↓. The point you pick determines the rectangle's orientation, as shown in Figure 9-22.

> **NOTE**
>
> AutoCAD remembers the length and width dimensions you enter so the next time you draw a rectangle using the **Dimensions** option you can simply press **<Enter>** to draw a rectangle the same size.

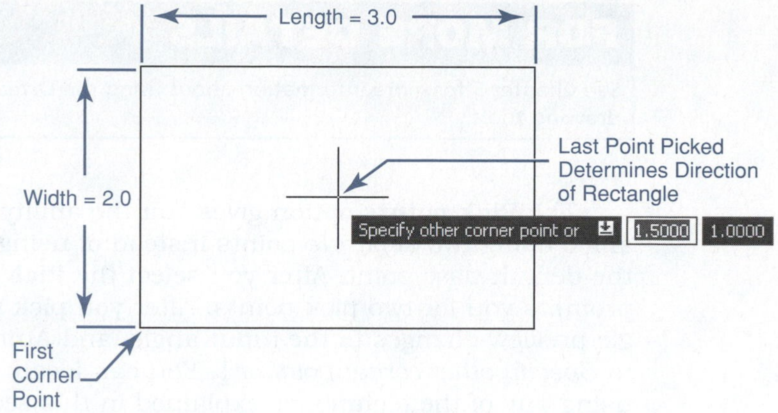

Figure 9-22
Drawing a rectangle by entering the length and width

Drawing a Rectangle at an Angle.

The **Rotation** option allows you to draw a rectangle at a user-specified angle. To use the **Rotation** option, you must pick the first corner point. You have three possible ways to input the rotation angle:

- Type the angle at the keyboard.
- Pick a point to define the angle using the first corner point as the base point.
- Use the **Points** option to pick two separate points to define the angle.

The first option requires that you enter the angle by typing it at the keyboard. For instance, to create a rectangle that is rotated 45°, you enter **45<Enter>.** After you enter the angle, the rectangle preview changes to the input angle, and AutoCAD again prompts you to *Specify other corner point or*↓. You can locate the second corner point using any of the techniques explained in this section, including using the **Dimensions** and **Area** options, as shown in Figure 9-23.

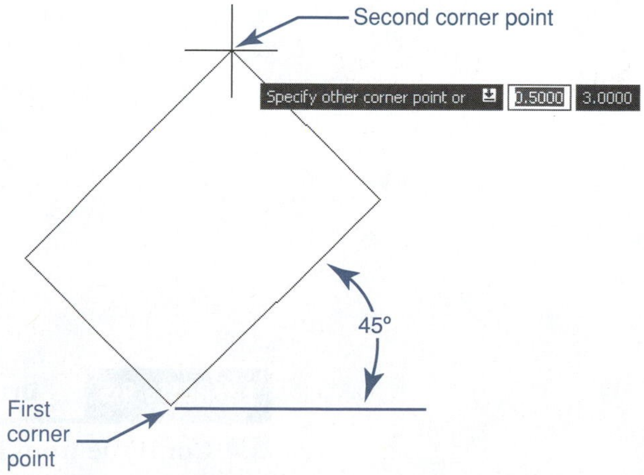

Figure 9-23
Drawing a rectangle at a 45° angle

You can also pick a point to define the angle using the first corner point as the base point, or vertex. When picking a point to define the angle, it is usually beneficial to use either the **Ortho Mode** or **Polar Tracking** drawing tool.

FOR MORE DETAILS

See Chapter 5 for more information about using the **Ortho Mode** and **Polar Tracking** drawing tools.

The **Pick points** option gives you the ability to define the rotation angle using two *separate* points instead of using the first corner point as the default base point. After you select the **Pick points** option, AutoCAD prompts you for two pick points. After you pick the two points, the rectangle preview changes to the input angle, and AutoCAD again prompts you to *Specify other corner point or* ↓. You can locate the second corner point using any of the techniques explained in this section.

NOTE

AutoCAD defaults to creating a rectangle at the same rotation angle the next time you use the command by displaying the current rotation angle at the command line:

Current rectangle modes: Rotation = 45

Drawing a Rectangle by Specifying the Area. The **Area** option allows you to draw a rectangle by specifying its area and either the length or the width. To use the **Area** option, you must pick the first corner point. After you select the **Area** option, enter the desired area and press **<Enter>**. AutoCAD then asks you whether you want to specify the length or width. Select the desired option and after you enter the distance, AutoCAD draws the rectangle automatically at the first corner point location, as shown in Figure 9-24.

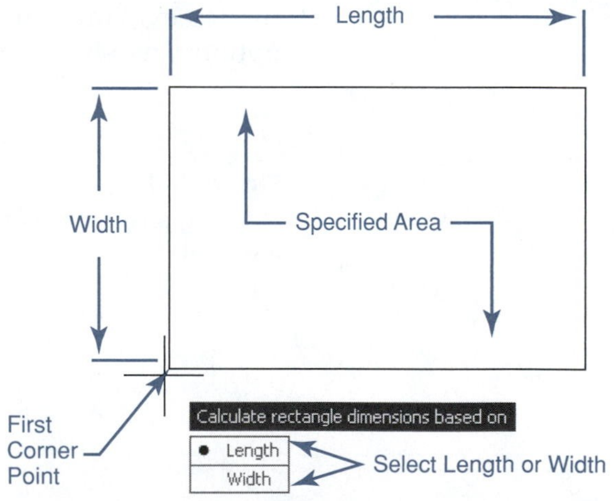

Figure 9-24
Drawing a rectangle by specifying the area

EXERCISE 9-5 **Drawing Rectangles**

1. Continue from Exercise 9-4.
2. Create a 3.000″ × 2.000″ rectangle similar to the rectangle shown in Figure 9-21 using the **RECTANG** command and relative coordinate entry.
3. Create a 3.000″ × 2.000″ rectangle similar to the rectangle shown in Figure 9-22 in another location using the **RECTANG** command and the **Dimensions** option to input the length and width.

4 Create a 3.000″ × 2.000″ rectangle at a 45° angle similar to the rectangle shown in Figure 9-23 in another location using the **RECTANG** command and the **Angle** option to input the 45° angle.

5 Save the drawing.

chamfer: To cut off a corner with a slight angle or bevel.

Chamfering Corners. The **Chamfer** option allows you to draw a rectangle with four beveled, or ***chamfered***, corners using the specified distance from the corner point to the beginning of each chamfer.

After you select the **Chamfer** option, enter the distance for the first leg of the chamfer and press **<Enter>**. AutoCAD then prompts you to *Specify second chamfer distance for rectangles <0.2500>:* using the first distance as the default. Typically, you want to simply press **<Enter>** to accept the default and create a rectangle with 45° chamfers, although you can specify a different distance. After entering the chamfer distances, you can create a rectangle with chamfered corners using any of the techniques already explained. Figure 9-25 shows a 3.000″ × 2.000″ rectangle drawn with .250″ × .250″ chamfered corners.

NOTE

AutoCAD defaults to creating a rectangle with chamfered corners the next time you use the command by displaying the current chamfer distances at the command line:

Current rectangle modes: Chamfer = 0.2500 × 0.2500

fillet: To round off an inside or outside corner at a specific radius.

Rounding Corners. The **Fillet** option allows you to draw a rectangle with four rounded, or ***filleted***, corners using the specified radius from the corner point.

After you select the **Fillet** option, enter the radius and press **<Enter>**. After entering the radius, you can create a rectangle using any of the techniques explained above. Figure 9-26 shows a 3.000″ × 2.000″ rectangle drawn with .250″ filleted corners.

NOTE

AutoCAD defaults to creating a rectangle with filleted corners the next time you use the command by displaying the current fillet radius at the command line:

Current rectangle modes: Fillet = 0.2500

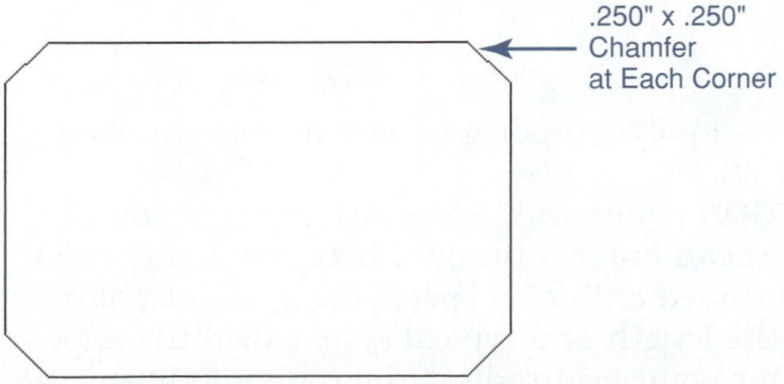

Figure 9-25
Drawing a rectangle with chamfered corners

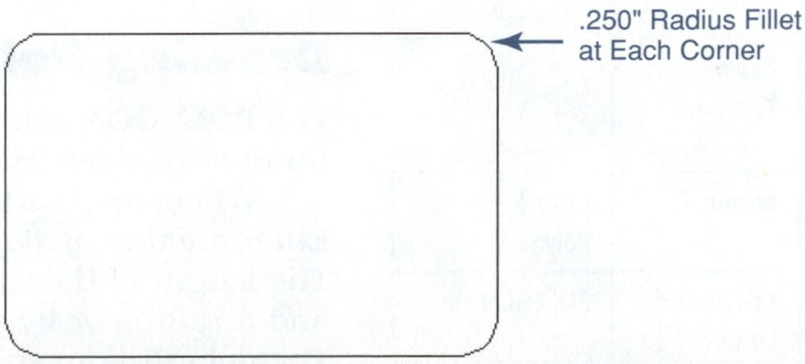

Figure 9-26
Drawing a rectangle with filleted corners

Drawing a Rectangle with a Width. The **Width** option allows you to draw a rectangle with a user-specified polyline width as explained earlier in the section "Drawing Polylines with a Width."

After you select the **Width** option, enter the line width and press **<Enter>**. After entering the width, you can create a rectangle using any of the techniques explained previously. Figure 9-27 shows a 3.000″ × 2.000″ rectangle drawn with a 0.100″ uniform line width.

> **NOTE**
>
> AutoCAD defaults to creating a rectangle with a width the next time you use the command by displaying the current line width at the command line:
>
> Current rectangle modes: Width = 0.1000

Figure 9-27
Drawing a rectangle with a uniform line width

EXERCISE 9-6 **Drawing Rectangles with Chamfered and Rounded Corners**

1. Continue from Exercise 9-5.
2. Draw a 3.000″ × 2.000″ rectangle with .250″ × .250″ chamfered corners similar to the rectangle shown in Figure 9-25 using the **RECTANG** command and the **Chamfer** option.
3. Draw a 3.000″ × 2.000″ rectangle in another location with .250″ rounded corners similar to the rectangle shown in Figure 9-26 using the **RECTANG** command and the **Fillet** option.
4. Draw a 3.000″ × 2.000″ rectangle with a 0.100″ uniform width similar to the rectangle shown in Figure 9-27 using the **RECTANG** command and the **Width** option.
5. Save the drawing.

POLYGON	
Ribbon & Panel:	Home | Draw 
Draw Toolbar:	
Menu:	Draw | Polygon
Command Line:	POLYGON
Command Alias:	POL

Drawing Polygons

The **POLYGON** command draws a polyline polygon with a user-supplied number of sides. See Figure 9-28.

When you start the **POLYGON** command, AutoCAD prompts you to *Enter number of sides <4>:*. You can enter a number between 3 and 1024. The length of the sides is determined either by specifying a center point and a radius or by indicating the length of a typical side, called the *edge*. The default is to specify a center point and radius; the radius indicates a circle that either inscribes or circumscribes the polygon, and the length of the sides is generated automatically.

Figure 9-28
Examples of polygons

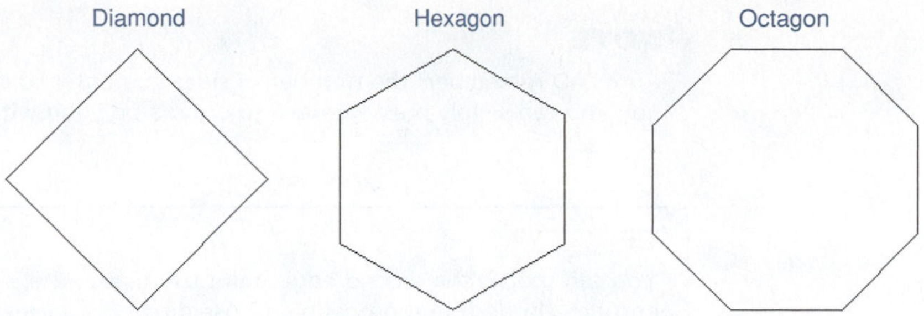

After you specify the number of sides, AutoCAD prompts you to *Specify center of polygon or*↓. The default is to locate a center point either by picking a point or by typing in a coordinate value. AutoCAD then asks you if you want to create the polygon inscribed inside a circle (see Figure 9-29A) with the specified radius or circumscribed on the outside of the circle (see Figure 9-29B) by prompting *Enter an option*↓. After selecting either option, AutoCAD then prompts you to *Specify radius of circle:*. You can either type a radius at the keyboard or pick a point as shown in Figures 9-29A and B.

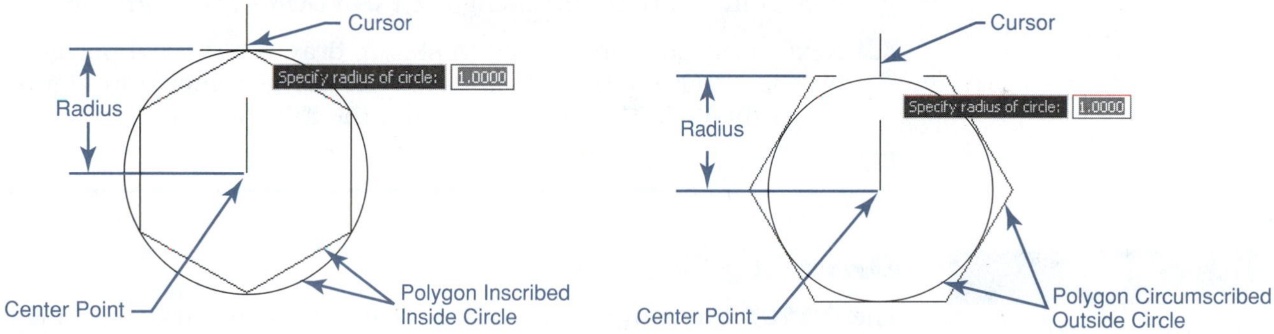

Figure 9-29
A Polygon with six sides inscribed in a circle **B** Polygon with six sides circumscribed outside a circle

Specifying the Length of a Side. The **Edge** option allows you to create a polygon by specifying the location and length of a side. AutoCAD uses the input length to automatically create the remaining specified number of sides.

After you select the **Edge** option, you can either pick a point or type in a coordinate value to locate the starting point of one of the sides. AutoCAD then prompts *Specify second endpoint of edge:*. The second point determines the length for all the sides specified *and* the rotation angle of the finished polygon, as shown in Figure 9-30.

Figure 9-30
Using the **Edge** option to draw a polygon

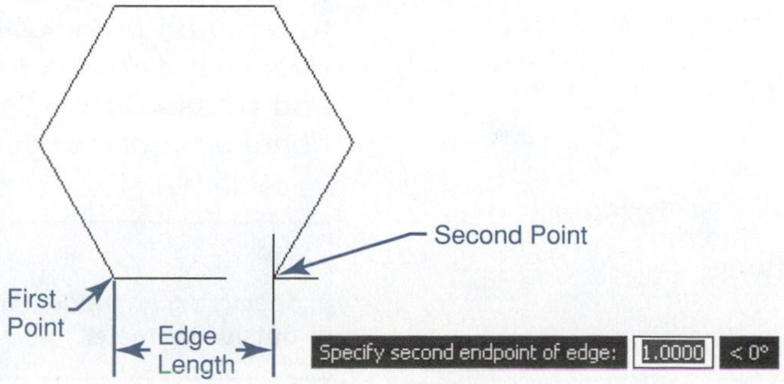

NOTE

AutoCAD remembers the number of sides you enter so the next time you draw a polygon you can simply press **<Enter>** to draw a polygon with the same number of sides.

TIP

You can specify the second edge point using absolute, relative, or polar coordinate entry methods. It is also possible to use direct distance entry with either the **Ortho Mode** or **Polar Tracking** drawing tool.

EXERCISE 9-7 Drawing Polygons

1. Continue from Exercise 9-6.
2. Draw a six-sided polygon *inscribed inside* a circle with a radius of 1.000″ similar to the polygon shown in Figure 9-29A using the **POLYGON** command.
3. Next to the polygon created in step 2, draw a six-sided polygon *circumscribed outside* a circle with a radius of 1.000″ similar to the polygon shown in Figure 9-29B using the **POLYGON** command.
4. Next to the polygon created in step 3, draw a six-sided polygon with an edge length of 0.500″ similar to the polygon shown in Figure 9-30 using the **POLYGON** command and the **Edge** option.
5. Save the drawing.

DONUT	
Ribbon & Panel:	Home | Draw 
Toolbar:	None
Menu:	Draw | Donut
Command Line:	DONUT
Command Alias:	DO

Drawing Donuts

The **DONUT** command draws a ring, or donut, with a user-specified inside diameter and outside diameter. The ring thickness equals the outside diameter minus the inside diameter. See Figure 9-31.

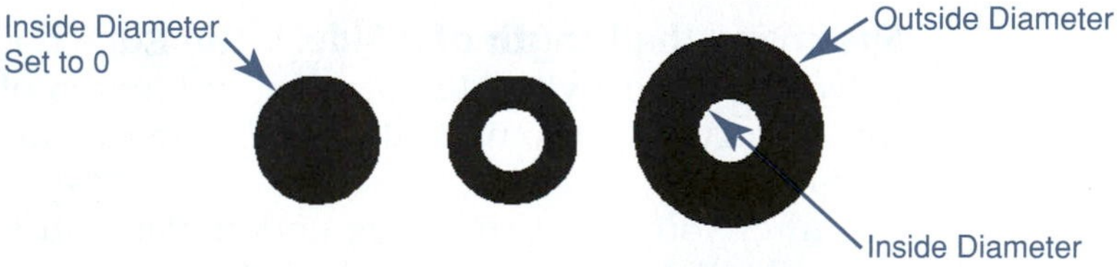

Figure 9-31
Examples of donuts

When you start the **DONUT** command, AutoCAD prompts you to *Specify inside diameter of donut <0.5000>:*. Enter a diameter greater than or equal to zero and press **<Enter>**. AutoCAD then prompts you to *Specify outside diameter of donut <1.0000>:*. Enter a value greater than the inside diameter and press **<Enter>**. AutoCAD repeatedly prompts you to *Specify center of donut or <exit>:* so you can locate multiple donuts, as shown in Figure 9-32.

TIP

Specifying an inside diameter equal to 0 creates a solid filled circle with the specified outside diameter.

Figure 9-32
Drawing donuts

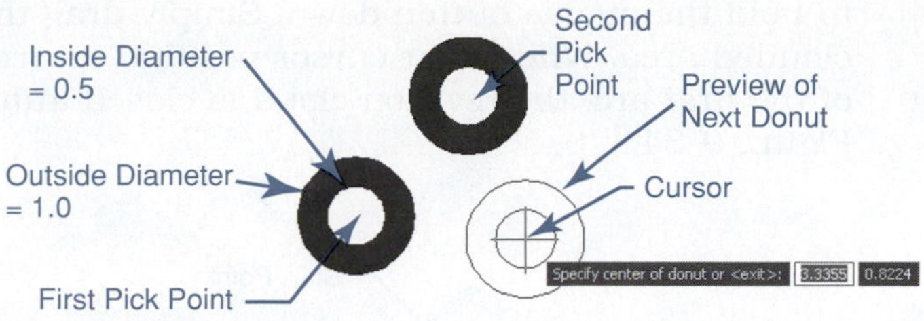

EXERCISE 9-8 **Drawing Donuts**

1. Continue from Exercise 9-7.
2. Create some donuts with an inside diameter of 0.500″ and an outside diameter of 1.000″ using the **DONUT** command.
3. Create some *solid* donuts with an inside diameter of 0.000″ and an outside diameter of 1.000″ using the **DONUT** command.
4. Save the drawing.

Drawing Revision Clouds

revision cloud: Continuous line made from arcs to resemble a cloud that is used to highlight markups and changes.

The **REVCLOUD** command draws a polyline of sequential arcs to form a cloud shape that can be used as a ***revision cloud*** on a drawing to highlight markups and changes (see Figure 9-33).

REVISION CLOUD	
Ribbon & Panel:	Home | Draw
Draw Toolbar:	
Menu:	Draw | Revision Cloud
Command Line:	REVCLOUD
Command Alias:	None

Figure 9-33
Example of revision cloud

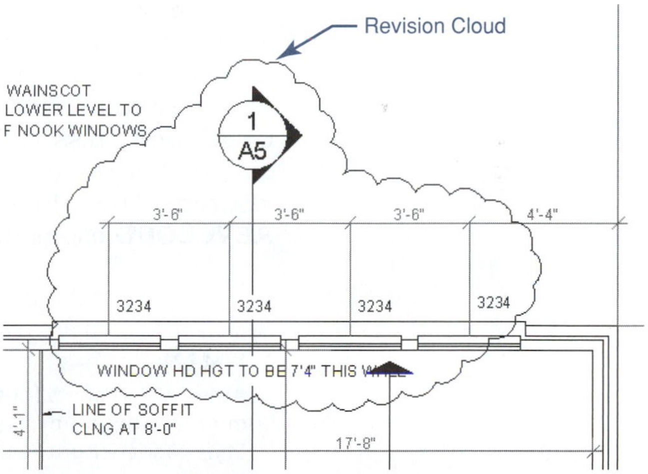

There are two different styles for a revision cloud: Normal or Calligraphy. The default style, Normal, draws the revision cloud using regular polyline arcs with no thickness. The Calligraphy style tapers the polyline arc thickness so the revision cloud looks as though it were drawn with a calligraphy pen.

When you start the **REVCLOUD** command, AutoCAD displays the default settings at the command line as follows:

Minimum arc length: 0.5000 Maximum arc length: 0.5000 Style: Normal

To create a revision cloud using the default settings, pick a point with your mouse and guide your mouse along the desired revision cloud path when AutoCAD prompts you to *Specify start point or* ↓. You *do not* need to hold the mouse button down. Simply drag the mouse to create the clouded area. When your cursor position returns to the beginning point of the first arc, the revision cloud is closed automatically, as shown in Figure 9-34.

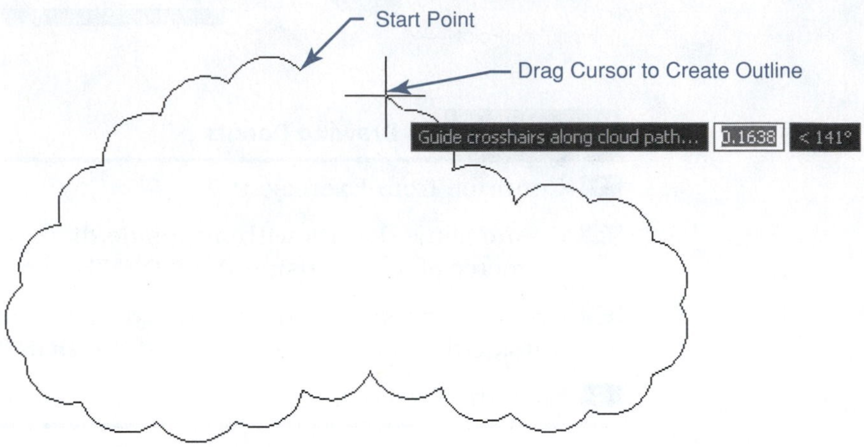

Figure 9-34
Drawing a revision cloud

AutoCAD interactively flips the arc direction based on the direction you drag your mouse after specifying the start point so that the arc bulge faces the proper way.

Changing the Arc Length

The **Arc length** option allows you to change the minimum and maximum arc length used to create the polyline arcs when the revision cloud is being drawn so that you can make them bigger or smaller.

After you select the **Arc length** option, enter the desired minimum length and press **<Enter>**. AutoCAD prompts you to *Specify maximum length of arc <0.5000>:*. Enter the desired maximum length and press **<Enter>**. The values become the default the next time you use the **REVCLOUD** command.

NOTE

AutoCAD accounts for the drawing scale factor by multiplying the minimum and maximum arc lengths by the current dimension scale factor, which is set via the **Dimension Style Manager** or the **DIMSCALE** system variable.

FOR MORE DETAILS

See page 529 in Chapter 13 for more information about setting the dimension scale factor. See page 8 in Chapter 1 for more information about the drawing scale factor.

Switching Styles

The **Style** option allows you to switch between the Normal style and the Calligraphy style. Figure 9-35 shows a revision cloud drawn using the Calligraphy style.

Figure 9-35
Revision cloud drawn using the Calligraphy style

Creating Revision Clouds from Existing Objects

You can convert existing objects such as a circles, ellipses, and polylines into a revision cloud using the **Object** option. After selecting the **Object** option, select the object you want to convert. After converting the object, AutoCAD allows you simply to change the direction of the arcs so they face in or out.

> **TIP**
> You can control whether the existing object is deleted after it is converted into a revision cloud via the **DELOBJ** system variable. Setting **DELOBJ** to **1** deletes the original object and setting **DELOBJ** to **0** maintains the original object.

EXERCISE 9-9 **Drawing Revision Clouds**

1. Continue from Exercise 9-8.
2. Create a revision cloud using the Calligraphy style similar to the one shown in Figure 9-35 using the **REVCLOUD** command and the **Style** option.
3. Create a circle using the **CIRCLE** command.
4. Convert the circle to a revision cloud using the **REVCLOUD** command and the **Object** option.
5. Save the drawing.

EDIT POLYLINE	
Ribbon & Panel:	Home | Modify 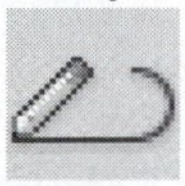
Modify II Toolbar:	
Menu:	Modify | Object | Polyline
Command Line:	PEDIT
Command Alias:	PE

Editing Polylines

You can edit polylines after they are created using the **PEDIT** command. The **PEDIT** command allows you to:

- Convert lines and arcs to polylines
- Close and open polylines
- Join multiple polylines together
- Change a polyline's width
- Edit polyline vertices so that you can move, add, and remove points
- Curve fit a polyline

- Control a polyline's linetype generation
- Reverse a polyline

When you start the **PEDIT** command, AutoCAD prompts you to *Select polyline or* ↓. You can then select a polyline, a line, or an arc. If you select an object that is not a polyline, AutoCAD displays the following at the command line so you can convert it:

Object selected is not a polyline

AutoCAD allows you to convert the object by prompting *Do you want to turn it into one?* ↓. The default is **Yes** so you can simply press **<Enter>** to convert the selected line or arc.

> **TIP**
>
> The **PEDITACCEPT** system variable allows you to suppress display of the *Object selected is not a polyline* prompt so that objects are automatically converted. Setting the **PEDITACCEPT** to **1** (on) suppresses the prompt. Setting **PEDITACCEPT** to **0** (off) turns the prompt back on.

You can edit multiple polylines using the **Multiple** option. You can use any of the selection options to select multiple objects. If any of the objects are not polylines, AutoCAD allows you to convert them using the same approach mentioned earlier.

After a polyline is selected, or converted, AutoCAD prompts you to *Enter an option* ↓ to allow you to select an editing option. All the **PEDIT** options are explored in the following sections.

Closing and Opening Polylines

You can close or open a polyline using either the **Close** or **Open** option. The **PEDIT** command provides one option or the other depending on the polyline's current open or closed status.

To close an open polyline so that a polyline segment is created between the first and last point, select the **Close** option. Figure 9-36 shows the result of selecting the **Close** option.

Figure 9-36
Closing an open polyline

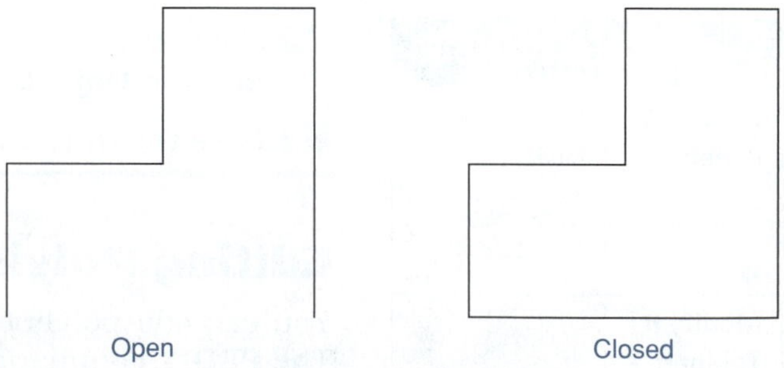

To open a closed polyline so that the polyline segment between the first and last point is removed, select the **Open** option.

fuzz distance: Distance used to determine whether polyline endpoints that are not connected can be connected by extending them or trimming them, or connecting them with a new polyline segment.

Joining Polylines

The **Join** option allows you to join a polyline, line, or arc to one or more open polylines either if their ends connect or if they are within a specified ***fuzz distance*** of each other.

NOTE

When you join objects using the **Join** option, the properties of the polyline selected first, including the polyline's ending width, are inherited by all the objects that are successfully joined.

Applying a fuzz distance is available only when you use the **Multiple** option and is explained in detail in the following section. After you select the **Join** option, you can then use any of the selection options to select one or more connected objects and press **<Enter>** as shown in Figure 9-37.

Figure 9-37
Joining an open polyline

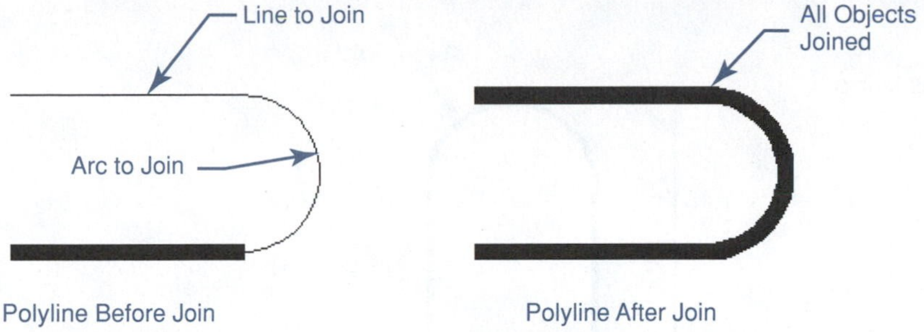

AutoCAD reports the success or failure of the join attempt by displaying how many objects were added to the original polyline at the command line:

2 segments added to polyline

It is your job to determine whether all the objects were joined based on how many objects you originally selected. For instance, if you selected three objects and AutoCAD says that only two segments were added, you have a problem. You then have to inspect visually the endpoints of each object that was not joined and connect any points that are not connected. This can become a very tedious process with a complex join operation that consists of many objects. Luckily, we can use the fuzz distance mentioned earlier.

Joining Polylines That Do Not Meet. As mentioned earlier, you can join polylines, lines, and arcs whose endpoints are not connected but are within a specified fuzz distance of each other. AutoCAD will either extend, trim, or insert a line segment in order to create the connection. To enter a fuzz distance, you *must* use the **Multiple** option explained earlier to select the objects you want to join first. If you then select the **Join** option using the same methods explained earlier, AutoCAD prompts you to *Enter fuzz distance or*↓ after you select the objects to join. You can then enter the distance you want to close and press **<Enter>**. AutoCAD displays how many segments were added at the command line in the same fashion as a regular join operation so you can determine whether all the objects were joined successfully.

You can set the method that AutoCAD uses to join polylines via the **Jointype** option. After selecting the **Jointype** option, you can choose one of the following options:

- **Extend** Joins by extending or trimming the segments to the nearest endpoints
- **Add** Joins by adding a straight segment between the nearest endpoints
- **Both** Joins by extending or trimming if possible. Otherwise joins by adding a straight segment between the nearest endpoints

TIP

Joining a polyline removes the curve fitting from a curve fit polyline. Curve fitting polylines are explained later in this section.

EXERCISE 9-10 **Joining Polylines Using PEDIT**

1. Start a new drawing using the **acad.dwt** drawing template.
2. Create the drawing shown in Figure 9-38 using only the **LINE** and **ARC** commands, making sure to connect all the line and arc segments.
3. Join all the line and arc segments using the **PEDIT** command and the **Join** option.
4. Save the drawing as ***CH9_EXERCISE10.***

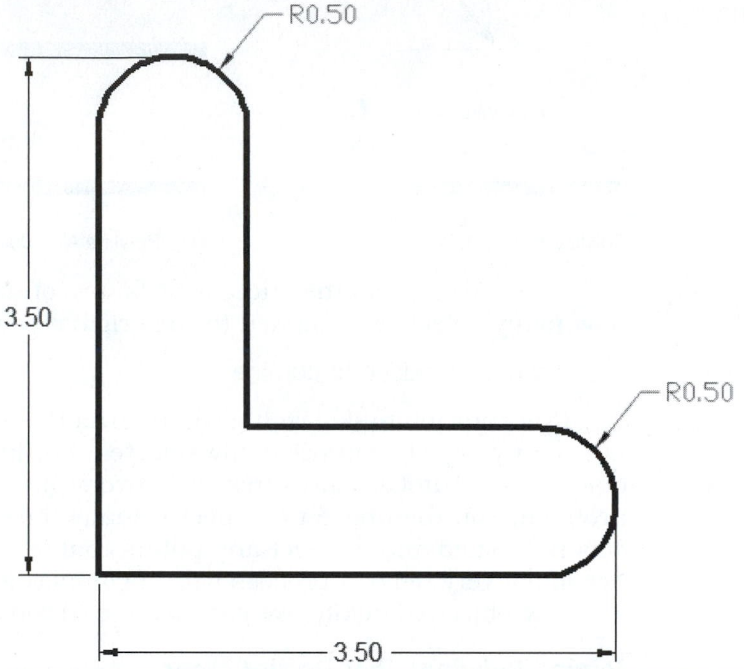

Figure 9-38
Joining polylines using **PEDIT**

Changing the Polyline Width

The **Width** option allows you to specify a new uniform width for all the polyline segments. After you select the **Width** option, enter the new uniform width and press **<Enter>** to change the width, as shown in Figure 9-39.

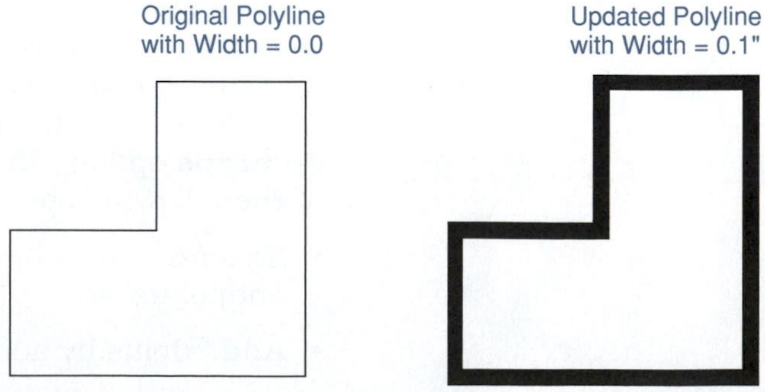

Figure 9-39
Changing the polyline width

> **TIP**
>
> You can vary the width from point to point using the **Properties** palette. The **Properties** palette allows you to step through each vertex of a polyline and set its width property individually.

EXERCISE 9-11 **Changing Polyline Width Using PEDIT**

1 Continue from Exercise 9-10.

2 Change the polyline width to a uniform width of **0.100″** using the **PEDIT** command and the **Width** option.

3 Save the drawing.

Editing Polyline Vertices

The **Edit vertex** option allows you to edit a polyline's vertex points individually so you can:

- Break one or more polyline segments
- Insert a vertex point
- Move a vertex point
- Regenerate the polyline
- Straighten two more polyline segments
- Attach a tangent direction
- Change the starting and ending width of a polyline segment

The **Edit vertex** option is considered a legacy option, and its use in editing vertex points is not recommended because of its complexity. Instead, it is suggested that you use multifunctional grips, which are discussed later in this chapter. They are much more user-friendly and easier to manipulate.

Converting Polylines into Smooth Curves

curve fit: The process of adding vertex points to a straight line segment polyline in order to create a smooth curve.

You can transform a polyline that is made up of straight line segments into a polyline with smooth curves using the **Fit** and **Spline** options. Both options allow you to ***curve fit*** a polyline with very different results.

After a polyline is curve fit using either option, it is possible to convert it back to straight polyline segments using the **Decurve** option. All the curve fit options are explained in detail in the following sections.

Fit Option. The **Fit** option creates an arc fit polyline. An arc fit polyline is a smooth curve consisting of arcs joining each pair of vertex points with the curve passing through all vertices of the polyline, as shown in Figure 9-40.

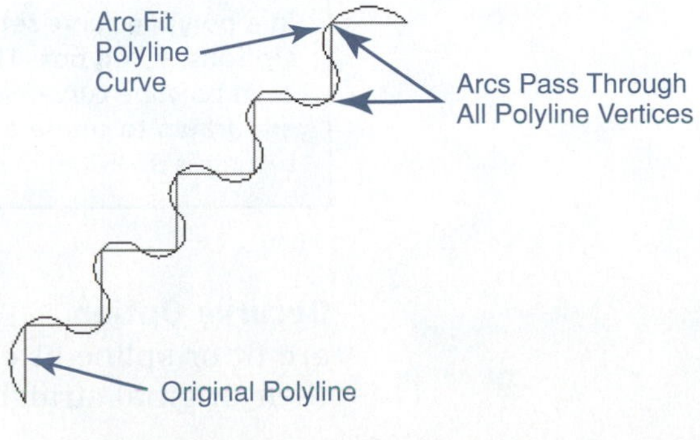

Figure 9-40
Arc fit polyline created using the **Fit** option

B-spline: An approximate spline curve also referred to as a nonuniform rational B-spline, or NURBS, curve.

Spline Option. The **Spline** option uses the vertices of the selected polyline as the control points to create a curve approximating a ***B-spline*** but is not as accurate as a true spline.

A spline fit polyline passes through the first and last polyline vertex points unless the original polyline was closed. The curve is pulled toward the other vertex points but does not pass through them, as shown in Figure 9-41. The more control points you specify, the more pull they exert on the curve.

> **TIP**
>
> Setting the **SPLFRAME** system variable to **1** (on) turns on the spline curve control point frame the next time the drawing is regenerated. AutoCAD draws both the frame and the spline curve. Setting **SPLFRAME** to **0** (off) turns off the spline curve control frame.

AutoCAD can generate either quadratic or cubic spline fit polylines. A cubic B-spline is very smooth, much smoother than a quadratic B-spline, as shown in Figure 9-42.

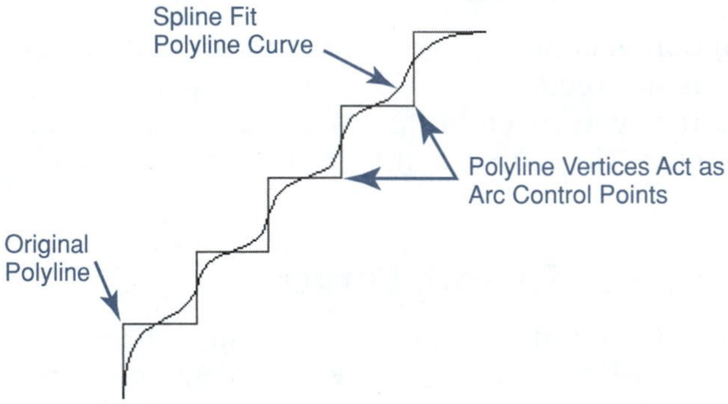

Figure 9-41
Spline fit polyline created using the **Spline** option

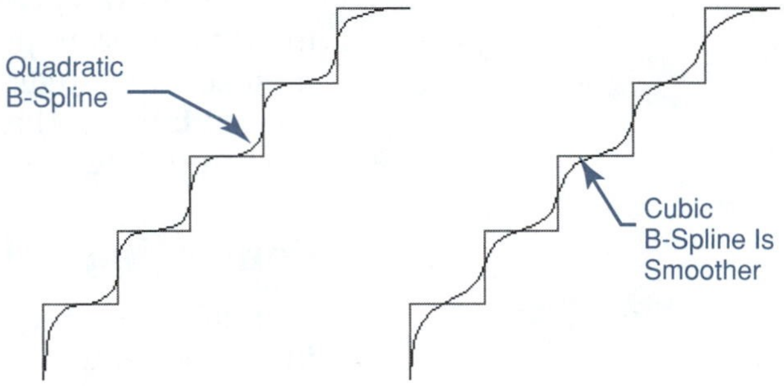

Figure 9-42
Quadratic and cubic B-splines compared

The default spline curve type is the smoother cubic B-spline. The **SPLINETYPE** system variable controls the type of spline curve created. Setting **SPLINETYPE** to **5** creates a quadratic B-spline. Setting **SPLINETYPE** to **6** creates a cubic B-spline.

> **TIP**
>
> You can also control the smoothness of a spline approximation via the **Segments in a polyline curve** setting in the **Display Resolution** area on the **Display** tab of the **Options** dialog box. This setting controls the number of line segments generated for each polyline curve. Setting this value higher means a greater number of line segments are drawn to create a more precise spline curve. The default value is 8. The maximum setting is 32767.

Decurve Option. The **Decurve** option removes extra points inserted by an arc fit or spline fit curve and straightens all the polyline segments back to their original straight line segments, as shown in Figure 9-43.

Figure 9-43
Curve fit polyline decurved using the **Decurve** option

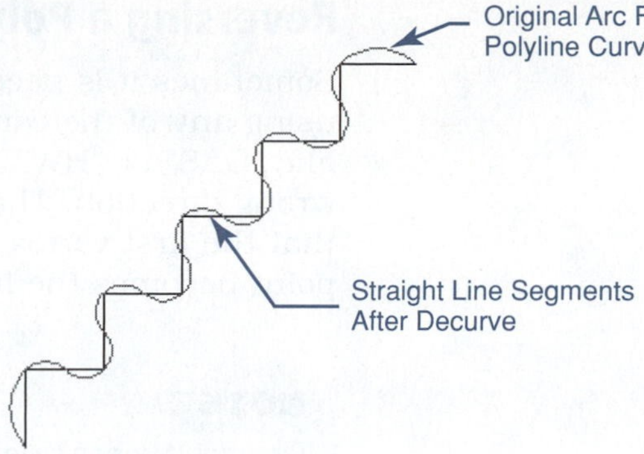

Chapter 9

TIP

You cannot use the **Decurve** option after you edit a spline fit polyline with either the **BREAK** or **TRIM** command.

EXERCISE 9-12 Converting Polylines into Smooth Curves

1. Continue from Exercise 9-11.
2. Create an arc fit polyline similar to the polyline shown in Figure 9-40 using the **PEDIT** command and the **Fit** option.
3. Create a cubic spline fit polyline in another location similar to the polyline shown in Figure 9-42 using the **PEDIT** command and the **Spline** option.
4. Convert both curve fit polylines created in steps 2 and 3 back into straight line segments similar to those shown in Figure 9-43 using the **PEDIT** command and the **Decurve** option.
5. Save the drawing.

Controlling Polyline Linetype Generation

The **Ltype gen** option allows you to generate the polyline's linetype definition in a continuous pattern through all the vertices of the polyline. When polyline linetype generation is turned off, the linetype definition is applied to each individual polyline segment so dashes, gaps, etc. are sometimes not displayed. Figure 9-44 shows a polyline with a **CENTER** linetype with linetype generation turned on and off.

NOTE

The **Ltype gen** option does not apply to polylines with tapered segments.

Figure 9-44
Polyline linetype generation turned on and turned off

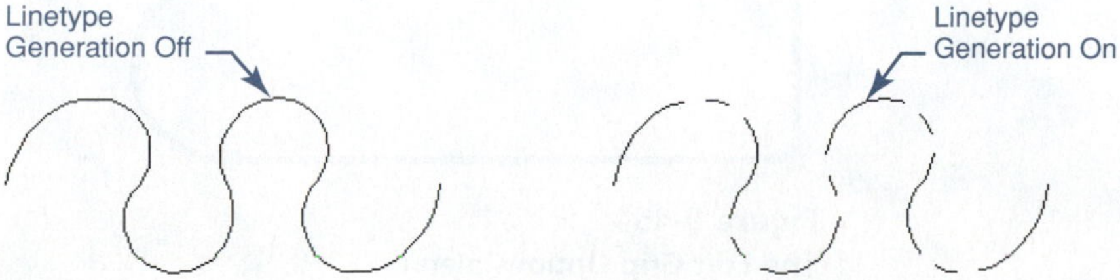

Reversing a Polyline

Sometimes it is necessary to reverse a polyline. For instance, if you are using any of the complex AutoCAD linetypes with words built into them like "GAS" or "HW", the words sometimes appear upside down or in the wrong direction. The **Reverse** option allows you to reverse a polyline so that the first vertex point becomes the last vertex point, the last vertex point becomes the first, and all vertex points in-between reverse order.

> **NOTE**
>
> By default, when reversing a polyline that has varying segment widths, all segment widths are updated when using the **Reverse** option so the polyline maintains its original appearance.

NEW to AutoCAD 2013

> **TIP**
>
> The **PLINEREVERSEWIDTHS** system variable provides increased flexibility when reversing the direction of polylines that have varying widths. When **PLINEREVERSEWIDTHS** is set to **0** (default), the start and end of the polyline are reversed and the segments with varying widths are unaffected. When **PLINEREVERSEWIDTHS** is set to **1**, the start and end of the polyline are reversed and widths of the segments are applied to the vertices starting in the opposite direction.

Editing Polylines Using Grips

One of the easiest ways to edit polylines is to use multifunctional polyline grips. If you select an existing polyline with your cursor, you'll see that, in addition to the familiar primary grips located at the end of each polyline segment, there are additional secondary grips located at each segment's midpoint. These are multifunctional grips whose available functions can be seen by hovering your cursor over a grip to display a menu of options, like the one shown in Figure 9-45, that you can use your mouse to select from.

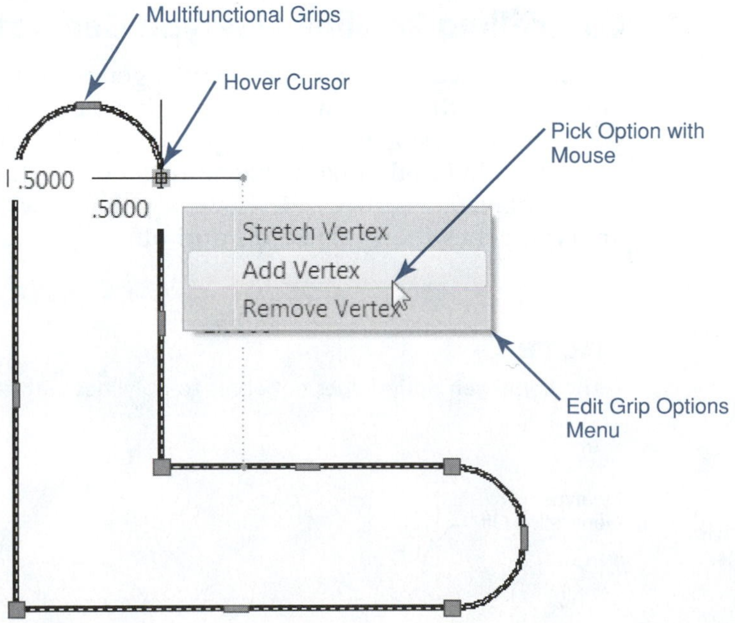

Figure 9-45
The **Edit Grip Options** menu

EXPLODE	
Ribbon & Panel:	Home | Modify 
Modify Toolbar:	
Pull-down Menu:	Modify | Explode
Command Line:	EXPLODE
Command Alias:	X

If you select a grip so that it is red (active), you can either cycle through the available functions by pressing the **<Ctrl>** key or choose one of the options from the menu by pressing the down arrow on your keyboard. Corresponding function icons appear next to the cursor in the AutoCAD drawing to indicate the active function.

To sub-select one or more segments of a polyline, hold down the **<Ctrl>** key while left-clicking on the polyline. Grip behavior for the sub-selected segments is the same as when an entire polyline is selected.

Exploding Complex Objects

You can explode any of the complex line objects discussed in this chapter and convert them into multiple individual line and arc segments using the **EXPLODE** command.

When you start the **EXPLODE** command, AutoCAD prompts you to *Select objects:* so that you can select one or more complex objects.

If you select one or more objects that cannot be exploded, AutoCAD displays how many objects could not be exploded at the command line:

1 was not able to be exploded.

NOTE

When you explode a polyline with a width, all the associated width information is discarded, and the resulting lines and arcs follow the polyline's centerline.

TIP

You can also explode other complex AutoCAD objects such as hatch objects, multiline text, dimensions, and blocks into their individual subobjects. These and other complex objects are discussed later in the textbook. Typically, it is wise not to explode complex objects unless it is absolutely necessary because it increases the amount of memory used by the drawing and makes editing drawing information more difficult.

Chapter Summary

This chapter explained how to create and edit the different complex polyline objects in AutoCAD. We learned that rectangles, polygons, donuts, and revision clouds are all constructed using polylines. We saw how it is possible for polylines to have a constant or varying width assigned to them so that you can create different visual effects.

We also explored different ways to edit a polyline after it has been created. The **PEDIT** command provides many of the necessary options but can be cumbersome to use, especially when editing point vertices. For this task, you should rely on a combination of the multifunctional grip editing tools and the **Properties** palette to get you through.

Finally, the **EXPLODE** command was introduced to show you that there is a way to break down complex polyline objects into individual line segments and arcs. It was also pointed out that this command should be used sparingly because it adds unnecessary data to your drawings and makes it harder to edit information later.

Chapter Test Questions

Multiple Choice

Circle the correct answer.

1. Complex line objects can be used for which of the following purposes?
   a. Drawing contour lines
   b. Calculating areas
   c. Drawing roadways
   d. All of the above
2. The command that breaks a complex line object down into individual lines and arcs is:
   a. **ERASE**
   b. **EXPLODE**
   c. **EXTEND**
   d. None of the above
3. The system variable that controls whether an old-format polyline is created or a new optimized polyline is created when you use the **PLINE** command is named:
   a. **PLTYPE**
   b. **PLINEWID**
   c. **PLINETYPE**
   d. **PTYPE**
4. By default, the polyline arcs created using the **PLINE** command's **Arc** option are:
   a. Created using three points
   b. Created using two points
   c. Tangent
   d. b and c

5. To create a clockwise polyline arc using the **Angle** option, you can:
   a. Enter an angle greater than 360°
   b. Enter an angle less than 0°
   c. Pick a point
   d. Change the base angle
6. You can use polyline widths to create:
   a. Arrowheads   c. Border lines
   b. Road signs   d. All of the above
7. You can draw a polyline rectangle with the **RECTANG** command by:
   a. Picking points
   b. Entering a length and width
   c. Specifying the total area and one side length
   d. All of the above
8. To draw a solid donut when using the **DONUT** command, specify an inside diameter:
   a. Greater than the outside diameter
   b. That is negative
   c. Of 0.000″
   d. Of 1.000″
9. The system variable that allows you to suppress the *Object selected is not a polyline* prompt when converting an arc or line into a polyline using the **PEDIT** command is named:
   a. **PEDITACCEPT**   c. **PLINEDIT**
   b. **ACCEPTPEDIT**   d. **APEDIT**
10. The maximum gap size that objects can be apart and still be joined using the **PEDIT** command's **Join** option is called:
   a. Join distance   c. Max gap
   b. Fuzz distance   d. Join gap

Matching

Write the number of the correct answer on the line.

a. Polyline ______
b. Rectangle ______
c. Polygon ______
d. Donut ______
e. Revision cloud ______
f. Arc fit polyline ______
g. Spline fit polyline ______

1. Multisided polyline object created by inputting the number of sides
2. Smooth polyline curve that uses the vertices of the selected polyline as the control points to create an approximate B-spline
3. Polyline object with four sides that can be created with two points
4. Smooth polyline curve consisting of arcs joining each pair of vertex points with the curve passing through all vertices
5. Complex line object made up of one or more connected line segments
6. Smoother of the B-spline curves
7. Continuous line made of arcs that resembles a cloud, used to highlight markups and changes

h. Quadratic B-spline _____

i. Cubic B-spline _____

8. Rougher of the B-spline curves

9. Round polyline object that can be a ring or a solid circle

True or False

Circle the correct answer.

1. **True or False:** Polylines can be used to calculate an enclosed area.
2. **True or False:** There are two different types of polylines.
3. **True or False:** Entering a negative angle when using the polyline arc **Angle** option creates a counterclockwise arc.
4. **True or False:** It is possible to create polylines that have a varying width from vertex point to vertex point.
5. **True or False:** Turning off the **Show/Hide Lineweight** button on the AutoCAD status bar turns off all polyline widths.
6. **True or False:** It is possible to draw a rectangle by specifying its total area.
7. **True or False:** You must specify a negative inside diameter to draw a solid (filled) donut using the **DONUT** command.
8. **True or False:** It is possible to join multiple objects together into one continuous polyline even when all the objects are not connected.
9. **True or False:** The **PEDIT** command's **Spline** option can be used to create a true B-spline.
10. **True or False:** It is possible to convert a curve fitted polyline back into its original straight line segments.

Chapter Projects

G Project 9-1: *Circuit Board* [BASIC]

1. Start a new drawing using the **acad.dwt** template. Set the grid spacing to **.1**, the snap spacing to **.025**, and turn both the grid display and **Snap** mode on.
2. Create the following layers:

Name	Color	Linetype	Lineweight	Description
Fab	7	Continuous	Default	Fabrication drawing
Top	5	Continuous	Default	Top layer of metal
Bottom	6	Continuous	Default	Bottom layer of metal
Drill	7	Continuous	Default	Via drill locations
Smask	3	Continuous	Default	Top layer solder mask
Silkscreen	7	Continuous	Default	Top layer silkscreen

3. With **Snap** mode turned on, draw the parts shown in Figure 9-46. Each round pad consists of a 0.060″-diameter circle on the **Top** layer, a 0.020″-diameter circle on the **Drill** layer, and another 0.060″-diameter circle on the **Bottom** layer. The center of each pad should be placed on a grid point.

Figure 9-46

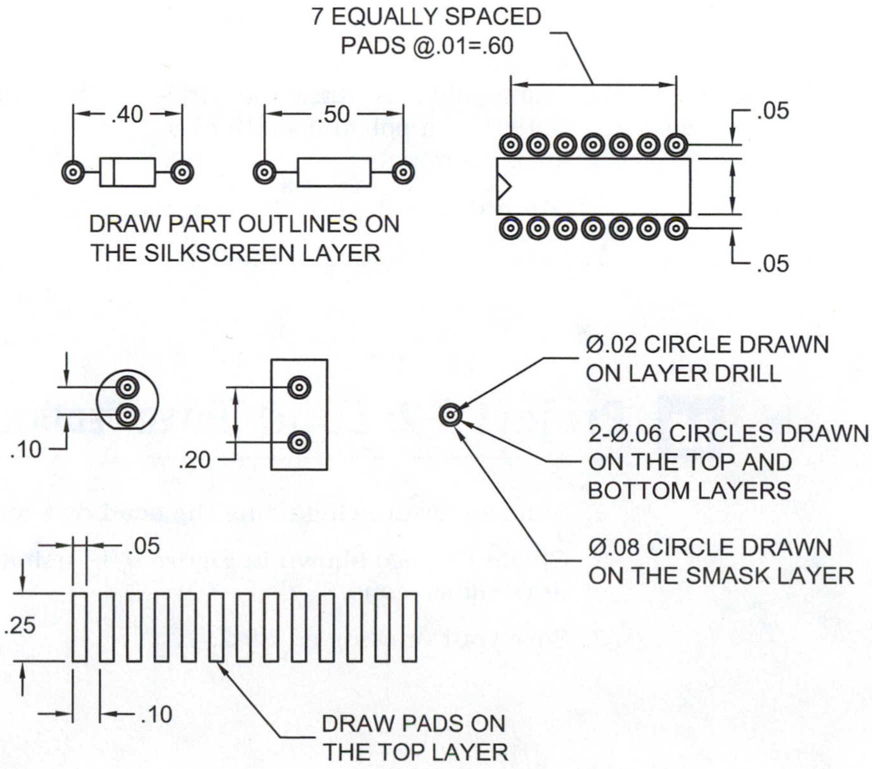

4. Create the board outline and move and copy the parts to arrange them as shown in Figure 9-47.

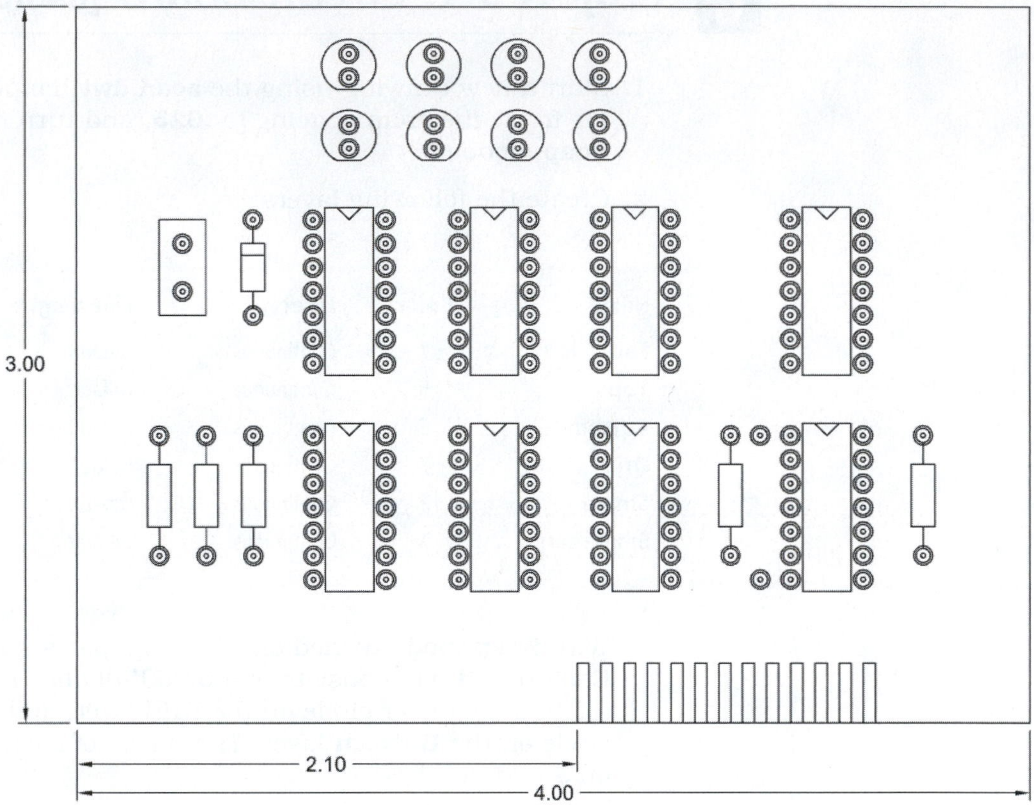

Figure 9-47

5. Using polylines, draw the wiring on the **Top** layer as shown in Figure 9-48. Use a polyline width of 0.006″. All points should be placed on snap coordinates.
6. **Do not** draw text or dimensions.
7. Save your drawing as ***P9-1***.

M Project 9-2: *Logo* [INTERMEDIATE]

1. Start a new drawing using the **acad.dwt** template.
2. Create the logo shown in Figure 9-49 using polyline objects. **Do not** draw dimensions.
3. Save your drawing as ***P9-2***.

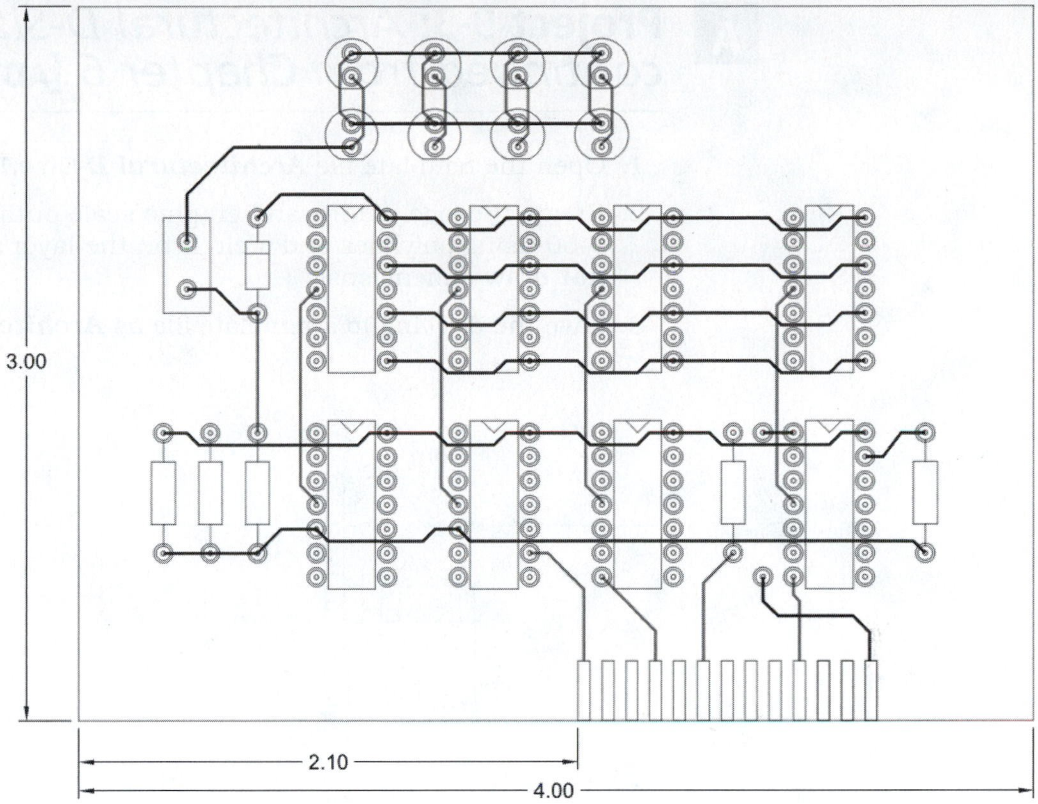

Figure 9-48

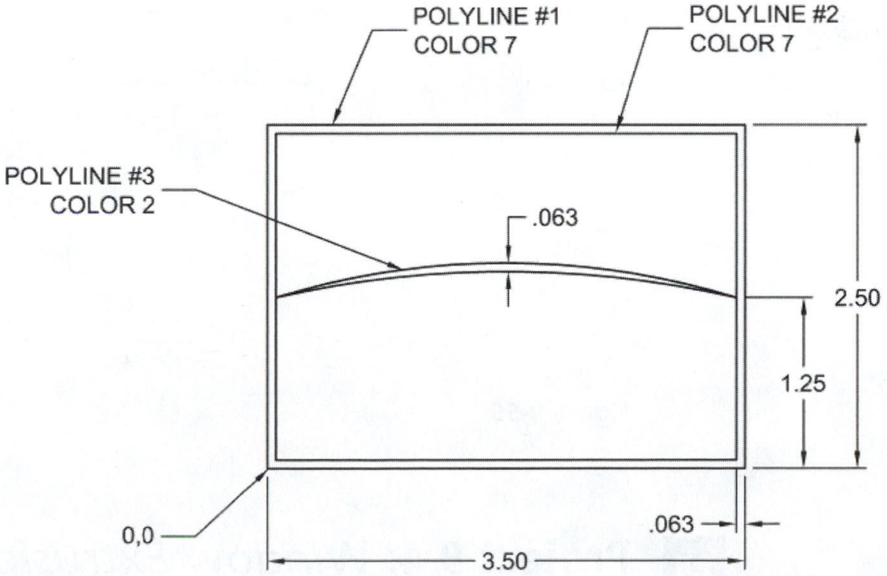

Figure 9-49

Project 9-3: *Architectural D-Size Border, continued from Chapter 6* [ADVANCED]

1. Open the template file ***Architectural D-Size.DWT*** from Chapter 6.
2. Create the logo outline and graphic scale outlines as shown in Figure 9-50 using polylines and a circle on the layer **A-Anno-Ttlb-Logo. Do not** draw dimensions.
3. Save the drawing to a template file as ***Architectural D-Size.DWT***.

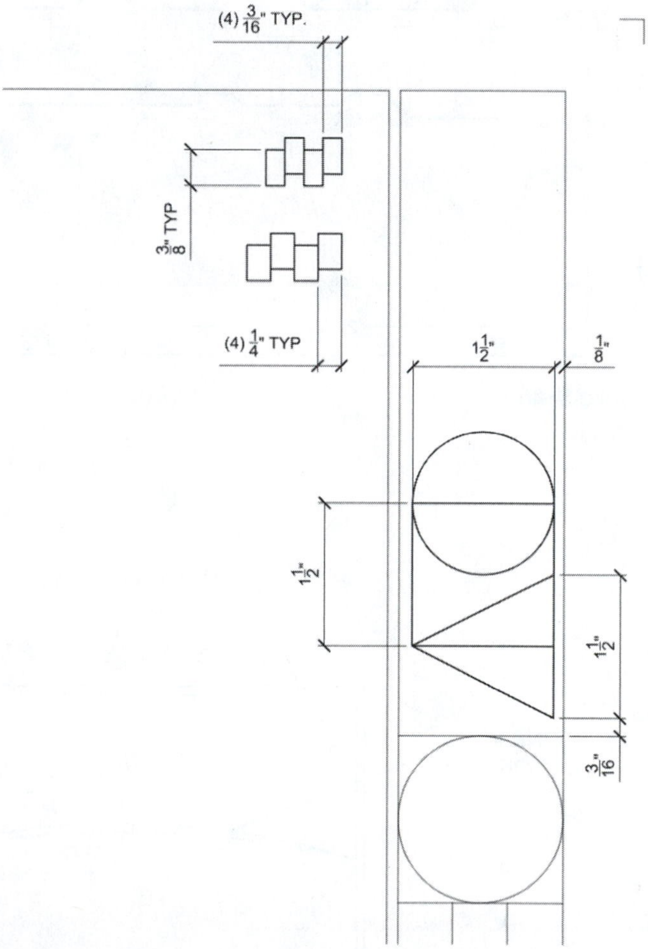

Figure 9-50

Project 9-4: *Window Extrusion—Metric* [BASIC]

1. Start a new drawing using the **acadiso.dwt** template.
2. Create the following layers:

Name	Color	Linetype	Lineweight	Description
Object	7	Continuous	0.60 mm	Object lines
Hidden	1	Hidden	0.30 mm	Hidden lines
Center	2	Center	0.30 mm	Centerlines
Hatch	4	Continuous	0.30 mm	Hatch patterns and fills
Notes	3	Continuous	0.30 mm	Text and notes
Dims	2	Continuous	0.30 mm	Dimensions

3. Draw the window extrusion as shown in Figure 9-51 using a single polyline on layer **Object**.
4. **Do not** draw enlarged detail in circle at top.
5. **Do not** include notes or dimensions.
6. Save the drawing as ***P9-4***.

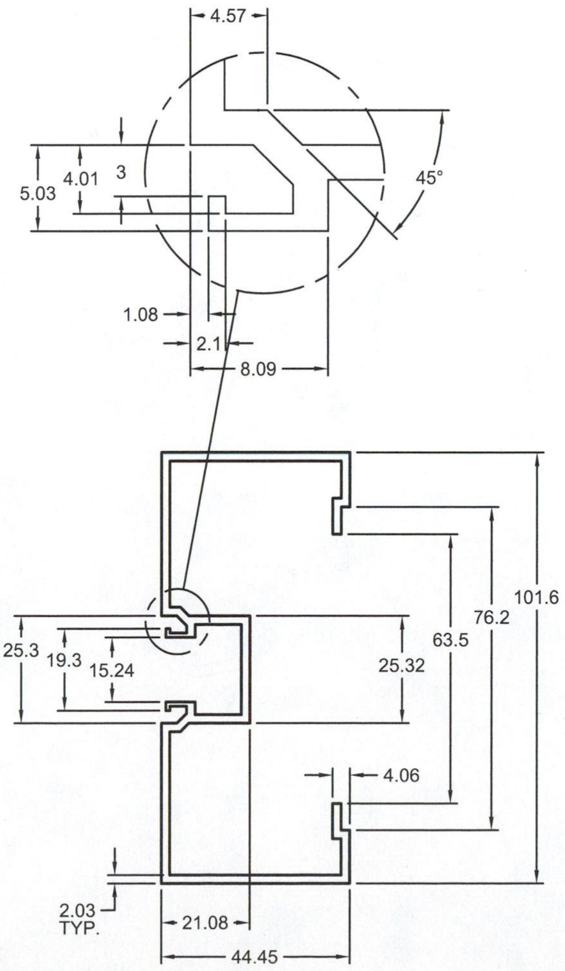

Figure 9-51

A Project 9-5: *Residential Architectural Plan, continued from Chapter 8* [ADVANCED]

1. Open drawing ***P8-5*** from Chapter 8.
2. Create the following layers:

Name	Color	Linetype	Lineweight	Plot/Noplot	Description
A-Eqpm-Fixd	White	Continuous	0.30 mm	Plot	Fixed equipment (fireplaces)
L-Walk	8	Continuous	0.50 mm	Plot	Driveway, patio, walkways, and steps
L-Walk-Pat	8	Continuous	Default 0.50 mm	Plot	Cross-hatch patterns for driveway, patio, walkways, and steps

3. Draw the patio and driveway as shown in Figure 9-52 using spline fit polylines. Use appropriate layers for all objects.
4. Save your drawing as ***P9-5***.

Figure 9-52

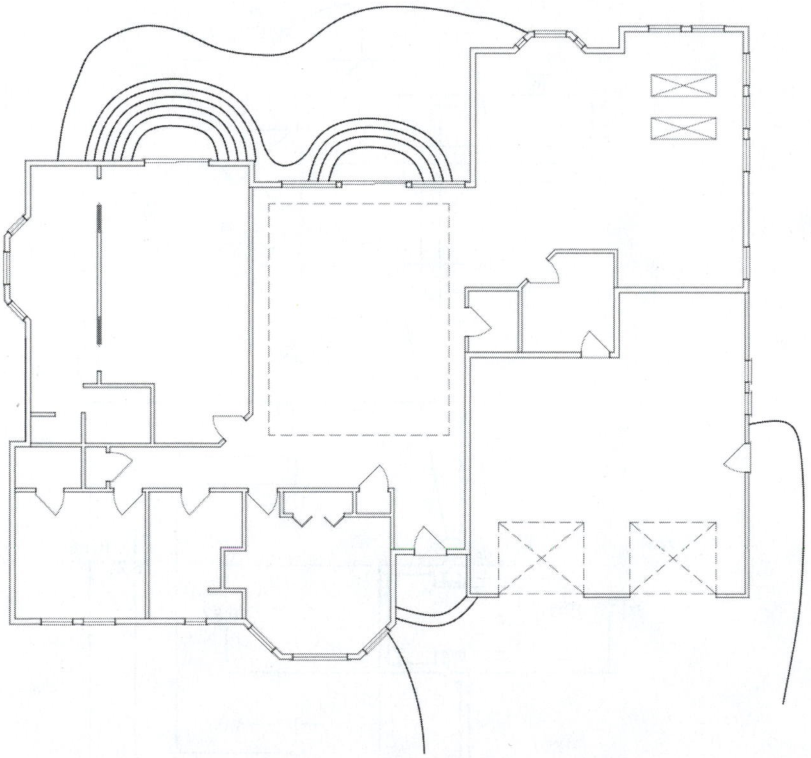

10 chapter ten
Pattern Fills and Hatching

CHAPTER OBJECTIVES

- Select a hatch boundary area
- Control hatch settings and options
- Modify hatched areas
- Match the settings of existing hatched areas
- Create solid and gradient fills
- Edit hatched areas
- Use **DesignCenter** to create hatch objects

Introduction

hatching: The process of filling in a closed area with a pattern.

Hatching is the process of filling in a closed area with a pattern. This is typically used in cross-section or elevation drawings to denote different material usage. Hatch patterns can consist of lines and dots as well as solid colors and gradient fill patterns. Hatching must be placed within a closed area, which means that the edges of the hatch area cannot contain any gaps or openings. AutoCAD provides a couple of different ways to create and select hatch boundaries. In this chapter, you'll look at how hatch patterns are created, controlled, and modified.

Hatching

hatch boundary: The edges of a hatched area.

hatch islands: Closed areas within a hatch boundary.

hatch pattern: The pattern used to fill a hatch boundary.

Figure 10-1 shows some different hatched areas. The ***hatch boundary*** defines the area of the hatch. ***Hatch islands*** are closed areas inside the outer hatch boundary. When you hatch an area, you can control how island areas are dealt with. The ***hatch pattern*** is the pattern used to fill in the boundary. The hatch pattern has a scale, rotation angle, and origin associated with it as well.

HATCH	
Ribbon & Panel:	Home Draw 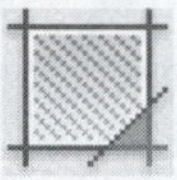
Draw Toolbar:	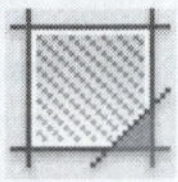
Menu:	Draw | Hatch...
Command Line:	HATCH/ BHATCH
Command Alias:	H

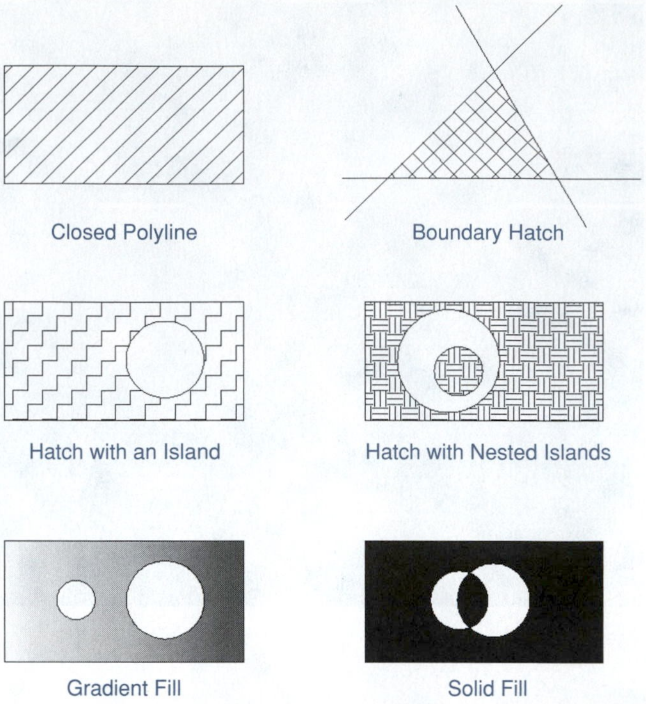

Figure 10-1
Hatch and gradient fill examples

The **HATCH** command is used to place different hatch patterns. All of the hatch settings and options are controlled via the **Hatch Creation** context tab of the ribbon shown in Figure 10-2, which is displayed after you start the command.

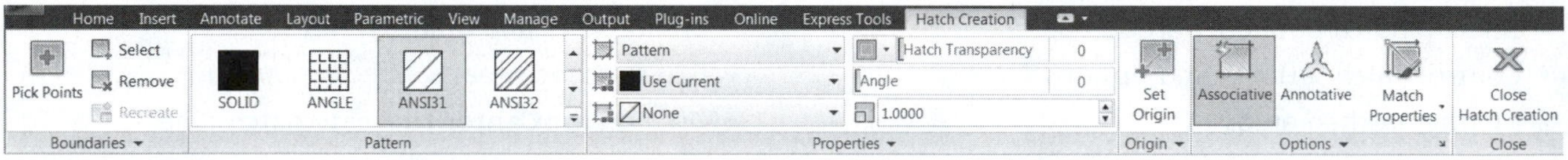

Figure 10-2
The **Hatch Creation** context tab of the ribbon

Selecting a Hatch Area

There are two ways to select hatch boundaries. The default method is to pick an internal point within a closed boundary area. The other method is to select objects that form a closed area such as circles and closed polylines.

Picking an Internal Point. When you pick an internal point, AutoCAD will search out from the point you pick and attempt to trace a closed area around the point you selected. If it's successful, AutoCAD will highlight the closed area and allow you to select additional points. This is a quick and easy way to create hatch areas.

Selecting Objects. If you select closed areas (such as circles or closed polylines) AutoCAD will simply hatch inside them. If you select open objects (such as lines, arcs, and open polylines), AutoCAD will attempt to calculate a hatch area. If the open objects are placed end to end and clearly define a closed area, then the results are predictable. However, if you choose overlapping objects, or if the objects don't clearly define a closed area, then your hatch area may not turn out the way you intend. Figure 10-3 shows some examples of selecting open and closed objects for hatch boundaries.

Chapter 10

Figure 10-3
Selecting hatch boundaries

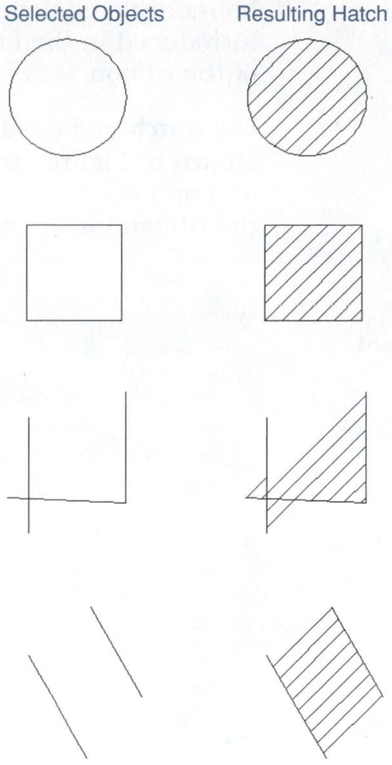

EXERCISE 10-1 Picking an Internal Boundary Point

To access student data files, go to **www.pearsondesigncentral.com.**

1. Open drawing ***EX10-1*** located in the student data files.
2. Start the **HATCH** command.
3. Place your cursor near where point 1 is shown in Figure 10-4 but do not pick a point yet. Notice the hatch preview.
4. Pick a point at the location indicated in Figure 10-4 and press **<Enter>** to accept the hatch pattern.
5. Save the drawing as ***CH10_EXERCISE1***. Your drawing should look like Figure 10-5.

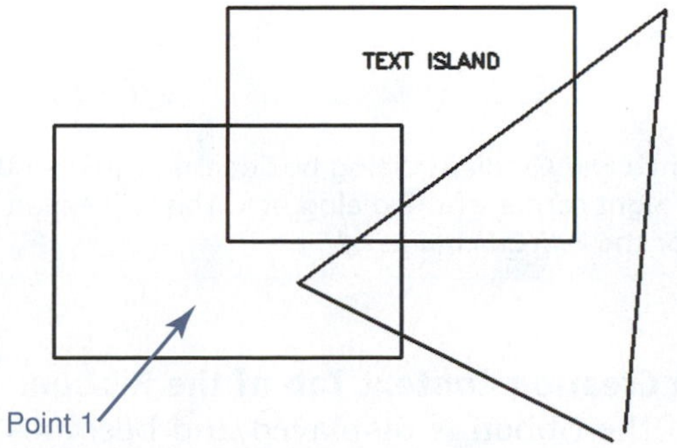

Figure 10-4
Picking boundary points

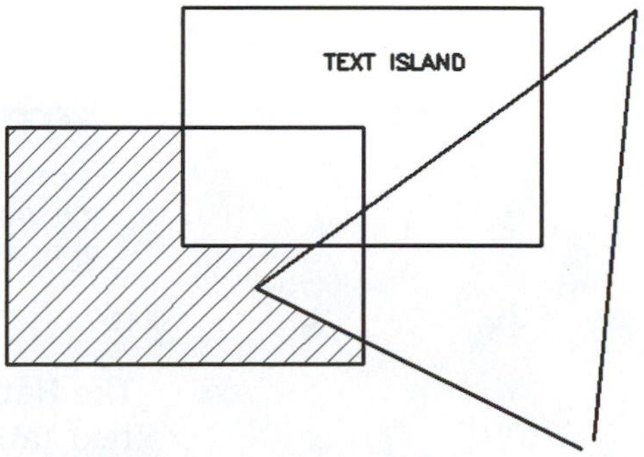

Figure 10-5
The hatched area

Controlling Hatch Settings and Options

There are two ways to control hatch settings and options. They are either by selecting the **seTtings** option at the command line before accepting the boundary area definition to display the **Hatch and Gradient** dialog box introduced in the next section or by using the **Hatch Creation** context tab of the ribbon shown in Figure 10-2.

The Hatch and Gradient Dialog Box. The **Hatch and Gradient** dialog box, shown in Figure 10-6, is a legacy method of controlling the hatch settings and options. It has been superseded by the **Hatch Creation** context tab of the ribbon for the most part. A brief overview is provided only.

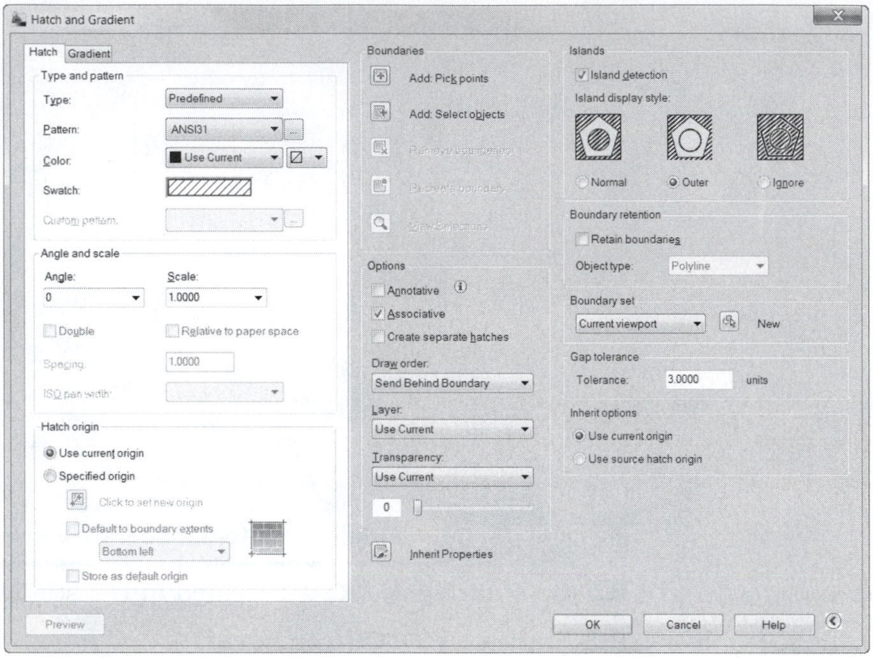

Figure 10-6
The **Hatch and Gradient** dialog box

The **Hatch and Gradient** dialog box is divided into three general sections. The **Hatch** and **Gradient** tabs on the left side of the dialog box allow you to control how the hatch looks. The **Boundaries** area in the center of the dialog box allows you to select or create a hatch area and controls how the hatch will behave. The right side of the dialog box allows you to control how hatch boundaries are created and how island areas are treated.

> **NOTE**
>
> If your **Hatch and Gradient** dialog box doesn't show all the options, select the arrow in the lower right corner of the dialog box. This will expand the dialog box to show all the options for the **HATCH** command.

The Hatch Creation Context Tab of the Ribbon. The **Hatch Creation** context tab of the ribbon is displayed and becomes the current tab when you start the **HATCH** command. You can change most settings and options on-the-fly either before or after defining the hatch boundary area. The different ribbon panels are explored in the following sections.

Boundaries Panel. The **Boundaries** panel provides different options for selecting and adjusting the boundary area. The different ways of selecting the boundary area were discussed earlier. The other boundary options are explained in the following sections.

Adding and Removing Boundaries. Once you have selected a hatch area, you can add additional boundaries by either selecting objects or picking additional points. You can also remove boundaries using the **Remove** button. You can simply select the boundary to remove from the selection when prompted.

Retaining the Boundary. When you create a boundary hatch, you have the option of keeping the boundary as either a polyline or a region. When either of the **Retain Boundaries** options is selected, AutoCAD will create a boundary on the same layer as the hatch pattern. By default, boundaries are not retained.

> **NOTE**
>
> You must select the down arrow at the bottom of the **Boundaries** panel to display the expanded panel for the **Retain Boundaries** and **Boundary Set** options.

> **TIP**
>
> If your drawing has a lot of hatching or contains complex boundaries, you may wish to retain your hatch boundaries and place the boundaries and hatch patterns on a separate layer. This allows you to make changes easily to the hatch patterns and boundaries and also allows you to turn off complex patterns that can sometimes get in the way when editing your drawing.

Boundary Sets. The **Boundary Set** options allow you to control which objects are used when detecting a boundary. The boundary set is a set of objects used to determine boundaries when picking points. By default, everything that is visible in the current viewport is used as the boundary set. If there are objects you wish to ignore or only certain objects you wish to use, select the **Select New Boundary Set** button on the left side of the list box to create a new boundary set. The boundary set is reset to all objects upon the completion of the **HATCH** command.

> **TIP**
>
> With large drawings, AutoCAD can sometimes take a while to calculate boundary areas. If this is the case, you may want to create a new boundary set or consider turning off or freezing layers to reduce the number of calculations needed to determine the boundary.

Pattern Panel. In addition to defining the boundary of the hatch area, you will also typically want to specify the hatch pattern appearance that is used to fill the defined area. AutoCAD comes with many predefined patterns that you can select from the **Pattern** panel. In fact, it is not obvious, but you can display most of them by selecting the arrow with the horizontal line on the bottom of the list box, as shown in Figure 10-7.

AutoCAD hatch patterns are similar to AutoCAD linetypes. By default, they are defined in an external text file named ACAD.PAT that can be either customized or completely replaced with another hatch pattern file. All of the hatch pattern definitions contained in the ACAD.PAT file are shown in Figure 10-8.

Figure 10-7
The expanded **Pattern** list

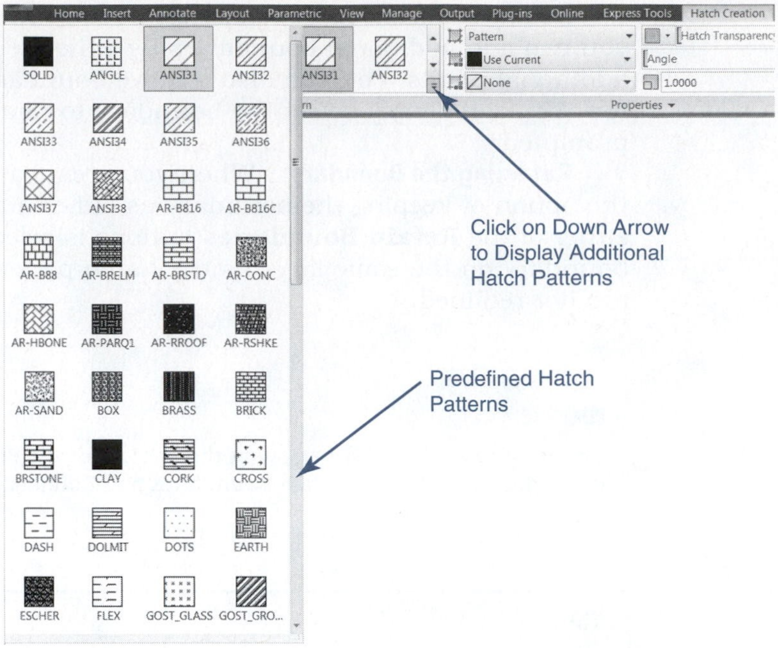

Figure 10-8
Hatch pattern definitions

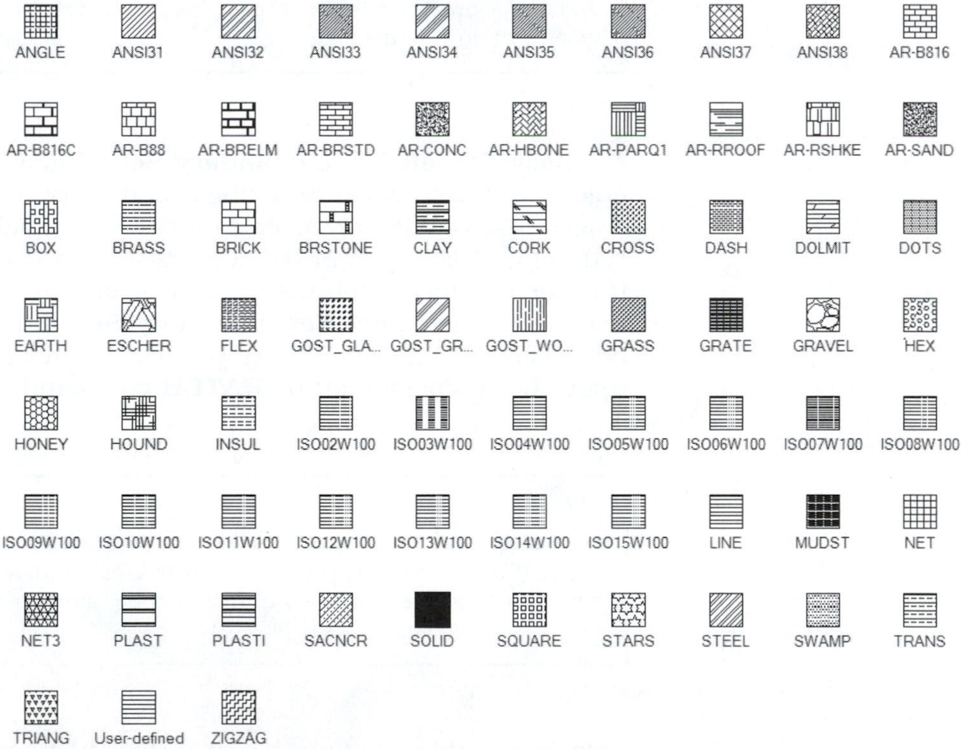

As you can see, there are many different types of hatch patterns for many different applications for various disciplines. The hatch patterns with the ANSI prefix are typically used to denote different materials in section on mechanical drawings. Each numbered pattern represents a specific type of material. For instance, the **ANSI32** hatch represents steel. The default is the **ANSI31** hatch type, which is represented with 45° lines spaced 1/8″ apart. Not only does this represent the material iron, but it is also the industry standard pattern for any material in section.

NOTE

There are actually two hatch pattern definition files: the default used for imperial units (ACAD.PAT) and another that is set up for metric units (ACADISO.PAT). The ACADISO.PAT hatch pattern file contains the same hatch definitions as the ACAD.PAT file, but they are scaled to appear correctly in a metric drawing. You can switch between imperial and metric units by setting the **MEASUREMENT** variable to **0** for imperial and **1** for metric.

The hatch patterns with the AR- prefix are architectural-type hatches and represent different brick patterns, concrete, and earth, just to name a few. These hatch types indicate the actual sizes of the material they represent, so they need to be scaled accordingly. For instance, the **AR-B816** hatch pattern represents an 8″ × 16″ block and is exactly 8″ tall by 16″ long. This allows you to hatch an exterior wall elevation for a building and show the block with the correct number of block courses.

Hatch patterns with the ISO prefix are metric patterns that are designed to comply with the ISO/DIS 12011 linetype specification. When you select an ISO pattern, the **ISO Pen Width** drop-down list is enabled on the **Properties** panel, explained later, so you can specify a pen width for the lines that make up the pattern.

TIP

You can select a hatch pattern either before or after defining the hatch boundary area. In fact, you can change most of the properties of a hatch pattern via the **Hatch Creation** context tab of the ribbon until you press **<Enter>** and accept your selections.

Properties Panel. The **Properties** panel shown in Figure 10-9 provides control over features that include hatch type, color, transparency, angle, scale, layer, and ISO pen width.

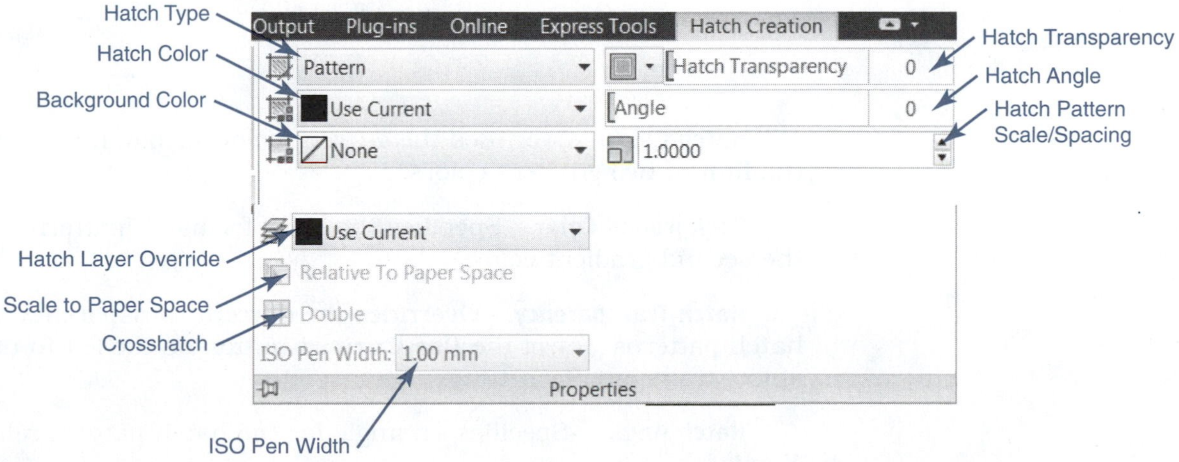

Figure 10-9
The **Properties** panel

Hatch Type. There are four different hatch types that you can choose from. The default **Pattern** hatch type provides access to all the built-in AutoCAD hatch pattern types discussed earlier, such as the ANSI standard and architectural (AR)-type hatches. The **Solid** hatch type allows you to hatch an area with a solid fill. The **Gradient** hatch type, discussed a little later in this chapter, allows you to apply one- and two-color solid fills with different shading effects.

The **User defined** hatch type allows you to define a hatch pattern consisting of straight lines at a defined angle and spacing. The user-defined pattern can have either a single set of parallel lines or a double set of perpendicular lines. The current linetype is used to draw the hatch pattern.

The appearance of the **User defined** hatch type is typically controlled via the **Hatch Angle** and **Hatch Spacing** options. **Hatch Angle** controls the angle of the lines (a setting of 0 produces horizontal lines; 90 produces vertical lines). **Hatch Spacing** is the spacing between the parallel lines. When the **Double** option is selected on the expanded **Properties** panel, an additional set of lines will be drawn perpendicular to the first set of hatch lines to create a crosshatch effect. The perpendicular hatch lines will have the same spacing as the parallel hatch lines. Figure 10-10 shows some examples of user-defined patterns.

Figure 10-10
User defined hatch patterns

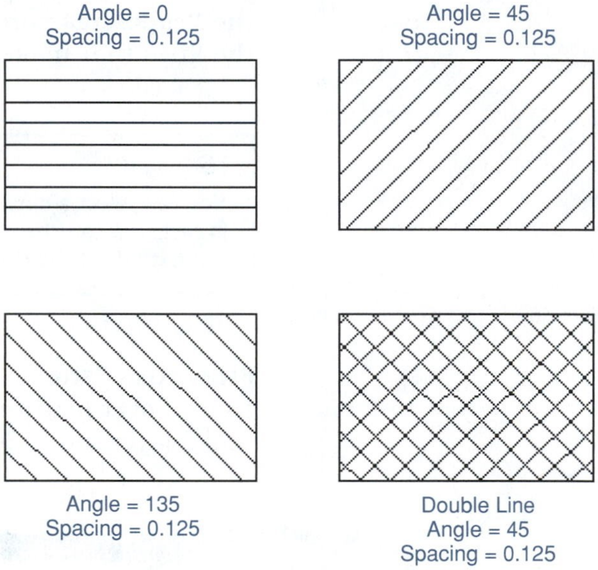

Hatch Color. Overrides the current color for hatch patterns or specifies the first of two gradient colors.

Background Color. Specifies the color for hatch pattern backgrounds or the second gradient color.

Hatch Transparency. Overrides the current transparency level for new hatch patterns. Select the **Use Current** button on the left to use the current object transparency setting.

Hatch Angle. Specifies an angle for the hatch pattern relative to the *X*-axis.

Hatch Pattern Scale/Spacing. Scales up or down predefined hatch patterns or sets the spacing for user-defined hatch patterns if the **User defined** pattern type is selected.

Hatch Layer Override. Overrides the current layer setting for new hatch patterns. Select the **Use Current** button on the left to use the current layer.

Scale to Paper Space. Automatically scales the hatch pattern relative to the current viewport scale in paper space. This option is available only from a layout.

Crosshatch. Creates a crosshatch by drawing a second set of lines at 90° to the original lines for user-defined hatch types. This option is available only when **Hatch Type** is set to **User defined.**

ISO Pen Width. Scales an ISO predefined pattern based on the selected pen width. This option is available only when an ISO type pattern has been selected.

EXERCISE 10-2 Hatch Pattern Properties

1. Continue from Exercise 10-1.
2. Start the **HATCH** command so the **Hatch Creation** context tab of the ribbon is displayed.
3. Select the **ANSI32** hatch pattern from the **Pattern** panel and pick a point where indicated in Figure 10-11 to create the hatch pattern. **Do not** press **<Enter>** yet.
4. Select the **ANSI37** hatch pattern from the **Pattern** panel.
5. Enter **2** in the **Hatch Pattern Scale** box on the **Properties** panel and press **<Enter>.**
6. Enter **45** in the **Hatch Angle** box on the **Properties** panel and press **<Enter>.**
7. Set the color to **red** in the **Hatch Color** list box on the **Properties** panel.
8. Press **<Enter>** to accept the hatch. Your drawing should look like Figure 10-12.
9. Save your drawing.

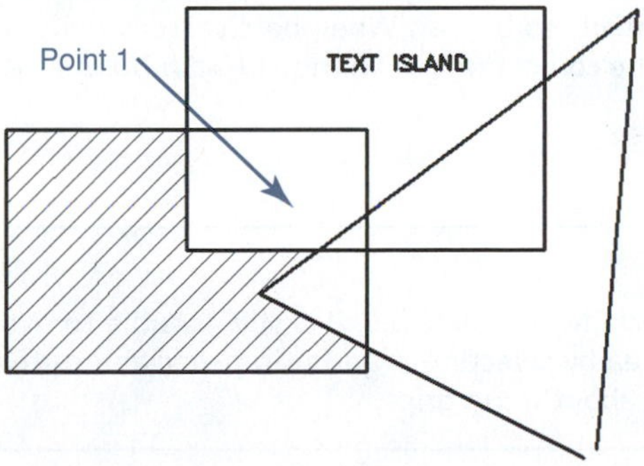

Figure 10-11
The boundary pick point

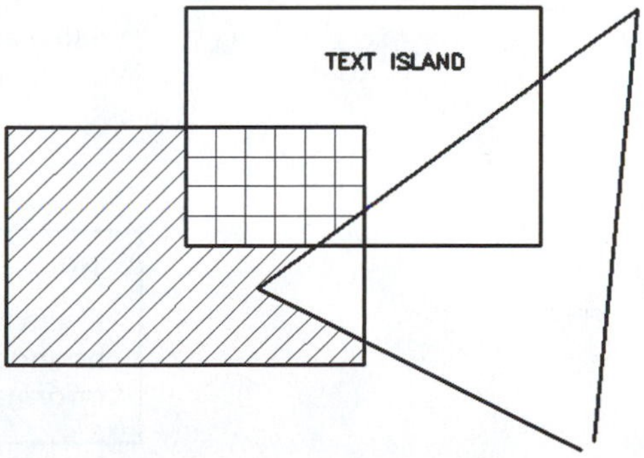

Figure 10-12
The completed hatch

Origin Panel. The **Origin** panel area allows you to control the starting point of the hatch pattern. By default, all hatch patterns are drawn using 0,0 as a base point. This means that AutoCAD calculates where the hatch pattern will be drawn based on the hatch pattern definition starting at the 0,0 coordinate. Typically that is what you want; however, there may be times when you want the hatch pattern to start at a specific coordinate. For example, if you are using a brick or tile pattern, you may want the pattern

Figure 10-13
Selecting a hatch origin

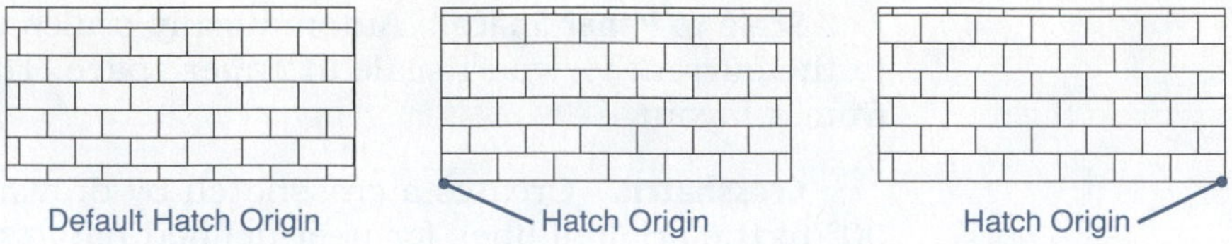

to start with a full brick or tile in the corner of the boundary. To do this, you select the hatch origin to be the corner of the hatch boundary. Figure 10-13 shows some examples of setting the hatch origin.

The **Set Origin** option allows you to select an origin point in your drawing. The **Use Current Origin** option simply uses the default hatch origin. By default this origin is 0,0 until you change it. It's also possible to set the origin to default to one of the four corners (or the center) of the boundary area. Once you specify a new origin, select the **Store as Default Origin** button to retain that point at the new default hatch origin.

Options Panel. The **Options** panel provides different options that control the appearance and behavior of hatch patterns.

Associative Hatching. In AutoCAD, *associativity* means a link between one drawing object and another. In Chapter 2, you saw an example of associative dimensioning. When you placed a dimension object, it was associated with the points on the objects you dimensioned. If those points moved, the dimension object moved along with it.

Associativity can also occur between a hatch object and its boundary. If the boundary edge is modified, its associated hatch objects will update and fill in the changed boundary. The **Associative** option turns associativity on and off.

NOTE

Hatch pattern associativity can be a fleeting thing. Associativity can be lost if the boundary edges change significantly. For example, if two overlapping objects were used to create a hatch boundary, modifying the objects so that they no longer overlap will cause the hatch associativity to be lost. When hatch associativity is lost, AutoCAD will display a message in the command line window: *Hatch boundary associativity removed*.

TIP

If hatch associativity is removed, it is still possible to dynamically change the hatch boundary area by selecting it and using special intuitive grips. See Chapter 7 for information about using grips.

Annotative Hatching. The **Annotative** button turns automated annotation scaling on and off. If **Annotative** is on, the hatch pattern is automatically scaled up or down based on the current annotation scale.

FOR MORE DETAILS

See page 8 in Chapter 1 for more information about the **Annotation Scale** feature.

Gap Tolerance. If a boundary area contains gaps and is therefore not closed, AutoCAD displays a **Boundary Definition Error** dialog box and displays red circles showing where the gaps are located on the drawing. You can either fix them or adjust the **Gap Tolerance.** The **Gap Tolerance** setting allows you to heal any gaps in a boundary. When the gap tolerance is set to 0, the boundary must be completely closed in order for a valid boundary to be created. When the gap tolerance is set greater than 0, AutoCAD will attempt to determine a boundary and will ignore any gaps that are smaller than or equal to the specified tolerance. When it finds a valid boundary with gaps smaller than the specified tolerance, AutoCAD will display the **Open Boundary Warning** box (see Figure 10-14) asking whether you'd like to continue to hatch the area.

> **NOTE**
>
> You must select the down arrow at the bottom of the **Options** panel to access the **Gap Tolerance** and the other options discussed in the following sections.

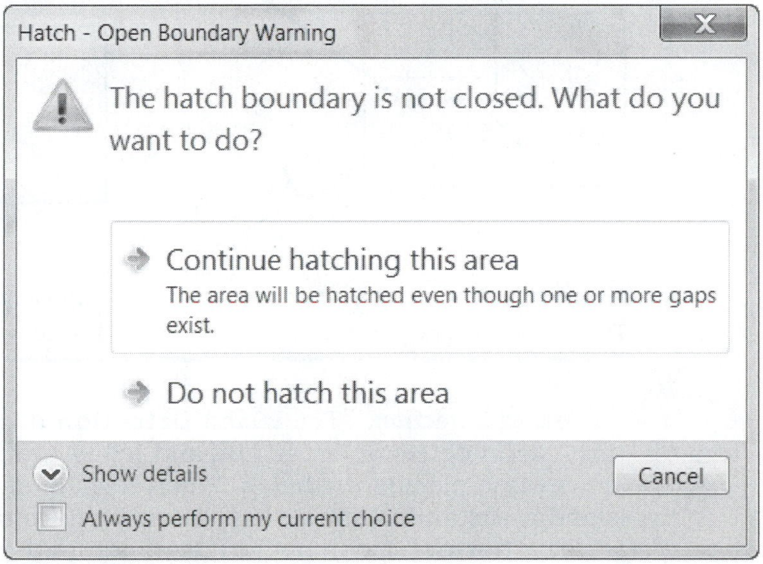

Figure 10-14
The **Open Boundary Warning** box

When AutoCAD detects a boundary with gaps, it will project the objects out to their intersection and use this point as the corner of the boundary.

Creating Separate Hatches. When you select or create more than one boundary, you have the option of creating a single hatch object that spans all the boundaries, or you can create separate hatch objects in each hatch area. The **Create separate hatches** option allows you to control this. Placing a check in the **Create separate hatches** box will create one hatch object for each closed boundary.

> **NOTE**
>
> Hatch boundaries don't have to touch in order to create hatch **objects**. You can create a single hatch object that spans multiple boundaries that don't physically overlap.

EXERCISE 10-3 Boundary Gaps

1. Continue from Exercise 10-2.
2. Start the **HATCH** command and select the **ANS31** hatch pattern.
3. Pick point 1 as shown in Figure 10-15. AutoCAD will display the **Boundary Definition Error** dialog box and place red circles on your drawing where gaps are located. Select **Close** to exit the dialog.
4. Set the **Gap Tolerance** option to **0.25** on the expanded **Options** panel and pick point 1 again. AutoCAD will display the **Open Boundary Warning** dialog box so you can select the **Continue hatching this area** option and create a closed boundary.
5. Press **<Enter>** to accept the hatch pattern and end the **HATCH** command.
6. Save your drawing. Your drawing should look like Figure 10-16.

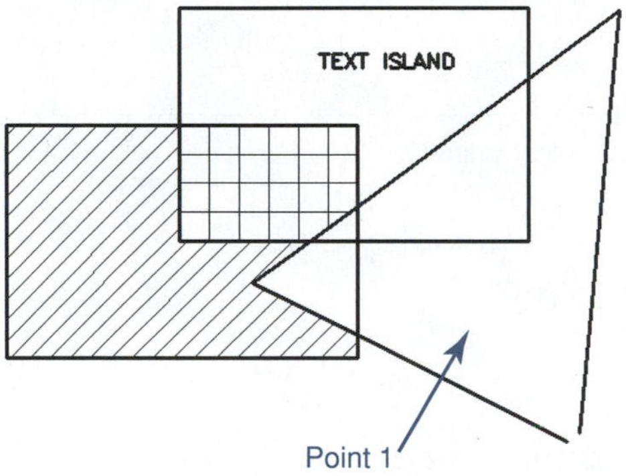

Figure 10-15
The boundary pick point

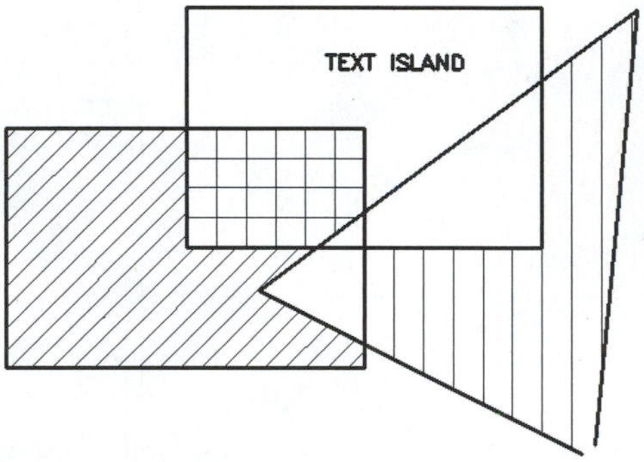

Figure 10-16
The completed hatch

Island Detection. The **Island Detection** drop-down list allows you to turn island detection on and off and tells AutoCAD how to deal with island areas when placing the hatch. When turned off, AutoCAD will ignore any island areas and create a single boundary around the point you pick.

The **Normal** option applies the hatch pattern to every other nesting level starting with the outer boundary. The **Outer** option applies the hatch pattern between the outer boundary and the first nesting level. All further nesting levels are ignored. The **Ignore** option simply ignores all internal islands and fills the entire outer boundary with the hatch pattern. Figure 10-17 shows the effect of the different **Island Detection** options.

Figure 10-17
Island Detection options

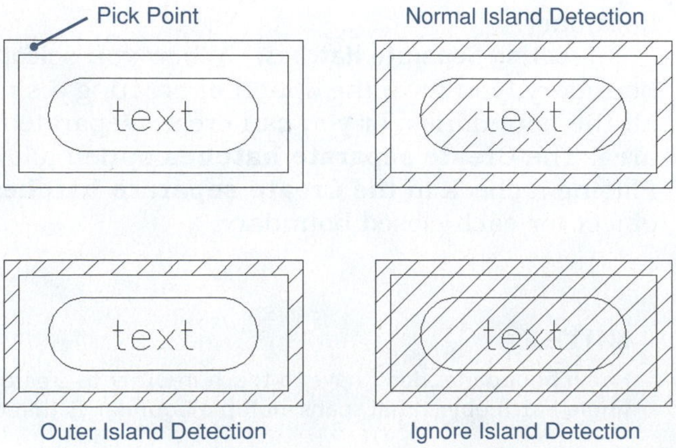

NOTE

Text objects (text, Mtext, and dimension text) are treated as though a closed box were drawn around the text. Selecting text inside a closed shape will result in the text being treated as an island within the boundary.

EXERCISE 10-4 Island Detection

1. Continue from Exercise 10-3.
2. Start the **HATCH** command and select the **SOLID** hatch pattern.
3. Pick point 1 shown in Figure 10-18. AutoCAD will detect the boundary along with the text island.
4. Select the **Ignore Island Detection** option on the **Options** panel. The hatch pattern will now fill over the text island.
5. Set the **Island Detection** back to **Normal** and press **<Enter>** to create the hatch pattern and end the **HATCH** command.
6. Save your drawing. Your drawing should look like Figure 10-19.

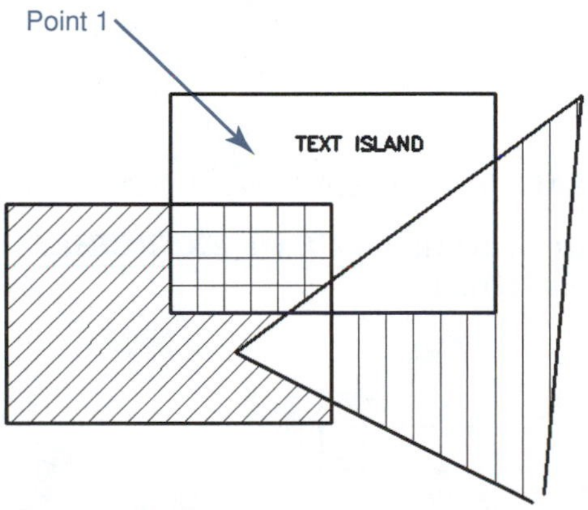

Figure 10-18
The boundary pick point

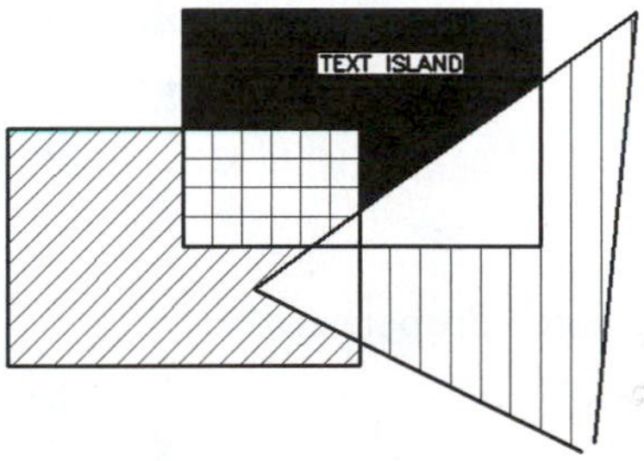

Figure 10-19
The completed hatch

Draw Order. The **Draw order** setting allows you to control the order in which the hatch pattern is drawn with respect to the boundary. The default option is to send the hatch pattern behind the boundary, which means that the boundary will be drawn on top of the hatch pattern. In most cases, the draw order doesn't matter; however, in cases where the boundary is on a different layer or is a different color from the hatch pattern, the draw order can affect the look of your drawing.

Matching Existing Hatch Patterns. If you have an existing hatch pattern in your drawing, AutoCAD can read the properties of the hatch pattern and use those settings to create a new hatch pattern. The **Match Properties** button allows you to select an existing hatch pattern from your drawing and will use the properties of the selected hatch as the default values in the dialog box. When you inherit hatch pattern properties, you have the option of inheriting the hatch origin of the selected hatch pattern or using the currently defined hatch origin. Selecting the down arrow to the right of the **Match Properties** button allows you to switch from the default **Use current origin** to the **Use source hatch origin** option, which will use the hatch origin of the selected hatch pattern.

EXERCISE 10-5 **Inheriting Hatch Patterns**

To access student data files, go to **www.pearsondesigncentral.com.**

1. Open drawing ***EX10-5*** located in the student data files. Set the layer **Fence** current.
2. Start the **HATCH** command and choose the **Match Properties** button on the **Options** panel. AutoCAD prompts you to *Select hatch object:*.
3. Pick the brick wall pattern on the left side of the drawing. AutoCAD now prompts you to *Pick internal point or* ↓. Pick the two points shown in Figure 10-20. Press **<Enter>**. All the settings for the selected hatch are now the default options for your new hatch.

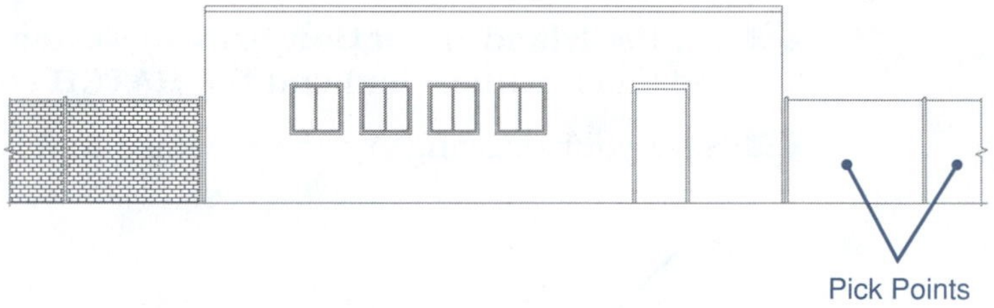

Figure 10-20
The boundary pick points

4. Press **<Enter>** to accept the pattern and end the **HATCH** command.
5. Save your drawing as ***CH10_EXERCISE5***. Your drawing should look like Figure 10-21.

Figure 10-21
Inheriting hatch properties

Gradient Fills

GRADIENT	
Ribbon & Panel:	Home Draw 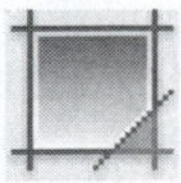
Draw Toolbar:	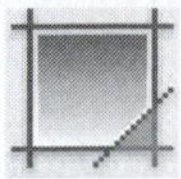
Menu:	Draw Gradient...
Command Line:	GRADIENT
Command Alias:	None

In addition to solid fills and hatch patterns, AutoCAD can also create gradient fills. Gradient fills create a smooth color transformation from either one color to light (or dark) or between two selected colors. Gradient fills can be created by selecting the **Gradient** hatch type from the **Properties** panel of the **Hatch Creation** context tab of the ribbon explained earlier or with the **GRADIENT** command.

The **GRADIENT** command displays the **Hatch Creation** context tab of the ribbon with the **Gradient** options. The **Gradient** options are similar to a solid hatch fill with two noticeable differences: the number of colors and the gradient pattern.

Two-Color Gradient

A two-color gradient fill transitions between the two colors selected for the **Gradient Color 1** and **Gradient Color 2** options on the **Properties** panel. When the **Two color** option is selected, the **Gradient Tint and Shade** slider bar is disabled. It is the default option.

One-Color Gradient

A one-color gradient fill creates a smooth color transition from a selected color to another shade of that color.

To create a one-color gradient, you must select the **Gradient Tint and Shade** option on the **Properties** panel. Selecting this option disables the **Gradient Color 2** option and turns on the **Gradient Tint and Shade** slider on the bottom right side of the **Properties** panel. This slider bar controls the shade of the transition color. With the slider at the left-hand side, the transition color is black. With the slider all the way to the right, the transition color is white.

Gradient Pattern

There are nine predefined gradient fill patterns to choose from on the **Pattern** panel. You choose the pattern you want and then optionally choose a rotation angle. You can also choose to have the fill centered within the boundary or generated from the edge of the boundary by turning on/off the **Centered** option on the **Origin** panel. With the **Centered** option turned off, you can use the **Hatch Angle** setting on the **Properties** panel to control which side the pattern generated from. Figure 10-22 shows some combinations of gradient patterns and rotation angles.

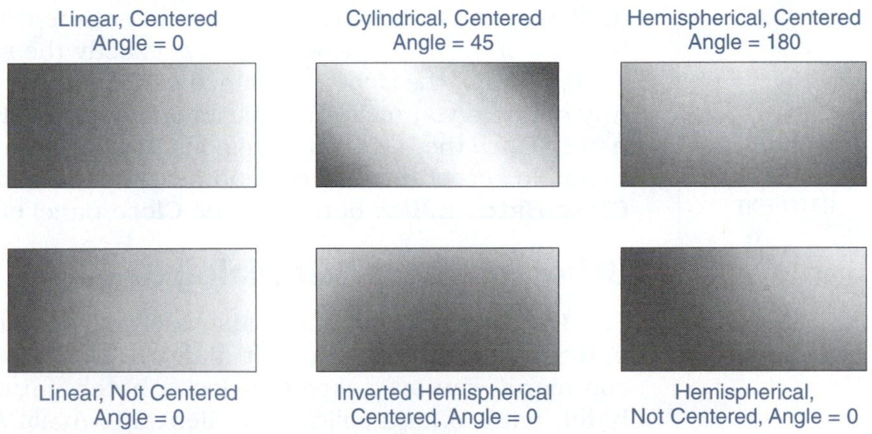

Figure 10-22
Gradient fill patterns

EXERCISE 10-6 **Creating a Gradient Fill**

1. Continue from Exercise 10-5 and set layer **Window** current.
2. Start the **GRADIENT** command and pick the points inside the eight window panes shown in Figure 10-23.

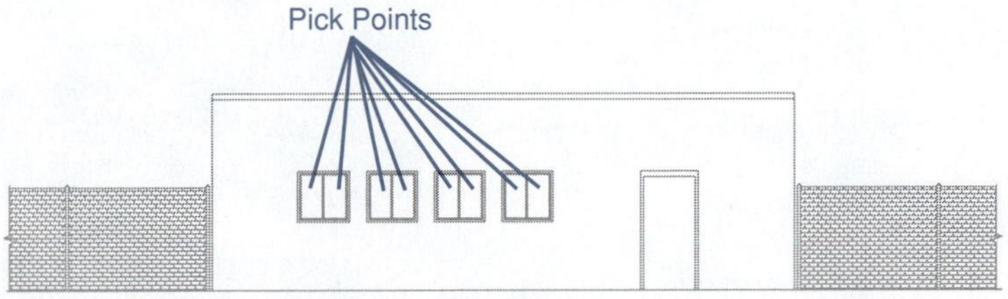

Figure 10-23
The boundary pick points

3. Select the **Gradient Tint and Shade** button on the **Properties** panel. Select the **Select Colors...** option from the **Gradient Color 1** drop-down list, and specify **ACI color 142** as the base color for the gradient fill. Choose **OK** to close the **Select Color** dialog box.

4. In the **Gradient Tint and Shade** slider, move the slider to the right end of the bar, so it is set to **90%.**
5. Select the linear pattern (the first pattern on the left) and set the **Angle** to **270** on the **Properties** panel.
6. Press **<Enter>** to accept the pattern and end the **GRADIENT** command.
7. Save your drawing. Your drawing should look like Figure 10-24.

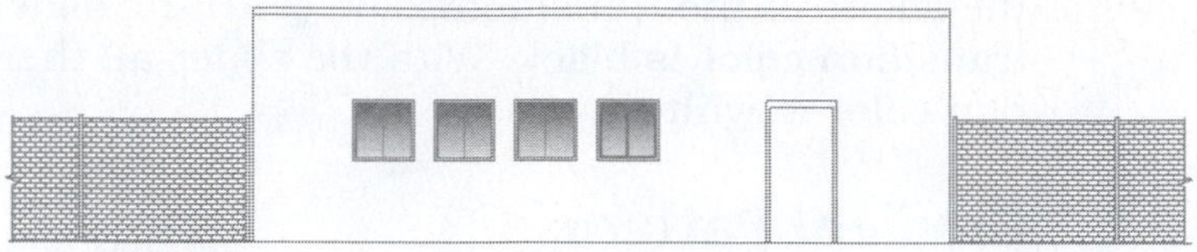

Figure 10-24
A gradient fill

EDIT HATCH	
Ribbon & Panel:	Home Modify 
Modify II Toolbar:	
Menu:	Modify Object | Hatch…
Command Line:	HATCHEDIT
Command Alias:	HE

Editing Hatch Patterns

Once a hatch object is created, there are a number of ways to modify it. You can change the hatch pattern along with any of the hatch options. You can even change a hatch pattern to a solid or gradient fill.

Using the Hatch Editor Context Tab of the Ribbon

The easiest way to edit a hatch pattern is to simply select it in your drawing to display the **Hatch Editor** context tab of the ribbon. The **Hatch Editor** context tab of the ribbon looks and acts exactly the same as the **Hatch Creation** context tab of the ribbon explained earlier in this chapter (see Figure 10-2). Any changes you make via the ribbon are applied directly to the selected hatch. Once the hatch pattern looks how you want it to, you can either press <**Esc**> to accept the changes and deselect the hatch pattern, or select the **Close Hatch Editor** button on the **Close** panel of the ribbon.

Using the Hatch Edit Dialog Box

The **HATCHEDIT** command allows you to modify any aspect of a hatch pattern using the **Hatch Edit** dialog box. When you start the **HATCHEDIT** command, you are asked to select a hatch pattern. Once you select a hatch pattern (or a solid or gradient fill), AutoCAD displays the **Hatch Edit** dialog box (see Figure 10-25).

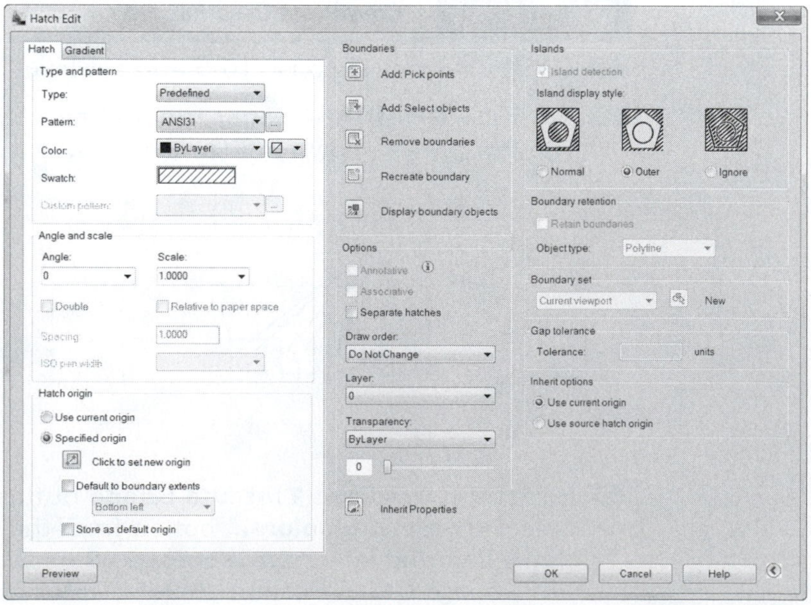

Figure 10-25
The **Hatch Edit** dialog box

NEW to AutoCAD 2013

> **TIP**
> It is possible to select more than one hatch boundary area at a time in your drawing and update them all simultaneously using the **Hatch Editor** context tab of the ribbon.

This dialog box is identical to the **Hatch and Gradient** dialog box used to create hatch objects if you use the **seTtings** option from the command line. When you select a hatch object, all of that object's settings are shown as the default values in the **Hatch Edit** dialog box. From this dialog box, you can change any aspect of the hatch object.

One option that is available in the **Hatch Edit** dialog box but is not available in the **Hatch and Gradient** dialog box is the **Recreate boundary** button. When you select this button, AutoCAD will create a new boundary for the hatch. If the hatch is associative, you have the option of keeping the association with the original boundary or reassociating the hatch with the new boundary. The **Recreate boundary** button always retains the new boundary as a new drawing object.

EXERCISE 10-7 **Editing Hatch Patterns**

1. Continue from Exercise 10-6.
2. Select the fence hatch pattern on the left side of the building to display the **Hatch Editor** context tab of the ribbon.
3. Select the **ANSI37** pattern from the **Pattern** panel and set the **Hatch Pattern Scale** to **30.** Press **<Enter>** to accept the pattern.
4. Select the brick pattern on the right side of the drawing to display the **Hatch Editor** context tab of the ribbon. Choose the **Match Properties** button and select the **ANSI37** pattern you just created.
5. Press **<Enter>** to accept the pattern.
6. Save your drawing. Your drawing should look like Figure 10-26.

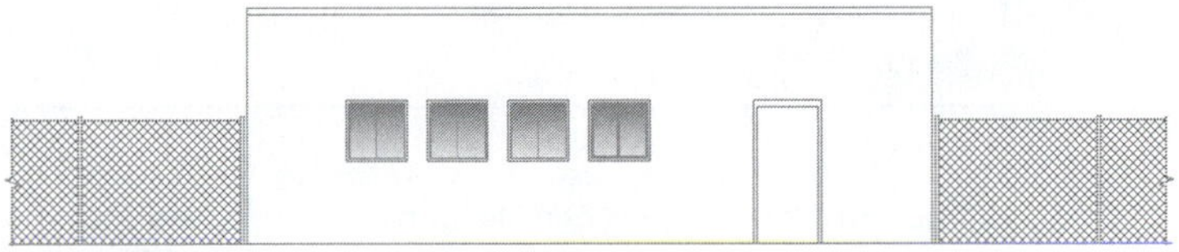

Figure 10-26
The modified hatch patterns

Using the Properties Palette

The **Properties** palette is another easy way to make changes to hatch objects. Although you can't make changes to the hatch boundaries, you can change the hatch pattern, scale, rotation angle, and hatch origin. You can also turn off the associativity and change the island detection method.

Trimming Hatches

When using the **TRIM** and **EXTEND** commands, you can select hatch objects as cutting/boundary edges. The edges of the individual hatch pattern lines will be used as stopping points. Only hatch patterns can be used in this manner; gradient and solid fill patterns will be ignored.

When using the **TRIM** command, you can trim hatch patterns back to selected cutting edges. When trimmed, the boundary edge of the hatch is trimmed back to the cutting edge, and the boundary is recalculated and reassociated if necessary. You cannot extend a hatch pattern out to a boundary edge.

EXERCISE 10-8 **Trimming Hatch Patterns**

1. Continue from Exercise 10-7 and thaw layer **Fence2.** Two new fence posts are displayed on the left and right sides of the drawing.
2. Zoom into the fence post on the left side and start the **TRIM** command. Select the new fence post as the cutting edge and press **<Enter>** to end the edge selection.
3. Pick the fence pattern in the middle of the post to trim the hatch pattern back to the new post. You can also select the boundary line near the top of the fence post to clean up the fence post. Repeat this process on the right-hand fence post.
4. Save your drawing. Your drawing should resemble Figure 10-27.

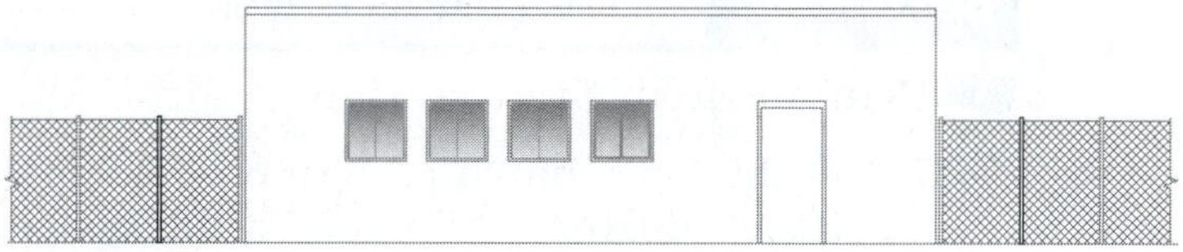

Figure 10-27
Trimming hatch objects

Exploding Hatches

There may be times when you need to modify the individual lines within a hatch pattern. To do this, you can use the **EXPLODE** command on hatch patterns. The **EXPLODE** command will convert hatch patterns to individual line segments.

> **TIP**
>
> You must take care when deciding to explode a hatch pattern. Exploding a hatch pattern can create a large number of individual objects and can greatly increase the size of your drawing. You may also have a hard time finding and cleaning up all the little line objects that the **EXPLODE** command creates.

Using DesignCenter with Hatch Patterns

AutoCAD's **DesignCenter** can also be used to create hatch patterns. When using **DesignCenter,** you can find and select .pat files on your hard drive or any accessible network drive. When you select a .pat file, **DesignCenter** will read the file and display a list of all hatch patterns defined within that file.

To create a hatch object with **DesignCenter,** you can simply drag and drop the desired hatch pattern into any closed area on your drawing. AutoCAD will create a simple boundary hatch using the default hatch settings. You can then double-click the hatch pattern to display the **Hatch Editor** context tab of the ribbon and make any desired changes.

FOR MORE DETAILS

See page 699 in Chapter 16 for more information about **DesignCenter**.

EXERCISE 10-9 Hatching with DesignCenter

1. Continue from Exercise 10-8 and set layer **Elevation** current.
2. Start the **ADCENTER** command to display the **DesignCenter** palette. Position the **DesignCenter** palette at a convenient location on your screen.
3. In the **DesignCenter** palette, choose the **Folders** palette and navigate to the **C:\Program Files\Autodesk\AutoCAD 2013\User Data Cache\Support** folder. Double-click on the **acad.pat** hatch pattern file. After a few moments, **DesignCenter** will show a list of all the hatch patterns defined in this file.
4. Scroll down the list and select the **AR-BRELM** pattern. Drag this hatch pattern onto your drawing and release it within the boundary of the building wall. AutoCAD will fill the building wall with this pattern. Close or hide the **DesignCenter** palette.
5. Select the pattern you just created to display the **Hatch Editor** tab of the context ribbon. Change the **Hatch Pattern Scale** to **2.0** and set the **Island Detection** to **Outer Island Detection** on the **Options** panel.
6. Press **<Enter>** to accept the pattern.
7. Save your drawing. Your drawing should resemble Figure 10-28.

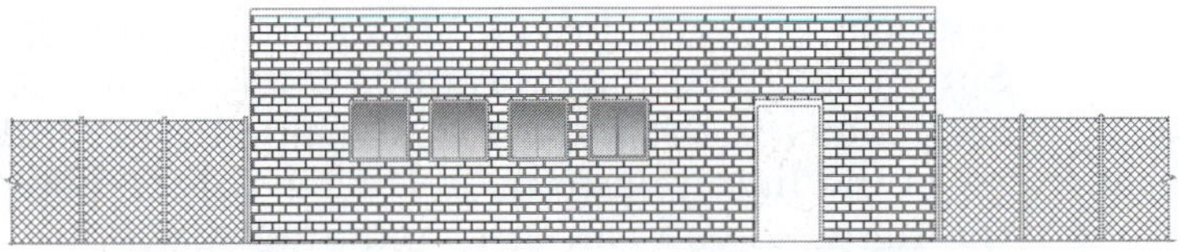

Figure 10-28
Hatching with **DesignCenter**

Chapter Summary

Creating hatch and fill patterns is an integral part of drafting and design. Not only do hatch patterns make a drawing look better, they also can provide needed clarity and even indicate the type of material something is constructed of.

AutoCAD makes the process of hatching simple, by allowing you simply to pick a point within the enclosed area you wish to hatch. AutoCAD calculates the hatch boundary area by casting a net outward to find the enclosed area and automatically displays the **Hatch Creation** context tab of the ribbon so you can select one of the many industry-standard patterns that come with AutoCAD or create your own user-defined pattern. Different properties such as color, angle, and scale can then be adjusted as necessary.

Solid fills and gradient fills allow you to apply different effects that can be used to create striking presentation drawings. Using two-color gradient fills, you can apply different shading techniques that represent spheres, cylinders, and boxes. If necessary, you can move the filled areas behind or in front of other objects in the drawing, thereby creating different overlap scenarios.

The best part is that hatch patterns remain associated with their boundary area by default, so if the boundary area changes, the hatch pattern is updated automatically to fill the new area. In addition, selecting an existing hatch pattern automatically displays the **Hatch Editor** context tab of the ribbon so you can make changes to the hatch pattern including the pattern type, rotation, scale, and any other property.

The **DesignCenter** tool, which is typically used to insert blocks and symbols, can also be used to insert hatch patterns using drag and drop. Simply locate any valid AutoCAD hatch pattern definition file with a .PAT extension via the **Explorer** navigation pane in **DesignCenter,** and open it. All of the hatch patterns in the file will be listed in the **Contents** pane on the right, so you can drag and drop them into a valid closed boundary area in your drawing and voilà!

Chapter Test Questions

Multiple Choice

Circle the correct answer.

1. A hatch boundary:
   a. Must consist of drawing objects connected end to end
   b. Cannot contain any islands
   c. Can consist of only straight line segments; curved boundaries are not allowed
   d. None of the above
2. The **Island Detection** option:
   a. Controls how island areas are hatched
   b. Allows you to ignore all island areas
   c. Allows you to hatch every other nested island area
   d. All of the above

3. A *solid* fill pattern:
   a. Can use only ACI color numbers
   b. Does not work with Color Book defined colors
   c. Can use any valid AutoCAD color
   d. Can use only RGB or HLS defined colors
4. The boundary set is:
   a. The set of objects used when detecting boundary edges
   b. The boundary edge of a hatched area
   c. Created when associative hatching is turned on
   d. None of the above
5. The **HATCHEDIT** command:
   a. Is used to explode hatch objects
   b. Is used to modify hatch patterns
   c. Does not work on gradient fills
   d. All of the above
6. If a predefined hatch pattern is defined as a set of parallel lines .5 unit apart at a 45° angle, applying a hatch scale of 2 and a hatch angle of 180° will result in an area hatch consisting of lines:
   a. 2 units apart at an angle of 45°
   b. 1 unit apart at an angle of 225°
   c. .5 unit apart at an angle of 180°
   d. 2 units apart at an angle of 180°
7. A one-color gradient fill transitions only between:
   a. Black and white
   b. A selected color and white
   c. A selected color and black
   d. None of the above
8. Hatch patterns can be:
   a. Exploded
   b. Used as edges in the **TRIM** and **EXTEND** commands
   c. Modified with the **TRIM** command
   d. All of the above

Matching

Write the number of the correct answer on the line.

a. Hatching ______
b. Gradient fill ______
c. Hatch boundary ______
d. Associativity ______
e. Hatch islands ______

1. A file that contains hatch pattern definitions
2. A link between two drawing objects so that when one changes, the other updates
3. A solid pattern with a smooth transition from one color to another
4. The allowable open area allowed when detecting boundary edges
5. Closed areas within a hatch boundary

f. Gap tolerance ______

g. Boundary set ______

h. Hatch pattern ______

i. ACAD.PAT ______

6. The process of filling in a closed area with a pattern

7. The set of objects used when detecting boundary edges

8. The edges of a hatched area

9. The pattern used to fill a hatched area

True or False

Circle the correct answer.

1. **True or False:** Hatch objects cannot be modified. You must delete and re-create them.
2. **True or False: DesignCenter** can be used to create hatch objects.
3. **True or False:** Objects must touch end to end to be used as hatch boundaries.
4. **True or False:** User-defined hatch patterns are always drawn with a continuous linetype.
5. **True or False:** Text objects are treated as closed objects when determining a boundary.
6. **True or False:** You can create only one hatch pattern at a time with the **HATCH** command.
7. **True or False:** Hatch patterns are defined in .pat files.
8. **True or False:** You cannot modify hatch pattern definitions.
9. **True or False:** Modifying hatch boundary objects can result in losing associativity with their hatch patterns.
10. **True or False:** AutoCAD can create one-, two-, and three-color gradient fills.

Chapter Projects

G Project 10-1: *Calculator, continued from Chapter 5* [BASIC]

1. Open drawing ***P5-1*** from Chapter 5.
2. Create the solid and gradient fill areas shown in Figure 10-29. Experiment with different gradient settings to achieve the desired effect.
3. Save your drawing as ***P10-1***.

Figure 10-29

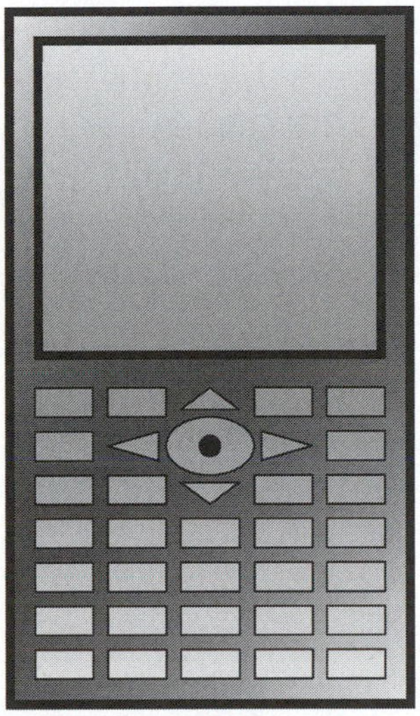

M Project 10-2: *Logo, continued from Chapter 9* [INTERMEDIATE]

1. Open drawing ***P9-2*** from Chapter 9.
2. Create the solid fill areas shown in Figure 10-30.
3. Save your drawing as ***P10-2***.

A Project 10-3: *Architectural D-Size Border, continued from Chapter 9* [ADVANCED]

1. Open the template file ***Architectural D-Size.DWT*** from Chapter 9.
2. Hatch the logo outline as shown in Figure 10-31 using a two-color gradient hatch on the layer **A-Anno-Ttlb-Logo**.
3. Hatch the graphic scale outline as shown in Figure 10-31 using the **SOLID** hatch on the layer **A-Anno-Ttlb-Text**.
4. Save the drawing to a template file as ***Architectural D-Size.DWT***.

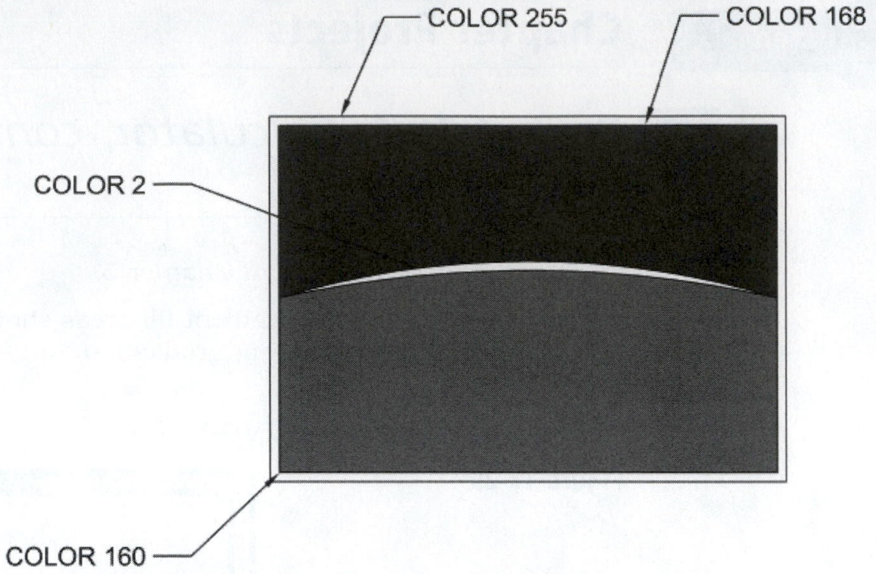

Figure 10-30

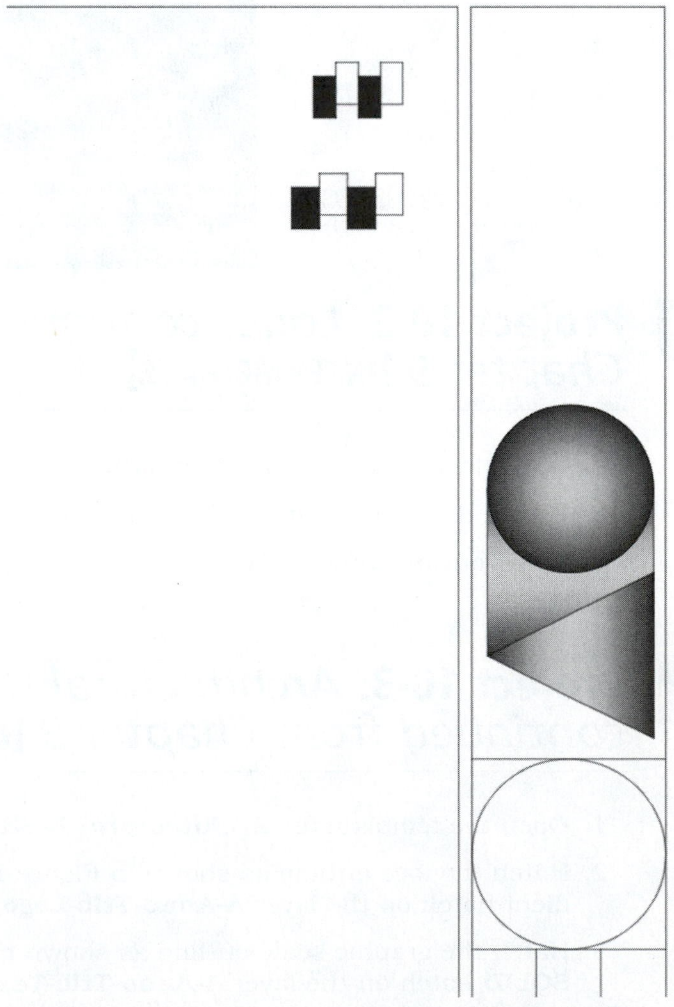
Figure 10-31

E Project 10-4: *Electrical Distribution Panel, continued from Chapter 7* [BASIC]

1. Open drawing ***P7-4*** from Chapter 7.
2. Add the hatching shown in Figure 10-32. Make sure the hatching is placed in back of the outlines.
3. Save your drawing as ***P10-4.***

Figure 10-32

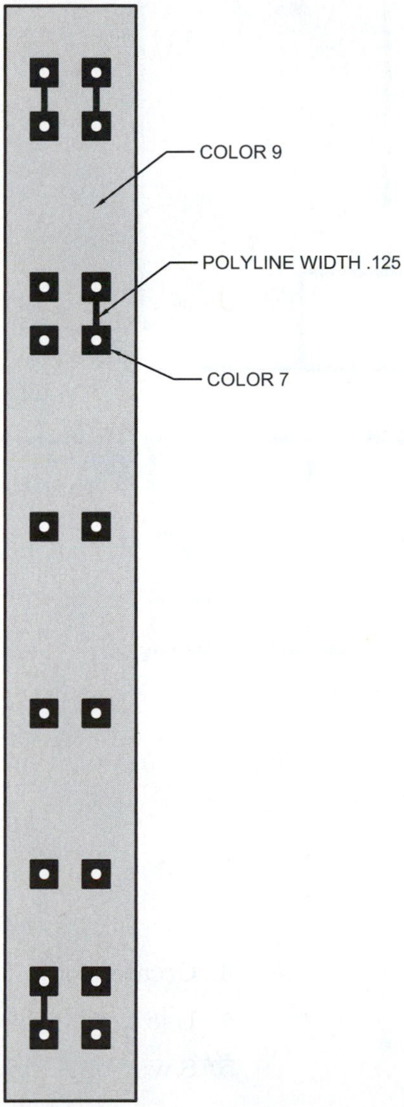

A Project 10-5: *Residential Architectural Plan, continued from Chapter 9* [ADVANCED]

1. Open drawing ***P9-5*** from Chapter 9.
2. Hatch the patio and driveway as shown in Figure 10-33. Use the **GRAVEL** hatch pattern. Experiment with the scale and rotation angle to achieve the desired stone pattern.

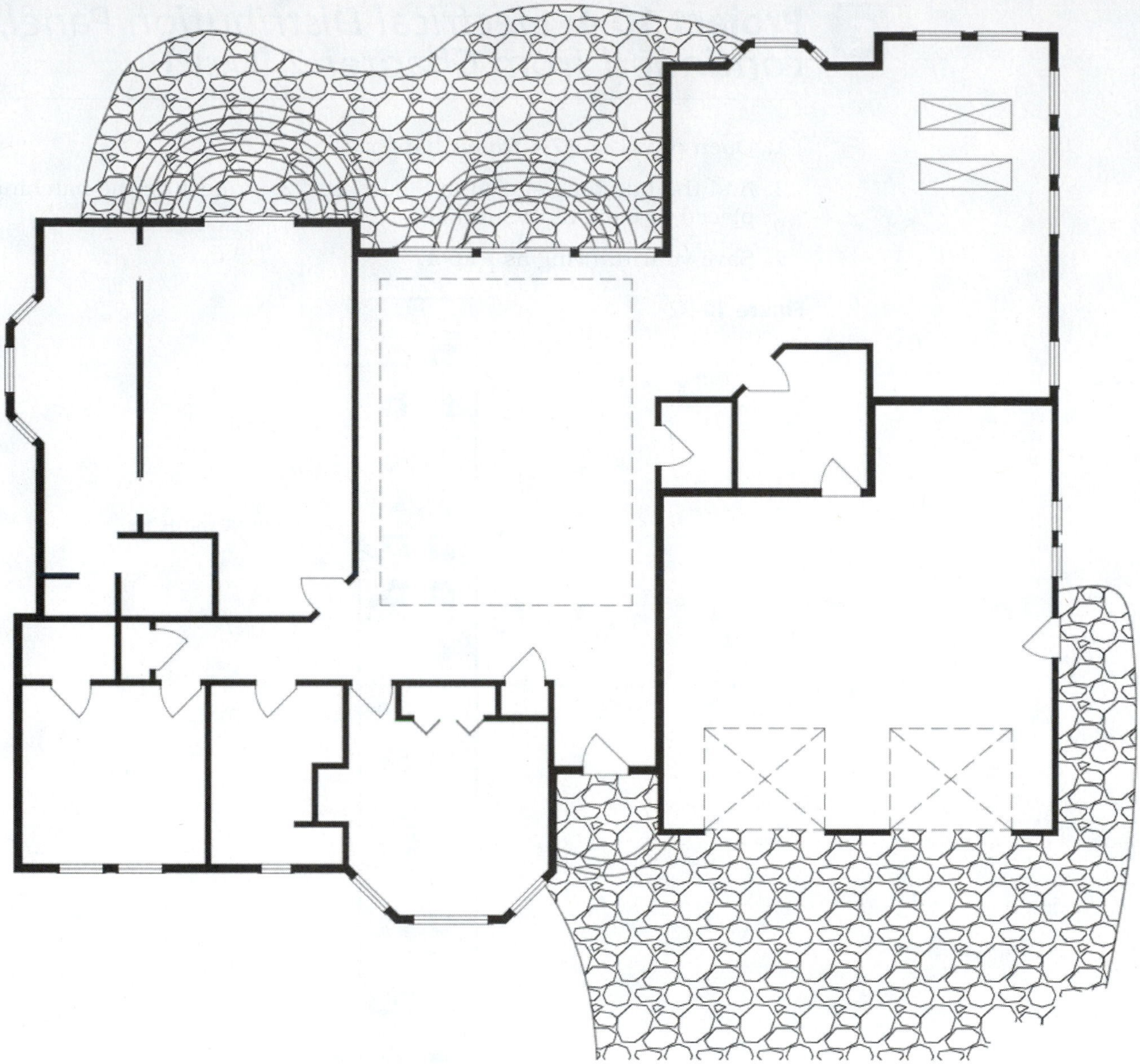

Figure 10-33

3. Create the solid fill areas in the walls.
4. Use appropriate layers for all objects.
5. Save your drawing as ***P10-5***.

11 chapter eleven
Adding Text

CHAPTER OBJECTIVES

- Control the appearance of text using text styles and fonts
- Understand the difference between TrueType fonts and AutoCAD SHX fonts
- Create and edit multiline text
- Create and automate horizontal, diagonal, and tolerance type stacked text
- Create and edit single-line text
- Insert intelligent text fields
- Find and replace text in a drawing
- Check text spelling for a whole drawing

Introduction

annotate: To add text, notes, and dimensions to a drawing.

They say a picture is worth a thousand words, and while the lines, arcs, and circles on a drawing can convey a great deal of design information, at the end of the day you will need to ***annotate*** your drawings in order to completely communicate your design.

Text on a drawing comes in many different shapes, sizes, and forms. It is used in a drawing's title block to tell the reader who created the drawing and when. Title block text might also provide information about who checked the drawing or what revision of a design you are viewing—both very important pieces of information. Of course, there is also the text that is created directly on a drawing in the form of notes, labels, and callouts with specific design instructions, references to other drawings, part numbers, and specifications, to name but a few. Figure 11-1 shows a few examples of different types of drawing annotation.

Manually annotating a drawing on the drafting board, originally referred to as *lettering*, was a tedious and time-consuming task. In fact,

Figure 11-1
Examples of drawing annotation

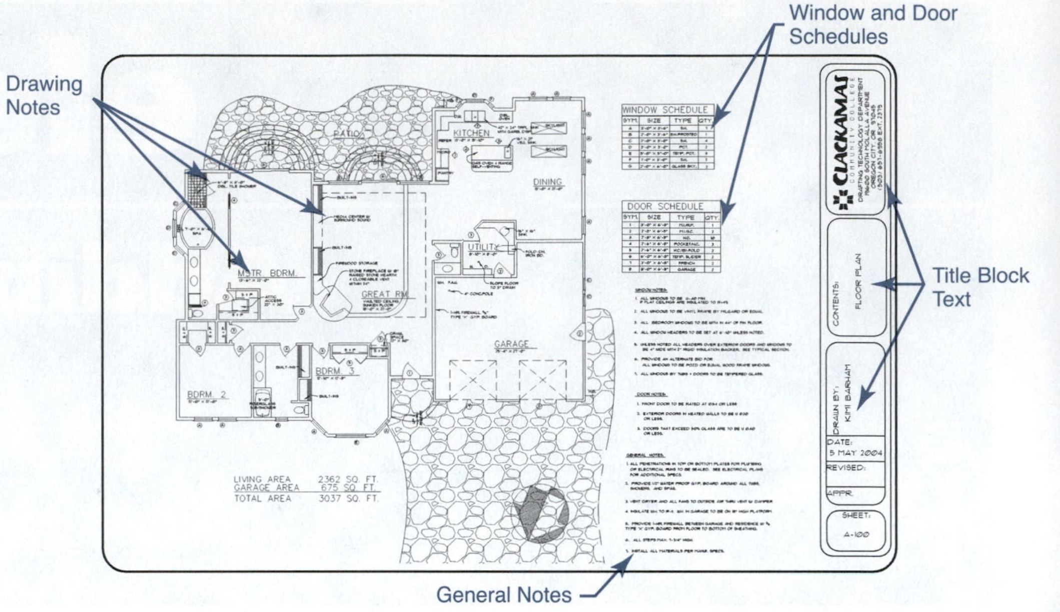

some considered it an art form because of the skill and dexterity needed to annotate a drawing properly.

Those days are long gone. AutoCAD provides a number of tools that allow you to annotate your drawings, in a fashion that meets or exceeds industry drafting standards quickly, and with minimum effort. You can add multiple lines of text by simply defining a boundary area that the text should fill so that as you type, AutoCAD automatically formats the text to fit. It is also possible to add text, known as a *field*, which can automatically update itself with the current date, the name of drawing file, or the properties of an object in a drawing!

In this chapter, we look at the tools AutoCAD provides for annotating your drawing. We also examine the tools used to *edit* annotation features. Once again, AutoCAD makes it quick and easy to change information once it is created in a drawing so that updating text is as simple as double-clicking with your mouse.

TIP

Text and other annotation features should be placed on a unique layer so that you can control their visibility. Text can be one of the most resource-intensive objects in a drawing. A drawing with a lot of text can become significantly bogged down. Being able to freeze text on its layer can significantly increase drawing performance.

Controlling the Appearance of Text

The appearance of text on a drawing is very important. Text should be created as legibly as possible so that it can be easily read and understood with minimum effort. Because of this, different standards have been established to control everything from the text font and height to how text should be located and oriented in a drawing.

FOR MORE DETAILS

See page 813 in Appendix A for detailed information about drafting industry text standards.

Fonts

typeface: The style or design of a font.

These days most people are familiar with text fonts. The font is what determines how text looks by defining its ***typeface***.

Some of the more popular TrueType® fonts are shown in Figure 11-2.

> **TIP**
>
> A drawing named ***TrueType.DWG,*** located in the AutoCAD Sample folder, shows the character map for many of the TrueType fonts.

Figure 11-2
Examples of TrueType fonts

Arial, **Arial Black**, Arial Narrow
City Blueprint, Country Blueprint, Stylus BT
Courier New, Times New Roman
Swis721 BT, Swiss721 Lt BT
Impact, Comic Sans MS, **Vineta BT**
SansSerif, Trebuchet MS, Verdana
Wingdings ♦✋☠✌☜♓■♑⬧☺

TrueType Fonts Versus AutoCAD Fonts. The fonts shown in Figure 11-2 are known as TrueType fonts. TrueType fonts are the standard font type provided as part of Microsoft® Windows. TrueType is actually a specification developed by Apple Computer and later adopted by Microsoft that allows for scalable text, meaning the same font can be displayed at any size and resolution. A TrueType font typically has a three-letter TTF filename extension.

> **NOTE**
>
> The **TEXTFILL** system variable controls the filling of TrueType fonts while plotting and rendering. Setting **TEXTFILL = 0** turns the solid fill off. Setting **TEXTFILL = 1** turns the solid fill on.

In addition to TrueType fonts, AutoCAD comes with its own set of fonts referred to as *SHX fonts* because of their three-letter SHX filename extension. Some of the standard AutoCAD SHX fonts are shown in Figure 11-3.

Figure 11-3
Examples of AutoCAD fonts

TXT	–	AaBbCcDdEe123456790
MONOTXT	–	AaBbCcDdEe123456790
SIMPLEX	–	AaBbCcDdEe123456790
ROMANS	–	AaBbCcDdEe123456790
ROMANC	–	AaBbCcDdEe123456790
ROMAND	–	AaBbCcDdEe123456790
ROMANT	–	AaBbCcDdEe123456790
BOLD	–	**AaBbCcDdEe123456790**
COMPLEX	–	AaBbCcDdEe123456790

As you can see from Figure 11-3, the AutoCAD fonts range from simple to complex. The most basic AutoCAD font is TXT.SHX. Text can be one of the most demanding factors on your computer system resources. Text with a complex font consumes more memory than text with a simple font. If you have a drawing with a lot of text, a complex double- or triple-line font takes much longer to regenerate than a simple font such as TXT.SHX.

TIP

A good balance of performance versus legibility is provided by both the ROMANS.SHX and SIMPLEX.SHX AutoCAD fonts.

Fonts are typically assigned to text styles because this provides the most control over the appearance of text in your drawing. It is possible to assign fonts directly to text objects using multiline text, but this approach is typically avoided because of the increased management needs. Text styles and multiline text are both discussed later in this chapter.

TIP

The **FONTALT** system variable specifies an alternate font to be used when a particular font file cannot be located on your system. By default, the **FONTALT** system variable is set to the AutoCAD SIMPLEX.SHX font.

Text Height

The height of text in a drawing is very important and, as mentioned earlier, is also determined by industry drafting standards. Text that is used for notes on a drawing is typically 0.100″ to 0.125″ (2 mm to 3 mm) tall, whereas text for titles is typically 0.188″ to 0.25″ (5 mm to 6 mm) tall. These are the standard heights that text should be on the final plotted or printed drawing, but they are not always the heights used when text is added to a drawing. Remember from Chapter 1 that if the final printed drawing is not at a scale of 1:1, you must scale annotation features up or down so that they plot at the correct size. This is accomplished by multiplying the desired printed text height by the reciprocal of the plot or viewport scale. This multiplier is referred to as the *drawing scale factor*.

TIP

The **TEXTSIZE** system variable controls the default text height used in a drawing. It is set to 0.20 by default.

FOR MORE DETAILS

See page 813 in Appendix A for more details about calculating the drawing scale factor manually.

Annotation Scale

Instead of calculating the scale factor manually as just described, it is possible to automate the process of scaling text so that it is created at the correct height for the final plotted drawing scale using the AutoCAD **Annotation Scale** feature located on the right side of the status bar.

NOTE

Remember that even though text with multiple annotation scales can be viewed at multiple scales, it is in reality represented by only one text object. AutoCAD does not make multiple copies for each scale representation. In fact, the **Annotation Scale** feature was developed to eliminate the need to create new text for each scale and to have to rely on layers to turn different scales off and on.

When text with its annotative property enabled is added to the drawing, it automatically scales up or down by the current annotation scale so that it is the correct height.

Taking it a step further, it is even possible to add additional different annotation scales to text automatically so that it can be viewed at different heights for different scale factors. Using this feature, each time the annotation scale is changed, all the text that has its annotative property enabled is resized accordingly.

FOR MORE DETAILS

See page 8 in Chapter 1 for a detailed description of the **Annotation Scale** feature. See Chapter 14 for an example of applying the annotation scale features using paper space layouts and viewports.

The best way to take advantage of the **Annotation Scale** feature when you are working with text is to enable the **Annotative** check box in the current text style. Text styles are explained in detail in the next section.

Text Styles

The font, height, and other characteristics that affect the appearance of text are typically managed using text styles. All text in a drawing has a text style associated with it. When you add text to a drawing, it is created using the current text style settings. The current text style can be set by selecting it from the text style list on the expanded **Annotation** panel on the **Home** tab of the ribbon or the **Text** panel on the **Annotate** tab of the ribbon shown in Figure 11-4, selecting it from the text style list in the multiline text editor explained later, or typed in if you are creating single-line text.

The default text style is named STANDARD, which is assigned the Arial TrueType font with a text height of 0.000″.

Figure 11-4
Text panel on the **Annotate** tab of the ribbon

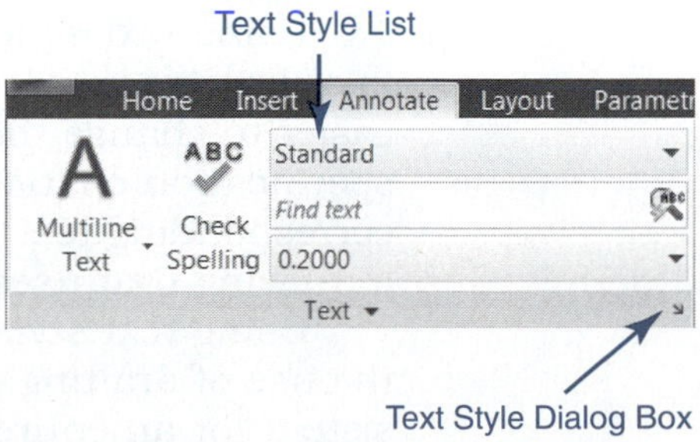

TIP

The **Annotate** tab of the ribbon provides quick and easy access to the most commonly used annotation tools. For this reason, you should select the **Annotate** tab to display the **Annotate** tools whenever you are adding text.

It is possible to modify the STANDARD text style or create one or more new text styles with user-defined names that can have different fonts, heights, or other properties.

Different text styles should be used to manage the different text types in a drawing. You might create a font named NOTES that is assigned the SIMPLEX.SHX font with a height set to 0.125″ that can be used for all note-type text in a drawing. You can then create another style named TITLES that is assigned the bold Arial TrueType font and a height of 0.25″ that can be used for all the title-type text in a drawing. See Figure 11-5.

NOTE

Text height either can be controlled by the text style height setting, or it can be specified when the text is created. If the text height is set to 0.000″ in the text style, you must specify the text height when text is added to a drawing. If the text style height is set to any value greater than 0.000″, the text height is set automatically when text is added to a drawing.

Figure 11-5
Examples of different text styles

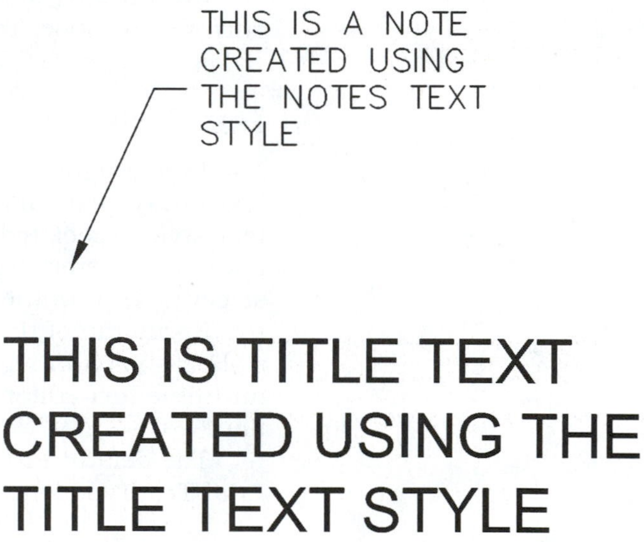

Using text styles to control the appearance of the different text types in a drawing provides a number of advantages. First, text styles make it easier to change the appearance of text if required. For instance, if the font specification changes for a certain type of text, you need to update only the corresponding text style. Otherwise, you must find every instance of text in a drawing that uses the old font and change it manually.

Using text styles to control the appearance of text also helps promote the use of drafting standards by providing the ability to have text look consistent for an entire project or organization.

NOTE

Text style names can be up to 255 characters long and can consist of letters, numbers, and a few other special characters such as underscores, hyphens, and even spaces. The default style name created by AutoCAD is "Style" followed by an integer value (i.e., Style1, Style2, etc.).

EXERCISE 11-1 **Creating and Modifying Text Styles**

1. Start a new drawing using the **acad.dwt** drawing template.
2. Update the STANDARD text style so that its font is set to the SIMPLEX.SHX AutoCAD font.
3. Create a text style named **NOTES** with the following settings:
   a. Font = **Simplex.shx**
   b. Height = **0.125″**
4. Create a text style named **TITLES** with the following settings:
   a. Font = **Arial**
   b. Height = **0.25″**
5. Create a text style named **ARCHITECTURAL** with the following settings:
   a. Font = **CityBlueprint**
   b. Height = **0.125″**
6. Create a text style named **MECHANICAL** with the following settings:
   a. Font = **GDT.shx**
   b. Height = **0.100″**
7. Save the drawing as ***CH11_EXERCISE 1***.

Creating Multiline Text

MULTILINE TEXT	
Ribbon & Panel:	Home Annotation 
Draw Toolbar:	
Menu:	Draw | Text Multiline Text...
Command Line:	MTEXT
Command Alias:	T or MT

Multiline text is a complex text object that can consist of multiple lines of text that you enter in paragraph form using an in-place text editor that resembles a simple word processing program. The text is automatically formatted to fit a rectangular boundary area that you define using two corner points before the text editor is displayed. AutoCAD automatically determines the horizontal length of the line of text by inserting soft returns similar to a word processor. The vertical height of the multiline text object depends on the amount of text, not the vertical height of the bounding box. See Figure 11-11.

The in-place text editor creates and edits the text in its current location and is transparent so you can see the drawing line work below to locate text accordingly. Some of the features and benefits of multiline text include:

- Setting tabs and indents
- Automated field insertion
- Importing external text files in ASCII or RTF format
- Enhanced symbol and special character insertion
- Bulleted and numbered list creation
- Creating stacked fractions and geometric tolerances
- Resizing the text boundary area using grips, and reformatting the text line length automatically
- The ability to switch selected text between uppercase and lowercase with the click of a mouse
- The ability to create multiple columns of text

Figure 11-11
Multiline text

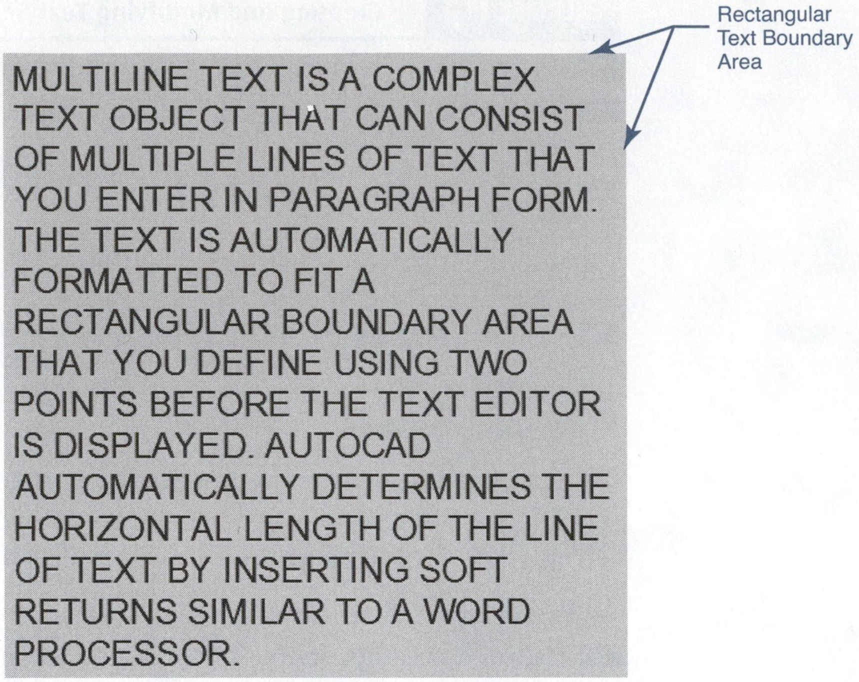

The **MTEXT** command is used to create multiline text using the in-place text editor. Editing multiline text using the in-place editor is explained later in this chapter.

When you start the **MTEXT** command, AutoCAD displays the current text style and height at the command line as follows:

Current text style: "Standard" Text height: 0.2000

AutoCAD prompts you to *Specify first corner:* and the text "abc" is displayed on the cursor crosshairs as shown in Figure 11-12.

Figure 11-12
First corner of the multiline text boundary area

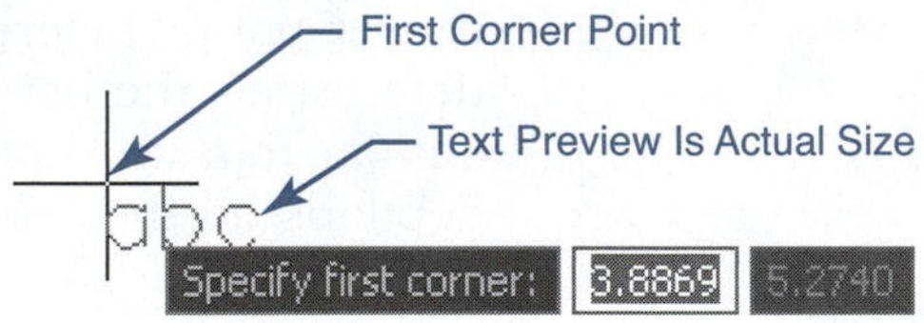

Because the size of the text is the *actual size* that the text will be created based on the current text height setting, it is affected by zooming in on and out of your drawing. Select the first corner of the rectangular area that you want to use to create the text. AutoCAD prompts you to *Specify opposite corner or* ↓ and displays a preview of the rectangular area as shown in Figure 11-13.

The arrow at the bottom of the rectangle indicates that the text flow is top to bottom. This is because the default justification for multiline text is the top left corner. It is possible to change the justification by selecting the **Justify** option when AutoCAD prompts you to *Specify opposite corner or* ↓. The different multiline justification options are shown in Figure 11-14.

NOTE

It is also possible to change the justification after you enter the in-place text editor using the **Text Editor** context tab of the ribbon explained later.

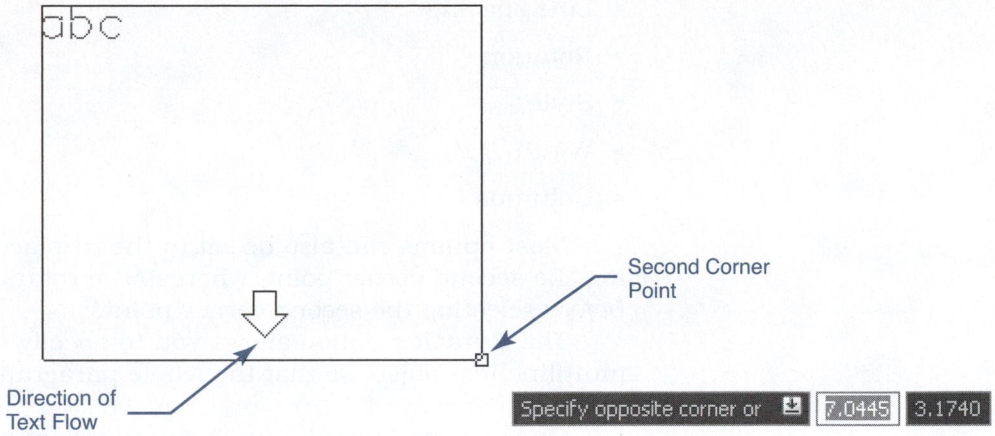

Figure 11-13
Second corner of the multiline text boundary area

Figure 11-14
Multiline text justification options

Notice how the arrows change to indicate how the justification affects the text flow.

The other options that are available before you select the second text boundary corner point are as follows:

- Height
- Justify

- Line spacing
- Rotation
- Style
- Width
- Columns

Most options can also be set in the in-place text editor *after* selecting the second corner point, whereas the rotation angle must be indicated *before* selecting the second corner point.

The **Rotation** option allows you to specify the angle for the complete multiline text object so that the whole paragraph of text is rotated at the angle you specify.

Once all the desired multiline options are set, select the second point to define the initial text boundary area. After you select the second point, AutoCAD displays the in-place multiline text editor shown in Figure 11-15 so you can start entering text. At the same time, the current tab of the ribbon at the top of the AutoCAD window switches to the **Text Editor** context tab of the ribbon shown in Figure 11-15 so you can access the multiline text tools and formatting options.

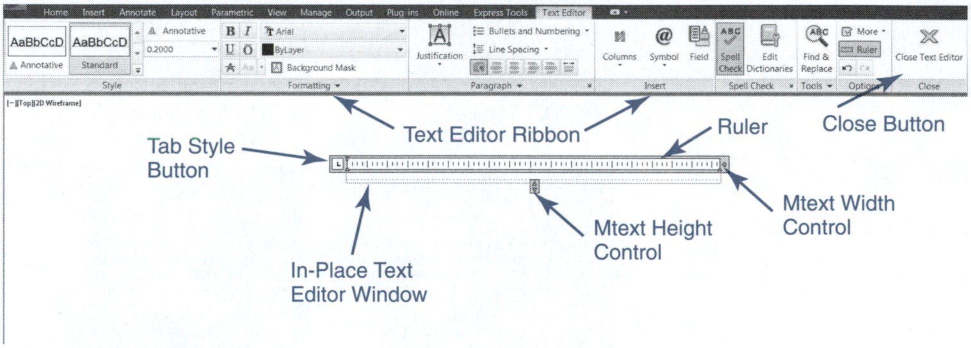

Figure 11-15
The in-place multiline text editor

The In-Place Multiline Text Editor

The in-place multiline text editor consists of the following components and features:

- In-place text editor window
- Ruler
- **Text Editor** context tab of the ribbon
- Right-click shortcut menu

The in-place text editor window is where you enter the text. As mentioned, it works like most text editors and word processor software. As you type and the text reaches the end of the text editor window, AutoCAD automatically enters what is commonly referred to as a “soft” return to break the line. You can also enter your own “hard” returns if you wish by pressing the **<Enter>** key. All the other common text editor keyboard controls are available to help you navigate, select, copy, paste, delete, and edit text as you type.

Multiline Text Editor Keyboard Controls	
Key or Key Combination	**Description**
Home	Moves cursor to the beginning of the current line
End	Moves cursor to the end of the current line
<Ctrl>+Home	Moves cursor to the first column of the first line
<Ctrl>+End	Moves cursor to the end of the last line
<Del>	Deletes character to the right of cursor
<Ctrl>+<Del>	Deletes complete word to the right of cursor
Page Up	Moves cursor to beginning of paragraph
Page Down	Moves cursor to end of paragraph
Arrow Keys	Moves cursor one position the direction of the arrow
<Shift> + Arrow Keys	Selects and highlights text under cursor as it moves
Backspace	Deletes character to the left of cursor
<Ctrl>+Backspace	Deletes word to the left of cursor
<Ctrl>+<Shift>+Space	Inserts a nonbreaking space
<Ctrl>+A	Selects all text
<Ctrl>+C	Copies selected text to the Windows Clipboard
<Ctrl>+V	Pastes text from Windows Clipboard at current cursor position
<Ctrl>+X	Cuts selected text so that the text is not copied to the Windows Clipboard
<Ctrl>+Z	Undoes last operation
<Ctrl>+<Shift>+U	Changes selected text to all uppercase
<Ctrl>+<Shift>+L	Changes selected text to all lowercase

TIP

You can use the Windows Clipboard to copy and paste text between other Windows applications and AutoCAD.

When you are finished entering text, you have three ways to exit the multiline text editor and create the text in the drawing:

- Select the **Close Text Editor** button on the **Text Editor** context tab of the ribbon.
- Click anywhere outside the text editor with your mouse.
- Hold down the **<Ctrl>** key and press **<Enter>.**

To close the text editor without saving the text or any changes, press the **<Esc>** key.

EXERCISE 11-2 Creating Multiline Text

1. Continue from Exercise 11-1.
2. Set the **NOTES** text style current.
3. Create the following paragraph of multiline text within an area that is 3″ wide and 3″ tall:

   The in-place text editor window is where you enter text. As mentioned, it works similarly to most text editors and word processor software you might be familiar with. As you type and the text reaches the end of the text editor window, AutoCAD automatically enters what is commonly referred to as a "soft" return to break the line.

4 Save the drawing.

The Ruler. The ruler indicates the width of the text using the current units setting. The diamond at the right end of the toolbar can be used to adjust the width of the multiline text boundary box by clicking and dragging with your mouse.

The arrow on the top left side of the ruler can be used to set the indent for the first line of a paragraph by clicking on it and dragging it to the desired position with your mouse as shown in Figure 11-16.

Figure 11-16
Setting the first line paragraph indent distance

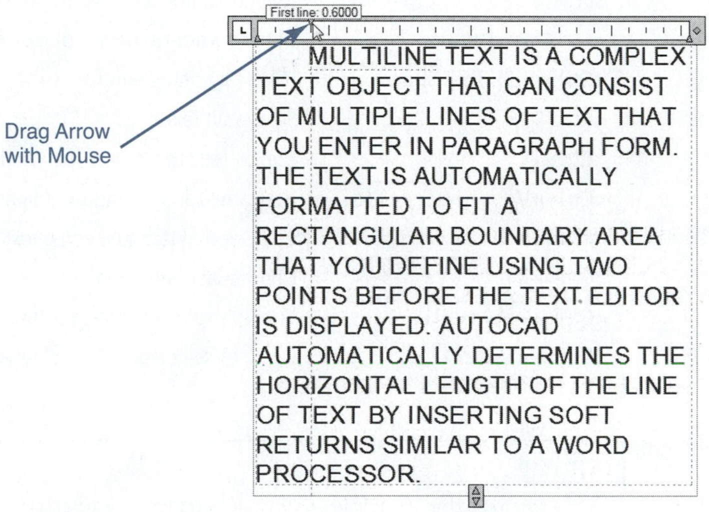

The arrow on the bottom left side of the ruler can be used to set the indent for the whole paragraph by clicking on it and dragging it to the desired position with your mouse as shown in Figure 11-17.

Figure 11-17
Setting the entire paragraph indent distance

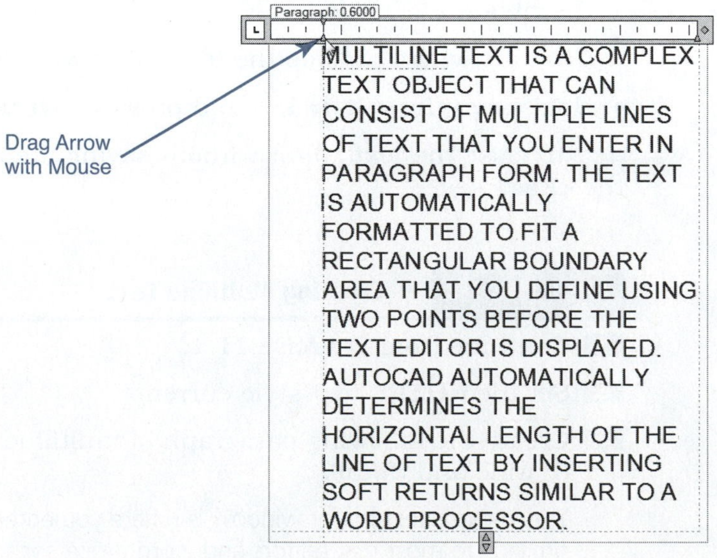

You can create one or more tab stops by clicking with your mouse in the ruler where you want to locate the tab stop as shown in Figure 11-18.

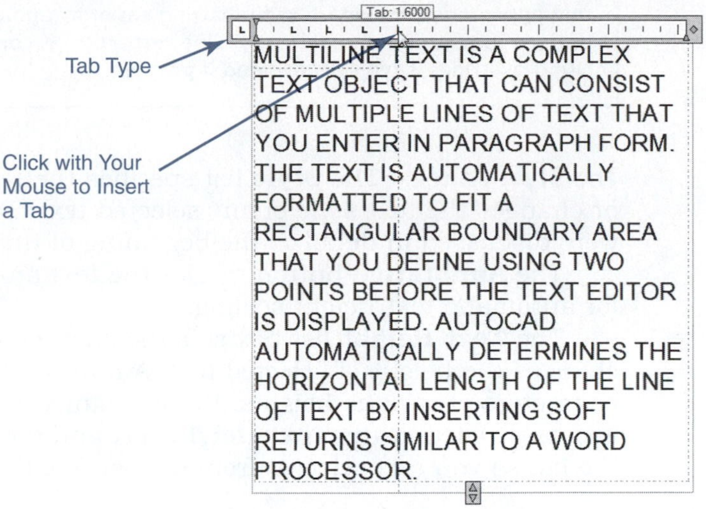

Figure 11-18
Setting tab stops

The button on the far left sets the tab type. Clicking on it goes through the left, center, right, and decimal tab types.

Once a tab stop is created, you can move it by placing your cursor over the top of it and dragging it when the cursor changes to a double horizontal arrow. To remove a tab stop, simply click on it with your cursor and drag it off the toolbar.

NOTE

You can turn the ruler off using the **Text Editor** context tab of the ribbon explained in the next section. The ruler stays off the next time you use the multiline text editor.

EXERCISE 11-3 **Using Tabs**

1. Continue from Exercise 11-2.
2. Make sure **NOTES** is the current text style.
3. Create the following table of multiline text within an area that is 4″ wide and 4″ tall with tab stops at every 1″:

1	2	3	4
5	6	7	8
9	10	11	12

4. Save the drawing.

The Text Editor Context Tab of the Ribbon

The **Text Editor** context tab of the ribbon shown in Figure 11-15 is used to control all aspects of the text's appearance ranging from the text style and font to the text height and justification. The various settings can be applied to new text or existing text that has already been selected (highlighted). The different **Text Editor** context ribbon panels are explained in the following sections.

TIP

Remember that it is common to control most of the different format settings using text styles as explained earlier in this chapter because it provides central control over the text appearance, making text formatting easier to update. Applying different format options to text directly in the multiline text editor is considered a text style override. Using overrides is typically avoided if possible.

The Style Panel. The **Style** list specifies the text style to use for new text or changes the text style of any selected text. Text styles and their usage were discussed in detail at the beginning of this chapter.

The **Annotative** button toggles the text annotative property on and off for automatic text height scaling.

The **Text Height** list box sets the character height for new text or changes the height of selected text. A multiline text object can contain characters of various heights. If the height you wish to use is not listed, you must click in the **Text Height** box and type it. It then becomes part of the list so you can select it from the list box the next time.

NOTE

Remember that text styles that have backward or upside-down effects do not work with multiline text and are not displayed.

TIP

If the current text style height is set to 0.0, you can change the default multiline text height displayed in the **Text Height** list box by setting the **TEXTSIZE** system variable. The default text height is 0.20.

The Formatting Panel. The **Bold** button turns bold formatting on and off for new or selected text. This option is available only for characters using TrueType fonts.

The **Italic** button turns italic formatting on and off for new or selected text. This option is available only for characters using TrueType fonts.

The **Underline** button turns underlining on and off for new or selected text.

The **Overline** button places a line over selected text.

The **Strikethrough** button puts a line through selected text.

NEW to AutoCAD 2013

The **Make Uppercase** button converts all selected text to uppercase.

The **Make Lowercase** button converts all selected text to lowercase.

The **Font** list specifies the font to use for new text or changes the font of any selected text. Both TrueType and the AutoCAD SHX fonts are listed. It is possible to mix different fonts within the same paragraph of multiline text.

The **Color** list specifies a color for new text or changes the color of selected text. You can also select one of the colors in the **Color** list or select the **Select Colors** option to display the **Select Color** dialog box.

The **Background Mask** button displays the **Background Mask** dialog box shown in Figure 11-19. This dialog box allows you to make the background of the finished multiline text boundary box opaque, as well as set its color. The **Use background mask** check box turns the background on and off. The **Border offset factor:** setting allows you to extend the background area beyond the original multiline text boundary area.

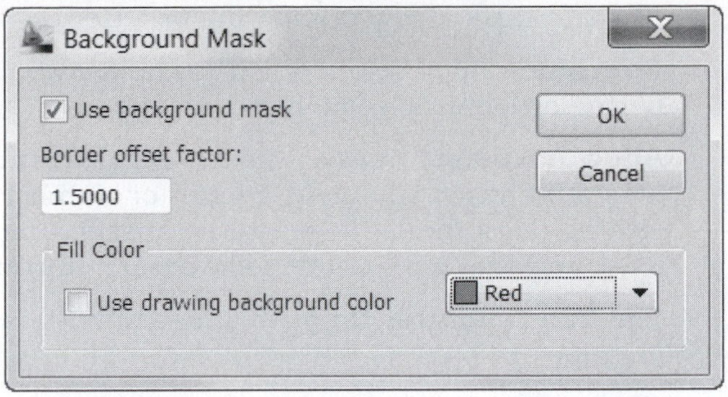

Figure 11-19
The **Background Mask** dialog box

You can either apply a fill color to the background area via the color list in the **Fill Color** area at the bottom of the dialog box, or you can elect to use the drawing background color by selecting the **Use drawing background color** check box. Using the drawing background color allows you to block out line work underneath the multiline text boundary box so you can't see it.

Certain features are displayed on the expanded panel. The **Oblique Angle** box controls the oblique angle, or slant, of new or selected text. The angle entered is measured from 90° vertical so that a positive angle slants text forward and a negative angle slants text backward. It is possible to enter a value between –85° and 85°. You can either type a value in the box or select the up and down arrows on the right to increase or decrease the value by 1. See Figure 11-10 for examples of text that has been obliqued.

The **Tracking** box decreases or increases the space between characters for new or selected text. You can either type a value in the box or select the up and down arrows on the right to increase or decrease the value by 0.1.

The **Width Factor** box controls the text character width. The default width is 1.0. Specifying a value greater than 1.0 expands the text so that it is wider. Specifying a value less than 1.0 condenses the text. You can either type a value in the box or select the up and down arrows on the right to increase or decrease the value by 0.1. See Figure 11-9 for examples of **Width Factor** settings.

The Paragraph Panel. The **Justification** button displays a menu with the same two-letter multiline text justification options shown earlier in Figure 11-14 (**Top Left TL, Middle Left ML,** etc.) when using the **Justify** option when you first start the **MTEXT** command. The **Justification** menu allows you to change the text justification within the multiline text editor.

The **Bullets and Numbering** button displays the menu shown in Figure 11-20 with the three different list formats (**Numbered, Lettered,** and **Bulleted**) along with various options:

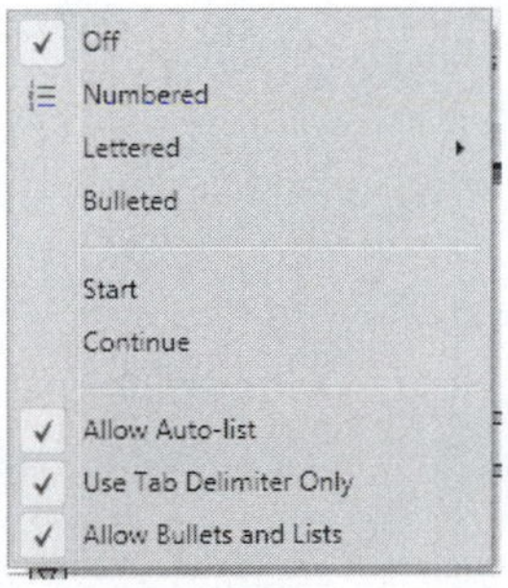

Figure 11-20
The **Bullets and Lists** menu

- **Off** Removes letters, numbers, and bullets from the selected text without changing the indentation
- **Numbered** Creates a numbered list using numbers with periods for each list item
- **Lettered** cascade menu Allows you to switch between uppercase and lowercase letters with periods for each list item. Double letters are used if the list has more items than the alphabet
- **Bulleted** Creates a bulleted list using round filled circles for each list item

- **Start** Starts a new numbering or lettering sequence
- **Continue** Adds selected text to the list above and continues the numbering or lettering sequence
- **Allow Auto-list** Toggles the **Auto-list** feature on and off. **Auto-list** creates a list when you enter a letter or number followed by a period "." or closing parenthesis ")", press the spacebar or **<Tab>** key, and enter at least one character of text followed by **<Enter>**
- **Use Tab Delimiter Only** Will use only the **<Tab>** key for automatic list creation
- **Allow Bullets and Lists** Disables the **Bullets and Numbering** feature

The **Line Spacing** button displays a menu that allows you to set the text line spacing for the multiline text object. Line spacing for multiline text is the distance between the bottom of one line of text and the bottom of the next line of text where single spacing is 1.66 times the text height. You can set the spacing increment to a multiple of single-line spacing using the following predefined scale factors:

- **1.0x** Single-line spacing
- **1.5x** One-and-a-half-line spacing
- **2.0x** Double-line spacing
- **2.5x** Two-and-a-half-line spacing

Selecting **More...** from the **Line Spacing** menu displays the **Paragraph** dialog box so you can make additional adjustments. The **Paragraph** dialog box is explained in detail next.

Selecting the angled down arrow on the far right of the panel title bar displays the **Paragraph** dialog box shown in Figure 11-21 so that you can do the following:

- Add and remove tab stops
- Set left and right indents

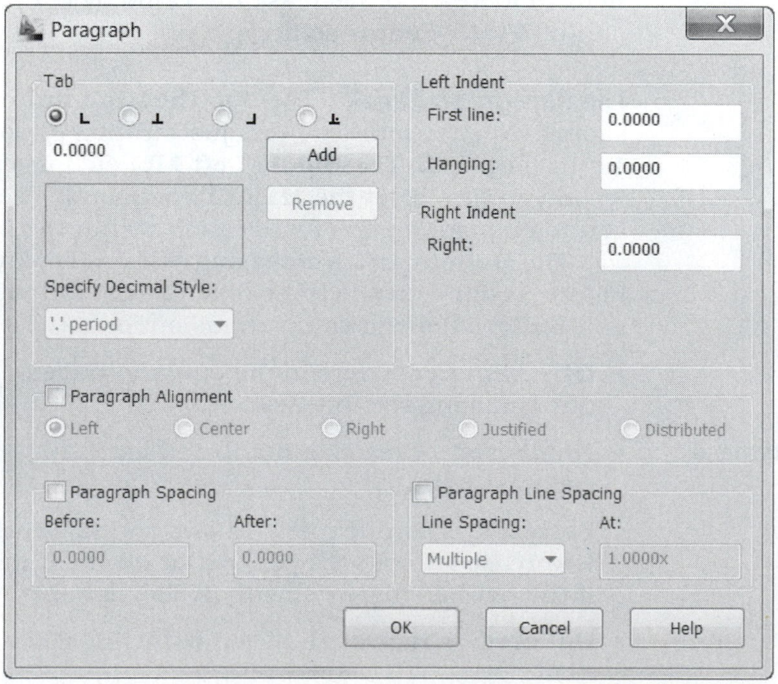

Figure 11-21
The **Paragraph** dialog box

- Set the horizontal paragraph justification
- Set the spacing between paragraphs
- Set the line spacing for the paragraph

The **Tab** area allows you to add and remove left, center, right, and decimal tab stops. To add a tab, enter the tab distance and select the **Add** button. To delete a tab, select it from the list and select the **Remove** button.

> **NOTE**
>
> Different tabs can also be selected from the **Tab** button on the left side of the ruler and then dragged into position.

The **Left Indent** area allows you to set the first line and hanging indent distances.

The **Right Indent** area allows you to set the right side indent distance.

The **Paragraph Alignment** area allows you to control the horizontal paragraph justification, text flow, and spacing using one of the following methods:

- The **Left** option aligns text on the left-hand margin so text flows right.
- The **Center** option centers text on the centerline of the text boundary and flows both directions.
- The **Right** option aligns text on the right-hand margin so text flows left.
- The **Justified** option spreads text out to fill the text boundary width by putting space between words.
- The **Distributed** option spreads text out to fill the text boundary width by putting space between letters.

The **Paragraph Spacing** area controls the spacing between paragraphs. Selecting the **Paragraph Spacing** check box enables the **Before:** and **After:** text boxes so that it is possible to set different spacing before and after a paragraph.

The **Paragraph Line Spacing** area controls the multiline line spacing. Line spacing for multiline text is the distance between the bottom of one line of text and the bottom of the next line. The default for single line spacing is 1.66 times the height of the text. The default spacing is **Multiple,** which is basically a multiplier that is applied to the preceding formula. The default setting is 1X, or one time. For double-line spacing, you would set **Multiple** to 2X and so on. The **Exactly** option maintains a consistent spacing using the absolute distance you specify. Using the **Exactly** option, it is possible to overlap rows. The **At least** line spacing option automatically increases line spacing to accommodate characters that are too large to fit.

Select **OK** in the **Paragraph** dialog box to exit and save your changes.

The five buttons to the right of the **Paragraph** button on the **Paragraph** panel control the horizontal justification and text spacing using the same **Paragraph Alignment** options provided in the **Paragraph** dialog box:

- The **Left** button aligns text on the left-hand margin so text flows right.
- The **Center** button centers text on the centerline of the text boundary and flows both directions.
- The **Right** button aligns text on the right-hand margin so text flows left.

- The **Justified** button spreads text out to fill the text boundary width by putting space between words.
- The **Distributed** button spreads text out to fill the text boundary width by putting space between letters.

EXERCISE 11-4 Formatting Multiline Text

1. Continue from Exercise 11-3.
2. Start the **MTEXT** command.
3. Define a text boundary area 3″ wide by 2″ tall.
4. Using the **Text Editor** context tab of the ribbon, do the following:
   a. Set the style to **TITLES.**
   b. Set the text height to **0.125″.**
   c. Turn on the **Italic** option.
   d. Set the justification to **Middle Center.**
5. Type the following paragraph:

   The in-place text editor window is where you enter text. As mentioned, it works similarly to most text editors and word processor software you might be familiar with. As you type and the text reaches the end of the text editor window, AutoCAD automatically enters what is commonly referred to as a "soft" return to break the line.
6. Save the drawing.

The Insert Panel. The **Columns** button displays the **Columns** menu shown in Figure 11-22, which allows you to format multiline text into multiple columns. You can use either a static approach in which you specify the number of columns explicitly or a dynamic approach that creates new columns automatically as you type. Both methods allow you to specify the width and height of each column, as well as the gutter width. Special grips allow you to edit the column width and height quickly after the text is added to the drawing.

Figure 11-22
Columns menu

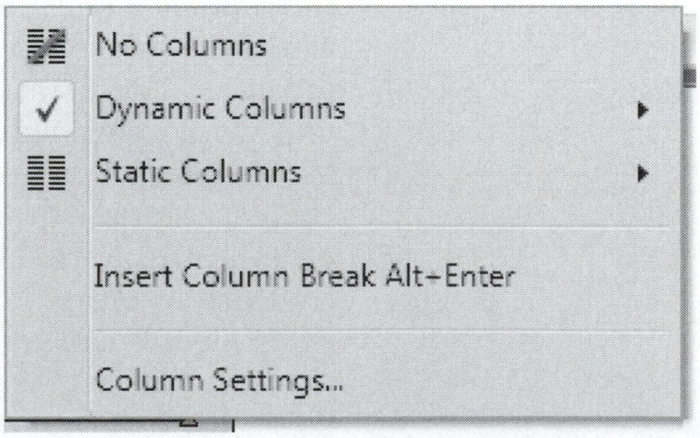

To use dynamic columns, select either **Auto height** or **Manual height** from the **Dynamic Columns** cascade menu. Both approaches use the current width of the multiline text boundary box that you defined for the initial column width. The difference is that the **Auto height** method uses the current height of the boundary box as the column height so that when text gets to the bottom of the boundary area it automatically jumps to the next column and starts at the top. When you select **Manual height,** the text boundary box height collapses to a single row with a double arrow size control at the bottom that you must click and drag to set the column height.

> **TIP**
>
> It is possible to ignore the column height and simply start entering text. The text will flow down in the same column using the current column width. You can then press **<Alt>+<Enter>** to jump to another column, and it will be created using the same width and height as the first column.

To use static columns, you must select the number of desired columns (2–6) from the **Static Columns** cascade menu. The column width is determined by the number of columns and the gutter width that can be fit within the defined text boundary area.

If you need to specify more than six columns, select the **More...** menu item on the **Static Columns** cascade menu to display the **Column Settings** dialog box shown in Figure 11-23.

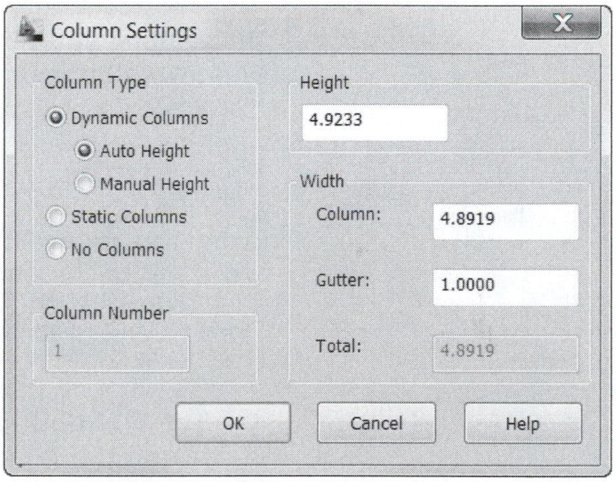

Figure 11-23
The **Column Settings** dialog box

As you can see, the **Column Settings** dialog box controls all the other main column settings such as the number of columns, column width, height, and gutter width. This is also where you can turn existing columns off by selecting **No Columns** in the **Column Type** area at the top left. The easiest way to display the **Column Settings** dialog box is to select **Column Settings** from the main **Columns** menu shown in Figure 11-22.

The **Symbol** button displays a menu that allows you to insert a symbol or a nonbreaking space at the current cursor position. Some of the more commonly used symbols are listed on the menu with either their AutoCAD %% control code or Unicode string as shown in Figure 11-24.

Selecting the **Other...** menu item at the bottom of the menu displays the **Character Map** dialog box shown in Figure 11-25 so you can insert symbols that are not included on the menu. This dialog box contains the entire character set for every available font. To insert a symbol from the **Character Map** dialog box, you must first select a symbol and then click the **Select** button to place it in the **Characters to copy** box. To insert

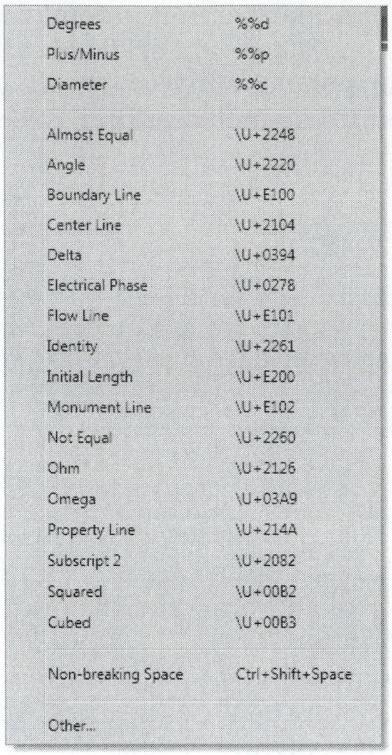

Figure 11-24
The **Symbols** menu

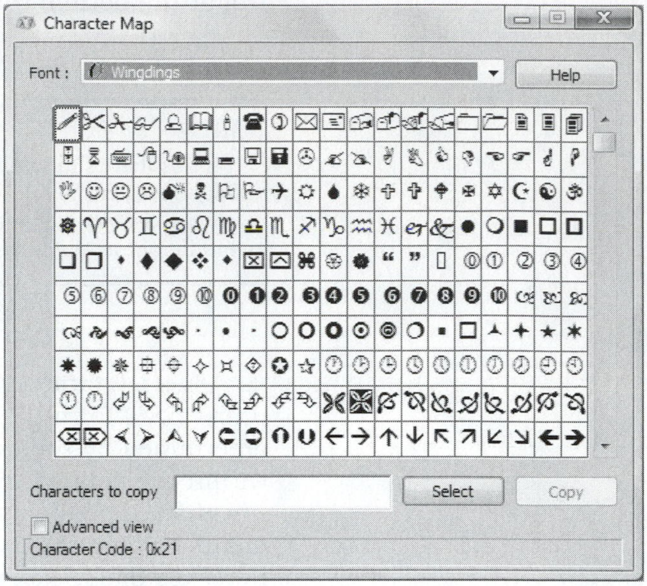

Figure 11-25
The **Character Map** dialog box

the symbol, you must select the **Copy** button to copy the symbol to the Windows Clipboard. You can then switch back to the multiline editor in AutoCAD and paste the selected symbol in the desired location.

> **NOTE**
> The **Character Map** dialog box is actually a separate program that shows up on the Windows taskbar when you display it. It must be closed and exited manually. If you do not close the dialog box, you might find yourself running multiple copies of the program if you repeatedly display it.

The **Field** button allows you to insert a field using the **Field** dialog box. Fields and the **Field** dialog box are explained in detail later in this chapter.

EXERCISE 11-5 Creating Lists and Inserting Symbols

1. Continue from Exercise 11-4.
2. Set the **NOTES** text style current.
3. Create the following bulleted list of multiline text within an area that is 4″ wide and 4″ tall:
   - This is a degree symbol °
   - This is a plus/minus symbol ±
   - This is a diameter symbol ∅
   - This is a boundary line symbol BL
   - This is a centerline symbol CL
   - This is a delta symbol Δ
   - This is a property line symbol PL

4 Change the bulleted list to a lettered list.

5 Change the lettered list to a numbered list.

6 Save the drawing.

The Spell Check Panel. The **Spell Check** button turns on and off the **Check Spelling As You Type** feature that allows you to check spelling as you enter text in the multiline text editor. Any word you enter is checked for spelling errors when it is completed so that any word that is misspelled is underlined in red. Spelling suggestions display when you right-click the underlined word.

The **Edit Dictionaries** button displays the **Dictionaries** dialog box explained later in "The Spell Checker" section so you can switch dictionaries to check spelling in other languages, add new words to a dictionary, and perform other dictionary management tasks.

The Tools Panel. The **Find & Replace** tool displays the **Find and Replace** dialog box shown in Figure 11-26 so you can search for a specific string of text and replace it with a new string of text.

- The **Find what:** text box is where you enter the text you want to search for.
- The **Replace with:** text box is where you enter the replacement text for the text entered in the **Find what:** text box.
- Selecting the **Match case** check box allows you to search for text that matches the uppercase and/or lowercase of the text entered in the **Find what:** text box exactly.
- Selecting the **Find whole words only** check box allows you to search only for text as a complete word with a space before and after; otherwise, the search will also find text that is part of a word.
- The **Use wildcards** check box allows the use of wildcard characters in searches. For more information on wildcard searches, see the "Finding and Replacing Text" section later in this chapter.
- The **Match diacritics** check box allows you to match diacritical marks, or accents, in search results.
- The **Match half/full width forms (East Asian languages)** check box matches half- and full-width Asian characters in search results.

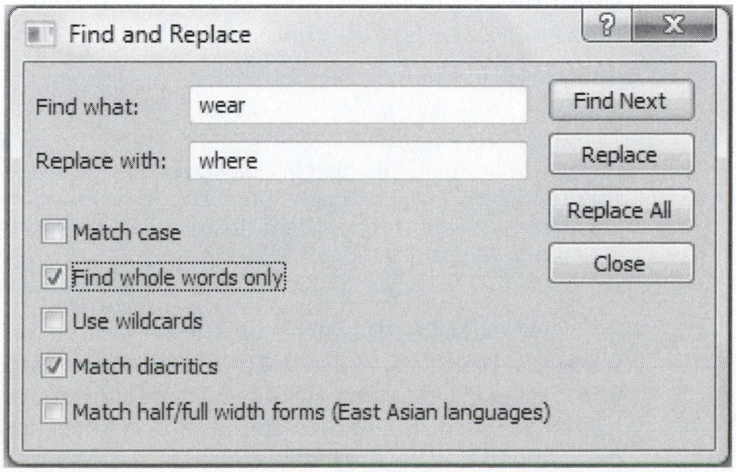

Figure 11-26
The **Find and Replace** dialog box

After all the search criteria are entered, you can choose one of three options:

- Select the **Find Next** button to search for and highlight the next occurrence of the search text.
- Select the **Replace** button to replace the highlighted text in the multiline text editor to update the text with the text entered in the **Replace with:** text box.
- Select the **Replace All** button to search for and replace all the text in the multiline text editor that matches the search criteria with the text entered in the **Replace with:** text box. A message box is displayed indicating how many occurrences were replaced so that you know whether, and how many, text strings were replaced.

The **Import Text...** button on the expanded panel allows you to import an ASCII (American Standard Code for Information Interchange) text file or an RTF (Rich Text Format) text file into the multiline text editor. Selecting the **Import Text...** button displays the **Select File** dialog box shown in Figure 11-27 so you can navigate your computer or network and find the text file to import.

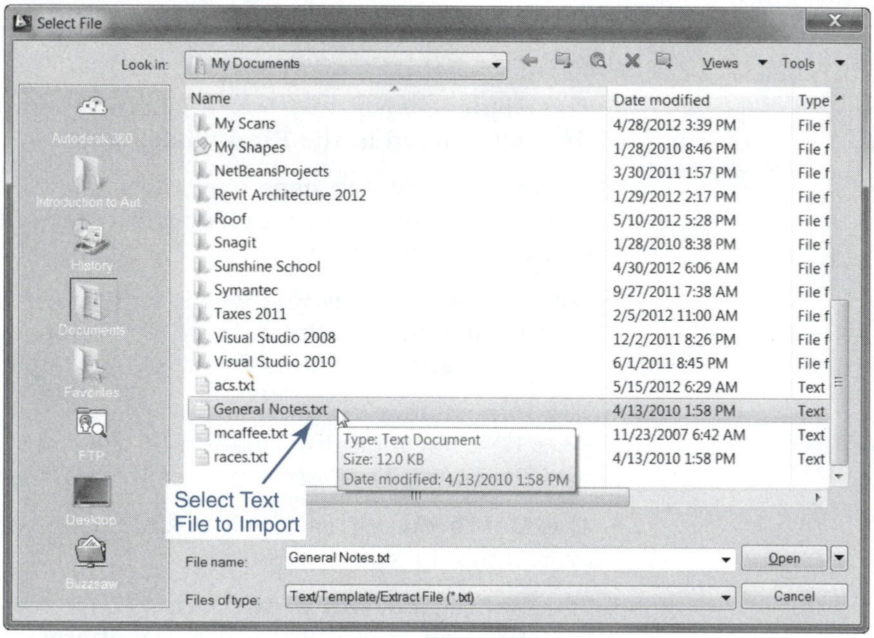

Figure 11-27
Importing a text file into the multiline text editor

Once you locate the file, select it so it is highlighted, and select the **Open** button to import the text. You can then edit the text if necessary using the standard methods explained in this chapter.

> **TIP**
>
> You can store text that is used in multiple drawings in an external text file so that you don't have to type the text in every drawing. For instance, you might store general notes in a file named General Notes.txt. If you locate the file on a network, all team members can then import the same text file. This approach both provides consistency and increases production.

The **AutoCAPS** button on the expanded panel turns the **AutoCAPS** feature on and off. **AutoCAPS** can be used much like the **<Caps Lock>** key to lock your keyboard so only uppercase letters can be entered. This is a handy feature in the drafting field because most drawing notes are uppercase according to industry standards.

> **NOTE**
>
> The **AutoCAPS** feature overrides the **<Caps Lock>** key so that it cannot be used to toggle uppercase on and off. You must turn **AutoCAPS** off in order to type lowercase.

The Options Panel. The **Ruler** tool toggles the ruler on and off. Once the ruler is turned off, it remains off the next time you display the in-place multiline text editor. See the preceding section "The Ruler" for detailed information about the ruler feature.

The **Undo** tool undoes actions in the multiline text editor, including changes to either text content or text formatting.

The **Redo** tool redoes actions in the multiline text editor, including changes to either text content or text formatting.

The **More** tool displays a menu with a few other multiline text options and features that are also located on the right-click menu explained in the next section.

The Right-Click Menu

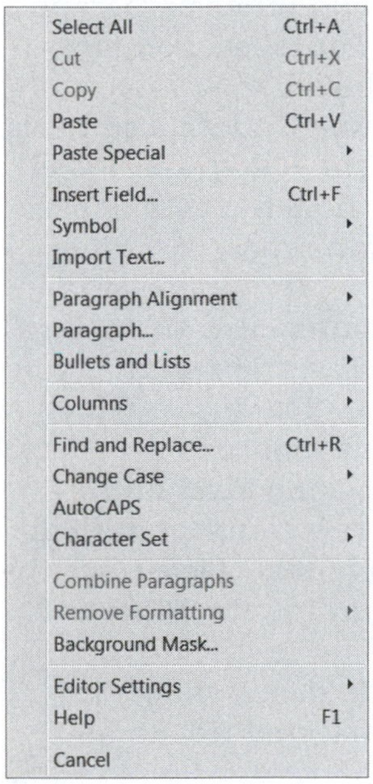

Figure 11-28
The right-click shortcut menu

The right-click shortcut menu shown in Figure 11-28 provides additional multiline text options and features, as well as access to some of the same features found on the **Text Editor** context tab of the ribbon explained earlier.

The right-click shortcut menu can be displayed by right-clicking with your mouse anywhere in the multiline text editor window. At the top of the menu are a few specific text-editing commands:

- **Select All** Selects all the text in the text editor
- **Cut** Deletes text and places it on the Windows Clipboard so you can paste it later
- **Copy** Copies text to the Windows Clipboard so you can paste it later
- **Paste** Inserts text that is currently on the Windows Clipboard
- **Paste Special** Displays a cascade menu that allows you to perform the following special paste operations:
  - **Paste without Character Formatting** Pastes and ignores any character-based formatting such as font, text height, etc. while maintaining any paragraph-based formatting such as justification, line spacing, etc.
  - **Paste without Paragraph Formatting** Pastes and ignores any paragraph-based formatting such as justification, line spacing, etc. while maintaining any character-based formatting such as font, text height, etc.
  - **Paste without Any Formatting** Ignores all original formatting and uses the current formatting

The **Insert Field...** menu item allows you to insert a field using the **Field** dialog box. Fields and the **Field** dialog box are explained in detail later in this chapter.

The **Symbol** menu item displays a cascade menu that allows you to insert a symbol or a nonbreaking space at the current cursor position. The **Symbol** cascade menu is the same as the **Symbols** menu displayed when you select the **Symbol** button on the **Insert** panel on the **Text Editor** context tab of the ribbon. See the preceding section "The Insert Panel" for complete information about using the **Symbols** menu.

The **Import Text...** menu item allows you to import a text file using the **Select File** dialog box shown in Figure 11-27.

The **Paragraph Alignment** menu item displays a cascade menu with the same horizontal paragraph justification, text flow, and spacing options found in the **Paragraph Alignment** area in the **Paragraph** dialog box shown earlier in Figure 11-21 in the "The Paragraph Panel" section:

- The **Left** option aligns text on the left-hand margin so text flows right.
- The **Center** option centers text on the centerline of the text boundary and flows both directions.
- The **Right** option aligns text on the right-hand margin so text flows left.
- The **Justified** option spreads text out to fill the text boundary width by putting space between words.
- The **Distributed** option spreads text out to fill the text boundary width by putting space between letters.

The **Paragraph...** menu item displays the same **Paragraph** dialog box shown earlier in Figure 11-21 in the "The Paragraph Panel" section so that you can control tabs, indents, paragraph alignment, and other paragraph features and settings. Please see the "The Paragraph Panel" section for detailed information regarding the **Paragraph** dialog box.

The **Bullets and Lists** menu item displays the same **Bullets and Lists** cascade menu shown earlier in Figure 11-20 in the "The Paragraph Panel" section so that you can create lettered, numbered, or bulleted lists. Please see the "The Paragraph Panel" section for detailed information regarding the **Bullets and Lists** menu.

The **Columns** menu item displays the same **Columns** cascade menu shown earlier in Figure 11-22 in the "The Insert Panel" section so that you can create dynamic and static columns. Please see the "The Insert Panel" section for detailed information regarding the **Columns** menu.

The **Find and Replace...** menu item displays the same **Find and Replace** dialog box shown earlier in Figure 11-26 so you can search for a specific string of text and replace it with a new string of text. Please see the "The Tools Panel" section for detailed information regarding the **Find and Replace** dialog box.

The **Change Case** menu item displays the cascade menu shown in Figure 11-29. This menu can be used to change the selected text to all uppercase or all lowercase.

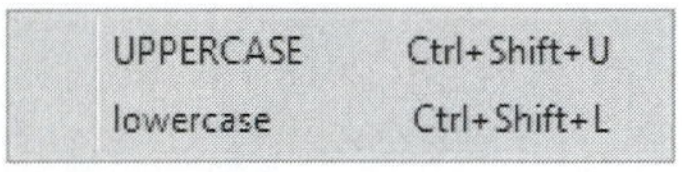

Figure 11-29
Change Case cascade menu

The **AutoCAPS** menu item turns the **AutoCAPS** feature explained earlier on and off.

The **Character Set** menu item displays the cascade menu shown in Figure 11-30. The **Character Set** menu item can be used to change the ***character set*** used so that text in other languages appears properly.

Figure 11-30
Character Set cascade menu

character set: The set of numeric codes used by a computer system to represent the characters (letters, numbers, punctuation, etc.) of a particular country or place.

The **Combine Paragraphs** menu item will combine multiple paragraphs of selected text together, removing any line feeds so that the selected text becomes one paragraph. The original text properties are retained.

The **Remove Formatting** menu item displays a cascade menu that provides different options for removing the formatting overrides for selected text so that those overrides revert back to the text's assigned text style:

- **Remove Character Formatting** Removes any character-based formatting such as font, text height, etc. while maintaining any paragraph-based formatting such as justification, line spacing, etc.

NOTE

The **Remove Formatting** menu item is displayed only when text is selected in the multiline text editor.

- **Remove Paragraph Formatting** Removes any paragraph-based formatting such as justification, line spacing, etc., while maintaining any character-based formatting such as font, text height, etc.
- **Remove All Formatting** Removes all formatting

The **Background Mask...** menu item displays the **Background Mask** dialog box shown earlier in Figure 11-19 so you can set the background of one text boundary box opaque and set its color.

The **Editor Settings** menu item displays a cascade menu that allows you to control the following multiline text editor display features:

- **Always Display as WYS/WYG**
- **Show Toolbar** Turns the **Text Formatting** toolbar on and off
- **Show Options** Turns the bottom portion of the **Text Formatting** toolbar on and off
- **Show Ruler** Turns the **Ruler** on and off
- **Opaque Background** Allows you to make the background of the editor opaque. By default, the editor is transparent
- **Check Spelling** Turns the **Check Spelling As You Type** feature on and off. This option is on by default
- **Check Spelling Settings...** Displays the **Check Spelling Settings** dialog box so you can specify text options that will be checked for spelling errors within your drawing
- **Dictionaries...** Displays the **Dictionaries** dialog box so you can control the dictionary that is checked against any found misspelled words
- **Text Highlight Color...** Allows you to change the color used to highlight text

Help displays the multiline text help topic.

EXERCISE 11-6 Using the Right-Click Menu

1. Continue from Exercise 11-5.
2. Using Windows Notepad, create a text file that contains the following text:

   This is text that is in an external file named Notes.txt that I am going to import into the multiline text editor and reformat.

3. Save the file as ***Notes.txt*** in a location where you can find it, and exit the Notepad program.

TIP

The Notepad program can typically be started by selecting the Windows **Start** button and navigating to the **Accessories** folder. You can also start Notepad by typing **Notepad<Enter>** in AutoCAD.

4 Switch back to AutoCAD and start the **MTEXT** command.

5 Define a text boundary area 2″ wide by 2″ tall.

6 Using the right-click menu, do the following:

a. Import the **Notes.txt** text file.

b. Set the background mask to **red.**

c. Set the paragraph alignment to **Center.**

d. Find all occurrences of the word "text" and replace it with "test".

e. Make all the text uppercase.

7 Save the drawing.

Creating Stacked Text

As mentioned earlier, it is possible to format text representing a fraction or tolerance so that the left character is placed on top of the right character as a horizontal fraction, diagonal fraction, or tolerance based on the following special stack characters:

- ^ Caret converts to left-justified tolerance values.
- / Forward slash converts to a center-justified fraction with a horizontal bar.
- \ Backward slash converts to a center-justified fraction with a horizontal bar.
- # Pound sign converts to a fraction with a diagonal bar the height of the two text strings.

This can be done manually using the **Stack** menu item located on the right-click shortcut menu or, even better, it can be automated using the **AutoStack** feature in the multiline text editor so that the desired fraction type is created automatically as you type. The **AutoStack** feature and properties are explained in the following section.

AutoStack Properties Dialog Box. The first time you type in a fraction or tolerance using the special characters listed in the previous section, AutoCAD displays the **AutoStack Properties** dialog box shown in Figure 11-31. This dialog box allows you to define specific text stacking properties

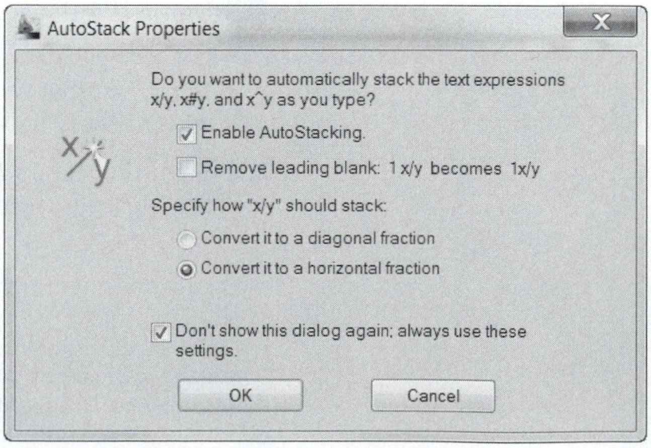

Figure 11-31
The **AutoStack Properties** dialog box

that can be applied automatically as you type when a number is entered followed by any of the special stacking characters.

The **Enable AutoStacking** check box allows you to turn **AutoStacking** on and off. If checked, text is automatically stacked when a number is typed in followed by any of the special characters.

The **Remove leading blank:** check box allows you to remove automatically any space between the whole number and the fraction if it is checked.

You can control whether a forward slash converts to a horizontal or diagonal fraction via the **Specify how "x/y" should stack:** radio buttons. If the **Convert it to a diagonal fraction** button is selected, diagonal fractions are created. If the **Convert it to a horizontal fraction** button is selected, horizontal fractions are created.

Selecting the **Don't show this dialog again; always use these settings** check box makes the **AutoStack** settings permanent so the **AutoStack Properties** dialog box is not displayed the next time you type a number followed by one of the special characters. The **AutoStack** properties are automatically applied as you type.

> **TIP**
> If you select the **Don't show this dialog again; always use these settings** check box, the only way to display the **AutoStack Properties** dialog box again is to select an existing fraction in the multiline text editor, right-click with your mouse, and select **Stack Properties** from the shortcut menu to display the **Stack Properties** dialog box. You can then select the **AutoStack...** button from the **Stack Properties** dialog box, explained in the next section.

Stack Properties Dialog Box. The **Stack Properties** dialog box shown in Figure 11-32 allows you to edit the text content, stack type, alignment, and size of stacked text. To display the dialog box, you must first select existing stacked text, right-click with your mouse, and select **Stack Properties** from the shortcut menu. The following options are available:

- The **Upper** and **Lower** text boxes in the **Text** section allow you to change the upper and lower numbers of a stacked fraction.
- The **Appearance** section allows you to edit the style, position, or text size of a stacked fraction.
- The **Style** list allows you to switch between the horizontal fraction, diagonal fraction, and tolerance stacking styles.

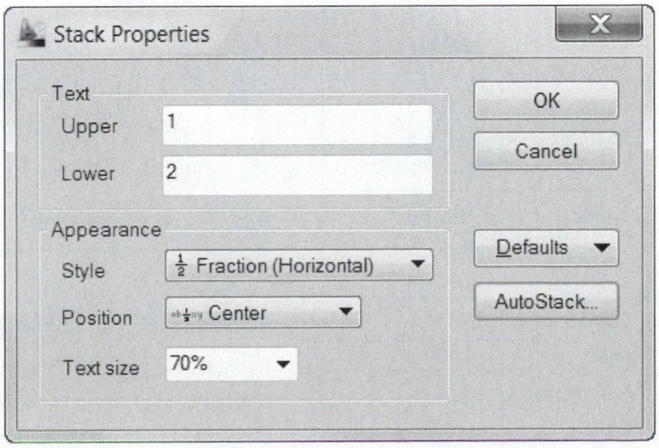

Figure 11-32
The **Stack Properties** dialog box

- The **Position** list allows you to switch between the following text alignments:
  - **Top** Aligns the top of the fraction with the top of the previous text
  - **Center** Centers the fraction vertically at the center of the previous text
  - **Bottom** Aligns the bottom of the fraction with the previous text

> **NOTE**
> Both the **Top** text and the **Bottom** text use the same alignment specified.

- The **Text size** list controls the size of the stacked text as a percentage relative to the size of the whole number text height. Valid values are between 25% and 125%. The default text size is 70%.
- The **Defaults** button allows you to either restore the default stacked text properties or save the current stacked text properties as the new default.
- The **AutoStack...** button displays the **AutoStack Properties** dialog box so you can either modify or turn off **AutoStack** properties.

EXERCISE 11-7 Creating Stacked Text

1. Continue from Exercise 11-6.
2. Start the **MTEXT** command.
3. Define a text boundary area 3″ wide by 3″ tall.
4. Enter the following line of text in the multiline text editor and press **<Enter>:**

   THIS IS A HORIZONTAL STACKED FRACTION 1/2
5. The **AutoStack Properties** dialog box shown in Figure 11-31 is displayed.
6. Select **Enable AutoStacking** so that "x/y" changes to a horizontal fraction.
7. Select the **Don't show this dialog again** check box.
8. Select **OK** to exit the **AutoStack Properties** dialog box.
9. Enter the following line of text in the multiline text editor and press **<Enter>:**

   THIS IS A DIAGONAL STACKED FRACTION 1#2
10. Enter the following line of text in the multiline text editor and press **<Enter>:**

    THIS IS A TOLERANCE VALUE 001^002
11. Save the drawing.

SINGLE-LINE TEXT	
Ribbon & Panel:	Home Annotation
Text Toolbar:	
Menu:	Draw|Text| Single Line Text
Command Line:	TEXT or DTEXT
Command Alias:	DT

Creating Single-Line Text

In addition to multiline text, you can also create what is referred to as *single-line text* to create one or more lines of text. Single-line text is the original text type in AutoCAD that preceded the more complex and feature-rich multiline text explored in the last section. With single-line text, each line of text is an independent object that can be modified. Multiple lines of single-line text *can be* entered at the same time in paragraph form with consistent vertical spacing between each line—it's just that you must break each line at the end using the **<Enter>** key. See Figure 11-33.

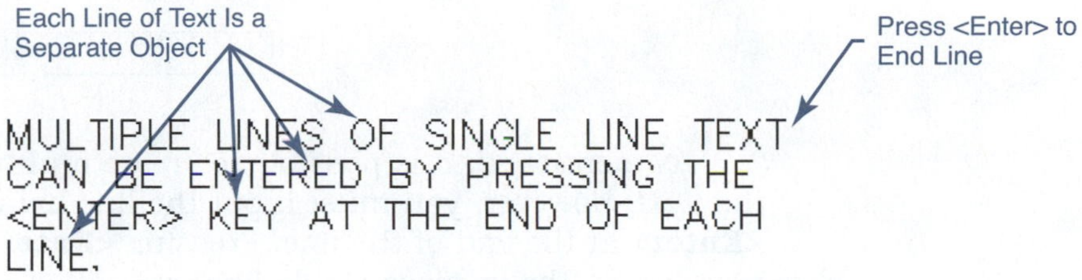

Figure 11-33
Single-line text

> **NOTE**
> Remember from the beginning of the chapter that if you set the current text style height to anything other than 0.00″ you will not be prompted for a text height when creating single-line text.

The **TEXT** command or the **DTEXT** command can be used to create single-line text.

When you start either command, AutoCAD displays the current text style and height at the command line as follows:

Current text style: "Standard" Text height: 0.2000

The text styles used for single-line text are the same as those used for multiline text, explained earlier. You can change the styles via the **Style** option explained below, although using the **Text Style** list box on the **Text** panel on the **Annotate** tab of the ribbon shown in Figure 11-4 is much easier as you will see. The text height can also be changed after you select the starting point for the text.

> **NOTE**
> By default, single-line text is left justified. This means that text that you type will flow to the right of the text start point. You can change the default justification using the justification options explained in one of the next sections.

After starting either command, AutoCAD prompts you to *Specify start point of text or* ↓. Select a starting point for the text either by picking a point in your drawing or by entering a coordinate location via the keyboard.

After locating the text start point, AutoCAD prompts you to *Specify height <0,2000>*:. Enter the desired text height and press **<Enter>.** The height entered becomes the default the next time you create single-line text.

After entering the height, AutoCAD prompts you to *Specify rotation angle of text <0>*:. Enter the desired text angle or press **<Enter>** to use the default.

> **TIP**
> You can also use your cursor to input the angle by selecting a point in response to the *Specify rotation angle of text <0>*: prompt. The text start point is used as the base point of the angle with the second point defining the angle. You can even utilize object snaps to align the text by snapping to points on existing objects.

After you enter the desired text angle, AutoCAD displays the no frills in-place single-line text editor, which is basically a dynamically sized box that grows longer as you type, as shown in Figure 11-34.

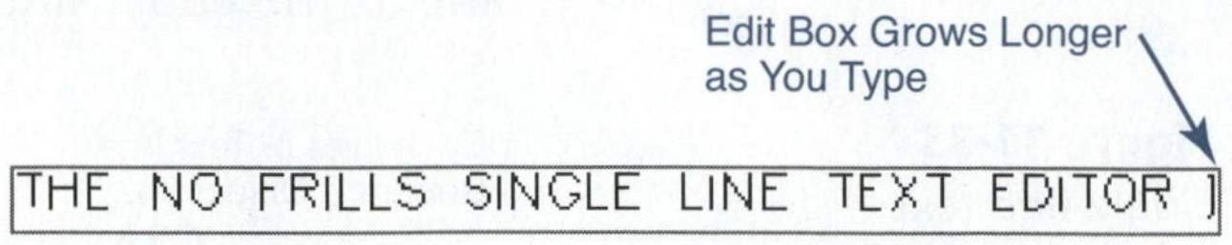

Figure 11-34
Entering single-line text

As mentioned, it is possible to create multiple lines of text using single-line text; however, you must input the line breaks manually by pressing **<Enter>** at the end of the line. Pressing **<Enter>** places the cursor on the next line in the in-place single-line text editor so you can continue typing as shown in Figure 11-35.

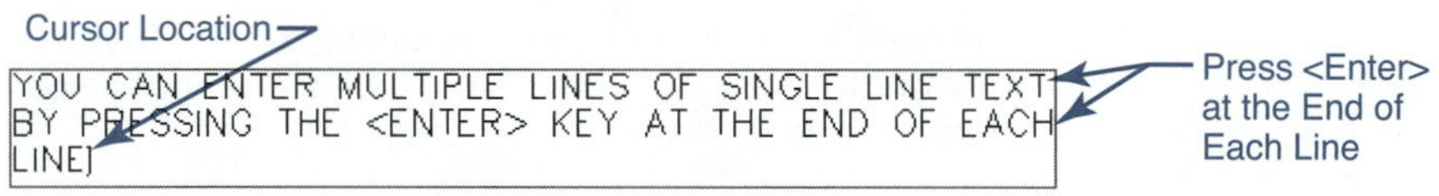

Figure 11-35
Entering multiple lines of single-line text

You can continue to add lines of text until you press the **<Enter>** key twice—meaning that you press **<Enter>** without entering any text on the current line. You can also pick a point outside the edit box with your mouse to end the command. Remember that each line of text is still a separate object even though it was all entered at the same time as shown in Figure 11-36.

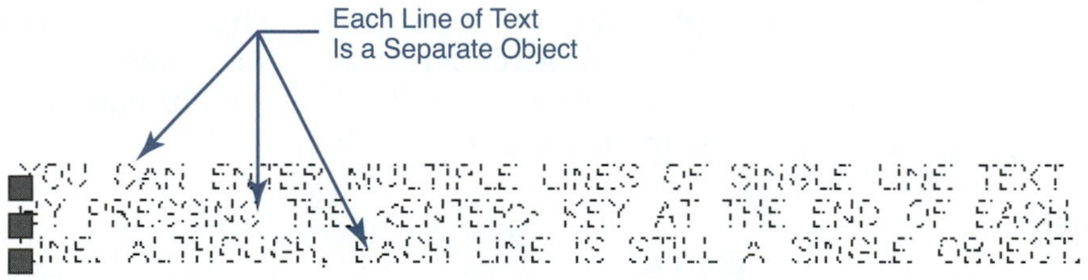

Figure 11-36
Multiple lines of single-line text

NOTE

The line spacing used for single-line text is 1.5 times the text height from the bottom of one line of text to the bottom of the next line.

TIP

If **TEXT** or **DTEXT** was the last command entered, when you create additional new single-line text you can simply press **<Enter>** at the *Specify start point of text or* ↓ prompt and skip the prompts for a text height and rotation angle. AutoCAD automatically displays the in-place single-line text editor directly below the last line of text created in the drawing using the same height, rotation angle, and justification so you can just start typing!

The Right-Click Menu

The single-line text editor also has the right-click menu shown in Figure 11-37, which provides additional functionality. The menu shares some of

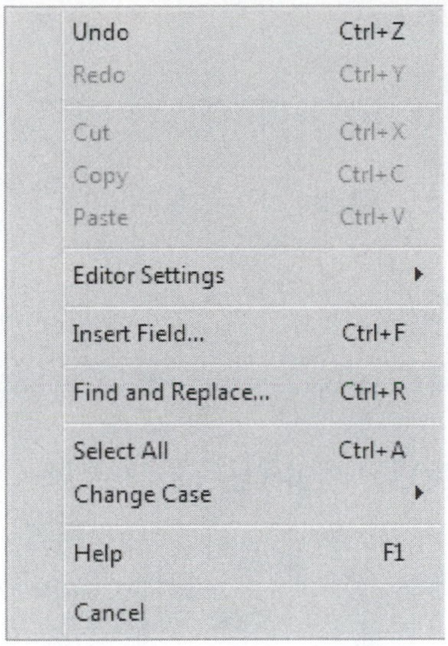

Figure 11-37
Single-line text editor right-click menu

the same tools and features found on the right-click menu in the multiline text editor explained earlier:

- **Undo/Redo** Allows you to undo/redo one or more actions in the text editor
- **Cut** Deletes text and places it on the Windows Clipboard so you can paste it later
- **Copy** Copies text to the Windows Clipboard so you can paste it later
- **Paste** Inserts text that is currently on the Windows Clipboard
- **Editor Settings** Cascade menu with the same editor options found in the multiline text editor
- **Insert Field...** Allows you to insert a field using the **Field** dialog box. Fields and the **Field** dialog box are explained in detail later in this chapter
- **Find and Replace...** Displays the **Find and Replace** dialog box so you can search for and replace text
- **Select All** Selects all the text in the single-line text editor
- **Change Case** Cascade menu that allows you to change the case of text
    - **UPPERCASE** Changes text to uppercase
    - **lowercase** Changes text to lowercase
- **Help** Displays the single-line text help topic
- **Cancel** Exits the single-line text editor

Single-Line Text Justification

Single-line text has a justification property similar to multiline text that determines how the text is aligned relative to the insertion point, although unlike multiline text, single-line justification affects only one line of text, not the complete paragraph. The different justification options are shown in Figure 11-38.

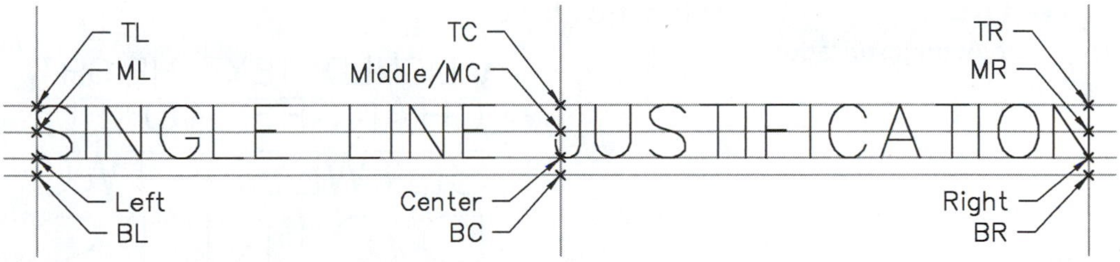

Figure 11-38
Single-line text justification options

The single-line text justification options can be used to specify any of the justifications shown in Figure 11-38. To change the text justification, start the **TEXT** or **DTEXT** command and select the justification option. AutoCAD prompts you to *Enter an option:*. After you select a justification, you specify a start point, height, and rotation angle using the methods explained earlier. The in-place single-line text editor is then displayed, and you can begin typing.

The text flow as you type is determined by the justification option chosen. Specifying **Right** justification makes text flow from the right to the left, whereas the **Center** justification option makes text spill out in both directions from the start point (see Figure 11-39).

Figure 11-39
Using the **Right** and **Center** justification options

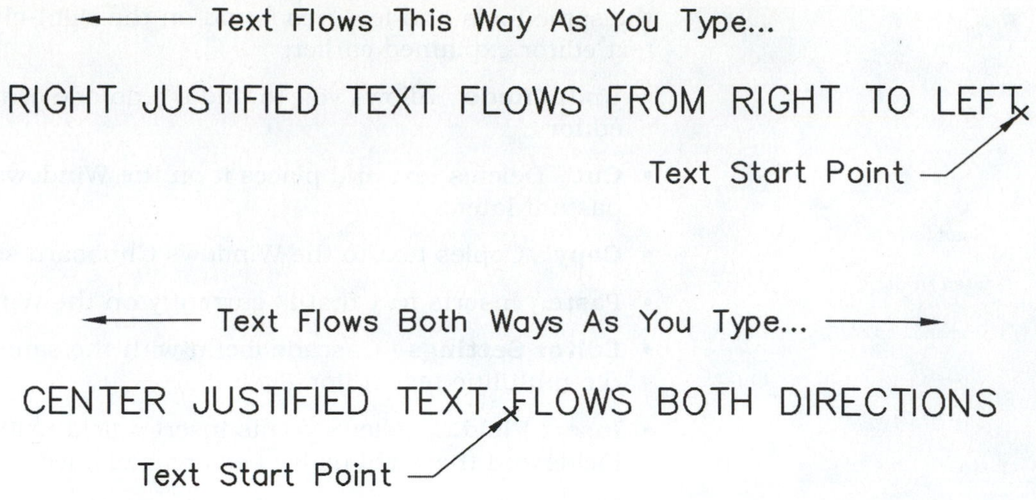

Except for the first two options, **Align** and **Fit,** most of the justification options are fairly self-explanatory. The **Align** and **Fit** justification options both allow you to locate text using two points to define the width and angle of the text. Both options force the text to fit between the two points specified—although with different methods. The **Align** option changes the height of the text (shorter or taller) to make the text fit, and the **Fit** option changes the text's width scale factor (narrower or wider) to make the text fit.

To use the **Align** option, start the **TEXT** or **DTEXT** command and select the **Align** option using the methods explained above. AutoCAD prompts you to *Specify first endpoint of text baseline:*. Select the starting point for the text. AutoCAD then prompts you to *Specify second endpoint of text baseline:*. This point determines both the angle and the final overall width of the text. Remember that the **Align** option changes the height of the text in order to make it fit between the two points. Because of this, the in-place single-line text editor box starts out tall and gets shorter as you type as shown in Figure 11-40.

Figure 11-40
Using the **Align** justification option

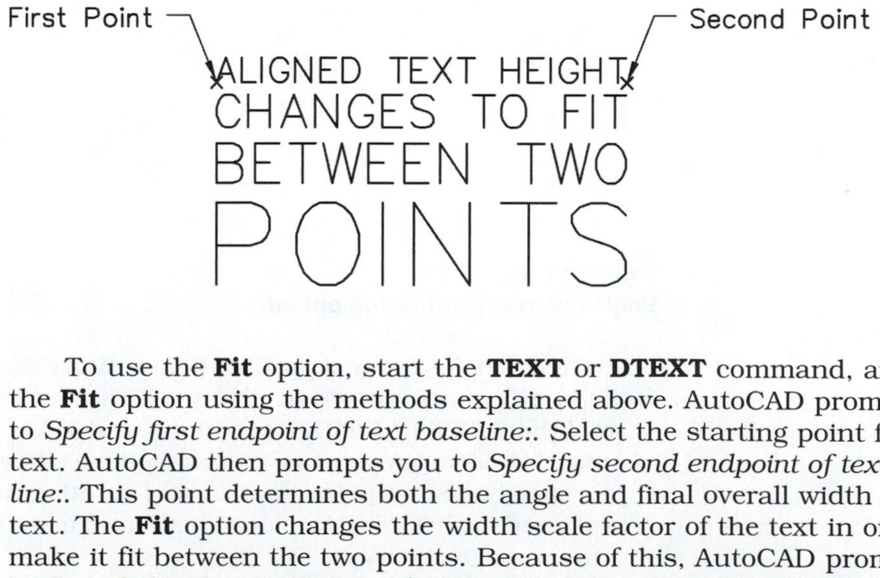

To use the **Fit** option, start the **TEXT** or **DTEXT** command, and select the **Fit** option using the methods explained above. AutoCAD prompts you to *Specify first endpoint of text baseline:*. Select the starting point for the text. AutoCAD then prompts you to *Specify second endpoint of text baseline:*. This point determines both the angle and final overall width of the text. The **Fit** option changes the width scale factor of the text in order to make it fit between the two points. Because of this, AutoCAD prompts you to *Specify height <0.1000>:*. After you enter the desired height, the in-place single-line text editor box is displayed and you can begin typing. The text is either expanded or compressed to fit between the two points as you type but the height is maintained as shown in Figure 11-41.

Figure 11-41
Using the **Fit** justification option

EXERCISE 11-8 **Creating Single-Line Text**

1. Continue from Exercise 11-7.
2. Create the single-line text shown in Figure 11-42 using the text style, height, and justification indicated.
3. Save the drawing.

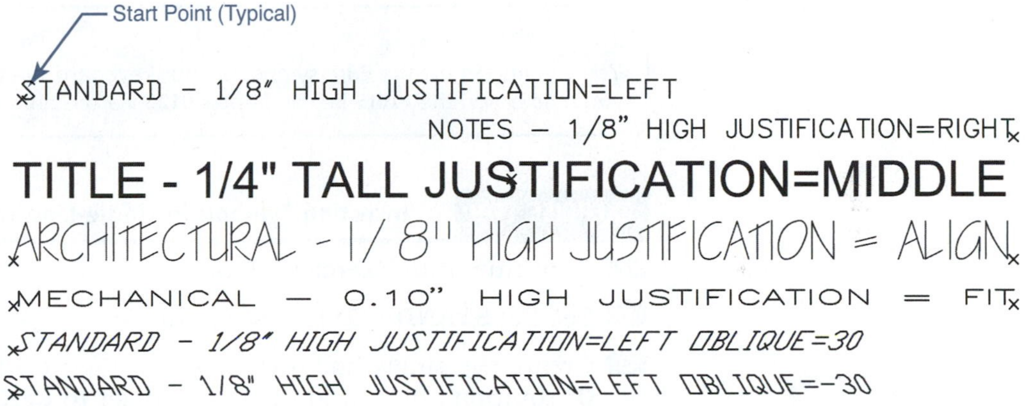

Figure 11-42
Creating single-line text

Inserting Special Symbols in Single-Line Text

You can insert a number of the same special symbols using the single-line text editor that you can insert using the multiline text editor, but your options are somewhat limited. There is no access to the **Character Map** dialog box, and the symbols you can use must be typed in using either their corresponding AutoCAD "%%" control code or their "\U+" Unicode string. The available AutoCAD control codes are as follows:

- **%%C** Draws circle diameter dimensioning symbol (∅)
- **%%D** Draws degree symbol (°)
- **%%P** Draws plus/minus tolerance symbol (±)
- **%%O** Toggles overscoring on and off
- **%%U** Toggles underscoring on and off
- **%%%** Draws a single percent sign (%)

The control codes are immediately converted into their corresponding symbols as you type. For instance, entering **%%D** in the single-line text editor inserts the degree symbol shown in Figure 11-43.

Figure 11-43
Using the %%D control code to insert a degree symbol

NOTE

You can use underscoring and overscoring at the same time.

The underscore (%%U) and overscore (%%O) control codes are toggles that can be turned on and off as shown in Figure 11-44.

TO OVERSCORE A WORD – ENTER %%O

TO UNDERSCORE A WORD – ENTER %%U

Figure 11-44
Using the %%U and %%O control codes to underscore and overscore text

TIP

You can also insert the Euro symbol. If your keyboard does not have a Euro symbol key, you hold down the **<Alt>** key and enter **0128** via the numeric keypad.

EXERCISE 11-9 **Inserting Symbols in Single-Line Text**

1. Continue from Exercise 11-8.
2. Set the **STANDARD** text style current.
3. Create the single-line text shown in Figure 11-45 at **0.125″** high, **0°** rotation angle, and justification set to **Left.**
4. Save the drawing.

Figure 11-45
Inserting symbols in single-line text

THIS IS A DIAMETER SYMBOL ∅
THIS IS A DEGREE SYMBOL °
THIS IS A PLUS/MINUS SYMBOL ±
THIS TEXT IS OVERSCORED AND UNDERSCORED
THIS IS A SINGLE PERCENT SIGN %

Text Fields

A field is intelligent text you can insert in your drawing that dynamically updates according to the data it is based on and/or represents. A classic example is the **Date** field. You can create a **Date** field in a drawing that automatically updates to reflect the current date, and even time, using a variety of different formats:

- 2/7/2012
- Tuesday, February 07, 2012
- 2012-02-07
- 7-Feb-12
- ...

Fields can be created by themselves, so they stand alone, or they can be inserted in any kind of text, attribute, or attribute definition. A field uses the same text style as the text object in which it is inserted and is displayed with a light gray background that is not plotted.

FOR MORE DETAILS

See Chapter 15 for more details about blocks and block attributes.

When a field is updated, the latest data are displayed. Fields can be set to update automatically via one or all of the following events and actions:

- When a drawing is opened
- When a drawing is saved
- When a drawing is plotted
- When you use eTransmit
- When a drawing is regenerated

It is also possible to turn off all the automatic update features so you must manually update any fields in a drawing. You can control how fields are updated, and then turn the field background display on and off, in the **Fields** area at the bottom left of the **User Preferences** tab of the **Options** dialog box shown in Figure 11-46.

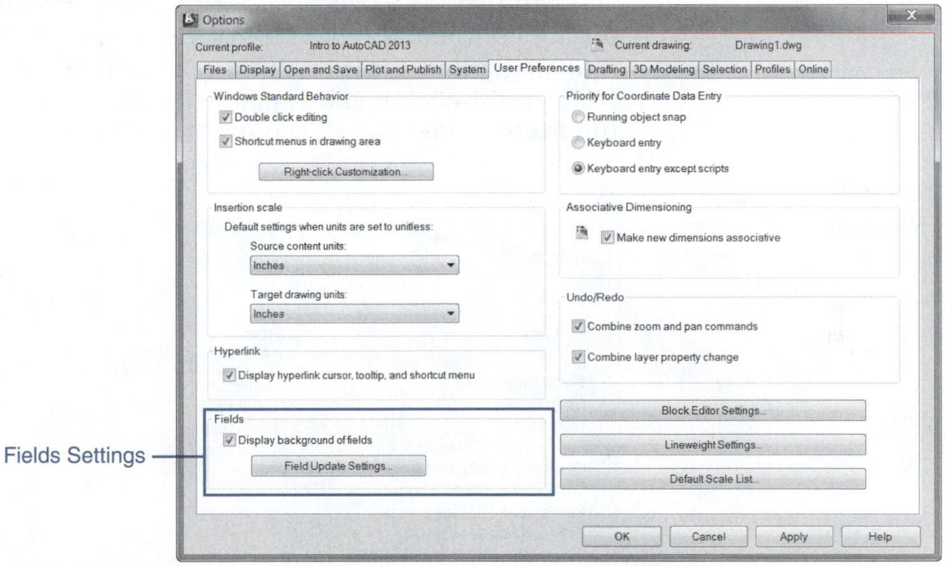

Figure 11-46
Fields settings on the **User Preferences** tab of the **Options** dialog box

Unchecking the **Display background of fields** check box turns off the light gray background. Selecting the **Field Update Settings...** button displays the **Field Update Settings** dialog box shown in Figure 11-47.

NOTE

A field that currently has no value displays all hyphens (--). For instance, the **PlotDate** field is not set to anything until a drawing is plotted. An invalid field displays all pound signs (####).

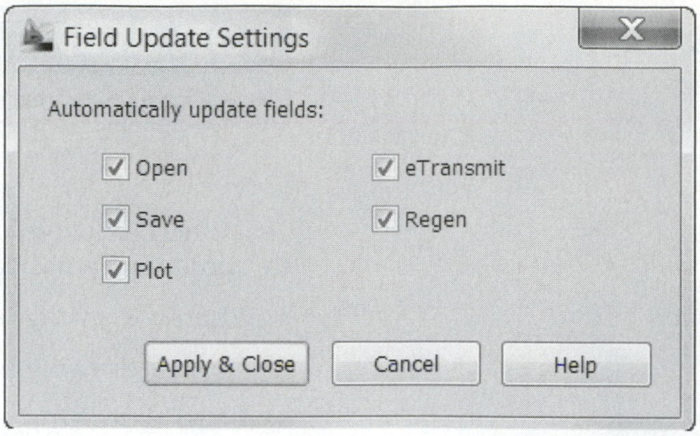

Figure 11-47
The **Field Update Settings** dialog box

INSERT FIELD	
Ribbon & Panel:	Insert Data Field
Text Editor:	
Toolbar:	None
Menu:	Insert Field...
Command Line:	FIELD
Command Alias:	None

This dialog box allows you to indicate what actions or events will automatically update fields. By default, they are all on. If you uncheck all the check boxes, you must update fields manually.

Inserting Text Fields

There are several different ways to insert a field. To create a single stand-alone field, you use the **FIELD** command.

To insert a field into multiline text, you can either select **Insert Field...** from the multiline editor right-click menu (see Figure 11-28), or you can use the **Field** button on the **Insert** panel on the **Text Editor** context tab of the ribbon explained earlier (see Figure 11-15). To insert a field into single-line text, you must select **Insert Field...** from the single-line editor right-click menu explained earlier. Any of these methods displays the **Field** dialog box shown in Figure 11-48.

Figure 11-48
The **Field** dialog box

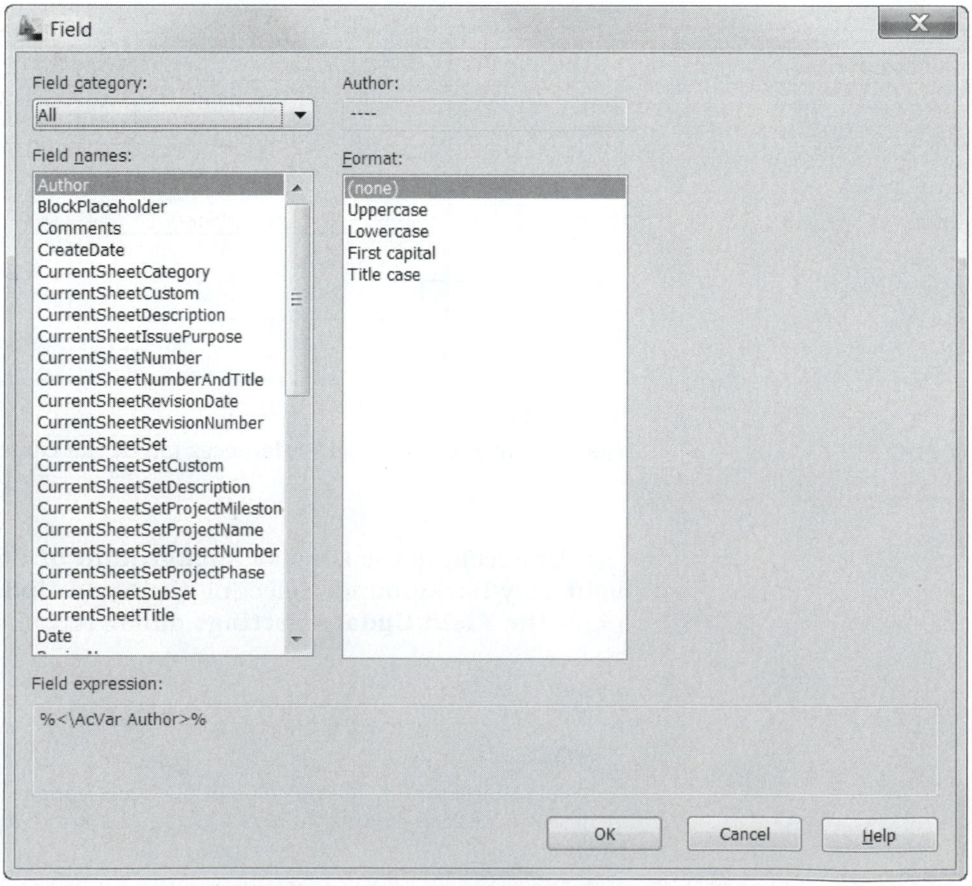

The **Field category:** list box lists the different types of fields available broken down into the following categories:

- **All** All fields
- **Date & Time** Date/time–related fields (created, saved, plotted)
- **Document** Drawing file–related fields (file name, size, saved by)
- **Linked** Hyperlink information
- **Objects** Object information (formulas, block names, drawing object properties)
- **Other** Miscellaneous information (diesel expressions, system variable values)
- **Plot** Plot information (plot device, paper size, scale)
- **Sheetset** Sheet set information

The **Field names:** list box changes based on the category selected. All the other options in the **Field** dialog box change based on the field category and field name that are selected. For instance, selecting the **Date & Time** field category displays a list of the following date-related field names:

- CreateDate
- Date
- PlotDate
- SaveDate

All the date fields allow you to specify a date format in the **Date format:** text box and control how the date appears in the drawing. You can either enter your own format via the keyboard using the control codes shown in the **Hints** area on the right side of the **Field** dialog box or, even easier, select a predefined format from the **Examples:** list in the middle of the dialog box shown in Figure 11-49.

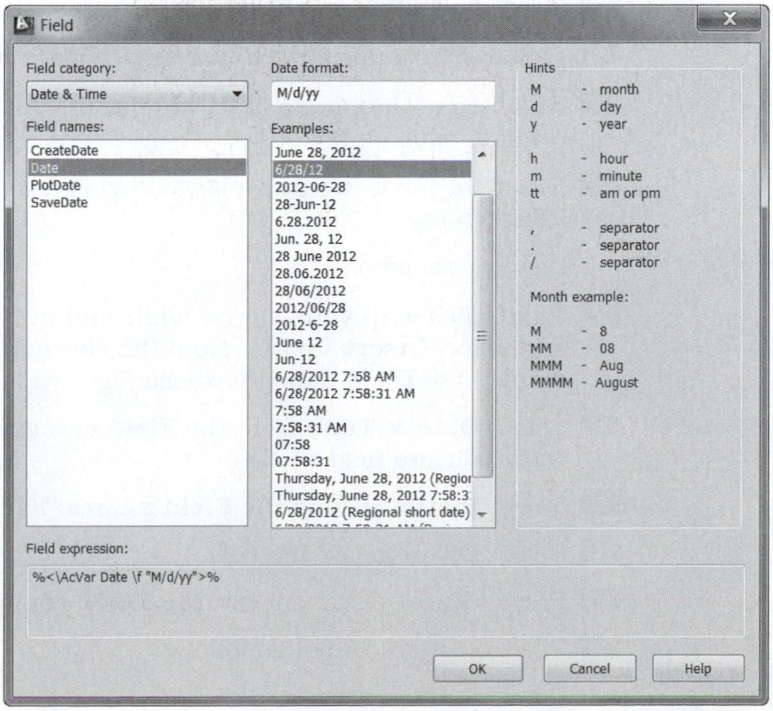

Figure 11-49
The **Field** dialog box with the **Date & Time** options

Figure 11-50
A **Date** field inserted into a paragraph of multiline text

The **Field expression:** box displays the actual field expression that underlies the field and cannot be edited. It is possible to use the field expression as a guide so that you can construct your own expressions in the **Date format:** text box.

When you have selected the desired field name and all its formatting options, you can select **OK** to insert the field. Figure 11-50 shows a **Date** field inserted in a multiline text object.

Editing Text Fields

Text fields are part of either a multiline or single-line text object. If you insert a stand-alone field as described earlier, it is created as multiline text. Because of this, you must use the same tools to edit a field as you do to edit multiline and single-line text. When a field is selected, the **Edit Field** option is available on the shortcut menu, or you can double-click the field to display the **Field** dialog box. Any changes are applied to all text in the field.

> **TIP**
> If you no longer want to update a field, you can preserve the value that is currently displayed by converting the field to text.

EXERCISE 11-10 Inserting Text Fields

1. Continue from Exercise 11-9.
2. Set the **NOTES** text style current.
3. Start the **TEXT** or **DTEXT** command to create single-line text.
4. Pick a start point for the text anywhere in your drawing.
5. Enter a rotation angle of **0°** when AutoCAD prompts you to *Specify rotation angle of text <0>:*.
6. Enter the following text followed by a space but *do not* press the **<Enter>** key:

   Drawing plotted on:
7. Right-click with your mouse while still in the single-line text editor, and select **Insert Field...** from the shortcut menu (see Figure 11-37) to display the **Field** dialog box (see Figure 11-48).
8. Select **Date & Time** from the **Field category:** list box to display the **Date & Time** field names.
9. Select **PlotDate** from the **Field names:** list box.
10. Select **OK** to insert the field.
11. Press **<Enter>** twice to exit the **TEXT** command.
12. The text should read as follows:

    Drawing plotted on: - - - -

13 Plot your drawing to any plotting device or file.

14 Text is updated so that it looks similar to the following, only with today's date:

Drawing plotted on: 3/10/2012

15 Save the drawing.

Editing Text

Both multiline and single-line text can be modified using any of the modify commands introduced earlier in the book. You can move, copy, rotate, scale, and array text just like any other drawing object. Multiline text can even be broken down into individual single-line text objects using the **EXPLODE** command.

You can also use grips to modify text. Both single-line text and multiline text can be moved using the grip located at the text insertion point. Multiline text also has grips that can be used to resize the boundary area using the **Stretch** option, as shown in Figure 11-51.

Figure 11-51
Using grips to resize the multiline text boundary

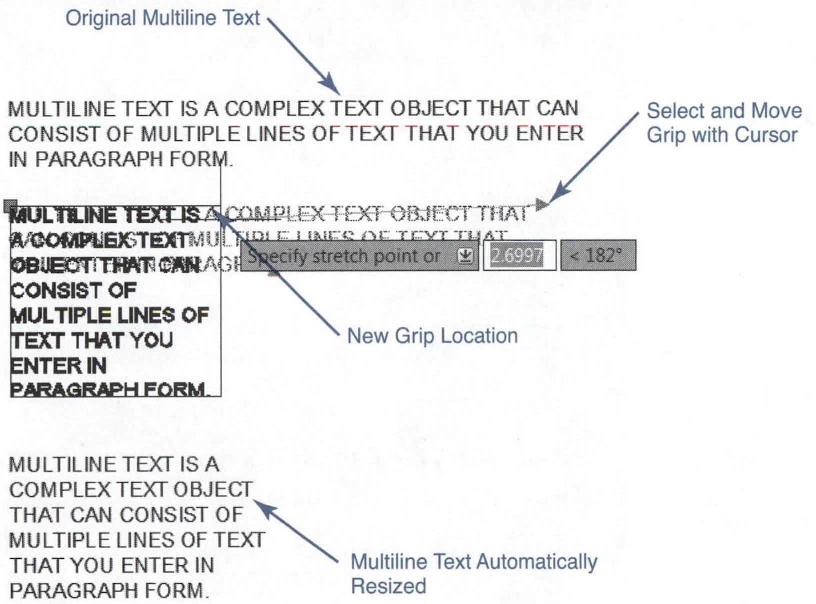

Editing Text Content

The easiest way to edit the text content is to simply double-click on the text you want to edit. If you double-click on multiline text, the same in-place multiline text editor used to create the text is displayed with the selected text, as shown in Figure 11-52. You can then update the text and any of its properties using the same methods and techniques introduced earlier.

Double-clicking on single-line text displays the in-place single-line text editor shown in Figure 11-53.

EDIT TEXT	
Ribbon & Panel:	None
Text Toolbar:	
Menu:	Modify Object Text | Edit
Command Line:	DDEDIT
Command Alias:	ED

Figure 11-52
Editing text using the multiline text editor

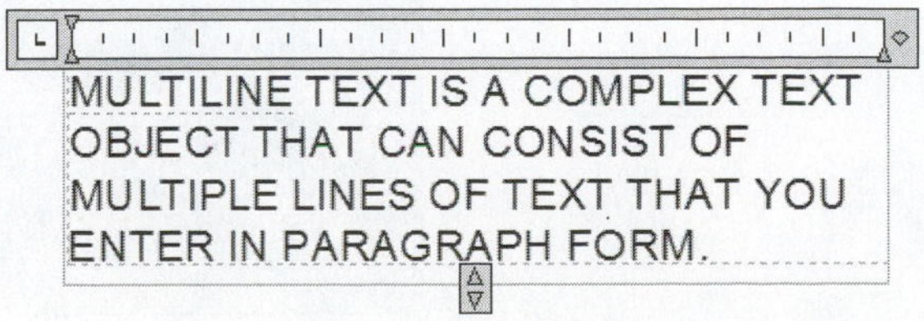

Figure 11-53
Editing text using the single-line text editor

You can also use the **DDEDIT** or **ED** command to edit text content. After starting the **DDEDIT** command, select the text to edit and press **<Enter>.** AutoCAD displays either the in-place multiline or single-line text editor depending on the type of text selected. You can then update the text using the methods and techniques explained earlier.

Editing Text Using the Properties Palette

The **Properties** palette allows you to change all facets of a text object, including text content, text style, height, justification, and rotation, to name but a few. Plus, using the **Properties** palette, you can also change the text's general properties, such as layer, color, and so on. It's the Swiss army knife of text-editing tools. The properties of a multiline text object are shown in Figure 11-54.

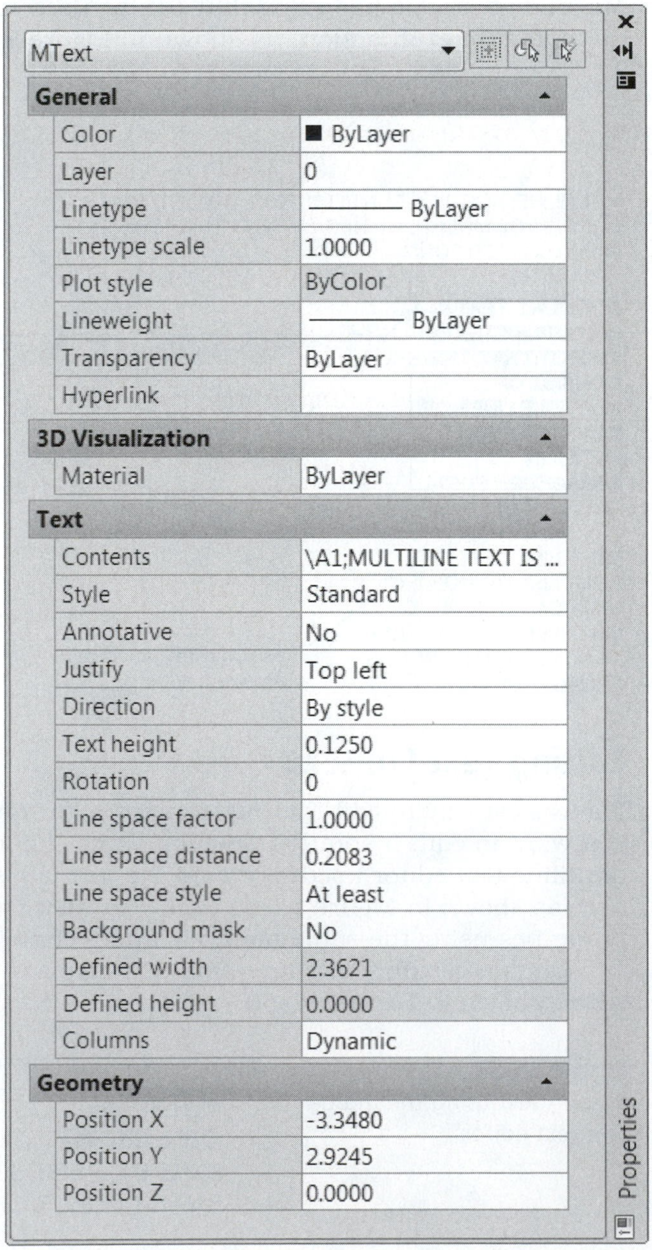

Figure 11-54
Properties of a multiline object

Selecting the button to the right of the **Contents** property displays the appropriate text editor so you can update the text contents as explained earlier.

> **TIP**
>
> You can update multiple text objects using the **Properties** palette. For instance, you can use the **Properties** palette to update the text height for all text in a drawing. In fact, you can even update the text height for both single-line and multiline text at the same time.

EXERCISE 11-11 **Editing Text**

1. Continue from Exercise 11-10.
2. Select the multiline text created in Exercise 11-2 so grips are displayed.
3. Select the top right corner grip and stretch the text boundary corner to the right (see Figure 11-51).
4. Press the **<Esc>** key to turn off grips.
5. Double-click on the multiline text object to display the in-place multiline text editor.
6. Resize the text width back to **3″** using the arrows on the right-hand side of the ruler (see Figure 11-15).
7. Press **<Ctrl>+A** to select all the text in the editor.
8. Use the **Text Editor** context tab of the ribbon to change the following:
   a. Set the style for all text to **ARCHITECTURAL.**
   b. Make all text uppercase.
   c. Deselect all text so nothing is highlighted by clicking anywhere in the text editor window with your cursor.
   d. Select the text "in-place editor" on the first line so it is highlighted.
   e. Change the selected text to **bold** and **italic.**
   f. Set the first line indent to **1″** and the paragraph indent to **0.5″** using the ruler.
9. Select **OK** or click outside the multiline text editor to exit and save your changes.
10. Double-click on any of the single-line text objects to display the in-place single-line text editor.
11. Type the following over the highlighted text:

    THIS IS SOME NEW TEXT!
12. Press **<Enter>** to exit the editor.
13. Hit **<Esc>** to exit the **DDEDIT** command.
14. Select all the text in the drawing and open the **Properties** palette (see Figure 11-54).
15. Change the height property to **0.1″** to update the text height for all the selected text.
16. Change the justification property to **Right** for all the selected text.
17. Press **<Esc>** to deselect all the text.
18. Save the drawing.

SCALE TEXT	
Ribbon & Panel:	Annotate Text | Scale
Text Toolbar:	
Menu:	Modify Object | Text |Scale
Command Line:	SCALE-TEXT
Command Alias:	NONE

Scaling Text

The **SCALETEXT** command allows you to change the height of one or more text objects using the following methods using a base point that you specify:

- Specifying a new height
- Specifying a scale factor
- Matching the height of an existing text object

You can elect to use each text object's insertion point as the base point about which the text is scaled, or you can select one of the different justification options explained earlier in the chapter. AutoCAD uses the base point to scale each text object, but it *doesn't change* the justification point for each object, as shown in Figure 11-55.

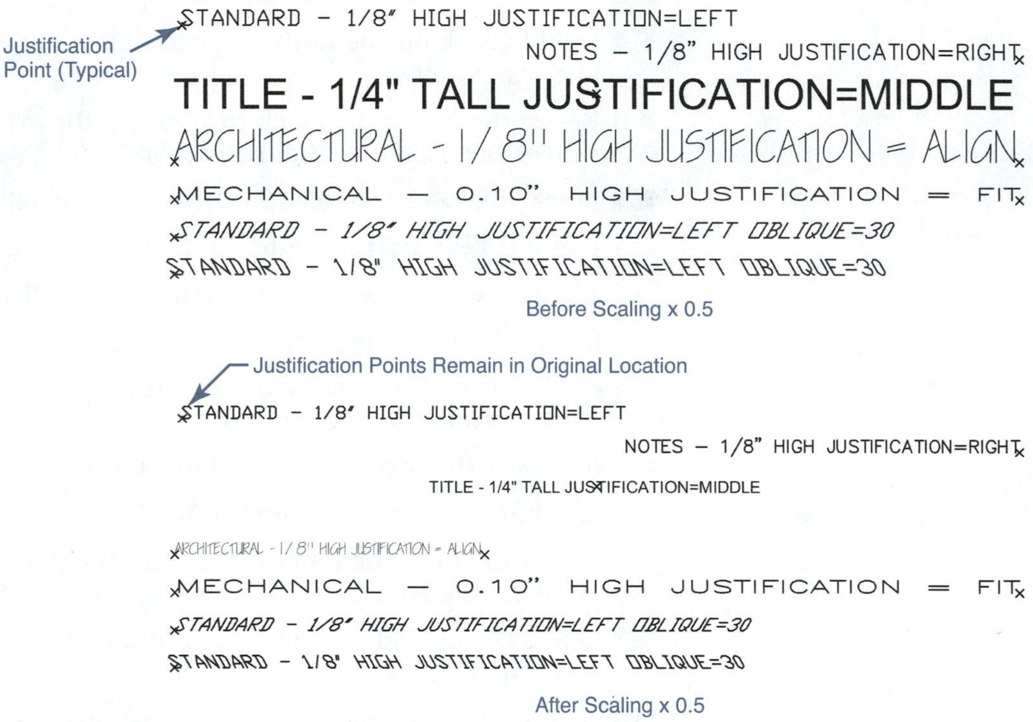

Figure 11-55
Changing text height using the **SCALETEXT** command

When you start the **SCALETEXT** command, AutoCAD prompts you to *Select objects:*. Select the text you want to update using any of the selection methods and press **<Enter>.** AutoCAD prompts you to *Enter a base point option for scaling:*. You can press **<Enter>** to use the existing text insertion points as base points, or you can select one of the different justification options. Remember that the justification point entered is used only as a temporary base point for each text object.

After you have selected a base point option, AutoCAD prompts you to *Specify new height or* ↓. You have three options: you can enter a new height, you can specify a scale factor to multiply each text height by, or you can match the height of an existing text object in the drawing. The default is to enter a new height.

EXERCISE 11-12 **Scaling Text**

1. Continue from Exercise 11-11.
2. Start the **SCALETEXT** command.
3. Type **ALL** and press **<Enter>** twice when AutoCAD prompts you to *Select objects:* to select everything in the drawing.
4. AutoCAD prompts you to *Enter a base point option for scaling* ↓.
5. Type **E<Enter>** or select the existing option using your arrow keys.
6. AutoCAD prompts you to *Specify new height or* ↓.
7. Type **.1<Enter>**.
8. All the text is resized to 0.1″ tall using its current insertion point.
9. Save the drawing.

JUSTIFY TEXT	
Ribbon & Panel:	Annotate Text Justify
Text Toolbar:	
Menu:	Modify Object | Text |Justify
Command Line:	JUSTIFY-TEXT
Command Alias:	NONE

Changing Text Justification

The **JUSTIFYTEXT** command allows you to change the justification property of one or more text objects without changing their location in the drawing. Typically, when you change the justification property of text using the **Properties** palette, the text is relocated about the new justification point as shown in Figure 11-56.

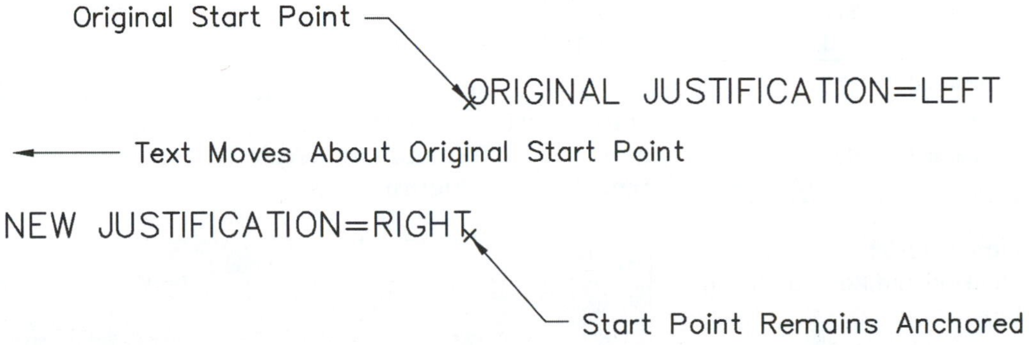

Figure 11-56
Changing text justification using the **Properties** palette

The **JUSTIFYTEXT** command provides a way around this problem. When you start the **JUSTIFYTEXT** command, AutoCAD prompts you to *Select objects:*. Select the text you want to update using any of the selection methods and press **<Enter>.** AutoCAD prompts you to *Enter a justification option:* so you can select one of the different justification options. The insertion points for all the selected text objects are changed to the justification point specified, but they remain in their original locations as shown in Figure 11-57.

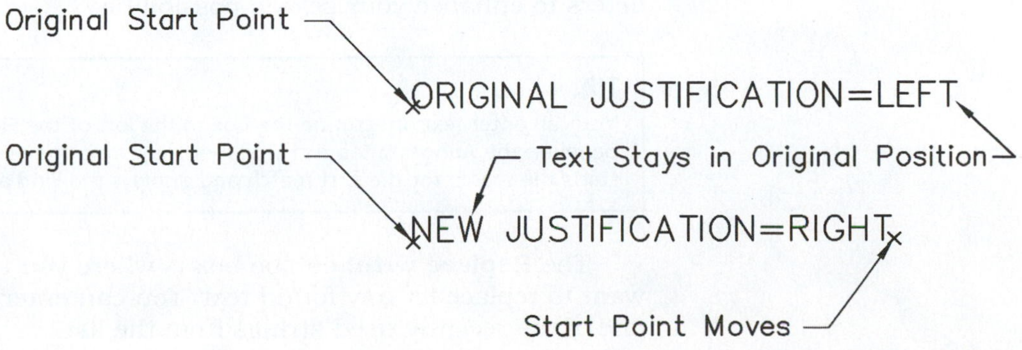

Figure 11-57
Changing text justification using the **JUSTIFYTEXT** command

EXERCISE 11-13 Changing Text Justification

1. Continue from Exercise 11-12.
2. Start the **JUSTIFYTEXT** command.
3. Type **ALL** and press **<Enter>** twice when AutoCAD prompts you to *Select objects:* to select everything in the drawing.
4. AutoCAD prompts you to *Enter a justification option* ↓.
5. Select the **Right** justification option.
6. All the text justification points are changed to **Right,** but the text remains in its original location.
7. Save the drawing.

FIND TEXT	
Ribbon & Panel:	Annotate Text 
Text Toolbar:	
Toolbar:	None
Menu:	Edit Find...
Command Line:	FIND
Command Alias:	None

Finding and Replacing Text

The **FIND** command allows you to find and replace text that you specify. AutoCAD searches through *all* the different text types in a drawing including:

- Single-line and multiline text
- Block attributes
- Dimensions
- Tables
- Hyperlinks

It is possible to limit what type of text to search for so you can refine your search via the **FIND** command's options explained later. When you start the **FIND** command, AutoCAD displays the **Find and Replace** dialog box shown in Figure 11-58.

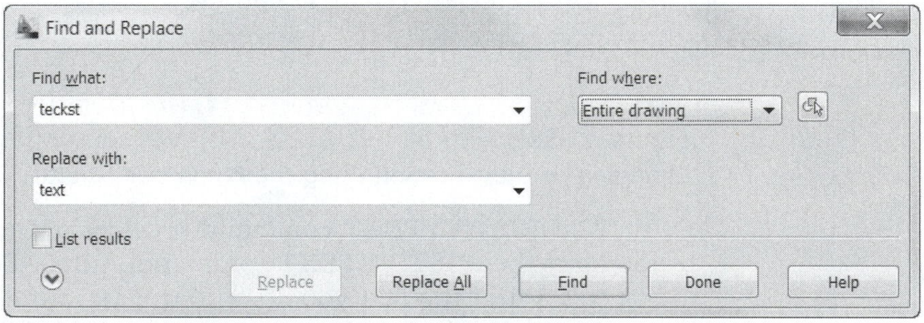

Figure 11-58
The **Find and Replace** dialog box

The **Find what:** combo box is where you type in the text string for which you want to search. You can enter a text string or choose one of the recently used strings from the list. It is also possible to use wildcard characters to enhance your search possibilities.

> **TIP**
>
> You can enter text directly via the box to the left of the **Find Text** button on the **Text** panel on the **Annotate** tab of the ribbon. Selecting the **Find Text** button automatically starts the search for the first match and displays the **Find and Replace** dialog box.

The **Replace with:** combo box is where you type in the text string you want to replace for any found text. You can enter a text string or choose one of the recently used strings from the list.

The **Find where:** list box allows you to specify where to search. You can search the current space/layout, the entire drawing, or selected objects. If one or more objects are already selected, the **Current selection** option is the default value; otherwise, the **Current space/layout** option is the default.

The **Select objects** button to the right of the **Find where:** list box closes the dialog box temporarily so that you can select objects in your drawing. Accepting the selection set by pressing **<Enter>** returns to the dialog box.

The **More Options** button on the lower left expands the dialog box as shown in Figure 11-59 so you can view and modify the search options and text types to search.

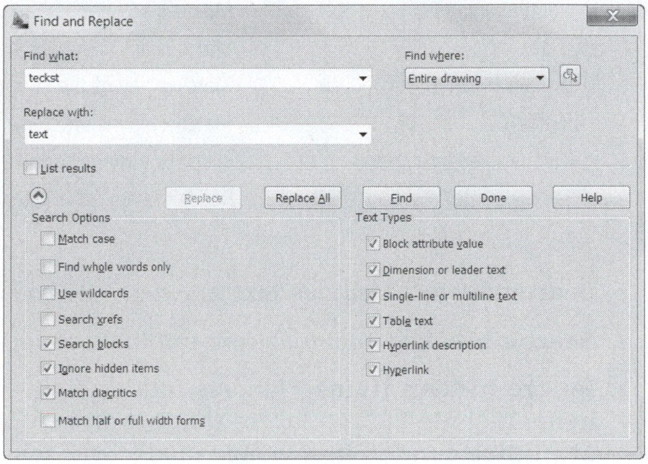

Figure 11-59
The **Find and Replace** dialog box with more options

The **Replace** button replaces the found text with the text that you enter in the **Replace with:** combo box.

The **Replace All** button finds *all* occurrences of the text entered in the **Find what:** combo box and replaces them with the text entered in the **Replace with:** combo box. AutoCAD reports the success or failure of the replacement attempt in a separate dialog box by indicating how many objects have been changed.

The **Find** button in the **Find and Replace** dialog box searches for the text that you enter in the **Find what:** combo box. Any text that is found is automatically zoomed into so you can see it in context. After finding the first occurrence of the text, the **Find** button becomes the **Find Next** button to allow you to search for the next text occurrence.

Selecting the **List results** check box displays a table with the text location (model or paper space), object type, and text string where the text was found showing it in context. Clicking on a column header in the table sorts the information based on the content in that column.

When **List results** are displayed, the **Zoom** button on the right allows you to zoom to the highlighted object. Additional buttons allow you to quickly create a selection set that includes all text objects in the list or only the highlighted items.

Selecting the **More Options** arrow button expands the dialog box so you can specify different search options and text types to search.

The different **Search Options** include:

- **Match case** Includes the case of the text in **Find what:** as part of the search criteria
- **Find whole words only** Finds only whole words that match the text in **Find what:**. For example, if you select **Find whole words only** and search for "is", **Find and Replace** does not locate the text string "this"

- **Use wildcards** Allows the use of the following wildcard characters in searches:

Find and Replace Wildcard Characters	
Wildcard Character	**Description**
* (Asterisk)	Matches any text string
@ (At)	Matches any letter *only*
# (Pound)	Matches any number *only*
? (Question mark)	Matches any single character (letters and numbers)
. (Period)	Matches any nonalphanumeric character
~ (Tilde)	Matches anything *but* the pattern
[ ] (Square brackets)	Matches any of the characters enclosed in the brackets
[~] (Tilde)	Matches any character not enclosed in the brackets
[-] (Hyphen and brackets)	Specifies a range for a single letter
' (Reverse quote)	Reads the next character literally

- **Search xrefs** Includes text in externally referenced files in search results
- **Search blocks** Includes text in blocks in search results
- **Ignore hidden items** Ignores hidden items in search results. Hidden items include text on layers that are frozen or turned off, text in block attributes created in invisible mode, and text in visibility states within dynamic blocks
- **Match diacritics** (Latin-based languages) Matches diacritical marks, or accents, in search results
- **Match half or full width forms** (East Asian Languages) Matches half- and full-width characters in search results

The **Text Types** area allows you to specify the type of text objects you want to include in the search. By default, all options are selected.

The **Done** button closes and exits the **Find and Replace** dialog box.

> **TIP**
>
> The **FIND** command can also be found near the bottom of many of the right-click menus for easy access.

EXERCISE 11-14 Finding and Replacing Text

1. Continue from Exercise 11-13.
2. Type the word **text** in the **Find Text** box on the **Text** panel of the **Annotate** tab.
3. Select the **Find Text** button on the right to display the **Find and Replace** dialog box shown in Figure 11-58.
4. Type the word **teckst** in the **Replace with:** list box.
5. Select the **Replace** button to replace the current text.
6. Select the **Find Next** button to find the next occurrence.
7. Select the **Replace All** button to replace all the text in the drawing.

8 Note how many matches were found and how many objects were changed and select the **OK** button.

9 Select the **Close** button to exit the dialog box.

10 Save the drawing.

CHECK SPELLING	
Ribbon & Panel:	Annotate Text Check Spelling
Text Toolbar:	ABC
Menu:	Tools Spelling...
Command Line:	SPELL
Command Alias:	SP

The Spell Checker

The **SPELL** command allows you to check and correct the spelling for the following text object types:

- Single-line and multiline text
- Dimensions
- Block attribute values
- External references

Entering the **SPELL** command displays the **Check Spelling** dialog box shown in Figure 11-60.

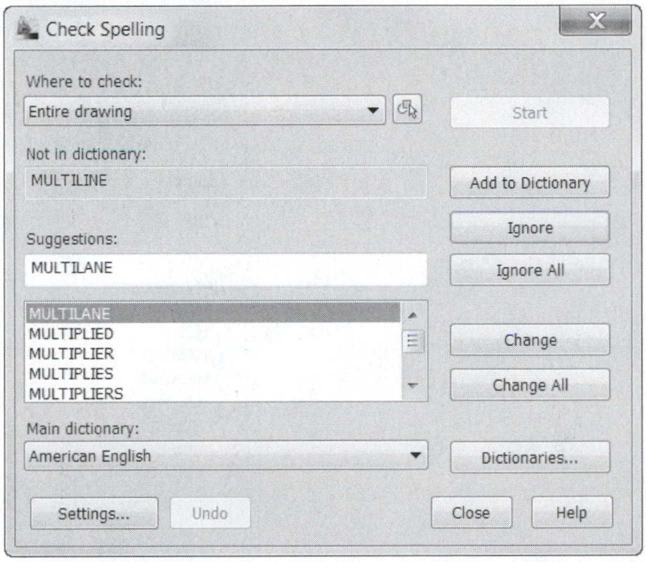

Figure 11-60
The **Check Spelling** dialog box

The **Where to check:** drop-down list allows you to limit where and what text AutoCAD checks for spelling errors. You have the following three options:

- Entire drawing
- Current space/layout
- Selected objects

By default, AutoCAD checks the entire drawing for spelling errors. If you select **Selected objects,** you must select some text objects in the drawing by selecting the **Select objects** button to the right of the **Where to check:** drop-down list. Otherwise, the **Start** button will be disabled.

Select the **Start** button to begin the spell-checking process. If no misspelled words are found, AutoCAD displays a message box indicating that the *Spelling Check is complete.* Otherwise, AutoCAD will automatically zoom to the first misspelled word in the drawing and highlight the offending text.

The **Not in dictionary:** area displays the highlighted word that is spelled incorrectly or was not found in the current dictionary. This is the text that will be updated if you select the **Change** or **Change All** button.

The **Suggestions:** box displays a list of suggested replacement words from the current dictionary. You can either select a replacement word from the list or type in a replacement word in the box.

The **Add to Dictionary** button adds the current word to the current custom dictionary. A different custom dictionary can be selected using the **Dictionaries...** button explained below.

The **Ignore** button skips the current word and begins searching for the next misspelled word.

The **Ignore All** button skips all the remaining occurrences of the misspelled word that match the current word.

The **Change** button replaces the current word with the word in the **Suggestions:** text box.

The **Change All** button replaces all occurrences of the misspelled word in the drawing based on the current **Where to check:** selection.

The **Dictionaries...** button displays the **Dictionaries** dialog box shown in Figure 11-61.

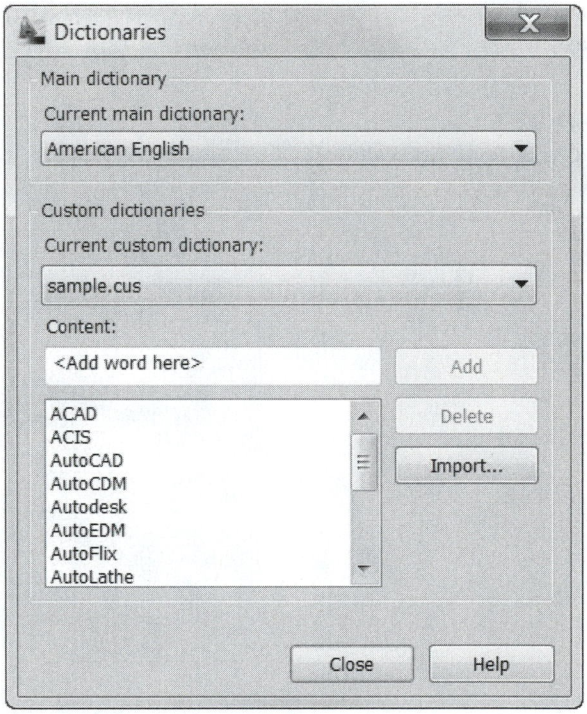

Figure 11-61
The **Dictionaries** dialog box

The **Dictionaries** dialog box allows you to switch dictionaries so you can check spelling in other languages. The default main dictionary is American English. To change to another language dictionary, select it from the **Current main dictionary:** list box at the top.

To add one or more words to the dictionary, enter it in the **Content:** text box and select the **Add** button. Any words you add in the **Check Spelling** dialog box or the **Dictionaries** dialog box are stored in the custom dictionary. By default, the custom dictionary is named sample.cus and is located in your AutoCAD Support folder.

NOTE

The maximum word length you can add to a custom dictionary is 63 characters.

You can manage custom dictionaries by selecting **Manage custom dictionaries...** from the **Current custom dictionary:** drop-down list to display the **Manage Custom Dictionaries** dialog box. The **Manage Custom**

Figure 11-62
The **Check Spelling Settings** dialog box

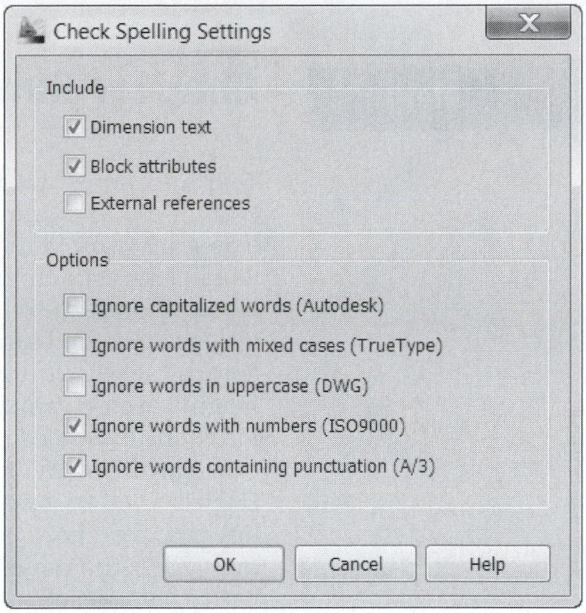

Dictionaries dialog box allows you to add dictionaries to check, create new dictionaries from scratch, and remove existing dictionaries.

The **Settings...** button in the **Check Spelling** dialog box displays the **Check Spelling Settings** dialog box shown in Figure 11-62, which allows you to control various aspects of the spell-checking behavior.

At the top of the **Check Spelling Settings** dialog box in the **Include** area, you can choose whether to check dimension text, block attributes, or external references.

At the bottom of the dialog box in the **Options** area, you can choose to ignore certain types of words commonly found in technical drawings such as words with numbers and words containing punctuation.

TIP

The **Undo** button allows you to undo changes if you change the wrong text.

EXERCISE 11-15 Using the Spell Checker

1. Continue from Exercise 11-14.
2. Start the **SPELL** command.
3. The **Check Spelling** dialog box is displayed.
4. Select the **Start** button.
5. AutoCAD zooms to the word "teckst" in your drawing while also displaying it in the **Not in dictionary:** text box.
6. **Suggestions:** is set to "text".
7. Select the **Change** button to update the current text.
8. The next occurrence of "teckst" is found.
9. Select the **Change All** button to update all occurrences of the misspelled word.
10. The "Spelling Check is complete" message box is displayed.
11. Select **OK.**
12. Save the drawing.

Chapter Summary

Text and notes are key features of any type of technical drawing. They literally help to communicate the idea that the drawings are trying to convey. It is important that text meet specific standards of appearance so that it is as clear and concise as possible, limiting the chance for errors or omissions. Standard fonts and heights must be applied on all drawings so that all text has the same look and feel. AutoCAD text styles provide the best control over text appearance because all of the settings, such as font and height, are centralized in one location instead of being applied individually for each text object in a drawing.

AutoCAD provides two different types of text: multiline and single line. Each serves its own purpose. Many times you will want to rely on single-line text for short notes, titles, and labels in a drawing. Other times you may want the benefits of multiline text, which allows you to create different list types, use multiple columns, and insert many different special symbols. Multiline text is the default used for most commands, but remember that you can always break multiline text up into multiple single-line text objects using the **EXPLODE** command. The easiest way to edit both types of text is simply to double-click on the text you want to change, and then AutoCAD will display the proper text-editing tool based on whether text is multiline or single line. Of course, you can always use the **Properties** palette to change the text content or any other property for that matter.

Advanced text tools help increase productivity and accuracy. Text fields allow you to automate text in a drawing so that you can insert text that will automatically update with the current date, when the drawing was plotted, the drawing name, and much more. The **Find and Replace** tool can be used to update text for an entire drawing in one step. The **Spell Checker** can scan and fix text for an entire drawing using a standard dictionary or a custom dictionary that can include your own key terms and abbreviations.

FOR MORE DETAILS

See page 683 in Chapter 16 for more information about extracting block attributes.

Chapter Test Questions

Multiple Choice

Circle the correct answer.

1. A font determines how text looks by defining its:
   - a. Boldness
   - b. Typeface
   - c. Language
   - d. All of the above
2. AutoCAD fonts have what three-letter file extension?
   - a. SHP
   - b. FNT
   - c. TTF
   - d. SHX

3. The system variable that controls the font substituted for a font not found on your system is named:

a. **ALTFONT** c. **SUBFONT**
b. **FONTSUB** d. **FONTALT**

4. To exit the in-place multiline text editor and save your text and any changes, you:

a. Select **Close Text Editor** on the **Text Editor** context tab of the ribbon
b. Press **<Ctrl>**+**<Enter>**
c. Click outside the editor window with your mouse
d. All of the above

5. The system variable that controls the default text height displayed in the multiline text editor **Text height** list box is:

a. **TEXTHEIGHT** c. **TXTHEIGHT**
b. **SIZETEXT** d. **TEXTSIZE**

6. The name of the feature in the multiline text editor that locks your keyboard so only uppercase letters can be typed is:

a. **CaseLock** c. **AutoCAPS**
b. **CapLocks** d. **CapAuto**

7. The **AutoStack** feature automatically stacks numeric text when what character is placed between two numbers?

a. / c. ^
b. # d. All of the above

8. What single-line justification option allows you to squeeze text between two points without changing the text height?

a. **Align** c. **Center**
b. **Fit** d. None of the above

9. The prefix used to insert special symbols into single-line text is:

a. @ c. \U++
b. %% d. b and c

10. To edit existing text, you can:

a. Double-click on the text
b. Use the **Properties** palette
c. Use the **DDEDIT** command
d. All of the above

Matching

Write the number of the correct answer on the line.

a. Annotate ______
b. Typeface ______
c. **TEXTFILL** ______

1. System variable that controls the filling of TrueType fonts while plotting and rendering
2. Locks your keyboard so only uppercase letters can be entered, similar to the **<Caps Lock>** key
3. The set of numeric codes used to represent the characters of a particular country or place

d. **FONTALT** ______	4. Controls the font, height, and other characteristics that affect the appearance of text
e. Text style ______	5. Creates different formats of stacked text as you type
f. Multiline text ______	6. To add text, notes, and dimensions to a drawing
g. **AutoCAPS** ______	7. Intelligent text that dynamically updates according to the data it is based on and/or represents
h. Character set ______	8. System variable that specifies an alternate font to be used when a particular font file cannot be located on your system
i. **AutoStack** ______	9. Complex text object that can consist of multiple lines of text that you enter in paragraph form
j. Field ______	10. The style or design of a font

True or False

Circle the correct answer.

1. **True or False:** The text font determines the height of the text in a drawing.
2. **True or False:** You can use both TrueType fonts and AutoCAD SHX fonts in a drawing at the same time.
3. **True or False:** You should always try to use text styles to control text fonts.
4. **True or False:** If you change a text style text height, all text of that style in a drawing is updated.
5. **True or False:** It is possible to resize a multiline text boundary size using grips.
6. **True or False:** You can copy text to and from the multiline text editor using the Windows Clipboard.
7. **True or False:** The **Import Text...** option in the multiline editor allows you to import a Microsoft Word document.
8. **True or False:** The **AutoCAPS** feature in the multiline editor can be turned off using your **<Caps Lock>** key.
9. **True or False:** If the current text style has a height assigned in the style that is greater than 0.0, you will be prompted for a text height when creating single-line text.
10. **True or False:** The single-line **Align** text justification option will change the text height in order to make the text entered fit between two selected points.

Chapter Projects

Project 11-1: *Calculator, continued from Chapter 10* [BASIC]

1. Open drawing ***P10-1*** from Chapter 10.
2. Add the text shown in Figure 11-63. *Hint:* Use multiline text with the **Middle Center** justification option.
3. Save your drawing as ***P11-1.***

Figure 11-63

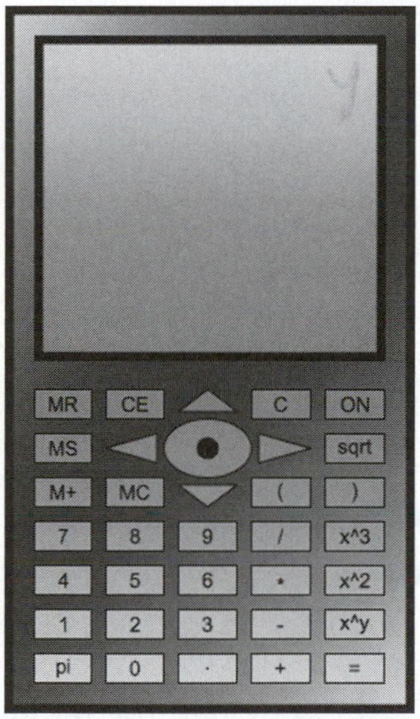

Project 11-2: *B-Size Mechanical Border, continued from Chapter 6* [INTERMEDIATE]

1. Open the template file ***Mechanical B-Size.DWT*** from Chapter 6.
2. Modify the **Standard** text style to use the **ROMANS.SHX** font file.
3. Set the snap to **1/16″** and add the text shown in Figure 11-64 on the layer **Title.** Large text is **1/8″** tall, and smaller text is **1/16″.** Use multiline text for the tolerance note and single-line text for all other text. Use text fields for the drawing name and plot date.
4. Save the drawing to a template file as ***Mechanical B-Size.DWT.***

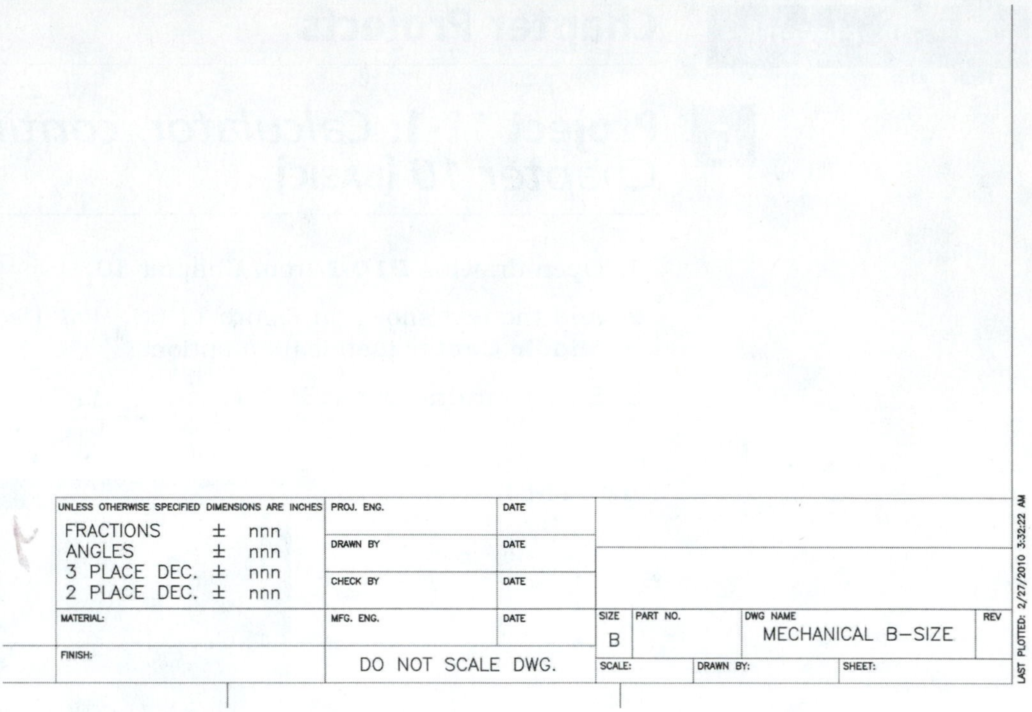

Figure 11-64

A **Project 11-3:** *Architectural D-Size Border, continued from Chapter 10* **[ADVANCED]**

1. Open the template file ***Architectural D-Size.DWT*** from Chapter 10.
2. Create a text style named **Border** assigned the text font **Simplex.shx.**
3. Create a text style named **Logo** assigned the text font **Century Gothic. ttf.**
4. Create a text style named **Arch** assigned the text font **CountryBlueprint. ttf.**
5. Create all text in the following steps at the approximate heights shown. Try to use standard heights when possible.
6. Create all the logo text as shown in Figure 11-65 using the text style **Logo** on the layer **A-Anno-Ttlb-Logo.**
7. Create the text on the bottom left that says, "Last plotted on MM/DD/YYYY" by inserting the date as a field using the **PlotDate** field so it updates each time the drawing is plotted.
8. Create all the remaining title border text as shown in Figure 11-65 using the text style **Border** on the layer **A-Anno-Ttlb-Text.**
9. Save the drawing to a template file as ***Architectural D-Size.DWT*.**

Figure 11-65

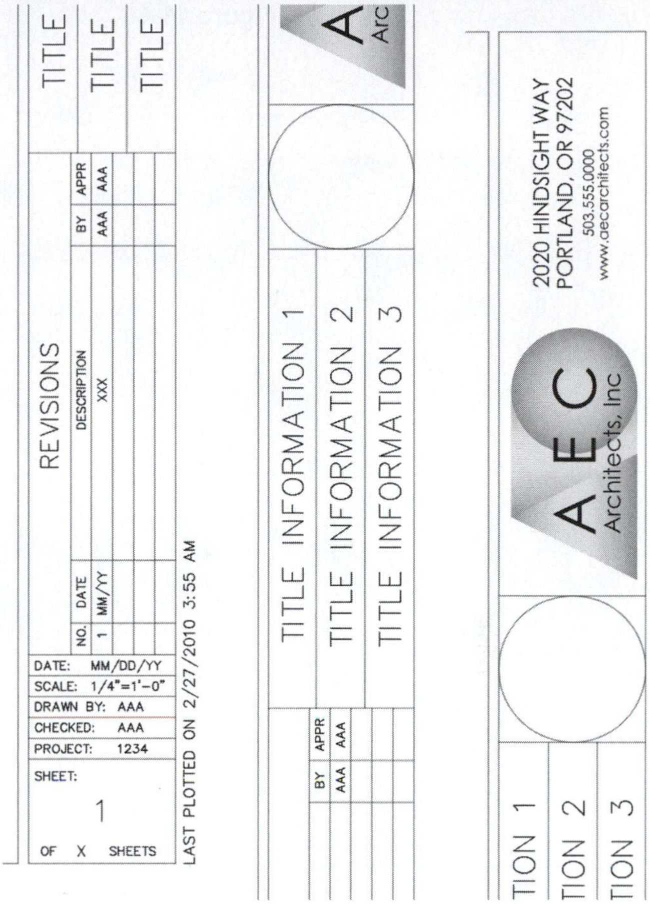

E Project 11-4: *Electrical Distribution Panel, continued from Chapter 10* [BASIC]

1. Open drawing ***P10-4*** from Chapter 10.
2. Add the electrical annotation shown in Figure 11-66. Place all annotation on the **E-Anno** layer.
3. Save your drawing as ***P11-4***.

Figure 11-66

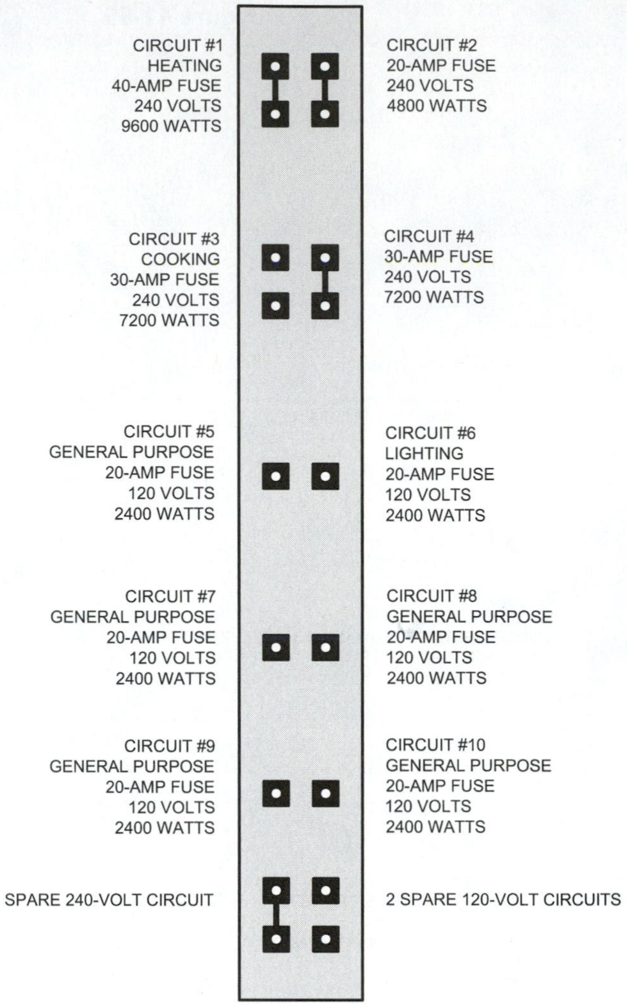

A Project 11-5: *Residential Architectural Plan, continued from Chapter 10* [ADVANCED]

1. Open drawing ***P10-5*** from Chapter 10.
2. Create the following layers:

Name	Color	Linetype	Lineweight	Description
A-Door-Iden	White	Continuous	0.30 mm	Door tags
A-Glaz-Iden	White	Continuous	0.30 mm	Window tags
A-Area-Iden	White	Continuous	0.30 mm	Room numbers, room identification, and area calculations
A-Anno-Legn	White	Continuous	0.30 mm	Door and window schedules
A-Anno-Note	White	Continuous	0.30 mm	General notes
A-Anno-Dims	White	Continuous	0.30 mm	Dimensioning

3. Create a text style called **A-SYMBOL** using the **ROMANS.SHX** font and set it current.

4. Create the door and window schedules and tags as shown in Figure 11-67 using lines and text. Use a text height of **6″** for the door and window tags and the small text in the schedule. Use a text height of **8″** for the column heads in the table and a text height of **12″** for the schedule titles.

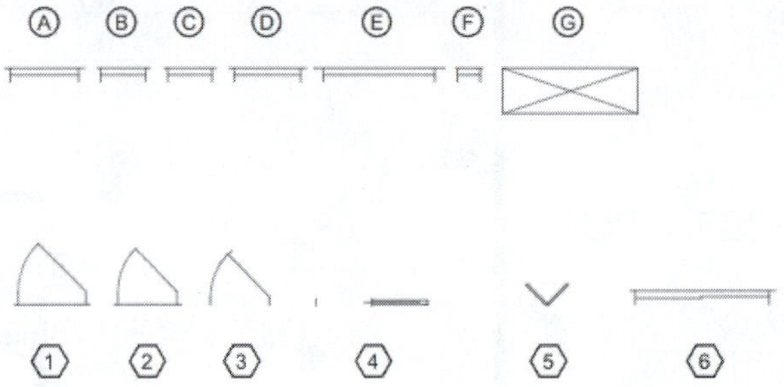

WINDOW SCHEDULE

SYM.	SIZE	TYPE	QTY.
A	3'-0" X 3'-6"	S.H.	10
B	2'-0" X 3'-6"	S.H./FROSTED	1
C	2'-0" X 3'-0"	S.H.	4
D	3'-0" X 3'-0"	PCT.	2
E	5'-0" X 5"-0"	TEMP. PCT.	3
F	1'-0" X 3'-0"	S.H.	2
G	2'-0" X 6'-0"	GLASS SKY.	2

DOOR SCHEDULE

SYM.	SIZE	TYPE	QTY.
1	3'-0" X 6'-8"	M.I./R.P.	1
2	2'-8" X 6'-8"	M.I./S.C.	2
3	2'-8" X 6'-8"	H.C.	8
4	2'-6" X 6'-8"	POCKET/H.C.	2
5	2'-6" X 6'-8"	H.C./BI-FOLD	2
6	6'-0" X 6'-8"	TEMP. SLIDER	2
7	8'-0" X 6'-8"	GARAGE	2

Figure 11-67

5. Place the door and window tags and add the room labels as shown in Figure 11-68. Place each object on its appropriate layer.

6. Save the drawing as ***P11-5***.

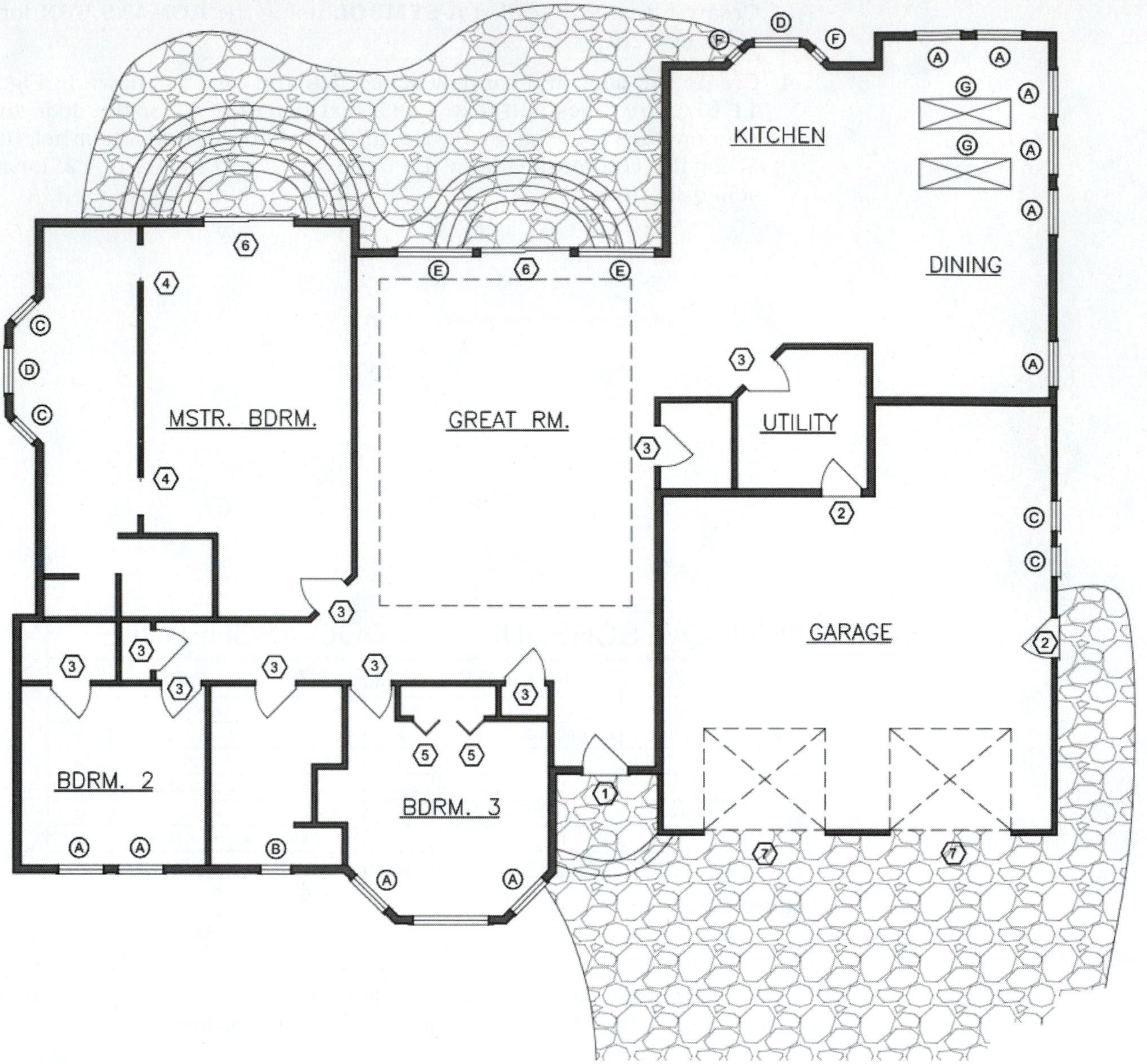
KITCHEN
DINING
MSTR. BDRM.
GREAT RM.
UTILITY
GARAGE
BDRM. 2
BDRM. 3

Figure 11-68

chapter twelve Working with Tables

CHAPTER OBJECTIVES

- Creating tables from scratch by entering the data manually
- Creating tables by linking with a Microsoft® Excel spreadsheet
- Managing data links using the **Data Link Manager**
- Controlling the appearance of tables using table styles
- Modifying tables using grips
- Inserting formulas in a table

Introduction

A table is an AutoCAD annotation object type that consists of data in rows and columns similar to an accounting spreadsheet. Many of the common spreadsheet features you may be familiar with work exactly the same in AutoCAD tables. It is even possible to paste a Microsoft Excel spreadsheet so that it converts directly into a static AutoCAD table with the desired formatting and fonts. Even better, you can link a dynamic AutoCAD table directly to an external Excel spreadsheet so that it updates automatically if the spreadsheet changes. Figure 12-1 shows an example of a table being used for an Architectural door schedule.

You can create a table based on three different types of data:

- **Static data** Manually enter data into a table created from scratch or from pasting Excel data using the Windows Clipboard
- **Externally linked data** Create a dynamic AutoCAD table by linking to an existing Excel spreadsheet

Figure 12-1
Table used for an Architectural window schedule

WINDOW SCHEDULE					
TAG	TYPE	MANUFACTURER	HEIGHT	WIDTH	COUNT
A	FIXED	ACME GLASS CO.	4'–0"	4'–0"	20
B	FIXED	ACME GLASS CO.	4'–0"	3'–6"	4
C	FIXED	ACME GLASS CO.	3'–0"	2'–6"	4
D	CASEMENT	GLASSARAMA, INC.	3'–0"	2'–0"	3
E	SIDELITE	SEASON ALL WINDOWS	4'–0"	1'–0"	1

- **Object data** Create an AutoCAD table from object data in the drawing using the **Data Extraction** wizard, which allows you to extract different object properties, including blocks and block attributes

FOR MORE DETAILS

See page 683 in Chapter 16 for detailed information about using the **Data Extraction** wizard.

cell: The box at the intersection of a table row and column that contains the table data or a formula. A cell is typically referenced using its column letter and row number separated with a colon. For example, the cell in column A and row 1 is referenced as A:1.

Using table styles, you can control all aspects of a table including the ***cell*** data format, the text and border properties, table direction, and other formatting options.

After the table has been created, the complete table, or individual rows and columns, can be resized using grips. Additional modifications can be made using the right-click shortcut menus or the **Table Cell** context tab of the ribbon explained later in the section on modifying tables.

Creating Tables from Scratch

TABLE	
Ribbon & Panel:	Home | Annotation 
Draw Toolbar:	
Menu:	Draw | Table...
Command Line:	TABLE
Command Alias:	TB

The **TABLE** command creates a table object by inserting an empty table in the drawing at a specified point or defined window area using the table style, number of rows, columns, and sizes you specify.

When you start the **TABLE** command, AutoCAD displays the **Insert Table** dialog box shown in Figure 12-2.

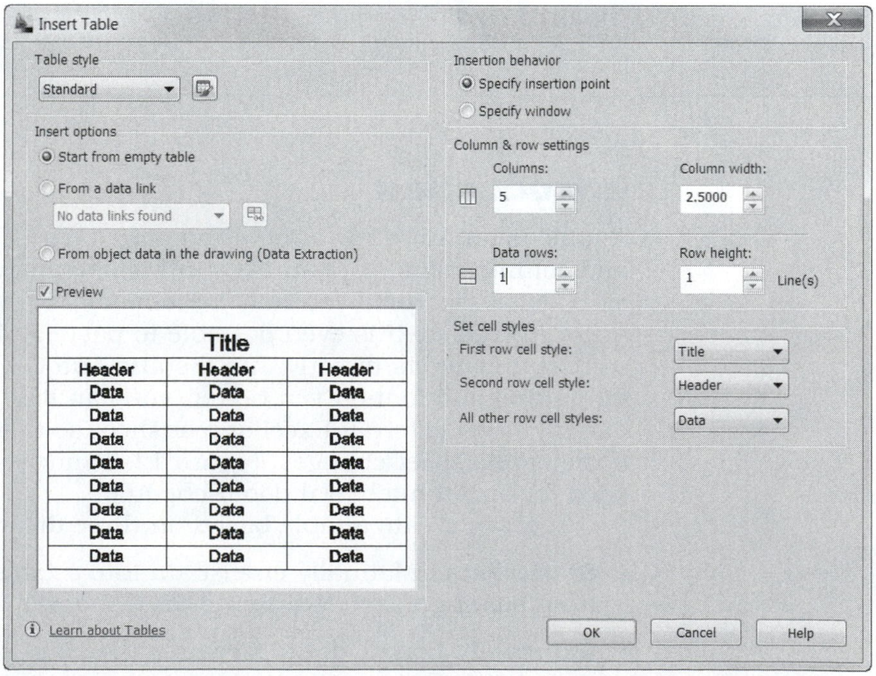

Figure 12-2
The **Insert Table** dialog box

The **Table style** area at the top left side of the dialog box is used to control the appearance of the table.

The drop-down list allows you to select an existing table style and make it current. The default style is Standard. Selecting the button to the right displays the **Table Style** dialog box so that you can update the current style or add a new table style. Table styles are discussed later in this chapter.

Below the **Table style** area is the **Insert options** area where you select one of the three ways to insert a table. The default method is **Start from empty table.** If you select any of the other table insert options, most of the other options on the right will be disabled.

The table **Preview** provides an example of what the current table style looks like.

The **Insertion behavior** section allows you to select how you want to locate the table. You can use an insertion point or specify a window boundary area.

The **Specify insertion point** option allows you to specify the location of the upper left corner of the table.

> **NOTE**
>
> - You can also set the current table style using the expanded **Annotation** panel on the **Home** tab of the ribbon.
> - If the table direction is set to **UP** in the current table style, the insertion point locates the *lower* left corner of the table.

The **Specify window** option allows you to locate and size the table by defining a rectangular window area. The specified column width and the final number of rows depend on the size of the boundary area.

> **NOTE**
>
> - When the **Specify window** option is used to locate the table and indicate its overall width, you can either specify the number of columns so that the column widths are set automatically, or you can specify the column width so that the number of columns is calculated automatically.
> - When the **Specify window** option is used to locate the table and indicate its overall height, you can either specify the number of rows so that the row height is set automatically, or you can specify the row height so that the number of rows is calculated automatically.

The table is sized using the number and size of the rows and columns specified in the **Column & row settings** area on the right side of the dialog box.

The **Columns:** box is used to specify the number of columns.

The **Column width:** box is used to specify the width of the columns.

The **Data rows:** box is used to specify the number of rows. A table style with a title row and a header row has a minimum of three rows.

The **Row height:** box is used to specify the row height in lines. The height of a line is based on the current text height and the cell margin settings in the current table style. Table styles are explored later in this section. The minimum row height is one line.

It is possible to create and apply different cell styles per row so that you can create different formatting for titles, headers, and data, if desired. The **Set cell styles** area allows you to assign the different styles independent of the current table style.

The **First row cell style** list box controls the cell style for the first row in the table. The **Title** cell style is used by default.

The **Second row cell style** list box controls the cell style for the second row in the table. The **Header** cell style is used by default.

The **All other row cell styles** list box controls the cell style for all other rows in the table. The **Data** cell style is used by default.

Selecting **OK** closes the dialog box, and AutoCAD prompts you to *Specify insertion point:* so you can locate the table. After the table is inserted, you are placed in **Edit** mode. The **Text Editor** context tab of the ribbon explained in Chapter 11 is displayed, and your cursor is in the first data cell ready for data entry. Adding and modifying table data are explained in the following section.

> **TIP**
>
> If you already have data in an Excel spreadsheet, you can copy and paste the Excel data as **AutoCAD Entities** by selecting **Paste Special** from the **Clipboard** panel on the **Home** tab of the ribbon and making sure the **Paste** option is selected. Pasting Excel data as **AutoCAD Entities** automatically creates a new table with the static values already entered.

Entering Table Data

When a table is inserted, you are placed in **Edit** mode so that the **Text Editor** context tab of the ribbon is displayed and the first data cell is highlighted so that you can begin entering data. To move to an adjacent cell in the same row, you can use the left and right arrow keys or press the **<Tab>** key to go to the cell on the right. To move to an adjacent cell in the same column, you can use the up and down arrow keys or press **<Enter>** to go to the cell directly below in the next row.

> **TIP**
>
> Table cells can contain text, fields, blocks, and even formulas. Inserting formulas is explored later in the section "Inserting Formulas."

You can use any of the text formatting features and options explained earlier in the "Creating Multiline Text" section in Chapter 11 to format the text in each cell. When you are editing text, the arrow keys move the text cursor and do not take you to another cell.

> **NOTE**
>
> The row height of a cell increases to accommodate multiple lines of text if the specified row height is exceeded.

When you are finished adding data to the table, you can use the same methods used for multiline text to close out of **Edit** mode and accept any additions and changes:

- Select **Close Text Editor** in the **Close** panel of the **Text Editor** context tab of the ribbon.
- Click anywhere outside the text editor with your mouse.
- Hold down the **<Ctrl>** key and press **<Enter>**.

> **TIP**
>
> By default, the in-place text editor displays column letters and row numbers when a table cell is selected for editing. Use the **TABLEINDICATOR** system variable to turn this display on and off. To set a new background color, select a table and click **Table Indicator Color** on the shortcut menu. The text color, size, style, and line color are controlled by the settings for column heads in the current table style.

Creating Tables by Inserting a Data Link

The second way to insert a table is to link it to an existing Microsoft Excel spreadsheet using the **From a data link** method in the **Insert options** area of the **Insert Table** dialog box shown in Figure 12-2. Using data links, you can display tabular data from a spreadsheet as an AutoCAD table. This allows you to take advantage of AutoCAD fonts, colors, text styles, and all of the other table formatting options while still maintaining a link to the original Excel data. If the Excel spreadsheet is updated, a notification balloon like the one shown in Figure 12-3 is displayed in the status tray on the right side of the status bar. It contains a link that lets you quickly update the table in the drawing so that it matches the Excel spreadsheet.

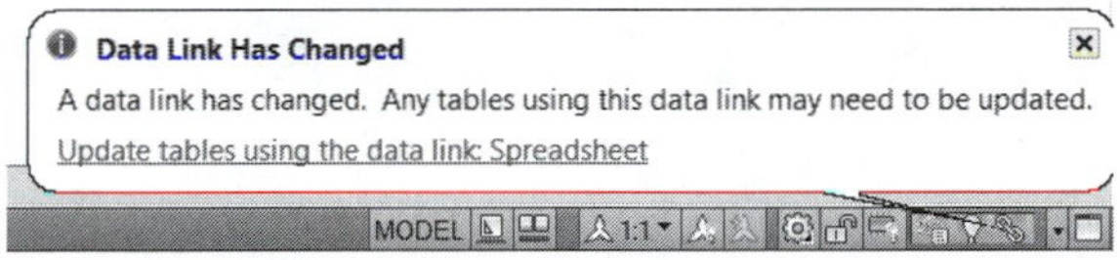

Figure 12-3
The **Data Link Notification** balloon

The Data Link Manager

When a new data link is created, you must give it a name, usually related to the type of data, and select the external file to which it links (XLS or CSV) using the **Data Link Manager** shown in Figure 12-4.

DATA LINK MANAGER	
Ribbon & Panel:	Insert Linking & Extraction 
Toolbar:	
Menu:	Tools | Data Links | Data Link Manager...
Command	DATALINK
Command Alias:	DL

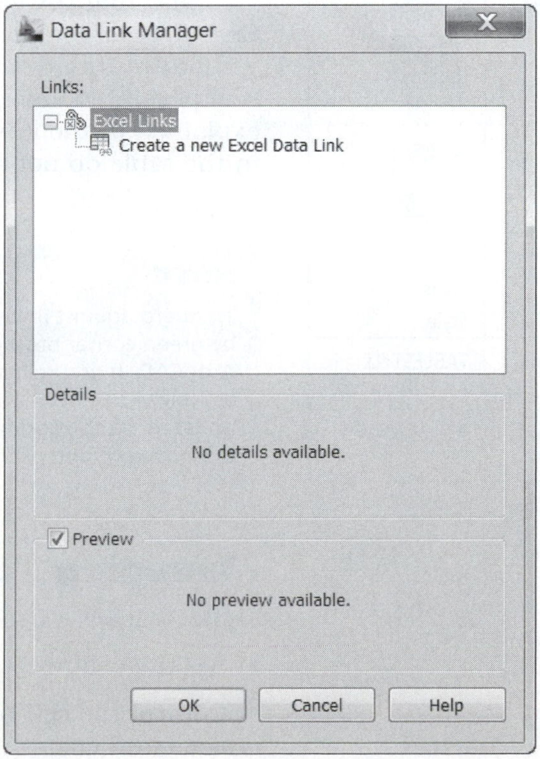

Figure 12-4
The **Data Link Manager** dialog box

Figure 12-5
The **New Excel Data Link** dialog box

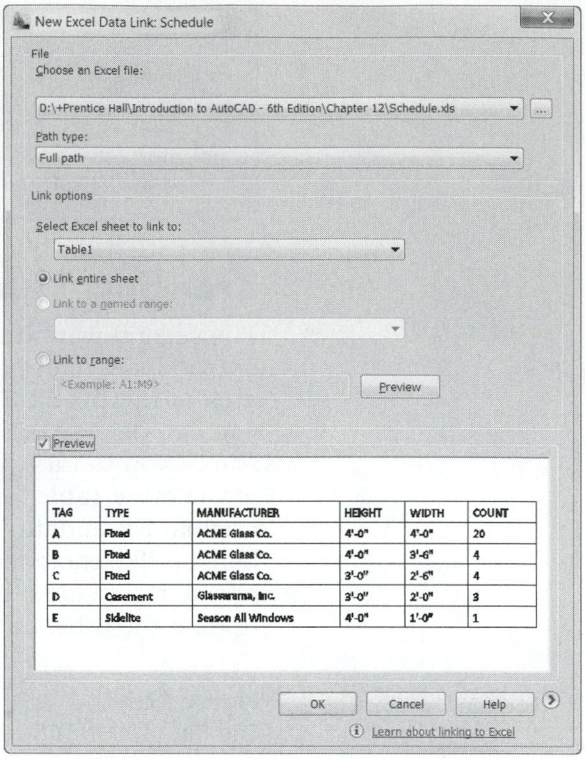

After entering a name and choosing a file, AutoCAD displays the **New Excel Data Link** dialog box shown in Figure 12-5. There you can choose which sheet in the file you want to link and whether you want to link to the entire sheet or just a specific range of cells.

Once the link has been established, select **OK** to close the **Data Link Manager** and return to the **Insert Table** dialog box. A preview of the linked table is shown at the bottom of the dialog box.

Selecting **OK** closes the dialog box, and AutoCAD prompts you to *Specify insertion point:* so you can locate the table. The table is inserted without putting you in **Edit** mode because the data are already created. It is possible to modify the table after it is inserted using the methods explained in the next section. Be careful, though, because changes made in the table do not automatically update the linked Excel spreadsheet.

TABLE STYLE	
Ribbon & Panel:	Home | Annotation 
Styles Toolbar:	
Menu:	Format | Table Style…
Command Line:	TABLESTYLE
Command Alias:	TS

NOTE

To guard against linked data getting out of sync, the range of linked cells is indicated by green corner brackets, and the linked cells are locked to prevent editing from within AutoCAD. If you select a linked cell, its status is indicated by the locked and linked icons as well as by information in a tooltip. It is possible to unlock a cell so that it can be updated via the **Locking** cascade menu on the right-click menu or the **Table Cell** context tab of the ribbon explained in the following section.

Managing Table Styles

Table styles are used to control the appearance of tables by allowing you to:

- Set the cell text style, height, data type, and alignment
- Control the cell border properties so you can set the border line thickness and color and turn border lines on and off

- Set the table text flow direction from top to bottom or bottom to top
- Set the horizontal and vertical cell margin distance

The **TABLESTYLE** command allows you to modify an existing table style or create a new one.

When you start the **TABLESTYLE** command, AutoCAD displays the **Table Style** dialog box shown in Figure 12-6.

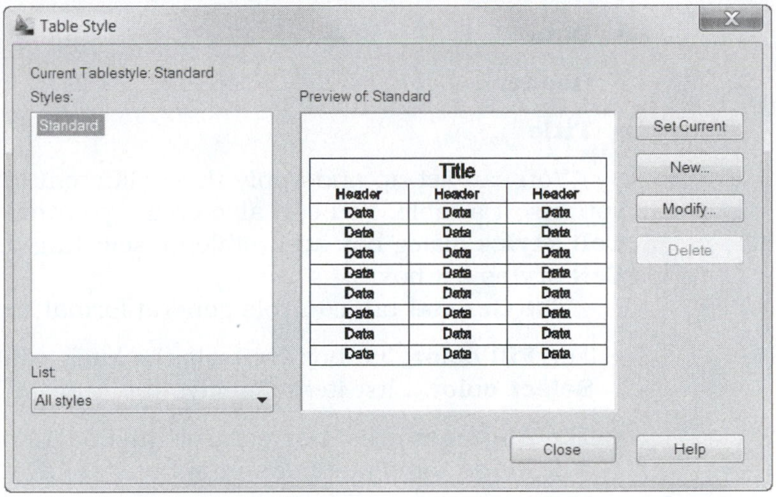

Figure 12-6
The **Table Style** dialog box

To create a new table style, select the **New...** button and enter the new table style name in the **Create New Table Style** dialog box. You can select an existing table style as a starting point by selecting it from the **Start With:** list. Selecting the **Continue...** button displays the **New Table Style** dialog box shown in Figure 12-7.

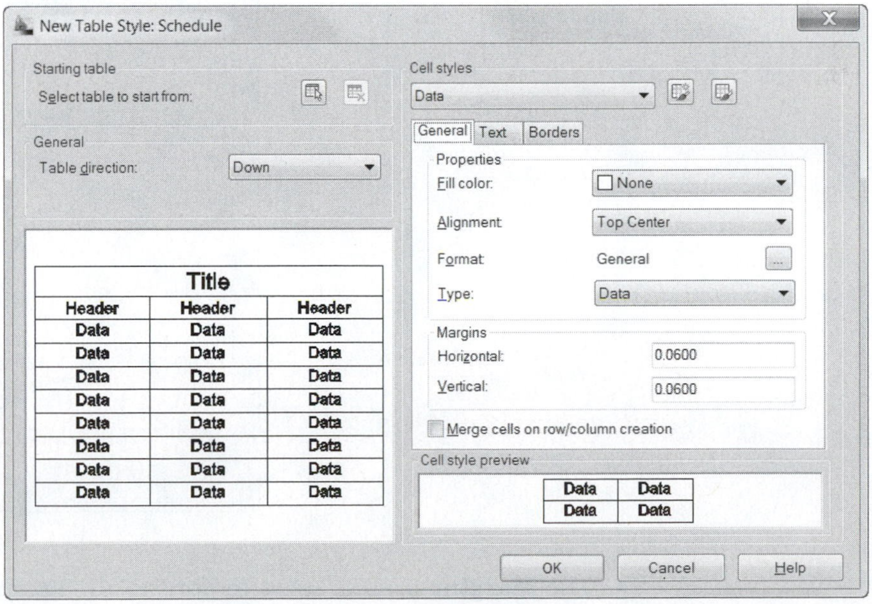

Figure 12-7
The **New Table Style** dialog box

The options in the **Modify Table Style** dialog box displayed when you select the **Modify...** button on the **Table Style** dialog are exactly the same as those in the **New Table Style** dialog box.

You can select a table in your drawing to use as a starting point for the new table style in the **Starting table** area at the top left of the dialog box.

The **Table direction:** list box controls the direction of the text flow for the table.

- **Down** Text reads from top to bottom (Default)
- **Up** Text reads from bottom to top. The title row and column heads row are located at the bottom of the table

On the right side of the dialog box, there are three tabs that control the properties for the three default cell types in the **Cell styles** list box at the top:

- **Data**
- **Header**
- **Title**

You can set up and apply these different cell types to any row when you insert a table. You can also create your own cell styles via the **Manage Cell Styles** dialog box accessible by selecting the button to the right of the **Cell styles** list box.

The **General** tab controls general formatting and data type settings:

- The **Fill color:** list box controls the background color of the cell. The **Select color...** list item displays the AutoCAD **Select Color** dialog box.
- The **Alignment:** list box controls justification and alignment for text in a cell. The same justification options are available as used for multiline text explained earlier in Chapter 11.
- The **Format:** setting controls the data type and display for the text in the cell. Selecting the **...** button to the right of the current **Format:** setting displays the **Table Cell Format** dialog box shown in Figure 12-8.

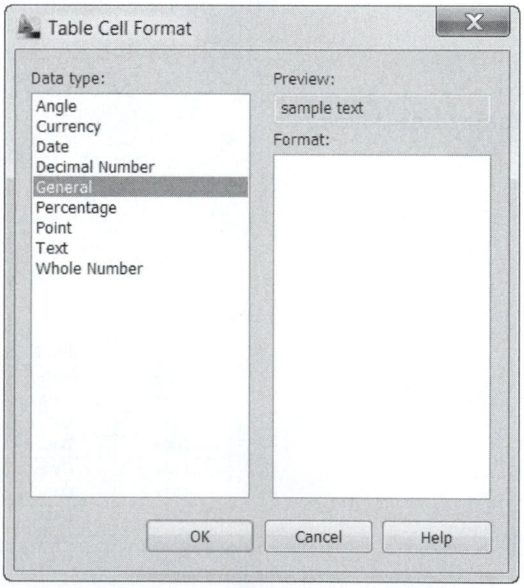

Figure 12-8
The **Table Cell Format** dialog box

- The **Margins** area is used to control the spacing, or margin, between the cell border and the cell content. The default margin setting is 0.06″.
  - The **Horizontal:** text box sets the distance between the cell text and the left and right cell borders.
  - The **Vertical:** text box sets the distance between the cell text and the top and bottom cell borders.

The **Text** tab controls different text formatting settings:

- The **Text style:** list box lists all of the text styles in the drawing. The **...** button to the right displays the **Text Style** dialog box so you can create a new text style.
- The **Text height:** box sets the text height. The default text height for data and column head cells is 0.1800. The default text height for the table title is 0.25.
- The **Text color:** list box controls the text color. The **Select color...** list item displays the AutoCAD **Select Color** dialog box.

The **Borders** tab allows you to control the lineweight, linetype, and color of all four cell borders:

- The **Lineweight:** list box controls the lineweight for the borders you specify by selecting a border button below.
- The **Linetype:** list box controls the linetype for the borders you specify by selecting a border button below.
- The **Color:** list box controls the color for the borders you specify by selecting a border button below. The **Select color...** list item displays the AutoCAD **Select Color** dialog box.
- Checking the **Double line** check box will draw a double line border using the spacing specified below.

The buttons across the bottom determine to which border lines the properties above are applied.

- The **All Borders** button applies the border property settings to all four cell borders.
- The **Outside Border** button applies the border property settings to just the outside border of all cells.
- The **Inside Border** button applies the border property settings to the inside border of all cells. This option does not apply to title row cells.
- The **Bottom Border** button applies the border property settings to the bottom borders of all cells.
- The **Left Border** button applies the border property settings to the left borders of all cells.
- The **Top Border** button applies the border property settings to the top borders of all cells.
- The **Right Border** button applies the border property settings to the right borders of all cells.
- The **No Border** button hides borders for all cells.

EXERCISE 12-1 Creating a Table from Scratch

1. Start a new drawing using the **acad.dwt** drawing template.
2. Create a text style named **Notes** with the following settings:

   a. Font = **Simplex.shx** AutoCAD font

   b. Height = **0.125″**
3. Create a text style named **Titles** with the following setting:

   a. Font = **Arial** TrueType font

4. Create a new table style named **Schedule** with the following settings:

   a. Set the **Data rows** text style to **Notes.**

   b. Set the **Title row** text style to **Titles.**

   c. Set the **Header row** text style to **Titles.**

   d. Set the text alignment to **Middle Center** for all rows.

   e. Set all border line lineweights to **0.50 mm** for all rows.

5. Create the window schedule shown in Figure 12-9 using the **TABLE** command with the **Schedule** table style you just created.

6. Save the drawing as ***CH12_EXERCISE***.

WINDOW SCHEDULE					
TAG	TYPE	MANUFACTURER	HEIGHT	WIDTH	COUNT
A	FIXED	ACME GLASS CO.	4'–0"	4'–0"	20
B	FIXED	ACME GLASS CO.	4'–0"	3'–6"	4
C	FIXED	ACME GLASS CO.	3'–0"	2'–6"	4
D	CASEMENT	GLASSARAMA, INC.	3'–0"	2'–0"	3
E	SIDELITE	SEASON ALL WINDOWS	4'–0"	1'–0"	1

Figure 12-9
Window schedule

Modifying Tables

There are two levels of modifying and editing an existing table: table level and cell level. Both methods rely on using grips.

> **FOR MORE DETAILS**
>
> See page 301 in Chapter 7 for more details about using grips.

You select a table by clicking directly on a table line so that the table level grips are displayed as shown in Figure 12-10.

	A	B	C	D	E	F
1	WINDOW SCHEDULE					
2	TAG	TYPE	MANUFACTURER	HEIGHT	WIDTH	COUNT
3	A	FIXED	ACME GLASS CO.	4'–0"	4'–0"	20
4	B	FIXED	ACME GLASS CO.	4'–0"	3'–6"	4
5	C	FIXED	ACME GLASS CO.	3'–0"	2'–6"	4
6	D	CASEMENT	GLASSARAMA, INC.	3'–0"	2'–0"	3
7	E	SIDELITE	SEASON ALL WINDOWS	4'–0"	1'–0"	1

Figure 12-10
Selecting a table for editing using grips

You can use the table grips to resize the table by stretching any corner except the insertion corner point. The insertion grip point moves the table. When you change the height or width of a table using grips, the rows and columns change proportionally.

You can change column widths by selecting a grip at the top of a column line and stretching it to another location. To also change the table width, press **<Ctrl>** while selecting the column grip.

The light blue triangle grip at the bottom center of the table is the table-breaking grip. A table with a large amount of data can be broken into primary and secondary table fragments. You can use the table-breaking grips found at the bottom of a table to make a table span multiple columns in your drawing or to manipulate the different table parts that have already been created.

The Right-Click Menu

All the other table level editing options are provided via the right-click menu shown in Figure 12-11.

Figure 12-11
The **Table Editing** right-click menu

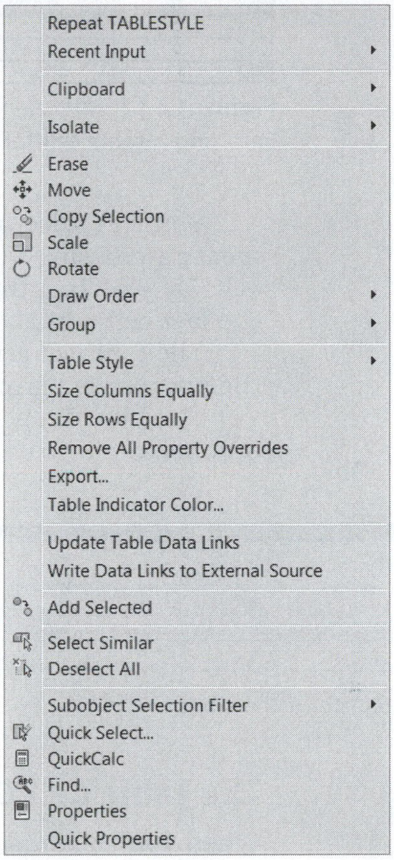

The **Table Style** menu item displays a cascade menu with the available table styles in the current drawing so you can change styles.

The **Size Columns Equally** menu item resizes all columns equally.

The **Size Rows Equally** menu item resizes all rows equally.

The **Remove All Property Overrides** menu item will reset the table back to its default format.

> **NOTE**
> You can also use the **TABLE-EXPORT** command to export a table to a comma-delimited file.

The **Export...** menu item allows you to export the table to a comma-delimited file via the **Export Data File** dialog box.

The **Table Indicator Color...** menu item allows you to change the color of the row/column indicators in the table editor using the standard AutoCAD **Select Color** dialog box.

The **Update Table Data Links** menu item updates the table with any changes in linked data if applicable.

The **Write Data Links to External Source** menu item writes any table data changes back to any linked source files.

Modifying Table Cells

To modify a table cell, you must click inside the cell with your mouse so the four cell grips display at the midpoints of each cell border line as shown in Figure 12-12.

	A	B	C	D	E	F
1	WINDOW SCHEDULE					
2	TAG	TYPE	MANUFACTURER	HEIGHT	WIDTH	COUNT
3	A	FIXED	ACME GLASS CO.	4'–0"	4'–0"	20
4	B	FIXED	ACME GLASS CO.	4'–0"	3'–6"	4
5	C	FIXED	ACME GLASS CO.	3'–0"	2'–6"	4
6	D	CASEMENT	GLASSARAMA, INC.	3'–0"	2'–0"	3
7	E	SIDELITE	SEASON ALL WINDOWS	4'–0"	1'–0"	1

Figure 12-12
Selecting a table cell for editing using grips

You can select multiple cells by clicking and dragging your cursor to create a crossing window over multiple cells. You can also select a range of cells by selecting the first cell and holding down the **<Shift>** key to select the last cell and all the cells in between.

The four cell grips can be used to resize a row or column by selecting the appropriate grip and dragging it to a new location.

The blue diamond in the bottom right corner can be dragged to copy and increment data automatically.

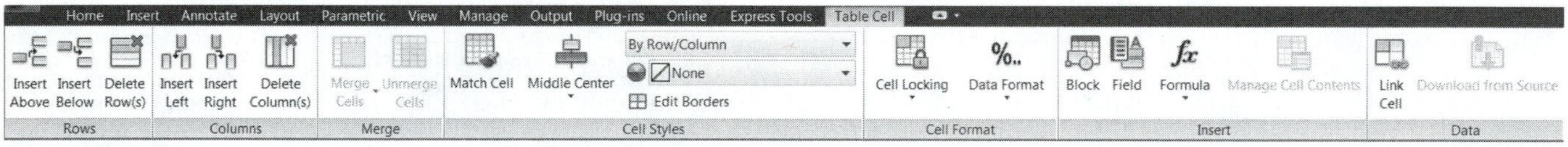

Figure 12-13
The **Table Cell** context tab of the ribbon

The Table Cell Context Tab of the Ribbon

When you click inside a table cell, the **Table Cell** context tab of the ribbon shown in Figure 12-13 is displayed.

Using the **Table Cell** context tab of the ribbon, you can do the following:

- Edit rows and columns
- Merge and unmerge cells
- Create and edit cell styles
- Alter the appearance of cell borders
- Edit data formatting and alignment
- Lock and unlock cells from editing
- Insert blocks, fields, and formulas
- Link the table to external data

The Right-Click Menu

With a cell selected, you can also right-click and use the options on the shortcut menu shown in Figure 12-14.

The **Cell Style** cascade menu allows you to change the cell style.

The **Background Fill** menu item allows you to specify the cell's fill color via the AutoCAD **Select Color** dialog box.

The **Alignment** cascade menu allows you to change the cell's text justification using one of the standard multiline text justification options.

The **Borders...** menu item displays the **Cell Border Properties** dialog box shown in Figure 12-15 so you can change the lineweight, linetype, and/or color of one or more of the cell border lines.

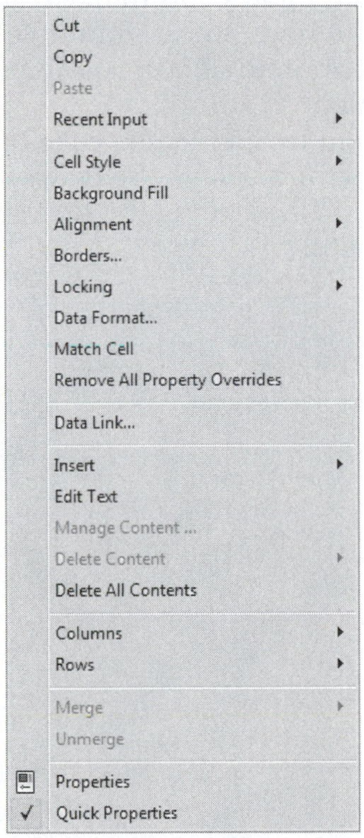

Figure 12-14
The **Cell Editing** right-click menu

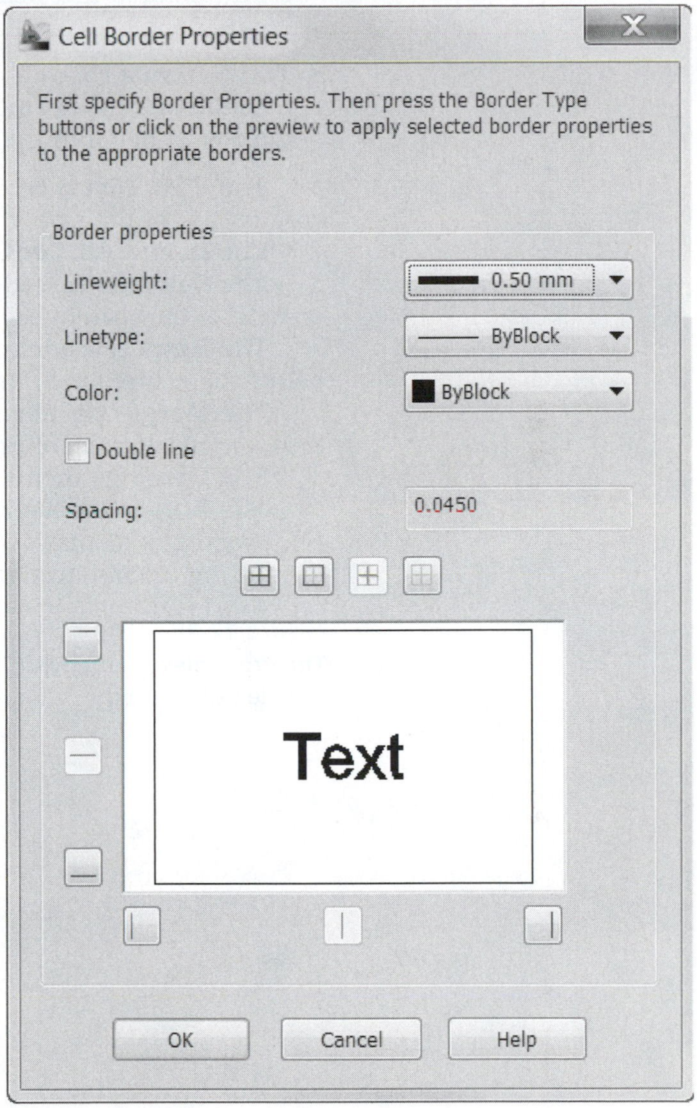

Figure 12-15
The **Cell Border Properties** dialog box

The **Locking** cascade menu allows you to lock and unlock data cell content and/or data cell formatting. Tables created using data linking or data extraction are automatically locked to prevent inadvertent changes and preserve data integrity.

The **Data Format...** menu item displays the **Table Cell Format** dialog box so that you can change the data type and format for a cell.

The **Match Cell** menu item allows you to copy the selected cell properties to one or more additional cells.

The **Remove All Property Overrides** will remove all property overrides and revert back to the original table style.

The **Data Link...** menu item allows you to create or edit data links using the **Data Link Manager.**

The **Insert** cascade menu allows you to insert the following items into a cell:

- The **Block...** menu item displays the **Insert a Block in a Table Cell** dialog box so you can insert a block in a cell.
- The **Field...** menu item displays the **Field** dialog box so you can insert an automated text field. See the "Text Fields" section in Chapter 11 for complete information about inserting and using fields.
- The **Formula** cascade menu allows you to insert a formula that does calculations using values in other table cells. Inserting formulas is discussed in detail in the next section.

The **Edit Text** menu item displays the table editor and **Text Editor** context tab of the ribbon so you can edit the cell text.

The **Delete All Contents** menu item deletes the cell contents.

The **Columns** cascade menu allows you to insert a new column to the left or right of the current cell, delete columns, or size multiple columns equally.

The **Rows** cascade menu allows you to insert a new row above or below the current cell, delete rows, or size multiple rows equally.

The **Merge** cascade menu item allows you to merge two or more cells into one block, row, or column.

The **Unmerge** menu item turns merged cells back into individual cells.

The **Properties** menu item displays the **Properties** palette with the cell properties displayed as shown in Figure 12-16 so you can make any formatting or content changes.

Figure 12-16
The **Properties** palette with a table cell selected

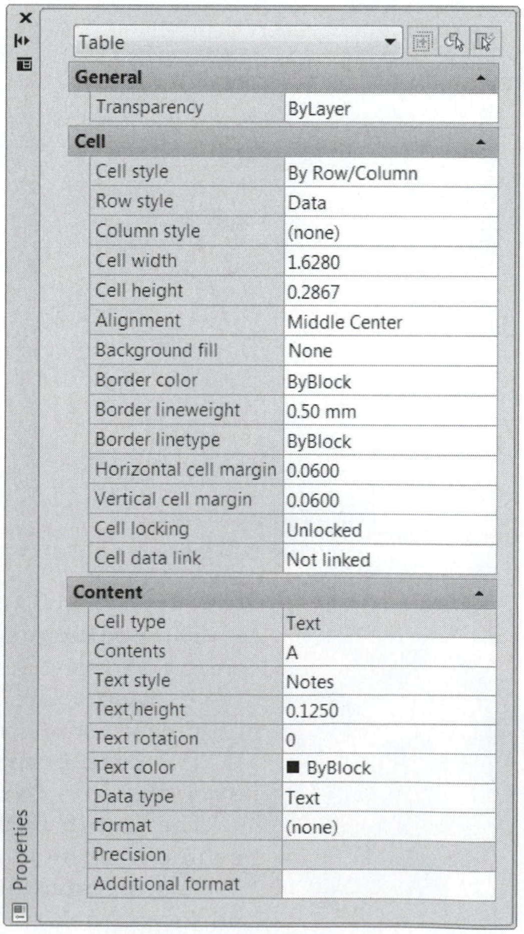

> **TIP**
> The **Properties** palette provides you with most of the editing features you might need, including access to many of the right-click shortcut menu items above.

Inserting Formulas

Table cells can contain formulas similar to an accounting spreadsheet program. AutoCAD provides the following spreadsheet type functions:

- **=Sum(A1:A10)** Sums the values in the first 10 rows in column A
- **=Average(A10:E10)** Calculates the average of the values in the first five columns in row 10
- =**Count(A1:D100)** Displays the total number of cells in columns A through D in rows 1 through 100
- **=A1+D1** Adds the values in A1 and D1
- **=A1−D1** Subtracts the value in D1 from the value in A1
- **=A1*D1** Multiplies the values in A1 and D1
- **=A1/D1** Divides the value in A1 by the value in D1
- **=A1^2** Squares the value in A1. The number after ^ is the exponent

All formulas must start with an equal sign (=). Formulas perform calculations using the values in other specified table cells by referencing their column letter and row number and/or constant values. The top left cell in a table is referenced using A1. A cell range is referenced using the first and last cells separated by a colon. For example, the range A1:D10 references the cells in rows one through 10 and columns A through D. Merged cells use the letter and number of the top left cell.

When you copy a formula from one cell to another, the range changes to reflect the new location. For example, if the formula in A11 sums A1 through A10, when you copy it to B11, the range changes so that the formula sums B1 through B10.

> **TIP**
> You can create an absolute cell address that doesn't change when it is copied by preceding the row and column with a dollar sign ($). For example, if you specify A1, the column and row will always stay the same.

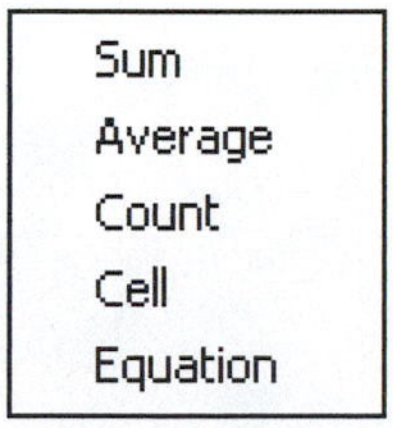

Figure 12-17
The **Insert Formula** cascade menu

You can insert a formula via the **Cell Editing** right-click menu shown in Figure 12-14, select it from the **Insert > Formula** cascade menu on the **Insert** panel shown in Figure 12-17, or enter it in manually using the in-place text editor.

> **NOTE**
> The **Sum, Average,** and **Count** formulas ignore empty cells and cells that do not contain a numeric value. The other mathematical formulas display pound signs (# # # #) when a formula references empty or nonnumeric data.

EXERCISE 12-2 Modifying a Table

1. Continue from Exercise 12-1.
2. Modify the window schedule as shown in Figure 12-18.
3. Save the drawing.

WINDOW SCHEDULE						
TAG	TYPE	MANUFACTURER	HEIGHT	WIDTH	SCREEN	COUNT
A	FIXED	ACME GLASS CO.	4'-0"	4'-0"	No	20
B	FIXED	ACME GLASS CO.	4'-0"	3'-6"	No	4
C	FIXED	ACME GLASS CO.	3'-0"	2'-6"	No	4
D	CASEMENT	GLASSARAMA, INC.	3'-0"	2'-0"	Yes	3
E	SIDELITE	SEASON ALL WINDOWS	4'-0"	1'-0"	No	1
F	SLIDER	ALUMICORE	7'-0"	8'-0"	Yes	1
G	DOUBLE HUNG	SEASON ALL WINDOWS	4'-0"	3'-0"	Yes	2
					TOTAL UNITS	35

Figure 12-18
Updated window schedule

chapter twelve

Chapter Summary

Tables can be used for many different purposes ranging from parts lists to door and window schedules. Using AutoCAD tables you have the choice of creating a static table from scratch or by copying and pasting from Excel. Dynamic tables can be created that are linked to external data sources that can be updated automatically. The **Data Link Manager** provides the ability to maintain and manage data links in one central location.

Table styles can be created to manage different table types in a drawing so you can control text and border formatting at at least three different levels: title, header, and data rows. Using the different cell styles you can set different text heights for the title, column headers, and all of the data. Additional formatting options can be applied using right-click menu options at the table (overall) level and for each individual cell selected. Grips can be used to resize columns and even resize complete tables.

Similar to Excel, you can also insert formulas that perform calculations such as sums and averages, making it possible to create a bill of materials that has an accurate count of parts or materials or a schedule with quantity takeoffs. As you will see, even these tables themselves can be created automatically using data extraction methods explained later in Chapter 16.

Chapter Test Questions

Multiple Choice

Circle the correct answer.

1. Tables in AutoCAD are created using what type of data?

a. Object
b. Static
c. Linked
d. All of the above

2. The box at the intersection of a row and column is referred to as:

a. Field
b. Square
c. Cell
d. A:1

3. The best way to modify a table after it is inserted is by using:

a. **Properties** palette
b. **Table Cell** context tab of the ribbon
c. Grips
d. All of the above

4. A table's appearance and formatting are typically controlled using:

a. Text styles
b. Table styles
c. Dimension styles
d. All of the above

5. The current table style can be set using:

a. **Annotation** panel
b. **Insert Table** dialog box
c. **Format** menu
d. a and b

6. Table cells can contain what type of data?

a. Text
b. Fields
c. Blocks
d. All of the above

7. The system variable that controls whether the in-place text editor displays column letters and row numbers is:

a. **TABLECOLS**
b. **TABLEROWS**
c. **TABLEDISPLAY**
d. **TABLEINDICATOR**

8. The **Data Link Manager** allows you to link to what file type?

a. XLS
b. CSV
c. MDB
d. a and b

9. The different options for starting a new table style include:

a. Copying an existing table style
b. Starting from scratch
c. Picking an existing table in the drawing
d. a and c

10. All table formulas start with:

a. Equal sign (=)
b. Parentheses
c. F
d. None of the above

Matching

Write the number of the correct answer on the line.

a. Table ______
b. Cell ______
c. Table styles ______
d. Cell style ______
e. **Paste Special** ______
f. **TABLEINDICATOR** ______
g. **Data Link Manager** ______
h. **TABLEEXPORT** ______
i. **Table Cell** ______

1. Controls individual cell characteristics that affect the appearance of cell text and borders
2. System variable that controls the display of column letters and row numbers in the table editor
3. Context tab of the ribbon used to modify tables
4. Command used to export a table to a comma-delimited file
5. Creates, edits, and manages data links
6. Command used to paste or link Excel data as an AutoCAD table
7. Controls the cell data format, the text and border properties, table direction, and other table formatting options
8. AutoCAD annotation object type that consists of data in rows and columns similar to an accounting spreadsheet
9. The box at the intersection of a table row and column that contains the table data or a formula

True or False

Circle the correct answer.

1. **True or False:** You can extract the lengths of all lines on a specified layer to an AutoCAD table that will update when a line changes length.
2. **True or False:** The best way to resize a table is by using grips.

3. **True or False:** It is possible to create and apply different cell styles per row so that you can create different formatting for titles, headers, and data.
4. **True or False:** You can create your own cell style if you want.
5. **True or False:** AutoCAD automatically updates an Excel spreadsheet that was pasted into your AutoCAD drawing.
6. **True or False:** Linked data cells are indicated by blue corner brackets.
7. **True or False:** The light blue triangle grip at the bottom center of a table that has grips on will copy data to adjacent cells when you drag it.
8. **True or False:** It is not possible to unlock and update data that are linked externally in a table.
9. **True or False:** All formulas must start with an open parenthesis.
10. **True or False:** The pound (#) symbol will create an absolute cell address.

Chapter Projects

G Project 12-1: *Parts List* [BASIC]

1. Start a new drawing using the **acad.dwt** template.
2. Create a table style named **Parts List** with the following settings:
   a. Text font—**Simplex.shx**
   b. Title row text height—**0.25**
   c. Header row text height—**0.125**
   d. Data row text height—**0.125**
   e. Border lineweight = **0.50 mm**
3. Create the Parts List table shown in Figure 12-19 using the **TABLE** command.
4. Save the drawing as ***P12-1***.

PARTS LIST			
ITEM	PART NUMBER	DESCRIPTION	QUANTITY
1	3VD-14602-01-00	EXHAUST PIPE COMP	1
2	92906-06600-00	WASHER	2
3	90101-06576-00	BOLT	2
4	3VD-14613-00-00	GASKET, EXHAUST PIPE	2
5	90179-08345-00	NUT, SPECIAL SHAPE	4
6	3VD-14710-03-00	MUFFLER ASSEMBLY	1
7	3VD-14755-00-00	GASKET, SILENCER	1
8	99999-01790-00	BOLT, FLANGE	1
9	90201-081H4-00	WASHER, PLATE	2
10	91316-08110-00	BOLT, HEXAGON	2

Figure 12-19

M Project 12-2: *Socket Head Cap Screws, continued from Chapter 7* [INTERMEDIATE]

1. Open drawing ***P7-2*** from Chapter 7.
2. Create a table style named **Screws** with the following settings:
   a. Text font—**Romans.shx**
   b. Title row text height—**0.25**
   c. Header row text height—**0.125**
   d. Data row text height—**0.125**
   e. Border lineweight = **0.50 mm**
3. Create the screw table shown in Figure 12-20 using the **TABLE** command.
4. Save the drawing as ***P12-2***.

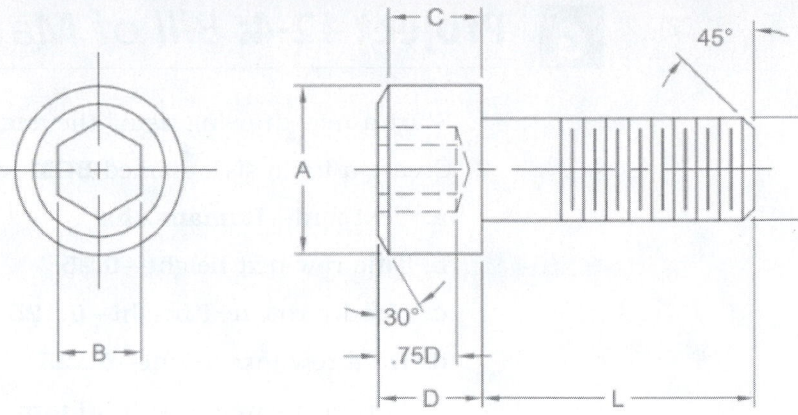

SOCKET HEAD CAP SCREW					
NOMINAL SIZE (D)	THREAD/IN	A	B	C	L
4 (.112)	40	.183	.09375	.103	1.00
5 (.125)	40	.205	.09375	.113	1.00
6 (.138)	32	.226	.109375	.125	1.25
8 (.164)	32	.270	.140625	.150	1.25
10 (.190)	24	.312	.15625	.171	1.50
¼ (.250)	20	.375	.1875	.225	1.50

Figure 12-20

A Project 12-3: *Residential Architectural Plan, continued from Chapter 11* [ADVANCED]

1. Open drawing ***P11-5*** from Chapter 11.
2. Create a table style named **Schedule** with the following settings:
   a. Text font—**Romans.shx**
   b. Title row text height—**12**
   c. Header row text height—**8**
   d. Data row text height—**6**
   e. Border lineweight = **0.50 mm**
3. Re-create the window schedule created for drawing ***P11-5*** using the **TABLE** command.
4. Save your drawing as ***P12-3***.

G Project 12-4: *Bill of Materials* [BASIC]

1. Start a new drawing using the **acad.dwt** template.
2. Create a table style named **BOM** with the following settings:
   a. Text font—**Romans.shx**
   b. Title row text height—**0.25**
   c. Header row text height—**0.125**
   d. Data row text height—**0.125**
   e. Border lineweight = **0.50 mm**
3. Create the Bill of Materials table shown in Figure 12-21 using the **TABLE** command.
4. Save the drawing as ***P12-4***.

BILL OF MATERIALS					
PART NUMBER	PART NAME	QUANTITY	DESCRIPTION	MATERIAL	PRICE
30431	TOP	1	6" X 9" SHEET METAL	STEEL	$3.00
34572	BODY	1	12" X 23 SHEET METAL	STEEL	$6.00
90321	HANDLES	2	C–TYPE	ALUMINUM	$12.00
36780	LATCHES	4	FRENCH MEDIUM	BRASS	$11.00
68857	FEET	4	ONE–INCH DIAMETER	RUBBER	$2.00
25410	SHELVES	5	5" X 11" SHEET METAL	STEEL	$6.00
20983	DIVIDERS	4	3" X 6" SHEET METAL	STEEL	$3.00
65382	HINGES	2	2" X 2"	BRASS	$2.00
76379	PADDING	5	5" X 11"	RUBBER	$6.00
98776	SCREWS	16	SHEET METAL SCREWS	STEEL	$2.00
TOTAL NUMBER OF ITEMS		44		TOTAL COST	$53.00

Figure 12-21

A Project 12-5: *Residential Architectural Plan, continued from Chapter 12* [ADVANCED]

1. Open drawing ***P12-3*** from Chapter 12.
2. Re-create the door schedule created for drawing ***P11-5*** using the **TABLE** command using the **Schedule** table style.
3. Save your drawing as ***P12-5***.

chapter thirteen Dimensioning Drawings

CHAPTER OBJECTIVES

- Create different types of dimension objects
- Create dimensions that match industry standards
- Control dimension associativity
- Create and manage dimension styles
- Create leader notes
- Update dimensions
- Match the settings of an existing dimension style

Introduction

Dimensioning drawings can be one of the more challenging aspects of using AutoCAD. Although creating dimension objects is fairly straightforward, controlling their look and behavior can be tricky. This is due to the many different types of dimension objects and the large number of variables that control how they look and behave. How you use dimensions and how they look and behave can also vary greatly depending on your industry (mechanical design, AEC, electronics, etc.). In this chapter, you'll examine how to place dimension objects as well as how to use dimension styles to control their look and behavior.

Dimension Tools

The most common dimension tools are located on the **Dimension** flyout menu on the **Annotation** panel on the **Home** tab of the ribbon for easy access (see Figure 13-1). These same tools and most of the other dimension tools are located on the **Dimensions** panel on the **Annotate** tab of the ribbon (see Figure 13-2).

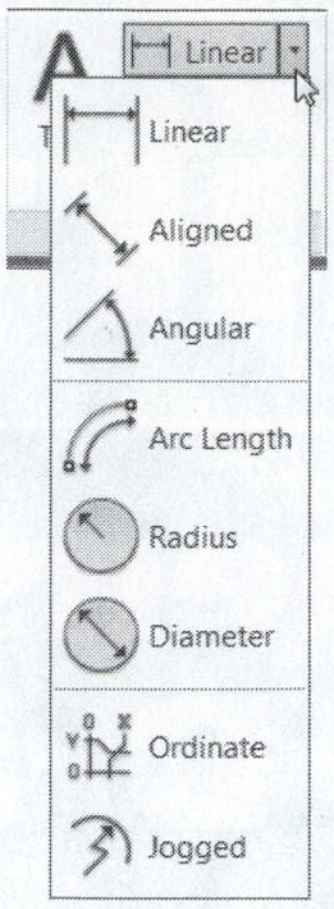

Figure 13-1
The **Dimension** tools on the **Annotation** panel on the **Home** tab of the ribbon

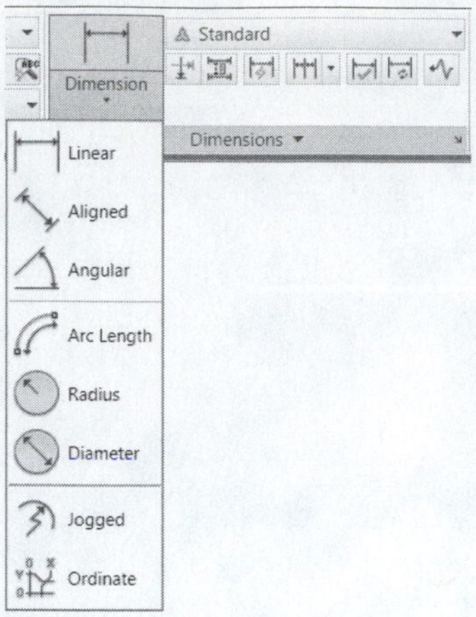

Figure 13-2
The **Dimension** tools on the **Dimensions** panel on the **Annotate** tab of the ribbon

Types of Dimensions

There are many types of dimension objects available in AutoCAD. Figure 13-3 shows some examples of the different types of dimension objects as well as some of the features found in a dimension object. The linear, radial, diameter, and angular dimensions are commonly used, but the type of dimensions you create will vary greatly based on your industry and discipline.

Figure 13-3
Types of dimension objects

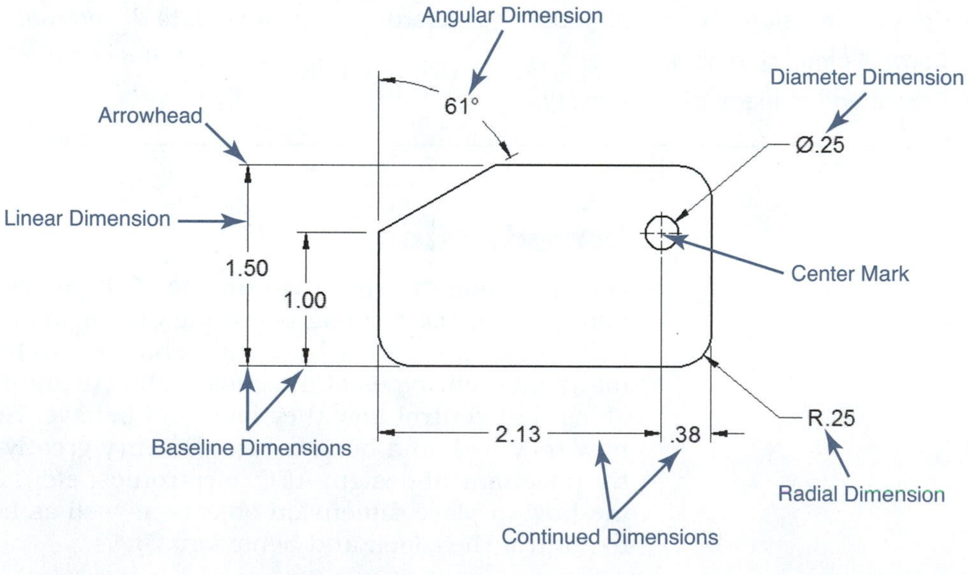

NOTE

Dimensions can be placed in either model space or layout (paper) space in AutoCAD. The decision of where to place dimensions (model or paper space) can be a hotly debated topic in the AutoCAD world. Regardless of how dimensioning is handled, the important thing is to maintain consistency among drawings for any given project. Your company's CAD standards should provide clear guidelines for how dimensioning should be handled and where dimensions should be placed.

Dimension Associativity

In Chapter 2, you saw briefly how associativity works with dimensioning. Dimension objects are linked to the geometry and update automatically when the geometry changes. AutoCAD has different levels of associativity depending on a number of factors. Sometimes AutoCAD will "flake out" and association will be lost. When this happens, it is sometimes possible to manually reassociate dimensions using the **REASSOCIATE** command. Controlling dimension associativity is discussed later in this chapter.

Definition Points

When you place dimension objects, you first choose the type of dimension you want to create, and then either pick points or select an object to define the placement of the dimension object. Using either method, AutoCAD automatically creates point objects that define the distance. These defining points are called ***defpoints.*** AutoCAD measures the distance between these defpoints and uses that distance as the default dimension text. For example, to dimension a line, you create a linear dimension. AutoCAD places defpoints at each end of the line and measures the distance between those defpoints. You then choose a location for the placement of the dimension text.

defpoint: Point created when placing dimensions that defines the measurement value of the dimension.

> **NOTE**
>
> The **Defpoints** layer is unique in that it doesn't plot, regardless of its **Plot/Noplot** layer setting. Also, once created, the **Defpoints** layer sometimes cannot be deleted with either the **PURGE** command or the **Delete Layer** button in the **LAYER** command.

When you create dimensions, AutoCAD automatically creates a layer called **Defpoints.** All defpoints are placed on the **Defpoints** layer.

> **TIP**
>
> If your drawing has a **Defpoints** layer, but no dimension objects, and you wish to get rid of the **Defpoints** layer but it will not purge, you can simply rename the layer. Once it is renamed, it will behave like any other layer and can be deleted or purged as needed.

LINEAR	
Ribbon & Panel:	Home | Annotation Linear
Dimension Toolbar:	
Menu:	Dimension | Linear
Command Line:	DIMLINEAR
Command Alias:	DIMLIN

Creating Horizontal and Vertical Dimensions

Vertical and horizontal dimensions are created with a single command, **DIMLINEAR.** The **DIMLINEAR** command measures the vertical or horizontal dimension between two definition points and allows you to pick the location of the dimension line.

Selecting Definition Points

There are two ways to create a linear dimension: pick points or select an object. Using the pick point method, you select any two points in your drawing and then select the location of the dimension text. Where you place the dimension text determines whether a vertical or horizontal dimension is created. If you place the dimension text above or below the points, AutoCAD will create a horizontal dimension. Selecting to the left or right of the selected points will create a vertical dimension (see Figure 13-4).

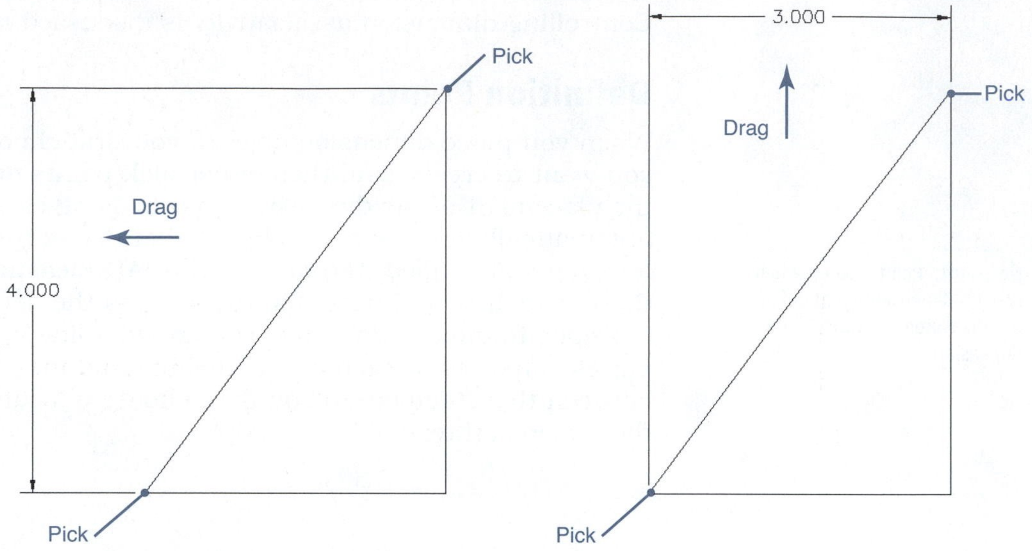

Figure 13-4
Placing a vertical or horizontal dimension

Selecting an Object

You can also create a linear dimension by selecting a line, arc, or circle. When you start the **DIMLINEAR** command, AutoCAD prompts you to *Specify first extension line origin or <select object>:*. Press **<Enter>** to select a line, arc, or circle. When you select an object, AutoCAD will select the two points at the ends of the object as the definition points. Figure 13-5 shows the results of selecting different objects.

> **NOTE**
>
> When selecting an object, you can select only line, arc, or circle objects. Ellipses, text points, or spline curves are not allowed. When you select a polyline object, AutoCAD will dimension the line or arc segment of the polyline at the point you selected.

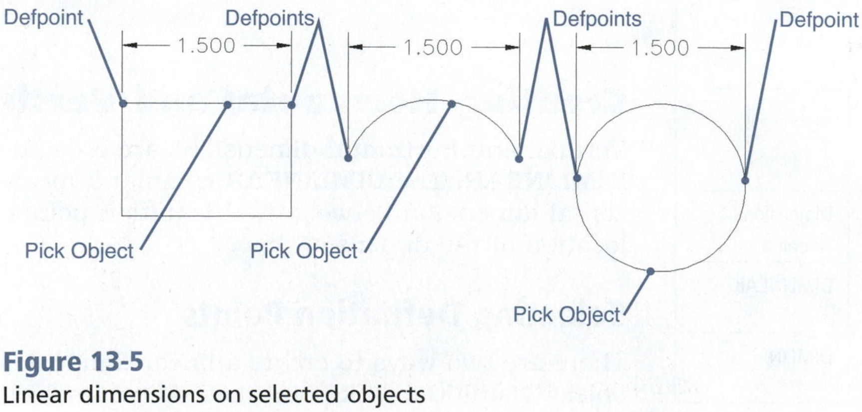

Figure 13-5
Linear dimensions on selected objects

The DIMLINEAR Options

After you select the definition points, AutoCAD provides a number of options for creating and placing the dimensions. These options are listed below.

Mtext	This option allows you to change the default dimension text using the mtext editor.
Text	The **Text** option allows you to modify the default dimension text at the command prompt. This is similar to the **Mtext** option, except you can place only a single line of text.
Angle	The **Angle** option allows you to specify the angle of the dimension text. The dimension text will be rotated to the specified angle.
Horizontal	By default, a horizontal or vertical dimension is placed depending on where you drag your cursor. This option allows you to override the cursor location and explicitly tell AutoCAD to place a horizontal dimension.
Vertical	This is like the **Horizontal** option, except you explicitly tell AutoCAD to place a vertical dimension.
Rotated	The **Rotated** option allows you to change the measurement angle of the dimension. For example, specifying an angle of 45 will cause AutoCAD to measure the distance between the two definition points along a 45° angled line (see Figure 13-6).

Figure 13-6
Rotated dimension text

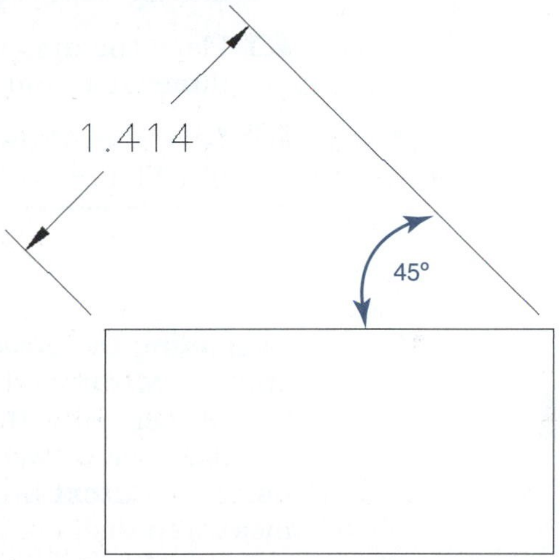

EXERCISE 13-1 **Creating Linear Dimensions**

To access student data files, go to **www.pearsondesigncentral.com.**

1. Open drawing ***EX13-1*** in the student data files. Make sure object snaps are turned on and set to detect **Endpoint** and **Center.**
2. Start the **DIMLINEAR** command. AutoCAD prompts you to *Specify first extension line origin or <select object>:.*
3. Pick the endpoint P1 shown in Figure 13-7. AutoCAD prompts you to *Specify second extension line origin:.*
4. Pick the endpoint P2 shown in Figure 13-7. AutoCAD prompts you to *Specify dimension line location or* ↓ and starts dragging the dimension line.
5. Place the dimension line as shown in Figure 13-8. AutoCAD places the dimension and ends the **DIMLINEAR** command.
6. Restart the **DIMLINEAR** command. AutoCAD prompts you to *Specify first extension line origin or <select object>:.*

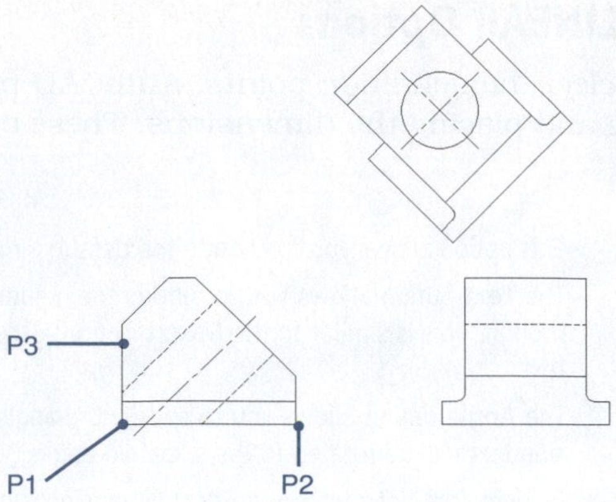

Figure 13-7
Selecting the definition points

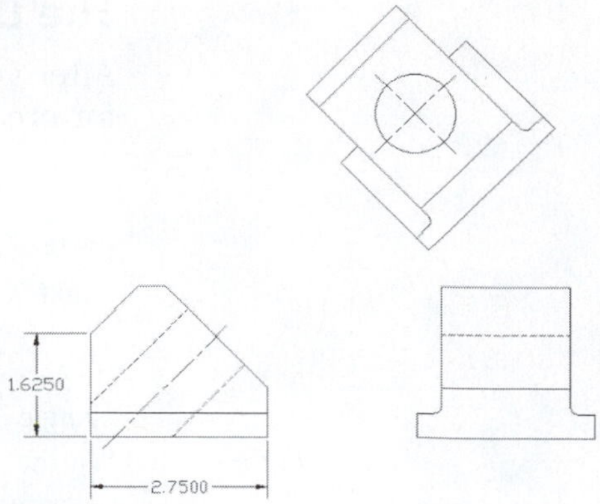

Figure 13-8
Linear dimensions

7. Press **<Enter>.** AutoCAD prompts you to *Select object to dimension.*
8. Pick the line at P3 shown in Figure 13-7. AutoCAD places the defpoints at the ends of the line and prompts you to *Specify dimension line location or* ↓.
9. Place the dimension line as shown in Figure 13-8. AutoCAD places the dimension and ends the **DIMLINEAR** command.
10. Save your drawing as ***CH13_EXERCISE1.*** Your drawing should look like Figure 13-8.

Overriding Dimension Text. The **DIMLINEAR** command has two text options: **Mtext** and **Text.** These options allow you to override the default text associated with the dimension. By default, AutoCAD places the numerical distance between the two definition points as the dimension text. By using the **Mtext** and **Text** options, you can modify or even override the measured distance. For example, you may want to include a note or other additional text along with the default dimension, or you may want to type in a specific dimension instead of using the measured dimension value.

The <> Brackets. When you use the **Mtext** option, AutoCAD displays the multiline text editor with the default dimension text highlighted (see Figure 13-9). The default dimension text is the measured distance between the definition points. You can type any text before or after the default dimension text or you can delete it, but you cannot modify the value of the highlighted text. If you remove the default text, AutoCAD will ignore the measured distance and display only the text you specify.

> **NOTE**
>
> Just because you can overwrite dimension text doesn't mean you should. When you overwrite the calculated dimension by either erasing or typing over the <> brackets, all dimension associativity is lost, so that if the drawing changes the dimension text remains the same and does not reflect the actual size of the object anymore. This situation should be avoided at all costs because eventually it will come back to haunt you.

Figure 13-9
The default dimension text

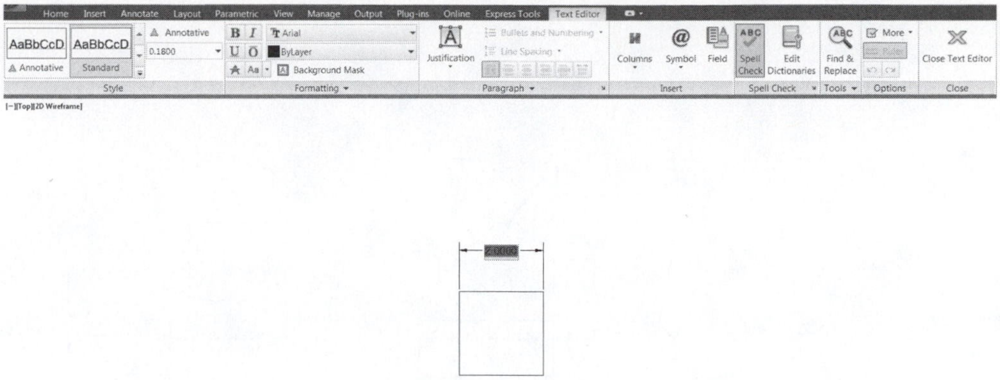

If you delete the default dimension text, you can re-create it by typing <>. When AutoCAD sees the <> brackets, it will replace it with the measured distance between the definition points.

You can use the <> brackets with the **Text** option as well. When you use the **Text** option, AutoCAD will display the measured dimension as a default and allow you to type a single line of text. You can type whatever text you want, using the <> brackets as a placeholder for the measured distance between the definition points.

> **TIP**
>
> You can also use the **DDEDIT** command to edit dimension text. Even easier, you can type in **ED** to use its command alias.

EXERCISE 13-2 Modifying Dimension Text

1. Continue from Exercise 13-1.
2. Start the **DIMLINEAR** command. AutoCAD prompts you to *Specify first extension line origin or <select object>:.*
3. Press **<Enter>.** AutoCAD prompts you to *Select object to dimension.*
4. Pick the line at P1 shown in Figure 13-10. AutoCAD places the defpoints at the ends of the line and prompts you to *Specify dimension line location or* ↓.
5. Choose the **Mtext** option. AutoCAD displays the multiline text editor with the default dimension text highlighted. Delete the default dimension text and type **1.00** in the mtext editor. Close the mtext editor. AutoCAD shows the dimension as 1.00.
6. Select the line you just dimensioned to activate its grips. Select the grip at one endpoint and drag it to a new location. Pick anywhere on the screen to place the end of the line. AutoCAD stretches the line and the dimension moves along with it, but the value of the dimension text does not update.
7. Start the **DDEDIT** command and select the **1.00** dimension text. Delete the **1.00** text and type <>. AutoCAD replaces the <> brackets with the measured length of the line.

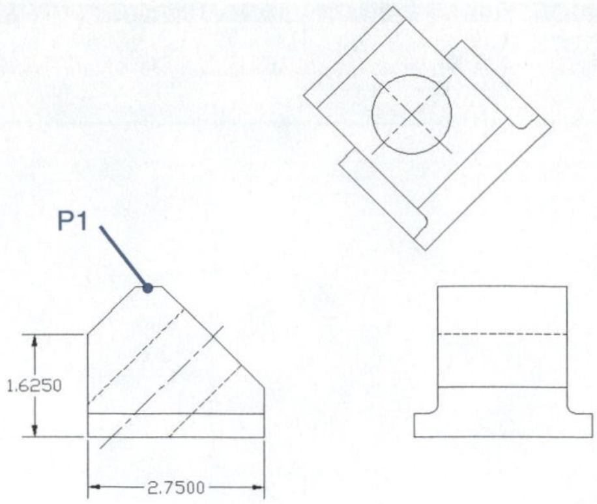

Figure 13-10
Specifying an object to dimension

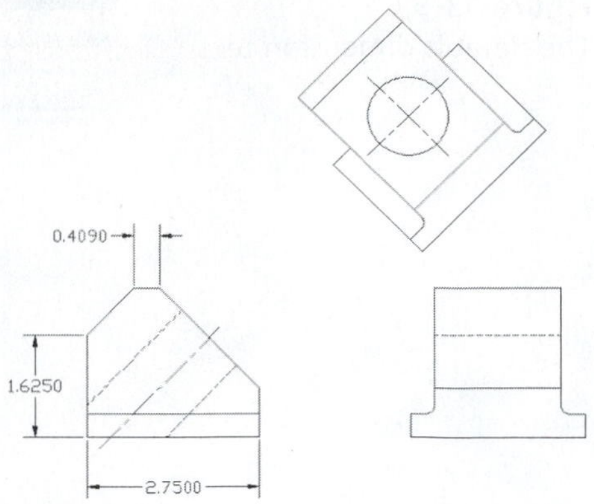

Figure 13-11
The modified dimension

8. Select the line to activate its grips and return the endpoint to its original location. AutoCAD stretches the line, and the dimension moves with it. The dimension text updates to show the change.
9. Save your drawing. Your drawing should look like Figure 13-11.

Creating Aligned Dimensions

ALIGNED	
Ribbon & Panel:	Home | Annotation Aligned
Toolbar:	
Menu:	Dimension | Aligned
Command Line:	DIMALIGNED
Command Alias:	DIMALI

An aligned dimension is another type of linear dimension. However, although horizontal and vertical dimensions measure distances along either the *X*- or *Y*-axis, respectively, an aligned dimension measures the true distance between any two points. The dimension text is placed parallel to a line between the two points (see Figure 13-12). Aligned dimensions are created with the **DIMALIGNED** command.

When using the **DIMALIGNED** command, you can select the two definition points, or you can select a line, arc, or circle. Once you specify the definition points, the **Mtext, Text,** and **Angle** options are available. These options are identical to the **Mtext, Text,** and **Angle** options in the **DIMLINEAR** command.

Figure 13-12
An aligned dimension

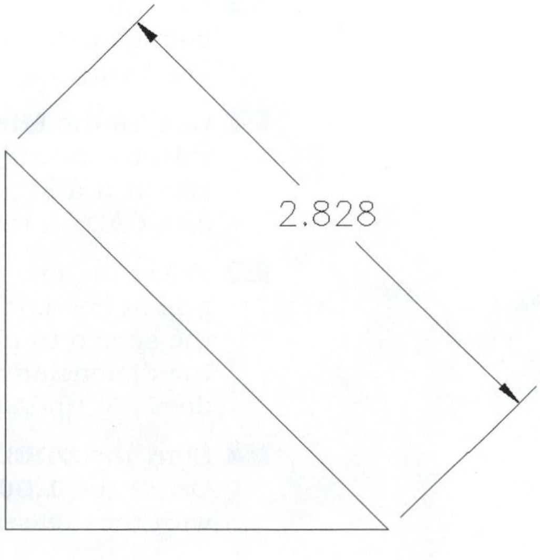

EXERCISE 13-3 **Creating Aligned Dimensions**

1. Continue from Exercise 13-2.
2. Start the **DIMALIGNED** command. AutoCAD prompts you to *Specify first extension line origin or <select object>:*.
3. Press **<Enter>.** AutoCAD prompts you to *Select object to dimension.*
4. Pick the line at P1 shown in Figure 13-13. AutoCAD places the defpoints at the ends of the line and prompts you to *Specify dimension line location or*↓.
5. Place the dimension line as shown in Figure 13-13.
6. Save your drawing. Your drawing should look like Figure 13-13.

Figure 13-13
An aligned dimension

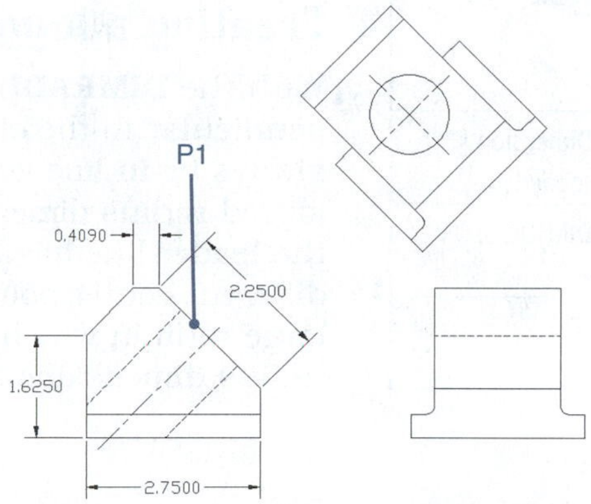

> **TIP**
>
> You can also select the extension line origin points to define the angle of the aligned dimension. Typically, you would rely on object snaps to snap to endpoints or intersections.

RADIUS	
Ribbon & Panel:	Home | Annotation  Radius
Dimension Toolbar:	
Menu:	Dimension | Radius
Command Line:	DIMRADIUS
Command Alias:	DIMRAD

Dimensioning Circles and Arcs

When dimensioning circles and arcs, you will typically be calling out either radius or diameter dimensions or, in the case of arcs, the length of an arc segment. AutoCAD provides a dimensioning command for each of these types of dimensions.

Radius Dimension

Radius dimensions are placed with the **DIMRADIUS** command. When you select this command, AutoCAD will prompt you to select an arc or circle. You can select circles, arcs, and polyline arc segments. Once you select an arc or circle, AutoCAD measures the radius of the arc and prompts you for the location of the text. You can place the text inside or outside the arc. AutoCAD will place a leader line perpendicular to the arc through the specified point on the arc and put a center mark in the center of the circle or arc. When you place the text, AutoCAD will automatically place an **R** prefix before the measured radius (see Figure 13-14). As with the **DIMLINEAR**

Figure 13-14
The radius prefix

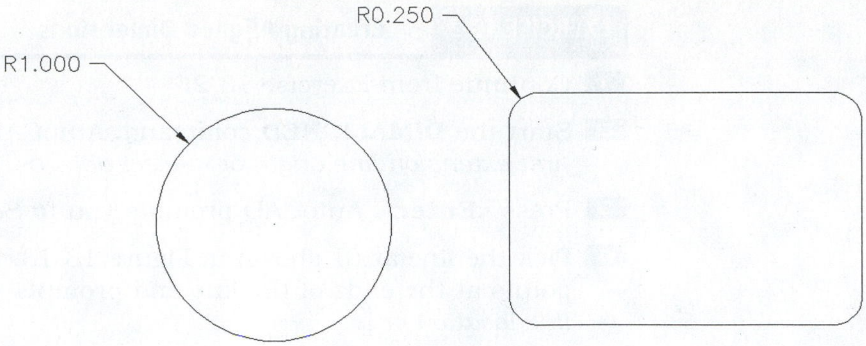

and **DIMALIGNED** commands, you have the **Mtext**, **Text**, and **Angle** options for modifying the dimension text.

JOGGED	
Ribbon & Panel:	Home | Annotation
	Jogged
Dimension Toolbar:	
Menu:	Dimension | Jogged
Command Line:	DIMJOGGED
Command Alias:	JOG

Creating a Jogged Radius Dimension

With the **DIMRADIUS** command, the leader line will always point perpendicular to the circle or arc segment. The start point of the leader will always be in line with the center point of the arc (see Figure 13-15). A jogged radius dimension is similar to a regular radius dimension except the leader line has an offset jog built into it. This allows you to specify a different center point for the leader. This can be useful when dimensioning large radii in which the center point lies outside your drawing area. Jogged radius dimensions are created with the **DIMJOGGED** command.

Figure 13-15
A radial and a jogged dimension

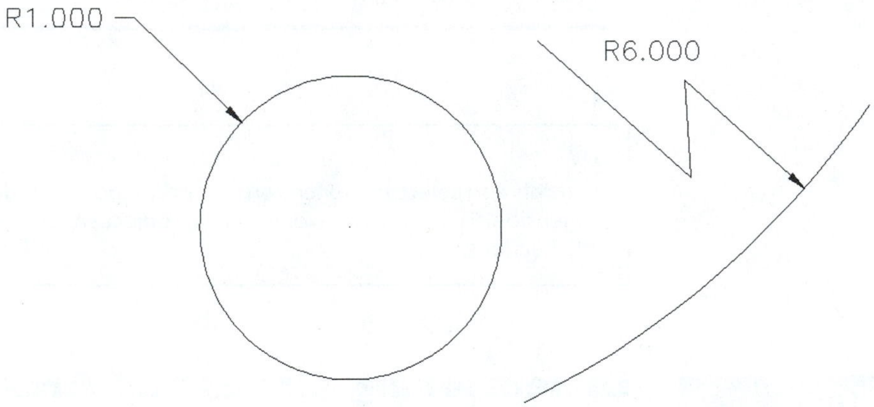

When you start the **DIMJOGGED** command, you are prompted to select a circle or arc. Once you select an object, AutoCAD prompts you to *Specify center location override:*. This is the location of the starting point (nonarrow end) of the leader line. The leader line is drawn from this point to a point on the circle or arc segment. You are then prompted for the location of the dimension text. Once you place the text, you can adjust the location of the jogged segment (see Figure 13-16).

DIAMETER	
Ribbon & Panel:	Home | Annotation
	Diameter
Dimension Toolbar:	
Menu:	Dimension | Diameter
Command Line:	DIMDIAMETER
Command Alias:	DIMDIA

Diameter Dimension

Diameter dimensions are placed with the **DIMDIAMETER** command. The **DIMDIAMETER** command behaves just like the **DIMRADIUS** command. The only difference is that text shown is the diameter of the arc or circle, and AutoCAD places the diameter symbol ∅ in front of the text.

Figure 13-16
The jogged segment

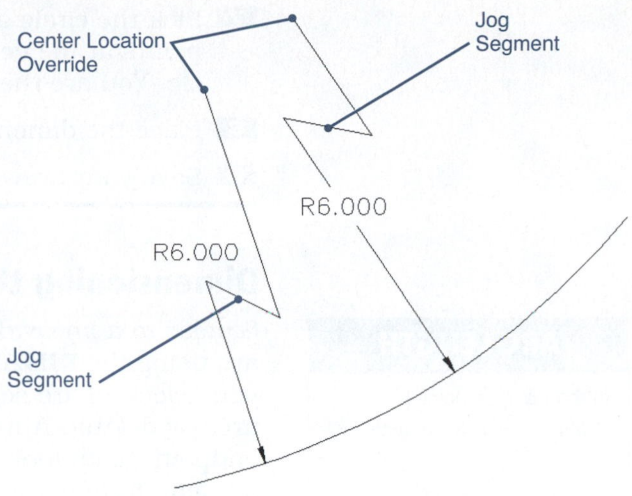

> **TIP**
> It is possible to dimension an arc beyond its endpoints. AutoCAD automatically creates an arc extension line.

EXERCISE 13-4 **Creating Radius and Diameter Dimensions**

1. Continue from Exercise 13-3.
2. Start the **DIMRADIUS** command. AutoCAD prompts you to *Select arc or circle:*.
3. Pick the arc at P1 shown in Figure 13-17. AutoCAD places the defpoints at the center of the arc and at the point you selected on the arc. You are then prompted to *Specify dimension line location or* ↓.
4. Choose the **Mtext** option and type **TYP.** after the default dimension text. Close the mtext editor.
5. Place the dimension line as shown in Figure 13-17.
6. Start the **DIMDIAMETER** command. AutoCAD prompts you to *Select arc or circle:*.

Figure 13-17
Radial and diameter dimensions

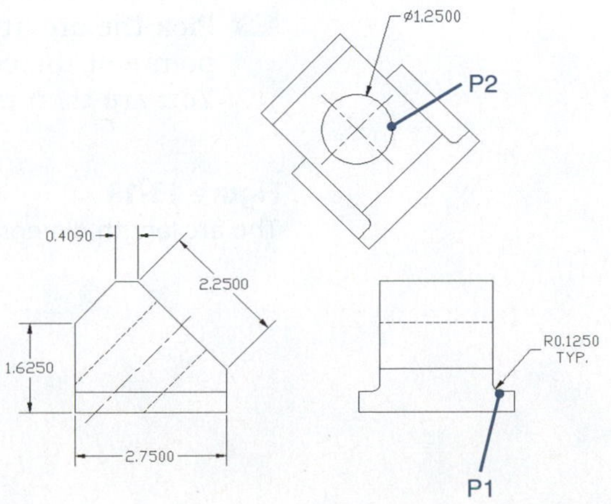

7 Pick the circle at P2 shown in Figure 13-17. AutoCAD places the defpoints at the center of the arc and at the point you selected on the circle. You are then prompted to *Specify dimension line location or* ↓.

8 Place the dimension line as shown in Figure 13-17.

9 Save your drawing. Your drawing should look like Figure 13-17.

Dimensioning the Length of an Arc

ARC LENGTH	
Ribbon & Panel:	Home | Annotation  Arc Length
Dimension Toolbar:	
Menu:	Dimension | Arc Length
Command Line:	DIMARC
Command Alias:	None

Similar to a linear dimension, AutoCAD can dimension the length of an arc using the **DIMARC** command. When using the **DIMARC** command, you select an arc segment, and AutoCAD measures the distance along the arc. By default, AutoCAD will dimension the entire length of the arc from endpoint to endpoint, but you can also opt to dimension a portion of the arc length. In addition to the **Mtext, Text,** and **Angle** options, the **Partial** option allows you to pick a start and endpoint along the arc segment and dimension only the portion of the arc between the two points.

When you place an arc length dimension, AutoCAD automatically places the arc symbol ∩ in front of the dimension value (see Figure 13-18).

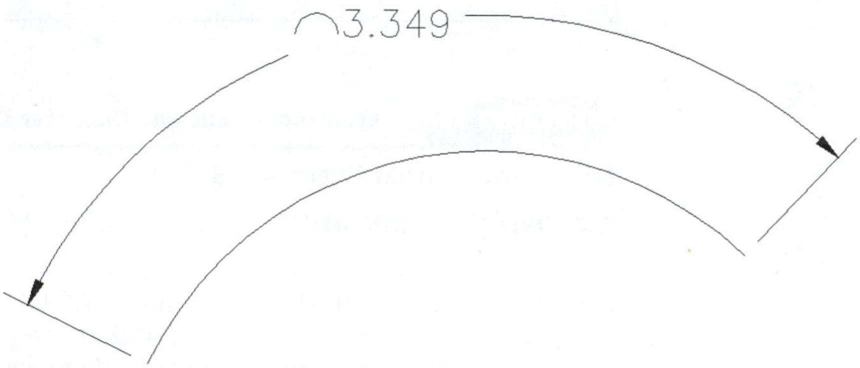

Figure 13-18
The ∩ symbol

EXERCISE 13-5 Creating an Arc Length Dimension

To access student data files, go to **www.pearsondesigncentral.com.**

1 Open drawing ***EX13-5*** in the student data files.

2 Start the **DIMARC** command. AutoCAD prompts you to *Select arc or polyline arc segment:*.

3 Pick the arc at P1 shown in Figure 13-19. AutoCAD places the defpoints at the center of the arc and at the point you selected on the arc. You are then prompted to *Specify dimension line location or* ↓.

Figure 13-19
The arc length dimension

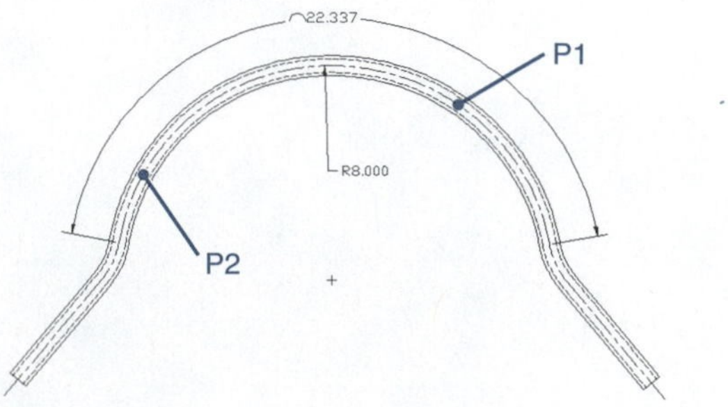

4. Place the dimension line as shown in Figure 13-19.
5. Start the **DIMRADIUS** command. AutoCAD prompts you to *Select arc or circle:*.
6. Pick the arc at P2 shown in Figure 13-19. You are prompted to *Specify arc length dimension location or* ↓.
7. Place the dimension line as shown in Figure 13-19.
8. Save your drawing as ***CH13_EXERCISE5.*** Your drawing should look like Figure 13-19.

CENTER MARK	
Ribbon & Panel:	Annotate | Dimensions
Dimension Toolbar:	
Menu:	Dimension | Center Mark
Command Line:	DIMCENTER
Command Alias:	None

Creating Center Marks

When dimensioning arcs and circles, AutoCAD places marks at the center of the dimensions (see Figure 13-20). You may have a need to place center marks on arcs and circles that are not dimensioned. AutoCAD has a number of ways to create center marks. One option is to simply draw center marks using either the **LINE** or **PLINE** command. Another way is to use the **DIMCENTER** command.

NOTE

When you use the **DIMCENTER** command, the resulting lines are not dimension objects but simply line segments.

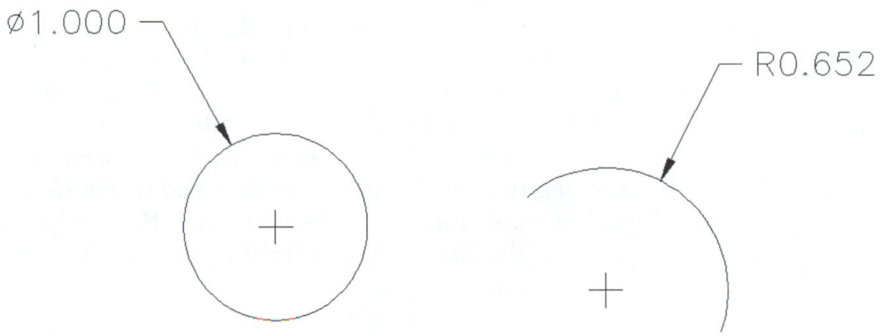

Figure 13-20
Center marks

The **DIMCENTER** command places orthogonal line segments at the center of a circle or arc segment. When you start the **DIMCENTER** command, AutoCAD prompts you to select a circle or an arc segment and then places center mark line segments.

FOR MORE DETAILS

The **DIMCEN** system variable controls the size of center marks. Dimension variables are typically controlled through dimension styles, which are covered later in this chapter. For more information on the **DIMCEN** system variable, see Appendix D.

ANGULAR	
Ribbon & Panel:	Home | Annotation Angular
Dimension Toolbar:	
Pull-down Menu:	Dimension | Angular
Command Line:	DIMANGULAR
Command Alias:	DIMANG

Angular Dimensions

With linear dimensions, AutoCAD needs to have two definition points in order to calculate the dimension value. With radius and diameter dimensions, AutoCAD can calculate the dimension value directly from the arcs and circles. When dimensioning angles, AutoCAD needs to know three points in order to define the angular dimension: a center vertex and two endpoints (see Figure 13-21). Angular dimensions are placed with the **DIMANGULAR** command. When using this command, you have three options for defining angular dimension: selecting an arc or circle, selecting two intersecting lines, or picking three points to define the vertex and the two endpoints.

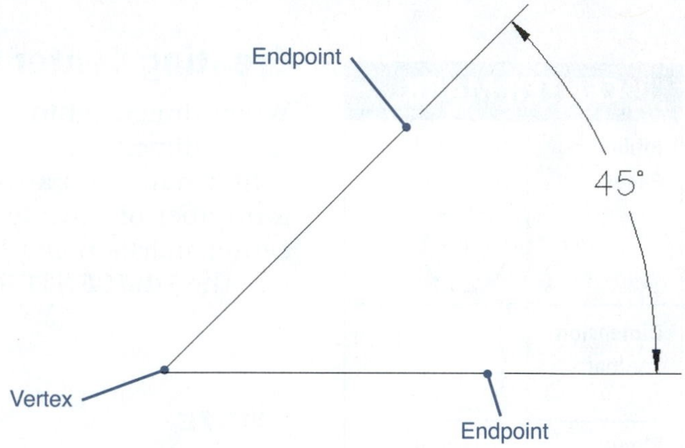

Figure 13-21
Angular dimension defpoints

Selecting Objects

When you start the **DIMANGULAR** command, AutoCAD prompts you to *Select arc, circle, line, or <specify vertex>*. If you select an arc, AutoCAD uses the center and ends of the arc to determine the angular dimensions.

If you select a circle, AutoCAD uses the selection point as one endpoint of the angle and the center of the circle as the vertex. AutoCAD then prompts you for a second endpoint and allows you to place the dimension text.

If you select a line segment, AutoCAD will ask you to select another line segment and will dimension the angle between endpoints of the first and second lines. AutoCAD will use the endpoints closest to the selection point of the line. Figure 13-22 shows the results of selecting two lines at various points.

Figure 13-22
Specifying angular defpoints

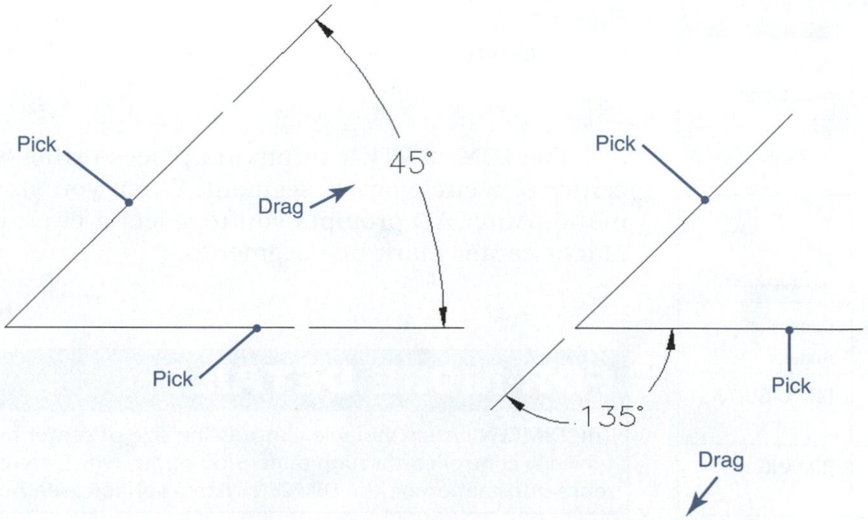

Selecting Vertex and Angle Endpoints

To specify the vertex and angle endpoints, press **<Enter>** when AutoCAD prompts you to *Select arc, circle, line, or <specify vertex>*. AutoCAD will prompt you for a vertex point and then prompt you for two endpoints.

The Quadrant Option

The **Quadrant** option allows you to place dimension text outside of the angle being measured. The only way to access the **Quadrant** option is from the right-click menu after selecting the angle to measure when AutoCAD prompts you: *Specify dimension arc line location or* ↓.

The **Quadrant** option prompts you to specify the quadrant that you want to dimension separate from specifying the dimension arc line location. If the dimension arc line is outside of the quadrant that is being measured, AutoCAD automatically creates an arc extension line using the current extension line settings.

EXERCISE 13-6 **Creating an Angular Dimension**

1. Continue from Exercise 13-5.
2. Start the **DIMANGULAR** command. AutoCAD prompts you to *Select arc, circle, line, or <specify vertex>*.
3. Pick the line at P1 shown in Figure 13-23. AutoCAD prompts you to *Select second line:*.

Figure 13-23
An angled dimension

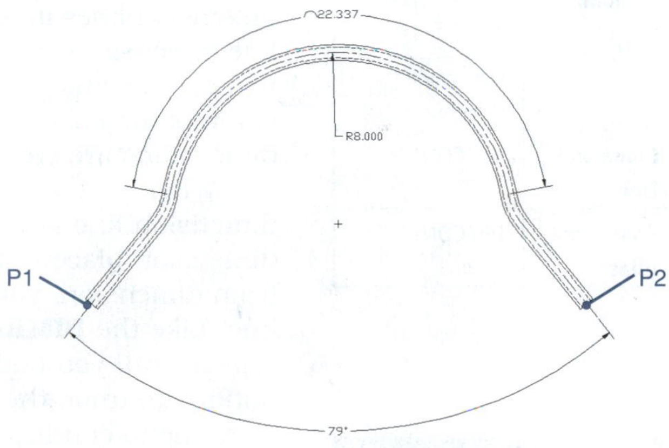

4. Pick the line at P2 shown in Figure 13-23. AutoCAD prompts you to *Specify dimension arc line location or* ↓.
5. Place the dimension line as shown in Figure 13-23. Notice that the angle that is dimensioned varies with your cursor location.
6. Save your drawing. Your drawing should look like Figure 13-23.

> **NOTE**
>
> If you select two parallel lines, AutoCAD will show you the message *Lines are parallel* in the command line and end the command. If you select anything but a line segment for the second line, AutoCAD will display the message *Object selected is not a line* in the command line and prompt you to *Select second line*.

Creating Datum and Chain Dimensions

Datum and chain dimensioning refers to linear dimensions that share common extension lines. A datum dimension is also known as a baseline dimension, in which multiple features are measured from a common feature. Chain dimensions are also known as continued dimensions, in which linear dimensions continue end to end. Figure 13-24 shows examples of continued and baseline dimensions.

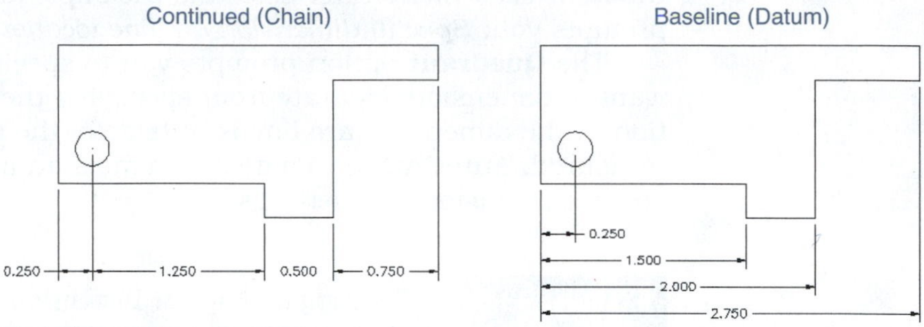

Figure 13-24
Continued and baseline dimensions

CONTINUE	
Ribbon & Panel:	Annotate | Dimensions Continue
Dimension Toolbar:	
Menu:	Dimension | Continue
Command Line:	DIMCONTINUE
Command Alias:	DIMCONT

Continued Dimension

A continued dimension is similar to a baseline dimension. It requires an existing linear or angular dimension, and it allows you to place multiple dimension lines in a single command. The only difference is that while baseline dimensions measure dimensions from a common extension line, continued dimensions measure from the last placed dimension line. The result is a chain of dimensions, each one measured from the last. Continued (or chain) dimensions are created with the **DIMCONTINUE** command.

When you start the **DIMCONTINUE** command, AutoCAD will place the dimension line at the second extension line of the last linear or angular dimension placed in the drawing. If you want to continue the dimension from dimension, you can press **<Enter>** to select a different extension line. Like the **DIMBASELINE** command, the **DIMCONTINUE** command will repeat until you end the command. You also have the **Undo** and **Select** options to undo the last continued dimension or to select a different extension line to continue from.

BASELINE	
Ribbon & Panel:	Annotate | Dimensions Baseline
Dimension Toolbar:	
Menu:	Dimension | Baseline
Command Line:	DIMBASELINE
Command Alias:	DIMBASE

Baseline Dimension

Baseline dimensions are measured from an extension line of an existing linear or angular dimension. When you place a baseline dimension, each dimension is measured from this extension line, and the dimension lines are spaced at a predefined distance. Baseline dimensions are created with the **DIMBASELINE** command.

FOR MORE DETAILS

The **DIMDLI** system variable controls the spacing of the baseline dimension lines. Dimension variables are typically controlled through dimension styles, which are covered later in this chapter. For more information on the **DIMDLI** system variable, see Appendix D.

The **DIMBASELINE** command requires an existing linear or angular dimension. By default, AutoCAD will use the first extension line of the last linear or angular dimension as the baseline. If you want to use a different extension line, you can press **<Enter>** to select a different extension line. If AutoCAD cannot locate or determine where the last dimension line is, it will prompt you to select an extension line to use for the baseline.

Once you've specified the extension line to use as the baseline, AutoCAD prompts you to pick a definition point for the next extension line. The **DIMBASELINE** command will continue to place baseline dimensions until you end the command. While placing baseline dimensions, you can use the **Undo** option to undo a dimension line placement or press **<Enter>** to select a different extension baseline.

EXERCISE 13-7 Creating Continued and Baseline Dimensions

To access student data files, go to **www.pearsondesigncentral.com.**

1. Open drawing ***EX13-7*** in the student data files.
2. Start the **DIMLINEAR** command and place the horizontal dimension between P1 and P2 as shown in Figure 13-25.
3. Start the **DIMCONTINUE** command. AutoCAD starts dragging a dimension from the previous dimension. You are prompted to *Specify a second extension line origin or* ↓.
4. Place the dimensions P3 and P4 as shown in Figure 13-25. Press **<Esc>** to exit the **DIMCONTINUE** command.
5. Start the **DIMBASELINE** command. AutoCAD starts dragging a dimension from the previous dimension. You are prompted to *Specify a second extension line origin or* ↓.
6. Press **<Enter>** to choose the **Select** option. AutoCAD prompts you to *Select base dimension:*.
7. Choose the extension line at P1 shown in Figure 13-26. AutoCAD prompts you to *Specify a second extension line origin or* ↓.

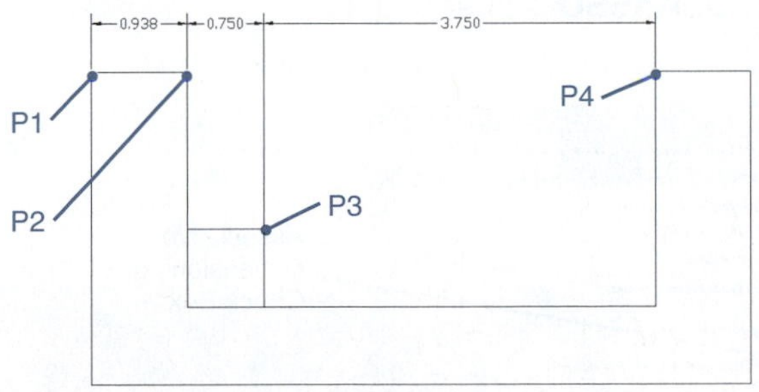

Figure 13-25
Specifying dimension points

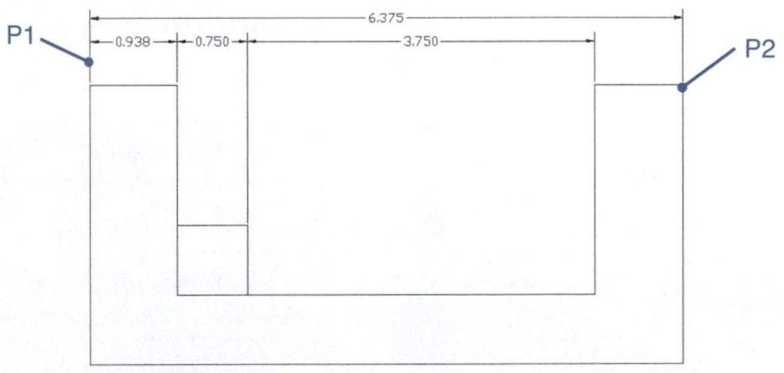

Figure 13-26
Continued and baseline dimensions

8. Select the end of the line at point P2 shown in Figure 13-26. AutoCAD automatically spaces the dimension above the selected dimension.
9. Save your drawing as ***CH13_EXERCISE7.*** Your drawing should look like Figure 13-26.

DIMASSOC System Variable

There are actually three levels of associativity for a dimension object. The **DIMASSOC** system variable controls which level of dimension associativity AutoCAD uses.

The **DIMASSOC** system variable can be set to a value of **0**, **1**, or **2**. When set to **2** (the default setting), dimension defpoints are associated with objects in the drawing. For example, if you dimension between the two endpoints of a line, AutoCAD will create defpoints at the endpoints of the line, and these defpoints will be associated with the line object. If the line moves, the dimension will move along with it. If an endpoint of the line is moved (stretched, trimmed, extended, etc.), the defpoint associated with that endpoint will move, and the dimension will update.

When **DIMASSOC** is set to **1**, AutoCAD still creates associative dimensions, but the defpoints are not associated with any particular geometry. To update a dimension, you must modify (move or stretch) the defpoints associated with the dimension explicitly. For example, if you dimension a line with **DIMASSOC** set to **1**, AutoCAD will create defpoints at the ends of the line. But if you move the line, the dimension will not follow it. You would have to select and move the dimension along with the line to keep them together. If you move the end of the line (by stretching, trimming, extending, etc.), you will need to move the defpoint located at the end of the line as well in order for the dimension to update.

When **DIMASSOC** is set to **0**, AutoCAD creates exploded dimensions with no associativity. No defpoints are created, and each part of the dimension is created as a separate object (lines and text).

> **TIP**
>
> Although it's possible to create exploded dimensions, it's considered bad practice in most CAD work environments. Exploded dimensions are difficult to manage and update and can lead to sloppy and inaccurate drawings.

You can toggle the **DIMASSOC** variable with the **Associative Dimensioning** check box in the **User Preferences** tab of the **Options** dialog box (see Figure 13-27). When this box is checked, **DIMASSOC** is set to **2**. With the check removed, **DIMASSOC** is set to **1**.

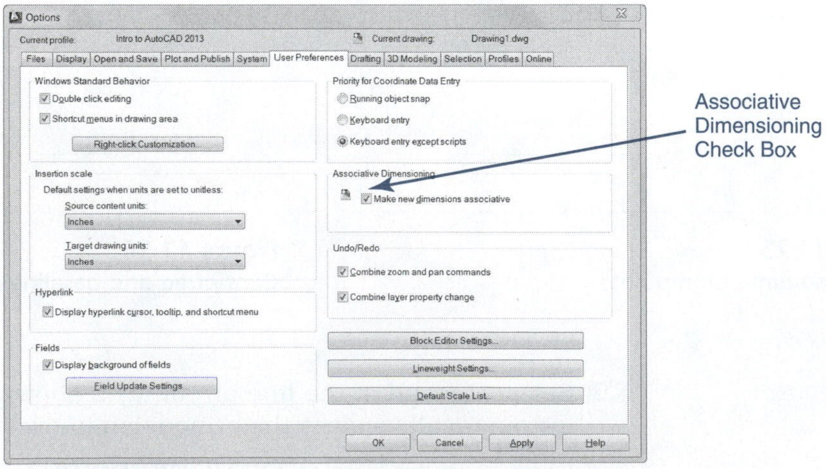

Figure 13-27

The **Associative Dimensioning** check box

ADJUST SPACE	
Ribbon & Panel:	Annotate | Dimensions 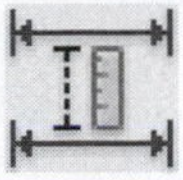
Dimension Toolbar:	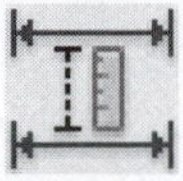
Menu:	Dimension | Dimension Space
Command Line:	DIMSPACE
Command Alias:	None

Dimension Tools

AutoCAD provides a few handy dimension tools that allow you to automate tasks that used to be much more time-consuming. There are tools to evenly space stacked dimensions and to break dimension lines and extension lines that cross other dimensions, as well as that have the ability to create jog lines in linear dimensions when a distance is too long to fit on the specified sheet size.

The Adjust Space Tool

The **Adjust Space** tool allows you to evenly space selected dimensions as shown in Figure 13-28. You can specify the spacing distance between dimension lines or let AutoCAD automatically determine a minimum spacing distance.

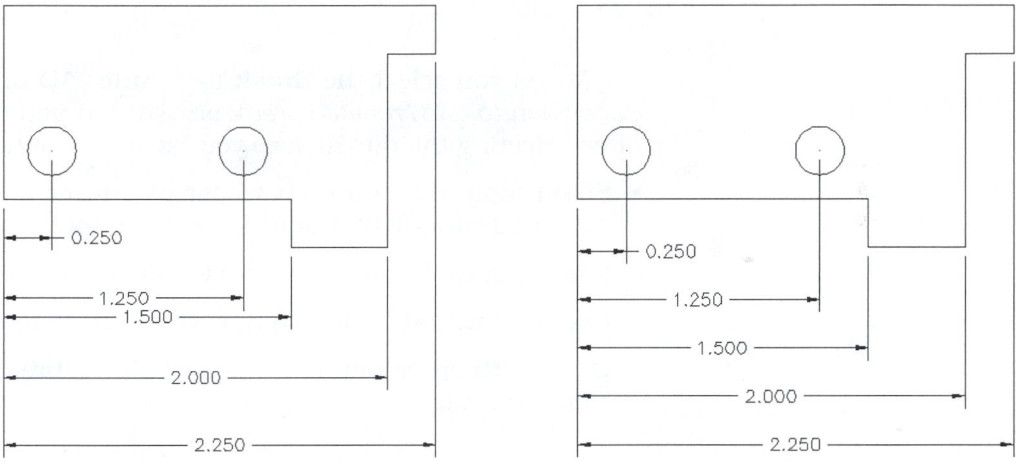

Dimensions Before Using Adjust Space Tool

Dimensions After Using Adjust Space Tool

Figure 13-28
The **Adjust Space** tool

When you select the **Adjust Space** tool, AutoCAD prompts you to *Select the base dimension:* so that you can select the first dimension in the stack. After selecting a base dimension, AutoCAD then prompts you to *Select dimensions to space:*. Select the dimensions you want to space, and either enter a distance or press **<Enter>** to select the **Auto** option. The **Auto** option automatically spaces the dimensions based on the current dimension text height.

BREAK	
Ribbon & Panel:	Annotate | Dimensions 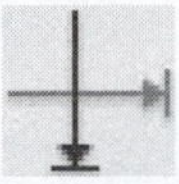
Dimension Toolbar:	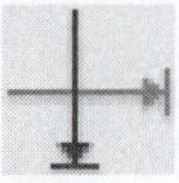
Menu:	Dimension | Dimension Break
Command Line:	DIMBREAK
Command Alias:	None

The Break Tool

The **Break** tool allows you to break dimension or extension lines where they intersect other dimensions or objects in your drawing as shown in Figure 13-29.

> **NOTE**
>
> When you break a dimension either by selecting objects or by using the **Auto** option, the breaks will automatically update when the intersection point moves. If the objects are moved so that they no longer intersect, the break will disappear; if they are moved back, the break will automatically return to the original location.

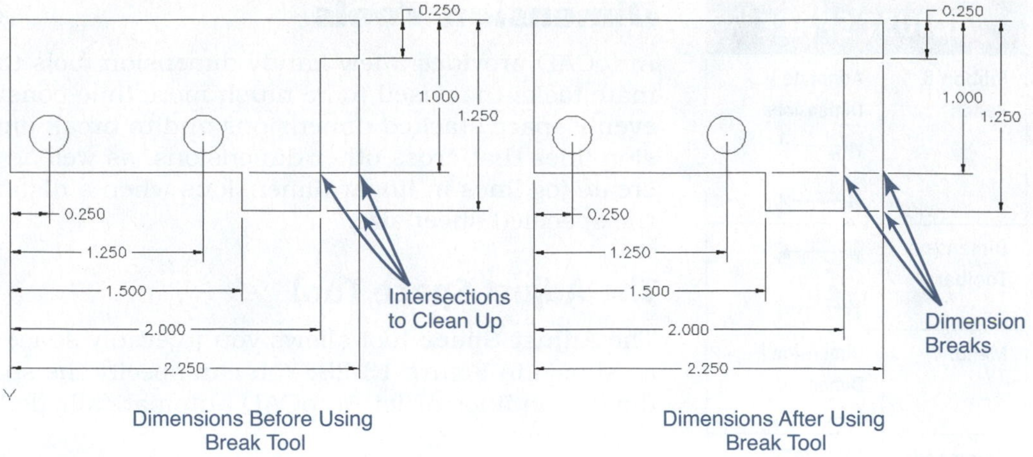

Figure 13-29
The **Break** tool

When you select the **Break** tool, AutoCAD prompts you to *Select dimension to add/remove break or* ↓ so that you can select the dimension. After selecting the dimension, you have four options:

- Select intersecting objects to use as cutting edges for the break. AutoCAD prompts for objects until you press **<Enter>**
- Use the **Auto** option to automatically trim around all intersecting objects
- Use the **Manual** option so that you have to manually pick break points
- Use the **Remove** option to remove all the breaks from selected dimensions or leaders

TIP

You can break more than one dimension at a time by selecting the **Multiple** option after the **Break** tool.

The Jog Line Tool

JOG LINE	
Ribbon & Panel:	Annotate | Dimensions 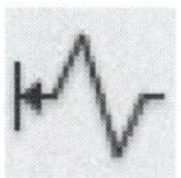
Dimension Toolbar:	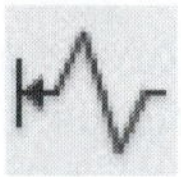
Menu:	Dimension | Jogged Linear
Command Line:	DIMJOGLINE
Command Alias:	None

The **Jog Line** tool allows you to add a jog, or breakline, to linear dimensions to represent measurements whose values are not the same length as the dimension line. Jogged dimension lines are typically used when a sheet is too small to display the true length of a dimension line as shown in Figure 13-30.

NOTE

The linear jog size can be specified on the **Symbols and Arrows** tab of the **Dimension Style Manager** dialog box explained later. The default is 1.5 x text height.

When you select the **Jog Line** tool, AutoCAD prompts you to *Select dimension to add jog or* ↓ so that you can select the dimension to add the jog. After selecting a dimension, AutoCAD then prompts you to *Specify jog location (or press Enter):*. You can either pick the location on the dimension line to locate the jog line or press **<Enter>** to place the jog line automatically based on the direction of the dimension definition points. The jog line is created closest to the first dimension definition point.

Figure 13-30
The **Jog Line** tool

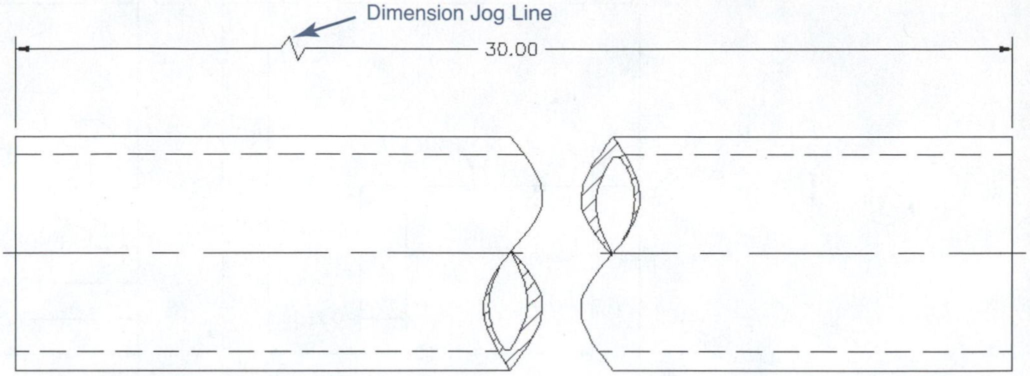

> **TIP**
> You can change the jog location using grips. You can turn off a jog line or edit its height using the **Properties** palette.

Quick Dimensioning

When creating dimension objects, you may find that placing dimensions can be a somewhat tedious, repetitive process. Many times you may wish to simply place some dimensions on the drawing and then go back and adjust their placement and orientation to suit your drawing. AutoCAD helps automate the process of placing dimensions by allowing you to create multiple dimensions at once. The **QDIM** command (quick dimension) allows you to select multiple objects and then select a type of dimension to place. AutoCAD will then automatically detect definition points and place the specified dimensions based on those points.

Quick Dimension

QUICK DIMENSION	
Ribbon & Panel:	Annotate | Dimensions 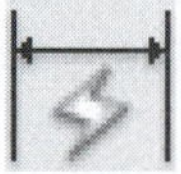
Dimension Toolbar:	
Menu:	Dimension | Quick Dimension
Command Line:	QDIM
Command Alias:	None

When you start the **QDIM** command, AutoCAD will prompt you to *Select geometry to dimension*:. Once you have built your selection set of objects, press **<Enter>,** and AutoCAD will provide a number of options. These options are described below.

Continuous. The **Continuous** option places continuous dimensions from the outermost points of the selected geometry. When you select this option, AutoCAD will place the dimension objects and allow you to select a placement point for the dimensions. The dimensions will be either vertical or horizontal based on where you drag your cursor.

Staggered. The **Staggered** option places a series of staggered or nested linear dimensions, starting from the innermost pair of definition points. From there, it will place a linear dimension on the next outer level of points and continue outward until the geometry is dimensioned. Figure 13-31 shows some examples of staggered dimensions placed with the **QDIM** command.

datumPoint. The **datumPoint** option sets a base point for the **Baseline** and **Ordinate** dimension options. By default, when you use the **Baseline** option, it places the datum or base point of the dimensions on the definition point nearest to 0,0. The **datumPoint** option allows you to override this and place the datum point at any point in the drawing.

Baseline. The **Baseline** option creates a series of baseline dimensions starting either at 0,0 or at the point specified with the **datumPoint** option. Figure 13-32 shows you some examples of baseline dimensions.

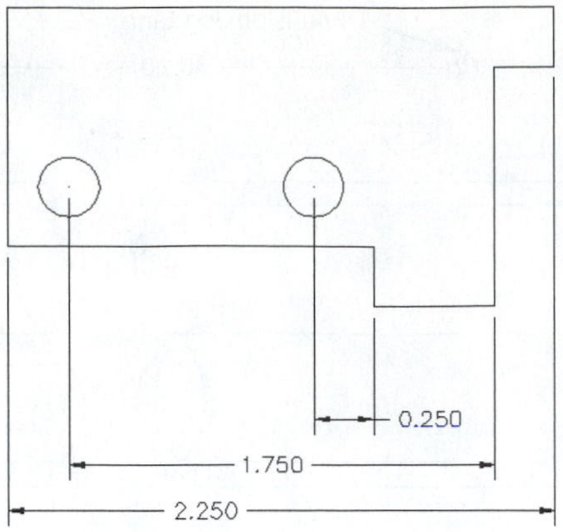

Figure 13-31
Staggered quick dimensions

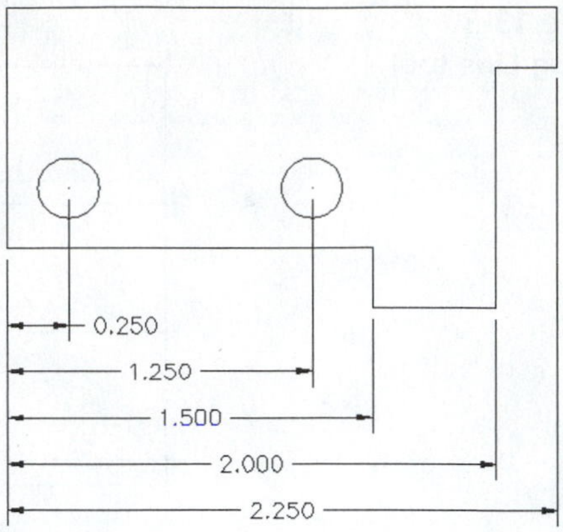

Figure 13-32
Baseline quick dimensions

Ordinate. Ordinate dimensioning displays *X*- and *Y*-datum coordinates based on an origin, or datum point. The datum point is typically located at a key point on the geometry such as the corner of a part. The **Ordinate** option of the **QDIM** command creates a set of ordinate dimensions with the origin being either 0,0 or a point specified with the **datumPoint** option.

> **TIP**
> Ordinate dimensions can also be created with the **DIMORDINATE** command. However, the **DIMORDINATE** command does not allow you to set a 0,0 datum point. To use the **DIMORDINATE** command, you must first establish a user coordinate system (UCS) with its origin located at your desired datum point, which is beyond the scope of this book. Using the **QDIM** command with the **datumPoint** and **Ordinate** options is a much quicker way of creating ordinate dimensions.

Radius. The **Radius** option will search through your selection of objects and find any circles or arcs. You are then prompted for a location for the leaders. The leaders are placed in the same relative position on each arc or circle. Figure 13-33 shows an example of using the **Radius** option.

Figure 13-33
Radius quick dimensions

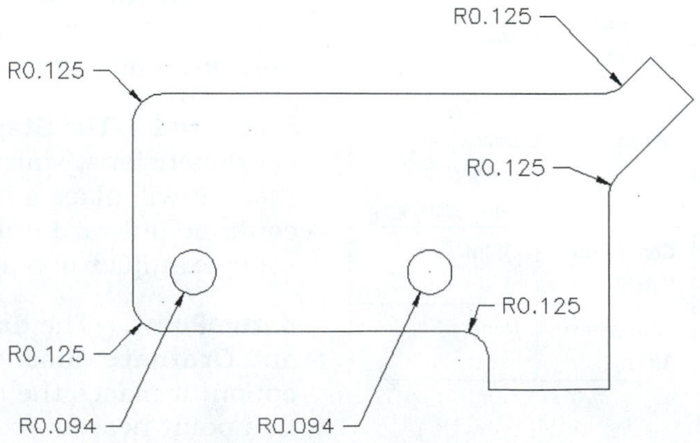

Diameter. The **Diameter** option works the same way as the **Radius** option. AutoCAD places diameter dimensions at the same relative points on each arc or circle.

Edit. The **Edit** option allows you to edit the definition points within the selection set. When you choose this option, AutoCAD will show you all the definition points found in the selection set. You can add or delete definition points prior to placing your dimensions.

seTtings. The **seTtings** option allows you to set the preference for determining definition points. By default, AutoCAD will look for endpoints of objects. You can set it to **Intersection** or **Endpoint**.

EXERCISE 13-8 **Creating Quick Dimensions**

To access student data files, go to **www.pearsondesigncentral.com.**

1. Open drawing ***EX13-8*** in the student data files.
2. Start the **QDIM** command. AutoCAD prompts you to *Select geometry to dimension:*.
3. Type **ALL<Enter>** to select all the geometry in the drawing. AutoCAD prompts you to *Specify dimension line position or* ↓.
4. Choose the **datumPoint** option and pick the endpoint P1 shown in Figure 13-34. AutoCAD prompts you to *Specify dimension line position or* ↓.
5. Choose the **Ordinate** option. AutoCAD prompts you to *Specify dimension line position or* ↓.
6. Place the *X*-datum dimensions as shown in Figure 13-34. AutoCAD prompts you to *Specify dimension line position or* ↓.
7. Restart the **QDIM** command. AutoCAD defaults to the **Ordinate** option. Place the *Y*-datum dimensions shown in Figure 13-35.
8. Save your drawing as ***CH13_EXERCISE8.*** Your drawing should look like Figure 13-35.

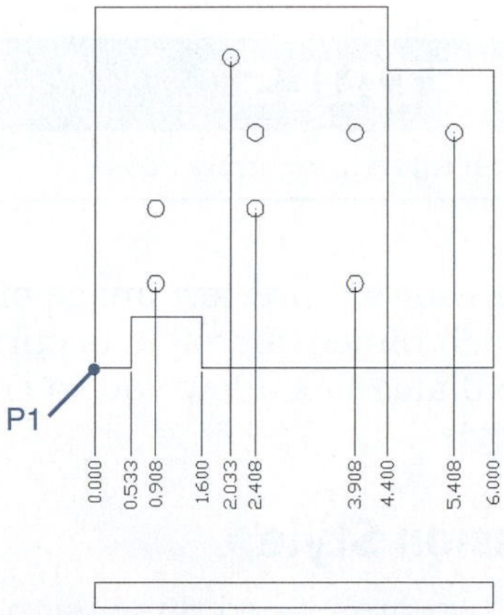

Figure 13-34
Selecting a datum point

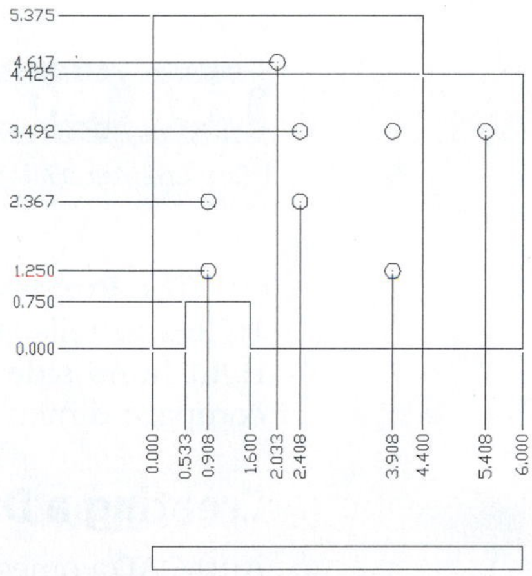

Figure 13-35
Ordinate quick dimensions

DIMENSION STYLE	
Ribbon & Panel:	Home | Annotation 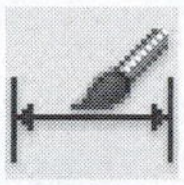
Dimension Toolbar:	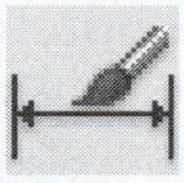
Menu:	Dimension | Dimension Style...
Command Line:	DIMSTYLE
Command Alias:	DDIM

Managing Dimension Styles

So far, we've looked at how to create and place dimension objects. Creating and placing dimension objects is only part of the process. In this section, you'll examine how to control the look of dimension objects through dimension styles.

A dimension style is a collection of dimension settings that is assigned a name and is applied as a group to dimension objects. Dimension styles control the look and behavior of dimension objects, such as the type of arrowhead used, the text style used in the dimensions, tolerance values and formatting, and the overall scale of the dimension.

Dimension styles work similarly to text styles or layers: you set a dimension style current and then any new objects are created using the settings contained within that style. Dimension styles are managed with the **DIMSTYLE** command.

When you start the **DIMSTYLE** command, AutoCAD displays the **Dimension Style Manager** dialog box (see Figure 13-36). From this dialog box, you can create dimension styles, modify dimension styles, compare dimension styles, and set a dimension style current. The **Styles:** list shows dimension styles defined in your drawing. The **List** options allow you to control which dimension styles are shown in the **Styles:** list. You can choose to show all dimension styles or only the ones currently used in the drawing. You can also choose to show or hide dimension styles contained in referenced drawings.

Figure 13-36
The **Dimension Style Manager** dialog box

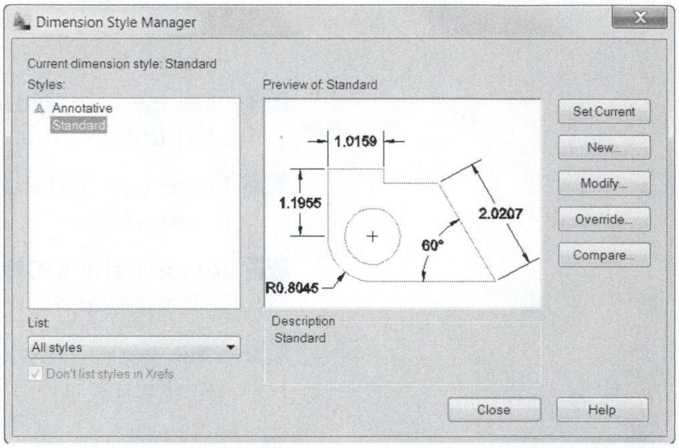

FOR MORE DETAILS

See Chapter 17 for more on referencing drawings.

The **Preview** area shows a preview image of the current dimension style and tells you which dimension style is current. The buttons along the right-hand side of the dialog box allow you to create, modify, override, and compare dimension styles.

Creating a Dimension Style

AutoCAD comes with two predefined dimension styles: Annotative and Standard. Standard is AutoCAD's default dimension style. Both can be modified, renamed, or even deleted if one is not the current style. The settings for the dimension styles are defined in the template file used to create the drawing. To create a new dimension style, choose the **New...** button. AutoCAD will display the **Create New Dimension Style** dialog box (see Figure 13-37).

When you create a new dimension style, AutoCAD will create a copy of an existing dimension style as the starting point. In the **Create New Dimension Style** dialog box, you specify the name for the new dimension style and tell AutoCAD which style to copy as the starting point. You can

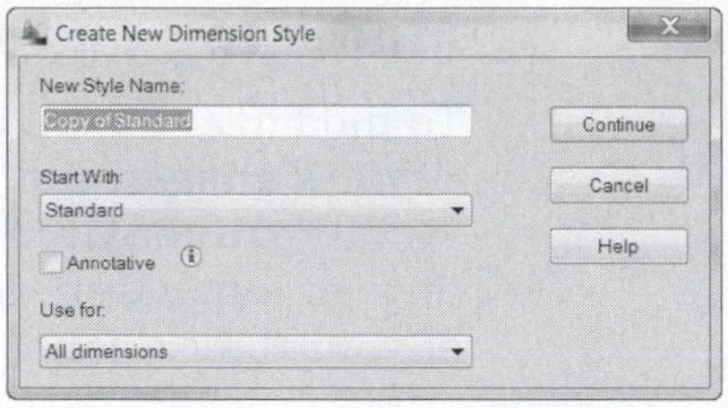

Figure 13-37
The **Create New Dimension Style** dialog box

also create a dimension style that applies only to a certain type of dimension. For example, you might want all your dimension text to align with the dimension line, except for radial and diameter dimensions, where you might want the text to be horizontal. These styles are known as *child dimension styles* and appear as a substyle of the parent dimension style.

> **TIP**
>
> When you select a child dimension style in the **Dimension Style Manager** dialog box, the **Preview** area shows you only the dimension settings that are different from the parent style, and the **Description** area lists the differences between the parent and child dimension styles.

EXERCISE 13-9 Creating a New Dimension Style

1. Continue from Exercise 13-8.
2. Start the **DIMSTYLE** command. AutoCAD displays the **Dimension Style Manager** dialog box. Choose **New...** to display the **Create New Dimension Style** dialog box.
3. Type **Mech** in the **New Style Name:** box, and make sure the **Start With:** box is set to **Standard** and the **Use for:** box is set to **All dimensions.** Choose **Continue** to create the new dimension style. AutoCAD displays the **New Dimension Style** dialog box.
4. Choose **OK** to accept the dimension style settings. AutoCAD returns you to the **Dimension Style Manager** dialog box. The new dimension style is listed in the **Styles:** list. Choose the **Close** button to end the **DIMSTYLE** command.
5. Start the **DIMLINEAR** command and place the dimension shown at P1 in Figure 13-38.
6. Save your drawing.

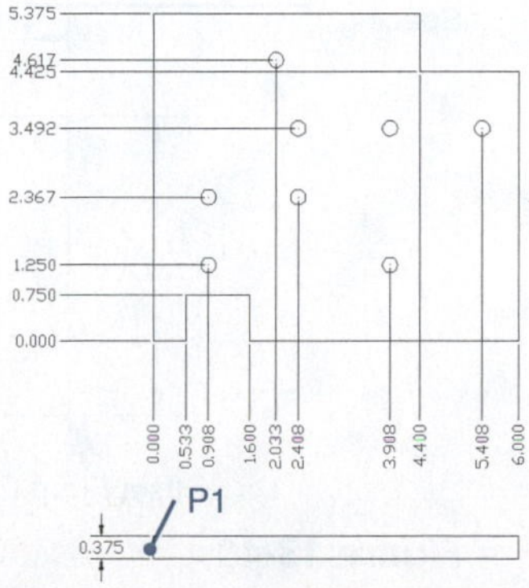

Figure 13-38
Creating a new dimension style

Modifying an Existing Dimension Style

To modify a dimension style, select the style name from the **Dimension Style Manager** and choose the **Modify...** button. This will display the **Modify Dimension Style** dialog box (see Figure 13-39). This dialog box is divided into seven different tabs that contain the settings for various aspects of your dimensions. These tabs are described in the following sections.

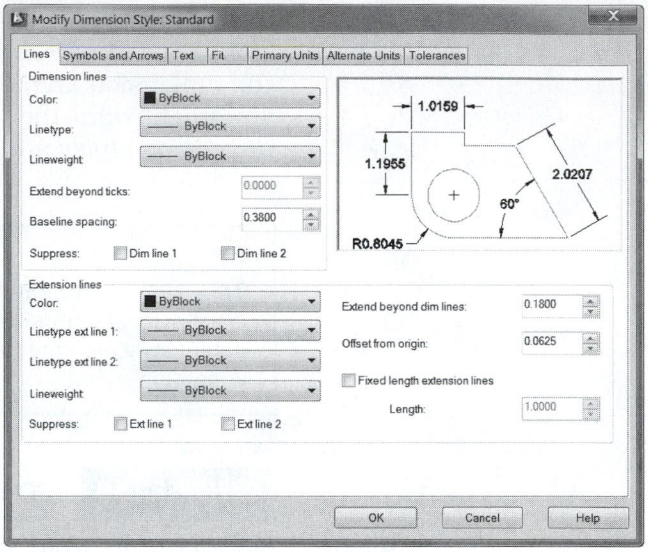

Figure 13-39
The **Modify Dimension Style** dialog box

Lines Settings. The **Lines** tab (see Figure 13-39) controls the dimension and extension lines within a dimension object. Figure 13-40 shows how these various settings map to dimension objects. The **Dimension lines** area allows you to set the color, linetype, and lineweight of the dimension lines as well as the spacing between dimension lines when creating baseline dimensions. The **Extend beyond ticks:** setting is available only when certain types of arrowheads are specified. For example, when an architectural tick is used, the **Extend beyond ticks:** setting controls how far past the tick to extend the dimension line. You can suppress the dimension line on either side of the text. This comes in handy when dimensioning in tight areas where the dimension lines tend to obscure dimension text.

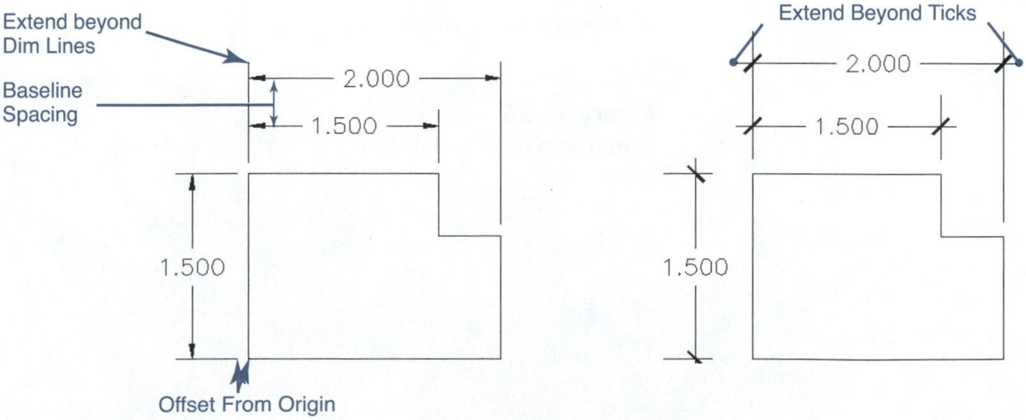

Figure 13-40
Dimension line settings

The **Extension lines** area has similar controls for extension lines. You can set the color, linetype, and lineweight of the extension lines as well as control the length of the extension line and the gap between the extension line and the object you are dimensioning.

Checking the **Fixed length extension lines** check box will create extension lines that are all the same length specified in the **Length:** box regardless of their origin point locations. The fixed length is calculated using the distance from the second extension line origin point (second pick point) to the dimension line location point (third pick point) minus the distance specified in the **Offset from origin:** box.

Symbols and Arrows. The **Symbols and Arrows** tab (see Figure 13-41) allows you to set the size and type of arrowheads used in dimensions. You can set different arrowheads for the first and second dimension lines as well as a separate arrowhead for leaders. The **Center marks** area allows you to set the size and type of center marks. This affects how center marks are shown in radial and diameter dimensions and also controls how center mark lines are created with the **DIMCENTER** command. The **Arc length symbol** area controls where the arc length symbol is displayed with the **DIMARC** command, and the **Jog angle:** setting controls the angle of the jogged segment in the **DIMJOGGED** command. Figure 13-42 shows examples of settings in the **Symbols and Arrows** tab.

> **NOTE**
>
> The **Leader:** arrowhead setting is used only by the old-style **QLEADER** command. Use the **Multileader Style Manager** introduced to control the arrowhead for the default leader type.

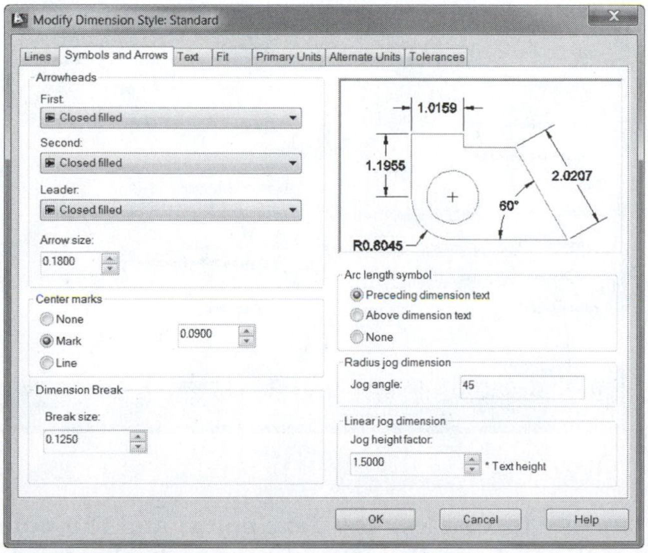

Figure 13-41
The **Symbols and Arrows** tab

The **Jog height factor:** setting controls the height of the jog created by the **Jog Line** tool explained earlier.

Text Settings. The **Text** tab (see Figure 13-43) controls how text is placed and how it looks. The **Text appearance** area allows you to set the text style used. The **...** button displays the **Style** dialog box to allow you to create and

Figure 13-42
Symbols and Arrows settings

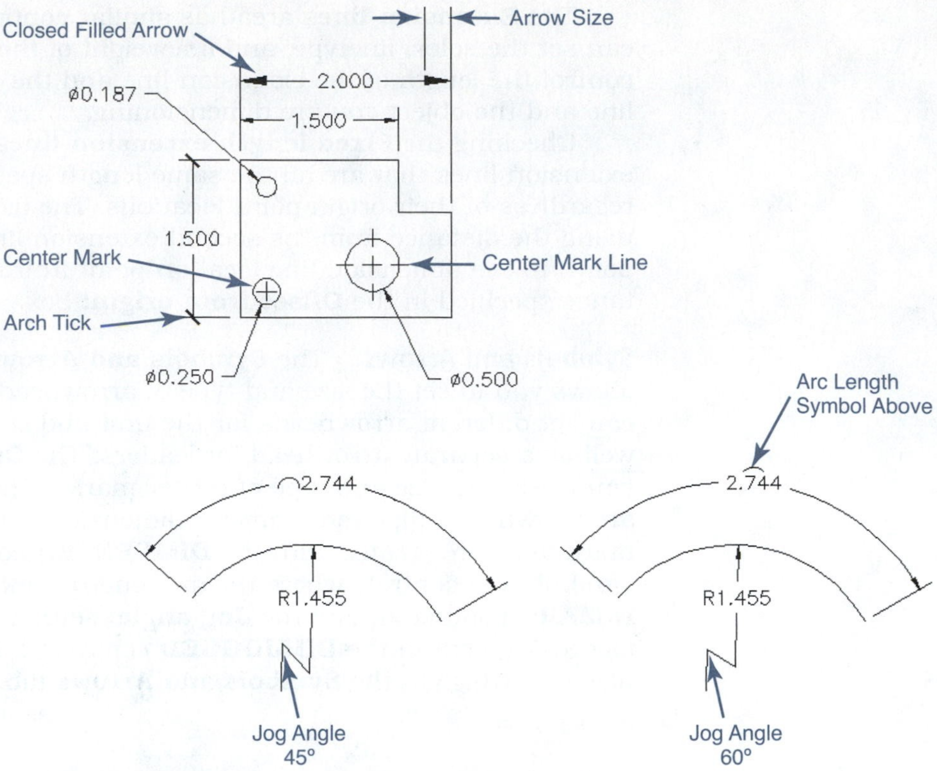

Figure 13-43
The **Text** tab

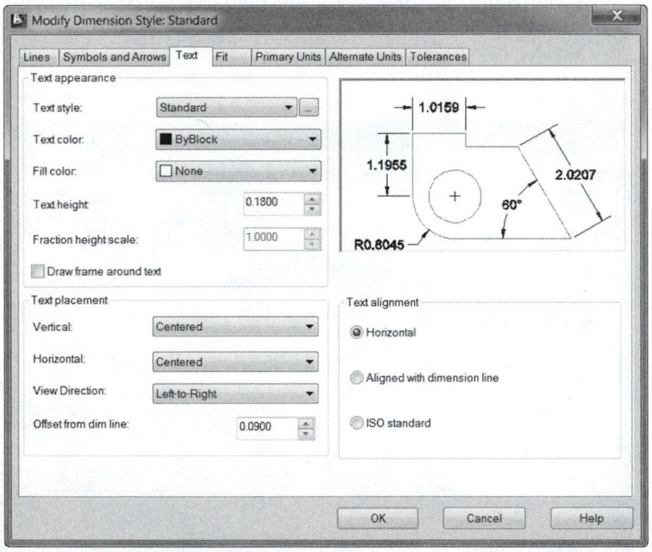

modify text styles. The **Text color:** and **Fill color:** buttons control the color of the text and the color of the text background. You can also draw a box around the text by turning on the **Draw frame around text** option.

The **Text height** and **Fraction height scale:** settings control text height. The **Fraction height scale** is a scale factor applied to numerator and denominator text in a fraction. For example, if the **Text height** is set to **.125** and the **Fraction height scale** is set to **.5**, the size of the numerator and denominator would be **.0625,** making the overall height of the fraction **.125.** Figure 13-44 shows examples of the **Text appearance** settings.

The **Text placement** area controls how text is placed in regard to the dimension lines and extension lines. The **Offset from dim line:** setting

Figure 13-44
Text appearance settings

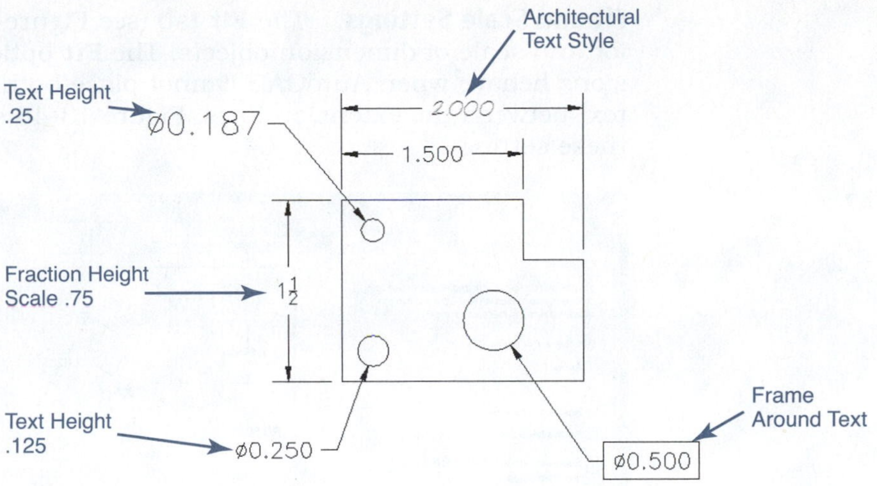

controls the gap between the dimension line and the dimension text. The **Vertical:** setting allows you to place the text above, below, or centered on the dimension line. You can also choose **JIS,** which places the dimension text to conform to the Japanese Industrial Standard. Figure 13-45 shows the effects of the **Vertical:** setting.

Figure 13-45
Vertical text settings

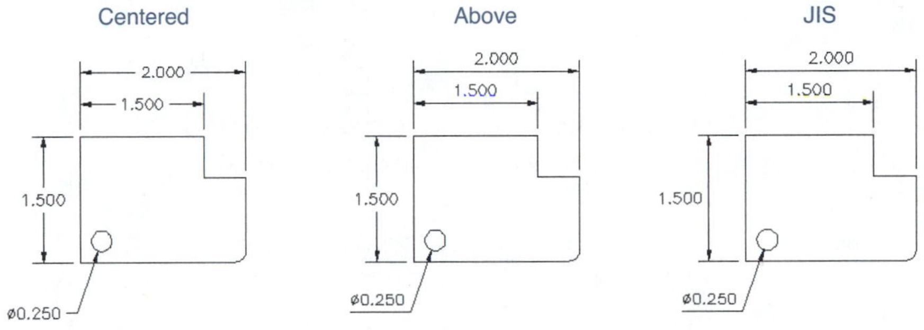

The **Horizontal:** setting controls where the text is placed in reference to the extension lines. You can place the text near the first or second extension line, or have the text drawn over the first or second extension line. Figure 13-46 shows the effects of the **Horizontal:** setting.

The **View Direction:** setting controls whether text reads from left-to-right or from right-to-left.

The **Text alignment** area controls whether text is always displayed horizontally or aligned with the dimension line. The **ISO standard** setting allows you to align text with one dimension line when text is inside the extension lines, but align it horizontally when it is outside the extension lines.

Figure 13-46
Horizontal text settings

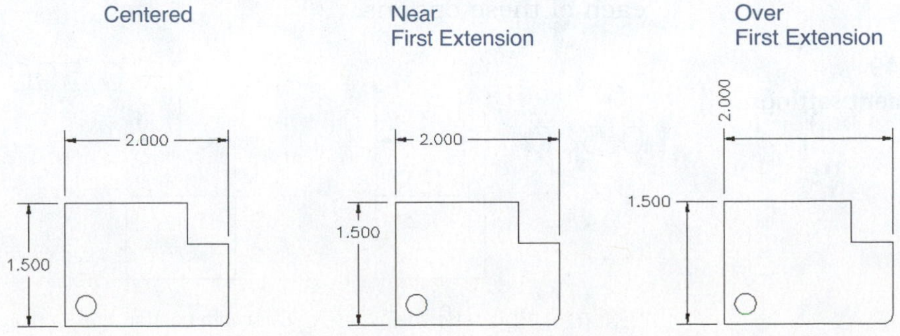

Fit and Scale Settings. The **Fit** tab (see Figure 13-47) controls the behavior and scale of dimension objects. The **Fit** options control how dimensions behave when AutoCAD cannot place both the dimension lines and text between the extension lines. Figure 13-48 shows examples of each of these settings.

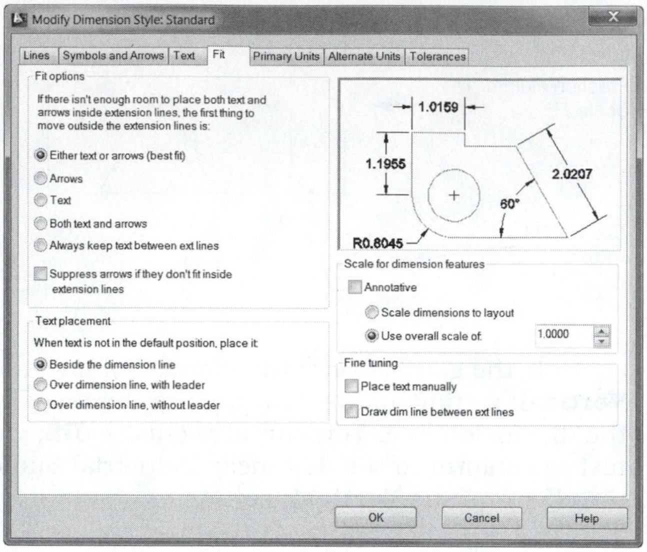

Figure 13-47
The **Fit** tab

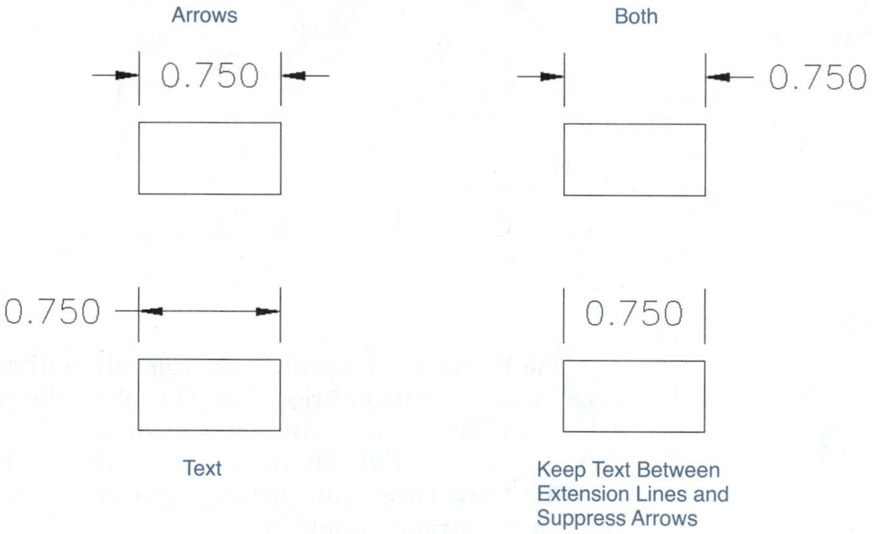

Figure 13-48
Fit options settings

The **Text placement** area controls where text is placed when it is not in its default position. You can choose to have AutoCAD move the text beside the dimension line (outside the extension line), over the dimension line with a leader line running between the text and the dimension line, or over the dimension line without a leader. Figure 13-49 shows the effect of each of these options.

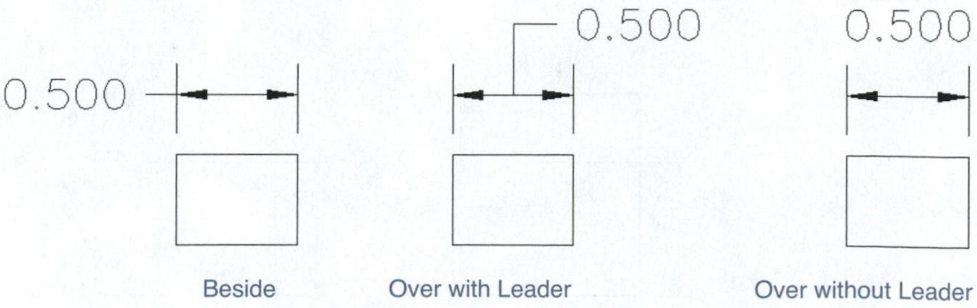

Figure 13-49
Text placement settings

Chapter 1 discussed annotation scale factors. For example, if you have a drawing plotted at a scale of 1/8″ = 1-0″, you need to scale all your model space annotation by a factor of 96. This ensures that as the drawing is scaled down for plotting, the annotation objects appear at the correct size because they have been scaled up. The **Scale for dimension features** area controls the overall annotation scale of dimension objects.

The **Annotative** scale setting utilizes the AutoCAD **Annotation Scale** feature located on the right side of the status bar so that dimension features are scaled automatically when dimensions are added to your drawing and you have calculated a scale factor.

NOTE

It's important to note that the **Scale for dimension features** setting affects only the size of dimension objects, *not* the values of the dimensions themselves.

FOR MORE DETAILS

See page 8 in Chapter 1 for a detailed description of the **Annotation Scale** feature.

The **Scale dimensions to layout** setting will automatically scale all your dimension features to match the scale of the layout viewport. This feature requires that you add dimensions through the paper space viewport so that AutoCAD knows what scale you are currently working in.

The **Use overall scale of:** setting is a manual scale factor that is applied to all dimension features. For example, if your text and arrowheads are set to a height of **.125** and the overall scale is set to **2,** AutoCAD will draw your text and arrowheads at a size of **.25.** Figure 13-50 shows an example of setting the overall dimension scale factor.

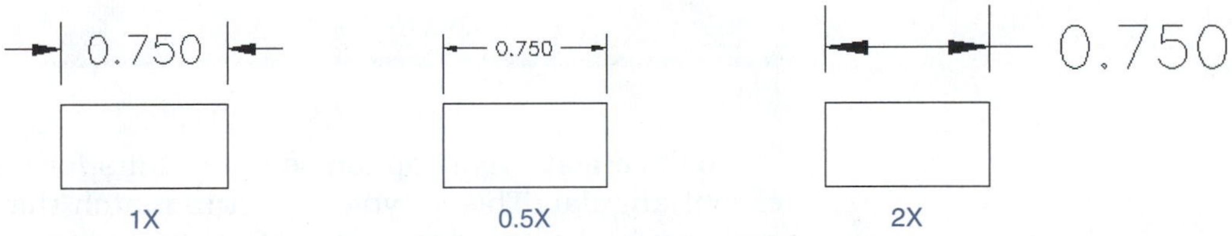

Figure 13-50
The overall dimension scale

FOR MORE DETAILS

See Chapter 14 for a detailed description of using paper space layouts and the different scale options for annotation features.

The **Fine tuning** area gives you some additional options for controlling the look of your dimension. When turned on, the **Place text manually** box adds an additional prompt when creating dimensions, which allows you to specify a location for the dimension text after you locate the dimension line.

The **Draw dim line between ext lines** option will force a dimension line to be placed between the extension lines, regardless of the location of the dimension text. Figure 13-51 shows some examples of turning on this option.

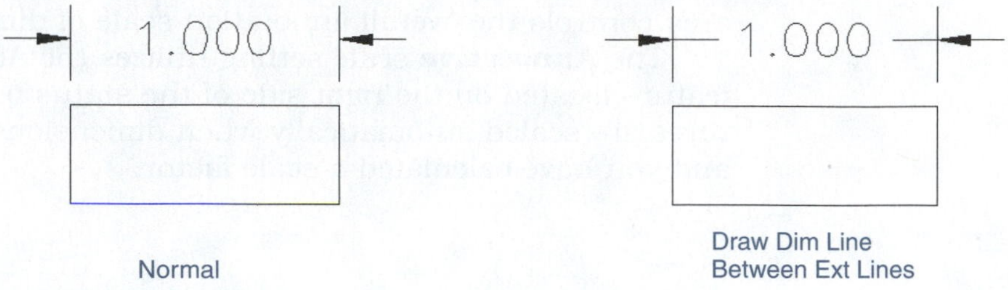

Figure 13-51
Draw dim line between ext lines options

Primary Units Tab. The **Primary Units** tab (see Figure 13-52) controls the formatting of the dimension text. The **Linear dimensions** area allows you to control how units are displayed; the **Angular dimensions** area controls the display of angular dimensions. The options are listed next.

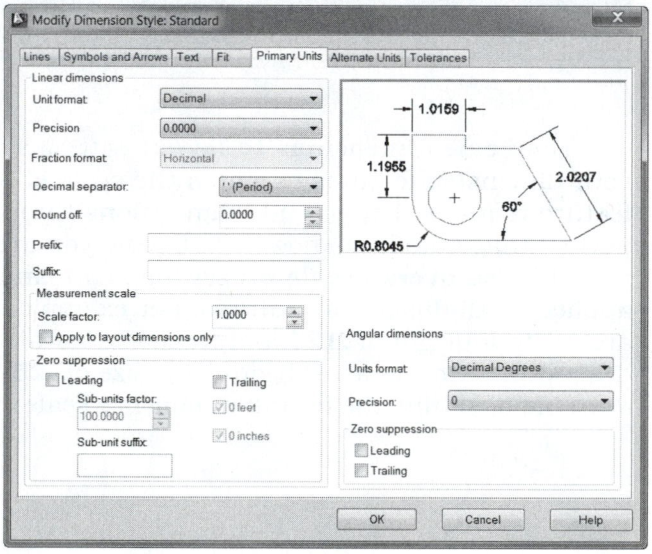

Figure 13-52
The **Primary Units** tab

Unit Format. This option sets the units format for all dimension types except angular. This is typically set to match the units of your drawing. In addition to the standard AutoCAD unit settings, you can also choose the **Windows Desktop** units, which use the settings contained in the **Region and Language** options in the Windows **Control Panel** (see Figure 13-53).

In the **Angular dimensions** area, the **Units format** list allows you to control how angular dimensions are displayed. You can choose from **Decimal Degrees, Degrees Minutes Seconds, Gradians,** or **Radian** units.

NOTE

Although it is common to set the dimension units of a dimension style the same as the display units used in the drawing, it is not required. As an example, you might have **Decimal** display units set in the drawing and **Architectural** units set in a dimension style. The separate unit settings also make it possible to create additional dimension styles with distinct dimension unit settings so that you can use different dimension standards in the same drawing.

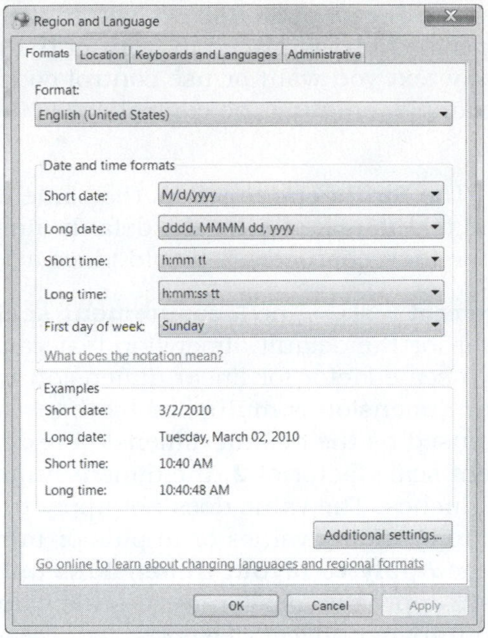

Figure 13-53
The Windows **Region and Language** dialog box

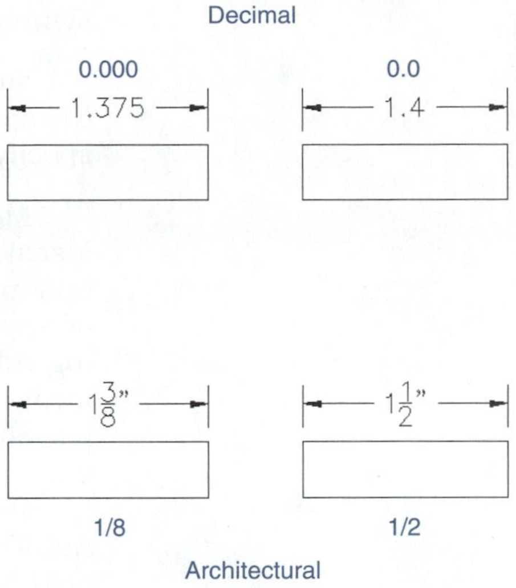

Figure 13-54
Primary Units Precision settings

Precision. This option controls the number of decimal places in the dimension text. This setting controls only how the dimension text is displayed; it does not change the drawing geometry or affect the actual measured value of the dimension. There are two settings: one for linear dimensions and one for angular dimensions. Figure 13-54 shows some examples of this setting.

Fraction Format. This controls how fractions are displayed. This option is available only when the **Unit format** is set to either **Architectural** or **Fractional.** This format is used in conjunction with the **Fraction height scale** in the **Text** tab. Figure 13-55 shows examples of these settings.

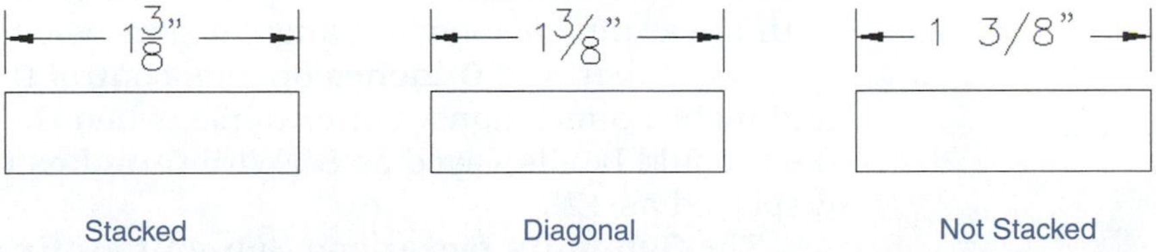

Figure 13-55
Fraction format settings

Decimal Separator. When the **Unit format** is set to **Decimal,** this option sets the character used for the decimal separator.

Round Off. This option sets the rounding rules for all dimension types except angular. If you enter a value of **0.25,** all distances are rounded to the nearest 0.25 unit. If you enter a value of **1.0,** all dimension distances are rounded to the nearest integer. The number of digits displayed after the decimal point depends on the **Precision** setting. Like the **Precision** setting, this setting affects only how dimensions are displayed; it does not change the geometry or the actual measured value of the dimension.

Prefix. The **Prefix** option allows you to set a prefix in the dimension text. The specified text is placed in front of the default dimension text. You can enter any text you want or use control codes to display special symbols. For example, entering the control code **%%c** displays the diameter symbol.

Suffix. The **Suffix** option works the same as the **Prefix** option except the specified text is placed after the default dimension text. For example, specifying the inch character (″) would place a ″ mark after each dimension.

Measurement Scale. The **Measurement scale** area allows you to define a scale factor for the default dimension text values. The **Scale factor** option sets a scale factor for linear dimension measurements. The value of any linear dimension is multiplied by this scale factor, and the resulting value is used as the default dimension text. For example, if you set a measurement scale factor of **2**, the dimension text for a 1-inch line is displayed as 2 inches. The value does not apply to angular dimensions and is not applied to rounding values or to plus or minus tolerance values.

When the **Apply to layout dimensions only** option is turned on, AutoCAD will apply the measurement scale value only to dimensions created in layout (paper space) viewports.

NOTE

- When you enter a prefix, it replaces any default prefixes such as those used in diameter and radius dimensioning. If you specify tolerance values, the prefix is added to the tolerance text as well as to the regular dimension text.
- Do not confuse the **Measurement scale** with the **Use overall scale of** setting located on the **Fit** tab discussed earlier. The **Measurement scale** factor changes the numerical value of a dimension so that it no longer represents the actual length in the drawing. The **Use overall scale of** setting, or dimension scale, affects only the appearance of dimension features such as arrowheads and text size. The numerical dimension value always reflects its true length.

Zero Suppression. These options control the display of leading and trailing zeros in dimension text. For example, when set to decimal units, turning on the **Leading** option means that a dimension value of 0.5000 would be shown as .5000. With the **Trailing** option turned on, a dimension of 12.5000 would be displayed as 12.5. There are separate settings for both linear dimensions and angular dimensions.

The **0 feet** and **0 inches** options control the display of zeros in feet and inches dimensions. For example, when the **0 feet** option is turned on, 0′-8″ would be displayed as 8″. With **0 inches** turned on, 12′-0″ would be displayed as 12′.

The **Sub-units factor** and **Sub-unit suffix** settings allow you to specify a subunits factor and suffix so that when a dimension value is less than 1, you can switch to smaller units instead of displaying a leading zero.

Alternate Units Tab. The **Alternate Units** tab (see Figure 13-56) allows you to show dimensions in two different formats. A typical example of this is to show both inch and millimeter dimensions such as **2.00 [50.8 mm].** The **Alternate Units** tab contains settings that are similar to the **Primary Units** tab. To enable alternate units, select the **Display alternate units** box. Once this is selected, the remaining options are enabled.

The **Unit format** and **Precision** options work the same as the **Primary Units** tab settings. When using fractional unit formats (**Architectural** and **Fractional**), you can choose between stacked or unstacked fractions.

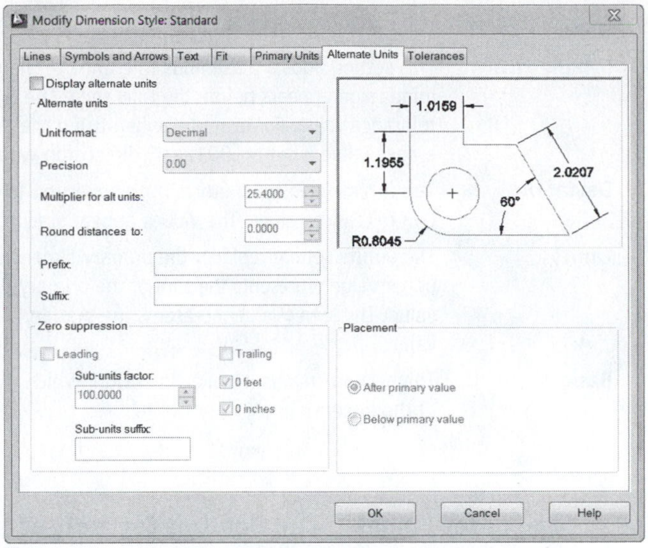

Figure 13-56
The **Alternate Units** tab

Multiplier for Alternate Units and Round Distances To. The **Multiplier for alt units:** setting specifies the conversion factor between the primary units and the alternate units. For example, to convert inches to millimeters, specify a multiplier of 25.4. The value has no effect on angular dimensions. The **Round distances to:** setting allows you to apply a rounding value to the alternate dimensions. This rounding value is independent of the primary units round-off value.

Prefix and Suffix and Zero Suppression. The **Prefix** and **Suffix** values work the same as for the primary units. To place an mm notation after the alternate dimensions, set the suffix to **mm.** The **Zero suppression** settings also work the same as the **Primary Units** tab settings.

Placement. This controls where the alternate units are displayed. You can choose between **After primary value** and **Below primary value.**

The Tolerances Tab. The **Tolerances** tab allows you to control the display and values of tolerances for both primary and alternate units. The **Zero suppression** and **Precision** settings work the same way as the primary and alternate units settings but control only the tolerance values. The **Upper** and **Lower** values control the upper and lower limits of the tolerance settings.

Method. The **Method** setting controls how the tolerances are displayed. These settings are described next. Figure 13-57 shows an example of each setting.

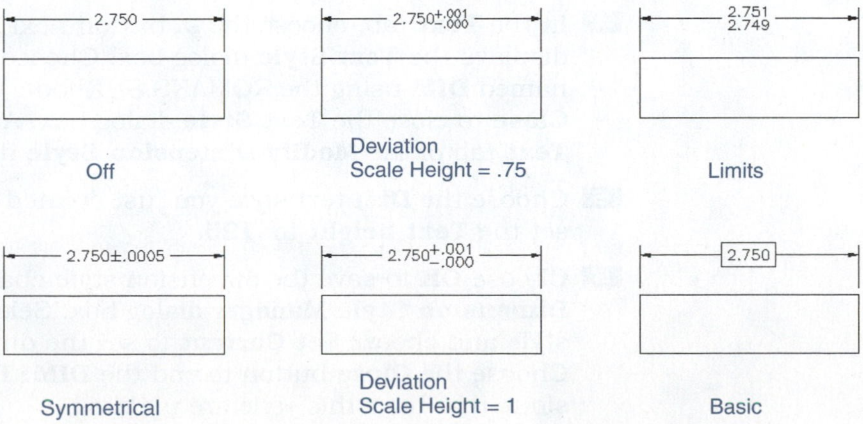

Figure 13-57
The tolerance **Method** settings

None	This setting turns off the tolerance display.
Symmetrical	This setting adds a plus/minus tolerance to the dimension measurement. A plus or minus sign appears before the tolerance. The **Symmetrical** setting uses the upper tolerance value. For example, when using the **Symmetrical** setting, if the upper tolerance value is set to **.001,** a 1″ dimension would be displayed as 1.0060.001.
Deviation	This is similar to symmetrical but allows you to display separate upper (+) and lower (−) tolerance values. The values appear stacked after the primary dimension.
Limits	The **Limits** setting replaces the primary dimension value with two stacked values. The upper value represents the sum of the primary dimension and the upper tolerance value. The lower value represents the primary dimension minus the lower tolerance value.
Basic	This setting creates a basic dimension, which displays a box around the full extents of the dimension.

Scaling for Height. The **Scaling for height** setting controls the relative size of the tolerance text. The value is a scale factor, which is multiplied by the primary unit text height. For example, if you set a **Scaling for height** value of **.5,** the tolerance text would be half the size of the primary units. This is primarily used with the **Deviation** and **Limits** methods.

Vertical Position. This option controls the vertical location of the primary dimension text in relation to the tolerance text. You can choose either **Top, Middle,** or **Bottom.** Figure 13-58 shows examples of the **Vertical position** setting.

Figure 13-58
Vertical position settings

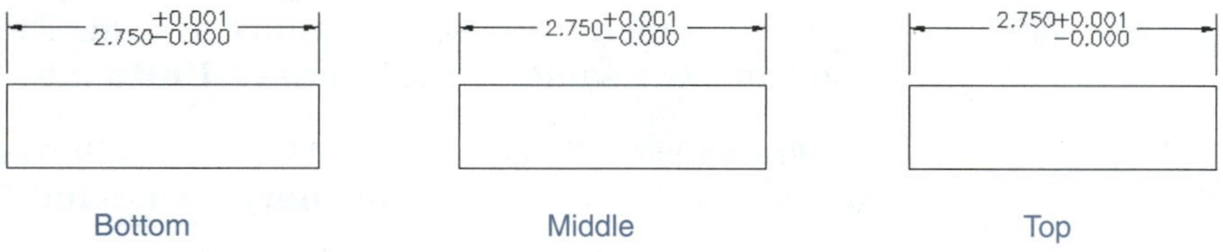

EXERCISE 13-10 Modifying an Existing Dimension Style

1. Continue from Exercise 13-9. Start the **DIMSTYLE** command to display the **Dimension Style Manager** dialog box.
2. Choose the **Mech** dimension style and choose the **Modify...** button. This will display the **Modify Dimension Style** dialog box.
3. In the **Symbols and Arrows** tab, set the **Arrow size** to **.125.**
4. In the **Text** tab, choose the **...** button next to the **Text style** list. This displays the **Text Style** dialog box. Choose **New** and create a text style named **DIM** using the ROMANS.SHX font. Choose **Apply** and then **Close** to close the **Text Style** dialog box. AutoCAD returns you to the **Text** tab of the **Modify Dimension Style** dialog box.
5. Choose the **Dim** text style you just created in the **Text style** list, and set the **Text height** to **.125.**
6. Choose **OK** to save the dimension style changes and return to the **Dimension Style Manager** dialog box. Select the **Mech** dimension style and choose **Set Current** to set the dimension style current. Choose the **Close** button to end the **DIMSTYLE** command. Any dimensions that have this style are updated.

7. Select the dimensions created in Exercises 13-8 and 13-9 and change their dimension styles to **Mech** by selecting the **Mech** style from the **Dimension Style** drop-down list on the expanded **Annotation** panel on the **Home** tab of the ribbon.

8. Save your drawing. Your drawing should resemble Figure 13-59.

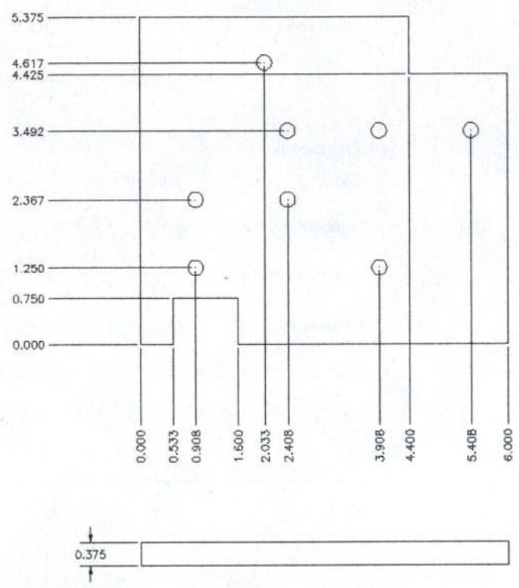

Figure 13-59
The modified dimension style

Modifying Dimension Styles Versus Overriding Dimension Styles

When modifying dimensions, any changes made to the dimension style will affect all the dimensions that use that style. There may be times when you want to change the settings for a single dimension without making changes to the dimension style. In this case, a dimension override is what you need.

A dimension override allows you to make changes to dimension settings without applying them to the dimension style. Once you make a dimension override, any new dimensions will be placed with the settings of the dimension override until that override is changed or deleted. The dimension objects created with the override will retain the override setting until the dimension style is reapplied to the dimension.

> **NOTE**
> A dimension override is similar to hard-coding object properties. For example, Chapter 6 showed how an object can have color, linetype, lineweight, and transparency settings that are different from the layer setting.

Overriding a Dimension Style. To create a dimension override, choose the **Override...** button from the **Dimension Style Manager** dialog box. When you choose this button, AutoCAD displays the **Override Current Style** dialog box (see Figure 13-60). This dialog box is the same as the **Modify Dimension Style** dialog box and allows you to make changes to the current dimension style settings. The difference is that the changes are not applied to the dimension style, but are stored in a **<style overrides>** setting that appears as a child style of the parent dimension (see Figure 13-61).

Once you create an override, the override settings are set current and are applied to all new dimensions.

Figure 13-60
The **Override Current Style** dialog box

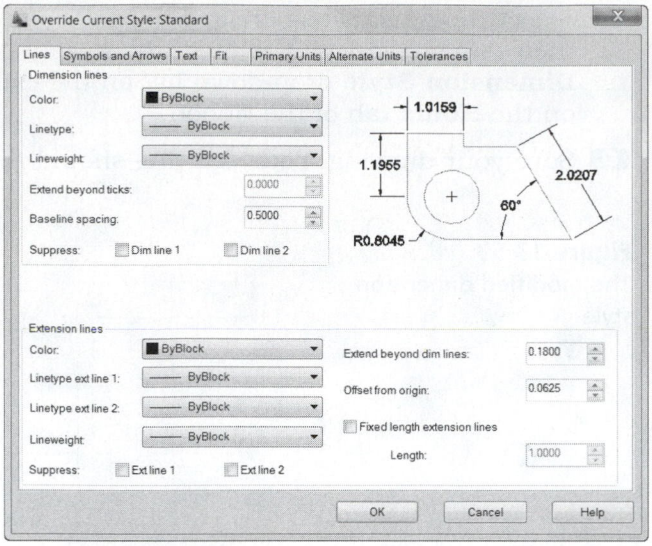

Figure 13-61
A dimension style override

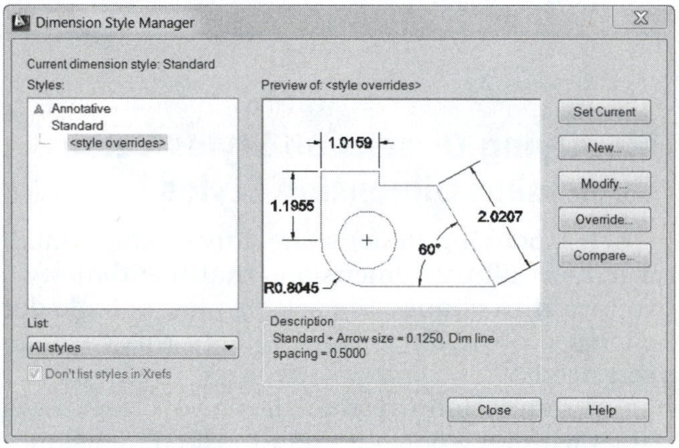

Dimension Variables. Another way to create a dimension override is to change the dimension variables directly. The dimension variables are system variables that control the dimension settings. When you make changes to the dimension style, its corresponding dimension variable is also set accordingly. A dimension style is basically a collection of these dimension variable settings. AutoCAD's dimension variables are listed in Appendix D. To change a dimension variable, just type the variable name and set the value. When you change a dimension variable, AutoCAD creates a dimension style override.

Saving an Override to a Style. If you decide you want to keep the override setting, you can save the setting to the current dimension style, making the changes permanent. To make the dimension overrides permanent, right-click on the **<style overrides>** in the **Dimension Style Manager** dialog box in the **DIMSTYLE** command, and choose **Save to current style** in the menu. Doing this will apply the dimension override settings to all the dimensions that use the current style.

NOTE

When you save a style override to a new dimension style, any dimensions created with the style overrides keep their original dimension style and the override settings. They are not changed to the new dimension style.

You can also save the dimension override settings to a new dimension style. To do this, right-click on the **<style overrides>** in the **Dimension Style Manager** dialog box in the **DIMSTYLE** command and choose **Rename.** You can then type in a name for the new dimension style. When you press **<Enter>,** AutoCAD will save the dimension style overrides to a new dimension style and move that style to the top level in the style list.

Deleting an Override. There are two ways to delete a style override. One way is to set another dimension style current. AutoCAD will display an **Alert box** stating that the overrides will be deleted (see Figure 13-62). Choose **Yes** to delete the current style override.

> **NOTE**
>
> When you delete a style override, any dimensions created with the style overrides keep their override settings.

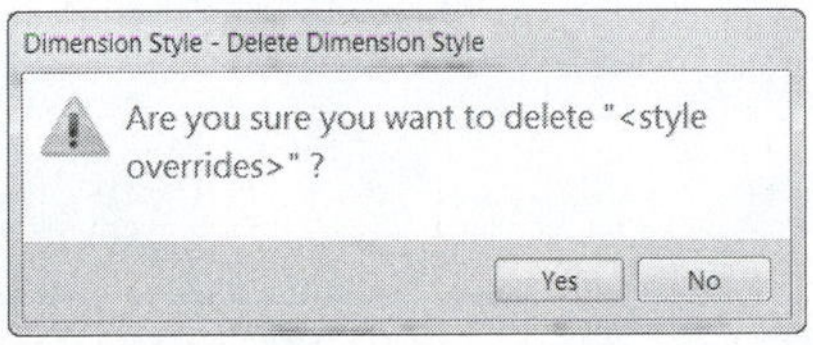

Figure 13-62
Delete overrides **Alert box**

Another way to delete an override is to select the override name in the **Dimension Style Manager** dialog box and press the **<Del>** key on your keyboard. You can also right-click on the override name and choose **Delete** from the menu. AutoCAD will ask whether you're sure you want to delete the override. Choose **Yes** to delete the override.

EXERCISE 13-11 Overriding a Dimension Style

1. Continue from Exercise 13-10.
2. Start the **DIMSTYLE** command. AutoCAD displays the **Dimension Style Manager** dialog box. Select the **Mech** dimension style and choose the **Override...** button. AutoCAD displays the **Override Current Style** dialog box.
3. In the **Tolerances** tab, set the **Method** to **Deviation.** Set the **Upper Value** to **.005** and the **Lower Value** to **0.** Set the **Scaling for height** to **.5** and turn on the **Leading** zero suppression. Choose **OK** to finish creating the overrides. AutoCAD returns you to the **Dimension Style Manager** dialog box. You should see the override listed as a child style of the **Mech** dimension style (see Figure 13-63). Choose **Close** to end the **DIMSTYLE** command.

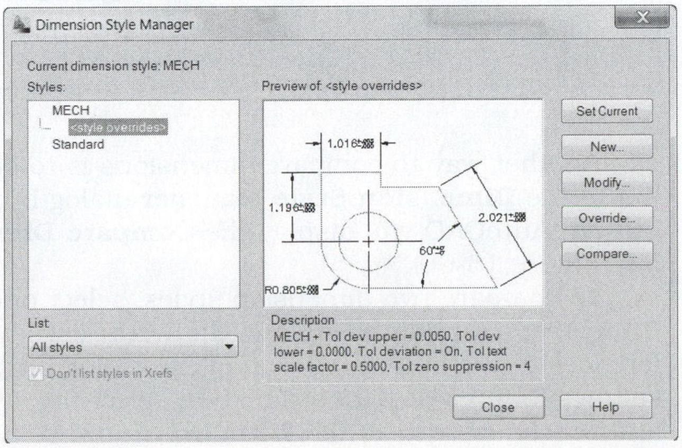

Figure 13-63
The **Mech** dimension style override

4 Start the **DIMDIAMETER** command and select the circle shown at P1 in Figure 13-64. Place the dimension as shown. The new dimension has the settings of the override while the existing dimensions remain unchanged.

5 Save your drawing. Your drawing should look like Figure 13-64.

Figure 13-64
Overriding a dimension style

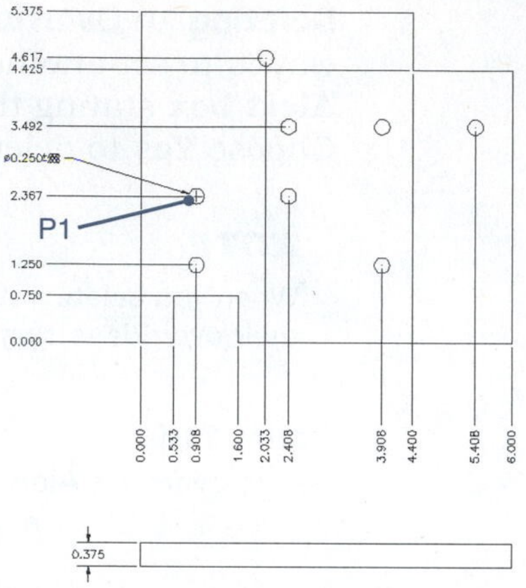

Comparing Dimension Styles

If you have a dimension style override or more than one dimension style, it is often helpful to know the differences between these styles. AutoCAD can compare two dimension styles and tell you which settings are different. When you select a dimension style in the **Dimension Style Manager** dialog box, AutoCAD will give you a description of the dimension style. If that style was based on an existing dimension style, AutoCAD will list the changes in the **Description** area (see Figure 13-65).

Figure 13-65
The **Description** area of the **Dimension Style Manager** dialog box

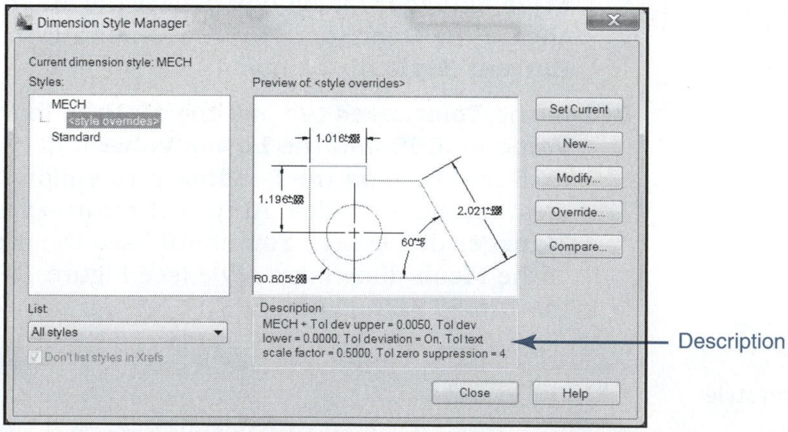

Another way to compare dimensions is to choose the **Compare...** button in the **Dimension Style Manager** dialog box. When you choose this button, AutoCAD will display the **Compare Dimension Styles** dialog box (see Figure 13-66).

To compare two dimension styles, select one dimension style in the **Compare:** list and one style in the **With:** list. AutoCAD will display the differences in the bottom portion of the dialog box. To see a listing of all the settings for a given dimension style, select the style in the **Compare:** list and choose **<none>** in the **With:** list. AutoCAD will list all the dimension

Figure 13-66
The **Compare Dimension Styles** dialog box

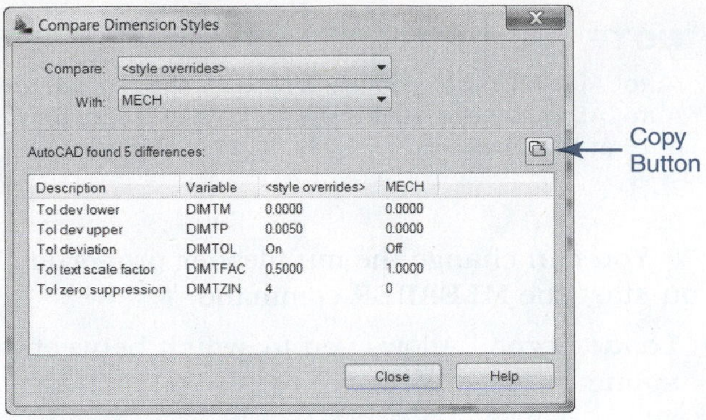

settings for that style. You can copy the list of results to the Windows Clipboard by choosing the **Copy** button (see Figure 13-66). The list is copied as tab-separated text, which can then be pasted into another Windows application.

Creating Leaders

Leaders are used for a variety of items when annotating a drawing, such as manufacturing notes, detail bubbles, etc. In general, a leader consists of an end symbol (arrowhead, dot, circle, etc.), a leader line (either curved or straight), and a callout (mtext, block, tolerance, etc.). Figure 13-67 shows some different examples of leaders. Leaders are created with the **MLEADER** command.

Figure 13-67
Different types of leaders

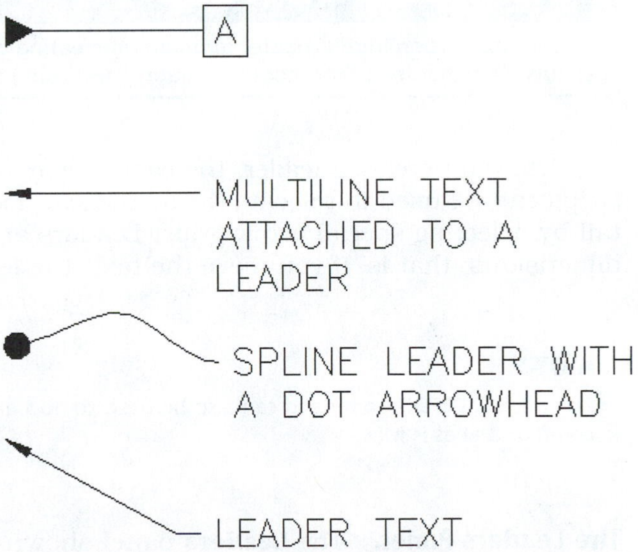

MULTILEADER	
Ribbon & Panel:	Home | Annotation Multileader
Multileader Toolbar:	
Menu:	Dimension | Multileader
Command Line:	MLEADER
Command Alias:	MLA

The Multileader Tool

By default, when you start the **MLEADER** command, AutoCAD prompts you to *Specify leader arrowhead location or* ↓ so that you first select the arrowhead location. AutoCAD then prompts you to *Specify leader landing location or* ↓. Picking a point creates the landing, or tail of the leader, and puts you in the multiline text editor so you can begin adding text.

It is possible to create a leader by locating either the arrowhead, the landing, or text first. You can specify which option to use via the command options when you start the **MLEADER** command or via a right-click menu. The method you specify remains in effect for subsequent leaders.

NOTE

AutoCAD's **MLEADER** command replaces the **QLEADER** command, which created AutoCAD quick leaders. It is still possible to create quick leaders by entering **QLEADER** or **LE** at the keyboard.

You can change the multileader properties by selecting **Options** when you start the **MLEADER** command:

- **Leader type** Allows you to switch between straight line segments and a spline
- **Leader landing** Turns the leader landing (tail) on or off
- **Content type** Allows you to specify whether to use text, a block, or nothing
- **Maxpoints** The maximum number of pick points used to create a leader. Default value is two points
- **First angle** Allows you to constrain the angle of the first line to a specific angle increment
- **Second angle** Allows you to constrain the angle of the second line to a specific angle increment

You must use the **Exit** option to exit the **Options** settings and begin drawing leaders.

FOR MORE DETAILS

See the next section in this chapter for more on creating geometric dimension and tolerance callouts. See Chapter 16 for more on creating and using blocks.

After you create a leader, the easiest way to edit it is by using grips. Grips can be used to relocate the arrowhead location and resize a leader tail by selecting special arrow grips. Leaders are associative just like dimensions; that is, if you move the text, the leader line will follow.

NOTE

The **MLEADEREDIT** command can also be used to add and remove leader lines. The command alias is **MLE**.

The Leaders Panel. The **Leaders** panel shown in Figure 13-68 provides quick access to all the commands and options discussed so far plus some additional useful multileader tools.

Using the **Leaders** panel, you can create new multileaders, add and remove leader lines, align multiple leaders, combine multiple block-type multileaders into a single multileader, and manage multileader styles.

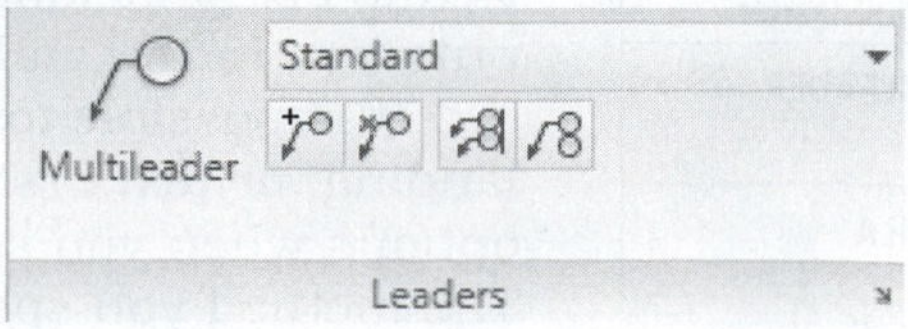

Figure 13-68
The **Leaders** panel

ADD LEADER	
Ribbon & Panel:	Home | Annotation Add Leader
Multileader Toolbar:	
Command Line:	None
Command Alias:	None

The Add Leader Tool.

You might be wondering about the word *multi* in the multileader name. The **Add Leader** tool allows you to add one or more leaders and arrowheads to an existing multileader object so that it points to multiple features. All the additional leader lines remain associated with the original leader so that if the text moves, so do the leader lines.

When you select the **Add Leader** tool, AutoCAD prompts you to *Specify leader arrowhead location:* so that you can select as many arrowhead locations as needed. You must press **<Enter>** to end the command.

> **TIP**
> It is also possible to add and remove multileaders by selecting the multileader and right-clicking to display the shortcut menu in Figure 13-69.

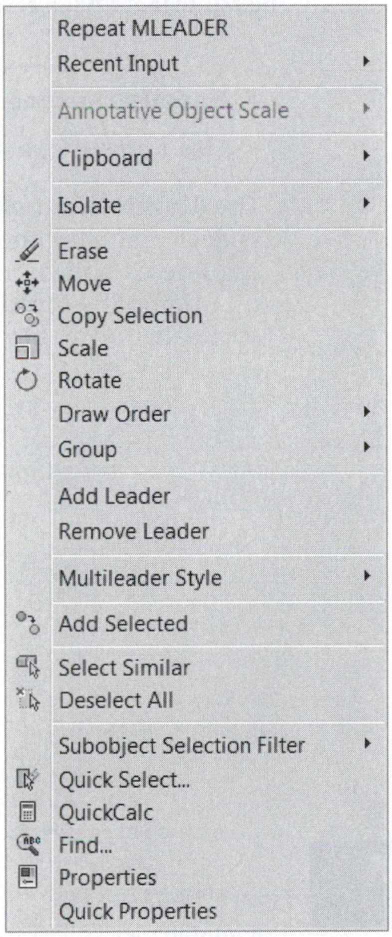

Figure 13-69
The **Multileader** right-click menu

REMOVE LEADER	
Ribbon & Panel:	Home | Annotation Remove Leader
Multileader Toolbar:	
Command Line:	None
Command Alias:	None

ALIGN	
Ribbon & Panel:	Home | Annotation Align
Multileader Toolbar:	
Menu:	None
Command Line:	MLEADERALIGN
Command Alias:	MLA

The Remove Leader Tool.

The **Remove Leader** tool allows you to remove one or more leaders from an existing multileader.

When you select the **Remove Leader** tool, AutoCAD prompts you to *Select a multileader:* so you can select the multileader to update. AutoCAD then prompts you to *Specify leaders to remove:* so that you can continue to remove leaders until you press **<Enter>** to end the command.

The Multileader Align Tool.

The **Multileader Align** tool allows you to quickly align a group of leaders along a line that you specify as shown in Figure 13-70.

You can control the leader spacing by selecting **Options** when you start the **Multileader Align** tool:

- **Distribute** Distributes leaders evenly (default)
- **Make leader segments Parallel** Makes angle portion of leader lines parallel

COLLECT	
Ribbon & Panel:	Home | Annotation  Collect
Multileader Toolbar:	
Menu:	None
Command Line:	MLEADERCOLLECT
Command Alias:	MLC

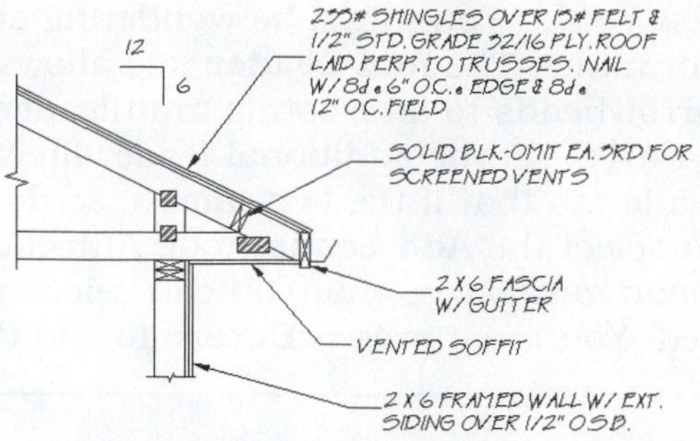

Leaders Before Using Multileader Align Tool

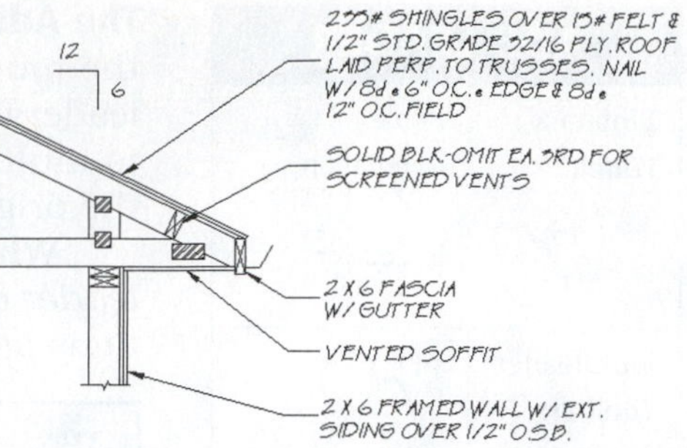

Leaders After Using Multileader Align Tool

Figure 13-70
The **Multileader Align** tool

- **Specify Spacing** Allows you to specify the spacing distance
- Use current spacing

The Multileader Collect Tool. The **Multileader Collect** tool allows you to collect and combine multiple blocks so that they are attached to one landing line as shown in Figure 13-71.

Using the **Multileader Collect** tool, blocks can be collected horizontally, vertically, or within a user-defined area.

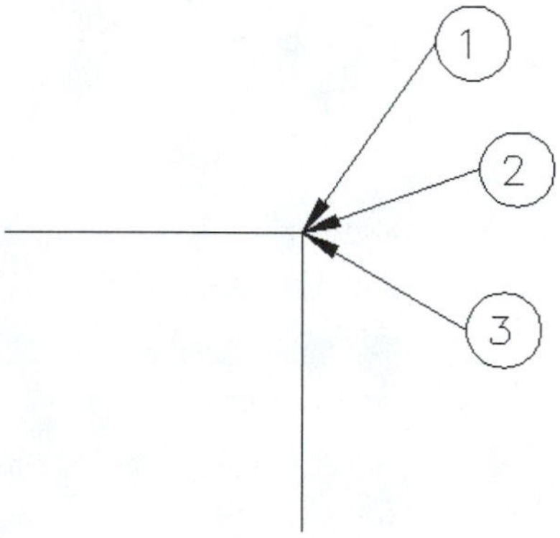

Leaders Before Using Multileader Collect Tool

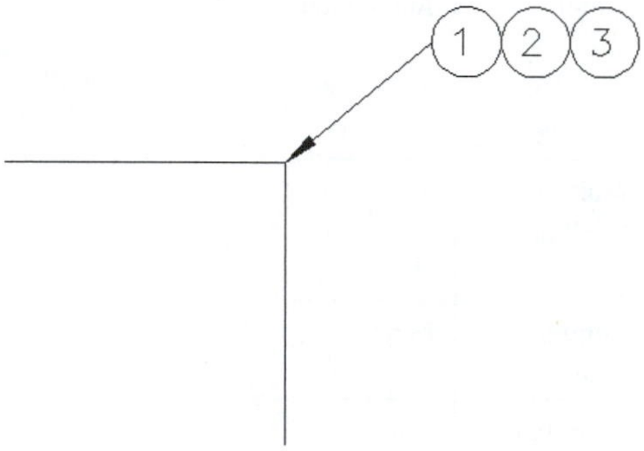

Leaders After Using Multileader Collect Tool

Figure 13-71
The **Multileader Collect** tool

MULTILEADER STYLE	
Ribbon & Panel:	Home | Annotation 
Multileader Toolbar:	
Menu:	None
Command Line:	MLEADERSTYLES
Command Alias:	MLS

FOR MORE DETAILS

See Chapter 16 for more on creating and using blocks.

Multileader Style. The **Multileader Style Manager** shown in Figure 13-72 allows you to control the multileader format and display options using a multileader style in a similar fashion to text styles, table styles, and dimension styles.

Selecting the **New...** or **Modify...** button displays the **Modify Multileader Style** dialog box shown in Figure 13-73.

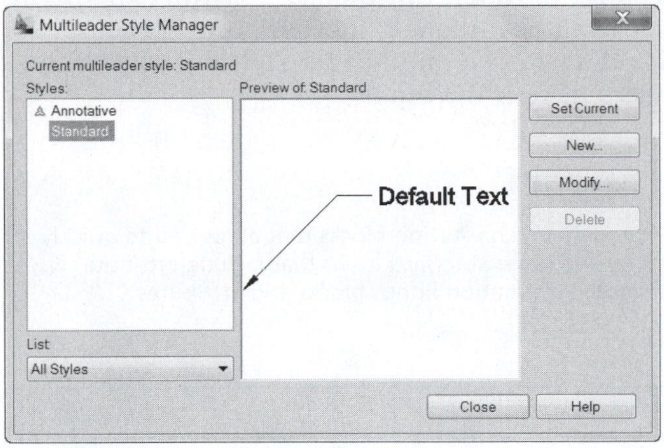

Figure 13-72
The **Multileader Style Manager**

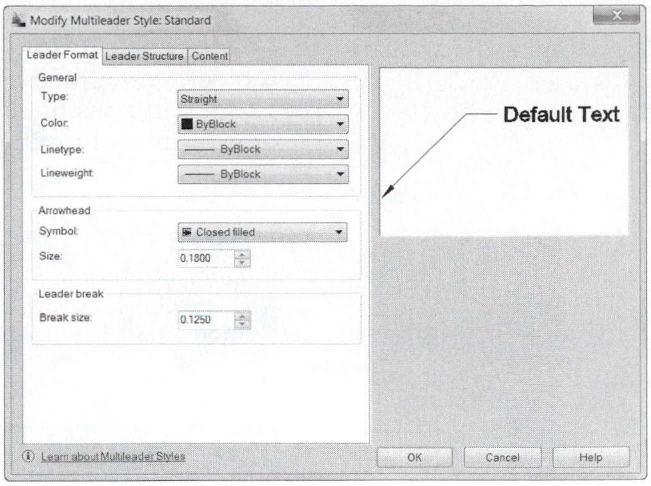

Figure 13-73
The **Modify Multileader Style** dialog box

The **Leader Format** tab (Figure 13-73) allows you to specify the type of leader line to use (straight or spline), control general properties (color, linetype, and lineweight), as well as specify the arrowhead type and size. The **Leader break** setting determines the break size for the selected multileader when the **DIMBREAK** command is used.

The **Leader Structure** tab (see Figure 13-74) allows you to control constraints such as the maximum number of points and the first and second segment angles. You can also turn the landing (tail) on and off, as well as specify its length. The **Scale** area allows you to take advantage of **Annotative** scaling, use the layout viewport scale, or specify the scale explicitly so text and arrows are created the correct size.

The **Content** tab (see Figure 13-75) allows you to indicate whether to use text, blocks, or nothing when creating leaders using the **Multileader type:** drop-down list. If you are using text, the **Text options** and **Leader connection** areas are enabled so that you can control default text, text style, angle, color, and height. The **Leader connection** area allows you to control where the text is attached and specify the gap distance between the end of the landing and the beginning of the text.

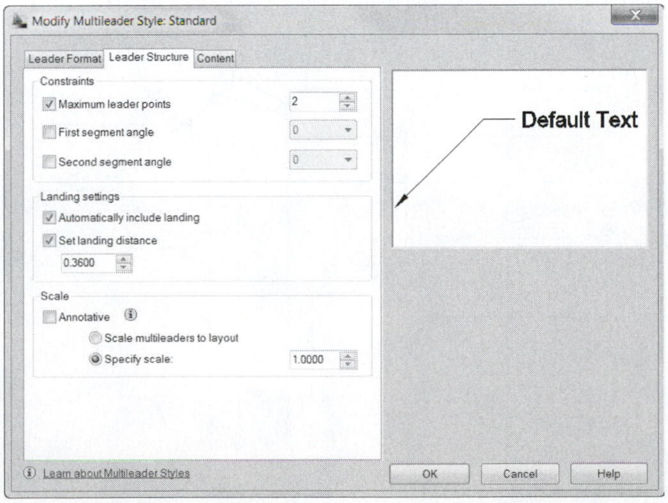

Figure 13-74
The **Leader Structure** tab

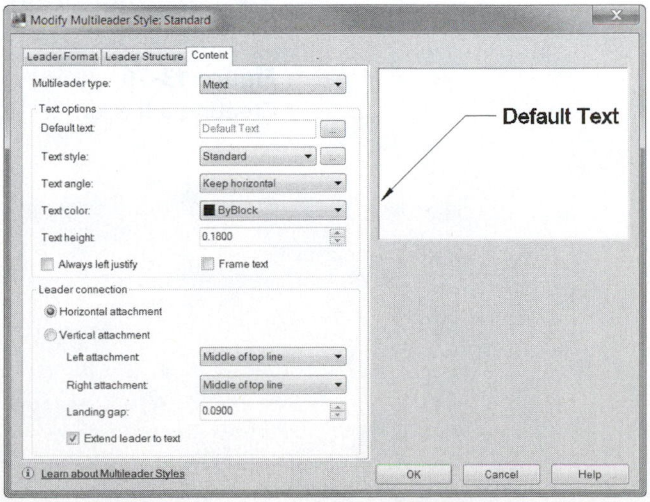

Figure 13-75
The **Content** tab

If you specify a block as the **Multileader type,** the **Text options** and **Leader connection** areas change to **Block options** so that you can specify a block name, where the block will be attached, its color, and scale.

When possible, you should try to use multileader styles to control the appearance of multiline leaders in your drawings.

> **NOTE**
>
> AutoCAD provides a number of predefined annotation blocks that allow you to quickly create detail callouts, circles, boxes, and other standard items that include attribute information. See Chapter 16 for more information about blocks and attributes.

> **TIP**
>
> The **Properties** palette also provides access to all the multileader settings discussed in this section for easy updating after a multileader is created.

EXERCISE 13-12 Creating a Leader

1. Continue from Exercise 13-11.
2. Display the **Multileader Style Manager** dialog box. Select the **Modify...** button, and on the **Leader Format** tab of the **Modify Multileader Style** dialog box, set the **Arrowhead** to **Dot** and the **Size:** to **0.125.**
3. On the **Content** tab, set the **Text height:** to **0.125** and the **Text style:** to **Dim.**
4. Choose **OK** to save the change, and close the **Multiline Style Manager** dialog box by selecting **Close.**
5. Start the **MLEADER** command. AutoCAD prompts you to *Specify leader arrowhead location or* ↓.
6. Pick the points P1 and P2 shown in Figure 13-76 and press **<Enter>** to end the point placement. AutoCAD starts the multiline text editor.
7. Type **SEE NOTE 1** and select **Close Text Editor** or click anywhere outside the multiline text editor to end the **MLEADER** command.
8. Save your drawing. Your drawing should look like Figure 13-76.

Figure 13-76
Creating a leader

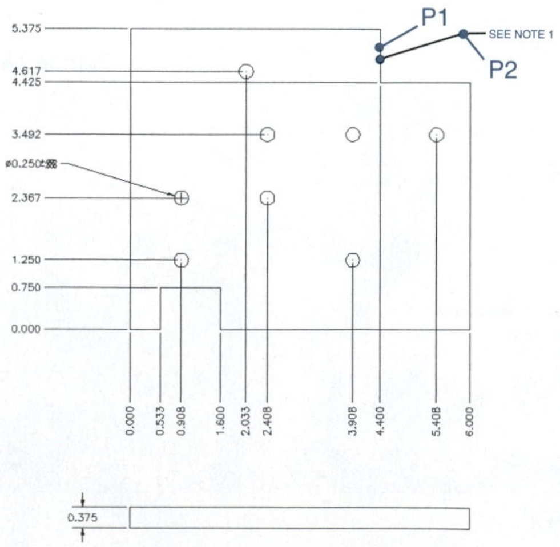

Creating Geometric Dimension and Tolerance Symbols (GD&T)

Geometric dimensioning and tolerancing (GD&T) is a method of specifying geometry requirements in mechanical engineering drawings. GD&T callouts use a series of symbols and numbers to convey specifications for mechanical parts and assemblies. Figure 13-77 shows an example of a GD&T callout (also called a *feature control frame*). GD&T is used primarily in mechanical design environments such as automotive, aerospace, electronic, and other manufacturing industries.

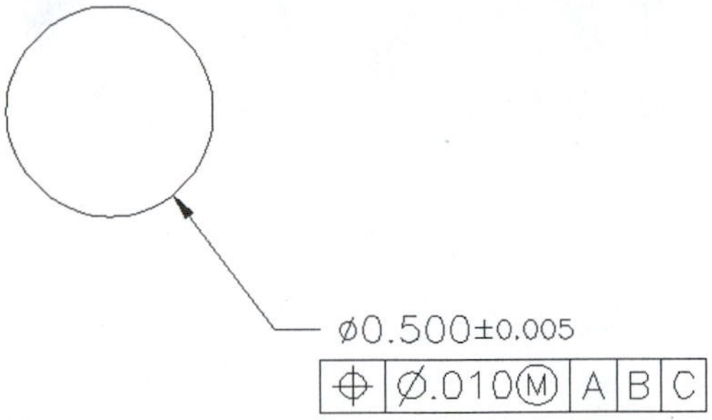

Figure 13-77
A feature control frame

TOLERANCE	
Ribbon & Panel:	Annotate | Dimensions 
Dimension Toolbar:	
Menu:	Dimension | Tolerance
Command Line:	TOLERANCE
Command Alias:	TOL

GD&T symbols denote acceptable variations in form, profile, orientation, location, and runout of a feature. You add GD&T callout symbols in feature control frames. These frames contain all the tolerance information for a single dimension. In AutoCAD, GD&T control feature frames are created with either the **LEADER** or **TOLERANCE** command. The **LEADER** command creates GD&T callouts with a leader attached to them, whereas the **TOLERANCE** command creates callouts without leaders.

FOR MORE DETAILS

Geometric tolerancing is covered by ASME Y14.5M—1994, which supersedes ANSI Y14.5M—1982. See Appendix A for more on drafting standards.

When you create a GD&T callout, AutoCAD displays the **Geometric Tolerance** dialog box (see Figure 13-78). With this dialog box, you can construct GD&T callouts. To construct a callout, work from left to right to specify the symbols and tolerance values that apply to the feature you are dimensioning. When you select the **Sym** box, AutoCAD displays the **Symbol** dialog box (see Figure 13-79).

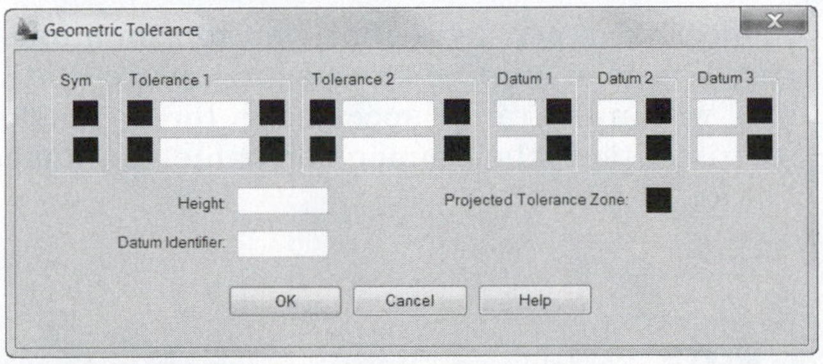

Figure 13-78
The **Geometric Tolerance** dialog box

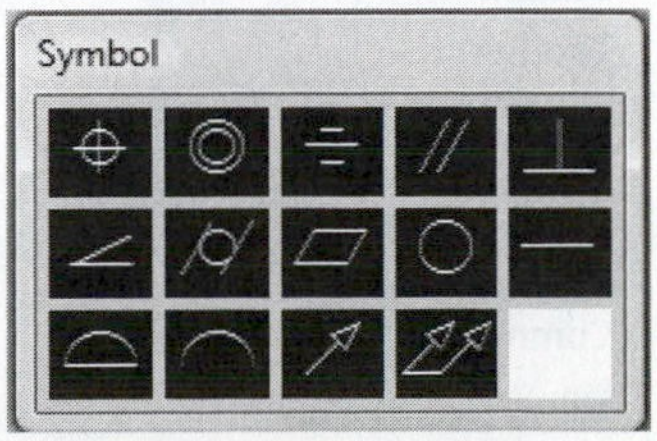

Figure 13-79
The **Symbol** dialog box

GDT Font

The GDT font used in the **TOLERANCE** command, as well as other mechanical callout symbols, can be found in the GDT.SHX font file. The GDT.SHX font uses geometric symbols for the lowercase letters a–z, and the capital roman simplex letters for the uppercase letters A–Z. The symbols used in the GDT.SHX font are shown in Figure 13-80 along with their corresponding lowercase letter representation.

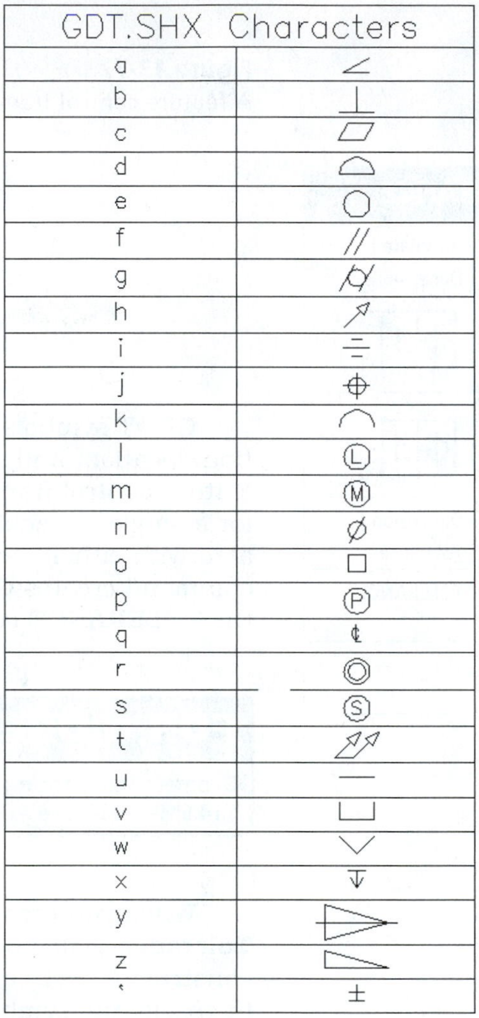

Figure 13-80
The GDT.SHX font characters

INSPECT	
Ribbon & Panel:	Annotate | Dimensions
Dimension Toolbar:	
Menu:	Dimension | Inspection
Command Line:	DIMINSPECT
Command Alias:	None

Inspection Dimensions

Inspection dimensions allow you to communicate how often manufactured parts should be checked to ensure that the tolerances of a part stay within the range specified in the dimension value. This is done using an inspection label, dimension value, and inspection rate as shown in Figure 13-81.

NOTE

You can add inspection dimensions to any type of dimension.

Figure 13-81
The **Inspection Dimension** dialog box

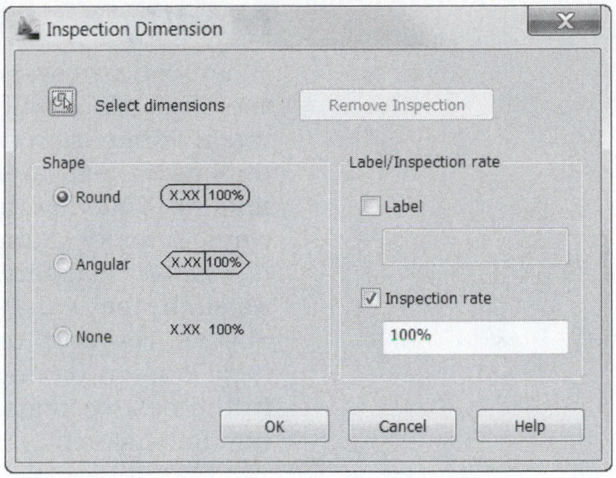

The dimension value is the value of the dimension before the inspection dimension is added. It can contain tolerances, text, and the measured value. The label and inspection rate fields are added using the **Inspection** tool explained below.

The **DIMINSPECT** command allows you to add or remove inspection dimensions and control their appearance including the shape, label, and inspection rate via the **Inspection Dimension** dialog box shown in Figure 13-81.

The **Shape** area allows you to control the type of inspection dimension shape used. You can switch between round, angular, and none.

The **Label** check box allows you to add a text label to the inspection dimensions. The label is located on the far left of the inspection dimension as shown in Figure 13-82.

The **Inspection rate** check box allows you to indicate the frequency that the dimension should be inspected and is typically expressed as a percentage. The inspection rate is located on the far right of the inspection dimension as shown in Figure 13-82.

Figure 13-82
Inspection dimension

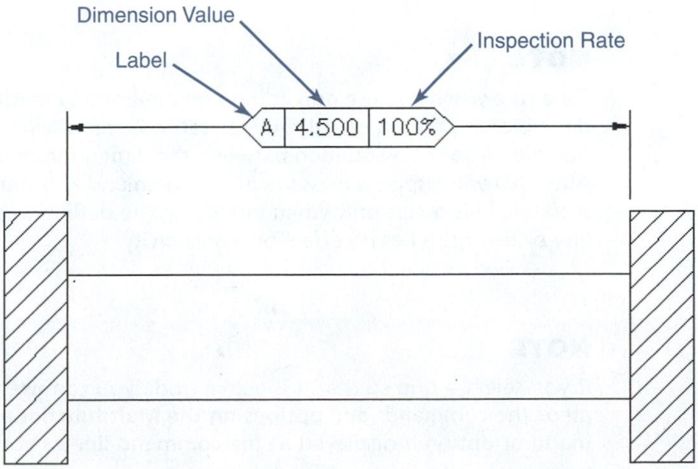

TIP

You can change the shape, label, and inspection rate of an inspection dimension after it is created using the **Properties** palette under the **Miscellaneous** category.

Modifying Dimensions

When you use associative dimensions and make changes to your geometry, the dimensions will change right along with it. However, you may need to modify dimension objects for a number of other reasons: to relocate the dimension text, to flip the arrowheads to the other side of the dimension line, or to modify the dimension text. In this section, you'll look at some ways to make changes to dimension objects.

Dimensions are objects, just as lines, arcs, circles, and text are objects. As such, they can be moved, copied, rotated, and so on just like other objects. However, unlike other objects, dimensions contain multiple parts (text, dimension lines, extension lines, etc.), and each part can be modified. In the next sections, you'll take a look at some different methods of modifying dimensions.

Grip Editing Dimensions

Grip editing is one of the easiest ways to modify dimensions. When you select a dimension object, AutoCAD will display grip edit points at the definition points, the ends of the dimension lines, and the insertion point of the dimension text. By selecting and moving these grips, you can quickly and easily modify dimension objects. Many grips are multifunctional so that if you hover your cursor over a grip, a shortcut menu similar to the one shown in Figure 13-83 is displayed. It provides access to many different dimension commands and options.

Figure 13-83
Multifunctional dimension grips

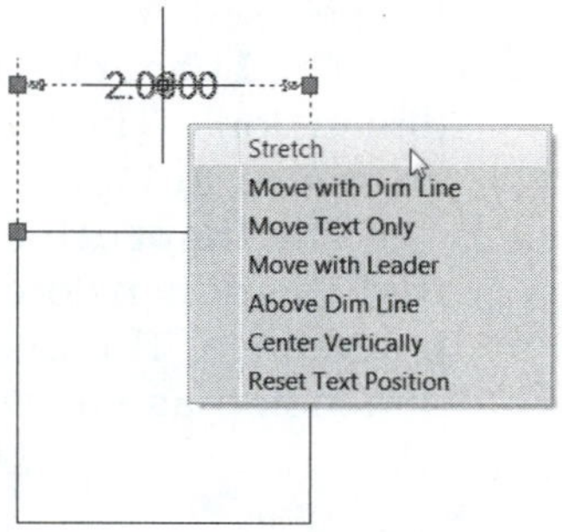

NOTE

Take care when you use grip editing on dimension definition points. If you have associate dimensioning turned on (**DIMASSOC** set to **2**), modifying the definition points of a dimension will drop the association between the dimension and its object. When this happens, AutoCAD will display a message at the command line stating: *Dimension extension disassociated*. This occurs only when modifying the definition points; modifying the dimension line or text grips has no effect on associativity.

NOTE

If you select a grip so that it is active (red), you can use the <Ctrl> key to cycle through all of the commands and options on the **Multifunctional Grip** menu. The current command or option is displayed at the command line as you cycle through.

TIP

The **Move Text Only** option found on the dimension text **Multifunctional Grip** menu is the only way to break text free from a dimension so that you can move it alone without affecting the dimension line appearance and configuration.

Right-Click Shortcut Menu

AutoCAD's right-click context menu also provides some editing abilities with dimensions. To activate the right-click menu, first select the dimension object(s) to activate its grips and then right-click anywhere on the drawing to display the menu. When dimensions are selected, the right-click menu will display the dimension-related menu options described in the following sections.

Dimension Style. This submenu allows you to apply a different dimension style to the selected dimensions. When you choose this option, you can select from a list of currently defined dimension styles. If you've made changes to the dimension and want to save those changes to a new style, choose the **Save as New Style** option. AutoCAD will display the **Save as New Dimension Style** dialog box, where you can type a new dimension style name or choose an existing dimension style name to overwrite.

Precision. This submenu allows you to modify the precision setting of the dimension text. The options for this menu change depending on the units set in the object's dimension style.

Remove Style Overrides. This submenu removes any dimension style overrides applied to the dimension.

Annotative Object Scale. This submenu is enabled only if you are using the **Annotation Scale** feature for dimensions. When enabled, this option displays a submenu with options to add or remove annotation scales so the same dimension can be used for multiple scale drawings. It is also possible to align multiple scale representations so they are in the same location using the **Synchronize Multiple-scale Positions** option.

FOR MORE DETAILS

See page 8 in Chapter 1 for a detailed description of the **Annotation Scale** feature.

EXERCISE 13-13 **Relocating Dimension Text**

To access student data files, go to **www.pearsondesigncentral.com.**

1. Open drawing ***EX13-13*** in the student data files. This drawing has a number of overlapping dimensions.
2. Select the dimension shown at P1 in Figure 13-84. Hover your cursor over the text grip to display the **Multifunctional Grip** menu, and select **Move with Leader.** AutoCAD will start dragging the dimension text. Place the dimension text as shown in Figure 13-85.

Figure 13-84
Relocating dimension text

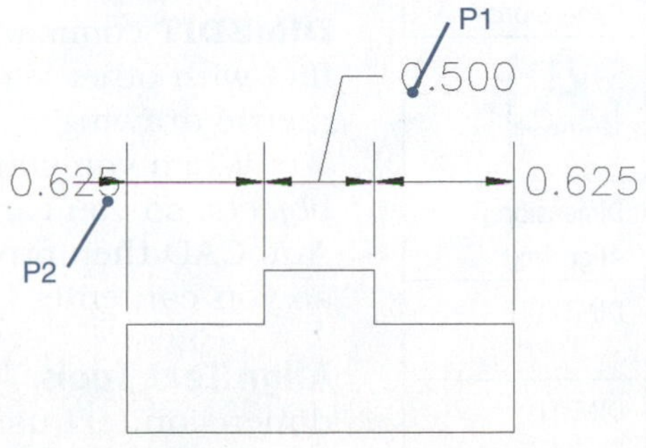

Figure 13-85
The modified dimensions

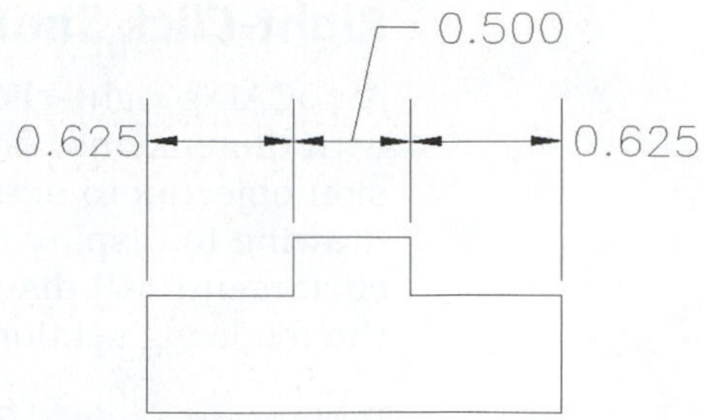

3 Select the arrowhead shown at P2 in Figure 13-84. Hover your cursor over the arrowhead grip to display the **Multifunctional Grip** menu, and select **Flip Arrow.** The arrowhead flips to the other side of the extension line.

4 Save your drawing as ***CH13_EXERCISE13.***

Modifying Dimension Text and Extension Lines

Sometimes it is necessary to modify dimension text and extension lines after a dimension has been created. The following sections provide an overview of some of the available tools and methods to replace, relocate, and modify dimension text, as well as change the angle of dimension extension lines in order to create oblique dimensions.

OBLIQUE	
Ribbon & Panel:	Annotate | Dimensions 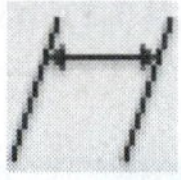
Dimension Toolbar:	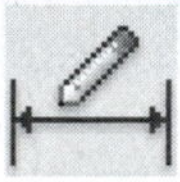
Menu:	Dimension | Oblique
Command Line:	DIMEDIT
Command Alias:	DIMED

The DDEDIT Command. The **DDEDIT** command works on dimension objects as well as regular text and mtext objects. Simply select the dimension object when you are prompted to *Select annotation object*:. AutoCAD will display the dimension text in the multiline text editor. AutoCAD's default dimension text will appear highlighted. You can place additional text before or after the default text, or replace it altogether.

If you delete the default dimension text, you can restore it by typing <> brackets in the mtext editor. AutoCAD will replace the <> brackets with the measured distance between the definition points.

> **TIP**
>
> If alternate dimensions are turned off, you can show the alternate dimension text by placing the square brackets [] along with the default brackets text <>. This works only if the default dimension text is present.

ALIGN TEXT	
Ribbon & Panel:	Annotate | Dimensions
Dimension Toolbar:	
Menu:	Dimension | Align Text
Command Line:	DIMTEDIT
Command Alias:	DIMTED

The Oblique Tool. The **Oblique** tool allows you to adjust the angle of the extension lines for linear dimensions using the **Oblique** option of the **DIMEDIT** command. The **Oblique** tool is useful when extension lines conflict with other features of the drawing or you need to dimension an isometric drawing.

When you start the **Oblique** tool, AutoCAD prompts you to *Select objects:* so you can select one or more dimensions and press **<Enter>.** AutoCAD then prompts you to *Enter obliquing angle (press Enter for none):* so you can enter the desired oblique angle.

Align Text Tools. The **Align Text** tools allow you to relocate or rotate dimension text using any of the **DIMTEDIT** command options described in the following table.

Home	This moves the dimension text back to its default position.
Angle	This changes the angle of the dimension text. Entering an angle of **0** degrees puts the text in its default orientation.
Left	This left-justifies the dimension text along the dimension line. This option works only with linear, radial, and diameter dimensions.
Center	This centers the dimension text on the dimension line.
Right	This right-justifies the dimension text along the dimension line. This option works only with linear, radial, and diameter dimensions.

EXERCISE 13-14 Editing Dimension Text and Extension Lines

To access student data files, go to **www.pearsondesigncentral.com.**

1. Open drawing ***EX13-14*** in the student data files.
2. Select the **Oblique** tool from the expanded **Dimensions** panel on the **Annotate** tab of the ribbon.
3. Select the dimensions shown at P1 and P2 in Figure 13-86 and press **<Enter>.** AutoCAD prompts you to *Enter obliquing angle (press ENTER for none):*.

Figure 13-86
Selecting dimension text

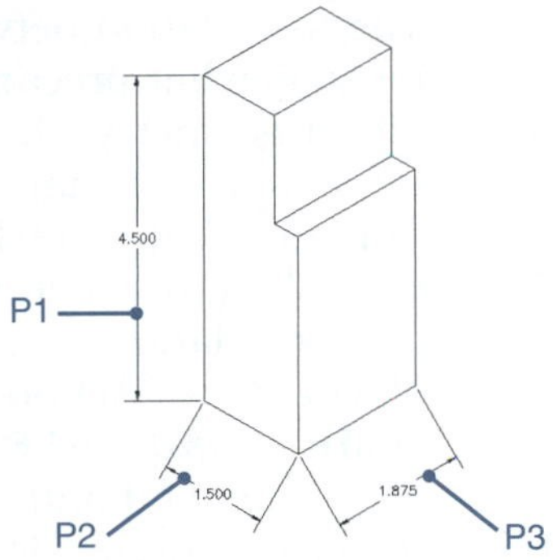

4. Type **30** and press **<Enter>.** AutoCAD adjusts the angle of the extension lines.
5. Select the **Oblique** tool again. Select the dimension shown at P3 in Figure 13-86 and press **<Enter>.**
6. Set the oblique angle to **150.** AutoCAD adjusts the extension line angle.
7. Select the **Text Angle** tool from the expanded **Dimensions** panel on the **Annotate** tab of the ribbon. AutoCAD prompts you to *Select dimension:*. Select the dimension text shown at P1 in Figure 13-86.
8. AutoCAD prompts you to *Specify angle for dimension text:*. Enter **–30** for the dimension text angle. AutoCAD rotates the dimension text.
9. Restart the **Text Angle** tool, and select the dimension shown at P2 in Figure 13-86. Enter **30** for the dimension text angle. AutoCAD rotates the dimension text.
10. Restart the **Text Angle** tool, and select the dimension shown at P3 in Figure 13-86. Enter **–30** for the dimension text angle. AutoCAD rotates the dimension text.
11. Start the **DDEDIT** command and select the dimension text P1. AutoCAD displays the multiline text editor with the default dimension

text shown. Highlight the dimension text and set the oblique angle to **30.** Choose **OK** to close the text editor.

12 Repeat step 11 with the text at points P2 and P3. Set the oblique angle to **30** and **–30**, respectively.

13 Save your drawing as ***CH13_EXERCISE14.*** Your drawing should resemble Figure 13-87.

Figure 13-87
The modified dimension text

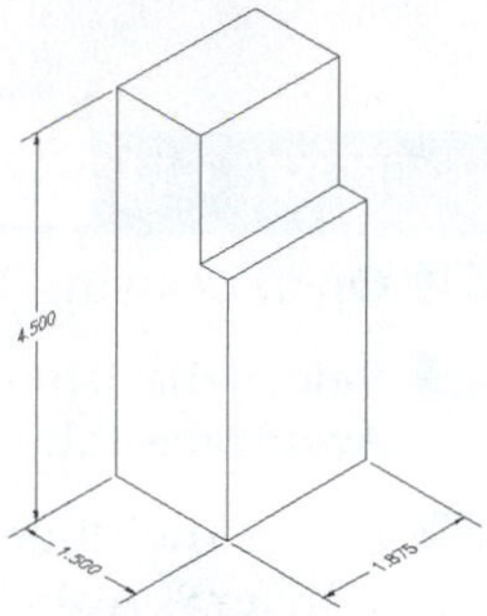

REASSOCIATE	
Ribbon & Panel:	Annotate | Dimensions 
Toolbar:	None
Menu:	Dimension | Reassociate Dimensions
Command Line:	DIMREASSOCIATE
Command Alias:	None

Reassociating Dimensions

The association between a dimension object and other drawing objects can be somewhat precarious. There are times when, in the course of editing object geometry, the original drawing objects may be redefined or modified in such a way that the objects' association with a dimension object is lost. This may happen when polylines are exploded, when objects are trimmed or broken, or when multiple objects are joined. You may want to change the association to have the dimension be associated with another drawing object. AutoCAD provides a way to change dimension associativity with the **DIMREASSOCIATE** command.

When you start the **DIMREASSOCIATE** command, AutoCAD asks you to select a dimension object. When you select a dimension object, AutoCAD places an X at the first definition point and asks you to specify a new location for it. You can simply pick a new location for the definition point or skip to the next definition point by pressing **<Enter>.** Depending on the type of dimension, AutoCAD will continue to prompt you for a new location for each definition point until the dimension is completely defined.

NOTE

The **DIMREASSOCIATE** command works only with dimension objects. If a dimension is exploded or created when the **DIMASSOC** system variable is set to **0,** the dimension text, lines, and arrows are no longer dimension objects and cannot be reassociated.

If you want to reassociate the dimension with a new object, use the **Select object** option and select a new object to associate with your dimension. The type of object you select will depend on the type of dimension you select.

EXERCISE 13-15 Reassociating a Dimension

1 Continue from Exercise 13-14.

2 Select the dimension shown at P1 in Figure 13-88. The grips for the dimension appear.

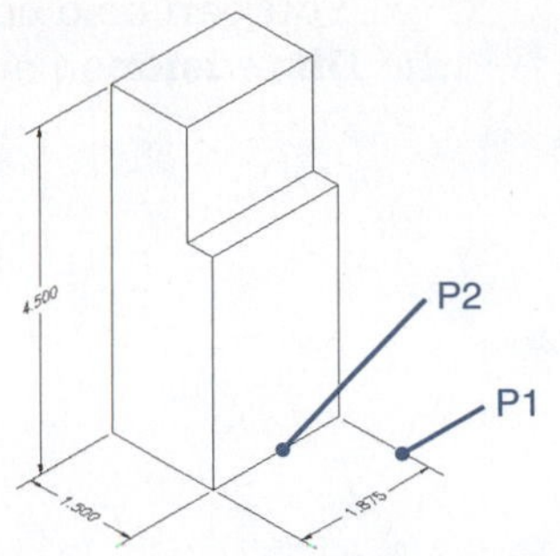

Figure 13-88
The reassociated dimension

3 Select the definition point grip shown at P1 and drag it off the object. AutoCAD displays the message *Dimension extension disassociated* at the command line. The dimension is no longer associated with the geometry.

4 Start the **DIMREASSOCIATE** command. Select the dimension you just modified and press **<Enter>.** AutoCAD places an X at the first defpoint and prompts you to *Specify first extension line origin or*↓.

5 Choose the **Select object** option and select the line shown at P2 in Figure 13-88. AutoCAD reassociates the dimension with the selected line.

6 Save your drawing.

Applying Dimension Styles

When working with multiple dimension styles, you may need to apply the settings on one style to an existing dimension. AutoCAD provides a number of ways to do this.

The Dimension Style Lists. One of the simplest ways to control the dimension styles in a drawing is via the **Dimension Style** list on the expanded **Annotation** panel on the **Home** tab of the ribbon (see Figure 13-89).

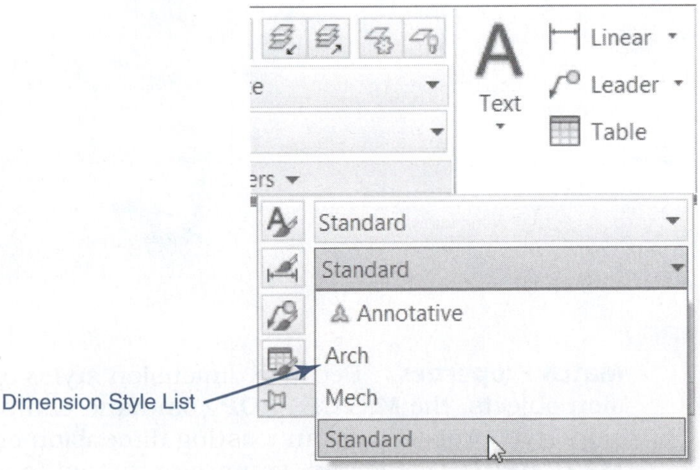

Figure 13-89
Using the **Dimension Style** list on the expanded **Annotation** panel

Selecting a dimension style from the **Dimension Style** drop-down list when no objects are selected will set the dimension style current so that any new dimensions will be created using that style. If one or more dimensions are selected so that their grips are displayed, selecting a different dimension style from the list will change the object's associated dimension styles to the new dimension style.

You can also control dimension styles via the **Dimension Style** list on the **Dimensions** panel on the **Annotate** tab of the ribbon (see Figure 13-90).

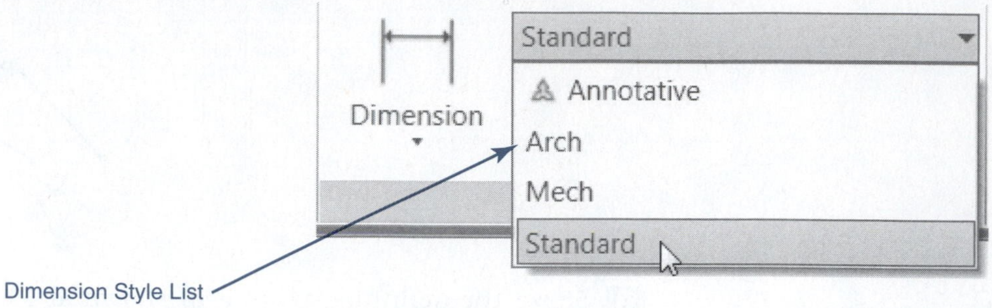

Figure 13-90
The **Dimension Style** list on the **Dimensions** panel

Properties Palette. A dimension style is simply an object property that applies only to dimension objects. Like other object properties, the **Properties** palette allows you to change the style of any selected dimension objects (see Figure 13-91). In addition to changing the style, you can also change the value of any style settings within the selected dimensions. This effectively creates dimension overrides for these dimension objects.

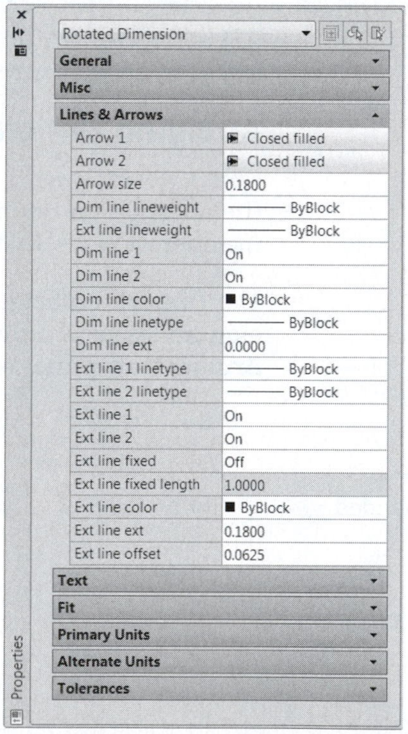

Figure 13-91
The **Properties** palette

Match Properties. Because dimension styles are just a property of dimension objects, the **MATCHPROP** command can be used to match the dimension style properties of an existing dimension object. When you start the **MATCHPROP** command, you are prompted to select a source object and then the destination object(s). The properties of the source object are applied to the destination objects.

When you use the **MATCHPROP** command, by default, all valid properties of the source object are applied to the destination objects, including layer, color, linetype, transparency, etc. To control which properties are applied, choose the **Settings** option of the **MATCHPROP** command. This will display the **Property Settings** dialog box (see Figure 13-92). This

Figure 13-92
The **Property Settings** dialog box

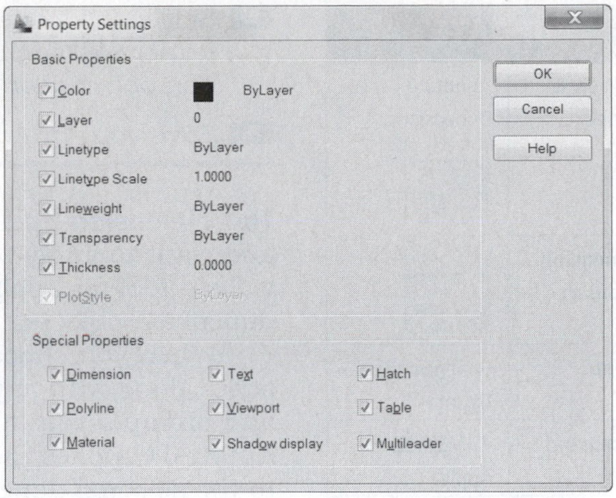

allows you to select which properties you want to apply to the destination objects. To apply only the dimension style properties, place a check in the **Dimension** box and remove the checks from all other boxes. Selecting only the **Dimension** option will filter the properties so that only the dimension style properties of the source object are applied to the destination objects.

> **TIP**
>
> It is possible to use the **MATCHPROP** command between drawings so you can select the source object in a drawing other than the destination object(s). This is a handy way to copy dimension style settings from one drawing to another without re-creating it from scratch or using **DesignCenter**.

EXERCISE 13-16 Using Match Properties to Update Dimension Styles

To access student data files, go to **www.pearsondesigncentral.com.**

1. Open drawing ***EX13-16*** in the student data files.
2. Start the **MATCHPROP** command. AutoCAD prompts you to *Select source object:*.
3. Select the leader shown at P1 in Figure 13-93. This dimension has a dimension style override for the arrowhead. AutoCAD prompts you to *Select destination object(s) or* ↓.

Figure 13-93
Matching dimension properties

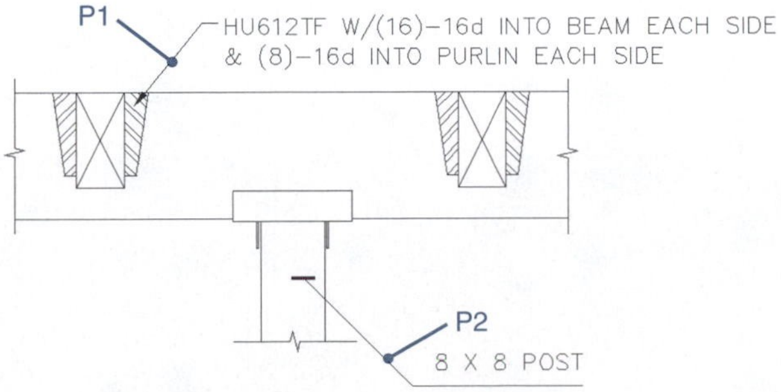

4. Choose the **Settings** option. AutoCAD displays the **Property Settings** dialog box. In the **Special Properties** area, remove the check from all the settings except **Dimension.** Press **OK** to close the dialog box. AutoCAD prompts you to *Select destination object(s) or* ↓.

UPDATE	
Ribbon & Panel:	Annotate | Dimensions 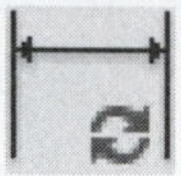
Dimension Toolbar:	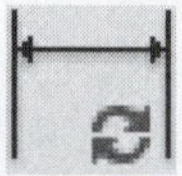
Menu:	Dimension | Update
Command Line:	-DIMSTYLE/ Apply
Command Alias:	None

5 Select the leader shown at P2 in Figure 13-93. AutoCAD updates the leader to match the source object and prompts you to *Select destination object(s) or* ↓. Press **<Enter>** to end the **MATCHPROP** command.

6 Save your drawing as ***CH13_EXERCISE16.***

The Dimension Update Tool. If you've created dimension style overrides and want to apply those overrides to an existing dimension, AutoCAD provides a tool for applying dimension styles (including overrides) to existing dimension objects.

When you choose this tool, AutoCAD lists the current dimension style, along with any overrides, at the command line (see Figure 13-94) and prompts you to *Select objects:*. Once you select the dimension object, AutoCAD applies the current dimension style settings, including overrides, to the selected dimensions.

NOTE

The **Dimension Update** tool is not technically a command. It is actually the **Apply** option of the **-DIMSTYLE** command, which is the command line version of the **DIMSTYLE** command. When you select this tool, AutoCAD starts the **-DIMSTYLE** command and automatically selects the **Apply** option.

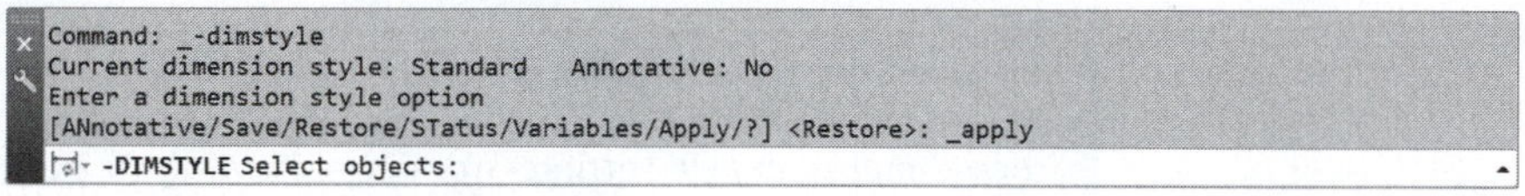

Figure 13-94
Updating dimensions

Chapter Summary

AutoCAD provides many different dimension types and settings to meet a wide array of industry standards. There are unidirectional dimensions for mechanical-type drawings and aligned dimensions for architectural standards. You can automatically insert a diameter or radial dimension with standard industry symbols by simply selecting circles or arcs. Linear dimensions can read either the actual length of objects or the distance between two points. Automatically stack dimensions using a specified spacing or chain strings of dimensions together using single pick points.

By default in AutoCAD, dimensions are associated with the geometry they are pointing to so that if the object changes, the dimensions update automatically to reflect the new size. Dimensions that are associated will even move with an object automatically when the object is moved in the drawing. Dimension associativity can be turned off, but it is not recommended because of all the benefits obtained by leaving it on.

Maintaining the appearance of dimensions on drawings so that they match industry standards is managed using dimension styles in AutoCAD. The **Dimension Style Manager** allows you to set and maintain the multitude of AutoCAD dimension settings. Dimension styles with different industry standards can be set up and stored in AutoCAD template (DWT) files so that they are instantly available when you start a new drawing. Occasionally, there is the need for an oddball dimension setting. Dimension overrides allow you to change a few dimension settings for a small number of dimensions without updating all of the dimensions in your drawing. Overrides can be set up in the **Dimension Style Manager,** or they can be applied directly to objects you select using the **Properties** palette. It is also possible to apply an override by using the **Dimension Update** tool to update any dimensions you select.

The **Multileader** tool allows you to quickly add feature notes with arrows to your drawings with a minimum of two pick points. The default is the arrowhead location and then location of the text, but it can be set to go the other direction. Multiple leader arrows can be added or removed with minimal effort. Multileader styles allow you to set up different leader types including splines and built-in part number bubbles, to name but a few.

As you have seen, controlling the appearance of dimensions and leader notes is a rather complex undertaking. There are literally hundreds of different dimension settings and controls to manage in order to get things to look just right. Fortunately, AutoCAD provides the ability to update and even match dimension styles to other existing dimensions in the current drawing or even between different drawings. This saves you the time-consuming process of going step-by-step through the **Dimension Style Manager.**

Chapter Test Questions

Multiple Choice

Circle the correct answer.

1. When using the **DIMLINEAR** command, which of the following is **not** a valid selection object?

   a. Line c. Ellipse

   b. Arc d. Circle

2. An arc length dimension:
   a. Is a linear dimension between the endpoints of an arc
   b. Measures the true distance along an arc segment
   c. Cannot be used on circles
   d. None of the above
3. To create a dimension with angled (oblique) extension lines you would:
   a. Use the **DIMOBLIQUE** command
   b. Use the **DIMEDIT** command and select the **Oblique** option
   c. Use grips to drag the extension lines to the desired angle
   d. None of the above; you cannot create angled extension lines
4. A dimension style override:
   a. Allows you to make temporary changes to a dimension style
   b. Is applied to all dimensions with the current dimension style
   c. Cannot be saved to a dimension style
   d. None of the above
5. Setting the **DIMASSOC** system variable to **1**:
   a. Creates exploded dimensions
   b. Creates dimensions that are not associated with other drawing objects
   c. Creates dimensions that are associated with other drawing objects
   d. You cannot set **DIMASSOC** to **1**
6. In the **Fit** tab of the **Modify Dimension Style** dialog box, the **Use overall scale of** setting:
   a. Controls the overall size of all elements of a dimension object
   b. Controls the value of dimension text
   c. Does not apply to dimensions placed in model space
   d. All of the above
7. The **Angle** option of the **DIMLINEAR** command:
   a. Creates an angular dimension instead of a linear dimension
   b. Creates extension lines at the specified angle
   c. Controls the angle of the dimension line
   d. Controls the angle of the dimension text
8. To flip a dimension arrowhead:
   a. Select the arrowhead and choose **Flip Arrow** from the **Multifunctional Grip** menu
   b. Delete the dimension and re-create it picking different defpoints
   c. Use the **MIRROR** command
   d. You cannot flip dimension arrowheads once they are placed
9. A baseline dimension:
   a. Creates dimensions that are aligned end to end
   b. Creates dimensions that are referenced from a common extension line
   c. Must be placed first before any other linear dimensions are created
   d. None of the above

10. Diameter dimensions:
    a. Automatically have the ∅ symbol placed in front of the dimension text
    b. Can be used with either arcs or circles
    c. Cannot be used on an ellipse
    d. All of the above

Matching

Write the number of the correct answer on the line.

a. Linear dimension ______
b. Angular dimension ______
c. **Defpoints** layer ______
d. Associativity ______
e. Aligned dimension ______
f. Radius dimension ______
g. Dimension style override ______
h. Diameter dimension ______
i. Arc length dimension ______
j. **DIMASSOC** ______

1. Layer automatically created for definition points
2. A link between two drawing objects so that when one changes, the other updates
3. A linear dimension between two points along an angled line
4. A dimension of an angle
5. A dimension from the center to the edge of an arc or circle
6. The system variable that controls dimension associativity
7. A link between dimension definition points and other drawing geometry
8. A dimension between two opposite points on a circle or arc
9. A temporary change to dimension style settings
10. A dimension of the true length of an arc segment

True or False

Circle the correct answer.

1. **True or False:** The **Defpoints** layer will never plot.
2. **True or False:** Dimensions cannot be exploded.
3. **True or False:** Dimension arrowheads can be flipped around the extension line.
4. **True or False:** The color and linetype of dimension lines are always BYLAYER.
5. **True or False:** You can override the default dimension text.
6. **True or False:** Centerline marks are created only with radius and diameter dimensions.
7. **True or False:** The **QDIM** command creates only linear dimensions.
8. **True or False:** Dimension style overrides are automatically applied to all existing dimension objects.
9. **True or False:** The **DDEDIT** command can be used to modify dimension objects.
10. **True or False:** The **DIMRADIUS** command can be used to dimension an ellipse.

Chapter Projects

Project 13-1: *Classroom Plan, continued from Chapter 8* [BASIC]

1. Open drawing ***P8-1*** from Chapter 8.
2. Create a text style named **ARCH** and assign it the TrueType font **Stylus_BT.**
3. Create a dimension style called **ARCH.** Use the settings shown in Figures 13-101 through 13-105.
4. Set the **Annotation Scale** to **1/2″ = 1′-0″** on the status bar.
5. Add the dimensions shown in Figure 13-95.
6. Save your drawing as ***P13-1.***

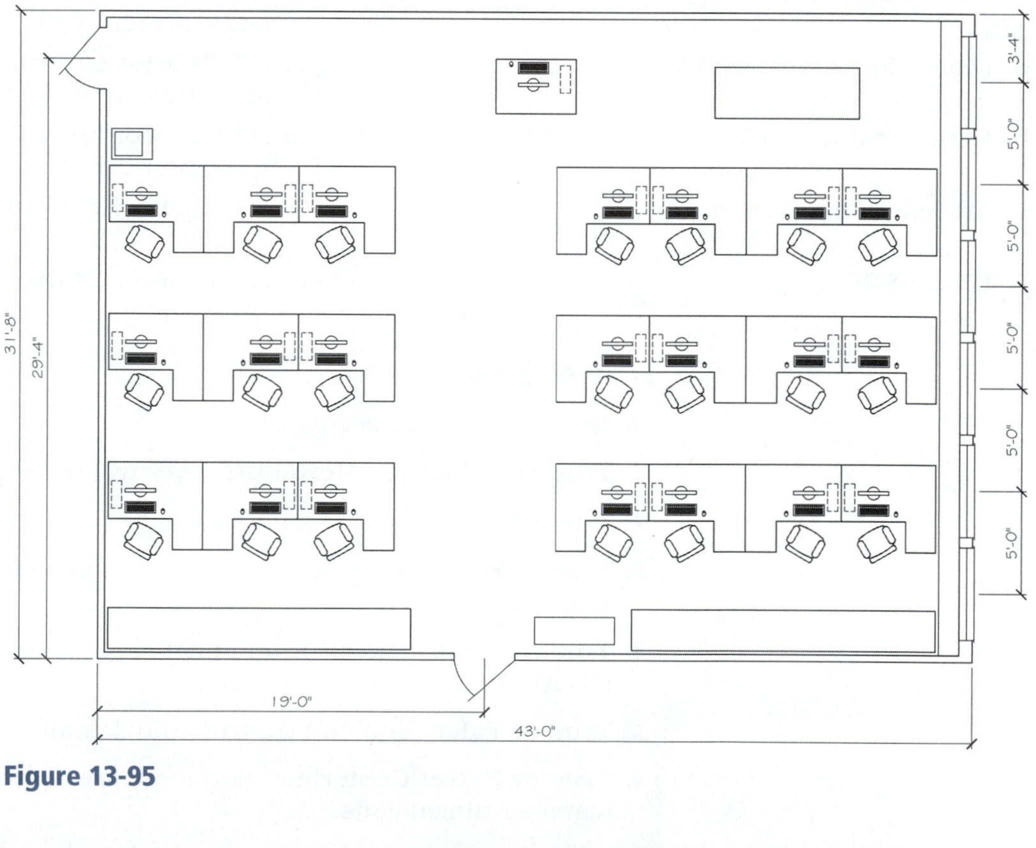

Figure 13-95

Project 13-2: *B-Size Mechanical Border, continued from Chapter 11* [INTERMEDIATE]

1. Open the template file ***Mechanical B-Size.DWT*** from Chapter 11.
2. Create a dimension style called **Mech** based on the **Standard** dimension style. Use the settings shown in Figures 13-96 through 13-100.

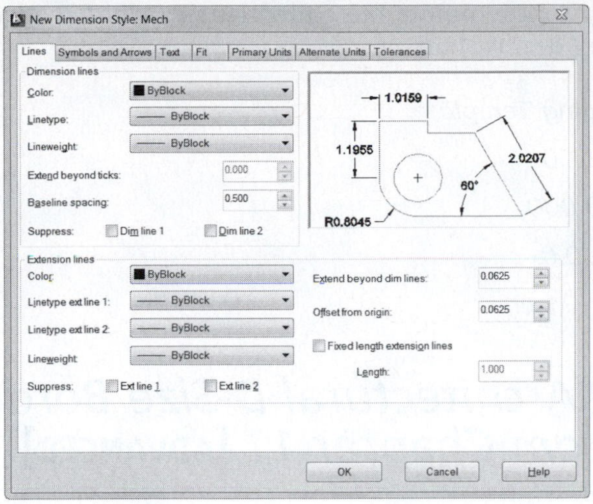

Figure 13-96

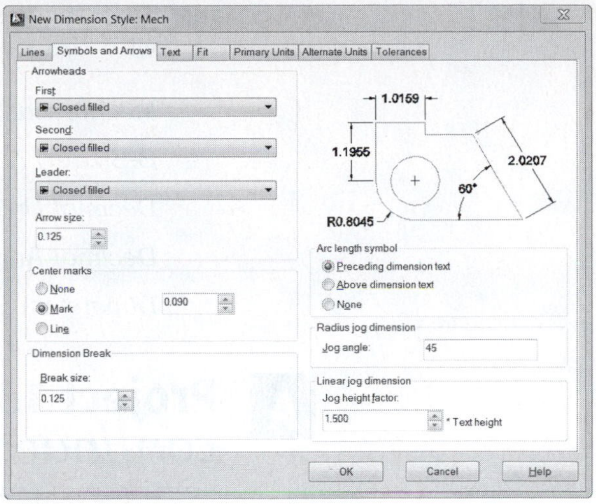

Figure 13-97

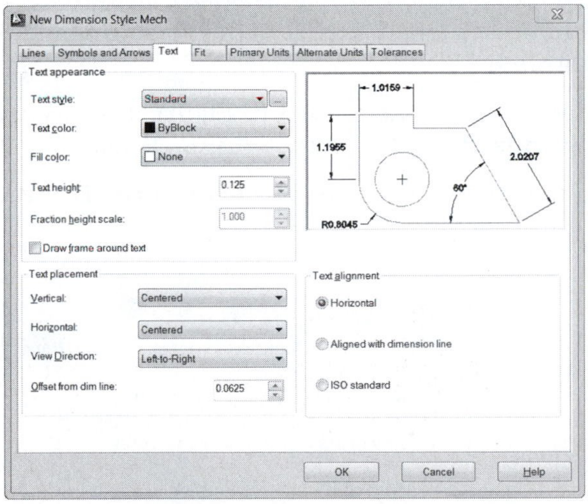

Figure 13-98

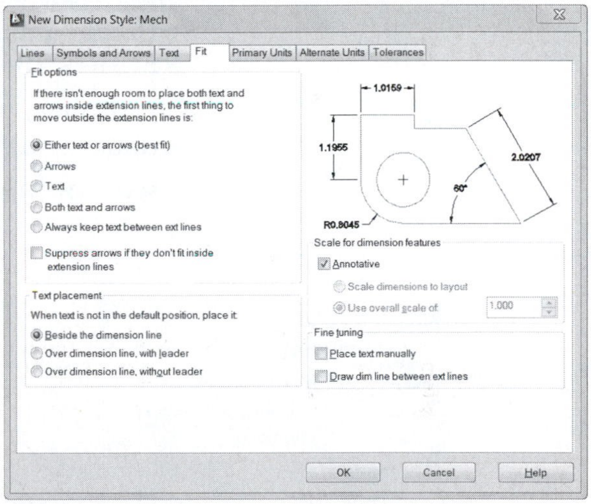

Figure 13-99

Figure 13-100

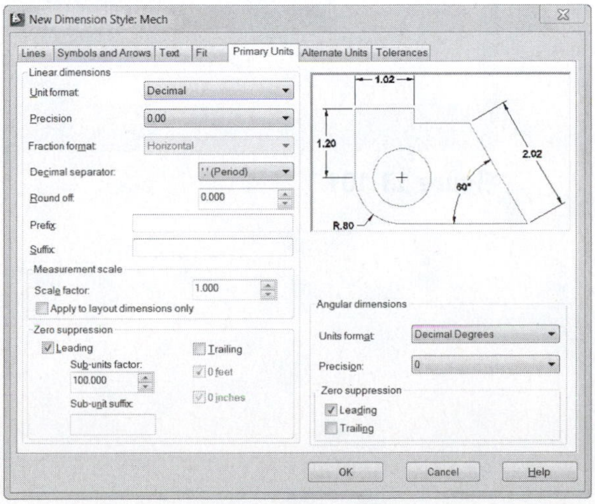

3. Save the drawing to a template file called ***Mechanical B-Size.DWT*** with the following description:

   Mechanical Drawing Template:

   B-Size - 17.0 × 11.0

   Decimal Units - 0.000

   Decimal Angles - 0.0

   Dimension Style - Mech

A Project 13-3: *Architectural D-Size Border, continued from Chapter 11* [ADVANCED]

1. Open the template file ***Architectural D-Size.DWT*** from Chapter 11.
2. Create a text style named **ARCH** and assign it the TrueType font **Stylus_BT.**
3. Create a dimension style named **ARCH** with the settings shown in Figures 13-101 through 13-105.
4. Dimension the graphic scales as shown in Figure 13-106 using the dimension style **Standard** on the layer **A-Anno-Dims.**
5. Save the drawing to a template file as ***Architectural D-Size.DWT.***

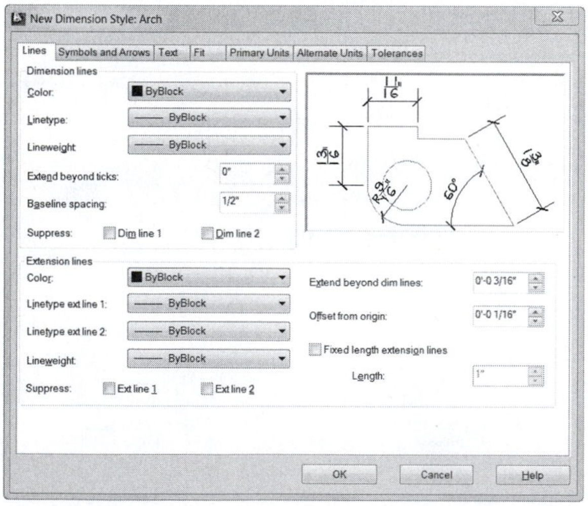

Figure 13-101

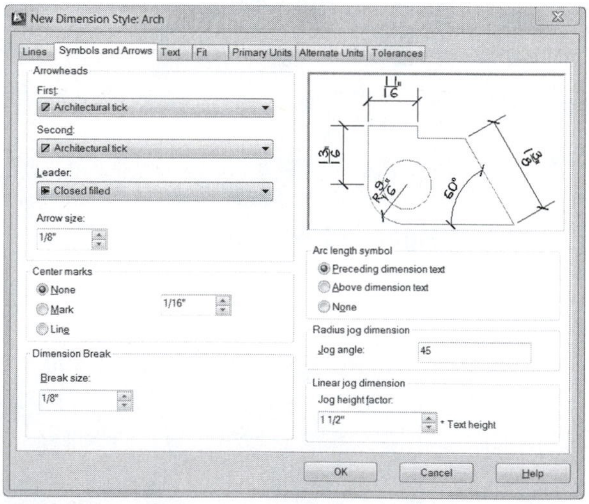

Figure 13-102

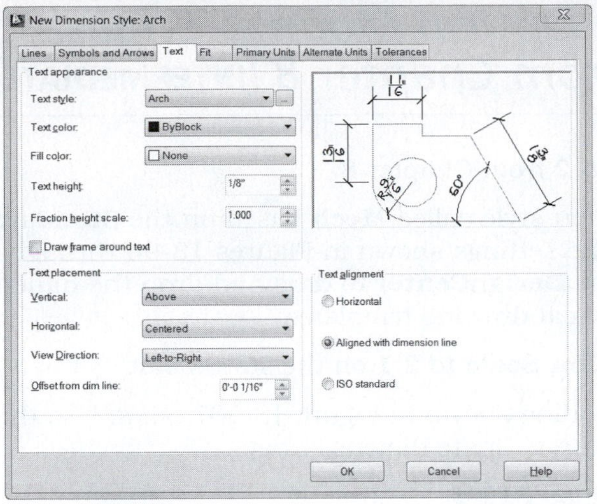

Figure 13-103

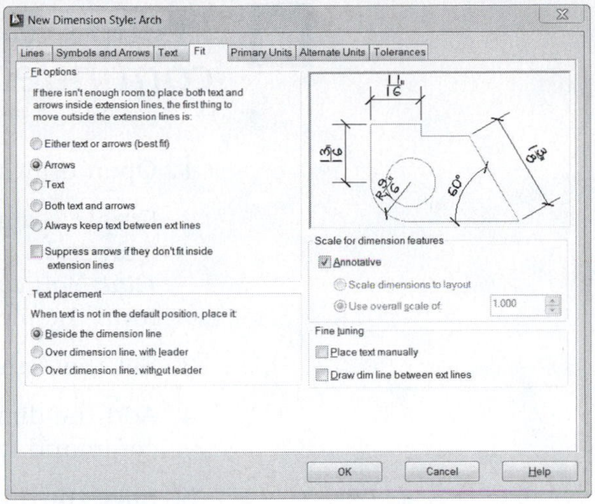

Figure 13-104

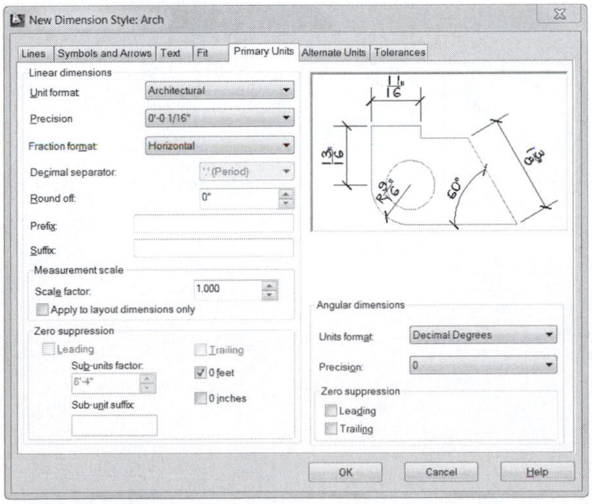

Figure 13-105

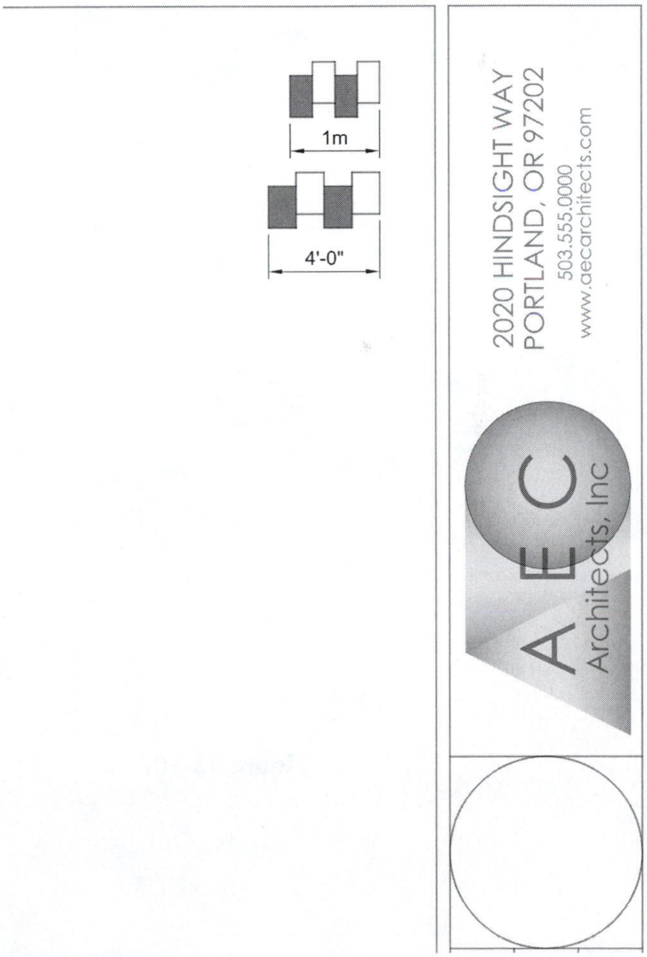

Figure 13-106

M Project 13-4: *Optical Mount—English Units, continued from Chapter 8* [INTERMEDIATE]

1. Open drawing ***P8-2*** from Chapter 8.
2. Create a dimension style called **Mech** based on the **Standard** dimension style. Use the settings shown in Figures 13-96 through 13-100. *Hint:* You can use **DesignCenter** to drag and drop the dimension style from the mechanical drawing templates.
3. Set the **Annotation Scale** to **2:1** on the status bar.
4. Add the dimensioning shown in Figure 13-107. *Hint:* Use the **QDIM** command to create ordinate dimensioning.
5. Save the drawing as ***P13-4.***

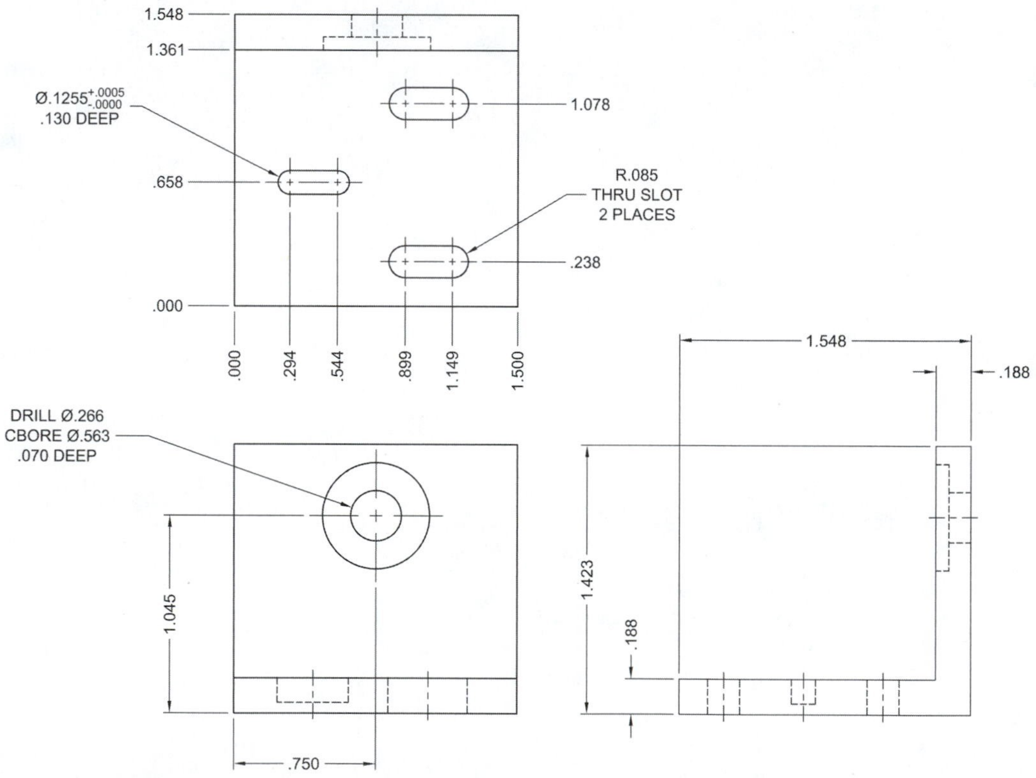

Figure 13-107

Project 13-5: *Residential Architectural Plan, continued from Chapter 11* [ADVANCED]

1. Open drawing ***P11-5*** from Chapter 11.
2. Create a dimension style called **ARCH.** Use the settings shown in Figures 13-101 through 13-105. On the **Fit** tab, select the **Annotative** scale setting check box in the **Scale for dimension features** area to turn on annotation scaling.
3. Set the **Annotation Scale** to **1/4″ = 1′-0″** on the status bar.
4. Add the dimensions shown in Figure 13-108.
5. Save your drawing as ***P13-5.***

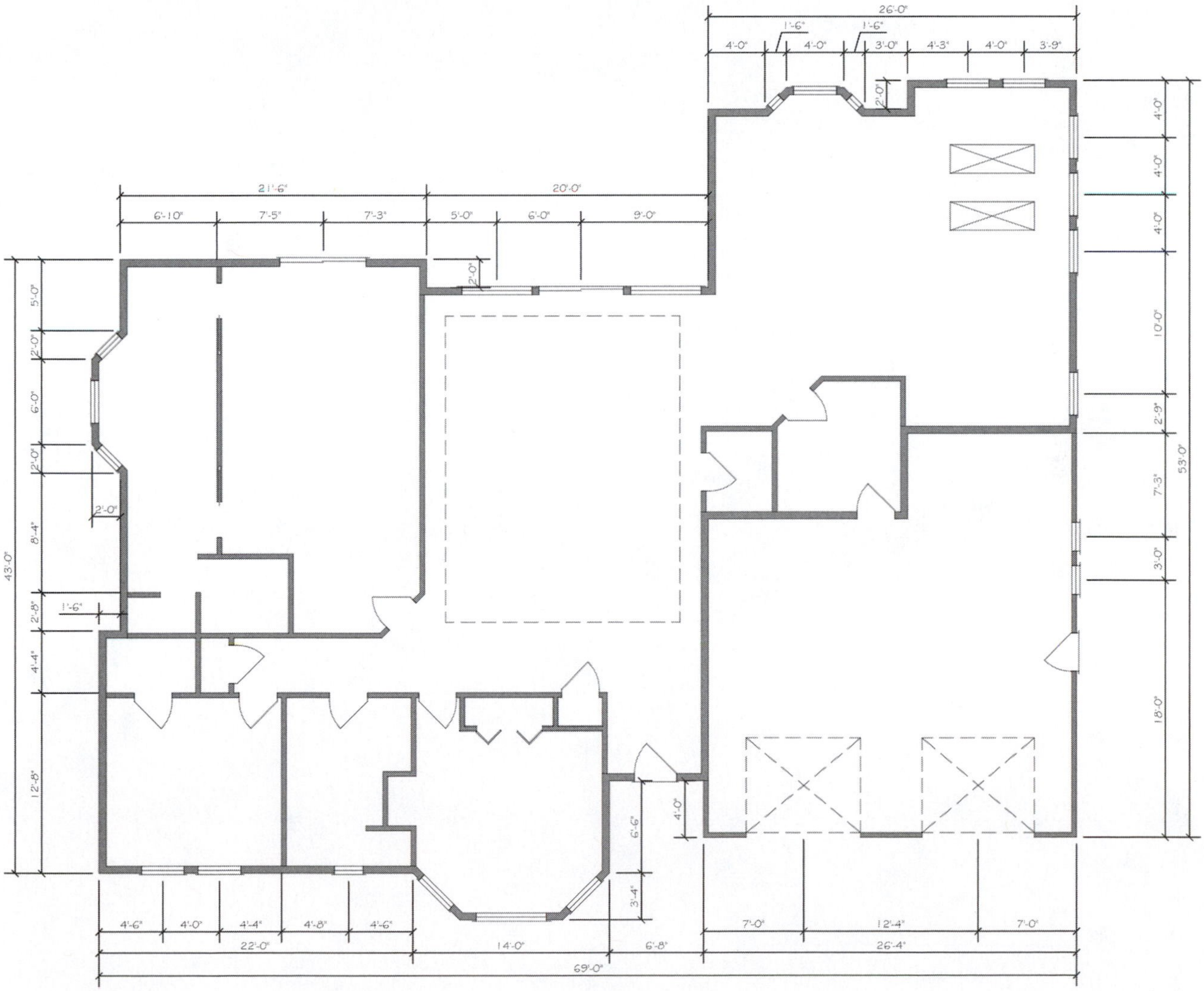

Figure 13-108

chapter fourteen

Managing Paper Space Layouts

CHAPTER OBJECTIVES

- Understand how and why paper space layouts are used
- Associate a printer/plotter with a layout
- Set the page size of a layout
- Create and import page setups
- Create layout viewports
- Set the viewport display scale
- Lock the viewport display
- Control layer visibility per viewport
- Modify viewports
- Create and manage layouts
- Explore the paper space linetype scaling feature

Introduction

In Chapter 1, we explained how AutoCAD has two distinct drawing environments: model space and paper space.

Remember that model space is the theoretically infinite 3D drawing environment where you locate most of the line work and annotation features that make up a drawing. To draw in model space, you select the **Model** tab at the bottom left of the drawing window as shown in Figure 14-1 to make it current.

> **NOTE**
>
> When model space is the active drawing environment, the UCS icon in the lower left-hand corner of the drawing window defaults to the icon shown in Figure 14-2.

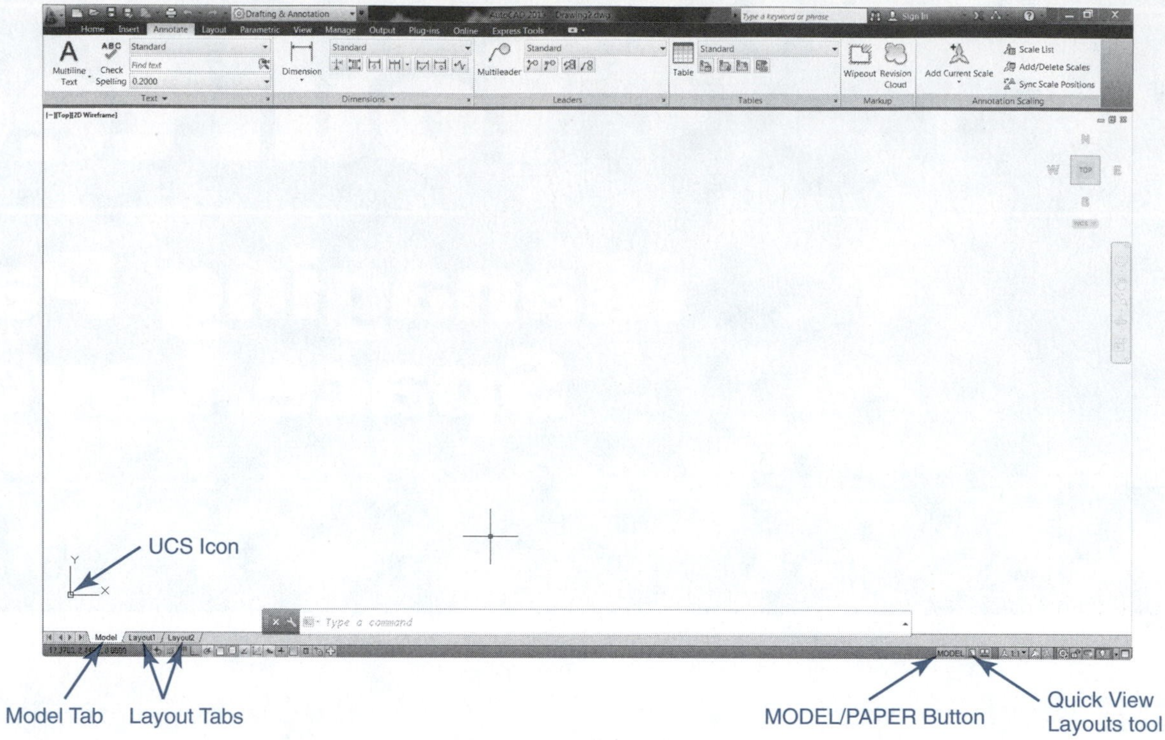

Figure 14-1

Switching between model space and paper space layouts

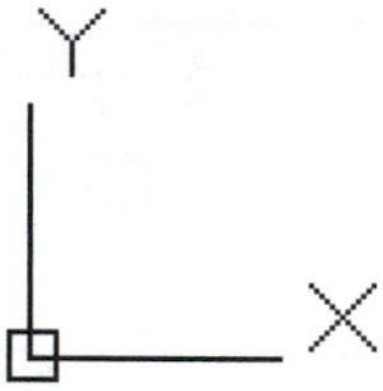

Figure 14-2

The model space UCS icon

To reiterate, paper space is the 2D environment where you lay out the drawing information created in model space for plotting/printing on the desired size of paper and at a specified scale factor. In effect, a layout represents what the drawing will look like when it is printed.

> **TIP**
>
> It is common to locate the title border information in a layout. Locating the border and title text in paper space allows them to be drawn at a scale of 1:1 because the plot scale in paper space is typically 1:1. Many of the default AutoCAD template files have the title border located in paper space.

It is possible to have multiple layouts in a drawing, each one a different paper size and scale. A new AutoCAD drawing that is based on the default template file **(acad.dwt)** contains two generic layouts named **Layout1** and **Layout2.**

The quickest and easiest way to switch between layouts is to select the desired layout tab on the bottom left of the drawing window shown in Figure 14-1.

Quick View Layouts

Another way to switch between model space and the paper space layouts is using the **Quick View Layouts** tool located on the right side of the status bar shown in Figure 14-1.

The **Quick View Layouts** tool displays a horizontal row of layout preview images at the bottom of the AutoCAD window so you can quickly switch between model space and all the layouts contained in a drawing (see Figure 14-3).

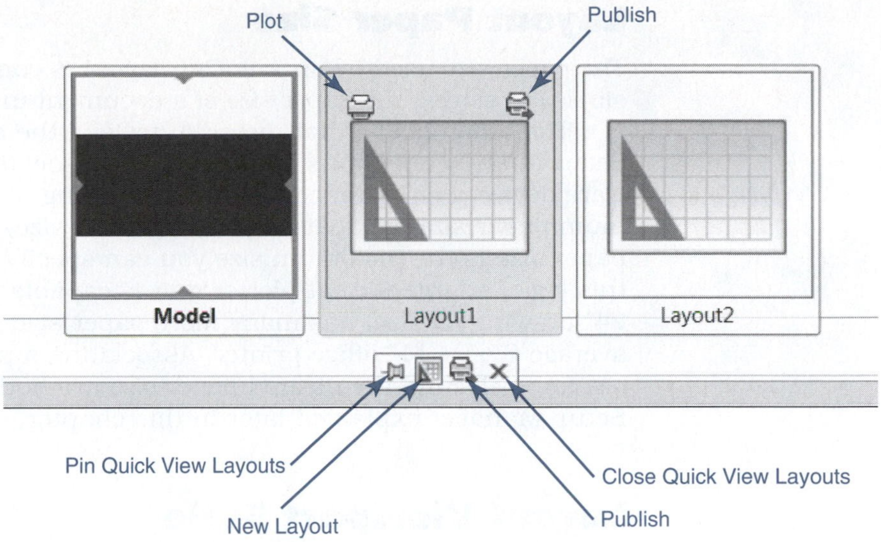

Figure 14-3

The **Quick View Layouts** tool

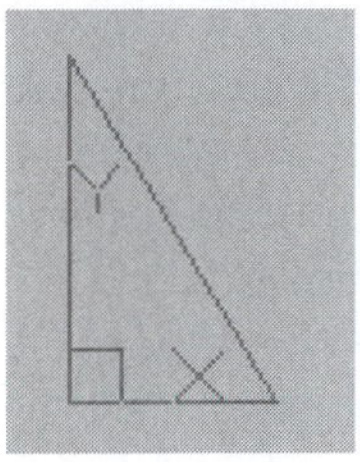

Figure 14-4

The paper space UCS icon

> **NOTE**
>
> When paper space is the active drawing environment, the UCS icon in the lower left-hand corner of the drawing window defaults to the icon shown in Figure 14-4.

In addition, moving your cursor over a layout preview displays **Plot** and **Publish** buttons in the upper corners of the image so that you can print directly from the **Quick View Layouts** tool.

> **NOTE**
>
> Move the mouse past the edge of the row of images to display layouts that extend beyond the edge of the screen.

> **TIP**
>
> You can increase or decrease the layout preview image size by holding down the **<Ctrl>** key while rolling the mouse wheel in and out.

Using the accompanying control panel displayed below the preview images, you can select the **Pin Quick View Layouts** button to keep the **Quick View Layouts** tool open so the previews are visible while you work. You can then select the **Close Quick View Layouts** button to turn off previews when you no longer want them displayed.

The **New Layout** button instantly creates a new generic layout in the drawing and displays its preview at the end of the current row of preview images. Creating and managing layouts is explained in detail later in this chapter.

The **Publish** button displays the **Publish** tool so you can quickly plot all the currently open drawings and layouts.

> **FOR MORE DETAILS**
>
> See page 639 in Chapter 15 for more detailed information about using the **PUBLISH** command for quickly plotting multiple drawings and layouts.

Layout Paper Size

The paper size used by an AutoCAD layout is controlled via its *page setup*, similar to setting the paper size of a document in a word processing program.

The difference is that, using AutoCAD, the available paper sizes are determined by the limits of the layout's associated plotting/printing hardware device. For instance, if you are printing on a printer whose maximum paper size capability is 8½″ × 11″ (A-size/letter), then an 8½″ × 11″ paper size is the maximum size you can specify for the layout. Applying this logic, a large-format plotter that is capable of printing up to a 36″ × 24″ drawing (D-size) has many more paper size settings available than the average 8½″ × 11″ office printer. Associating a printer/plotter with a layout and selecting the desired paper size are both controlled using the Page Setup Manager explained later in this chapter.

Layout Viewport Scale

layout viewport: The user-defined window created in a paper space layout that allows you to view drawing information that resides in model space.

The scale of a drawing is controlled via one or more ***layout viewports*** created in a layout.

In Chapter 1 we used the analogy that an AutoCAD paper space layout can be thought of as a 2D sheet of paper that hovers over your 3D model space drawing information. Views of the model space information are created by cutting one or more holes referred to as layout viewports in the paper so that you can see the drawing model below. You scale the model space information displayed in the viewport by zooming in and out at a specific scale factor. It is even possible to create multiple viewports and specify a different scale factor for each individual viewport, as shown in Figure 14-5, allowing you to easily create multiscaled drawings.

Figure 14-5

Paper space layout with multiple scaled viewports

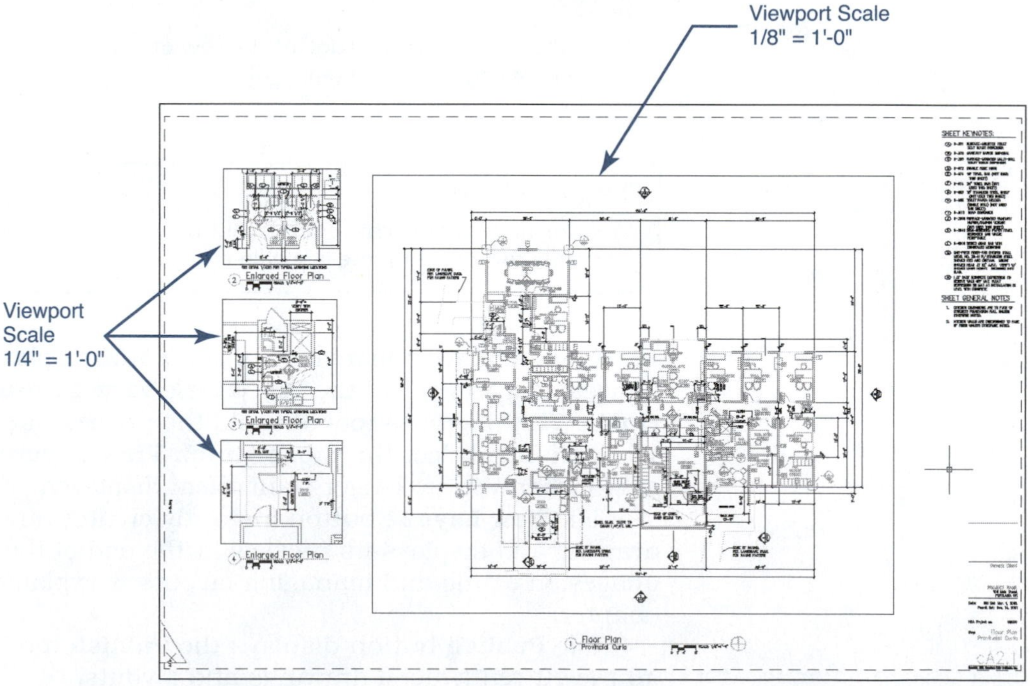

TIP

AutoCAD provides a list of all of the standard viewport scales on the status bar so that you can quickly set a viewport scale without having to calculate the zoom scale factor each time. Both methods are described later in this chapter.

Being able to create plots with differently scaled viewports is one of the primary benefits of using paper space layouts. This is something you simply can't do in model space unless you scale the actual drawing information—which should be avoided at all costs. Remember that in AutoCAD, the key is to draw everything exactly as it exists in the real world.

Controlling Layers per Layout Viewport

Another very useful capability of layout viewports is that you can freeze and thaw layers per viewport using the viewport layer freeze option introduced in Chapter 6. This allows you to create multiple viewports on one or more layouts that each display different model space drawing information.

You can also control the layer color, linetype, lineweight, transparency, and plot style properties per viewport using viewport layer overrides. Viewport layer overrides allow you to change the layer color, linetype, lineweight, transparency, and plot style properties in each viewport while retaining the original layer properties in model space and in the other layout viewports. Viewport layer overrides are discussed in detail later in this chapter.

FOR MORE DETAILS

See Chapter 6 for more information about using layers to organize drawing information.

Setting Up a Layout

Once you are ready to lay out a drawing for plotting from paper space, select one of the default layouts **(Layout1** or **Layout2).**

When you switch to a layout for the first time, a single layout viewport is displayed on the page with a dashed line indicating the ***printable area*** as shown in Figure 14-6.

printable area: The actual physical area that can be printed for the currently specified plotting device and paper size.

PAGE SETUP MANAGER	
Ribbon & Panel:	Output | Plot
Layouts Toolbar:	
Menu:	File | Page Setup Manager…
Command Line:	PAGESETUP
Command Alias:	None

The first thing you need to do when you are setting up a layout is to specify the desired printer/plotter output device. Once you specify an output device, *then* you can select a paper size. Remember that the two are intimately related because the available paper sizes are determined by the capabilities of the currently associated printer/plotter. The printer/plotter, paper size, and most of the other plot settings are controlled via the page setup associated with the layout.

To modify the settings for the page setup, you use the Page Setup Manager, which is explained in the next section.

The Page Setup Manager

The Page Setup Manager allows you to do the following:

- Display details of the current page setup
- Set another page setup current
- Modify an existing page setup
- Create a new page setup
- Import a page setup from another drawing

Figure 14-6
Switching to a layout the first time

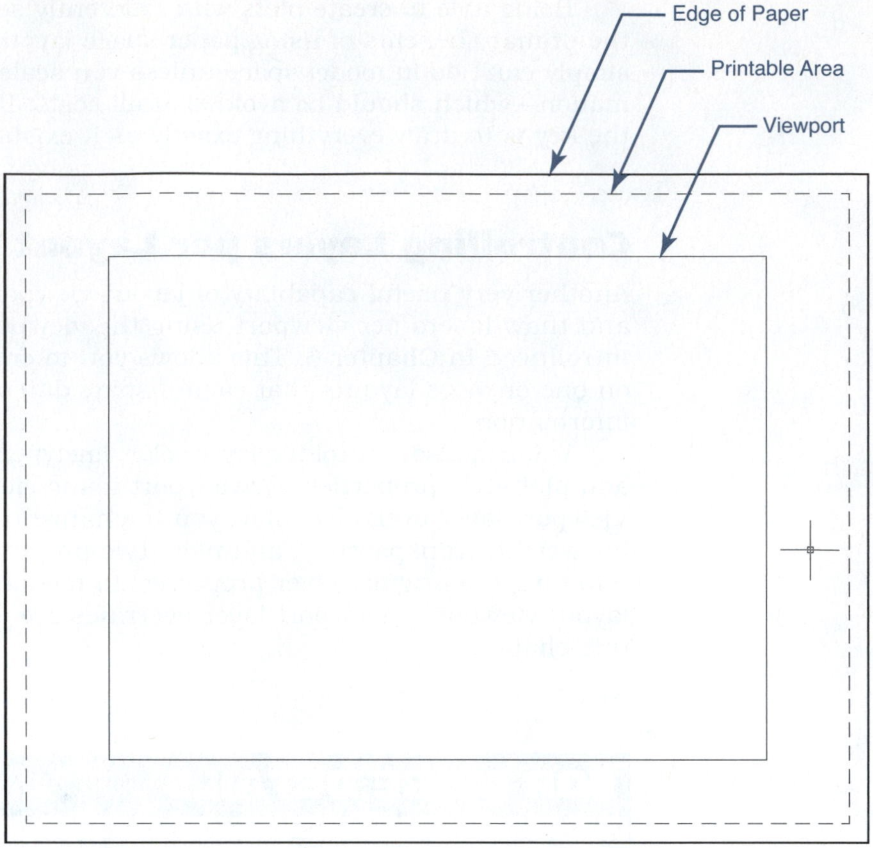

The **Page Setup Manager** dialog box is shown in Figure 14-7.

Current page displays the page setup that is applied to the current layout. By default it is set to **<None>.**

The **Page setups** box lists the page setups that can be modified or applied to the current layout.

Figure 14-7
The **Page Setup Manager** dialog box

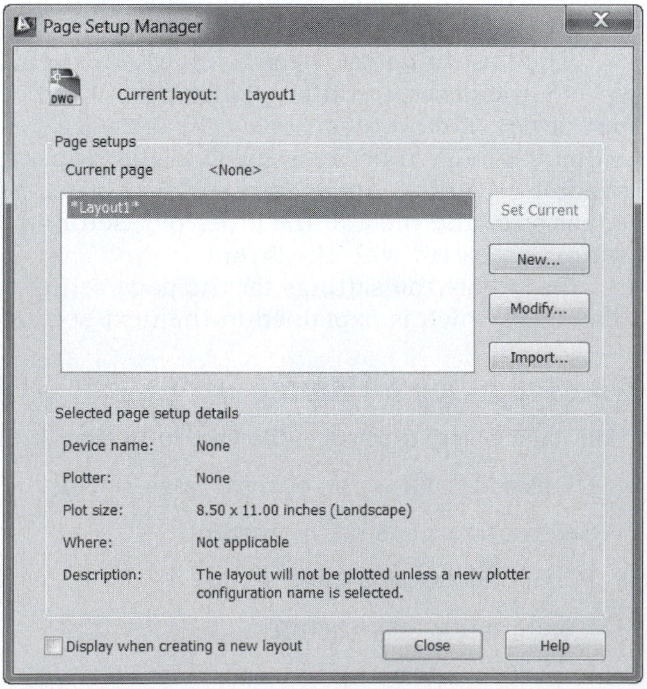

By default, a page setup is automatically applied to each layout with the same name as the layout with an asterisk (*) added to the beginning and end of the layout name. For instance, the default page setups for the **Layout1** and **Layout2** layouts are ***Layout1*** and ***Layout2***, respectively.

Any new or imported page setups are automatically added to the **Page setups** list. You can make a page setup current by double-clicking on it in the list or by highlighting the page setup and selecting the **Set Current** button.

> **TIP**
>
> If you right-click in the **Page setups** list box, a shortcut menu is displayed that allows you to set current, rename, or delete a page setup.

> **NOTE**
>
> It is not possible to set current, rename, or delete any of the default page setups that begin and end with an asterisk.

The **Selected page setup details** area at the bottom of the dialog box displays the following information about the currently selected page setup:

- **Device name** Name of the plot device specified in the currently selected page setup
- **Plotter** Type of plot device specified in the currently selected page setup
- **Plot size** Plot size and orientation specified in the currently selected page setup
- **Where** Physical location of the output device specified in the currently selected page setup
- **Description** Description of the output device specified in the currently selected page setup

The **Display when creating a new layout** check box allows you to control whether the **Page Setup Manager** is displayed when a new layout tab is selected or a new layout is created.

> **TIP**
>
> You can also control whether the **Page Setup Manager** is displayed for new layouts via the **Show Page Setup Manager for new layouts** option on the **Display** tab of the **Options** dialog box.

Modifying a Page Setup. You can modify the settings of a page setup at any time. In order to modify any default page setup, the layout the page setup is associated with must first be set current. Selecting the **Modify...** button in the **Page Setup Manager** dialog box displays the **Page Setup** dialog box shown in Figure 14-8.

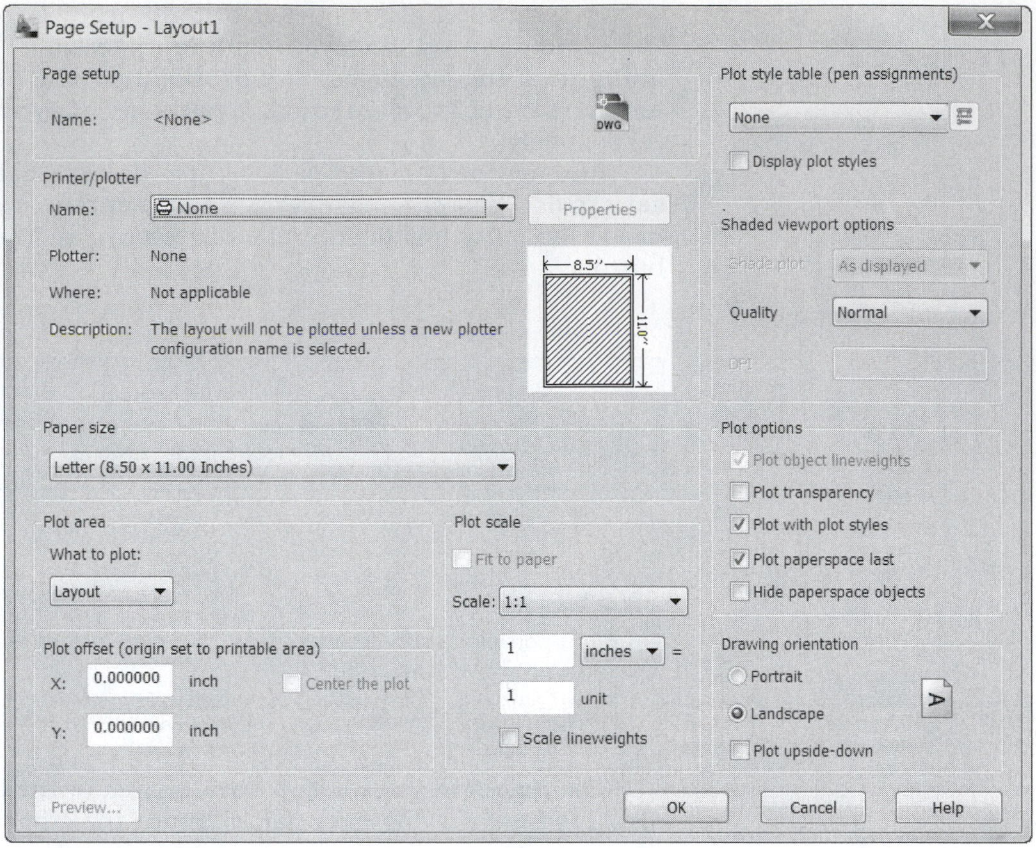

Figure 14-8
The **Page Setup** dialog box

The **Page Setup** dialog box is almost exactly the same as the **Plot** dialog box shown in Figure 14-9. In fact, the two dialog boxes control the same settings. The only differences between the two are:

- Changes made in the **Page Setup** dialog box are saved with the layout. Changes made in the **Plot** dialog box are *not* saved, unless you select the **Apply to Layout** button.
- You can plot from the **Plot** dialog box. You *cannot* plot from the **Page Setup** dialog box.
- The **Plot** dialog box can be toggled to display more plot options using the **More Options** arrow button at the bottom right of the dialog box as shown in Figure 14-9, or it can be set to display a limited number of options.

In this chapter, the main concern is controlling the paper size of the layout so that you can properly set up a drawing for plotting (discussed in Chapter 15). For this reason, most of the other plot-related page setup settings are mentioned only briefly. The following sections explain primarily how to associate an output device so that you can select the desired layout paper size.

Selecting a Printer/Plotter Device. The **Printer/plotter** area of the **Page Setup** dialog box allows you to specify a printer/plotter by selecting it from the **Name:** list box shown in Figure 14-10.

The **Name:** list box provides a list of the available printers/plotters you can associate with a layout. The list includes both ***.PC3 files*** and system printers that are prefixed with different icons—a plotter icon for a .PC3 file and a printer icon for a system printer.

.PC3 file: Plotter configuration file used to store and manage printer/plotter settings.

Figure 14-9
The **Plot** dialog box

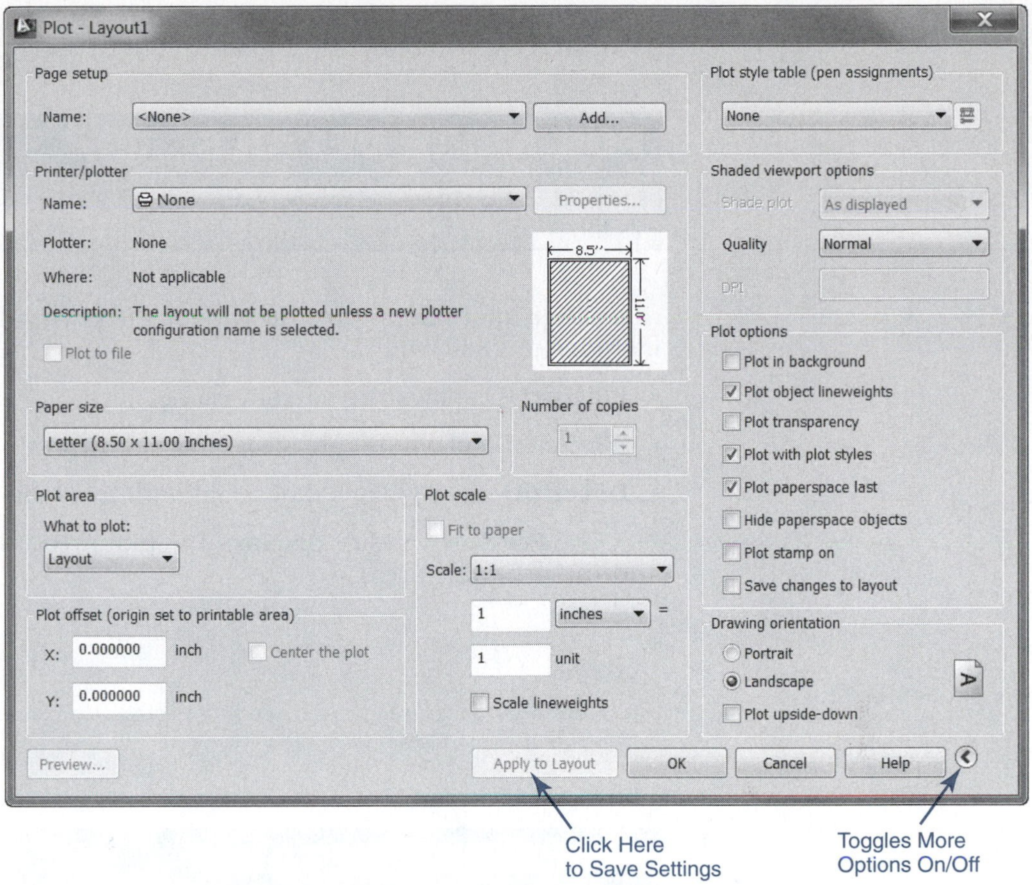

Figure 14-10
Selecting a printer/plotter from the **Name:** list box

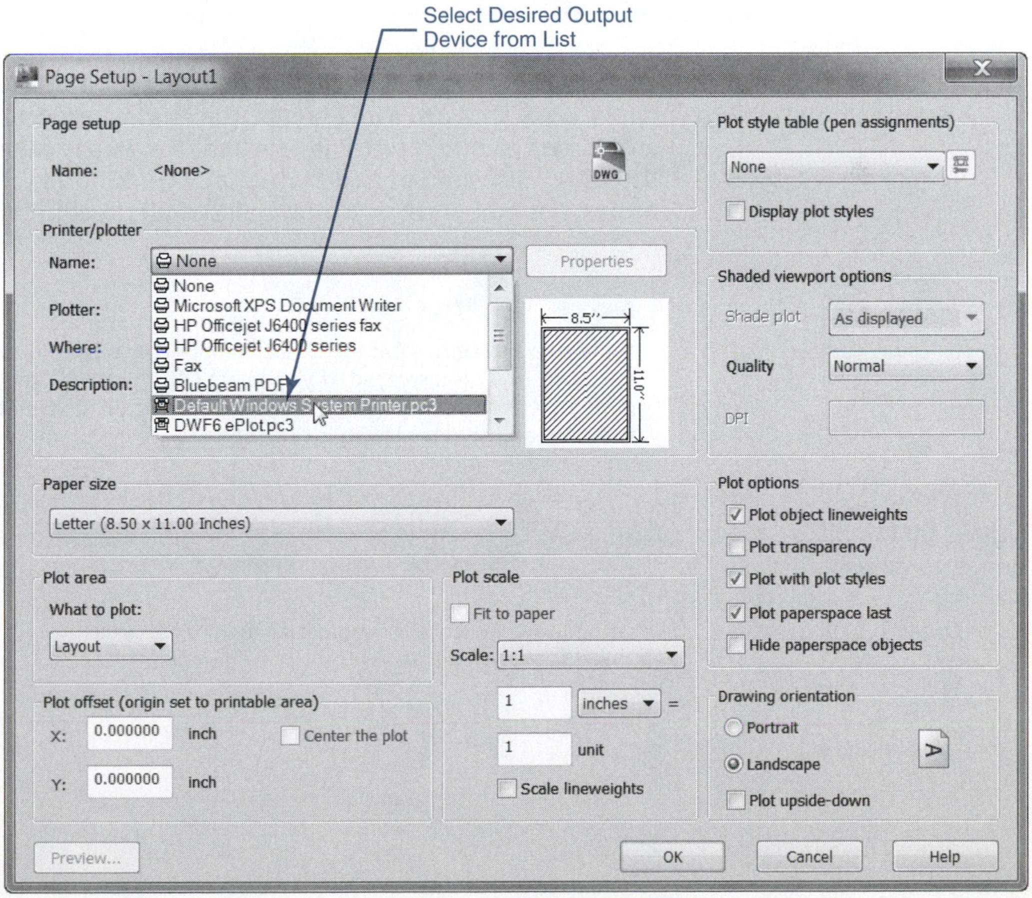

The **Properties...** button displays the **Plotter Configuration Editor** so you can view or modify the current plotter configuration.

FOR MORE DETAILS

See page 634 in Chapter 15 for more on using the **Plotter Configuration Editor** to manage .PC3 files.

Other information provided about the currently selected printer/plotter includes the following:

- **Plotter** Displays the current name
- **Where** Displays the physical location or port
- **Description** Displays a description if available

The **Preview** window displays the plot area relative to the paper size and the printable area.

NOTE

If the printer/plotter you wish to use is not listed, you can add it using the **Plotter Manager**'s **Add-a-Plotter** wizard.

FOR MORE DETAILS

See page 634 in Chapter 15 for more on using the **Add-a-Plotter** wizard.

Selecting a Paper Size. The **Paper size** list box displays the standard paper sizes that are available for the associated printer/plotter. Every time a different printer/plotter is selected, the **Paper size** list is updated with the paper sizes supported by that device. If no plotter is selected so that the **Name:** list box is set to **None,** a list of all the standard paper sizes is provided.

NOTE

If the selected printer/plotter doesn't support the current paper size, the warning shown in Figure 14-11 is displayed. If you select **OK,** the paper size is changed to the default paper size for the new printer/plotter. If you select **Cancel,** the printer/plotter is changed to **None,** and the paper size is not changed.

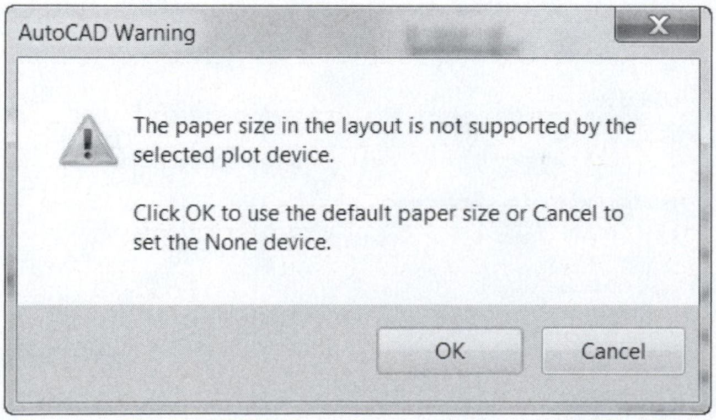

Figure 14-11
Unsupported paper size warning

If you are plotting a raster image, such as a BMP or TIFF file, the size of the plot is specified in pixels, not in inches or millimeters.

> **TIP**
>
> If you are unsure what printer/plotter to specify, you can set the plotter to **None** so that it is still possible to select the desired paper size.

Other Page Setup Settings. The following is a brief overview of a few of the other page setup settings.

The **Plot area** settings determine the area of the drawing to plot. The **What to plot:** list box provides five different options:

- **Display** The current screen display
- **Extents** The extents of the drawing
- **Layout** The current layout
- **View** A named view (must have at least one named view to be enabled)
- **Window** User-specified window area

The **Plot area** is typically set to **Layout** for a paper space layout. The other **Plot area** settings are more commonly used when plotting in model space.

The **Plot offset** area allows you to offset the plot area relative to the lower-left corner of the printable area or the edge of the paper.

> **NOTE**
>
> You can change what the offset is relative to via the **Specify plot offset relative to** options on the **Plot and Publish** tab of the **Options** dialog box.

> **FOR MORE DETAILS**
>
> See Chapter 15 for more detailed information about controlling the other plot settings and plotting your drawing.

The **Plot scale** area controls the ratio of the plotted units to the drawing units. Most of the standard drafting scales are listed in the **Scale:** list box. The default scale is 1:1 when plotting a layout.

Creating a New Page Setup. If you think that you might use the same page setup settings in another layout in the current drawing or even in a layout in another drawing, you can create a named page setup. Named page setups are saved in the drawing file so that they can be applied to other layouts or imported into other drawing files. Importing page setups is explained in the next section.

Using named page setups also allows you to plot the same layout more than one way. You can apply different named page setups to the same layout so that there are different output results each time. For example, you might create different named page setups to plot to printers/plotters that are in different locations.

To create a new named page setup, select the **New...** button in the **Page Setup Manager** dialog box. The **New Page Setup** dialog box shown in Figure 14-12 is displayed.

Figure 14-12
The **New Page Setup** dialog box

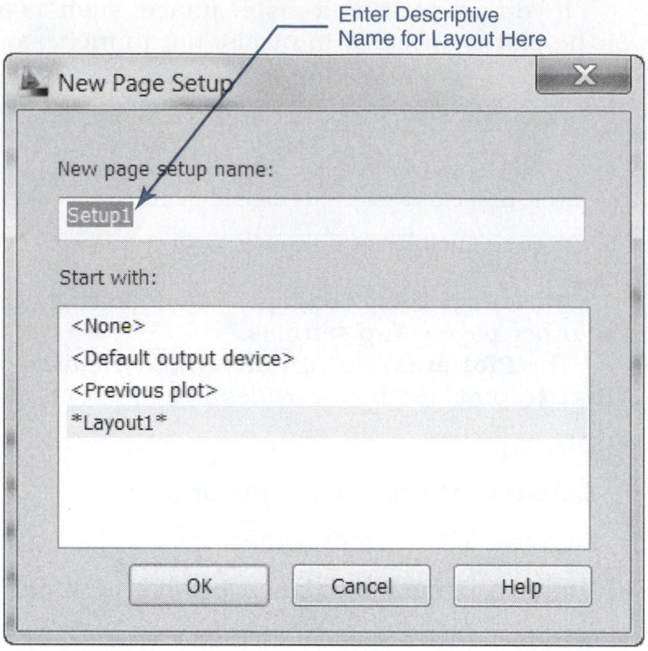

Enter the name for the new page setup in the **New page setup name:** text box. The default name is **Setup** followed by an integer representing a sequential number (i.e., **Setup1, Setup2,** etc.). You should enter a descriptive name indicating the page setup's purpose.

The **Start with:** list allows you to select a page setup to use as a starting point for the new page setup:

- **<None>** No page setup is used as a starting point.
- **<Default output device>** The default output device specified on the **Plot and Publish** tab of the **Options** dialog box is set as the printer in the new page setup.
- **<Previous plot>** The new page setup uses the settings specified in the last plot.

When you select the **OK** button at the bottom of the **New Page Setup** dialog box, the **Page Setup** dialog box shown earlier in Figure 14-8 is displayed using the settings saved with the selected starting point page setup. You can then modify any settings if necessary. When you exit the **Page Setup** dialog box, the new named page setup is displayed in the list of page setups in the **Page Setup Manager** as shown in Figure 14-13.

Importing a Page Setup from Another Drawing. A named page setup can be imported from another drawing file (DWG), drawing template file (DWT), or drawing exchange format file (DXF). To import a named page setup, select the **Import...** button in the **Page Setup Manager** shown in Figure 14-7. The **Select Page Setup from File** dialog box is displayed so that you can select the source file from which you want to import. After you locate the file and select the **Open** button, the **Import Page Setups** dialog box shown in Figure 14-14 is displayed so you can select one or more page setups.

The **Page setups** list box lists the page setups that can be imported from the selected drawing and whether they are located in model space or paper space. The **Name** column lists the name of the page setup, and the **Location** column lists the page setup location (model or layout).

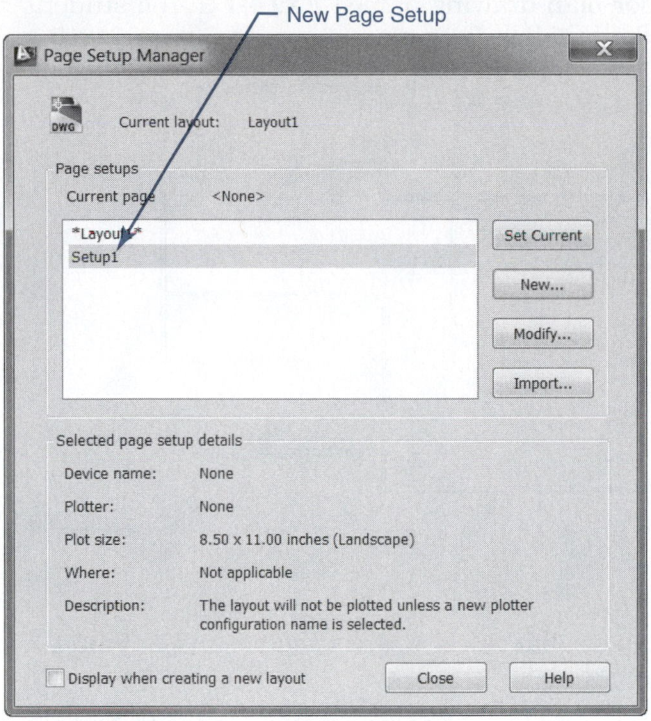

Figure 14-13
The **Page Setup Manager** with new page setup

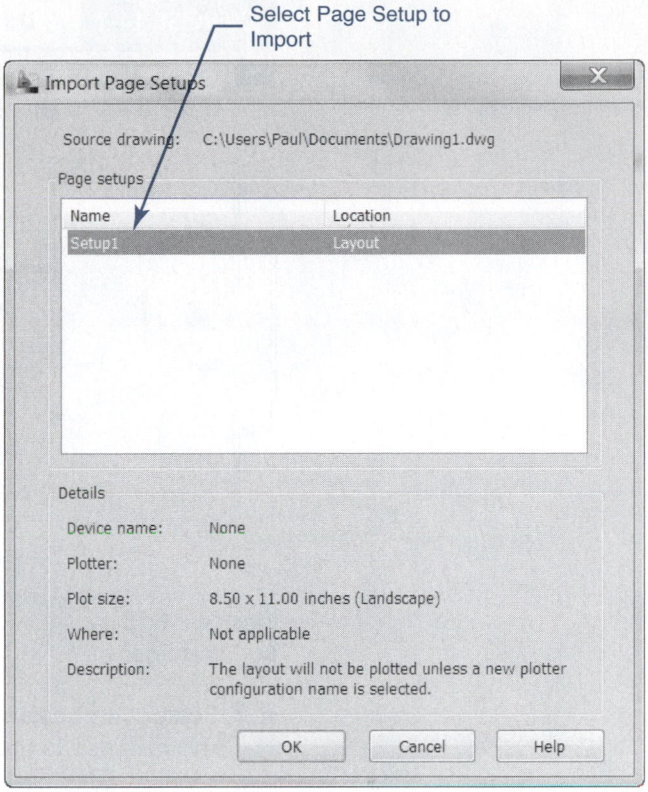

Figure 14-14
The **Import Page Setups** dialog box

NOTE

If a page setup with the name selected already exists in the drawing, a warning is displayed asking you whether you want to redefine it. Selecting **OK** overwrites the page setup with the new page setup settings.

The **Details** area at the bottom of the dialog box displays information about the selected page setup.

- **Device name** The name of the plot device specified in the currently selected page setup
- **Plotter** The type of plot device specified in the currently selected page setup
- **Plot size** The plot size and orientation specified in the currently selected page setup
- **Where** Physical location of the output device specified in the currently selected page setup
- **Description** Description of the output device specified in the currently selected page setup

Select **OK** to import the selected page setup.

Setting a Page Setup Current. The **Set Current** button on the **Page Setup Manager** dialog box sets the selected page setup current for the active layout so that all the page setup settings are updated to match the selected page setup.

EXERCISE 14-1 Using the Page Setup Manager

To access student data files, go to **www.pearsondesigncentral.com.**

1 Open the building floor plan drawing named ***EX14-1*** in the student data files to display the building floor plan shown in Figure 14-15.

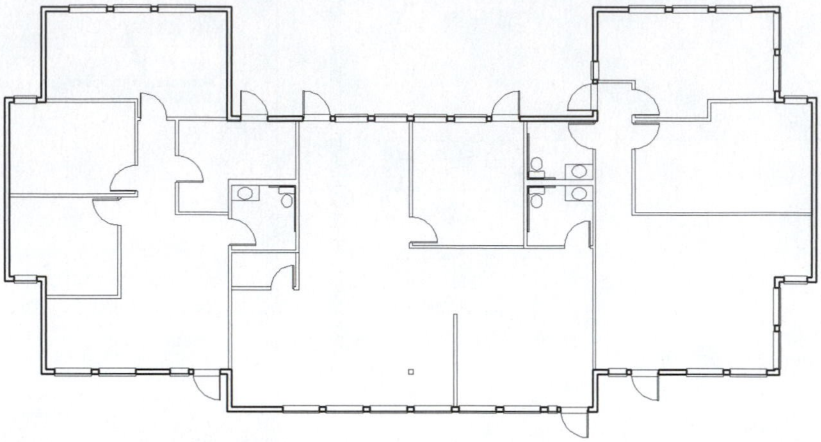

Figure 14-15
Building floor plan

2 Select the **Layout1** tab so that paper space is active and **Layout1** is the current layout.

3 Use the Page Setup Manager to set the associated plotter to **None** and the paper size to **ARCH D (36.00 × 24.00 Inches).**

4 Select the **Layout2** tab and switch to the **Layout2** layout.

5 Use the Page Setup Manager to set the associated plotter to **None** and the paper size to **ANSI B (17.00 × 11.00 Inches).**

6 Save the drawing as ***CH14_EXERCISE.***

Creating Layout Viewports

Layout viewports are the windows that you create in paper space that allow you to view the drawing information in model space at a specified scale (refer to Figure 14-5). Just like the windows in a building, layout viewports can be many different shapes and sizes. A layout viewport can be rectangular, polygonal, or even circular! You can create a single viewport that fits the paper size of the layout, or you can create multiple viewports. Each viewport is controlled independently so that different model space information can be displayed in each viewport, even at different scales if necessary.

NOTE

Do not attempt to create one layout viewport completely within the borders of another layout viewport because unpredictable results can occur. It is possible, though, to overlap viewports.

A layout viewport is treated just like other basic AutoCAD drawing objects such as lines, circles, and arcs. Similar to drawing other AutoCAD objects, a new viewport assumes the current object properties such as layer, color, and linetype when it is created.

After a viewport is created, you can modify it using any of the standard modify commands (**ERASE, MOVE, COPY, SCALE,** etc.). You can even use grips to resize a viewport quickly using the **STRETCH** option.

> **TIP**
>
> Typically, you do not want viewports to be displayed on the final plotted drawing. Because of this, layout viewports should be created on a unique layer so that you can control their visibility. The best approach is to create layout viewports on a layer whose **Plot** property is set to **No plot** so that you can see the viewports in the AutoCAD drawing window, but they do not plot.

SINGLE VIEWPORT

Ribbon & Panel:	Layout | Layout Viewports  Rectangular
Viewports Toolbar:	
Menu:	Views | Viewports | 1 Viewport
Command Line:	MVIEW VPORTS -VPORTS
Command Alias:	MV

You can create one or more layout viewports using the **MVIEW, -VPORTS,** or **VPORTS** command. Creating layout viewports using each of these commands is explained in the following sections.

Creating a Single Rectangular Viewport. The most common type of layout viewport is a single rectangular viewport. A single rectangular viewport is created by selecting two corner points. It is the default viewport option when you use either the **MVIEW** or **-VPORTS** command.

> **TIP**
>
> Do not forget to create a unique viewport layer set to **No plot** and make it current before you create a viewport using the **MVIEW** or **-VPORTS** command. Some typical layer names used include **Viewport** or **Vport.**

When you start either command, AutoCAD prompts you to *Specify corner of viewport or* ↓ as shown in Figure 14-16.

Figure 14-16
Locating the first corner point of a layout viewport

Select the first corner of the viewport or enter a coordinate value at the keyboard. AutoCAD then prompts you to *Specify opposite corner:* as shown in Figure 14-17 so you can specify the second point.

Figure 14-17
Locating the opposite corner point of a layout viewport

The viewport is immediately zoomed to the extents of the model space drawing information as shown in Figure 14-18.

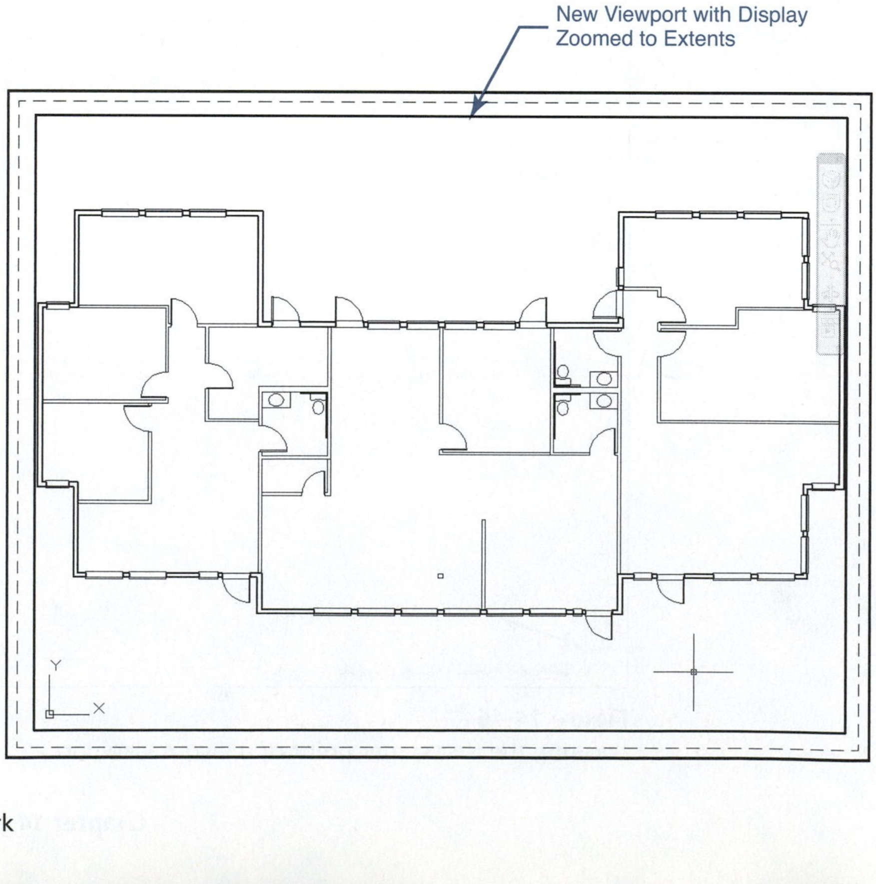

Figure 14-18
New layout viewport defaults to zoom extents

At this point, the viewport is not set at any standard scale. You must manually set the viewport scale factor using the techniques explained later in this chapter.

> **TIP**
>
> You can create a rectangular viewport that is the exact size of the layout's printable area using the **Fit** option. **Fit** is the default option so that you can simply press the <Enter> key when you run either the **MVIEW** or **-VPORTS** command before specifying the first viewport corner point.

POLYGONAL VIEWPORT	
Ribbon & Panel:	Layout | Layout Viewports 
Viewports Toolbar:	
Menu:	Views | Viewports | Polygonal Viewport
Command Line:	MVIEW VPORTS
Command Alias:	MV

Creating a Polygonal Viewport. You can create an irregularly shaped viewport with three or more sides using the **Polygonal** option of the **MVIEW** or **-VPORTS** command. A polygonal viewport is created by selecting multiple points.

To create a polygonal viewport, start the **MVIEW** or **-VPORTS** command and select the **Polygonal** option. AutoCAD prompts you to *Specify start point:*. After selecting the first point, AutoCAD prompts you to *Specify next point or* ↓ so you can start selecting points and define the viewport polygon as shown in Figure 14-19.

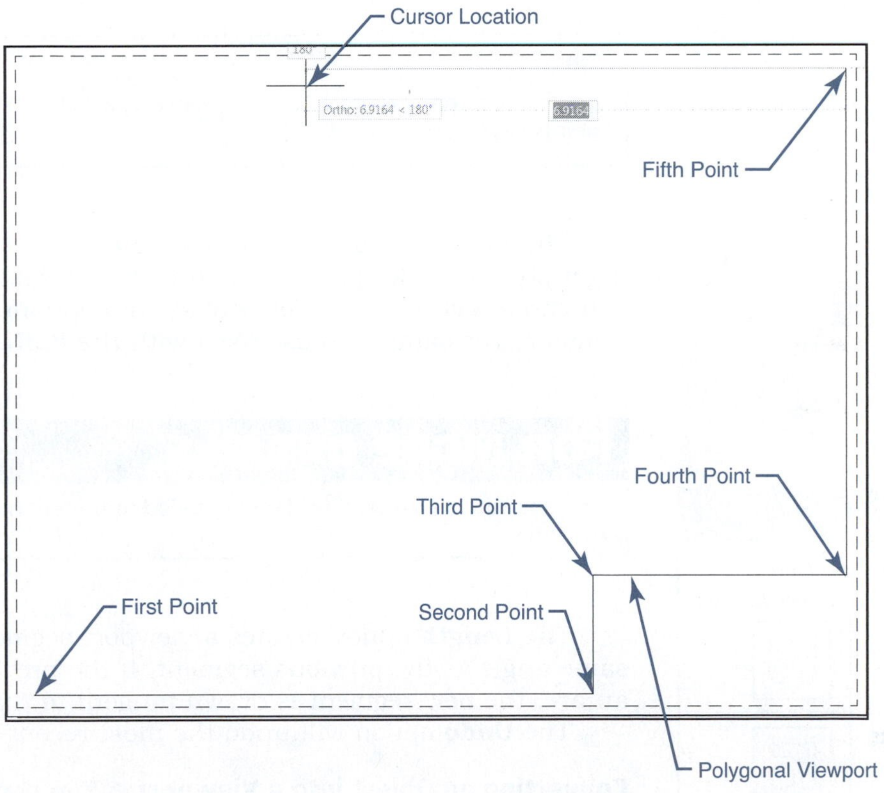

Figure 14-19
Creating a polygonal viewport

To finish the polygon viewport, you close it by selecting the **Close** option. The **Close** option draws a viewport segment from the last current point to the start point and exits the command. Similar to a rectangular viewport, a polygonal viewport is immediately zoomed to the extents of the model space drawing information as shown in Figure 14-20.

Figure 14-20
Using the **Close** option to complete a polygonal viewport

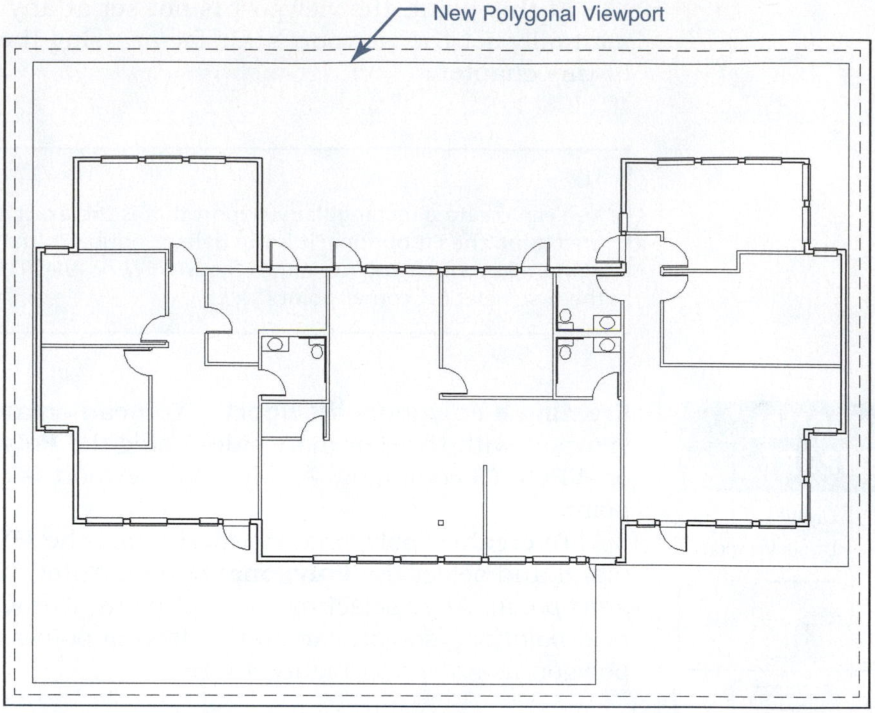

> **TIP**
>
> You can also press <**Enter**> to close a polygonal viewport after three or more viewport points have been defined.

The **Arc** option allows you to create arc segments when you are defining a polygonal viewport. You can pick a second point to define the arc, or you can select from a number of arc suboptions. The arc creation suboptions are the same as those used with the **PLINE** command.

> **FOR MORE DETAILS**
>
> See page 356 in Chapter 9 for more detailed information about using the **PLINE** command **Arc** options.

OBJECT	
Ribbon & Panel:	Layout | Layout Viewports
Viewports Toolbar:	
Menu:	Views | Viewports | Object
Command Line:	MVIEW, VPORTS
Command Alias:	MV

The **Length** option creates a viewport segment a specified length at the same angle as the previous segment. If the previous viewport segment is an arc, the new segment is drawn tangent to that arc segment.

The **Undo** option will undo the most recent viewport segment.

Converting an Object into a Viewport. You can convert any of the following objects into a layout viewport:

- Polyline
- Circle
- Ellipse
- Region
- Spline

NOTE

In order to convert a polyline into a viewport, the polyline must be closed, and it must have more than three vertices.

To convert an object into a layout viewport, start the **MVIEW** or **-VPORTS** command and select the **Object** option. AutoCAD prompts you to *Select object to clip viewport:* so you can pick the object to convert. A circle is shown converted to a viewport in Figure 14-21.

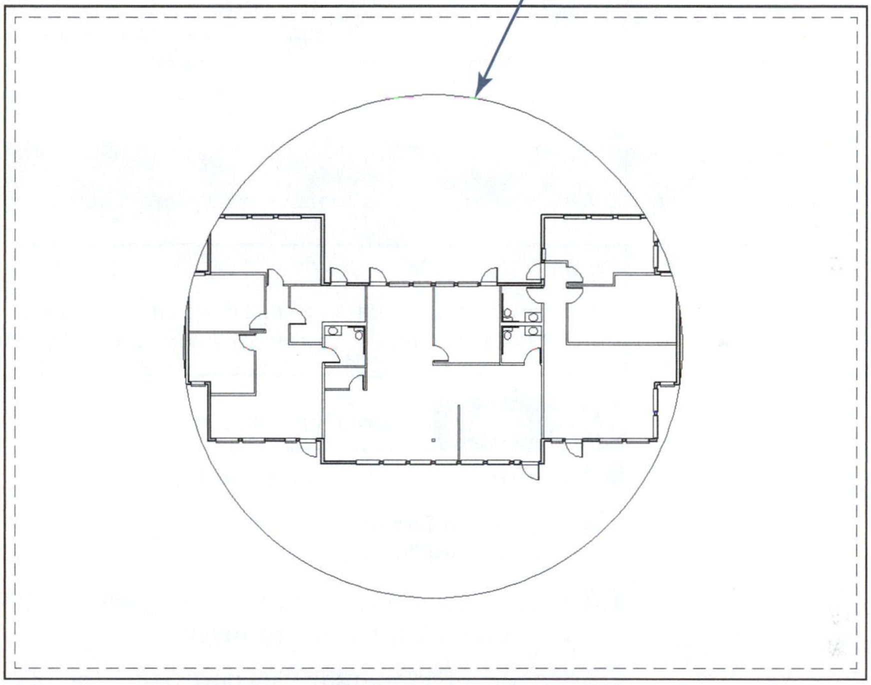

Figure 14-21
Converting a circle to a viewport

NEW VIEWPORT	
Ribbon & Panel:	Layout | Layout Viewports Named
Viewports Toolbar:	
Menu:	Views | Viewports | New Viewports...
Command Line:	VPORTS
Command Alias:	None

Using the Viewports Dialog Box. You can automatically create one or more rectangular viewports using the **Viewports** dialog box. The **VPORTS** command displays the **Viewports** dialog box shown in Figure 14-22.

The **Standard viewports:** box on the left displays a list of standard viewport configurations that you can select. The **Preview** window displays a preview of the selected viewport configuration.

The **Viewport Spacing:** box allows you to specify the spacing you want to apply between the viewports for the selected configuration. The **Preview** window is updated to show the results of the spacing indicated.

The **Setup:** list box allows you to switch between a 2D and a 3D viewport setup. When you select 3D, standard orthogonal 3D views are applied to the selected viewport configuration. The **Change view to:** list box replaces the view in the selected viewport with the view you select from the list. The **Visual Style:** list box allows you to change the visual style used for the viewport. It should typically be set to **2D Wireframe,** unless you are working in 3D.

Select **OK** after you have specified the desired configuration and spacing to exit the **Viewports** dialog box. After the dialog box is closed, AutoCAD asks you to specify the rectangular area within which to fit the viewport configuration by prompting you to pick two corner points.

Figure 14-22
The **Viewports** dialog box

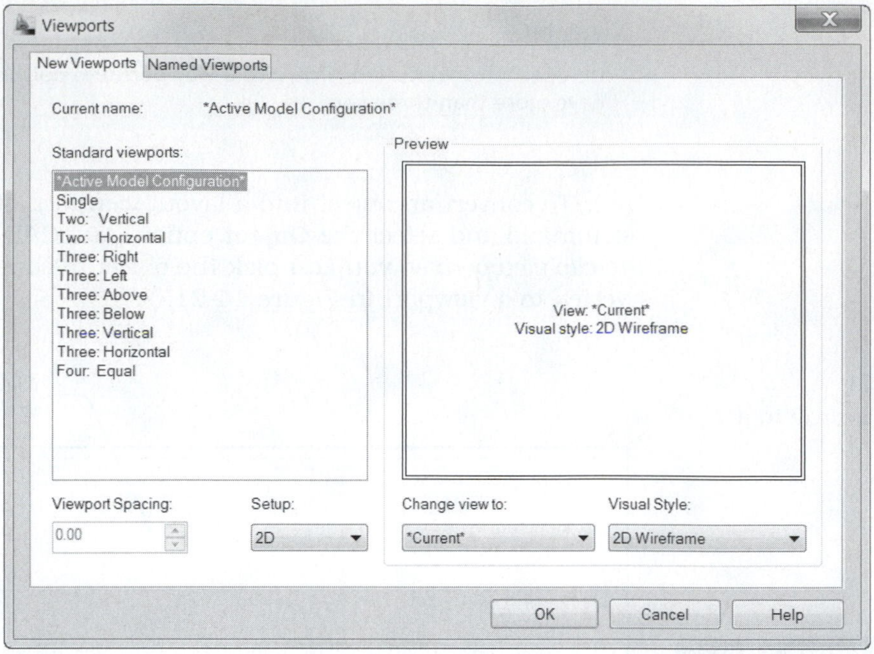

TIP

You can use the **Fit** option to make the viewport configuration fill the layout's printable area by pressing the **<Enter>** key when AutoCAD prompts for the first corner point.

EXERCISE 14-2 Creating Layout Viewports

1. Continue from Exercise 14-1.
2. Select the **Layout1** tab so that paper space is active and **Layout1** is the current layout.
3. Create a new layer named **Viewport,** set its **Plot** property to **No plot,** and make it the current layer.
4. Create a rectangular viewport using the **MVIEW** or **-VPORTS** command that is the same size as the printable area. *Hint:* The **Fit** option creates a viewport the same size as the printable area.
5. Select the **Layout2** tab and switch to the **Layout2** layout.
6. Create a rectangular viewport using the **MVIEW** or **-VPORTS** command that is the same size as the printable area.
7. Save the drawing.

NOTE

Double-clicking with your mouse directly on the viewport border maximizes the viewport so it fills the entire drawing window. You can double-click on the maximized border to return to the regular layout view. Maximizing viewports is covered later in this chapter.

Making a Viewport Current

There are three ways to make a layout viewport current:

- Select the **PAPER** button on the status bar.
- Enter the **MSPACE** or **MS** command.
- Double-click with your mouse inside a viewport.

The first two methods work best when you are working with a single layout viewport. If you have more than one viewport, you must double-click with your mouse inside the viewport you want to make current. When a viewport is current, its borderline becomes bold, and your mouse pointer changes to the cursor crosshairs mode as shown in Figure 14-23.

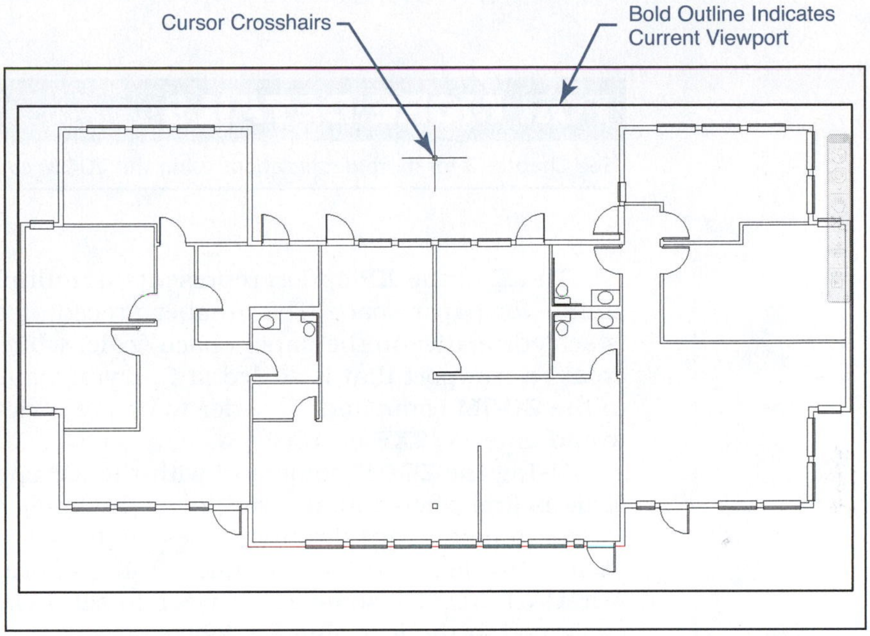

Figure 14-23
Making a layout viewport current

When a viewport is current, you can work on the model space drawing just like you are in model space—although it can be somewhat cumbersome working "through" the viewport. The ability to maximize viewports, which is discussed later in the chapter, makes this process much more user-friendly.

Switching Back to Paper Space. There are three ways to switch back to paper space so that no viewports are current:

- Select the **MODEL** button on the status bar.
- Enter the **PSPACE** or **PS** command.
- Double-click with your mouse outside all viewports.

All information that is created when paper space is active and no viewports are current is added to paper space exclusively **(TILEMODE = 0)**. In this mode, it is possible to add information (such as titles and drawing scales) directly above a viewport. This approach allows you to add information to your drawing that is displayed on the plotted drawing but does not need to be part of the model space design.

Setting the Viewport Scale

As explained in the introduction to the chapter, the scale of the drawing information displayed in a layout viewport is controlled by zooming in on and out of the active viewport. If you zoom in, the drawing gets larger, and the scale is increased. If you zoom out, the drawing gets smaller, and the scale is decreased. To set a viewport to a standard drafting scale, you must zoom in or out in the viewport at a zoom scale factor equal to the scale you want the drawing information to plot. For instance, if you want the drawing information in a viewport to plot at a scale of 2:1, you must zoom in by a scale factor of 2 in the viewport so that everything appears twice as large as actual size. To plot at a scale of 1:2, you zoom out by a scale factor of 1/2 so that everything is half of its actual size.

Zooming in on and out of a layout viewport to a specific scale factor is done using the **XP** option of the **ZOOM** command.

FOR MORE DETAILS

See Chapter 3 for more details about using the **ZOOM** command.

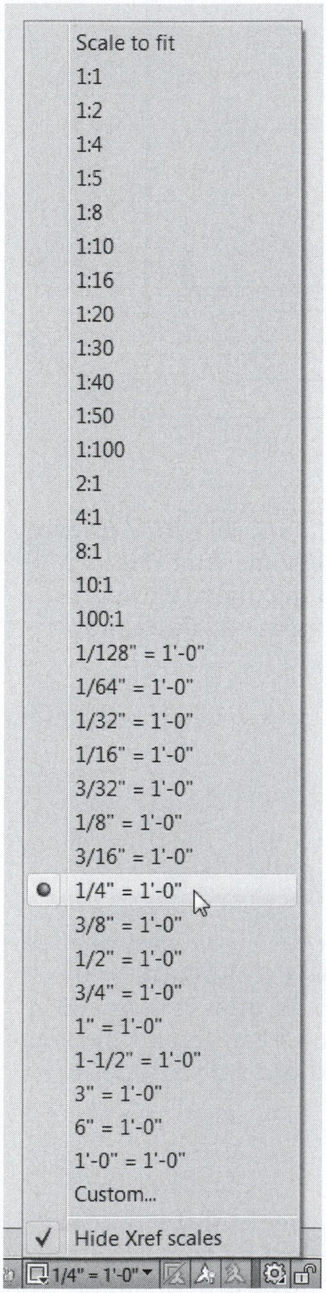

Figure 14-24
Setting the viewport scale

The **X** in the **XP** option represents a multiplication sign, and the **P** stands for paper space. The number preceding the **XP** is the value the view is scaled relative to the paper space scale, which is 1:1. For example, to create a viewport that is scaled at 2:1, you would enter **2XP** in response to the **ZOOM** command. In order to create a view that is scaled 1:2, you would enter **1/2XP** or **.5XP.**

Using the **ZOOM** command with the **XP** option to set the viewport scale is fine when you are working with simple scales such as 2:1 or 1:2. Converting standard drafting scales such as 1/4″=1′-0″ or 1–12″=1′-0″ to their equivalent scale factors takes a little more time and effort. Luckily, AutoCAD provides some easier ways to set a viewport's scale, which are explained in the following sections.

Setting the Viewport Scale on the Status Bar. The easiest way to set the viewport scale is via the **Viewport Scale** button on the right side of the AutoCAD status bar. Clicking anywhere on the **Viewport Scale** button displays a list of standard drafting scales that you can use to set the zoom scale factor of the current viewport as shown in Figure 14-24.

The viewport scale is displayed on the status bar only when a viewport is current. You can make a viewport current by double-clicking in the viewport with your mouse. Select the desired scale factor from the list, and the viewport is zoomed in or out by the preestablished scale factor.

TIP

After the viewport scale is set, zooming in and out using any **Zoom** tools should be avoided. Any incremental zoom is enough to change the zoom scale factor so that it is no longer correct. Panning the display is not a problem because the zoom factor remains the same. The easiest way to prevent inadvertent zooms is to lock the viewport by selecting the **Lock/Unlock Viewport** button to the left of the **Viewport Scale** button on the status bar when the viewport is current and toggling it so the **Lock** icon is closed.

Using the Properties Palette to Set the Viewport Scale. You can also control the viewport scale factor via the **Properties** palette. Setting the viewport scale using the **Properties** palette requires that you be in paper space in order to select the viewport object. Selecting a viewport displays the properties shown in Figure 14-25 so that you can select a **Standard scale** from the list.

Figure 14-25
Setting the viewport scale via the **Properties** palette

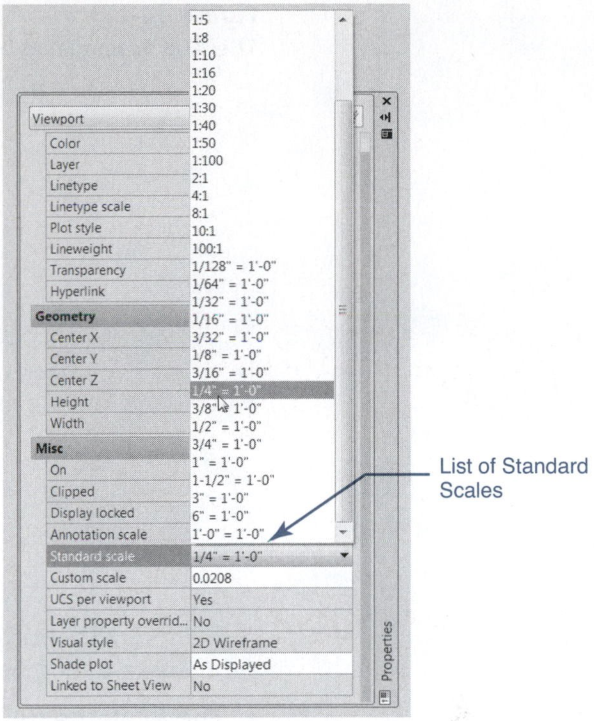

> **TIP**
>
> You can also set a custom scale using the **Properties** palette if the scale you need is not in the **Standard scale** list. To specify a custom scale, enter the desired scale factor in the **Custom scale** property text field.

Adding and Editing Scales in the Standard Scale List. The **SCALELISTEDIT** command allows you to add new scales or edit existing scales that appear in the **Scale List** box. You can either type in the command, or you can select **Custom...** from the bottom of the scale list. The **Edit Drawing Scales** dialog box shown in Figure 14-26 is displayed.

The **Scale List** on the left displays the list of currently defined scales. Selecting a scale from the list displays the ratio of paper units to drawing units at the bottom of the **Scale List.**

Figure 14-26
The **Edit Drawing Scales** dialog box

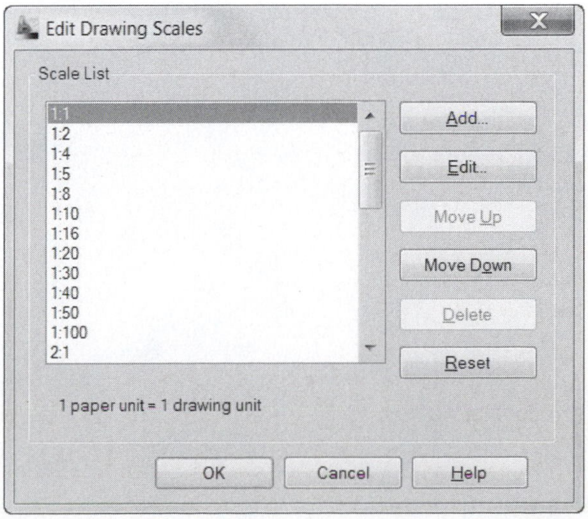

Figure 14-27
The **Add Scale** dialog box

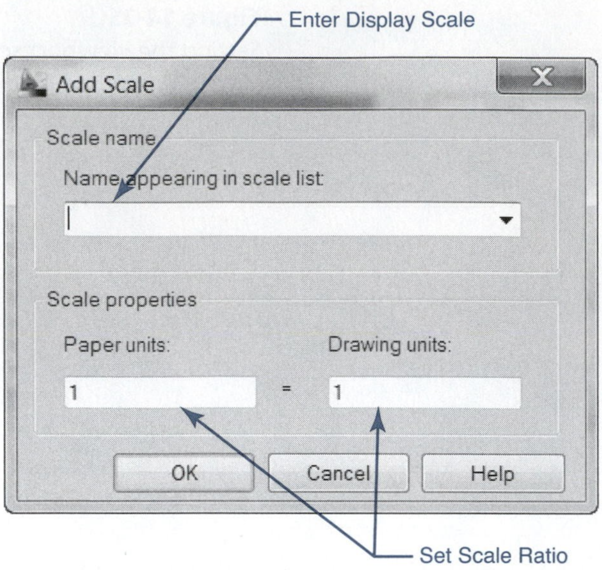

The **Add...** button allows you to add a custom scale to the list via the **Add Scale** dialog box shown in Figure 14-27. In this dialog box:

- The **Scale name** area is where you enter the descriptive or numeric name as you want it to appear in the list in the **Name appearing in scale list:** text box.
- The **Scale properties** area is where you set the ratio of paper units to drawing units by entering the numeric values in the **Paper units:** and **Drawing units:** text boxes.

The **Edit...** button in the **Edit Drawing Scales** dialog box allows you to edit an existing scale via the **Edit Scale** dialog box shown in Figure 14-28. In this dialog box:

- The **Scale name** area is where you update the descriptive or numeric name as you want it to appear in the list in the **Name appearing in scale list:** text box.

Figure 14-28
The **Edit Scale** dialog box

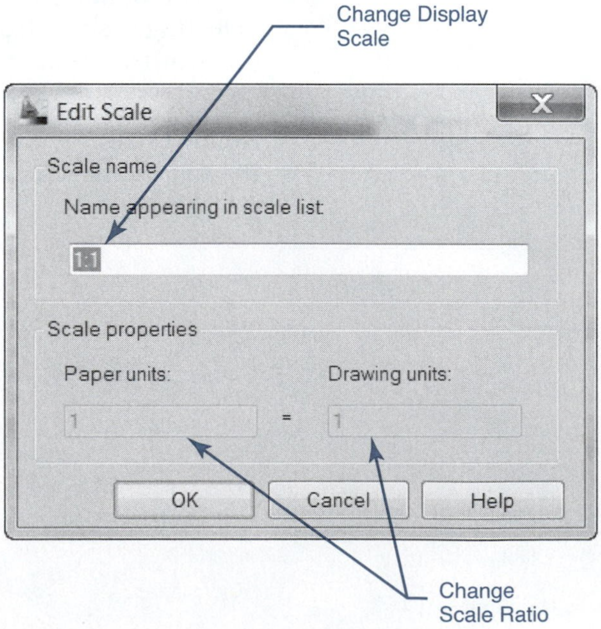

- The **Scale properties** area is where you change the ratio of paper units to drawing units by entering new numeric values in the **Paper units:** and **Drawing units:** text boxes.

The **Move Up** button in the **Edit Drawing Scales** dialog box moves the currently selected scale in the **Scale List** up one position so that it appears in that position in all scale list boxes. The **Move Down** button moves the currently selected scale in the **Scale List** down one position so that it appears in that position in all scale list boxes.

The **Delete** button permanently removes the currently selected scale from the **Scale List.** The **Reset** button deletes any custom scales that were added and restores the default list of standard AutoCAD scales.

Locking the Viewport Display

You can protect the viewport scale from being accidentally changed by locking the viewport display so it is impossible to zoom or pan inside the viewport when it is current. When a viewport is locked, any attempt to zoom or pan affects the entire paper space layout similarly to if you were working in paper space. The current viewport remains active; it is just temporarily disabled during the zoom or pan process. The easiest way to lock a viewport is to select the **Lock/Unlock Viewport** button on the status bar as shown in Figure 14-29. In addition, you can also use the following methods:

- Select viewport and right-click to display the shortcut menu and set the **Display locked** menu item to **Yes.**
- Set the **Display locked** property to **Yes** via the **Properties** palette.
- Use the **MVIEW** command's **Lock** option and select the viewport.

To unlock a viewport, select the **Lock/Unlock Viewport** button or use any of the options listed above and set the **Locked** property to **Off** or **No.**

Figure 14-29
The **Lock/Unlock Viewport** button on the status bar

EXERCISE 14-3 **Setting the Viewport Scale**

1. Continue from Exercise 14-2.
2. Select the **Layout1** tab so that paper space is active and **Layout1** is the current layout.
3. Make the viewport created in Exercise 14-2 the active viewport, and **Zoom Extents** so that the entire floor plan fills the viewport.
4. Set the viewport scale to **1/4″ = 1′-0″** by selecting it from the **Viewport Scale** list on the right side of the status bar.
5. Select the **Lock/Unlock Viewport** button to the left of the **Viewport Scale** list to lock the viewport.
6. Make paper space the active drawing environment by selecting the **MODEL** button on the status bar and toggling it to **PAPER.**
7. **Layout1** should now look similar to Figure 14-30. It now is 1/4″ = 1′-0″ scale drawing on a D-size sheet (36″ × 24″).

Figure 14-30
Layout1 with **1/4″ = 1′-0″** scale viewport on D-size paper (36″ × 24″)

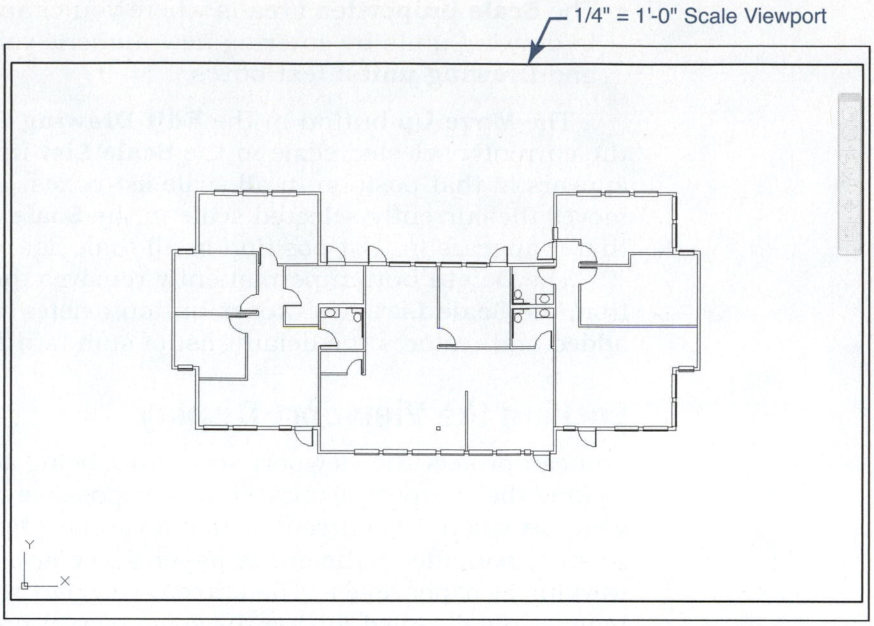

8 Select the **Layout2** tab and switch to the **Layout2** layout.

9 Make the viewport created in Exercise 14-2 the active viewport, and **Zoom Extents** so that the entire floor plan fills the viewport.

10 Set the viewport scale to **1/8″ = 1′-0″** by selecting it from the **Viewport Scale** list on the right side of the status bar.

11 Select the **Lock/Unlock Viewport** button to the left of the **Viewport Scale** list to lock the viewport.

12 **Layout2** should now look similar to Figure 14-31. It is now a 1/8″ = 1′-0″ scale drawing on a B-size sheet (17″ × 11″).

Figure 14-31
Layout2 with **1/8″ = 1′-0″** scale viewport on B-size paper (17″ × 11″)

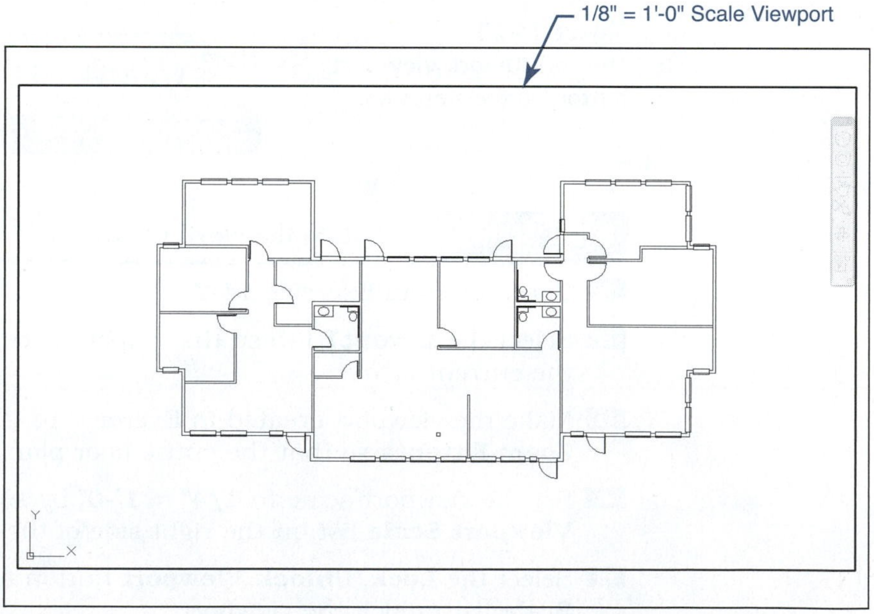

13 Make paper space the active drawing environment by selecting the **MODEL** button on the status bar and toggling it to **PAPER**.

14 Save the drawing.

Controlling Layers per Layout Viewport

As mentioned earlier, it is possible to control layers per layout viewport so that you can display different model space drawing information in each individual viewport while not affecting the information in model space. You can freeze and thaw layers in individual viewports, as well as control the color, linetype, lineweight, and transparency level used. These individual viewport specific layer settings are referred to as *viewport layer overrides*.

The most popular viewport layer override is the ability to freeze a layer in an individual viewport. This allows you to leave all of the layers on (thawed) in model space but then freeze different layers in each viewport to create multiple views of the same model space information and create different drawings. For example, one layout could be used to display the electrical plan information, and another layout might display only the HVAC plan information. The possibilities are endless, especially when combined with the concept of external reference drawings.

> **FOR MORE DETAILS**
>
> See Chapter 17 for more information about using external reference drawings (xrefs).

There are two different ways to freeze layers per viewport: in the current viewport or in any new viewports. Freezing layers in the **New VP Freeze** column means that any information on the selected layers will not be displayed when you create any new layout viewports in the future.

Freezing layers in the current viewport is most common. Obviously, to freeze layers in the current viewport, you must first make the viewport current. After the viewport is current, start the **LAYER** command to display the **Layer Properties Manager**.

The viewport layer override columns are displayed at the right before the **Description** column as shown in Figure 14-32.

To freeze a layer in the current viewport, click on the sun icon in the **VP Freeze** column and change it to a snowflake icon, just as with the regular **Freeze** option. The selected layer is frozen in the current viewport as shown in Figure 14-33.

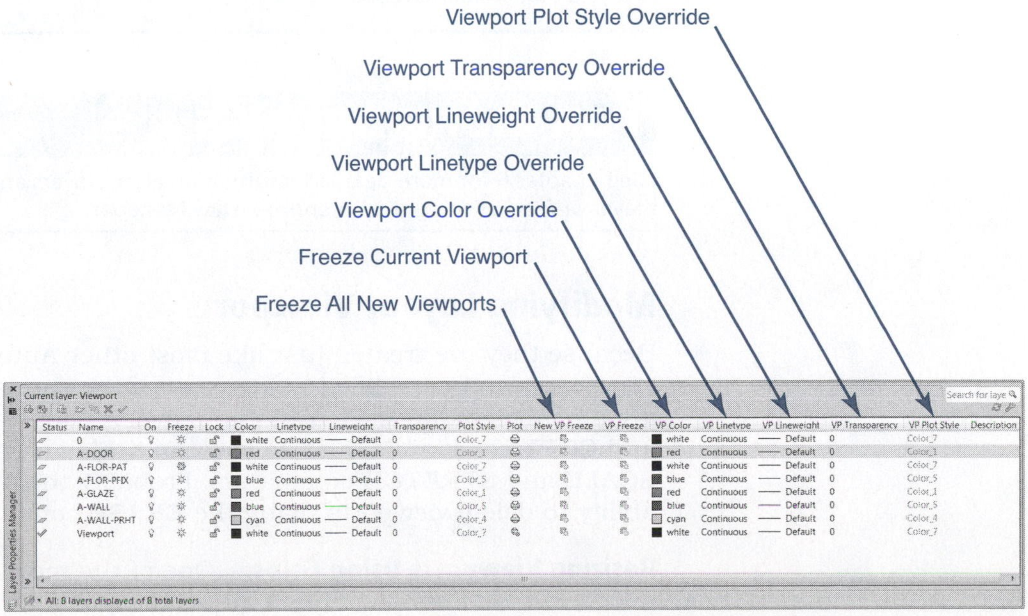

Figure 14-32
The **Layer Properties Manager** in paper space

Figure 14-33
Viewport with **A-DOOR** layer frozen

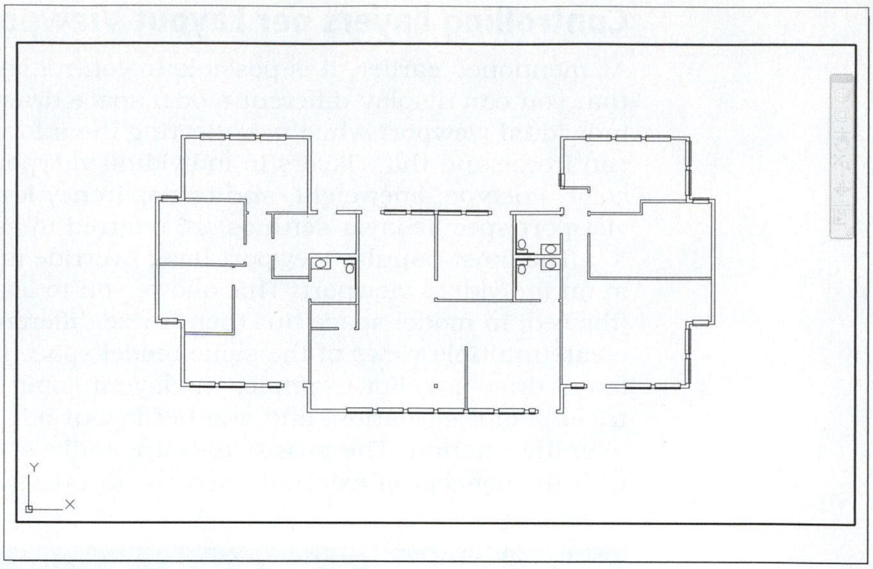

> **NOTE**
>
> When any viewport layer override is applied, a different background color is used in the **Layer Properties Manager.**

The same technique can be used to override the other layer settings (color, linetype, lineweight, transparency, and plot style). Simply make the viewport current and select the desired overrides.

You can remove viewport layer overrides using the right-click menu in the **Layer** list in the **Layer Properties Manager**. The **VPLAYEROVERRIDESMODE** system variable allows you to temporarily turn off all viewport layer overrides.

> **TIP**
>
> When a viewport contains layer overrides, a **Viewport Overrides** property filter is automatically created so that you can select the **Viewport Overrides** filter and view only the layers that contain overrides.

> **FOR MORE DETAILS**
>
> See Chapter 6 for more detailed information about layers and controlling the different layer properties using the **Layer Properties Manager.**

Modifying Layout Viewports

Because they are treated just like most other AutoCAD objects, layout viewports can be modified using most of the same modify commands you are already familiar with. You can move or copy viewports using the **MOVE** and **COPY** commands, just as you can scale and stretch viewports via the **SCALE** and **STRETCH** commands. Probably the most important is the ability to delete viewports using the **ERASE** command.

Resizing Viewports Using Grips. One of the most common ways to resize a viewport is to simply rely on grips. Using a viewport's grips and the

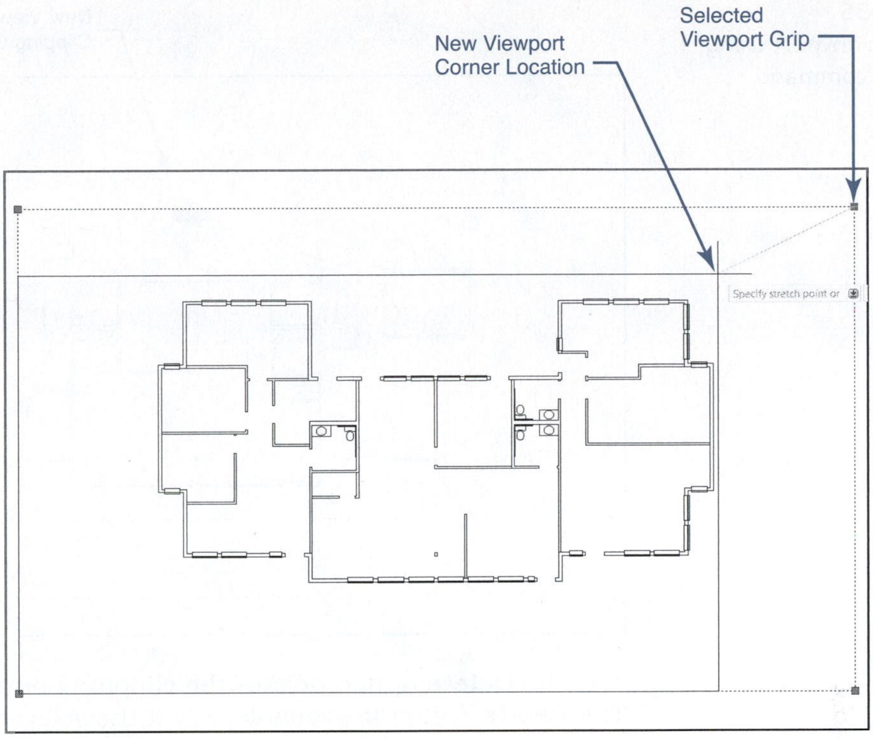

Figure 14-34
Using grips to resize a viewport

Stretch option allows you to modify a viewport quickly and make it the size needed as shown in Figure 14-34.

FOR MORE DETAILS

See page 301 in Chapter 7 for detailed information about using grips.

Clipping Viewports. You can change the shape of a viewport using the **VPCLIP** command.

Using the **VPCLIP** command, you can either select a different object to convert into a viewport, or you can redefine the viewport using a new polygon viewport.

VIEWPORT CLIP	
Ribbon & Panel:	Layout | Layout Viewports  Clip
Viewports Toolbar:	
Pull-down Menu:	None
Command Line:	VPCLIP
Command Alias:	None

NOTE

It is possible to convert circles, closed polylines, ellipses, closed splines, and regions into a layout viewport.

When you start the **VPCLIP** command and a viewport is not already selected, AutoCAD prompts you to *Select viewport to clip:* so you can select a viewport. Once a viewport is selected, AutoCAD prompts you to *Select clipping object or* ↓. You can either select an object to convert into a viewport, or you can define a new polygon window by selecting the **Polygon** option. The options for creating a polygon viewport are the same as explained earlier in the chapter. The new viewport that is created to replace the existing viewport is referred to as a *clipping boundary*, as shown in Figure 14-35.

Figure 14-35
Clipping a viewport using the **VPCLIP** command

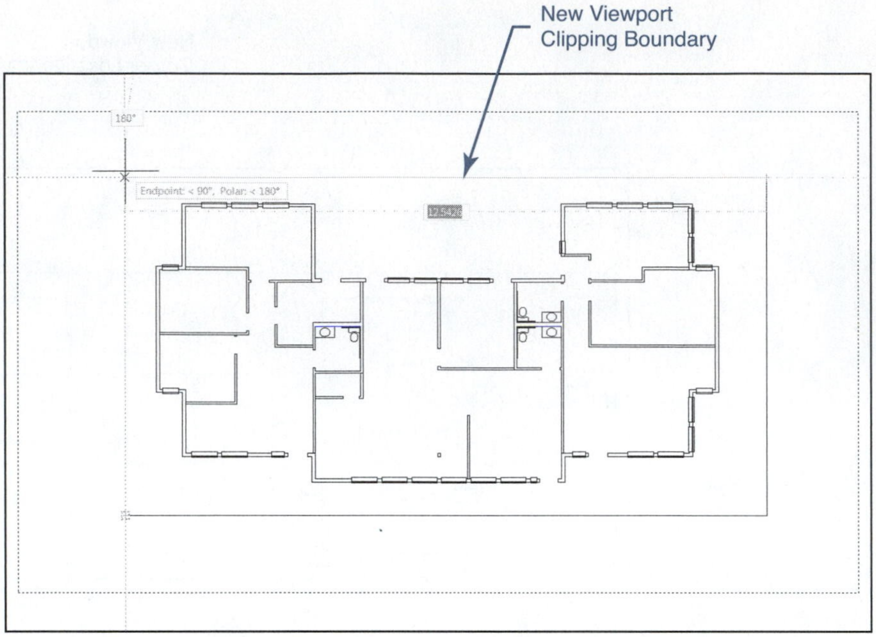

The **Delete** option deletes the clipping boundary of a selected viewport. The **Delete** option is available only if the selected viewport has already been clipped once using the **VPCLIP** command.

> **TIP**
>
> You can determine whether a viewport has been clipped using the **VPCLIP** command by checking the viewport's **Clipped** property via the **Properties** palette. If it is set to **Yes,** the viewport has been clipped.

Turning Viewport Display Off and On

You can turn the viewport display on and off temporarily so that the model space objects displayed in the viewport are no longer visible. This can be used to either speed up drawing regeneration time or control what drawing information is plotted. There are three ways to turn a viewport off:

- Select the viewport, right-click to display the shortcut menu, and set the **Display Viewport Objects** menu item to **No**.
- Set the viewport's **On** property to **No** via the **Properties** palette.
- Use the **MVIEW** command's **Off** option and select the viewport.

> **NOTE**
>
> The viewport boundary is still displayed if a viewport is turned off. Only the model space information is turned off.

A viewport that has been turned off is considered inactive. You can only have up to 64 viewports active at one time.

To make a viewport active again, use any of the options listed above to toggle the viewport's **Display** property to **On** or **Yes.**

> **TIP**
>
> The maximum number of active viewports is controlled using the **MAXACTVP** system variable. The maximum value is 64.

Maximizing a Viewport

You can maximize a layout viewport so that it fills the entire drawing window area, which makes it easier to work on your model space design without switching entirely from paper space to model space. This feature was introduced to get around the complications of working "through" a layout viewport to get to the model space drawing information while you were still in paper space. There are four ways to maximize a layout viewport:

- Select the **Maximize Viewport** button on the status bar.
- Double-click on the viewport outline.
- Select the viewport, right-click to display the shortcut menu, and select the **Maximize Viewport** menu item.
- Type **VPMAX<Enter>.**

Any method enlarges the viewport to fit the drawing window display area and changes the border to a thick red hashed line (see Figure 14-36).

To pan and zoom when a viewport is maximized and not change the original viewport display when you switch back to the viewport, use the **Minimize Viewport** options below. When a viewport is maximized, it is almost as though you were working in model space on the **Model** tab.

Figure 14-36
Drawing display with a layout viewport maximized

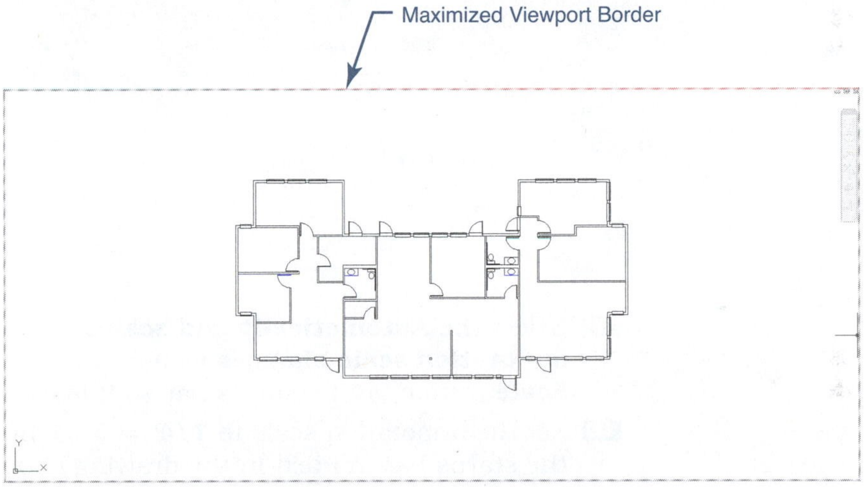

There are four ways to restore the maximized layout viewport back to its original size and display:

- Select the **Minimize Viewport** button on the status bar.
- Double-click on the maximized viewport.
- Select the viewport, right-click to display the shortcut menu, and select the **Minimize Viewport** menu item.
- Type **VPMIN<Enter>.**

EXERCISE 14-4 **Working with Multiple Annotation Scales**

1. Continue from Exercise 14-3.
2. Create a text style named **Notes** with the following settings:
   a. Font = **Simplex.shx** AutoCAD font
   b. **Annotative** should be checked
   c. Paper text height = **0.125″**

3 Create the following layer:

Name	Color	Linetype	Lineweight	Description
A-Anno-Note	3	Continuous	0.30 mm	Drawing note text

4 Select the **Model** tab so that model space is active.

5 Set the **Notes** text style current on the **Annotation** panel.

6 Set the **A-Anno-Note** layer current in the **Layer** list box.

7 Set the annotation scale to **1/8″ = 1′-0″** by selecting it from the **Annotation Scale** list on the status bar.

8 Create the text shown in Figure 14-37 using the **Center** justification option.

Figure 14-37
1/8″ = 1′-0″ scale view with 12″ high text

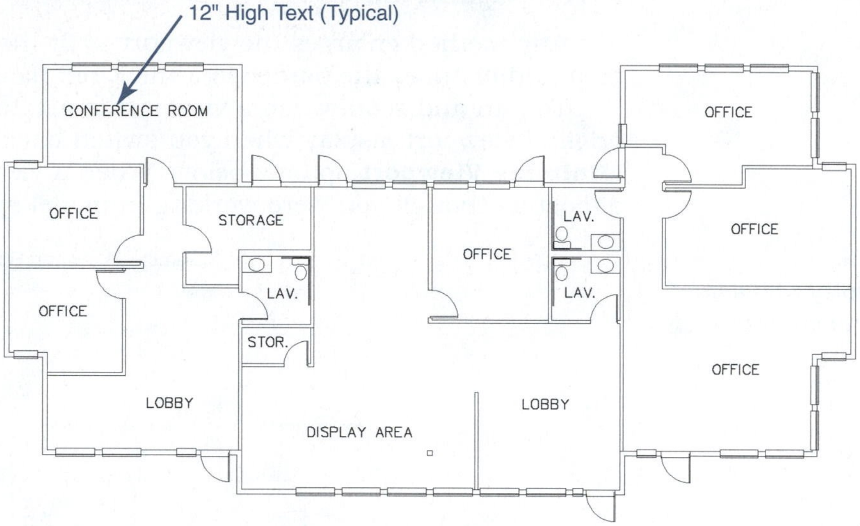

9 Select the **Automatically add scales to annotative objects when the annotation scale changes** icon on the far right of the **Annotation Scale** button on the status bar so it is on.

10 Set the annotation scale to **1/4″ = 1′-0″** by selecting it from the list on the status bar. All text in the drawing should scale down by 1/2.

11 Center the 1/4″ = 1′-0″ text in each room by using the upper left grip to move each piece of text individually of its 1/8″ = 1′-0″ scale representation as shown in Figure 14-38.

Figure 14-38
1/4″ = 1′-0″ scale view with 6″ high text

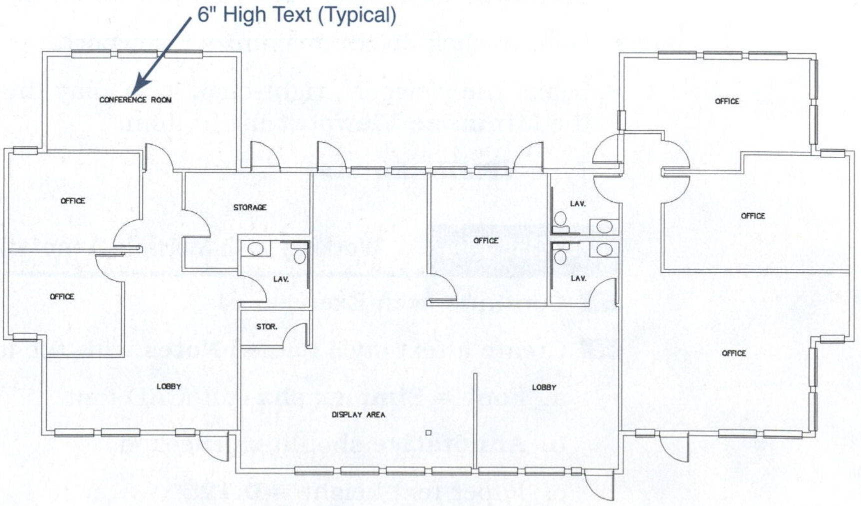

12 Select the **Layout1** tab so that paper space is active and **Layout1** is the current layout. Only the 1/4″ = 1′-0″ text is visible.

13 Select the **Layout2** tab and switch to the **Layout2** layout. Only the 1/8″ = 1′-0″ text is visible.

14 Make paper space the active drawing environment by double-clicking outside the viewport.

15 Save the drawing.

Managing Layouts

The following sections describe how to manage layouts so that you can do the following:

- Create a new layout
- Rename a layout
- Move or copy a layout
- Delete a layout

One of the easiest ways to accomplish any of these tasks is to rely on the layout's right-click shortcut menu. Right-clicking with your mouse on any layout tab displays the shortcut menu shown in Figure 14-39.

Figure 14-39
The **Layout** right-click shortcut menu

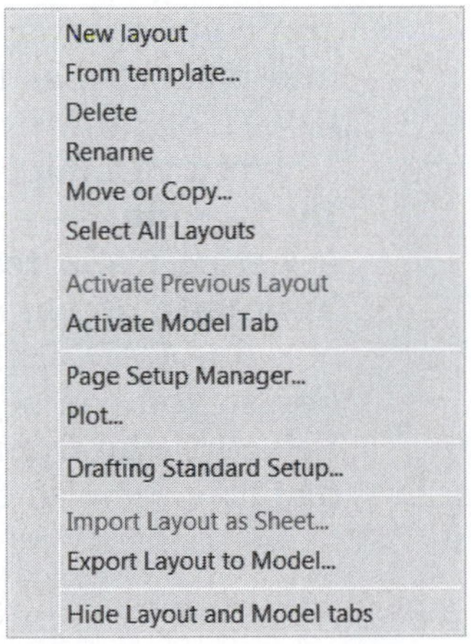

NEW LAYOUT	
Ribbon & Panel:	None
Layouts Toolbar:	
Menu:	Insert| Layout| New Layout
Command Line:	LAYOUT
Command Alias:	LO

TIP

The **Select All Layouts** menu item on the **Layout** right-click menu provides a quick way to perform a task on all the layouts at one time.

The **LAYOUT** command also provides most of the same functionality, but as you might expect, it's not quite as user-friendly. Emphasis is placed on using the right-click menu where appropriate in the following sections.

Creating a New Layout

There are four ways to create a new layout:

- Add a new generic layout tab with the default settings so that the settings must be updated via the Page Setup Manager.

- Import a layout from an existing drawing file (DWG), drawing template file (DWT), or drawing exchange format file (DXF).
- Use the **Create Layout** wizard that steps you through the layout setup.
- Copy an existing layout tab in the current drawing file and rename it.

The first three methods are described in the following sections. Copying a layout is covered a little later.

Adding a Generic Layout with Default Settings. You can quickly add a generic layout with default page setup settings. You must then use the Page Setup Manager described earlier in this chapter to set up the layout as required.

You can add a generic layout by selecting **New layout** from the **Layout** cascade menu on the **Insert** menu, by right-clicking and selecting **New layout** from the shortcut menu, or by using the **New** option of the **LAYOUT** command.

AutoCAD prompts you to *Enter new Layout name <Layout3>:* if you add a new layout via the **Insert** menu or the **LAYOUT** command. The default layout name is "Layout" followed by an integer representing the layout number in the sequence.

When you select **New layout** from the right-click shortcut menu, a layout is added with the default name, and you must rename it. Renaming layouts is covered later in this chapter.

LAYOUT FROM TEMPLATE	
Ribbon & Panel:	None
Layouts Toolbar:	
Menu:	Insert | Layout | Layout from Template
Command Line:	LAYOUT
Command Alias:	LO

Importing a Layout from a Drawing Template. To save time and effort, you can import a layout that is already set up with the correct paper size and plot settings from an existing drawing file (DWG), drawing template file (DWT), or drawing exchange format file (DXF).

You can import a layout by selecting **Layout from Template...** from the **Layout** cascade menu on the **Insert** menu, by right-clicking and selecting **From template...** from the shortcut menu, or by using the **Template** option of the **LAYOUT** command.

AutoCAD displays the **Select Template From File** standard file dialog box so you can select the file from which you want to import the layout. Selecting the **Open** button gets a list of the layouts in the selected file and displays them in the **Insert Layout(s)** dialog box shown in Figure 14-40.

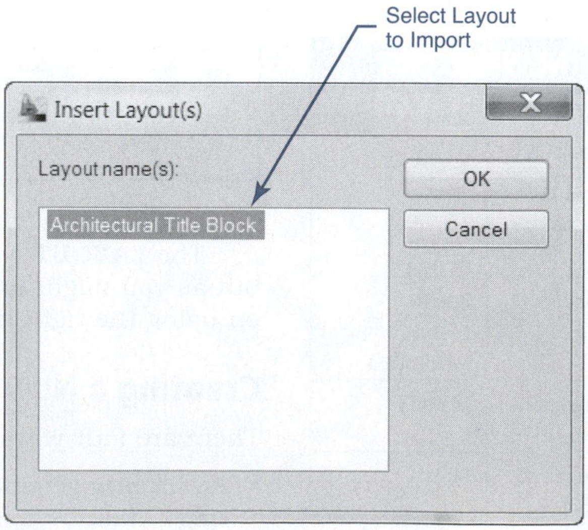

Figure 14-40
The **Insert Layout(s)** dialog box

CREATE LAYOUT WIZARD	
Ribbon & Panel:	None
Layouts Toolbar:	None
Menu:	Insert | Layout | Create Layout Wizard
Command Line:	LAYOUTWIZARD
Command Alias:	None

NOTE

If a layout with the same name already exists in the current drawing during the import process, the layout is still added, but it is renamed by prefixing the layout name with a default layout name and a dash (-).

Select one or more layouts you want to import in the **Layout name(s):** list box and select **OK.** The selected layout(s) are imported with all their settings and drawing information and added to the right end of the layout tabs at the bottom of the drawing window.

Creating a New Layout Using the Layout Wizard. The **Create Layout** wizard automates the process of creating, *and setting up*, a new layout by prompting you for information about the different layout settings in a series of preprogrammed steps.

You can start the **Create Layout** wizard by selecting **Create Layout Wizard** from the **Layout** cascade menu on the **Insert** menu or by using the **LAYOUTWIZARD** command. The **Create Layout** dialog box is displayed with the **Begin** step displayed as shown in Figure 14-41.

The steps that the wizard will take you through are listed on the left in sequence from top to bottom with the arrow to the left indicating the current step. Select the **Next** button to continue to the next step or the **Back** button to return to a previous step if you want to verify or change anything. The setup steps and options are as follows:

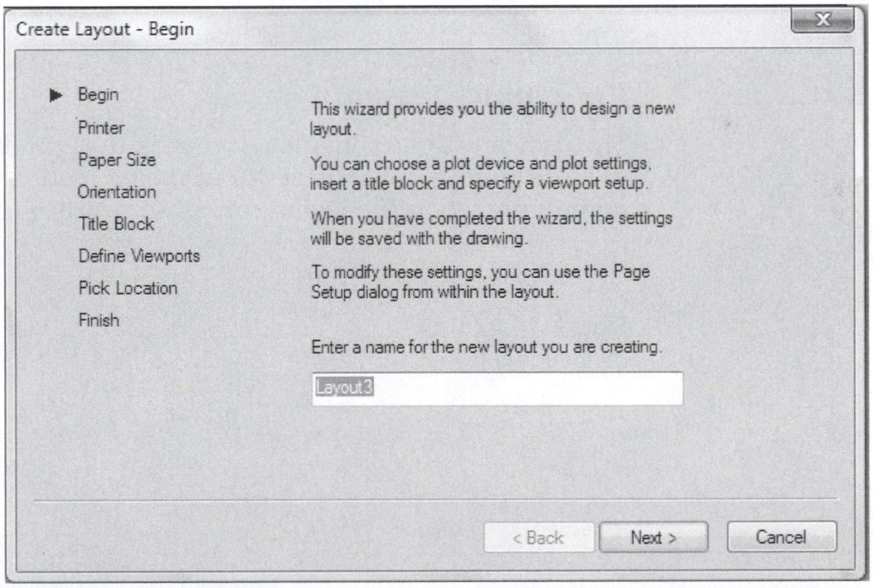

Figure 14-41
The **Create Layout—Begin** step

- **Begin** Allows you to enter the desired name for the new layout
- **Printer** Allows you to select a system printer/plotter output device
- **Paper Size** Allows you to specify a paper size based on the printer selected in the previous step and switch drawing units between millimeters and inches
- **Orientation** Allows you to switch between the portrait and landscape paper orientation modes

- **Title Block** Allows you to insert a predefined title block in the layout as a block or an xref. The title block drawings listed are located in the default AutoCAD **Template** folder

FOR MORE DETAILS

See Chapter 16 for more information about blocks. See Chapter 17 for more information about external references (xrefs).

- **Define Viewports** Allows you to select a layout viewport configuration and set the viewport scale from a list of predefined standard scales
- **Pick Location** Allows you to define the area to fill with the viewport configuration selected in the previous step by picking two corner points. If no location is selected, AutoCAD uses the layout's printable area
- **Finish** Exits the **Create Layout** wizard and creates the new layout with the selected settings

NOTE

You can always change the information entered in the **Create Layout** wizard later by selecting the layout and using the Page Setup Manager explained earlier in the chapter.

Renaming a Layout

The easiest way to rename a layout is to right-click on the layout tab and select **Rename** from the shortcut menu. You can then update the layout name directly on the layout tab as shown in Figure 14-42.

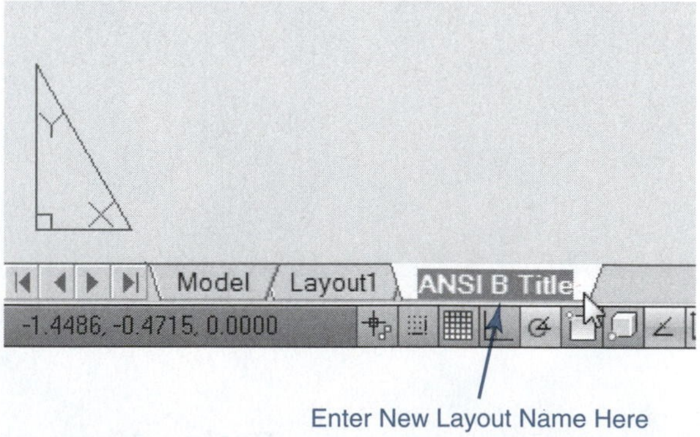

Figure 14-42
Renaming a layout

You can also rename a layout using the **Rename** option of the **LAYOUT** command. Using the **LAYOUT** command requires that you enter the layout to change in response to *Enter layout to rename <Layout1>:* where the current layout is the default name. AutoCAD then prompts you to *Enter new layout name:* so you can enter the new name.

TIP

You can double-click on a layout tab to automatically rename a layout.

Moving and Copying a Layout

The easiest way to move or copy a layout is to right-click on the layout tab and select **Move or Copy...** from the shortcut menu to display the **Move or Copy** dialog box shown in Figure 14-43.

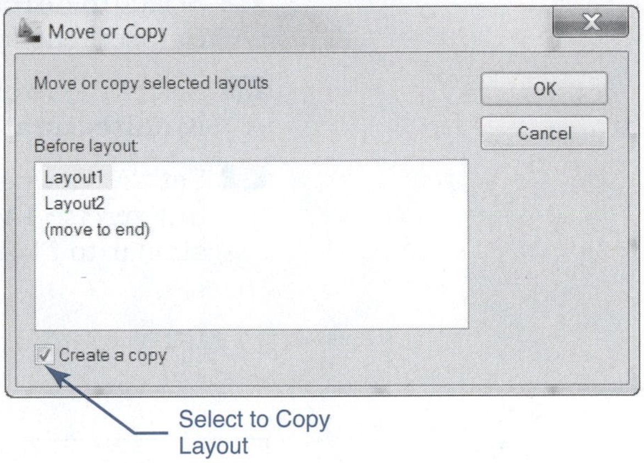

Figure 14-43
The **Move or Copy** dialog box

Select the layout from the list in the **Before layout:** list box that you want to locate the current layout *before*. When you select **OK,** the layout will be moved or copied so it appears as the layout tab directly preceding, or to the left of, the selected tab.

If you want to make a copy of a layout and move it at the same time, select the **Create a copy** check box on the bottom of the dialog box. AutoCAD creates a copy of the layout with the same name as the current layout with a numerical suffix representing the sequence appended in parentheses. For instance, **Layout1** becomes **Layout1(2).**

TIP

It is possible to select a layout tab and drag it into another position with your mouse.

Deleting a Layout

The easiest way to delete a layout is to right-click on the layout tab and select **Delete** from the shortcut menu. AutoCAD displays a warning before deleting the layout so you can cancel the operation or select **OK** to continue.

NOTE

You cannot delete the **Model** tab.

You can also delete a layout using the **Delete** option of the **LAYOUT** command. Using the **LAYOUT** command requires that you enter the layout to delete in response to *Enter name of layout to delete <Layout1>:* where the current layout is the default name.

EXERCISE 14-5 Managing Layouts

To access student data files, go to **www.pearsondesigncentral.com.**

1. Continue from Exercise 14-4.
2. Right-click on a layout tab and select the **From template...** menu item on the **Layout** right-click menu in order to insert a new **Architectural D-Size** layout from an existing AutoCAD drawing template file.
3. Select the **Architectural D-Size.dwt** template file in the student data files in the **Select Template From File** dialog box and the **Open** button to display the **Insert Layout(s)** dialog box.
4. Select the **Architectural Title Block** layout and select the **OK** button to insert the layout.
5. Select the **Architectural Title Block** tab and switch to the **Architectural Title Block** layout.
6. Set the viewport scale to **1/4″ = 1′-0″** using the techniques learned in Exercise 14-3 and center the floor plan in the viewport so it looks similar to Figure 14-44.

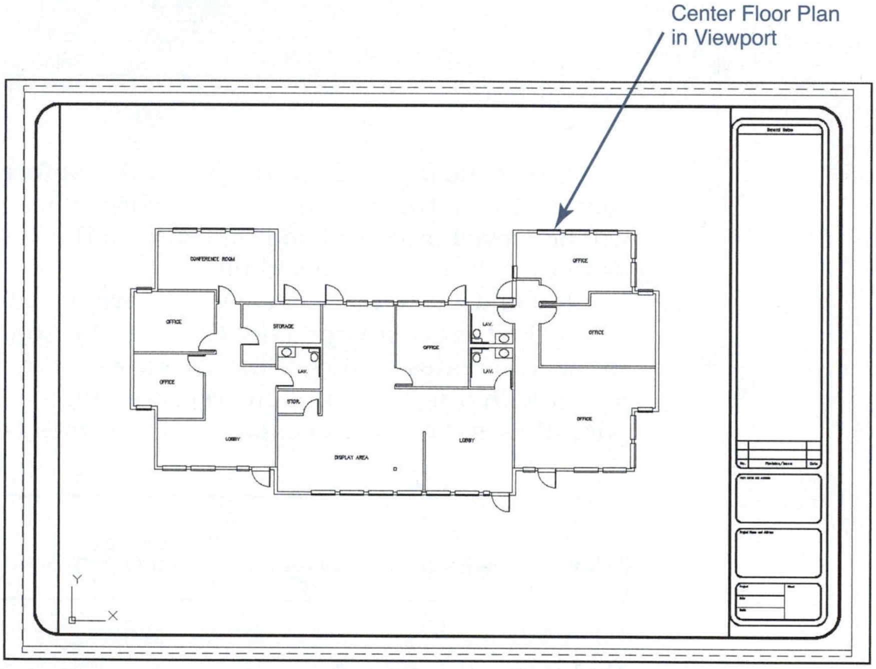

Figure 14-44
The **Architectural Title Block** layout with **1/4″** = **1′-0″** viewport

7. Rename the **Architectural Title Block** layout to **ANSI D Title Block** by right-clicking with your mouse on the **Architectural Title Block** tab and selecting **Rename** from the shortcut menu.
8. Rename the **Layout2** layout to **ANSI B Title Block** by right-clicking with your mouse on the **Layout2** tab and selecting **Rename** from the shortcut menu.
9. Delete the **Layout1** layout by right-clicking with your mouse on the **Layout1** tab and selecting **Delete** from the shortcut menu.
10. Save the drawing.

Paper Space Linetype Scale

The **PSLTSCALE** system variable allows you to scale linetype definitions based on the viewport scale so that linetype definitions will display the same in multiple viewports that have different scale factors. Without paper space linetype scaling, the same linetype definition will appear at different scales in each viewport as shown in Figure 14-45.

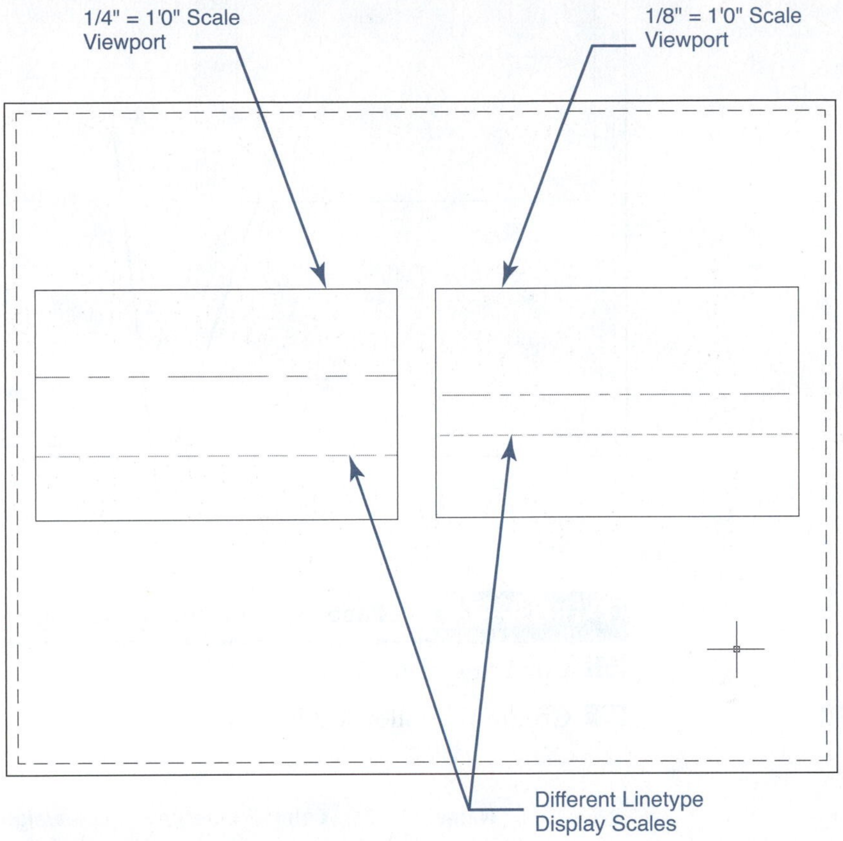

Figure 14-45
Paper space linetype scaling not turned on

Setting **PSLTSCALE** to **1** (on) tells AutoCAD to scale the linetype definitions of all the objects displayed in a viewport by the inverse of the viewport scale factor as shown in Figure 14-46.

Be aware that the global linetype scale controlled using the **LTSCALE** system variable is still in effect when paper space linetype scale is turned on and can have some unintended effects. Typically, the **LTSCALE** system variable is set to **1** when paper space linetype scale is being used **(PSLTSCALE = 1)**.

FOR MORE DETAILS

See page 238 in Chapter 6 for more information about linetype definitions and the **LTSCALE** system variable.

Figure 14-46
Paper space linetype scaling turned on

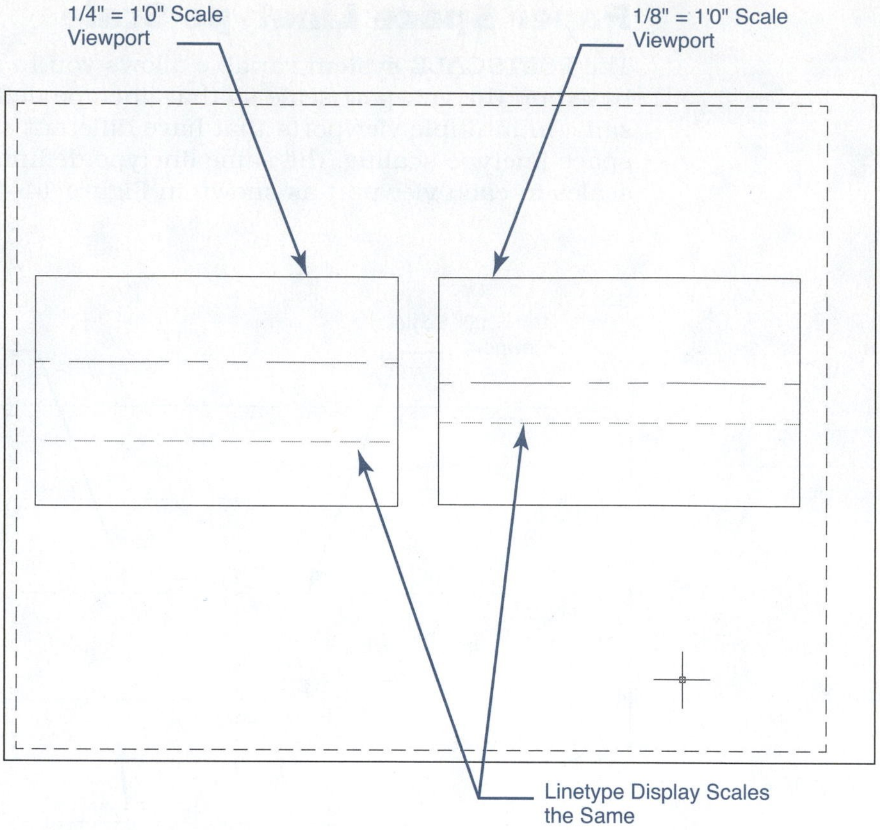

EXERCISE 14-6 Paper Space Linetype Scaling

1. Continue from Exercise 14-5.
2. Create the following layers:

Name	Color	Linetype	Lineweight	Description
A-Roof-Otln	1	Hidden	Default	Roof outline
A-Site-Prop	5	Phantom	Default	Property line

3. Set the **PSLTSCALE** system variable to **1** so paper space linetype scaling is turned on.
4. Set the **LTSCALE** system variable to **1** to so that global linetype scaling is turned off.
5. Switch to the **ANSI D Title Block** layout.
6. Maximize the viewport using the **Maximize Viewport** button on the status bar so you can work in model space through the viewport.
7. Set the **A-Roof-Otln** layer current in the **Layer** list box.
8. Create the roof outline as shown in Figure 14-47. **Do not** draw dimensions.
9. Set the **A-Site-Prop** layer current in the **Layer** list box.
10. Create the property line as shown in Figure 14-47. **Do not** draw dimensions.

11 Switch to the **ANSI B Title Block** layout.

12 The roof outline and property line should also appear scaled correctly in the 1/8″ = 1′-0″ viewport.

13 Save the drawing.

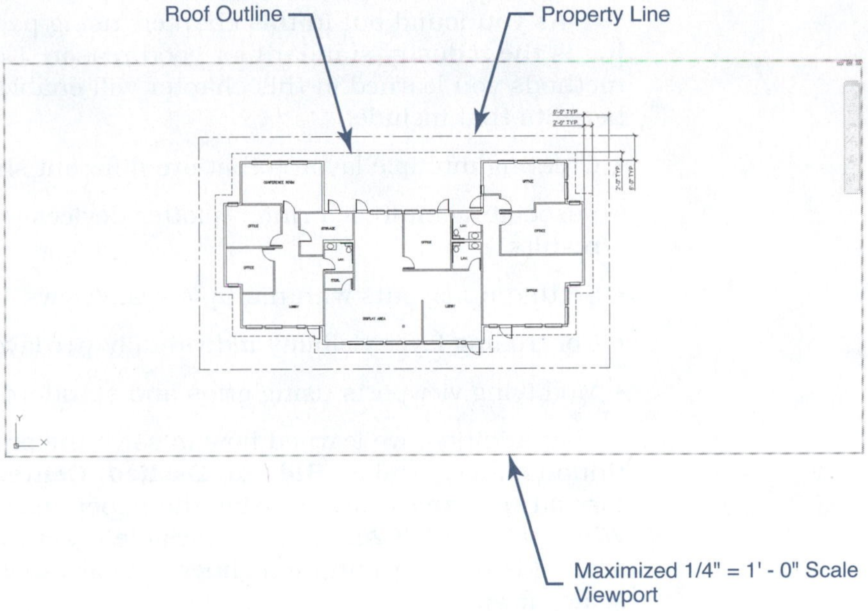

Figure 14-47
Using paper space linetype scaling

Chapter Summary

In this chapter, we explained the different ways to set up and lay out a drawing using paper space techniques so that it is ready for output to the associated printer, plotter, or other output device.

As you found out in this chapter, using paper space to lay out a drawing is the industry standard for good reason. Using the techniques and methods you learned in this chapter will enable you to take advantage of benefits that include:

- Creating multiple layouts that are different sheet sizes
- Associating multiple printer/plotter devices to create different output results
- Setting up layouts with multiple scale views
- Controlling layer visibility individually per layout viewport
- Modifying viewports using grips and standard AutoCAD commands

In addition, we learned how to solve the problem of displaying noncontinuous linetypes (i.e., **Hidden, Dashed, Center,** etc.) at different scale factors on the same drawing using the paper space linetype scaling feature. When the **PSLTSCALE** system variable is set to **1** and paper space linetype scaling is on, noncontinuous lines appear exactly the same in different scale viewports.

FOR MORE DETAILS

See Chapter 15 for more information about plotting to different output devices.

Chapter Test Questions

Multiple Choice

Circle the correct answer.

1. Most of a drawing's line work and annotation features are drawn in:
   a. Paper space
   b. Model space
   c. Drawing space
   d. None of the above
2. The paper size of a layout is controlled via its:
   a. Drawing limits
   b. Associated plotting device
   c. b and d
   d. Page setup
3. The user-defined window created in a paper space layout that allows you to view and scale information in model space is referred to as a:
   a. Layout portal
   b. Layout viewport

c. Layout window
d. Layout aperture

4. The printable area of a layout is represented by:
   a. Shadow
   b. Edge of the layout
   c. Dashed line
   d. Drawing limits
5. The command used to create a layout viewport is:
   a. **MVIEW**
   b. **VPORTS**
   c. **-VPORTS**
   d. All of the above
6. The layout viewport creation option that creates a viewport the same size as a layout's printable area is:
   a. **Polygonal**
   b. **Object**
   c. **Fit**
   d. **Restore**
7. To make a layout viewport current:
   a. Double-click with the mouse inside the viewport
   b. Type **MS<Enter>**
   c. Type **PS<Enter>**
   d. a and b
8. The scale of a layout viewport can be set using:
   a. The **Viewport Scale** list on the status bar
   b. The **ZOOM** command to specify a zoom scale factor
   c. The **Properties** palette
   d. All of the above
9. To prevent a viewport scale from changing accidentally, it is best to:
   a. Turn the viewport off
   b. Work only in model space
   c. Freeze the viewport layer
   d. Lock the viewport display
10. The system variable used to control whether paper space linetype scaling is on or off is:
    a. **PSLTSCALE**
    b. **LTSCALE**
    c. **PAPERSCALE**
    d. All of the above

Matching

Write the number of the correct answer on the line.

a. **TILEMODE** ______

b. Page setup ______

c. Layout viewport ______

d. Printable area ______

e. Page Setup Manager ______

f. .PC3 file ______

g. **MVIEW** command ______

h. **-VPORTS** command ______

i. **VCLIP** command ______

j. **PSLTSCALE** ______

1. Displays details of the current page setup, creates new page setups, and modifies existing page setups
2. System variable that controls whether paper space linetype scaling is on or off
3. Command used to create one or more layout viewports
4. Plotter configuration file used to store and manage printer/plotter settings
5. Command used to create one or more layout viewports
6. System variable that controls whether you are working in model space or paper space
7. User-defined window created in a paper space layout that allows you to view drawing information in model space
8. Controls the settings that affect the appearance of a plotted drawing
9. Actual physical area that can be printed for the currently specified plotting device and paper size
10. Command used to change the shape of a viewport

True or False

Circle the correct answer.

1. **True or False:** Most drawing line work and annotation features are drawn in model space.
2. **True or False:** You cannot locate any drawing information in a paper space layout.
3. **True or False:** The associated printer/plotter device determines what paper sizes are available.
4. **True or False:** Layout viewport scale is controlled by zooming in and out in a viewport.
5. **True or False:** Setting the associated plot device to **None** allows you select any standard paper size.
6. **True or False:** A layout viewport is treated like most other AutoCAD drawing objects (lines, circles, etc.).
7. **True or False:** It is not possible to create circular viewports.
8. **True or False:** It is possible to add your own custom scales to the AutoCAD standard **Scale List.**
9. **True or False:** It is possible to freeze and thaw layer information in each individual viewport.
10. **True or False:** The shape of a viewport cannot be changed; it must be deleted and then re-created in the new shape.

chapterfourteen

Chapter Projects

G Project 14-1: *Classroom Plan, continued from Chapter 13* [BASIC]

To access student data files, go to **www.pearsondesigncentral.com.**

1. Open drawing ***P13-1*** from Chapter 13.
2. Right-click on a layout tab and select **From template...** from the shortcut menu to import a layout.
3. Open the **Architectural D-Size.dwt** drawing template in the student data files, and import the **Architectural Title Block** layout from the template.
4. Select the **Architectural Title Block** layout to set it current. There is a single viewport in this layout. Make the viewport current by double-clicking inside the viewport boundary.
5. **Zoom Extents** so the drawing fills the viewport and set the **Viewport Scale** to **1/2″ = 1′-0″**. Position the drawing within the viewport so it matches Figure 14-48.
6. Switch back to paper space by double-clicking outside the viewport.
7. Delete the **Layout1** and **Layout2** layouts.
8. Save the drawing as ***P14-1***.

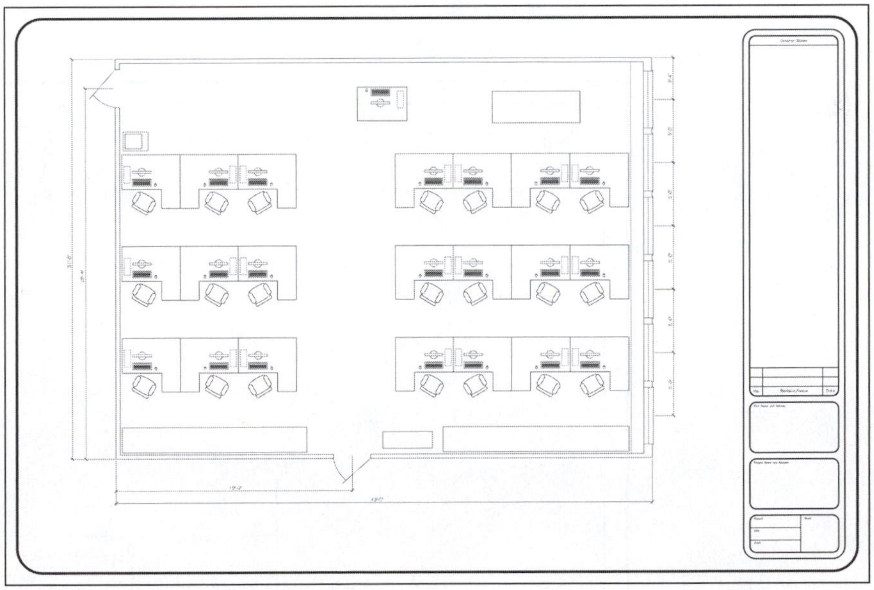

Figure 14-48

M Project 14-2: *B-Size Mechanical Border, continued from Chapter 13* [INTERMEDIATE]

1. Open template file ***Mechanical B-Size.DWT*** from Chapter 13.
2. Press the **<Ctrl>+A** keyboard combination to select everything in the drawing.
3. Press the **<Ctrl>+<Shift>+C** keyboard combination, and specify **0,0** as the base point.
4. Press the **<Del>** key or use the **ERASE** command to delete all the selected objects.
5. Select the **Layout1** tab to switch to paper space.
6. Erase the existing default viewport.
7. Use the Page Setup Manager to set the associated plotter to **None** and the paper size to **ANSI B (17.00 × 11.00 Inches).**
8. Press the **<Ctrl>+V** keyboard combination and enter **–.25,–.75** when AutoCAD prompts you to *Specify insertion point:* to paste the title border in paper space.
9. Create a polygonal viewport on layer **Viewport** at the inside border edges as shown in Figure 14-49.
10. Rename the **Layout1** layout to **Mechanical B-Size** and delete the **Layout2** layout.
11. Save the drawing as a template file named ***Mechanical B-Size.DWT.***

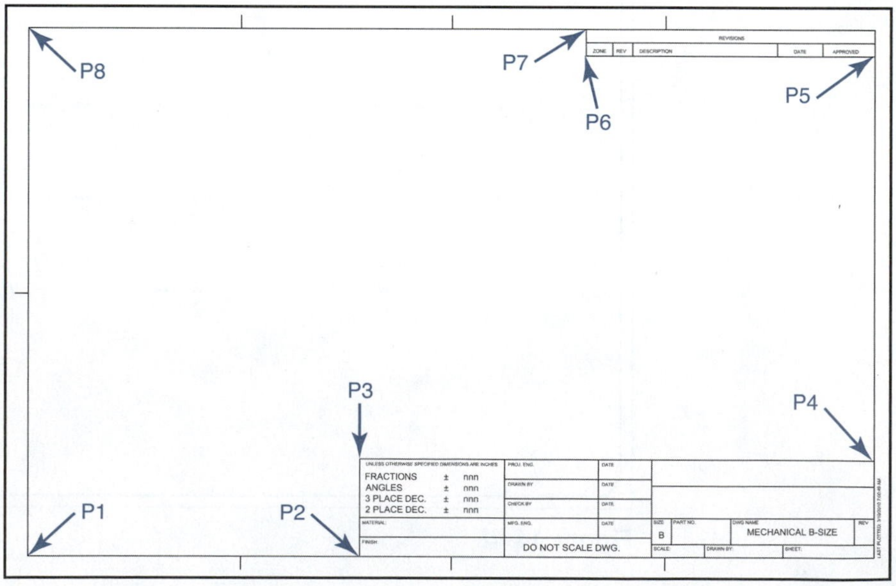

Figure 14-49

A Project 14-3: *Architectural D-Size Border, continued from Chapter 13* [ADVANCED]

1. Open template file ***Architectural D-Size.DWT*** from Chapter 13.
2. Press the **<Ctrl>+A** keyboard combination to select everything in the drawing.
3. Press the **<Ctrl>+<Shift>+C** keyboard combination, and select the bottom left corner of the border corner tick marks using the **Endpoint** object snap.
4. Press the **<Del>** key or use the **ERASE** command to delete all the selected objects.
5. Select the **Layout1** tab to switch to paper space.
6. Erase the existing default viewport.
7. Use the Page Setup Manager to set the associated plotter to **None** and the paper size to **ARCH D (36.00 × 24.00 Inches).**
8. Press the **<Ctrl>+V** keyboard combination and enter **–.25, –.75** when AutoCAD prompts you to *Specify insertion point:* to paste the title border in paper space.
9. Create a rectangular viewport on layer **A-Anno-Vprt** at the inside border edges as shown in Figure 14-50.

Figure 14-50

10. Rename the **Layout1** layout to **Architectural D-Size** and delete the **Layout2** layout.
11. Make sure that paper space is the current drawing environment by double-clicking outside the viewport.
12. Save the drawing to a template file as ***Architectural D-Size.DWT***.

M Project 14-4: *Optical Mount—English Units, continued from Chapter 13* [INTERMEDIATE]

1. Open drawing ***P13-4*** from Chapter 13.
2. Select **From template...** from the **Layout** right-click menu to import a layout.
3. Import the **Mechanical B-Size** layout and border from the **Mechanical B-Size.dwt** template file created in Project 14-2.
4. Select the **Mechanical B-Size** layout to make it current.
5. Set the viewport scale to **2:1** and center the view as shown in Figure 14-51.
6. Lock the viewport display so the view scale doesn't change.
7. Delete the **Layout1** and **Layout2** layouts.
8. Save the drawing as ***P14-4***.

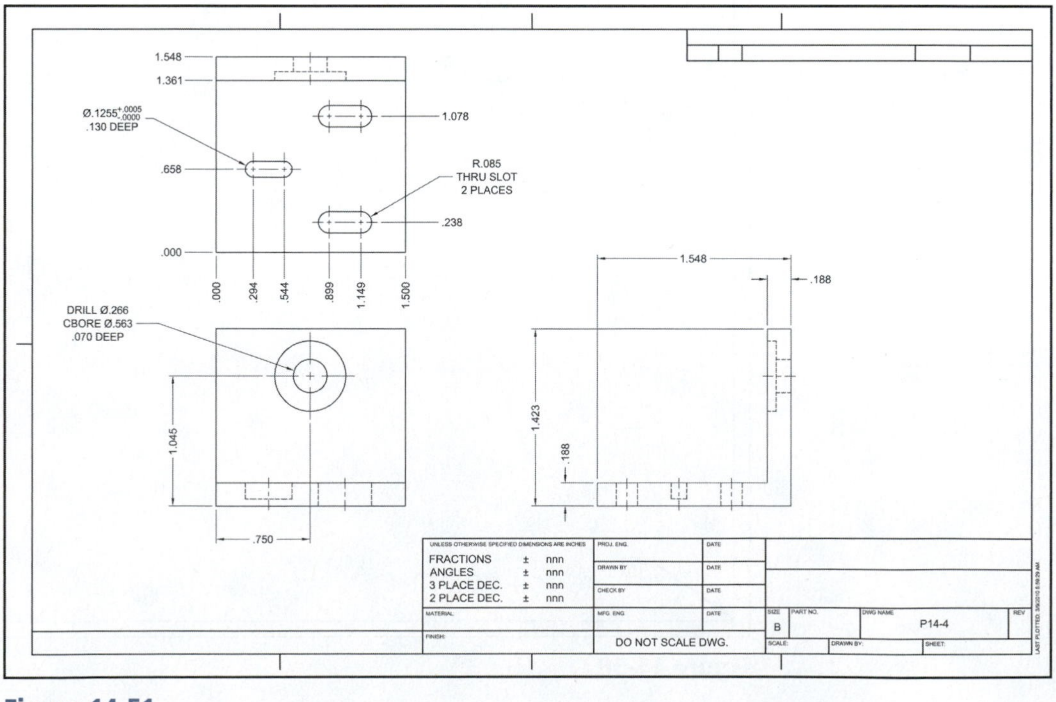

Figure 14-51

A Project 14-5: *Residential Architectural Plan, continued from Chapter 13* [ADVANCED]

1. Open drawing ***P13-5*** from Chapter 13.
2. Select **From template...** from the **Layout** right-click menu to import a layout.
3. Import the **Architectural D-Size** layout and border from the **Architectural D-Size.dwt** template file created in Project 14-3.
4. Select the **Architectural D-Size** layout to make it current.
5. Set the viewport scale to **1/4″ = 1′-0″** and center the view as shown in Figure 14-52.
6. Lock the viewport display so the view scale doesn't change.
7. Delete the **Layout1** and **Layout2** layouts.
8. Save the drawing as ***P14-5.***

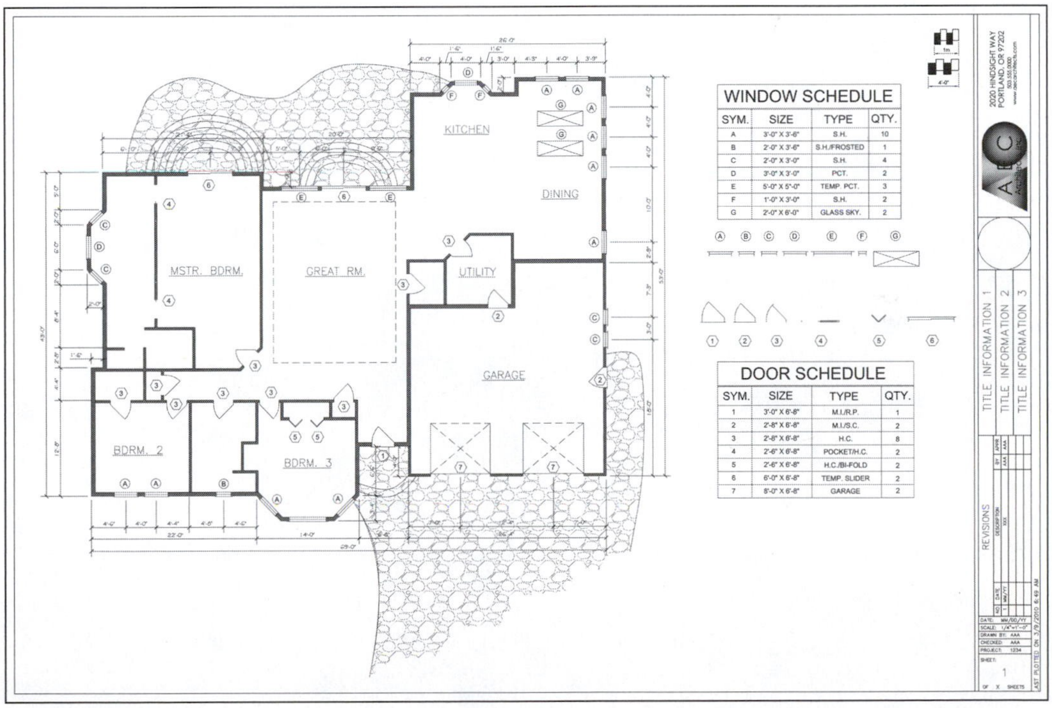

Figure 14-52

chapter fifteen
Plotting and Publishing

CHAPTER OBJECTIVES

- Plot from both model space and paper space
- Manage page setups using plot styles
- Control the final look of a plotted sheet
- Select, add, and configure various plotting devices
- Create electronic plot files including DWF, PDF, and other raster file formats
- View and mark up DWF files in the Autodesk Design Review application

plotting: The process of printing a drawing in AutoCAD.

PLOT	
Ribbon & Panel:	Output | Plot 
Standard Toolbar:	
Menu:	File | Plot...
Command Line:	PLOT/PRINT
Command Alias:	CTRL+P

Introduction

In most cases, the purpose of creating AutoCAD drawings is to create a set of printed hard-copy drawings. In AutoCAD, this process is called ***plotting.*** In Chapter 14, we looked at how to create and manage paper space layouts, which (among other things) allow you to define the default settings for a plot. In this chapter, we examine various ways of outputting drawings, including how to plot from model space and how to plot to various file formats.

Page Setups and Plotting

In Chapter 14, we looked at how to create a page setup using the **PAGESETUP** command. Page setups are simply collections of plot settings that have a name assigned to them. When creating a page setup, you specify the default printer/plotter, the default paper size, and other default output options. Each drawing space (model space and each paper space layout) has a default page setup assigned to it that contains all the default plot settings for that drawing space.

NOTE

In the early days of AutoCAD, drawings were typically output to pen plotters, which would create hard-copy prints by physically grabbing a pen and moving it around a piece of paper or Mylar. Although these types of plotters are rarely used today, the terminology has remained. Today, the terms *print* and *plot* are synonymous in AutoCAD.

Plotting is done with the **PLOT** command. When you start the **PLOT** command, AutoCAD looks at the current page setup and displays those settings in the **Plot** dialog box (see Figure 15-1).

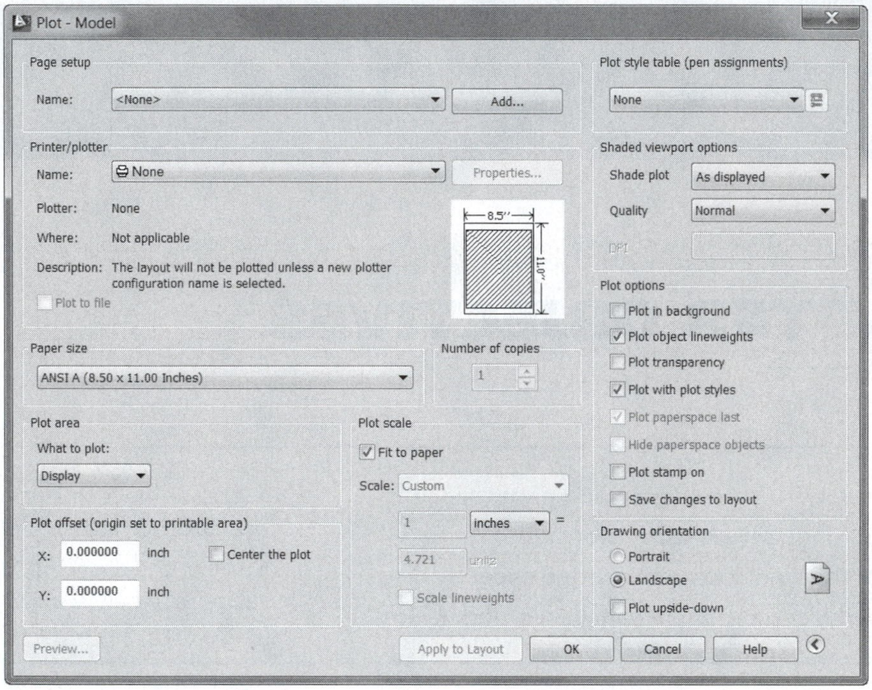

Figure 15-1
The **Plot** dialog box

TIP

The quickest way to start the **PLOT** command is by selecting the **Plot . . .** button on the **Quick Access** toolbar, which is always displayed on the top left of the AutoCAD window.

The **Plot** dialog box has the same settings as the **Page Setup** dialog box and allows you to make any final adjustments to your plot settings before outputting your drawing. The **Plot** dialog box also has additional controls that allow you to create and modify page setups.

NOTE

The main difference between the **Plot** dialog box and the **Page Setup** dialog box is that any changes are discarded when you select **OK** in the **Plot** dialog box unless you select the **Apply to Layout** button.

PREVIEW	
Ribbon & Panel:	Output | Plot 
Standard Toolbar:	
Menu:	File | Plot Preview
Command Line:	PREVIEW
Command Alias:	None

To create a plot using the default page setup values, you can simply start the **PLOT** command and choose **OK.** However, before you commit your drawing to paper, it's a good idea to check over your default settings and preview your plot.

Previewing Your Plot

The **Preview...** button in the **Plot** dialog box allows you to see a preview of the final output before you commit it to paper. When you select the **Preview...** button, AutoCAD switches to plot preview mode (see Figure 15-2). In preview mode, the AutoCAD toolbars and pull-down menus are replaced with the **Preview** toolbar. These tools allow you to zoom in on and pan around the drawing to inspect it before you send it to the printer. If you are satisfied with the preview, you can choose the **Plot** button to send the drawing to the printer. Otherwise, you can choose **Cancel** to return to the **Plot** dialog box. The tools available in the **Preview** toolbar are also available in the **Preview Mode** right-click menu (see Figure 15-3).

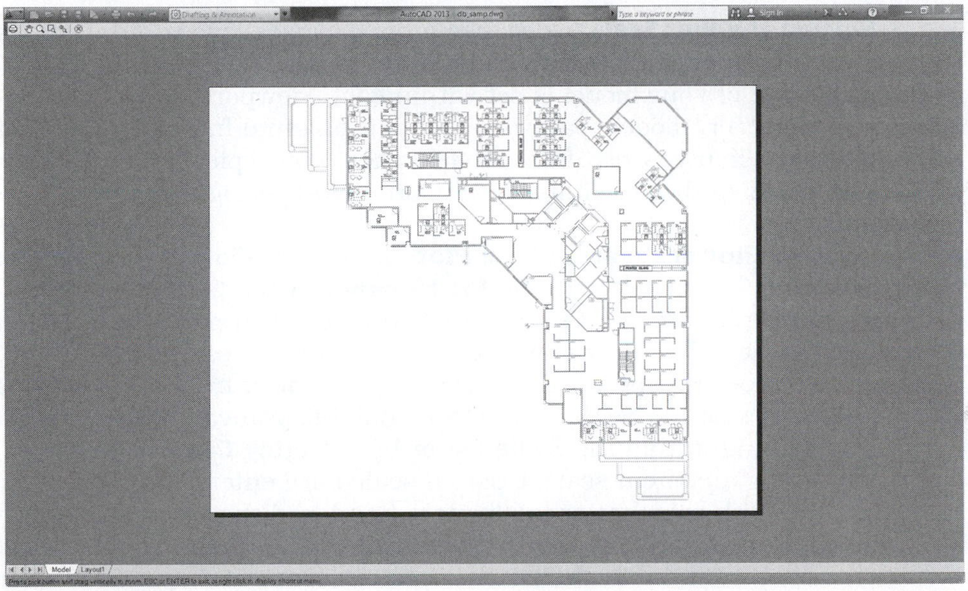

Figure 15-2
Plot preview mode

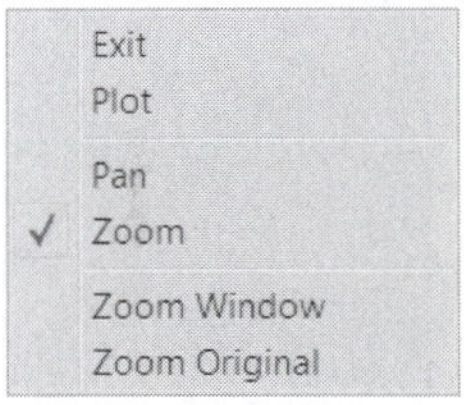

Figure 15-3
The **Preview Mode** right-click menu

The PREVIEW Command. If you're confident in your plot settings, you can go directly to a plot preview with the **PREVIEW** command. The **PREVIEW** command bypasses the **PLOT** command and goes directly to plot preview mode. If you're satisfied with the plot preview, you can choose the **Plot** button and output your drawing. However, if you need to make changes, choosing **Cancel** will return you to your drawing. You then have to use the **PLOT** or **PAGESETUP** command to make changes to your default plot settings.

Plotting from Model Space

The process of plotting is the same whether you plot from model space or paper space. However, there are some things to keep in mind when plotting from model space, particularly with regard to plot scale.

Specifying the Plot Area. When plotting a paper space layout, you will typically plot the entire layout. Selecting the **Layout** option in the **What to**

plot: list tells AutoCAD to plot the area defined in the paper space layout. When plotting from model space, the **Layout** option is not available, and you must choose a specific area to plot. The **What to plot:** drop-down list allows you to specify a number of different plot areas. The options are described below.

Display	Plots the objects currently displayed on the screen.
Extents	Plots all the objects currently visible in the drawing. Does not include objects on frozen layers but does include objects on layers that are turned off.
Limits	Plots objects located within the drawing limits.
View	Plots named views saved with the **VIEW** command. When selected, a list of named views is enabled, allowing you to select the view you wish to plot.
Window	Allows you to select a plot area by picking a window area. When selected, a **Window** button is enabled. Picking the **Window** button temporarily hides the dialog box and allows you to pick a window area to plot.

Setting the Plot Scale. Because a paper space layout represents an actual piece of paper, the plot scale of a paper space layout is typically 1:1. The plot scale of your model is set within each viewport.

However, model space represents the actual full-size version of your design. When you plot from model space, you typically need to adjust the plot scale so that the full-size version of your design will fit on a piece of paper.

The **Plot scale** area of the **Plot** dialog box allows you to set the drawing scale. When selected, the **Fit to paper** check box will examine the specified plot area and scale it to fit the specified paper size. The calculated scale will appear grayed out in the **Scale** area.

To plot at a specific scale, remove the check from the **Fit to paper** box to enable the **Scale** area. Once enabled, you can specify a plot scale by selecting it from the **Scale** list or by selecting **Custom** from the list and specifying a custom scale. Custom scales are entered as plotted (paper) units in either inches or millimeters (mm) and their equivalent drawing units. For example, to specify a scale of 1/4″ = 1′–0″, you could either choose it from the **Scale** list or choose **Custom** and specify **.25 inch = 12 units,** or **1 inch = 48 units.**

> **TIP**
>
> You can add to and modify the list of available plot scales with the **SCALELISTEDIT** command. See page 589 in Chapter 14 for more information about the **SCALELISTEDIT** command.

Setting the Plot Offset. The **Plot offset** area allows you to position your plot area on your paper. When set to **X: 0** and **Y: 0,** AutoCAD will place the specified plot area of your drawing at the lower left corner of the printable area of your paper. Recall from Chapter 14 that the printable area is the actual physical area that can be printed for a specified plotting device and paper size. This area varies with the printer and paper size you select.

By changing the X and Y offset values, you can reposition the drawing plot area on the paper. If your plot area goes outside the printable area, AutoCAD will warn you by showing a red line in the preview area of the **Plot** dialog box (see Figure 15-4).

Figure 15-4
The preview area of the **Plot** dialog box

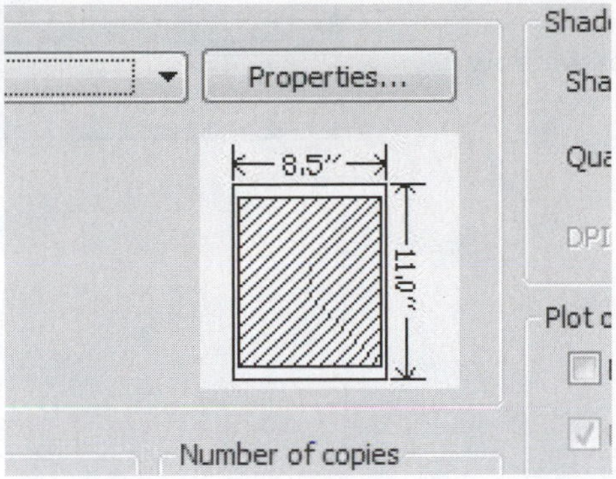

TIP

You can change the plot offset to be relative to the edge of the paper instead of the printable area on the **Plot and Publish** tab of the **Options** dialog box.

The **Center the plot** check box will compare the printable area of your paper to the plot area of your drawing and calculate the appropriate X and Y offset values to center the plot area in the printable area of your paper.

EXERCISE 15-1 Plotting from Model Space

To access student data files, go to **www.pearsondesigncentral.com.**

1. Open drawing ***db_samp*** located in the student data files.
2. Start the **PLOT** command to display the **Plot** dialog box.
3. Select the **DWF6 ePlot.pc3** printer and then select the **ARCH D (36.00 × 24.00 Inches)** paper size.
4. Select **Extents** from the **What to plot:** list.
5. Remove the check from the **Fit to paper** box and choose **3/32″ = 1′-0″** from the **Scale** list.
6. Choose **Center the plot** option in the **Plot offset** area.
7. Select the **Preview...** button.
8. AutoCAD will display the plot preview shown earlier in Figure 15-2. You can zoom and pan to examine the plot preview. When done, choose the **Close Preview Window** button to return to the **Plot** dialog box.
9. In the **What to plot:** list, choose **Window.** AutoCAD will close the dialog box and prompt you to *Specify first corner:*.
10. Draw a window around the upper right corner of the building as shown in Figure 15-5. After drawing the window, AutoCAD returns you to the **Plot** dialog box.
11. Choose **1/4″ = 1′-0″** from the **Scale** list. Select the **Preview...** button. AutoCAD displays the plot preview as shown in Figure 15-6.
12. Choose the **Close Preview Window** button to exit the plot preview, and choose **Cancel** to close the **Plot** dialog box. **Do not** save the drawing.

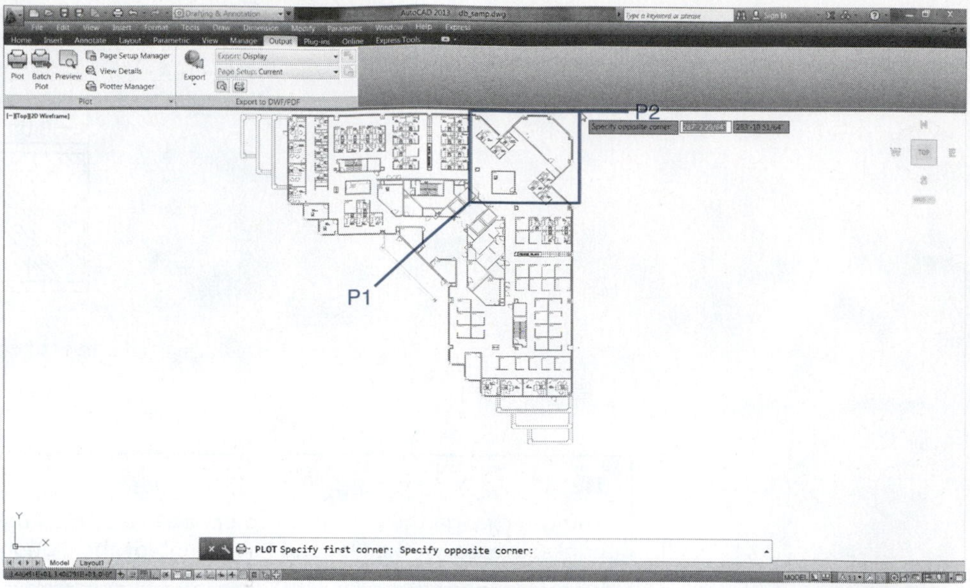

Figure 15-5
Selecting a plot window

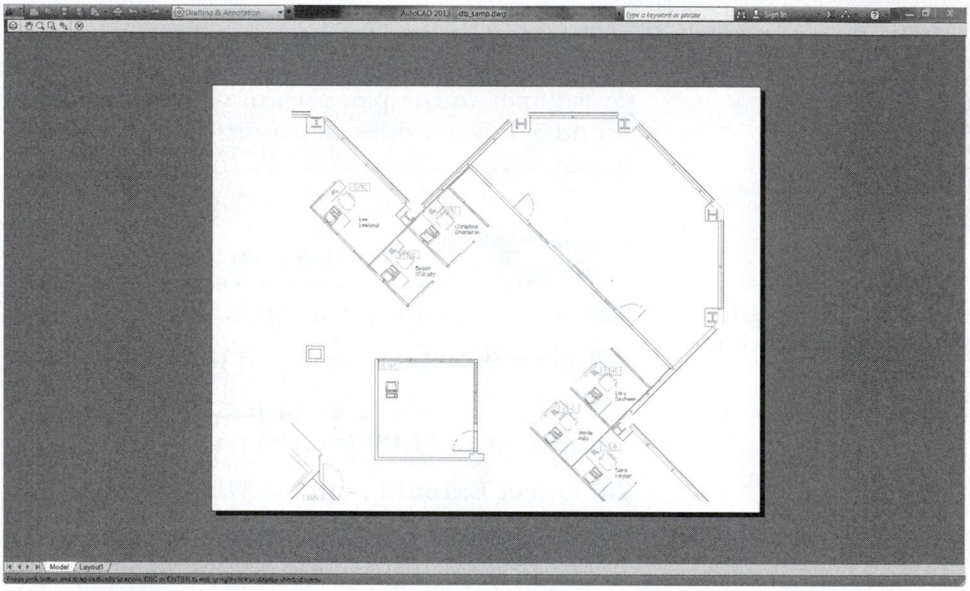

Figure 15-6
The plot preview of the selected area

Plotting a Page Layout

Plotting a page layout is in many aspects simpler than plotting from model space. In setting up the page layout, you will typically define many or all of the plotting defaults. However, when you plot, you will still want to double-check your plot settings and do a plot preview before sending it to the printer. This also gives you the opportunity to temporarily override plot settings for any given plot.

EXERCISE 15-2 **Plotting a Page Layout**

To access student data files, go to **www.pearsondesigncentral.com.**

1. Open drawing ***Welding Fixture-1*** in the student data files.
2. Select the **Mounting Bar Casting Support** page layout tab.
3. Start the **PLOT** command to display the **Plot** dialog box and select the **Preview...** button to display the plot preview. Notice that the viewports are displayed on the plot preview (see Figure 15-7). This is because the viewports are currently on a plotting layer.

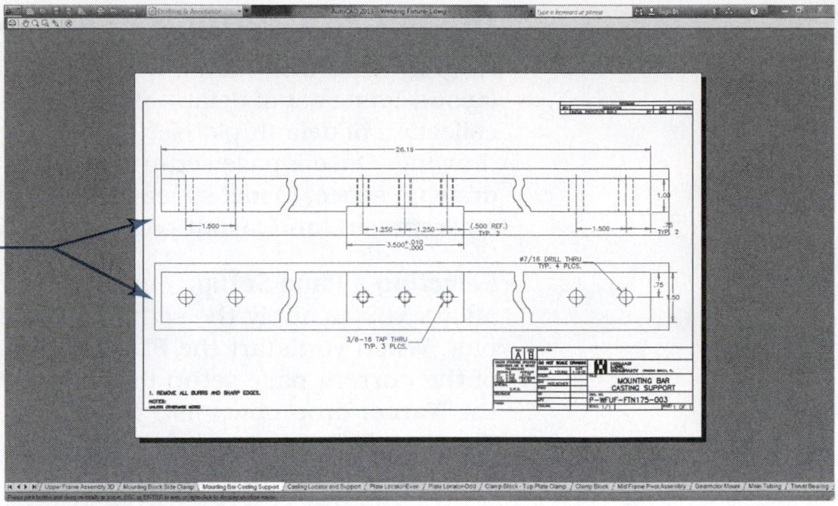

Figure 15-7
Viewport outlines in the plot preview

4. Choose the **Close Preview Window** button to exit the plot preview, and choose **Cancel** to close the **Plot** dialog box.
5. Select the two viewports and choose **Viewport** from the **Layer** drop-down list. This places the viewports on the nonplotting **Viewport** layer.
6. Restart the **PLOT** command. Notice that the plot preview area shows a red bar on the right-hand side of the page. This is because the **Plot offset X** value is set to **0.010.**
7. Set the **X** value in the **Plot offset** to **0.00** and select the **Preview...** button. This displays the plot preview. The plot preview now looks correct, and the drawing is ready to plot (see Figure 15-8).
8. Choose the **Close Preview Window** button to exit the plot preview, and choose **Cancel** to close the **Plot** dialog box. **Do not** save the drawing file.

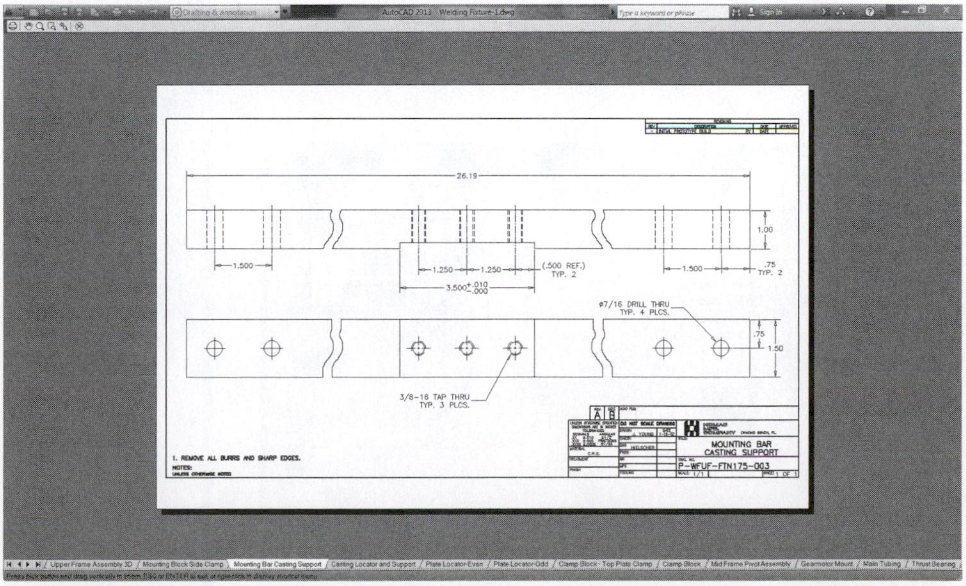

Figure 15-8
The corrected plot preview

Default Plot Settings and Page Setups

Keep in mind that each drawing environment (model space and each layout) has a set of default plot settings associated with it. A page setup is a collection of default plot settings that are assigned a name and saved in the drawing. Once a page setup is created, its settings can be applied to a given drawing space. Model space page setups can be applied to the model space environment, and layout page setups can be applied to layout (paper) spaces.

Selecting a Page Setup. In the **Plot** dialog box, the **Page setup** area allows you to apply the settings stored in a page setup to the current plot. When you start the **PLOT** command, AutoCAD displays the name of the current page setup in the **Name:** drop-down list. When you select the **Name:** drop-down list, you'll see a list of page setups stored in the drawing. Selecting one of these page setups will apply the settings stored in the page setup to the current plot.

In addition to page setups, there are three additional items in the **Name** list: **<None>, <Previous plot>,** and **Import...**. The **<None>** setting tells you that the current plot settings do not match any stored page setups. If you are using a page setup and make any changes to the setting in the **Plot** dialog box, the **Name** setting will change to **<None>,** noting that the current plot settings no longer match the settings stored in the page setup.

The **<Previous plot>** setting will reuse the settings from the last successful **PLOT** command.

Importing a Page Setup. Selecting **Import...** from the **Name** list allows you to import a page setup from another drawing. When you select **Import...,** AutoCAD displays the **Select Page Setup From File** dialog box (see Figure 15-9), which allows you to select a drawing file. Once you select a drawing file, AutoCAD will display the **Import Page Setups** dialog box (see Figure 15-10), which displays all the saved page setups within a drawing. Select a page setup from the dialog box, and choose **OK** to import the page setup into your current drawing. The imported page setup will now be listed in the **Name** drop-down list so you can select it.

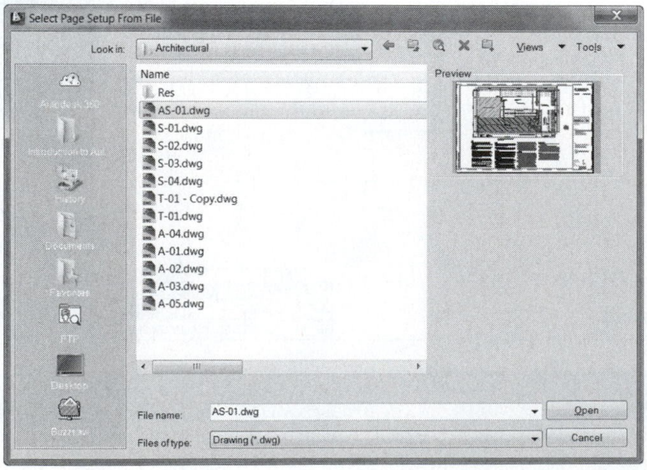

Figure 15-9
The **Select Page Setup From File** dialog box

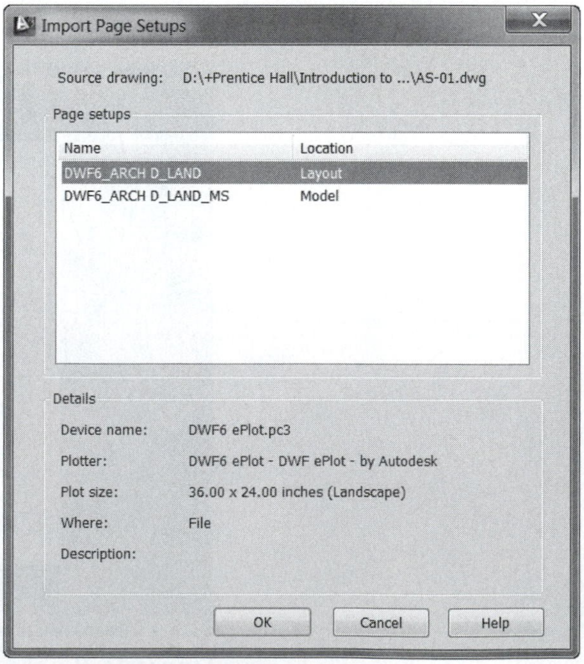

Figure 15-10
The **Import Page Setups** dialog box

Creating a Page Setup. AutoCAD also allows you to save your current plot settings to a page setup. Once you have your plot settings to your liking, choose the **Add...** button in the **Page setup** area. AutoCAD will display the **Add Page Setup** dialog box (see Figure 15-11). Simply type a name and choose **OK** to save the current plot settings to the new page setup.

You can update an existing page setup by entering the existing page setup name into the **Add Page Setup** dialog box. AutoCAD will display a **Question** dialog box (see Figure 15-12) telling you the page setup already exists and asking whether you'd like to redefine it. Choose **Yes** to update the existing page setup with the current plot settings.

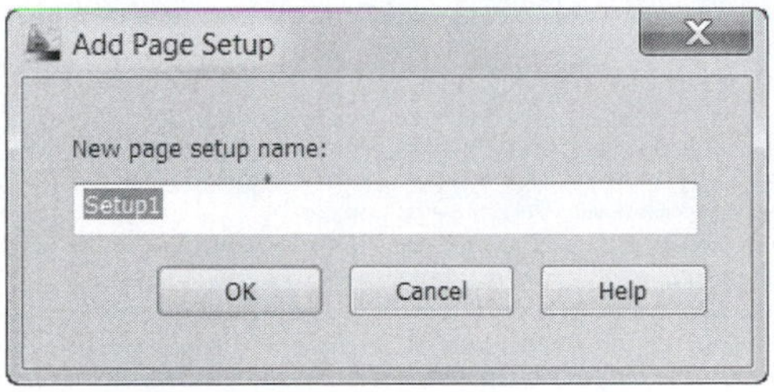

Figure 15-11
The **Add Page Setup** dialog box

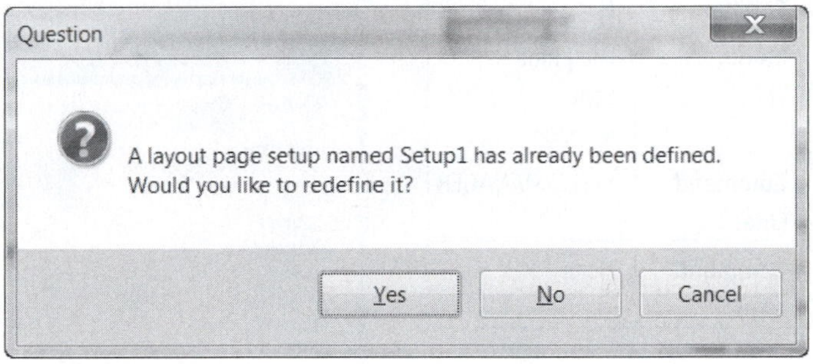

Figure 15-12
The **Add Page Setup Question** dialog box

Applying Plot Settings to the Current Layout. As we mentioned earlier, each drawing space has a set of default plot settings. The **Apply to Layout** button allows you to take the settings displayed in the **Plot** dialog box and apply them to the current layout. These settings then become the default plot settings for that layout or model space.

Plot Styles and Lineweights

As noted earlier in the chapter, in the early days of AutoCAD, pen plotters were commonly used. These plotters typically had a pen carousel in which you loaded pens. You would load pens with different pen widths or different colors in each position in the carousel. You would also have a pen table that would tell AutoCAD which pen to use for each AutoCAD color. For example, use pen 4 for color 1, pen 2 for colors 2 and 3, etc. Modern printers no longer use physical pens, but AutoCAD still allows you to use pen tables to control the final look of your plot. Today, AutoCAD refers to these pen tables as *plot styles*.

A plot style is a table of settings that allows you to control all aspects of your plotted output. For example, you may have a plot table that converts AutoCAD colors to grayscale colors or a plot table that allows you to screen back certain colors.

named plot style: Plot style that is organized by a user-defined name. Named plot styles are stored in .STB files.

color-dependent plot style: Plot style that is organized by the AutoCAD Color Index (ACI) number. Color-dependent plot styles are stored in .CTB files.

There are two types of plot styles: ***named plot styles*** and ***color-dependent plot styles.*** Named plot styles are stored in .STB files. Color-dependent plot styles are stored in .CTB files. A drawing can use either color-dependent plot styles or named plot styles, but not both. By default, color-dependent plot styles are used for new drawings.

> **NOTE**
>
> You can change the default plot style type used for new drawings by selecting the **Plot Style Table Settings** button on the **Plot and Publish** tab of the **Options** dialog box.

PLOT STYLE MANAGER	
Ribbon & Panel:	
Toolbar:	None
Menu:	File | Plot Style Manager…
Command Line:	STYLESMANAGER
Command Alias:	None

Plot Style Manager

The **STYLESMANAGER** command will open the folder where the plot style table files are stored (see Figure 15-13). From this folder, double-clicking on a .CTB or an .STB file will start the **Plot Style Table Editor** application (see Figure 15-14). This is a stand-alone Windows program that runs outside of AutoCAD. This program allows you to create and modify AutoCAD

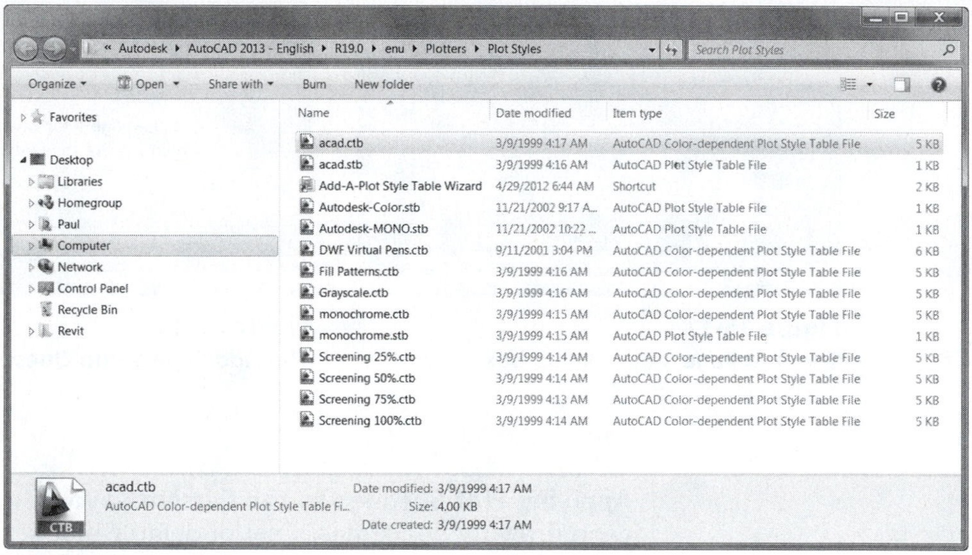

Figure 15-13
Plot Styles folder

Figure 15-14
The **Plot Style Table Editor**

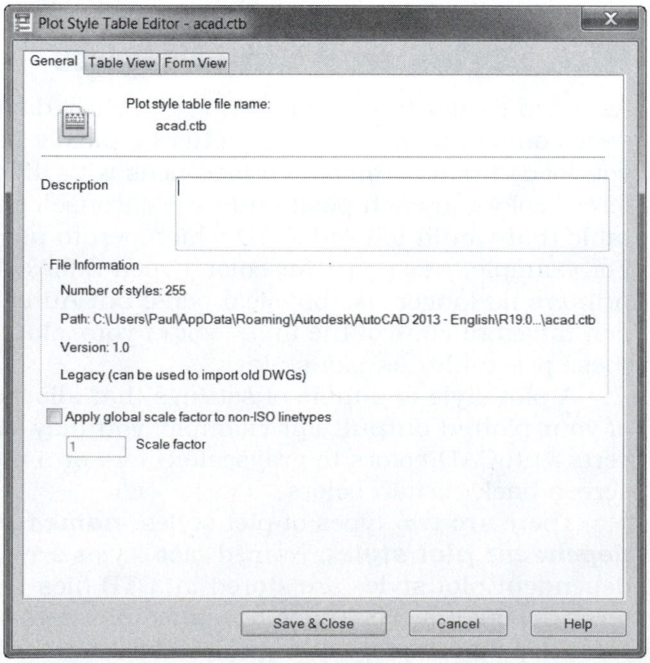

plot style tables. The **General** tab displays information about the plot style. The **Table View** and **Form View** tabs display the table settings in different formats. The **Form View** tab (see Figure 15-15) is useful for setting the properties of multiple colors at once. In this view, you can select multiple pens and apply settings to them in a single step.

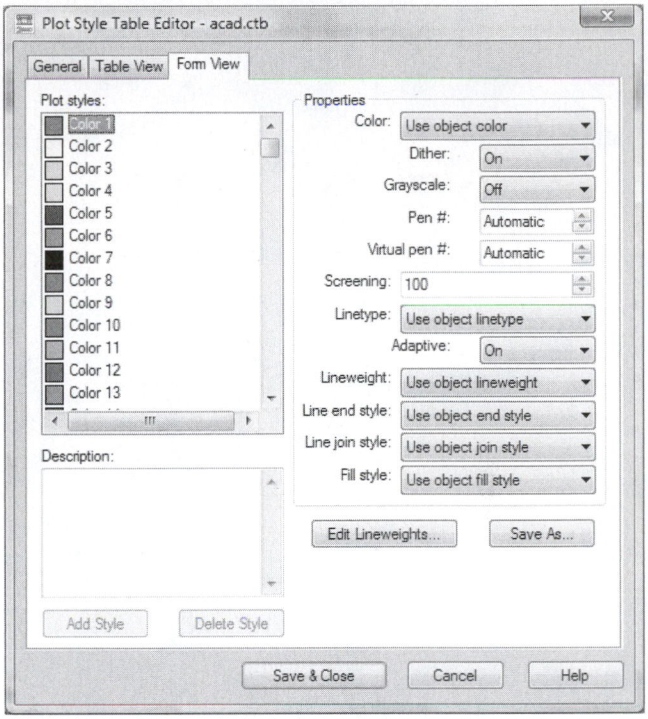

Figure 15-15
The **Form View** tab of the **Plot Style Table Editor**

Color-Dependent Plot Styles

Color-dependent plot styles map AutoCAD colors within your drawing to specific plotter settings. When you use color-dependent plot styles, all objects with the same color are plotted with the same plotter settings.

> **NOTE**
>
> The specifics of each of these settings are beyond the scope of this book. For detailed information on these settings, choose the **Help** button on the **Plot Style Table Editor** application. Keep in mind that some settings (such as pen numbers and virtual pen numbers) may not be supported by your specific printer. Refer to your printer documentation to see which features are supported.

Named Plot Styles

Named plot styles allow you to assign plotter settings directly to AutoCAD objects or AutoCAD layers. Within each .STB file, plotter settings are assigned to plot style names (see Figure 15-16). These plot styles are then assigned to each drawing layer and therefore to each object in the drawing. When named plot styles are used in a drawing, the **Plot Style** column is enabled in the **Layer Properties Manager** palette (see Figure 15-17). This allows you to assign a named plot style to a layer.

> **NOTE**
>
> When using named plot styles, the plot style name behaves like other object properties. By default, plot styles are assigned by layer, but you can hard-code a plot style for any specific object.

Figure 15-16
Named plot styles

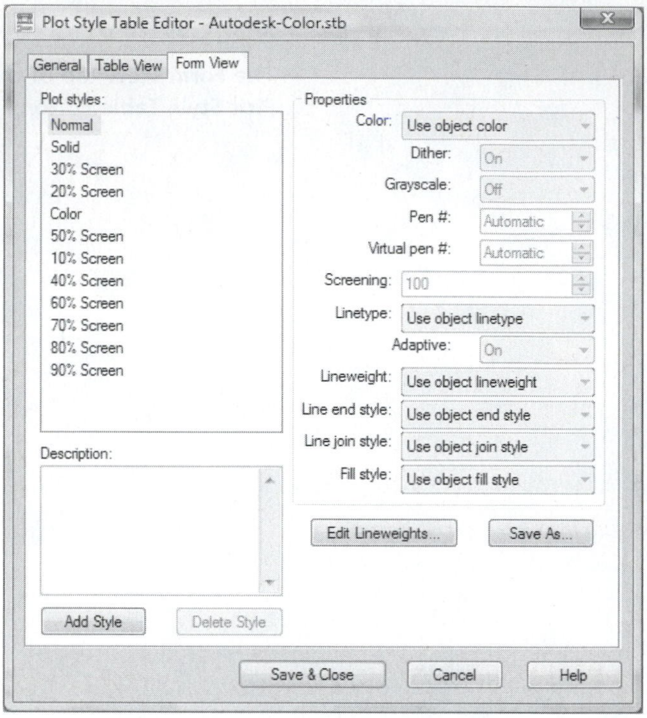

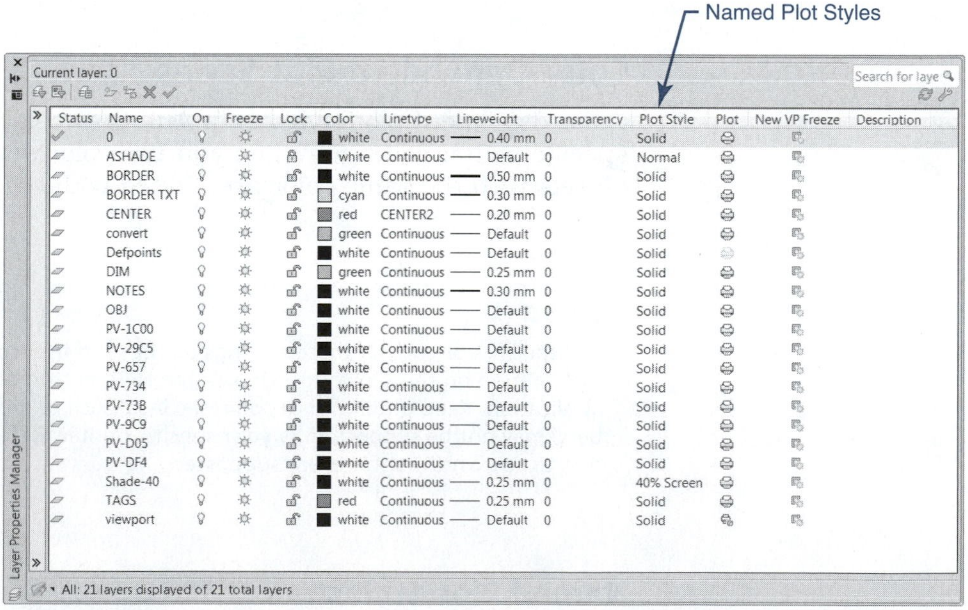

Figure 15-17
The **Plot Style** column of the **Layer Properties Manager** palette

When using named plot styles, AutoCAD creates a plot style called **Normal.** This is AutoCAD's default named plot style name and is included in each .STB file. This is similar to the **0** layer name and the **Continuous** linetype. It cannot be deleted and is always available.

Using Plot Styles

As mentioned earlier, an AutoCAD drawing can use either color-dependent plot styles or named plot styles but not both. When you create a new drawing file, the drawing template typically determines whether AutoCAD uses color-dependent plot styles or named plot styles as well as the default plot style file (see Figure 15-18).

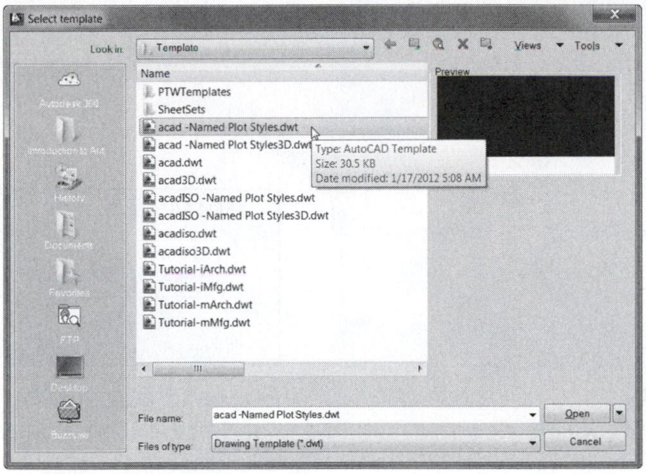

Figure 15-18
Drawing templates with various plot styles

> **NOTE**
>
> When plotting from model space, selecting a plot style table will cause AutoCAD to ask whether you want this plot style table applied to all paper space layouts. If you answer **Yes,** AutoCAD will update the default plot settings for each layout to use the selected plot style table.

Once a drawing has been created and the type of plot styles has been set, the **Plot style table** area of the **Plot** dialog box will show either .STB or .CTB files. From this list, you can tell AutoCAD which plot style table to use for your plot.

When working with named plot styles, it is possible to assign a plot style table that does not include plot styles that are used in your drawing. For example, say you create a drawing and assign the plot style named **40% Screen** that's defined in the **Autodesk-MONO.STB** file. If you then select the **ACAD.STB** plot style table, the **40% Screen** style is not defined in that .STB file. When this happens, AutoCAD will display the **Select Plot Style** dialog box (see Figure 15-19) and ask you to select a different plot style for that layer.

When you select a plot style table, the **Edit plot styles** button is enabled (see Figure 15-20), which starts the **Plot Style Table Editor** application (see Figure 15-14). This allows you to view and/or modify the selected plot style table.

> **TIP**
>
> You can use the **CONVERTPSTYLES** command to convert a named plot style drawing to a color-dependent plot style drawing or vice versa.

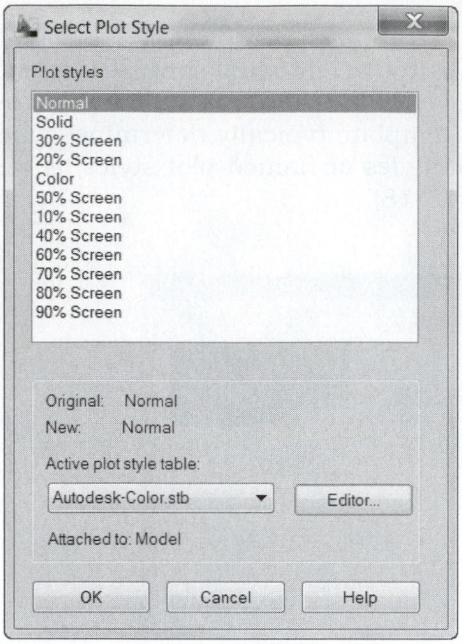

Figure 15-19
The **Select Plot Style** dialog box

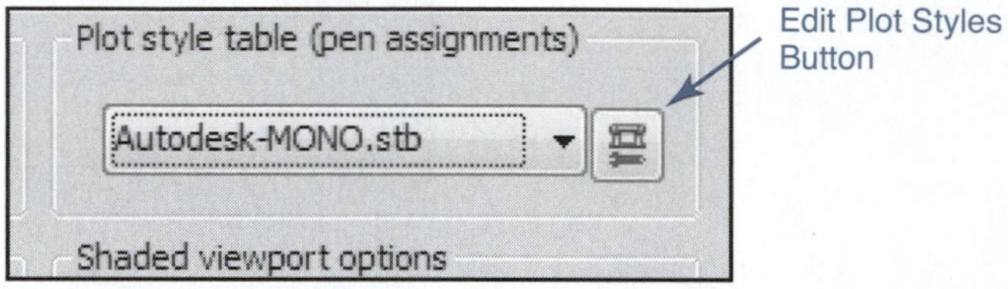

Figure 15-20
The **Edit Plot Styles** button

Plot Options

The **Plot options** area of the **Plot** dialog box allows you to specify options for plotting lineweights, transparency, plot styles, shaded plots, and the order in which objects are plotted.

Plot in Background. This option specifies that the plot is processed in the background. Typically, when you plot, AutoCAD stops all other activity while the drawing is plotting and will show you a plotting progress bar (see Figure 15-21).

Figure 15-21
The **Plot Job Progress** bar

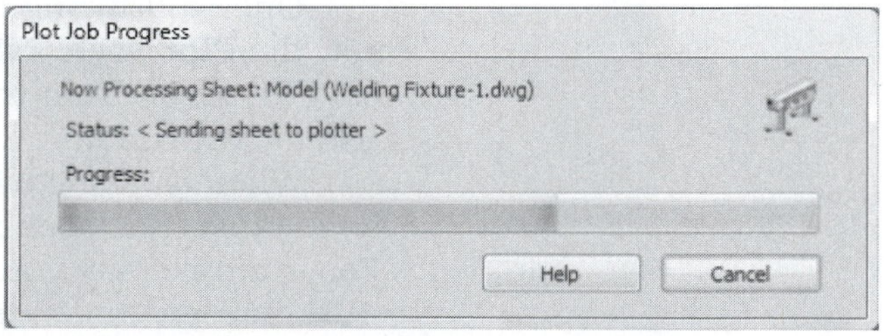

When the **Plot in background** option is turned on, AutoCAD will return you to the drawing environment and process the plot in the background. This allows you to work while the plot is being generated, but may also increase the time it takes to plot the drawing.

Plot Object Lineweights. This option specifies whether lineweights assigned to objects and layers are plotted. When turned on, any lineweight information assigned in your drawing will be applied to the plot. When turned off, a lineweight of **0** will be applied to all objects in the plot, which results in all objects being plotted with a very thin lineweight.

Plot Transparency. This option specifies whether any objects with transparency levels greater than **0** get plotted with solid or transparent settings.

Plot with Plot Styles. This option specifies whether plot styles applied to objects and layers are plotted. This means that the plot style settings contained in the specified .CTB or .STB file will be applied to the plot. When you select this option, the **Plot object lineweights** option is automatically enabled.

Plot Paperspace Last. This option allows you to control which space is plotted first. Generally, paper space geometry is usually plotted before model space geometry. Turning this option on will force AutoCAD to plot the model space geometry first.

Hide Paperspace Objects. This option typically affects only 3D drawings and is available only when plotting from a paper space layout. When plotting a 3D object, you may want to have AutoCAD do a hidden line removal, which eliminates any lines appearing behind a 3D object. This option tells AutoCAD whether the hidden line removal process applies to objects in paper space as well as objects in model space.

Plot Stamp On. Turning this option on places a plot stamp on a specified corner of each drawing and/or logs it to a file.

Save Changes to Layout. This option saves the changes that you make to the layout in the **Plot** dialog box.

Plot stamp settings are specified in the **Plot Stamp** dialog box (see Figure 15-22), which allows you to control the information that you want to appear in the plot stamp, such as drawing name, date and time, plot scale, and so on. To open the **Plot Stamp** dialog box, turn on the **Plot stamp on** option and then click the **Plot Stamp Settings** button, which is displayed on the right.

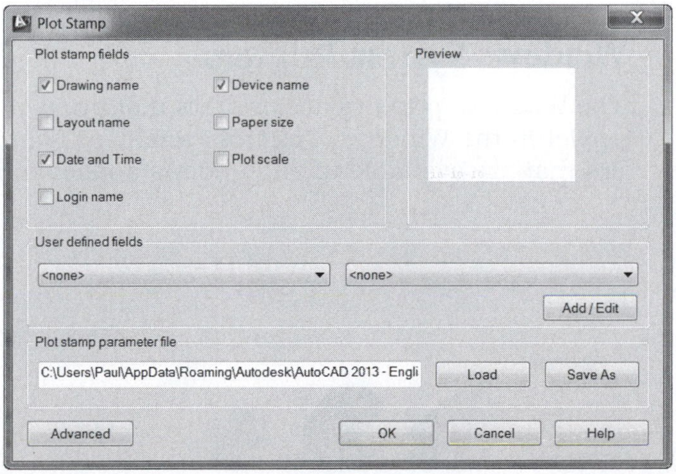

Figure 15-22
The **Plot Stamp** dialog box

> **TIP**
>
> You can also open the **Plot Stamp** dialog box by clicking the **Plot Stamp Settings** button on the **Plot and Publish** tab of the **Options** dialog box.

From the **Plot Stamp** dialog box, you can select what information you want to display, and you can also create user-defined text to display a custom plot stamp.

Selecting the **Advanced** button displays the **Advanced Options** dialog box (see Figure 15-23), which allows you to control the placement and orientation of the plot stamp as well as the font and height of the plot stamp text.

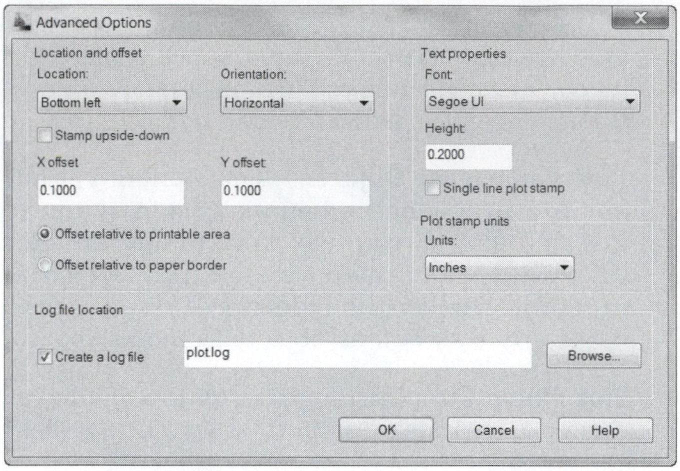

Figure 15-23
The **Advanced Options** dialog box

Plotter Setup

The **Printer/plotter** area of the **Plot** dialog box lists all the printers available when plotting a drawing. To select a printer, simply select it from the **Name:** list. Once selected, AutoCAD will display information about the printer beneath the name, including the name of the printer driver, the printer port, and any description about the printer. The list of printers is divided into two types: Windows-configured printers and AutoCAD-configured printers.

Windows System Printers

The Windows printers are printers that are configured with the **Printers** applet in the Windows **Control Panel** (see Figure 15-24). These are printers that are available to all Windows applications.

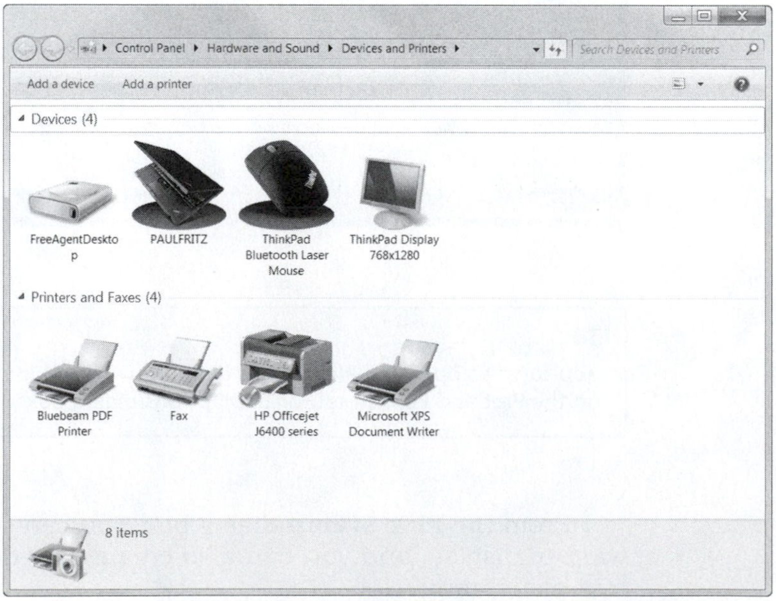

Figure 15-24
The **Printers** control window

AutoCAD Printers

AutoCAD printers are configured and controlled by AutoCAD directly. They bypass the Windows printing system and allow AutoCAD to print directly to the printer. AutoCAD-configured printers may also have features available that are not available in a Windows printer. There are also AutoCAD printer drivers that allow you to convert AutoCAD drawings to various raster and vector file formats, such as JPG, BMP, or HPGL.

.PC3 and .PMP Files. AutoCAD-configured printers are stored in plotter configuration files (.PC3 files). These files are also listed in the **Printer/plotter Name** list (see Figure 15-25).

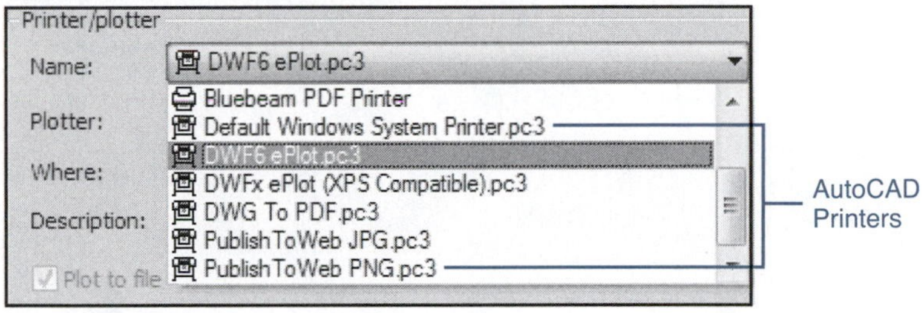

Figure 15-25
The **Printer/plotter Name** list

In addition to .PC3 files, AutoCAD also uses plot model parameter (.PMP) files to store custom plotter calibration settings as well as user-defined custom paper sizes.

Plotter Manager

PLOTTER MANAGER	
Ribbon & Panel:	Output | Plot
Toolbar:	None
Menu:	File | Plotter Manager...
Command Line:	PLOTTERMANAGER
Command Alias:	None

The **PLOTTERMANAGER** command displays the folder containing AutoCAD .PC3 files (see Figure 15-26). From this folder, you can create new plotter configurations and modify existing ones.

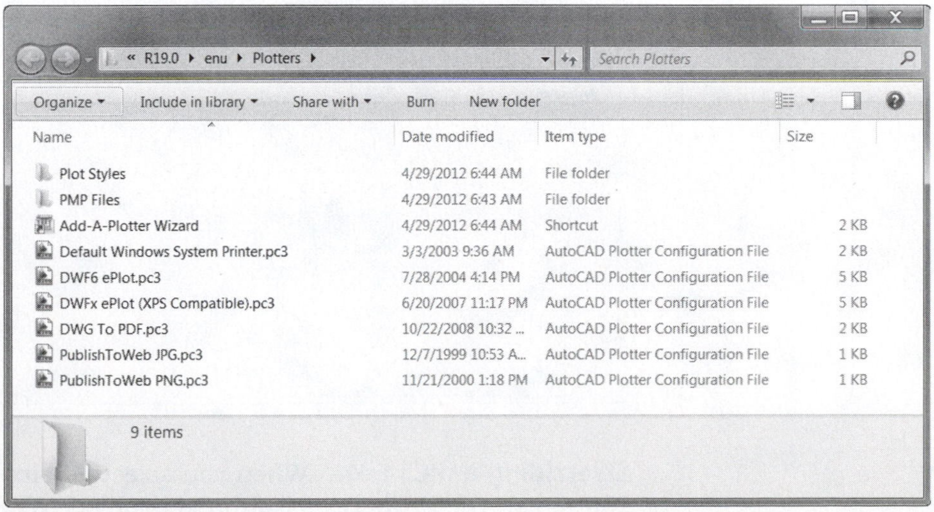

Figure 15-26
AutoCAD's **Plotters** folder

Plotter Configuration Editor. To modify an existing .PC3 file, simply double-click the file. This displays the **Plotter Configuration Editor** (see Figure 15-27). From this dialog box, you can view and modify settings specific to the printer such as the printer port, custom page sizes, and printable areas.

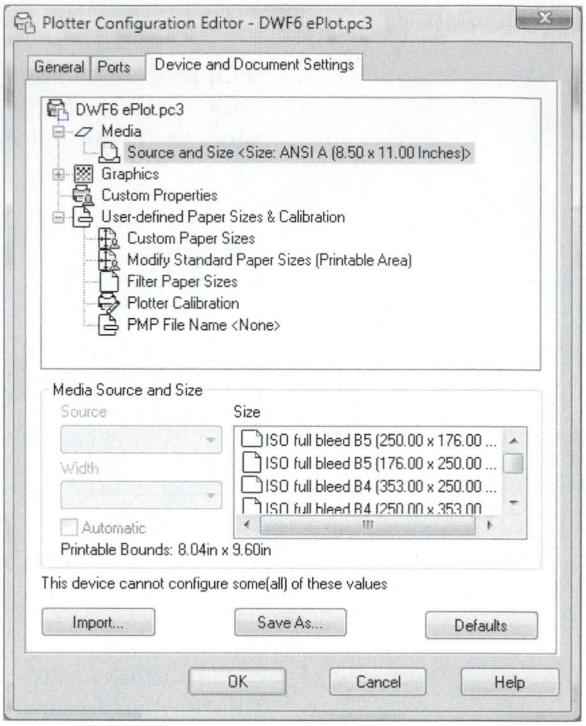

Figure 15-27
The **Plotter Configuration Editor**

Add-a-Plotter Wizard. The **Add-a-Plotter** wizard walks you through the process of creating a new plotter configuration file (see Figure 15-28). This wizard allows you to create a new plotter configuration using either AutoCAD-supplied print drivers, or drivers supplied by the printer manufacturer, or by importing a plotter configuration file from an earlier version of AutoCAD (.PCP or .PC2 files).

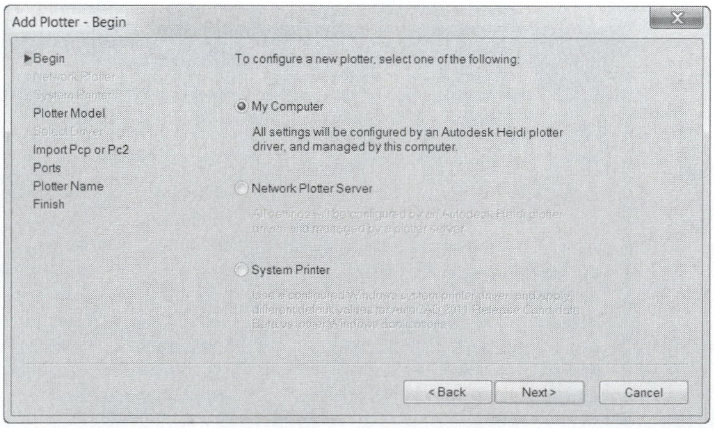

Figure 15-28
The **Add-a-Plotter** wizard

Overriding a .PC3 File. When you select a printer from the **Printer/plotter Name** list, the **Properties** button is enabled. When you select this button, AutoCAD displays the **Plotter Configuration Editor** (see Figure 15-27). This allows you to make changes to the plotter configuration within the

PLOT command. When you make changes to the plotter configuration from within the **PLOT** command, AutoCAD will ask you whether you want to save the changes to the .PC3 file or make the changes only for the current plot (see Figure 15-29).

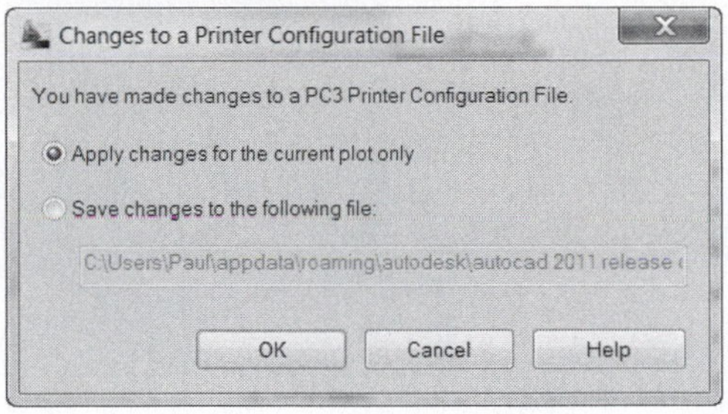

Figure 15-29
The **Changes to a Printer Configuration File** dialog box

EXERCISE 15-3 Adding a New Plotter

To access student data files, go to **www.pearsondesigncentral.com.**

1. Open drawing ***db_samp*** located in the student data files.
2. Start the **PLOTTERMANAGER** command to display the **Plotters** folder.
3. Double-click the **Add-a-Plotter** wizard. AutoCAD displays the **Add Plotter** dialog box. Choose **Next** to begin the wizard.
4. Choose **My Computer** to tell AutoCAD that the printer will be controlled locally from your computer (see Figure 15-28). Choose **Next** to continue to the **Plotter Model** step.
5. Choose **Hewlett-Packard** in the **Manufacturers** list and **Draftpro (7570A)** in the **Models** list (see Figure 15-30). Choose **Next** to continue to the **Import Pcp or Pc2** step.

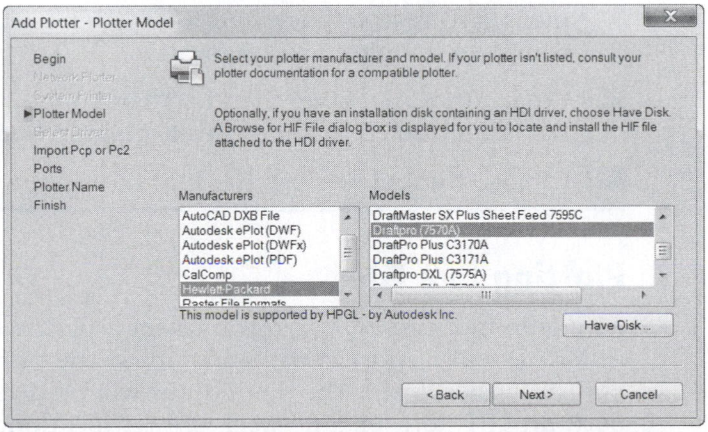

Figure 15-30
Selecting a plotter

6. You are given the opportunity to import a .PCP or .PC2 file from an older version of AutoCAD. Choose **Next** to continue to the **Ports** step.
7. Because this plotter is not actually hooked up to your computer, select the **Plot to File** option (see Figure 15-31). This will redirect the printer output to a file. Choose **Next** to continue to the **Plotter Name** step.
8. Accept the default name of **DraftPro (7570A).** Choose **Next** to continue to the **Finish** step.
9. At this point, you can modify the plotter defaults by choosing the **Edit Plotter Configuration...** button (see Figure 15-32). The **Calibrate**

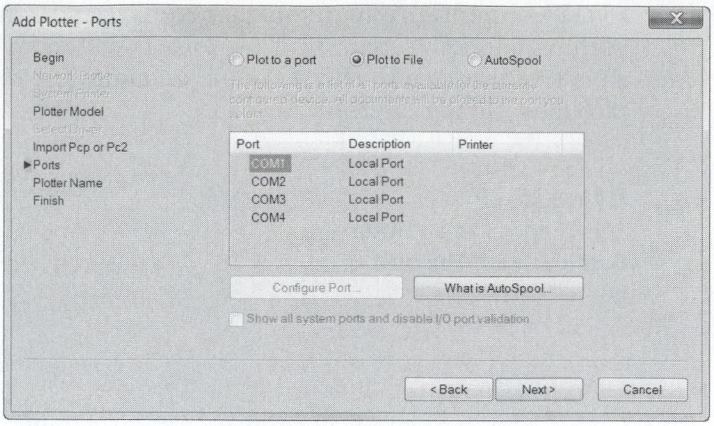

Figure 15-31
Specifying a port

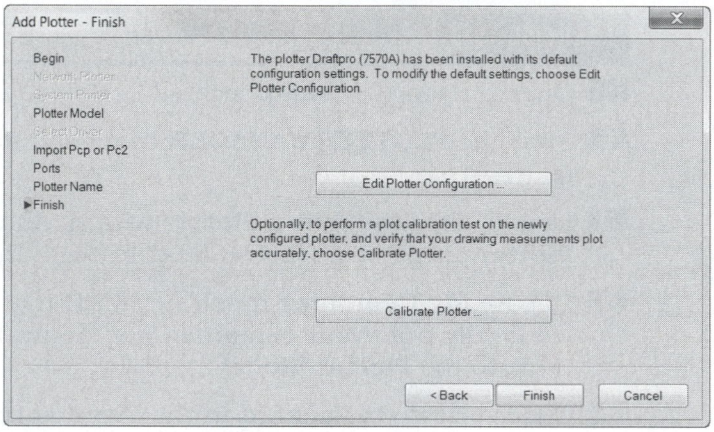

Figure 15-32
The configured plotter

Plotter... button allows you to verify the accuracy of the plotter output by creating a sample plot, measuring the output, and inputting the measured results back into the plotter calibration. Choose **Finish** to complete the plotter configuration.

10 From AutoCAD, start the **PLOT** command. The **Draftpro (7570A).PC3** file is now listed in the **Printer/plotter Name** list.

11 Choose **Cancel** to close the **Plot** dialog box. **Do not** save the drawing.

Plotting to a File

As mentioned earlier, when you select a plotter in the **Plot** dialog box, AutoCAD will display information about the printer, including the port. The port describes where the plot output will be directed—for example, a USB port, an LPT port, or a network printer location. The output port for any particular printer is defined within the plotter configuration (.PC3) file for the printer and is displayed next to the **Where:** label in the plotter description in the **Printer/plotter** area of the **Plot** dialog box.

It is possible to redirect the output to a file by selecting the **Plot to file** check box directly below the plotter description.

In addition, it is possible to create other file formats via the **PLOT** command by selecting their corresponding .PC3 file, such as DWF and PDF files. They are all explained in the following sections.

Plot File—PLT. The **Plot to file** box in the **Plot** dialog box allows you to redirect the output from the specified port to a plot file. Plot files can be used in various ways. Some office environments use plot management software that may require plot files. Some plot files can be used in other programs. The Hewlett-Packard Graphics Language (HPGL or HPGL/2) is a plot file format used in many Hewlett-Packard plotters. Some graphics programs support HPGL files instead of AutoCAD files. If you have a need to create a plot file, select the **Plot to file** option in the **Plot** dialog box. When you plot, AutoCAD will ask you for the name and location of the plot file. Plot files typically use a .PLT file extension.

Design Web Format File—DWF/DWFx. The Design Web Format (DWF) is a file format developed by Autodesk that allows you to publish your drawing on the World Wide Web or an intranet network. DWF files can contain one or more drawing sheets (layouts) and also support real-time panning and zooming as well as control over the display of layers and named views. DWF files cannot be opened in AutoCAD, but they can be attached as underlays.

> **NOTE**
>
> The DWFx format allows you to view drawings using Microsoft's XPS Viewer, which is automatically installed with Windows and Internet Explorer version 7 and higher.

DWF files can be reviewed, marked up, and plotted using the free Autodesk® Design Review software. DWF files can also be viewed and shared using Autodesk's free Web service named Freewheel at http://freewheel.autodesk.com.

To plot to a DWF file, select either the **DWF6 ePlot.pc3** or the **DWFx ePlot (XPS compatible).pc3** plot configuration in the **Printer/plotter Name** list. To change the DWF preferences, choose the **Properties** button in the **Plot** dialog box, choose the **Custom Properties** on the **Device and Document Settings** tab of the **Plotter Configuration Editor** dialog box, and then select the **Custom Properties...** button (see Figure 15-33). The **DWF6 ePlot Properties** dialog box is shown in Figure 15-34.

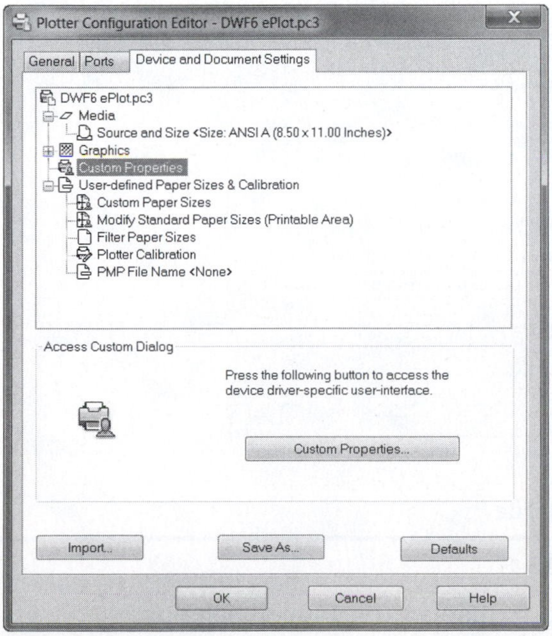

Figure 15-33
The **Device and Document Settings** tab

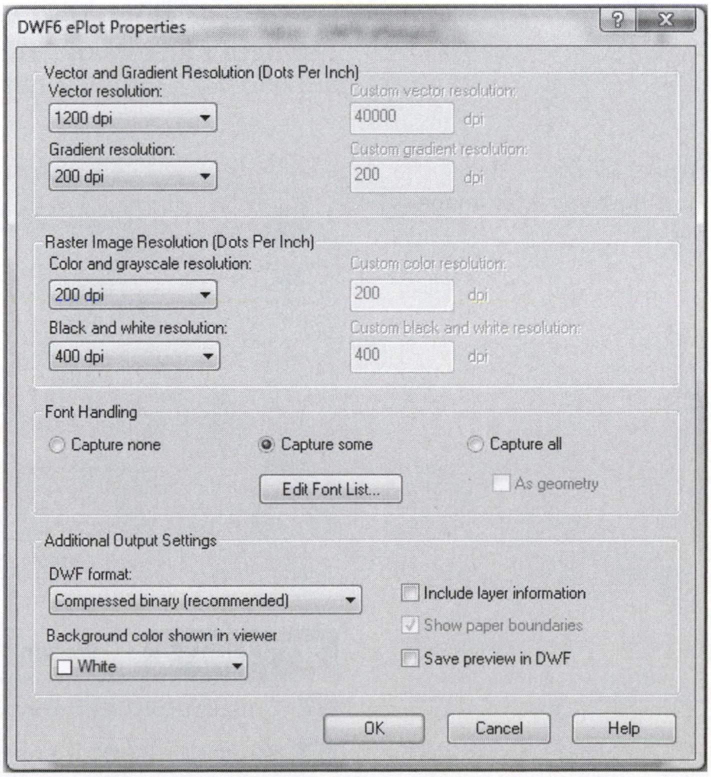

Figure 15-34
The **DWF6 ePlot Properties** dialog box

In this dialog box, you can set the resolution of the raster and vector components of the DWF file, control which fonts are embedded in the DWF file, set the background color, and control whether layer control is included in the DWF file.

Adobe® Portable Document Format—PDF. PDF files are the industry standard for sharing graphical information. Using PDF files, you can share drawings with almost anyone because the Adobe Reader® is already installed on most computers. If the Adobe Reader is not installed, it can be easily downloaded and installed for free from the Internet, most of the time, automatically.

To plot to a PDF file, select the **DWG to PDF.PC3** plot configuration in the **Printer/plotter Name** list. When you plot, the standard Windows file dialog box is displayed so that you can specify a file name and location to save the PDF file.

> **TIP**
>
> It is possible to skip the **PLOT** command and export one or more layouts directly to a DWF or PDF file via the **Export to DWF/PDF** panel on the **Output** tab of the ribbon.

Raster Image File—BMP/CALS/JPEG/PNG/TIFF. AutoCAD comes with a number of plot drivers that allow you to plot to various raster file formats. When you plot a drawing to a raster file, AutoCAD objects are converted to a series of pixels. When plotting to a raster image file, sheet size is measured in pixels instead of inches or millimeters. The resolution and color depth of the raster file determines the quality of the final output and also affects the size of the final file.

To configure AutoCAD to plot to a raster image file, run the **Add-a-Plotter** wizard, select **My Computer, Next,** and choose **Raster File Formats** in the **Manufacturers** list (see Figure 15-35). AutoCAD provides support for a number of raster file formats.

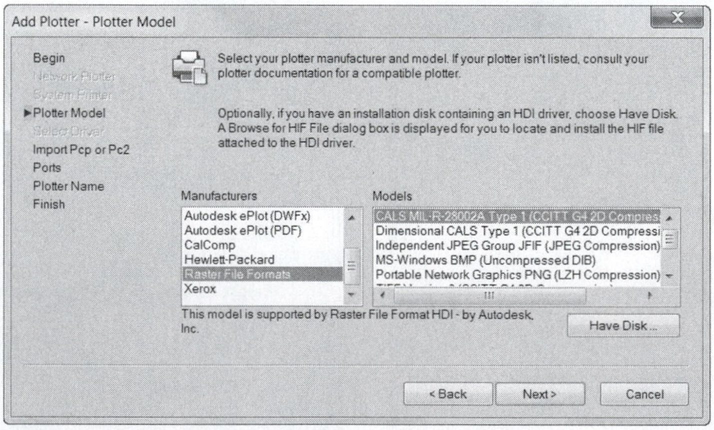

Figure 15-35
Plotting to a raster image file

EXERCISE 15-4 Plotting to a File

1. Continue from Exercise 15-3.
2. Start the **PLOT** command to display the **Plot** dialog box.
3. Select the **DWF6 ePlot.pc3** printer and then select the **ARCH D (36.00 × 24.00 Inches)** paper size.

4. Select **Extents** from the **What to plot:** list.
5. Remove the check from the **Fit to paper** box and choose **3/32″ = 1′-0″** from the **Scale** list.
6. Choose the **Center the plot** option in the **Plot offset** area, and select the **Preview...** button.
7. AutoCAD will display the plot preview. You can zoom and pan to examine the plot preview. When done, choose the **Plot** button to create the plot.
8. AutoCAD prompts you for the name and location of the plot file. Save the plot as ***CH15_EXERCISE4.DWF*** and choose **Save** to create the DWF file. AutoCAD plots the drawing and ends the **PLOT** command.

BATCH PLOT	
Ribbon & Panel:	Output | Plot 
Standard Toolbar:	
Menu:	File | Plot...
Command Line:	PUBLISH
Command Alias:	None

Plotting a Set of Drawings

Although the **PLOT** command allows you to create a single plot, there are many times when you need to create a set of drawings. This might include multiple layouts within a single drawing or include layouts from other drawing files. You may even need to mix model space plots with paper space layout plots. AutoCAD's **PUBLISH** command allows you to create multiple plots and to save the settings so the plot set can be re-created.

Batch Plotting

When you start the **PUBLISH** command, AutoCAD displays the **Publish** dialog box (see Figure 15-36).

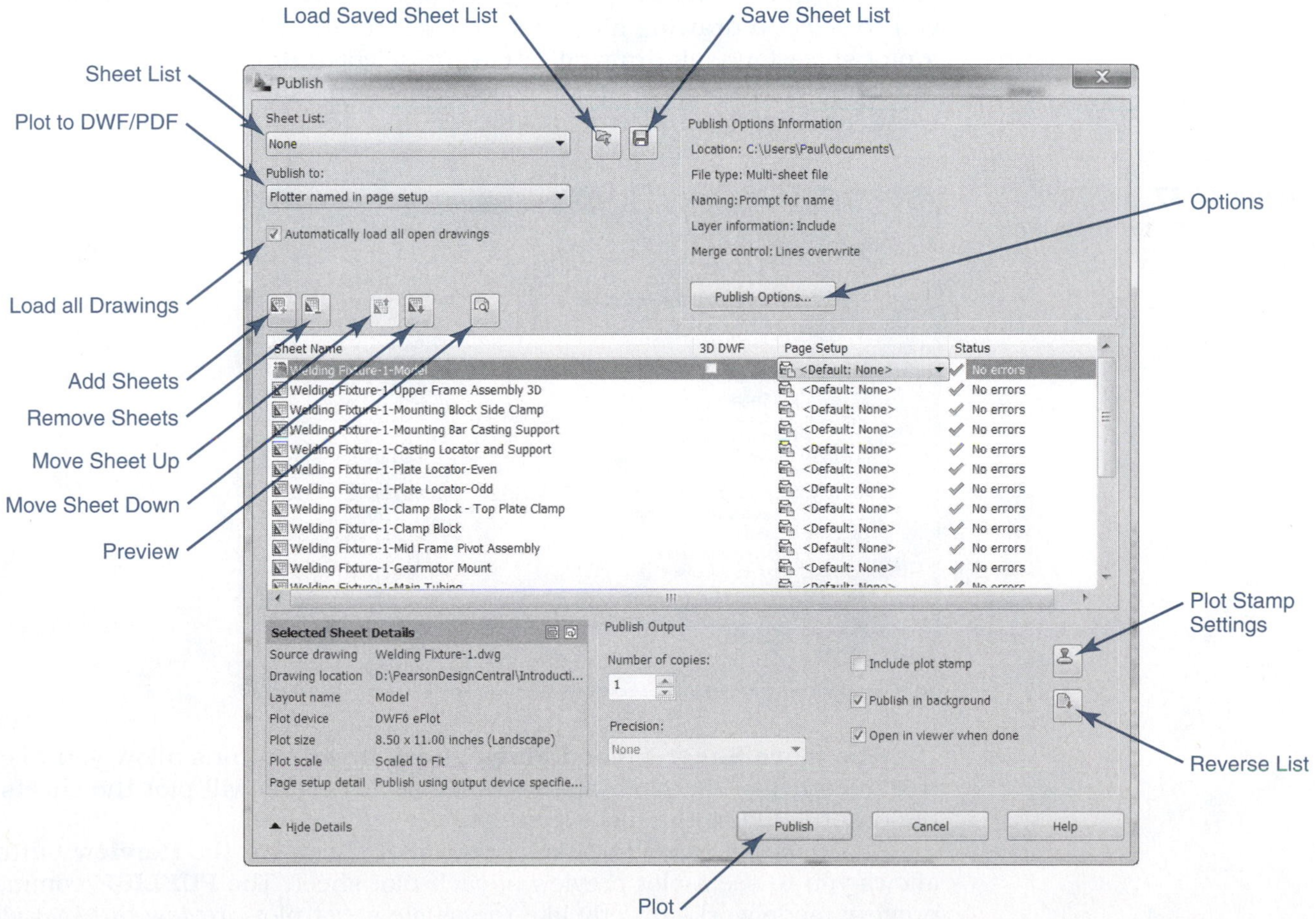

Figure 15-36
The **Publish** dialog box

When the **PUBLISH** command starts, AutoCAD automatically imports all the currently open drawings and shows them in the list. The drawings are listed by their file name and drawing tab name and also show the current page setup and the status of the last plot. You can change the page setup used for a plot sheet by selecting the page setup and selecting an available page setup from the drop-down list. You can also import page setups from other drawings to use in your plot sheet set.

NOTE

You can set the **PUBLISH** command not to automatically load all open drawings by unchecking **Automatically load all open drawings** at the upper left of the dialog box.

TIP

It is possible to save a list of sheets to a .dsd (Drawing set Description) file so that you can plot the same list of sheets again in the future by selecting the **Save Sheet List** button. Select the **Load Saved Sheet List** button to load a previously saved list. The **Sheet List:** drop-down list allows you to quickly select previous sheet lists.

Creating a Plot File Drawing Set. The **Add** and **Remove** buttons allow you to make changes to the list of plot sheets. To remove a plot sheet from the list, simply select the plot sheet(s) and choose the **Remove** button.

To add plot sheets to the list, choose the **Add** button. AutoCAD displays the **Select Drawings** dialog box (see Figure 15-37), which allows you to select a drawing file. Once you select a drawing, AutoCAD will add a plot sheet for each drawing tab in the selected drawing. You can control whether AutoCAD imports model space and/or layout tabs using the **Include:** drop-down list.

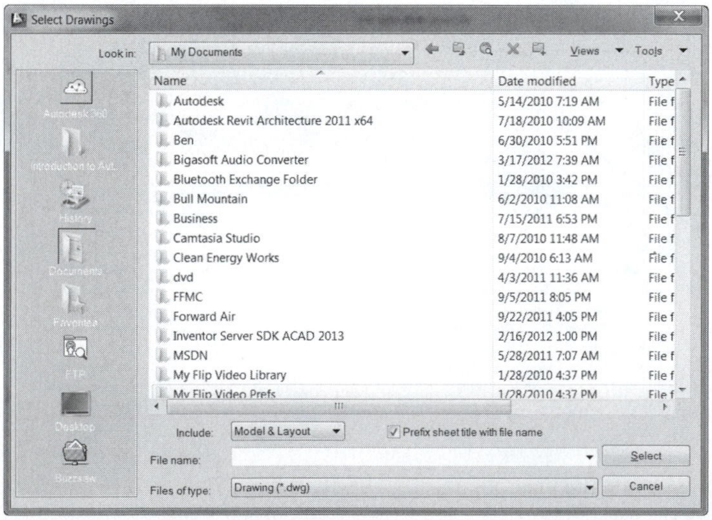

Figure 15-37
The **Select Drawings** dialog box

The **Move Sheet Up** and **Move Sheet Down** buttons allow you to control the order of the plot sheets in the list. AutoCAD will plot the sheets in the order listed in the plot sheet list.

When you're ready to publish your plot sheet list, the **Preview** button allows you to see a plot preview of each plot sheet. The **PUBLISH** command preview mode works exactly like the single sheet plot preview but includes forward and back arrows (see Figure 15-38) that allow you to move through the plot sheet previews.

Figure 15-38
The **Publish** preview controls

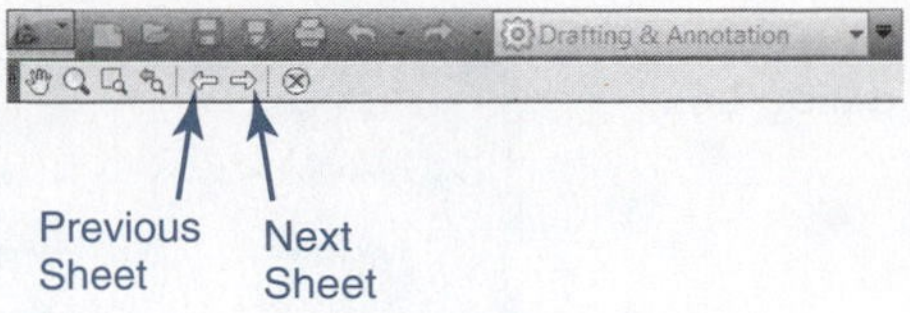

Creating an Electronic Drawing Set. When you publish a set of plot sheets, you have the option of plotting to the printer defined in the layout or overriding that printer and creating an electronic drawing set in either a DWF, DWFx, or PDF format via the **Publish to:** drop-down list at the top of the **Publish** dialog box. When you select either option, AutoCAD will ignore the printer specified in the page setup and create the selected file type. DWF/DWFx files can be viewed and marked up using Autodesk Design Review introduced later in this chapter. PDF files can be viewed using the ubiquitous Adobe Reader, version 7 or later.

The **Publish Options...** button displays the **Publish Options** dialog box shown in Figure 15-39 and enables you to view and modify settings for the DWF/PDF output.

Figure 15-39
The **Publish Options** dialog box

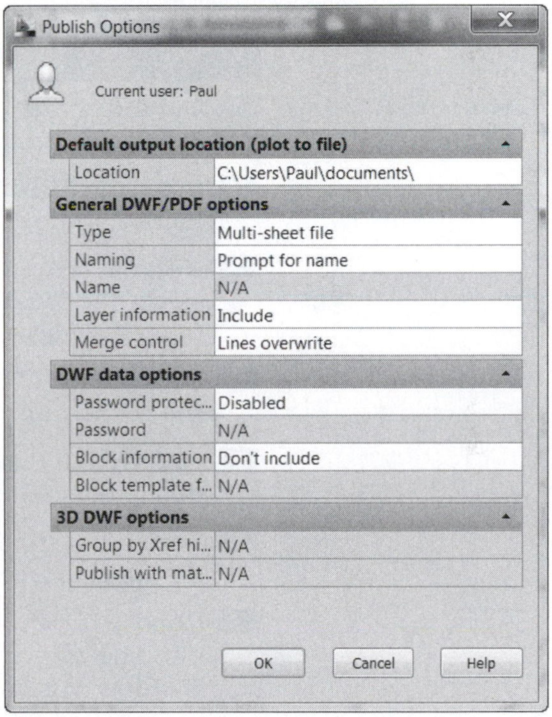

Because DWF/PDF files support multiple sheets, you have the options of printing each sheet to a separate file or plotting all sheets to a single, multisheet file. You also have the option of including layer and block information and enabling password protection.

Publish Output. The **Include plot stamp** option allows you to turn plot stamping on and off. Selecting the **Plot Stamp Settings** button displays the **Plot Stamp** dialog box (see Figure 15-40), which allows you to change the plot stamp options.

The **Publish in background** option allows you to process the list of drawings and layouts in the background so that you can continue to work in AutoCAD. A notification balloon is displayed in the AutoCAD status tray on the right side of the status bar when plotting is complete.

Figure 15-40
The **Plot Stamp** dialog box

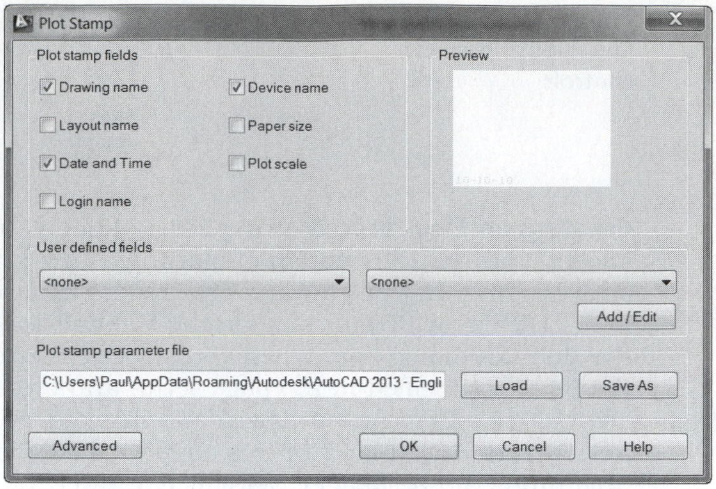

The **Open in viewer when done** option allows you to view DWF, DWFx, or PDF files in their respective viewer programs when plotting is complete.

EXERCISE 15-5 Publishing an Electronic Drawing Set

To access student data files, go to **www.pearsondesigncentral.com.**

1. Open drawing ***Welding Fixture-1*** in the student data files. This drawing contains multiple paper space layouts for a welding fixture.
2. Start the **PUBLISH** command to display the **Publish** dialog box (see Figure 15-36).
3. Because we're interested in plotting only the paper space layouts, select the **Welding Fixture-1-Model** sheet from the list of sheet names. Choose the **Remove** button to remove this sheet from the list.
4. Select the **DWF** option from the **Publish to:** drop-down list to direct the results to a DWF file.
5. Choose the **Publish Options...** button to display the **Publish Options** dialog box (see Figure 15-39).
6. Verify that the DWF type is set to **Multi-sheet file.** Choose **Include** in the **Layer information** list and choose **OK** to close the dialog box.
7. Choose the **Preview** button to switch to preview mode. Examine the plot sheets to make sure they look correct. Choose the **Close Preview Window** button to end the preview.
8. Choose **Publish** to create the DWF file. AutoCAD will prompt you for the name of the DWF file. Specify ***CH15_EXERCISE5.DWF*** and choose **Select** to create the DWF file.
9. AutoCAD will publish the DWF file and ask you whether you'd like to save the plot sheet list. Choose **No** to return to the drawing. **Do not** save the drawing file.

Working with DWF Files

Once you've created a DWF file, you have a couple of options for viewing and sharing them. Autodesk Design Review is installed when AutoCAD is installed and is also available as a free download from the Autodesk website for those who do not have AutoCAD.

> **TIP**
>
> It is possible to view and share DWF files without Autodesk Design Review software by uploading your file to the Autodesk Freewheel website located at http://freewheel.autodesk.com.

Autodesk Design Review

Autodesk Design Review allows you to view, measure, mark up, and print AutoCAD DWF files, making it possible to share your drawings with others who may not have AutoCAD while also maintaining your intellectual property because DWF files cannot be edited. The best part is that Autodesk Design Review is free and easily available at www.autodesk.com. The multisheet DWF file of the ***Welding Fixture-1*** drawing from the last exercise is shown open in Autodesk Design Review in Figure 15-41.

> **NOTE**
>
> For additional information about the Autodesk Design Review program, please refer to the Autodesk Design Review online help information or go to www.autodesk.com.

Figure 15-41
Autodesk Design Review

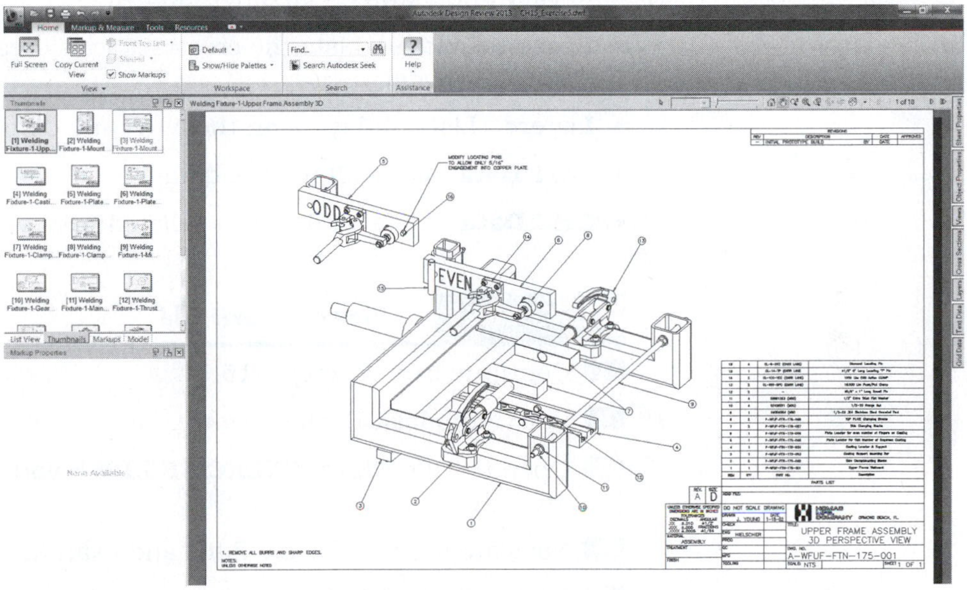

Most of the **Autodesk Design Review** tools are provided on the ribbon at the top of the screen, which has four tabs:

- **Home** Controls views, workspaces, searching for text, getting help
- **Markup & Measure** Clipboard, formatting, add callouts, draw tools, measure tools, stamps, and symbols
- **Tools** Compare sheets, 3D tools, create new sheets by taking snapshot
- **Resources** Access online resources such as discussion groups, video tutorials, blogs, and additional tools

Navigation tools are located on the toolbar at the upper right of the drawing window so you can pan, zoom, and navigate to the previous or next sheet using the **Previous Page** or **Next Page** arrow buttons. The palette at the top left displays all of the open sheet information and has four tabs:

- **List View** List of sheets
- **Thumbnails** Previews of sheets
- **Markups** List of marked-up sheets
- **Model** Model view

NOTE

Autodesk Design Review comes with AutoCAD so that you can install it from the AutoCAD installation CD. It is typically installed by default.

Properties for the selected tab are displayed on the palette below. The tabs along the right side of the window display the following information about the drawing in a palette format that is set to **Auto-hide** by default:

- **Sheet Properties** Lists the properties for the selected sheet
- **Object Properties** Lists the properties for the selected object
- **Views** Lists standard 2D and 3D views created in Autodesk Design Review and views created by AutoCAD
- **Cross Sections** Lists the cross sections created by you or the publisher of the 3D model
- **Layers** Lists all layers on the currently displayed sheet
- **Text Data** Lists all textual data
- **Grid Data** Lists all detail associated with a selection

EXERCISE 15-6 **Viewing a DWF File**

1. Continue from Exercise 15-5.
2. Start Autodesk Design Review.
3. Open the file ***CH15_EXERCISE5.DWF*** you created in the previous exercise.
4. Navigate around the DWF file and examine the multiple plot sheets.
5. Switch to the **Markup & Measure** tab and try the different tools.

Autodesk DWF Writer

The Autodesk DWF Writer is a Windows system printer driver that allows you to publish DWF files by simply selecting **Autodesk DWF Writer** from your standard **Printer Name** drop-down list in any Windows application. The DWF Writer allows you to create DWF files from any application that does not offer built-in DWF publishing. The DWF Writer is available as a free download from the Autodesk website (www.autodesk.com).

Chapter Summary

Whether you do quick and dirty check plots to verify your work, create drawing sets to send to contractors, produce full-color presentation drawings, or create electronic plots to share and collaborate with others over the Internet, plotting is an integral part of using AutoCAD. AutoCAD provides a large number of options to precisely control the look and format of your output.

We looked at how page setups are used to manage different plot settings when a drawing is plotted and how they are stored in the drawing. The ability to import page setups means you can set up standard page setups in one or more drawings or template files and then import them on an as-needed basis when you must get a drawing ready to plot.

The use of plot styles to control the output appearance of drawings was introduced. We saw that there are two different approaches to applying plot styles: color dependent and named. The most prevalent is the color-dependent plot styles (.CTB) that allow you to control object output appearance according to its color in a drawing. Named plot styles (.STB) afford you more control because you can assign a different plot style to anything in a drawing regardless of its color, but they also take a lot more work to manage.

An overview of the **Plotter Manager** to create and manage AutoCAD's plotter configuration (.PC3) files was provided so that you can add different physical printing devices or the ability to output to different raster file formats.

The ability to output directly to industry standard plot files using the Design Web Format (DWF) and Portable Document Format (PDF) format was explored so that you can share your AutoCAD designs directly with other clients and consultants without the need to print any hard-copy output. Using AutoCAD's **Batch Plotting** utility it is even possible to create a complete electronic drawing set in one step.

The best part is, using Autodesk's free downloadable Design Review software (available at www.autodesk.com), clients and consultants do not even have to have AutoCAD to view, print, and even mark up their drawings.

Chapter Test Questions

Multiple Choice

Circle the correct answer.

1. A page setup is:

a. A paper space layout

b. A set of default plot settings

c. A way to assign lineweights to AutoCAD objects

d. A print driver

2. Which of the following model space plot scales will result in a drawing scaled to 1/2″ = 1′-0″?

a. .5 = 1

b. 1 = 24

c. 24 = 1

d. 1 = .5

3. Named plot style tables are stored in:
   a. .CTB files c. .DWF files
   b. .PC3 files d. .STB files
4. Plotter configurations are stored in:
   a. .CTB files c. .DWF files
   b. .PC3 files d. .STB files
5. To plot everything visible in the drawing, you would set the plot area to:
   a. Limits c. Layout
   b. Extents d. Display
6. A DWF file:
   a. Is a Design Web Format file
   b. Can be viewed only electronically; it cannot be printed
   c. Can be opened in AutoCAD
   d. Does not show layer information
7. Which of the following AutoCAD commands does **not** print drawings?
   a. **PREVIEW** c. **SAVEAS**
   b. **PLOT** d. **PUBLISH**
8. Color-dependent plot style tables are stored in:
   a. .CTB files c. .DWF files
   b. .PC3 files d. .STB files
9. Plot stamps:
   a. Can contain only specific preset information
   b. Always appear in the lower left corner of the plot
   c. Use only the TXT.SHX text font
   d. None of the above
10. Raster files:
   a. Contain only pixels, no actual AutoCAD objects
   b. Are not supported in AutoCAD
   c. Must not exceed 640 × 480 resolution
   d. None of the above

Matching

Write the number of the correct answer on the line.

a. .PC3 ______
b. DWF ______
c. Page setup ______
d. .STB ______
e. .CTB ______
f. **PLOT** ______
g. **PUBLISH** ______
h. **Plot Stamp** ______
i. PLT ______
j. BMP ______

1. Plotter configuration file
2. Text added to a drawing at plot time
3. Command used to print multiple plot sheets
4. Color-dependent style table file
5. Command used to print a single plot sheet
6. An electronic plot file format
7. A group of default plot settings
8. A type of raster file
9. Named plot style table file
10. An AutoCAD plot file

True or False

Circle the correct answer.

1. **True or False:** Page setups are used only in layout space.
2. **True or False:** You can use both color-dependent plot styles and named plot styles within a single drawing.
3. **True or False:** Page setups can be created with the **PLOT** command.
4. **True or False:** DWF files cannot be opened in AutoCAD.
5. **True or False:** DWF files can contain only a single plot sheet.
6. **True or False:** DWF files do not support AutoCAD layers.
7. **True or False:** .PC3 files cannot be modified.
8. **True or False:** Objects in paper space are always plotted first.
9. **True or False:** You can publish layouts from multiple drawing files.
10. **True or False:** Color-dependent plot styles are assigned by layer name.

Chapter Projects

G Project 15-1: *Classroom Plan, continued from Chapter 14* [BASIC]

1. Open drawing ***P14-1*** from Chapter 14.
2. Start the **PLOT** command so that the **Plot** dialog box is displayed.
3. Set the **Printer/plotter Name** to a large-format plotter capable of printing on 36″ × 24″ paper (D-size). If you do not have access to a large-format plotter, set the **Printer/plotter Name** to **DWF6 ePlot.pc3** to create a Design Web Format (DWF) file.
4. Make sure the paper size is correct.
5. Make sure that the **Plot area** is set to **Extents.**
6. Select the **Center the plot** check box in the **Plot offset** area.
7. Make sure that the **Plot scale** is set to **1:1.**
8. Select the **More Options** arrow button at the bottom right of the dialog box to display the additional plotting options.
9. Select the **monochrome.ctb** plot style table.
10. Select the **Preview** button at the bottom left of the dialog box to preview the plot and make sure that everything is OK.
11. Select the **Apply to Layout** button at the bottom of the dialog box to save the changes with the layout.
12. Select **OK** to plot the drawing.
13. Save the drawing as ***P15-1.***

M Project 15-2: *B-Size Mechanical Border, continued from Chapter 14* [INTERMEDIATE]

1. Open template file ***Mechanical B-Size.DWT*** from Chapter 14.
2. Start the **PLOT** command so that the **Plot** dialog box is displayed.
3. Set the **Printer/plotter Name** to a printer or plotter capable of printing on 11″ × 17″ paper (B-size). If you do not have access to a printer/plotter that can print 11″ × 17″, set the **Printer/plotter Name** to **DWF6 ePlot.pc3** to create a Design Web Format (DWF) file.
4. Make sure the paper size is correct.
5. Make sure that the **Plot area** is set to **Layout.**
6. Make sure that the **Plot scale** is set to **1:1.**
7. Select the **More Options** arrow button at the bottom right of the dialog box to display the additional plotting options.
8. Select the **monochrome.ctb** plot style table.

9. Select the **Preview** button at the bottom left of the dialog box to preview the plot and make sure that everything is OK.
10. Select the **Apply to Layout** button at the bottom of the dialog box to save the changes with the layout.
11. Select **OK** to plot the drawing.
12. Save the drawing as a template file named ***Mechanical B-Size.DWT.***

A Project 15-3: *Architectural D-Size Border, continued from Chapter 14* [ADVANCED]

1. Open template file ***Architectural D-Size.DWT*** from Chapter 14.
2. Start the **PLOT** command so that the **Plot** dialog box is displayed.
3. Set the **Printer/plotter Name** to a large-format plotter capable of printing on 36″ × 24″ paper (D-size). If you do not have access to a large-format plotter, set the **Printer/plotter Name** to **DWF6 ePlot.pc3** to create a Design Web Format (DWF) file.
4. Make sure the paper size is correct.
5. Make sure that the **Plot area** is set to **Layout.**
6. Make sure that the **Plot scale** is set to **1:1.**
7. Select the **More Options** arrow button at the bottom right of the dialog box to display the additional plotting options.
8. Select the **monochrome.ctb** plot style table.
9. Select the **Preview** button at the bottom left of the dialog box to preview the plot and make sure that everything is OK.
10. Select the **Apply to Layout** button at the bottom of the dialog box to save the changes with the layout.
11. Select **OK** to plot the drawing.
12. Save the drawing to a template file as ***Architectural D-Size.DWT.***

M Project 15-4: *Optical Mount—English Units, continued from Chapter 14* [INTERMEDIATE]

1. Open drawing ***P14-4*** from Chapter 14.
2. Start the **PLOT** command so that the **Plot** dialog box is displayed.
3. Set the **Printer/plotter Name** to a large-format plotter capable of printing on 36″ × 24″ paper (D-size). If you do not have access to a large-format plotter, set the **Printer/plotter Name** to **DWF6 ePlot.pc3** to create a Design Web Format (DWF) file.
4. Make sure the paper size is correct.
5. Make sure that the **Plot area** is set to **Layout.**

6. Make sure that the **Plot scale** is set to **1:1.**
7. Select the **More Options** arrow button at the bottom right of the dialog box to display the additional plotting options.
8. Select the **monochrome.ctb** plot style table.
9. Select the **Preview** button at the bottom left of the dialog box to preview the plot and make sure that everything is OK.
10. Select the **Apply to Layout** button at the bottom of the dialog box to save the changes with the layout.
11. Select **OK** to plot the drawing.
12. Save the drawing as ***P15-4.***

A Project 15-5: *Residential Architectural Plan, continued from Chapter 14* [ADVANCED]

1. Open drawing ***P14-5*** from Chapter 14.
2. Start the **PLOT** command so that the **Plot** dialog box is displayed.
3. Set the **Printer/plotter Name** to a large-format plotter capable of printing on 36″ × 24″ paper (D-size). If you do not have access to a large-format plotter, set the **Printer/plotter Name** to **DWF6 ePlot.pc3** to create a Design Web Format (DWF) file.
4. Make sure the paper size is correct.
5. Make sure that the **Plot area** is set to **Layout.**
6. Make sure that the **Plot scale** is set to **1:1.**
7. Select the **More Options** arrow button at the bottom right of the dialog box to display the additional plotting options.
8. Select the **monochrome.ctb** plot style table.
9. Select the **Preview** button at the bottom left of the dialog box to preview the plot and make sure that everything is OK.
10. Select the **Apply to Layout** button at the bottom of the dialog box to save the changes with the layout.
11. Select **OK** to plot the drawing.
12. Save the drawing as ***P15-5.***

16 chapter sixteen
Blocks and Block Attributes

CHAPTER OBJECTIVES

- Create and insert blocks
- Understand the difference between a block definition and a block reference
- Explore the different types of blocks
- Create unit blocks that can be inserted with different *x* and *y* scale factors
- Manage block object properties such as layer, color, linetype, and lineweight
- Understand the significance of creating blocks on Layer **0**
- Insert drawing files as blocks using Windows Explorer
- Create a drawing file (DWG) out of an internal block
- Create and update block attributes
- Extract block attributes to an AutoCAD table or external file
- Use **DesignCenter** to insert blocks
- Use and customize tool palettes
- Introduction to dynamic blocks
- Use **Content Explorer** to browse DWG files to locate and insert drawing information

Introduction

Blocks, also referred to as *symbols*, are one of the most valuable features in AutoCAD. A block is a named collection of AutoCAD objects treated as a single complex object that can be inserted in a drawing one or more times. Blocks provide the following benefits and features:

- Provide the ability to reuse drawing information repeatedly in one or more drawings
- Increase drawing uniformity and consistency
- Promote and help maintain drafting standards

- Reduce drawing size
- Reduce amount of time and effort to update and revise drawings
- Add intelligence to drawings

Blocks can be made from practically any type of AutoCAD objects including lines, circles, text, dimensions, and even hatching. They may be as simple as a single line or as complex as a complete drawing. There are three basic types of blocks as shown in Figure 16-1:

- **Annotation** Detail bubbles, section marks, door/window tags
- **Schematic** Electrical symbols, plumbing symbols, weld symbols
- **Real-Size** Furniture, doors/windows, plumbing fixtures

Figure 16-1
Examples of block types

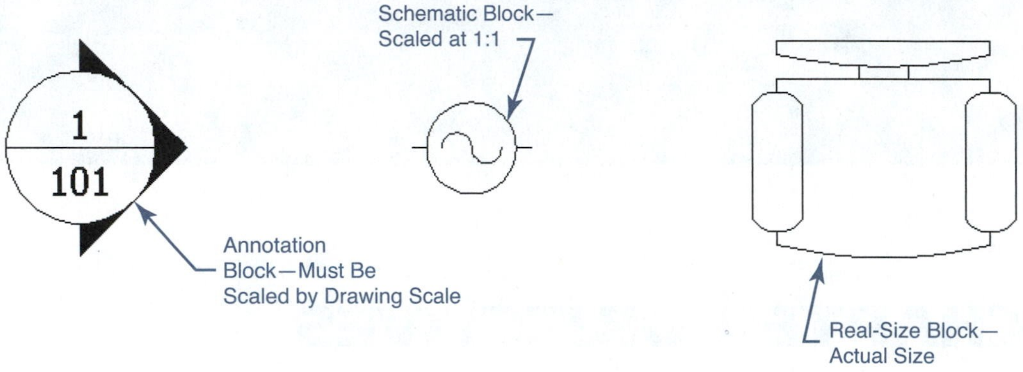

Annotation blocks need to be scaled up or down when they are inserted to account for the drawing scale, just like text and dimensions. For instance, a detail bubble drawn with a 1/2″-diameter circle as shown in Figure 16-1 would have to be scaled up by 48 in a drawing with the scale of 1/4″ = 1′-0″ in order to plot at the correct size.

> **TIP**
> It is possible to make a block annotative so it scales up or down automatically using the current annotation scale.

Schematic blocks are created at the size they will plot so that you can create schematic drawings at a scale of 1:1. For instance, the electrical symbol in Figure 16-1 is drawn with a 1/4″ diameter so that it can easily be located in a schematic drawing created on a 1/4″ or 1/8″ grid layout.

Real-size blocks are created at the actual size that the objects exist in the real world so that they can be used to accurately lay out a drawing. For instance, a 2′-0″ wide chair is drawn 24″ wide so that when it is located on a floor plan it represents the actual furniture.

block attribute: A dynamic text-like object that can be included in a block definition to store alphanumeric data.

It is even possible to attach dynamic intelligent text referred to as a ***block attribute*** that can be updated when a block is inserted or anytime later.

> **NOTE**
> Like other complex objects, a block can be converted back into its original subobjects using the **EXPLODE** command. Using the **EXPLODE** command with blocks is examined later in this chapter.

Existing block attributes can be extracted directly to an AutoCAD table so that you can automatically create schedules, parts lists, bills of materials, and other tabular type information. In fact, block attributes can even be extracted to an external text file, spreadsheet, or database so that the attribute information can be shared with others, used to generate reports, and used to perform other tasks.

As you can see, blocks are very useful. The following sections explain how to exploit the power of blocks and block attributes in your AutoCAD drawings.

Creating Blocks

The named group of AutoCAD objects that make up a block is referred to as a ***block definition***.

block definition: A user-defined collection of drawing objects assigned a base point and a name that is stored centrally in a drawing.

block reference: An instance of a block definition inserted in a drawing that references the central block definition drawing data.

Every time a block is inserted in a drawing it refers back to the centrally located block definition. In fact, when a block is inserted in a drawing, it is referred to as a ***block reference*** because it refers back to the block definition to determine its appearance and other properties.

CREATE BLOCK	
Ribbon & Panel:	Insert Block Definition Create Block
Draw Toolbar:	
Menu:	Draw Block | Make…
Command Line:	BLOCK BMAKE
Command Alias:	B

NOTE

It is possible to create blocks that are made up of other blocks. Creating a block within a block is a concept referred to as *block nesting* because one block is nested inside another block.

All that is stored with the block reference is the block's insertion point, scale (*x*, *y*, and *z*), and rotation angle. The rest of the information is derived from the block definition. This arrangement provides a couple of advantages. One advantage is that the drawing size is reduced because the block definition is centrally stored in *one* place, regardless of how many references of the block exist in a drawing. The other advantage is that if you update a block definition, all references to that block definition in a drawing are automatically updated, regardless of how many references there are.

Creating a new block definition is easy. You simply draw the objects you want the block to consist of using standard drawing techniques and then start the **BLOCK** command so you can select the objects and give them a descriptive name that you can reference later.

The BLOCK Command

The **BLOCK** command creates a block definition using the objects you select with the name specified via the **Block Definition** dialog box shown in Figure 16-2.

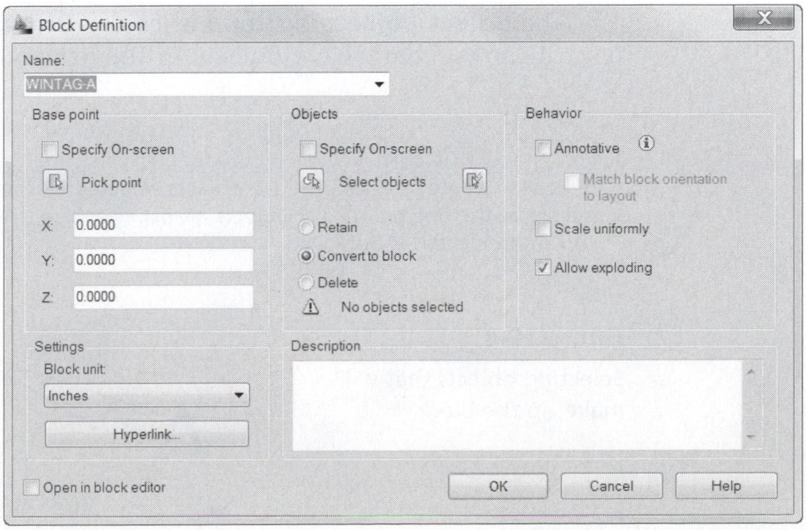

Figure 16-2
The **Block Definition** dialog box

The **Name:** list box is where you enter the desired block name. The name can be up to 255 characters long and can include letters, numbers, or blank spaces. Typically, you want to use a descriptive name that reflects the block's contents and/or usage.

> **NOTE**
>
> Do not use the block names **AVE_RENDER, DIRECT, LIGHT, OVERHEAD, RM_SDB,** or **SH_SPOT.** These names are reserved for special AutoCAD objects.

Selecting an existing block name from the list will redefine all references to that block in the drawing if you make any changes. Redefining blocks is explained later in this chapter.

The **Base point** area allows you to specify an insertion point for the block. This point is used to locate the block in the drawing when it is inserted later. The default insertion point is 0,0,0. You can either enter the *x*, *y*, and *z* coordinate values directly in their respective text boxes or pick a point in your drawing by selecting the **Pick point** button. The **Pick point** button temporarily closes the **Block Definition** dialog box so that you can pick a point in the drawing as shown in Figure 16-3.

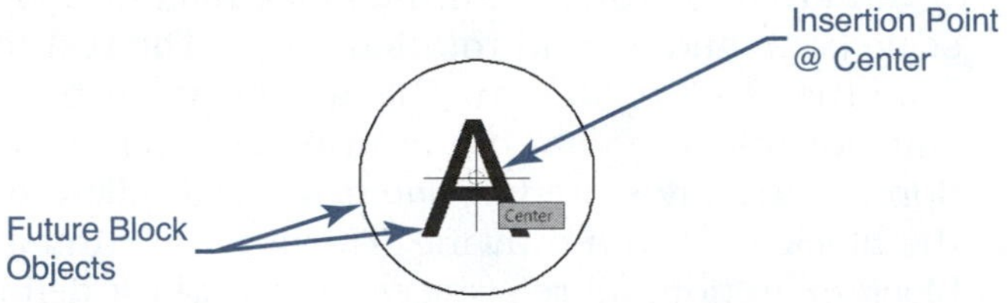

Figure 16-3

Selecting a block insertion point

> **TIP**
>
> Typically, you should rely on object snaps to snap to a key point on the objects that comprise the block. For instance, you might select the center point if you were creating a detail bubble block or the endpoint at a corner of a desk block.

The **Objects** area allows you to select the objects to include in the new block definition if there are none already selected in the drawing, as well as to indicate what to do with the selected objects after the block definition is created.

The **Select objects** button closes the **Block Definition** dialog box temporarily so you can select objects in the drawing as shown in Figure 16-4.

> **NOTE**
>
> If no objects are selected, the **No objects selected** warning shown in Figure 16-2 is displayed at the bottom of the **Objects** area. Otherwise, the number of objects that are currently selected is displayed.

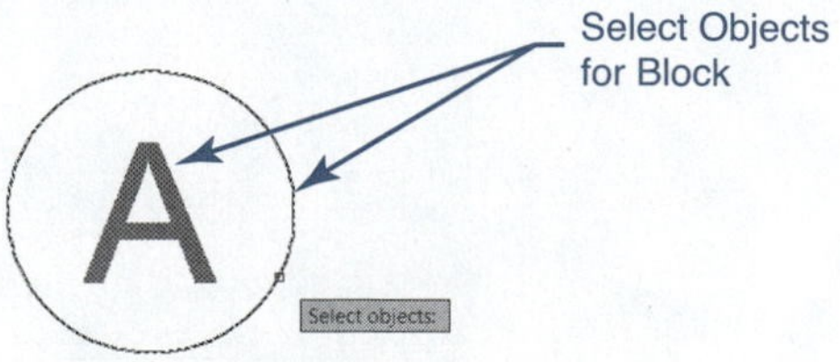

Figure 16-4

Selecting objects that will make up the block

You can use any standard selection process. When you finish selecting objects, press **<Enter>** to redisplay the **Block Definition** dialog box and continue defining the block. Pressing the <**Esc**> key when selecting objects will deselect the objects so that nothing is selected and redisplay the **Block Definition** dialog box.

The **QuickSelect** button closes the **Block Definition** dialog box temporarily and displays the **Quick Select** dialog box shown in Figure 16-5 so you can select objects by filtering one or more object properties.

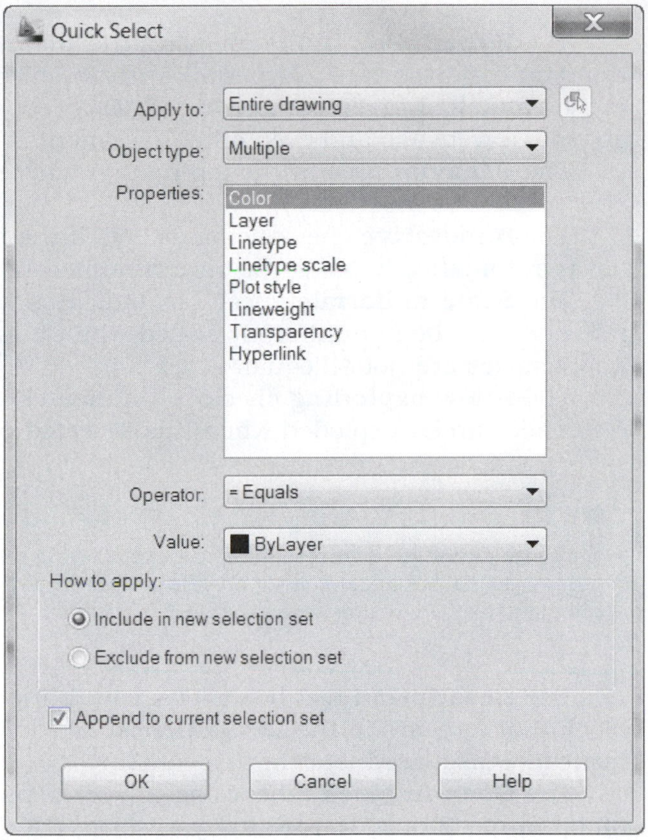

Figure 16-5
The **Quick Select** dialog box

The other three options in the **Objects** area directly below the **Select objects** button determine what happens to the selected objects after the block is created:

- **Retain** Retains the original selected objects in the drawing without doing anything
- **Convert to block (default)** Converts the selected objects to a block reference "in-place"
- **Delete** Deletes all the selected objects after the block is created so that they no longer exist

> **TIP**
> If you use the **Delete** option by accident, you can use the **OOPS** command to undelete the block subobjects. Type **OOPS<Enter>** immediately after the block is created in order to return the original block subobjects to your drawing.

The **Settings** area at the bottom left is where you specify different settings for the block.

The **Block unit:** list box lists the different possible insertion units for the block. If you insert a block that is created with different block drawing units than the insertion scale units currently set for the drawing, the block is automatically scaled up or down according to the scale factor equivalent of the ratio between the different unit systems.

> **NOTE**
>
> The insertion scale units are set via the **Drawing Units** dialog box, which can be displayed by selecting **Units** from the **Drawing Utilitues** menu on the big **A** application menu or using the **UNITS** command.

The **Hyperlink...** button displays the **Insert Hyperlink** dialog box so that you can associate a hyperlink with the block definition. Hyperlinks can be attached to almost any AutoCAD object so that it is possible to link objects to websites and even other documents.

The **Behavior** area at the top right is where you control what happens after a block is inserted.

The **Annotative** check box indicates if the block can be scaled up and down automatically using the current annotation scale.

The **Scale uniformly** check box indicates whether or not the block reference can be nonuniformly scaled when it is inserted so that the *x*, *y*, and *z* scales are not all equal.

The **Allow exploding** check box indicates whether or not the block reference can be exploded when it is inserted or afterward.

> **NOTE**
>
> The block definition is created in the current drawing *only*. To use the block in any other drawing, you must first export it to a separate drawing file using the **WBLOCK** command explained later in this chapter.

The **Description** text box allows you to input a text description for the block that appears in the **DesignCenter** block drawing content management tool discussed later in this chapter.

The **Open in block editor** check box opens the current block definition in the **Block Editor** after you select **OK.** The **Block Editor** is described briefly later in this chapter.

After you have entered a name for the block, selected one or more objects, and specified the desired settings described above, select **OK** to close the dialog box and create the block.

Block Object Properties

When you insert a block, the block reference assumes the current object properties (layer, color, linetype, lineweight) just like other AutoCAD objects. Be aware that the current properties are assigned to the overall complex block reference *only*. The object properties of the subobjects that make up the block are determined by how the objects were originally created before they were made into a block.

There are three different techniques for controlling the properties of a block's subobjects that result in the following effects when the block is inserted:

- Create subobjects on Layer **0** with the color, linetype, and lineweight set to **ByLayer**
- Create subobjects on any layer other than **0**
- Create subobjects using the ByBlock property set for color, linetype, or lineweight

Creating Blocks on Layer 0. Creating block subobjects on Layer **0** with object properties set to **ByLayer** is the most popular approach to creating blocks because it provides the most flexibility. Blocks with subobjects created on Layer **0** have the special ability to assume the current object properties when they are inserted. This allows you to create one block that can be used in multiple scenarios based on the layer that is current when the block is inserted.

Hard-Coding a Block's Object Properties. Creating block subobjects on any layer other than **0** locks the subobjects on the layer on which they were created so that the subobjects always maintain their original properties regardless of what layer or other properties are current when the block is inserted. This approach provides the least amount of flexibility because the block's subobjects are always located on the layer on which they were created regardless of the current layer and object properties in the drawing when the block is inserted. However, this hard-coded approach can have its uses, especially if standards dictate that a particular layer should be maintained for the life of a drawing.

Using the ByBlock Object Property. The ByBlock property allows you to create block subobjects that will assume the current color, linetype, lineweight, or transparency property when the block is inserted. Normally, a block and its subobjects ignore the color, linetype, lineweight, and transparency properties when the block is inserted. If you create a block subobject with any of these properties set to **ByBlock**, the subobject will assume the current setting for the property during the insertion process. For instance, setting a line's color property to **ByBlock** and including it in a block definition forces the line to assume the current color when the block is inserted. If the current color setting is **red**, then the line subobject is **red.** The same logic applies to the linetype and lineweight properties.

EXERCISE 16-1 Creating Blocks

1. Start a new drawing using the **acad.dwt** drawing template.
2. Create the following layers:

Name	Color	Linetype	Lineweight	Description
WINTAG-B	1	Continuous	Default	Layer used for all WINTAG-B block subobjects
A-Glaze-Iden	3	Continuous	Default	Window tag layer

3. Create the "A" window tag shown in Figure 16-6 on Layer **0**.
4. Create the "B" window tag shown in Figure 16-6 on layer **WINTAG-B**.
5. Create the "C" window tag shown in Figure 16-6 on Layer **0** with the color, linetype, and lineweight properties all set to **ByBlock**.
6. Start the **BLOCK** command to display the **Block Definition** dialog box.

Figure 16-6
Window tag blocks

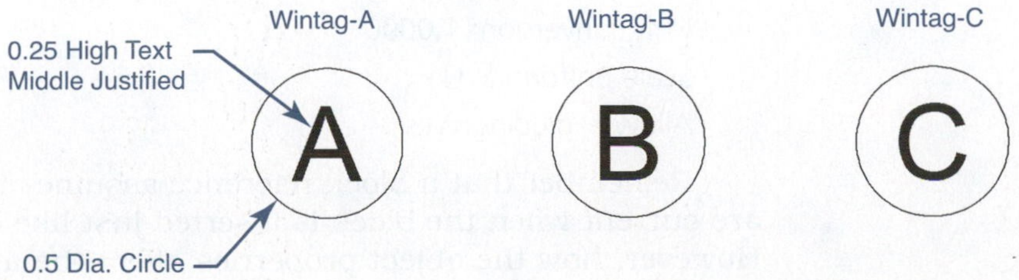

7. Enter the name **WINTAG-A** in the **Name:** list box.
8. Select the **Pick point** button in the **Base point** area.
9. Select the center point of the "A" window tag circle using the **Center** object snap.
10. Select the **Select objects** button in the **Objects** area.
11. Select the "A" window tag circle and text, and press **<Enter>** to return to the **Block Definition** dialog box.
12. Make sure that the **Convert to block** button is selected.
13. Select the **Annotative** check box in the **Behavior** area.
14. Select **OK** to create the block.
15. Repeat steps 6 through 14 to create blocks named **WINTAG-B** and **WINTAG-C** for the "B" window tag and the "C" window tag, respectively.
16. Save the drawing as ***CH16_EXERCISE1.***

Inserting Blocks

As mentioned earlier, when you insert a block, it creates a block reference. Remember that the information about the objects that make up the block and what the block looks like is determined by the block definition explained in the previous section. All that you need to specify when inserting a block is the following:

- Block name
- Insertion point
- *x*, *y*, and *z* scale
- Rotation angle

In fact, besides the standard object properties such as layer, color, linetype, and transparency discussed later, this constitutes the majority of the information that is stored with the block reference. This is evident when you list a block reference using the AutoCAD **LIST** command:

```
BLOCK REFERENCE Layer: "0"
Space: Model space
Handle = a4
Block Name: "WINTAG-A"
at point, X= 0.0000 Y= 0.0000 Z= 0.0000
X scale factor: 1.0000
Y scale factor: 1.0000
rotation angle: 0
Z scale factor: 1.0000
InsUnits: Inches
Unit conversion: 1.0000
Scale uniformly: No
Allow exploding: Yes
```

Remember that a block reference assumes the object properties that are current when the block is inserted just like any other AutoCAD object. However, how the object properties affect the appearance of the block

INSERT BLOCK	
Ribbon & Panel:	Insert Block  Insert
Draw Toolbar:	
Menu:	Insert Block…
Command Line:	INSERT
Command Alias:	I

reference is dependent on how the block was created as explained earlier in the section "Creating Blocks."

The INSERT Command

The **INSERT** command allows you to insert a block reference by specifying the block name, insertion point, scale, and rotation angle via the **Insert** dialog box shown in Figure 16-7.

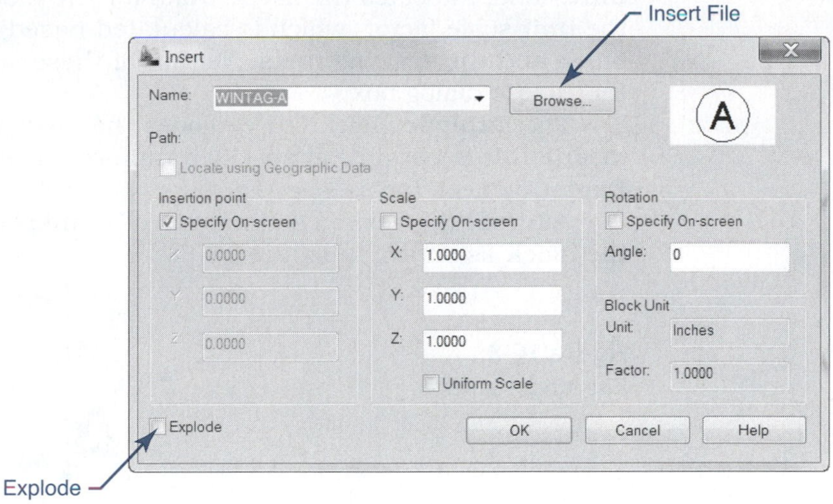

Figure 16-7
The **Insert** dialog box

The **Name:** list box lists the names of all the blocks defined in a drawing that can be inserted.

The **Browse…** button displays the standard **Select Drawing File** dialog box so you can select a block or drawing file to insert.

The **Path:** label specifies the path to the block if you select an external drawing file using the **Browse…** button above.

The **Locate using Geographic Data** check box will insert the block using geographic data as the reference. This option is enabled only if both the block and the current drawing have geographic data.

The **Preview** window displays a preview of the specified block to insert. A lightning bolt icon in the lower-right corner of the preview indicates that the block is dynamic.

The **Insertion point** area allows you to specify the insertion point for the block. You can either pick a point in the drawing after you select **OK** (default), or you can specify the coordinate position in the **X:, Y:,** and **Z:** text boxes. The **Specify On-screen** check box toggles between the two methods.

The **Scale** area allows you to specify the *x*, *y*, and *z* scale factors for the inserted block. You can either enter the scale factors in the **X:, Y:,** and **Z:** text boxes (default), or you can enter the scale factors after you select **OK.** The **Specify On-screen** check box toggles between the two methods.

> **NOTE**
>
> It is possible to insert an external drawing file (DWG) file from anywhere on your computer or network using the **Browse…** button. Inserting external drawing files is explained in detail later in this chapter.

The **Uniform Scale** check box forces a single scale value for the *X*-, *Y*-, and *Z*-axes. When the **Uniform Scale** check box is selected, the *y* and *z* scales default to the value specified for *x*.

The **Rotation** area allows you to specify the rotation angle for the inserted block in the current UCS. You can either enter the rotation angle in the **Angle:** text box (default), or you can enter the rotation angle after you select **OK.** The **Specify On-screen** check box toggles between the two methods.

The **Block Unit** area displays information about the block units. The **Unit:** label indicates the insert units for the block. The **Factor:** displays the unit scale factor, which is calculated based on the insert units of the block and the drawing units. Neither of these settings can be changed in the **Insert** dialog box.

The **Explode** check box explodes the block immediately after it is inserted. It is possible to specify a uniform scale factor only when the **Explode** check box is selected.

After all the desired settings have been specified, select **OK** to insert the block as shown in Figure 16-8.

Figure 16-8
Inserting a block

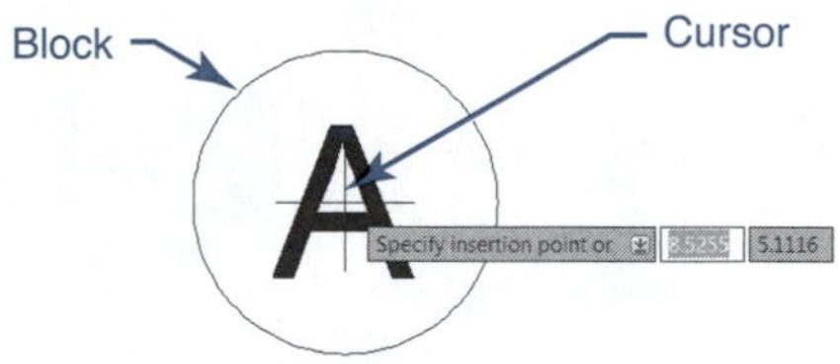

Figure 16-8 shows a block being inserted using the default settings, which prompt you to *Specify insertion point or* ↓ on-screen during the insertion process.

If the **Specify On-screen** check box is selected for the **Scale** settings, AutoCAD prompts you to *Enter X scale factor, specify opposite corner, or* ↓ so that you can either enter the desired scale for the *X*-axis at the keyboard or pick a corner point in your drawing that dynamically defines both the *x* and *y* scales. The default scale factor is always **1.**

If you enter an *x* scale and press **<Enter>,** AutoCAD then prompts you to *Enter Y scale factor <use X scale factor>:* ↓. You can either press **<Enter>** so that the *x* and *y* scales are equal, or you can enter a different scale factor to create a nonuniformly scaled block. Nonuniformly scaled blocks are discussed in the next section.

If the **Specify On-screen** check box is selected for the **Rotation** settings, AutoCAD prompts you to *Specify rotation angle <0>:* so that you can either enter the desired rotation angle at the keyboard or pick a point in your drawing that dynamically defines the angle using the insertion point as the angle base point as shown in Figure 16-9.

Figure 16-9
Inserting a block and specifying the rotation angle on-screen

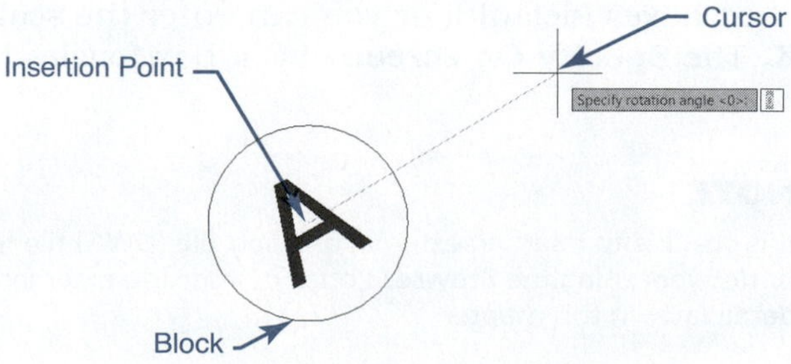

EXERCISE 16-2 **Inserting Blocks**

1 Continue from Exercise 16-1.

2 Set the current layer to **A-Glaze-Iden** via the **Layers** drop-down list.

3 Set the current color to **Blue** via the **Properties** panel on the **Home** tab of the ribbon.

4 Use the **INSERT** command to insert the **WINTAG-A, WINTAG-B**, and **WINTAG-C** blocks anywhere in the drawing so that you can see all three block references in the drawing window.

5 Compare how the object properties are different for each block reference.

6 Turn on the **Automatically add scales to annotative objects when the annotation scale changes** button on the right side of the status bar.

7 Change the **Annotation Scale** to **1:2**.

8 Insert one of the WINTAG blocks.

9 Change the **Annotation Scale** to **2:1**.

10 Insert another WINTAG block.

11 Save the drawing.

Nonuniformly Scaled Unit Blocks

unit block: A block or symbol drawn within a 1 × 1 unit square that is inserted in the drawing with different *x* and *y* scales to achieve different final sizes.

If the **Uniform Scale** check box was not selected when the block was created, you can specify different *x*, *y*, and *z* scale factors when a block is inserted so that the block can be scaled along a single axis. In fact, this is a technique that is used to create what are known as ***unit blocks***.

Unit blocks can be scaled along one axis so that one block definition can serve multiple purposes. A classic example is a structural lumber section, which is typically represented by a nominally sized rectangle with a cross through it (see Figure 16-10). Creating the lumber section as a unit block allows you to specify different *x* and *y* scales when the block is inserted so that different lumber sizes can be created as shown in Figure 16-10.

Figure 16-10
Structural lumber section inserted as a unit block with nonuniform scales

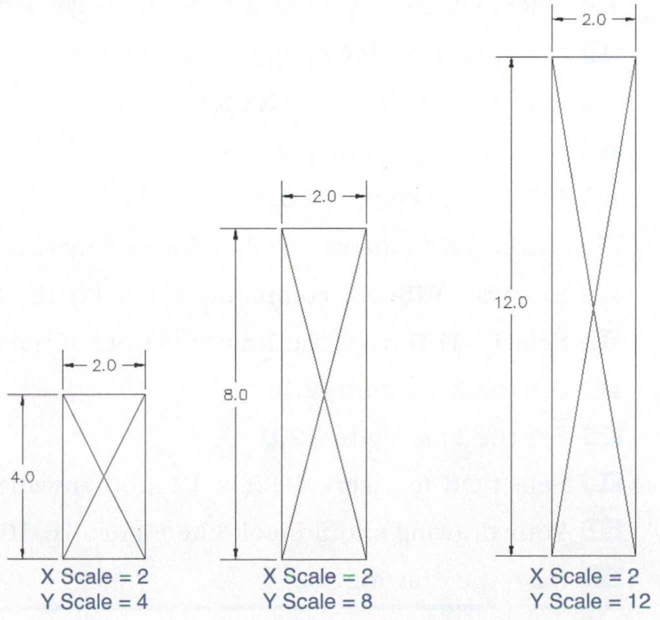

EXERCISE 16-3 Nonuniformly Scaled Unit Blocks

1. Start a new drawing using the **acad.dwt** drawing template.
2. Create the unit block drawing shown in Figure 16-11.

Figure 16-11
1 × 1 unit block

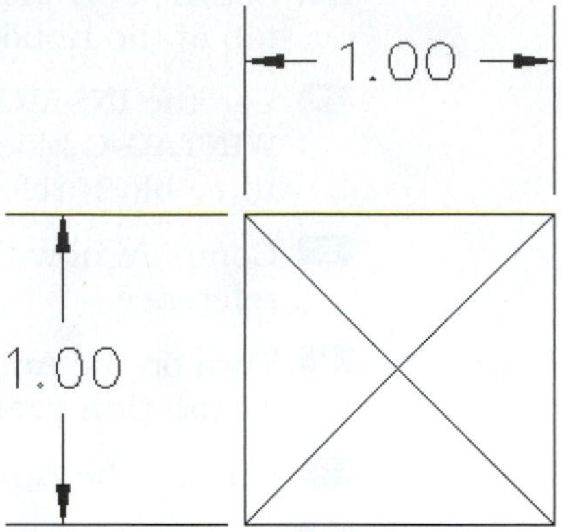

3. Use the **BLOCK** command to create a block named **STUD** that consists of the line work created in step 2 with a base point at the lower left-hand corner.
4. Start the **INSERT** command to display the **Insert** dialog box.

> **NOTE**
> The lumber sizes used in the examples in this section are shown as nominal sizes and not actual sizes for the sake of simplicity.

5. Select **STUD** from the **Name:** list box.
6. Make sure the **Specify On-screen** check box is unselected in the **Scale** area.
7. Set the **X:** scale to **2.0**.
8. Set the **Y:** scale to **4.0**.
9. Select **OK** to insert the 2 × 4 stud anywhere in your drawing.
10. Start the **INSERT** command to display the **Insert** dialog box.
11. Select **STUD** from the **Name:** list box if not selected.
12. Set the **X:** scale to **2.0**.
13. Set the **Y:** scale to **8.0**.
14. Select **OK** to insert the 2 × 8 stud anywhere in your drawing.
15. Start the **INSERT** command to display the **Insert** dialog box.
16. Select **STUD** from the **Name:** list box if not selected.
17. Set the **X:** scale to **2.0**.
18. Set the **Y:** scale to **12.0**.
19. Select **OK** to insert the 2 × 12 stud anywhere in your drawing.
20. Your drawing should look like Figure 16-10.
21. Save the drawing.

Exploding Blocks

As mentioned earlier in the Introduction, a block reference is considered a complex object just like a polyline, boundary hatch, or dimension. If the **Allow exploding** check box was selected when the block was created, you can explode a block back into its original individual subobjects either after it is inserted using the **EXPLODE** command or when it is inserted by selecting the **Explode** check box in the **Insert** dialog box shown in Figure 16-7.

> **TIP**
>
> Typically, you do not want to explode blocks because you lose all the advantages of using them in the first place. Not only can you no longer automatically update an exploded block using the techniques explained later in this chapter, but you also increase the size of the drawing because each subobject is added as a new object and is no longer simply a reference.

Inserting a Drawing File as a Block

It is possible, and actually quite common, to insert an entire drawing file (DWG) as a block. When you insert a drawing file, a block definition with the same name as the file is automatically created using all the information in the drawing file.

> **NOTE**
>
> When you insert a drawing file as a block, only model space information is included. Objects located in paper space are ignored.

There are a couple of ways to insert a drawing file as a block. To insert a drawing file via the **Insert** dialog box explained earlier, select the **Browse...** button shown in Figure 16-7 to display the **Select Drawing File** dialog box shown in Figure 16-12.

Find the file you want to insert and select the **Open** button. A block definition with the same name as the drawing file is added to the **Name** list box, and it becomes the current block to insert as shown in Figure 16-13.

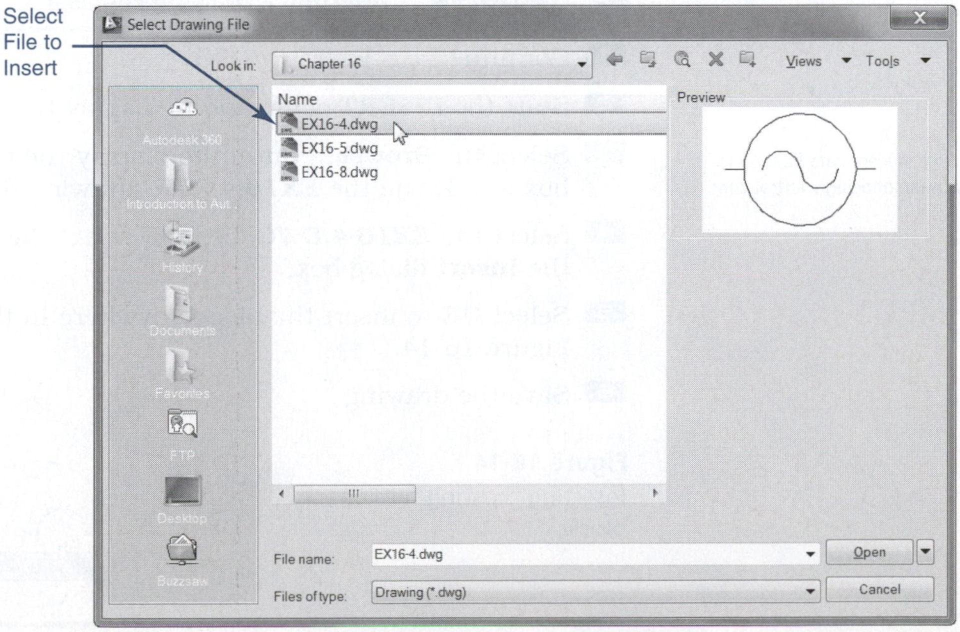

Figure 16-12
Selecting a drawing file to insert as a block

Figure 16-13
New block definition added to list

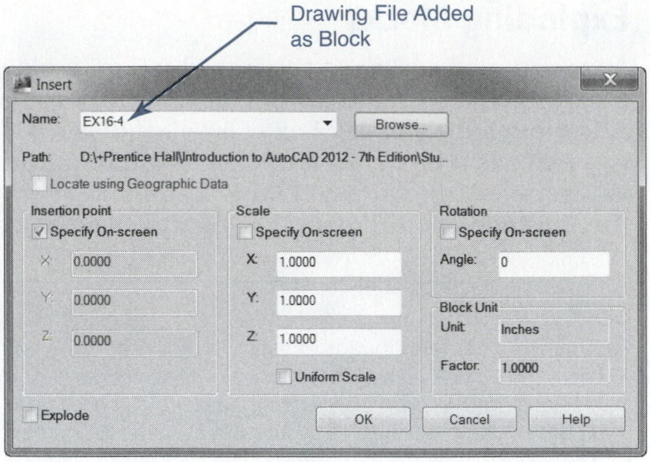

Once a drawing has been selected and it has been made a block definition, the exact same settings can be specified. You can select **OK** to insert the block.

NOTE

When you insert a drawing file, all the nongraphical named information defined in the drawing, such as layers, linetypes, text styles, dimension styles, etc., comes along for the ride so that *any* named information defined in the original drawing becomes part of the current drawing.

TIP

By default, the insertion base point for a drawing file inserted as a block is the coordinate location 0,0,0 in the original drawing file. You can change the insertion base point by opening the drawing file and using the **BASE** command to set it to another location. Don't forget to save the drawing.

EXERCISE 16-4 Inserting a Drawing File as a Block

1. Continue from Exercise 16-3.
2. Start the **INSERT** command to display the **Insert** dialog box.
3. Select the **Browse...** button to display the **Select Drawing File** dialog box and locate the ***EX16-4.DWG*** drawing file in the student data files.
4. Select the ***EX16-4.DWG*** file, and select the **Open** button to return to the **Insert** dialog box.
5. Select **OK** to insert the block anywhere in the drawing as shown in Figure 16-14.
6. Save the drawing.

To access student data files, go to **www.pearsondesigncentral.com.**

Figure 16-14
Inserting drawing files as blocks

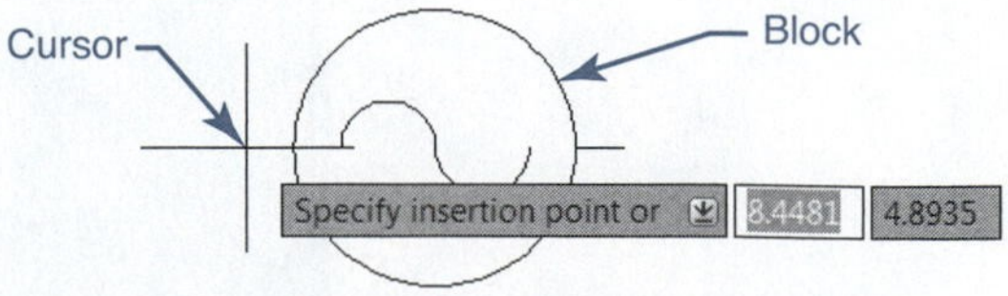

Using Windows Explorer to Insert a Drawing File

You can use Windows® Explorer to drag and drop a drawing file directly into the current drawing. You can start Windows Explorer a number of ways including by double-clicking on the **My Computer** icon on the Windows desktop, by right-clicking on the Windows **Start** button and selecting **Explore** from the menu, or even by typing the **EXPLORE** command in AutoCAD.

In order to use drag-and-drop techniques, you must be able to have both AutoCAD and Explorer visible on your computer at the same time, as shown in Figure 16-15.

Figure 16-15
Using Windows Explorer to insert files

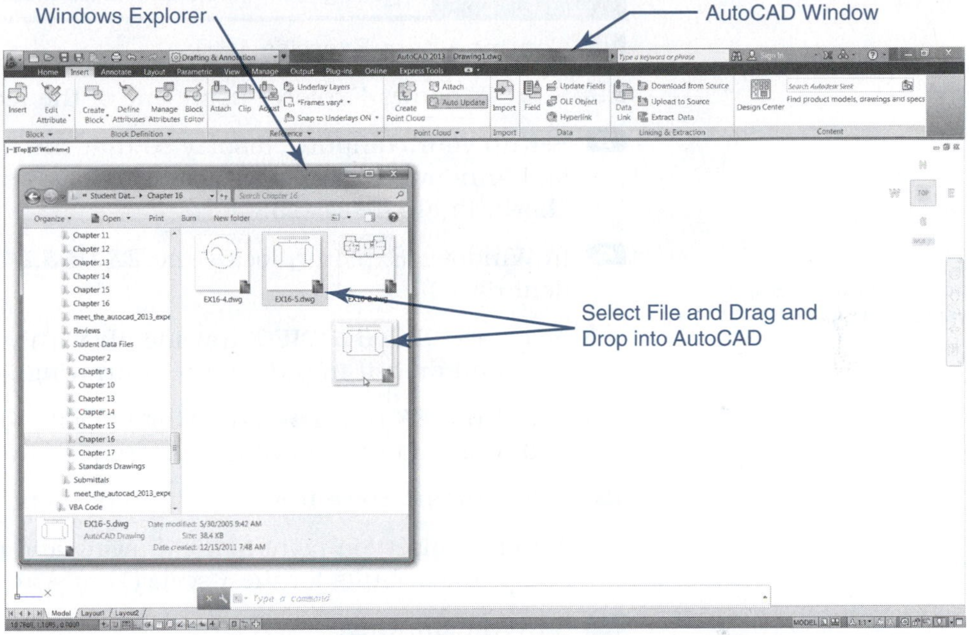

If you select a file with the *left* mouse button and drag and drop it into your drawing, the same insertion point, scale factor, and rotation angle command prompts are displayed as if the **Specify On-screen** check boxes were selected in the **Insert** dialog box described earlier.

If you select a file with the *right* mouse button and drag and drop it into your drawing, the shortcut menu shown in Figure 16-16 is displayed.

Figure 16-16
Right-click **Drag-and-Drop** shortcut menu

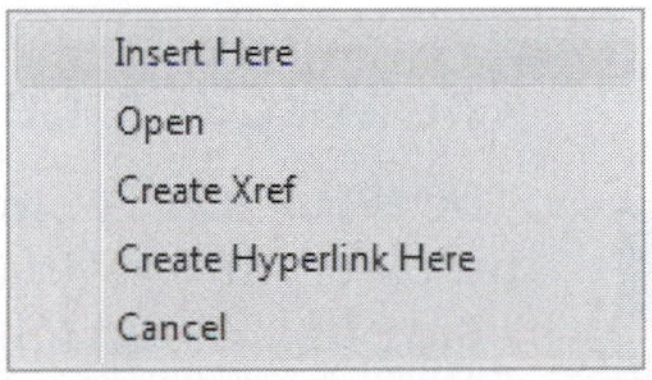

Using the shortcut menu, you can elect to do one of the following:

- **Insert Here** Inserts the file as a block the same as above
- **Open** Opens the drawing file in a new window
- **Create Xref** Attaches the drawing as an xref
- **Create Hyperlink Here** Creates a hyperlink to the drawing on the object you select
- **Cancel** Cancels drag-and-drop operation

> **NOTE**
>
> It is possible to drag and drop only one drawing file at a time.

> **FOR MORE DETAILS**
>
> See Chapter 17 for more details about using xrefs (external references).

EXERCISE 16-5 Using Windows Explorer to Insert a Drawing File

1. Continue from Exercise 16-4.
2. Start Windows Explorer using one of the techniques explained above.
3. Set up your computer display so that the AutoCAD drawing window and Windows Explorer window are both visible, similar to the display shown in Figure 16-15.
4. In Windows Explorer, locate the ***EX16-5.DWG*** drawing file in the student data files.
5. Select the ***EX16-5.DWG*** drawing file with your *left* mouse button, and drag and drop it into the current drawing.
6. Select the ***EX16-5.DWG*** drawing file with your *right* mouse button, and drag and drop it into the current drawing.
7. Select **Insert Here** from the shortcut menu.
8. Select an insertion point in the drawing and press **<Enter>** three times to accept the defaults for the *x* scale **(1)**, *y* scale **(1)**, and rotation angle **(0)**.
9. Save the drawing.

To access student data files, go to **www.pearsondesigncentral.com.**

Exporting Blocks

As mentioned earlier in the "Creating Blocks" section, by default, a block definition is stored *only* in the drawing in which it is created. In order to use the block in another drawing, you must first export it to a drawing file (DWG). You can then insert it using the techniques explained above.

The WBLOCK Command

WRITE BLOCK

Ribbon & Panel:	Insert | Block Definition

Write Block

Toolbar:	None
Menu:	None
Command Line:	WBLOCK
Command Alias:	W

The **WBLOCK** command, short for "write block," writes a block definition to an external drawing file (DWG) with the file name and location you specify using any of the following methods:

- Write an existing block definition that is already defined internally in a drawing
- Create a new block definition *and* write the block to an external drawing file
- Create a new block definition using *all* the information in the drawing, and write the block to an external drawing file

Starting the **WBLOCK** command displays the **Write Block** dialog box shown in Figure 16-17. The **Source** area is the main area of the dialog box used to specify how to create the block.

Figure 16-17
The **Write Block** dialog box

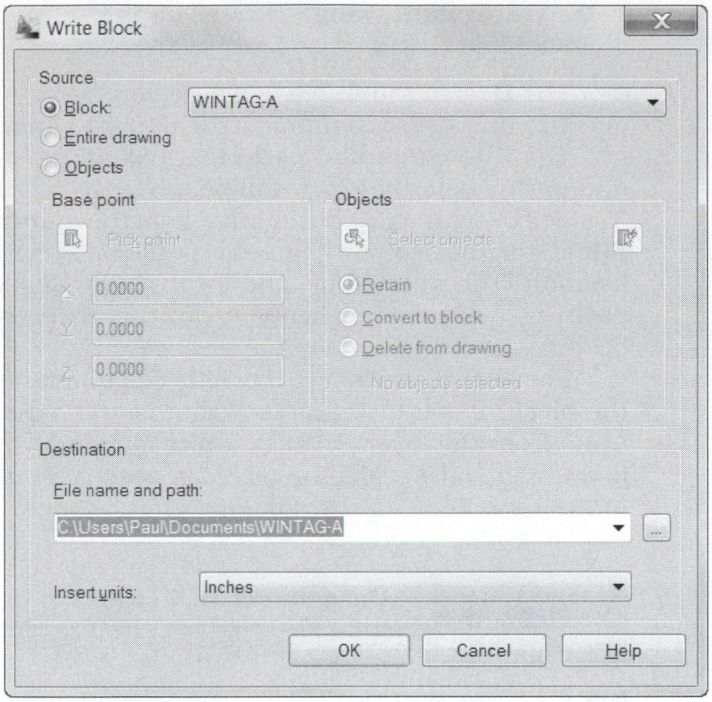

The **Block** option allows you to select a block that has already been defined in the drawing from the list on the right. This option and the list are disabled if there are no blocks defined in the drawing. The **Entire drawing** option creates a block out of the entire drawing and writes it out to a file.

> **TIP**
>
> Using **WBLOCK** to create a block out of the entire drawing and write it to a file is an old trick used to quickly purge a drawing of all its unreferenced drawing information such as layers, linetypes, text styles, dimension styles, other blocks, and so on, so that the file size is reduced.

The **Objects** option allows you to create a new block on the fly and write it out to an external file using the exact same techniques as the **BLOCK** command explained earlier in the chapter. See the earlier section "Creating Blocks" for complete, detailed information about creating a block from scratch.

The **Base point** area allows you to specify a base point for the block. The default value is 0,0,0.

The **Select objects** button closes the **Write Block** dialog box temporarily so you can select objects in the drawing as shown earlier in Figure 16-4. The **QuickSelect** button closes the **Write Block** dialog box temporarily and displays the **Quick Select** dialog box shown earlier in Figure 16-5 so you can select objects by filtering on one or more object properties.

The other three options in the **Objects** area directly below the **Select objects** button determine what happens to the selected objects after the block is created:

- **Retain (default)** Retains the original selected objects in the drawing without doing anything
- **Convert to block** Converts the selected objects to a block reference "in-place"

- **Delete from drawing** Deletes all the selected objects after the block is created so that they no longer exist

The **Destination** area is where you specify the file name and location and the units of measurement to be used when the block is inserted.

The **File name and path:** text box allows you to enter the file name and path where the block will be saved.

Selecting the **[...]** button displays the standard **Browse for Drawing File** dialog box so you can select a file or specify another drive and folder location. The selected file and location are displayed in the **File name and path:** text box above when you exit the dialog box by selecting the **Save** button.

The **Insert units:** list box lists the different possible insertion units for the block. If you insert a block that is created with different block drawing units from the insertion scale units currently set for the drawing, the block is automatically scaled up or down according to the scale factor equivalent of the ratio between the different unit systems.

EXERCISE 16-6 Using the WBLOCK Command to Export a Block

1. Continue from Exercise 16-5.
2. Start the **WBLOCK** command to display the **Write Block** dialog box.
3. Select the **Block** option in the **Source** area at the top of the dialog box.
4. Select the **WINTAG-A** block from the **Block** list box.
5. Set the **File name and path:** setting in the **Destination** area to a folder location of your choice using the **WINTAG-A.DWG** file name, and select **OK** to export the block.
6. Draw a "D" window tag similar to the others with the same circle diameter and text height somewhere in the drawing.
7. Start the **WBLOCK** command to display the **Write Block** dialog box again.
8. Select the **Objects** option in the **Source** area at the top of the dialog box.
9. Select the **Pick point** button in the **Base point** area.
10. Select the center point of the "D" window tag circle you just created using the **Center** object snap.
11. Select the **Select objects** button in the **Objects** area.
12. Select the "D" window tag circle and text, and press **<Enter>** to return to the **Write Block** dialog box.
13. Set the **File name and path:** setting in the **Destination** area to a folder location of your choice with the file name ***WINTAG-D.DWG*** and select **OK** to export the block.
14. Save the drawing.

Block Attributes

As explained in the Introduction, an attribute is a text-like object included in a block definition that is used to store alphanumeric information. It can be either updated dynamically when a block is inserted or updated manually after the block is inserted later by selecting the block. Updated attribute data can then be used to automatically create tables or exported to external files using the **Data Extraction** wizard explained later in this chapter.

The key to an attribute is its tag, which is used to store and retrieve the attribute data. A tag is an attribute's unique identifier, similar to a field in a database or a row/column in a spreadsheet. The tag allows you to specify which attributes to extract when you use the **Data Extraction** wizard. Tags are typically all uppercase and cannot include any spaces or special characters. They are typically given a descriptive name indicating the type of data they are storing. For example, the attribute tags for a window tag block that contains information about the window type, width, height, and manufacturer might be defined as shown in Figure 16-18.

> **NOTE**
>
> Attributes can be set to be invisible so that you can attach nongraphical information to a block that can be updated and extracted even though you can't see it in the drawing and it doesn't plot. This and other special attribute properties are discussed later in the section "Creating Attributes."

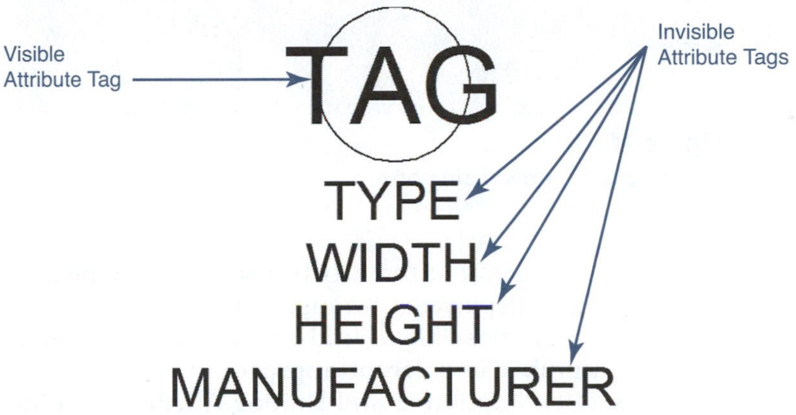

Figure 16-18
Window tag block with attribute tags—before block definition

Figure 16-18 shows what the window tag block looks like prior to being defined. Attributes that are defined to be invisible are not turned off until the block is defined and inserted as a block reference in the drawing as shown later in Figure 16-21.

The other key parts of an attribute definition are its prompt and default value. The prompt is what you see when you insert the block so you know what type of information to enter. The default value is what the attribute is automatically set to if no information is entered. The attribute tag, prompt, and default value for the window tag block's manufacturer attribute are shown in Figure 16-19.

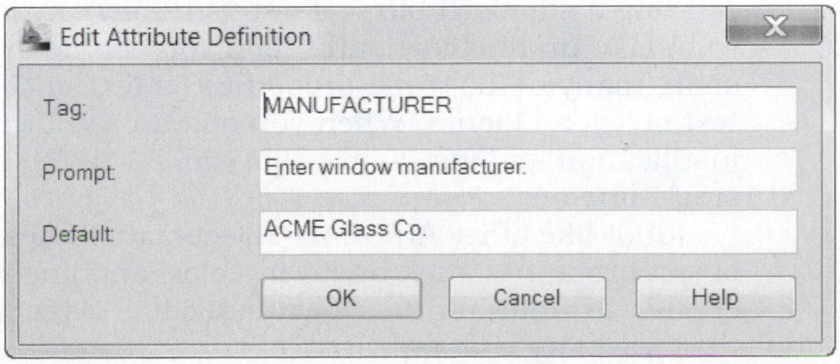

Figure 16-19
Manufacturer attribute tag, prompt, and default value

After the block is defined and you insert it, you are automatically prompted to enter the attribute values either individually at the command prompt or en masse via the **Edit Attributes** dialog box shown in Figure 16-20.

After the attribute values have been entered either via the **Edit Attributes** dialog box or at the command prompt, a block reference is created as shown in Figure 16-21.

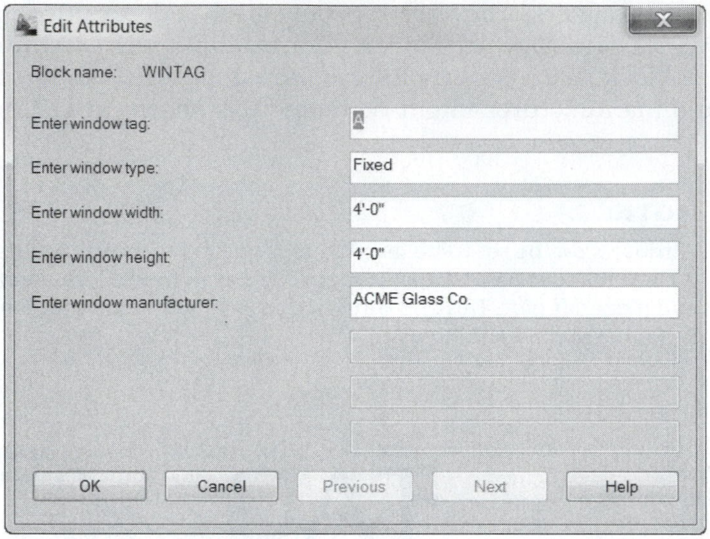

Figure 16-20
The **Edit Attributes** dialog box

Figure 16-21
The inserted block reference with attributes

Notice that the attributes that were defined as invisible are now no longer displayed, although it is possible to turn them on if necessary.

It is possible to update the attributes after the block is inserted using a number of different approaches, all of which are explained later in the section "Updating and Editing Attributes." First, though, we need to create a block with some attributes.

NOTE

Attribute display is controlled via the **Attributes** panel on the **Insert** tab of the ribbon. The **Display All** setting turns all invisible attributes on and the **Hide All** setting turns off all attributes. The **Retain Display** setting displays attributes as they were originally defined. You can also use the **ATTDISP** command to control the same settings.

Creating Attributes

When working with attributes, you follow the same steps you would for creating a standard block. First you draw any line work and/or text that will make up the block, and then you can define the attributes. Attributes share many of the same properties as text, including the ability to assign text styles and fonts. When you add an attribute, you must also specify a justification and insertion point, similar to the manner in which you add single-line text.

Just like other AutoCAD objects, attributes also assume the current object properties such as layer, color, and linetype. Some organizations create attributes on their own individual layer so you can further control their visibility and appearance.

> **FOR MORE DETAILS**
>
> See Chapter 11 for more details about the different text properties and effects. See Chapter 6 for more details about managing object properties.

Attribute Definition

DEFINE ATTRIBUTES	
Ribbon & Panel:	Insert Block Definition  Define Attributes
Toolbar:	None
Menu:	Draw | Block | Define Attributes...
Command Line:	ATTDEF
Command Alias:	ATT

The **ATTDEF** command creates an attribute definition via the **Attribute Definition** dialog box shown in Figure 16-22.

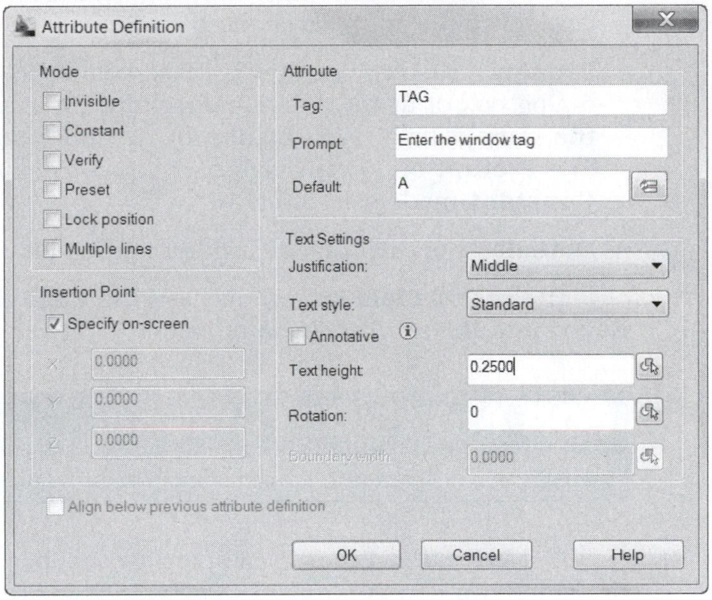

Figure 16-22
The **Attribute Definition** dialog box

The **Mode** area is where you control the visibility and other attribute options that are set when you insert the block. The **Mode** options are as follows:

- **Invisible** Specifies that attribute values are not displayed or printed when you insert the block
- **Constant** Makes the attribute a constant value so that it cannot be updated either when it is inserted or anytime later
- **Verify** Has you verify that the attribute value is correct when you insert the block by prompting you for the attribute information twice
- **Preset** Sets the attribute to its default value and does not prompt you for the attribute information, although it is still possible to update the attribute after it is inserted using the techniques explained in the following section
- **Lock position** Locks the position of the attribute definition in the block so that it cannot be moved after the block is inserted using grips
- **Multiple lines** Allows you to create multiple line attributes by selecting the **[...]** button next to the **Default** value (changed from the **Insert Field** button when this option is selected) to display a stripped-down version of the multiline text editor introduced in Chapter 11 and add multiple lines of text

NOTE

The **Verify** and **Preset** attribute modes work only when you enter attributes at the command prompt. They have no effect whenever the **Edit Attributes** dialog box is used to update attribute information.

The **Attribute** area is where you define the attribute tag, prompt, and default value:

- **Tag** The unique alphanumeric key used to identify the attribute. Enter a descriptive name using any combination of characters except spaces. Lowercase letters are automatically changed to uppercase. Attribute tags can contain up to 256 characters
- **Prompt** The prompt that is displayed either in the **Edit Attributes** dialog box or at the command prompt when you insert the block. If the prompt field is left blank, the attribute tag is used as a prompt. The **Prompt** option is disabled if you are defining an attribute with the **Constant** mode selected
- **Default** Specifies the default attribute value used

The **Insert Field** button displays the **Field** dialog box so you can insert a field into the attribute default value.

FOR MORE DETAILS

See page 452 in Chapter 11 for more details about using text fields.

The **Insertion Point** area specifies the location for the attribute in the drawing. You can enter coordinate values via the keyboard, or if you select the **Specify on-screen** check box, you can pick a point in your drawing after you select **OK** and the dialog box closes.

The **Text Settings** area sets the justification, text style, height, and rotation of the attribute text:

- **Justification** Allows you to set the attribute justification from a list of standard single-line text justification options
- **Text style** Allows you to assign a text style from a list of text styles defined in the current drawing
- **Annotative** Allows you to make the attribute **Annotative** so that it scales up and down automatically based on the current annotation scale
- **Text height** Allows you to specify the height of the attribute text. You can enter a height value via the keyboard, or select the **Text height** button to define the height by picking points with your mouse. The **Text height:** option is disabled if a text style with a height greater than 0.0 is selected or if the justification is set to **Align**
- **Rotation** Allows you to specify the rotation angle of the attribute text. You can enter a value via that keyboard or select the **Rotation** button to define the rotation angle by picking points with your mouse. The **Rotation:** option is disabled if the justification is set to **Align** or **Fit**

FOR MORE DETAILS

See Chapter 11 for more details about the different text options.

The **Align below previous attribute definition** check box allows you to automatically locate an attribute tag directly below the previously defined attribute using all of the same text options. If selected, both the **Insertion Point** and **Text Settings** areas of the dialog box are disabled. This option is disabled if you have not previously created an attribute definition.

Selecting **OK** closes the dialog box, and AutoCAD prompts you to *Specify start point:* so you can locate the attribute in the drawing. If the **Align below previous attribute definition** check box is selected, the attribute is automatically located directly below the last attribute that was defined.

> **TIP**
> Although you can change the prompt order of the attributes after a block is defined, it is best to select the attributes individually in the order you want to be prompted. If you select all the attributes using any of the window selection methods, the ordering of the attributes can be random.

EXERCISE 16-7 **Creating a Block with Attributes**

1. Start a new drawing using the **acad.dwt** drawing template.
2. Create the window tag drawing shown in Figure 16-23 on Layer **0** at 0,0,0 with the following attributes and settings:

Tag	Prompt	Default	Mode
TAG	Enter window tag:	A	Visible
TYPE	Enter window type:	Fixed	Invisible
WIDTH	Enter window width:	4′-0″	Invisible/Verify
HEIGHT	Enter window height:	4′-0″	Invisible/Verify
MANUFACTURER	Enter window manufacturer:	ACME Glass Co.	Invisible/Preset

3. Save the drawing as ***Wintag***.

Figure 16-23
Window tag block definition with attributes

Updating and Editing Attributes

By default, when you insert a block with attributes, you automatically get prompted to update the attribute values individually at the command prompt in the order in which the attributes were created. The alternate **Edit Attributes** dialog box can be displayed during the insertion process by setting the **ATTDIA** system variable to **1** (on). Setting **ATTDIA** to **0** (off) turns the **Edit Attributes** dialog box off.

> **TIP**
>
> It is possible to turn attribute prompts off temporarily when you are inserting a block by setting the **ATTREQ** system variable to **0** (off). When **ATTREQ = 0,** an attributed block is inserted as though there are no attributes attached. The attributes can still be updated after the block is inserted using the techniques explained below. Set **ATTREQ** to **1** (on) to turn attribute prompts back on.

The easiest way to update attributes after they are inserted is to simply double-click on the attributed block. Double-clicking on a block with attributes displays the **Enhanced Attribute Editor** dialog box discussed in the next section so that you can update attribute values, as well as change attribute text options and attribute object properties.

> **NOTE**
>
> Changes made to attribute properties using the **Enhanced Attribute Editor** affect only the individually selected block reference.

The **Block Attribute Manager** discussed a little later in this section allows you to edit block attribute definitions on a global scale so that you can change the attribute modes, the attribute prompt order, and even remove attributes, so that *all* existing and future block references in the drawing are updated.

> **TIP**
>
> It is possible to use grips to modify attributes so that you can perform basic editing tasks such as moving, rotating, and scaling attributes. Any changes affect the whole block if the **Lock position** check box was selected when the block was created.

FOR MORE DETAILS

See page 301 in Chapter 7 for more details about using grips.

EDIT ATTRIBUTE SINGLE	
Ribbon & Panel:	Insert | Block  Single
Modify II Toolbar:	
Menu:	Modify | Object | Attribute | Single
Command Line:	EATTEDIT
Command Alias:	None

Editing Attributes Individually

The **EATTEDIT** command allows you to update attributes via the **Enhanced Attribute Editor** dialog box so that you can do the following:

- Update attribute values
- Control attribute text options (text style, height, etc.)
- Manage attribute object properties (layer, color, linetype, etc.)

After starting the **EATTEDIT** command, AutoCAD prompts you to *Select a block:*. Select the block to update and press **<Enter>** to display the **Enhanced Attribute Editor** dialog box shown in Figure 16-24.

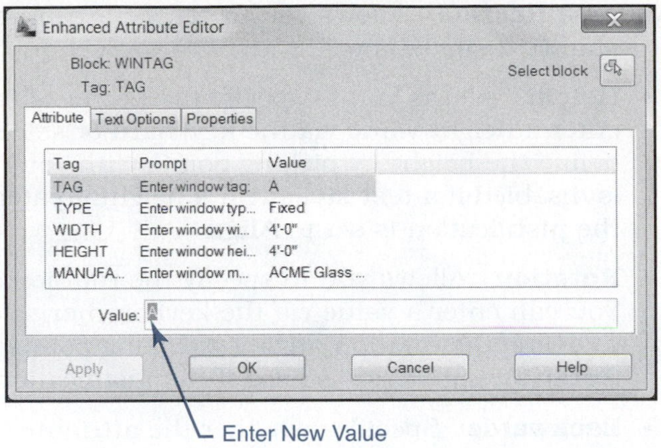

Figure 16-24 The **Enhanced Attribute Editor** dialog box—**Attribute** tab

The name of the selected block along with the current attribute tag is displayed at the top left of the dialog box. The **Select block** button on the right temporarily closes the dialog box so you can select another block to update.

The **Attribute** tab is the default tab shown in Figure 16-24 that allows you to update attribute values. All the block's attribute tags and their corresponding prompts and values are displayed in a tabulated list that you can navigate by selecting an attribute with your mouse or by pressing **<Enter>** while the **Value:** text box below is selected.

NOTE

If you modify a block and then select another block before saving the changes, you are prompted to save the changes first. To save changes and update the selected block, select the **Apply** button at the bottom of the dialog box.

The **Value:** text box displays the current value assigned to the attribute highlighted in the list box above. Enter a new value and press **<Enter>** to update the attribute and proceed to the next attribute in the list.

TIP

You can insert a field in a value by right-clicking and selecting **Insert Field...** on the shortcut menu to display the **Field** dialog box.

If a multiline attribute is selected, the **[...]** button is displayed to the right of the **Value:** text box so you can select it to display the stripped-down multiline text editor and edit multiline attribute values.

The **Text Options** tab shown in Figure 16-25 allows you to control the text properties of the currently selected attribute:

- **Text Style** Allows you to assign a text style from a list of text styles defined in the current drawing

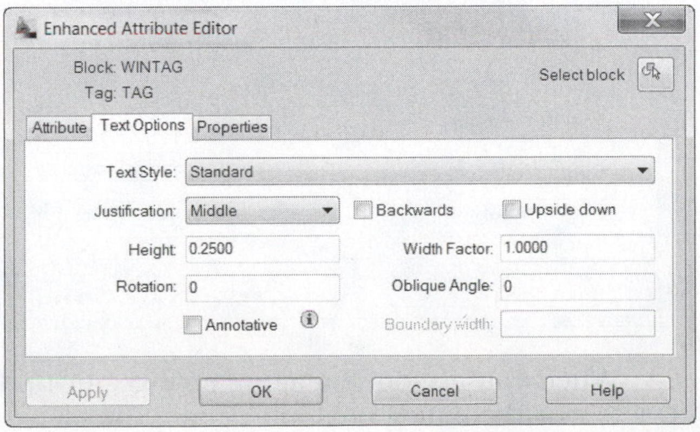

Figure 16-25 The **Enhanced Attribute Editor** dialog box—**Text Options** tab

- **Justification** Allows you to set the attribute justification from a list of standard single-line text justification options
- **Height** Allows you to specify the height of the attribute text. You can enter a height value via the keyboard or select the **Height** button to define the height by picking points with your mouse. The **Height** option is disabled if a text style with a height greater than 0.0 is selected or if the justification is set to **Align**
- **Rotation** Allows you to specify the rotation angle of the attribute text. You can enter a value via the keyboard or select the **Rotation** button to define the rotation angle by picking points with your mouse. The **Rotation** option is disabled if the justification is set to **Align** or **Fit**
- **Backwards** Specifies whether the attribute text is displayed backward
- **Upside down** Specifies whether the attribute text is displayed upside down
- **Width Factor** Sets the character spacing for the attribute text. Entering a value less than 1.0 condenses the text. Entering a value greater than 1.0 expands it
- **Oblique Angle** Specifies the angle that the attribute text is slanted
- **Annotative** Specifies whether annotation scaling is on or off

FOR MORE DETAILS

See Chapter 11 for more details about the different text properties and effects.

NOTE

If the current drawing uses color-dependent plot styles, the **Plot style** list is disabled.

The **Properties** tab shown in Figure 16-26 allows you to control the general object properties of the currently selected attribute:

- **Layer** Specifies the attribute layer
- **Linetype** Specifies the attribute linetype
- **Color** Specifies the attribute color
- **Lineweight** Specifies the attribute lineweight
- **Plot style** Specifies the attribute plot style

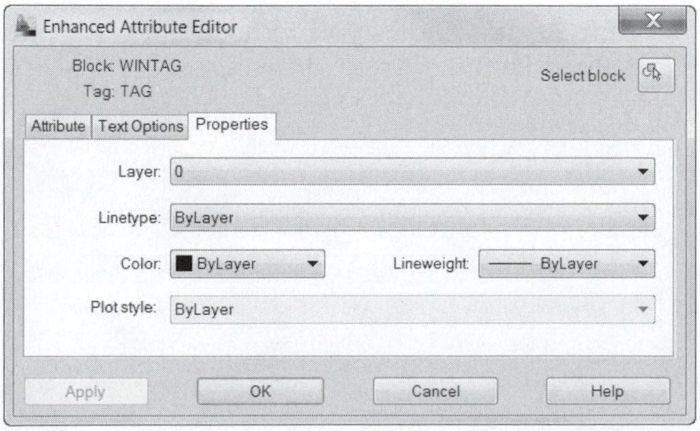

Figure 16-26 The **Enhanced Attribute Editor** dialog box—**Properties** tab

When you are done making changes or updates, you can either select **OK** to exit the dialog box and update the block, or you can select **Apply** to update the block and keep the **Enhanced Attribute Editor** dialog box open so you can make more changes.

Editing Attributes Globally

EDIT ATTRIBUTES MULTIPLE	
Ribbon & Panel:	Insert | Block Multiple
Toolbar:	None
Menu:	Modify | Object | Attribute | Global
Command Line:	-ATTEDIT
Command Alias:	-ATE

The **-ATTEDIT** command allows you to quickly update attribute values globally throughout an entire drawing at the same time.

The **-ATTEDIT** command is rather archaic. In fact, the **-ATTEDIT** command is actually just the old command line version of the **ATTEDIT** dialog box–driven command. It may be an old, clunky command, but it is the only way to update more than one attribute at a time in a drawing so that you don't have to select and update each block individually.

After starting the **-ATTEDIT** command, AutoCAD prompts: *Edit attributes one at a time?*↓. Enter **N** or **No <Enter>** to update attributes globally. AutoCAD then prompts: *Edit only attributes visible on screen?*↓ Typically, you should enter **No <Enter>** to ensure all attributes in the drawing are updated accordingly and not just those shown in the drawing window.

AutoCAD then prompts you for the block name, attribute tag, and attribute value to be found. The default asterisk (*) value represents a wildcard, meaning that all blocks that match that category will be processed. If you know the block name, attribute tag, or attribute value for the block you want to update, you can enter the information to limit the number of blocks that are processed. Pressing **<Enter>** in response to all these prompts forces AutoCAD to process all the attributed blocks in the drawing.

AutoCAD then requests the original value of the attribute text value to change by prompting *Enter string to change:* so you can enter the current attribute value. You are then prompted for a new attribute value *Enter new string:* so you can enter a new value. Immediately after you press **<Enter>**, AutoCAD searches the drawing for all the attributes with a value of the text to change and updates the attribute with the new value as shown in Figure 16-27.

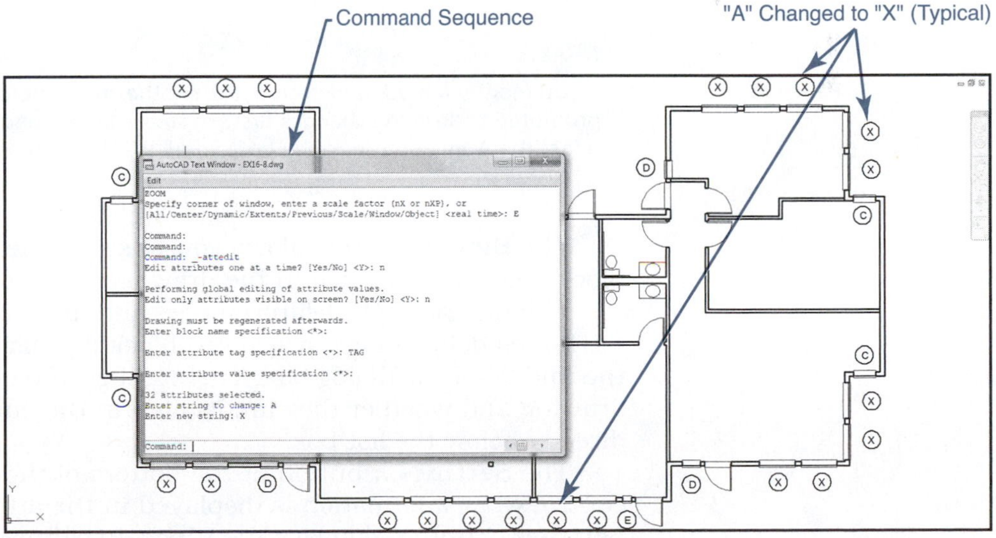

Figure 16-27
Updating attributes globally in a drawing

Managing Attributes

The **BATTMAN** command allows you to update one or more block attribute definitions via the **Block Attribute Manager** dialog box so that you can do the following:

- Edit attribute definitions so that you can change the tag, prompt, default, and even the modes (invisible, constant, verify, preset)

BLOCK ATTRIBUTE MANAGER	
Ribbon & Panel:	Insert | Block  Manage Attributes
Modify II Toolbar:	
Menu:	Modify | Object | Attribute | Block Attribute Manager
Command Line:	BATTMAN
Command Alias:	None

- Control attribute definition text options (text style, height, etc.)
- Manage attribute definition object properties (layer, color, linetype, etc.)
- Change the attribute prompt order
- Remove attribute definitions

Changes made with the **Block Attribute Manager** update the block definition so that all future block insertions reflect the changes. It is also possible to synchronize the changes with blocks that have already been inserted.

Starting the **BATTMAN** command displays the **Block Attribute Manager** dialog box shown in Figure 16-28.

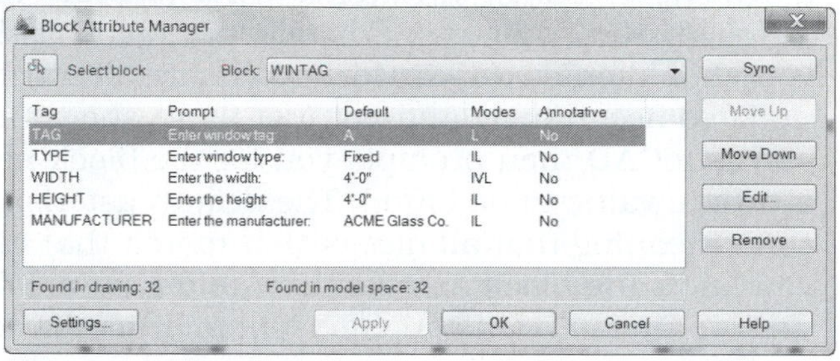

Figure 16-28
The **Block Attribute Manager** dialog box

The **Select block** button allows you to choose a block definition to edit by selecting a corresponding block reference in the current drawing. Selecting the **Select block** button temporarily closes the **Block Attribute Manager** dialog box and prompts you to *Select a block:*. Select the block to update, and the dialog box is redisplayed.

NOTE

If you modify a block and then select another block before saving the changes, you are prompted to save the changes first. To save changes and update the selected block, select the **Apply** button at the bottom of the dialog box.

The **Block:** list box allows you to select the block from the list of blocks currently defined in the drawing.

The tag, prompt, default, mode, and annotative properties of all the attributes defined for the selected block are displayed in the list box in the middle of the dialog box. The number of block references found in the drawing and whether they are located in the current layout are displayed directly below the list box.

The **Settings...** button at the bottom of the dialog box allows you to control what information is displayed in the attribute list box. Selecting the **Settings...** button displays the **Block Attribute Settings** dialog box shown in Figure 16-29.

The following options are available:

- The **Display in list** area is where you select which properties you want to display in the attribute list. Selected properties are displayed as an additional column in the list. The **Tag** property is always displayed.
- The **Select All** button selects all of the properties in the **Display in list** area above.

Figure 16-29
The **Block Attribute Settings** dialog box

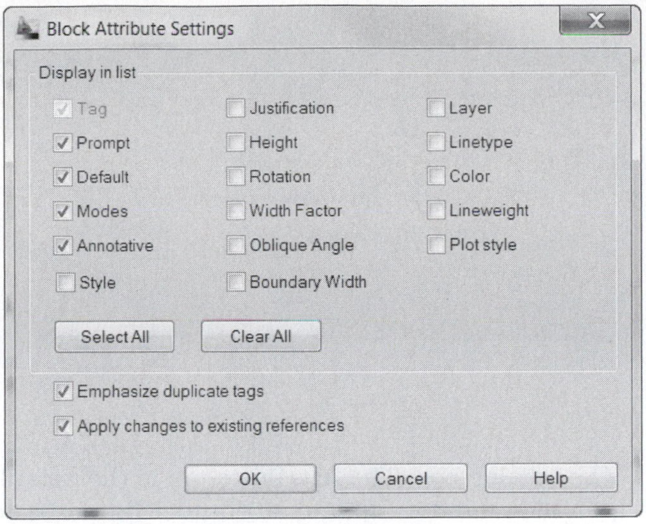

- The **Clear All** button clears all of the properties in the **Display in list** area above.
- The **Emphasize duplicate tags** check box turns duplicate tag emphasis on and off. When the **Emphasize duplicate tags** check box is selected, duplicate tag names are changed to red in the attribute list in the **Block Attribute Manager** dialog box so they can be easily identified.
- The **Apply changes to existing references** check box indicates whether to update all the existing block references in the drawing when any changes are made. When the **Apply changes to existing references** check box is selected, all existing and new block references are updated with the new attribute definitions. If it is not selected, only new block references have the new attribute definitions.
- The **OK** button accepts any setting changes, closes the **Block Attribute Settings** dialog box, and returns you to the **Block Attribute Manager** so you can continue to make any changes.

In the **Block Attribute Manager** dialog box, there are several more options:

- The **Sync** button updates all block references in the drawing with the currently defined attribute properties. Attribute values are not affected by any changes.
- The **Move Up** button moves the selected attribute tag up in the prompt order.
- The **Move Down** button moves the selected attribute tag down in the prompt order.
- The **Edit...** button displays the **Edit Attribute** dialog box shown in Figure 16-30.

NOTE

The **Move Up** and **Move Down** buttons are both disabled when a constant attribute is selected.

Using the **Edit Attribute** dialog box, you can modify the attribute definition properties. The name of the selected block is displayed at the top left

Figure 16-30
The **Edit Attribute** dialog box—**Attribute** tab

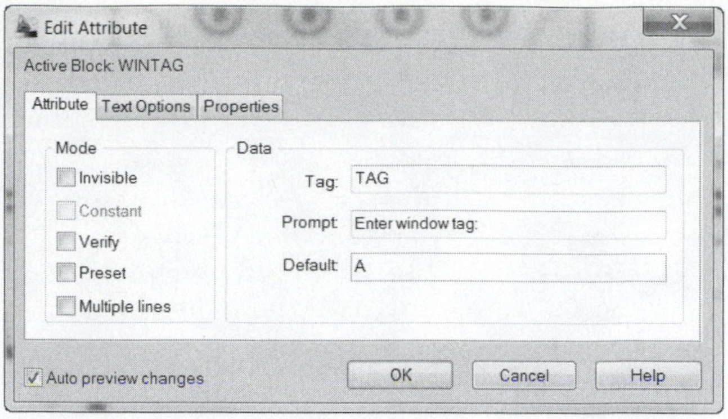

of the dialog box. The **Attribute** tab is the default tab shown in Figure 16-30 that allows you to update attribute definitions; you can control:

- The **Mode** area is where you update the visibility and other attribute options that are set when you insert the block. There are five different options:
  - **Invisible** Specifies that attribute values are not displayed or printed when you insert the block
  - **Constant** Makes attribute a constant value so that it cannot be updated either when it is inserted or anytime later. This option is disabled when using the **Block Attribute Manager**. The **Constant** option can be used only when an attribute is first defined
  - **Verify** Has you verify that the attribute value is correct when you insert the block by prompting you for the attribute information twice
  - **Preset** Sets the attribute to its default value and does not prompt you for the attribute information although it is possible to still update the attribute after it is inserted using the techniques explained in the following section
  - **Multiple lines** Allows you to use multiline attributes
- The **Data** area is where you update the attribute tag, prompt, and default value:
  - **Tag** The unique alphanumeric key used to identify the attribute. Enter a descriptive name using any combination of characters except spaces. Lowercase letters are automatically changed to uppercase. Attribute tags can be up to 256 characters long
  - **Prompt** The prompt that is displayed either in the **Edit Attribute** dialog box or at the command prompt when you insert the block. If the prompt field is left blank, the attribute tag is used as a prompt. The **Prompt** option is disabled if you are defining an attribute with the **Constant** mode selected
  - **Default** Specifies the default attribute value used

The **Text Options** tab shown in Figure 16-31 allows you to control the text properties of the currently selected attribute definition:

- **Text Style** Allows you to assign a text style from a list of text styles defined in the current drawing
- **Justification** Allows you to set the attribute justification from a list of standard single-line text justification options

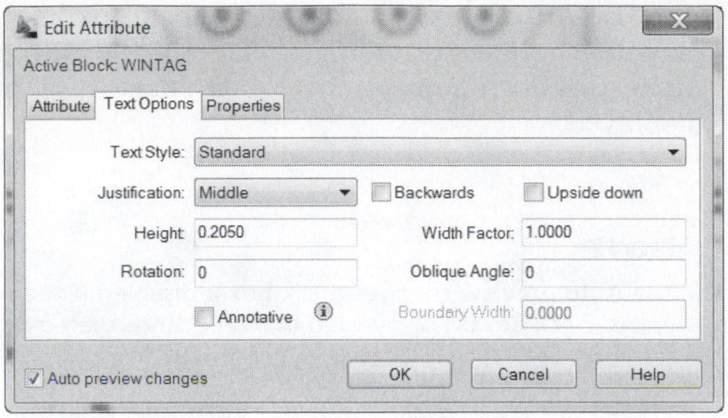

Figure 16-31
The **Edit Attribute** dialog box—**Text Options** tab

- **Height** Allows you to specify the height of the attribute text. The **Height** option is disabled if a text style with a height greater than 0.0 is selected or if the justification is set to **Align**
- **Rotation** Allows you to specify the rotation angle of the attribute text. The **Rotation** option is disabled if the justification is set to **Align** or **Fit**
- **Backwards** Specifies whether the attribute text is displayed backward
- **Upside down** Specifies whether the attribute text is displayed upside down
- **Width Factor** Sets the character spacing for the attribute text. Entering a value less than 1.0 condenses the text. Entering a value greater than 1.0 expands it
- **Oblique Angle** Specifies the angle that the attribute text is slanted
- **Annotative** Specifies whether the attribute scales up and down using the current annotation scale

FOR MORE DETAILS

See Chapter 11 for more details about the different text properties and effects.

The **Properties** tab shown in Figure 16-32 allows you to control the general object properties of the currently selected attribute definition:

- **Layer** Specifies the attribute layer
- **Linetype** Specifies the attribute linetype
- **Color** Specifies the attribute color
- **Lineweight** Specifies the attribute lineweight
- **Plot style** Specifies the attribute plot style

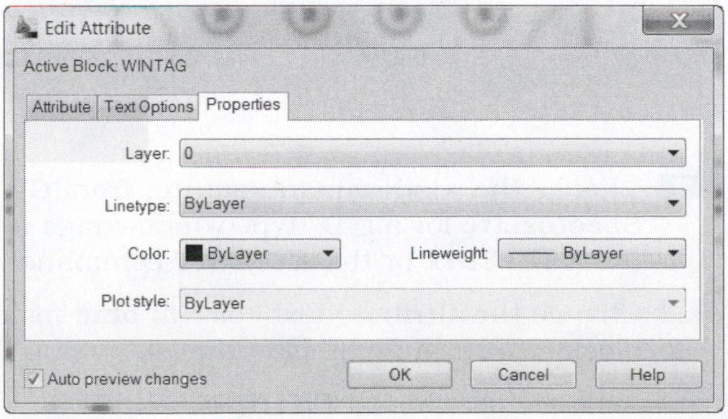

Figure 16-32
The **Edit Attribute** dialog box—**Properties** tab

The **Auto preview changes** check box allows you to immediately display any updates or changes made in the **Edit Attribute** dialog box. If the **Auto preview changes** check box is selected, any changes are immediately displayed.

NOTE

The **Auto preview changes** check box is disabled if the **Apply changes to existing references** check box is not selected in the **Settings** dialog box described earlier.

The **OK** button accepts any setting changes, closes the **Edit Attribute** dialog box, and returns you to the **Block Attribute Manager** so you can continue to make any changes.

The **Remove** button removes the selected attribute from the block definition. The **Remove** button is disabled when a block has only one attribute.

The **Apply** button applies the changes you made to all block references in the drawing but does not close the **Block Attribute Manager.**

Select **OK** to accept any updates and close the **Block Attribute Manager** dialog box.

EXERCISE 16-8 Updating and Editing Attributes

To access student data files, go to **www.pearsondesigncentral.com.**

1. Open the building floor plan drawing named ***EX16-8*** in the student data files.
2. Set layer **A-Glaze-Iden** current.
3. Start the **INSERT** command.
4. Select the **Uniform Scale** check box and set the **X Scale** to **48**.
5. Insert the ***WINTAG.DWG*** file created in Exercise 16-7 as a block using the **Browse...** button.
6. Locate the window tags as shown in Figure 16-33 and update them with the following attribute values:

Attribute	Window Type				
TAG	A	B	C	D	E
TYPE	Fixed	Fixed	Fixed	Casement	Sidelite
WIDTH	4′-0″	3′-6″	2′-6″	2′-0″	1′-0″
HEIGHT	4′-0″	4′-0″	3′-0″	3′-0″	4′-0″
MANUFACTURER	ACME Glass Co.	ACME Glass Co.	ACME Glass Co.	Glassarama, Inc.	Season All Windows

7. Change the window manufacturer from **Glassarama, Inc.** to **SpectorLite** for all "D" type window tags in the drawing using either the **EATTEDIT** or the **ATTEDIT** command.
8. Change the attribute text color to **blue** for the **TAG** attribute for all blocks in the building plan drawing using the **BATTMAN** command.
9. Save the drawing as ***CH16_EXERCISE8***.

Figure 16-33
Building floor plan with window tags

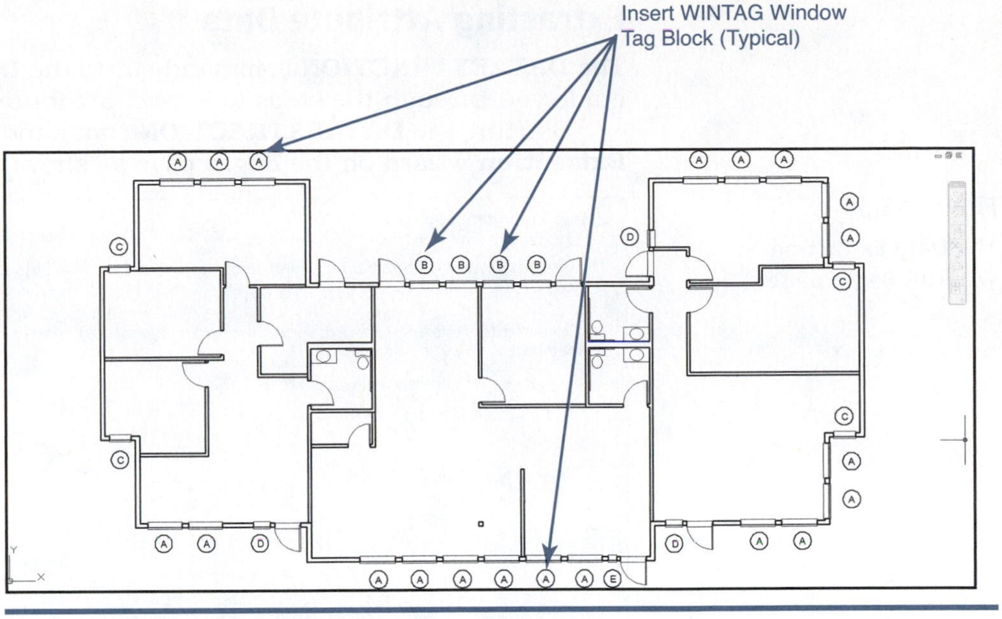

Extracting Attributes

It is possible to extract property information from objects in drawings, including blocks and their attributes, to a formatted table in the current drawing or to an external file so that you can quickly create schedules, parts lists, bills of materials, and other tabular-type information based on the current drawing, or even multiple drawings.

> **TIP**
> The extracted data can even be merged and linked with information in a Microsoft Excel® spreadsheet so that is possible to include additional external information.

EXTRACT DATA	
Ribbon & Panel:	Insert | Linking & Extraction Extract Data
Modify II Toolbar:	
Menu:	Tools | Data Extraction...
Command Line:	DATA-EXTRACTION
Command Alias:	DX

To make the extraction process as easy as possible, AutoCAD provides the **Data Extraction** wizard, which guides you through a series of preprogrammed steps so that you can provide the following information.

- Data source for information to extract
  - Current drawing
  - Multiple drawings or sheet set
  - Selected objects
- The block names and attribute tags to extract
- Whether to output the attribute information to an AutoCAD table or to output the information to one of the following external file types:
  - Comma-delimited text file (CSV)
  - Microsoft Excel® spreadsheet (XLS)
  - Microsoft Access® database (MDB)
- Generic text file (TXT)

The **Data Extraction** wizard saves all the settings you specify in each step to an external file (DXE) so that you can use it the next time you use the **Data Extraction** wizard.

Extracting Attribute Data

The **DATAEXTRACTION** command starts the **Data Extraction** wizard to guide you through the steps to extract attribute information.

Starting the **DATAEXTRACTION** command displays the **Data Extraction** wizard on the **Begin** page as shown in Figure 16-34.

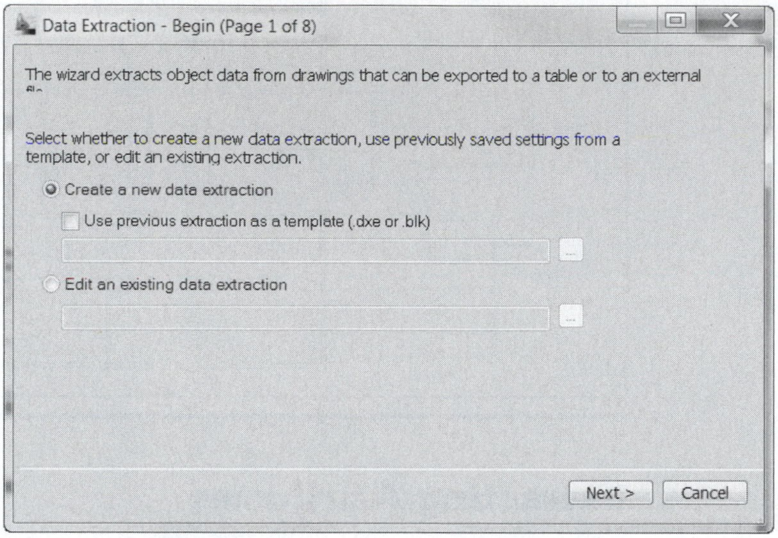

Figure 16-34
The **Data Extraction** wizard—**Begin** page

The **Begin** page allows you to select whether you want to specify new extraction settings from scratch or use settings previously saved in an attribute extraction file (DXE or BLK).

If you select the **Use previous extraction as a template** option, you must select the **[...]** button on the right to select a file using the standard file selection dialog box.

> **NOTE**
>
> If you are creating a new data extraction, you must create a data extraction template file (DXE) before proceeding to the **Define Data Source** page.

The **Edit an existing data extraction** option allows you to modify an existing data extraction (DXE) file. You must select the **[...]** button on the right to select a file using the standard file selection dialog box.

Select the **Next >** button on the bottom to proceed to the **Define Data Source** page shown in Figure 16-35 or the **Cancel** button to close the wizard.

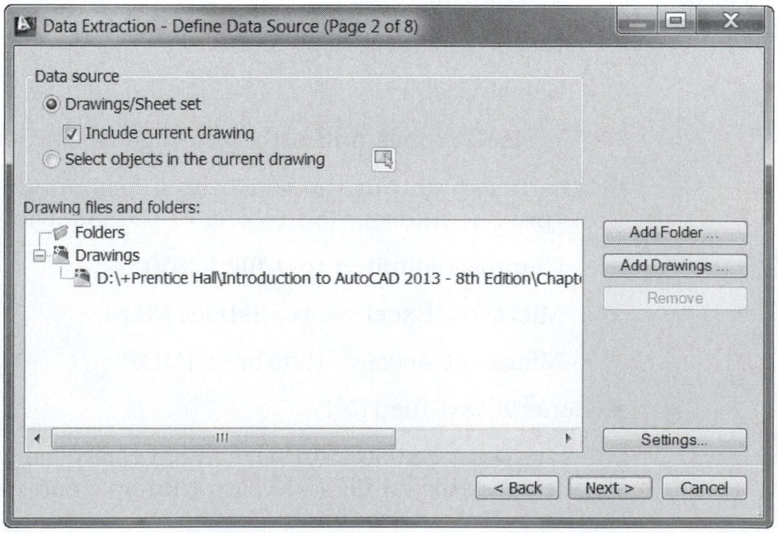

Figure 16-35
The **Data Extraction** wizard—**Define Data Source** page

The **Define Data Source** page allows you to select one of the following data sources from which to extract the attribute information:

- **Drawings/Sheet set** Enables the **Add Folder...** and **Add Drawings...** buttons so you can add a folder or more drawings (DWG) or sheet sets (DST) using the standard file selection dialog box. The current drawing is included by default
- **Select objects in the current drawing** Enables the **Select objects** button so you can select one or more blocks in the current drawing

NOTE

You can delete one or more files from the list by selecting the file(s) and selecting the **Remove** button on the right.

The **Drawing files and folders:** list box lists all the drawing files or sheets in the selected sheet set from which attributes will be extracted.

The **Settings...** button displays the **Data Extraction—Additional Settings** dialog box shown in Figure 16-36.

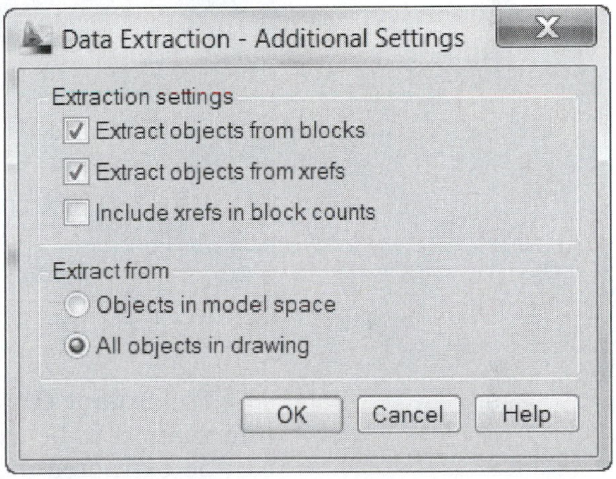

Figure 16-36
The **Data Extraction—Additional Settings** dialog box

The **Additional Settings** dialog box allows you specify whether to include nested blocks and xrefs, as well as specify which types of blocks should be included in the overall block count.

The **Extraction settings** area allows you to control which blocks are included in the attribute extraction process and whether to include xrefs in the block count.

- **Extract objects from blocks** Includes blocks nested within other blocks
- **Extract objects from xrefs** Includes blocks located in any attached xrefs
- **Include xrefs in block counts** Includes attached xrefs as blocks in block counts

FOR MORE DETAILS

See Chapter 17 for more details about xrefs.

The **Extract from** area provides options for which objects to include in the extraction process.

- **Objects in model space** Extracts from only block references in model space and ignores any blocks located in paper space layouts
- **All objects in drawing** Extracts from all block references in the entire drawing (model space and paper space)

The **OK** button accepts any setting changes, closes the **Additional Settings** dialog box, and returns you to the **Data Extraction** wizard so you can continue to the next step.

Select the **Next >** button on the bottom to proceed to the **Select Objects** page shown in Figure 16-37, the **Cancel** button to close the wizard, or the <**Back** button to return to the previous page.

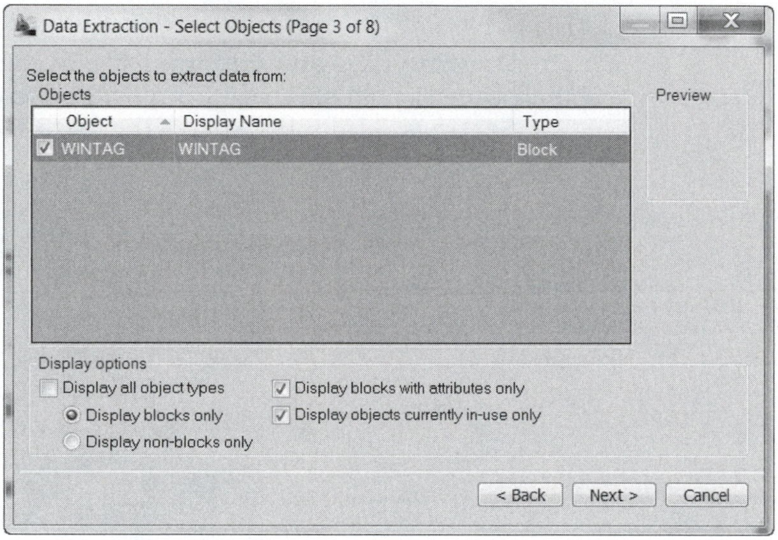

Figure 16-37
The **Data Extraction** wizard—**Select Objects** page

The **Select Objects** page allows you to select the objects and drawing information to be extracted. Just about any AutoCAD object information can be extracted including blocks and non-blocks.

> **TIP**
>
> It is possible to resize columns with your mouse and reverse the sort order by clicking on the column header. You can also select or unselect all objects via a right-click shortcut menu.

The **Objects** list displays each object by its name in the **Object** column. Blocks are listed by block name, and non-blocks are listed by their object name.

The **Display Name** column allows you to enter an optional alternative name for an object as it will appear in the extracted information. To change a display name, right-click in the **Display Name** column and select **Edit Display Name** from the shortcut menu.

The **Type** column indicates whether the object is a block or non-block.

The **Preview** area displays a preview image of the checked block in the **Objects** list.

You can limit the types of objects displayed in the **Objects** list in the **Display options** area at the bottom.

The **Display all object types** option displays a list of all object types (blocks and non-blocks) in the **Objects** list. It is on by default.

Turning off the **Display all object types** option allows you to toggle between the **Display blocks only** option and the **Display non-blocks only** option so you can further filter the **Objects** list.

The **Display blocks with attributes only** option displays only those blocks that have attributes in the **Objects** list.

The **Display objects currently in-use only** will limit the **Objects** list to objects that exist in the selected drawings.

Select the **Next >** button at the bottom to proceed to the **Select Properties** page shown in Figure 16-38, the **Cancel** button to close the wizard, or the **<Back** button to return to the previous page.

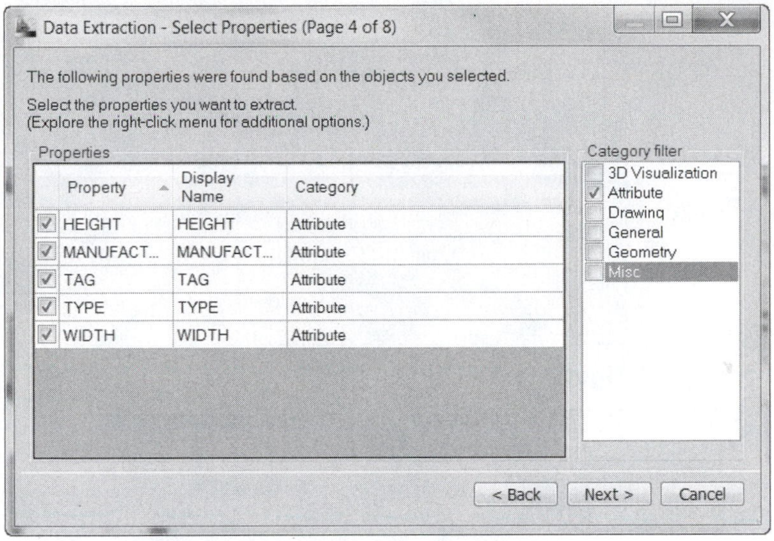

Figure 16-38

The **Data Extraction** wizard—**Select Properties** page

The **Select Properties** page allows you to control the object, block, and drawing properties to extract.

Each row in the **Properties** list displays a property name, display name, and category.

> **TIP**
>
> It is possible to resize columns with your mouse and reverse the sort order by clicking on the column header. You can also select or unselect all properties via a right-click shortcut menu.

The **Property** column displays the properties of all the objects selected on the **Select Objects** page in the previous step. These are the same object properties displayed in the **Properties** palette in AutoCAD.

The **Display Name** column allows you to enter an optional alternative name for a property as it will appear in the extracted information. To change a display name, right-click in the **Display Name** column and select **Edit Display Name** from the shortcut menu.

The **Category** column displays a category for each property. For example, **General** designates ordinary object properties, such as color or layer. **Attribute** designates user-defined attributes. These are the same object categories displayed in the **Properties** palette in AutoCAD.

The **Category filter** check box list allows you to filter the list of properties shown in the **Properties** list based on the category listed in the **Category** column. Only checked categories are displayed.

Select the **Next >** button on the bottom to proceed to the **Refine Data** page shown in Figure 16-39, the **Cancel** button to close the wizard, or the **<Back** button to return to the previous page.

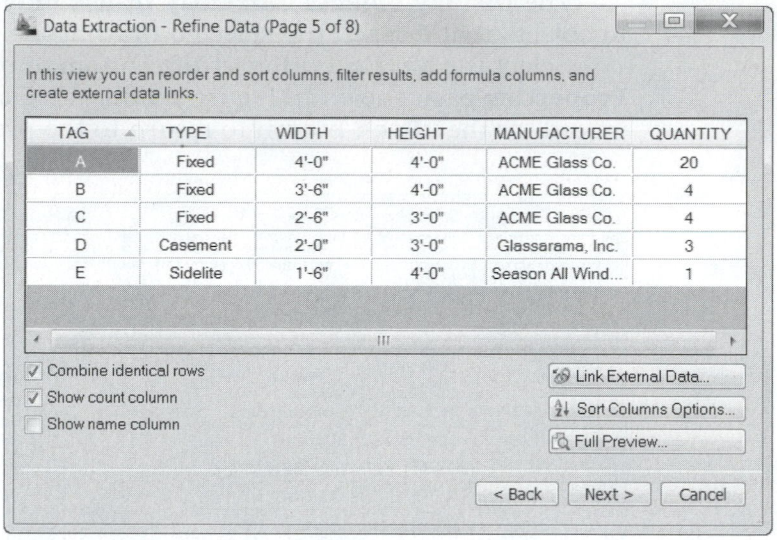

Figure 16-39

The **Data Extraction** wizard—**Refine Data** page

> **NOTE**
>
> Special icons are displayed in the column header for inserted formula columns and columns extracted from a Microsoft Excel spreadsheet.

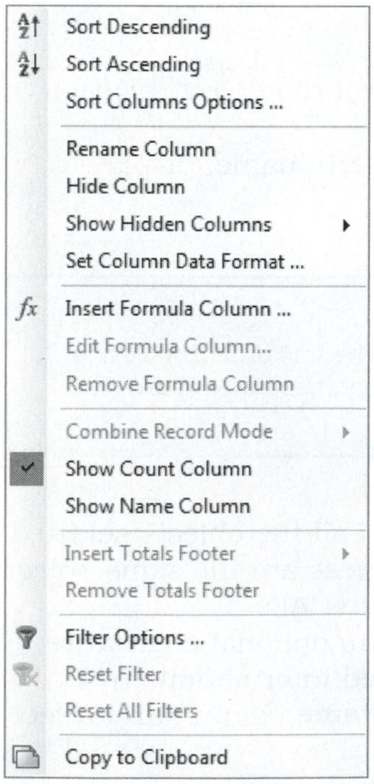

Figure 16-40

The **Data Extraction** wizard—**Refine Data** shortcut menu

The **Refine Data** page allows you to modify the structure of the data extraction table. You can reorder and sort columns, filter results, add formula columns and footer rows, and even create a link to data in a Microsoft Excel spreadsheet.

The grid in the middle of the dialog box displays properties that were selected in the **Select Properties** page in the previous step in a tabular format. The **Quantity** and **Name** columns display by default and can be turned off as explained below.

The **Combine identical rows** check box groups identical records by row in the table and updates the **Quantity** column with the sum total.

The **Show count column** check box toggles the **Quantity** column on and off in the table display.

The **Show name column** check box toggles the **Name** column on and off in the table display.

The **Link External Data...** button displays the **Link External Data** dialog box, where you can create a link between the extracted drawing data and data in an Excel spreadsheet.

The **Sort Columns Options...** button displays the **Sort Columns** dialog box, where you can sort data across multiple columns.

The **Full Preview...** button displays a full preview of the final output, including linked external data. The preview is for viewing only.

Right-clicking in a column displays the shortcut menu shown in Figure 16-40, which gives you the following options:

Option	Description
Sort Descending	Sorts column data in a descending order
Sort Ascending	Sorts column data in an ascending order
Sort Column Options...	Displays the **Sort Columns** dialog box so you can sort data across multiple columns
Rename Column	Allows in-place editing of the selected column name
Hide Column	Hides the selected column
Show Hidden Columns	Displays the hidden column. The cascade menu allows you to **Display All Hidden Columns**
Set Column Data Format...	Displays the **Set Cell Format** dialog box so you can set a data type for cells in the selected column
Insert Formula Column...	Displays the **Insert Formula Column** dialog box so you can insert a formula into the table to the right of the selected column
Edit Formula Column...	Displays the **Edit Formula Column** dialog box. Available only when a formula column is selected
Remove Formula Column	Removes the selected formula column. Available only when a formula column is selected
Combine Record Mode	Displays numeric data in the selected column as separate values or collapses identical property rows into one row and displays the sum of all the numeric data in the selected column. This option is available when the **Combine Identical Rows** is checked and the selected column contains numerical data
Show Count Column	Displays a **Count** column that lists the quantity of each property
Show Name Column	Displays a **Name** column that displays the name of each property
Insert Totals Footer	Displays a cascade menu with options for **Sum, Max, Min,** and **Average** formulas. Creates a footer row for the selected column that is placed below all data rows and displays values based on the selected arithmetic function. Available only for columns that have a numeric data type
Sum	Displays a sum of all the values in the selected column in a footer row
Max	Displays the maximum value in the selected column in a footer row
Min	Displays the minimum value in the selected column in a footer row
Average	Displays the average value in the selected column in a footer row
Remove Totals Footer	Removes the **Totals** footer. Available only when a footer row exists
Filter Options...	Displays the **Filter Column** dialog box so you can specify filter conditions for the selected column
Reset Filter	Restores the default filter for the selected column
Reset All Filters	Restores default filters for all columns that have filters
Copy to Clipboard	Copies selected data cells to the Clipboard

Select the **Next >** button at the bottom to proceed to the **Choose Output** page shown in Figure 16-41, the **Cancel** button to close the wizard, or the **<Back** button to return to the previous page.

The **Choose Output** page allows you to select the type of output to which the data are extracted.

The **Insert data extraction table into drawing** check box allows you to extract the attribute information to an AutoCAD table.

The **Output data to external file** check box allows you to export the attribute information to the file type and location you specify. Selecting the **[...]** button displays the standard **Save As** file dialog box so you can select the file type via the **File of type:** list box at the bottom of the dialog box and the folder location to save the file. By default, the file name is the

Figure 16-41

The **Data Extraction** wizard—**Choose Output** page

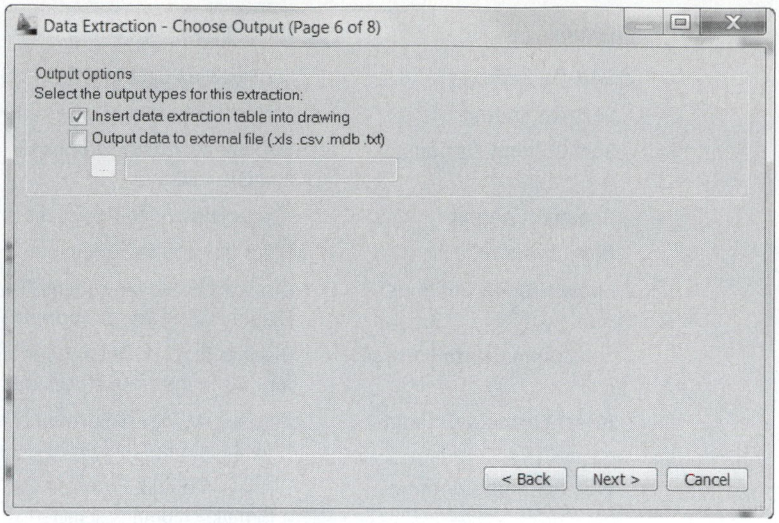

same name as the current drawing file. The three-character file extension is determined by the file type selected. The four file output options are as follows:

- XLS Microsoft Excel spreadsheet
- MDB Microsoft Access database
- CSV Comma-separated file format
- TXT Tab-separated file format

Select the **Next >** button at the bottom to proceed to either the **Table Style** page shown in Figure 16-42 or the **Finish** page shown in Figure 16-43, the **Cancel** button to close the wizard, or the **<Back** button to return to the previous page.

Figure 16-42

The **Data Extraction** wizard—**Table Style** page

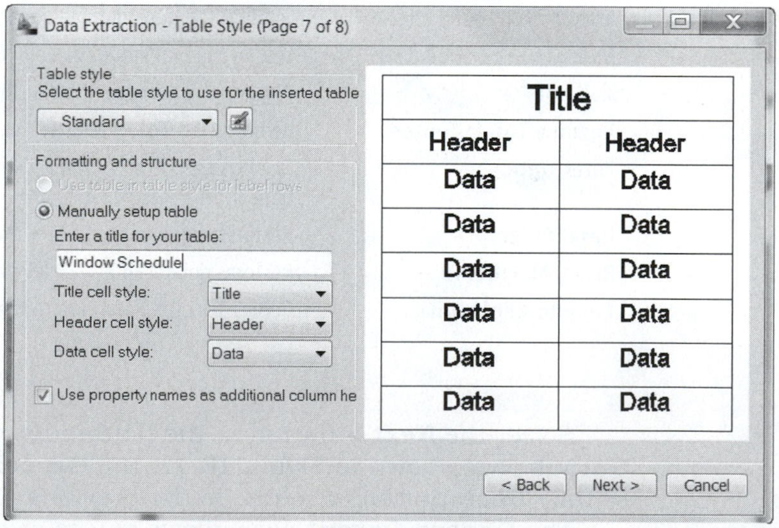

The **Table Style** page allows you to control the appearance of the table before it is inserted in the drawing.

> **NOTE**
>
> The **Table Style** step is displayed only if the **Insert data extraction table into drawing** check box was selected previously on the **Choose Output** page.

The **Table style** area at the top allows you to control the table style used for the extracted data. The **Select the table style to use for the inserted table** list box allows you to select an existing table style. You can also select the **Table Style** button to the right to display the **Table Style** dialog box to modify an existing table style or create a new one.

The **Formatting and structure** area allows you to fine-tune the final table structure and format.

The **Use table in table style for label rows** option creates the data extraction table with a set of top rows that contain label cells and a bottom set of label rows that contain header and footer cells. Extracted data are inserted between the top and bottom label rows.

The **Manually setup table** option allows you to manually enter a title and select a specific title, header, and data cell style.

The **Enter a title for your table:** text box allows you to enter a title for the table. This row is not overwritten when the table is updated. If the selected table style does not include a title row, this option is not available. The default table style, **Standard**, includes a title row.

The **Title cell style:** list allows you to select a separate style for the title cell. Select the drop-down list to select a title cell style defined in the selected table style.

The **Header cell style:** list allows you to select a separate style for the header row. Select the drop-down list to select a cell style defined in the selected table style.

The **Data cell style:** list allows you to select a separate style for data cells. Select the drop-down list to select a cell style defined in the selected table style.

The **Use property names as additional column headers** check box includes column headers and uses the **Display Name** property as the header row.

FOR MORE DETAILS

See page 482 in Chapter 12 for more details about controlling table format using table styles.

Select the **Next >** button at the bottom to proceed to the **Finish** page shown in Figure 16-43, the **Cancel** button to close the wizard, or the **<Back** button to return to the previous page.

The **Finish** page allows you to complete the process of extracting object property data that was specified in the wizard and creates the output type that was specified on the **Choose Output** page.

NOTE

If data linking and column matching to an Excel spreadsheet was defined in the **Link External Data** dialog box, the selected data in the spreadsheet are also extracted.

If you select the **Insert data extraction table into drawing** check box on the **Choose Output** page, when you select the **Finish** button, a table will be attached to your mouse cursor. AutoCAD then prompts you to *Specify insertion point:* so you can locate the table as shown in Figure 16-44.

If the **Output data to external file** option was selected, the extracted data are saved to the specified file type.

Figure 16-43

The **Data Extraction** wizard—**Finish** page

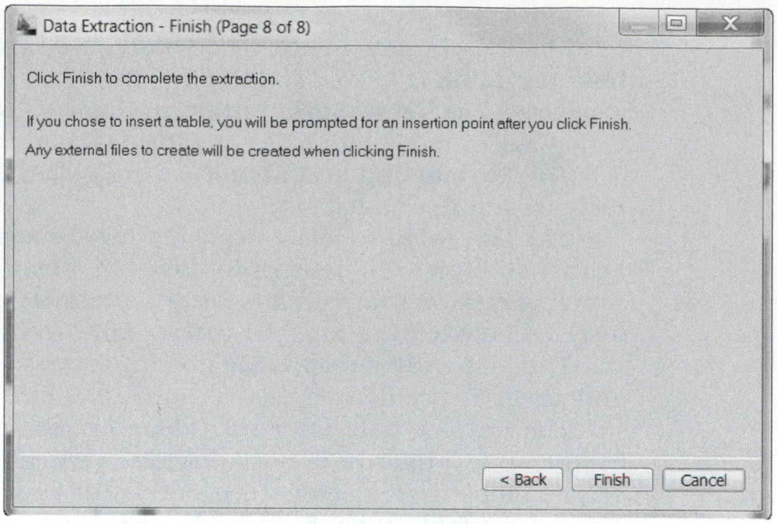

Figure 16-44

Table created using the **Data Extraction** wizard

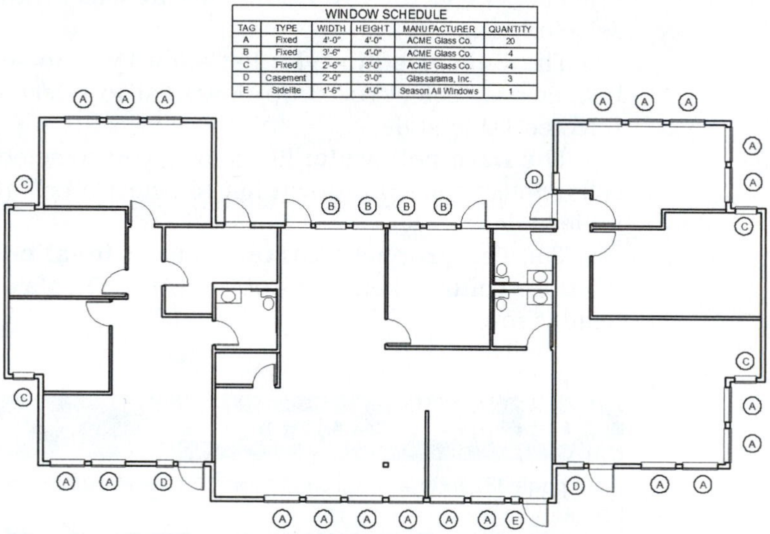

Updating Data Extraction Table Data Manually

Data extraction table data are locked by default to prevent the data from being updated and possibly getting out of sync with the source data (attributes). When you click on a table cell, a **Lock** icon is displayed along with the data extraction information as shown in Figure 16-45.

Figure 16-45

Locked cell in a data extraction table

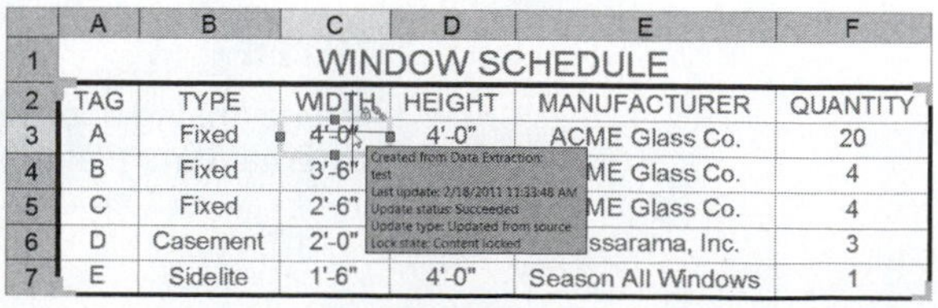

You can unlock a cell by selecting **Locking** from the right-click menu and checking the **Unlocked** cascade menu item. Table data that are overwritten manually will be updated when the table data are updated using the automated update data links options explained in the following section.

Updating Data Extraction Table Data Automatically

You can update data extraction table data automatically when the extracted source data (attributes) change.

AutoCAD locates a **Data Link** icon in the status tray on the far right of the status bar any time a data extraction table is located in your drawing. You can right-click on the icon and select **Update All Data Links...** from the shortcut menu shown in Figure 16-46, and AutoCAD will read all the attributes in the drawing and update the table data with any changes.

> **NOTE**
>
> You can also update links from the **Tools** menu on the **Data Links** cascade menu.

Figure 16-46

Updating data links via the **Data Link** shortcut menu

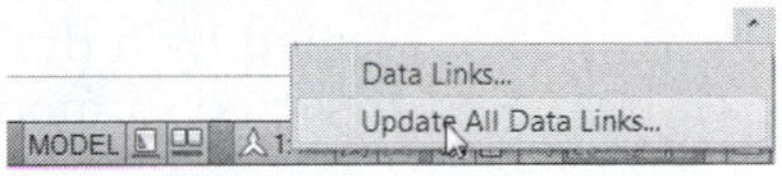

You can select to be notified when extracted data have changed. When information in the data source has changed that affects the extracted data in a table, the **Data Extraction—Outdated Table** dialog box is displayed so that you can update the table data automatically (see Figure 16-47).

Figure 16-47

The **Data Extraction—Outdated Table** dialog box

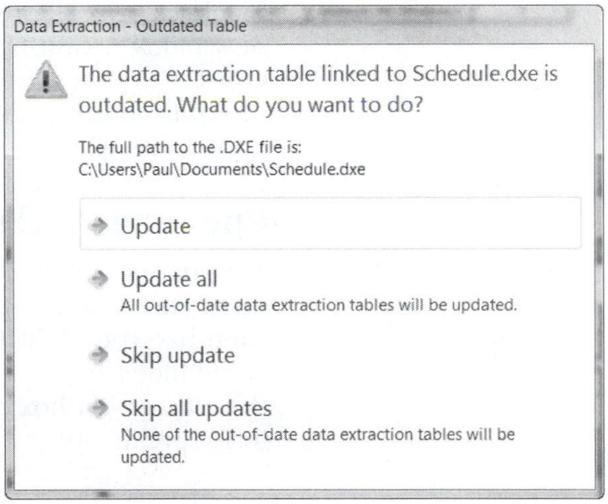

Notification is controlled by the current **DXEVAL** system variable setting. By default, **DXEVAL** is set to check whether the extracted data are not current only when the **PLOT** or **PUBLISH** command is used. It can also be set to occur with the **OPEN, SAVE,** and **ETRANSMIT** commands. The **DXEVAL** system is stored as an integer using the sum of the following values:

- **0** No notification
- **1** Open
- **2** Save
- **4** Plot
- **8** Publish
- **16** eTransmit/Archive
- **32** Save with Automatic Update
- **64** Plot with Automatic Update

- **128** Publish with Automatic Update
- **256** eTransmit/Archive with Automatic Update

The default value of **DXEVAL** is **12**, which enables notification for the **PLOT** and **PUBLISH** commands.

EXERCISE 16-9 **Extracting Attributes**

1. Continue from Exercise 16-8.
2. Use the **Data Extraction** wizard and extract all the block attributes to create the window schedule shown in Figure 16-44 using the AutoCAD table option.
   Hint: Use your mouse to reorder and sort the columns as needed in the **Refine Data** page shown in Figure 16-39. The table must be scaled by a drawing scale factor of **48** after the table is inserted if it is inserted in model space.
3. Save the drawing.

Redefining Blocks

One of the greatest benefits of using blocks in your drawings is that it makes it possible to quickly redefine a block so that all existing and future block references are automatically updated in the drawing to match the new block definition. You may have hundreds, or even thousands, of references of a block in a drawing, and they will all be updated. Think how much time it would take to update each one manually, and it's easy to appreciate why it is such a great feature.

Updating Blocks Created in the Current Drawing

To redefine a block in the current drawing, you simply follow the steps outlined earlier in the chapter to create the updated block information. You then use the **BLOCK** command to save the drawing information with the same block name as the existing block name to update by selecting it from the **Name:** list box at the top of the **Block Definition** dialog box, as shown in Figure 16-48.

Figure 16-48

Redefining an existing block

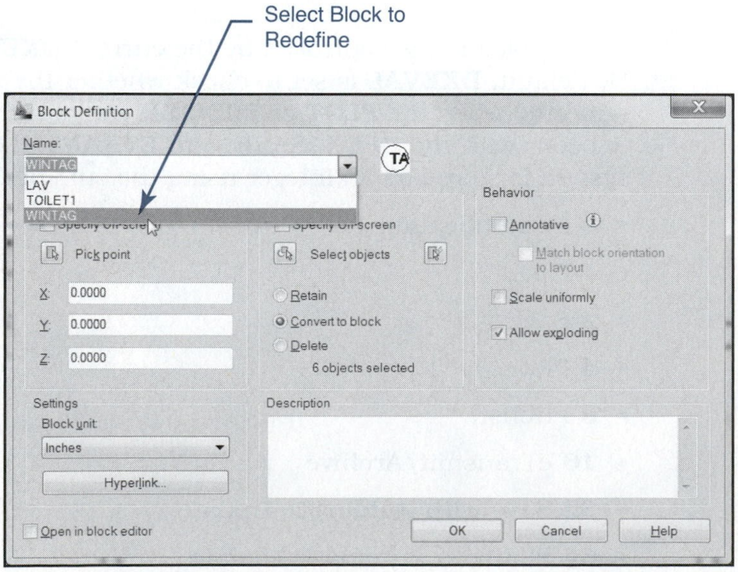

When you select **OK** to update the block information, AutoCAD displays a message like the one shown in Figure 16-49. This informs you that the block definition already exists and asks you whether you want to update it.

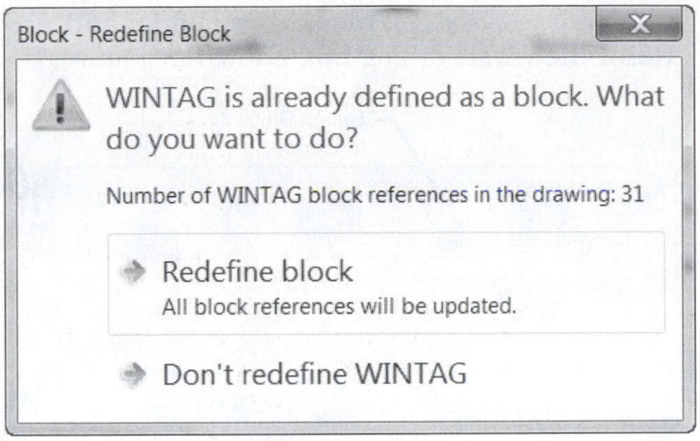

Figure 16-49
Updating a block definition

Selecting the **Redefine block** button replaces the existing block definition with the new one, and all the existing block references in the drawing are immediately updated to reflect the new definition. All future block insertions will also refer to the new block definition.

The easiest way to update a block is to insert the original block and explode it so that you can update its subobjects and then redefine it using the **BLOCK** command as explained above.

> **TIP**
> Be sure that when you insert the original block that you specify a base point that you can remember, a uniform scale of **1.0**, and a rotation angle of **0.0.** If the base point, scale, or rotation angle is different from the original when you redefine the block, all block references will be updated to reflect the change, causing unpredictable results.

Updating Blocks Inserted from an External Drawing File

EDIT REFERENCE	
Ribbon & Panel:	Insert | Reference Edit Reference
Toolbar:	Refedit
Menu:	Tools | Xref and In-place Block Editing | Edit Reference In-Place
Command Line:	REFEDIT
Command Alias:	None

Block definitions created by inserting an external drawing file are not automatically updated when the original drawing file is modified. The easiest way to update a block definition created by inserting a drawing file is to simply reinsert the updated drawing file using the **INSERT** command explained earlier to display the **Insert** dialog box shown in Figure 16-7 and select the **Browse...** button to select the updated drawing file using the standard **Select Drawing File** dialog box.

When you select **OK** to exit the **Insert** dialog box and insert the updated block, AutoCAD displays a message like the one shown in Figure 16-49. This informs you that the block definition already exists and asks whether you want to update it. Rather than insert another block reference by picking a point in the drawing, you can press the <**Esc**> key to cancel the insertion process. All the existing block references are still updated, but you don't end up with a new, unwanted block reference in your drawing.

Editing Blocks In-Place

The **REFEDIT** command, which was originally created to edit xrefs, can be used to quickly redefine a block "in-place" without having to explode the block and re-create it using the **BLOCK** command as explained above.

FOR MORE DETAILS

See page 743 in Chapter 17 for more details about xrefs and using the **REFEDIT** command.

After starting the **REFEDIT** command, AutoCAD prompts you to *Select reference:*. Select the block to redefine, and press **<Enter>** to display the **Reference Edit** dialog box shown in Figure 16-50.

Figure 16-50
The **Reference Edit** dialog box

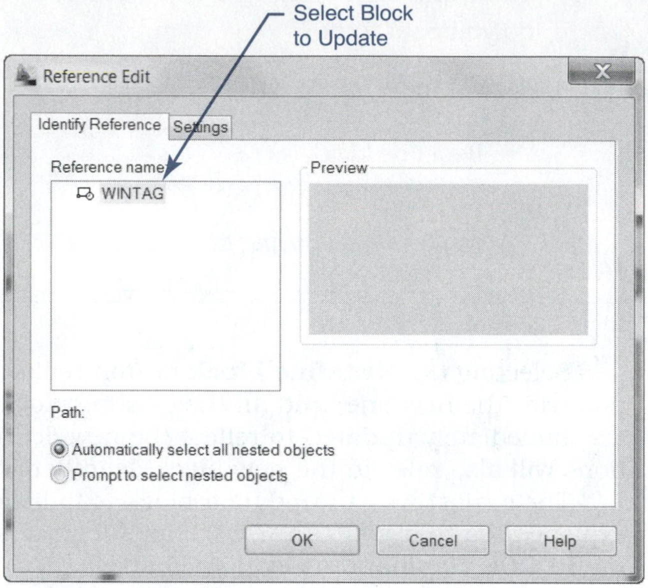

This dialog box provides the following options:

- The **Identify Reference** tab is used to identify and select the block definition you want to edit.
  - The block name is listed on the left in the **Reference name:** box along with any blocks that might be nested within the block. If multiple blocks are displayed, you must select the block you want to modify from the list. Only one block can be edited in place at a time.
  - The **Preview** window displays a preview image of the currently selected block.
  - The **Automatically select all nested objects** option controls whether nested blocks are included automatically in the block editing session.
  - The **Prompt to select nested objects** option controls whether nested blocks must be selected individually in the block editing session.
- The **Settings** tab is used to control various block editing settings.
  - The **Create unique layer, style, and block names** check box allows you to control how xref layers and other named objects are managed.
  - The **Display attribute definitions for editing** check box allows you to control whether all the attribute definitions in a block reference are displayed during the block editing session.

NOTE

When **Display attribute definitions for editing** is selected, attribute *values* are turned off, and all the block attribute *definitions* are displayed so that they can be edited. The updated attribute definitions affect only future block insertions—the attributes in existing block references are unchanged. Attributes defined as **Constant** cannot be updated.

working set: The group of objects selected for in-place editing using the **REFEDIT** command.

Additionally, the **Lock objects not in working set** check box allows you to lock all objects not in the ***working set*** so that you don't inadvertently modify other objects in the drawing while in a block editing session. Locked objects behave similarly to objects on a locked layer—they can be viewed, but they cannot be selected.

Selecting **OK** puts you in the block editing mode where all the objects that are not part of the working set are locked *and* faded back so that the objects to edit in the working set stand out as shown in Figure 16-51.

When you are in block editing mode, the **Edit Reference** panel shown in Figure 16-52 is turned on to allow you to manage the working set and save or discard any changes made to the block definition.

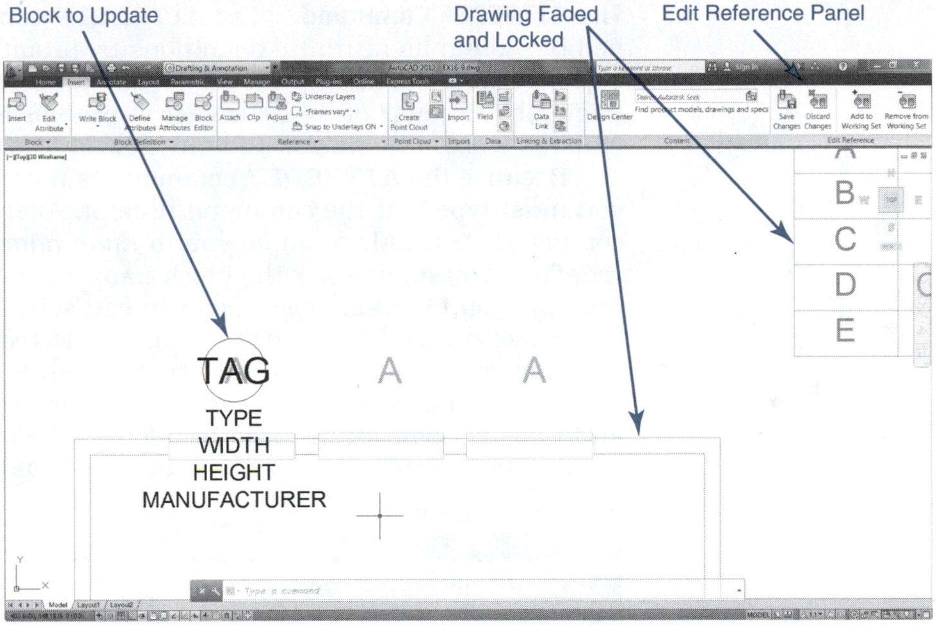

Figure 16-51
Drawing display in block editing mode

Figure 16-52
The **Edit Reference** panel

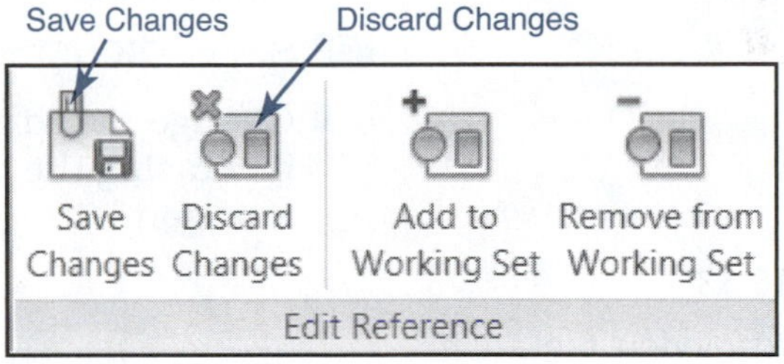

In block editing mode, you can edit the block definition using any of the standard AutoCAD drawing and editing commands. You can add information, erase information, and change object properties—almost anything you would normally do in the AutoCAD drawing editor.

When you are done updating the block definition, select the **Save Changes** button on the left side of the **Edit Reference** panel shown in Figure 16-52 to save the changes and exit block editing mode. You can discard any changes and exit block editing mode by selecting the **Discard Changes** button shown in Figure 16-52.

Redefining Blocks with Attributes

It is possible to redefine block attributes using any of the standard techniques explained so far, but there are a few idiosyncrasies to be aware of. For the most part, only future block references will reflect the changes made to the attribute definition properties and modes—existing block references do not get updated.

Adding new attribute definitions is even more problematic—adding a new attribute to a block affects only future block insertions. Not even the **BATTMAN** command described earlier allows you to add new attributes. Fortunately, AutoCAD provides the **ATTREDEF** command to solve the issues surrounding updating blocks with attributes.

> **NOTE**
>
> When an attribute definition is updated, the current attribute value remains the same; only the attribute properties are updated.

The ATTREDEF Command. The **ATTREDEF** command redefines the specified block and its attribute definitions by prompting you to select the objects that will make up the block, similar to when you created the block originally. Because of this, the easiest process is to explode the block to make any changes and/or add any new attribute definitions.

Because the **ATTREDEF** command is not on any menu or ribbon, you must type it at the command prompt. After starting the **ATTREDEF** command, AutoCAD prompts you to *Enter name of the block you wish to redefine:*. You must enter the block name at the keyboard. AutoCAD then prompts you to *Select objects:* so you can select the objects and attributes that make up the block. After you have selected all the block objects, press the **<Enter>** key, and AutoCAD prompts you to *Specify insertion base point of new Block:* so you can select the insertion point. You should select an insertion point in the exact location as the original base point, or any existing block references in the drawing will move.

EXERCISE 16-10 Redefining Blocks

1. Continue from Exercise 16-9.
2. Start the **REFEDIT** command and select any one of the **WINTAG** window tag blocks.
3. Select **OK** in the **Reference Edit** dialog box to enter block editing mode.
4. Change the window tag circle to a hexagon as shown in Figure 16-53 by erasing the circle and using the **POLYGON** command to create the hexagon.

Figure 16-53

Redefined window tag blocks

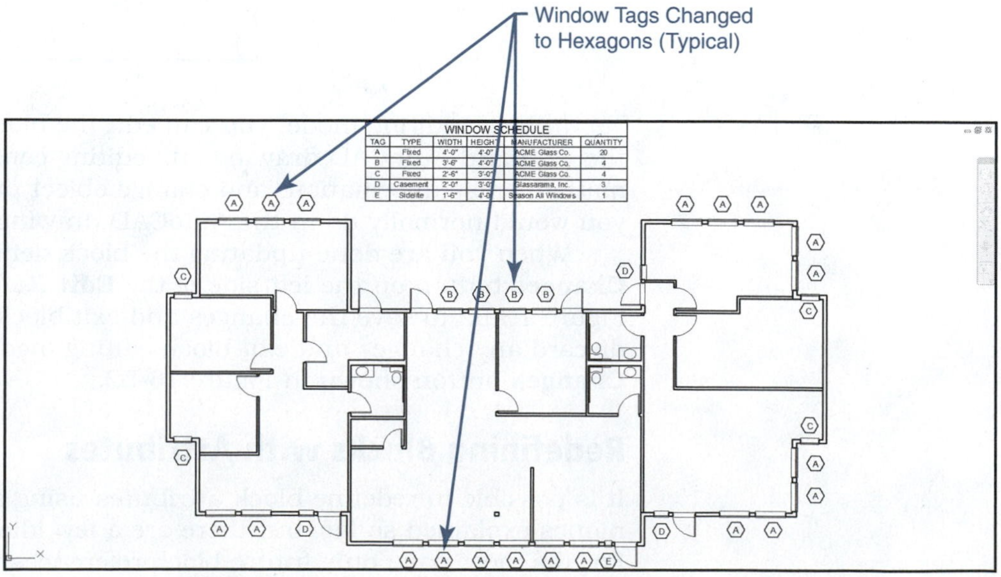

5 Select the **Save Changes** button on the **Edit Reference** panel to save your changes. All window tags in the drawing should immediately change to hexagons.

6 Save the drawing.

Using DesignCenter to Manage Blocks

AutoCAD's **DesignCenter** is a multipurpose tool that provides easy access to blocks, hatch patterns, layers, linetypes, text styles, dimension styles, and other named object information contained in other drawings on your computer, on a network location, or even on the Internet.

DesignCenter allows you to "open" another drawing so that you can view the drawing's named objects, referred to as *drawing content,* in list or icon form. You can then copy any of the drawing content from the source drawing to your current drawing by simply dragging and dropping it with your mouse. You can even select multiple objects, making it possible to copy a group of named objects as one. For instance, using this approach, you could copy all the layer definitions from one drawing to another, saving a lot of time. In addition to layers, **DesignCenter** provides access to the following drawing content:

- Blocks
- Dimension styles
- Layers
- Linetypes
- Table styles
- Text styles
- Xrefs

For the purpose of this chapter, we are going to concentrate on using **DesignCenter** to manage and insert blocks.

> **TIP**
>
> Using **DesignCenter,** you can create a standard drawing, or drawings, that contains all of your organization's standard layers, linetypes, text styles, and so on. Then you can locate it centrally on a network drive, giving your coworkers access to it so all they have to do is drag and drop to set up their drawings.

DESIGNCENTER

Ribbon & Panel:	Insert | Content

Standard Toolbar:	
Menu:	Tools | Design Center
Command Line:	ADCENTER
Command Alias:	ADC

The DesignCenter Window

The **ADCENTER** command displays the **DesignCenter** window so that you can locate and insert drawing content from other drawings located on your computer, a network, or the Internet.

Starting the **ADCENTER** command displays the **DesignCenter** window shown in Figure 16-54.

The **DesignCenter** window consists of three parts:

- **Tree view** (left pane) Navigation tools used to locate drawing files and Web-based content
- **Content area** (right pane) Displays the contents of a drawing or Web content once it is located
- **Toolbar** (top) Additional navigation and display tools

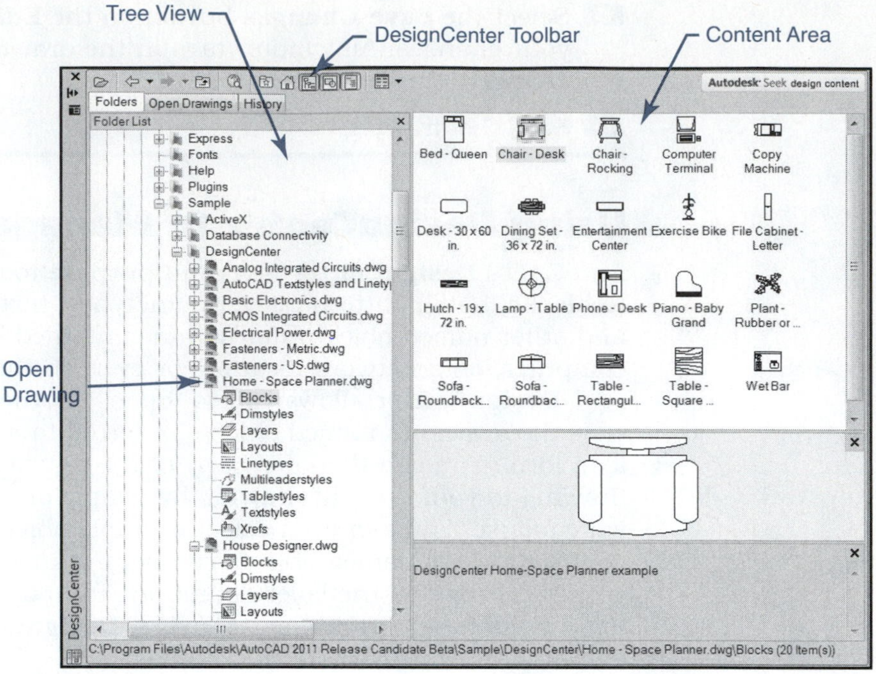

Figure 16-54

The **DesignCenter** window

> **NOTE**
>
> If the tree view is not displayed, select the **Tree View Toggle** button on the **DesignCenter** toolbar at the top of the **DesignCenter** window shown in Figure 16-54.

The following sections explain each of these parts as well as other **DesignCenter** features.

Tree View. The tree view on the left allows you to locate a drawing file using the following methods so that you can display the drawing's contents in the content area on the right:

- **Folders** tab Explorer-like interface that allows you to navigate the hierarchy of files and folders on your computer or attached network drives (see Figure 16-54)
- **Open Drawings** tab List of all currently open drawings
- **History** tab History of the last drawings accessed

> **TIP**
>
> You can remove a file from the **History** tab by selecting the file, right-clicking, and selecting **Delete** from the shortcut menu.

Content Area. The content area on the right side of the window displays the contents of the drawing or the named object collection currently selected in the tree view on the left. When a block is selected, it is possible to display a preview and a description as shown in Figure 16-55.

Figure 16-55
The content area

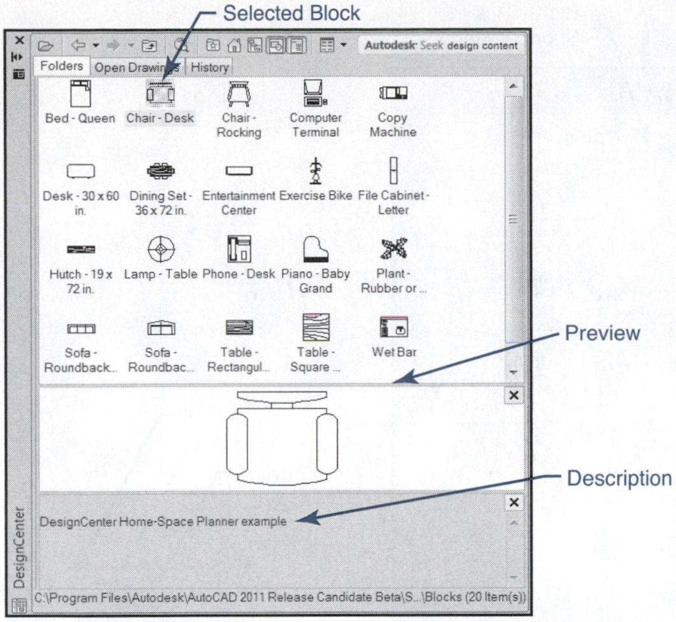

The preview window and description window can be toggled on and off by selecting the **Preview** and **Description** buttons on the **DesignCenter** toolbar shown in Figure 16-57. It is also possible to switch how the information is viewed in the content pane via the **Views** flyout menu on the right side of the **DesignCenter** toolbar shown in Figure 16-57 to one of the following standard Explorer-type formats:

- Large icons
- Small icons
- List
- Details

You can navigate in the content area by double-clicking an icon with your mouse to display its contents. You can then select the **Up** arrow on the **DesignCenter** toolbar shown in Figure 16-57 to go back up one level in the hierarchy.

Right-clicking on a block icon displays the shortcut menu shown in Figure 16-56 so that you can do the following:

- **Insert Block...** Displays the **Insert** dialog box
- **Insert and Redefine** Inserts the selected block and redefines all block definitions in the drawing
- **Redefine only** Redefines a block in the drawing but does not insert a copy
- **Block Editor** Displays the dynamic block editor
- **Copy** Copies the block to the Windows Clipboard
- **Create Tool Palette** Creates a custom tool palette

DesignCenter Toolbar. The **DesignCenter** toolbar shown in Figure 16-57 provides the following navigation tools and display options:

- **Load** Displays the standard file selection dialog box so you can locate a file and load its information in the content area

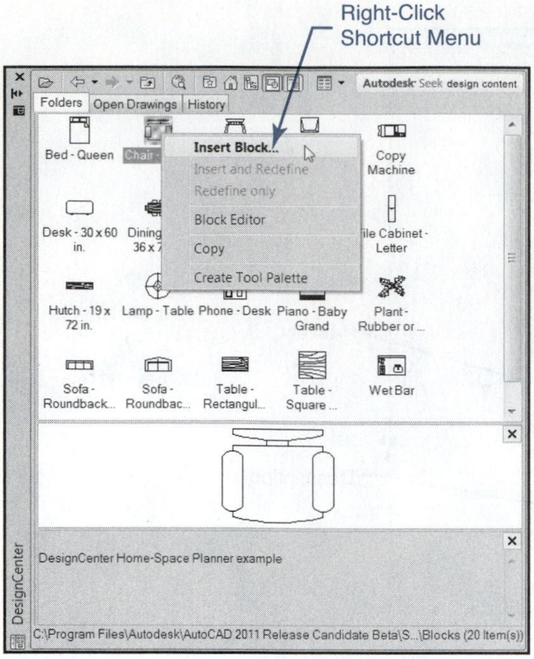

Figure 16-56

The content area shortcut menu

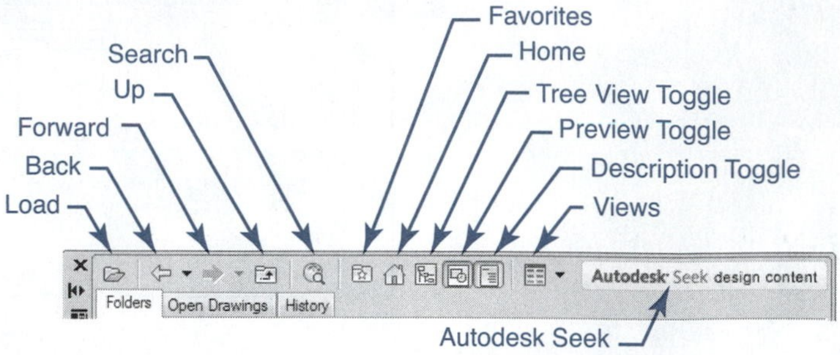

Figure 16-57

The **DesignCenter** toolbar

- **Back** Returns to the most recent location in the history list
- **Forward** Moves forward to a recent location in the history list
- **Up** Displays the contents of the next level up in the hierarchy
- **Search** Displays the **Search** dialog box so you can enter search criteria to locate drawings, blocks, and other named objects within drawings
- **Favorites** Displays the contents of the **Favorites** folder in the content area. You can add items to the **Favorites** folder by right-clicking and selecting **Add to Favorites** from the shortcut menu
- **Home** Returns **DesignCenter** to the home folder. You can change the home folder by navigating to the desired folder in the tree view, right-clicking, and selecting **Set as Home** from the shortcut menu
- **Tree View Toggle** Displays and hides the tree view. When the tree view is hidden, you can still navigate in the content area using the techniques described earlier
- **Preview Toggle** Toggles the preview window on and off in the content area
- **Description Toggle** Toggles the description window on and off in the content area
- **Views** Allows you to switch between different display formats in the content area

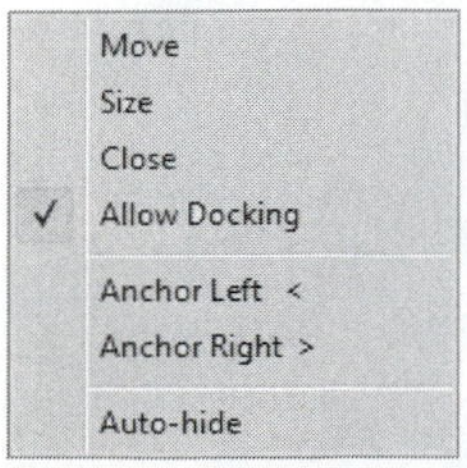

Figure 16-58

The **DesignCenter Properties** shortcut menu

DesignCenter Properties. Just like other AutoCAD windows and palettes, the **DesignCenter** window can be moved, resized, and docked using your mouse. You can also control these and other features by selecting the **Properties** button on the window title bar to display the shortcut menu shown in Figure 16-58.

Using the shortcut menu, you can prevent the **DesignCenter** window from being docked. You can also toggle on and off the **Auto-hide** feature that collapses the window, so that only the title bar is visible when the mouse pointer is not directly over the window.

TIP

The <Ctrl>+2 keyboard combination can be used to quickly toggle **DesignCenter** on and off.

Inserting Blocks. Once you locate a block using one of the methods described above and it is visible in the content area, there are three ways you can insert the block into the current drawing using **DesignCenter**:

- Drag and drop the block into the current drawing using your mouse.
- Double-click on the block in the content area to display the **Insert** dialog box.
- Right-click on the block in the content area to display the shortcut menu shown earlier in Figure 16-56.

NOTE

The following exercise requires that you install the sample **DesignCenter** drawing files that come with AutoCAD 2013. By default, the sample drawings are located in the ***C:\Program Files\AutoCAD 2013\Sample\DesignCenter*** folder.

Each method has its merits. Dragging and dropping a block is obviously the fastest method, while double-clicking on a block provides the most control because you can specify different block settings in the **Insert** dialog box. Finally, right-clicking provides the only option to redefine a block. Practice using each method so that you are prepared for any situation.

Autodesk Seek. Autodesk **Seek** is an online utility that allows you to search product information and drawings from the Web and download them directly into your AutoCAD drawing. It can be accessed either from the right side of the **DesignCenter** toolbar shown in Figure 16-57 or by entering your search criteria directly on the **Content** panel on the **Insert** tab of the ribbon in the **Seek design content** search box.

Either method will launch your Internet browser and take you to the http://seek.autodesk.com website so you can find the product you are searching for. Once you locate a drawing, you can drag and drop the content into the current AutoCAD drawing.

It is also possible to share your blocks and other content with other Autodesk **Seek** users by selecting the **Share with Autodesk Seek** tool on the **Autodesk Seek** panel on the **Output** tab of the ribbon. Selecting the **Share with Autodesk Seek** tool asks you what content you want to share and then takes you through an online submittal process where the selected content is then uploaded to the Autodesk **Seek** website.

EXERCISE 16-11 Using DesignCenter

1. Continue from Exercise 16-10.
2. Set layer **A-Furn** current.
3. Start **DesignCenter** and navigate to the ***Home-Space Planner.dwg*** file located in the **DesignCenter** folder as shown in Figure 16-54.
4. Select the **Blocks** icon so you can see the blocks defined in the drawing in the content area on the right as shown in Figure 16-55.

5 Select the **Tree View Toggle** button on the **DesignCenter** toolbar shown in Figure 16-57 to turn off the tree view.

6 Insert blocks using the techniques explained above, and furnish the floor plan in a manner similar to Figure 16-59.

7 Save the drawing.

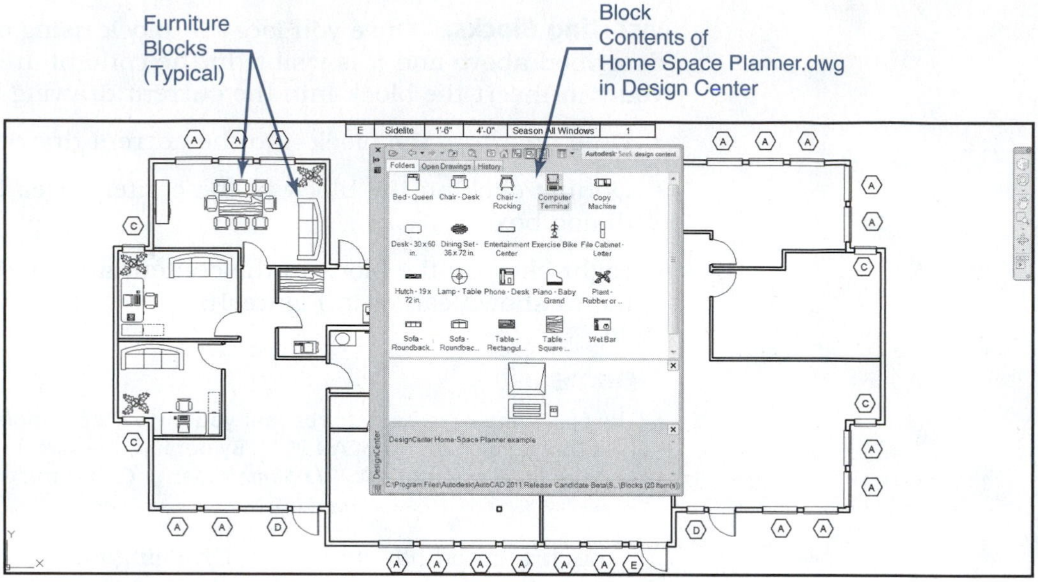

Figure 16-59

Building floor plan with office furniture and equipment blocks inserted using **DesignCenter**

Tool Palettes and Dynamic Blocks

TOOL PALETTES	
Ribbon & Panel:	View | Palettes Tool Palettes
Standard Toolbar:	
Menu:	Tools | Palettes | Tool Palettes
Command Line:	TOOL PALETTES
Command Alias:	TP

Tool palettes are highly customizable palette-type windows that allow you to group and organize blocks, hatch patterns, and even commands, using graphical icons on easily accessible palettes organized in a series of named tabs.

Dynamic blocks are multipurpose blocks that can be changed after they are inserted using special grips that allow you to display multiple block views, sizes, block behavior, and more. Using dynamic blocks, one block definition can be used for a myriad of different scenarios and situations. Dynamic blocks are covered in detail later in this section. The AutoCAD tool palettes are shown in Figure 16-60.

NOTE

All dynamic blocks have a lightning bolt in the lower right corner of their tool palette icon as shown in Figure 16-60 to indicate that they can be dynamically updated after they are inserted. Inserting and updating dynamic blocks is explained later in this section.

Tool palette tools can be either dragged and dropped directly into your drawing to perform the associated action or selected by clicking on the tool's icon with your mouse. Figure 16-61 shows the **Door-Imperial** block being inserted in the drawing by dragging and dropping it from the sample **Architectural** palette.

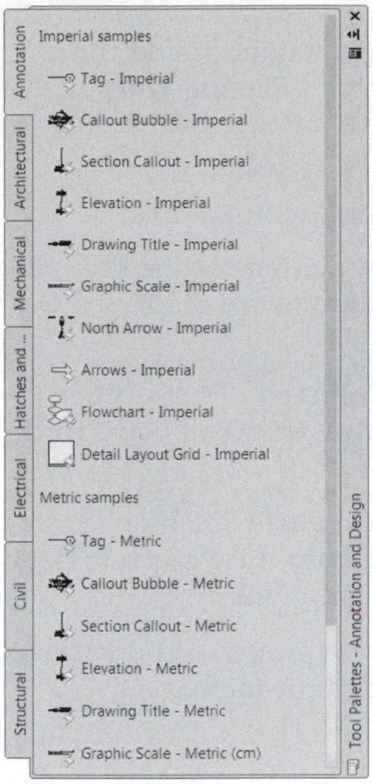

Figure 16-60

AutoCAD tool palettes

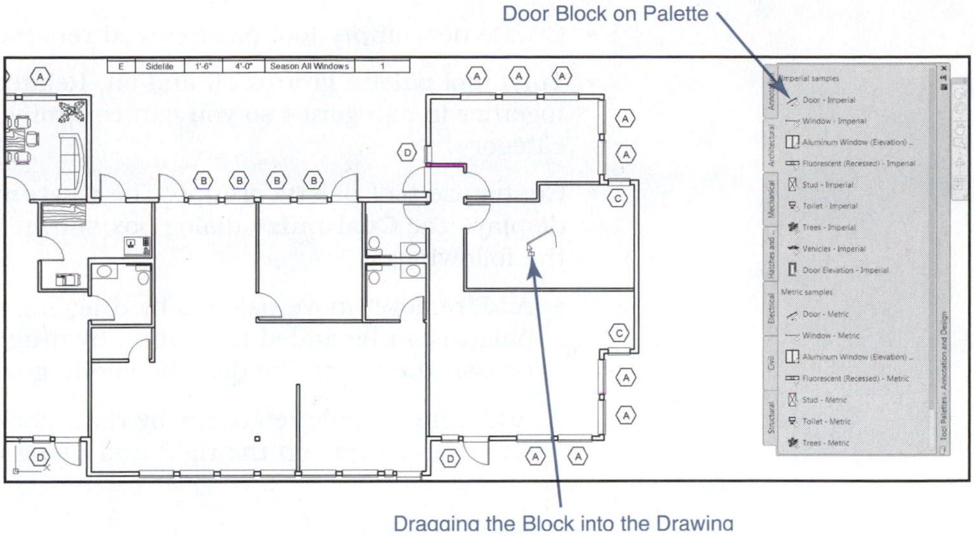

Figure 16-61

Inserting the **Door-Imperial** block from the sample **Architectural** palette

Controlling Tool Palettes

Because they utilize the palette-type window, tool palettes can be hidden when you are not using them via the **Auto-hide** palette feature, as well as made transparent so that you can see through them to your drawing below using the **Transparency** palette feature. These and other features can be controlled via the **Properties** shortcut menu that can be displayed by clicking on the **Properties** button at the top of the palette title bar (see Figure 16-60).

> **TIP**
>
> The **Auto-hide** feature can also be quickly turned on and off via the **Auto-hide** button located directly above the **Properties** button (see Figure 16-60).

> **FOR MORE DETAILS**
>
> See Chapter 1 for more information about controlling different palette properties such as **Auto-hide** and transparency.

More options are available by right-clicking anywhere on the title bar to display the shortcut menu shown in Figure 16-62.

In addition to the **Auto-hide** and **Transparency** palette features, the tool palette title bar right-click menu allows you to do the following:

- Turn tool palette docking off so that if you drag a palette to the far left or right side of your screen, the palette will remain in a floating state and not attach itself to the AutoCAD window.

- Anchor tool palettes on the left or right side of the AutoCAD window. Anchored palettes are palettes that are docked but hidden using the **Auto-hide** feature so that only the title bar is visible. Placing your mouse over the palette title bar displays the entire palette, but it remains anchored.
- Create new empty tool palettes and rename existing tool palettes.
- Turn tool palette groups off and on. Related tool palettes can be grouped together in categories so you can control what palettes are displayed by category.
- Customize tool palette groups. The **Customize Palettes...** menu item displays the **Customize** dialog box shown in Figure 16-63 so you can do the following:
  - Add/remove/move palettes by dragging palettes with your mouse. A palette can be added to a group by dragging it from the **Palettes:** list box on the left to the desired palette group on the right.
  - Add/remove palette groups by right-clicking on a group in the **Palette Groups:** list box on the right and using the shortcut menu.

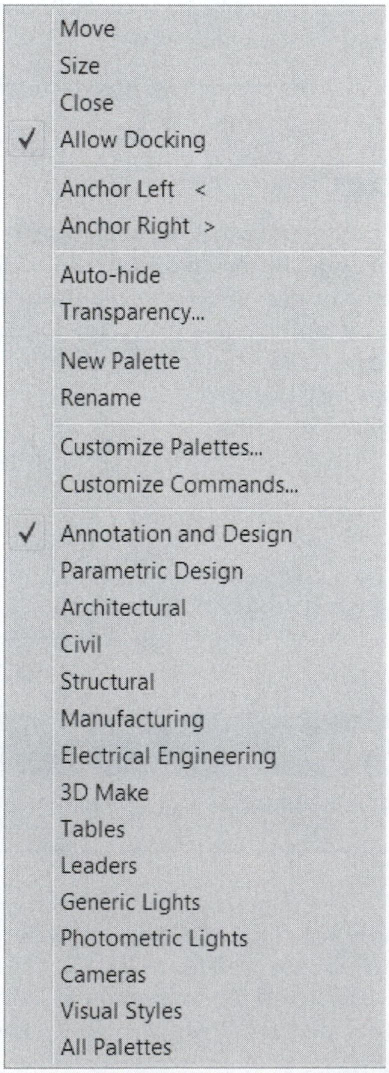

Figure 16-62

Tool palette title bar right-click menu

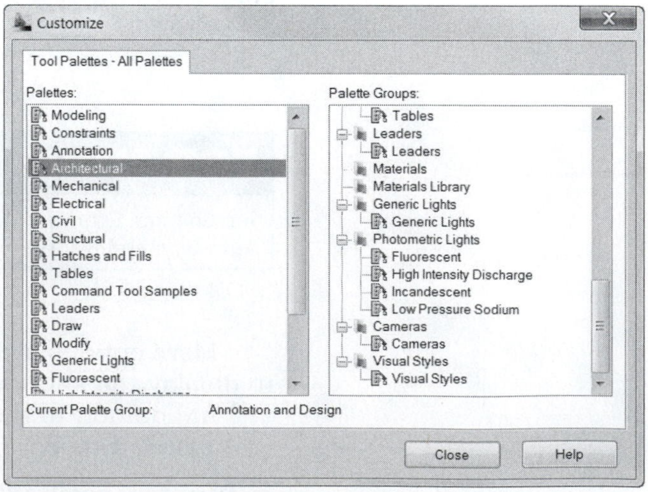

Figure 16-63

The **Customize** dialog box

- Export and import tool palettes using the XTP file format so that palettes can be shared with other users by right-clicking on a palette in the **Palettes:** list box on the left and selecting **Export...** or **Import...** from the shortcut menu to display the Windows file dialog box.

- Add custom commands. The **Customize Commands...** menu item displays the **Customize User Interface** dialog box with a list of all the AutoCAD commands. To add a command to a tool palette, you simply drag it from the **Command List:** and drop it onto the tool palette of your choice.

But wait, there's more. There are a total of four different tool palette right-click shortcut menus depending on where you right-click with your mouse. If you right-click on a tool palette anywhere between toolbar icons on an empty space on the palette background, the shortcut menu in Figure 16-64 is displayed.

Figure 16-64

Tool palette background right-click menu

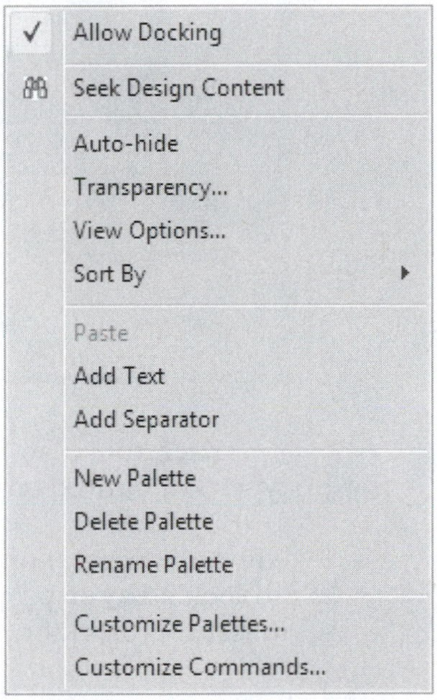

In addition to most of the commands and features already discussed, this menu also allows you to control different display options. The **View Options...** menu item displays the **View Options** dialog box so that you can switch between icon and list view, as well as control the size of the images used for the icons. The **Sort By** cascade menu allows you to automatically sort tool icons by name or type.

Right-clicking on the named tab on a tool palette displays yet another shortcut menu. This menu allows you to move a palette up and down in the palette order, rename a palette, or create a new palette.

Finally, right-clicking directly over a tool palette icon displays a shortcut menu that allows you to cut, copy, delete, rename, and control the selected tool's properties.

Tool Properties

The **Properties...** menu item located on the bottom of a tool's right-click shortcut menu displays the **Tool Properties** dialog box shown in Figure 16-65 so you can edit the tool's name and description, as well as control tool-specific properties such as block locations, hatch pattern names, and command macros depending on the tool type selected. The properties for a block are shown in Figure 16-65.

Figure 16-65

The **Tool Properties** dialog box for a block

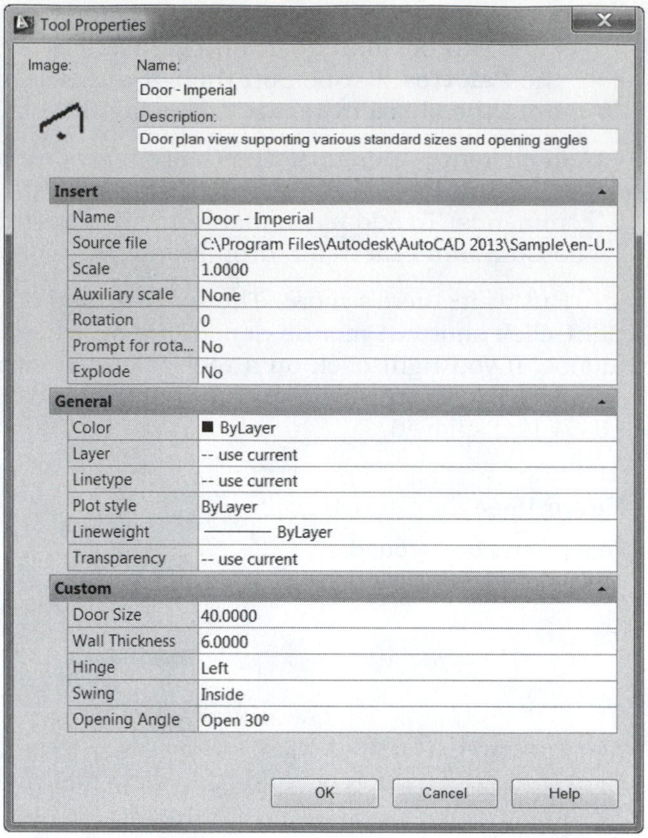

Each tool also has general properties such as layer, color, and linetype that can be controlled via the **Tool Properties** dialog box (see Figure 16-65). These properties are applied to any object type that is created when the corresponding tool palette icon is selected. For instance, setting a block's **Layer** property to any layer setting other than **—use current** will insert the block on the layer specified.

> **TIP**
>
> It is possible to rearrange the order of the tools on a tool palette by left-clicking a tool icon and dragging it to another location.

EXERCISE 16-12 Using Tool Palettes

1. Continue from Exercise 16-11.
2. Turn on tool palettes via the **Palettes** panel on the **View** tab of the ribbon.
3. Right-click anywhere on the **Tool Palettes** title bar and select **Annotation and Design** from the shortcut menu to turn on only the **Annotation and Design** tool palettes shown in Figure 16-60.
4. Size and position the palettes on the screen using your mouse.
5. Turn the **Auto-hide** feature on by selecting the **Auto-hide** button at the top of the palette title bar directly above the **Properties** button.
6. Move your mouse off the palette so that the palette closes and only the palette title bar is visible.
7. Right-click anywhere on the **Tool Palettes** title bar again, and select **Anchor Right >** to anchor the tool palette on the right side of the screen.

8 Put your cursor over the anchored tool palette to display it, and select the **Architectural** palette tab to make it active.

9 Select the **Door-Imperial** block at the top of the **Architectural** palette by clicking on it with your left mouse button. AutoCAD should prompt you to *Specify insertion point or* ↓.

10 Pick a point to locate the block anywhere on the floor plan.

11 Select the **Fluorescent (Recessed)-Imperial** block, hold your mouse button down, and drag-and-drop the light fixture block anywhere in the drawing.

12 Right-click on the **Door-Imperial** block on the **Architectural** palette and select **Properties...** from the shortcut menu to display the **Tool Properties** dialog box.

13 Change the **Layer** property under the **General** category from **—use current** to **A-DOOR,** and select **OK** to close the dialog box.

14 Insert another **Door-Imperial** block. It should now always insert on the **A-DOOR** layer regardless of what layer is current.

15 Save the drawing.

Adding Tools to Tool Palettes

One of the coolest things about tool palettes is that you can add information to a palette by simply selecting an object in your drawing and dragging it onto the tool palette where you want it to be located. If the object is a block, it is added to the palette as a block. If the object is a hatch pattern, the hatch pattern is added to the palette. If the object selected is not a block or a hatch pattern, the command used to create the object is added to the palette. For instance, dragging a piece of multiline text from a drawing onto a tool palette will add the **MTEXT** command using the default multiline text icon as shown in Figure 16-66.

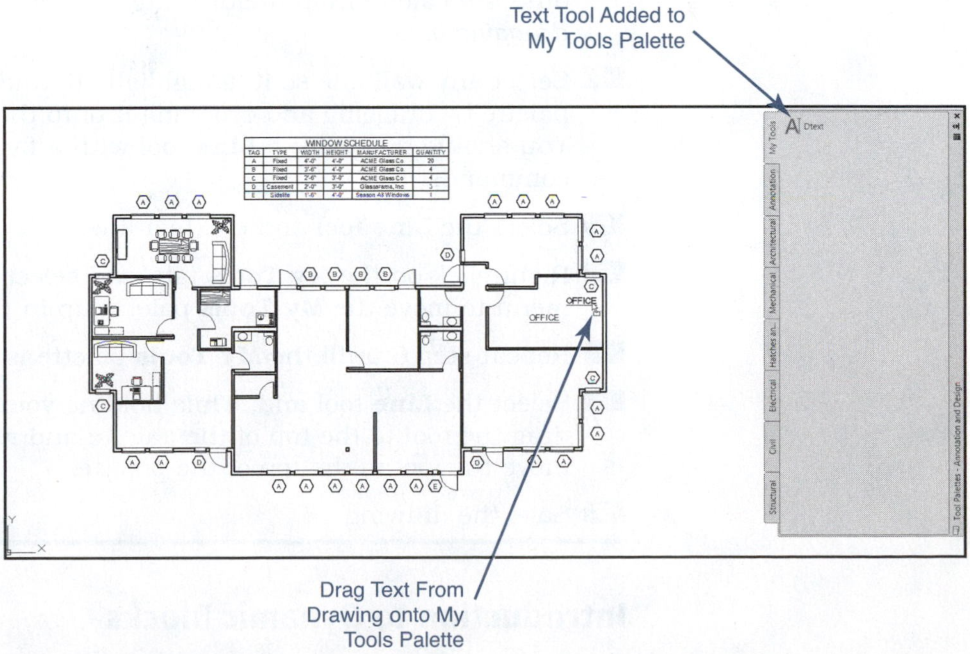

Figure 16-66

Adding tools by dragging and dropping them from the drawing

There are a couple of different ways to add blocks to a palette besides dragging them from the drawing.

Using the **DesignCenter** palette described earlier, it is possible to automatically create a new palette that contains all the blocks in a drawing by right-clicking on a drawing on the **DesignCenter Folders** tab and selecting the **Create Tool Palette** menu item from the shortcut menu. A new palette with the same name as the drawing is added to the current palette group with blocks and tool icons generated for each block.

DesignCenter can also create a new palette that consists of all the drawing files located in a folder. If you right-click on a folder that contains drawing (DWG) files and select **Create Tool Palette of Blocks** from the shortcut menu, AutoCAD will create a new tool palette with the same name as the folder with blocks and icons for each drawing file in the folder.

> **TIP**
> Drawing (DWG) files can also be added to a tool palette by dragging and dropping them from Windows Explorer onto the desired palette. It is even possible to add multiple drawings at the same time using the **<Ctrl>** and **<Shift>** keys to select multiple files.

EXERCISE 16-13 **Adding Tools to Tool Palettes**

1. Continue from Exercise 16-12.
2. Right-click anywhere on the **Tool Palettes** title bar, and select **New Palette** from the shortcut menu to create a new palette. Name the new palette **My Tools**.
3. Select any toilet block on the floor plan in the drawing so it is highlighted, and add it to the **My Tools** palette by dragging and dropping it onto the palette from the drawing. *Be careful not to select a grip when dragging it.*
4. Select any wall line so it is highlighted, and add it to the **My Tools** palette by dragging and dropping it onto the palette from the drawing. You should now have a **Line** tool with a flyout of assorted drawing commands.
5. Select the **Line** tool and create a line.
6. Right-click on the **My Tools** tab, and select **Move Up** from the shortcut menu to move the **My Tools** palette up in the palette order.
7. Repeat step 6 until the **My Tools** palette is the top-level palette.
8. Select the **Line** tool and, while holding your left mouse button down, drag the tool to the top of the palette and release the mouse button to move the tool to the top of the palette.
9. Save the drawing.

Introduction to Dynamic Blocks

As mentioned earlier, dynamic blocks are multipurpose blocks that allow you to use a single block to represent many different variations, sizes, and typical actions that would normally require a block library consisting of numerous different block definitions. Using dynamic blocks, you typically insert a generic version of the block and then use the special grips shown in the following table to update it dynamically:

Dynamic Block Grips

	Grip	Description
	List Arrow	Selecting grip displays a list of block options such as size, configuration, number, or views to choose from.
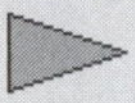	Stretch Arrow	Dragging grip allows you to stretch, scale, and array a block to predefined sizes and configurations.
	Locator Box	Dragging grip allows you to stretch or move a block or block subcomponent.
	Flip Arrow	Selecting grip flips a block in the direction of the arrow.
	Alignment	Dragging grip aligns a block with existing objects in the drawing.
	Rotate	Selecting grip allows you to rotate a block to predefined angles using your cursor.

For example, using dynamic block technology, one single block of an architectural-type door for a floor plan can be updated so that you can:

- Switch between different standard door opening angles
- Resize the door using standard door opening and frame widths
- Flip the door horizontally or vertically about the center of the door opening
- Automatically align the door along a wall

FOR MORE DETAILS

See page 301 in Chapter 7 for more information about using grips to modify objects.

TIP

Many of a block's dynamic options and features can be set *prior* to inserting the block using the **Properties** palette instead of using grips after the block is inserted. If you turn on the **Properties** palette and select a dynamic block on a tool palette, the dynamic block options that can be updated prior to insertion are listed under the **Custom** category.

Using the **List Arrow** grip, the door opening angle can be set to 30°, 45°, 60°, 90°, or even appear closed as shown in Figure 16-67.

Using the **Stretch Arrow** grip, you can resize the door to any predefined opening size (24″, 28″, 30″, 32″, 36″, or 40″) as shown in Figure 16-68.

Using the **Flip Arrow** grip, you can mirror the door about the center of the opening either horizontally or vertically as shown in Figure 16-69.

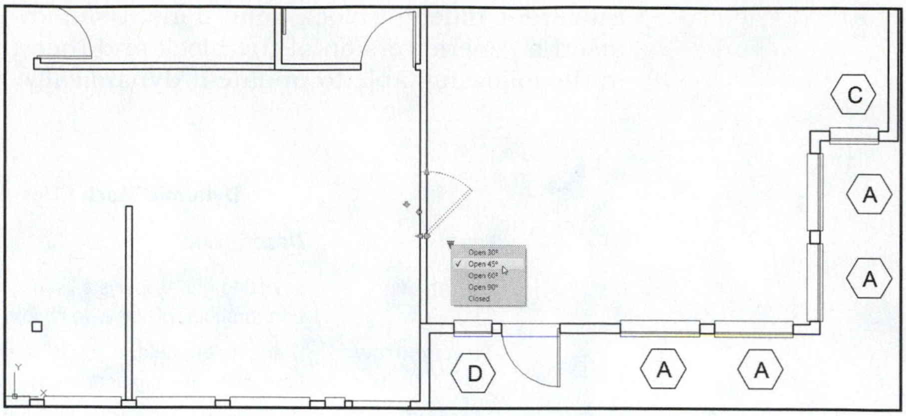

Figure 16-67

Using the dynamic **List Arrow** grip to change the door opening angle

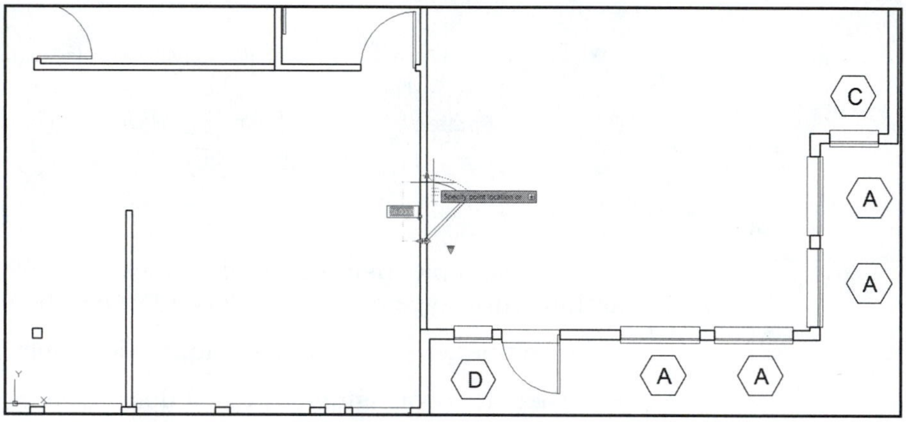

Figure 16-68

Using the dynamic **Stretch Arrow** grip to change the door opening size

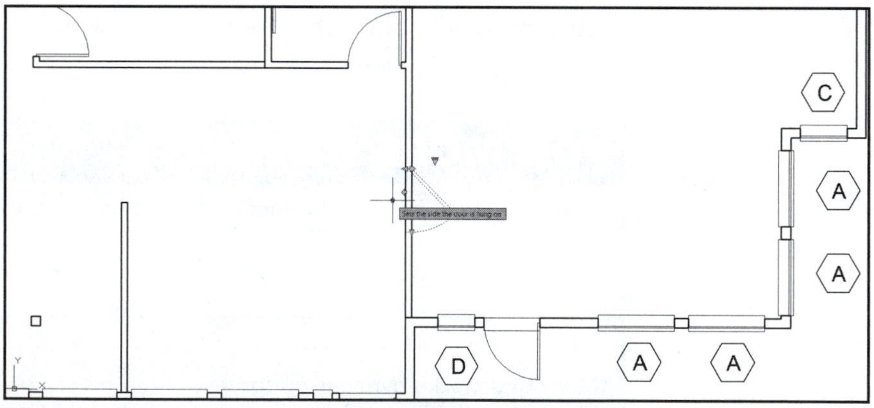

Figure 16-69

Using the dynamic **Flip Arrow** grip to mirror the door

With the **Alignment** grip, you can drag the door near a wall, and it will automatically align itself along the same angle as the wall as shown in Figure 16-70.

> **TIP**
>
> The dynamic block alignment feature also works as the dynamic block is inserted so that you can instantly align doors, windows, and other blocks with existing objects in your drawing.

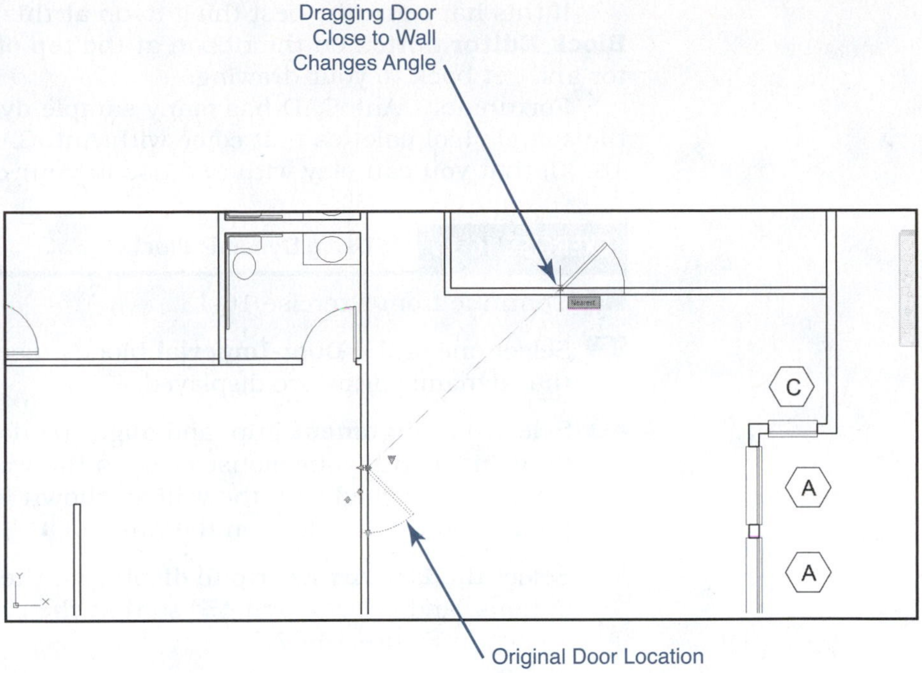

Figure 16-70

Using the **Alignment** grip to align the door with the wall

Unfortunately, covering all the dynamic block update options and features is beyond the scope of this textbook, as is the complex process involved in creating a dynamic block. Because of their complex nature, AutoCAD includes a special **Block Editor** environment for creating and updating dynamic blocks that has its own set of "authoring" palettes where you define parameters and actions. You might have started it accidentally at some point and wondered what it was because it changes the ribbon and the color of the AutoCAD background as shown in Figure 16-71.

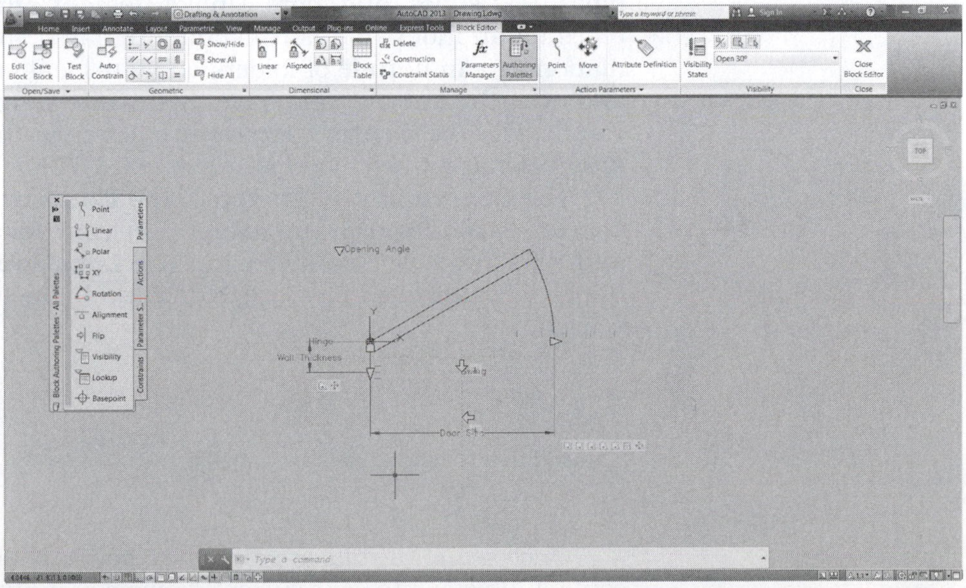

Figure 16-71

The AutoCAD dynamic **Block Editor**

If this happens, the best thing to do at this point is to select the **Close Block Editor** button on the ribbon at the top of the screen to exit the editor and get back to your drawing.

Fortunately, AutoCAD has many sample dynamic blocks available on the sample tool palettes that come with AutoCAD (shown earlier in Figure 16-60) that you can play with and use in your drawings.

EXERCISE 16-14 Using Dynamic Blocks

1. Continue from Exercise 16-13.
2. Select one of the **Door-Imperial** blocks inserted in Exercise 16-12 so that dynamic grips are displayed.
3. Select the **Alignment** grip, and align the door with the vertical wall by dragging it with your mouse close to the wall until the block rotates 90° and is aligned with the wall as shown in Figure 16-70. Select a point to locate the door on the wall.
4. Select the **List Arrow** grip to display all the door opening angle options, and select **Open 45°** so that the door angle is updated as shown in Figure 16-67.
5. Select the vertical **Stretch Arrow** grip, and stretch the door so that the door opening is 36″ wide as shown in Figure 16-68.
6. Select the horizontal **Stretch Arrow** grip, and stretch the door so the door frame width is 4″ wide, the same as the wall thickness.
7. Select the vertical **Flip Arrow** grip, and mirror the door horizontally as shown in Figure 16-69.
8. Save the drawing.

Autodesk Content Explorer

Autodesk **Content Explorer** allows you to instantly access one or more drawings to find different drawing content such as blocks, layers, linetypes, text styles, and more. Unlike **DesignCenter, Content Explorer** relies on an index that is constantly updated so you can search for information in a multitude of folders on your local computer, network servers, and even the Internet and have the results returned instantaneously. You can display the **Content Explorer** palette via the **Explore** button on the **Plug-ins** tab of the ribbon (see Figure 16-72).

The **Search** box at the top of the **Content Explorer** palette allows you to search for drawing content on your local computer, network, and the Autodesk **Seek** website. The **Location** drop-down menu on the upper left shown in Figure 16-72 allows you to select which location to search.

NOTE

In addition to blocks, you can search for text strings and even block attributes.

Once search results are displayed, you can simply drag and drop selected content directly into your current drawing just like you do with **DesignCenter**. Right-clicking on content will display a shortcut menu similar to the one shown in Figure 16-73 with different options depending on the content type.

Figure 16-72
The **Content Explorer** palette

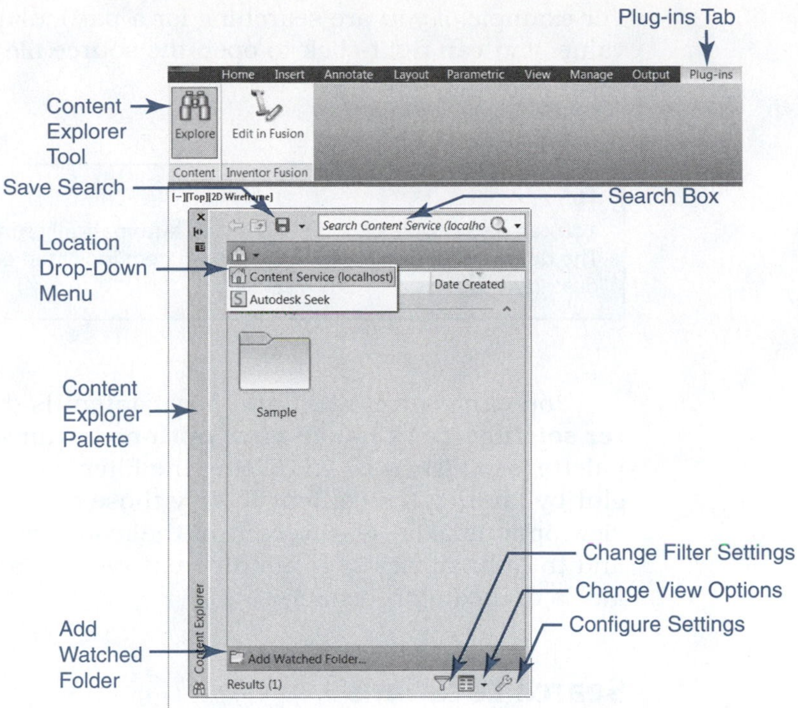

Figure 16-73
The **Content Explorer** right-click menu

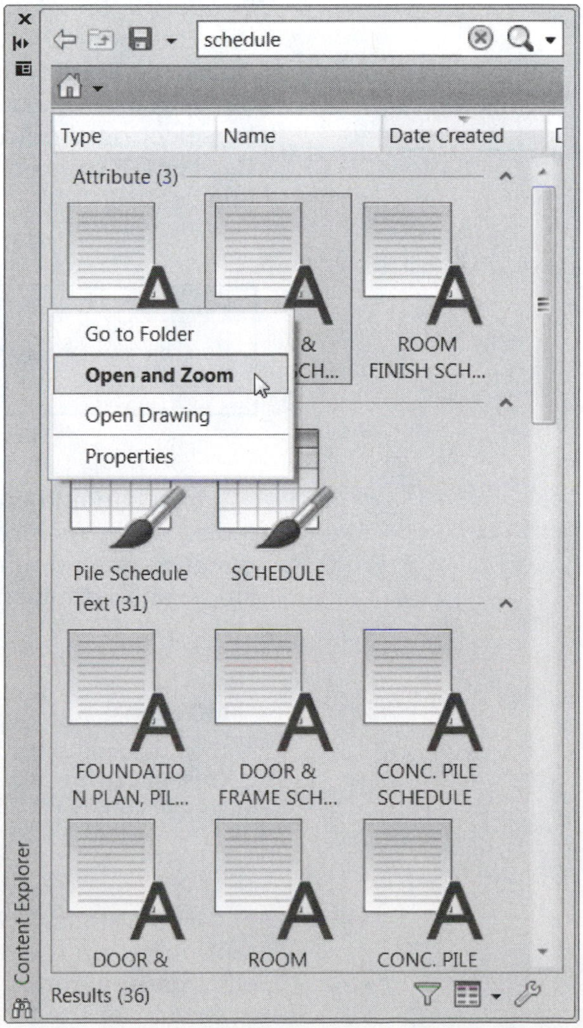

For example, if you are searching for a particular text string or attribute value, you can right-click to open the source file and zoom directly to the found text.

> **TIP**
>
> You can also double-click on content to automatically run its default command or option. The default command is always the bold item indicated on the right-click shortcut menu described above.

You can control what and how content is displayed via the **Change filter settings** and **Change view options** buttons on the bottom right of the palette (see Figure 16-72). Using the filter options you can reduce the info glut by limiting the content to only those objects you're interested in. The view options allow you to control the icon size, switch between detailed and thumbnail views, group different results, and turn on/off the text labels and column headers.

Search Locations

In order to provide the optimum performance when doing complex searches, Autodesk **Content Explorer** searches for information only in specific locations that have been included in an index that is constantly updated to reflect any changes. Default locations include the AutoCAD **Sample** folder, downloaded content folders, and the Autodesk **Seek** website. You can add your own local folder(s) to the search index by selecting the **Add Watched Folder...** button at the bottom of the **Content Explorer** palette when you are at the **Home** location (see Figure 16-72).

> **TIP**
>
> You can also include local folders by dragging and dropping them from Windows Explorer into **Content Explorer.**

You can add one or more network folders to the **Content Explorer** index, but it requires that the Autodesk **Content Service** software be installed and running on that network computer in order to maintain a single shared index that everyone can access and search.

> **NOTE**
>
> The Autodesk **Content Service** software required to add networked locations to the **Content Explorer** index can be installed separately via the **AutoCAD 2013** installation program under the **Tools and Utilities** options.

The Autodesk **Seek** location allows you to browse and search for content online on the Autodesk **Seek** website so you can find files from specific manufacturers or about different product types without going to an external website as shown in Figure 16-74.

Figure 16-74
Autodesk **Seek** content

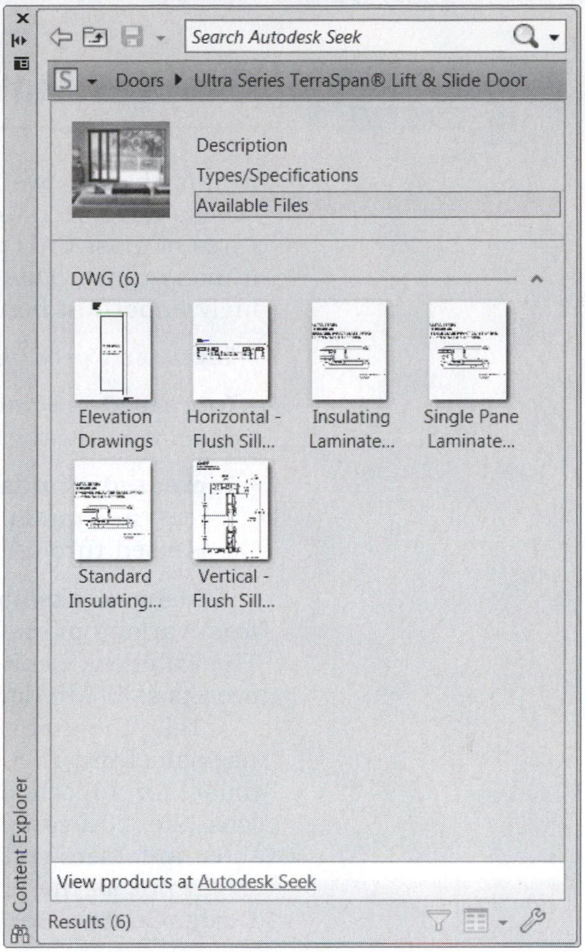

Chapter Summary

In this chapter, we learned how to create, insert, and manage blocks. Blocks have been around for a long time and are one of the primary features of most CAD software because you can draw something once and use it many times. This simple capability provides three basic but overwhelmingly important benefits:

- **Increased productivity** Draw it once and use it over and over again.
- **Increased precision** If you take the time to draw a block right the first time, it is always correct for each subsequent insertion.
- **Increased standards compliance** Draw a block that you are sure meets the standards of your organization, and then distribute it so that it is used throughout a project.

Many blocks already exist that can be downloaded from the Internet from various manufacturers, suppliers, trade organizations, and others. The Autodesk **Seek** feature provides access to much of this content. It is even possible to download complete symbol libraries of blocks.

Take the time to consider when to make a block. If you are going to use something in a drawing more than three times, it might be a good candidate for a block. Think about creating a block library and what it might look like. You can create several separate block drawing files and organize them in folders so they can be inserted using Windows Explorer, or you might put all the blocks in a single drawing file and access them using **DesignCenter**. Each approach has its pros and cons.

The ability to add nongraphical alphanumeric intelligence to your drawings in the form of block attributes is another huge productivity enhancer. Now you can create a single block definition and assign different alphanumeric information each time it is inserted—visible or invisible! Using invisible attributes, you can attach important alphanumeric information to blocks that will not plot but can be extracted to an AutoCAD table, text file, spreadsheet, or even database. What you do with this information is up to your own imagination.

Accessibility is the key to utilizing blocks productively. There are many different ways to organize and provide blocks. Tool palettes are convenient and highly customizable, whereas **DesignCenter** is unwieldy but it provides access to information that tool palettes can't. Alternatively, sometimes dragging and dropping a file from Windows Explorer is the way to go. Autodesk **Content Explorer** can do all of the above, usually quicker too, but you must first create an index of all the information you wish to access. You will find yourself mixing and matching different block tools to meet your needs at the moment. Take time to investigate AutoCAD's dynamic block samples and glimpse the symbol libraries of the future. Now one block can provide a complete symbol library that is just a click away!

> **TIP**
>
> Be careful when downloading any information from the Internet. You will want to examine any blocks you download and check them for accuracy and standards compliance. Just like anything on the Internet, there is some bad information to be found—you must take the time to separate the wheat from the chaff.

Chapter Test Questions

Multiple Choice

Circle the correct answer.

1. An AutoCAD block is best described as a:
   a. Hatch pattern
   b. Named collection of AutoCAD objects treated as a single complex object
   c. Title border
   d. Group of layers

2. The advantage of using blocks in a drawing is:
   a. Reduced drawing size
   b. Increased accuracy
   c. Ease of updating drawings
   d. All of the above

3. When inserting an annotation-type block, it is necessary to:
   a. Put it on a text layer
   b. Scale the block by the drawing scale
   c. Set the text style
   d. All of the above

4. A block attribute is:
   a. An object property such as layer, color, linetype, or lineweight
   b. A scale
   c. A rotation
   d. Dynamic text used to store alphanumeric data

5. Defining a block within another block is referred to as:
   a. Block assembly
   b. Impossible
   c. Block reference
   d. Block nesting

6. Block subobjects created on Layer **0** with all their object properties set to **ByLayer** assume what current object property when the block is inserted?
   a. Color
   b. Lineweight
   c. Layer
   d. All of the above

7. Unit blocks allow you to:
   a. Maintain consistent grid and snap settings
   b. Scale a block differently in the *x* and *y* scale for different results
   c. Transfer blocks from one unit system to another
   d. All of the above

8. Dragging and dropping a drawing from Windows Explorer into a drawing using the right mouse button allows you to:
   a. Open a drawing
   b. Insert a drawing as a block
   c. Attach an xref
   d. All of the above
9. The command that allows you to turn invisible attributes on so they are displayed in the drawing is:
   a. **ATTREQ** c. **ATTDISP**
   b. **ATTDIA** d. **-ATTEDIT**
10. The command that allows you to update the value of an attribute is:
   a. **-ATTEDIT** c. **EATTEDIT**
   b. **BATTMAN** d. a and c

Matching

Write the number of the correct answer on the line.

a. Block attribute ______
b. Block definition ______
c. Block reference ______
d. **BLOCK** command ______
e. ByBlock property ______
f. **INSERT** command ______
g. Unit block ______
h. **WBLOCK** command ______
i. **ATTDIA** system variable ______
j. **REFEDIT** command ______

1. Block drawn within a 1 × 1 unit square that is inserted in the drawing with different *x* and *y* scales
2. Writes a block definition to an external drawing file (DWG)
3. Dynamic text-like object that can be included in a block definition to store alphanumeric data
4. User-defined collection of drawing objects stored centrally in a drawing
5. Controls whether the **Edit Attributes** dialog box is displayed during the insertion process
6. Creates a block definition using the objects you select with the name specified
7. Property that will assume the current color, linetype, or lineweight property when a block is inserted
8. Redefines a block "in-place" without having to explode the block
9. Inserts a block reference by specifying the block name, insertion point, scale, and rotation angle
10. Instance of a block definition inserted in a drawing that references the central block definition drawing data

True or False

Circle the correct answer.

1. **True or False:** Blocks can be defined so that they cannot be exploded.
2. **True or False:** It is not possible to create a block with the same name as a block already defined in a drawing.

3. **True or False:** A block definition cannot be inserted in another drawing until it is exported as a drawing file.
4. **True or False:** It is possible to *always* specify a different *x*, *y*, and *z* scale when inserting a block.
5. **True or False:** When inserting a drawing file (DWG) as a block, both model space and paper space information are included.
6. **True or False:** It is possible to export all the objects in a drawing automatically using the **WBLOCK** command.
7. **True or False:** Attributes can be located automatically so that they align below the previous attribute.
8. **True or False:** It is possible to insert an AutoCAD field in an attribute value.
9. **True or False:** The **-ATTEDIT** command allows you to update multiple attributes with the same value at one time.
10. **True or False:** A table created using the **Data Extraction** wizard can be set to update automatically if a referenced attribute value changes.

Chapter Projects

G Project 16-1: *Classroom Plan, continued from Chapter 15* [BASIC]

1. Open drawing ***P15-1*** from Chapter 15.
2. Create separate blocks for each of the items shown in Figure 16-75 using the insertion points indicated by the "X" symbol.
3. Create blocks for the left- and right-hand workstations as shown in Figure 16-75 using the insertion points shown. Use the blocks created in the previous step as components of the workstation blocks.
4. Replace the original workstations with the new workstation blocks.
5. Save your drawing as ***P16-1***.

Figure 16-75

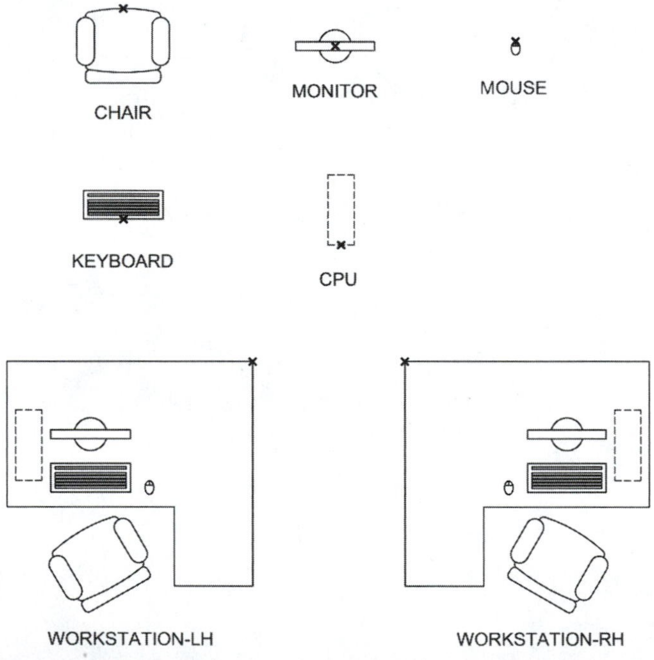

M Project 16-2: *B-Size Mechanical Border, continued from Chapter 15* [INTERMEDIATE]

1. Open template file ***Mechanical B-Size.DWT*** from Chapter 15.
2. Create the title block attribute definitions shown in Figure 16-76. Place the attributes on the **Title** layer. Use the definitions shown in the following table:

Tag	Prompt	Default	Justification	Height
TITLE	Drawing Title	Title	Center	0.2
DESCRIPTION	Description	Description	Center	0.125
PARTNO	Part Number	xxx	Left	0.125
SCALE	Drawing Scale	1:1	Left	0.09375
DWN	Drawn By	AAA	Left	0.09375
SHEET	Sheet Number	1 of 1	Left	0.09375
REV	Revision Number	0	Center	0.125
PROJ_ENG	Project Engineer	AAA	Left	0.09375
PE_DATE	Date	mm/dd/yy	Left	0.09375
DWN_BY	Drawn By	AAA	Left	0.09375
DWN_DATE	Date	mm/dd/yy	Left	0.09375
CHK_BY	Checked By	AAA	Left	0.09375
CHK_DATE	Date	mm/dd/yy	Left	0.09375
MFG_ENG	Manufacturing Engineer	AAA	Left	0.09375
ME_DATE	Date	mm/dd/yy	Left	0.09375

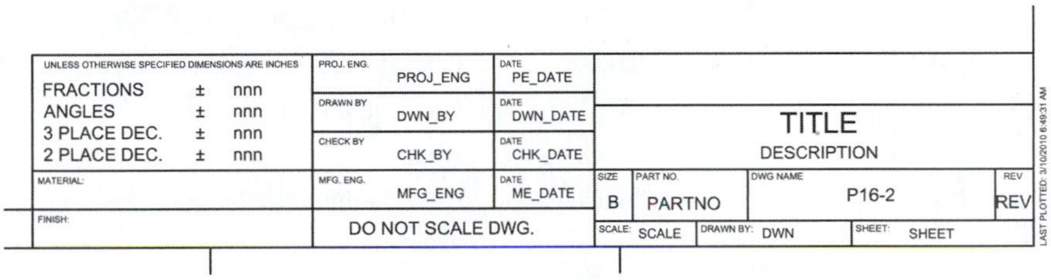

Title Attributes Mechanical B-size

Figure 16-76

3. Use the **WBLOCK** command to create a block/drawing named ***Title Attributes Mechanical B-Size.DWG*** by selecting the attributes defined above and shown in Figure 16-76 using the following settings:
   a. Set the **Base point** to **0,0,0**.
   b. Set the **Objects** option to the **Delete from drawing** setting so the attributes are deleted.
   c. Set **Insert units** to **Unitless**.
4. Use the **WBLOCK** command to create a block/drawing named ***Mechanical B-Size.DWG*** by selecting all the remaining title border line work and static text that never changes using the following settings:
   a. Set the **Base point** to **0,0,0**.
   b. Set the **Objects** option to the **Delete from drawing** setting so the attributes are deleted.
   c. Set **Insert units** to **Unitless**.
5. Close the drawing template. **Do not** save changes to the drawing template.

A Project 16-3: *Architectural D-Size Border, continued from Chapter 15* [ADVANCED]

1. Open template file ***Architectural D-Size.DWT*** from Chapter 15.
2. Create a layer named **A-ANNO-TTLB-ATTS** with default properties. Set its color to **red** and make it the current layer.
3. Replace all the updateable title block text with the attribute definitions shown in Figure 16-77 and defined in the following table:

Tag	Prompt	Default
DATE	Enter the date:	MM/DD/YY
SCALE	Enter the scale:	1/4" = 1'-0:
DRNBY	Enter drawn by initials:	AAA
CHKBY	Enter checked by initials:	AAA
PROJECT	Enter project number:	1234
SHTNO	Enter the sheet number:	1
TOTAL	Enter the total number of sheets:	100
TITLE1	Enter the first title line:	TITLE
TITLE2	Enter the second title line:	INTRODUCTION TO AUTOCAD
TITLE3	Enter the third title line:	PRENTICE HALL

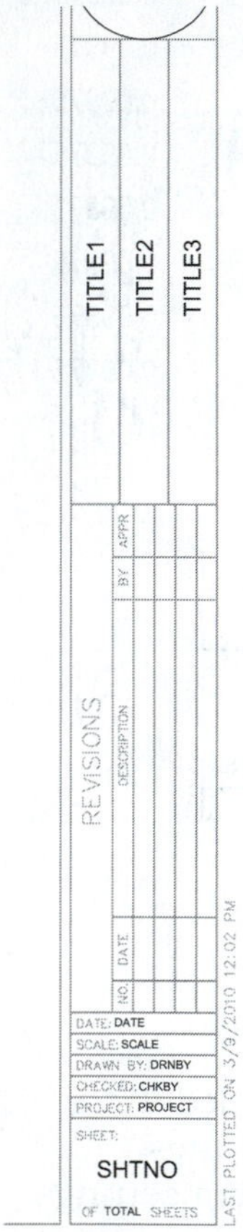

Figure 16-77

4. Use the **WBLOCK** command to create a block/drawing named ***Title Attributes Architectural D-Size.DWG*** by selecting the attributes defined above and shown in Figure 16-77 using the following settings:
   a. Set the **Base point** to **0,0,0**.
   b. Set the **Objects** option to the **Delete from drawing** setting so the attributes are deleted.
   c. Set **Insert units** to **Unitless**.
5. Use the **WBLOCK** command to create a block/drawing named ***Architectural D-Size.DWG*** by selecting all the remaining title border line work and static text that never changes using the following settings.
   a. Set the **Base point** to **0,0,0**.
   b. Set the **Objects** option to the **Delete from drawing** setting so the objects are deleted.
   c. Set **Insert units** to **Unitless**.

   Note: **Do not** include the graphic scale in the upper right-hand corner as part of title block definition!
6. Close the drawing template. **Do not** save changes to the drawing template.

M Project 16-4: *Socket Head Cap Screws—English Units, continued from Chapter 12* [INTERMEDIATE]

1. Open drawing ***P12-2*** from Chapter 12.
2. Create blocks from the fasteners created for Chapter 12 using the following settings:
   a. Name the block as indicated in the table shown in Figure 16-78. Do not include any text in the block definition.
   b. Specify the base point shown with "X" in Figure 16-78.
   c. Select the **Convert to block** option so the block is converted in place.
   d. Select the **Allow exploding** option.

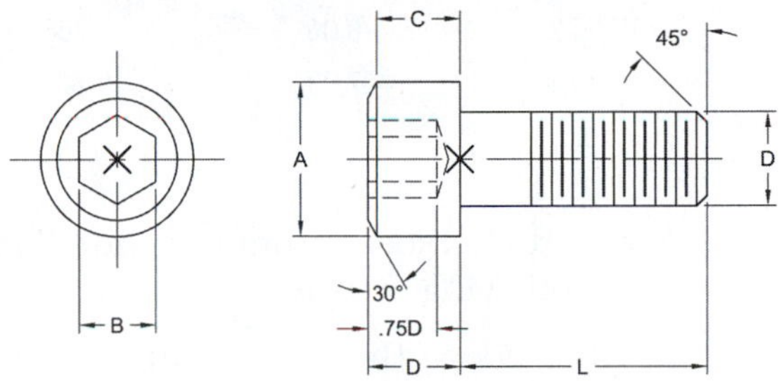

SOCKET HEAD CAP SCREW BLOCK TABLE						
BLOCK NAMES	NOMINAL SIZE (D)	THREAD/IN	A	B	C	L
M4_PLAN & M4_ELEV	4 (.112)	40	.183	.09375	.103	1.00
M5_PLAN & M5_ELEV	5 (.125)	40	.205	.09375	.113	1.00
M6_PLAN & M6_ELEV	6 (.138)	32	.226	.109375	.125	1.25
M8_PLAN & M8_ELEV	8 (.164)	32	.270	.140625	.150	1.25
M10_PLAN & M10_ELEV	10 (.190)	24	.312	.15625	.171	1.50

Figure 16-78

3. Save the drawing as **Socket Head Cap Screws** but leave the drawing open.
4. Start a new drawing using the **acad.dwt** template.
5. Start **DesignCenter** and select the **Open Drawings** tab.
6. Select the plus symbol (+) next to **Socket Head Cap Screws.dwg** to expand the tree.
7. Select the **Blocks** icon so that the fastener blocks you created in step 2 are displayed in the content area on the right.
8. Practice dragging and dropping fastener symbols into your drawing using both the left and right mouse buttons.
9. Double-click on a block to display the **Insert** dialog box.

A Project 16-5: *Structural Steel Symbol Library* [ADVANCED]

1. Start a new drawing using the **acad.dwt** template.
2. Draw eight wide flange shapes using the designation and dimensions in the following steel table using the wide flange profile shown in Figure 16-79.

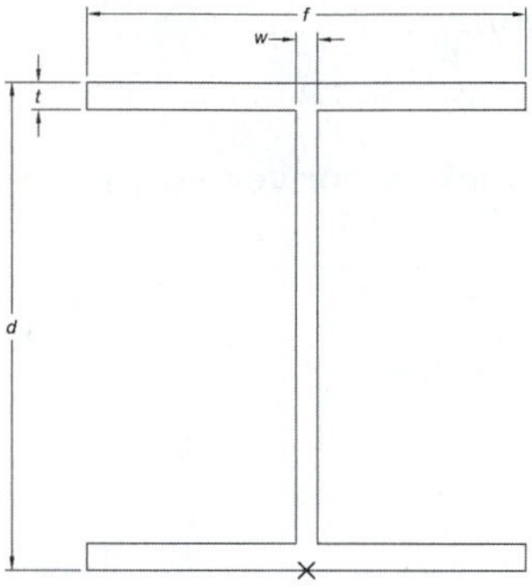

Figure 16-79

Designation	Depth—*d*	Web Thickness—*w*	Flange Width—*f*	Flange Thickness—*t*
W8x67	9.00	0.570	8.280	0.935
W8x58	8.75	0.510	8.220	0.810
W8x48	8.50	0.400	8.110	0.685
W8x40	8.25	0.360	8.070	0.560
W8x35	8.12	0.310	8.020	0.495
W8x31	8.00	0.285	7.995	0.435
W8x28	8.06	0.285	6.535	0.465
W8x24	7.93	0.245	6.495	0.400

3. Create blocks from the wide flange shapes drawn in step 2 using the following settings:
   a. Name the block using its corresponding steel designation (i.e., **W8x67**). **Do not** include text or dimensions in the block definition.
   b. Specify the base point shown with "X" in Figure 16-79.
   c. Select the **Convert to block** option so the block is converted in place.
   d. Select the **Allow exploding** option.
4. Save the drawing as **Structural Steel Symbols** but leave the drawing open.
5. Start a new drawing using the **acad.dwt** template.
6. Start **DesignCenter** and select the **Open Drawings** tab.
7. Select the plus symbol (+) next to **Structural Steel Symbols.dwg** to expand the tree.
8. Select the **Blocks** icon so that the structural steel blocks you created in step 3 are displayed in the content area on the right.
9. Practice dragging and dropping structural steel symbols into your drawing using both the left and right mouse buttons.
10. Double-click on a block to display the **Insert** dialog box.

chapter seventeen

Working with External References

CHAPTER OBJECTIVES

- Reference an external drawing
- Use *attachment* versus *overlay* attachment types
- Control the path stored with an xref
- Load and unload xrefs
- Bind an xref
- Edit xrefs
- Attach raster images
- Control the brightness and contrast of a raster image
- Use DWF underlays
- Use DGN underlays
- Use PDF underlays
- Create a transmittal set of drawings

Introduction

Rapidly produced, high-quality drawings are the objective of any drafter or designer. When changes are made to a design, drawings must be updated to reflect the changes. Opening and editing each drawing affected by a change can be a time-consuming process. AutoCAD can help with this process by allowing changes in one drawing to be automatically reflected in other files. This is done through the use of externally referenced drawings, called ***xrefs***.

xref: A drawing that is referenced by another drawing. The drawing references are updated when the source drawing is modified.

When you create an xref, you are placing a reference to another drawing into your drawing. When changes are made to the referenced drawing, your drawing is updated to reflect the changes.

For example, consider the design of a building where multiple people are working on various aspects of the building at once. People working on the HVAC, piping, and electrical systems need to see where the walls, doors, and windows are located. In this situation, the HVAC, piping, and electrical designers could place an xref of the floor plan into their drawings.

That way, when changes are made to the floor plan, the xref will update to show those changes, and they can adjust their design as needed.

AutoCAD also allows you to create similar references to raster images. Raster images can enhance your drawing by providing additional visual information to your drawing. Civil or architectural drawings can use an image as a background to locate placement points or structural positions. Satellite or aerial views can be used to trace or locate utilities or roadways. Raster images can also be used to enhance the appearance of your company name or logo. Images are similar to xrefs in that AutoCAD creates a reference to the raster image file. If and when the raster image updates, the changes are automatically reflected in your drawing.

In many design environments, design data can come from many different sources and in different formats. Often, vector drawing data may be provided in a format that you only wish to view, but not modify. To accommodate this, AutoCAD provides a way to display and view this type of CAD information, called ***underlays***. An underlay is similar to both xref drawings and raster images.

underlay: A CAD file that is not directly modifiable by AutoCAD but is still displayed within a drawing and updated when the source data are changed.

AutoCAD allows you to display DWF (Design Web Format), DGN (MicroStation Design), and PDF (Adobe Portable Document Format) files as underlays. The DWF file format is a compressed vector-based drawing file format developed by Autodesk that allows you to share your drawings with other individuals who do not have AutoCAD and/or who should not have access to sensitive, proprietary design information.

DWF files cannot be modified; they can only be viewed and marked up. Autodesk provides free downloadable software, called Design Review, on its website that allows you to view, mark up, and print DWF files. Another advantage of DWF files is that DWF file sizes are significantly smaller than the original drawing files (DWG) so that they take up less room and can be transferred faster electronically via email or the Internet.

DGN files are vector-based drawing files created by MicroStation, a CAD package similar to AutoCAD. AutoCAD currently supports DGN files created by version 8 (V8) of MicroStation. DGN files cannot be modified by AutoCAD directly; however, AutoCAD can convert DGN files to the DWG file format. AutoCAD can also export drawing data to the DGN file format. See Chapter 18 for more on importing and exporting drawing data.

PDF files, which are also a vector-based format, are the industry standard for sharing electronic information because they can be easily viewed and printed using the free Adobe Reader software (version 7 or later) that is installed on most computers. Using PDF files, you can share drawings with practically anyone. You can download the Adobe Reader software at www.Adobe.com if you do not have it installed. Although it is not possible to convert a PDF file into the AutoCAD DWG format, you can create PDF files from your AutoCAD drawings. See Chapter 15 for more information about plotting and the procedure for creating PDF files.

In this chapter, we'll examine xrefs, images, and underlays, the different ways they can be embedded in a drawing, how they are updated, and how to manage and keep track of their relationships.

The Reference Panel

Located on the **Insert** tab of the ribbon, the **Reference** panel shown in Figure 17-1 provides most of the tools needed to work with the different types of reference files described above. The **Attach** tool allows you to create a reference to any of the different file types using one standard file selection dialog box. The **Clip** tool helps you reduce visual clutter and increase drawing performance by allowing you to "clip," or cut out, portions of a reference file that do not need to be viewed in your drawing. The **Adjust** tool allows you to adjust the fade, contrast, and monochrome settings of referenced images and underlays. Other tools allow you to control reference layer settings, whether a frame or border is displayed around the edges of a reference, and turn on/off the ability to snap to reference features using AutoCAD's object snap feature. All these tools and more are covered in detail in the following sections.

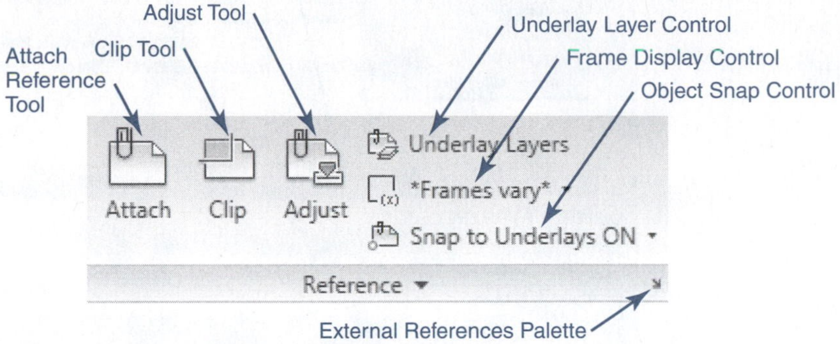

Figure 17-1
The **Reference** panel

> **NOTE**
>
> By default, xrefs appear lighter than nonreferenced drawing information so that you can distinguish information that is part of your drawing and can be modified from information that is part of a reference file and cannot be modified unless you open the xref or use one of the xref editing tools explained later.

> **TIP**
>
> The xref fade level can be adjusted using the **Xref fading** slider control that can be displayed by clicking on the down arrow on the bottom of the **Reference** panel to display the expanded panel. It is set to 70% by default.

External References Palette

EXTERNAL REFERENCES	
Ribbon & Panel:	Insert | Reference
Reference Toolbar:	
Menu:	Insert | External Reference
Command Line:	XREF
Command Alias:	XR

Xrefs, raster images, and underlay files are all managed using the **External References** palette shown in Figure 17-2. The **External References** palette can be displayed by selecting the angled down arrow on the right side of the **Reference** panel shown in Figure 17-1.

The toolbar on the top of the **External References** palette allows you to create new file references and refresh the status of existing file references. The button on the left of the toolbar displays a drop-down menu with the following reference attachment options:

- **Attach DWG...** References another drawing file (DWG) using the **XATTACH** command
- **Attach Image...** References a raster image file (BMP, JPG, GIF, etc.) using the **IMAGEATTACH** command
- **Attach DWF...** References a Design Web Format file (DWF) using the **DWFATTACH** command
- **Attach DGN...** References a DGN file using the **DGNATTACH** command
- **Attach PDF...** References a PDF file using the **PDFATTACH** command
- **Attach Point Cloud...** References a point cloud file using the **POINTCLOUDATTACH** command

NEW to AutoCAD 2013

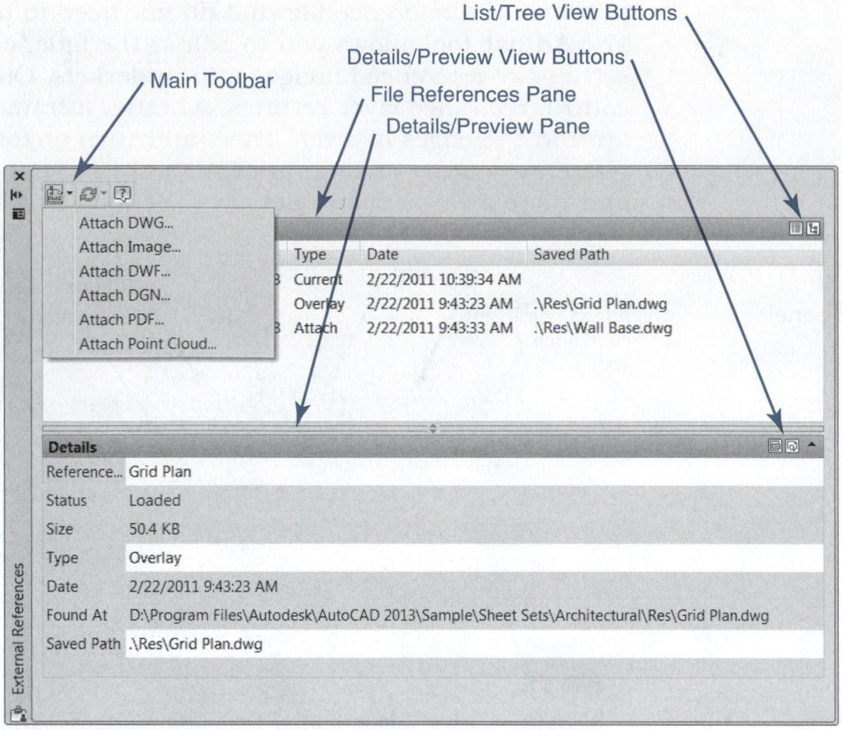

Figure 17-2

The **External References** palette

Whichever of these attachment options is selected becomes the default button displayed on the toolbar.

The **Refresh** button in the middle updates the status of reference files so that they are current, and the question mark (**?**) button displays the AutoCAD Help topic for External References.

The **File References** pane lists the current drawing, referred to as the *master drawing*, and any referenced drawings, raster images, or underlays along with their current status, size, type, and the date/time they were last updated. Files can be displayed in the default **List View** mode (F3) or in **Tree View** mode (F4) using the buttons at the top right of the **File References** pane or their corresponding function key. The **Tree View** mode makes it possible to view any nested references and how they are related.

> **TIP**
>
> In the **List View** mode, you can select two or more files using the standard Windows **<Shift>** and **<Ctrl>** key methods.

Right-click shortcut menus provide most of the options for working with the files in the **File References** pane. If you right-click when no files are selected, a shortcut menu with the following options is displayed:

- **Reload All References** Reloads all referenced files
- **Select All** Selects all file references except the current drawing
- **Attach DWG...** References another drawing using the **XATTACH** command

- **Attach Image...** References an image file using the **IMAGEATTACH** command
- **Attach DWF...** References a DWF file using the **DWFATTACH** command
- **Attach DGN...** References a DGN file using the **DGNATTACH** command
- **Attach PDF...** References a PDF file using the **PDFATTACH** command
- **Attach Point Cloud...** References a point cloud file using the **POINTCLOUDATTACH** command

NEW to AutoCAD 2013

- **Tooltip Style** Allows you to set the tooltip style shown when you hover your mouse pointer over a reference name to display either the file name of the reference, a graphical preview in one of three sizes, or a list of details as shown in Figure 17-3
- **Details/Preview Pane** Toggles the **Details/Preview** pane at the bottom of the palette on and off

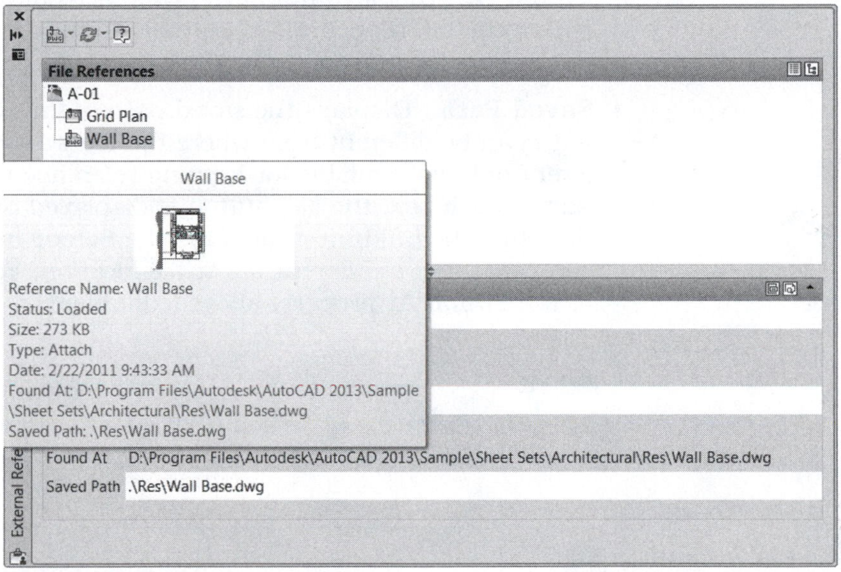

Figure 17-3

Tooltip style set to **Details** mode

Right-clicking when one or more files are selected displays a shortcut menu with some or all of the following options, depending on the file type(s) selected:

- **Open** Opens the selected file reference using the associated application
- **Attach...** Displays the **Attach** dialog box corresponding to the selected reference type
- **Unload** Unloads the selected file reference
- **Reload** Reloads the selected file reference
- **Detach** Detaches the selected file reference
- **Bind...** Displays the **Bind Xrefs** dialog box so that you can make an xref part of the current drawing (available only for referenced DWG files)

The **Details/Preview** pane on the bottom can display either properties for the selected file references or a thumbnail preview if available. Use the buttons on the top right of the **Details/Preview** pane to switch between the two different modes. The default **Details** pane displays the following properties for all reference file types:

- **Reference Name** File reference name in drawing. Displays *Varies* if multiple file references are selected (editable)
- **Status** Displays whether file reference is loaded, unloaded, or not found (read-only)
- **Size** Displays the file size of selected file reference (read-only)
- **Type** Indicates whether a DWG file reference is an attachment or overlay, the image file type or underlay (editable for DWG files/read-only for images, DWF, DGN, and PDF files). You can use this property to quickly switch referenced drawings between the **Attachment** and **Overlay** attachment types after an xref has been attached without having to detach and reattach it again
- **Date** Displays last date the file reference was modified (read-only)

NEW to AutoCAD 2013

- **Found At** Displays full path of the selected file reference. This path is where the referenced file is actually found and might not be the same as the **Saved Path** property below (read-only)

NEW to AutoCAD 2013

- **Saved Path** Displays the saved path of the selected file reference. This path can be different from where the file was found because of the different options available for locating reference files. If you click in the **Saved Path** box, the [...] button is displayed on the right side of the box. Selecting the [...] button displays the **Select new path** dialog box where you can select a different file or file location. Valid path changes are stored to the **Found At** property above (editable)

NOTE

The majority of reference file properties are read-only and cannot be edited unless otherwise noted.

TIP

It is possible to specify a different reference file using the [...] button on the right. When you do this, AutoCAD simply references the specified file instead of the file specified in the **Reference Name**. This allows you to quickly swap one reference file for another.

If you select a referenced raster image file, additional image-specific properties are displayed such as the image size and resolution. All the additional image properties are read-only and cannot be edited.

The specifics of using the **External References** palette to reference and manage file types are detailed in the following sections beginning with the first, and arguably the most popular, of the reference file types, external drawing (DWG) references. These are commonly referred to in the industry as *xrefs*.

Blocks Versus Xrefs

Xrefs are similar to blocks but with a few notable exceptions.

Blocks

When you insert a block, you are creating a reference to a block definition that exists entirely inside the drawing file. When you insert an external drawing file with the **INSERT** command, AutoCAD converts the external drawing file into an internal block definition. Changes to the original drawing file are not reflected in the drawings containing the inserted blocks.

Xrefs

When you attach an xref, you are directly referencing an external drawing file. Whenever changes are made to the external drawing file, all the references to that drawing are updated as well. Because xrefs point to external drawings, the location of the drawing file (the file path) is important.

Nested Xrefs

Any drawing can be attached as an xref to another xref, a concept known as nesting. To view nested xrefs, select the **Tree View** button on the **File References** pane of the **External References** palette.

nested xref: An xref within an xref. This occurs when the drawing you are referencing contains a reference to another drawing.

It is possible to place a drawing that contains an xref as an xref. For example, say you have a drawing called *MASTER* that contains a reference to drawing A, and drawing A contains a reference to drawing B (see Figure 17-4). In this example, drawing B is referred to as a ***nested xref***.

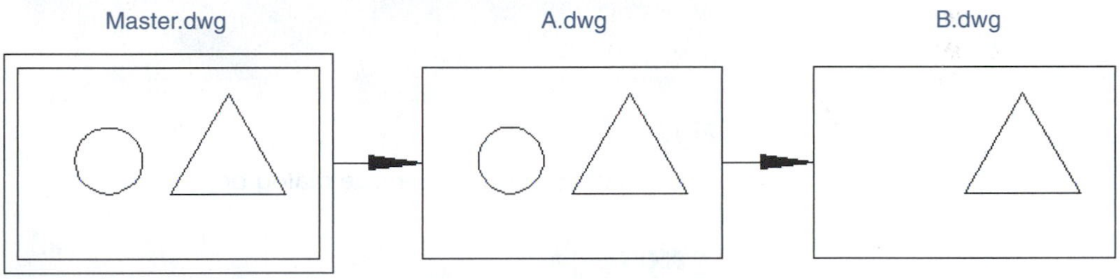

Figure 17-4
Nested xrefs

Xref nesting can lead to some interesting or unexpected results. In the preceding example, when you reference drawing A, drawing B comes along as a nested xref. However, drawing B could also contain an xref (drawing C), and drawing C might also contain an xref, and the nesting could go on and on. You can also create circular xrefs where drawings reference one another. For example, drawing A could reference drawing B, and drawing B could reference drawing A.

If AutoCAD detects circular xrefs, it will display a warning that circular references are detected (see Figure 17-5) and ask whether you want to continue. If you choose **Yes**, AutoCAD will break the circular reference and proceed with loading the xref.

Figure 17-5
Circular xrefs warning

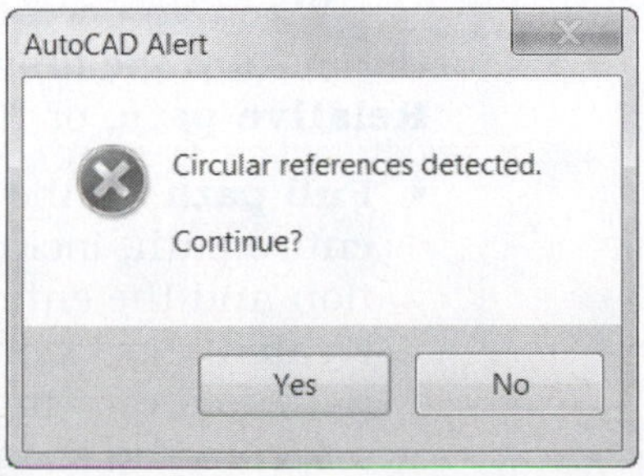

DWG REFERENCE	
Ribbon & Panel:	Insert | Reference 
Reference Toolbar:	
Menu:	Insert | DWG Reference…
Command Line:	XATTACH
Command Alias:	XA

Attaching an Xref

When you attach an xref, you create a link to an external drawing file in your drawing. You can attach an xref either by selecting **Attach DWG…** from the drop-down or right-click menu in the **External References** palette or via the **Attach** tool on the **Reference** panel. Once you've selected a drawing, and select **OPEN**, AutoCAD displays the **Attach External Reference** dialog box (shown in Figure 17-6).

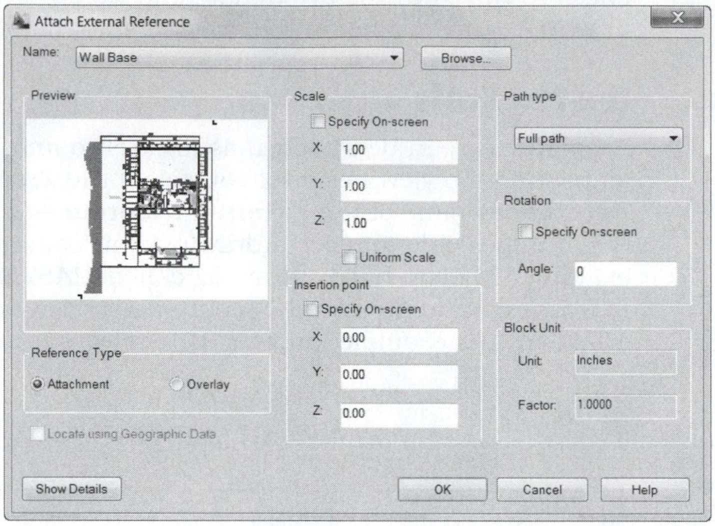

Figure 17-6

The **Attach External Reference** dialog box

> **NOTE**
>
> When AutoCAD references a drawing, only model space objects are included. Objects in paper space are ignored.

Attachment Versus Overlay

When you attach an xref, you can tell AutoCAD how you want that xref to behave when referenced in other drawings. The **Attachment** option tells AutoCAD to load this drawing and any nested xrefs. The **Overlay** option tells AutoCAD to ignore any nested xrefs and load only the top-level drawing.

The **Attachment** and **Overlay** options control only how nested xrefs behave when the drawing is referenced in another drawing.

Setting the Path Type

When AutoCAD loads an xref, it must locate the drawing on your computer or network. The file path is the location of the drawing file on your system. It includes the drive letter or server name along with the list of folders and subfolders where the drawing file is located.

When you create an xref, you can tell AutoCAD how you want to store the path to the drawing file. You have the option of saving the **Full path, Relative path**, or **No path:**

- **Full path** If the **Path type** is set to **Full path**, AutoCAD stores the entire path, including the local hard drive name or the network location and the entire list of folders and subfolders where the drawing is located. For example, *C:\Design\Projects\8013\arch* describes the full path to a drawing file. In this example, the xref is located on the local *C:* drive, in the *Design\Projects\8013\arch* folder.

- **Relative path** Using the **Relative path** option, AutoCAD automatically updates the xref path to assume the current path of the master, or host, drawing so that drive letters and network server names are not a factor as long as the subfolder structure stays the same. AutoCAD replaces the period (.) in the relative path with the path to the master drawing file. For example, if the relative path is set to *.\Xrefs*, the referenced drawings can be located at *C:\Design\Projects\8013\Xrefs* on one computer or at the network location *N:\Consultants\AEC Architects\Projects\8013\Xrefs* on another computer. The only requirement is that the master drawing be located in the *8013* folder on both computers so that the subfolder structure is the same.
- **No path** Using **No path**, AutoCAD will store only the xref drawing name and no path information. When AutoCAD opens the drawing, it will look for the xref in the current drawing folder. If it doesn't find the xref there, it will then search the folders defined in the AutoCAD **Support File Search Path**. The **Support File Search Path** is defined in the **Files** tab of the **Options** dialog box. If it still doesn't find the xref, it will display a note at the command line that the xref cannot be found.

> **TIP**
>
> You can also use the **Project Files Search Path** setting on the **Files** tab of the **Options** dialog box to locate xrefs that rely on the **No path** option, create a project, and provide one or more paths to search. You must first set the **PROJECTNAME** system variable to the name of the project you created.

If your drawing files remain at a single location and are never moved or sent to another site, the drawing file paths will remain the same every time you load a drawing file. However, if you send your drawings to others (to a contractor, client, manufacturer, etc.), you need to consider how your drawings will be loaded at these remote sites. Using the **Relative path** or **No path** option will make it easier for others to locate the xref drawings.

Insertion Point, Scale, and Rotation

Once you set the reference type and the path type, the rest of the attachment process is identical to inserting a block. The **Insertion point, Scale**, and **Rotation** options work exactly like those in the **INSERT** command. You can specify these values in the dialog box or by selecting them in the drawing.

Manage Xrefs Icon

When xrefs are attached to a drawing, the **Manage Xrefs** icon is displayed in the system tray in the lower-right corner (see Figure 17-7). Clicking on the icon displays the **External References** palette, providing a quick way to check xrefs and their status in the current drawing. If an attached xref changes, a notification balloon is also displayed in the system tray, indicating that the xref needs to be reloaded with a link to reload it (see Figure 17-13).

Figure 17-7
The **Manage Xrefs** icon

EXERCISE 17-1 **Attaching an Xref**

To access student data files, go to **www.pearsondesigncentral.com.**

1. Start a new drawing using the ***Architectural D-size.DWT*** drawing template located in the student data files.
2. Switch to the **Model** tab.

3. Create a layer named **References** and assign a **Continuous** linetype and color **7.** Set this layer **Current.**

4. Select the **Insert** tab to display the **Reference** panel, and select the **External References** button to display the **External References** palette.

5. Select **Attach DWG...** from the **External References** palette toolbar. Select the ***Grid Plan.dwg*** located in AutoCAD's ***\Sample\Sheet Sets\Architectural\Res*** folder.

6. Set the **Reference Type** to **Attachment.** Set the **Insertion point** to **0,0**, the **Scale** to **1**, and the **Rotation** to **0**. Choose **OK** to place the xref in your drawing. Do a **Zoom Extents** to see the entire xref.

7. Select **Attach DWG...** from the **External References** palette toolbar again. Select the ***Wall Base.dwg*** located in the ***\Sample\Sheet Sets\Architectural\Res*** folder.

8. Set the **Reference Type** to **Attachment**. Set the **Insertion point** to **0,0**, the **Scale** to **1**, and the **Rotation** to **0**. Choose **OK** to place the xref in your drawing. Do another **Zoom Extents** to see the entire xref.

9. Save the drawing as ***CH17_EXERCISE1***. Your drawing should resemble Figure 17-8.

Figure 17-8

The attached xrefs

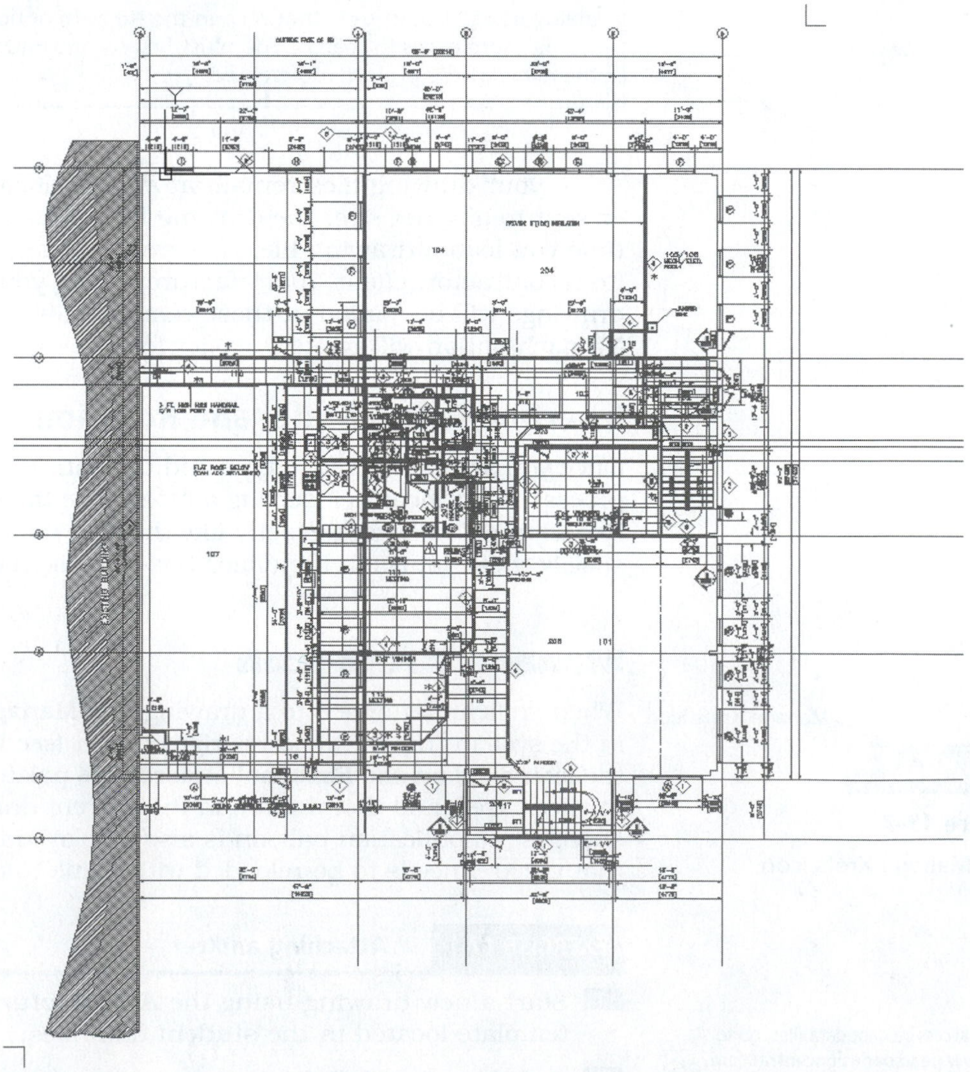

Layers and Xrefs

When you attach an xref to a drawing, all the drawing's layers come with it. However, AutoCAD distinguishes between layers in the current drawing and layers in an xref by appending the file name along with the pipe (|) character to the layer name. For example, if you reference a drawing called ***Grid***, which contains a layer called **S-Grid,** AutoCAD will display the layer name as **Grid|S-Grid** in the **Layer Properties Manager** palette.

If your drawing contains multiple references to the same drawing file, AutoCAD will assign a number to each reference and append it along with the file name. For example, if you have two references to the drawing ***Grid*** in your drawing, AutoCAD will display the layers **Grid|1_S-Grid** and **Grid|2_S-Grid** in the **Layer Properties Manager** palette. The **Layer Properties Manager** palette also gives you filters for displaying the layers for any given xref.

Changing Xref Layers

The initial state of the xref layers will be the state in which the source drawing was saved. A layer that was frozen in a drawing will initially appear frozen when that drawing is referenced. You can make changes to xref layers, but there are some limitations on what you can do. You cannot set an xref layer as the current layer, and you cannot rename xref layers. However, you can change the color, linetype, lineweight, and visibility of xref layers. This allows you to change how xref layers are displayed and plotted within your drawing.

When you make changes to xref layer settings, AutoCAD will retain any changes to the layer settings the next time the drawing is loaded.

> **TIP**
>
> You can control the retention of xref layer settings with the **VISRETAIN** system variable. Setting **VISRETAIN** to **1** tells AutoCAD to retain any changes made to xref layers. Setting **VISRETAIN** to **0** tells AutoCAD to ignore changes made to xref layers and use the setting stored in the reference drawing each time the reference is loaded. This variable can also be set with the **Retain changes to Xref layers** box in the **Open and Save** tab of the **Options** dialog box.

EXERCISE 17-2 Xref Layers

1. Continue from Exercise 17-1.
2. Start the **LAYER** command. AutoCAD displays the **Layer Properties Manager** palette.
3. Expand the **Xref** tree in the filters on the left side of the palette. You'll see the loaded xrefs listed in the tree. Choose the **Wall Base** xref to show only the layers in that xref.
4. Freeze all the layers that start with **Wall Base|1_**. Thaw all the **Wall Base|2_** layers. Freeze all the **Wall Base|2_Arch_Reflected_ Ceiling_ Plan_** layers. This isolates the second-floor layers for this building. Choose **OK** to close the **Layer Properties Manager** palette.
5. Save the drawing. Your drawing should resemble Figure 17-9.

Figure 17-9

The modified xref layers

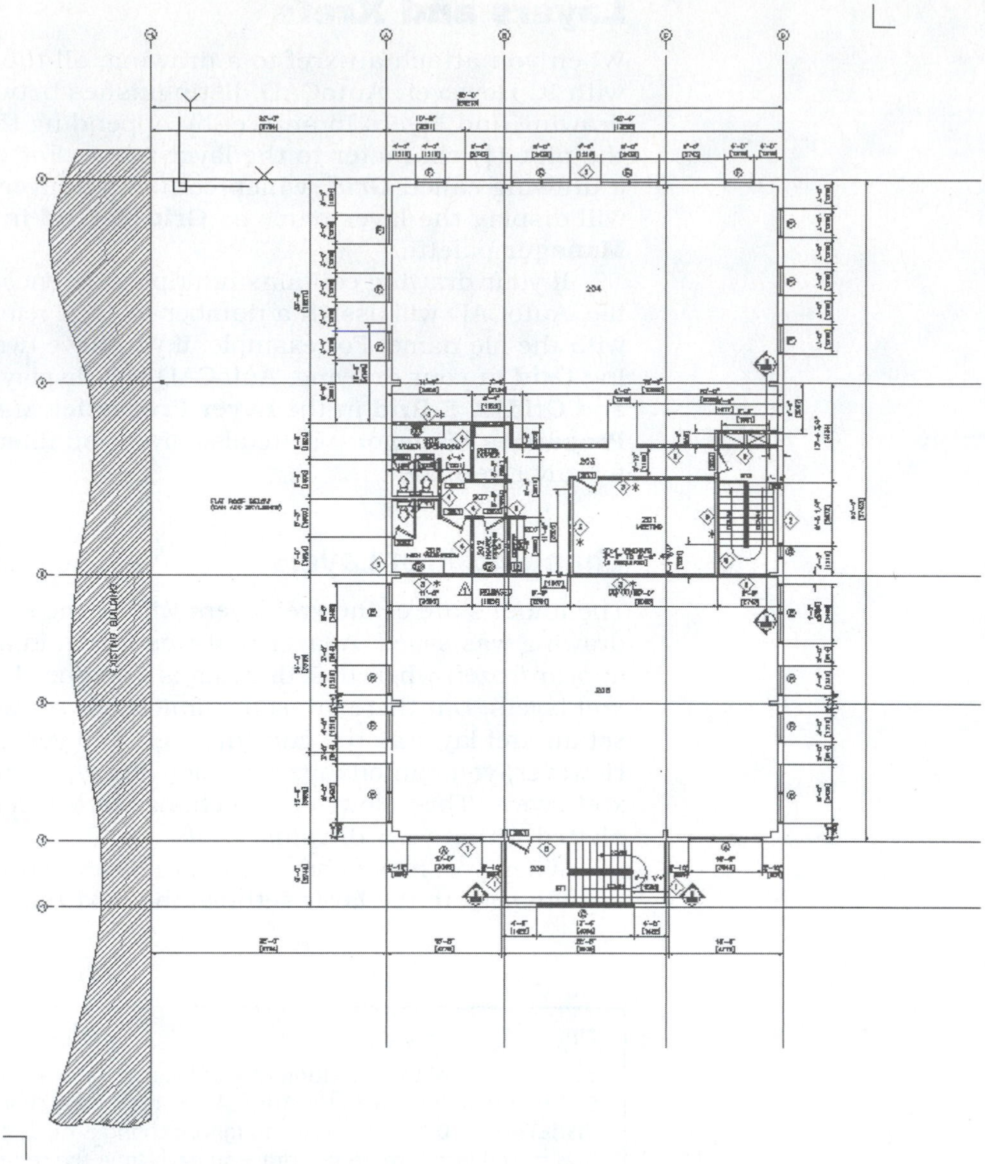

Managing Xrefs

The **External References** palette discussed earlier is the main xref management tool (see Figure 17-10).

The default list view shows each reference along with its status (loaded or unloaded), file size, attachment type (attach or overlay), file date, and the full path to where the reference is located. The list can be sorted by any column type by selecting the column header at the top of the list as shown in Figure 17-10.

The tree view shows the hierarchy of the loaded xrefs. This allows you to see nested xrefs and their relationship with other xrefs in the drawing as shown in Figure 17-11.

The Right-Click Menu

As mentioned earlier, most of the xref options and settings are provided via a shortcut menu that is displayed when you right-click on an xref in the **File References** pane as shown in Figure 17-12.

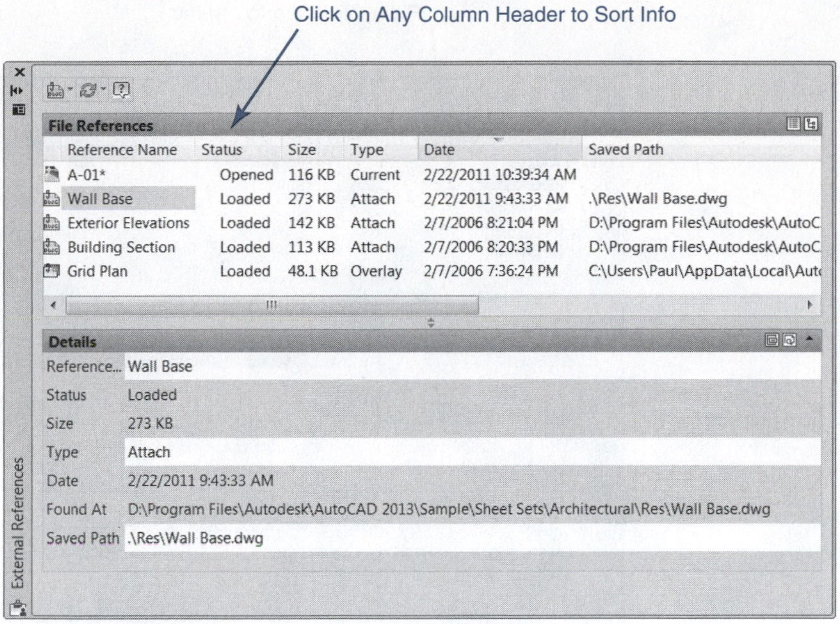

Figure 17-10

The **External References** palette—**List View** mode

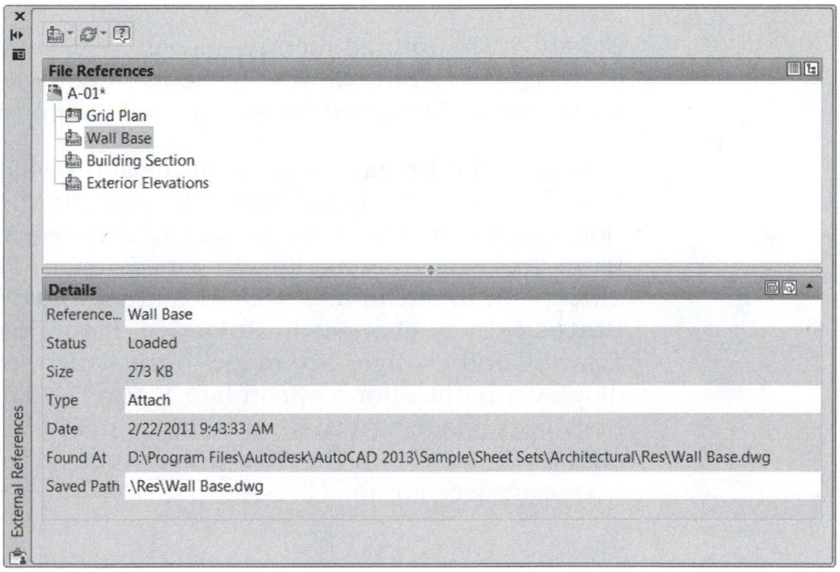

Figure 17-11

The **External References** palette—**Tree View** mode

Open. The **Open** menu item will open the selected referenced drawing(s) in a new drawing window. When you select **Open**, AutoCAD changes the status of the drawing(s) to **Opened** in the **External References** palette. This is the same as choosing **Open** from the **File** pull-down menu and opening the referenced file directly. The advantage of using **Open** from the **File References** pane is that AutoCAD will locate the drawing and open it automatically. It also allows you to open multiple drawings at the same time.

Attach.... The **Attach...** menu item will display the corresponding attach-type dialog box for the currently selected file type so you can attach another reference file of the same type. This option is unavailable when more than one file is selected.

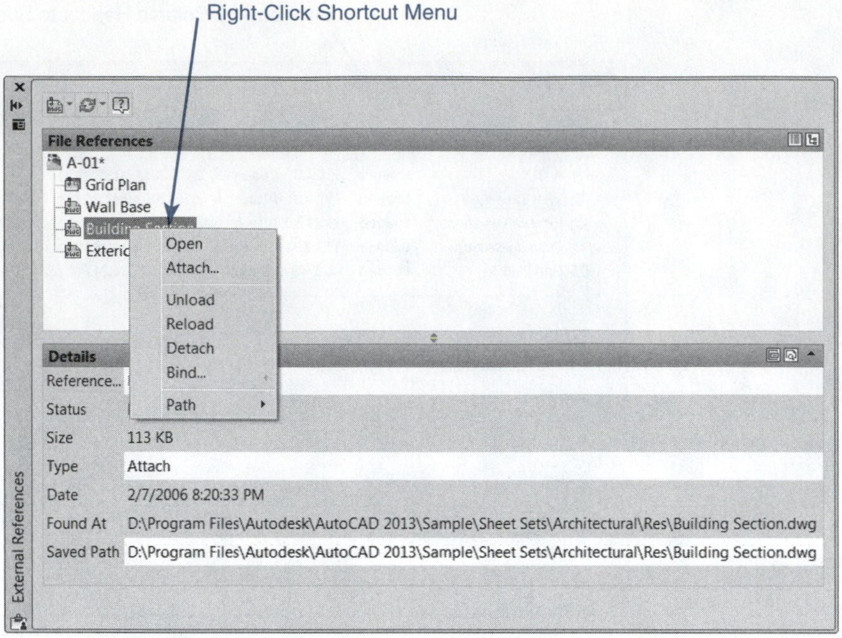

Figure 17-12

The **External References** palette—right-click menu

Unload. The **Unload** menu item will remove the selected xref(s) from the drawing screen but will retain the reference within the drawing. The xref layers are still retained but the drawing is not displayed.

Reload. The **Reload** menu item reloads xref(s) in the current drawing. When you reload an xref, AutoCAD reopens the drawing from the location specified in the path. Reloading is necessary when changes are made to an xref while the current drawing is open. The **Reload** menu item also allows you to reload any unloaded xrefs. Once you reload an xref, the **Status** column changes to **Reloaded**. If you have an xref loaded into your drawing and changes are made to the source of the xref, AutoCAD will display a notification balloon (see Figure 17-13) telling you that changes have been made and that reloading is necessary. AutoCAD will also change the status in the **File References** pane to note that reloading is necessary (see Figure 17-14).

Figure 17-13

The xref notification balloon

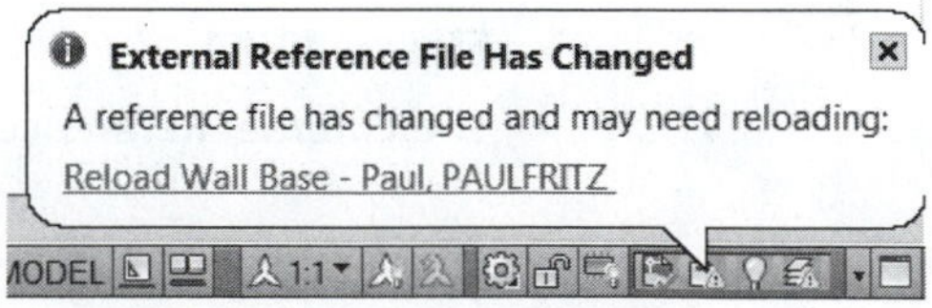

Detach. The **Detach** menu item will remove attached xref(s). This completely removes the xref and any nested xrefs from your drawing. All xref layer information is also removed from your drawing.

Bind.... The **Bind...** menu item converts an externally referenced drawing to an AutoCAD block in the master drawing. When you bind an xref, the xref becomes a permanent part of the current drawing, and any link to the referenced file is broken. The file is removed from the **File References** pane, and changes made to the original referenced drawing will not be updated.

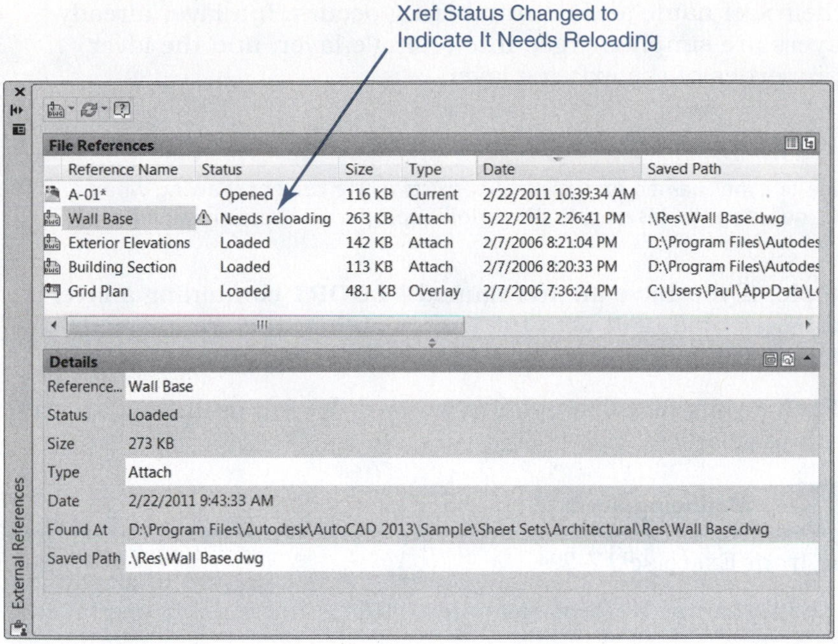

Figure 17-14

The xref status

Figure 17-15

The **Bind Xrefs** dialog box

When you bind an xref, you have some options for how to deal with layer names. When you choose the **Bind...** menu item, AutoCAD displays the **Bind Xrefs** dialog box (see Figure 17-15), which allows you to control how the xrefs are bound.

The Bind Option. The **Bind** option binds the selected xref to the current drawing. Xref layers are converted from the format *xref|layer* to the format *xref%n%*layer, where the number *n* is assigned automatically. This allows xref-dependent layers to retain their unique identity.

For example, if you have an xref named **FLOOR1** containing a layer named **WALL**, this layer would appear as **FLOOR1|WALL** while the drawing is an xref. Once you bind the xref using the **Bind** option, the layer name is converted to **FLOOR1$0$WALL**. If the layer **FLOOR1$0$WALL** already existed, the layer **FLOOR1|WALL** would be converted to **FLOOR1$1$WALL.**

NOTE

Other named objects (i.e., dimension styles, block definitions, text styles, etc.) are renamed in a similar fashion. For example, if the ***FLOOR1*** drawing contained a block named **DOOR**, the block definition would be renamed **FLOOR1$0$DOOR.**

TIP

The **BINDTYPE** system variable controls the default bind type used. When **BINDTYPE** is set to **0** (the default), object definitions are renamed using the numbering convention. For example, **FLOOR1|WALL** is converted to **FLOOR1$0$WALL**. When **BINDTYPE** is set to **1**, object definitions are not renamed, and the xref name is ignored. For example, **FLOOR1|WALL** is converted to **WALL**.

The Insert Option. The **Insert** option binds the xref to the current drawing in a way similar to detaching and inserting the reference drawing as a regular block. Rather than renaming xref layers, the layers are stripped of their xref name and no numbering occurs. If a layer already exists, the layers are simply merged into a single layer, and the layer retains the properties of the existing layer.

> **NOTE**
>
> If a layer name or other named symbol already exists in the current drawing when a drawing is bound using the **Insert** type, the original properties are maintained.

For example, if you have an xref named **FLOOR1** containing a layer named **WALL**, after binding it with the **Insert** option, the xref-dependent layer **FLOOR1|WALL** becomes layer **WALL**.

NEW to AutoCAD 2013

Path. The **Path** submenu allows you to remove the full path from an xref or set the path to relative.

EXERCISE 17-3 Managing Xrefs

1. Continue from Exercise 17-2.
2. Display the **External References** palette if it is not already displayed.
3. Select the **Grid Plan** reference. In the **Type** property, select **Attach** and change the attachment type to **Overlay**. Repeat this for the **Wall Base** reference.
4. Select the **Wall Base** reference, right-click, and select **Unload** from the shortcut menu. The **Status** column changes to **Unloaded.**
5. The **Wall Base** reference drawing is unloaded and disappears from your drawing.
6. The **Wall Base** drawing is shown as unloaded but is still referenced in the drawing (see Figure 17-16). Select the **Wall Base** drawing and choose **Reload** from the right-click shortcut menu. The status changes to **Loaded.**
7. AutoCAD reloads the reference drawing, and it is displayed in its original location.
8. Save your drawing.

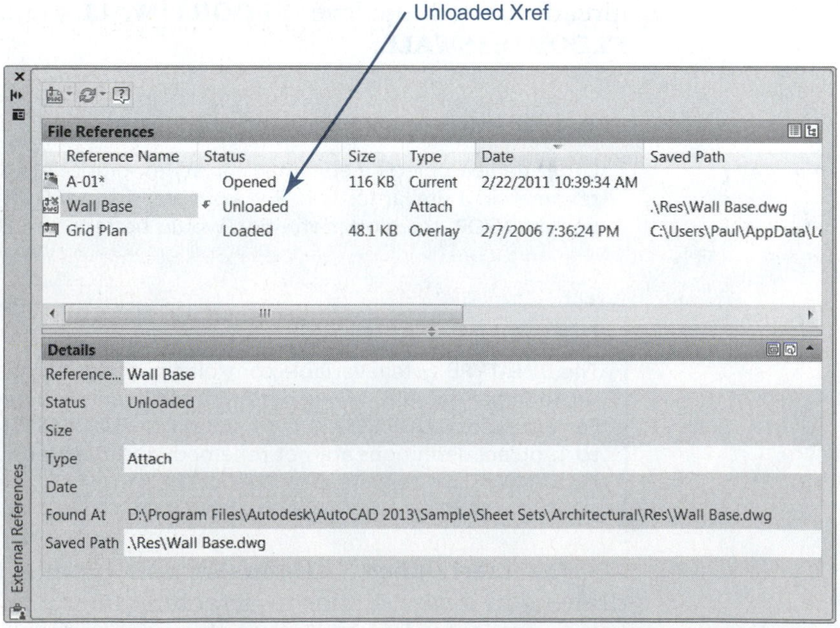

Figure 17-16
The unloaded xref

Editing Xrefs

The easiest way to modify an xref is to select it in the drawing so that the **External Reference** context tab of the ribbon shown in Figure 17-17 is displayed, allowing you to easily access the most useful xref modification tools and controls.

Figure 17-17
The **External Reference** context tab of the ribbon

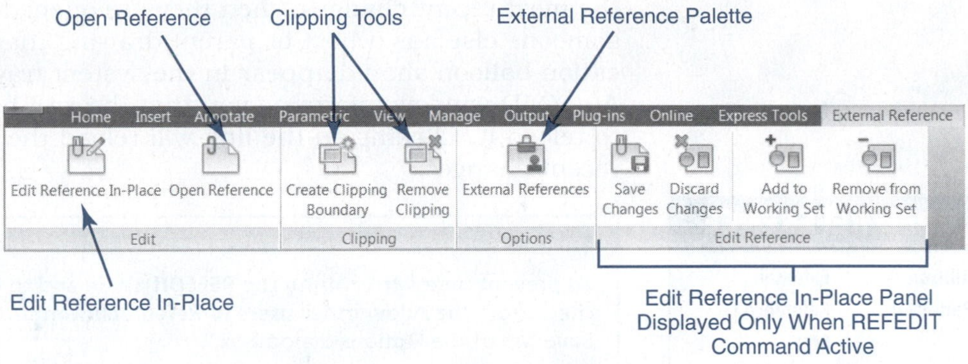

The **External Reference** context tab of the ribbon provides tools to perform the following tasks:

- Edit the xref in-place so that you do not have to open the xref drawing file in a separate window.
- Open the attached xref in a new AutoCAD drawing window so that you can make any changes and updates as you normally would in AutoCAD, and then save the drawing.
- Cut out, or clip, an xref so that only the portion of the xref you need to see is loaded and displayed.

The following sections explore these xref editing tools in detail.

edit reference in-place: Using the **REFEDIT** command to make changes to an externally referenced drawing.

EDIT REFERENCE IN-PLACE	
Ribbon & Panel:	External Reference | Edit  Edit Reference In-Place
Refedit Toolbar:	
Menu:	Xref and Block In-Place Editing | Edit Reference In-Place
Command Line:	REFEDIT
Command Alias:	None

Edit Reference In-Place

It is possible to edit an xref directly within the host drawing. In Chapter 16, you looked at how to use the **REFEDIT** command to modify block definitions. The **REFEDIT** command also allows you to modify an xref from within your current drawing. This is known as ***edit reference in-place***.

FOR MORE DETAILS

See Chapter 16 for more on using the **REFEDIT** command.

Selecting the **Edit Reference In-Place** tool on the **Edit** panel on the **External Reference** context tab of the ribbon displays the **Reference Edit** dialog box and displays the selected reference drawing along with any blocks or nested xrefs contained in the reference drawing. Selecting the **OK** button will put you in edit mode so that the reference drawing is no longer one complex block-type object, and you can modify the individual drawing objects using the regular AutoCAD modify commands.

NOTE

You need to have the proper access privileges to the disk where the reference is stored in order to use the **REFEDIT** command on an xref. If you are referencing a read-only drawing from a CD or network drive, you will not be able to make changes to the xref.

After you have completed modifying the drawing and you save it, all the host or parent drawings that reference the modified drawing will show the most recent changes when they are opened the next time. If you or someone else has a host or parent drawing that is currently open, a notification balloon should appear in the system tray on the bottom right of the AutoCAD window informing you that the xref has been changed with a link to reload it. Clicking on the link will reload the xref and display the most recent changes.

OPEN REFERENCE	
Ribbon & Panel:	External Reference | Edit
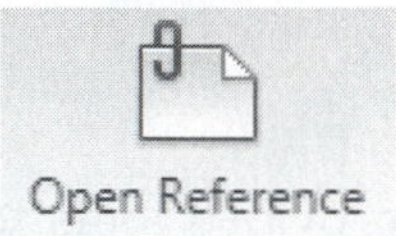	
Toolbar:	None
Menu:	Tools | Xref and Block In-place Editing | Open Reference
Command Line:	XOPEN
Command Alias:	None

TIP

To prevent others from using the **REFEDIT** command to edit your drawing, remove the check from the **Allow other users to Refedit current drawing** option in the **Open and Save** tab of the **Options** dialog box.

Opening Xrefs

Of course, one of the easiest ways to make changes to an xref is to simply open the referenced drawing file with the **OPEN** command. When you make changes to the referenced drawing and save them, AutoCAD will notify you that changes have been made to the referenced drawing and allow you to update the xref by reloading it.

The **Open** option on the right-click menu in the **External References** palette allows you to open referenced drawings directly, bypassing the **Select File** dialog box. As we discussed in the previous section, selecting one or more xrefs in the **External References** palette and choosing **Open** from the right-click menu will cause AutoCAD to open each xref in a separate drawing window.

The **Open Reference** tool on the **External Reference** context tab of the ribbon also allows you to open referenced drawings directly. Selecting the **Open Reference** tool simply opens the selected xref. Like the **REFEDIT** command, saving the xref will ensure that all host drawings that reference the modified file are updated as well.

CLIP XREF	
Ribbon & Panel:	External Reference | Clipping

Reference Toolbar:	
Menu:	Modify | Clip | Xref
Command Line:	XCLIP
Command Alias:	XC

EXERCISE 17-4 **Editing Xrefs**

1. Continue from Exercise 17-3.
2. Display the **External References** palette if it is not already displayed.
3. Select the **Grid Plan** reference and choose **Open** from the right-click shortcut menu. The status changes to **Open**.
4. AutoCAD opens the ***Grid Plan.dwg*** file in a new window.
5. Close the ***Grid Plan*** drawing. **Do not** save any changes.

Clipping an Xref

There may be times when you want to view only a portion of an xref. The **XCLIP** command allows you to "clip out" part of the displayed xref. The drawing or xref is not altered, but the xref is clipped to limit the display to only a portion of the xref. Clipping xrefs also speeds up the performance of a drawing. Information that is outside the clipping boundary is not processed by AutoCAD.

When you start the **XCLIP** command, AutoCAD asks you to select an xref and then presents a number of options. These are described in the following table:

On/Off	Turns clipping on and off for a given xref. Turning clipping off will cause AutoCAD to ignore any clipping boundaries assigned the xref.
Clip Depth	This option is used in 3D xrefs. The **Clip Depth** allows you to set the viewing depth of 3D models.
Delete	Deletes any xclip boundaries associated with an xref.
Generate Polyline	Draws a polyline around the edge of an xclip area. When you choose this option AutoCAD will create a polyline along the outline of a clipped xref. Once the polyline is created it has no association with the xref. It is simply a polyline object in the drawing.
New Boundary	Defines a new clipping area. If the xref has an existing clipping boundary, AutoCAD will ask you whether you want to delete the old boundary. You then have three methods for defining a new clipping area.
Select Polyline	Uses an existing polyline to define a new clipping area. The existing polyline remains after the new clipping area is defined.
Polygonal	Allows you to draw a polygon to define the clip area. The polygon does not remain after the clipping area is defined.
Rectangular	Allows you to draw a box or rectangle to define the clipping area. The rectangle does not remain after the clipping area is defined.
Invert Clip	Inverts the clipping boundary. Clipped objects are shown, and shown objects are hidden.

Xref clipping is similar to cropping an image in other Windows applications. When you clip an xref, you are simply selecting an area of the xref to display.

It is possible to edit the boundary of a clipped xref using grips to resize the area, as well as invert the clipping area. Before editing a clipping boundary it must first be visible, so you can select it. The easiest way to control the visibility of xref clipping boundaries is via the **Reference** panel on the **Insert** tab on the ribbon. Reference clipping boundaries are referred to as *frames*. By default, frames are hidden and do not display. You can turn them on so they are visible in the drawing by clicking on the **Hide frames** option on the **Reference** panel and selecting either the **Display and plot frames** or the **Display but don't plot frames** option from the flyout menu.

NOTE

You can also change the visibility of an xref clipping boundary by changing the **XCLIPFRAME** system variable. Setting the **XCLIPFRAME** variable to **1** makes xref clipping boundaries visible. Setting it to **0** hides xref clipping frames.

EXERCISE 17-5 Clipping Xrefs

1. Continue from Exercise 17-4.
2. Start the **XCLIP** command and select both the ***Grid Base*** and ***Wall Base*** drawings and press **<Enter>**.

3 Select the **New Boundary** option and then choose **Rectangular** to create a rectangular clipping boundary.

4 Pick the endpoints at P1 and P2 as shown in Figure 17-18. AutoCAD clips the xrefs around the rectangular area.

5 Save your drawing.

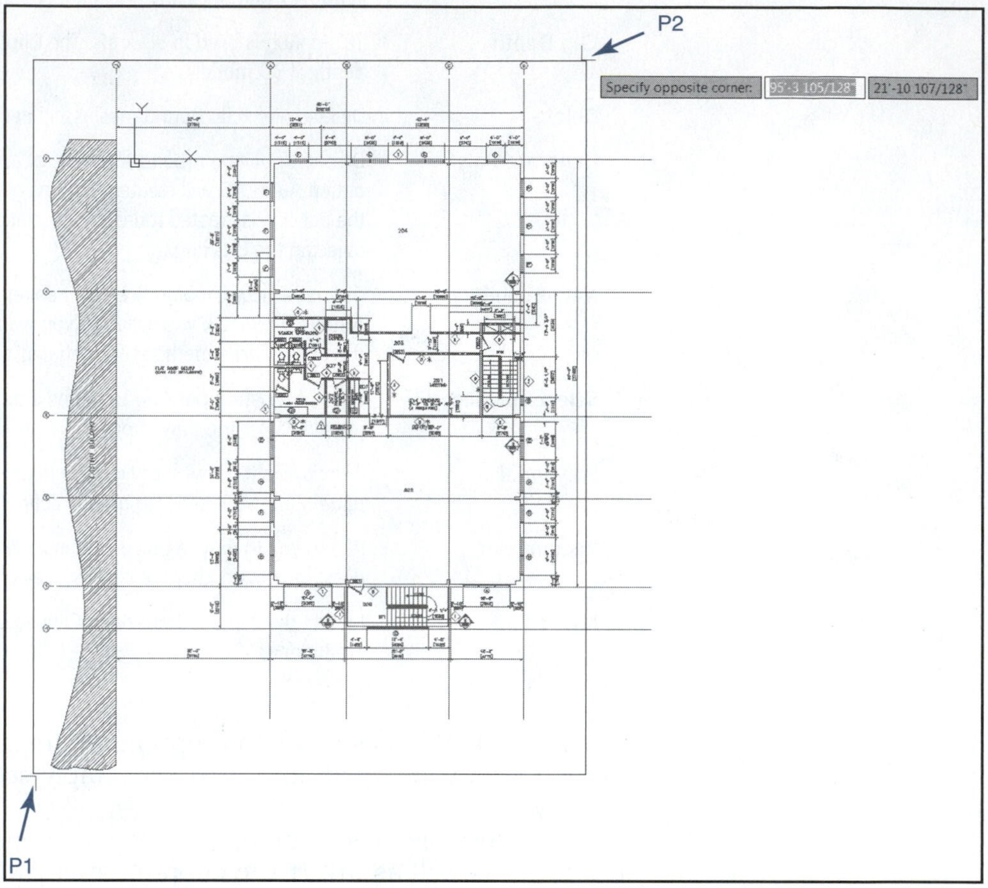

Figure 17-18
Xref clipping area

BIND	
Ribbon & Panel:	None
Reference Toolbar:	
Menu:	Modify | Object | External Reference | Bind...
Command Line:	XBIND
Command Alias:	XB

Binding Parts of an Xref

Using the **Bind...** option within the **External References** palette allows you to bind an entire reference file to your current drawing. This results in the entire drawing being converted to a block and inserted into your drawing. The **XBIND** command allows you to selectively bind individual named objects (layers, blocks, text styles, etc.) to your current drawing.

When you start the **XBIND** command, AutoCAD displays the **Xbind** dialog box (see Figure 17-19). The **Xrefs** area displays all the xrefs in the drawing. Clicking on an xref name will display a list of all the named objects within the xref. To bind an individual object, select the object and choose the **Add->** button to add it to the **Definitions to Bind** list. You can add and remove objects from the list. When you are satisfied with the list of object definitions, choose **OK** to bind those object definitions to your current drawing.

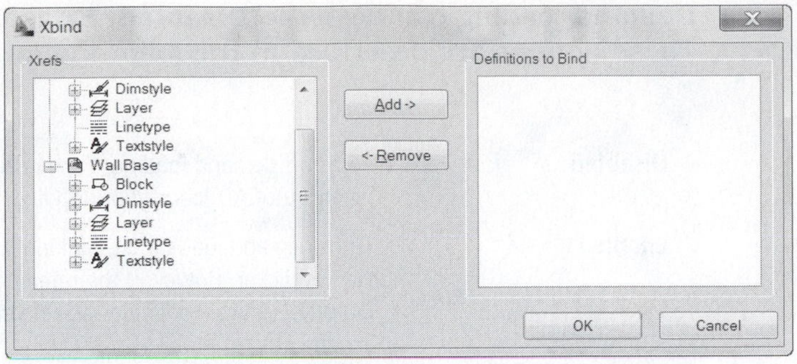

Figure 17-19
The **Xbind** dialog box

Demand Loading Xrefs

Demand loading is designed to help make AutoCAD run faster and more efficiently. If you have a number of xrefs loaded, or your referenced drawings are large and complex, you may notice slower system performance. To help with this, AutoCAD uses a method called ***demand loading***.

demand loading: Loading only the visible part of a referenced drawing.

Demand loading works by loading only the parts of an xref that AutoCAD is actually showing. Layers that are turned off or frozen or any geometry hidden by a clipping boundary are not loaded into your drawing until they are needed. When a layer state or a clipping boundary changes, AutoCAD loads the geometry from the referenced drawing. AutoCAD gives you some options for controlling demand loading. These options are found in the **Open and Save** tab of the **Options** dialog box (see Figure 17-20).

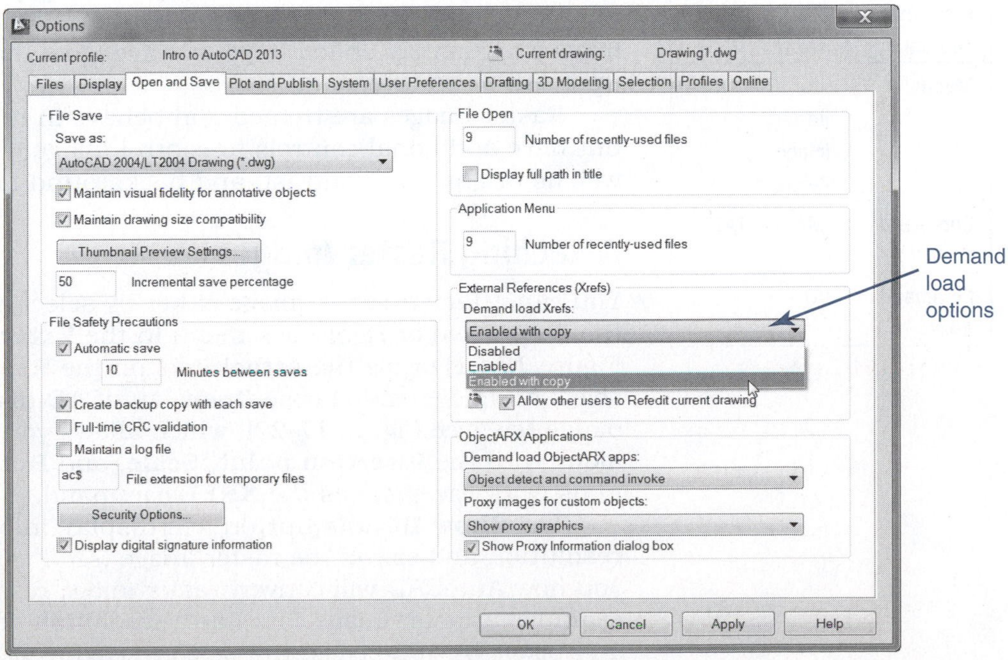

Figure 17-20
Options for demand load xrefs

Demand loading can be set to **Disabled, Enabled**, or **Enabled with copy**. These options are described in the following table:

Disabled	Turns off demand loading. Each referenced drawing is completely loaded when AutoCAD loads your drawing.
Enabled	Turns demand loading on, making AutoCAD run faster and regenerate views quicker. However, the referenced drawings will be locked, preventing others from modifying the referenced drawing while your drawing is open.
Enabled with copy	This is AutoCAD's default setting. AutoCAD will make a temporary copy of any referenced drawings and load this copy into your drawing. This enables demand loading while still allowing other users to modify the referenced drawings.

The **Enabled with copy** option provides the benefits of demand loading while still allowing others to work on the referenced drawings. If you use the **REFEDIT** command while the **Enabled with copy** option is set, AutoCAD will save the changes back to the original referenced file, not the temporary copy.

Working with Raster Images

RASTER IMAGE REFERENCE	
Ribbon & Panel:	Insert | Reference  Attach
Reference Toolbar:	
Menu:	Insert | Raster Image Reference...
Command Line:	IMAGEATTACH
Command Alias:	IAT

Raster images can enhance your drawings in a number of ways. They can provide colorful backgrounds with a company logo or background images for accurately tracing shapes. Architectural and civil drawings can benefit greatly by attaching satellite or aerial images to show site locations or conditions.

These views can then serve as backgrounds to help the reader visualize locations or to help the designer to locate utility points for xrefs or inserts. An image can also help provide vital information about your drawing or the function of your part.

An image can be just about any of the popular raster image formats including .BMP, .GIF, .PNG, .TIF, and others. Much like xrefs, the images are simply linked to your drawing so they can be quickly changed, updated, or removed.

Raster images are treated and behave in much the same way as xrefs but have additional controls to control image quality and transparency as well as brightness, contrast, and background fading.

Attaching Raster Images

You can attach a raster image either by selecting **Attach Image...** from the drop-down or right-click menu in the **External References** palette (see Figure 17-21) or via the **Attach** tool on the **Reference** panel. Once you select an image and choose **Open**, AutoCAD displays the **Attach Image** dialog box (see Figure 17-22), which allows you to set the type of path along with the **Insertion point, Scale**, and **Rotation** angle. All these functions work the same as the **XREF** command.

The **Show Details** button will display information about the resolution and size of the raster image (see Figure 17-23). This will tell you how AutoCAD will convert raster image resolution to physical size. For example, a raster image that has a resolution of 72 pixels per inch, and is 144 pixels by 108 pixels, will be converted to 2″ × 1.5″ in AutoCAD. The **Show Details** button displays information about the image resolution, AutoCAD units, and the image size in both pixels and AutoCAD units.

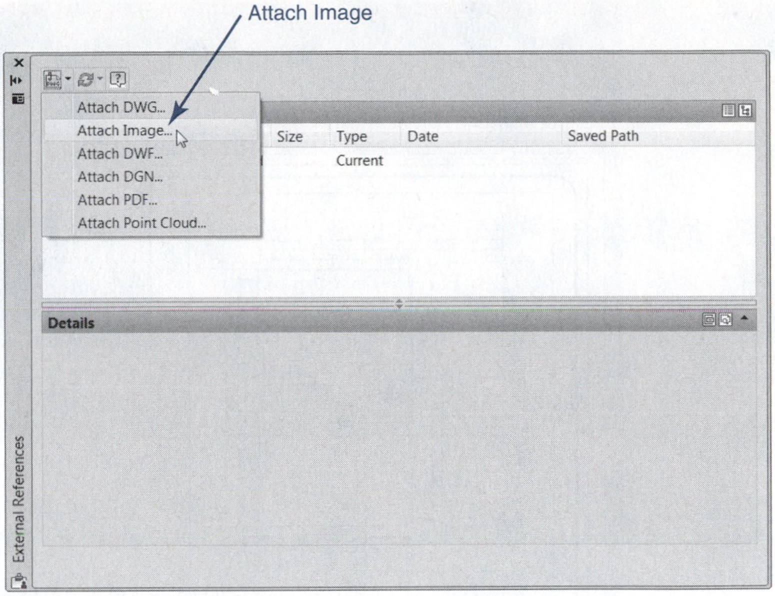

Figure 17-21
The **External References** palette

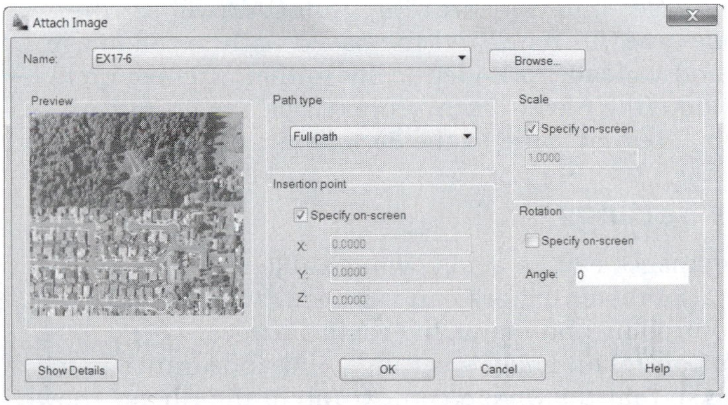

Figure 17-22
The **Attach Image** dialog box

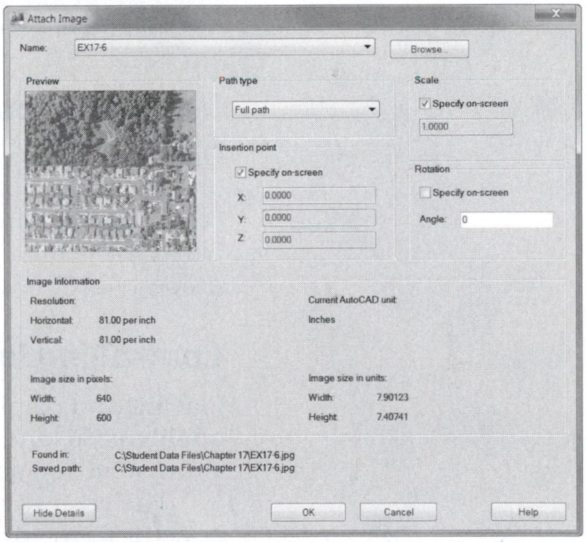

Figure 17-23
Raster image details

EXERCISE 17-6 Attaching Raster Images

1. Continue from Exercise 17-5.
2. Switch to the **Architectural Title Block** layout. Use grips to move and resize the viewport as shown in Figure 17-24. Set the viewport scale to **1/8″ = 1′–0″**.
3. Display the **External References** palette if it is not already displayed.
4. Choose **Attach Image...** and select the image ***EX17-6.jpg*** in the student data files. Check the **Specify on-screen** option for the **Insertion point** and set the **Scale** at **2**. Choose **OK** and place the image as shown in Figure 17-24.
5. Save the drawing.

To access student data files, go to **www.pearsondesigncentral.com**.

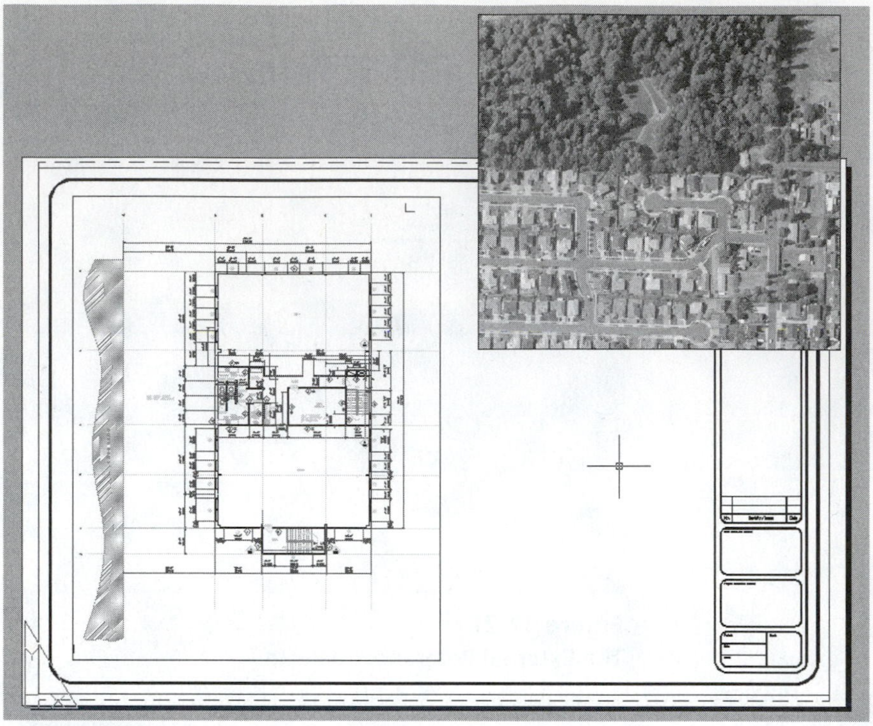

Figure 17-24
The attached image

Managing Images

Once you have loaded images into your drawing, AutoCAD will list the images, their status, file type, file date, and the saved path to the image file. **Detach, Reload**, and **Unload** work identically to their xref counterparts. You can also update the **Saved Path** property via the **Found At** property on the **Details/Preview** pane in the **External References** palette.

Controlling Image Settings

Placing and displaying images can be a somewhat subjective process. The quality, size, and format of raster images can vary widely. AutoCAD provides some tools for controlling and managing raster images.

The easiest way to control an image's settings and appearance is to select it in the drawing so that the **Image** context tab of the ribbon shown in Figure 17-25 is displayed, allowing you easy access to the most useful image settings.

IMAGE ADJUST	
Ribbon & Panel:	Image | Adjust
Reference Toolbar:	
Menu:	Modify | Object | Image | Adjust...
Command Line:	IMAGEADJUST
Command Alias:	IAD

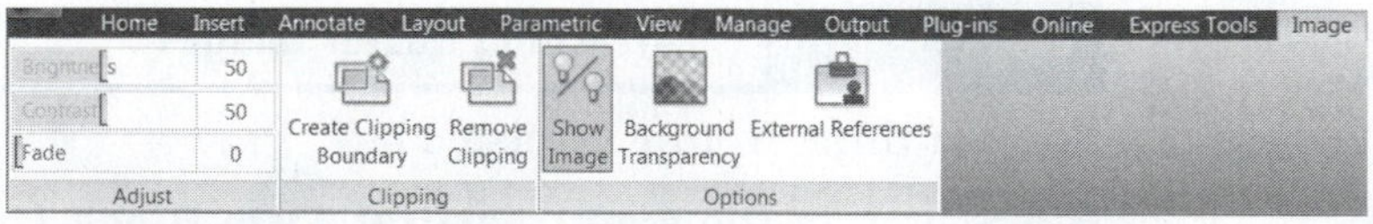

Figure 17-25
The **Image** context tab of the ribbon

Controlling Image Frames. Before you can select an image in a drawing, you must first turn on the image borders or frames. The easiest way to do that is via the **Reference** panel on the **Insert** tab of the ribbon. Click on the **Hide frames** option, and select either the **Display and plot frames** or the **Display but don't plot frames** option from the flyout menu. The **IMAGEFRAME** system variable also controls the display of the image outline.

CLIP IMAGE	
Ribbon & Panel:	Image | Clipping  Create Clipping Boundary
Reference Toolbar:	
Menu:	Modify | Clip | Image
Command Line:	IMAGECLIP
Command Alias:	ICL

IMAGE TRANSPARENCY	
Ribbon & Panel:	Image | Options  Background Transparency
Reference Toolbar:	
Menu:	Modify | Object | Image | Transparency
Command Line:	TRANSPARENCY
Command Alias:	IAD

If an image is clipped, it controls the display of the clipping boundary. There are three settings for the **IMAGEFRAME** variable: **0**, **1**, and **2**. These are described in the following table:

IMAGEFRAME = 0	Image frames are not displayed or plotted.
IMAGEFRAME = 1	Image frames are both displayed and plotted.
IMAGEFRAME = 2	Image frames are displayed but not plotted.

Adjusting Image Brightness, Contrast, and Fade Settings. The **Brightness** adjustment changes the brightness of an image. This can range from completely black to completely white.

The **Contrast** adjustment allows you to control the relative difference between dark and light areas of the image.

NOTE

Many of the image settings discussed in this section can also be controlled via the **Image** cascade menu located on the right-click menu displayed when an image is selected, as well as in the **Properties** palette.

The **Fade** adjustment allows you to blend the image into the background. Moving the **Fade** control toward the right will adjust the overall color of the image to match the background color. If AutoCAD's background is set to black, increasing the **Fade** setting causes the image to fade to black. If the background color is set to white, increasing the **Fade** setting causes the image to fade to white.

Image Clipping. As with xrefs, you can apply clipping boundaries to images. The **Create Clipping Boundary** tool allows you to define and control clipping boundaries associated with images. The options are identical to the **XCLIP** command discussed earlier.

Image clipping boundaries can be modified directly using grips. When you select a clipped image, AutoCAD displays grips at the corners of the clipping boundary. If the clipping boundary is rectangular, moving a grip changes the length and width of the clipping boundary. If the boundary is polygonal, moving a grip will change the shape of the clipping boundary.

Transparency. Some image file formats (such as GIF or PNG) support transparent pixels. When using images with transparency, you can turn the transparency on and off by selecting the **Background Transparency** button on the **Options** panel. If your image file format supports transparency, setting it to on will allow objects behind the image to be seen through the transparent pixels in the image.

EXERCISE 17-7 Controlling Image Settings

1. Continue from Exercise 17-6.
2. Select the raster image so the **Image** context tab of the ribbon is displayed.
3. Select the **Create Clipping Boundary** tool on the **Clipping** panel. Select the **Rectangular** option and clip the image as shown in Figure 17-26. Position the image as necessary to match Figure 17-26.

Figure 17-26
The clipped image

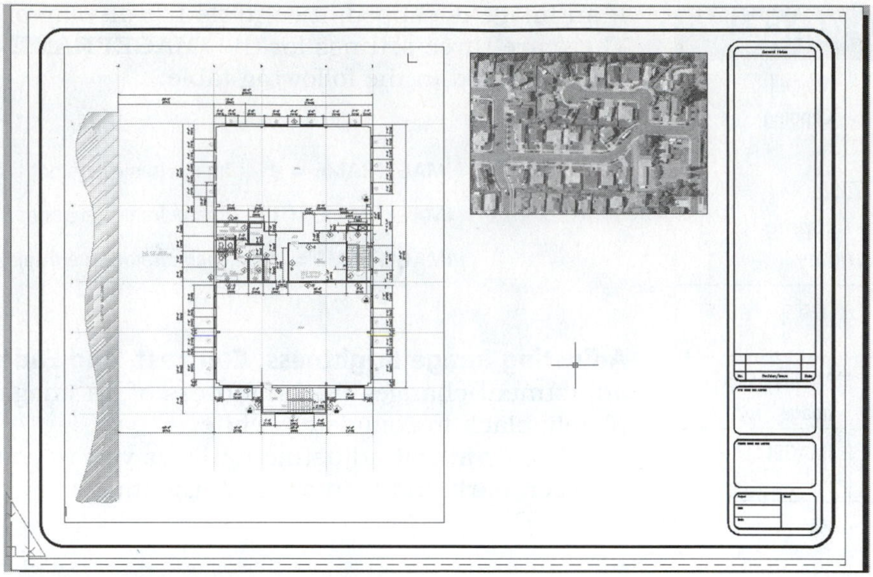

4 Adjust the **Brightness** and **Contrast** settings to your liking using the settings on the **Adjust** panel.

5 Save your drawing.

Working with DWF Underlays

DWF UNDERLAY	
Ribbon & Panel:	Insert | Reference  Attach
Insert Toolbar:	
Menu:	Insert | DWF Underlay...
Command Line:	DWFATTACH
Command Alias:	None

Remember from the beginning of the chapter that the DWF file format is a compressed vector-based drawing file format that allows you to share your drawings with other individuals who should not have access to sensitive, proprietary design information.

It is possible to reference DWF files in a similar fashion as xref drawings and raster images using the **DWF Underlay** feature by specifying a file path, insertion point, scale, and rotation angle.

You can modify the appearance of a DWF underlay after it is attached so that it is possible to change the DWF underlay from color-based to monochrome, adjust its fade and contrast, as well as automatically adjust the DWF colors to match the drawing background. It is also possible to define a clipping boundary to limit the visible area of the DWF underlay in a fashion similar to xrefs and images.

Attaching DWF Underlays

You can attach a DWF underlay either by selecting **Attach DWF...** from the drop-down or right-click menu in the **External References** palette or by selecting the **Attach** tool on the **Reference** panel on the **Insert** tab of the ribbon.

Either method displays the **Select Reference File** dialog box so you can select a DWF file to attach to your drawing. After you select a file and choose **Open**, AutoCAD displays the **Attach DWF Underlay** dialog box shown in Figure 17-27 where you set the type of path along with the **Insertion point, Scale**, and **Rotation** angle. These options are the same as those for the **XREF** command.

If the DWF file consists of multiple sheets, you must select the sheet to attach from the **Select one or more sheets from the DWF file:** list box on the left.

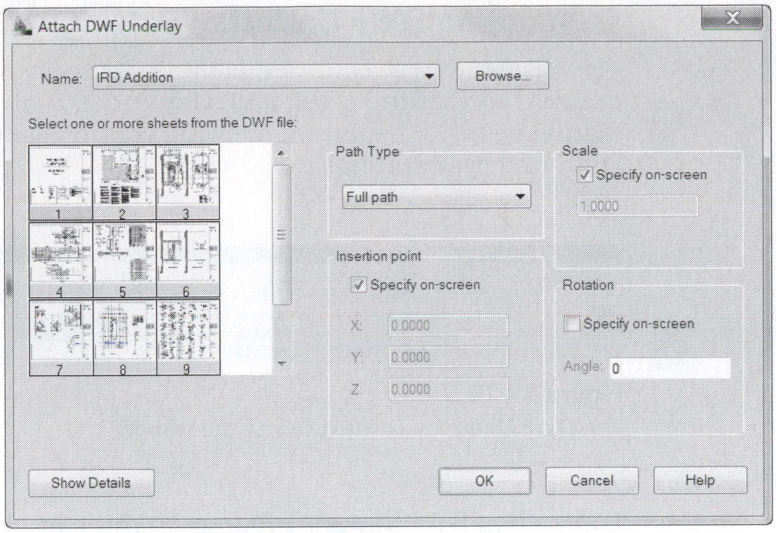

Figure 17-27
The **Attach DWF Underlay** dialog box

Managing DWF Underlays

Once you attach one or more DWF underlays in your drawing, AutoCAD will list the DWF file names, their status, file type, file date, and the saved path to the DWF file in the **External References** palette as shown in Figure 17-28.

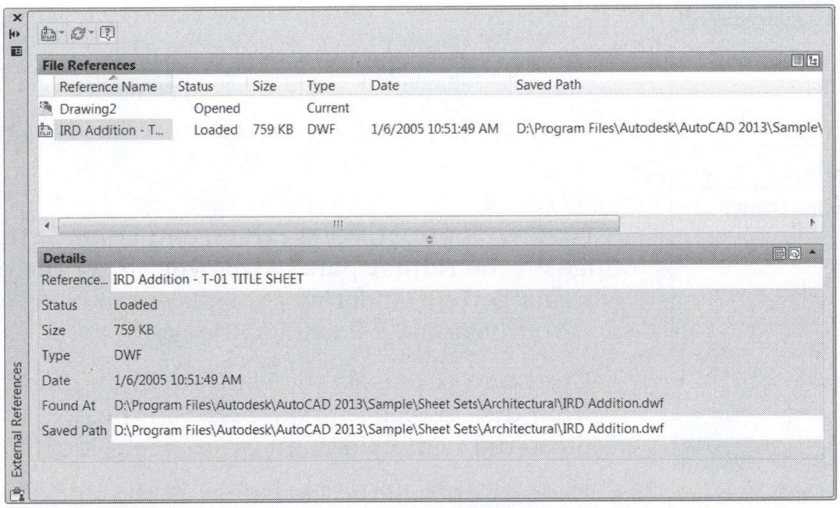

Figure 17-28
The **External References** palette with a DWF underlay attached

Similar to xrefs, most of the DWF underlay options and settings are provided via a right-click shortcut menu similar to the xref shortcut menu shown earlier in Figure 17-12. The DWF underlay options work the same as the xref file options, with a few subtle differences.

Selecting **Open** from the shortcut menu will open the DWF file using the downloadable Autodesk Design Review software mentioned earlier so that you can view, *but not edit*, the DWF file.

The **Attach...** menu item displays the **Select DWF File** dialog box so that you can attach another DWF file; the other DWF underlay options, **Unload**, **Reload**, and **Detach**, work the same as their xref counterparts.

Controlling DWF Underlay Settings

The easiest way to control a DWF underlay's settings is to select it in the drawing so that the **DWF Underlay** context tab of the ribbon shown in Figure 17-29 is displayed, allowing you to easily access the most useful DWF underlay settings and options.

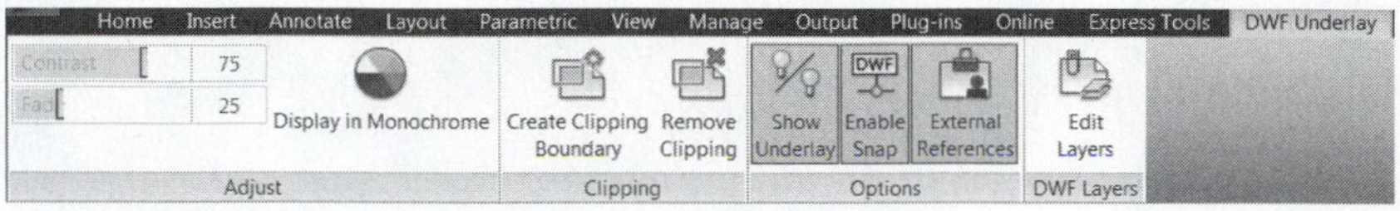

Figure 17-29
The **DWF Underlay** context tab of the ribbon

Controlling DWF Underlay Frames. You can control whether a border outline is displayed around the edges of a DWF underlay via the **Hide frames** flyout menu on the **Reference** panel on the **Insert** tab of the ribbon. Unlike raster images, DWF frames do not need to be on in order to select a DWF underlay. To turn frames on, select either the **Display and plot frames** or the **Display but don't plot frames** option from the flyout menu.

The **DWFFRAME** system variable also controls the display of the DWF underlay outline. If a DWF underlay is clipped, it controls the display of the clipping boundary. There are three settings for the **DWFFRAME** variable: **0**, **1**, and **2**. These are described in the following table:

DWF ADJUST	
Ribbon & Panel:	DWF Underlay | Adjust
Toolbar:	None
Menu:	None
Command Line:	DWFADJUST
Command Alias:	None

DWFFRAME = 0	DWF underlay frames are not displayed and are not plotted.
DWFFRAME = 1	DWF underlay frames are both displayed and plotted.
DWFFRAME = 2	DWF underlay frames are displayed but not plotted (default).

Adjusting Contrast, Fade Effect, and Color Settings. The options and settings on the **Adjust** panel allow you to set the contrast, fade effect, and whether a DWF underlay is displayed in color or monochrome.

You have the following options:

- **Contrast** Controls the contrast of the underlay. Values settings are from 0 to 100. The greater the setting, the higher the contrast between dark and light colors, and vice versa. (default = 75)
- **Fade** Controls the fade effect of the underlay. Values settings are from 0 to 80. The higher the setting, the lighter the line work in the underlay. The lower the setting, the darker the line work. (default = 25)
- **Monochrome** Toggles the DWF underlay between color display and monochrome display (black and white). (default = On)

DWF CLIP	
Ribbon & Panel:	DWF Underlay | Clipping  Create Clipping Boundary
Toolbar:	None
Menu:	None
Command Line:	DWFCLIP
Command Alias:	None

DWF Underlay Clipping. Similar to both xrefs and images, you can apply clipping boundaries to DWF underlays. The **Create Clipping Boundary** tool allows you to define and control clipping boundaries associated with DWF files. The options are identical to the **XCLIP** and **IMAGECLIP** commands.

Adjusting Colors for the Current Background. The **Adjust Colors for Background** option controls whether the DWF underlay colors are visible against the current drawing background color. The option is accessible only via the **Properties** palette under the **Underlay Adjust** category.

The default setting of **Yes** forces AutoCAD to analyze the background colors of the DWF underlay and the drawing environment to determine whether they are both light or both dark. If necessary, the colors of the DWF underlay are adjusted so the underlay is visible.

If the **Adjust Colors for Background** option is changed to **No**, the original colors of the underlay are always used regardless of the current background color. If you use this setting, the DWF underlay might not always be visible.

Turning Object Snaps On and Off. You can control whether object snapping is enabled for the DWF underlay geometry by selecting the **Enable Snap** button on the **DWF Underlay** context tab of the ribbon and toggling on or off.

> **NOTE**
>
> The **DWFOSNAP** system variable allows you to control whether object snapping to objects that are part of a DWF file is enabled. Setting **DWFOSNAP = 1** (default) allows you to snap to DWF underlay objects. Setting **DWFOSNAP = 0** turns DWF underlay object snaps off.

> **NOTE**
>
> You can control layers in other attached xrefs by selecting them in the **Reference Name:** list box at the top.

DWF Layer Control

DWF LAYERS	
Ribbon & Panel:	DWF Underlay | DWF Layers

Reference Toolbar:	None
Menu:	None
Command Line:	DWFLAYERS
Command Alias:	None

When a DWF file is created, the user has the option of including layer information within the DWF file. This allows people viewing the DWF file to turn layers on and off. People viewing the DWF file cannot control the name, color, linetype, etc., of DWF layers, only the layer visibility.

When you attach a DWF underlay, if the DWF file contains layer information, AutoCAD allows you this same ability. The **DWFLAYERS** command allows you to turn on and off the layers within a DWF file. The **DWFLAYERS** command is also available by selecting a DWF underlay and choosing **DWF Layers...** from the right-click menu or the **DWF Underlay** context tab of the ribbon.

When you start the **DWFLAYERS** command, AutoCAD will prompt you to select the DWF underlay. If the DWF underlay contains layer information, AutoCAD will display the layer names in the **Underlay Layers** dialog box (see Figure 17-30). In this dialog box, you can turn DWF layers on and off by clicking the lightbulb icon next to each layer. You can select multiple layers by pressing the **<Ctrl>** or **<Shift>** key while clicking layer names. You can also turn layers on and off by right-clicking highlighted layers and choosing **Layer(s) On** or **Layer(s) Off** from the right-click menu.

Figure 17-30 The **Underlay Layers** dialog box

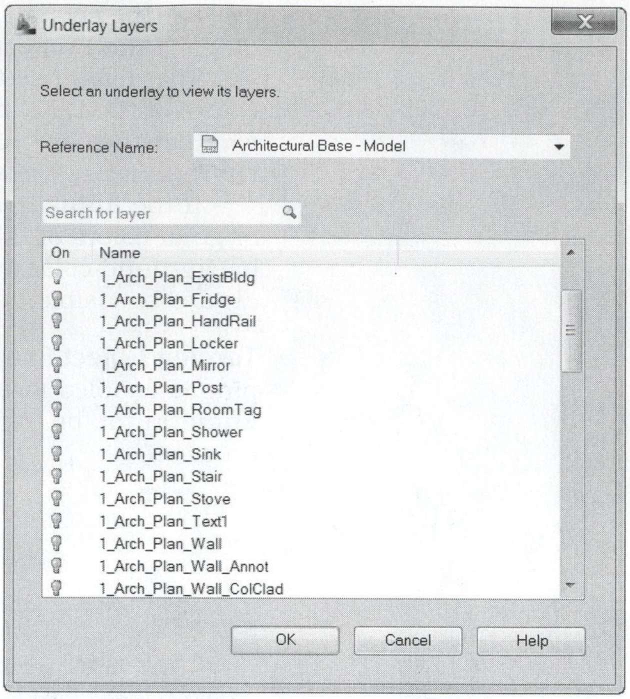

Working with DGN Underlays

Similar to the DWF underlay, AutoCAD supports the referencing of MicroStation V8 DGN design files. Like a DWF underlay, a DGN underlay is a view-only version of the design data contained in the DGN file. DGN underlays are attached in the same way DWF files are, with some minor differences. You can also control the DGN underlay settings via a context ribbon tab and panels that are displayed when you select a DGN file in a drawing.

Attaching DGN Underlays

DGN UNDERLAY	
Ribbon & Panel:	Insert | Reference 
Insert Toolbar:	
Menu:	Insert | DGN Underlay...
Command Line:	DGNATTACH
Command Alias:	None

You can attach a DGN underlay either by selecting **Attach DGN...** from the drop-down or right-click menu in the **External References** palette or by selecting the **Attach** tool on the **Reference** panel on the **Insert** tab of the ribbon.

Either method displays the **Select Reference File** dialog box so you can select a DGN file. After you select a file and choose **Open**, AutoCAD displays the **Attach DGN Underlay** dialog box shown in Figure 17-31 where you set the type of **Path Type** along with the **Insertion point, Scale,** and **Rotation** angle.

Unlike AutoCAD, which has only one model design space, DGN files can contain multiple design models. Select the desired design model from the **Select a design model from the DGN file:** list. Only a single design model can be displayed per underlay. Sheet models within a DGN file (similar to DWF sheets) are not listed.

The **Conversion Units** area of the dialog box allows you to control how units are converted in the DGN file. DGN files use *working units* (imperial or metric) called *master units* and *subunits*. Some number of subunits is equal to one master unit. Select the unit you wish to use in your AutoCAD drawing. For example, if master units are set to feet and subunits are set to inches, then 12 subunits would equal 1 master unit (feet). Selecting master units in the **Conversion Units** area would convert DGN master units (feet) to AutoCAD's unit of measurement.

Figure 17-31
The **Attach DGN Underlay** dialog box

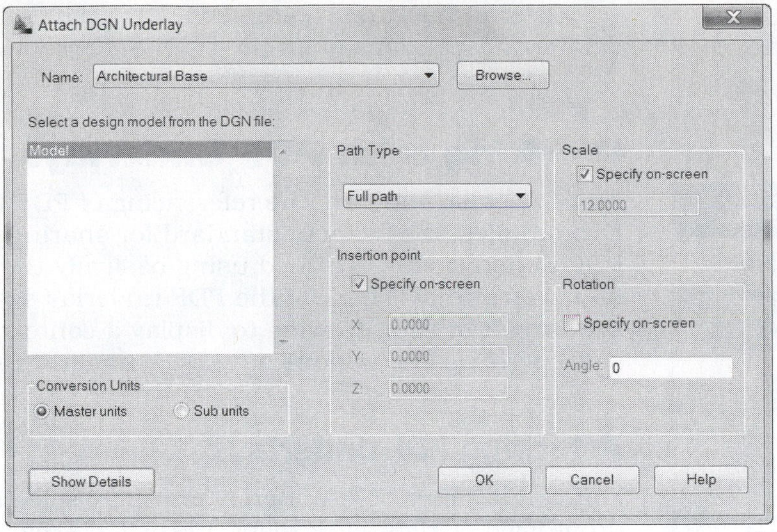

DGN ADJUST	
Ribbon & Panel:	DGN Underlay | Adjust
Toolbar:	None
Menu:	None
Command Line:	DGNADJUST
Command Alias:	None

DGN CLIP	
Ribbon & Panel:	DGN Underlay | Clipping  Create Clipping Boundary
Toolbar:	None
Menu:	None
Command Line:	DGNCLIP
Command Alias:	None

The **Insertion Point, Scale**, and **Rotation** settings are the same as those for xrefs and DWF underlays.

Managing DGN Underlays

Once you attach one or more DGN underlays in your drawing, AutoCAD will list all of them along with all the other xrefs, images, and DWF underlays in the **External References** palette.

Like DWF underlays, the different DGN underlay options and settings are provided via a right-click shortcut menu. The DGN underlay options work exactly the same as their DWF underlay counterparts with some slight differences.

The **Open** option from the shortcut menu is not selectable. This is because AutoCAD does not include a DGN file viewer with AutoCAD.

The **Attach...** menu item displays the **Select DGN File** dialog box so that you can attach another DGN file; all the other DGN underlay options—**Unload, Reload**, and **Detach**—work exactly the same as their xref counterparts and DWF underlay.

Controlling DGN Underlay Settings. The easiest way to control a DGN underlay's settings is to select it in the drawing so that the **DGN Underlay** context tab of the ribbon shown in Figure 17-32 is displayed, allowing you to easily access the most useful DGN underlay settings and options.

Figure 17-32
The **DGN Underlay** context tab of the ribbon

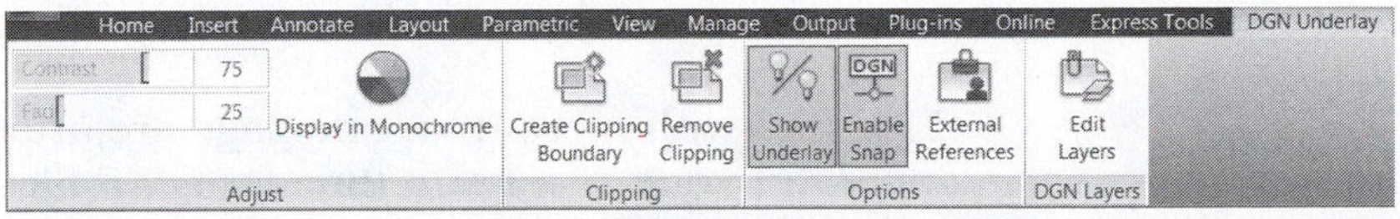

DGN underlays share all the same settings and options as DWF underlays, so that you can do the following:

- Adjust the contrast, fade, and monochrome settings
- Clip portions of a DGN underlay so it is not displayed
- Enable/disable object snapping to the DGN underlay geometry
- Turn on/off DGN underlay layers if they are included

Refer to the "Controlling DWF Underlay Settings" section earlier for detailed descriptions of all the DGN underlay options.

Working with PDF Underlays

PDF UNDERLAY	
Ribbon & Panel:	Insert | Reference 
Insert Toolbar:	
Menu:	Insert | PDF Underlay
Command Line:	PDFATTACH
Command Alias:	None

AutoCAD also supports the referencing of PDF (Adobe Portable Document Format) files, the de facto standard for sharing electronic information. PDF underlays are attached using basically the same methods as DGN files. You can also control the PDF underlay settings after it is attached by selecting it in your drawing to display a context tab of the ribbon with the same settings and options as a DGN underlay.

Attaching PDF Underlays

You can attach a PDF underlay either by selecting **Attach PDF...** from the drop-down or right-click menu in the **External References** palette or by selecting the **Attach** tool on the **Reference** panel on the **Insert** tab of the ribbon.

Either method displays the **Select Reference File** dialog box so you can select a PDF file. After you select a file and choose **Open**, AutoCAD displays the **Attach PDF Underlay** dialog box shown in Figure 17-33 where you set the **Path Type** along with the **Insertion point, Scale**, and **Rotation** angle.

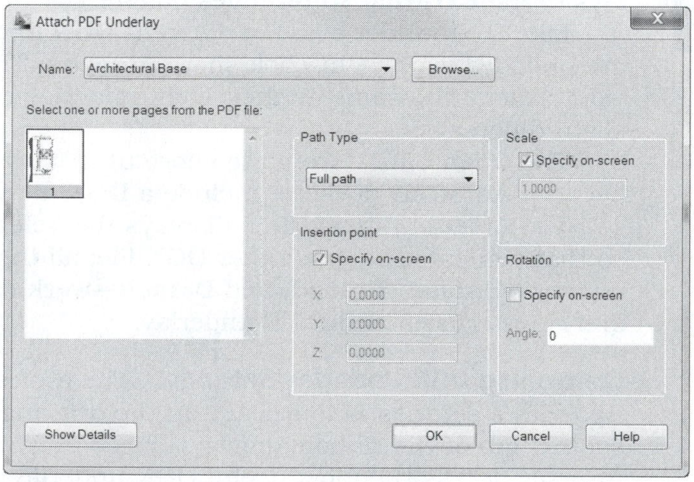

Figure 17-33
The **Attach PDF Underlay** dialog box

PDF files with more than one page are attached one *page* at a time (as opposed to one *sheet* at a time for DWF files or one *model* at a time for DGN files). If the PDF file has more than one page, you must select the desired page from the **Select one or more pages from the PDF file:** list.

The **Insertion point, Scale**, and **Rotation** settings work the same as for the other types of underlays.

> **NOTE**
>
> Hypertext links in PDF files are converted to straight text and digital signatures are not supported.

PDF ADJUST	
Ribbon & Panel:	PDF Underlay | Adjust
Toolbar:	None
Pull-down Menu:	PDFADJUST
Command Line:	None
Command Alias:	None

Managing PDF Underlays

Once you attach one or more PDF underlays in your drawing, AutoCAD will list them along with all the other xrefs, images, and underlays in the **External References** palette.

Like the other underlays, the different PDF underlay options and settings are provided via a right-click shortcut menu.

Controlling PDF Underlay Settings. The easiest way to control a PDF underlay's settings is to select it in the drawing so that the **PDF Underlay** context tab of the ribbon shown in Figure 17-34 is displayed, allowing you to easily access the most useful PDF underlay settings and options.

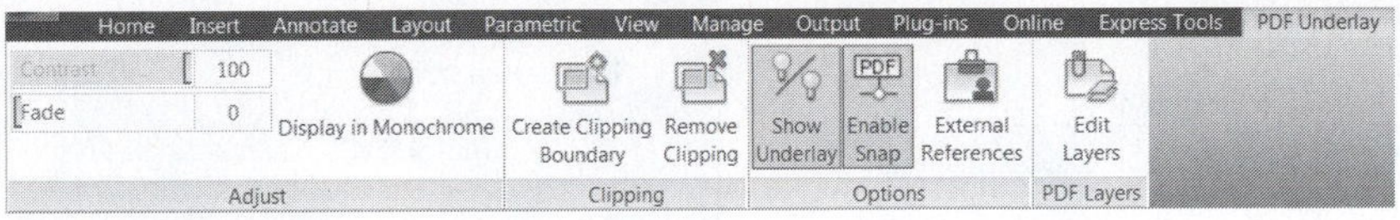

Figure 17-34
The **PDF Underlay** context tab of the ribbon

PDF underlays share all the same settings and options as DGN underlays so that you can do the following:

- Adjust the contrast, fade, and monochrome settings
- Clip portions of a PDF underlay so it is not displayed
- Enable/disable object snapping to the PDF underlay geometry
- Turn on/off PDF underlay layers if they are included

Refer to the "Controlling DGN Underlay Settings" section earlier for detailed descriptions of all the PDF underlay options.

PDF CLIP	
Ribbon & Panel:	PDF Underlay | Clipping
 Create Clipping Boundary	
Toolbar:	None
Pull-down Menu:	None
Command Line:	PDFCLIP
Command Alias:	None

Transmitting Drawings with References

When creating drawings that use referenced drawings or images, it's important to consider what happens to those drawings when they are given to others (clients, contractors, vendors, etc.). When you provide drawings to others, any referenced files must be supplied as well. This can be a difficult task when there are multiple references stored in different locations. The problem is compounded if nested xrefs are used.

Fortunately, AutoCAD provides the **ETRANSMIT** command to help manage these external files. The **ETRANSMIT** command helps solve the problem of sending incomplete files by compiling all external files into a separate folder or zip file. You can also create an email and automatically attach the files to the email.

ETRANSMIT	
Application Menu:	Publish | eTransmit 
Toolbar:	None
Menu:	File | eTransmit...
Command Line:	ETRANSMIT
Command Alias:	None

Using eTransmit

Before using the **ETRANSMIT** command, you need to save any changes to your drawing. If you start the command before you save any changes, AutoCAD will ask you to save the changes before continuing (see Figure 17-35).

Selecting Files. When you start the **ETRANSMIT** command, AutoCAD displays the **Create Transmittal** dialog box (see Figure 17-36). The **Files Tree** tab shows you a hierarchical tree view of your drawing and any files that are associated with it. From this view, you can see the relationships of the files and also which files are attached to which.

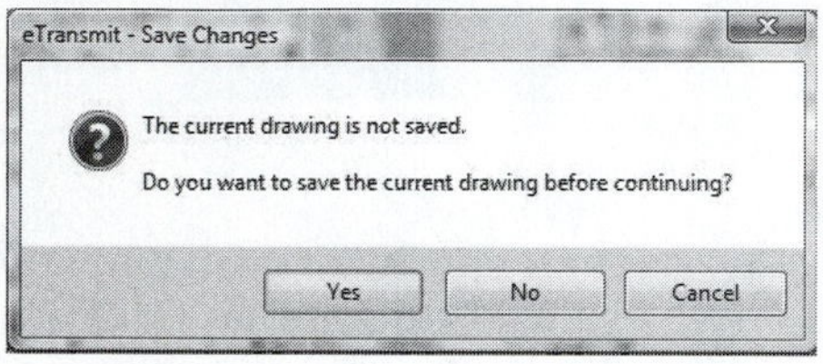

Figure 17-35
The **Save Changes** notification

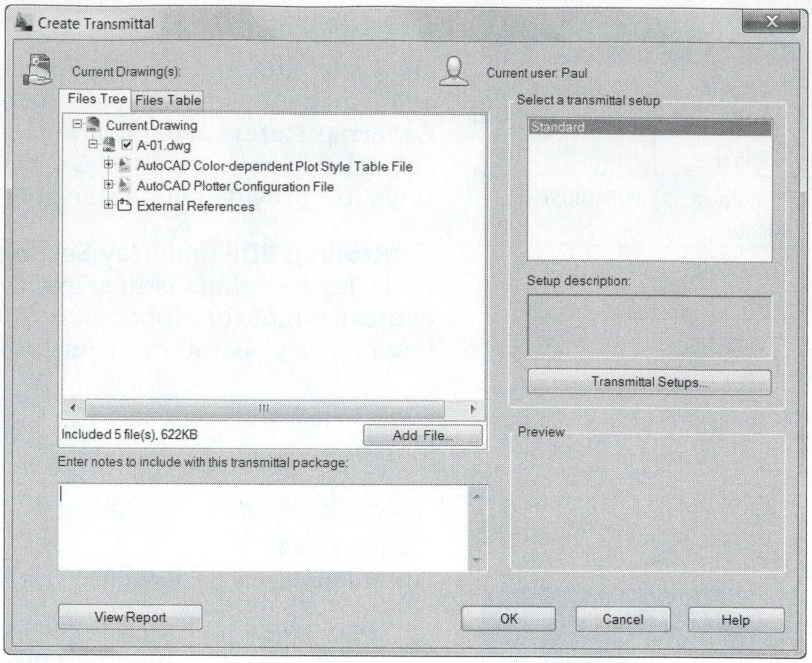

Figure 17-36
The **Create Transmittal** dialog box

The **Files Table** tab (see Figure 17-37) shows you a flattened list of all files associated with your drawing. This view does not show file relationships but may be easier to work with because all the files are displayed in a single list.

Figure 17-37
The **Files Table** tab

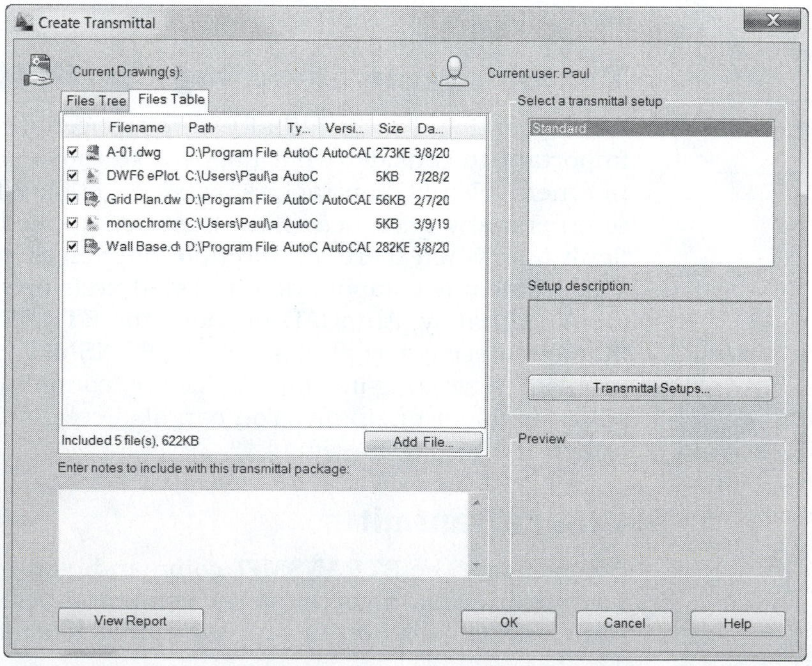

With either view, you can select the files you wish to include in your transmittal by checking or unchecking the box next to the file.

The **Add File...** button allows you to specify additional files you wish to include in your transmittal, such as design specifications, product data sheets, or cover letters.

The Transmittal Report. When you create your transmittal, AutoCAD will create a transmittal report to include with the transmittal. The **View Report** button displays the **View Transmittal Report** dialog box, which shows you a copy of the information that will be included in this report. The **Save As...** button allows you to save this report to a text file. The **Close** button closes the **View Transmittal Report** dialog box.

You can add additional information to this report by typing it into the text area above the **View Report** button. Any text typed here will be added to the transmittal report (see Figure 17-38).

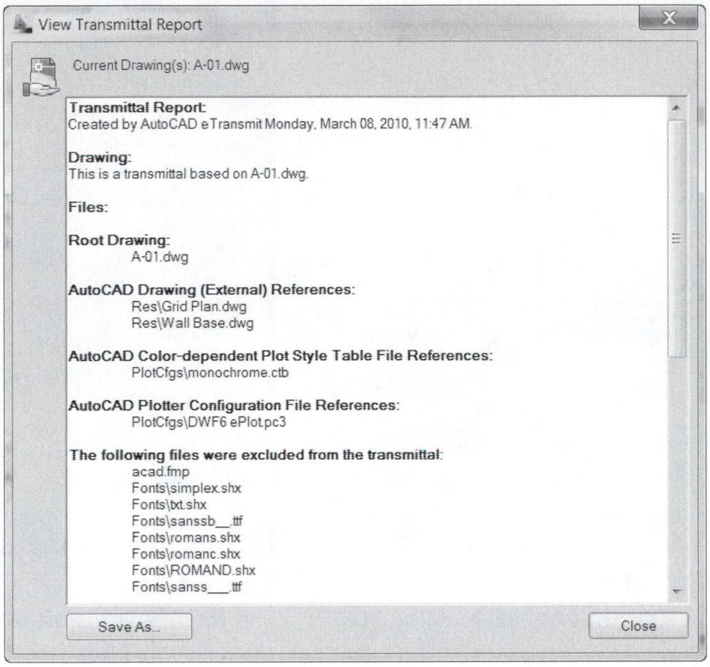

Figure 17-38
The sample transmittal report

Configuring the Transmittal

A transmittal setup contains all the settings for the transmittal, including which files to include, how the files are organized, and how xrefs are included with the drawing. Multiple transmittal setups can be created and saved. This allows you to create different setups for different clients or needs. When you choose the **Transmittal Setups...** button, AutoCAD displays the **Transmittal Setups** dialog box (see Figure 17-39). This allows you to modify, rename, or delete an existing setup or create a new transmittal setup. Transmittal setups are similar to page setups or dimension styles in that they simply assign a name to a collection of settings.

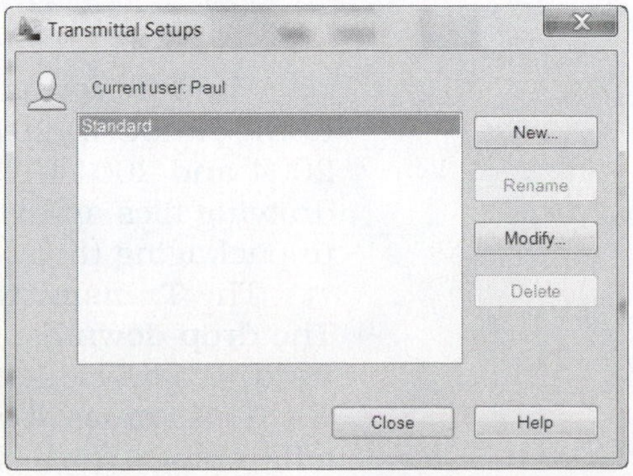

Figure 17-39
The **Transmittal Setups** dialog box

To create a new setup, choose the **New...** button in the **Transmittal Setups** dialog box. This displays the **New Transmittal Setup** dialog box (see Figure 17-40) where you can assign a name to your new transmittal setup. Each new transmittal setup is created from an existing setup. The **Based on:** list allows you to choose which setup to use as a basis for your new setup.

Once you create a new setup or choose the **Modify...** button, AutoCAD will display the **Modify Transmittal Setup** dialog box (see Figure 17-41). This dialog box allows you to modify the setting for the transmittal.

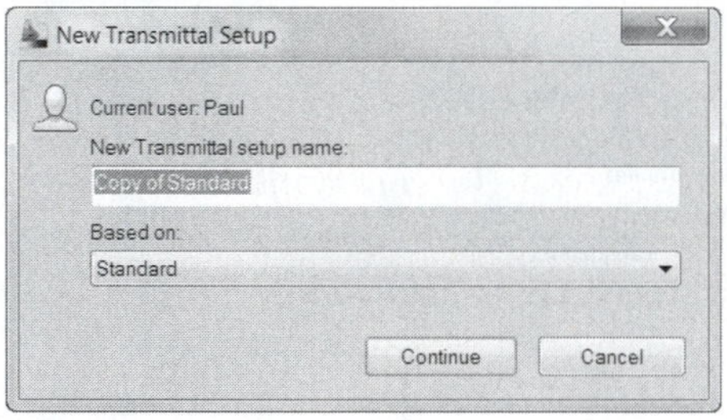

Figure 17-40
The **New Transmittal Setup** dialog box

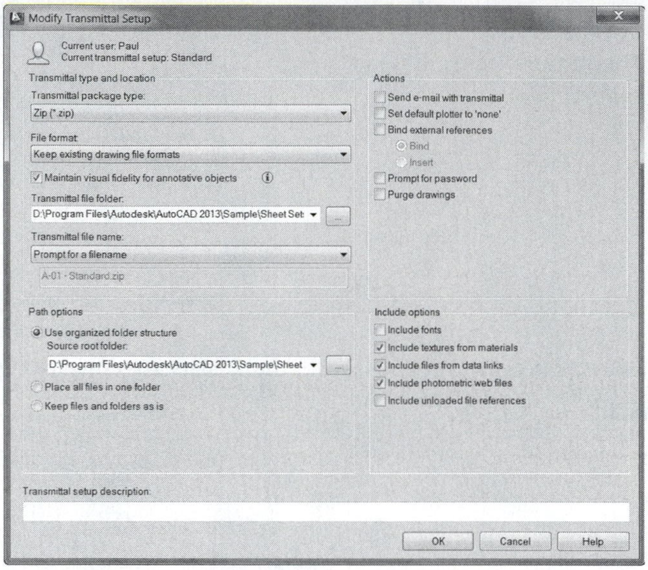

Figure 17-41
The **Modify Transmittal Setup** dialog box

Transmittal Settings. The **Transmittal package type:** allows you to select how the files will be stored. The options are described in the following table:

Folder (Set of Files)	Packages the files in a single file folder. The **Transmittal file folder:** setting specifies the location of the folder. You may want to create a new folder to store the transmittal files.
Self-extracting Executable (.exe)	Packages the files in a self-extracting file. This is similar to a zip file but does not require a separate zip program to open the files. The user can simply double-click on the files to open, decompress, and extract them.
Zip (*.zip)	Packages the files in a compressed zip file. All files are compressed into a single file, which makes them easy to send electronically. Windows XP systems have built-in support for zip files. Earlier versions of Windows may require a zip program such as Winzip.

The **File format:** option lets you convert AutoCAD 2013 drawings back to the AutoCAD 2010 and 2010 LT, AutoCAD 2007 and 2007 LT, AutoCAD 2004 and 2004 LT, or AutoCAD 2000 and 2000 LT release formats. All drawing files and xrefs are converted back to the selected file format prior to packaging them.

The **Transmittal file folder:** is the location for the transmitted files. The drop-down list will display the nine previous locations that have been used, or you can choose the **Browse** button to specify a new location.

The **Transmittal file name:** determines the ZIP or EXE file name and tells AutoCAD which method is used for naming. By default, AutoCAD combines the drawing file name with the transmittal setup name. For example, a drawing called **Plan.dwg** using the **Standard** transmittal setup with the **Zip** package option would have a transmittal file name called **Plan-Standard.zip**. You can change the default file name by typing a new name in the space below the **Transmittal file name:**. This option is disabled if the **Folder** package type is used. These options are described in the following table:

Prompt for a filename	This method will prompt you for a file name each time you create a transmittal. The file will be stored in the folder set in the **Transmittal file folder:** setting.
Overwrite if necessary	This option will automatically name the file. If that file already exists, AutoCAD will automatically overwrite the existing file.
Increment file name if necessary	This option will automatically name the file. If the file already exists, AutoCAD will create a new file name by adding a number to the end of the file name. For example, a zip file called **Plan-Standard.zip** would be incremented to **Plan-Standard 1.zip**.

The **Path options** area allows you to choose how the files are organized within the package. These are described in the following table:

Use organized folder structure	This method duplicates the folder structure for the files being transmitted. The root folder is the top-level folder for the transmittal. For files that lie within the root folder path, a folder is created for each file's parent folder. Files that are outside the root folder path are placed in the root folder. Other folders are created as needed for fonts and plot configurations.
Place all files in one folder:	This option places all files in a single folder defined in the **Transmittal file folder** option. No subfolders are created.
Keep files and folders as is	This option replicates the existing folder structure of all the files included in the transmittal. This option works well when you have xrefs or images stored with full paths because it retains the complete folder structure for all files.

The **Send e-mail with transmittal** option will cause AutoCAD to start a new email message with the transmittal files included as attachments.

The **Set default plotter to 'none'** option changes the default plotter for all model and paper space layouts to **None**. This prevents AutoCAD from trying to communicate with plotters that may not be configured on another user's system.

The **Bind external references** option causes AutoCAD to bind all xrefs in the transmittal drawing file. This means that no xref files are included with the transmittal and that all xrefs are automatically bound before packaging. This does not affect the source drawing file, only the transmittal copy. The advantage of using this option is that the person receiving the transmittal will not have to deal with xref paths or missing files. The disadvantage is that for large or complex drawings, binding xrefs may cause the file size to increase significantly.

The **Prompt for password** option is available only when packaging the transmittal as a ZIP or EXE file. When this option is selected, AutoCAD will password-protect the ZIP or EXE file. When using this option to create the transmittal package, AutoCAD will display the **Transmittal-Set Password** dialog box (see Figure 17-42) that will prompt you for a password and ask you to confirm that password. The recipient of the transmittal package will need to type in the password to gain access to the files.

The **Purge drawings** option will do a complete purge of all the drawings in the transmittal package.

Figure 17-42
The **Set Password** dialog box

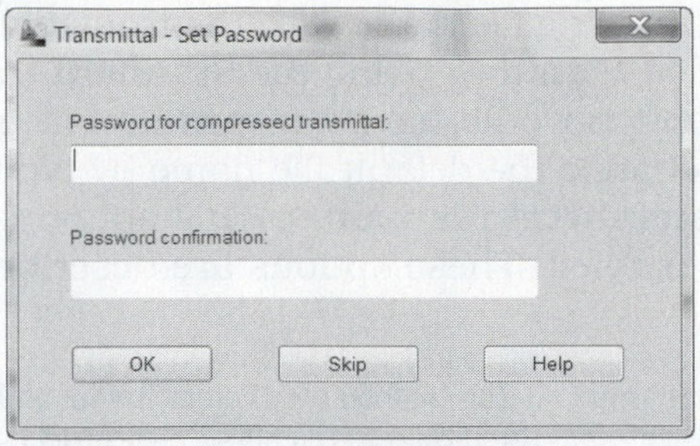

The **Include options** area allows you to specify whether to include associated fonts, textures from materials, external files referenced by a data link, photometric web files that are associated with web lights, and unloaded file references.

EXERCISE 17-8 Transmitting Xrefs

1. Continue from Exercise 17-7.
2. Start the **ETRANSMIT** command. If you have any unsaved changes, AutoCAD will ask whether you want to save them. Choose **OK** to save any changes.
3. Look at the **Files Tree** and **Files Table** tabs to see which files are going to be included in the transmittal.
4. Choose the **Transmittal Setups...** button and choose **New...** to create a new transmittal setup. Name the transmittal setup **Chapter 17** and choose **Continue** to continue setting up the transmittal.
5. Set the **Transmittal package type:** to **Zip** and **Keep existing drawing file formats**. Select a location from the **Transmittal file folder:** and choose **Prompt for a filename**.
6. Choose **Place all files in one folder** and **Include fonts.** Turn all other options off. Choose **OK** to save the transmittal setup and **Close** to return to the **Create Transmittal** dialog box. Your settings should be set to match Figure 17-43.
7. Choose **OK** to create the transmittal. Save the transmittal as ***CH17_EXERCISE8***.

Figure 17-43
Transmittal settings

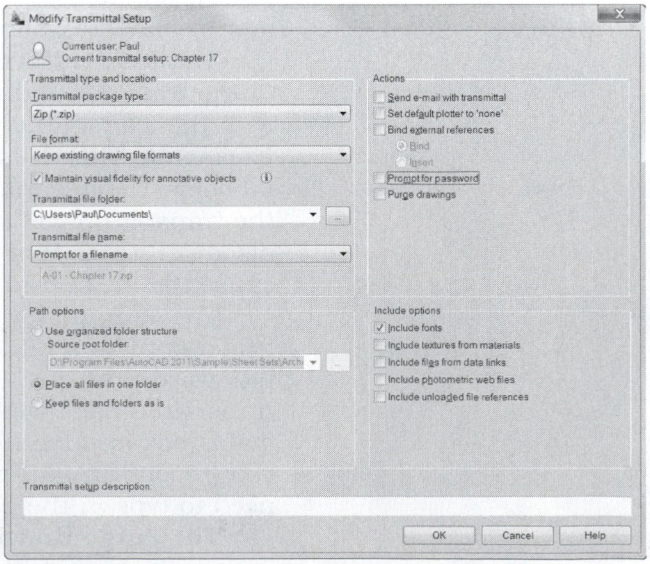

Chapter Summary

Referencing external drawings is a key feature in environments in which multiple people are working on a project and coordination is crucial. In fact, there is really no other easy way for more than one person to access a drawing file at the same time and maintain data integrity. Sooner or later someone is going to overwrite another person's changes. That is why if you try to open a drawing that someone else already has open, AutoCAD will only let you open it in read-only mode.

Using external references, you split up a drawing into logical chunks (files) so everyone can work on his or her own stuff and then reference them back together so everyone can coordinate his or her work with that of the others. Obviously, file and document management is critical, hence the importance of how you set up and manage xref paths in your drawings. The editing and update process is also of primary concern. People need the ability to always see the latest information when changes are made, and access needs to be controlled. The good thing is that AutoCAD notifies when changes are made to xrefs in your drawing so that they can be reloaded with the latest information.

This ability to always have the latest information applies to the other types of files that can be referenced in AutoCAD, too. Raster image references allow you to place photos and other images in your drawings while maintaining a link back to the original. The ability to reference DWF, DGN, and PDF files allows you to share and coordinate your drawing information with many different sources that might not have AutoCAD. Context tabs of the ribbon that display whenever you select one of the different reference types allow you to easily control the appearance and behavior of reference files in your drawings.

When you need to send a drawing that has one or more references to someone else, the AutoCAD **eTransmit** utility allows you to automatically gather up all of the referenced files and package them together in one zip file for easy transfer. It even has the ability to automatically create an email and attach the zip file in one step. Alternatively, you can also bind referenced files so that they become part of the original drawing and all reference links are broken. This is typically done as a last resort because you lose all the benefits of using xrefs in the first place.

Chapter Test Questions

Multiple Choice

Circle the correct answer.

1. Which of the following statements best defines an xref?
   a. A drawing that is independent of all other drawings
   b. A drawing attached to the current or host drawing with a link back to the original drawing
   c. A drawing that can bind only to the current drawing
   d. All of the above

2. Why would "Reload" be needed when using xrefs?
   a. To lock changes out of the current drawing
   b. To check updates to a current attached drawing

c. To bind changes to a current drawing
d. All of the above

3. Binding an attached xref drawing will:
   a. Isolate the drawing from any more updates
   b. Make the attached drawing more editable
   c. Bind it somewhat permanently to the current drawing
   d. All of the above

4. Which bind-type option will bind named xref objects such as layers, linetypes, and textstyles and **not** rename them with the xref name and a "0" prefix?
   a. **Bind** option
   b. **Insert** option
   c. Setting **BINDTYPE** system variable to **0**
   d. None of the above

5. The **XOPEN** command is used for:
   a. Opening a deleted drawing
   b. Opening a new drawing
   c. Directly opening an attached xref
   d. All of the above

6. The **XBIND** command is used for:
   a. Adding or removing individual dependent definitions from the xrefed drawing to the host drawing
   b. Managing xref layer settings
   c. Adding or removing layer definitions to the current host drawing
   d. All of the above

7. An eTransmit report contains the following information:
   a. Date and drawing name
   b. File paths and xref file paths
   c. Any excluded files
   d. All of the above

8. eTransmit files can be which of the following?
   a. .exe (self-extracting executable files)
   b. .zip (zip files)
   c. Folder (set of files)
   d. All of the above

9. Why would "demand loading" be applied to xrefs?
   a. To automatically load your drawing when AutoCAD is opened
   b. To speed up AutoCAD and make it run more efficiently
   c. To block others from using your xrefs
   d. All of the above

10. Why would raster images be applied to a drawing?
    a. To provide a company logo background image
    b. To provide location points for satellite topographical drawings
    c. To trace shapes or profiles
    d. All of the above

Matching

Write the letter of the correct answer on the line.

a. **External Reference** _____
b. **ETRANSMIT** _____
c. **IMAGEATTACH** _____
d. **XCLIP** _____
e. **REFEDIT** _____
f. **XATTACH** _____
g. **XBIND** _____
h. **IMAGEADJUST** _____
i. **XOPEN** _____
j. **IMAGEQUALITY** _____

1. Displays the **Select Image File** dialog box
2. Bypasses the **External References** palette and directly attaches an xref
3. A reference to a drawing file that retains a link back to the original drawing file
4. Opens an attached xref directly in your current drawing
5. Packages drawing and dependent files for file transfer
6. Binds individual named object definitions from an xref drawing
7. Toggles an image between draft and high-quality mode
8. Opens a referenced drawing in a new drawing window
9. Sets contrast, brightness, and fade on an attached image
10. Crops an external reference to a defined boundary

True or False

Circle the correct answer.

1. **True or False:** Changes to "attached" drawings are not shown on the host drawing.
2. **True or False:** Changes to "bound" drawings are not shown on the host drawing.
3. **True or False:** "Detach" removes an xref attached drawing.
4. **True or False:** "Reloading" an xref is done to remove any changes made to the attached drawing.
5. **True or False:** Layers can be included in attached drawings.
6. **True or False:** When binding an xref, named objects such as layers, linetypes, and textstyles are always renamed by prefixing the named object with the xref file name followed by "0".
7. **True or False:** eTransmit can also provide a report and other files along with the drawing file to be transmitted.
8. **True or False:** With demand loading, "Enabled with Copy" lets others use your drawing while you continue to edit it.
9. **True or False:** The resolution can be adjusted on an attached image on your AutoCAD drawing.
10. **True or False:** Image quality cannot be adjusted on an attached image on your AutoCAD drawing.

chapter seventeen

Chapter Projects

G Project 17-1: *Classroom Plan, continued from Chapter 16* [BASIC]

1. Open drawing ***P16-1*** from Chapter 16.
2. Switch to the **Architectural Title Block** layout and erase the existing title block information.
3. Attach the drawing ***Architectural D-Size.dwg*** created in Chapter 16 as an overlay xref. Place the xref at the coordinates **-.75,-.5**.
4. Insert the drawing ***Title Attributes Architectural D-Size.dwg*** as a block. Use an insertion point of **-.5,.25**. Fill in appropriate values for the attributes. Your drawing should resemble Figure 17-44.
5. Save your drawing as ***P17-1***.

Figure 17-44

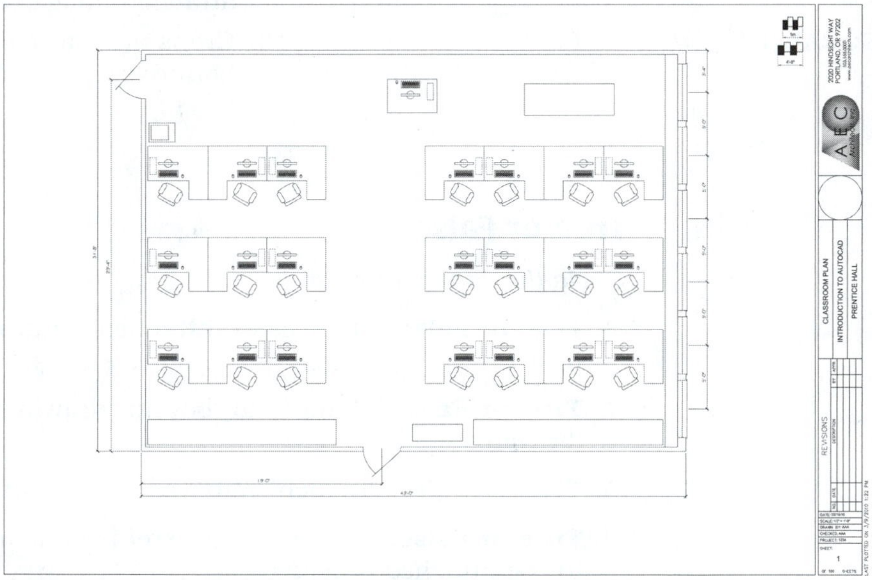

M Project 17-2: *Logo/B-Size Mechanical Border, continued from Chapters 10 & 16* [INTERMEDIATE]

1. Open drawing ***P10-2***. Move the geometry so the lower left corner of the logo is located at **0,0**.
2. Create a new text style called **PEARSON** using the Arial.ttf font. Assign a width of **1.25** to the style.
3. Create a second text style called **PH** using the Times New Roman.ttf font.

Figure 17-45

4. Add the text shown in Figure 17-45. All text is **0.375** high. Assign the color **255** directly to the text.

   Hint: Use the **DRAWORDER** command to send the fill areas behind.

5. Scale the logo so the height is **.375**, as shown in Figure 17-45.
6. Save the drawing as ***PH-Logo***.
7. Open the template file ***Mechanical B-Size.DWT*** from Chapter 16.
8. Set the **Mechanical B-Size** layout current and attach the drawing ***PH-Logo*** as an overlay reference. Place the drawing as shown in Figure 17-46.
9. Save the drawing template as ***Mechanical B-Size.DWG***.

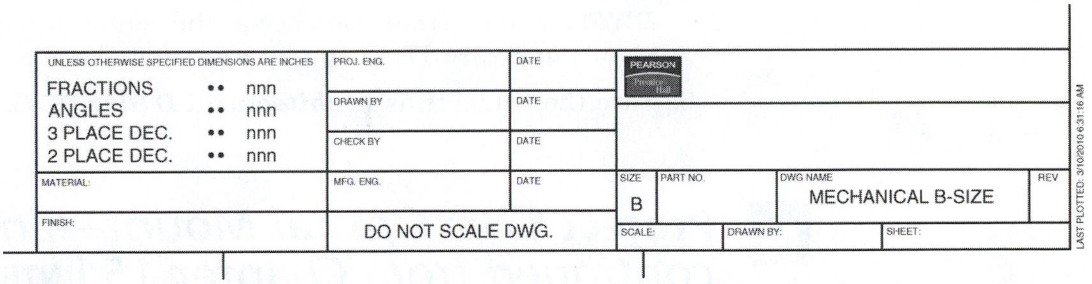

Figure 17-46

A Project 17-3: *Architectural D-Size Border, continued from Chapter 16* [ADVANCED]

1. Start a new drawing using the **acad.dwt** template.
2. Create the architect's professional seal shown in Figure 17-47 as follows:
   a. Draw all information on Layer **0**.
   b. Use the **DONUT** command to create a donut at **0,0** with an inside diameter of **1.70″** and an outside diameter of **1.75″**.

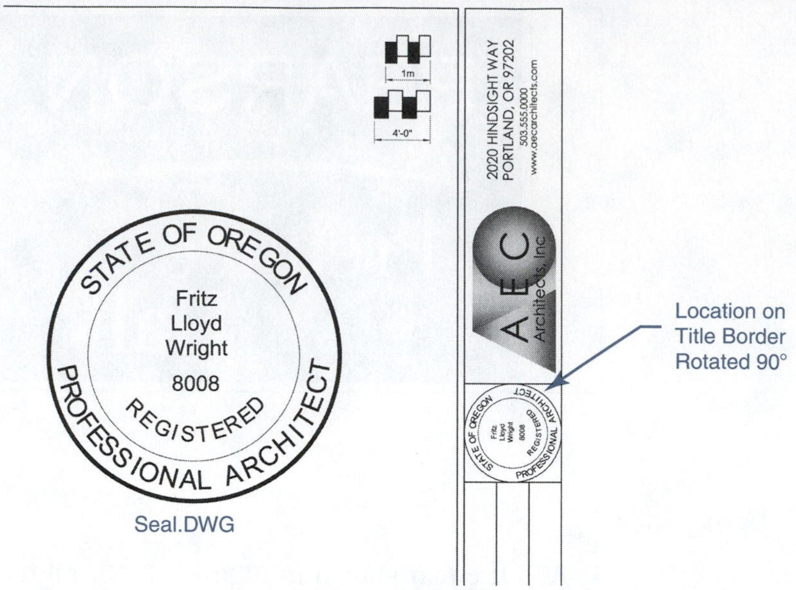

Figure 17-47

c. Use the **CIRCLE** command to create the inside circle with a diameter of **1.25″**.

d. Use the **TEXT** command to create all text as single-line text. Outside curved text is **0.125″** high. Inside text is **0.093″**.

e. Save the drawing as ***Seal.DWG***.

3. Open template file ***Architectural D-Size.DWT*** from Chapter 16.
4. Attach the architect's professional seal drawing created above (***Seal.DWG***) as an external reference at the center of the title border circle as shown in Figure 17-47 so that it is rotated **90°**.
5. Save the template as ***Architectural D-Size.DWG***.

M **Project 17-4:** *Optical Mount—English Units, continued from Chapter 15* [INTERMEDIATE]

1. Open drawing ***P15-4*** from Chapter 15.
2. Switch to the **Mechanical B-Size** layout. Erase the existing title block geometry, leaving only the viewport.
3. Attach the drawing ***Mechanical B-Size.DWG*** as an overlay xref. Place the reference at **0,0** at a scale of **1** and a rotation angle of **0**.
4. Insert the drawing ***Title Attributes Mechanical B-Size.dwg*** as a block. Place the block at **0,0** at a scale of **1** and a rotation angle of **0**. Enter appropriate values for the title block attributes. Your drawing should look like Figure 17-48.
5. Save the drawing as ***P17-4***.

Figure 17-48

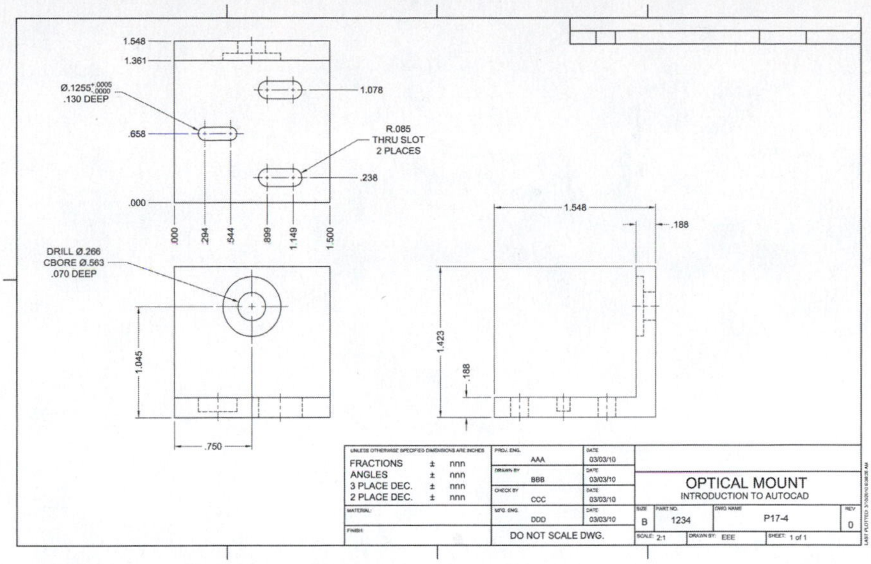

Project 17-5: *Residential Architectural Plan, continued from Chapter 15* [ADVANCED]

1. Open drawing ***P15-5*** from Chapter 15.
2. Switch to the **Architectural D-Size** layout. Erase the existing title block geometry, leaving only the viewport.
3. Attach the drawing ***Architectural D-Size.DWG*** as an overlay xref. Place the reference at **0,0** at a scale of **1** and a rotation angle of **0**.
4. Insert the drawing ***Title Attributes D-Size.dwg*** as a block. Place the block at **0,0** at a scale of **1** and a rotation angle of **0**. Enter appropriate values for the title block attributes. Your drawing should look like Figure 17-49.
5. Save the drawing as ***P17-5***.

Figure 17-49

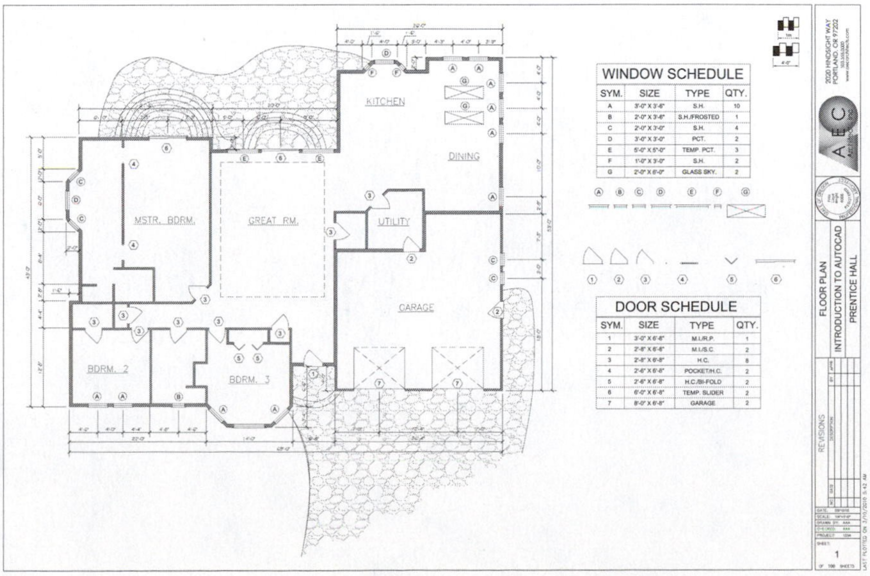

chapter eighteen
Drawing Management Tools and Utilities

CHAPTER OBJECTIVES

- Understand the backup and autosave settings
- Fix a corrupt drawing
- Purge a drawing of unused data
- Import and export different drawing file types
- Copy and paste information between different software applications
- Use object linking and embedding objects in AutoCAD drawings
- Automate repetitive tasks using the **Action Recorder**
- Use the **Measure** tools
- Use the **QuickCalc** calculator
- Delete duplicate objects
- Use web-based collaboration tools

Introduction

Successful AutoCAD drawing management requires thorough attention to drawing file creation, maintenance, saving, and naming conventions. Drawing management also includes addressing corrupt drawing files, importing and exporting various CAD drawing formats, as well as combining and sharing data using the Windows Clipboard feature or object linking and embedding (OLE). In this chapter, we will examine the AutoCAD drawing utilities and additional drawing management procedures to use when different source applications are needed to increase productivity. We will also look at automating repetitive tasks using the **Action Recorder,** retrieve useful info about your drawing using the **Measure** tools, and introduce AutoCAD's **QuickCalc** calculator. In addition, preserving the data integrity of your drawings by deleting unnecessary duplicate objects is explored, and we take a look at AutoCAD's online collaboration tools.

Drawing File Backup and Recovery

Anyone who has used a computer has undoubtedly experienced computer problems. Operating systems that lock up, programs that stop responding, viruses, power outages, and equipment failures are a routine part of working with computers. How do you protect your drawings, which represent many hours of valuable work? For starters, safe computing practices such as regular backups, up-to-date antivirus and anti-spyware software scans, and routine computer maintenance can greatly reduce the risk of data loss. AutoCAD offers some additional ways of backing up your design data as well as some tools to help monitor file integrity and recover lost design data.

File Safety Precautions

The **File Safety Precautions** area of the **Open and Save** tab of the **Options** dialog box allows you to control some of these backup and file recovery options (see Figure 18-1).

Figure 18-1
The **Open and Save** tab of the **Options** dialog box

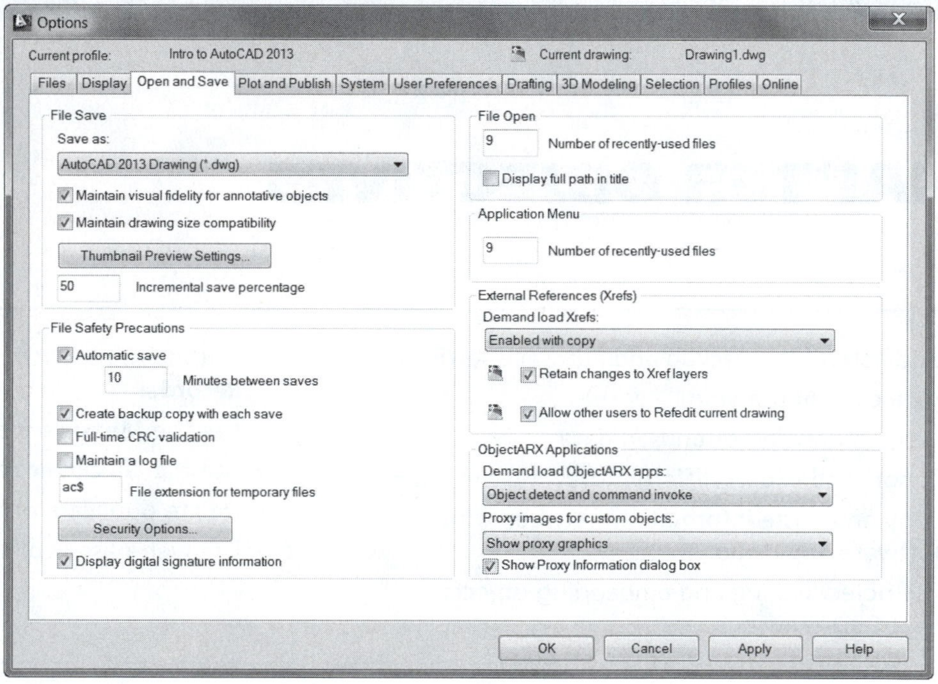

Backup Files. By default, when you save a drawing in AutoCAD, the file is saved with a DWG file extension. The previously saved version of that drawing is renamed with a BAK file extension. For example, you have a drawing called ***A-06.DWG***. When you open that drawing, make changes to it, and then save your drawing, the previously saved file is renamed ***A-06.BAK***, and the new changes are saved to ***A-06.DWG***. If a BAK file already exists, it is overwritten with the new BAK file.

If you are unable to open your current drawing, or if you need to recover changes made to your drawing, you can simply rename the BAK file extension to DWG and open the backup file in AutoCAD. You may want to change the file name as well to avoid confusion. For example, you have two files: ***A-06.BAK*** and ***A-06.DWG***. You wish to open the BAK file to recover some objects you deleted. To avoid confusing the two files, you can rename the BAK file to ***A-06-Backup.DWG*** and then open the backup file in AutoCAD.

By default, AutoCAD has backup files enabled. To disable the backup file creation, remove the check from the **Create backup copy with each save** box in the **Open and Save** tab of the **Options** dialog box (see Figure 18-1).

Autosave Files. Backup files (BAK) are created only when you save your drawing. For this reason, it's considered good practice to save your drawing often. However, there are times when AutoCAD quits before you have the opportunity to save. To help recover from these instances, AutoCAD can automatically save your drawing file at regular intervals. This is known as an ***autosave***. By default, AutoCAD does this every 10 minutes.

autosave: The automatic saving of your drawing by AutoCAD at regular intervals. The default save interval is 10 minutes.

Files created with the **Autosave** feature are considered temporary files. When AutoCAD performs an autosave, it assigns a name consisting of the file name combined with a random number and the file extension .SV$. These files are placed in the **Windows Temp** folder and are created as a failsafe to recover drawing information in the event of a program failure or power failure. If your drawing is closed normally, these temporary save files are deleted. If the drawing does not close normally, the temporary files are retained and can be renamed and opened in AutoCAD.

When you start a command, AutoCAD looks at the time since the last autosave was done. If the time is greater than the autosave interval, AutoCAD will do an autosave before it starts your command. AutoCAD displays a message when it is performing an automatic save while you are working. Following is an example:

```
Automatic save to C:\Users\Paul\appdata\local\temp\AS-01_1_1_7542.sv$
```

If you do not see a message from AutoCAD, you should check that the **Autosave** feature is enabled and that a reasonable save interval is set. You can set this in the **Automatic save** box in the **Open and Save** tab of the **Options** dialog box (see Figure 18-1). The **Automatic Save File Location** setting in the **Files** tab of the **Options** dialog box allows you to change the location where the files are saved.

Temporary Files. In addition to the autosave files, AutoCAD also creates temporary files in the **Windows Temp** folder. These temporary files are used by AutoCAD and Windows to manage data while your drawing file is open. These keep track of undo and redo information as well as store changes to your drawing in between saves. These files are given a random name with an .AC$ file extension.

As with the autosave files (.sv$), when a drawing is closed normally, these temporary files are deleted. However, if a drawing is not closed properly, these temporary files are retained. They can also be renamed as .DWG and opened in AutoCAD. Since these files are randomly named, finding the exact file you are looking for can be hit-or-miss. Also, there is no guarantee that the information you're seeking will be contained in these files, but it does give you some additional places to look if you lose valuable design information.

The **File extension for temporary files** box in the **Open and Save** tab of the **Options** dialog box (see Figure 18-1) allows you to change the file extension of these temporary files. Also, the **Temporary Drawing File Location** setting in the **Files** tab of the **Options** dialog box allows you to change the location where these temporary files are stored (see Figure 18-2).

Corrupt Drawing Objects. Drawing corruption can occur when a drawing object is not defined properly within the drawing file. This can happen when importing drawing information from other CAD applications, if you are using custom software applications inside AutoCAD, or if AutoCAD closes without saving your drawing.

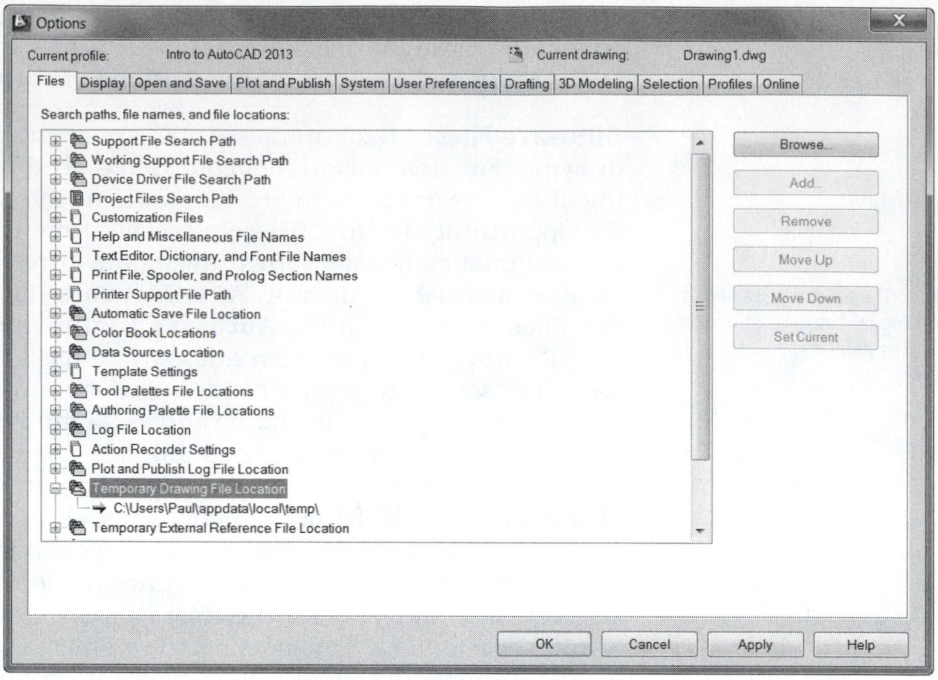

Figure 18-2
The **Files** tab of the **Options** dialog box

Corrupt objects can cause a variety of problems from AutoCAD locking up to a drawing failing to load properly. When you consider that drawings can be used as xrefs and that nested references may be used, a single corrupt object can wreck havoc on a design project.

If you suspect that corrupt objects may be causing a problem, AutoCAD allows you to turn on a cyclic redundancy check (CRC) to monitor all new objects created during the drawing session. This option will check all new objects to ensure they are well defined before AutoCAD adds them to the drawing. This is set by checking the **Full-time CRC validation** box in the **Open and Save** tab of the **Options** dialog box (see Figure 18-1). This checking can slow down the drawing process slightly, so this option should be turned on only as needed to help track down the source of corrupt drawing objects.

DRAWING RECOVERY MANAGER	
Application Menu:	Drawing Utilities 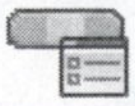
Toolbar:	None
Menu:	File | Drawing Utilities | Drawing Recovery Manager...
Command Line:	DRAWINGRECOVERY
Command Alias:	None

Recovering Lost or Corrupt Drawings

If your AutoCAD session locks up or closes before you can save your drawing, AutoCAD provides some tools for recovering lost drawing information and fixing corrupt drawings.

> **NOTE**
> Although these tools can recover many damaged or corrupt drawings, they are not guaranteed to recover all lost information. Remember to save often and back up critical drawing files on a regular basis.

The Drawing Recovery Manager. If your AutoCAD session ends prematurely, the next time you start AutoCAD, it will display a message about drawing recovery (see Figure 18-3), and the **Drawing Recovery Manager** (see Figure 18-4) will start automatically. You can also start the **Drawing Recovery Manager** with the **DRAWINGRECOVERY** command.

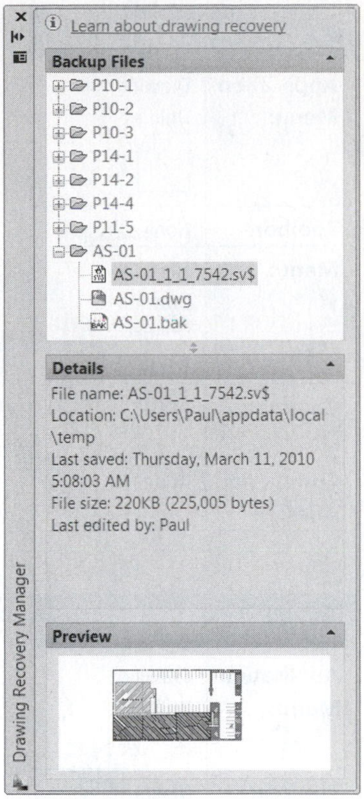

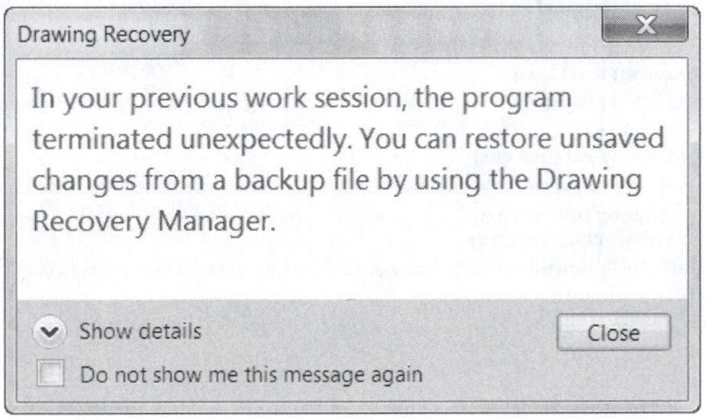

Figure 18-3
The **Drawing Recovery** message

Figure 18-4
The **Drawing Recovery Manager** palette

The **Drawing Recovery Manager** provides an easy way to examine backup and autosave files. When the **Drawing Recovery Manager** starts, it searches for backup (BAK) and autosave (SV$) files along with their associated DWG files and displays them in the **Drawing Recovery Manager** palette (see Figure 18-4).

> **NOTE**
> The **Drawing Recovery Manager** will start automatically every time you start AutoCAD until you remove the drawings from the **Backup Files** area.

The **Backup Files** area displays all the backup, autosave, and drawing files associated with a given drawing. Selecting one of the listed files will display information about the file in the **Details** area and a preview of the file in the **Preview** area.

You can open the selected file by double-clicking it or choosing **Open** from the right-click menu. This allows you to examine in detail the various backup files. When you find the one you want to keep, save it using the file name of your choosing. You can then remove the drawing from the **Drawing Recovery Manager** by selecting the drawing file name folder in the **Backup Files** area and choosing **Remove** from the right-click menu (see Figure 18-5).

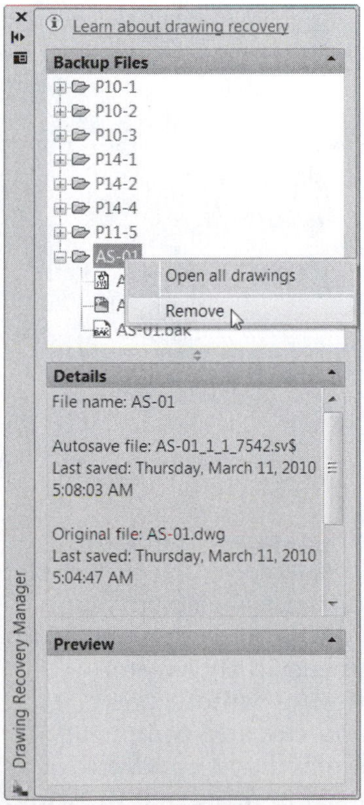

Figure 18-5
Removing drawings from the **Drawing Recovery Manager**

Fixing Corrupt Drawings. AutoCAD provides two commands to examine and repair corrupt drawing files: **AUDIT** and **RECOVER.**

The **AUDIT** and **RECOVER** commands will both scan a drawing for any corruption and allow you to attempt to correct any problems they find.

AUDIT	
Application Menu:	Drawing Utilities
Toolbar:	None
Menu:	File | Drawing Utilities | Audit
Command Line:	AUDIT
Command Alias:	None

RECOVER	
Application Menu:	Drawing Utilities Recover
Toolbar:	None
Pull-down Menu:	File | Drawing Utilities | Recover...
Command Line:	RECOVER
Command Alias:	None

The **RECOVER** command allows you to select any drawing file to scan. The **AUDIT** command scans only the currently open drawing file. In addition, the **AUDIT** command gives you the option of just scanning the file without attempting to correct the problems.

The **AUDIT** and **RECOVER** commands operate only on a single drawing file. If the drawing has any xrefs, the xrefs will not be scanned for problems. If you wish to scan a drawing and all of its associated xrefs, you should use the **RECOVERALL** command. The **RECOVERALL** command scans the drawing and any xrefs attached to the drawing. The **RECOVERALL** command also displays a report at the end of the command showing the results for each drawing it scans (see Figure 18-6).

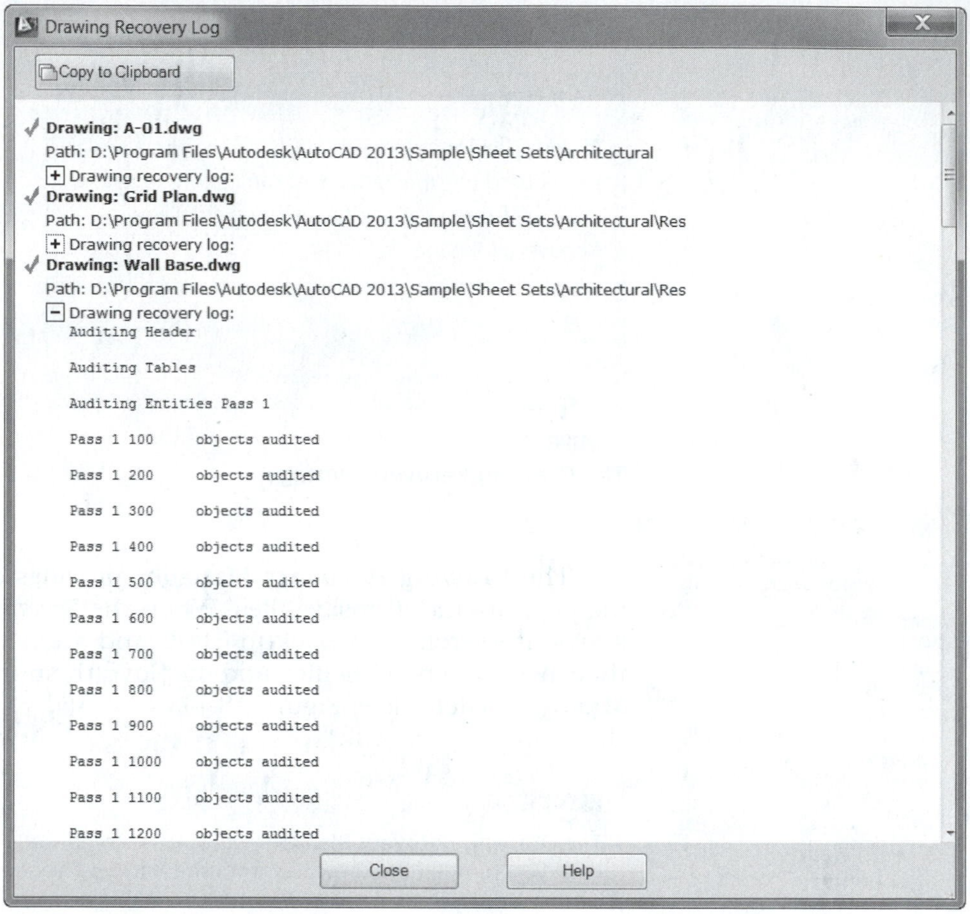

Figure 18-6
The **RECOVERALL** error report

Cleaning Up Drawing Files

As you have seen, AutoCAD drawings consist of both graphical and nongraphical elements. Layer settings, block definitions, linetypes, text styles, plot styles, table styles, dimension styles, and other nongraphical elements can be stored in a drawing, even if they may not be used within the drawing. It is possible to have empty layers, unused linetypes, dimension styles, etc.

Although these elements can reside in the drawing without being used, they do add to the size of the drawing file and can add complexity to a drawing. For example, a CAD layering standard may have hundreds of potential layers, but only a handful of them are used in any given drawing. Similarly, you may have a block library that consists of many symbols, but you may use only a few in any single drawing. There is no need to have all of these extra settings and block definitions stored with every drawing.

RECOVER WITH XREFS	
Application Menu:	Drawing Utilities | Recover with Xrefs
Toolbar:	None
Menu:	File | Drawing Utilities | Recover drawing and xrefs…
Command Line:	RECOVERALL
Command Alias:	None

PURGE	
Application Menu:	Drawing Utilities
Toolbar:	None
Menu:	File | Drawing Utilities | Purge
Command Line:	PURGE
Command Alias:	None

To help manage these various definitions and style settings, AutoCAD provides the **PURGE** command to view unused styles and definitions and remove them from the drawing.

The PURGE Command. When you start the **PURGE** command, AutoCAD displays the **Purge** dialog box (see Figure 18-7). This dialog box has a list of the various items that can be purged from a drawing. By default, AutoCAD shows you all the items that can be purged. A plus (+) symbol next to any item denotes a category that contains items that can be purged. Clicking on the + symbol expands the tree to show you the specific items. To purge an item, simply select the object from the list and choose the **Purge** button. You can select multiple items using either **<Ctrl>** or **<Shift>** while selecting items. To purge all unused objects from a drawing, choose the **Purge All** button. Placing a check in the **Confirm each item to be purged** check box will cause AutoCAD to prompt you before it purges each object.

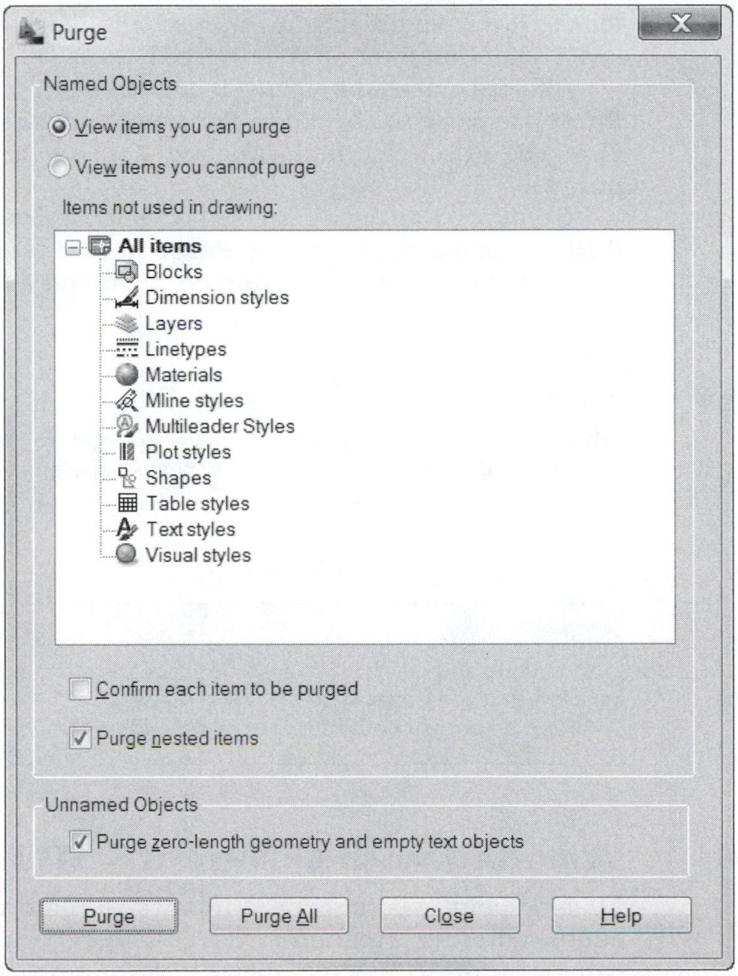

Figure 18-7
The **Purge** dialog box

You can also choose to display items that cannot be purged by selecting the **View items you cannot purge** button. Keep in mind that only unused objects can be purged from the drawing. When the **View items you cannot purge** button is selected, you will not be able to purge any objects. In addition, the following default AutoCAD objects cannot be purged from a drawing.

Default Objects	Name
Layers	**0**, Defpoints
Linetypes	ByLayer, Continous, ByBlock
Multileader Style	Standard
Multiline Style	Standard
Dimension Style	Standard
Plot Style	Normal
Table Style	Standard
Text Style	Standard

Purging Nested Items. Some objects may be nested, meaning that unused objects are dependent on other unused objects. For example, you may have a block definition that contains an unused layer definition. In order for the layer definition to be purged, the block definition containing the layer definition must first be purged.

To purge nested items, you can keep selecting items and choosing **Purge,** or you can check the **Purge nested items** box. When this box is checked, all selected items and any items nested below them will also be purged.

To quickly purge all unused objects from your drawing, start the **PURGE** command, check the **Purge nested items** box, turn off the **Confirm each item to be purged** item, and choose **Purge All.**

NOTE

It is possible to purge zero-length geometry and text objects that consist only of spaces by selecting the check box in the **Unamed Objects** area at the bottom of the **Purge** dialog box.

TIP

Sometimes you may have a layer that appears to be unused but cannot be purged. Layers that are frozen within a layout viewport (**VP Freeze** in the **Layer** dialog box) cannot be purged until they are thawed within that viewport.

Working with Different CAD File Formats

At some point, you may need to work with a drawing file created in another drafting program or use AutoCAD data in another software application. AutoCAD has the ability to read and write a number of different raster and vector file formats. Importing and exporting various file formats can be done in a variety of ways.

Exporting to DWF/PDF Files

In Chapter 15, we saw how it is possible to create DWF/DWFx (Design Web Format) and PDF (Adobe Portable Document Format) files using the **PLOT** command. It is also possible to export a file directly to the DWF/DWFx and PDF formats using the tools and settings on the **Export to DWF/PDF** panel on the **Output** tab of the ribbon shown in Figure 18-8.

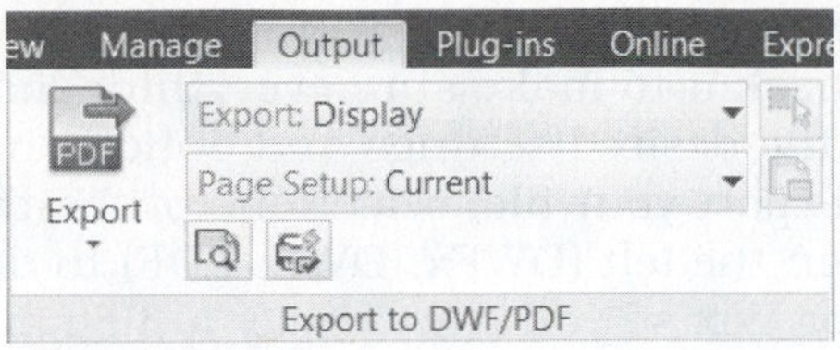

Figure 18-8
The **Export to DWF/PDF** panel

FOR MORE DETAILS

See page 637 in Chapter 15 for more information about the DWF/DWFx and PDF file formats.

The **Export** list box at the top of the panel allows you to specify what information to export. In a paper space layout, you can export the current layout or all layouts at one time. In model space, you can export what is currently displayed, the drawing extents, or pick a window area.

The **Page Setup** list box allows you to control what page setup settings to apply. By default, the current page setup is used. The **Override** option displays the **Page Setup Override** dialog box so you can change the paper size, the plot style table (pen assignments), the plot scale, and other plot settings.

The **Export to DWF/PDF Options** button displays the **Export to DWF/PDF Options** dialog box shown in Figure 18-9 so you can control the output settings, such as whether to create a multisheet file or to include layer information.

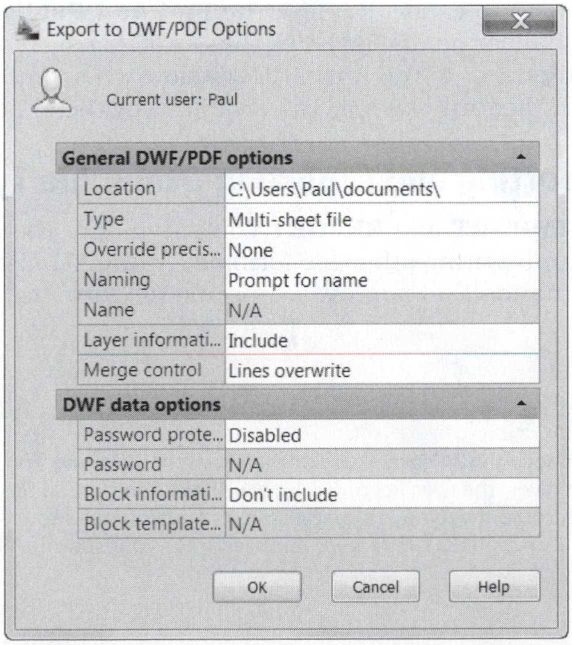

Figure 18-9
The **Export to DWF/PDF Options** dialog box

The **Preview** button allows you to preview the file before exporting it so you can check it to make sure everything looks correct.

Once all the desired settings and options have been selected and you are ready to export your file, select one of the three export types from the flyout menu on the left (DWFx, DWF, PDF) to display its corresponding **Save As** dialog box so you can specify a file name and location. All three output formats share a dialog box similar to the **Save As PDF** dialog box shown in Figure 18-10.

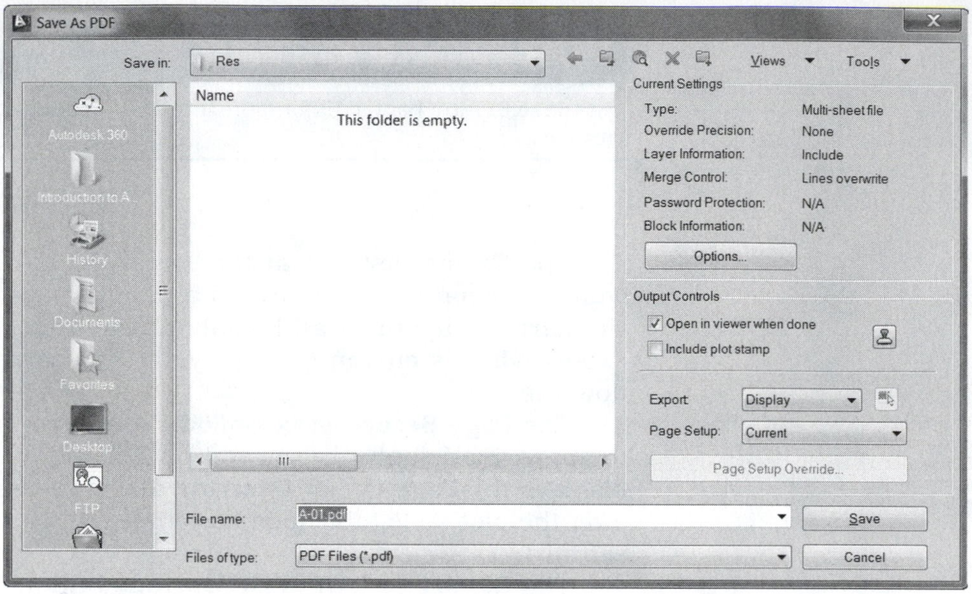

Figure 18-10
The **Save As PDF** dialog box

Select the **Save** button once the file name and location have been specified to export the file. The **Plot and Publish Job Complete** notification balloon is displayed in the AutoCAD system tray in the lower right-hand corner of the AutoCAD window when AutoCAD is done exporting the file, indicating the success or failure of the export process.

Importing and Exporting Other File Types

The **IMPORT** and **EXPORT** commands are the most common ways of reading and writing other file formats. AutoCAD also provides a number of commands that work with specific file formats.

NOTE

This section will cover some of the basics of importing and exporting various file formats. However, the specifics of working with each individual file type are beyond the scope of this book. If you have a specific file format you need to read or write, please consult the AutoCAD 2013 Help feature and search for your specific file format.

The following table describes the various file formats that AutoCAD supports and the commands that are available to read or write.

File Format	Description	Import Commands	Export Commands
DXF	Design Exchange File. A text file used by Autodesk to exchange CAD information. The most common way of exchanging AutoCAD drawing information between various CAD packages.	**OPEN, DXFIN**	**SAVEAS, DXFOUT**
DGN	MicroStation Design file. A 2D/3D vector file format created by MicroStation.	**IMPORT, DGNIMPORT**	**EXPORT, DGNEXPORT**
DXB	Design Exchange Binary file. A binary version of the DXF file. This file is typically used to flatten 3D models to 2D drawings. 3D models are plotted to a flat 2D DXB file.	**DXBIN**	**PLOT**
ACIS/SAT	Standard Acis Text. A 3D solid file format. Only **REGION** or **3DSOLID** objects are supported in this file format.	**IMPORT, ACISIN**	**EXPORT, ACISOUT**
STL	Stereolithography file. A 3D solid file format typically used in rapid prototyping applications. Only **REGION** or **3DSOLID** objects are supported in this file format.	Not Supported	**STLOUT**
3DS	3D Studio file. Typically a 3D file format used primarily with rendering and animation applications.	Not Supported	**3DSOUT**
DXX	Attribute extract DXF file. An abbreviated type of DXF file created by the **ATTEXT** command in AutoCAD. Only block and attribute information is included in a DXX file.	Not Supported	**EXPORT, ATTEXT**
EPS	Encapsulated Postscript file. Used in a variety of desktop publishing applications and maintains a high-resolution print capability.	Not Supported	**EXPORT, PSOUT**
FBX	Open framework for 3D data transfer that allows importing and exporting 3D objects, 2D objects with thickness, lights, cameras, and materials from one Autodesk program to another.	**IMPORT**	**FBXEXPORT**
WMF	Windows Metafile. A combination of raster and vector formats used in Microsoft Windows and Office applications.	**IMPORT, WMFIN**	**EXPORT, WMFOUT**
BMP, JPG, PNG, TIF	Various raster file formats.	Not Supported	**BMPOUT, JPGOUT, PNGOUT, TIFOUT**

EXPORT	
Application Menu:	Other Formats
Toolbar:	None
Menu:	File | Export...
Command Line:	EXPORT
Command Alias:	EXP

The EXPORT Command. The **EXPORT** command allows you to export AutoCAD drawing information to various file formats. When you start the **EXPORT** command, AutoCAD will display the **Export Data** dialog box (see Figure 18-11) where you can specify the output file type as well as the file name.

Once you specify the file name and file type, AutoCAD will prompt you to select the objects you want to export. Once you select the objects to export, press **<Enter>** to export the objects to the specified file.

NOTE

The **PLOT** command also provides some additional ways to export your file to various raster and vector file formats. These file formats include JPG, BMP, PNG, CALS, TIF, TGA, PDF, PCX, and HPGL. These formats require the configuration of plotters via the **Add-a-Plotter** wizard, which can be accessed with the **Add or Configure Plotters...** button in the **Plot and Publish** tab of the **Options** dialog box.

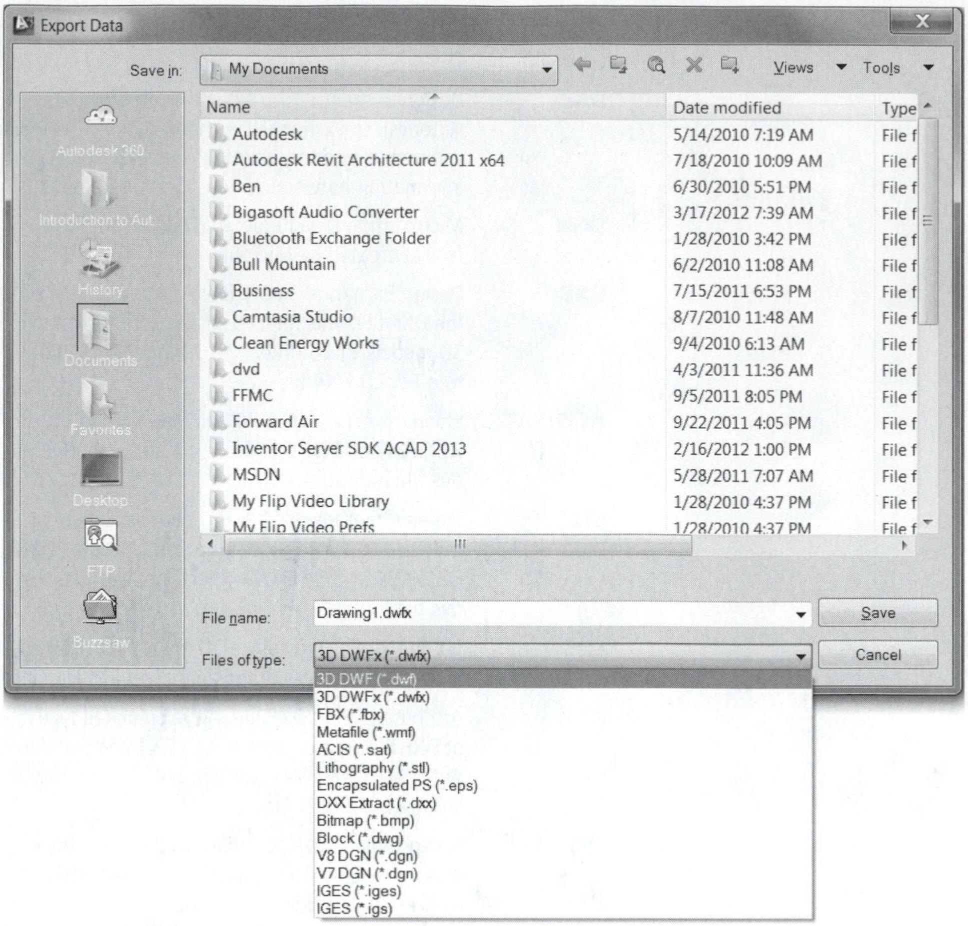

Figure 18-11
The **Export Data** dialog box

IMPORT	
Ribbon & Panel:	Insert | Import
Insert Toolbar:	
Menu:	File | Import...
Command Line:	IMPORT
Command Alias:	IMP

The IMPORT Command. The **IMPORT** command allows you to convert various file formats to AutoCAD objects. When you start the **IMPORT** command, AutoCAD will display the **Import File** dialog box (see Figure 18-12) and allow you to specify the file type as well as the file name.

NOTE

Take care when exporting objects from paper space layouts. Because you are prompted to select objects, only selected objects in the current drawing space will be exported. Exporting objects from both model space and paper space is not allowed.

After you specify the file name and file type, AutoCAD imports the data and places it in the drawing. The imported objects are typically converted to a block and placed as a single object, which can then be exploded.

Working with DXF Files

DXF stands for *Design Exchange File* and is the primary method that AutoCAD uses for importing and exporting data between CAD applications. A DXF file can be either binary or ASCII text (most commonly used) and is widely used and supported by most CAD applications. DXF files can be created in AutoCAD with the **SAVEAS** or **DXFOUT** command. The **DXFOUT** command is actually a command alias for the **SAVEAS** command.

NOTE

The specifics of importing a file will vary depending on the type of file selected. See the AutoCAD 2013 Help file for the specifics of importing each type of file.

Figure 18-12
The **Import File** dialog box

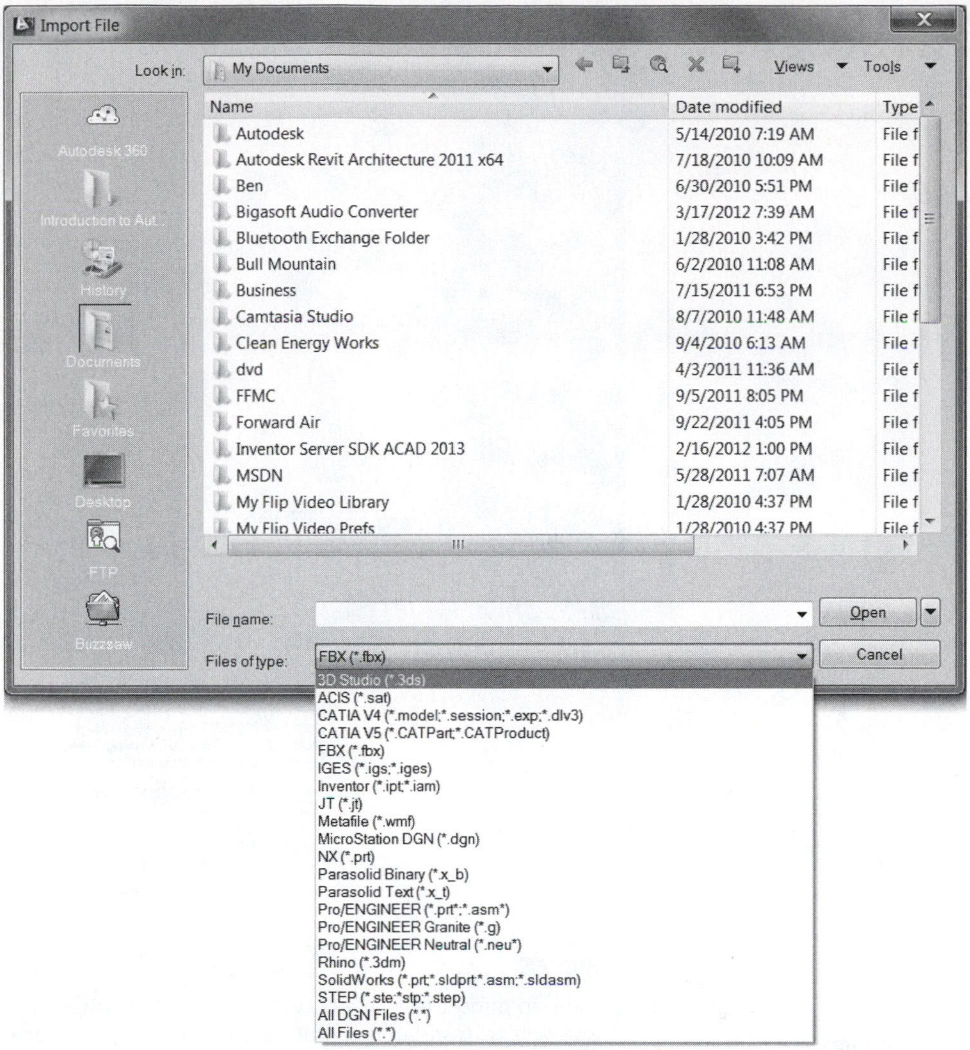

Creating a DXF File. Although the **EXPORT** command only allows you to export selected objects within a drawing, a DXF file represents the entire drawing (paper space, model space, layers, blocks, etc.). Like the DWG file format, the DXF file format has changed over the various releases of AutoCAD. AutoCAD can currently create DXF files in the following formats: AutoCAD 2013, AutoCAD 2010, AutoCAD 2007, AutoCAD 2004, AutoCAD 2000, and AutoCAD R12.

NOTE

The DXF file format is defined in the AutoCAD Customization Guide section of the AutoCAD 2013 Help.

When you start the **SAVEAS** command, AutoCAD displays the **Save Drawing As** dialog box (see Figure 18-13). Specify the file name, location, and type of file you wish to create and choose **Save.**

DWG CONVERT	
Application Menu:	Save As
Toolbar:	None
Menu:	File | DWG Convert
Command Line:	DWGCONVERT
Command Alias:	None

DWG Convert Tool

The **DWG Convert** tool allows you to convert a group of drawings to the following AutoCAD DWG release formats: AutoCAD 2013, AutoCAD 2010, AutoCAD 2007, AutoCAD 2004, AutoCAD 2000, and AutoCAD R14.

Figure 18-13
The **Save Drawing As** dialog box

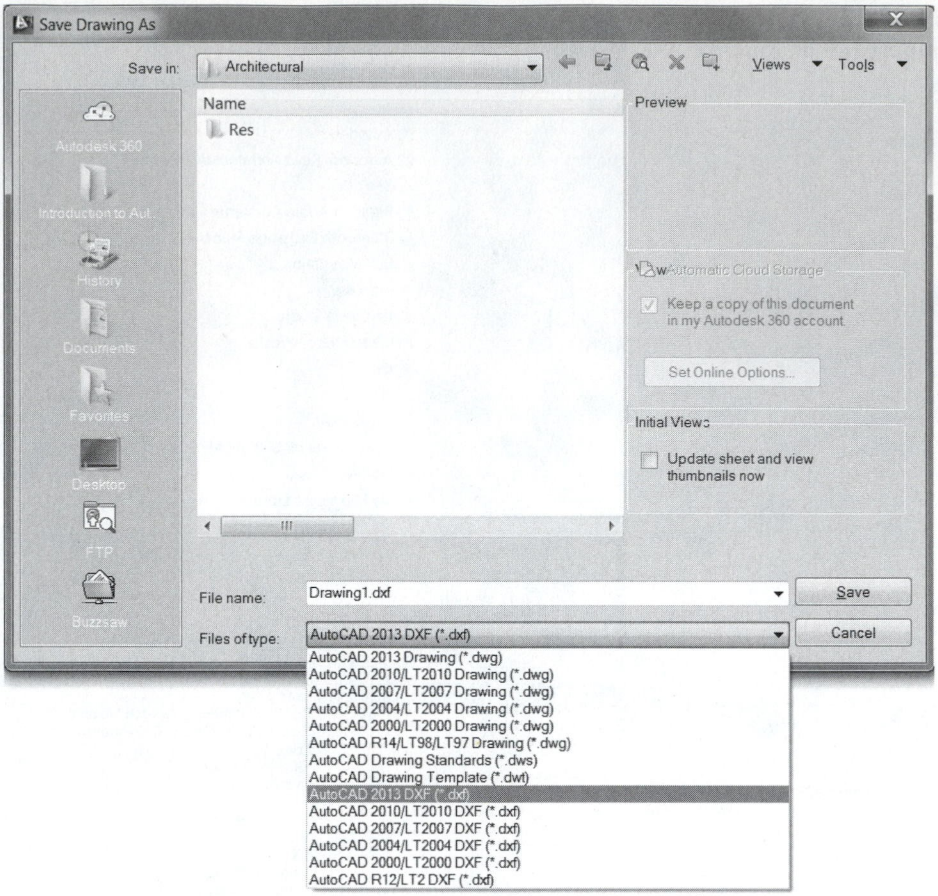

NOTE

Keep in mind that some object types are not supported in earlier versions of AutoCAD and will be translated to their earlier object types. For example, ellipses and spline curves are converted to polylines in the R12 file format.

Select the **DWG Convert** tool to display the **DWG Convert** dialog box shown in Figure 18-14.

In the **DWG Convert** dialog box, you select the files you wish to convert along with a conversion setup that controls all of the conversion properties. The buttons along the bottom of the file list box shown in Figure 18-14 allow you to add one or more drawings to convert, make a new list of files, save a list of files, as well as open or append existing file lists. The **Conversion Setups...** button allows you to add, delete, rename, or modify conversion setups so you can manage and maintain multiple setups for multiple clients and/or consultants.

The **Modify Conversion Setup** dialog box shown in Figure 18-15 controls all of the conversion settings.

In the **Conversion type and location** area at the top of the dialog box, you select the desired file format to convert to, as well as whether to save the converted files in-place, to a specific folder, or to either a compressed zip file or a self-extracting .exe file.

The **Actions** area on the right side of the dialog box allows you to include one or more of the following actions to be performed during the conversion:

- **Create backup (*.bak) files** Backup files are automatically created during the conversion
- **Convert digitally signed files** Controls whether digitally signed drawings are converted

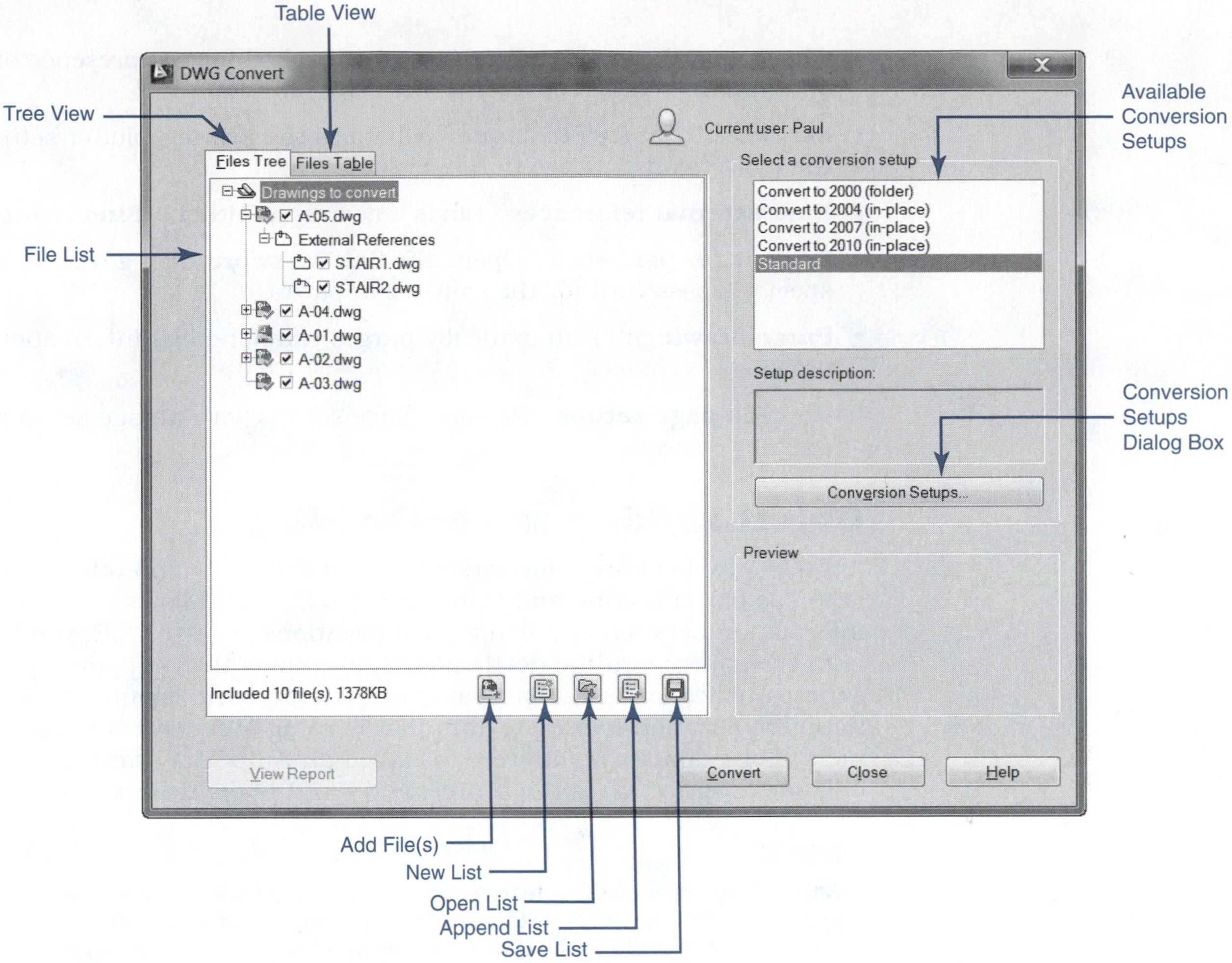

Figure 18-14
The **DWG Convert** dialog box

Figure 18-15
The **Modify Conversion Setup** dialog box

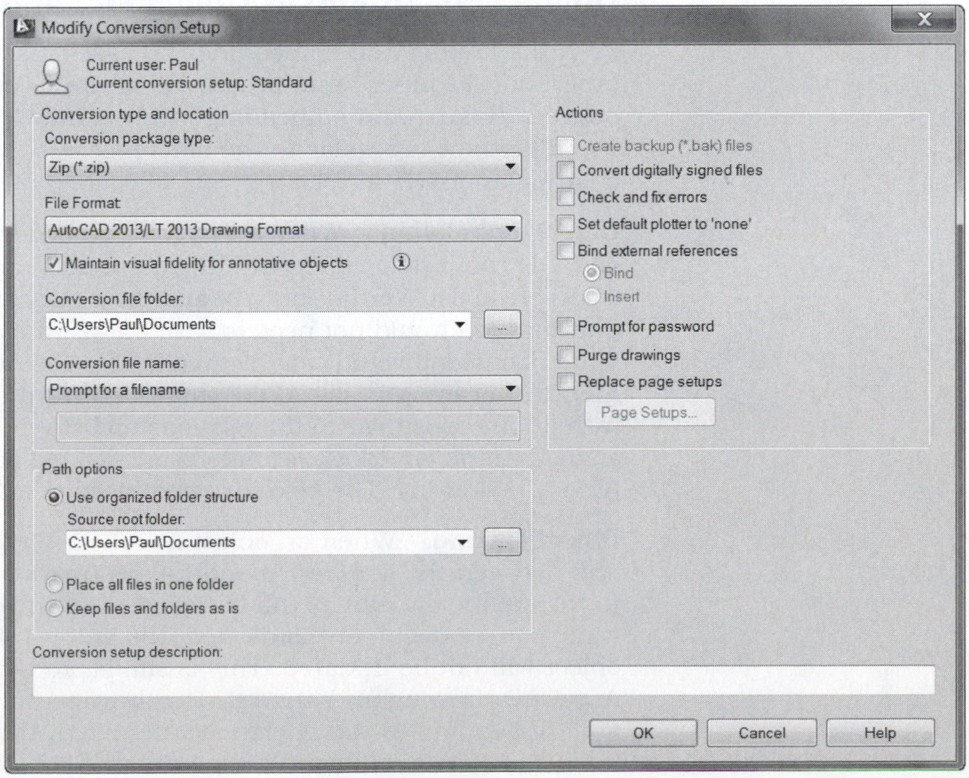

- **Check and fix errors** Drawings are checked for the presence of errors and automatically recovered if any errors are found
- **Set default plotter to 'none'** Changes the printer/plotter setting in the conversion package to **None**
- **Bind external references** Binds any xrefs as either a **Bind** or **Insert** type
- **Prompt for password** Opens the **Set Password** dialog box so you can specify a password for the conversion package
- **Purge drawings** Automatically purges unreferenced information from drawings
- **Replace page setups** Replaces page setups with a page setup from another drawing

Object Linking and Embedding

Another way to share information between AutoCAD and other applications is to use object linking and embedding (OLE). OLE allows you to share information between two Windows applications. To use OLE, you need both the source and the destination applications that support OLE. The source application is the program used to create the document. The destination application is the program that is going to receive the source document. For example, if you were to embed an AutoCAD drawing in a Word document, AutoCAD is the source, and Word is the destination.

NOTE

Although the Windows OLE feature can use AutoCAD as either a source or a destination application, this chapter focuses primarily on placing OLE objects in AutoCAD drawings. Keep in mind that the behavior of data from other applications will vary from program to program. To link or embed AutoCAD drawings in other applications, refer to the documentation for that application for specifics on using OLE within that program.

Object Linking Versus Object Embedding

Both the linking and embedding processes insert information from one program's document into another program's document. The difference between linking and embedding involves how the information is stored. The difference is similar to the difference between inserting a block and creating an external reference.

Object Embedding. When an object is embedded into a document, that object is completely stored with the destination application. For example, if you created a Word document and then embedded it into an AutoCAD drawing, you would not need to save the Word file to a separate file. That Word document would exist entirely within the AutoCAD drawing. When the AutoCAD drawing is saved, the embedded Word document is saved along with it. This is similar to the relationship between an AutoCAD drawing and a block definition. Block definitions are defined and stored entirely within the AutoCAD drawing. The block does not need to exist as a separate drawing file.

Object Linking. When an object is linked, Windows simply creates a link between the source file and the destination file. Any changes made to the source document will be reflected in the destination document. If the source document is deleted, the link will be broken, and the OLE object will not be updated. This is similar to the relationship between an AutoCAD drawing and an xref. The drawing file does not store the entire xref, only a link to the referenced file. When the referenced file is updated, the AutoCAD drawing containing the xref is also updated.

INSERT OLE OBJECT	
Ribbon & Panel:	Insert | Data
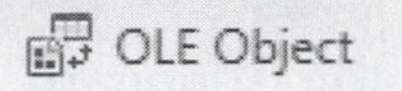	
Insert Toolbar:	
Menu:	Insert | OLE Object...
Command Line:	INSERTOBJ
Command Alias:	None

Inserting OLE Objects

There are a number of ways to create and insert OLE objects within an AutoCAD drawing. The method you use will depend primarily on whether you want to link or embed the OLE object and how you want the OLE object to be displayed within the drawing.

The INSERTOBJ Command. The **INSERTOBJ** command allows you to create a linked or embedded object. When the command starts, AutoCAD displays the **Insert Object** dialog box (see Figure 18-16).

From this dialog box, you can choose whether you want to create a new OLE source document or use an existing file as the source document. Select the **Create New** button to create a new embedded document. Selecting this will only allow you to embed a new file. Once you select the type of file you wish to embed, Windows will launch that application with a new document for you to modify. Once you are done modifying the embedded object, select **File | Update Drawing** in the source application, and the embedded object will appear in your drawing. Because the object is now embedded in the AutoCAD drawing, you can close the source application.

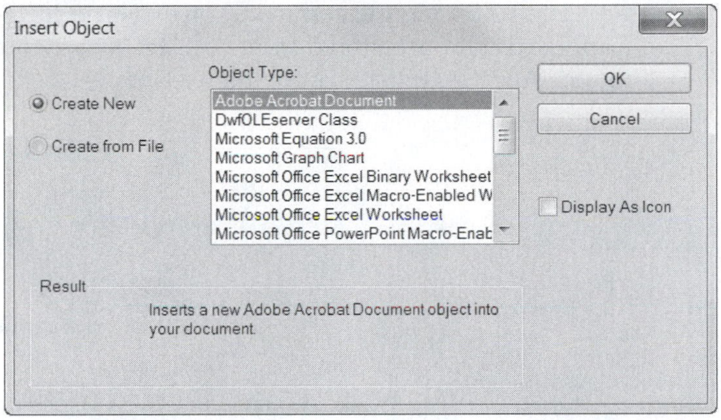

Figure 18-16
The **Insert Object** dialog box

NOTE

The **Object Type:** list in the **Insert Object** dialog box will vary depending on the software you have installed on your computer. Also, the exact method of updating the AutoCAD drawing may vary depending on the source application.

PASTE	
Ribbon & Panel:	Home | Clipboard 
Standard Toolbar:	
Menu:	Edit | Paste
Command Line:	PASTECLIP
Command Alias:	Ctrl+V

If you want to insert an existing document as an OLE object, select the **Create from File** button and then choose **Browse...** to select the source document. Once you select the source file, you can choose whether you want to link to the source file by putting a check in the **Link** box. Not checking the **Link** box will embed the source file in your drawing.

Placing a check in the **Display As Icon** box will display the OLE object as an icon within the drawing. This affects only how the OLE object is displayed in AutoCAD and does not affect the contents of the OLE object.

Using the Windows Clipboard. The Windows Clipboard feature can also be used to link and embed data from other applications. The Windows Clipboard provides a way to store data temporarily from most Windows programs. In most Windows applications, you can select data and choose **Copy** from the **Edit** pull-down menu or press **<Ctrl>+C** within that application. Once information is copied to the Windows Clipboard, it can be pasted into other locations within the same program or into other Windows applications.

PASTE SPECIAL	
Ribbon & Panel:	Home | Clipboard Paste Special
Toolbar:	None
Menu:	Edit | Paste Special…
Command Line:	PASTESPEC
Command Alias:	None

The Windows Clipboard can be used to store information from within a file or to copy entire files or multiple files and folders.

When data are stored in the Windows Clipboard, they can be placed into an AutoCAD drawing using either the **PASTECLIP** or **PASTESPEC** command.

The **PASTECLIP** command will place the contents of the Clipboard as an embedded OLE object. When you start the **PASTECLIP** command, AutoCAD will prompt you for an insertion point. Depending on the type of data in the Clipboard, AutoCAD may display the **OLE Text Size** dialog box (see Figure 18-17). This dialog box allows you to control how Windows fonts are displayed within AutoCAD and allows you to convert the Windows text point size to AutoCAD text height.

> **TIP**
>
> You can also display the **OLE Text Size** dialog box by selecting an OLE object after it is inserted and right-clicking to display a shortcut menu with an OLE submenu with different OLE options including **Text Size…**.

The **PASTESPEC** command gives you a little more control over how the Clipboard data are stored in AutoCAD. When you start the **PASTESPEC** command, AutoCAD displays the **Paste Special** dialog box (see Figure 18-18).

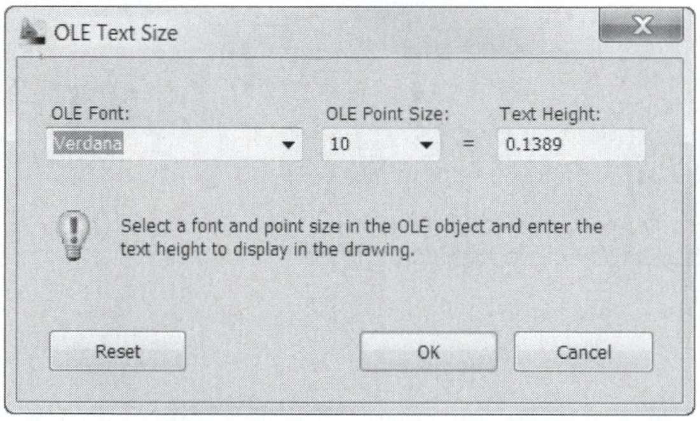

Figure 18-17
The **OLE Text Size** dialog box

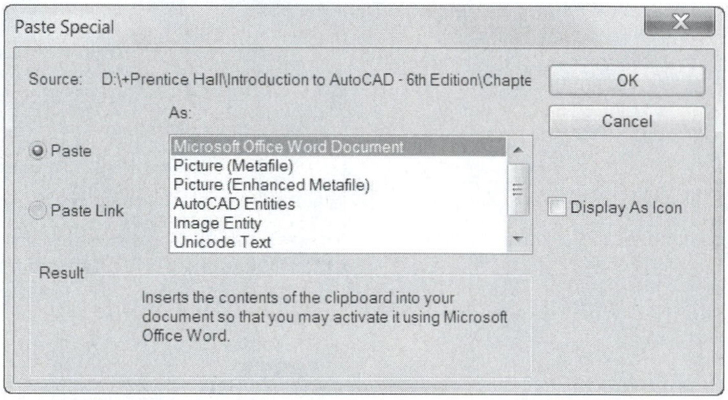

Figure 18-18
The **Paste Special** dialog box

The **PASTESPEC** command allows you to place an OLE object as either a linked or embedded object. It also gives you the ability to convert the Clipboard contents to AutoCAD entities. The types of entities created depend on the type of data in the Clipboard. AutoCAD will automatically convert the Clipboard data to the most appropriate AutoCAD object. For example, Excel spreadsheet data are converted to an AutoCAD table, Word data are converted to AutoCAD text, raster image data are converted to AutoCAD image overlays, etc.

Drag and Drop. Another feature of Windows is the ability to drag and drop data between Windows applications. Drag and drop involves selecting data in the source application and, while holding your left mouse button down, dragging the data onto your AutoCAD drawing. This can take a little practice and preplanning because both applications must be visible and accessible.

Drag and drop works the same as **PASTECLIP;** the only difference is that drag and drop bypasses the Windows Clipboard.

Editing OLE Objects

The nature of OLE objects is that they are edited in their source application. Double-clicking an OLE object will launch the source application with the OLE data. You can make changes to the source data and then either close the source application or, in most applications, choose **Close and Return to Drawing** from the **File** menu in the source application.

Managing Linked Objects. Linked objects, because they rely on the coordination of multiple files, require a little more attention than embedded objects. The location of the linked file is critical to updating and maintaining the information in the OLE object. The way in which you want the information updated and the ability to terminate a link are also part of maintaining an OLE linked object. The **OLELINKS** command allows you to manage linked OLE objects from within AutoCAD.

OLE LINKS	
Ribbon & Panel:	None
Toolbar:	None
Menu:	Edit | OLE Links
Command Line:	OLELINKS
Command Alias:	None

The **OLELINKS** command works only if you have linked OLE objects in your AutoCAD drawing. When you start the **OLELINKS** command, AutoCAD displays the **Links** dialog box (see Figure 18-19). The **Update Now** button will refresh the OLE object from the source file. The **Open Source** button will open the source file and allow you to make changes. The **Change Source...** button allows you to specify a different source file for the OLE object. When you change the source file, the new source file must be the same type of file as the original source file. The **Break Link** button will terminate the link between AutoCAD and the source file and turn the linked object into an embedded object.

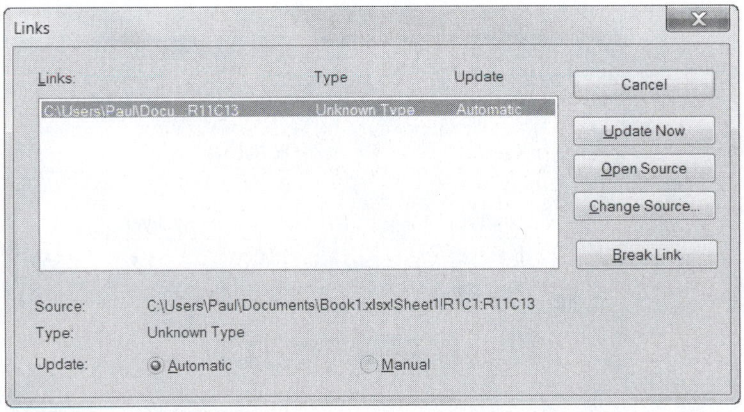

Figure 18-19
The **Links** dialog box

At the bottom of the **Links** dialog box are two buttons that allow you to control how the OLE objects are updated. Choosing **Automatic** causes AutoCAD to update the OLE object whenever the source file changes. Choosing **Manual** tells AutoCAD not to update the OLE object until you choose the **Update Now** button.

Plot Quality. OLE objects are treated as raster objects when a raster plotter is used. Because large, high-resolution, color-rich rasters can be expensive to plot, you can set the **OLEQUALITY** system variable to control how each OLE object is plotted. There are four possible settings: **0** (Monochrome), **1** (Low Quality), **2** (High Quality), and **3** (Automatically Select). The default setting, **Automatically Select,** assigns a plot-quality level based on the type of object. The higher the plot-quality setting, the more time and memory are used to plot. The **OLEQUALITY** variable can be applied separately to each OLE object in the drawing.

Controlling the Visibility of OLE Objects. While working on a drawing, you may want to suppress the display or plotting of OLE objects. The **OLEHIDE** system variable allows you to control the visibility and plotting of OLE objects in model space, paper space, or both. The default setting is **0,** which displays and plots all OLE objects in both model and paper space. Setting **OLEHIDE** to **1** displays and plots OLE objects in paper space only. Setting **OLEHIDE** to **2** displays and plots OLE objects in model space only. Setting **OLEHIDE** to **3** suppresses the display and plotting of all OLE objects in both model and paper space. The **OLEHIDE** variable applies globally to all OLE objects in a drawing.

OLEFRAME System Variable. When OLE objects are placed in AutoCAD, they behave like other AutoCAD objects in that they have default properties, such as layer color and linetype, associated with them. Like raster image overlays, these properties apply to the frame surrounding the OLE objects. The **OLEFRAME** system variable controls the display and plotting of the OLE object frame. Setting **OLEFRAME** to **0** turns off the OLE frame, and it will not be displayed or plotted. Setting **OLEFRAME** to **1** displays the OLE frame both on screen and in plots. Setting **OLEFRAME** to **2** displays the OLE frame in the display but suppresses it in plots. The **OLEFRAME** variable applies globally to all OLE objects in a drawing.

OLE Properties. As stated earlier, OLE objects behave similarly to other objects in a drawing. They can be moved, copied, resized, etc. The **Properties** palette (see Figure 18-20) displays information specific to OLE objects, such as the location and the height and width scale of the OLE object. You can also control the plot quality of the OLE object.

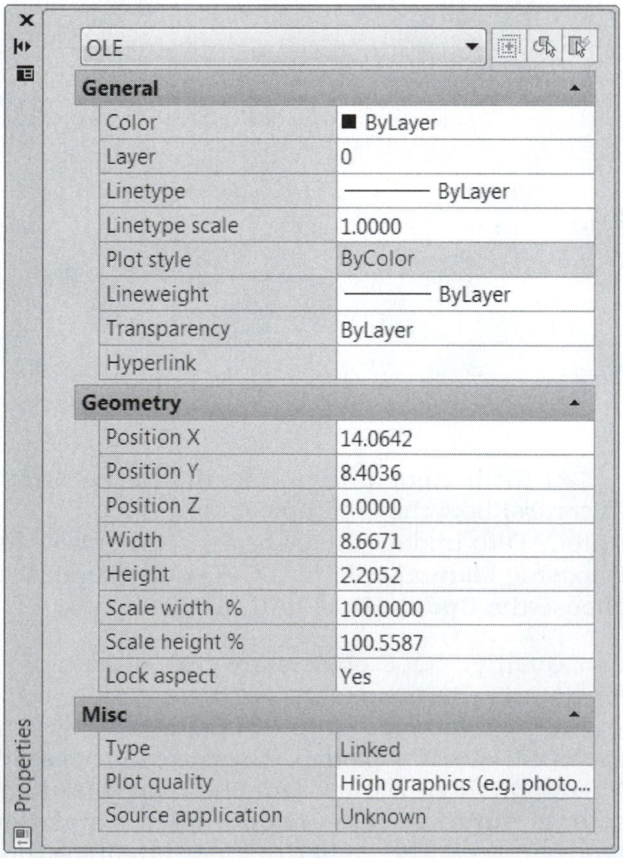

Figure 18-20
The **Properties** palette

Action Recorder

The **Action Recorder** tool allows you to automate repetitive tasks by recording the AutoCAD commands, inputs, and options you enter as an action macro that you, or anyone else, can replay later. If you find yourself doing the same series of steps over and over again, the **Action Recorder** can help by recording them so that the next time you need to do the same thing, all you have to do is press the **Play** button. The **Play** button and all the other **Action Recorder** tools and features are located on the **Action Recorder** panel on the **Manage** tab of the ribbon shown in Figure 18-21.

> **NOTE**
>
> There are certain actions that cannot be recorded—specifically, file operation commands such as **OPEN** and **CLOSE,** as well as any type of grip editing. Although it is possible to display a dialog box, it is not possible to track and record your actions once it is displayed. Additionally, the **Quick Properties** palette is not recognized and certain tool palette commands cannot be recorded.

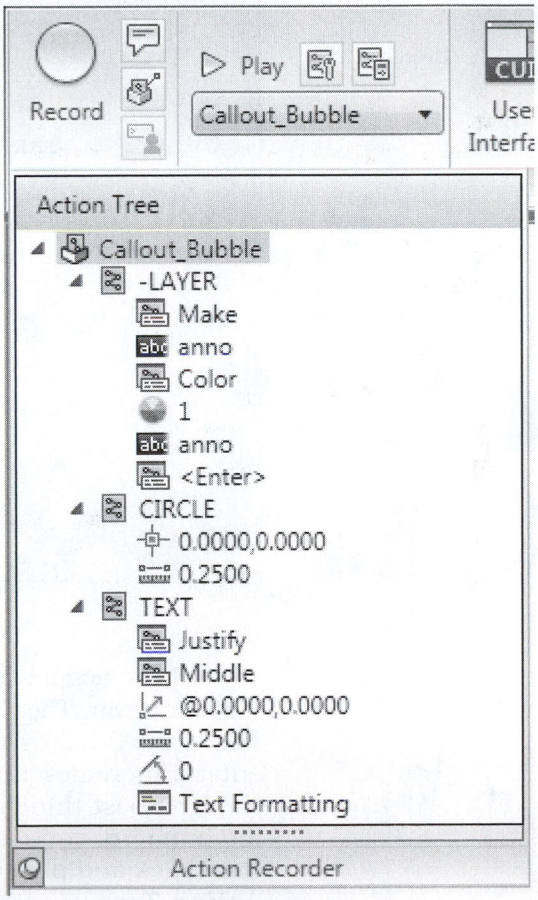

Figure 18-21
The **Action Recorder** panel

To use the **Action Recorder** you simply press the **Record** button, step through the series of commands that you would normally go through to complete a task, and push the **Stop** button when you are done. The **Action Recorder** can record actions entered via the command line window, ribbon panels, menus, the **Layer Properties Manager,** the **Properties** palette, tool palettes, and even toolbars. While recording an action macro, the **Red Recording Circle** icon is displayed near the crosshairs to indicate that the **Action Recorder** is running and any commands and input are being recorded.

> **TIP**
>
> Many commands have an alternate command line–only version that can be accessed by prefixing the command with a hyphen (-) that allows you to work around the **Action Recorder**'s inability to record dialog box actions. For instance, whereas the **HATCH** command displays the **Hatch and Gradient** dialog box, which cannot be recorded, the **-HATCH** command allows you to place hatches by entering all the command options via the keyboard so that the **Action Recorder** can record them.

When you press the **Stop** button, the **Action Macro** dialog box shown in Figure 18-22 is displayed so you can enter a command name for the macro.

Figure 18-22
The **Action Macro** dialog box

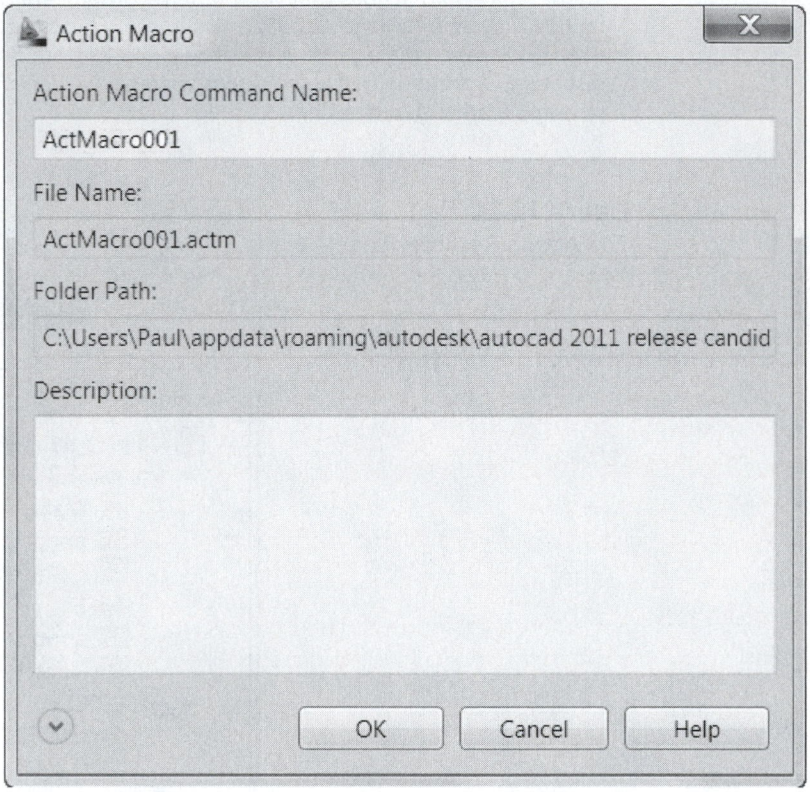

All the actions entered are saved to an action macro file with an **.ACTM** file extension. The default macro and file name provided is ***ActMacro001,*** where the 3-digit suffix is incremented each time. It is suggested that you enter a more descriptive name that better indicates the nature of the macro.

The best thing about action macros is that, after you are done recording a macro, you can go back and customize it by adding your own text messages and pauses for user input by right-clicking on an action in the **Action Tree** window and using the shortcut menu shown in Figure 18-23.

> **NOTE**
>
> There are a few limitations when naming an action macro. An action macro cannot have the same name as an AutoCAD command. For instance, you cannot create a macro named **LINE.** It is also not possible to use spaces or special characters. It is suggested you substitute a dash (-) or an underscore (_) when a space is required.

Figure 18-23
Adding messages and pauses for user input

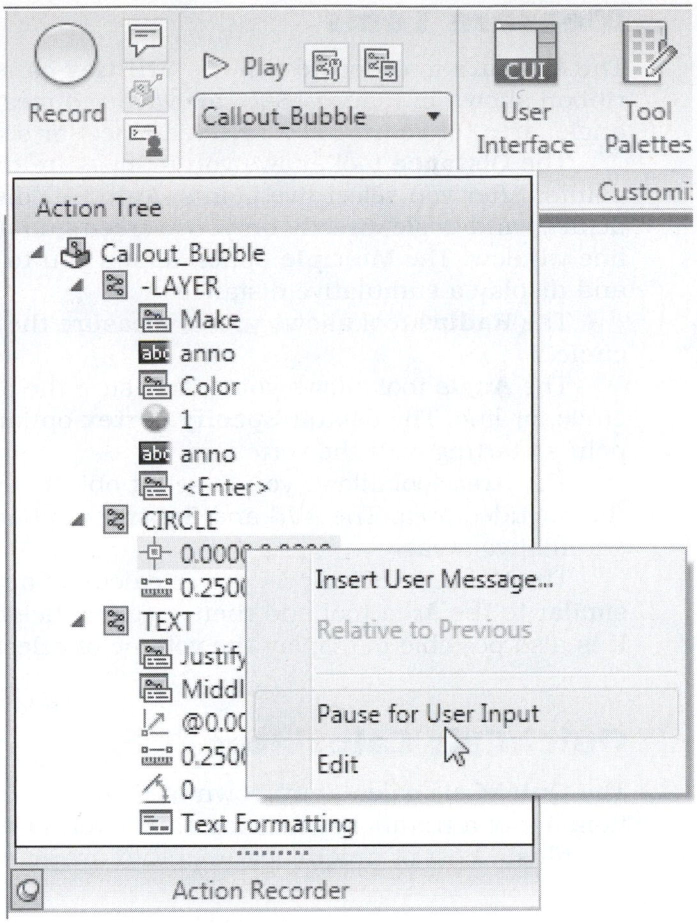

The **Preferences** button on the **Action Recorder** panel displays the **Action Recorder Preferences** dialog box shown in Figure 18-24, which allows you to control whether the **Action Recorder** panel expands when recording or playing back an action macro, and if you are prompted to provide a command name for the action macro when you press the **Stop** button and recording is stopped.

Figure 18-24
The **Action Recorder Preferences** dialog box

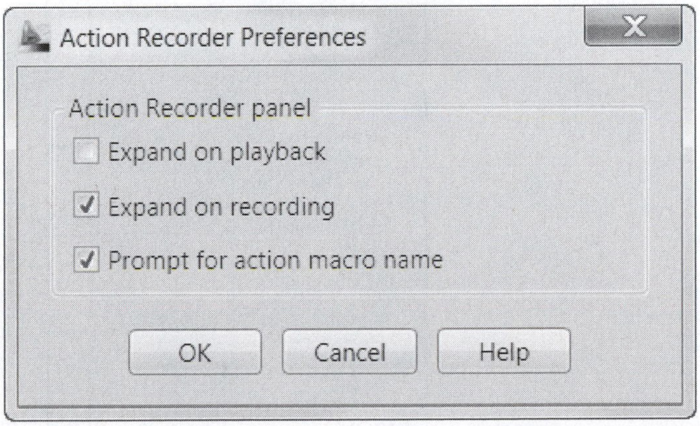

TIP

By default, action macro files are stored in the folder specified in the **Actions Recording File Location** setting under **Action Recorder Settings** on the **Files** tab of the **Options** dialog box. The **Additional Actions Reading File Locations** setting allows you to share action macro files in a network location so multiple people on different computers can access and run them.

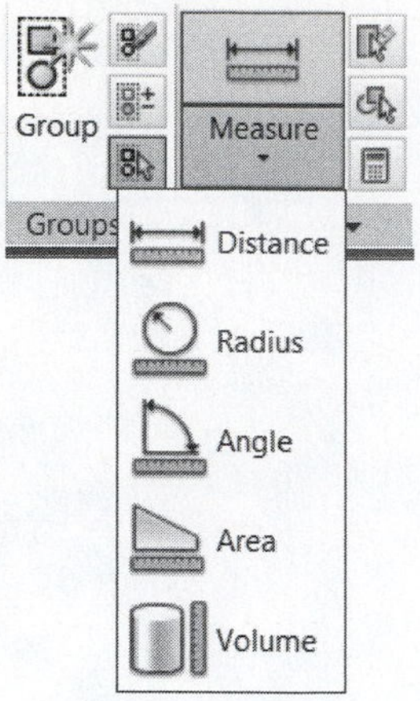

Figure 18-25
The **Measure** tools on the **Utilities** panel

Measure Tools

The **Measure** tools located on the **Utilities** panel on the **Home** tab of the ribbon shown in Figure 18-25 allow you to measure the distance, radius, angle, area, or volume of a selected object or sequence of points.

The **Distance** tool allows you to measure the distance between two points. After you select two points, AutoCAD displays the distance, delta x, delta y, and angle directly on your screen and at the AutoCAD command line window. The **Multiple** option allows you to continue picking points and display a cumulative distance.

The **Radius** tool allows you to measure the radius of a selected arc or circle.

The **Angle** tool allows you to measure the angle of a selected arc, circle, or line. The default **Specify vertex** option allows you to pick three points starting with the vertex.

The **Area** tool allows you to select objects or pick points and display the included area. The **Add** and **Subtract** options allow you to calculate cumulative areas.

The **Volume** tool allows you to calculate an area using techniques similar to the **Area** tool and then specify a height to determine the volume. It is also possible to display the volume of selected solids or regions.

QuickCalc Calculator

The **QuickCalc** calculator shown in Figure 18-26 provides all of the functionality of a traditional desktop calculator, or even the Windows calculator, plus a host of unique features that are specific to AutoCAD.

Figure 18-26
The **QuickCalc** calculator

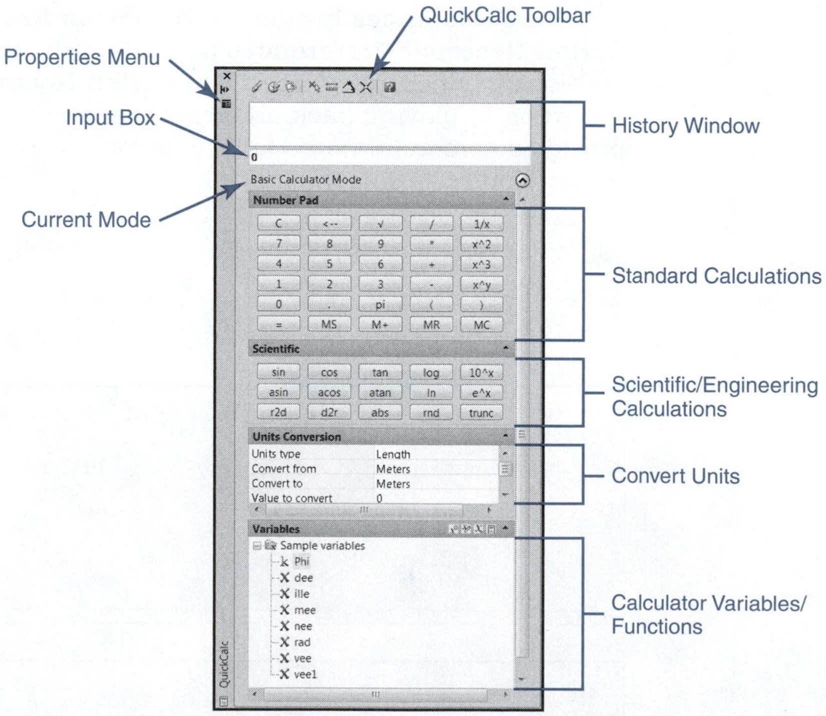

In addition to standard mathematical calculations, the **QuickCalc** calculator provides the ability to select points, distances, and angles in your drawing; perform scientific and engineering calculations; convert units;

and store/retrieve variables. Some of the different **QuickCalc** calculator capabilities and features include:

- Running **History** window that allows you to see, and even reevaluate, previously entered expressions and calculations
- Ability to share calculations with the **Properties** palette and automatically update/modify object properties in your drawing
- Perform complex mathematical and trigonometric calculations
- Convert between different unit systems using AutoCAD data values
- Perform geometric calculations based on specific object types
- Copy and paste values/expressions to and from the command prompt
- Compute both feet/inch and fractional values in stacked or decimal format
- Define, store, and retrieve built-in and user-defined calculator variables

NOTE

The Windows calculator can typically be found in the **Accessories** folder if you go to the Windows **Start** button and select **All Programs.**

TIP

The **QuickCalc** calculator is an AutoCAD palette so it shares many of the interface features you should now be familiar with. It can be easily resized and placed anywhere on your screen. In addition, it is possible to turn on its **Auto-hide** feature so the palette collapses when not in use. These and other features can be easily accessed via the palette **Properties** menu that is displayed when you select the **Properties** button on the palette title bar.

Using QuickCalc

There are a few different ways to use the **QuickCalc** calculator in AutoCAD:

- Directly, by displaying the **QuickCalc** palette using one of the following methods:
  - Select **QuickCalc** from the **Palettes** panel on the **View** tab of the ribbon.
  - Right-click with your mouse and select **QuickCalc** from the shortcut menu.
  - Enter the command **QUICKCALC** or its alias **QC** at the command prompt.
- Interacting with the **Properties** palette
- Within a command from a shortcut menu or via the command prompt

The first method is pretty self-explanatory. When you interact with **QuickCalc** directly, you are using it basically as a regular calculator, similar to the calculator that comes with Windows. You can copy and paste numerical values back and forth between AutoCAD and the calculator using the Windows Clipboard, but nothing that happens in **QuickCalc** affects your drawing.

You interact with the **Properties** palette by selecting the **QuickCalc** button that is displayed next to the property value you are working with. Clicking on **QuickCalc** displays the current property value in **QuickCalc** so you can calculate a value. After you are done calculating a value, you can transfer the result back to the **Properties** palette by selecting the **Apply** button. The property is updated and any associated object(s) are changed in the drawing.

When a command is active, you can access **QuickCalc** either by right-clicking to display the shortcut menu and select **QuickCalc** or by entering **QUICKCALC** or **QC** at the command prompt and preceding it with an apostrophe ('). Using the apostrophe (') prefix allows **QUICKCALC** to run transparently within the command. If you omit the prefix, you will receive an error. After you are done calculating a value, you can transfer the result back to the active command by selecting the **Apply** button. Calculations that you transfer back to the command will update the drawing accordingly.

> **NOTE**
>
> If you are using **QuickCalc** within a command to calculate a value for direct distance entry, you must first position the cursor to determine the desired direction and then press the **<Enter>** key.

> **TIP**
>
> The current **QuickCalc** mode indicating whether you started **QuickCalc** directly (Basic Calculator Mode), via the **Properties** palette (Property Calculation), or within a command (Active Command) is always displayed directly below the **Input** box, as shown in Figure 18-26.

Entering and Evaluating Expressions. Expressions are entered in the **Input** box shown in Figure 18-26 via the keyboard, the **QuickCalc** number pad, or a combination of both. **QuickCalc** evaluates expressions according to the standard mathematical rules of precedence:

- Expressions in parentheses are evaluated first, starting with the innermost set of parentheses and working out.
- Mathematical operators are processed in standard order (exponents, multiply/divide, add/subtract).
- Operators of equal precedence are evaluated from left to right.

You can either press the **<Enter>** key on your keyboard or click on the equal sign (=) on the **QuickCalc** number pad to evaluate an expression entered in the **Input** box.

All expressions that you enter are stored in the **History** window at the top of the palette so that you can review and retrieve them for reevaluation using different input values if you want. The right-click menu in the **History** window provides the ability to paste expressions and their values back to the **Input** box or to the AutoCAD command prompt.

If units are currently set to **Architectural,** the calculator displays the results of calculations entered in imperial units in the architectural format and rounds them to the current linear precision set in the drawing. The results for all other calculations display in decimal format with full precision.

It is possible to enter feet (') and inch (") units anytime in the **Input** box, even if the units are not currently set to **Architectural** or **Engineering** in the drawing. Unlike when entering distances at the command prompt, you can separate feet, inches, and fractional inches with a dash, a space, or nothing. The following are all valid feet-inch formatted values:

4′ or 48″
4′-7″ or 4′ 7″ or 4′7″
4′-1/2″ or 4′ 1/2″ or 4′1/2″

4′-7-1/2″ or 4′ 7-1/2″ or 4′7-1/2″
4′-7 1/2″ or 4′ 7 1/2″ or 4′7 1/2″

Similar to entering inches at the command prompt, in **QuickCalc,** you have the option of either entering double quotes (") when specifying inches or simply omitting them.

> **NOTE**
> If you are using imperial units, **QuickCalc** interprets the dash (-) as a unit separator rather than a subtraction operator. To indicate subtraction, you must include at least one space before or after the minus sign in your expressions.

> **TIP**
> You can use **QuickCalc** to calculate square feet and cubic feet using the following abbreviations:
>
> sq. ft. or sq ft
>
> cu. ft. or cu ft

The QuickCalc Toolbar. The toolbar at the top of the **QuickCalc** palette shown in Figure 18-27 provides a variety of useful tools and functions.

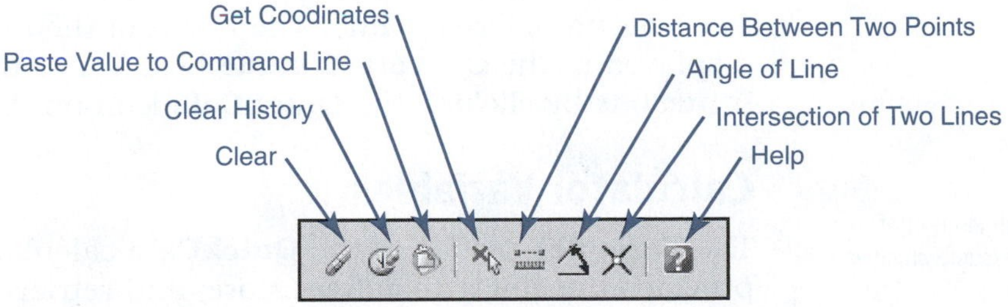

Figure 18-27
The **QuickCalc** toolbar buttons

The different tools and their descriptions are as follows:

- **Clear** Clears the **Input** box similar to selecting **C** on the number pad
- **Clear History** Clears the **History** area
- **Paste Value to Command Line** Pastes the value currently displayed in the **Input** box to the command prompt. When **QuickCalc** is used transparently within a command, this button is removed from the toolbar and replaced by the **Apply** button at the bottom of the calculator so you can apply results directly to the active command
- **Get Coordinates** Returns the coordinate value of a point selected in the drawing
- **Distance Between Two Points** Calculates the distance between two points selected in the drawing. The distance is always returned as a unitless decimal value regardless of the current unit settings

- **Angle of Line Defined by Two Points** Calculates the angle of the line defined by two points selected in the drawing
- **Intersection of Two Lines Defined by Four Points** Calculates the intersection of two lines defined by four points selected in the drawing

As you can see, a number of the tools interact with your AutoCAD drawing so that you can retrieve drawing information such as point coordinates, distances, and angles and input them directly into **QuickCalc.** You can then use **QuickCalc** to perform complex calculations using the drawing data and then, if you want, you can send the results back to AutoCAD by using copy and paste techniques or by using the **Apply** button, depending on how you started **QuickCalc.**

Converting Units

The **Units Conversion** section of the **QuickCalc** calculator shown in Figure 18-26 allows you to quickly convert length, area, volume, and angular values between different unit systems. The list of units in the **Convert from** and **Convert to** drop-down lists is determined by the unit type currently selected at the top in the **Units type** drop-down list.

NOTE

You should always enter decimal values without any units in the **Value to convert** box.

The number in the **Value to convert** box automatically displays the current value in the **Input** box, but you can simply overwrite it if you want to convert a different value. The result of the units conversion is instantly displayed in the **Converted value** box. You can copy the result to the **Input** box by clicking the **QuickCalc** icon on the right side of the box.

Calculator Variables

variable: User-defined unit of storage that may assume any given value or set of values.

The **Variables** section of the **QuickCalc** calculator shown in Figure 18-28 provides the ability to define, store, and retrieve calculator ***variables***.

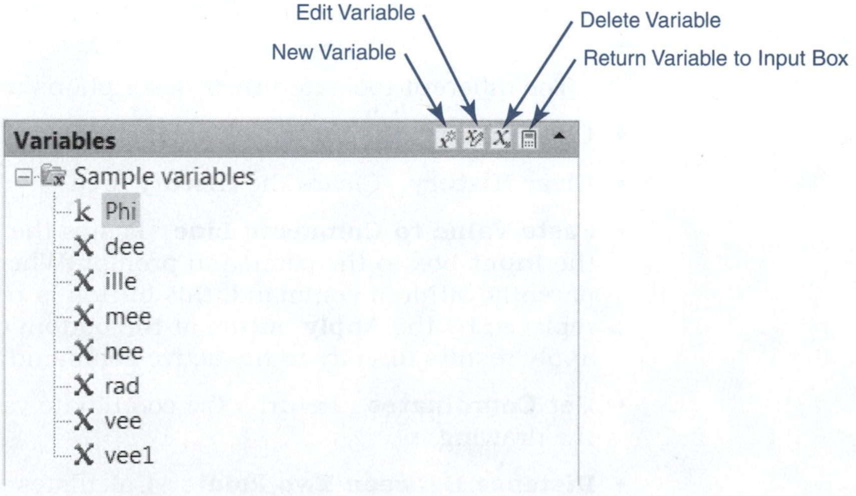

Figure 18-28
The **Variables** section of the **QuickCalc** calculator

Variables can be either constant values (coordinates, real numbers, or integers) or functions. When you hover your mouse over a variable, a tooltip displays with the variable's current value, type, and description. Double-clicking on a variable places its value in the **QuickCalc Input** box. The toolbar at the top of the **Variables** section and a right-click menu provide the following capabilities:

- Create a new variable or category
- Edit an existing variable
- Rename a variable
- Delete a variable
- Return variable value to **Input** box

AutoCAD provides a number of sample variables and functions. Most of these are expressions that combine the AutoCAD CAL functions with the **Endpoint** object snap mode. The following table provides a list of the sample variables/functions:

Variable or Function	Value or Expression	Description
Phi	1.61803399	Golden ratio
dee	dist(end,end)	Distance between two endpoints
ille	ill(end,end,end)	Intersection of two lines defined by four endpoints
mee	(end+end)/2	Midpoint between two endpoints
nee	nor(end,end)	Unit vector in the XY plane and normal to two endpoints
rad	rad	Radius of a selected circle, arc, or polyline arc
vee	vee(end,end)	Vector from two endpoints
vee1	vec1(end,end)	Unit vector from two endpoints

You can either modify the sample variables/functions or create your own.

Creating and Editing Calculator Variables. You create and edit calculator variables using the **Variable Definition** dialog box shown in Figure 18-29.

The following rules apply when defining new variables:

- **Constants** Expressions entered in the **Value or expression:** text box are evaluated before they are stored. Variables that are defined as constants are accessible in other drawings and between AutoCAD sessions.
- **Functions** Expressions entered in the **Value or expression:** text box are stored as text. Functions are evaluated when they are used in the **QuickCalc Input** box.

NOTE

The **CAL** command is the original command line version of the **QuickCalc** calculator that is typically referred to as the geometry calculator. The CAL functions allow you to evaluate point, real, or integer expressions that incorporate existing AutoCAD drawing geometry and the object snap functions. For more information about the **CAL** command, please consult the AutoCAD Help.

Figure 18-29
The **Variable Definition** dialog box

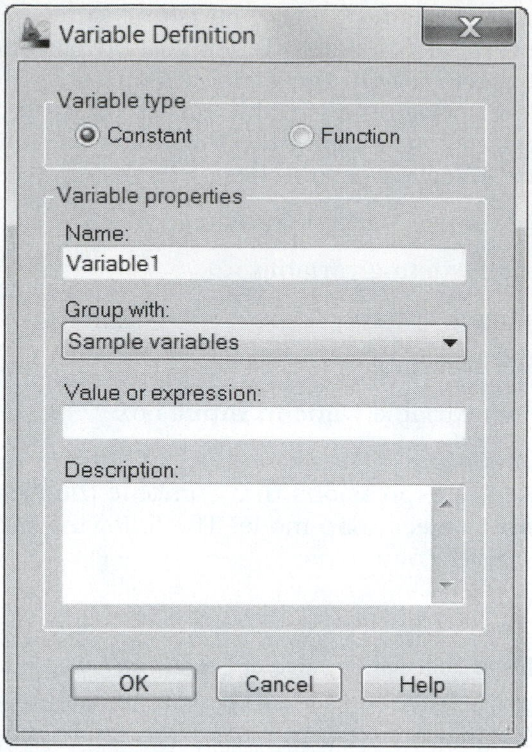

Deleting Duplicate Objects

The **Delete Duplicate Objects** tool helps you clean up your drawings by removing duplicate or unnecessary drawing objects (lines, arcs, polylines) so that you can enhance and preserve the data integrity of your drawings.

DELETE DUPLICATE OBJECTS	
Ribbon & Panel:	Home | Modify 
Toolbar:	Modify II 
Menu:	Modify
Command Line:	OVERKILL
Command Alias:	None

NOTE

The **Delete Duplicate Objects** tool can be set to combine partially overlapping or contiguous objects.

The first thing that you do after starting the **Delete Duplicate Objects** tool is select the objects in the drawing that you want to process.

TIP

You can type **All<Enter>** to quickly select everything in the drawing.

After the desired objects are selected and you press **<Enter>** to accept the selection set, the **Delete Duplicate Objects** dialog box shown in Figure 18-30 is displayed so you can refine the deletion process.

The **Delete Duplicate Objects** dialog box allows you to control the following settings and options:

- **Tolerance** Controls the precision with which the **OVERKILL** command makes numeric comparisons
- **Ignore object property** Determines which object properties are ignored during comparison

Figure 18-30
The **Delete Duplicate Objects** dialog box

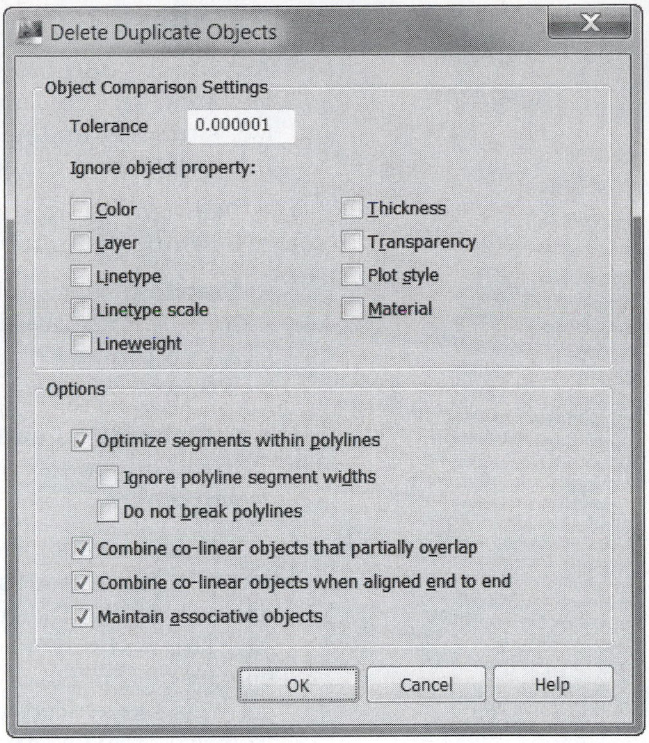

- **Optimize segments within polylines** Individual line and arc segments within selected polylines are examined so that duplicate vertices and segments are removed
- **Combine co-linear objects that partially overlap** Overlapping objects are combined into single objects
- **Combine co-linear objects when aligned end to end** Objects that have common endpoints are combined into single objects
- **Maintain associative objects** Associative objects are not deleted or modified

Web-Based Collaboration Tools

AutoCAD is integrated directly with the Internet and the **Autodesk 360** web and mobile applications. **Autodesk 360** lets you view, edit, and share drawings using the web or a mobile device. The **Autodesk 360** options are located on the **Autodesk 360** drop-down menu on the **InfoCenter** toolbar shown in Figure 18-31.

Figure 18-31
The **Autodesk 360** drop-down menu on the **InfoCenter** toolbar

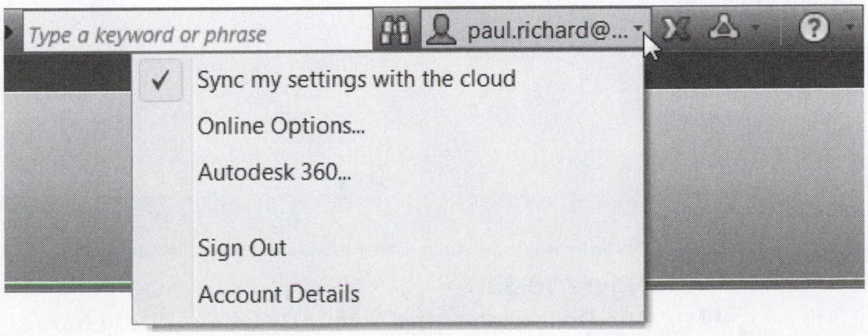

NEW to AutoCAD 2013

Autodesk 360

Autodesk® 360 provides web-enabled, typically referred to as cloud-based, features, services, and other products that allow you to design, visualize, simulate, and share your work with others anytime, anywhere via the Internet. Features include:

- **Storage** Store your design files online through an **Autodesk 360** account that allows you to access them anytime, anywhere
- **Viewing** Allow others to view your design files—even if they do not have AutoCAD. Users can view and edit 2D and 3D design files through a web browser or via a mobile device using **Autodesk 360**, **AutoCAD WS**, and Autodesk Design Review
- **Collaboration and Sharing** Share files, keep track of file updates, and invite others to comment on designs in the **Autodesk 360** collaboration workspace

You can quickly sign into your **Autodesk 360** account and access many of the **Autodesk 360** tools and options via the **AutoDesk 360** drop-down menu on the **InfoCenter** toolbar as shown in Figure 18-31.

The first time you access **Autodesk 360**, you have the opportunity to specify default cloud settings to control when your design data and custom settings are synced with the cloud. When you upload drawings directly from AutoCAD to **Autodesk 360**, external references and other dependent files are automatically included with the upload.

You can also choose to automatically sync your program appearance, profiles, workspaces, options, and support files so that you can restore them on any computer. You can modify the default cloud settings by selecting **Online Options...** on the drop-down menu on the **InfoCenter** toolbar shown in Figure 18-31, which displays the **Online** tab of the AutoCAD **Options** dialog box shown in Figure 18-32.

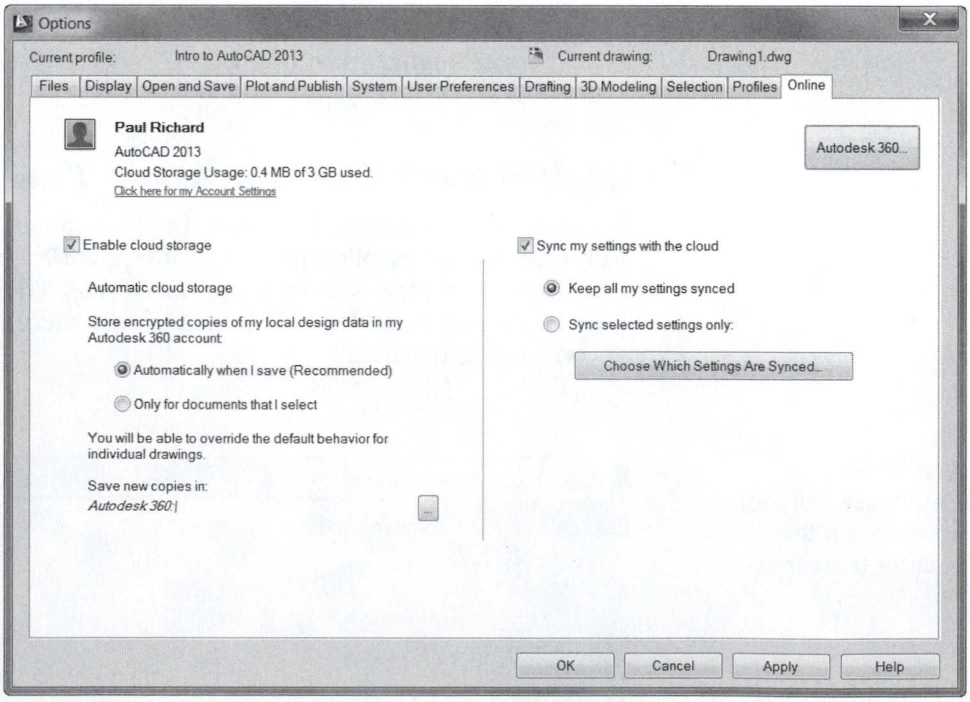

Figure 18-32
The **Online** tab of the AutoCAD **Options** dialog box

The Online Tab

The **Autodesk 360** tools are located on the **Online** tab of the ribbon shown in Figure 18-33.

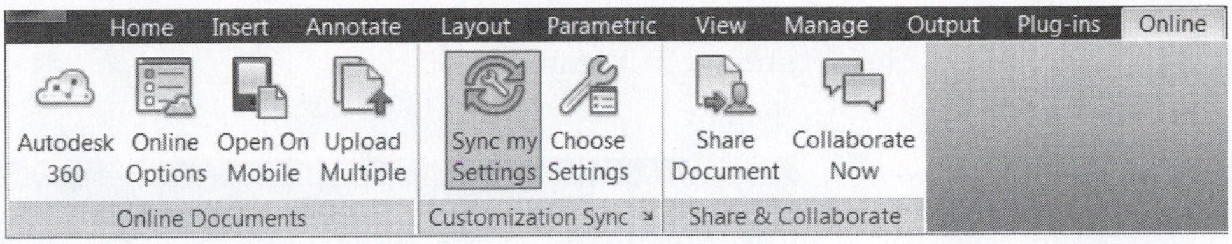

Figure 18-33
The **Online** tab of the ribbon

The **Online** tab tools are explained in the following sections.

The Autodesk 360 Tool. The **Autodesk 360** tool opens your **Autodesk 360** documents list and folders in a browser as shown in Figure 18-34. If you are not already logged in, you're prompted to do so.

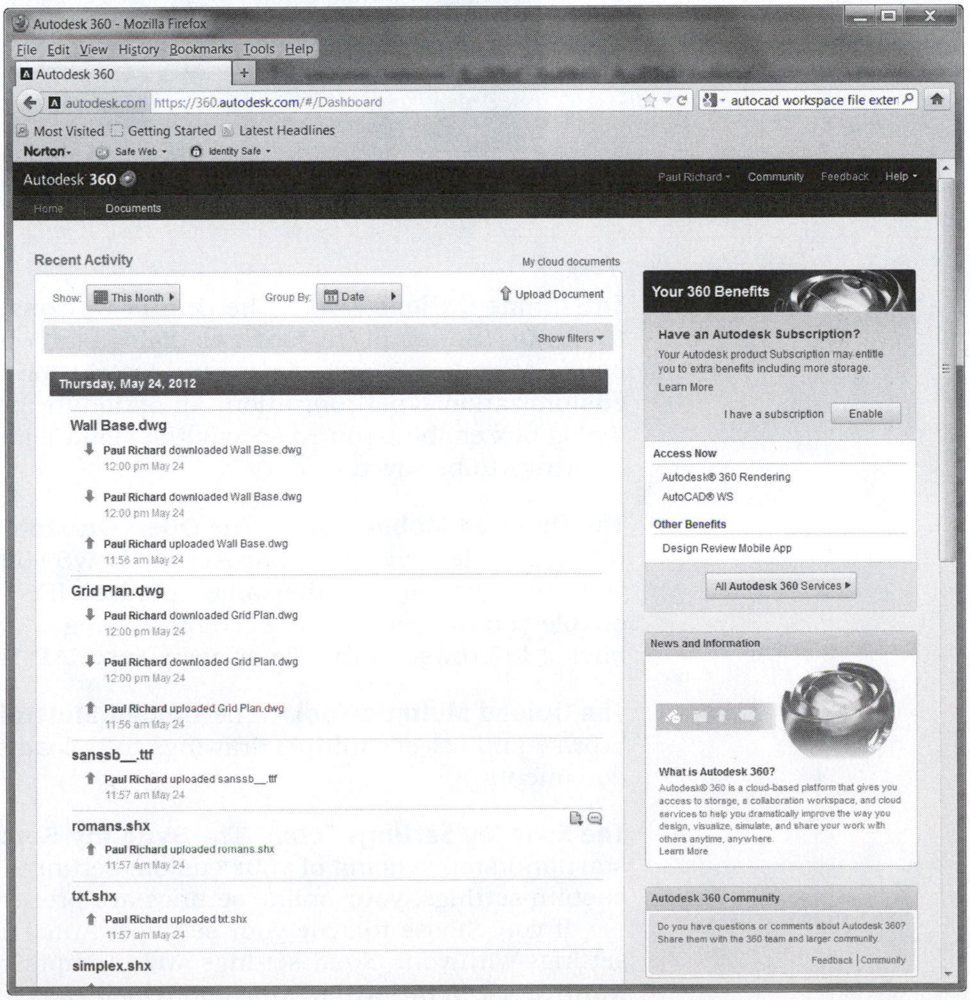

Figure 18-34
The **Autodesk 360** website

Your **Autodesk 360** documents are also available from many of the common **Select File** dialog boxes throughout AutoCAD such as **Save As** and **Open**. For example, when you open, save, or attach a file, you can access **Autodesk 360** directly from the **Places** list on the left side of the dialog box.

Once a drawing has been uploaded, you can edit it online using **AutoCAD WS**, the browser-based drawing editor provided by Autodesk shown in Figure 18-35.

Figure 18-35
The **AutoCAD WS** online drawing editor

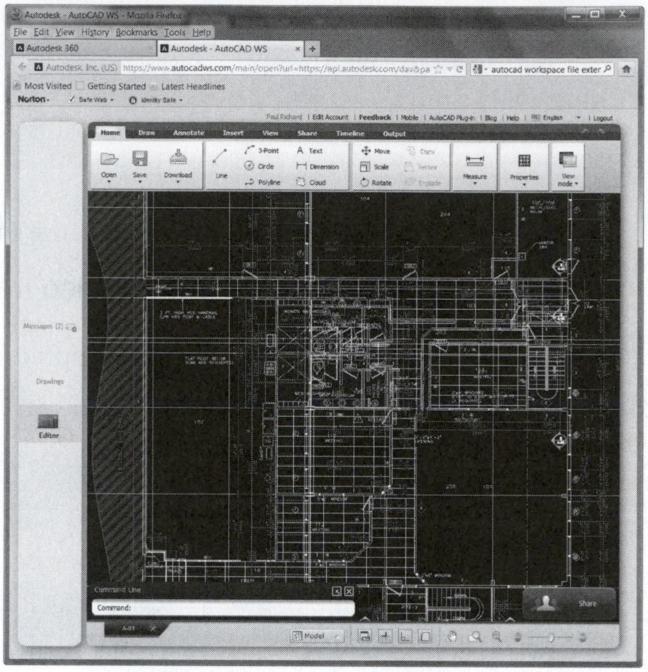

The Online Options Tool. The **Online Options** tool provides easy access to the **Online** tab of the **Options** dialog box, where you can monitor your online storage capacity and control interaction with cloud documents and customization synchronization. An option in the lower left corner of the dialog box enables you to specify the cloud folder in which you want your drawings to be saved.

The Open On Mobile Tool. The **Open On Mobile** tool sends notifications to any mobile device that has **AutoCAD WS** software installed and where you are signed in with the same Autodesk ID. These notifications will enable you to open up the current drawing on your mobile device without having to browse to the file or open **AutoCAD WS** first.

The Upload Multiple Tool. The **Upload Multiple** tool enables you to browse and select multiple drawings to upload to your **Autodesk 360** documents.

The Sync My Settings Tool. The **Sync my Settings** tool enables you to start and stop syncing of your custom settings. If you stop syncing your custom settings, your online settings are preserved but no longer updated.

If you choose to sync your settings, AutoCAD compares your local settings with your cloud settings and prompts you to choose whether you want to use your local settings, in which case it will upload them to the cloud, or your online settings, in which case it will download them from the cloud.

Bubble notifications indicate when settings are being uploaded to or downloaded from the cloud.

The Choose Settings Tool. Use the **Choose Settings** tool to specify which settings to include in the customization sync:

- The **Options** setting includes almost all the controls in the **Options** dialog box.
- The **Customization Files** setting includes custom menu files, workspace files, and more (.cuix, .aws).
- The **Printer support files** setting includes copies of printer support files (.pc3, .ctb, and .stb).
- The **Custom hatch patterns** setting includes your custom hatch pattern files (.pat).
- The **Tool Palettes** setting includes tool palette files and groups (.atc, .xtp).
- The **Drawing template files** setting includes your drawing templates (.dwt).
- The **Custom fonts, shapes, and linetypes** setting requires that AutoCAD be restarted.

When you make changes to your customization settings with synchronization enabled, a bubble notification in the upper right corner notifies you that the changes are being uploaded.

When you sign out of **Autodesk 360**, a dialog box asks you to choose whether you want to keep your custom settings or restore the previous settings.

The Customization Sync Tool. The **Customization Sync** tool displays the **Online** tab of the AutoCAD **Options** dialog box.

The Share Document Tool. Use the **Share Document** tool to share your current drawing with other users. If the current drawing is saved locally only, a copy of the drawing is uploaded to the cloud and shared. It is possible to control the access level of shared documents.

The Collaborate Now Tool. The **Collaborate Now** tool will launch **AutoCAD WS** in the user's default browser and initiate a collaboration session with another **WS** user.

NOTE

The **CAD Manager Control Utility** includes additional manager level controls for **Autodesk 360**. You can install the **CAD Manager Control Utility** via the **Install Tools & Utilities** option of the AutoCAD installation program.

chapter eighteen

Chapter Summary

This chapter explored additional drawing management techniques that include recovering and fixing corrupt files and changing settings in AutoCAD to create backup files. Remember that AutoCAD drawings can be shared with other CAD programs and viewed in other software applications. In turn, other CAD and Windows-based files can be translated into AutoCAD. Sharing data from one software application to another is cost efficient, productive, and becoming commonplace in the design industry. AutoCAD has internal tools to assist with these file translations. As with most Windows software, AutoCAD provides all the object linking and embedding tools such as **Copy**, **Cut**, and **Paste**, as well as ways to enhance OLE objects with system variables that control display, plotting, and editing options. Automating repetitive tasks using the **Action Recorder** tool saves an enormous amount of time and helps to promote standards. The **Measure** tools allow you to quickly check your work and that of others, as well as instantly ascertain areas and volumes. The **QuickCalc** calculator is integrated into AutoCAD so you can perform complex mathematical expressions and convert units, then apply the results directly in your drawing. The **Delete Duplicate Objects** tool not only helps you to maintain data integrity in your drawings but also helps reduce file sizes. Finally, the online collaboration tools provided by **Autodesk 360** and **AutoCAD WS** allow you to share and update your drawing files in real time on the web and on mobile devices so that everyone on the team always has access to the latest and greatest information wherever he or she is located.

Chapter Test Questions

Multiple Choice

Circle the correct answer.

1. The **PURGE** command can remove unused:
   a. Layers
   b. Linetypes
   c. Blocks
   d. All of the above
2. The **EXPORT** command supports the following file types:
   a. WMF, JPG, EPS, DXX, BMP, DWG, 3DS
   b. WMF, SAT, EPS, DXX, BMP, 3DS, DWG
   c. JPG, PNG, DXX, BMP, DXX, EPS, SAT
   d. None of the above
3. The command that saves and exports an AutoCAD object into a drawing file is:
   a. **WBLOCK**
   b. **WMFOUT**
   c. **JPGOUT**
   d. **DWGOUT**
4. The backup file extension is:
   a. AC$
   b. BAC
   c. SV$
   d. BAK

5. A DXF file can be created by:

a. Pasting a DWG file into Word

b. Using the **SAVE** or **SAVEAS** command

c. Using the **XREF** command

d. None of the above

6. A source application file:

a. Is where an object is linked

b. Can never be changed or edited

c. Is the same as a destination file

d. None of the above

7. Dragging and dropping objects is the same as:

a. Embedding and linking

b. Copying and pasting

c. Cutting and pasting

d. All of the above

8. An AutoCAD file with linked objects:

a. Can be automatically updated if there are changes to the source file

b. Tends to be smaller in file size than files with embedded objects

c. Must be updated if either the source or the destination file is moved to another drive or directory

d. All of the above

9. An embedded object can be changed or edited in an AutoCAD file:

a. By right-clicking on the object and selecting **Edit**

b. By double-clicking on the object to bring up the source application

c. By deleting the object, re-creating an updated version in the source file, and bringing it back into AutoCAD through the Clipboard

d. Is not allowed

10. The **QuickCalc** calculator can be displayed by:

a. Right-clicking and selecting it from the shortcut menu

b. Selecting it from the **Palettes** panel on the **View** tab of the ribbon

c. Entering **QC** at the command prompt

d. All of the above

Matching

Write the number of the correct answer on the line.

a. BAK ______	1. Eliminates unused lines, blocks, and layers
b. **PASTECLIP** ______	2. Pastes copied objects
c. **AUDIT** ______	3. Automates repetitive tasks
d. **Drawing Recovery Manager** ______	4. AutoCAD backup file
e. **Action Recorder** ______	5. Attribute extract DXF file
f. **OLELINKS** ______	6. Changes other file types into an AutoCAD drawing file
g. **PURGE** ______	7. Modifies existing OLE links

h. DXX _____

i. **IMPORT** _____

j. **EXPORT** _____

8. Changes AutoCAD drawing file types into a specific file format
9. Checks and fixes errors in a drawing file
10. Attempts to restore or retrieve open and backup drawing files

True or False

Circle the correct answer.

1. **True or False:** The **RECOVER** command can be used on open drawings.
2. **True or False:** The **AUDIT** command can be used on closed drawings.
3. **True or False:** The **Drawing Recovery Manager** can restore an unsaved drawing file.
4. **True or False:** The **PURGE** command is used to erase unused named objects.
5. **True or False:** The **INSERTOBJ** command can be used to create a table from scratch in Word and link it into AutoCAD.
6. **True or False:** The **OLE Links** dialog box is used to update, change, or break a linked object in AutoCAD.
7. **True or False:** The **OLEFRAME** system variable when set to **2** will display a frame around an OLE object on the screen and a plot.
8. **True or False:** The **Action Recorder** can record selections made in a dialog box.
9. **True or False:** The BMP export file is a raster image.
10. **True or False:** OLE also means object linking and editing.

appendix A Drafting Standards Overview

Standards Organizations

Standards provide a basis for uniformity in engineering drawing. Many industries and governments can use these standards as a guideline to develop their documents. It is not the intent of recognized national standards organizations to prevent individual organizations from designing specific formats. The intent is to provide common engineering standards to aid the interchange of drawings between companies, governments, and other users.

The following organizations are three leaders in drafting standards.

American National Standards Institute (ANSI)

ANSI has been a leader in the voluntary standards system of the United States. This organization has provided a forum for private and public sectors to collectively work together toward the development of national standards. Efforts to coordinate national standards date back to 1911. In 1916, the following agencies were instrumental in establishing a national body to oversee the development of national standards:

1. The American Institute of Electrical Engineers (now IEEE)
2. The American Society of Mechanical Engineers (ASME)
3. The American Society of Civil Engineers (ASCE)
4. The American Institute of Mining, Metallurgical, and Petroleum Engineers (AIME)
5. The American Society for Testing and Materials (ASTM)

These organizations along with the U.S. Departments of War, Navy, and Commerce were the founders of the American Engineering Standards Committee (AESC). This organization led to the formation of the American National Standards Institute (ANSI) in 1969. Throughout its history, ANSI has continued to coordinate national and international efforts to approve voluntary standards. Over the past 85 years, this organization has maintained its strong ties with the original founding organizations and others to become one of the most highly regarded standards systems in the world.

Specific standards are revised periodically by a committee of industrial leaders who also serve as representatives of various industrial service organizations. For example, the vice president of engineering at Xerox Corporation might serve on the board of the American Society of Mechanical Engineers (ASME). These committee members revise such standards as Drawing Sheet Size and Format, Dimensioning and Tolerancing, and Line Conventions and Lettering. The standards should be readily available in the classroom so that students can develop engineering drawings that adhere to these standards. Specific standards need to be available for each content area—mechanical, electrical, or civil. The following is an example of some commonly used mechanical engineering standards.

American Society of Mechanical Engineers (ASME)

The American Society of Mechanical Engineers conducts one of the world's largest publishing operations to produce technical and engineering documents to establish standards. ASME documents are recognized worldwide for industrial and manufacturing codes and standards. Some of the popular documents on engineering standards include:

Y14.2M-1992 Line Conventions and Lettering

Y14.5.2-2000-2001 Certification of Geometric Dimensioning and Tolerancing

Y14.38-1999 Abbreviations and Acronyms

Y14.1-1980 (R1987) Drawing Sheet Size and Format

Y14.1M-1992 Metric Drawing Sheet Size and Format

Y14.3M-1994 Multiview and Sectional View Drawings

International Organization for Standardization (ISO)

The International Organization for Standardization is an organized network of the national standards institutes of 148 countries. It is a nongovernmental organization, but its members are not. ISO has a unique mission in acting as a bridge between business/industry and consumers/users. ISO has published more than 13,700 International Standards ranging from engineering drawing to medical devices. ISO is also responsible for providing a framework for quality management throughout the processes of producing and delivering products and services by implementing ISO 9000.

Some of the more commonly used ISO drawing standards are:

ISO 10135:1994

Technical drawings—Simplified representation of molded, cast, and forged parts

ISO 10209-1:1992

Technical product documentation—Vocabulary—Part 1: Terms relating to technical drawings: general and types of drawings

ISO 10209-2:1993

Technical product documentation—Vocabulary—Part 2: Terms relating to projection methods

Many companies, such as General Electric and General Motors, develop their own standards by incorporating the use of ANSI, ASME, and ISO criteria. In this way, national standards can be incorporated with company standards to meet specific requirements.

Text

Text can be inserted into the model space or into paper space layouts. When inserting text into a layout, the height of the text is equal to the printed or plotted size. Layouts are normally printed or plotted on a one-to-one scale. If the text height is inserted at 0.125 into the layout and printed at 1:1, the printed text height will be 0.125.

When text is entered into model space, consideration must be given to the drawing scale factor. See the following section for additional information about standard model space text heights.

Standard Text Heights

The typical standard height for text on a drawing is 1/8″. Fractions need to be created 1/4″ tall. These are general guidelines for text height. Text height should be increased or decreased based on individual situations.

To achieve these final printed and plotted text sizes, it is necessary to create the text within the AutoCAD drawing at the correct size. The following table lists examples of the relationship between sheet size, plot scale, scale factor, model space drawing area, and text height.

	Sheet Size	Plot Scale	Scale Factor	Model Space Drawing Area	Text Height
Architect's Scale	12″ × 9″	1/8″ = 1′-0″	96	96′ × 72′	1′-0″
	24″ × 18″	1/2″ = 1′-0″	24	48′ × 36′	3″
Engineer's Scale (Civil)	18″ × 12″	1″ = 200′	2400	3600′ × 2400′	25′
	36″ × 24″	1″ = 50′	600	1800′ × 1200′	6.25′
Engineer's Scale (Mech.)	11″ × 8.5″	1″ = 2″	2	22″ × 17″	.25″
	34″ × 22″	1″ = 1.5″	1.5	51″ × 33″	3/16″
Metric Scale	279 mm × 216 mm	1 mm = 5 mm	5	1395 mm × 1080 mm	15.875 mm
	432 mm × 279 mm	1 mm = 20 mm	20	7620 mm × 5080 mm	63.5 mm

Calculating the Scale Factor

The drawing scale factor used to scale annotation features up and down is always the reciprocal of the plot or viewport scale. The easiest way to calculate the reciprocal value of the plot/viewport scale is to first put all values into the same units and then cross-multiply. For example, to calculate the drawing scale factor for the Architectural scale 1/8″ = 1′-0″, you would first convert all values to inches and display them all as stacked fractions:

$$\tfrac{1}{8}'' = \frac{12''}{1}$$

Then cross-multiply by multiplying the denominator on the left side of the equal sign (=) (8) times the numerator on the right side (12) and then the numerator on the left (1) times the denominator on the right (1) for a result of 96/1. The last step is to reduce the fraction by dividing the denominator (1) into the numerator (96) for a scale factor of 96.

Notes and Locating Text on a Drawing

Notes and text are necessary to supplement a fully dimensioned engineering drawing. Notes should be clear and concise to avoid any misinterpretation. Notes are always lettered horizontally on the sheet and systematically organized. Do not place notes and text in crowded or busy locations on the drawing. Avoid placing notes in between orthographic views. Use only standard ANSI or ASME abbreviations with a note.

Notes are classified as General Notes or Local/Specific Notes.

General Notes. General notes apply to the entire drawing. General notes are typically placed in the lower right-hand corner of the drawing above or to the left of the title block. Title blocks may provide general information about the drawing such as tolerance, material, or treatment. General notes may be placed below the view to which the note applies.

Local/Specific Notes. Local notes provide specific detailed information. These notes are placed adjacent to the specific feature they describe. Local notes may be connected with a leader. The leader arrow or dot will touch the detail and end with a note.

Leaders

Leaders should be attached at the middle front of the first word of the note or after the last word of the note. Leaders to a circle should be developed radially. The slanted line of the leader should be aimed at the center of the circle or arc. A shoulder or horizontal line of the leader is optional. Leader lines should not cross each other. Refer to the following standard for additional information:

Y14.5.2-2000-2001 Certification of Geometric Dimensioning and Tolerancing

Sheet Layouts

A convenient code to identify American National Standard sheet sizes and forms suggested by the authors for title, parts or materials list, and revision blocks, for use of instructors in making assignments, is shown here. All dimensions are in inches.

Three sizes of sheets are illustrated: Size A, Figure A-1, Size B, Figure A-5, and Size C, Figure A-6. Metric size sheets are not shown.

Eight forms of lettering arrangements are suggested, known as Forms 1, 2, 3, 4, 5, 6, 7, and 8, as shown below and on the next page (see Figures A-2, A-3, A-4, A-7, A-8, and A-9). The total length of Forms 1, 2, 3, and 4 may be adjusted to fit Sizes A4, A3, and A2.

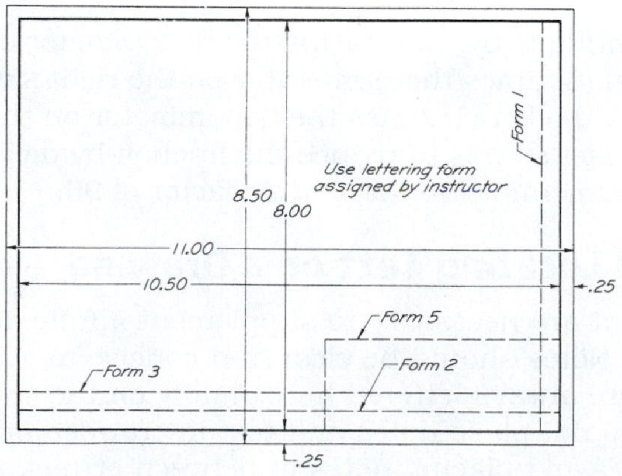

Figure A-1
Size A sheet (8.50″ × 11.00″)

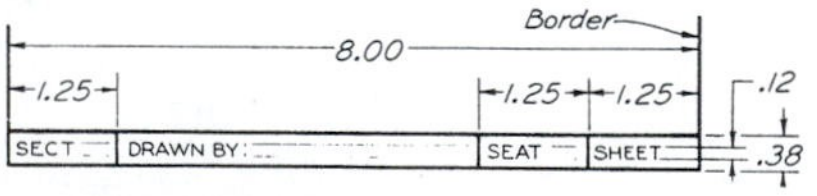

Figure A-2
Form 1. Title block

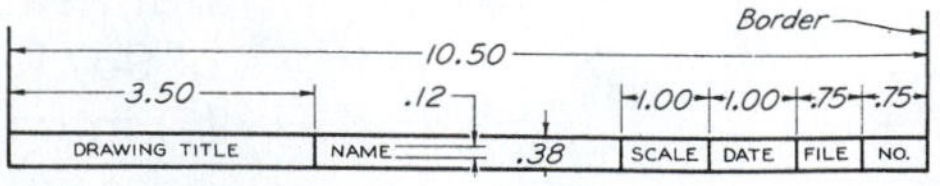

Figure A-3
Form 2. Title block

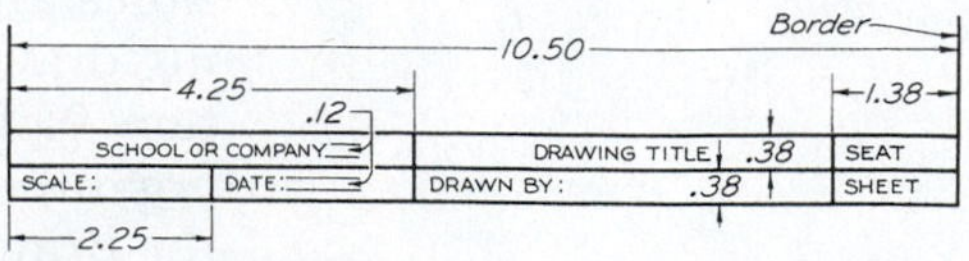

Figure A-4
Form 3. Title block

Sheet Sizes

American National Standard

A – 8.50″ × 11.00″
B – 11.00″ × 17.00″
C – 17.00″ × 22.00″
D – 22.00″ × 34.00″
E – 34.00″ × 44.00″

International Standard

A4 – 210 mm × 297 mm
A3 – 297 mm × 420 mm
A2 – 420 mm × 594 mm
A1 – 594 mm × 841 mm
A0 – 841 mm × 1189 mm
(25.4 mm = 1.00″)

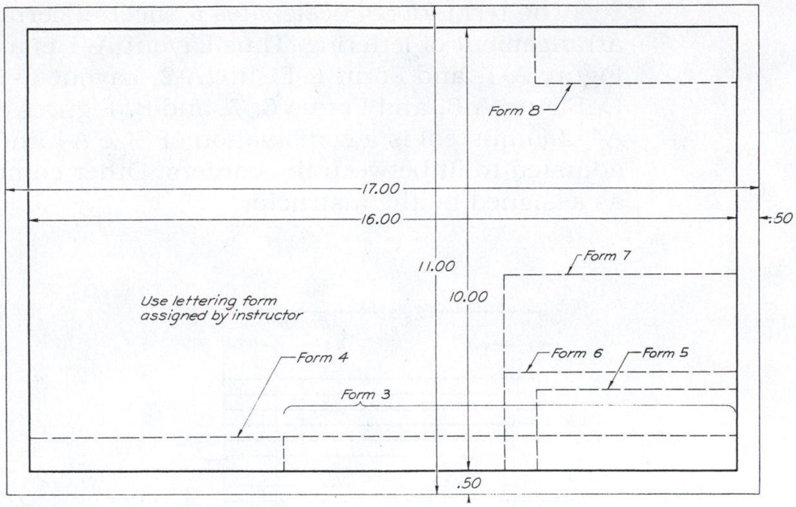

Figure A-5
Size B sheet (11.00″ × 17.00″)

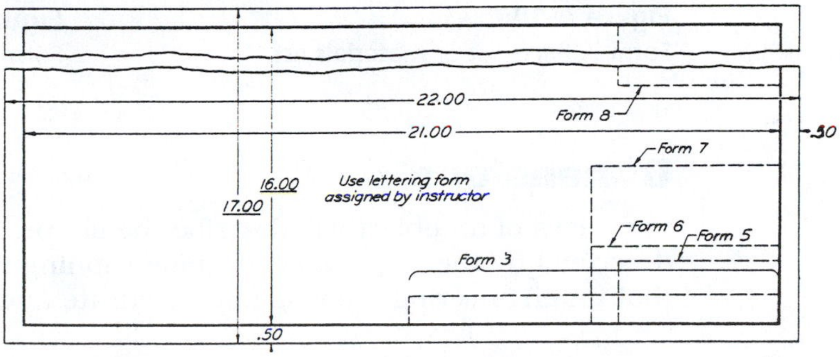

Figure A-6
Size C sheet (17.00″ × 22.00″)

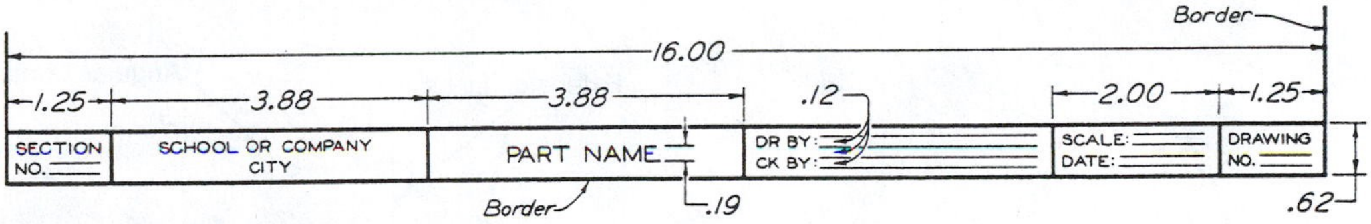

Figure A-7
Form 4. Title block

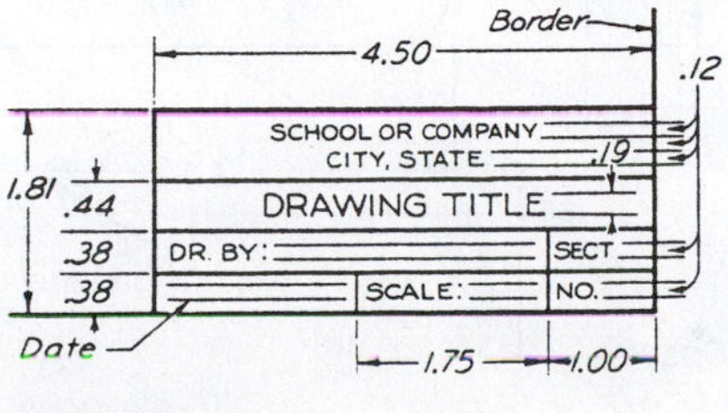

Figure A-8
Form 5. Title block

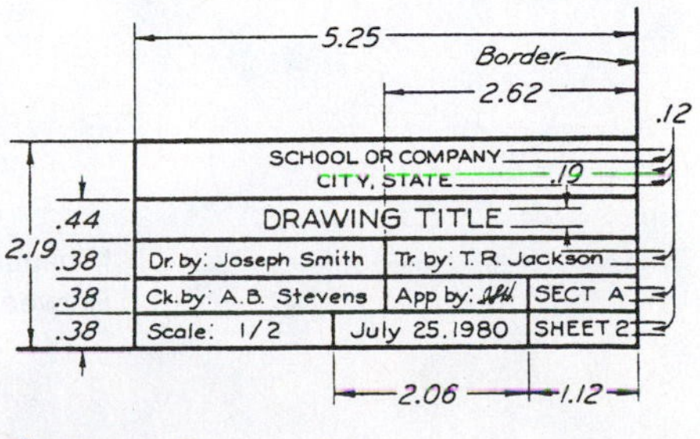

Figure A-9
Form 6. Title block

The term *layout* designates a sheet of certain size plus a certain arrangement of lettering. Thus Layout A–1 is a combination of Size A, Figure A-1, and Form 1, Figure A-2. Layout C–678 is a combination of Size C, Figure A-6, and Forms 6, 7, and 8, Figures A-9, A-10, and A-11. Layout A4–2 (adjusted) is a combination of Size A4 and Form 2, Figure A-3, adjusted to fit between the borders. Other combinations may be employed as assigned by the instructor.

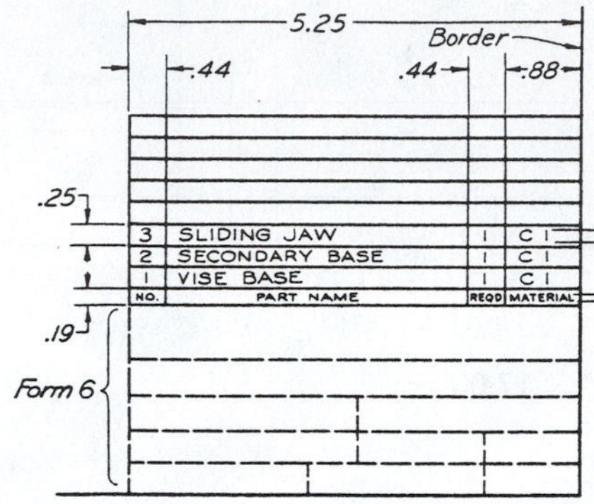

Figure A-10
Form 7. Parts list or materials list

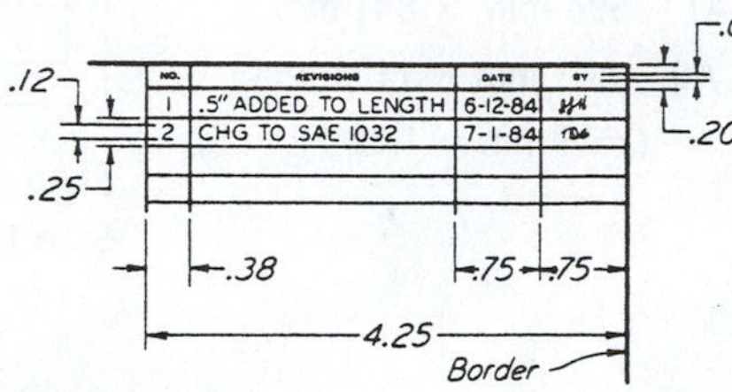

Figure A-11
Form 8. Revision block

Dimensions

The views of an object will describe the shape. The size of the object is described by the use of modern dimensioning techniques. It is important that an engineering drawing have accurate and functional dimensions.

Standard Feature Sizes

Figure A-12 illustrates some common terms and distances to consider when dimensioning standard feature sizes.

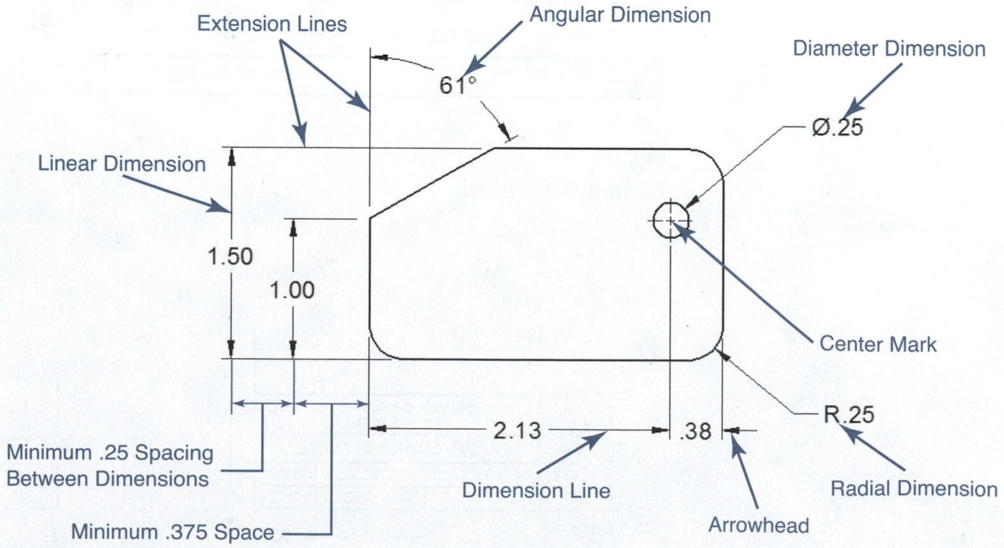

Figure A-12
Linear dimension features

Mechanical Style versus Architectural Style

Mechanical Style

There are two systems of placing dimensions on a drawing, the *unidirectional system* and the *aligned system*. In the unidirectional system, all the dimension figures and notes are lettered horizontally on the sheet (see Figure A-12). This is the preferred system of the American National Standards Institute. The mechanical style of dimensioning illustrates the unidirectional system. The unidirectional system is widely used because it is easy to read and interpret on large drawings. The unidirectional system is the standard default dimensioning system in AutoCAD.

Architectural Style

The architectural style of dimensioning (see Figure A-13) illustrates the aligned system. The aligned system has all the dimension figures aligned with the dimension line. Many of the dimension figures are horizontal on the sheet and some are aligned or turned. Any rotated figures are to be read from the right side of the sheet.

Figure A-13
Architectural dimension style

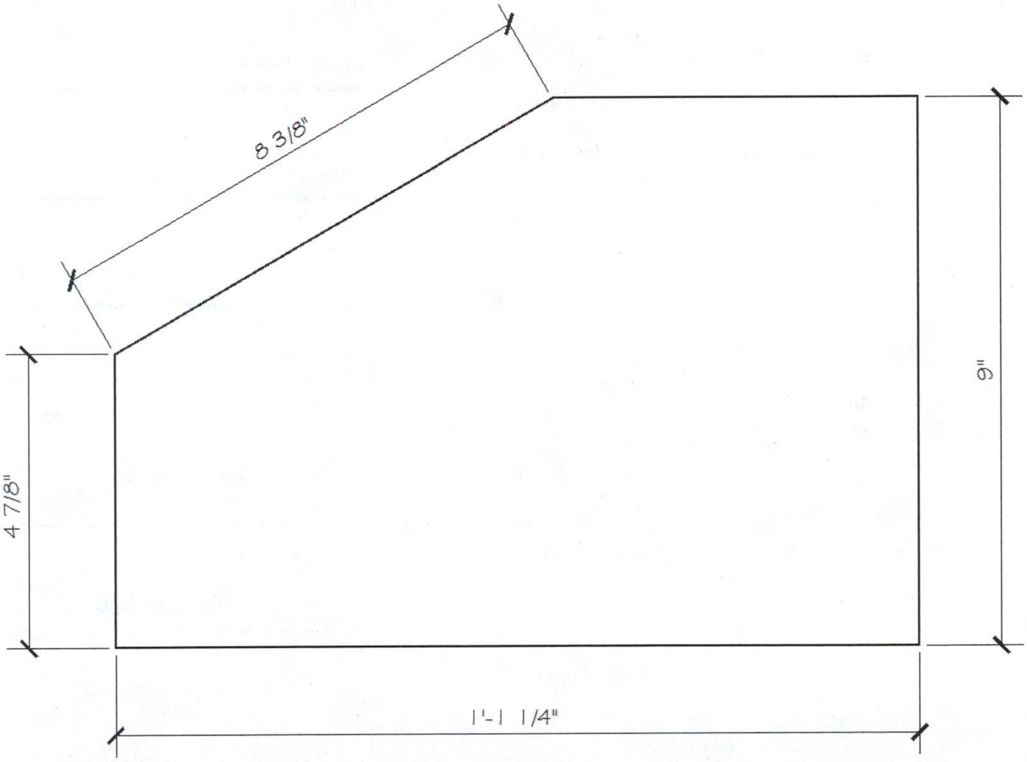

The architectural style of dimensioning has numbers placed on top of an unbroken dimension line. The dimension line typically ends with a slash, dot, or arrowhead. The numbers normally are designated with inch (") and foot (') symbols.

Linetypes and Thicknesses

Linetypes that are used within AutoCAD should correspond with the standard ANSI linetypes and thicknesses. Every line that is used on a technical drawing has a specific meaning and needs to be illustrated in a certain way. The American National Standards Institute has established the Line Conventions and Lettering standard ANSI Y-14.2M-1992. This standard describes the size, application, and construction of various lines that are used in creating engineering drawings. Figure A-14 details various linetypes and their applications.

Figure A-14
Alphabet of lines (full-size)

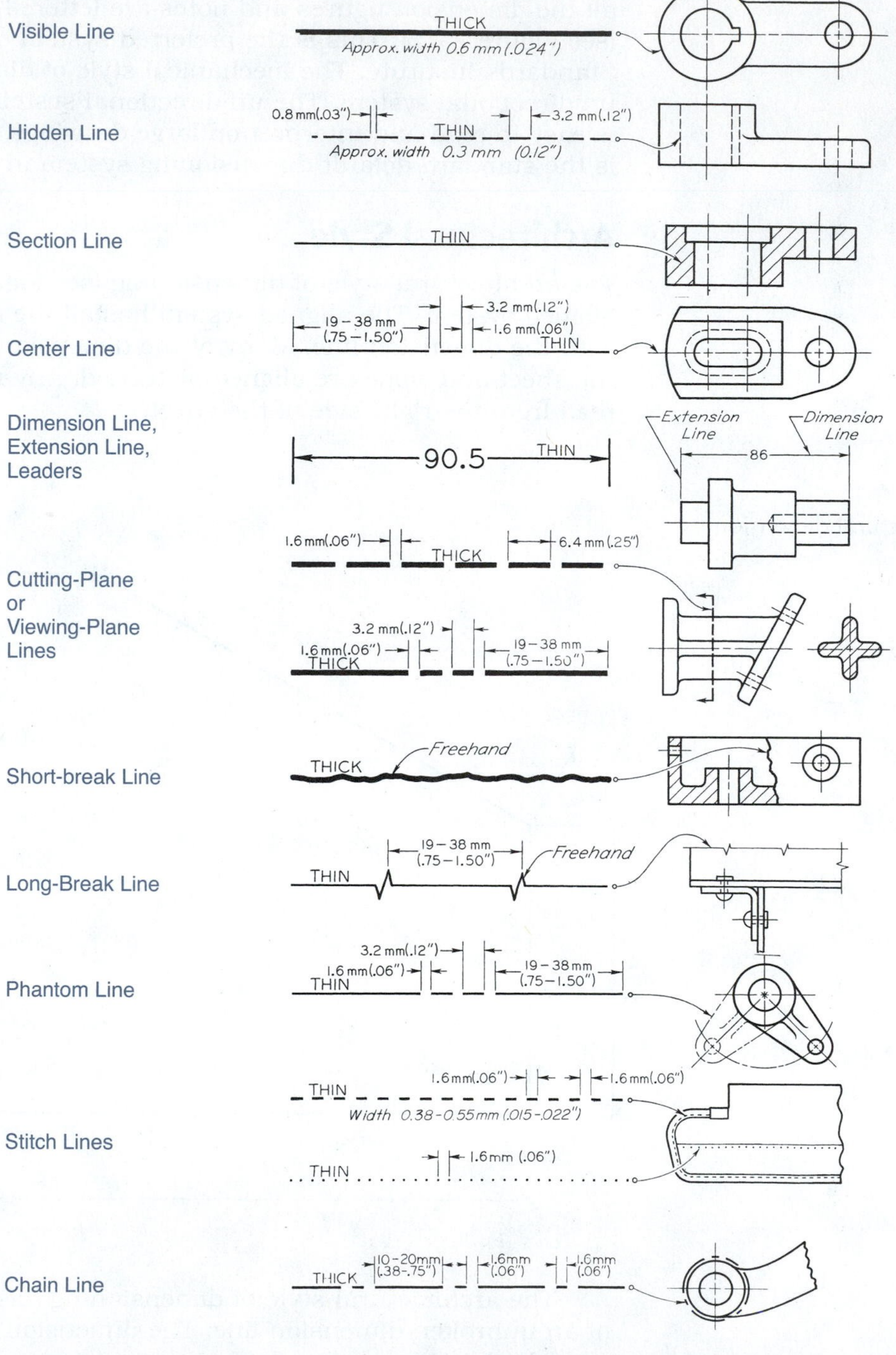

It should be noted that the line widths established in this illustration are approximate and the actual width is governed by the size and style of the drawing. Large drawings will need to have wider lines, and drawings that are reduced in size will need to have smaller line widths than specified in this illustration. The ANSI Y14.2M standard and this illustration should be used as a guide to produce crisp and legible engineering drawings from AutoCAD.

Linetypes are described in an AutoCAD file called ACAD.LIN. These linetypes should be loaded into the AutoCAD drawing file and assigned correct lineweights that correspond with the ANSI standards. The AutoCAD command **LTSCALE** should be used to adjust the size of the linetypes to match the size of the drawing area in AutoCAD. Figure A-15 shows examples of AutoCAD's standard linetypes, which are defined in the ACAD.LIN file.

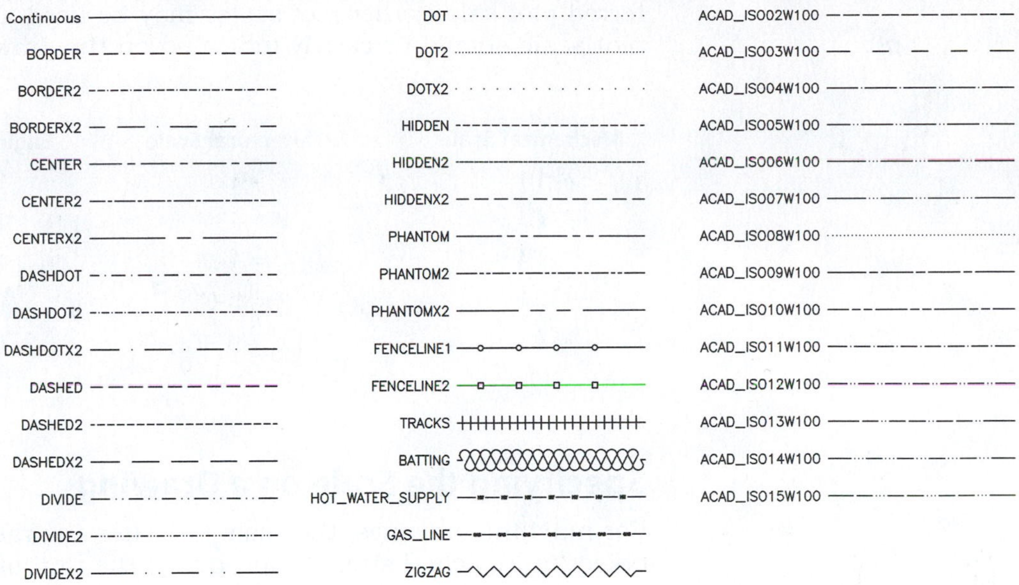

Figure A-15
Standard AutoCAD linetypes

Standard Sheet Sizes and Scales

The use of standard sheet sizes and the uniform location of the title block, revision block, and bill of materials provide definite advantages for engineering drawings. These advantages include readability, handling, filing, and reproduction. As drawings are shared between organizations and companies, an advantage is realized when information is located in the same location on all drawings.

Standard sheet size also provides consistency between hand-drawn and printer/plotter-created engineering drawings. Drawings that are created on printers can use standard engineering sheet sizes of 8.5″ × 11″ or 17″ × 11″. Drawings that are created with plotters that use rolls of various media need to be trimmed to final standard size such as 17″ × 22″ or 22″ × 34″. International sheet sizes based on millimeters would need to be trimmed to final standard size such as 420 mm × 594 mm or 594 mm × 841 mm. (See Figure A-16.)

Figure A-16
Standard U.S. and metric paper sizes

Nearest International Size[a] (millimeter)	Standard U.S. Size[a] (inch)
A4 210 × 297	A 8.5 × 11.0
A3 297 × 420	B 11.0 × 17.0
A2 420 × 594	C 17.0 × 22.0
A1 594 × 841	D 22.0 × 34.0
A0 841 × 1189	E 34.0 × 44.0

[a] ANSI Y14.1m-1992.

Standard Plot Scales

Each drafting discipline has plot scales that are commonly used within that discipline. The following table lists standard plot scales for the mechanical, architectural, and civil engineering disciplines. These are preferred plot sales; other plot scales may be used as needed. In all cases, the plot scale should be clearly indicated on the drawing.

Mechanical Scale	Architectural Scale	Engineers' Scale
1:1	1/8″ = 1′-0″	1″ = 10′
1:2	1/4″ = 1′-0″	1″ = 20′
1:4	1/2″ = 1′-0″	1″ = 30′
2:1	1″ = 1′-0″	1″ = 50′
4:1	1 1/2″ = 1′-0″	1″ = 60′
10:1	3″ = 1′-0″	1″ = 100′

Specifying the Scale on a Drawing

For machine drawings, the scale indicates the ratio of the size of the drawn object to its actual size, irrespective of the unit of measurement used. The recommended practice is to letter full-size or 1:1; half-size or 1:2; and similarly for other reductions. Expansion or enlargement scales are given as 2:1 or 2:3; 3:1 or 3:3; 5:1 or 5:3; 10:1 or 10:3; and so on.

The various scale calibrations available on the metric scale and the engineers' scale provide almost unlimited scale ratios. The preferred metric scale ratios appear to be 1:1, 1:2, 1:5, 1:10, 1:20, 1:50, 1:100, and 1:200.

Map scales are indicated in terms of fractions, such as scale $\frac{1}{62500}$, or graphically, such as 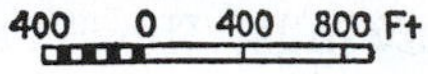

.

Standard ANSI Hatch Patterns

Section Lining

Section-lining symbols (see Figure A-17) have been used to indicate specific materials. These symbols represent general material types only, such as cast iron, brass, and steel. Now, however, because there are so many different types of materials, and each has so many subtypes, a general name or symbol is not enough. For example, there are hundreds of different kinds of steel. Since detailed specifications of material must be lettered in the form of a note or in the title strip, the general-purpose (cast-iron) section lining may be used for all materials on detail drawings (single parts).

Section-lining symbols may be used in assembly drawings in cases where it is desirable to distinguish different materials; otherwise, the general-purpose symbol is used for all parts.

CAD programs usually include a library that allows the user to select from a variety of section-lining patterns, making it easy to indicate various types of material rather than using the generic cast-iron symbol for all sectioned parts.

ANSI has standardized many section lines that are used for sectional drawing. AutoCAD uses the **HATCH** command to insert hatch patterns that are used to illustrate these section lines. The following table lists the ANSI section line with corresponding AutoCAD hatch pattern, as seen in Figure A-17.

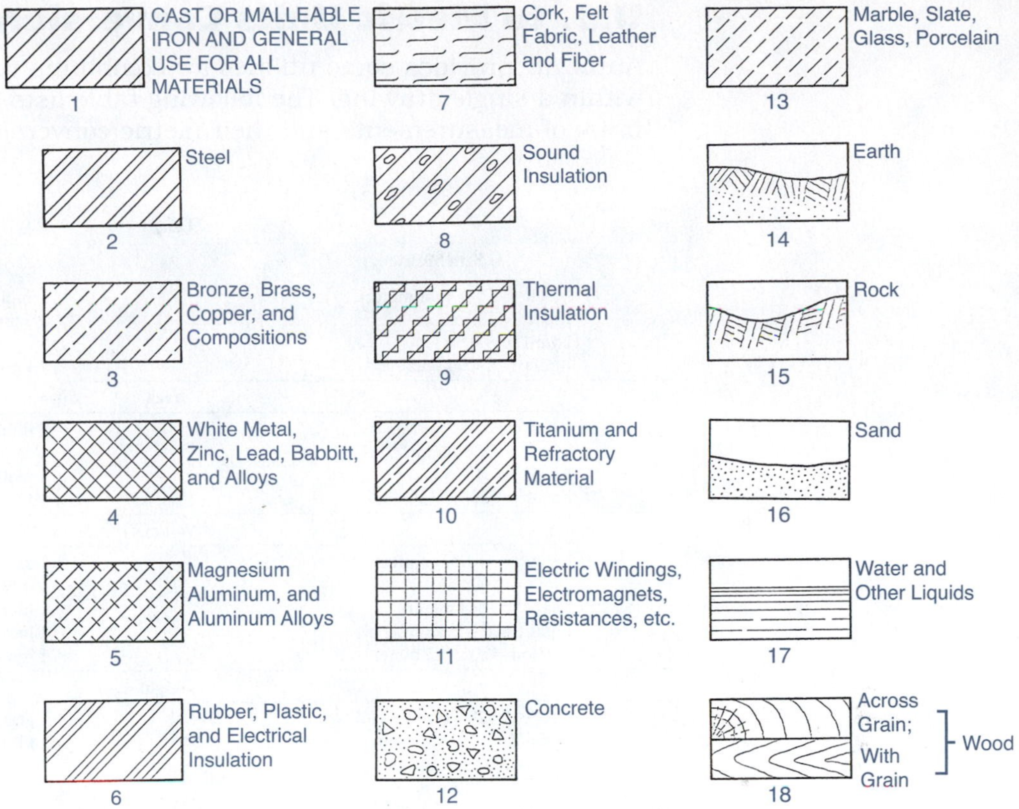

Figure A-17
Symbols for section lining

Figure Number	ANSI Pattern Name	AutoCAD Hatch Pattern
A-17 (1)	Cast/General Use	ANSI 31
A-17 (2)	Steel	ANSI 32 or Steel
A-17 (3)	Bronze, brass, copper, etc.	ANSI 33
A-17 (4)	White metal, zinc, lead, etc.	ANSI 37
A-17 (5)	Magnesium, aluminum, etc.	ANSI 38 (include a material note)
A-17 (6)	Rubber, plastic, electrical insulation	ANSI 34
A-17 (7)	Cork, felt, fabric, leather, fiber	Cork
A-17 (8)	Sound insulation	Insulation (include a material note)
A-17 (9)	Thermal insulation	Insulation (include a material note)
A-17 (10)	Titanium/refractory material	
A-17 (11)	Electric windings, electromagnets, etc.	ANSI 37 (rotate 45°)
A-17 (12)	Concrete	AR-CONC
A-17 (13)	Marble, slate, glass, porcelain	Dash (rotate 45°)
A-17 (14)	Earth	Earth (rotate angle)
A-17 (15)	Rock	
A-17 (16)	Sand	AR-SAND
A-17 (17)	Water and other liquids	
A-17 (18)	Wood	

U.S. to Metric Units Conversions

AutoCAD provides some utilities for combining metric and imperial units within a single drawing. The following table lists standard U.S. (imperial) units of measurements and their metric conversions.

U.S. to Metric	Metric to U.S.
Length	
1 inch = 2.540 centimeters 1 foot = .305 meter 1 yard = .914 meter 1 mile = 1.609 kilometers	1 millimeter = .039 inch 1 centimeter = .394 inch 1 meter = 3.281 feet or 1.094 yards 1 kilometer = .621 mile
Area	
1 inch^2 = 6.451 centimeter^2 1 foot^2 = .093 meter^2 1 yard^2 = .836 meter^2 1 acre^2 = 4,046.873 meter^2	1 millimeter^2 = .00155 inch^2 1 centimeter^2 = .155 inch^2 1 meter^2 = 10.764 foot^2 or 1.196 yard^2 1 kilometer^2 = .386 mile^2 or 247.04 acre^2
Volume	
1 inch^3 = 16.387 centimeter^3 1 foot^3 = .028 meter^3 1 yard^3 = .764 meter^3 1 quart = 0.946 liter 1 gallon = .003785 meter^3	1 centimeter^3 = .061 inch^3 1 meter^3 = 35.314 foot^3 or 1.308 yard^3 1 liter = .2642 gallons 1 liter = 1.057 quarts 1 meter^3 = 264.02 gallons
Weight	
1 ounce = 28.349 grams 1 pound = .454 kilogram 1 ton = .907 metric ton	1 gram = .035 ounce 1 kilogram = 2.205 pounds 1 metric ton = 1.102 tons
Velocity	
1 foot/second = .305 meter/second 1 mile/hour = .447 meter/second	1 meter/second = 3.281 feet/second 1 kilometer/hour = .621 mile/second
Acceleration	
1 inch/second^2 = .0254 meter/second^2 1 foot/second^2 = .305 meter/second^2	1 meter/second^2 = 3.278 feet/second^2
Force	
N (newton) = basic unit of force, kg-m/s^2. A mass of one kilogram (1 kg) exerts a gravitational force of 9.8 N (theoretically 9.80665 N) at mean sea level.	

appendix B
Command Reference

Use the Help feature of AutoCAD for additional information about commands and their options.

Command	Description
3D	Creates 3D surfaced objects.
3DALIGN	Aligns objects with other objects in 2D and 3D environment.
3DARRAY	Copies objects in a rectangular or polar 3D array.
3DCLIP	Opens the Adjust Clipping Planes window and starts the 3D Orbit view.
3DCONFIG	Allows user to specify 3D graphics system configuration settings.
-3DCONFIG	Provides a command line interface to 3D graphics system's configuration settings.
3DCORBIT	Opens the 3D Orbit view and places selected objects in continuous orbit based on mouse click and drag direction and speed.
3DDISTANCE	Opens the 3D Orbit view and allows user to move camera relative to object either increasing or decreasing object's apparent size without changing perspective.
3DDWF	Displays **Export 3D DWF** dialog box.
3DEDITBAR	Reshapes, scales, and edits the tangency of NURBS surfaces.
3DFACE	Creates a three- or four-sided surface.
3DFLY	Activates fly-through mode and enables you to navigate in any direction, including off XY plane.
3DFORBIT	Controls interactive viewing of objects in 3D, using an unconstrained orbit.

Command	Description
3DMESH	Creates a free-form polygon mesh on an M×N grid.
3DMOVE	Displays move grip tool in a 3D view and moves objects a specified distance in a specified direction.
3DORBIT	Allows interactive viewing of selected 3D objects by clicking and dragging the mouse.
3DORBITCTR	Allows user selection of a center of rotation for the 3D Orbit view.
3DOSNAP	Sets the object snap modes for 3D objects via dialog box.
-3DOSNAP	Sets the object snap modes for 3D objects from the command line.
3DPAN	Initiates interactive viewing of selected 3D objects and enables dragging the view.
3DPOLY	Creates a polyline with 3D line segments.
3DPRINT	Sends a 3D model to a 3D printing service.
3DROTATE	Displays rotate grip tool in a 3D view and revolves objects around a base point.
3DSCALE	In a 3D view, displays the 3D Scale gizmo to aid in resizing 3D objects.
3DSIN	Starts import process for a 3D Studio file.
3DSWIVEL	Initiates interactive viewing of selected 3D objects and moves the camera based on cursor movement.
3DWALK	Interactively changes view of a 3D drawing so that you appear to be walking through the model.
3DZOOM	Initiates interactive viewing of selected 3D objects and allows zooming in or out.
ABOUT	Displays information about the software such as version number and the license agreement.
ACISIN	Imports an SAT ACIS file into the drawing.
ACISOUT	Exports an AutoCAD body, solid, or region to an SAT ACIS file.
ACTBASEPOINT	Inserts a base point in an action macro.
ACTMANAGER	Manages action macro files.
ACTRECORD	Starts the recording of an action macro.
ACTSTOP	Stops the recording of an action macro.
-ACTSTOP	Stops the recording of an action macro.
ACTUSERINPUT	Requests a user input during playback.
ACTUSERMESSAGE	Inserts a message that will be viewed during playback.
-ACTUSERMESSAGE	Inserts a message that will be viewed during playback.
ADCCLOSE	Closes **DesignCenter** window.
ADCENTER	Opens **DesignCenter** window.
ADCNAVIGATE	Loads a specified path or drawing file name into the tree view of **DesignCenter**.
ADDSELECTED	Creates a new object based on the object type and general properties of a selected object.

Command	Description
ADJUST	Adjusts the fade, contrast, and monochrome settings of the selected image or underlay (DWF, DWFx, PDF, or DGN).
ALIGN	Aligns two objects in either 2D or 3D using one, two, or three pairs of source and destination points.
ALLPLAY	Plays all named views in current drawing.
AMECONVERT	Converts Advanced Modeling Extension (AME) regions or solids to AutoCAD solid models.
ANALYSISCURVATURE	Displays a color gradient onto a surface to evaluate different aspects of its curvature.
ANALYSISDRAFT	Displays a color gradient onto a 3D model to evaluate whether there is adequate space between a part and its mold.
ANALYSISOPTIONS	Sets the display options for zebra, curvature, and draft analysis.
ANALYSISZEBRA	Projects stripes onto a 3D model to analyze surface continuity.
ANIPATH	Saves an animation along a path in a 3D model.
ANNORESET	Resets the location of all scale representations for an annotative object to that of the current scale representation.
ANNOUPDATE	Updates existing annotative objects to match the current properties of their styles.
APERTURE	Specifies size of the object snap target box.
APPLOAD	Opens **Load/Unload Applications** dialog box.
ARC	Draws an arc based on specified points.
ARCHIVE	Opens the **Archive Sheet Set** dialog box, which packages the current sheet set files to be archived.
AREA	Calculates area and perimeter of specified objects or areas.
ARRAY	Copies selected objects arranged in a rectangular, path, or polar pattern.
ARRAYCLASSIC	Displays the legacy **Array** dialog box.
ARRAYCLOSE	Saves back or discards changes made to an array's source objects and exits the array editing state.
ARRAYEDIT	Edits associative array objects and their source objects.
ARRAYPATH	Evenly distributes object copies along a path or a portion of a path.
ARRAYPOLAR	Evenly distributes object copies in a circular pattern around a center point or axis of rotation.
ARRAYRECT	Distributes object copies into any combination of rows, columns, and levels.
ARX	Loads and unloads ObjectARX applications.
ATTACH	Inserts an external reference, image, or underlay (DWF, DWFx, PDF, or DGN files) in the current drawing.

Command	Description
ATTACHURL	Associates hyperlinks with selected objects or areas in a drawing.
ATTDEF	Opens the **Attribute Definition** dialog box.
ATTDISP	Controls visibility of block attributes in a drawing.
ATTEDIT	Opens **Edit Attributes** dialog box, which permits editing of attribute values for a selected block.
ATTEXT	Opens **Attribute Extraction** dialog box, which permits informational text stored in blocks to be saved to a file.
ATTIPEDIT	Changes the textual content of an attribute within a block.
ATTREDEF	Redefines an existing block and updates attribute definitions.
ATTSYNC	Updates all occurrences of a specified block with the current attributes.
AUDIT	Finds and attempts to correct errors in a drawing.
AUTOCOMPLETE	Controls what types of automated keyboard features are available at the command prompt.
AUTOCONSTRAIN	Applies geometric constraints to a selection set of objects based on orientation of the objects relative to one another.
AUTOPUBLISH	Publishes drawings to DWF, DWFx, or PDF files automatically to a specified location.
BACKGROUND	Reintroduction of **BACKGROUND** command.
BACTION	Associates an action with a parameter in a dynamic block definition.
BACTIONBAR	Displays or hides action bars for a selection set of parameter objects.
BACTIONSET	Enables user to specify objects associated with an action in a dynamic block.
BACTIONTOOL	Adds an action to a dynamic block.
BASE	Sets the insertion base point coordinates of a drawing in the current UCS.
BASSOCIATE	Associates an action whose parameter has been removed with a new parameter in a dynamic block definition.
BATTMAN	Displays the **Block Attribute Manager**, which permits block attribute property edits.
BATTORDER	Controls order in which block attributes are listed when the block is inserted or edited.
BAUTHORPALETTE	Opens Block Authoring Palettes window.
BAUTHORPALETTECLOSE	Closes Block Authoring Palettes window.
BCLOSE	Closes the **Block Editor**.
BCONSTRUCTION	Converts geometry into construction geometry.

Command	Description
BCPARAMETER	Applies constraint parameters to selected objects, or converts dimensional constraints to parameter constraints.
-BCPARAMETER	Applies constraint parameters to selected objects, or converts dimensional constraints to parameter constraints from the command line.
BCYCLEORDER	Displays **Insertion Cycling Order** dialog box allowing user to change the cycling order of grips in a dynamic block.
BEDIT	Opens the **Edit Block Definition** dialog box.
BESETTINGS	Displays the **Block Editor Settings** dialog box.
BGRIPSET	Controls number and position of grips for a parameter in a dynamic block.
BHATCH	See **HATCH**.
BLEND	Creates a spline in the gap between two selected lines or curves.
BLOCK	A group of reusable objects with flexible insert options.
BLOCKICON	Creates preview images for blocks displayed in **DesignCenter.**
BLOOKUPTABLE	Displays **Property Lookup Table** dialog box.
BMPOUT	Creates a bitmap file from selected objects.
BOUNDARY	Converts an enclosed area into a region or a polyline.
BOX	Draws a solid 3-dimensional box.
BPARAMETER	Adds a parameter to a dynamic block.
BREAK	Splits the selected object into two parts.
BREP	Removes history from 3D solid primitives and composite solids.
BROWSER	Launches the default web browser.
BSAVE	Saves changes to the current block definition and retains the same name.
BSAVEAS	Saves a copy of a block definition under a new name.
BTABLE	Displays a dialog box to define variations of a block.
BTESTBLOCK	Displays a window within the **Block Editor** to test a dynamic block.
BVHIDE	Makes selected objects invisible in a visibility state.
BVSHOW	Controls visibility of objects in a dynamic block.
BVSTATE	Manages visibility states in a dynamic block.
CAL	Calculates mathematical and geometric expressions.
CAMERA	Sets position of camera and target for viewing.
CHAMFER	Draws an angled corner between two lines.
CHAMFEREDGE	Bevels the edges of 3D solids and surfaces.

Command	Description
CHANGE	Changes the properties of selected objects.
CHECKSTANDARDS	Compares the current drawing with a standards file and notes violations.
CHPROP	Enables changing the color, layer, linetype, linetype scale factor, lineweight, and thickness of a selected object.
CHSPACE	Moves objects from model space to paper space, or vice versa. (former Express Tool)
CIRCLE	Draws a circle.
CLASSICGROUP	Opens the legacy **Object Grouping** dialog box.
CLEANSCREENOFF	Restores all toolbars and dockable windows cleared by the **CLEANSCREENON** command.
CLEANSCREENON	Clears the screen of all toolbars and dockable windows.
CLIP	Crops a selected external reference, image, viewport, or underlay (DWF, DWFx, PDF, or DGN) to a specified boundary.
CLOSE	Closes current active drawing.
CLOSEALL	Closes all open drawings.
COLOR	Specifies color for new objects.
COMMANDLINE	Restores the command line.
COMMANDLINEHIDE	Hides the command line.
COMPILE	Compiles PostScript font and shape files.
CONE	Draws a 3D solid cone with a circular or elliptical base.
CONSTRAINTBAR	A toolbar-like UI element that displays the available geometric constraints on an object.
CONSTRAINTSETTINGS	Controls the display of geometric constraints on constraint bars.
CONTENTEXPLORER	Finds and inserts content such as drawing files, blocks, and styles.
CONTENTEXPLORERCLOSE	Closes the **Content Explorer** window.
CONVERT	Updates 2D polylines and associative hatches created in AutoCAD Release 13 or earlier.
CONVERTCTB	Changes a color-dependent plot style table to a named plot style table.
CONVERTOLDLIGHTS	Converts lights created in previous releases to lights in AutoCAD 2007 format.
CONVERTOLDMATERIALS	Converts materials created in previous releases to materials in AutoCAD 2007 format.
CONVERTPSTYLES	Changes current drawing to either a named or color-dependent plot style.
CONVTOMESH	Converts 3D objects such as polygon meshes, surfaces, and solids to mesh objects.
CONVTONURBS	Converts 3D solids and surfaces into NURBS surfaces.
CONVTOSOLID	Converts polylines and circles with thickness to 3D solids.
CONVTOSURFACE	Converts objects to surfaces.

Command	Description
COPY	Creates copies of selected objects at a specified location.
COPYBASE	Copies selected objects with a user-defined base point.
COPYCLIP	Copies all selected objects to the Clipboard.
COPYHIST	Copies command line text to the Clipboard.
COPYLINK	Copies the current view to the Clipboard for inclusion in other OLE applications.
COPYTOLAYER	Copies one or more objects to another layer. (former Express Tool)
-COPYTOLAYER	Copies one or more objects to another layer from the command line.
CUI	Allows customization of workspaces, toolbars, menus, shortcut menus, and keyboard shortcuts.
CUIEXPORT	Exports customized settings.
CUIIMPORT	Imports customized settings.
CUILOAD	Loads a CUIx file.
CUIUNLOAD	Unloads a CUIx file.
CUSTOMIZE	Allows customization of tool palettes.
CUTCLIP	Removes objects from the drawing and places them on the Clipboard.
CVADD	Adds control vertices to NURBS surfaces and splines.
CVHIDE	Turns off the display of control vertices for all NURBS surfaces and curves.
CVREBUILD	Rebuilds the shape of NURBS surfaces and curves.
-CVREBUILD	Rebuilds the shape of NURBS surfaces and curves.
CVREMOVE	Removes the shape of NURBS surfaces and curves.
CVSHOW	Displays the control vertices for specified NURBS surfaces or curves.
CYLINDER	Draws a solid 3D cylinder with either a circular or elliptical cross section.
DASHBOARD	Opens Dashboard window.
DASHBOARDCLOSE	Closes Dashboard window. Routed to the **RIBBONCLOSE** command.
DATAEXTRACTION	Exports object property, block attribute, and drawing information to a data extraction table or to an external file and specifies a data link to an Excel spreadsheet.
-DATAEXTRACTION	Exports object property, block attribute, and drawing information to a data extraction table or to an external file and specifies a data link to an Excel spreadsheet from the command line.
DATALINK	Displays the **Data Link Manager**.
DATALINKUPDATE	Updates data to or from an established external data link.

Command	Description
DBCLOSE	Closes the dbConnect Manager and removes the **dbConnect** menu from the menu bar.
DBCONNECT	Opens dbConnect Manager and adds **dbConnect** menu to the menu bar, establishing an interface with external database tables.
DBLIST	Displays database information about drawing objects in the text window.
DCALIGNED	Constrains the distance between two points on different objects.
DCANGULAR	Constrains the angle between line or polyline segments, the angle swept out by an arc or a polyline arc segment, or the angle between three points on objects.
DCCONVERT	Converts associative dimensions to dimensional constraints.
DCDIAMETER	Constrains the diameter of a circle or an arc.
DCDISPLAY	Displays or hides the dynamic constraints associated with a selection set of objects.
DCFORM	Specifies whether the dimensional constraint being created is dynamic or annotational.
DCHORIZONTAL	Constrains the X distance between points on an object, or between two points on different objects.
DCLINEAR	Creates a horizontal, vertical, or rotated constraint based on the locations of the extension line origins and the dimension line.
DCRADIUS	Constrains the radius of a circle or an arc.
DCVERTICAL	Constrains the Y distance between points on an object, or between two points on different objects.
DDEDIT	Enables editing of single-line text, dimension text, attribute definitions, and feature control frames.
DDPTYPE	Specifies point display style and size.
DDVPOINT	Specification 3D viewing direction.
DELAY	Specifies the length of a timed pause in a script.
DELCONSTRAINT	Removes all geometric and dimensional constraints from a selection set of objects.
DETACHURL	Removes hyperlinks from selected objects.
DGNADJUST	Changes the display options of selected DGN underlays.
-DGNADJUST	Provides a command line interface to the DGN underlay display options.
DGNATTACH	Attaches a DGN underlay to the current drawing.
-DGNATTACH	Attaches a DGN underlay to the current drawing from the command line.
DGNBIND	Binds DGN underlays to the current drawing.

Command	Description
-DGNBIND	Binds DGN underlays to the current drawing from the command line.
DGNCLIP	Defines a clipping boundary for a selected DGN underlay.
DGNEXPORT	Creates one or more DGN files from the current drawing. You will be able to attach DGN files with non-DGN extensions.
-DGNEXPORT	Creates one or more DGN files from the current drawing from the command line.
DGNIMPORT	Creates one or more DGN files from the current drawing. You will be able to attach DGN files with non-DGN extensions.
-DGNIMPORT	Creates one or more DGN files from the current drawing from the command line.
DGNMAPPING	Opens the **DGN Mapping Setups Manager** dialog box.
DIM and DIM1	Initiates **Dimensioning** mode. **DIM1** allows user to execute a single dimensioning command before returning to the command prompt.
DIMALIGNED	Creates a linear dimension parallel to an angled edge.
DIMANGULAR	Creates an angular dimension between two lines or three points.
DIMARC	Creates an arc length dimension.
DIMBASELINE	Creates a linear, angular, or ordinate dimension from a selected baseline.
DIMBREAK	Adds or removes a dimension break.
DIMCENTER	Creates center marks or centerlines of circles and arcs.
DIMCONSTRAINT	Applies dimensional constraints to selected objects or points on objects.
DIMCONTINUE	Creates a chained linear, angular, or ordinate dimension.
DIMDIAMETER	Creates diameter dimensions for circles and arcs, which include the diameter symbol.
DIMDISASSOCIATE	Removes associativity from specified dimensions.
DIMEDIT	Edits dimension extension lines and text.
DIMINSPECT	Creates or removes inspection dimensions.
-DIMINSPECT	Provides a command line interface to create or remove inspection dimensions.
DIMJOGGED	Creates a foreshortened radius dimension.
DIMJOGLINE	Adds or removes a jog line on a linear or aligned dimension.
DIMLINEAR	Creates horizontal or vertical linear dimensions.
DIMORDINATE	Creates ordinate dimensions based on specified *x* and *y* data.
DIMOVERRIDE	Temporarily changes a dimension system variable without changing the dimension style.
DIMRADIUS	Creates a radius dimension for a circle or arc, which includes a radius symbol.

Command	Description
DIMREASSOCIATE	Links selected dimensions to association points on objects.
DIMREGEN	Updates the locations of associative dimensions.
DIMSPACE	Adjusts the spacing equally between parallel linear and angular dimensions.
DIMSTYLE	Manages dimension styles.
DIMTEDIT	Permits moving and rotating dimension text.
DIST	Measures the distance and angle between two specified points.
DISTANTLIGHT	Creates a distant light.
DIVIDE	Divides an object into evenly spaced segments marked by points.
DONUT	Draws filled rings and circles.
DRAGMODE	Controls display of dragged objects.
DRAWINGRECOVERY	Displays list of files open during a system failure and offers options for recovery.
DRAWINGRECOVERYHIDE	Closes the **Drawing Recovery Manager**.
DRAWORDER	Changes the draw order of drawing objects.
DSETTINGS	Sets snap, grid, polar tracking, object snap, and dynamic input.
DVIEW	Creates parallel projection or perspective views in 3D.
DWFADJUST	Allows adjustment of a DWF underlay from the command line.
DWFATTACH	Attaches a DWF underlay to current drawing.
DWFCLIP	Uses clipping boundaries to define a subregion of a DWF underlay.
DWFFORMAT	Sets the default DWF format to the selected format to DWF or DWFx for the **PUBLISH**, **3DDWF**, and **EXPORT** commands.
DWFLAYERS	Controls the display of layers in a DWF underlay.
DWGCONVERT	Converts drawing format version for one or more selected drawing files.
DWGPROPS	Sets and displays the properties of the current drawing.
DXBIN	Imports Drawing Exchange Binary format files.
EATTEDIT	Edits block attributes.
EATTEXT	Extracts block attribute data to a table or to an external file.
EDGE	Changes display visibility of 3D Face edges.
EDGESURF	Creates a 3D mesh conforming to four selected edges.
EDITSHOT	Opens the **Edit View** dialog box with the **Shot Properties** tab active.
ELEV	Sets elevation and extrusion thickness for new objects.
ELLIPSE	Draws an ellipse or an elliptical arc.

Command	Description
ERASE	Removes selected objects.
ETRANSMIT	Packages files for Internet transmission.
EXPLODE	Breaks a selected compound object into component parts.
EXPORT	Saves object to other file formats.
EXPORTDWF	Creates a DWF file and allows you to set individual page setup overrides on a sheet-by-sheet basis.
EXPORTDWFX	Creates a DWFx file where you can set individual page setup overrides on a sheet-by-sheet basis.
EXPORTLAYOUT	Exports all visible objects from current layout to the model space of a new drawing.
EXPORTPDF	Creates a PDF file where you can set individual page setup overrides on a sheet-by-sheet basis.
EXPORTTOAUTOCAD	Creates a new DWG file with all AEC objects exploded.
-EXPORTTOUTOCAD	Provides a command line interface to create a new DWG file with all AEC objects exploded.
EXTEND	Extends selected object to meet a selected boundary edge.
EXTERNALREFERENCES	Displays **External References** palette.
EXTERNALREFERENCESCLOSE	Closes **External References** palette.
EXTRUDE	Creates a solid by extruding a cross section to a specified height.
FBXEXPORT	Creates an Autodesk® FBX file containing selected objects in the current drawing.
-FBXEXPORT	Creates an Autodesk® FBX file containing selected objects in the current drawing from the command line.
FBXIMPORT	Imports an Autodesk® FBX file, which can contain objects, lights, cameras, and materials.
-FBXIMPORT	Imports an Autodesk® FBX file, which can contain objects, lights, cameras, and materials, from the command line.
FIELD	Creates a multiline text object, which can be updated automatically when the field value changes.
FILL	Controls the display of filled areas in hatches, 2D solids, and polylines.
FILLET	Creates a rounded corner tangent to two objects with a specified radius.
FILLETEDGE	Rounds and fillets the edges of solid objects.
FILTER	Allows creation of a list of criteria for creating a selection set.
FIND	Enables finding, selecting, and replacing specified text.
FLATSHOT	Creates a 2D representation of all 3D objects in the current view.

Command	Description
FREESPOT	Creates a free spotlight, which is similar to a spotlight without a specified target.
FREEWEB	Creates a free web light, which is similar to a web light without a specified target.
GCCOINCIDENT	Constrains two points together or a point to a curve (or an extension of a curve).
GCCOLLINEAR	Causes two or more line segments to lie along the same line.
GCCONCENTRIC	Constrains two arcs, circles, or ellipses to the same center point.
GCEQUAL	Constrains two arcs, circles, or ellipses to the same center point.
GCFIX	Locks points and curves in position.
GCHORIZONTAL	Causes lines or pairs of points to lie parallel to the *X*-axis of the current coordinate system.
GCPARALLEL	Causes selected lines to lie parallel to each other.
GCPERPENDICULAR	Causes selected lines to lie 90 degrees to one another.
GCSMOOTH	Constrains a spline to be contiguous and maintain G2 continuity with another spline, line, arc, or polyline.
GCSYMMETRIC	Causes selected objects to become symmetrically constrained about a selected line.
GCTANGENT	Constrains two curves to maintain a point of tangency to each other or their extensions.
GCVERTICAL	Causes lines or pairs of points to lie parallel to the *Y*-axis of the current coordinate system.
GEOGRAPHICLOCATION	Specifies latitude and longitude of a location.
GEOMCONSTRAINT	Applies or persists geometric relationships between objects or points on objects.
GOTOURL	Opens the file or web page associated with a hyperlink in the drawing.
GRADIENT	Fills a closed area with a gradient fill pattern.
GRAPHICSCONFIG	Sets options for 3D display performance.
GRAPHSCR	Closes the text window.
GRID	Displays a reference pattern of dots at user-specified spacing.
GROUP	Creates and manages sets of grouped objects.
GROUPEDIT	Adds and removes objects from the selected group, or renames a selected group.
HATCH	Creates a hatch pattern, solid fill, or gradient fill inside a closed area.
HATCHEDIT	Changes existing hatches or fills.
HATCHGENERATEBOUNDARY	Creates a nonassociated polyline around a selected hatch.

Command	Description
HATCHSETBOUNDARY	Redefines a selected hatch or fill to conform to a different closed boundary.
HATCHSETORIGIN	Controls the starting location of hatch pattern generation for a selected hatch.
HATCHTOBACK	Sets the draw order for all hatches in the drawing to be behind all other objects.
HELIX	Creates a 2D or 3D spiral.
HELP	Displays explanation of concepts, commands, and procedures.
HIDE	Regenerates model and suppresses hidden lines.
HIDEOBJECTS	Hides selected objects.
HIDEPALETTES	Hides all currently displayed palettes such as the command line, **DesignCenter**, and properties, keeping track of their positions.
HLSETTINGS	Controls hidden line display properties.
HYPERLINK	Attaches or modifies a hyperlink to a drawing object.
HYPERLINKOPTIONS	Manages display of hyperlink properties.
ID	Displays coordinates of selected point.
IMAGE	Opens **Image Manager**.
IMAGEADJUST	Controls image brightness, contrast, and fade values.
IMAGEATTACH	Attaches image to drawing.
IMAGECLIP	Creates clipping boundaries for images.
IMAGEFRAME	Controls image frame display and plotting.
IMAGEQUALITY	Controls image display quality.
IMPORT	Imports files from other applications.
IMPRINT	Imprints an edge on a 3D solid.
INSERT	Places drawings or blocks into drawing.
INSERTOBJ	Inserts a linked or embedded object.
INTERFERE	Determines whether two solid objects overlap.
-INTERFERE	Highlights 3D solids that overlap from the command line.
INTERSECT	Creates a new solid from the area common to two or more solids or regions.
ISOLATEOBJECTS	Displays selected objects across layers; unselected objects are hidden.
ISOPLANE	Selects active isometric plane.
JOGSECTION	Adds a jogged segment to a section object.
JOIN	Combines similar objects into a single object.
JPGOUT	Saves selected objects to a JPEG file format.
JUSTIFYTEXT	Changes the justification point of text.
LAYCUR	Changes layer of selected objects to current layer. (former Express Tool)
LAYDEL	Deletes layer of a selected object and all objects on layer, and purges layer from drawing. (former Express Tool)
-LAYDEL	Deletes layer of a selected object and all objects on layer, and purges layer from drawing from the command line.

Command	Description
LAYER	Manages layers. The **Layer Properties Manager** dialog is a modeless dialog.
LAYERCLOSE	Closes the **Layer Properties Manager** dialog from the command line.
LAYERP	Undoes changes to layer settings.
LAYERPMODE	Controls tracking of layer setting changes.
LAYERSTATE	Saves, restores, and manages named layer states.
LAYFRZ	Freezes layer of selected objects. (former Express Tool)
LAYISO	Isolates layer of selected objects so that all other layers are turned off. (former Express Tool)
LAYLCK	Locks layer of selected objects. (former Express Tool)
LAYMCH	Changes layer of a selected object to match destination layer. (former Express Tool)
-LAYMCH	Changes layer of a selected object to match destination layer from the command line.
LAYMCUR	Makes layer of a selected object current. (renamed **AI_MOLC**)
LAYMRG	Merges selected layers onto a destination layer. (former Express Tool)
-LAYMRG	Merges selected layers onto a destination layer from the command line.
LAYOFF	Turns off layer of selected object. (former Express Tool)
LAYON	Turns on all layers. (former Express Tool)
LAYOUT	Manages drawing layout tabs.
LAYOUTWIZARD	Starts layout wizard.
LAYTHW	Thaws all layers. (former Express Tool)
LAYTRANS	Converts drawing layers to specified standards.
LAYULK	Unlocks layer of a selected object. (former Express Tool)
LAYUNISO	Turns on layers that were turned off with last **LAYISO** command. (former Express Tool)
LAYVPI	Isolates an object's layer to the current viewport. (former Express Tool)
LAYWALK	Dynamically displays layers in a drawing. (former Express Tool)
LEADER	Creates leader lines for notes and dimensions.
LENGTHEN	Modifies object length.
LIGHT	Controls lights in rendered scenes.
LIGHTLIST	Opens Lights in Model window to add and modify lights.
LIGHTLISTCLOSE	Closes Lights in Model window.
LIMITS	Sets drawing size.
LINE	Draws straight line segments.
LINETYPE	Manages linetypes.
LIST	Displays database information.

Command	Description
LIVESECTION	Turns on live sectioning for a selected section object.
LOAD	Loads shapes for use by the **SHAPE** command.
LOFT	Creates a 3D solid or surface by lofting through a set of two or more curves.
LOGFILEOFF	Closes the log file.
LOGFILEON	Records contents of text window to a file.
LTSCALE	Sets drawing linetype scale.
LWEIGHT	Manages lineweights.
MACROTRACE	Evaluates DIESEL expressions.
MARKUP	Manages markup sets.
MARKUPCLOSE	Closes **Markup Set Manager**.
MASSPROP	Displays mass properties of solids and regions.
MATBROWSERCLOSE	Closes the Materials Browser.
MATBROWSEROPEN	Opens the Materials Browser.
MATEDITORCLOSE	Closes the Materials Editor.
MATEDITOROPEN	Opens the Materials Editor.
MATCHCELL	Copies the properties of one table cell to other selected table cells.
MATCHPROP	Copies the properties of one object to other selected objects.
MATERIALATTACH	Attaches materials to objects by layer.
MATERIALMAP	Displays a material mapper grip tool to adjust mapping on a face or an object.
MATERIALS	Manages, applies, and modifies materials.
MATERIALSCLOSE	Closes Materials window.
MEASURE	Marks segments of a specified length on an object.
MEASUREGEOM	Measures the distance, radius, angle, area, and volume of selected objects or sequence of points.
MENU	Loads a customizable XML-based file containing menus, toolbars, tool palettes, and other interface elements.
MESH	Creates a 3D mesh primitive object such as a box, cone, cylinder, pyramid, sphere, wedge, or torus.
MESHCAP	Creates a mesh face that connects open edges.
MESHCOLLAPSE	Merges the vertices of selected mesh faces or edges.
MESHCREASE	Sharpens the edges of selected mesh subobjects.
MESHEXTRUDE	Extends a mesh face into 3D space.
MESHMERGE	Merges adjacent faces into a single face.
MESHOPTIONS	Displays the **Mesh Tessellation Options** dialog box, which controls default settings for converting existing objects to mesh objects.

Command	Description
MESHPRIMITIVEOPTIONS	Displays the **Mesh Primitive Options** dialog box, which sets the tessellation defaults for primitive mesh objects.
MESHREFINE	Multiplies the number of faces in selected mesh objects or faces.
MESHSMOOTHLESS	Decreases the level of smoothness for mesh objects by one level.
MESHSMOOTHMORE	Increases the level of smoothness for mesh objects by one level.
MESHSPIN	Spins the adjoining edge of two triangular mesh faces.
MESHSPLIT	Splits a mesh face into two faces.
MESHUNCREASE	Removes the crease from selected mesh faces, edges, or vertices.
MIGRATEMATERIALS	Finds any legacy materials in tool palettes and converts them to generic type.
MINSERT	Inserts copies of a block in a rectangular array.
MIRROR	Creates a mirror image about an axis.
MIRROR3D	Creates a mirror image about a plane.
MLEADER	Creates a line that connects annotation to a feature.
MLEADERALIGN	Organizes selected multileaders along a specified line.
MLEADERCOLLECT	Organizes selected multileaders containing blocks as content into a group attached to a single leader line.
MLEADEREDIT	Adds leader lines to, or removes leader lines from, a multileader object.
MLEADERSTYLE	Defines a new multileader style.
MLEDIT	Modifies multiline vertices, breaks, and intersections.
MLINE	Creates multiple parallel lines.
MLSTYLE	Controls multiline styles.
MODEL	Enters model space.
MOVE	Moves objects from one location to another.
MREDO	Reverses multiple **UNDO** commands.
MSLIDE	Makes a slide file of current model viewport or layout.
MSPACE	Enters model space for active viewport in layout space.
MTEDIT	Modifies multiline text.
MTEXT	Creates multiple lines of text as a single object.
MULTIPLE	Repeats the next command until you enter **<Esc>**.
MVIEW	Creates and manages layout viewports.
MVSETUP	Helps set up drawing views.
NAVBAR	Provides access to navigation and orientation tools from a toolbar type interface.
NAVSMOTION	Displays the ShowMotion interface.
NAVSMOTIONCLOSE	Closes the ShowMotion interface.

Command	Description
NAVSWHEEL	Displays the SteeringWheel.
NAVVCUBE	Shows/hides the ViewCube.
NCOPY	Copies objects that are contained in an xref, block, or DGN underlay.
NETLOAD	Loads a .NET application.
NEW	Starts a new drawing.
NEWSHEETSET	Creates a new sheet set.
NEWSHOT	Opens the **New View** dialog box with the **Shot Properties** tab active.
OBJECTSCALE	Adds or deletes supported scales for annotative objects.
-OBJECTSCALE	Provides a command line interface to add or delete supported scales for annotative objects.
OFFSET	Draws objects parallel to a specified object.
OFFSETEDGE	Creates a closed polyline or spline object that is offset by a specified distance from the edges of a selected face on a 3D solid or a planar surface.
OLELINKS	Manages OLE (object linking and embedding) links.
OLESCALE	Manages OLE (object linking and embedding) object properties.
ONLINECOLNOW	Starts an online session with **AutoCAD WS**, in which people that you invite can simultaneously view and edit your current drawing.
ONLINEDOCS	Opens your **Autodesk 360** documents list and folders in a browser.
ONLINEOPTIONS	Opens the **Online** tab of the **Options** dialog box.
ONLINESHARE	Designates who can access the current document from your **Autodesk 360**.
ONLINESYNC	Starts or stops syncing your custom settings with your **Autodesk 360** account.
ONLINESYNCSETTINGS	Displays the **Choose Which Settings Are Synced** dialog box where you can specify selected settings to be synced.
ONLINETOMOBILE	Sends a notification to your mobile devices, enabling you to find and open the current drawing on your mobile devices quickly.
ONLINEUPLOAD	Uploads specified drawing files to your **Autodesk 360** account.
OOPS	Restores objects removed by the last **ERASE** command.
OPEN	Opens a previously created drawing file.
OPENDWFMARKUP	Opens a DWF or DWFx file that contains markups.
OPENSHEETSET	Opens a specified sheet set.
OPTIONS	Controls AutoCAD settings.
ORTHO	Limits cursor movement to horizontal and vertical directions while in drawing and editing commands.

Command	Description
OSNAP	Sets running object snaps.
OVERKILL	Removes duplicate or overlapping lines, arcs, and polylines. Also combines partially overlapping or contiguous ones.
-OVERKILL	Removes duplicate or overlapping lines, arcs, and polylines from the command line. Also combines partially overlapping or contiguous ones.
PAGESETUP	Manages page layout, plotting device, paper size, and other layout settings.
PAN	Moves drawing on screen without changing zoom factor.
PARAMETERS	Controls the associative parameters used in the drawing.
PARAMETERSCLOSE	Closes the **Parameters Manager** palette.
PARTIALOAD	Loads additional components into a partially opened drawing.
PARTIALOPEN	Opens selected views and layers from a drawing file.
PASTEASHYPERLINK	Pastes information from the Clipboard as a hyperlink.
PASTEBLOCK	Pastes objects from the Clipboard as a block.
PASTECLIP	Pastes data from the Clipboard.
PASTEORIG	Pastes objects from the Clipboard retaining coordinate information from original drawing.
PASTESPEC	Sets file formats and linking options for pasted objects.
PCINWIZARD	Opens wizard to import PCP and PC2 configuration file plot settings.
PDFADJUST	Adjusts the fade, contrast, and monochrome settings of a PDF underlay.
PDFATTACH	Inserts a PDF file as an underlay into the current drawing.
PDFCLIP	Crops the display of a selected PDF underlay to a specified boundary.
PDFLAYERS	Controls the display of layers in a PDF underlay.
PEDIT	Modifies polylines and 3D meshes.
PFACE	Creates a 3D mesh by entering vertices.
PLAN	Creates a view looking down the current UCS *Z*-axis toward the origin.
PLANESURF	Creates a planar surface.
PLINE	Creates a connected sequence of line and arc segments as a single object.
PLOT	Prints a drawing to a plotter, printer, or file.
PLOTSTAMP	Places information on corner of drawing and creates a log file.
PLOTSTYLE	Manages plot styles for new or selected objects.
PLOTTERMANAGER	Adds or modifies a plotter configuration.
PNGOUT	Saves to a Portable Network Graphics format file.

Command	Description
POINT	Draws a point.
POINTCLOUD	Provides options to create and attach an indexed point cloud file.
POINTCLOUDATTACH	Inserts an indexed point cloud (PCG or ISD) file into the current drawing.
-POINTCLOUDATTACH	Inserts an indexed point cloud (PCG or ISD) file into the current drawing from the command line.
POINTCLOUDCLIP	Crops the display of a selected point cloud to specified boundaries.
POINTCLOUDINDEX	Creates an indexed point cloud (PCG or ISD) file from a scan file.
POINTCLOUDINTENSITYEDIT	Opens the **Point Cloud Intensity Color Mapping** dialog box that specifies intensity color mapping for eligible point clouds.
POINTLIGHT	Creates a point light.
POLYGON	Draws regular polygons with up to 1024 sides.
POLYSOLID	Creates a 3D polysolid.
PRESSPULL	Presses or pulls bounded areas.
PREVIEW	Shows plot appearance.
PROJECTGEOMETRY	Projects points, lines, or curves onto a 3D solid or surface from different directions.
PROPERTIES	Used to view or change object properties.
PROPERTIESCLOSE	Closes **Properties** palette.
PSETUPIN	Imports a page setup.
PSPACE	Enters paper space.
PUBLISH	Publishes drawings to DWF, DWFx, and PDF files, or to plotters.
PUBLISHTOWEB	Converts drawings to HTML pages.
PURGE	Removes unused items from the drawing database.
-PURGE	Removes unused items from the drawing database from the command line.
PYRAMID	Creates a 3D solid pyramid.
QCCLOSE	Closes the **QuickCalc** calculator.
QDIM	Quickly creates or edits a series of dimensions.
QLEADER	Quickly creates leader line and text.
QNEW	Starts a new drawing from the default template file.
QSAVE	Saves the current drawing.
QSELECT	Quickly creates a selection set based on filtering criteria.
QTEXT	Controls text and attribute display and plotting.
QUICKCALC	Opens the **QuickCalc** calculator.
QUICKCUI	Displays the CUI editor in a collapsed state. Additional support for enhanced tooltips, quick access panel, and ribbons.
QUIT	Exits AutoCAD and prompts to save or discard changes.

Command	Description
QVDRAWING	Displays a two-level structure of preview images at the bottom of the application. The first level displays the images of open drawings, and the second level displays the images for model space and layouts in a drawing.
QVDRAWINGCLOSE	Closes preview images of open drawings and layouts in a drawing.
RAY	Creates a line extending to infinity in one direction.
RECOVER	Repairs a damaged drawing.
RECOVERALL	Repairs a damaged drawing and xrefs.
RECTANG	Creates rectangles.
REDEFINE	Restores AutoCAD commands previously changed by the **UNDEFINE** command.
REDO	Reverses the effects of a single **UNDO** command.
REDRAW	Refreshes current viewport display.
REDRAWALL	Refreshes display in all viewports.
REFCLOSE	Saves or discards changes made during in-place editing of an xref or block.
REFEDIT	Selects a reference for editing.
REFSET	Modifies working set during in-place editing of a reference.
REGEN	Regenerates the entire drawing and recomputes geometry for objects in the current viewport.
REGENALL	Regenerates and recomputes geometry for all viewports.
REGENAUTO	Controls automatic regeneration of a drawing.
REGION	Creates a 2-dimensional area object from a closed shape or loop.
REINIT	Reinitializes digitizer, digitizer input/output port, and program parameters file.
RENAME	Changes object names.
RENDER	Produces a realistically shaded view of a 3D model.
RENDERCROP	Selects a specific region in an image for rendering.
RENDERENVIRONMENT	Provides visual cues for the apparent distance of objects.
RENDEREXPOSURE	Provides settings to interactively adjust the lighting global for the most recent rendered output.
RENDERONLINE	Uses the online resources in your **Autodesk 360** account to create an image of a 3D solid or surface model.
RENDERPRESETS	Specifies render presets, reusable rendering parameters for rendering an image.
RENDERWIN	Displays Render window without starting a render task.
RESETBLOCK	Restores dynamic block references to the default value.
RESUME	Restarts an interrupted script.

Command	Description
REVCLOUD	Creates a cloud-shaped polyline.
REVERSE	Reverses the order of vertices of the selected lines, polylines, splines, and helixes.
REVOLVE	Creates a solid by revolving a closed 2-dimensional shape around an axis.
REVSURF	Creates a rotated surface about an axis.
RIBBON	Opens the Ribbon window.
RIBBONCLOSE	Closes the Ribbon window.
ROTATE	Rotates selected objects around a specified base point.
ROTATE3D	Rotates an object in a 3D coordinate system.
RPREF	Controls rendering preferences.
RPREFCLOSE	Closes **Advanced Render Settings** palette, if it is displayed.
RSCRIPT	Creates a continuously running script.
RULESURF	Creates a polygon mesh between two curves.
SAVE	Saves a drawing.
SAVEAS	Saves current drawing with options for renaming file, changing file type, or changing file location.
SAVEIMG	Saves a rendered image to a BMP, TGA, or TIFF file.
SCALE	Proportionally enlarges or reduces objects relative to a base point.
SCALELISTEDIT	Manages scales available for layout viewports, page layouts, and plotting.
SCALETEXT	Enlarges or reduces text objects while maintaining location.
SCRIPT	Executes a sequence of commands from a script file.
SECTION	Creates a cross section through a solid.
SECTIONPLANE	Creates a section object that acts as a cutting plane through a 3D object.
SECTIONPLANEJOG	Adds a jogged segment to a section object.
SECTIONPLANESETTINGS	Sets display options for the selected section plane.
SECTIONPLANETOBLOCK	Saves selected section planes as 2D or 3D blocks.
SECURITYOPTIONS	Controls drawing security settings.
SEEK	Opens a web browser and displays the Autodesk **Seek** home page.
SELECT	Places objects in the previous selection set.
SELECTSIMILAR	Adds similar objects to the selection set based on selected objects.
SEQUENCEPLAY	Plays the named views in one view category.
SETBYLAYER	Changes property and ByBlock settings for selected objects to ByLayer.
SETIDROPHANDLER	Sets i-drop content default type.
SETVAR	Lists or changes system variable values.
SHADEMODE	Controls solid model shading.

Command	Description
SHAPE	Inserts a shape into the current drawing.
SHEETSET	Opens the **Sheet Set Manager**.
SHEETSETHIDE	Closes the **Sheet Set Manager**.
SHELL	Allows execution of operating system commands within AutoCAD.
SHOWPALETTES	Restores the state of the display and position of palettes hidden by **HIDEPALETTES**. Press **<Ctrl>+<Shift>+H** to switch between **HIDEPALETTES** and **SHOWPALETTES**.
SHOWRENDERGALLERY	Displays the images that were previously rendered and stored in your **Autodesk 360** account.
SIGVALIDATE	Displays digital signature information.
SKETCH	Draws a freehand line composed of segments.
SLICE	Divides a solid along a specified plane.
SNAP	Limits cursor movement to specified intervals.
SOLDRAW	Generates visible and hidden lines for viewports created with **SOLVIEW**.
SOLID	Creates 2D filled triangles and four-sided polygons.
SOLIDEDIT	Edits faces and edges of 3D solid objects.
SOLPROF	Creates a 2D profile of a 3D solid.
SOLVIEW	Creates orthographic, auxiliary, and sectional views of 3D solids.
SPACETRANS	Converts lengths between model space units and paper space units.
SPELL	Checks spelling of selected objects in a drawing.
SPHERE	Creates a solid sphere.
SPLINE	Creates a smooth curve fit to a sequence of points within a specified tolerance.
SPLINEDIT	Modifies splines or spline-fit polylines.
SPOTLIGHT	Creates a spotlight.
STANDARDS	Associates the current drawing with a Standards file.
STATUS	Displays drawing statistics, modes, and extents.
STLOUT	Stores solid data in a STL file format for stereo lithography.
STRETCH	Stretches selected objects.
STYLE	Manages text styles.
STYLESMANAGER	Manages plot styles.
SUBTRACT	Creates composite solid or region by subtracting selected objects or regions.
SUNPROPERTIES	Opens **Sun** palette and sets properties of the sun.
SUNPROPERTIESCLOSE	Closes Sun Properties window.
SURFBLEND	Creates a continuous blend surface between two existing surfaces.
SURFEXTEND	Lengthens a surface by a specified distance.
SURFEXTRACTCURVE	Extracts isoline curves from a surface.

Command	Description
SURFFILLET	Creates a filleted surface between two other surfaces.
SURFNETWORK	Creates a surface in the space between several curves in the U and V directions (including surface and solid edge subobjects).
SURFOFFSET	Creates a parallel surface a specified distance from the original surface.
SURFPATCH	Creates a new surface by fitting a cap over a surface edge that forms a closed loop.
SURFSCULPT	Trims and combines surfaces that bound a watertight area to create a solid.
SURFTRIM	Trims portions of a surface where it meets another surface or type of geometry.
SURFUNTRIM	Replaces surface areas removed by the **SURFTRIM** command.
SWEEP	Creates a 3D solid or surface by sweeping a 2D curve along a path.
SYSWINDOWS	Arranges windows and icons when the application window is shared with external applications.
TABLE	Creates an empty table in the drawing.
TABLEDIT	Edits text in a selected table cell.
TABLEEXPORT	Exports data from a table object in comma-separated file format.
TABLESTYLE	Sets the current table style. Creates, modifies, and deletes table styles.
TABLET	Turns on and off, calibrates, and configures an attached digitizing tablet input device.
TABSURF	Creates a surfaced polygon mesh by specifying a path curve and direction vector.
TASKBAR	Controls drawing display mode on the Windows taskbar.
TEXT	Creates a single line of user-entered text.
TEXTEDIT	Edits a dimensional constraint, dimension, or text object.
TEXTSCR	Opens the command line in a separate window.
TEXTTOFRONT	Brings text and/or dimensions in front of other drawing objects.
THICKEN	Creates a 3D solid by thickening a surface.
TIFOUT	Creates a TIFF file from selected objects.
TIME	Displays drawing date and time statistics.
TIMELINE	Provides access to previous versions of the **AutoCAD WS** online copy of the current drawing.
TINSERT	Inserts a block in a table cell.
TOLERANCE	Adds geometric tolerances in feature control frames.
TOOLBAR	Manages toolbar display and customization.
TOOLPALETTES	Opens **Tool Palettes** window.
TOOLPALETTESCLOSE	Closes **Tool Palettes** window.
TORUS	Creates a donut-shaped solid.
TPNAVIGATE	Displays a specified tool palette or palette group.

Command	Description
TRACE	Creates solid lines.
TRANSPARENCY	Controls transparency of background in images.
TRAYSETTINGS	Controls status bar tray content.
TREESTAT	Displays information about a drawing's spatial index.
TRIM	Removes part of an object at a selected cutting edge.
U	Undo.
UCS	Creates and manages user coordinate systems.
UCSICON	Controls display and location of UCS icon.
UCSMAN	Manages defined user coordinate systems.
ULAYERS	Controls the display of layers in a DWF, DWFx, PDF, or DGN underlay.
UNDEFINE	Allows an application-defined command to override an AutoCAD command.
UNDO	Reverses previous commands.
UNGROUP	Explodes a group.
UNION	Adds selected regions or solids.
UNISOLATEOBJECTS	Displays previously hidden objects.
UNITS	Sets coordinate and angle display precision and formats.
UPDATEFIELD	Updates fields for selected items.
UPDATETHUMBSNOW	Updates thumbnail previews in the **Sheet Set Manager**.
VBAIDE	Edits code, forms, and references for any loaded or embedded VBA projects in the current drawing.
VBALOAD	Loads a VBA (Visual Basic for Applications) project into the current work session.
VBAMAN	Loads, unloads, saves, creates, embeds, and extracts VBA projects.
VBARUN	Runs a VBA macro.
VBASTMT	Executes a Visual Basic complete instruction in the context of the current drawing on the AutoCAD command line.
VBAUNLOAD	Unloads a VBA (Visual Basic for Applications) project.
VIEW	Saves and restores named views.
VIEWBASE	Creates a base view from model space or Autodesk Inventor models.
VIEWCOMPONENT	Selects drawing view components for editing.
VIEWDETAIL	Supports the creation of detail views by selecting an existing drawing view
VIEWDETAILSTYLE	Supports the creation or modification of detail view styles.
VIEWEDIT	Edits an existing 2D view.
VIEWGO	Navigates to a named view.
VIEWPLAY	Plays the ShowMotion animation for the named view.
VIEWPLOTDETAILS	Displays information about completed plot and publish jobs.
VIEWPROJ	Creates one or more projected views from an existing 2D view.

Command	Description
VIEWRES	Sets resolution for objects in the current viewport.
VIEWSECTION	Supports the creation of section views by selecting a drawing view to cut.
VIEWSECTIONSTYLE	Supports the creation and editing of section view styles.
VIEWSETPROJ	Specifies the active project file for drawings containing drawing views from Inventor models.
VIEWSKETCH	Activates model space for a view and enters a "view sketching" state to edit and constrain a section line or detail boundary.
VIEWSKETCHCLOSE	Exits a "view sketching" state and makes paper space current.
VIEWSTD	Defines the default settings for 2D views.
VIEWSYMBOLSKETCH	Constrains the section line and detail boundaries to the drawing view geometry.
VISUALSTYLES	Creates and modifies visual styles and applies a visual style to a viewport.
-VISUALSTYLES	Creates and modifies visual styles and applies a visual style to a viewport from the command line.
VISUALSTYLESCLOSE	Closes **Visual Styles Manager** dialog box.
VLISP	Opens the Visual Lisp Console window to develop, test, and debug AutoLISP programs.
VPCLIP	Clips viewport objects and modifies viewport boundary.
VPLAYER	Sets layer visibility within viewports. **VPLAYER** can now run in the **Model** tab with a limited set of options.
VPMAX	Enlarges current viewport to full screen and switches to model space for editing.
VPMIN	Restores viewport to settings prior to maximizing.
VPOINT	Sets 3D viewing direction.
VPORTS	Creates viewports in model or paper space.
VSCURRENT	Sets visual style in current viewport.
VSLIDE	Opens an image slide file for viewing in the current viewport.
VSSAVE	Saves a visual style.
VTOPTIONS	Controls view transitions.
WALKFLYSETTINGS	Specifies walk and fly settings.
WBLOCK	Saves a block to a new drawing file.
WEBLIGHT	Creates a web light.
WEDGE	Creates a 3D solid wedge.
WELCOMESCREEN	Displays the **Welcome Screen** when you start the program.
WHOHAS	Displays the current user's computer name, login ID, and full name (if available) and the date and time the drawing file was opened.
WIPEOUT	Creates a polygonal area that covers existing objects with the current background color.

Command	Description
WMFIN	Imports a Windows metafile as a block.
WMFOPTS	Sets options for the **WMFIN** command.
WMFOUT	Saves selected objects to a Windows metafile format.
WORKSPACE	Manages workspaces.
WSSAVE	Saves a workspace scheme and settings.
WSSETTINGS	Sets workspace options.
XATTACH	Attaches a drawing as an external reference to the current drawing.
XBIND	Adds specified xref-dependent named objects to the drawing.
XCLIP	Defines an external reference display clipping boundary.
XEDGES	Creates wireframe geometry by extracting edges from a 3D solid or surface.
XLINE	Creates a line that is infinite in both directions.
XOPEN	Opens an external reference for editing in a new window.
XPLODE	Disassembles a block into its component objects for editing.
XREF	Manages external references.
ZOOM	Changes the magnification of objects in the current viewport.

appendix C
Command Aliases

Command aliases are shortcuts for commands that you enter at the keyboard. *Note:* Command aliases beginning with a dash (-) suppress display of dialog box windows and force input entry from the command line.

Command	Alias
3DALIGN	3AL
3DARRAY	3A
3DFACE	3F
3DMOVE	3M
3DORBIT	3DO, ORBIT
3DPOLY	3P
3DPRINT	3DP, 3DPLOT, RAPIDPROTOTYPE
3DROTATE	3R
3DSCALE	3S
3DWALK	3DNAVIGATE, 3DW
ACTRECORD	ARR
ACTSTOP	ARS
-ACTSTOP	-ARS
ACTUSERINPUT	ARU
ACTUSERMESSAGE	ARM
-ACTUSERMESSAGE	-ARM
ADCENTER	ADC, DC, DCENTER
ALIGN	AL
ANALYSISCURVATURE	CURVATUREANALYSIS
ANALYSISDRAFTANGLE	DRAFTANGLEANALYSIS
ANALYSISZEBRA	ZEBRA
APPLOAD	AP
ARC	A
AREA	AA
ARRAY	AR
-ARRAY	-AR
ATTDEF	ATT
-ATTDEF	-ATT
ATTEDIT	ATE
-ATTEDIT	-ATE, ATTE
ATTIPE	ATI
BACTION	AC
BCLOSE	BC
BCPARAMETER	CPARAM
BEDIT	BE
BLOCK	B
-BLOCK	-B
BOUNDARY	BO
-BOUNDARY	-BO
BPARAMETER	PARAM
BREAK	BR
BSAVE	BS
BVSTATE	VS
CAMERA	CAM
CHAMFER	CHA
CHANGE	-CH
CHECKSTANDARDS	CHK
CIRCLE	C
COLOR	COL, COLOUR
COMMANDLINE	CLI
CONSTRAINTBAR	CBAR
CONSTRAINTSETTINGS	CSETTINGS
COPY	CO, CP

Command	Alias
CTABLESTYLE	CT
CVADD	INSERTCONTROLPOINT
CVHIDE	POINTOFF
CVREBUILD	REBUILD
CVREMOVE	REMOVECONTROL-POINT
CVSHOW	POINTON
CYLINDER	CYL
DATAEXTRACTION	DX
DATALINK	DL
DATALINKUPDATE	DLU
DBCONNECT	DBC
DDEDIT	ED
DDGRIPS	GR
DDVPOINT	VP
DELCONSTRAINT	DELCON
DIMALIGNED	DAL
DIMANGULAR	DAN
DIMARC	DAR
DIMBASELINE	DBA
DIMCENTER	DCE
DIMCONSTRAINT	DCON
DIMCONTINUE	DCO
DIMDIAMETER	DDI
DIMDISASSOCIATE	DDA
DIMEDIT	DED
DIMJOGGED	DJO, JOG
DIMJOGLINE	DJL
DIMLINEAR	DLI
DIMORDINATE	DOR
DIMOVERRIDE	DOV
DIMRADIUS	DRA
DIMREASSOCIATE	DRE
DIMSTYLE	D, DST
DIST	DI
DIVIDE	DIV
DONUT	DO
DRAWINGRECOVERY	DRM
DRAWORDER	DR
DSETTINGS	DS, SE
DVIEW	DV
EDITSHOT	ESHOT
ELLIPSE	EL
ERASE	E
EXPLODE	X
EXPORT	EXP
-EXPORTTOAUTOCAD	AECTOACAD
EXTEND	EX
EXTERNALREFERENCES	ER
EXTRUDE	EXT
FILLET	F
FILTER	FI
FLATSHOT	FSHOT
GEOGRAPHICLOCATION	GEO, NORTH, NORTHDIR

Command	Alias
GEOMCONSTRAINT	GCON
GRADIENT	GD
GROUP	G
-GROUP	-G
HATCH	BH, H
-HATCH	-H
HATCHEDIT	HE
HATCHTOBACK	HB
HIDE	HI
HIDEPALETTES	POFF
IMAGE	IM
-IMAGE	-IM
IMAGEADJUST	IAD
IMAGEATTACH	IAT
IMAGECLIP	ICL
IMPORT	IMP
INSERT	I
-INSERT	-I
INSERTOBJ	IO
INTERFERE	INF
INTERSECT	IN
ISOLATEOBJECTS	ISOLATE
JOIN	J
LAYER	LA
-LAYER	-LA
-LAYOUT	LO
LAYERSTATE	LAS, LMAN
LENGTHEN	LEN
LINE	L
LINETYPE	LT, LTYPE
-LINETYPE	-LT, -LTYPE
LIST	LI, LS, SHOWMAT
LTSCALE	LTS
LINEWEIGHT	LW, LWEIGHT
MARKUP	MSM
MATBROWSEROPEN	MAT
MATCHPROP	MA
MEASURE	ME
MEASUREGEOM	MEA
MESHCREASE	CREASE
MESHREFINE	REFINE
MESHSMOOTH	CONVTOMESH, SMOOTH
MESHSMOOTHLESS	LESS
MESHSPLIT	SPLIT
MESHUNCREASE	UNCREASE
MIRROR	MI
MLEADER	MLD
MLEADERALIGN	MLA
MLEADERCOLLECT	MLC
MLEADEREDIT	MLE
MLEADERSTYLE	MLS
MLINE	ML
MOVE	M
MSPACE	MS

Command	Alias
MTEXT	MT, T
-MTEXT	-T
MVIEW	MV
NAVSMOTION	MOTION
NAVSMOTIONCLOSE	MOTIONCLS
NAVSWHEEL	WHEEL
NAVVCUBE	CUBE
NEWSHOT	NSHOT
NEWVIEW	NVIEW
OFFSET	O
OPTIONS	OP
OSNAP	OS
-OSNAP	-OS
PAN	P
-PAN	-P
PARAMETERS	PAR
-PARAMETERS	-PAR
-PARTIALOPEN	PARTIALOPEN
PASTESPEC	PA
PEDIT	PE
PLINE	PL
PLOT	PRINT
POINT	PO
POINTCLOUD	PC
POINTCLOUDATTACH	PCATTACH
POINTCLOUDINDEX	PCINDEX
POINTLIGHT	FREEPOINT
POLYGON	POL
POLYSOLID	PSOLID
PREVIEW	PRE
PROPERTIES	CH, MO, PR, PROPS
PROPERTIESCLOSE	PRCLOSE
PSPACE	PS
PUBLISHTOWEB	PTW
PURGE	PU
-PURGE	-PU
PYRAMID	PYR
QLEADER	LE
QUICKCALC	QC
QUICKCUI	QCUI
QUIT	EXIT
QVDRAWING	QVD
QVDRAWINGCLOSE	QVDC
QVLAYOUT	QVL
QVLAYOUTCLOSE	QVLC
RECTANG	REC
REDRAW	R
REDRAWALL	RA
REGEN	RE
REGENALL	REA
REGION	REG
RENAME	REN
-RENAME	-REN
RENDER	RR
RENDERCROP	RC

Command	Alias
RENDERPRESETS	RFILEOPT, RP
RENDERWIN	RENDSCR, RW
REVOLVE	REV
ROTATE	RO
RPREF	RPR
SCALE	SC
SCRIPT	SCR
SECTION	SEC
SECTIONPLANE	SPLANE
SECTIONPLANEJOG	JOGSECTION
SECTIONPLANETO-BLOCK	GENERATESECTION
SEQUENCEPLAY	SPLAY
SETVAR	SET
SHADEMODE	SHA
SHEETSET	SSM
SHOWPALETTES	PON
SLICE	SL
SNAP	SN
SOLID	SO
SPELL	SP
SPLINE	SPL
SPLINEDIT	SPE
STANDARDS	STA
STRETCH	S
STYLE	ST
SUBTRACT	SU
SURFBLEND	BLENDSRF
SURFEXTEND	EXTENDSRF
SURFFILLET	FILLETSRF
SURFNETWORK	NETWORKSRF
SURFOFFSET	OFFSETSRF
SURFPATCH	PATCH
SURFSCULPT	CREATESOLID
TABLE	TB
TABLESTYLE	TS
TABLET	TA
TEXT	DT
THICKNESS	TH
TILEMODE	TI
TOLERANCE	TOL
TOOLBAR	TO
TOOLPALETTES	TP
TORUS	TOR
TRIM	TR
UCSMAN	UC
UNION	UNI
UNISOLATEOBJECTS	UNHIDE, UNISOLATE
UNITS	UN
-UNITS	-UN
VIEW	V
-VIEW	-V
VIEWGO	VGO
VIEWPLAY	VPLAY

Command	Alias	Command	Alias
VISUALSTYLES	VSM	XATTACH	XA
-VISUALSTYLES	-VSM	XBIND	XB
VPOINT	VP	-XBIND	-XB
-VPOINT	-VP	XCLIP	XC
VSCURRENT	VS	XLINE	XL
WBLOCK	W	XREF	XR
-WBLOCK	-W	-XREF	-XR
WEDGE	WE	ZOOM	Z

appendix D System Variables

AutoCAD stores the values for its operating environment and some of its commands in system variables. System variables control how the commands work. They also set default colors, sizes, and values. They store information about the drawing and the software configuration. Some system variables can be changed by the user; others are read-only.

To see a list of all system variables and their current settings, type **SETVAR** at the command line, type "?", and then "*".

Use AutoCAD's Help feature for additional information about system variables and their options.

Name	Description	Type	Storage Location	Initial Value
3DCONVERSIONMODE	Converts material and light definitions to the current product release.	Integer	Drawing	1
3DDWFPREC	Controls the precision of 3D DWF publishing.	Integer	Drawing	2
3DOSMODE	Controls the settings for the 3D object snaps.	Integer	Registry	11
3DSELECTIONMODE	Controls the selection precedence of visually overlapping objects when using 3D visual styles.	Integer	User-settings	1
ACADLSPACDOC	Controls loading of acad.lsp file.	Integer	Registry	0
ACADPREFIX	Stores directory path.	String	Not-Saved	pathname
ACADVER	Stores AutoCAD version number.	String	Not-Saved	(Read-only)
ACTPATH	Stores the paths where additional Action Scripts can be found.	String	Registry	" "
ACTRECORDSTATE	Specifies the current state of the **Action Recorder**.	Integer	Not-Saved	0

Name	Description	Type	Storage Location	Initial Value
ACTRECPATH	Stores the path where the Action Scripts are saved.	String	Registry	pathname
ACTUI	Controls the type and level of user UI feedback provided during the playback and recording phase.	Bitcode	Registry	6
ADCSTATE	Indicates whether **DesignCenter™** is active.	Integer	Not-Saved	varies
AFLAGS	Sets options for attributes.	Integer	Not-Saved	16
ANGBASE	Sets base angle relative to current UCS.	Real	Drawing	0.0000
ANGDIR	Sets direction of positive angle measurement.	Integer	Drawing	0
ANNOALLVISIBLE	Hides or displays annotative objects that do not support the current annotation scale.	Integer	Drawing	1
ANNOAUTOSCALE	Updates annotative objects to support the annotation scale when the annotation scale is changed.	Integer	Registry	-4
ANNOMONITOR	Turns the annotation monitor on and off.	Integer	Registry	-2
ANNOTATIVEDWG	Specifies whether or not the drawing will behave as an annotative block when inserted into another drawing.	Integer	Drawing	0
APBOX	Controls display of AutoSnap™ aperture box.	Integer	Registry	0
APERTURE	Controls display size for object snap target box in pixels (1–50).	Integer	Registry	10
APPAUTOLOAD	Controls when plug-in applications are loaded.	Bitcode	User-settings	14
APPLYGLOBALOPACITIES	Applies transparency settings to all palettes.	Switch	Registry	0
AREA	Stores last area computed by **AREA** command.	Real	Not-Saved	(Read-only)
ARRAYASSOCIATIVITY	Sets the default behavior of new arrays to be associative or non-associative.	Integer	Registry	1
ARRAYEDITSTATE	Indicates whether the drawing is in the array editing state.	Integer	Not-Saved	0
ARRAYTYPE	Specifies the default array type.	Integer	Registry	0
ATTDIA	Controls whether **INSERT** command uses dialog box.	Integer	Registry	0
ATTIPE	Controls the display of the in-place editor used to create multiline attributes.	Integer	Registry	0
ATTMODE	Controls attribute display.	Integer	Drawing	1
ATTMULTI	Controls whether multiline attributes can be created.	Integer	Registry	1
ATTREQ	Controls whether **INSERT** command uses default attribute settings.	Integer	Registry	1

Name	Description	Type	Storage Location	Initial Value
AUDITCTL	Controls writing of audit report files.	Integer	Registry	0
AUNITS	Sets angle units.	Integer	Drawing	0
AUPREC	Sets precision of angular units.	Integer	Drawing	0
AUTOCOMPLETEDELAY	Controls the amount of time that elapses before automated keyboard features display at the command prompt.	Integer	Drawing	0.3
AUTOCOMPLETEMODE	Controls what types of automated keyboard features are available at the command prompt.	Integer	Drawing	15
AUTODWFPUBLISH	Controls whether the **AutoPublish** feature is on or off.	Bitcode	Registry	0
AUTOSNAP	Controls display of AutoSnap marker, tooltip, and magnet. Turns on and off polar and object snap tracking. Controls display of polar and object snap tracking tooltips.	Integer	Registry	63
BACKGROUNDPLOT	Controls background plotting.	Integer	Registry	2
BACTIONBARMODE	Indicates whether the action bars or the legacy action objects are displayed in the **Block Editor**.	Integer	Registry	1
BACTIONCOLOR	Sets text color for **Block Editor** actions.	String	Registry	7
BACZ	Controls location of back clipping plane.	Real	Drawing	None
BCONSTATUSMODE	Turns the constraint display status on and off and controls the shading of objects based on their constraint level.	Integer	Not-Saved	0
BDEPENDENCYHIGHLIGHT	Controls highlighting of dependent objects when editing blocks.	Integer	Registry	1
BGRIPOBJCOLOR	Sets grip color in **Block Editor**.	String	Registry	141
BGRIPOBJSIZE	Sets custom grip size in **Block Editor** relative to screen display (1–256).	Integer	Registry	8
BINDTYPE	Controls naming of xrefs when binding or editing in place.	Integer	Not-Saved	0
BLOCKEDITLOCK	Controls opening **Block Editor**.	Integer	Registry	0
BLOCKEDITOR	Indicates whether **Block Editor** is open.	Integer	Not-Saved	0
BLOCKTESTWINDOW	Indicates whether or not a test block window is current.	Integer	Not-Saved	0
BPARAMETERCOLOR	Sets parameter color in **Block Editor**.	String	Registry	7
BPARAMETERFONT	Sets font for parameters and action in **Block Editor**.	String	Registry	Simplex.shx

Name	Description	Type	Storage Location	Initial Value
BPARAMETERSIZE	Sets parameter and feature text size in **Block Editor** relative to screen display (1–256).	Integer	Registry	12
BPTEXTHORIZONTAL	Forces the text displayed for action parameters and constraint parameters in the **Block Editor** to be horizontal.	Integer	Registry	1
BTMARKDISPLAY	Controls display of value set markers.	Integer	Registry	1
BVMODE	Controls display of hidden objects in **Block Editor**.	Integer	Not-Saved	0
CACHEMAXFILES	Sets the maximum number of graphics cache files saved in the local configured temporary folder for the product.	Integer	Registry	256
CACHEMAXTOTALSIZE	Sets the maximum total size of all graphics cache files saved in the local configured temporary folder for the product.	Integer	Registry	1024
CALCINPUT	Controls evaluation of mathematical expressions and global constants in windows and dialog boxes.	Integer	Registry	1
CAMERADISPLAY	Toggle whether camera objects are displayed in the current drawing.	Integer	Drawing	0
CAMERAHEIGHT	Stores the default height for newly created camera objects.	Integer	Drawing	0
CANNOSCALE	Sets the name of the current annotation scale for the current space.	String	Drawing	1:1
CANNOSCALEVALUE	Returns the value to the current annotation scale.	Real	Drawing	1
CAPTURETHUMBNAILS	Controls whether thumbnails are generated for the **Rewind** tool when a view is changed by a navigation tool, except **ViewCube**, **SteeringWheels**, and **ShowMotion**, and when to generate this type of thumbnail.	Integer	Registry	1
CCONSTRAINTFORM	Controls whether annotational or dynamic constraints are applied to objects.	Integer	Registry	0
CDATE	Reads calendar date and time.	Real	Not-Saved	(Read-only)
CECOLOR	Sets new object color.	String	Drawing	BYLAYER
CELTSCALE	Sets object linetype scaling factor relative to **LTSCALE** setting.	Real	Drawing	1.0000

Name	Description	Type	Storage Location	Initial Value
CELTYPE	Sets new object linetype.	String	Drawing	BYLAYER
CELWEIGHT	Sets new object lineweight.	Integer	Drawing	-1
CENTERMT	Controls grip stretching of horizontally centered multiline text.	Switch	User-settings	0
CETRANSPARENCY	Sets the transparency level for new objects.	String	Drawing	BYLAYER
CHAMFERA	Sets first chamfer distance.	Real	Drawing	0.0000
CHAMFERB	Sets second chamfer distance.	Real	Drawing	0.0000
CHAMFERC	Sets chamfer length.	Real	Drawing	0.0000
CHAMFERD	Sets chamfer angle.	Real	Drawing	0.0000
CHAMMODE	Sets chamfer input method.	Integer	Not-Saved	0
CIRCLERAD	Sets circle radius default value.	Real	Not-Saved	0.0000
CLASSICKEYS	Sets shortcuts to pre-Windows AutoCAD shortcuts or Windows shortcuts.	Switch	Registry	0
CLAYER	Sets current layer.	String	Drawing	0
CLEANSCREENSTATE	Stores a value that indicates whether the clean screen state is on or off.	Integer	Not-Saved	0
CLIPROMPTLINES	Sets the number of lines displayed in the temporary prompt history when the command window is set to display one line.	Integer	Registry	3
CLIPROMPTUPDATE	Controls whether the command line displays the progress as a command or script is run.	Integer	Registry	0
CLISTATE	Controls display of command window.	Integer	Not-Saved	1
CMATERIAL	Sets the material of new objects.	String	Drawing	BYLAYER
CMDACTIVE	Indicates whether ordinary command, transparent command, script, or dialog box is active.	Integer	Not-Saved	None
CMDDIA	Controls command dialog box display.	Integer	Registry	1
CMDECHO	Controls echoing of prompts and input during scripts.	Integer	Not-Saved	1
CMDINPUTHISTORYMAX	Sets maximum number of previous input values stored in command prompt.	Integer	Registry	20
CMDNAMES	Displays names of active and transparent commands.	String	Not-Saved	None
CMLEADERSTYLE	Sets the name of the current multileader style.	String	Drawing	STANDARD
CMLJUST	Specifies multiline justification.	Integer	Drawing	0
CMLSCALE	Controls multiline overall width.	Real	Drawing	1.0000 (imperial) 20.0000 (metric)

Name	Description	Type	Storage Location	Initial Value
CMLSTYLE	Sets multiline style.	String	Drawing	STANDARD
COMPASS	Controls display of 3D compass in current viewport.	Integer	Not-Saved	0
CONSTRAINTBARDISPLAY	Displays constraint bars for objects after you manually apply a constraint or autoconstrain them.	Bitcode	Registry	1
CONSTRAINTBARMODE	Controls the display of geometrical constraints on constraint bars.	Bitcode	Registry	4095
CONSTRAINTINFER	Controls whether the geometric constraints are inferred while drawing and editing geometry.	Bitcode	Registry	0
CONSTRAINTNAMEFORMAT	Controls the text format for dimensional constraints.	Integer	Registry	2
CONSTRAINTRELAX	Indicates whether constraints are enforced or relaxed when editing an object.	Integer	Not-Saved	0
CONSTRAINTSOLVEMODE	Controls constraint behavior when applying or editing constraints.	Bitcode	Registry	1
CONTENTEXPLORERSTATE	Indicates whether the **Content Explorer** window is open or closed.	Integer	Not-Saved	Varies
COORDS	Controls updating of coordinates on status line.	Integer	Registry	1
COPYMODE	Controls whether the **COPY** command repeats automatically.	Integer	Registry	0
CPLOTSTYLE	Controls new object plot style.	String	Drawing	Varies
CPROFILE	Displays current profile name.	String	Registry	(Read-only) <Unnamed Profile>
CROSSINGAREACOLOR	Controls the color of the selection area during crossing selection.	Integer	Registry	100
CSHADOW	Sets the shadow display property for a 3D object.	Integer	Drawing	0
CTAB	Stores name of current tab in drawing (**Model** or **Layout**).	String	Drawing	Varies
CTABLESTYLE	Sets current table style name.	String	Drawing	STANDARD
CULLINGOBJ	Controls whether 3D subobjects that are hidden from view can be highlighted or selected.	Integer	Registry	0
CULLINGOBJSELECTION	Controls whether 3D objects that are hidden from view can be highlighted or selected.	Integer	Registry	1
CURSORSIZE	Sets crosshair size as percentage of screen size (1–100%).	Integer	Registry	5

Name	Description	Type	Storage Location	Initial Value
CVIEWDETAILSTYLE	Sets the name of the current detail view style. The current detail view style controls the appearance of all new model documentation detail views, detail boundaries, and leader lines you create.	String	Drawing	24 (imperial) or 50 (metric)
CVIEWSECTIONSTYLE	Sets the name of the current section view style. The current section view style controls the appearance of all new model documentation section views, section boundaries, and leader lines you create.	String	Drawing	24 (imperial) or 50 (metric)
CVPORT	Sets identification number of current viewport.	Integer	Drawing	2
DASHBOARDSTATE	Determines whether the Dashboard window is active or not.	Integer	Not-Saved	Varies
DATALINKNOTIFY	Controls the notification for updated or missing data.links.	Integer	Registry	2
DATE	Stores current date and time in Modified Julian format.	Real	Not-Saved	Varies
DBCSTATE	Stores status of dbConnect Manager.	Integer	Drawing	(Read-only) 0
DBLCLKEDIT	Controls the double-click editing behavior in the drawing area. Double-click actions can be customized using the Customize User Interface (CUI) editor. The system variable can accept the values of on and off in place of 1 and 0.	Integer	Registry	1
DBMOD	Indicates drawing modification status.	Integer	Not-Saved	(Read-only) 0
DCTCUST	Displays path and file name of current custom spelling dictionary.	String	Registry	pathname
DCTMAIN	Displays file name of current main spelling dictionary.	String	Registry	Varies by country/region
DEFAULTGIZMO	Sets the 3D Move, 3D Rotate, or 3D Scale gizmo as the default during subobject selection.	Integer	Not-Saved	0
DEFAULTLIGHTING	Turns default lighting on and off.	Integer	Drawing	1
DEFAULTLIGHTINGTYPE	Specifies the type of default lighting.	Integer	Drawing	1
DEFLPLSTYLE	Specifies Layer **0** default plot style.	String	Registry	Varies

Name	Description	Type	Storage Location	Initial Value
DEFPLYSTYLE	Specifies new object default plot style.	String	Registry	None
DELOBJ	Controls whether source objects for new object creation are retained or deleted.	Integer	Registry	1
DEMANDLOAD	Specifies if and when to demand load certain applications.	Integer	Registry	3
DGNFRAME	Determines whether DGN underlay frames are visible or plotted in the current drawing.	Integer	Drawing	0
DGNIMPORTMAX	Controls the maximum number of elements translated during **DGNIMPORT**.	Real	Registry	10000000
DGNIMPORTMODE	Controls the default behavior of the **DGNIMPORT** command.	Integer	User-settings	0
DGNMAPPINGPATH	Stores the location of the DGNSetups.INI file, which stores the DGN mapping setups.	String	Registry	C:\Documents <username>\ and Settings\ Application Data\ Autodesk\ AutoCAD\ R17.2\enu\ Support
DGNOSNAP	Controls object snapping for geometry in DGN underlays.	Integer	Registry	1
DIASTAT	Specifies exit method for most recently used dialog box.	Integer	Not-Saved	None
DIGITIZER	Identifies digitizers connected to the system.	Integer	Registry	0
DIMADEC	Controls angular dimension precision display.	Integer	Drawing	0
DIMALT	Controls display of dimension alternate units.	Switch	Drawing	Off
DIMALTD	Controls precision of alternate units.	Integer	Drawing	2
DIMALTF	Controls multiplier for alternate units.	Real	Drawing	25.4
DIMALTRND	Rounds off alternate dimension units.	Real	Drawing	0.00
DIMALTTD	Sets tolerance value precision for alternate dimension units.	Integer	Drawing	2
DIMALTTZ	Controls tolerance value zero suppression.	Integer	Drawing	0
DIMALTU	Sets units format for alternate units of all secondary dimension styles except Angular.	Integer	Drawing	2
DIMALTZ	Controls alternate unit dimension value zero suppression.	Integer	Drawing	0
DIMANNO	Indicates whether or not the current dimension style is annotative.	Integer	Drawing	Based on current style

Name	Description	Type	Storage Location	Initial Value
DIMAPOST	Specifies text prefix or suffix for alternate dimension values, except for angular dimensions.	String	Drawing	None
DIMARCSYM	Controls display of the arc symbol in an arc length dimension.	Integer	Drawing	0
DIMASO	Controls dimension object associativity. Obsolete—replaced by **DIMASSOC**.	Switch	Drawing	On
DIMASSOC	Controls dimension object associativity.	Integer	Drawing	2
DIMASZ	Controls dimension line and leader line arrowhead size.	Real	Drawing	0.1800
DIMATFIT	Controls spacing of dimension text and arrows when both will not fit between extension lines.	Integer	Drawing	3
DIMAUNIT	Sets angular dimension unit format.	Integer	Drawing	0
DIMAZIN	Suppresses angular dimension zeros.	Integer	Drawing	0
DIMBLK	Controls arrowhead style.	String	Drawing	None
DIMBLK1	Controls arrowhead style for first end of dimension line when **DIMSAH** is on.	String	Drawing	None
DIMBLK2	Controls arrowhead style for second end of dimension line when **DIMSAH** is on.	String	Drawing	None
DIMCEN	Controls drawing of circle and arc center marks or centerlines.	Real	Drawing	0.0900
DIMCLRD	Controls colors of dimension lines, arrowheads, and leader lines.	Integer	Drawing	0
DIMCLRE	Controls colors of dimension extension lines.	Integer	Drawing	0
DIMCLRT	Controls color of dimension text.	Integer	Drawing	0
DIMCONSTRAINTICON	Displays the lock icon next to the text for dimensional constraints.	Bitcode	Registry	3
DIMDEC	Sets precision of primary dimension units.	Integer	Drawing	4
DIMDLE	Sets dimension line extension beyond extension line for oblique line arrowhead style.	Real	Drawing	0.0000
DIMDLI	Controls dimension line spacing for baseline dimensions.	Real	Drawing	0.3800
DIMDSEP	Specifies decimal format dimension separator.	Single-character	Drawing	Decimal point
DIMEXE	Specifies distance extension line extends beyond dimension line.	Real	Drawing	0.1800
DIMEXO	Specifies extension line offset distance from origin points.	Real	Drawing	0.0625

Name	Description	Type	Storage Location	Initial Value
DIMFIT	Preserves script integrity. Replaced by **DIMATFIT** and **DIMTMOVE**.	Integer	Drawing	3
DIMFRAC	Sets fraction format for architectural or fractional dimensions.	Integer	Drawing	0
DIMFXL	Sets the total length of the extension lines starting from the dimension line toward the dimension origin.	Real	Drawing	1
DIMFXLON	Controls whether extension lines are set to a fixed length.	Switch	Drawing	Off
DIMGAP	Sets distance around dimension text when text is between dimension lines.	Real	Drawing	0.0900
DIMJOGANG	Determines the angle of the transverse segment of the dimension line in a jogged radius dimension.	Real	Drawing	45° (90° Metric)
DIMJUST	Controls horizontal placement of dimension text.	Integer	Drawing	0
DIMLDRBLK	Specifies leader arrow type.	String	Drawing	None
DIMLFAC	Sets linear dimension measurement scale factor.	Real	Drawing	1.0000
DIMLIM	Generates dimension limits as default text.	Switch	Drawing	Off
DIMLTEX1	Sets the linetype of the first extension line.	String	Drawing	" "
DIMLTEX2	Sets the linetype of the second extension line.	String	Drawing	" "
DIMLTYPE	Sets the linetype of the dimension line.	String	Drawing	" "
DIMLUNIT	Sets units for all dimension types, except Angular.	Integer	Drawing	2
DIMLWD	Assigns dimension line lineweight.	Enum	Drawing	-2
DIMLWE	Assigns extension line lineweight.	Enum	Drawing	-2
DIMPOST	Specifies text prefix or suffix for dimension measurements.	String	Drawing	None
DIMRND	Sets rounding increment for dimension distances.	Real	Drawing	0.0000
DIMSAH	Controls dimension line arrowhead display.	Switch	Drawing	Off
DIMSCALE	Sets overall dimensioning variable scale factor.	Real	Drawing	1.0000
DIMSD1	Controls first dimension line suppression.	Switch	Drawing	Off
DIMSD2	Controls second dimension line suppression.	Switch	Drawing	Off
DIMSE1	Controls first extension line suppression.	Switch	Drawing	Off
DIMSE2	Controls second extension line suppression.	Switch	Drawing	Off

Name	Description	Type	Storage Location	Initial Value
DIMSHO	Preserves script integrity.	Switch	Drawing	On
DIMSOXD	Controls display of dimension lines outside extension lines.	Switch	Drawing	Off
DIMSTYLE	Stores name of current dimension style.	String	Drawing	(Read-only) STANDARD
DIMTAD	Controls vertical location of dimension text relative to dimension line.	Integer	Drawing	0
DIMTDEC	Sets precision of tolerance value display for primary dimension units.	Integer	Drawing	4
DIMTFAC	Specifies scale factor for fraction and tolerance value text relative to dimension text height.	Real	Drawing	1.0000
DIMTFILL	Controls the background of dimension text.	Integer	Drawing	0
DIMTFILLCLR	Sets the color for the text background in dimensions.	Integer	Drawing	0
DIMTIH	Controls dimension text position inside extension lines, except for ordinate dimensioning.	Switch	Drawing	On
DIMTIX	Positions dimension text between extension lines.	Switch	Drawing	Off
DIMTM	Sets lower tolerance limit for dimension text when **DIMTOL** or **DIMLIM** is on.	Real	Drawing	0.0000
DIMTMOVE	Sets dimension text movement rules.	Integer	Drawing	0
DIMTOFL	Controls drawing of dimension line between extension lines.	Switch	Drawing	Off
DIMTOH	Controls dimension text position outside extension lines.	Switch	Drawing	Off
DIMTOL	Adds tolerances to dimension text.	Switch	Drawing	Off
DIMTOLJ	Sets tolerance value vertical justification relative to nominal dimension text.	Integer	Drawing	1
DIMTP	Sets upper tolerance limit for dimension text when **DIMTOL** or **DIMLIM** is on.	Real	Drawing	0.0000
DIMTSZ	Specifies size of oblique line arrowhead style.	Real	Drawing	0.0000
DIMTVP	Controls vertical placement of dimension text relative to dimension line.	Real	Drawing	0.0000
DIMTXSTY	Specifies dimension text style.	String	Drawing	STANDARD
DIMTXT	Specifies dimension text height unless current text style has fixed height.	Real	Drawing	0.1800
DIMTXTDIRECTION	Specifies the reading direction of the dimension text.	Integer	Drawing	0
DIMTZIN	Controls zero suppression in tolerance values.	Integer	Drawing	0

Name	Description	Type	Storage Location	Initial Value
DIMUNIT	Obsolete—replaced by **DIMLUNIT** and **DIMFRAC**. Retained to preserve script integrity.	Integer	Drawing	2
DIMUPT	Controls options for dimension user-positioned text.	Switch	Drawing	Off
DIMZIN	Controls zero suppression in primary dimension unit values.	Integer	Drawing	0
DISPSLIH	Controls silhouette curve display for solid objects in wireframe display mode.	Integer	Drawing	0
DISTANCE	Stores value computed by **DIST** command.	Real	Not-Saved	None
DIVMESHBOXHEIGHT	Sets the number of sub-divisions for the height of a mesh box along the *Z*-axis.	Integer	User-settings	3
DIVMESHBOXLENGTH	Sets the number of sub-divisions for the length of a mesh box along the *X*-axis.	Integer	User-settings	3
DIVMESHBOXWIDTH	Sets the number of subdivisions for the width of a mesh box along the *Y*-axis.	Integer	User-settings	3
DIVMESHCONEAXIS	Sets the number of subdivisions around the perimeter of the mesh cone base.	Integer	User-settings	8
DIVMESHCONEBASE	Sets the number of sub-divisions between the perimeter and the center point of the mesh cone base.	Integer	User-settings	3
DIVMESHCONEHEIGHT	Sets the number of sub-divisions between the base and the point or top of the mesh cone.	Integer	User-settings	3
DIVMESHCYLAXIS	Sets the number of sub-divisions around the perimeter of the mesh cylinder base.	Integer	User-settings	8
DIVMESHCYLBASE	Sets the number of radial subdivisions from the center of the mesh cylinder base to its perimeter.	Integer	User-settings	3
DIVMESHCYLHEIGHT	Sets the number of sub-divisions between the base and the top of the mesh cylinder.	Integer	User-settings	3
DIVMESHPYRBASE	Sets the number of radial subdivisions between the center of the mesh pyramid base and its perimeter.	Integer	User-settings	3
DIVMESHPYRHEIGHT	Sets the number of subdivisions between the base and the top of the mesh pyramid.	Integer	User-settings	3

Name	Description	Type	Storage Location	Initial Value
DIVMESHPYRLENGTH	Sets the number of subdivisions along each dimension of a mesh pyramid base.	Integer	User-settings	3
DIVMESHSPHEREAXIS	Sets the number of radial subdivisions around the axis endpoint of the mesh sphere.	Integer	User-settings	12
DIVMESHSPHEREHEIGHT	Sets the number of subdivisions between the two axis endpoints of the mesh sphere.	Integer	User-settings	6
DIVMESHTORUSPATH	Sets the number of subdivisions in the path that is swept by the profile of a mesh torus.	Integer	User-settings	8
DIVMESHTORUSECTION	Sets the number of subdivisions in the profile that sweeps the path of a mesh torus.	Integer	User-settings	8
DIVMESHWEDGEBASE	Sets the number of subdivisions between the midpoint of the perimeter of the triangular dimension of the mesh wedge.	Integer	User-settings	3
DIVMESHWEDGEHEIGHT	Sets the number of subdivisions for the height of the mesh wedge along the *Z*-axis.	Integer	User-settings	3
DIVMESHWEDGELENGTH	Sets the number of subdivisions for the length of a mesh wedge along the *X*-axis.	Integer	User-settings	4
DIVMESHWEDGESLOPE	Sets the number of subdivisions in the slope that extends from the apex of the wedge to the edge of the base.	Integer	User-settings	3
DIVMESHWEDGEWIDTH	Sets the number of subdivisions for the width of the mesh wedge along the *Y*-axis.	Integer	User-settings	3
DONUTID	Sets default value for donut inside diameter.	Real	Not-Saved	0.5000
DONUTOD	Sets default value for donut outside diameter.	Real	Not-Saved	1.0000
DRAGMODE	Controls visibility of objects during dragging.	Integer	Registry	2
DRAGP1	Sets regen-drag input sampling rate.	Integer	Registry	10
DRAGP2	Sets fast-drag input sampling rate.	Integer	Registry	25
DRAGVS	Sets the visual style while creating 3D objects.	String	Drawing	Current visual style
DRAWORDERCTL	Controls draw order functionality.	Integer	Drawing	3

Name	Description	Type	Storage Location	Initial Value
DRSTATE	Controls Drawing Recovery window.	Integer	Not-Saved	Varies
DTEXTED	Controls user interface for editing text.	Integer	Registry	0
DWFFRAME	Determines whether the DWF frame is visible and whether it will plot.	Integer	Drawing	2
DWFOSNAP	Determines whether object snapping is enabled for DWF underlays.	Integer	Registry	1
DWGCHECK	Checks drawings for problems when opening.	Integer	Registry	0
DWGCODEPAGE	Stores same value as **SYSCODEPAGE** (for compatibility reasons).	String	Drawing	(Read-only)
DWGNAME	Stores drawing name entered by user.	String	Not-Saved	Drawing.dwg
DWGPREFIX	Stores drive/directory prefix for drawing.	String	Not-Saved	(Read-only)
DWGTITLED	Indicates current drawing naming status.	Integer	Not-Saved	0
DXEVAL	Controls when data extraction tables are compared against the data source, and if the data are not current, displays an update notification.	Integer	Drawing	12
DYNCONSTRAINTDISPLAY	Displays or hides dynamic constraints.	Integer	Registry	1
DYNDIGRIP	Controls dynamic dimension display during grip stretch editing.	Bitcode	Registry	31
DYNDIVIS	Controls number of dynamic dimensions displayed during grip stretch editing.	Integer	User-settings	1
DYNINFOTIPS	Turns cycling tips for grip manipulation on and off.	Integer	Registry	1
DYNMODE	Turns **Dynamic Input** features on and off.	Integer	User-settings	3
DYNPICOORDS	Controls type of coordinate, relative or absolute, used for pointer input.	Switch	User-settings	0
DYNPIFORMAT	Controls type of coordinate, polar or Cartesian, used for pointer input.	Switch	User-settings	0
DYNPIVIS	Controls pointer input display.	Integer	User-settings	1
DYNPROMPT	Controls **Dynamic Input** tooltip prompt display.	Integer	User-settings	1
DYNTOOLTIPS	Controls which tooltips are impacted by tooltip appearance settings.	Switch	User-settings	0
EDGEMODE	Controls cutting and boundary edge behavior in **TRIM** and **EXTEND** commands.	Integer	Registry	0

Name	Description	Type	Storage Location	Initial Value
ELEVATION	Stores current elevation of new objects relative to active UCS.	Real	Drawing	0.0000
ENTERPRISEMENU	Stores CUI file name including path.	String	Registry	(Read-only) "."
ERHIGHLIGHT	Controls whether reference names or reference objects are highlighted when their counterparts are selected in the **External References** palette or in the drawing window.	Integer	Registry	1
ERRNO	Displays error code number when AutoLISP function causes error detected by AutoCAD.	Integer	Not-Saved	(Read-only) 0
ERSTATE	Determines whether the External References window is inactive, active/visible, or active/auto-hidden.	Integer	Not-Saved	Varies
EXPERT	Controls display of selected warning prompts.	Integer	Not-Saved	0
EXPLMODE	Controls whether **EXPLODE** command supports nonuniformly scaled blocks.	Integer	Not-Saved	1
EXTMAX	Stores upper-right coordinates of drawing extents.	3D-point	Drawing	Varies
EXTMIN	Stores lower-left coordinates of drawing extents.	3D-point	Drawing	Varies
EXTNAMES	Sets named object name parameters.	Integer	Drawing	1
FACETERDEVNORMAL	Sets the maximum angle between the surface normal and contiguous mesh faces.	Real	User-settings	40
FACETERDEVSURFACE	Sets how closely the converted mesh object adheres to the original shape of the solid or surface.	Real	User-settings	0.001
FACETERGRIDRATIO	Sets the maximum aspect ratio for the mesh subdivisions that are created for solids and surfaces converted to mesh.	Real	User-settings	0.0000
FACETERMAXEDGE-LENGTH	Sets the maximum length of edges for mesh objects that are created by conversion from solids and surfaces.	Real	User-settings	0.0000
FACETERMAXGRID	Sets the maximum number of U and V grid lines for solids and surfaces converted to mesh.	Integer	User-settings	4096
FACETERMESHTYPE	Sets the type of mesh to be created.	Integer	User-settings	0
FACETERMINUGRID	Sets the minimum number of U grid lines for solids and surfaces that are converted to mesh.	Integer	User-settings	0

Name	Description	Type	Storage Location	Initial Value
FACETERMINVGRID	Sets the minimum number of V grid lines for solids and surfaces that are converted to mesh.	Integer	User-settings	0
FACETERPRIMITIVEMODE	Specifies whether smoothness settings for objects that are converted to mesh are derived from the **Mesh Tessellation Options** or the **Mesh Primitive Options** dialog box.	Bitcode	User-settings	1
FACETERSMOOTHLEV	Sets the default level of smoothness for objects that are converted to mesh.	Integer	User-settings	1
FACETRATIO	Controls faceting aspect ratio for cylindrical and conic ShapeManager solids.	Integer	Not-Saved	0
FACETRES	Adjusts smoothness of shaded and rendered objects and objects with hidden lines removed (0.01–10.0).	Real	Drawing	0.5
FIELDDISPLAY	Controls field background display.	Integer	Registry	1
FIELDEVAL	Controls timing of field updates.	Integer	Drawing	31
FILEDIA	Controls display of file navigation dialog boxes.	Integer	Registry	1
FILLETRAD	Stores current fillet radius.	Real	Drawing	0.0000
FILLETRAD3D	Stores the current fillet radius for 3D objects.	Real	Drawing	1.0000
FILLMODE	Controls display of filled objects.	Integer	Drawing	1
FONTALT	Specifies alternate font used when specified font cannot be found.	String	Registry	Simplex.shx
FONTMAP	Specifies font mapping file.	String	Registry	acad.fmp
FRAME	Turns the display of frames on and off for all external references; images; and DWF, DWFx, PDF, and DGN underlays.	Integer	Drawing	3
FRAMESELECTION	Controls whether the frame of an image, underlay, or clipped xref can be selected.	Integer	Registry	1
FRONTZ	Stores back clipping plane location.	Real	Drawing	None
FULLOPEN	Indicates whether drawing is partially open.	Integer	Not-Saved	(Read-only)
FULLPLOTPATH	Controls whether plot spooler is sent full path of drawing file.	Integer	Registry	1
GEOLATLONGFORMAT	Controls the format of the latitude/longitude representation in the drawing.	Integer	Drawing	0
GEOMARKERVISIBILITY	Controls the visibility of geographic markers.	Integer	Drawing	1
GFCLRSTATE	Specifies whether a gradient fill uses one color or two colors.	Integer	Not-saved	0

Name	Description	Type	Storage Location	Initial Value
GLOBALOPACITY	Controls transparency level for all palettes.	Integer	Registry	100
GRIDDISPLAY	Controls the display behavior and display limits of the grid.	Bitcode	Drawing	3
GRIDMAJOR	Controls the frequency of major grid lines compared to minor grid lines.	Integer	Drawing	5
GRIDMODE	Controls grid display.	Integer	Drawing	0
GRIDUNIT	Specifies the grid spacing (X and Y) for the current viewport.	2D-point	Drawing	0.500,0.500 (Imperial) or 10,10 (Metric)
GRIPBLOCK	Controls block grip locations.	Integer	Registry	0
GRIPCOLOR	Controls the color of nonselected grips.	Integer	Registry	150
GRIPCONTOUR	Controls the color of the grip contour.	Integer	Registry	251
GRIPDYNCOLOR	Controls dynamic block custom grip color.	Integer	Registry	140
GRIPHOT	Controls the color of selected grips (drawn as filled boxes).	Integer	Registry	12
GRIPHOVER	Controls the color of hover grips (drawn as filled boxes).	Integer	Registry	11
GRIPMULTIFUNCTIONAL	Specifies the access methods to multifunctional grips.	Bitcode	Registry	3
GRIPOBJLIMIT	Sets object number limit for selection set and suppresses grip display when limit is exceeded (1–32,767).	Integer	Registry	100
GRIPS	Turns grips on and off.	Integer	Registry	1
GRIPSIZE	Sets size of grip box in pixels (1–255).	Integer	Registry	5
GRIPSUBOBJECTMODE	Controls whether grips are automatically made hot when subobjects are selected.	Bitcode	Registry	1
GRIPTIPS	Controls display of grip tips.	Integer	Registry	1
GROUPDISPLAYMODE	Controls the display and grips on groups when group selection is on.	Integer	Registry	2
GTAUTO	Controls whether or not grip tools display automatically when selecting objects in 3D space.	Integer	Registry	1
GTDEFAULT	Controls whether or not the **3DMOVE**, **3DROTATE**, and **3DSCALE** commands start automatically when the **MOVE**, **ROTATE**, and **SCALE** commands (respectively) are started in a 3D view.	Integer	Registry	0
GTLOCATION	Sets the default location for grip tools.	Integer	Registry	0
HALOGAP	Sets size of gap to be displayed when an object is hidden by another.	Integer	Drawing	0
HANDLES	Preserves integrity of scripts. Handles are always on.	Integer	Drawing	(Read-only) On

Name	Description	Type	Storage Location	Initial Value
HELPPREFIX	Sets the file path for the help system.	String	Registry	C:\Program Files\ Autodesk\ AutoCAD
HIDEPRECISION	Controls hide and shade accuracy.	Integer	Not-Saved	0
HIDETEXT	Specifies whether text objects are included in **HIDE** command.	Integer	Drawing	1
HIDEXREFSCALES	Controls the display of Xref scales. 0—Xref scales are Displayed; 1—Xref scales are hidden.	Integer	Registry	1
HIGHLIGHT	Controls object highlighting.	Integer	Not-saved	1
HPANG	Specifies hatch pattern angle.	Real	Not-saved	0
HPANNOTATIVE	Controls whether a new hatch pattern is annotative.	Integer	Drawing	0
HPASSOC	Controls associativity of hatch patterns and gradient fills.	Integer	Registry	1
HPBACKGROUNDCOLOR	Controls the background color for hatch patterns.	String	Drawing	None
HPBOUND	Controls object type created by **BHATCH** and **BOUNDARY** commands.	Integer	Not-Saved	1
HPBOUNDRETAIN	Controls whether boundary objects are created for new hatches and fills.	Integer	Drawing	0
HPCOLOR	Sets a default color for new hatches.	String	Drawing	Use current
HPDLGMODE	Controls the display of the **Hatch and Gradient** dialog box and the **Hatch Edit** dialog box.	String	User-settings	2
HPDOUBLE	Specifies hatch pattern doubling for user-created patterns.	Integer	Not-Saved	0
HPDRAWORDER	Controls draw order of hatches and fills.	Integer	Not-Saved	3
HPGAPTOL	Sets allowable gap in hatch boundary.	Real	Registry	0
HPINHERIT	Controls how **MATCHPROP** copies hatch origin from source to destination object.	Integer	Drawing	0
HPISLANDDETECTION	Controls how islands within the hatch boundary are treated.	Integer	Drawing	1
HPISLANDDETECTION-MODE	Controls how islands within the hatch boundary are treated.	Integer	Drawing	1
HPLAYER	Specifies a default layer for new hatches and fills.	String	Drawing	Use current
HPMAXLINES	Controls the maximum number of hatch lines that will generate. Values can be set at a minimum of 100 and a maximum of 10,000,000.	Real	Registry	1000000

Name	Description	Type	Storage Location	Initial Value
HPNAME	Creates default hatch pattern name.	String	Not-Saved	ANSI131
HPOBJWARNING	Sets number of hatch boundary objects that can be selected before triggering a warning message.	Integer	Registry	10000
HPORIGIN	Sets hatch origin point for new hatch objects.	2D-point	Drawing	0,0
HPORIGINMODE	Controls determination of default hatch origin point.	Integer	Registry	0
HPQUICKPREVIEW	Controls whether to display a preview when specifying internal points for a hatch.	Switch	User-settings	1
HPQUICKPREVTIMEOUT	Sets the maximum duration that AutoCAD tries to generate a hatch preview when using the **HATCH** command.	Integer	Registry	2
HPSCALE	Specifies hatch pattern scale factor.	Real	Not-Saved	1.0000
HPSEPARATE	Controls number of hatch objects created when **HATCH** operates on multiple closed boundaries.	Integer	Registry	0
HPSPACE	Specifies pattern line spacing for user-created hatch patterns.	Real	Not-Saved	1.0000
HPTRANSPARENCY	Sets the default transparency for new hatches and fills.	String	Drawing	Use current
HYPERLINKBASE	Specifies the path used for all relative hyperlinks in the drawing. If no value is specified, the drawing path is used for all relative hyperlinks.	String	Drawing	" "
IMAGEFRAME	Controls whether image frames are displayed and plotted.	Integer	Drawing	1
IMAGEHLT	Controls highlighting of raster images.	Integer	Registry	0
IMPLIEDFACE	Controls the detection of implied faces.	Integer	Registry	1
INDEXCTL	Controls whether layer and spatial indexes are created and saved in drawing files.	Integer	Registry	0
INETLOCATION	Stores Internet location used by **BROWSER** command and **Browse the Web** dialog box.	String	Registry	http://www.autodesk.com
INPUTHISTORYMODE	Controls the content and location of the display of a history of user input.	Bitcode	Registry	15
INSBASE	Stores insertion base point set by **BASE**.	3D-point	Drawing	0.0000, 0.0000
INSNAME	Sets default block name for **INSERT** command.	String	Not-Saved	" "]"
INSUNITS	Specifies drawing units value for automatic scaling of blocks, images, or xrefs inserted or attached to a drawing.	Integer	Drawing	1

Name	Description	Type	Storage Location	Initial Value
INSUNITSDEFSOURCE	Sets source content units value (0–20).	Integer	Registry	1
INSUNITSDEFTARGET	Sets target drawing units value (0–20).	Integer	Registry	1
INTELLIGENTUPDATE	Controls graphic refresh rate.	Integer	Registry	20
INTERFERECOLOR	Sets the color of interference objects.	Integer	Drawing	1
INTERFEREOBJVS	Sets the visual style for interference objects.	String	Drawing	Realistic
INTERFEREVPVS	Sets the visual style for the current viewport while using the **INTERFERENCE** command.	String	Drawing	Wireframe
INTERSECTIONCOLOR	Sets color of intersection polylines.	Integer	Drawing	257
INTERSECTIONDISPLAY	Controls display of intersection polylines.	Switch	Drawing	Off
ISAVEBAK	Controls creation of backup files (BAK).	Integer	Registry	1
ISAVEPERCENT	Sets allowable amount of wasted space in a drawing file (0–100).	Integer	Registry	50
ISOLINES	Sets number of contour lines on surfaced objects (0–2047).	Integer	Drawing	4
LARGEOBJECTSUPPORT	Controls large object size limit support when you open and save drawings.	Integer	Registry	0
LASTANGLE	Stores end angle of last arc created.	Real	Not-Saved	(Read-only) 0
LASTPOINT	Stores last point entered.	3D-point	Not-Saved	0.0000, 0.0000
LASTPROMPT	Stores last string echoed to the command line.	String	Not-Saved	" "
LATITUDE	Specifies the latitude of the drawing model.	Real	Drawing	Varies
LAYEREVAL	Controls when the **Unreconciled New Layer** filter list in the **Layer Properties Manager** is evaluated for new layers.	Integer	Drawing	1
LAYERFILTERALERT	Controls layer filters.	Integer	Registry	2
LAYERNOTIFY	Specifies when an alert displays for new layers that have not yet been reconciled.	Bitcode	Drawing	15
LAYLOCKFADECTL	Controls the dimming for objects on locked layers.	Integer	Registry	50
LAYOUTCREATEVIEWPORT	Specifies whether a single viewport should be created on each new layout added to a drawing.	Integer	Registry	1
LAYOUTREGENCTL	Controls display list updates in model and layout tabs.	Integer	Registry	2
LEGACYCTRLPICK	Specifies the keys for selection cycling and the behavior for **<Ctrl>** + left click.	Integer	Registry	0

Name	Description	Type	Storage Location	Initial Value
LENSLENGTH	Stores lens length used if perspective viewing.	Real	Drawing	(Read-only) 50.0000
LIGHTGLYPHDISPLAY	Controls whether light glyphs are displayed.	Integer	Drawing	1
LIGHTINGUNITS	Controls whether generic or photometric lights are used, and indicates the current lighting units.	Integer	Drawing	0
LIGHTLISTSTATE	Indicates whether the Lights in Model window is open or closed.	Integer	Not-Saved	0
LIGHTSINBLOCKS	Controls whether lights contained in blocks are used when rendering.	Integer	Drawing	0
LIMCHECK	Controls object creation outside grid limits.	Integer	Drawing	0
LIMMAX	Stores coordinates of upper-right grid limits.	2D-point	Drawing	12.0000, 9.0000
LIMMIN	Stores coordinates of lower-left grid limits.	2D-point	Drawing	0.0000, 0.0000
LINEARBRIGHTNESS	Controls the global brightness level of the drawing in the standard lighting workflow.	Integer	Drawing	0
LINEARCONTRAST	Controls the global contrast level of the drawing in the standard lighting workflow.	Integer	Drawing	0
LOCALE	Returns code indicating current locale.	String	Not-Saved	(Read-only) " "
LOCALROOTPREFIX	Stores path to root folder where local customizable files installed.	String	Registry	(Read-only) "pathname"
LOCKUI	Locks position and size of toolbars and windows.	Bitcode	Registry	0
LOFTANG1	Sets the draft angle through the first cross section in a loft operation.	Real	Drawing	90
LOFTANG2	Sets the draft angle through the last cross section in a loft operation.	Real	Drawing	90
LOFTMAG1	Sets the magnitude of draft angle through the first cross section in a loft operation.	Integer	Drawing	1
LOFTMAG2	Sets the magnitude of draft angle through the last cross section in a loft operation.	Integer	Drawing	1
LOFTNORMALS	Controls the normals of a lofted object where it passes through cross sections.	Integer	Drawing	1
LOFTPARAM	Controls the shape of lofted solids and surfaces.	Bitcode	Drawing	7
LOGEXPBRIGHTNESS	Controls the global brightness level of the drawing when using photometric lighting.	Real	Drawing	65.0
LOGEXPCONTRAST	Controls the global contrast level of the drawing when using photometric lighting.	Real	Drawing	50.0

Name	Description	Type	Storage Location	Initial Value
LOGEXPDAYLIGHT	Controls whether exterior daylight is used when using photometric lighting.	Integer	Drawing	2
LOGEXPMIDTONES	Controls the global midtones level of the drawing when using photometric lighting.	Real	Drawing	1.0
LOGFILEMODE	Controls creation of log file.	Integer	Registry	0
LOGFILENAME	Specifies path and name of log file for current drawing.	String	Drawing	(Read-only) Varies
LOGFILEPATH	Specifies path for log files for all session drawings.	String	Drawing	"c:\ Documents and Settings\ username\ LocalSettings\ Application Data\ Autodesk\ application_ name\ release_ number\ locale_code"
LOGINNAME	Displays user's name.	String	Not-Saved	" "
LONGITUDE	Specifies the longitude of the drawing model.	Real	Drawing	Varies
LTSCALE	Sets global linetype scale factor.	Real	Drawing	1.0000
LUNITS	Sets linear unit type.	Integer	Drawing	2
LUPREC	Sets precision for all read-only linear units.	Integer	Drawing	4
LWDEFAULT	Sets default lineweight value.	Enum	Registry	25
LWDISPLAY	Controls lineweight display.	Integer	Drawing	0
LWUNITS	Sets lineweight display unit as inches or millimeters.	Integer	Registry	1
MATBROWSERSTATE	Controls the state of the Materials Browser.	Switch	User-settings	0
MATEDITORSTATE	Indicates whether the Materials Editor is open or closed.	Integer	Drawing	1
MAXACTVP	Sets maximum number of active layout viewports.	Integer	Drawing	64
MAXSORT	Sets maximum number of symbol or block names sorted by listing commands.	Integer	Registry	1000
MAXTOUCHES	Identifies the number of touch points supported by connected digitizers.	Integer	Not-Saved	0
MBUTTONPAN	Controls pointing device third button or wheel behavior.	Integer	Registry	1
MEASUREINIT	Sets default units, imperial or metric, for drawing started from scratch.	Integer	Registry	Varies by country/ region
MEASUREMENT	Sets units, imperial or metric, for hatch patterns and linetype files.	Integer	Drawing	0

Name	Description	Type	Storage Location	Initial Value
MENUBAR	Controls the display of the menu bar.	Integer	Registry	0
MENUCTL	Controls screen menu page switching.	Integer	Registry	1
MENUECHO	Sets menu echo and prompt control bits.	Integer	Not-Saved	0
MENUNAME	Stores customization file name and path.	String	Registry	(Read-only) "customization_file_name"
MESHTYPE	Controls the type of mesh that is created by **REVSURF**, **TABSURF**, **RULESURF**, and **EDGESURF**.	Bitcode	Drawing	1
MIRRHATCH	Controls how **MIRROR** reflects hatch patterns.	Integer	Drawing	0
MIRRTEXT	Controls text mirroring.	Integer	Drawing	0
MODEMACRO	Displays a text string on the status line.	String	Not-Saved	" "
MSLTSCALE	Scales linetypes displayed on the **Model** tab by the annotation scale.	Real	Drawing	1
MSMSTATE	Stores a value that indicates whether the **Markup Set Manager** is open or closed.	Integer	Not-Saved	0
MSOLESCALE	Controls scale of an OLE object pasted into model space.	Real	Drawing	1.0
MTEXTCOLUMN	Sets the default column setting for an mtext object.	Integer	Drawing	2
MTEXTED	Defines application for editing multiline text.	String	Registry	"Internal"
MTEXTFIXED	Obsolete.	Integer	Registry	0
MTEXTTOOLBAR	Controls the display of the **In-Place Text Editor**.	Integer	User-settings	2
MTJIGSTRING	Sets content of sample text for **MTEXT** command.	String	Registry	"abc"
MYDOCUMENTSPREFIX	Stores full path to **My Documents** folder for current user.	String	Registry	(Read-only) "pathname"
NAVBARDISPLAY	Controls the display of the navigation bar in all viewports.	Integer	Registry	1
NAVSWHEELMODE	Mode of the SteeringWheels.	Integer	Registry	0
NAVSWHEELOPACITYBIG	Controls the opacity of the big SteeringWheels.	Integer	Registry	50
NAVSWHEELOPACITYMINI	Controls the size of the mini SteeringWheels.	Integer	Registry	50
NAVVCUBEDISPLAY	Controls the display of the ViewCube on the canvas when the 3D graphic system is active.	Integer	Drawing	1
NAVVCUBELOCATION	Controls the display location of the ViewCube.	Integer	Registry	0
NAVVCUBEORIENT	Controls whether the ViewCube always reflects the WCS.	Integer	Registry	1

Name	Description	Type	Storage Location	Initial Value
NAVVCUBESIZE	Controls the display size of the ViewCube.	Integer	Registry	1
NAVVCUBOPACITY	Controls the opacity of ViewCube when it is inactive.	Integer	Registry	50
NEWTRANSIENTAPI	Controls which version of APIs is used for 2D and 3D objects.	Integer	Registry	1
NOMUTT	Controls message display.	Short	Not-Saved	0
NORTHDIRECTION	Specifies the angle of the Sun from north.	Real	Drawing	Varies
OBJECTISOLATIONMODE	Controls whether hidden objects remain hidden between drawing sessions.	Integer	User-settings	0
OBSCUREDCOLOR	Sets obscured line color.	Integer	Drawing	257
OBSCUREDLTYPE	Sets obscured line linetype.	Integer	Drawing	0
OFFSETDIST	Sets offset distance default value.	Real	Not-Saved	1.0000
OFFSETGAPTYPE	Controls polyline gaps when polyline is offset.	Integer	Registry	0
OLEFRAME	Controls OLE object frame display and plotting.	Integer	Drawing	2
OLEHIDE	Controls OLE object display and plotting.	Integer	Registry	0
OLEQUALITY	Sets OLE object default plot quality.	Integer	Registry	3
OLESTARTUP	Controls loading of OLE source applications.	Integer	Drawing	0
ONLINEDOCMODE	Indicates whether a copy of a new drawing is saved automatically to your **Autodesk 360** account.	Integer	Registry	1
ONLINEDOCUMENTS	Stores whether you can open and save drawing files directly to your **Autodesk 360** account.	Integer	Registry	1
ONLINESYNCTIME	Controls the time interval for synchronizing current customization settings with a local cache, which then are stored in your **Autodesk 360** account.	Integer	Registry	5
OPENPARTIAL	Controls whether visible objects in a layout display as a drawing is being opened.	Integer	Registry	1
OPMSTATE	Stores a value that indicates whether the **Properties** palette is open, closed, or hidden.	Integer	Not-Saved	0
ORTHOMODE	Controls **Ortho** mode.	Integer	Drawing	0
OSMODE	Sets running object snap modes using the following bitcodes.	Integer	Registry	4133
OSNAPCOORD	Controls conflicts between running object snaps and entered coordinates.	Integer	Registry	2

Name	Description	Type	Storage Location	Initial Value
OSNAPNODELEGACY	Controls whether the **Node** object snap can be used to snap to multiline text objects.	Integer	Registry	0
OSNAPZ	Controls projection of object snaps.	Integer	Not-Saved	0
OSOPTIONS	Automatically suppresses object snaps on hatch objects and when using a dynamic UCS.	Bitcode	Registry	3
PALETTEOPAQUE	Controls window transparency.	Integer	Registry	0
PAPERUPDATE	Controls print warning dialog display.	Integer	Registry	0
PARAMETERCOPYMODE	Controls how constraints and referenced variables are copied when replicating constrained geometry.	Integer	Registry	1
PARAMETERSSTATUS	Indicates whether the **Parameters Manager** palette is displayed or hidden.	Integer	Registry	0
PDFFRAME	Determines whether the PDF underlay frame is visible.	Integer	Drawing	1
PDFOSNAP	Determines whether object snapping is active for geometry in PDF underlays that are attached to the drawing.	Integer	Registry	1
PDMODE	Sets point object symbol.	Integer	Drawing	0
PDSIZE	Sets point object display size.	Real	Drawing	0.0000
PEDITACCEPT	Controls display of **PEDIT** prompt.	Integer	Registry	0
PELLIPSE	Controls ellipse type.	Integer	Drawing	0
PERIMETER	Stores last perimeter computed by **AREA** or **LIST** command.	Real	Not-Saved	0.0000
PERSPECTIVE	Specifies whether the current viewport displays a perspective working view.	Integer	Drawing	Varies
PERSPECTIVECLIP	Determines the location of eyepoint clipping. The value determines where the eyepoint clipping occurs as a percentage. Values can range between 0.01 and 10.0. If you select a small value, the *z* values of objects will be compressed at the target view and beyond. If you select a value such as 0.5%, the clipping will appear very close to the eyepoint of the view. In some extreme cases, it might be appropriate to use 0.1%, but it is recommended to change the setting to a higher value such as 5%.	Real	User-settings	5

Name	Description	Type	Storage Location	Initial Value
PFACEVMAX	Sets maximum vertices per face.	Integer	Not-Saved	(Read-only) 4
PICKADD	Controls object selection.	Integer	Registry	1
PICKAUTO	Controls automatic windowing for object selection.	Integer	Registry	1
PICKBOX	Sets object selection target height in pixels.	Integer	Registry	3
PICKDRAG	Controls selection window drawing method.	Integer	Registry	0
PICKFIRST	Controls object selection order.	Integer	Registry	1
PICKSTYLE	Controls group and associative hatch selection.	Integer	Registry	1
PLATFORM	Stores name of platform in use.	String	Not-Saved	(Read-only) Varies
PLINEGEN	Controls polyline linetype generation around vertices.	Integer	Drawing	0
PLINEREVERSEWIDTHS	Controls the appearance of a polyline when it is reversed.	Integer	Registry	0
PLINETYPE	Controls type of polyline.	Integer	Registry	2
PLINEWID	Stores default polyline width.	Real	Drawing	0.0000
PLOTOFFSET	Controls location of plot offset.	Integer	Registry	0
PLOTROTMODE	Controls plot orientation.	Integer	Registry	2
PLOTTRANSPARENCY-OVERRIDE	Controls whether object transparency is plotted.	Integer	User-settings	1
PLQUIET	Controls display of plot dialog boxes and nonfatal errors.	Integer	Registry	0
POINTCLOUDAUTOUPDATE	Controls whether a point cloud is regenerated automatically after manipulation, panning, zooming, or orbiting.	Integer	Registry	1
POINTCLOUDBOUNDARY	Turns the display of a point cloud bounding box on and off.	Integer	User-settings	1
POINTCLOUDCLIPFRAME	Determines whether point cloud clipping boundaries are visible or plotted in the current drawing.	Integer	Drawing	2
POINTCLOUDDENSITY	Controls the number of points displayed at once for all point clouds in the drawing view.	Integer	Drawing	15
POINTCLOUDLOCK	Controls whether an attached point cloud can be manipulated, moved, or rotated.	Integer	Registry	0
POINTCLOUDPOINTMAX	Sets the maximum number of point cloud points that can exist in a drawing.	Integer	Registry	1500000
POINTCLOUDRTDENSITY	Improves performance by degrading the number of points displayed in the drawing view zooming, panning, or orbiting in real time.	Integer	Drawing	5

Name	Description	Type	Storage Location	Initial Value
POLARADDANG	Controls user-defined polar angles.	String	Registry	" "
POLARANG	Sets polar angle increment.	Real	Registry	90
POLARDIST	Sets polar snap increment.	Real	Registry	0.0000
POLARMODE	Controls polar and object snap tracking settings.	Integer	Registry	0
POLYSIDES	Sets **POLYGON** default side number (3–1024).	Integer	Not-Saved	4
POPUPS	Displays status of current display driver.	Integer	Not-Saved	(Read-only) 1
PREVIEWCREATION-TRANSPARENCY	Controls the transparency of the preview generated while using **SURFBLEND**, **SURFPATCH**, **SURFFILLET**, **FILLETEDGE**, **CHAMFEREDGE**, and **LOFT** commands.	Integer	Registry	60
PREVIEWEFFECT	Specifies display method for previewing selection of objects.	Integer	Registry	2
PREVIEWFACEEFFECT	Specifies the visual effect used for previewing selection of face subobjects.	Integer	Registry	1
PREVIEWFILTER	Controls object types included in selection previewing.	Bitcode	Registry	1
PREVIEWTYPE	Controls the view to use for generating the thumbnail when the drawing is saved.	Integer	Drawing	0
PRODUCT	Returns product name.	String	Not-Saved	(Read-only) "AutoCAD"
PROGRAM	Returns program name.	String	Not-Saved	(Read-only) "acad"
PROJECTNAME	Assigns project name to current drawing.	String	Drawing	" "
PROJMODE	Sets projection mode for trimming or extending.	Integer	Registry	1
PROPERTYPREVIEW	Controls whether in-canvas preview of property editing, through object or style, is enabled.	Integer	Registry	1
PROPOBJLIMIT	Limits the number of objects that can be changed at one time with the **Properties** and **Quick Properties** palettes.	Integer	User-settings	25000
PROPPREVTIMEOUT	Sets the maximum number of seconds for a property preview to display before the preview is automatically cancelled.	Integer	Registry	1
PROXYGRAPHICS	Controls saving of proxy object images.	Integer	Drawing	1
PROXYNOTICE	Controls proxy warning display.	Integer	Registry	1
PROXYSHOW	Controls proxy object display.	Integer	Registry	1
PSLTSCALE	Controls paper space linetype scaling.	Integer	Drawing	1

Name	Description	Type	Storage Location	Initial Value
PSOLHEIGHT	Sets the default height for a swept solid object created with the **POLYSOLID** command.	Real	Drawing	4 (imperial) or 80 (metric)
PSOLWIDTH	Sets the default width for a swept solid object created with the **POLYSOLID** command.	Real	Registry	0.25 (imperial) or 5 (metric)
PSTYLEMODE	Controls plot style table type.	Integer	Drawing	(Read-only) 1
PSTYLEPOLICY	Controls association of color with plot style.	Integer	Registry	1
PSVPSCALE	Sets view scale factor for new viewports.	Real	Drawing	0
PUBLISHALLSHEETS	Controls how the **Publish** dialog list is populated.	Integer	Registry	1
PUBLISHCOLLATE	Controls whether sheets are published as a single job.	Integer	User-settings	1
PUBLISHHATCH	Controls whether hatch patterns published to DWF format are treated as a single object when they are opened in Autodesk Impression.	Integer	Registry	1
PUCSBASE	Stores UCS name defining origin and orientation of orthographic UCS settings in paper space.	String	Drawing	" "
QCSTATE	Activates **QuickCalc** calculator.	Integer	Not-Saved	(Read-only) Varies
QPLOCATION	Sets the location mode of **Quick Properties** panel.	Integer	Registry	0
QPMODE	Sets the on or off state of **Quick Properties** panel.	Integer	Registry	1
QTEXTMODE	Controls text display.	Integer	Drawing	0
QVDRAWINGPIN	Controls the default display state of preview images of drawings.	Integer	Registry	0
QVLAYOUTPIN	Controls the default display state of preview images of model space and layouts in a drawing.	Integer	Registry	0
RASTERDPI	Controls paper size and plot scaling when converting from dimensional to dimensionless output devices (100–32,767).	Integer	Registry	300
REBUILD2DCV	Sets the number of control vertices when rebuilding a spline.	Integer	Registry	6
REBUILD2DDEGREE	Sets the global degree when rebuilding a spline.	Integer	Registry	1
REBUILD2DOPTION	Sets the global degree when rebuilding a spline.	Switch	Registry	1
REBUILDDEGREEU	Sets the degree in the U direction when rebuilding a NURBS surface.	Integer	Registry	3

Name	Description	Type	Storage Location	Initial Value
REBUILDDEGREEV	Sets the degree in the V direction when rebuilding a NURBS surface.	Integer	Registry	3
REBUILDOPTIONS	Controls deletion and trimming options when rebuilding a NURBS surface.	Integer	Registry	1
REBUILDU	Sets the number of grid lines in the U direction when rebuilding a NURBS surface.	Integer	Registry	6
REBUILDV	Sets the number of grid lines in the V direction when rebuilding a NURBS surface.	Integer	Registry	6
RECOVERAUTO	Controls the display of recovery notifications before or after opening a damaged drawing file.	Bitcode	Registry	0
RECOVERYMODE	Controls recording of drawing recovery information after system failure.	Integer	Registry	2
REFEDITNAME	Displays name of edited reference.	String	Not-Saved	" "
REGENMODE	Controls automatic drawing regeneration.	Integer	Drawing	1
RE-INIT	Reinitializes digitizer, digitizer port, and acad.pgp file.	Integer	Not-Saved	0
REMEMBERFOLDERS	Controls default path stored in standard file selection dialog boxes.	Integer	Registry	1
RENDERPREFSSTATE	Stores a value that indicates whether the **Advanced Render Settings** palette is open.	Integer	Not-Saved	0
RENDERUSERLIGHTS	Controls whether user lights are translated during rendering.	Integer	Drawing	1
REPORTERROR	Controls reporting of errors to Autodesk.	Integer	Registry	1
RIBBONCONTEXTSELECT	Controls how ribbon context tabs are displayed when you single-or double-click an object.	Integer	User-settings	1
RIBBONCONTEXTSELLIM	Suppresses the display of ribbon context tabs when the selection set includes more than the specified number of objects.	Integer	User-settings	2500
RIBBONICONRESIZE	Controls the resizing of images on the ribbon to standard sizes.	Integer	Registry	1
RIBBONSELECTMODE	Determines whether a pick first selection set remains selected after a ribbon context tab is invoked and the command is completed.	Integer	User-setting	1

Name	Description	Type	Storage Location	Initial Value
RIBBONSTATE	Determines whether the ribbon window is active or not.	Integer	Not-Saved	1
ROAMABLEROOTPREFIX	Stores path to folder where roamable customizable files are stored.	String	Registry	(Read-only) "pathname"
ROLLOVEROPACITY	Controls the transparency of a palette while the cursor moves over the palette.	Integer	Registry	100
ROLLOVERTIPS	Controls the display of rollover tooltips in the application.	Integer	Registry	1
RTDISPLAY	Controls raster image and OLE content display during Realtime **ZOOM** and **PAN**.	Integer	Registry	1
SAVEFIDELITY	Controls whether the drawing is saved with visual fidelity.	Bitcode	Registry	1
SAVEFILE	Saves name of current automatic save file.	String	Registry	(Read-only) "c:\ Documents and Settings\ username\ Local Settings\ TEMP\ Drawing1. dwg"
SAVEFILEPATH	Specifies path to directory for all automatic save files in current session.	String	Registry	"c:\ Documents and Settings\ username\ Local Settings\ TEMP\"
SAVENAME	Stores file name and directory path for most recently saved drawing.	String	Not-Saved	(Read-only) " "
SAVETIME	Sets automatic save interval, in minutes.	Integer	Registry	10
SCREENMODE	Indicates display state.	Integer	Not-Saved	(Read-only) 3
SCREENSIZE	Stores current viewport size in pixels.	2D-point	Not-Saved	(Read-only) Varies
SELECTIONANNODISPLAY	Controls whether alternate scale representations are temporarily displayed in a dimmed state when an annotative object is selected.	Integer	Registry	1
SELECTIONAREA	Controls display effects for selection areas.	Integer	Registry	1
SELECTIONAREAOPACITY	Controls selection area opacity during window and crossing selection (0–100).	Integer	Registry	25
SELECTIONCYCLING	Controls selection cycling and whether the **Selection** dialog box is displayed.	Integer	Registry	1

Name	Description	Type	Storage Location	Initial Value
SELECTIONPREVIEW	Controls selection previewing display.	Bitcode	Registry	3
SELECTIONPREVIEWLIMIT	Limits the number of objects that can display preview highlighting during a window or crossing selection.	Integer	Registry	2000
SELECTSIMILARMODE	Controls which properties must match for an object of the same type to be selected with **SELECTSIMILAR**.	Bitcode	User-settings	130
SETBYLAYERMODE	Controls which properties are selected for **SETBYLAYER**.	Integer	User-settings	127
SHADEDGE	Controls edge shading in rendering.	Integer	Drawing	3
SHADEDIF	Sets ratio of diffuse reflective light to ambient light.	Integer	Drawing	70
SHADOWPLANELOCATION	Controls the location of an invisible ground plane used to display shadows.	Integer	Drawing	0
SHORTCUTMENU	Controls display of **Default**, **Edit**, and **Command mode** shortcut menus.	Integer	Registry	11
SHORTCUTMENU-DURATION	Specifies how long (in milliseconds) the right button on a pointing device must be pressed to display a shortcut menu in the drawing area.	Integer	Registry	250
SHOWHIST	Controls the Show History property for solids in a drawing.	Integer	Drawing	1
SHOWLAYERUSAGE	Controls **Layer Properties Manager** layer icon display.	Integer	Registry	1
SHOWMOTIONPIN	Controls the default state for **ShowMotion**. The setting of this system variable is cross session.	Integer	Registry	1
SHOWPAGESETUP-FORNEWLAYOUTS	Specifies whether the Page Setup Manager is displayed when a new layout is created.	Integer	Registry	0
SHPNAME	Sets default shape name.	String	Not-Saved	" "
SIGWARN	Controls digital signature warning.	Integer	Registry	1
SKETCHIN	Sets **SKETCH** command record increment.	Real	Drawing	0.1000
SKPOLY	Sets **SKETCH** command to create lines, polylines, or splines.	Integer	Drawing	0
SKTOLERANCE	Determines how closely the spline fits to the freehand sketch.	Real	Drawing	0.5
SMOOTHMESHCONVERT	Sets whether mesh objects that you convert to 3D solids or surfaces are smoothed or faceted, and whether their faces are merged.	Bitcode	User-settings	0

Name	Description	Type	Storage Location	Initial Value
SMOOTHMESHGRID	Sets the maximum level of smoothness at which the underlying mesh facet grid is displayed on 3D mesh objects.	Integer	User-settings	3
SMOOTHMESHMAXFACE	Sets the maximum number of faces permitted for mesh objects.	Integer	User-settings	1000000
SMOOTHMESHMAXLEV	Sets the maximum smoothness level for mesh objects.	Integer	User-settings	4
SNAPANG	Sets snap and grid rotation angle for current viewport.	Real	Drawing	0
SNAPBASE	Sets snap and grid origin point for current viewport.	2D-point	Drawing	0.0000, 0.0000
SNAPGRIDLEGACY	Specifies whether the grid snap is active only when specifying a point, or also during object selection.	Integer	Registry	0
SNAPISOPAIR	Controls isometric plane for current viewport.	Integer	Drawing	0
SNAPMODE	Turns **Snap** on and off.	Integer	Drawing	0
SNAPSTYLE	Sets snap style for current viewport.	Integer	Drawing	0
SNAPTYPE	Sets snap type for current viewport.	Integer	Registry	0
SNAPUNIT	Sets snap spacing for current viewport.	2D-point	Drawing	0.5000, 0.5000
SOLIDCHECK	Controls solid validation.	Integer	Not-Saved	1
SOLIDHIST	Controls the default History property setting for new and existing objects.	Integer	Drawing	1
SPLDEGREE	Stores the last-used degree setting for splines and sets the default degree setting for the **SPLINE** command when specifying control vertices.	Integer	Not-saved	3
SPLFRAME	Controls spline and spline-fit polyline display.	Integer	Drawing	0
SPLINESEGS	Sets number of segments in each spline-fit polyline.	Integer	Drawing	8
SPLINETYPE	Sets curve type for spline-fit polylines.	Integer	Drawing	6
SPLKNOTS	Stores the last-used knot parameterization for splines and sets the default knot setting for the **SPLINE** command when specifying fit points.	Integer	Not-Saved	0
SPLMETHOD	Stores the last-used spline method and sets the default method for the **SPLINE** command.	Integer	Not-Saved	0

Name	Description	Type	Storage Location	Initial Value
SPLPERIODIC	Controls whether splines and NURBS surfaces are generated with periodic properties when they are closed, or whether they exhibit legacy behavior.	Integer	User-settings	1
SSFOUND	Displays sheet set path and file name.	String	Not-Saved	(Read-only) " "
SSLOCATE	Controls opening of associated sheet sets when drawing is opened.	Integer	User-settings	1
SSMAUTOOPEN	Controls **Sheet Set Manager** display when drawing is opened.	Integer	User-settings	1
SSMPOLLTIME	Sets time interval for automatic refreshes of sheet set status data.	Integer	Registry	60
SSMSHEETSTATUS	Controls refreshing of sheet set status data.	Integer	Registry	2
SSMSTATE	Activates **Sheet Set Manager**.	Integer	Not-Saved	(Read-only) Varies
STANDARDSVIOLATION	Controls standards violation notification.	Integer	Registry	2
STARTUP	Controls display of **Create New Drawing** dialog box.	Integer	Registry	0
STATUSBAR	Controls the display of the application and drawing status bars.	Integer	Registry	1
STEPSIZE	Specifies the step size in current units when users are in **Walk** mode.	Real	Drawing	6.000
STEPSPERSEC	Specifies the number of steps taken per second when users are in **Walk** mode.	Real	Drawing	2
SUBOBJSELECTIONMODE	Filters whether a face, edge, or vertex is selected with **<Ctrl>**+Click.	Integer	Not-Saved	0
SUNPROPERTIESSTATE	Indicates whether the Sun Properties window is open or closed.	Integer	Not-Saved	0
SUNSTATUS	Controls whether the Sun is casting light in the viewport.	Integer	Drawing	1
SUPPRESSALERTS	Controls alerts about potential data loss when opening and saving newer drawings in older versions of the product.	Integer	Not-Saved	0
SURFACEASSOCIATIVITY	Controls whether surfaces maintain a relationship with the objects from which they were created.	Integer	Drawing	1
SURFACEASSOCIATIVITY-DRAG	Sets the dragging preview behavior of associative surfaces to increase performance.	Switch	Registry	1

Name	Description	Type	Storage Location	Initial Value
SURFACEAUTOTRIM	Controls whether surfaces are automatically trimmed when you project geometry onto them.	Integer	Registry	0
SURFACEMODELINGMODE	Controls whether surfaces are created as procedural surfaces or NURBS surfaces.	Switch	Not-Saved	0
SURFTAB1	Sets tabulation number for **RULESURF** and **TABSURF** commands and M mesh density for **REVSURF** and **EDGESURF**.	Integer	Drawing	6
SURFTAB2	Sets N mesh density for **REVSURF** and **EDGESURF**.	Integer	Drawing	6
SURFTYPE	Controls surface type for **PEDIT** smooth option.	Integer	Drawing	6
SURFU	Sets M surface density for **PEDIT** smooth.	Integer	Drawing	6
SURFV	Sets N surface density for **PEDIT** smooth.	Integer	Drawing	6
SYSCODEPAGE	Returns system code page.	String	Not-Saved	(Read-only) " "
TABLEINDICATOR	Controls row and column label display for table cell text editor.	Integer	User-settings	1
TABLETOOLBAR	Controls the display of the **Table** toolbar.	Integer	Registry	2
TABMODE	Controls tablet use.	Integer	Not-Saved	0
TARGET	Stores location of target point for current viewport.	3D-point	Drawing	(Read-only) 0.0000, 0.0000
TBCUSTOMIZE	Controls customization of toolbars.	Switch	Registry	1
TBSHOWSHORTCUTS	Specifies whether shortcut keys are displayed in tooltips.	String	Registry	yes
TDCREATE	Stores local time and date of drawing creation.	Real	Drawing	(Read-only) Varies
TDINDWG	Stores total drawing editing time.	Read	Drawing	(Read-only) Varies
TDUCREATE	Stores universal time and date of drawing creation.	Real	Drawing	(Read-only) Varies
TDUPDATE	Stores local time and date of last drawing update/save.	Real	Drawing	(Read-only) Varies
TDUSRTIMER	Stores user-elapsed timer.	Real	Drawing	(Read-only) Varies
TDUUPDATE	Stores universal time and date of last drawing update/save.	Real	Drawing	(Read-only) Varies
TEMPOVERRIDES	Controls temporary override keys.	Integer	Registry	1

Name	Description	Type	Storage Location	Initial Value
TEMPREFIX	Contains directory name for temporary file placement.	String	Not-Saved	(Read-only) "c:\ Documents and Settings\ username\ Local Settings\ Temp\"
TEXTEVAL	Controls evaluation of text strings entered with **TEXT** or **-TEXT**.	Integer	Not-Saved	0
TEXTFILL	Controls TrueType font fill when plotting and rendering.	Integer	Registry	1
TEXTOUTPUTFILEFORMAT	Provides Unicode options for plot and text window log files.	Integer	Registry	0
TEXTQLTY	Sets TrueType font outline resolution tessellation fineness for plotting and rendering (0–100).	Integer	Not-Saved	50
TEXTSIZE	Sets default text height for current style.	Real	Drawing	0.2000
TEXTSTYLE	Sets name of current text style.	String	Drawing	STANDARD
THICKNESS	Sets current 3D thickness.	Real	Drawing	0.0000
THUMBSAVE	Controls whether BMP preview mages are saved with the drawing.	Integer	Registry	1
THUMBSIZE	Controls the display of the ViewCube on the canvas when the 3D graphic system is active.	Integer	Registry	1
TILEMODE	Makes **Model** tab or last **Layout** tab active.	Integer	Drawing	1
TIMEZONE	Sets the time zone for a sun study.	Enum	Drawing	-8000
TOOLTIPMERGE	Combines drafting tooltips into a single tooltip. The appearance of the merged tooltip is controlled by the settings in the **Tooltip Appearance** dialog box.	Switch	User-settings	0
TOOLTIPS	Controls tooltip display.	Integer	Registry	1
TOOLTIPSIZE	Sets the display size for tooltips.	Integer	Registry	0
TOOLTIPTRANSPARENCY	Sets the transparency for tooltips.	Integer	Registry	0
TPSTATE	Indicates whether **Tool Palettes** window is active.	Integer	Not-Saved	(Read-only) Varies
TRACKPATH	Controls polar and object snap tracking alignment path display.	Integer	Registry	0
TRANSPARENCYDISPLAY	Controls whether the object transparency is displayed.	Integer	Registry	1
TRAYICONS	Controls status bar tray display.	Integer	Registry	1

Appendix D

Name	Description	Type	Storage Location	Initial Value
TRAYNOTIFY	Controls display of service notifications in status bar tray.	Integer	Registry	1
TRAYTIMEOUT	Controls display time for service notifications.	Integer	Registry	5
TREEDEPTH	Controls spatial index tree branches.	Integer	Drawing	3020
TREEMAX	Controls number of nodes in spatial index.	Integer	Registry	10000000
TRIMMODE	Controls trimming of chamfers and fillets.	Integer	Registry	1
TSPACEFAC	Controls multiline line spacing expressed as a factor of text height (.25–4.0).	Real	Not-Saved	1.0
TSPACETYPE	Controls multiline line spacing type.	Integer	Registry	1
TSTACKALIGN	Controls stacked text vertical alignment.	Integer	Drawing	1
TSTACKSIZE	Controls stacked text fraction height expressed as percentage of text height (25–125).	Integer	Drawing	70
UCS2DDISPLAYSETTING	Displays the UCS icon when the **2D Wireframe** visual style is current.	Integer	Registry	1
UCS3DPARADISPLAY-SETTING	Displays the UCS icon when perspective view is off and a 3D visual style is current.	Integer	Registry	1
UCS3DPERPDISPLAY-SETTING	Displays the UCS icon when perspective view is on and a 3D visual style is current.	Integer	Registry	1
UCSAXISANG	Stores default UCS rotation angle for *X*, *Y*, *Z* option of UCS command.	Integer	Registry	90
UCSBASE	Stores name of UCS that defines origin and orientation of orthographic UCS settings.	String	Drawing	WORLD
UCSDETECT	Controls whether dynamic UCS acquisition is active or not.	Integer	Drawing	1
UCSFOLLOW	Generates a plan view when UCS changes.	Integer	Drawing	0
UCSICON	Controls UCS icon display.	Integer	Drawing	3
UCSNAME	Stores name of current coordinate system for current viewport in current space.	String	Drawing	(Read-only)
UCSORG	Stores origin point of current coordinate system for current viewport in current space.	3D-point	Drawing	(Read-only)
UCSORTHO	Determines whether related UCS is restored when an orthographic view is restored.	Integer	Registry	1
UCSSELECTMODE	Controls whether the UCS icon is highlighted when the cursor moves over it and whether you can click to select the icon.	Integer	Registry	1

Name	Description	Type	Storage Location	Initial Value
UCSVIEW	Determines whether current UCS is saved with named view.	Integer	Registry	1
UCSVP	Determines whether UCS in viewports remains fixed or changes to reflect the UCS of the current viewport.	Integer	Drawing	1
UCSXDIR	Stores X direction of current UCS for current viewport in current space.	3D-point	Drawing	(Read-only) 1.0000, 0.0000, 0.0000
UCSYDIR	Stores Y direction of current UCS for current viewport in current space.	3D-point	Drawing	(Read-only) 0.0000, 1.0000, 0.0000
UNDOCTL	Stores state of **Auto**, **Control**, and **Group** options of **UNDO** command.	Integer	Not-Saved	(Read-only) 21
UNDOMARKS	Stores number of marks set in **UNDO** command by **Mark** option.	Integer	Not-Saved	(Read-only) 0
UNITMODE	Controls unit display format.	Integer	Drawing	0
UOSNAP	Determines whether object snapping is active for geometry in DWF, DWFx, PDF, and DGN underlays that are attached to the drawing.	Integer	Registry	1
UPDATETHUMBNAIL	Controls **Sheet Set Manager** thumbnail preview updates.	Bitcode	Drawing	15
USERI1-5	Provides storage and retrieval of integer values.	Integer	Drawing	0
USERR1-5	Provides storage and retrieval or real numbers.	Real	Drawing	0.0000
USERS1-5	Provides storage and retrieval of text string data.	String	Not-Saved	" "
VIEWCTR	Stores current viewport center.	3D-point	Drawing	(Read-only) Varies
VIEWDIR	Stores current viewport viewing direction.	3D-vector	Drawing	(Read-only) None
VIEWMODE	Stores current viewport **View** mode.	Integer	Drawing	(Read-only)
VIEWSIZE	Stores current viewport view height.	Real	Drawing	(Read-only) Varies
VIEWSKETCHMODE	Turns the view sketching state on or off.	Integer	Registry	0
VIEWTWIST	Stores current viewport twist angle.	Real	Drawing	(Read-only) 0
VIEWUPDATEAUTO	Specifies whether Model Documentation views are updated automatically when changes are pending.	Integer	Drawing	1
VISRETAIN	Controls x-ref dependent layer properties.	Integer	Drawing	1

Name	Description	Type	Storage Location	Initial Value
VPCONTROL	Controls whether the **Viewport** label menus are displayed in all viewports.	Integer	Registry	1
VPLAYEROVERRIDES	Indicates whether there are any layers with viewport (VP) property overrides for the current layout viewport.	Integer	Drawing	1
VPLAYEROVERRIDESMODE	Controls whether layer property overrides associated with layout viewports are displayed and plotted.	Integer	Registry	1
VPMAXIMIZEDSTATE	Indicates whether viewport is maximized.	Integer	Not-Saved	(Read-only) 0
VPROTATEASSOC	Controls whether the view within a viewport is rotated with the viewport when the viewport is rotated.	Integer	User-settings	1
VSACURVATUREHIGH	Sets the value at which a surface displays as green during curvature analysis.	Real	Drawing	1
VSACURVATURELOW	Sets the value at which a surface displays as blue during curvature analysis.	Real	Drawing	-1
VSACURVATURETYPE	Controls which type of curvature analysis is used.	Integer	Drawing	0
VSADRAFTANGLEHIGH	Sets the value at which a model displays as green during draft analysis.	Real	Drawing	3
VSADRAFTANGLELOW	Sets the value at which a model displays as blue during draft analysis.	Real	Drawing	-3
VSAZEBRACOLOR1	Sets the first color of the zebra stripes displayed during zebra analysis.	String	Drawing	255,255,255
VSAZEBRACOLOR2	Sets the second (contrasting) color of the zebra stripes displayed during zebra analysis.	String	Drawing	0,0,0
VSAZEBRADIRECTION	Controls whether zebra stripes display horizontally, vertically, or at an angle during zebra analysis.	Integer	Drawing	90
VSAZEBRASIZE	Controls the width of the zebra stripes displayed during zebra analysis.	Integer	Drawing	45
VSAZEBRATYPE	Sets the type of zebra display when using zebra analysis.	Integer	Drawing	1
VSBACKGROUNDS	Controls whether backgrounds are displayed in the current viewport.	Integer	Drawing	1
VSEDGECOLOR	Sets the color of edges.	String	Drawing	7
VSEDGEJITTER	Controls the degree to which lines are made to appear as though sketched with a pencil.	String	Drawing	-2

Name	Description	Type	Storage Location	Initial Value
VSEDGELEX	Makes edges on 3D objects extend beyond their intersection for a hand-drawn effect.	Integer	Drawing	-6
VSEDGEOVERHANG	Makes lines extend beyond their intersection for a hand-drawn effect.	Integer	Drawing	-6
VSEDGES	Controls the types of edges that are displayed in the viewport.	Integer	Drawing	1
VSEDGESMOOTH	Specifies the angle at which crease edges are displayed.	Integer	Drawing	1
VSFACECOLORMODE	Controls how the color of faces is calculated.	Integer	Drawing	0
VSFACEHIGHLIGHT	Controls the display of specular highlights on faces without materials in the current viewport. The range is –100 to 100. The higher the number, the larger the highlight. Objects with materials attached ignore the setting of **VSFACEHIGHLIGHT** when **VSMATERIALMODE** is on.	Integer	Drawing	-30
VSFACEOPACITY	Controls the transparency of faces in the current viewport. The range is –100 to 100. At 100, the face is completely opaque. At 0, the face is completely transparent. Negative values set the transparency level but turn off the effect in the drawing.	Integer	Drawing	-60
VSFACESTYLE	Controls how faces are displayed in the current viewport.	Integer	Drawing	1
VSHALOGAP	Sets the halo gap in the visual style applied to the current viewport.	Integer	Drawing	1
VSHIDEPRECISION	Controls the accuracy of hides and shades in the visual style applied to the current viewport.	Integer	Not-Saved	0
VSINTERSECTIONCOLOR	Specifies the color of intersection polylines in the visual style applied to the current viewport.	Integer	Drawing	7
VSINTERSECTIONEDGES	Specifies the display of intersection edges in the visual style applied to the current viewport.	Switch	Drawing	0

Name	Description	Type	Storage Location	Initial Value
VSINTERSECTIONLTYPE	Controls whether obscured lines are displayed in the current viewport and sets their linetype.	Integer	Drawing	1
VSISOONTOP	Displays isolines on top of shaded objects in the visual style applied to the current viewport.	Integer	Drawing	0
VSLIGHTINGQUALITY	Sets the lighting quality in the current viewport.	Integer	Drawing	1
VSMATERIALMODE	Controls the display of materials in the current viewport.	Integer	Drawing	0
VSMAX	Stores coordinate of upper-right corner of current viewport's virtual screen.	3D-point	Drawing	(Read-only) Varies
VSMIN	Stores coordinate of lower-left corner of current viewport's virtual screen.	3D-point	Drawing	(Read-only) Varies
VSMONOCOLOR	Sets the color for monochrome display of faces.	String	Drawing	255,255,255
VSOBSCUREDCOLOR	Specifies the color of obscured lines in the visual style applied to the current viewport.	String	Drawing	BYENTITY
VSOBSCUREDEDGES	Controls whether obscured (hidden) edges are displayed.	Integer	Drawing	1
VSOBSCUREDLTYPE	Specifies the linetype of obscured lines in the visual style applied to the current viewport.	Integer	Drawing	1
VSOCCLUDEDCOLOR	Specifies the color of occluded (hidden) lines in the visual style applied to the current viewport.	String	Drawing	BYENTITY
VSOCCLUDEDEDGES	Controls whether occluded (hidden) edges are displayed.	Integer	Drawing	1
VSOCCLUDEDLTYPE	Specifies the linetype of occluded (hidden) lines in the visual style applied to the current viewport.	Integer	Drawing	1
VSSHADOWS	Controls whether a visual style displays shadows.	Integer	Drawing	0
VSSILHEDGES	Controls display of silhouette curves of solid objects in the visual style applied to the current viewport.	Integer	Drawing	0
VSSILHWIDTH	Specifies the width in pixels for display of silhouette edges in the current viewport.	Integer	Drawing	5
VSSTATE	Stores a value that indicates whether the Visual Styles window is open.	Integer	Not-Saved	0

Name	Description	Type	Storage Location	Initial Value
VTDURATION	Sets smooth view transition duration (0–5000).	Integer	Registry	750
VTENABLE	Controls use of smooth view transitions.	Integer	Registry	3
VTFPS	Sets smooth view transition minimum speed (1.0–30.0).	Real	Registry	7.0
WHIPARC	Controls circle and arc display smoothness.	Integer	Registry	0
WHIPTHREAD	Controls multithreaded processing.	Integer	Registry	1
WINDOWAREACOLOR	Controls the color of the transparent selection area during window selection. The valid range is 1 to 255. **SELECTIONAREA** must be on.	Integer	Registry	150
WIPEOUTFRAME	Controls the display of frames for wipeout objects.	Integer	Drawing	1
WMFBKGND	Controls background display of Windows metafile objects.	Integer	Not-Saved	Off
WMFFORGND	Controls foreground color for Windows metafile objects.	Integer	Not-Saved	Off
WORKSPACELABEL	Controls the display of the workspace label in the status bar.	Integer	Registry	0
WORLDUCS	Indicates whether UCS is same as WCS.	Integer	Not-Saved	(Read-only) 1
WORLDVIEW	Determines whether input to **DVIEW**, **VPOINT**, **3DORBIT** is relative to WCS or current UCS.	Integer	Drawing	1
WRITESTAT	Indicates write status of drawing file.	Integer	Not-Saved	(Read-only) 1
WSAUTOSAVE	Saves changes you made to a workspace when you switch to another workspace.	Switch	Registry	0
WSCURRENT	Returns name of current workspace and sets workspace to current.	String	Not-Saved	AutoCAD Default
XCLIPFRAME	Controls xref clipping boundary visibility.	Integer	Drawing	0
XDWGFADECTL	Controls the dimming for all DWG xref objects.	Integer	Registry	70
XEDIT	Controls availability of in-place reference editing.	Integer	Drawing	1
XFADECTL	Controls fading intensity percentage for references edited in place (0–90).	Integer	Registry	50
XLOADCTL	Controls xref demand loading.	Integer	Registry	2
XLOADPATH	Creates path for storing temporary copies of demand-loaded xref files.	String	Registry	"pathname"
XREFCTL	Controls creation of external reference log files.	Integer	Registry	0

Name	Description	Type	Storage Location	Initial Value
XREFNOTIFY	Controls notification for updated or missing xrefs.	Integer	Registry	2
XREFTTYPE	Controls default reference type when attaching or overlaying an xref.	Integer	Registry	0
ZOOMFACTOR	Controls magnification changes when mouse wheel moves (3–100).	Integer	Registry	60
ZOOMWHEEL	Allows users to toggle the behavior of mouse wheel zoom operations.	Integer	Registry	0

appendix E
Express Tools

Express Tools are additional productivity tools originally developed by users and unsupported by Autodesk, which extend the power of AutoCAD's basic commands. They cover a wide range of functions. All Express Tools can be entered at the command line; some are accessible through the **Express Tools** tab of the ribbon, the **Express** pull-down menu, and the **Express** toolbars.

Express Tools are automatically installed with a full software installation or a custom installation with the **Express Tool** option selected. To activate Express Tools, enter **EXPRESSTOOLS** at the command line to load the library of tools. If the **Express** menu is not present, enter **EXPRESSMENU** to display the menu.

Tool Name	Description	Ribbon	Command Line	Toolbar	Express Menu
ALIASEDIT	Creates, modifies, and deletes command aliases.	Express Tools	ALIASEDIT	N/A	Tools – Command Alias Editor
ALIGNSPACE	Adjusts a viewport's zoom factor and position based on model space and/or paper space alignment points.	Express Tools	ALIGNSPACE	N/A	Layout – Align Space
ARCTEXT	Aligns text with a specified arc.	Express Tools	ARCTEXT	Express Tools Text	Text – Arc Aligned Text
ATTIN	Imports block attribute values from an external file.	Express Tools	ATTIN	N/A	Blocks – Import Attribute Information
ATTOUT	Exports block attribute values to an external file.	Express Tools	ATTOUT	N/A	Blocks – Export Attribute Information
BCOUNT	Counts blocks.	N/A	BCOUNT	N/A	N/A
BLOCK?	Lists objects in block.	Express Tools	BLOCK?	N/A	N/A

Tool Name	Description	Ribbon	Command Line	Toolbar	Express Menu
BLOCKREPLACE	Replaces block with another.	Express Tools	BLOCKREPLACE	N/A	Blocks – Replace block with another block
BLOCKTOXREF	Replaces block with xref.	Express Tools	BLOCKTOXREF	N/A	Blocks – Convert block to xref
BREAKLINE	Draws a breakline.	Express Tools	BREAKLINE	Express Tools Standard	Draw – Break line Symbol
BSCALE	Scales blocks.	N/A	BSCALE	N/A	Blocks – Scale blocks
BURST	Explodes block and converts attribute values to text.	Express Tools	BURST	Express Tools Block	Blocks – Explode Attributes to Text
CDORDER	Arranges object draw order based on color number.	Express Tools	CDORDER	N/A	N/A
CHURLS	Changes a URL.	Express Tools	CHURLS	N/A	Web – Change URLs
CLIPIT	Clips xrefs or images with curves or lines.	N/A	CLIPIT	Express Tools Block	Modify – Extended Clip
CLOSEALL	Closes all open drawings prompting to save changes.	N/A	CLOSEALL	N/A	File tools – Close All Drawings
COPYM	Copies objects with options for repeat, array, divide, and measure.	N/A	COPYM	Express Tools Standard	Modify – Multiple copy
DIMEX	Exports dimension style to an external file.	Express Tools	DIMEX	N/A	Dimension – Dimstyle Export
DIMIN	Imports named dimension styles to drawing.	Express Tools	DIMIN	N/A	Dimstyle – Import
DIMREASSOC	Restores dimension value to measured value.	Express Tools	DIMREASSOC	N/A	Dimension – Reset Dim Text Value
DUMPSHX	Converts SHX files to SHP files.	N/A	See Express Help. This is an Operating System command.	N/A	N/A
EDITTIME	Tracks active editing time.	N/A	EDITTIME	N/A	Tools – Dwg Editing Time
EXOFFSET	Enhanced offset command.	Express Tools	EXOFFSET	N/A	Modify – Extended Offset
EXPLAN	Enhanced plan command.	Express Tools	EXPLAN	N/A	Tools – Plan View
EXPRESSMENU	Loads **Express Tool** menu and displays menu on menu bar.	N/A	EXPRESSMENU	N/A	N/A
EXPRESSTOOLS	Loads Express Tools libraries. Adds Express directory to search path. Enables **Express** menu.	N/A	EXPRESSTOOLS	N/A	N/A

Tool Name	Description	Ribbon	Command Line	Toolbar	Express Menu
EXTRIM	Enhanced trim command. Extends cutting edge options.	Express Tools	EXTRIM	N/A	N/A
FASTSELECT	Creates selection set from objects touching selected object.	N/A	FS	Express Tools Standard	Selection – Fast Select
FLATTEN	Creates 2D drawing from 3D object.	Express Tools	FLATTEN	N/A	N/A
FULLSCREEN	Hides title and menu bars to maximize drawing area.	N/A	FULLSCREEN, FULLSCREENON, FULLSCREENOFF, FULLSCREEN-OPTIONS	N/A	Tools – Full Screen AutoCAD
GATTE	Globally edits attribute values for selected block.	Express Tools	GATTE	N/A	N/A
GETSEL	Creates temporary selection set.	Express Tools	GETSEL	N/A	Selection – Get Selection Set
IMAGEDIT	Launches image editing program.	N/A	IMAGEDIT	N/A	File tools – Image edit
JULIAN	Performs calendar conversions.	N/A	DATE	N/A	N/A
LAYOUTMERGE	Merges selected layouts into one.	Express Tools	LAYOUTMERGE, -LAYOUTMERGE	N/A	Layout – Merge layout(s)
LSP	Displays AutoLISP commands.	N/A	LSP	N/A	N/A
LSPSURF	Displays AutoLISP file contents.	N/A	LSPSURF	N/A	N/A
MKLTYPE	Makes a linetype from selected objects.	Express Tools	MKLTYPE	N/A	Tools – Make Linetype
MKSHAPE	Makes an AutoCAD shape from selected objects.	Express Tools	MKSHAPE	N/A	Tools – Make Shape
MOCORO	Moves, copies, rotates, and scales with a single command.	Express Tools	MOCORO	Express Tools Standard	Modify – Move Copy Rotate
MOVEBAK	Changes storage location for BAK files.	N/A	MOVEBAK	N/A	N/A
MPEDIT	Like **PEDIT** but with multiple polyline capabilities.	N/A	MPEDIT	N/A	N/A
MSTRETCH	Allows more than one crossing window or polygon selection for a stretch operation.	Express Tools	MSTRETCH	Express Tools Standards	Modify – Multiple Object Stretch
NCOPY	Copies nested objects in an xref or block.	Express Tools	NCOPY	Express Tools Block	Blocks – Copy Nested Objects
PLT2DWG	Imports HPGL files retaining colors.	N/A	PLT2DWG	N/A	File tools – Convert PLT to DWG

Tool Name	Description	Ribbon	Command Line	Toolbar	Express Menu
PROPULATE	Manages Drawing Properties data.	N/A	PROPULATE	N/A	File tools – Updates Drawing Properties data
PSBSCALE	Scales blocks relative to paper space.	N/A	PSBSCALE	N/A	Blocks – Paper space block scale
PSTSCALE	Scales model space text to correct height in paper space.	N/A	PSTSCALE	N/A	Text – Paper space text height
QLATTACH	Attaches leader line to mtext, tolerance, or a block.	Express Tools	QLATTACH	N/A	Dimension – Leader Tools – Attach Leader to Annotation
QLATTACHSET	Attaches leader lines to AutoCAD 13 objects.	Express Tools	QLATTACHSET	N/A	Dimension – Leader Tools – Global Attach Leader to Annotation
QLDETACHSET	Globally detaches leaders from annotation objects.	Express Tools	QLDETACHSET	N/A	Dimension – Leader Tools – Detach Leaders from Annotation
QQUIT	Closes all open drawings and exits AutoCAD.	N/A	QQUIT	N/A	File tools – Quick ext
REDIR	Redefines file paths in xrefs, images, shapes, styles, and text.	N/A	REDIR	N/A	File tools – Path Substitution
REDIRMODE	Sets object types or **REDIR** command.	N/A	REDIRMODE, -REDIRMODE	N/A	N/A
REPURLS	Find and replace function for URL addresses.	Express Tools	REPURLS	N/A	Web – Replace URLs
REVERT	Closes and reopens current drawing saving changes.	N/A	REVERT	N/A	File – Revert
RTEDIT	Edit remote text objects.	N/A	RTEDIT	N/A	N/A
RTEXT	Creates reactive text.	Express Tools	RTEXT	N/A	Text – Remote Text
RTUCS	Rotates UCS dynamically.	N/A	RTUCS	Express Tools UCS	Tools – Realtime UCS
SAVEALL	Saves all open drawings keeping drawings open.	N/A	SAVEALL	N/A	File tools – Save All Drawings
SHOWURLS	Displays all embedded URLs for viewing or editing.	Express Tools	SHOWURLS	Express Tools Standard	Web – Show URLs
SHP2BLK	Converts existing shape to block.	Express Tools	SHP2BLK	N/A	Modify – Convert Shape to Block
SSX	Creates a selected set.	N/A	SSX	N/A	N/A

Tool Name	Description	Ribbon	Command Line	Toolbar	Express Menu
SUPERHATCH	Extends **HATCH** command to permit use of additional types of hatch patterns.	Express Tools	SUPERHATCH	Express Tools Standard	Draw – Super Hatch
SYSVDLG	Manages system variable settings.	Express Tools	SYSVDLG	N/A	Tools – System Variable Editor
TCASE	Changes case of text.	Express Tools	TCASE, -TCASE	N/A	Text – Change text case
TCIRCLE	Encloses selected text with a circle, slot, or rectangle.	Express Tools	TCIRCLE	N/A	Text – Enclose Text with Object
TCOUNT	Adds numbering to text objects.	Express Tools	TCOUNT	N/A	Text – Automatic Text Numbering
TEXTFIT	Fits text to selected Start and end points.	Express Tools	TEXTFIT	Express Tools Text	Text – Text Fit
TEXTMASK	Places a mask behind selected text.	Express Tools	TEXTMASK	Express Tools Text	Text – Text Mask
TEXTUNMASK	Removes mask created by TEXTMASK.	Express Tools	TEXTUNMASK	N/A	Text – Unmask Text
TFRAMES	Toggles frames for wipeout and image objects on and off.	N/A	TFRAMES	Express Tools Standard	N/A
TJUST	Changes justification for text without moving text.	Express Tools	TJUST	N/A	Text – Justify Text
TORIENT	Adjusts rotated block text to horizontal or right-read.	Express Tools	TORIENT	N/A	Text – Orient Text
TREX	Combines **TRIM** and **EXTEND** commands.	N/A	TREX	N/A	N/A
TSCALE	Scales text, mtext, attributes, and attribute definitions.	N/A	TSCALE	N/A	Text – Scale Text
TXT2MTXT	Converts **TEXT** or **DTEXT** objects to **MTEXT**.	Express Tools	TXT2MTXT	N/A	Text – Convert Text to Mtext
TXTEXP	Explodes text into lines and arcs.	Express Tools	TXTEXP	Express Tools Text	Text – Explode Text
VPSCALE	Displays viewport scale factor.	Express Tools	VPSCALE	N/A	Layout – List Viewport Scale
VPSYNC	Synchronizes one or more viewports with a master.	Express Tools	VPSYNC	N/A	Layout – Synchronize Viewports
XDLIST	Lists extended object data for selected object.	Express Tools	XDLIST	N/A	Tools – List Object Xdata

Tool Name	Description	Ribbon	Command Line	Toolbar	Express Menu
XLIST	Extends **LIST** command to nested objects in blocks or xrefs.	Express Tools	XLIST, -XLIST	Express Tools Block	Blocks – List Xref/ Block Objects
XDATA	Attaches extended object data to an object.	Express Tools	XDATA	N/A	Tools – Xdata Attachment

Glossary

absolute coordinate entry The process of specifying a point by typing in a coordinate. The coordinate is measured from the origin or 0,0 point in the drawing.

acquired point Object tracking feature used to locate a point as an intermediate location in order to locate temporary alignment paths. Acquired points show up as a small cross in the drawing. Some points are acquired by simply placing your cursor over key object definition points while other acquired points require selecting a point with your mouse.

annotate To add text, notes, and dimensions to a drawing to communicate a complete design by indicating materials, locations, distances, and other key information.

array A rectangular, circular, or linear pattern of objects.

associativity A link between drawing objects and dimension objects. Associative dimensions will update and follow the drawing objects to which they are linked.

autosave The automatic saving of your drawing by AutoCAD at regular intervals. The default save interval is 10 minutes. Autosave files have a .SV$ file extension by default and are automatically deleted when the drawing is closed normally.

AutoTracking AutoCAD feature that helps you to draw objects at specific angles or in specific relationships to other objects. When you turn on AutoTracking, temporary alignment paths help you create objects at precise positions and angles. Both orthogonal and polar tracking are available.

block attribute A dynamic text-like object that can be included in a block definition to store alphanumeric data. Attribute values can be preset, specified when the block is inserted, or updated anytime during the life of a drawing. Attribute data can be automatically extracted from a drawing and output to an AutoCAD table or an external file.

block definition A user-defined collection of drawing objects assigned a base point and a name that is stored centrally in a drawing. A block can be inserted in a drawing multiple times as a block reference. When a block definition is updated, all block references with the same name are automatically updated.

block reference An instance of a block definition inserted in a drawing that references the central block definition drawing data. All that is stored with the block reference is an insertion point, scale, and rotation angle. All other data are derived from the block definition.

B-spline An approximate spline curve also referred to as a nonuniform rational B-spline, or NURBS, curve.

building a selection set The process of specifying the objects you wish to edit. You can add and remove objects to a selection set and reuse previous selection sets.

cell The box at the intersection of a table row and column that contains the table data or a formula. A cell is typically referenced using its column letter and row number separated with a colon. For example, the cell in column A and row 1 is referenced as A:1.

chamfer To cut off a corner with a slight angle or bevel.

character set The set of numeric codes used by a computer system to represent the characters (letters, numbers, punctuation, etc.) of a particular country or place. The most common character set in use today is ASCII (American Standard Code for Information Interchange).

color-dependent plot style Plot style that is organized by the AutoCAD Color Index (ACI) number. Color-dependent plot styles are automatically assigned by the color of the AutoCAD object. All objects with the same color are assigned the same plot style settings. Color-dependent plot styles are stored in .CTB files.

command alias An abbreviated definition of a command name that enables you to enter commands more quickly at the keyboard by entering the first one or two letters of the command name. Appendix C contains a complete list of the default AutoCAD command aliases.

contour line A line on a map that joins points of equal elevation. On a single contour line, all points have the same elevation. Contour lines are typically placed at designated vertical intervals to indicate elevation changes.

coordinate entry The process of specifying point locations.

crossing window A method of selecting objects in a selection set by specifying a rectangular area. Anything that touches the crossing window area is selected.

curve fit The process of adding vertex points to a straight line segment polyline in order to create a smooth curve. Adding more points creates a smoother curve fit.

deferred point Object snap feature that allows you to "build" the object snap point using multiple point selection input by deferring the first point selected so that it can be used in conjunction with other point or object selections. For example, to find the intersection of two lines that don't physically intersect but that would intersect if they were extended in the same direction requires that you pick both lines. The first point selection is deferred while you pick the second line. Deferred point AutoSnap markers are followed by an ellipsis (...), indicating that more information is needed.

defpoint Point created when placing dimensions that defines the measurement value of the dimension. AutoCAD measures the distance between the defpoints and uses the value as the default dimension text.

demand loading Loading only the visible part of a referenced drawing. Other parts of the drawing are loaded only when necessary. AutoCAD uses demand loading to increase system performance when xrefs are used.

dimension style A collection of dimension settings that control how dimension objects act and are displayed.

direct distance entry The process of specifying a point by dragging the AutoCAD cursor to specify direction and typing in a distance.

drawing template A drawing used as a starting point when creating a new drawing. Drawing templates can contain page layouts, borders, title blocks, layer settings, and many other settings or drawing objects you use on a regular basis. Drawing templates have a file extension of .DWT.

edit reference in-place Using the **REFEDIT** command to make changes to an externally referenced drawing. This allows you to make changes to one drawing from within another drawing.

fillet To round off an inside or outside corner at a specific radius.

freeze/thaw Hiding or displaying the contents of a drawing layer. Objects on a frozen layer are ignored by AutoCAD, are not shown in the drawing, and cannot be edited.

fuzz distance Distance used to determine whether polyline endpoints that are not connected can be connected by extending them, trimming them, or connecting them with a new polyline segment.

grips Editing points that appear at key locations on drawing objects. Once grips are activated, you can directly modify drawing objects by selecting their grips.

hatch boundary The edges of a hatched area. These edges can be closed objects (such as a circle or closed polyline) or a combination of objects that define a closed area.

hatch islands Closed areas within a hatch boundary. You have the option of telling AutoCAD how to deal with island areas when creating hatch objects.

hatch pattern The pattern used to fill a hatch boundary. Hatch patterns are defined in .pat files and also include solid and gradient fill patterns.

hatching The process of filling in a closed area with a pattern. Hatching can consist of solid filled areas, gradient filled areas, or areas filled with patterns of lines.

implied windowing Feature that allows you to create a window or a crossing selection automatically by picking an empty space in a drawing to define the first corner point. The opposite corner point defines a window selection if it is picked to the right of the first corner point and a crossing selection if it is picked to the left.

layer A collection of object properties and display settings that are applied to objects.

layout 2D page setup created in paper space that represents the paper size and what the drawing will look like when it is printed.

layout viewport The user-defined window created in a paper space layout that allows you to view drawing information that resides in model space. Layout viewports are sometimes referred to as "floating" viewports because they can be moved, copied, and resized unlike the "tiled" viewports created in model space that are static and must abut each other.

model The geometry (lines, circles, etc.) created in a drawing that defines the object or objects drawn. The graphical representation of the real-world object or part.

named plot style Plot style that is organized by a user-defined name. Named plot styles can be assigned to AutoCAD layers or hard-coded to individual drawing objects. Named plot styles are stored in .STB files.

nested xref An xref within an xref. This occurs when the drawing you are referencing contains a reference to another drawing. For example, you reference drawing A, and drawing A contains a reference to drawing B; drawing B is the nested xref.

objects Graphical drawing elements, such as lines, arcs, circles, polylines, and text.

object snaps/osnaps Geometric points on objects such as the endpoints or midpoint of a line or the center of an arc of a circle. Object snaps can be construction points on objects or calculated points such as a point of tangency, a perpendicular point, or the projected intersection of two drawing objects.

offset To create a parallel copy of an object.

orthographic 90° increments. When the **Ortho** mode is turned on, AutoCAD locks the cursor movement to 0°, 90°, 180°, and 270° angles.

orthographic projection The two-dimensional graphic representation of an object formed by the perpendicular intersections of lines drawn from points on the object to a plane of projection. Orthographic projection is a drafting technique commonly used to create multiple view drawings by creating one view, then projecting perpendicular lines from the complete view to create the other views. This approach limits the number of times you need to measure in your drawing, reducing errors and increasing productivity.

page setup A collection of plot settings that are applied to a drawing layout. Page setups can be used and shared among multiple drawings.

pan The process of moving your drawing from side to side in the display window so the location of the view changes without affecting the zoom scale.

parametric Automated creation of a drawing based on a given set of dimensions referred to as *parameters*. These input parameters are applied against algorithms that create points, distances, and angles for the creation of drawing geometry. A simple example of creating a drawing parametrically is entering a width (*X*) and a height (*Y*) to create a rectangle.

parametric design Design process that utilizes both variable and constrained dimensions that automatically update the drawing objects they are assigned to so that many different variations of a base design can be accurately represented.

parsec A unit of astronomical length based on the distance from Earth at which stellar parallax is one second of arc and equal to 3.258 light-years, 3.086×10^{13} kilometers, or 1.918×10^{13} miles.

.PC3 file Plotter configuration file used to store and manage printer/plotter settings. .PC3 files control plot device settings such as port connections and output settings, media, graphics, physical pen configuration, custom properties, initialization strings, calibration, and user-defined paper sizes.

pickbox Square box that replaces the cursor crosshairs whenever AutoCAD prompts you to *Select objects:*. It is used to pick objects in a drawing to create a selection set.

plot style A collection of property settings defined in a plot style table that is applied when the drawing is plotted to control the appearance of the drawing objects on the printed drawing. Plot styles can be used to control line thickness, grayscale, screening, and other plot features.

plotting The process of printing a drawing in AutoCAD. Plotting includes outputting your drawing to printers and plotters as well as various electronic file formats.

point A one-dimensional object that is defined as a single coordinate in space. Points have no length or width, only a coordinate location. Points are referenced with the **Node** object snap.

polar tracking A process where AutoCAD will lock the cursor movement to predefined angles. When the cursor gets close to one of these predefined angles, AutoCAD will lock onto that angle and display the angle measurement at the cursor.

printable area The actual physical area that can be printed for the currently specified plotting device and paper size. Most printers cannot print to the very edge of the paper because of mechanical limitations.

properties The settings that control how and where a drawing object is shown in the drawing. Some properties are common to all objects (layer, color, linetype, and lineweight) or specific to a particular type of drawing object (the radius of a circle or the endpoint of a line).

revision cloud Continuous line made from arcs to resemble a cloud that is used to highlight markups and changes. Sometimes marked with a delta triangle indicating the revision number or letter.

right-hand rule Easy-to-understand reference that can be used to determine the positive and negative direction of the *X*-, *Y*-, and *Z*-axes. To use the right-hand rule, you clench your right hand into a fist with your palm facing toward you and extend your thumb to the right, point your pointer finger straight up, and point your middle finger toward you. If your palm is the origin at 0,0,0, then your thumb represents positive *X*, your pointer finger represents positive *Y*, and your middle finger represents positive *Z*.

rubber band A live preview of a drawing object as it is being drawn. The rubber-band preview allows you to see objects as they are being created.

scale factor Multiplier that determines the size of annotation features such as text height, dimension features, and linetype appearance when a drawing is plotted or printed. The scale factor is typically the reciprocal of the plot scale or view scale.

selection set One or more selected objects that are treated as one unit by an AutoCAD command. Objects in a selection set are typically highlighted (dashed).

sheet set An organized and named collection of sheets created from multiple AutoCAD drawing files.

sheet size The size of the paper on which a drawing is printed or plotted.

standard colors Colors 1–9 of the AutoCAD Color Index.

system variable A named setting maintained by AutoCAD that controls an aspect of a drawing or the drawing environment. Most system variables can be changed by entering the variable name at the command line, although some variables are read-only and cannot be changed.

transparent command A command that can be used without interrupting the currently active command. Most display commands can be used transparently so that you can pan and zoom in a drawing while simultaneously using the drawing and editing commands. Transparent commands are run by entering an apostrophe (') before the command name.

typeface The style or design of a font. Other unique properties include size, boldness (line thickness), and obliqueness (an angle applied to the characters, not to be confused with an italic font).

underlay A CAD file that is not directly modifiable by AutoCAD but is still displayed within a drawing and updated when the source data are changed. AutoCAD currently supports the display of DWF and DGN files as underlays.

unit block A block or symbol drawn within a 1 × 1 unit square that is inserted in the drawing with different *x* and *y* scales to achieve different final sizes.

user coordinate system (UCS) A user-defined variation of the world coordinate system. Variations in the coordinate system range from moving the default drawing origin (0,0,0) to another location to changing orientations for the *X*-, *Y*-, and *Z*-axes. It is possible to rotate the WCS on any axis to create a UCS with a different two-dimensional XY plane—a technique commonly used to create multiview 3D drawings.

user interface The commands and mechanisms the user interacts with to control a program's operation and input data.

variable User-defined unit of storage that may assume any given value or set of values. Variable values are dynamic and can change at any time. Often variables are assigned data types so that they can store only specific types and amounts of data.

viewport A window in the paper space environment that shows the view of the model space environment.

working set The group of objects selected for in-place editing using the **REFEDIT** command. Objects can be added to and removed from the working set using the **Refedit** toolbar during the in-place editing process.

workspace A named configuration of menus, toolbars, and palettes that are grouped and organized so that you can work in a custom, task-oriented drawing environment.

world coordinate system (WCS) The default coordinate system in AutoCAD upon which all objects and user coordinate systems are based.

xref A drawing that is referenced by another drawing. The drawing references are updated when the source drawing is modified.

Index

D

E

I

J

K

L

Q

U

V